A Software Laboratory Manual and Workbook

STRATEGIES for the Technical Professional

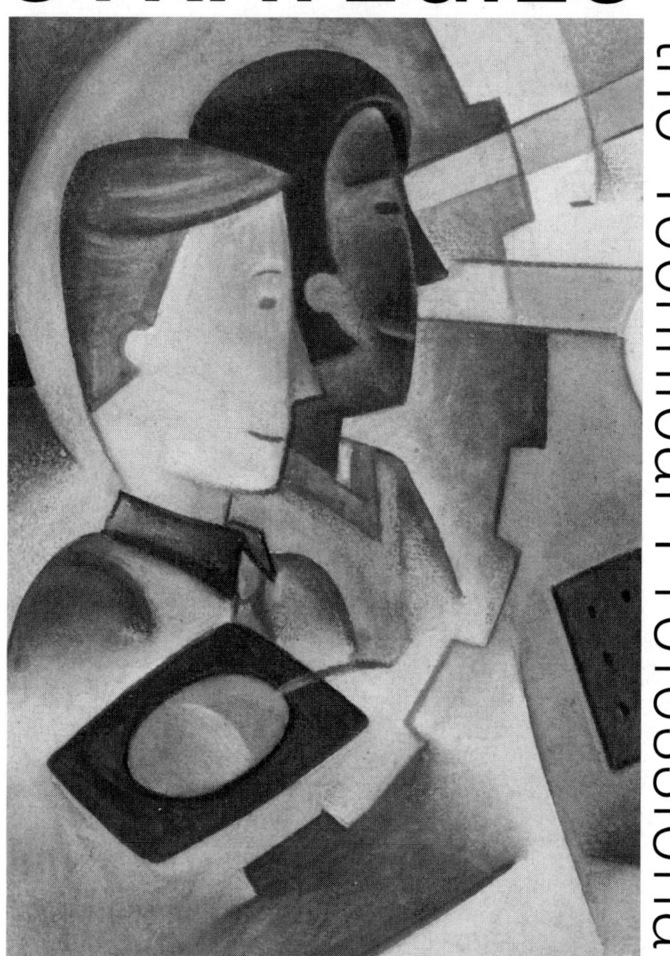

Edited by
James L. Antonakos
Kenneth C. Mansfield Jr.

Broome Community College

Custom Edition containing material taken from:

Office 2000 Essentials
by Robert Ferrett, John Preston, and Sally Preston

Computer Applications in Technology
by James L. Antonakos and Kenneth C. Mansfield Jr.

Instant AutoCAD: Essentials for AutoCAD 2000
by Stephen J. Ethier and Christine A. Ethier

Internet Essentials, Fourth Edition
by David Clark

Cover art courtesy of Stock Illustration Source.
Excerpts taken from:
Office 2000 Essentials
by Robert Ferrett, John Preston, and Sally Preston
Copyright © 2000 by Prentice-Hall, Inc.
A Pearson Education Company
Upper Saddle River, New Jersey 07458

Computer Applications in Technology
by James L. Antonakos and Kenneth C. Mansfield, Jr.
Copyright © 2000 by Pearson Custom Publishing.
A Pearson Education Company
Boston, Massachusetts 02116

Instant AutoCAD: Essentials for AutoCAD 2000
by Stephen J. Ethier and Christine A. Ethier
Copyright © 2001 by Prentice-Hall, Inc.

Internet Essentials, Fourth Edition
by David Clark
Copyright © 2000 by Prentice-Hall, Inc.

Access 2000 Essentials Basic
by Robert Ferrett, John Preston, and Sally Preston
Copyright © 2000 by Prentice-Hall, Inc.

Access 2000 Essentials Intermediate
by Robert Ferrett, John Preston, and Sally Preston
Copyright © 2000 by Prentice-Hall, Inc.

Strategies for Problem Solving Workbook (revised printing)
by Brian K. Saltzer
Copyright © 2000 by Pearson Custom Publishing

This special edition published in cooperation with Pearson Custom Publishing.

Printed in the United States of America

10 9 8 7 6 5 4 3 2 1

Please visit our web site at www.pearsoncustom.com

ISBN 0-536-70651-4

BA 995773

PEARSON CUSTOM PUBLISHING
75 Arlington Street, Boston, MA 02116
A Pearson Education Company

Dedication

To all the students who are beginning
their journey into the world of technology.

Contents at a Glance

Introduction v

Part I **Internet Essentials** 1
Getting Started with the Internet 3
Using Email 21
Searching the World Wide Web 47

Part II **Word** 69
Getting Started with Word 71
Editing a Document 91
Formatting Text 113
Formatting a Document 141
Working with Tables 167

Part III **Excel** 183
Introduction to Excel 185
Enhancing the Appearance of the Worksheet 205
Techniques for Working Efficiently in Excel 227
Making the Computer Do the Math 247
Understanding the Numbers by Using a Chart 277
Using Excel's Interactive Features 301

Part IV **PowerPoint** 323
Getting Started with PowerPoint 325
Improving the Design of the Presentation 345
Charting Numerical Data 369
Adding Animations for the Slide Show 387

Part V **Access** 401
Creating a Database 403
Entering and Editing Data 423
Querying Your Database 443
Creating and Using Forms 463
Creating and Printing Reports 485
Interacting and Connecting 507
Customizing Fields and Tables 529
Making Data Entry Easier and More Accurate 559

Part VI **ACTRIX** 589
Drawing Skill Opportunities 591

Part VII **Instant AutoCAD Essentials for AutoCAD 2000** 605
Introduction 606
The Big Picture: Ready. . . 607
Always Be Prepared: . . . Set . . . 627
Every Journey Begins with a Single Line: . . . *Go!* 647
Alterations Done Here: Modifying 669
WYSIWYG (What You See Is What You Get): Viewing 687

Part VIII Electronics Workbench/MultiSIM 701
Introduction to MultiSIM 703
Power Supply Circuits 717
The Transistor Amplifier 721
Operational Amplifiers 725
Digital Logic Circuitry 729

Appendices

Appendix A Basics
Working with Windows 737
Windows Disk and File Management 753
Working with Office 2000 769

Appendix B Microcomputer Hardware
Microcomputer Hardware 787

Appendix C MathPro
MathPro 889

Appendix D Office 2000 Task Guide
Task Guide 893

Appendix E Glossary 913

Index

Introduction

Essentials courseware from Prentice Hall is anchored in the practical and professional needs of all types of students.

The *Essentials* series has been conceived around a "learning-by-doing" approach that encourages you to grasp application-related concepts as you expand your skills through hands-on tutorials. As such, it consists of modular lessons that are built around a series of numbered, step-by-step procedures that are clear, concise, and easy to review. Explicatory material is interwoven before each lesson and between the steps. Additional features, tips, pitfalls, and other related information are provided at exactly the place where you would most expect them. They are easily recognizable elements that stand out from the main flow of the tutorial. We have even designed our icons to match the Microsoft Office theme. The end-of-chapter exercises have likewise been carefully graded from the routine Checking Concepts and Terms to tasks in the Discovery Zone that gently prod you into extending what you've learned into areas beyond the explicit scope of the lessons proper. In the following pages, you'll find out more about the rationale behind each book element and how to use each to your maximum benefit.

How to Use This Book

This book is divided into several sections that cover different topics. Each of the major sections is divided into two to six projects. A project covers one area (or a few closely related areas) of application functionality. For example, the Word projects cover such topics as formatting text, editing a document, and working with tables. Each project is then divided into seven to nine lessons that are related to that topic. For example, a PowerPoint project on animations is divided into lessons explaining how to create transitions between slides, make bulleted points appear one at a time, and dim previous points. Each lesson presents a specific task or closely related set of tasks in a manageable chunk that is easy to assimilate and retain.

Each element in *this book* is designed to maximize your learning experience. Following is a list of the *Essentials* project elements and a description of how each element can help you:

- **Project Objectives.** Starting with an objective gives you short-term, attainable goals. Using project objectives that closely match the titles of the step-by-step tutorials breaks down the possibly overwhelming prospect of learning several new features of Office into small, attainable, bite-sized tasks. Look over the objectives on the opening page of the project before you begin, and review them after completing the project to identify the main goals for each project.
- **Key Terms.** This book includes a limited number of useful vocabulary words and definitions, such as ***word wrap***, ***primary key***, ***shortcut menu***, and ***cell***. Key terms introduced in each project are listed in alphabetical order immediately after the objectives on the opening page of the project. These key terms are shown in bold italic and are defined during their first use within the text. Definitions of key terms are also included in the Glossary.
- **Why Would I Do This?** You are studying Office so that you can accomplish useful tasks in the real world. This brief section tells you why these tasks or procedures are important. What can you do with the knowledge? How can these application features be applied to everyday tasks?
- **Visual Summary.** This opening section graphically illustrates the concepts and features that you will learn in the project. One or more figures, with ample callouts, show the final result of completing the project. This road map to your destination keeps you motivated as you work through the individual steps of each task.
- **Lessons.** Each lesson contains one or more tasks that correspond to an objective on the opening page of the project. A lesson consists of step-by-step tutorials, their associated data files, screen shots, and the special notes described as follows. Although each lesson often builds on the previous one, the lessons (and the exercises) have been made as modular

as possible. For example, you can skip tasks that you have already mastered, and begin a later lesson using a data file provided specifically for its task(s).

- **Step-by-Step Tutorial.** The lessons consist of numbered, bold, step-by-step instructions that show you in a clear, concise, and direct manner how to perform the procedures. These hands-on tutorials, which are the "essentials" of each project, let you "learn by doing." Regular paragraphs between the steps clarify the results of each step. Also, screen shots are introduced after key steps for you to check against the results on your monitor. To preview or review the lesson, you can easily scan the bold numbered steps. Quick (or impatient!) learners may likewise ignore the intervening paragraphs.

- **Need to Know.** These sidebars provide essential tips for performing the task and using the application more effectively. You can easily recognize them by their distinctive icon and bold headings. It is well worth the effort to review these crucial notes again after completing the project.

- **Nice to Know.** Nice to Know comments provide extra tips, shortcuts, alternative ways to complete a process, and special hints about using the software. You may safely ignore these for the moment to focus on the main task at hand, or you may pause to learn and appreciate these tidbits. Here, you find neat tricks and special insights to impress your friends and coworkers!

- **If You Have Problems...** These short troubleshooting notes help you anticipate or solve common problems quickly and effectively. Even if you do not encounter the problem at this time, make a mental note of it so that you know where to look when you find yourself (or others) in difficulty.
- **Summary.** This section provides a brief recap of the tasks learned in the project. The summary guides you to places where you can expand your knowledge, which may include references to specific Help topics or the Prentice Hall *Essentials* Web site (`http://www.prenhall.com/essentials`).
- **Checking Concepts and Terms.** This section offers optional True/False, Multiple Choice, Screen ID, and Discussion questions that are designed to check your comprehension and assess retention. If you need to refresh your memory, the relevant lesson number is provided after each True/False and Multiple Choice question. For example, [L5] directs you to review Lesson 5 for the answer. Lesson numbers may be provided—where relevant—for other types of exercises as well.

- **Skill Drill Exercises.** This section enables you to check your comprehension, evaluate your progress, and practice what you've learned. The exercises in this section build on and reinforce what was learned in each project. Generally, the Skill Drill exercises include step-by-step instructions.

- **Challenge Exercises.** These exercises, included in all but the Basics section, expand on or relate to the skills practiced in the project. Each exercise provides a brief narrative introduction, followed by instructions. Although the instructions are often written in a step-by-step format, the steps are not as detailed as those in the Skill Drill section. Providing less-specific steps helps you learn to think on your own. These exercises foster the "near transfer" of learning.

- **Discovery Zone Exercises.** These exercises, included in all but the Basics section, require advanced knowledge of project topics or the application of skills from multiple lessons. Additionally, these exercises might require you to research topics in Help or on the Web to complete them. This self-directed method of learning new skills emulates real-world experience. We provide the cues, and you do the exploring!

- **Learning to Learn.** Throughout this book, you will find lessons, exercises, and other elements highlighted by this icon. For the most part, they involve using or exploring the built-in Help system or Web-based Help, which is also accessible from the application. However, their significance is much greater. Microsoft Office has become so rich in features that cater to so many diverse needs that it is no longer possible to anticipate and teach you everything that you might need to know. It is becoming increasingly important that, as you learn from this book, you also "learn to learn" on your own. These elements help you identify related—perhaps more specialized—tasks or questions, and show you how to discover the right procedures or answers by exploiting the many resources that are already within the application.

- **Task Guide.** The Task Guide comprising Appendix D lists all the procedures and shortcuts you have learned in this book. It can be used in two complementary ways to enhance your learning experience. You can refer to it, while progressing through the book, to refresh your memory on procedures learned in a previous lesson. Or, you can keep it as a handy real-world reference while using the applications for your daily work.
- **Glossary.** Here, you find the definitions—collected in one place—of all the key terms defined throughout the book and listed on the opening page of each project. Use it to refresh your memory.

Typeface Conventions Used in This Book

We have used the following conventions throughout this book to make it easier for you to understand the material:

- Key terms appear in ***italic and bold*** the first time that they are defined in a project.
- Text that you type, as well as text that appears on your computer screen as warning, confirmation, or general information, appears in a special `monospace` typeface.
- Hotkeys, the underlined keys onscreen that activate commands and options, are also underlined in this book. Hotkeys offer a quick way to bring up frequently used commands.

CD-ROM Contents for Strategies for Technical Professionals

The CD-ROM for *Strategies for Technical Professionals* contains hundreds of files used to support instruction in each Part of the lab manual. The files are distributed over four directories on the CD-ROM, as indicated in the table below. The majority of the files are found in the **office2000** directory. You should look there first whenever you need an Access, Word, Excel, or PowerPoint file. These files start with the following letters:

- **AO** - Access
- **WO** - Word
- **EO** - Excel
- **PO** - PowerPoint

Some Access files are also located in two other directories. Access files beginning with the characters **AC1** are found in **access2000basic**. Access files beginning with **AC2** are found in the **access2000essentials** project subdirectories.

CD-ROM Directory	Files	Where Files are Used
access2000basic	Access	Part V
access2000essentials	Access	Part V
iae2000	AutoCAD	Part VII
office2000	Access, Word, Excel, PowerPoint	Part II, III, IV, V

Notes:

1. There are no files required for Parts I, VI, and VIII.
2. All directories except **iae2000** contain a subdirectory called **student** where the files reside.
3. **access2000essentials** contains seven subdirectories in its **student** folder: **project01** through **project07**. Each of the seven subdirectories contain files beginning with the characters **AC2**.
4. If you encounter pathnames such as **student/excel/project**, or **PowerPoint/student** when asked to open a file, simply look in the **office2000/Student** directory.

How to Use the CD-ROM

The CD-ROM that accompanies this book contains all the data files for you to use as you work through the step-by-step tutorials, and the Skill Drill, Challenge, and Discovery Zone exercises provided at the end of each textbook project. The CD has several Student folders containing all of the files for all of the projects.

The filenames correspond to the filenames called for in the textbook. The files are named in the following manner: The first two characters represent the software and the book (such as A for Access and O for Office). The last four digits indicate the project number and the file number within the project. For example, the first file used in the Word Project 1 section is 0101. Therefore, the complete name for the first Word file is WO-0101, while the third PowerPoint file in the fourth PowerPoint project is PO-0403.

Files on a CD-ROM are read-only; they cannot be modified in any way. To use the provided data files while working through this book, you are instructed to open a file and then save it to your floppy disk, where you can modify it.

You do not have to copy the files on the CD to the hard drive. Each time you need to use one of these files, you are told how to transfer a copy to a floppy disk where you can make your modifications as instructed in the text.

If you are working on your own computer, or have permission to save files to your own folder on a lab computer's hard disk, you may save your files to the hard drive instead of a floppy disk. It is usually much faster to work on the hard drive and it does not require the use of multiple floppy disks.

Since many computer labs do not allow you to save files to the hard disk that is shared with other users, this book assumes that you will be transferring the files from the CD to a floppy disk where you will make the modifications described in the text.

In the Word, Excel, and PowerPoint projects, you will open the file from the CD and then save it with a different name to a floppy disk. In Access, the process is similar, except you transfer the file first, remove its read-only property, rename the file, and then open it from the floppy disk.

It is easy to forget your CD in the drive at a computer lab or it may get damaged. You may want to copy the files to a set of floppy disks or to the hard drive of your home computer to protect against accidental loss.

- **Saving to a 3.5 inch floppy-disk.** For security or space reasons, many labs do not allow you to save to the hard drive at all. The third lesson in Project 2 of Appendix A shows you how to copy a file to a 3.5-inch floppy disk from the CD-ROM.
- **Copying to a 3.5-inch floppy disk**. The only way you can transfer Microsoft Access databases to a floppy disk is to manually copy the files. You can copy any, including non-Access, files in the manner described below, but Access requires an extra step. Unlike the other Office applications, Access does not have a Save As command for databases. This means that you cannot open and save each data file individually with a different name, as you can while working with Word, Excel, or PowerPoint.

  First, select the files on the CD that you want to copy and ensure that their combined size (shown on the status bar of the Explorer window) will fit on a 1.44MB floppy disk. Right-click on the selection, choose Send To on the shortcut menu that appears, and then choose 3 1/2 Floppy on the submenu. After copying, select the copied files on the floppy disk and right-click the selection. This time, choose Properties, choose the General tab on the Properties dialog box that appears, and then uncheck the read-only attribute at the bottom of this page. Because the original files on the CD-ROM were read-only, the files were copied with this attribute turned on. You can rename files copied in this manner after you have turned off the read-only attribute.

  Although you can use the same method to copy the entire CD contents to a large-capacity drive, it is much simpler to use the installation routine in the CD-ROM for this purpose. This automatically removes the read-only attribute while transferring the files.
- **Installing to a hard drive or Zip drive**. The CD-ROM contains an installation routine that automatically copies all the contents to a local or networked hard drive, or to a remov-

able large-capacity drive (for example, an Iomega Zip drive). If you are working in the classroom, your instructor may have installed the files to a network drive and can tell you where the files are located.

Otherwise, run the installation routine yourself to transfer all the files to the hard drive (for example, if you are working at home or working on your own computer at work) or to your personal Zip drive.

The Instructor's Manual

An Instructor's Manual is available that contains answers to the Checking Concepts and Terms self-tests at the end of each major section, as well as other aids for the instructor. A CD-ROM is included that contains Office files supporting the work in each section.

Part I Internet Essentials

Internet Essentials

1 Getting Started with the Internet

2 Using Email

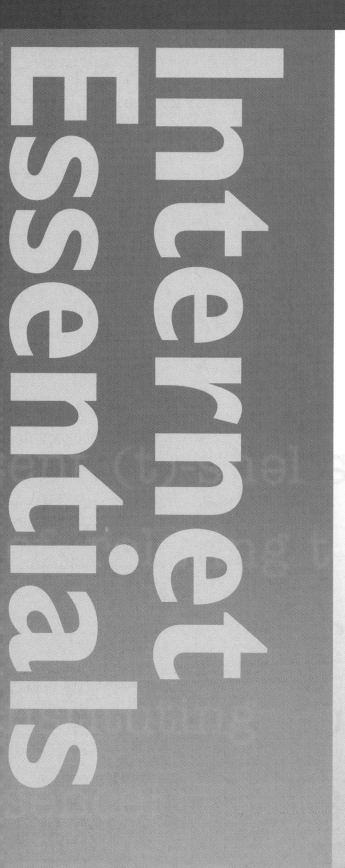

3 Searching the World Wide Web

Project 1

Getting Started with the Internet

Objectives

In this project, you learn how to

- **Start Internet Explorer**
- **Configure Internet Explorer**
- **Navigate the World Wide Web Using Hyperlinks**
- **Navigate the World Wide Web Using URLs**

Key terms introduced in this project include

- browser
- dial-up connections
- dedicated connections
- ethernet
- home page
- hyperlink
- Internet Service Provider (ISP)
- modem
- server
- URL
- Web site
- World Wide Web

SOURCE: *Essentials: Internet, 4/e, Clark*

Why Would I Do This?

You can't open a newspaper, turn on your television, or pick up a magazine without seeing something about the Internet. In just a few short years, we have seen an exponential number of new users coming online, and the trend isn't slowing down. Everybody from the President of the United States to the Rolling Stones to the guy next door can be found on the Internet. What are they doing?

Being connected to the Internet gives you the capability to do the following:

- Communicate with anyone in the world who has a link to the Net
- Download software
- Conduct research and search a wide range of online databases
- Join in international discussion groups about almost any topic under the sun
- Publish your accomplishments on the Net and share them with an audience of millions
- Shop for books, music, flowers, and lots more
- Play chess, cards, or a variety of other online games
- Watch online broadcasts

The Net has made these options, and more, available to millions of users worldwide.

For roughly 25 years, the Internet was the virtual home of research scientists and academia's elite. Access wasn't for just anybody. You had to be affiliated with an educational institution or government lab to get online. Even then, you needed to be able to navigate the cryptic structure of the Internet by using confusing command-line codes that took a degree in computer science to understand. The Internet was not a particularly friendly place.

Then, two things happened. First, the Internet opened its doors to the general public. This took care of the access problem, and the Internet began to grow. The general public started using the email on the Internet to communicate with friends, family, and colleagues. People started to share files using file transfer protocols, and they debated the hot topics of the day using Internet newsgroups.

The next development revolutionized the Internet. That development was the World Wide Web. The World Wide Web and the software to access the Web made navigating the Internet a snap. Using programs such as Netscape Navigator and Internet Explorer, any three-year-old could now surf the Web. The Internet (specifically, the World Wide Web) was now ready to become a presence in the homes of anyone with a computer, a modem, and an open phone line.

We'll start our exploration of the Internet with a look at the World Wide Web and see what all the fuss is about.

Visual Summary

Microsoft's Internet Explorer is the software we will be using to access the World Wide Web, as shown in Figure 1.1. Using Internet Explorer, we will be able to perform a variety of functions via the Internet.

But let's talk about connections for a moment. In order to follow the exercises in this book, you will first have to establish a connection to the Internet. You can connect to the Internet in one of two basic ways: dedicated connections and dial-up connections.

Dedicated connections, which you tend to see only in computer labs or offices, are permanently wired to the Internet. So, you don't have to use a modem to make the connection. A ***modem*** is a device that enables a computer to send and receive data over regular phone lines. With a dedicated connection, your computer becomes part of the Internet. You have a direct link from your computer to the rest of the world. This line is piped into the lab through an ***ethernet*** or another networking scheme. Ethernet is a common networking scheme used to link computers so that they can share data. These lines have the potential to move data back and forth quickly.

Dial-up connections are connections that you make by dialing a server with a modem connected to your desktop computer. A ***server*** is a computer that offers a service to another computer. In this case, it offers access to the Internet. These accounts let you connect to the server just as if you had a dedicated connection; the only differences are that it's slower and you have to use a modem to connect to the server. To establish a dial-up connection you need an agreement with an ***Internet Service Provider (ISP)***. An ISP is an organization that provides you with access to the Internet. This may be an online service such as America Online, an educational institution, a business, or a private company that supplies Internet connections. ISPs have sprung up all over the country in the past few years, so finding one shouldn't be difficult. These providers usually charge for their services, so shopping around for the best deal is a good idea.

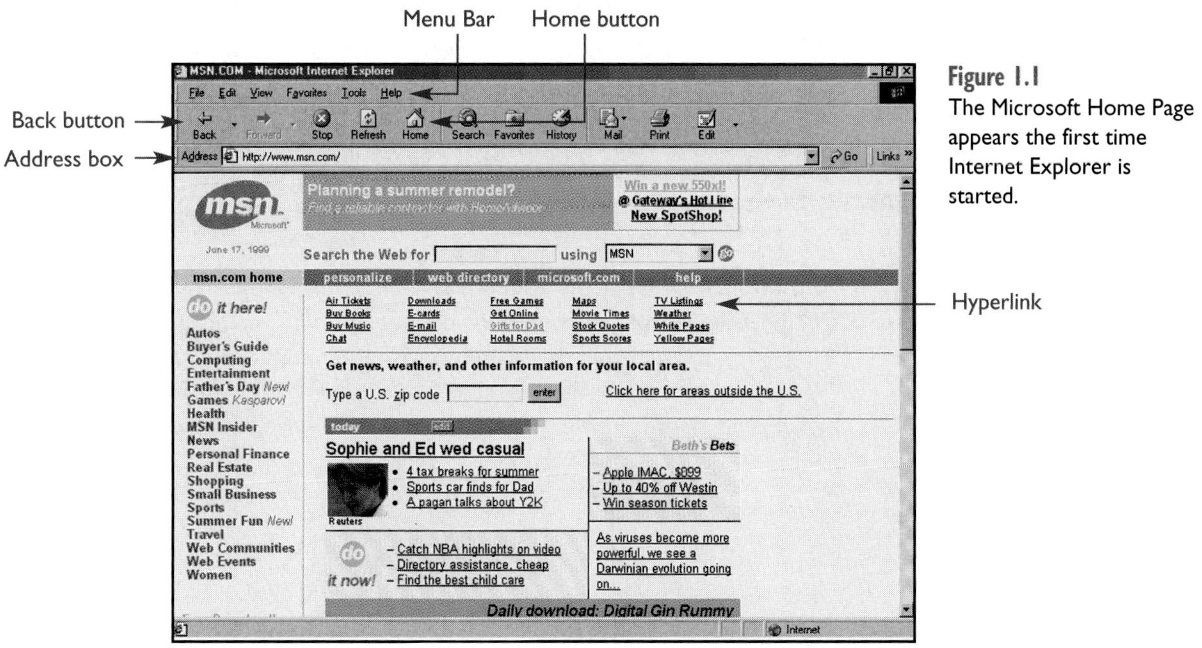

Figure 1.1
The Microsoft Home Page appears the first time Internet Explorer is started.

To find an ISP that meets your needs, talk with friends who are connected, call a local computer users group, or check in the Yellow Pages under Internet Access Providers. After you have settled on a provider, you will get everything you need to get online—including software and specific instructions to dial into its network. You're then ready to start exploring the Internet.

Lesson 1: Starting Internet Explorer

Microsoft's Internet Explorer 5 comes prepackaged with Windows 98, the second edition. If you have an earlier version of Windows 98, you may need to upgrade. Using Internet Explorer, you can jump into the World Wide Web to explore all the possibilities the Internet has to offer.

To Start Internet Explorer

1 Locate the Internet Explore icon on the desktop (see Figure 1.2).
By default, this icon is placed on the desktop during installation of Windows software.

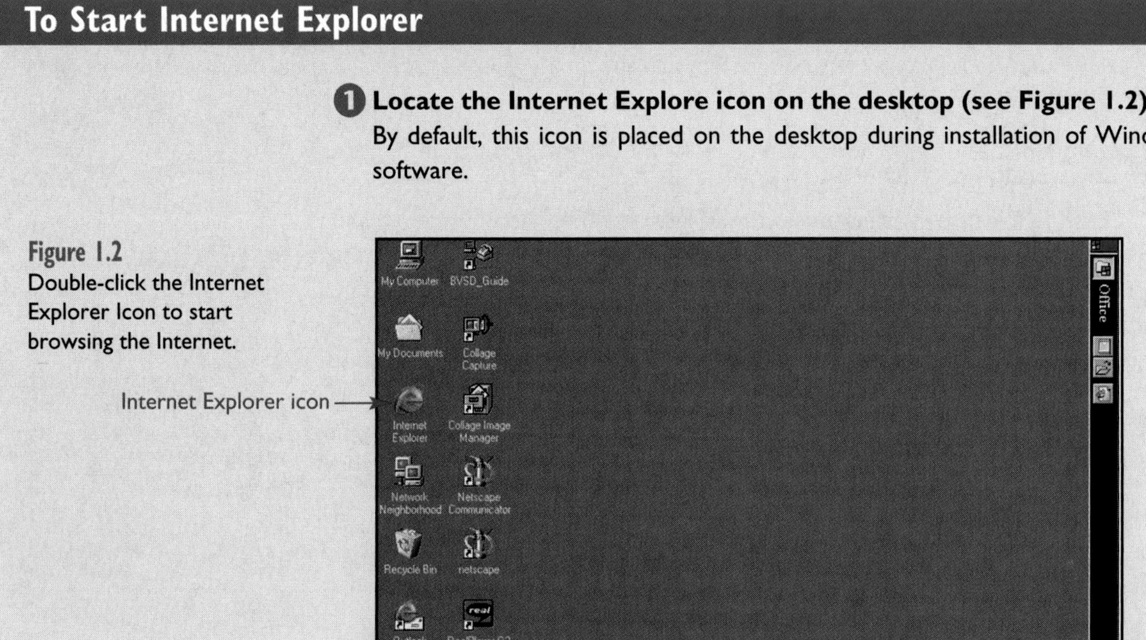

Figure 1.2
Double-click the Internet Explorer Icon to start browsing the Internet.

2 Double-click the icon to activate Internet Explorer.
A home page opens when you are connected to the Internet, as shown in Figure 1.3. If this is the first time Internet Explorer starts on your machine, the Microsoft Home Page will appear. You'll have a chance to change this option in the following lessons. Leave this page open and continue with the next lesson.

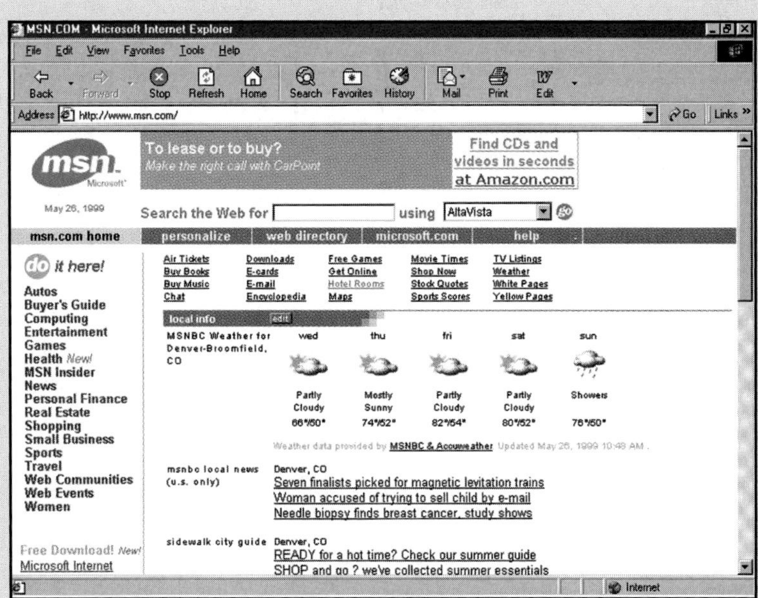

Figure 1.3
The Microsoft Network's Home Page.

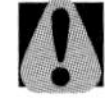

Changing Your Start Page
The page you see when you start Internet Explorer can be changed to a different page, so don't be alarmed if yours looks different from what you see in Figure 1.3. You will learn some of the customization options in the next lesson. Also, be aware that Web page content and look frequently change as the page evolves.

Lesson 2: Configuring Internet Explorer

Internet Explorer allows you to customize several options to be better able meet your needs. In this lesson, you'll look at some of these options. These options include ways to change your start-up page and to configure Internet Explorer to work with other programs (such as Outlook Express) that you'll use to send and receive email.

To Configure Internet Explorer

1. **Select Internet Options from the Tools menu to open the Internet Options dialog box, as shown in Figure 1.4.**

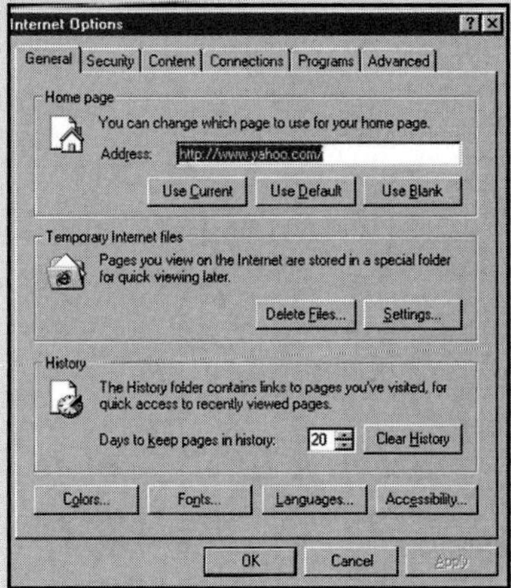

Figure 1.4
Internet Explorer allows you to customize your start-up options from the Internet Options dialog box.

continues ▶

To Configure Internet Explorer (continued)

2 In the section labeled Home page, type in the address of a page you would like to have as your default page. If you don't know of an address to use, type `http://www.yahoo.com`.

This sets the default home page to be that of Yahoo!, which is a popular Internet starting point.

3 Click OK to close the dialog box and return to the Microsoft Internet Explorer Home Page.

4 Locate the Home button in the toolbar, as shown in Figure 1.5

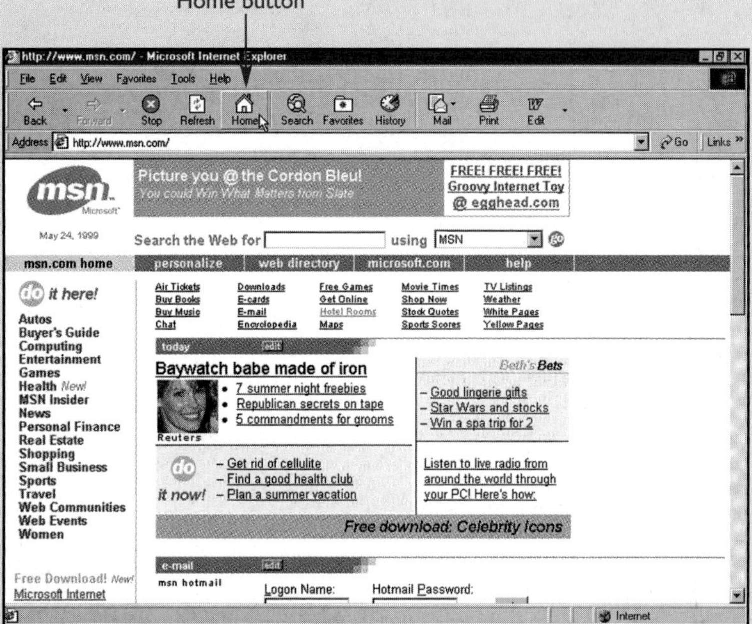

Figure 1.5
Clicking the Home button takes you to the home page you set in Step 2.

5 Click the Home button.

Internet Explorer takes you to the default home page you chose, in this case, Yahoo!

6 Select Internet Options from the Tools menu again to choose more customization options.

7 Click the Programs tab of the Internet Options dialog box, as shown in Figure 1.6.

As you work your way through this workbook, you'll call on many of the programs seen in this dialog box. Internet Explorer works with a variety of other programs to extend its functionality, and you should make sure that its options are set correctly now to avoid any confusion later.

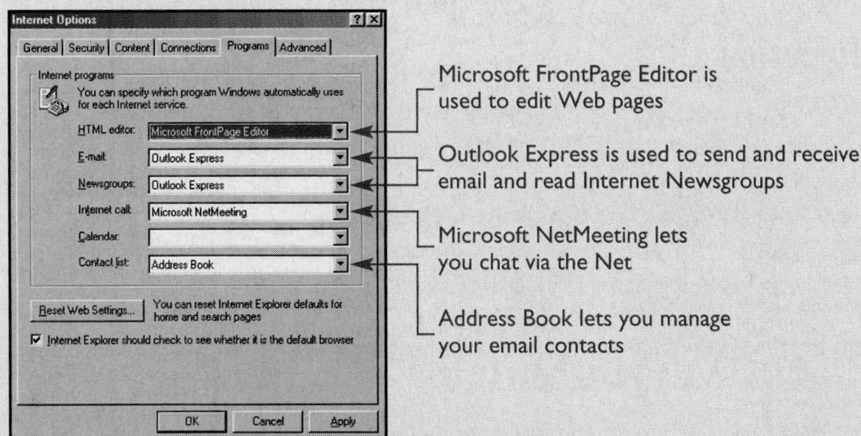

Figure 1.6
Select the Programs tab to view program options for Internet Explorer.

8 Use the drop-down menus to select the following options:

Table 1.1 Configuration Options for Internet Explorer

HTML Editor	FrontPage Editor
Email	Outlook Express
Newsgroups	Outlook Express
Internet Call	NetMeeting
Contact List	Address Book

You can leave the Calendar entry blank. When you are finished, your screen should look like Figure 1.6.

If you don't see some of these options in the drop-down menus, they may not have been installed during the installation of Windows 98. You will need to reinstall these components by using the original Windows 98 CD-ROM that came with your computer.

9 Click OK to close the dialog box and return to the home page.
Leave the home page onscreen and continue with the next lesson.

Using the Internet Options Dialog Box
There are a variety of other settings that you can explore from the Internet Options dialog box. Internet Explorer should work fine with the changes that you made. Feel free to explore other options in this dialog box.

Lesson 3: Navigating the World Wide Web Using Hyperlinks

With so much to see and so many places to go on the World Wide Web, how do you get from one site to another? One of the easiest and fastest ways is to use ***hyperlinks***. A hyperlink is a selectable piece of text found on a Web page. When a hyperlink is selected and activated (by clicking it with the mouse), it connects you to another World Wide Web page. When you navigate from one site to another by clicking a hyperlink, you are taken from page to page quickly and efficiently.

To Navigate the World Wide Web Using Hyperlinks

1. **Click the Home button found in the toolbar.**
   Because you set Yahoo! as your default home page, Internet Explorer opens that page. Yahoo! is a good jumping-off place for people who want to surf the Web. You'll use Yahoo! to learn how to navigate the Internet by using hyperlinks.

2. **Move the cursor over the words `Business & Economy`, as shown in Figure 1.7, and then click.**
   You will know that the cursor is in the correct place because it changes into a hand.

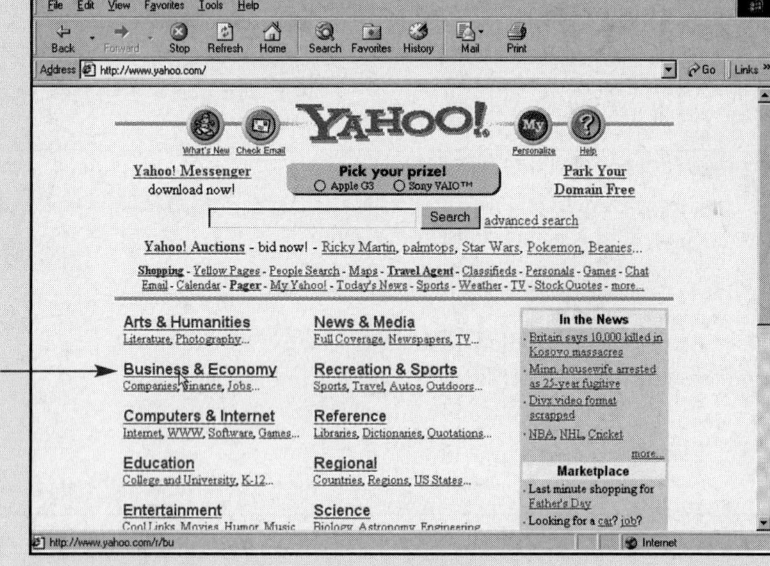

Figure 1.7
Clicking a hyperlink takes you to another page on the Web.

The Business & Economy hyperlink enables you to move to a topic-related Web page

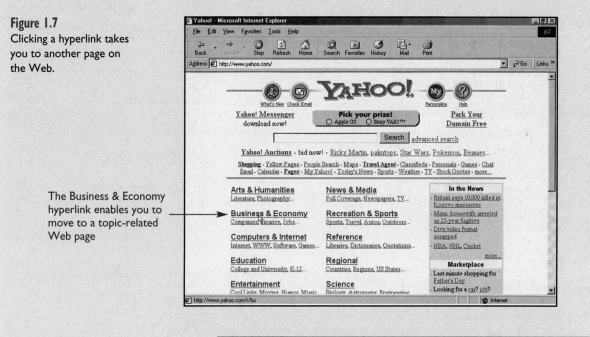

Identifying a Hyperlink
Notice that the words are blue and are underlined, signifying that this is a link to another page. Many (but not all) hyperlinks will appear this way.

A new page filled with more hyperlinks appears (see Figure 1.8).

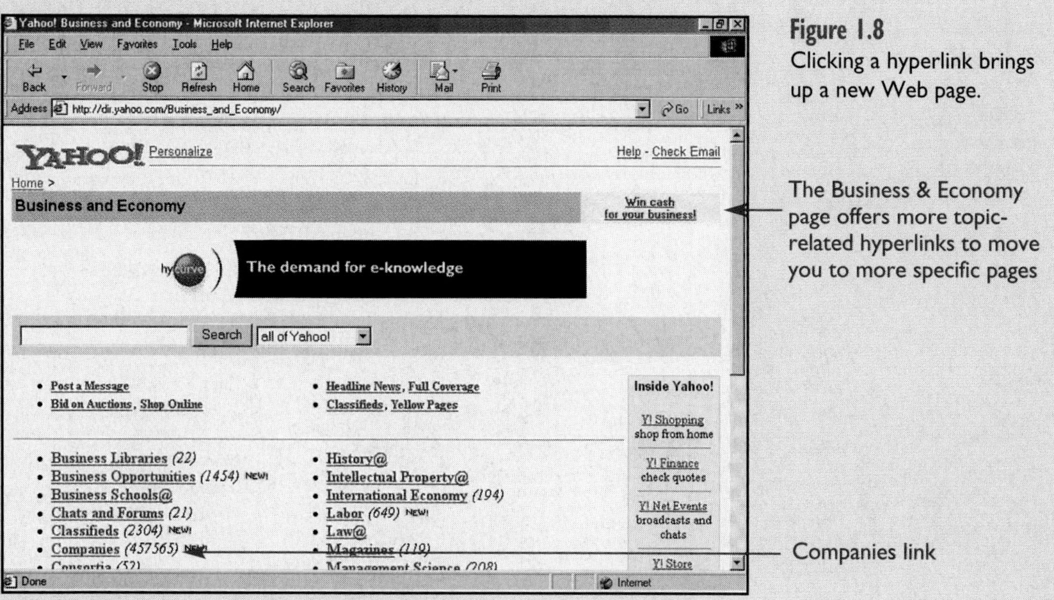

Figure 1.8
Clicking a hyperlink brings up a new Web page.

If you ever accidentally click a hyperlink and want to return to your original page, don't panic. Simply click the Back button found on the toolbar and you return to the previous page.

3. **Locate the Companies link on the page that appears, and then place your cursor over it and click (refer to Figure 1.8).**
   Nearly every page on the Web has a hyperlink on it, so there's always someplace new to go. Continue looking for links until you find the Prentice Hall home page.
4. **Find the Publishing link on the new page, and click again.**
5. **Scroll down the page, find the link that says `Prentice Hall`, and click one more time.**

   You're almost there. Because Prentice Hall has several different Web pages you can connect to, you have one more click to make.
6. **Click the link labeled `Home` to connect with the Prentice Hall Web page, as shown in Figure 1.9.**
   Take some time to explore the offerings there.

Pages Will Change
Web pages are constantly changing as the content is updated and designs are altered to make them more accessible. Don't be alarmed if the pages that you see look somewhat different from those shown in the figures in this workbook.

When you finish, click the Home button on the toolbar to return to the Yahoo! home page. Leave that page open and continue with the next lesson.

continues ▶

To Navigate the World Wide Web Using Hyperlinks (continued)

Figure 1.9
Follow the links to connect with the Prentice Hall Web page.

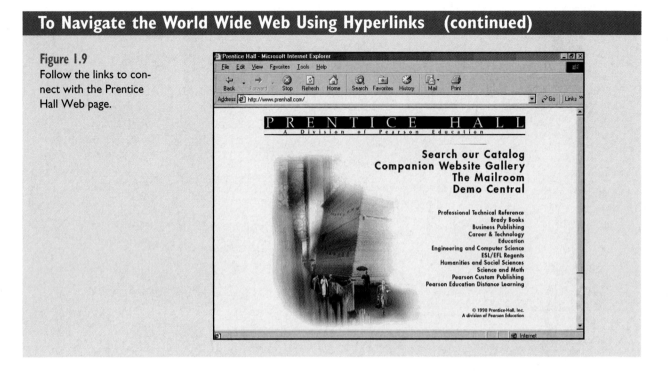

Lesson 4: Navigating the World Wide Web Using URLs

Sometimes, it is fine to explore the Internet by simply clicking hyperlinks and hoping to find something interesting. More often than not, you will. There will be other times, however, when you want to connect with a specific site identified by its ***URL***, or Uniform Resource Locator. This is an address on the World Wide Web that usually begins with `http://`.

To Navigate the World Wide Web Using URLs

1. **Place the cursor in the Address box in Internet Explorer, and click (see Figure 1.10).**
   This box is also known as the location box, and it is where you type in the address of a site you want to visit.
2. **Select the existing text in the address box by holding down the mouse button and dragging the cursor over the text. Then, press Del.**
   This erases the existing text and you are ready to type in a new address.
3. **Type `http://www.colorado.edu`, and press ↵Enter.**
   The home page of the University of Colorado in Boulder appears on your screen, as shown in Figure 1.11.

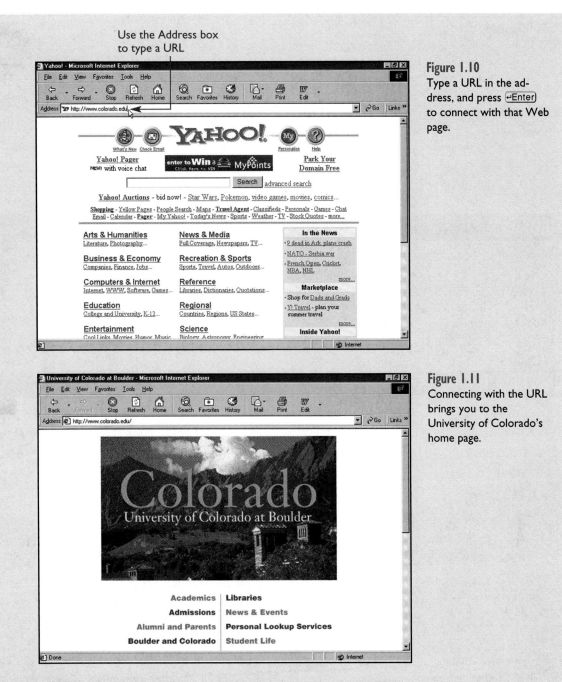

Figure 1.10
Type a URL in the address, and press ↵Enter to connect with that Web page.

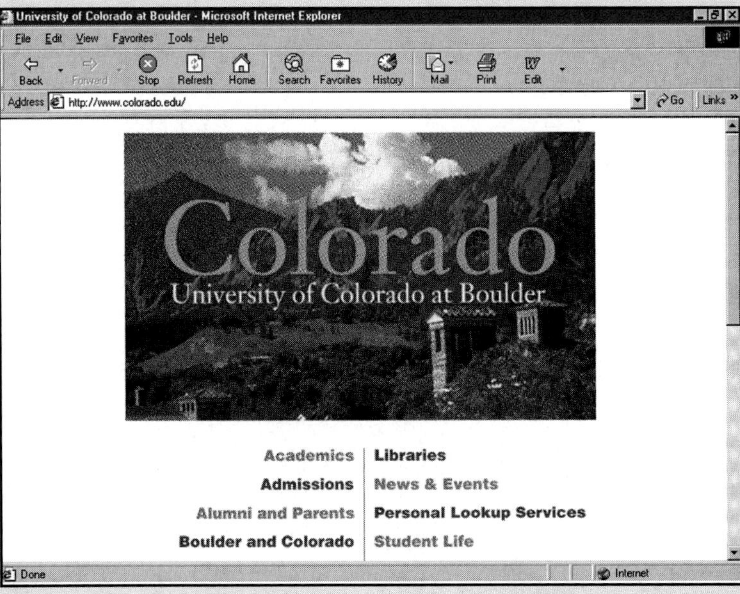

Figure 1.11
Connecting with the URL brings you to the University of Colorado's home page.

4 Use the URLs supplied in Table 1.2 to practice connecting to Web sites by typing in URLs in the Address box. Press ↵Enter after you type in each one to move to that location.

Table 1.2 Some Useful Internet Addresses to Visit

http://www.excite.com	Excite.com—another useful jumping-off point
http://www.msn.com	Microsoft home page
http://www.mcp.com	Home page of Macmillan Computer Publishing
http://www.whitehouse.gov	The White House home page
http://www.billboard.com	Billboard Online

Entering a URL

Although the http:// is an official part of the Internet address of these sites, it is not necessary to type that part of the address. Simply typing www.whitehouse.gov in the address box is enough to get you to the White House Web page. Your Web browser will complete the address for you and include the http://.

Summary

Congratulations! You successfully learned how to surf the Internet using Internet Explorer. You learned that there are different ways of getting around the Web, either by clicking hyperlinks that are a part of every Web page, or by typing in a URL in the address box. To expand on your knowledge, spend a few minutes exploring Help on these topics. Additionally, complete some of the Skill Drills, Challenge, and Discovery Zone exercises.

Checking Concepts and Terms

True/False

For each of the following, check *T* or *F* to indicate whether the statement is true or false.

__T __F **1.** Hyperlinks are always blue and underlined. [L3]

__T __F **2.** It is not necessary to type in the http:// when entering a URL in Internet Explorer's Address box. [L4]

__T __F **3.** You know that you've placed the cursor correctly over a hyperlink because it changes into a hand. [L3]

__T __F **4.** Web page content never changes and always looks the same. [L1]

__T __F **5.** To connect directly with an Internet site, you can type the URL directly in the address box. [L4]

Multiple Choice

Circle the letter of the correct answer for each of the following.

1. Internet Explorer works with other programs to do what? [L2]

a. send and receive email

b. read discussion newsgroups

c. chat

d. all of the above

2. What is a URL? [L4]

a. an Internet Browser

b. a graphics file type commonly found on the Web

c. an Internet Web address

d. an email address

3. The Address box is also sometimes referred to as what? [L4]
   a. Universal Resource Locator
   b. URL box
   c. location box
   d. none of the above

4. How do you recognize an Internet Web address? [L4]
   a. It always begins with Internet.
   b. It contains the @ character.
   c. It begins with http://.
   d. all of the above

5. Which of the following is an example of a valid URL? [L4]
   a. http://www.yahoo.com
   b. clarkd@bvsd.k12.co.us
   c. http://www.yahoo com
   d. all of the above

Screen ID

Identify each of the items shown in Figure 1.12.

Figure 1.12

A. Address box
B. Hyperlinks
C. Menu bar
D. Toolbar
E. URL

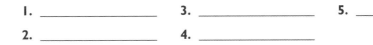

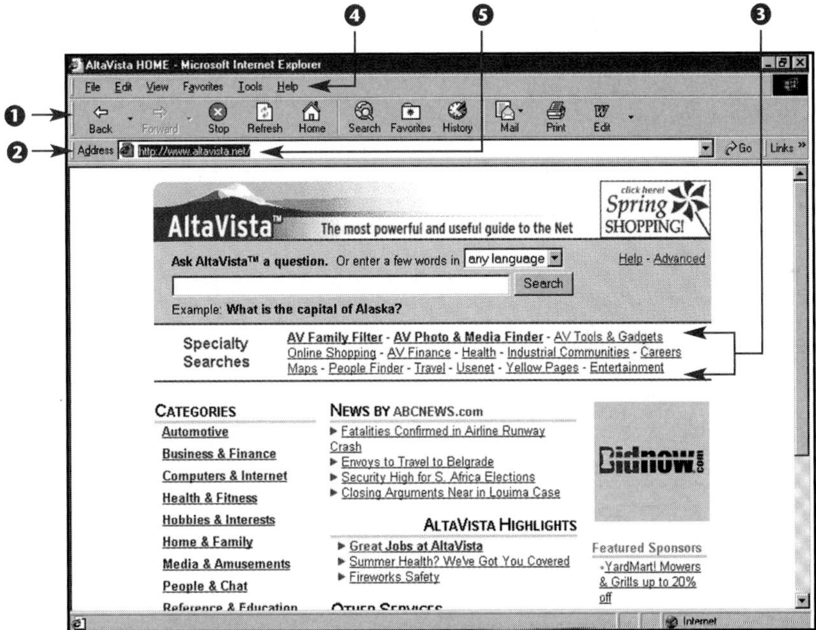

1. ____________ 3. ____________ 5. ____________

2. ____________ 4. ____________

Discussion Questions

1. What kind of topics might you want to have as part of your customized start-up page?
2. Why would a Web page look different from the last time you visited it? Who might have changed the page?
3. How do hyperlinks make your Web search easier? What is an alternative to using hyperlinks?

Skill Drill

Skill Drill exercises reinforce project skills. Each skill that is reinforced is the same, or nearly the same, as a skill presented in the project. Detailed instructions are provided in a step-by-step format.

1. Starting a Web Browser

There is more than one way to open Internet Explorer. If you are unable to locate a desktop icon, don't panic.

1. Move the mouse until it reaches the Start button in the lower-left corner of your screen.
2. Click once.
3. Using the mouse, highlight Programs in the pop-up menu that appears.
4. In the next menu that appears, search for Internet Explorer.
5. Move the mouse to highlight Internet Explorer.
6. Click once.

2. Configuring Internet Explorer

Internet Explorer has a nifty feature called AutoComplete. When this is enabled, Explorer tries to guess what you are trying to type in the address box and other places, and fills in the rest for you. This is especially useful for those long URLs that never seem to end.

1. Select Internet Options from the Tools Menu.
2. Click the Content tab.
3. Click the AutoComplete button under the Personal Information section.
4. Make sure that the box next to Web Address is checked.
5. If you are on a shared computer, uncheck the box next to usernames and passwords on forms. You don't want this information stored on a computer that is used by someone else.

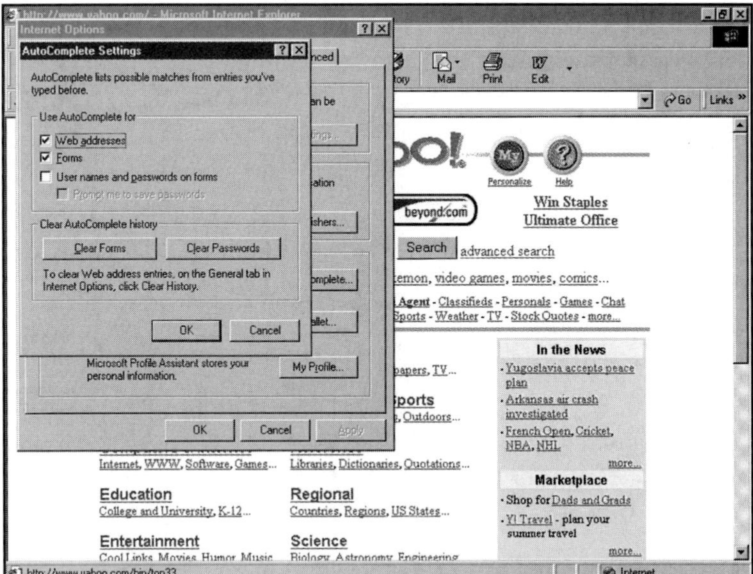

Figure 1.13
AutoComplete makes your online life much easier.

6. Click OK. You return to the Internet Options window.
7. Click OK again to close the Internet Options.

3. Navigating the World Wide Web via Hyperlinks

1. Start Internet Explorer if it is not already open.
2. Locate at least three hyperlinks on the page that appears.
3. Select one and click it. You will go to that link's location.
4. Click the Back button in the Internet Explorer's toolbar. You return to the original page.
5. Repeat this procedure with the two other hyperlinks you identified on the page.

4. Navigating the World Wide Web via URLs

1. Start Internet Explorer if it is not already open.
2. Locate the Address box just below the Toolbar.
3. Type `http://www.amazon.com` and press ↵Enter. You go to the Amazon.com Web site.
4. Practice this procedure with other URLs you have seen in this book or elsewhere.

Challenge

Challenge exercises expand on or are somewhat related to skills presented in the lessons. Each exercise provides a brief narrative introduction, followed by instructions in a numbered-step format that are not as detailed as those in the Skill Drill section.

1. Using the Help Files in Internet Explorer

Internet Explorer provides online help if you encounter a problem whose answer isn't obvious. You can access this help utility from the Internet Explorer menu bar. Using the Help window, find answers to the following.

- How to browse Web pages while not being connected to the Internet
- How to protect yourself and your computer from software that is potentially damaging
- How to quickly find Web pages that you recently visited
- How to print the contents of a Web page

2. Exploring the Internet Explorer Toolbar

Internet Explorer has a variety of buttons on the toolbar that perform different functions. Getting familiar with the toolbar functions can make your browsing experience a good deal easier and more pleasant.

1. Using the mouse, place the cursor over each of the buttons available in the toolbar and click. Observe what happens.
2. Place the cursor in the toolbar, and hold down the right mouse button. A pop-up menu appears. Explore the options for customizing the look and feel of the toolbar.

3. Creating an Offline Presentation

You need to do a presentation of ways to navigate the Internet by using Internet Explorer. However, you are not sure that you will have an active Internet connection. You decide to download several Web pages onto your local hard drive for viewing.

1. Open Internet Explorer if it isn't already open.
2. Click the Home button found on the toolbar return to your default home page. You'll save this site for offline browsing.
3. Select Add to Favorites from the Favorites menu item.
4. Make sure that the box next to Make Available Offline is checked, as shown in Figure 1.14.
5. Click OK. For more advanced options, click the customize button and explore the offerings found there.

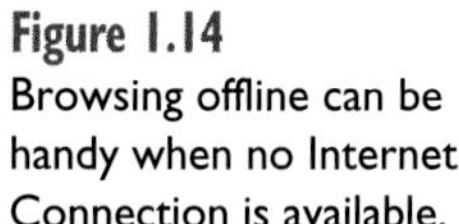

Figure 1.14
Browsing offline can be handy when no Internet Connection is available.

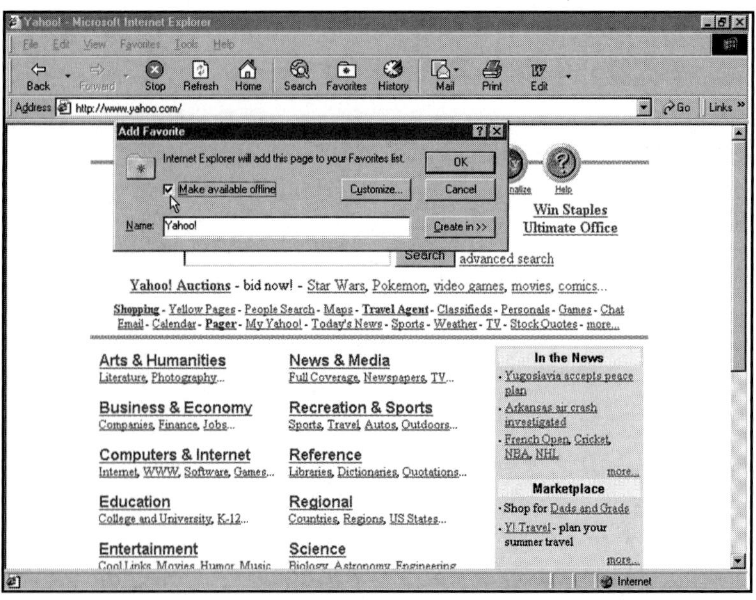

Discovery Zone

Discovery Zone exercises require an advanced knowledge of topics presented in *Essentials* lessons, the application of skills from multiple lessons, or self-directed learning of new skills.

1. Working with Keyboard Shortcuts

By learning keyboard shortcuts, you can make more efficient use of your time while in Internet Explorer. Spend some time exploring how to navigate the Internet without using the mouse.

By using keyboard shortcuts, you can perform the following functions:

- Save the contents of a Web page to your local hard drive.
- Print the contents of a Web page.
- Refresh the current window.
- Scroll through the contents of the current page without using the mouse. (*Hint*: Look in the Help Utility to find a list of keyboard shortcuts.)

2. Preparing a News Summary of the Day

You need to create a summary of the news of the day for a class project. You know that by customizing your start-up page at msn.com you will have access to a variety of offerings by some of the best news organizations in the world. Spend some time reorganizing your start-up page to display the news.

Next, browse through the news from these different organizations and save/print items that you think might be useful for preparing your summary.

3. Check the Weather in Istanbul (or Anywhere)

You're being sent out of town and want to find out the weather and local happenings in Miami (you can choose another town located far from where you are). Use the options available on the msn.com page to explore the local news and weather in that area. Look for entertainment and restaurant listings, as well.

Project 2

Using Email

Objectives

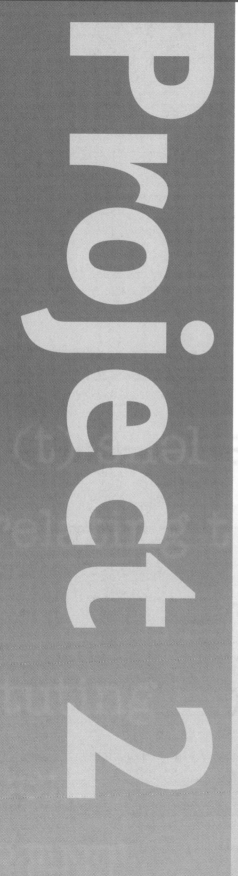

In this project, you learn how to

- ➤ Start Outlook Express
- ➤ Configure Outlook Express
- ➤ Compose and Send an Email Message
- ➤ Read the Mail in Your Inbox
- ➤ Reply, Forward, Save, and Delete Mail
- ➤ Manage an Address Book

Key terms introduced in this project include

- HTTP
- Inbox
- IMAP
- mail server
- pane
- POP

SOURCE: *Essentials: Internet, 4/e, Clark*

Why Would I Do This?

Without the communications aspect, the Internet is nothing but a big shopping mall. The capability to communicate with anyone who has an email address and to do it with the immediacy that email provides is nothing short of a revolution. It has changed the way we do business, the way we study, and the way we learn.

Email is the primary tool you use to communicate with other people on the Internet. Using email, you can correspond with friends and relatives. You can also ask for advice on a variety of topics—from pet care to the purchase of a new car.

An email message can travel from North America to Antarctica in less than a second. It doesn't take much longer that that for a message to travel all around the world with optimum conditions and connections. When set up properly, email is more immediate and more precise than other forms of communication.

Many different programs are used to send and receive email. In this project, you learn how to send and receive email by using Outlook Express 5. Outlook Express 5 comes prepackaged with the second edition of Windows 98. If you have an earlier version of Windows 98, you may need to upgrade.

Visual Summary

To get started with reading and sending email, you need to know your way around the Outlook Express program. There are three basic panes you should learn how to navigate. The Mail Account pane (also called the Folder list) lists your email accounts and folders. The Message List lists the emails waiting to be read, and the Preview pane displays your email message. These three basic panes are shown in Figure 2.1.

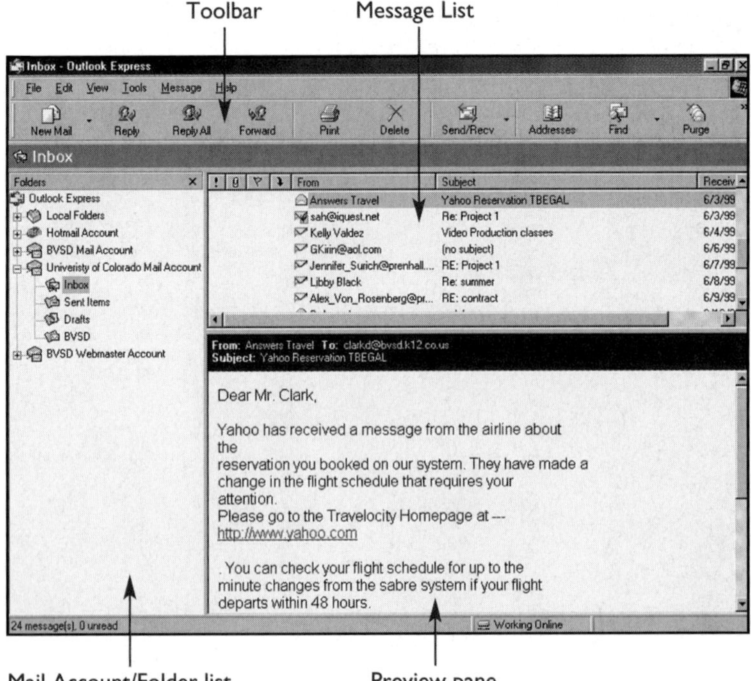

Figure 2.1
You can use Outlook Express to send and receive email.

Lesson 1: Starting Outlook Express

To use Outlook Express to send and receive email over the Internet, you need to first establish an email account, which is provided by your Internet Service Provider. Your email address will look something like this:

```
clarkd@bvsd.k12.co.us
```

Sending email is a simple task, as long as you know the address of the person you want to send it to. Not all email addresses are easy to read, but they make sense if you know how to break them down. An email address is a combination of letters, numbers, and symbols. They always include an @ sign and at least one period. Table 2.1 breaks down an email address within the Boulder Valley School District.

Table 2.1 Examination of the Email Address clarkd@bvsd.k12.co.us

Address Part	What It Means
clarkd	The login name used to connect to the Internet.
@	Every Internet email address has one of these symbols, called an "at" sign.
bvsd	The name of the computer that this user connects to.
k12	The school district of this email address services kindergarten through 12th grade.
co	That school district is in Colorado.
us	It is also in the United States.

The information before the @ sign is the username; the information after @ gives the location. There should never be a space in an email address.

You can tell a lot from an email address. For example, sometimes you can tell which country someone is from by the suffix in the address. Table 2.2 lists just a few geographical email suffixes.

Table 2.2 Geographical Explanation of Email Suffixes

Suffix	Location
au	Australia
at	Austria
ca	Canada
de	Germany
dk	Denmark
fi	Finland
fr	France
uk	United Kingdom
us	United States

Not all addresses are geographically designed. Some email addresses tell you the nature of the organization. For example, the following address is a valid email address:

```
dclark@mcp.com
```

The .com at the end tells you that mcp is a commercial site on the Internet. (In this case, it's Macmillan Computer Publishing.) If your connection is through your school or university, there is a good chance that your email address ends in .edu, which stands for education.

For example, the following email address tells you that the address is housed at an educational institution:

```
dclark@stripe.colorado.edu
```

Table 2.3 lists some other common email suffixes, by usage.

Table 2.3 Meanings of Common Email Suffixes

Suffix	Use
.gov	Government
.com	Commercial organization
.mil	Military
.net	Network resources
.org	Nonprofit organizations (usually)
.edu	Educational institution

To continue with this project, you need to know your email address.

If you don't have an email address or aren't sure what it is, don't panic. Outlook Express can help you create one with hotmail.com. Select Hotmail from the Tools/New Account Signup menu item. Follow the dialog boxes as they appear and provide the information when asked.

If you go this route, you can skip Lesson 2 because your account will be automatically configured for you.

To Start Outlook Express

1. **To Start Outlook Express, locate the Outlook Express icon on your desktop, as shown in Figure 2.2.**
   During the installation process, Windows 98 automatically created a shortcut to Outlook Express on the desktop.

If you can't locate a shortcut to Outlook Express on the desktop, look under the Start Menu/Programs items in the lower-left corner of your screen. There may be an option to start Outlook Express there as well.

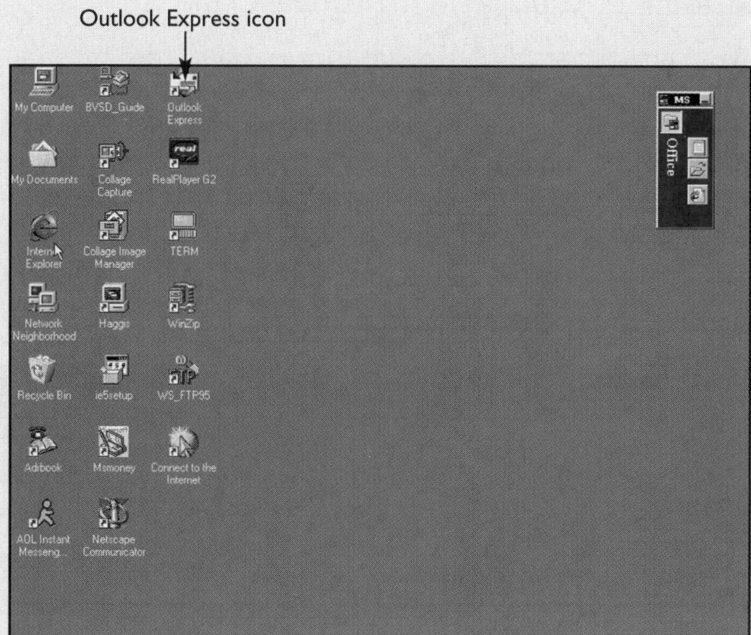

Figure 2.2
Look for the Outlook Express icon on your desktop.

Outlook Express versus Outlook
Outlook Express comes bundled with the Windows 98 Operating system. Another program, Microsoft Outlook, also is used to send and receive email. This program is the commercial version of Outlook and comes bundled with Microsoft Office. Microsoft Outlook looks and feels very different from Outlook Express.

2 Double-click the icon to activate the program. In a few seconds Outlook Express will appear. Your window should look similar to Figure 2.3.

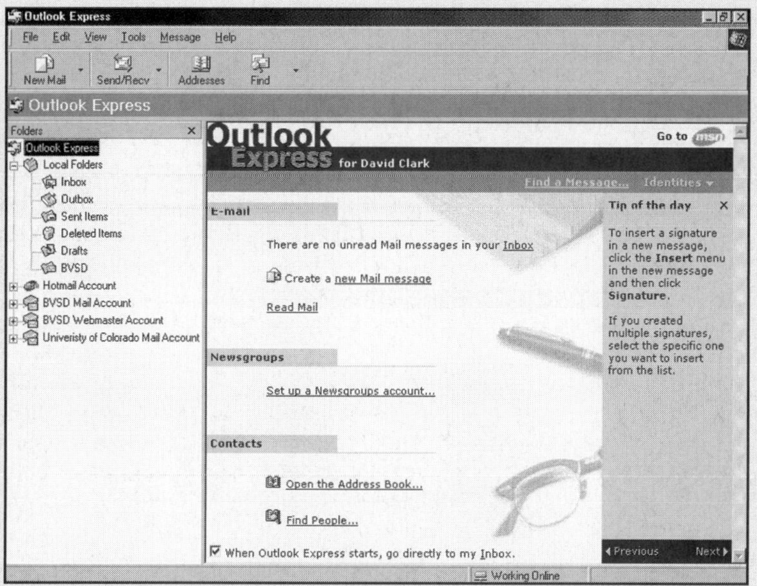

Figure 2.3
Outlook Express makes it simple to send and receive email.

Lesson 2: Configuring Outlook Express

Before you can start sending and receiving email, you need to supply Outlook Express with some information. Specifically, it needs to know where to look for your email. To check your email, you need to first establish a connection with the server, as described in Project 1, "Getting Started with the Internet." You also need to know the address of your mail server. A ***mail server*** is a computer on the Internet, where your email will be delivered. It is always active, so email can be delivered any time day or night.

The address of your mail server will be supplied by your Internet Service Provider. It will most likely be the latter part of your email address, following the @ sign.

To Configure Outlook Express

1 Select Accounts from the Tools menu to open the Internet Accounts dialog box, as shown in Figure 2.4.

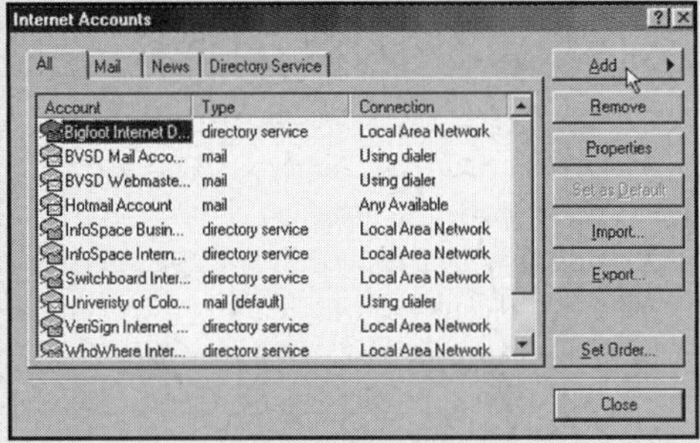

Figure 2.4
Click the Add button to add a new mail account.

2 Click the Add button.
A popup menu appears.

3 Because you are creating a mail account, select Mail from the options that appear. By doing so, you activate the Internet Connection Wizard.
This handy utility walks you through the steps of configuring Outlook Express so you can read your email.

4 Fill in your name in the first Internet Connection Wizard dialog box, as shown in Figure 2.5.
This is the name that will appear in the From: field in email you send.

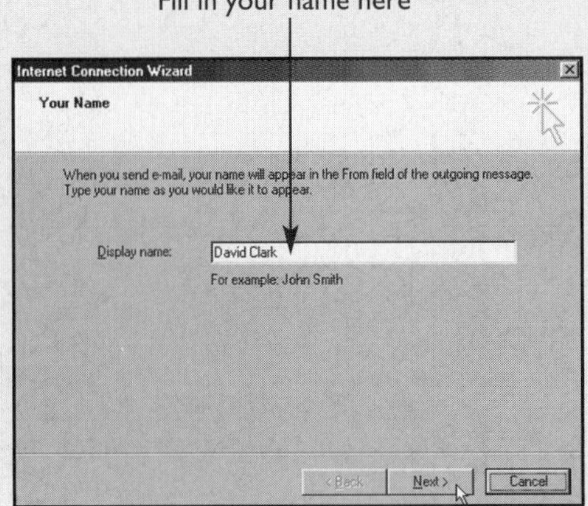

Figure 2.5
The name you fill in appears in the From: field when you send email.

5 Click Next to move to the next dialog box in the Internet Connection Wizard.

6 Fill in your email address in the dialog box that appears, and then click Next.

In the next dialog box that appears, you have an email server decision to make. You need to make this decision based on the service provided by your Internet Service Provider. Do you want to use IMAP, POP, or HTTP as your mail service? And what's the difference between them?

POP Goes Your Email

Selecting ***POP*** allows you to download all of your email to your local hard drive. (POP stands for Post Office Protocol.) It removes the email from the server (unless specifically told to leave copies of the mail on the server). You can then read your mail without being connected to the Internet. If you read your email from only a single connected computer, this is a good option.

An ***IMAP*** server downloads only the headers of the email stored on the server, such as the subject, sender's name, and so on. (IMAP stands for Internet Message Access Protocol.) After you select an email message, the IMAP client (in this case, Outlook Express) transfers a copy of that message, leaving it on the server. IMAP clients start more quickly because they retrieve only the headers of your messages. When you delete a message from your Inbox, it deletes it off the server. IMAP is a good choice if you read your mail from multiple computers (for example, one at home and one at work), because the mail stays on the server until you delete it. It also does not use as much local hard drive space.

HTTP servers are used for Web-based email services such as hotmail.com. HTTP, which stands for Hypertext Transfer Protocol, is the way information is transferred via the World Wide Web. This type of email can be checked via the Web by connecting with the site's URL.

Many Internet service providers offer both IMAP and POP. The rest of this project uses IMAP as the example. If this option isn't supported by your Internet Service Provider, you may need to switch over to POP.

7 Select IMAP from the drop-down menu, as shown in Figure 2.6.

Make your email server choice here

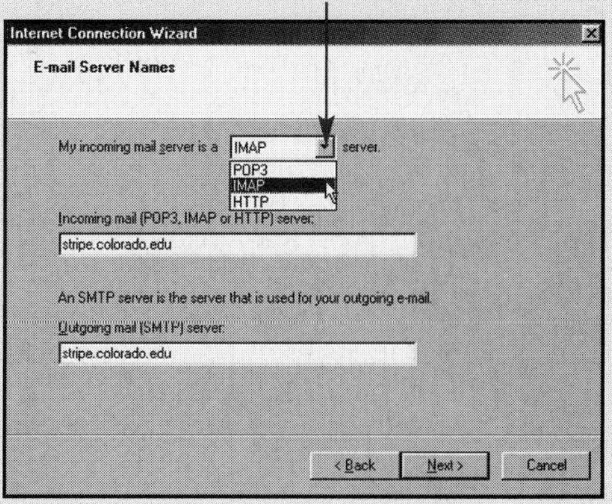

Figure 2.6
You have three choices of mail server types.

continues ▶

To Configure Outlook Express (continued)

8 Fill in the name of your IMAP server.

In most cases, this is the last part of your email address. For example, if your email address is bclinton@whitehouse.gov, use whitehouse.gov as your IMAP server.

9 Fill in your Outgoing mail (SMTP) server.

In most cases, this is the same value as your POP or IMAP server. Click Next to advance to the next Internet Connection Wizard dialog box, as shown in Figure 2.7.

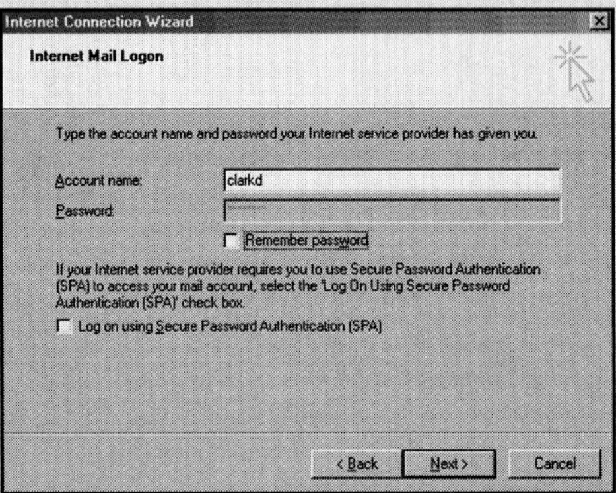

Figure 2.7
Enter your account name and password.

10 Add your login and password, and then click Next.

Your login is the first part of your email address. Using the previous example, you would fill in bclinton. Your Internet Service Provider supplies you with your password when you first create your Internet access account. Click Next to advance to the next dialog box, as shown in Figure 2.8.

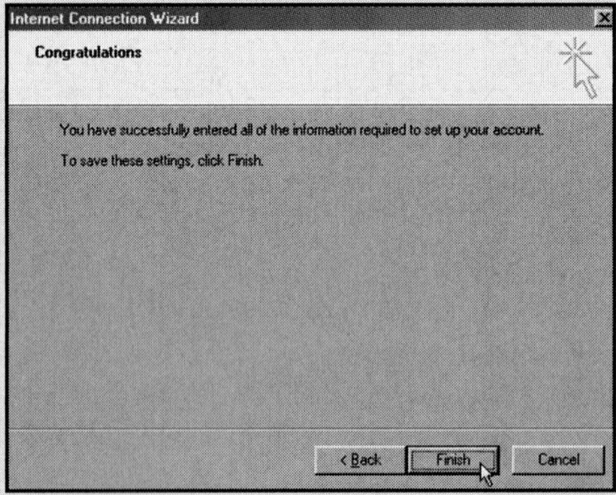

Figure 2.8
Click Finish to create your account.

11 Click Finish. Outlook Express creates your mail account. You are now asked ask you if you want it to download the folder list for your IMAP account. Click Yes.

Outlook Express creates a connection with your server, and downloads the folders and mail that already may exist on your account.

Protecting Your Privacy

If you are using a shared computer, such as one in a computer lab, be sure to erase the information you placed in the configuration windows (especially your login name and password) before you leave. Otherwise, anyone can read your email from this machine.

Leave Outlook Express onscreen and continue with the next lesson.

Lesson 3: Composing and Sending an Email Message

You now use Outlook Express to create an email message and send it. Before you can send email, you need to make sure that you have an active connection to the Internet. This means that you are in a networked lab with a direct connection to the Internet or you have established a dialup connection in accordance with the instructions provided by your Internet Service Provider.

Choosing Your Email Format

Before composing email, decide what format you want your email to be in. Under the Format menu item, you have two choices: Rich Text (HTML) and Plain Text.

If you select Rich Text, you can use different fonts and colors and a variety of other effects. However, not all email programs can view these effects, so the resulting email message may appear with a good deal of garbage included. If you're not sure what email program your recipient is using or if it is capable of reading all the whistles and bells that Outlook Express has to offer, make sure that the Plain Text option is selected.

To Compose and Send an Email Message

1. **In the Mail Account pane on the left-hand side of the screen, click once on your new email account name, as shown in Figure 2.9 (this step is only necessary if you have multiple email accounts). Click the New Message button.**
2. **The New Message window displays (see Figure 2.10), for you to type in your email information.**
   The From: field is filled in with your own email address.
3. **In the To: field, type in your own email address.**
   Because this may be your first email message, you can send one to yourself for practice. This will also give you an email in your Inbox for later, when you learn how to read your email.
4. **Place the cursor in the Subject: field and fill in a subject.**
   The subject contains a few words to give the recipient an idea of what the message is about. If you can't think of anything to put there, type `Hello`.

continues ▶

To Compose and Send an Email Message (continued)

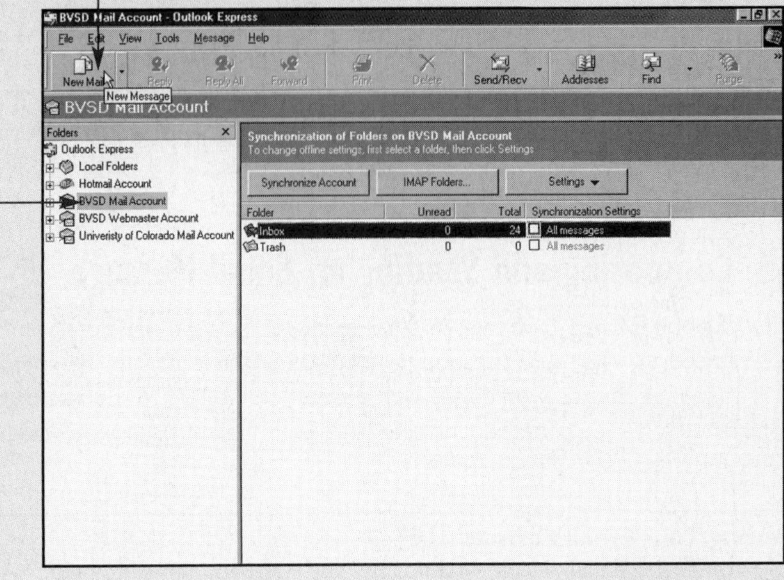

Figure 2.9
Click Compose New Mail to create a new email message.

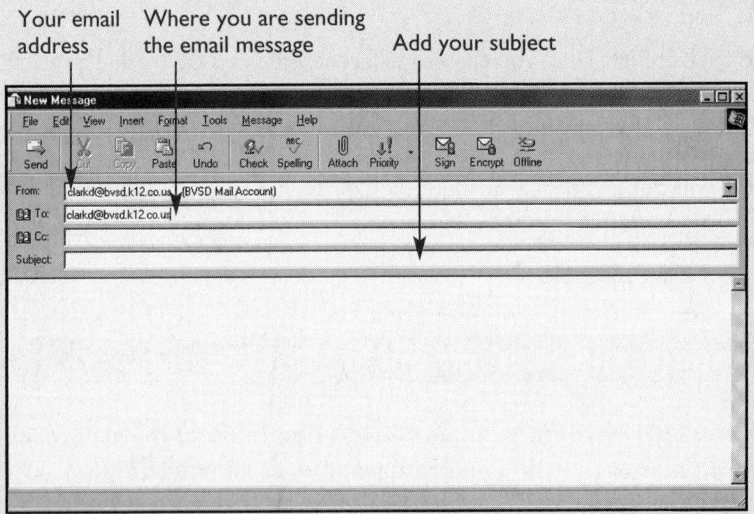

Figure 2.10
Type your recipient's address in the To: field.

Sending Carbon Copy Emails

The cc: field refers to carbon copy, and it's used just like with business letters. You can enter a second address in this field, and a copy of the message will be sent to it.

The bcc: field stands for blind carbon copy. You can enter an address in here as well. However, the original recipient will not be able to tell that a copy of your email has been sent to the second address. The bcc: address will not be visible in his or her message.

5 **Place the cursor in the message body, directly below the Subject: field, and type `This is my first email!!!`.**

When you finish, the window should look like Figure 2.11.

Click here to send   Your email message displays here

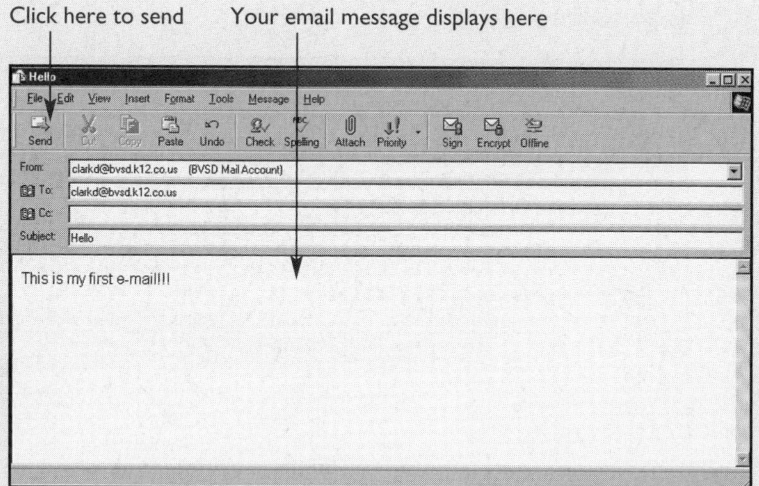

Figure 2.11
Your message appears in the message window.

6 Click the Send button.
Your first email message is on its way!

If you receive an error message, saying that your email is undeliverable, check first to make sure that the email address was entered correctly. Check also to make sure that the SMTP and IMAP/POP server information was entered correctly. To check that information do the following:

1. Right-click on your connection name in the Mail Account/Folder pane.
2. Select Properties from the pop-up menu.
3. Click on the Servers Tab in the window that appears.
4. Check to make sure the information is correct.
5. Click OK to close the window.

Leave Outlook Express onscreen and continue with the next lesson.

Lesson 4: Reading the Mail in Your Inbox

You should now have an email in your ***Inbox***, which is the listing of email messages you have waiting to be read. Use the email you sent to yourself in the last lesson to learn how to access your email.

Looking Through the Outlook Panes
By default, the Outlook Express window divides itself into three sections called ***panes***. The pane on the left lists your mail accounts and folders. The upper-right pane contains a list of the mail in your mailbox. The lower-right pane shows a preview of the message itself. These panes can be resized by placing the cursor on the dividing line between the sections until the cursor becomes a double arrow. Drag the mouse to resize the pane, as shown in Figure 2.12.

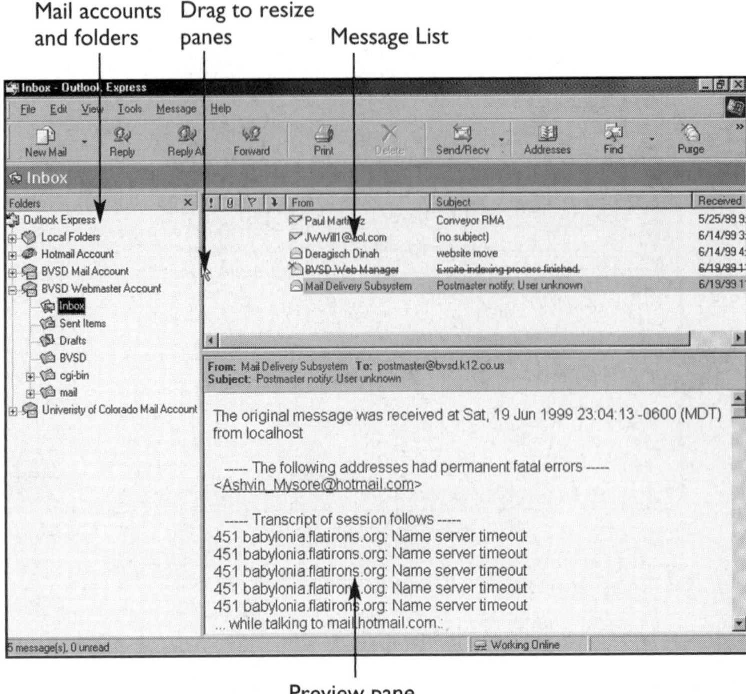

Figure 2.12
Drag to resize the panes.

To Read the Mail in Your Inbox

1. **Locate your email account in the mail accounts and folder pane. Click once on the plus symbol next to it.**
   A list of the available folders appears, including Inbox. If a minus symbol exists instead of a plus sign, your folders are already visible, so you can skip this step.

2. **Click Inbox one time.**
   A list of available messages appears in the Message List pane, as shown in Figure 2.13.

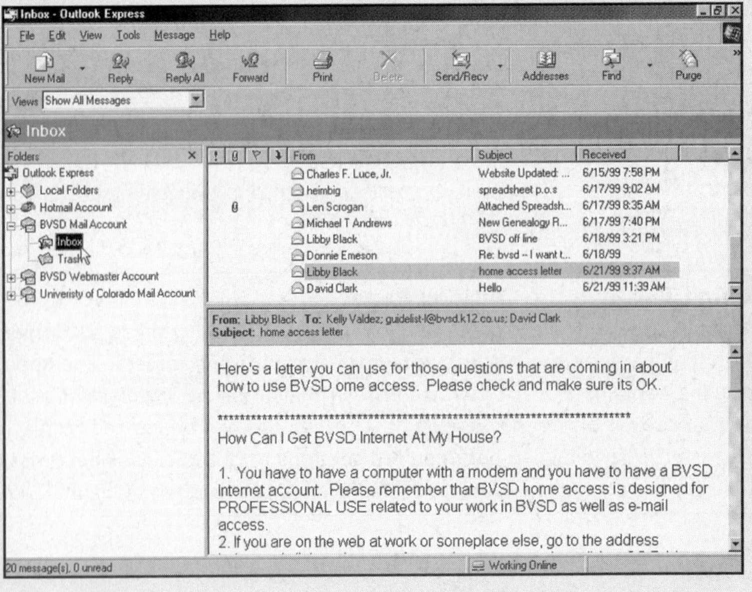

Figure 2.13
Click on Inbox to bring up a list of messages waiting to be read.

❸ **Click the message you sent to yourself in Lesson 3.**
You recognize this message because it has your name in the From: column. The message appears in the pane directly below.

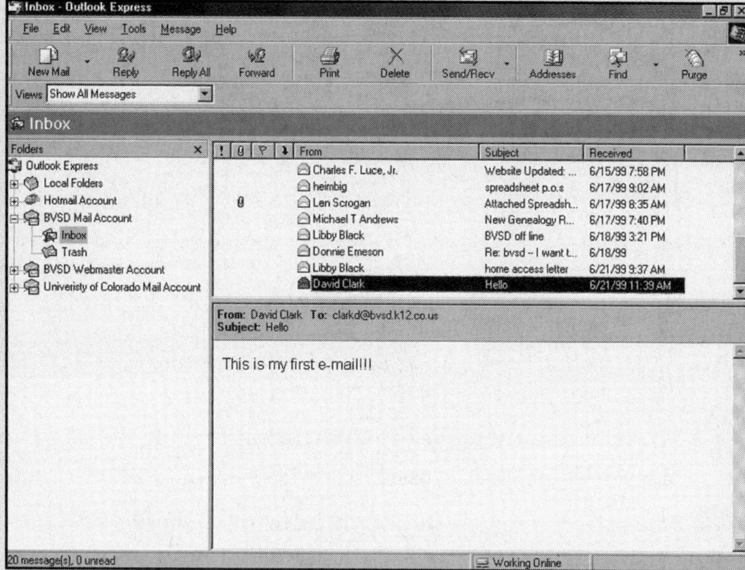

Figure 2.14
Reading your mail.

❹ **Double-click the message name in the Message List.**
It appears in a new window for easier reading this time, as shown in Figure 2.15. If the message is short, reading it in the preview pane will do just fine, but for longer messages, a full window works better.

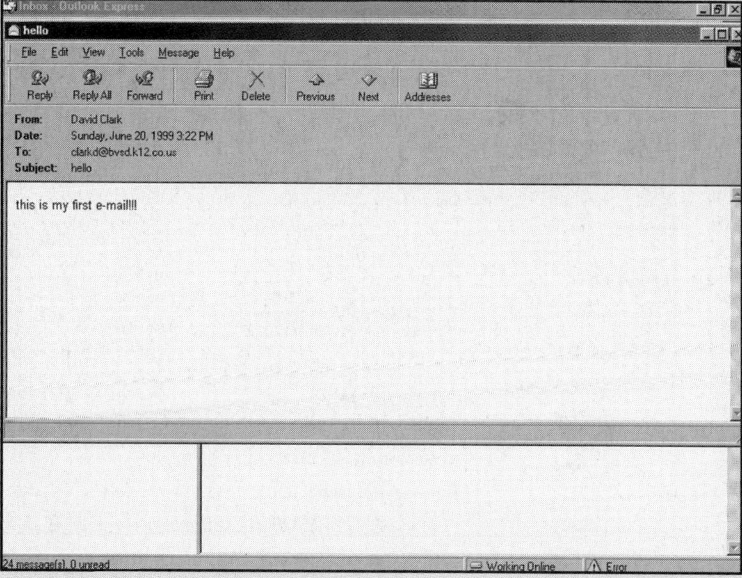

Figure 2.15
Double-clicking the message brings up a new window.

Leave Outlook Express onscreen and continue with the next lesson.

Lesson 5: Replying, Forwarding, Saving, and Deleting Mail

Now that you have started to receive email, the next step is to figure out what to do with it. You have several options, as shown in Table 2.4.

Table 2.4 Email Options

Option	Use
Reply	Respond to the author of the message
Forward	Send the message to a different user
Save	Copy the message into a folder for future reference
Delete	Get rid of the message altogether

To Reply, Forward, Save, and Delete Mail

1. **To reply to a message, double-click it in your Message List.**
   A new window opens, displaying the message.

2. **Place the cursor on the Reply button, as shown in Figure 2.16, and click once.**
   The To: field is filled in for you, as is the Subject: field. The cursor is placed in the message field, and you are ready to start typing your reply.

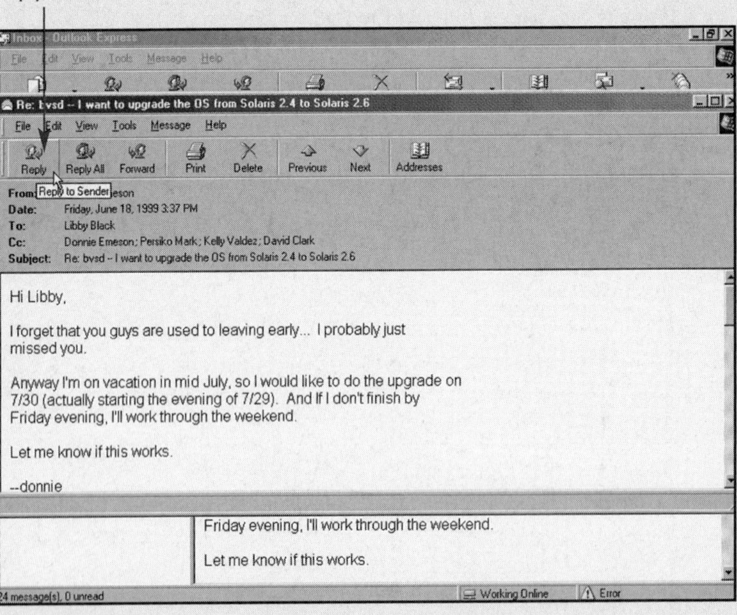

Figure 2.16
Click the Reply button to respond to an email.

Changing the Subject
Although the Subject: field is automatically filled in for you, you can change what is there by placing the cursor in the field, erasing the contents, and filling in a new subject.

❸ **Type a reply in the message body.**
Notice that the original message is included in your reply. You can erase it by highlighting it and pressing (Del).

❹ **Click Send.**
The message is sent.

❺ **To forward a message, double-click it in your Inbox.**
A new window opens up, displaying the message.

❻ **Place the cursor on the forward icon, as shown in Figure 2.17, and click.**
The cursor is placed in the To: field. The Subject: field is filled in for you.

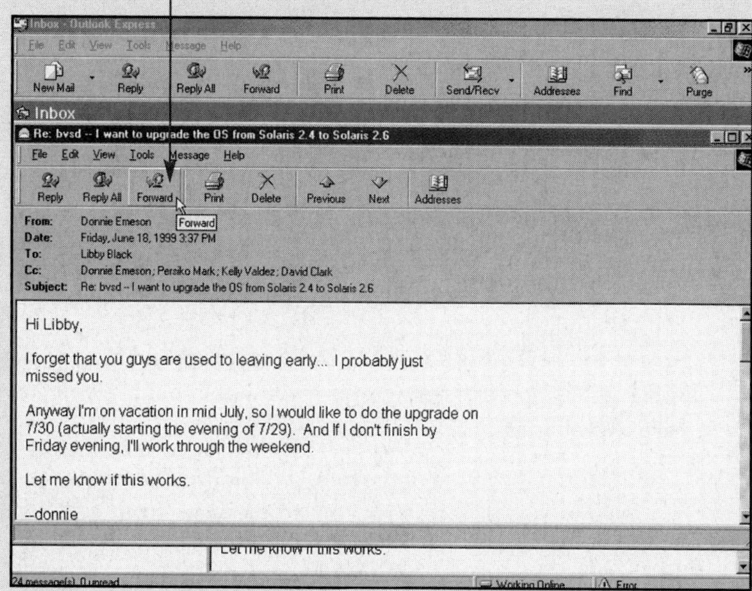

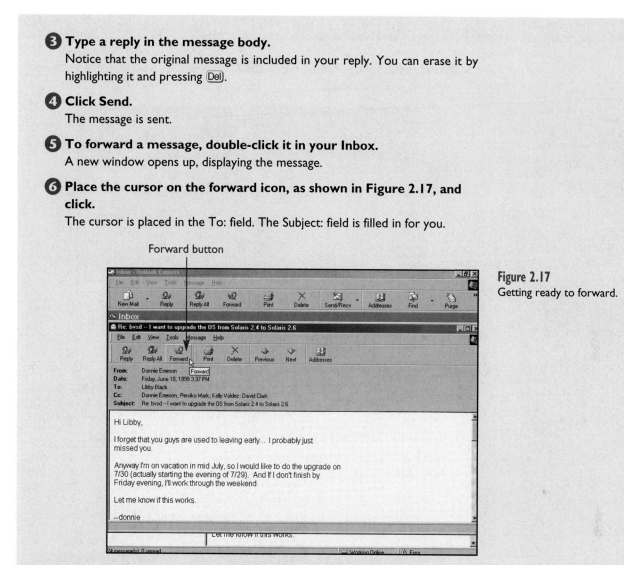

Figure 2.17
Getting ready to forward.

❼ **Fill in an email address that you want to forward the message to and click Send.**
The message is forwarded to the new recipient. If you can't think of an address of someone who might want to receive this message, forward the message to yourself.

Changing the Reply
You can change the contents of the Subject: field in the same way as when you reply to a message. You can also place the cursor in the message window and add your own personal comments before forwarding it to the new recipient.

You'll often receive email that you don't want to delete, yet you don't want to see it in your Inbox each time you check your mail. The solution is to move it to a folder.

continues ▶

To Reply, Forward, Save, and Delete Mail (continued)

8 With your Inbox visible, right-click the message you want to save, as shown in Figure 2.18.

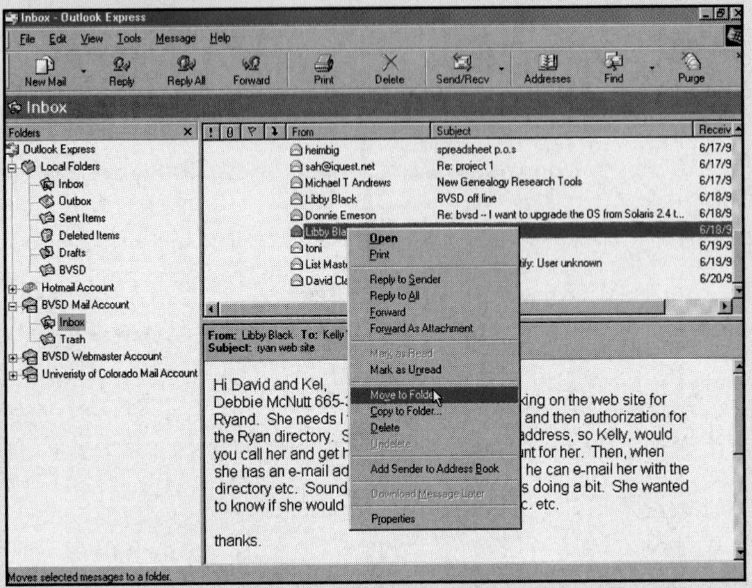

Figure 2.18
Moving mail to a folder starts with a right-click.

9 Select Move To Folder from the pop-up menu that appears.
A dialog box appears, asking where you want to move your message to. You have two options:

- You can move the message to a folder on the remote server. Doing this allows you to access your saved messages from different machines you may check your email from.
- You can save the message to a local folder. This way, you will be able to read your message offline, but only from the computer you are presently using.

For this lesson, save the message onto your email account on your remote server.

10 Click the name of your email account, as shown in Figure 2.19.
This tells Outlook Express that you are saving this email message in a folder on the remote server.

11 Click on New Folder. You will be prompted for the name of your new folder.
This name can be anything you like. You can create different folders for different purposes—one for saved email from family members, another for school-related messages, and so on.

12 Type in the name of the folder, and then click OK.
The folder will be created and appear under the email account you selected in Step 3.

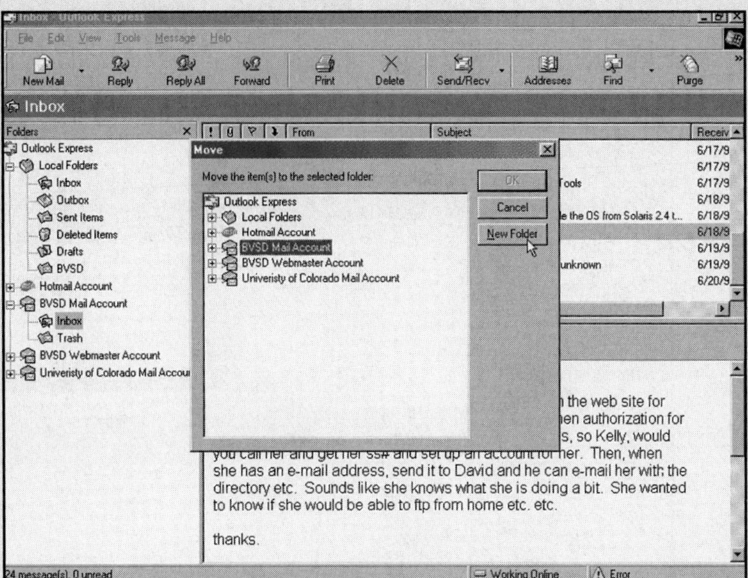

Figure 2.19
Select the account where you want to move the message.

13 **Click once on the new folder's name to select it.**
This lets Outlook Express know that you are saving the new message in that folder.

14 **Click OK.**
The message is moved into the new folder and marked for deletion from your Inbox.

15 **To access your saved message, click the new folder one time from in the Mail Account pane.**
Your message appears in the Message List.

After people know you are online, you'll start receiving a lot of email. Just like regular mail, you'll start receiving junk mail as well. The delete function provides the perfect solution to unwanted and old email.

16 **To delete a message, click it one time to select it.**
If there are no messages you want to delete at this time, simply email yourself a new message with the subject `Delete me!`.

17 **Click the Delete button on the toolbar, as shown in Figure 2.20.**
This marks the message for deletion, but is not removed from your Inbox—at least, not yet.

18 **Select Purge Deleted Messages from the Edit menu.**
This removes the message from your Inbox. It is no longer available for reading.

Leave Outlook Express onscreen and continue with the next lesson.

continues ▶

To Reply, Forward, Save, and Delete Mail (continued)

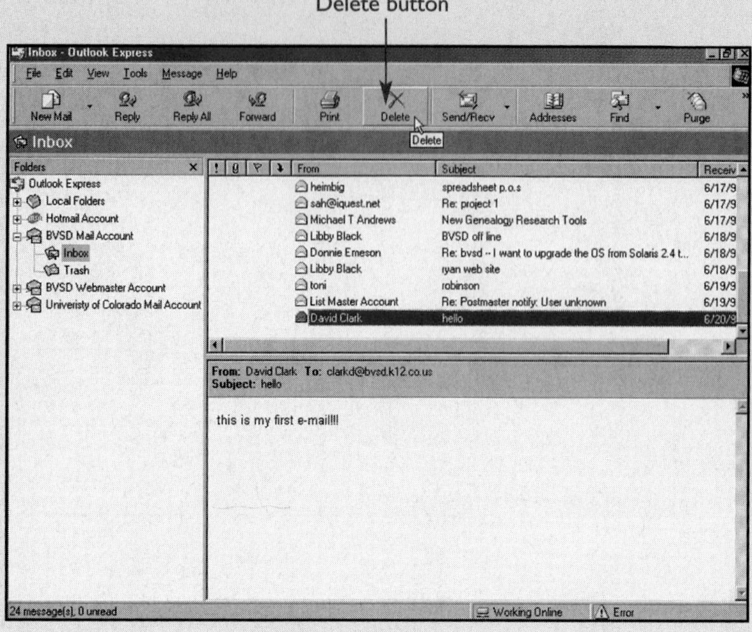

Figure 2.20
Click the Delete button to get rid of unwanted mail.

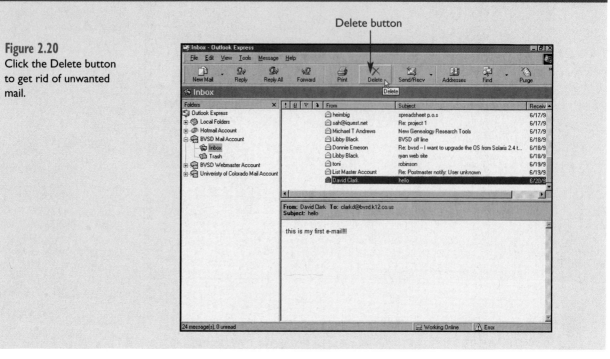

Lesson 6: Managing an Address Book

After you start making online contacts, keeping track of all those email addresses can be quite a chore. Luckily, most email programs have a built-in address book that helps you keep track of your correspondents and makes it easier for you to remember their email addresses.

To Manage an Address Book

1. **Select an email message from the message pane by clicking on it once.**
   The message opens up in a new window.

2. **Select Add Sender to Address Book from the Tools menu, as shown in Figure 2.21.**
   The sender's address is added to your address book.

   From now on, whenever you want to send email to this person, you can simply fill in his or her first name or whatever appears in the From: field when you receive email from that person.

Adding an Email Address to Your Address Book
You don't have to wait for an email message from someone to add that person to your address book. Click the Address icon on the toolbar, and then click on New. Select New Contact in the pop-up menu that appears, and enter the information yourself.

You can also edit the information for contacts you've already added. Select a name by clicking on it once. Then, click the Properties button.

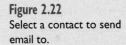

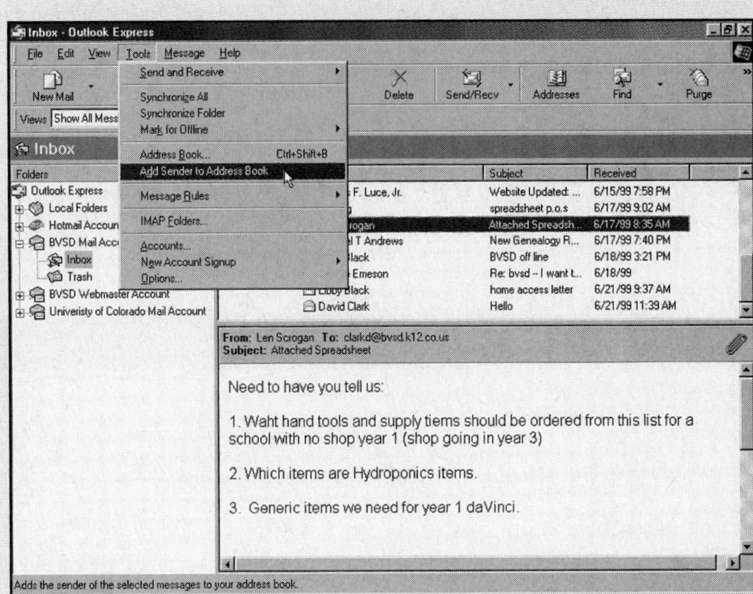

Figure 2.21
Select Add Sender to Address Book.

❸ **Another way to use your address book entries is to click New Mail to open the Select Recipient's dialog box, in which you can compose a new email message.**

❹ **Click on the Address Book icon next to the To: field, as shown in Figure 2.22.**

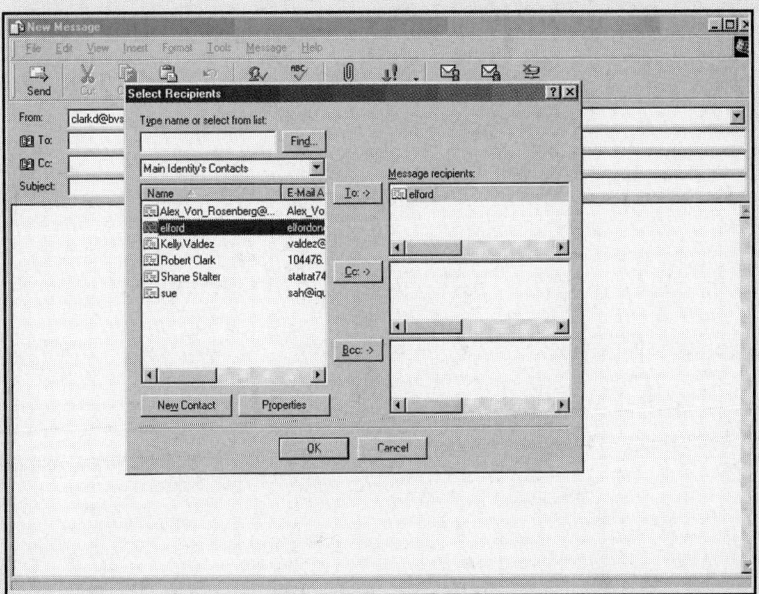

Figure 2.22
Select a contact to send email to.

❺ **Double-click the name of someone you'd like to send email to and click OK.**

The name and address are automatically filled in for you.

Summary

In this lesson, you learned how to use Outlook Express to read, send, and receive email. You acquired some valuable skills for organizing your email, such as saving to folders and creating an address book.

To expand on your knowledge, spend a few minutes exploring Help on these topics. Additionally, complete some of the Skill Drill, Challenge, and Discovery Zone exercises.

Checking Concepts and Terms

True/False

For each of the following, check *T* or *F* to indicate whether the statement is true or false.

__T __F **1.** An email address can have a maximum of one space. [L1]

__T __F **2.** To check your email, you need to know your password. [L2]

__T __F **3.** To send and receive email, you need to have an account on a computer directly tied into the Internet. [L1]

__T __F **4.** Forwarding means that you are replying to the original author of the message. [L5]

__T __F **5.** You can't change the subject heading in a message you are replying to. [L5]

Multiple Choice

Circle the letter of the correct answer for each of the following.

1. What is available on the Outlook Express toolbar? [L5]

a. Forward button

b. Reply button

c. Send button

d. all of the above

2. When forwarding a message, you can't change which of the following? [L5]

a. Subject: field

b. From: field

c. the message itself

d. all of the above

3. Which of the following is *not* a valid email address? [L1]

a. clarkd@bvsd.k12.co.us

b. CLARKD@COLORADO.EDU

c. david clark@mcp.com

d. dclark@mcp.com

4. Which of the following can you do while viewing your email? [L5]

a. delete the message

b. reply to the message

c. forward the message

d. all of the above

5. A deleted message is gone when you do which of the following? [L5]

a. exit Outlook Express

b. select Purge Deleted Messages from the Edit menu

c. click the Delete button

d. none of the above

Screen ID

Identify each of the items shown in Figure 2.23.

Figure 2.23

A. Toolbar
B. Message List
C. Mail Accounts
D. Preview pane
E. Inbox
F. Saved Mail folder
G. New Mail button

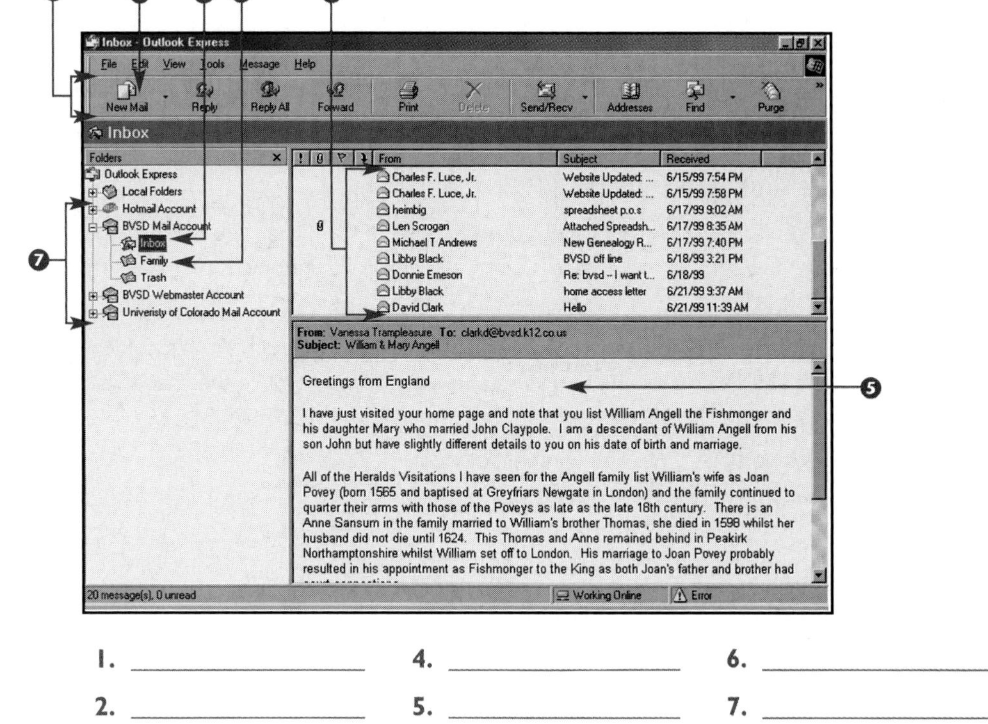

1. ____________________
2. ____________________
3. ____________________
4. ____________________
5. ____________________
6. ____________________
7. ____________________

Discussion Questions

1. How has email changed the way companies do business? How has it changed the way people communicate worldwide?
2. Why would you want to keep an up-to-date address book in your email program?

Skill Drill

Skill Drill exercises reinforce project skills. Each skill that is reinforced is the same, or nearly the same, as a skill presented in the project. Detailed instructions are provided in a step-by-step format.

1. Starting Your Email Program

There is more than one way to open Outlook Express. If you are unable to locate a desktop icon, don't panic.

1. Move the mouse until it reaches the Start button in the lower-left corner of your screen.
2. Click once.
3. In the next menu, search for Outlook Express.
4. Select it with your mouse and release the mouse button.

2. Double-checking Your Configuration

There may be times when you need to change your configuration settings. This could be because you changed your password, you want to rename your account, or for other reasons. Here's how.

1. Start Outlook Express.
2. Select Properties from the File menu.
3. Click on each tab, and check to make sure that your email account is set up the way you want it.

3. Working with Your Mail Folders

It is quite easy to confuse which mail folder you are currently viewing. You need to be careful to make sure the correct mail folder is open. Spend some time practicing opening your Inbox.

1. Click once on the plus sign (+) next to your email account in the Mail Account pane so you can view your folders.
2. Click on your Inbox one time. The contents of your Inbox will appear in the Message List pane.
3. Select another folder by clicking on it one time. Notice the change in the Message List pane.

As you create more and more folders to better organize your email, knowing how to move between then effectively will be an important skill to have.

4. Replying, Forwarding, Saving, and Deleting Mail

Knowing just exactly what to do with your email is vital for maintaining a manageable Inbox. Email can pile up quickly, especially if you join some email discussion groups, as will be discussed in the next project. Take some time to make sure that you thoroughly understand your options when it comes to email. Review the following options.

- Replying: To send a reply to the author of the message. The email address is filled in for you, as is the subject line. You can change the subject line, if you want. The original email can be included in your reply.
- Forwarding: To send a copy of a received email to another user. The subject line is filled in for you, although you may change it if you wish. You can also include your own personal comments in the email if you want.
- Saving: To move a copy of received email to a folder. You can create folders on your local machine or server. Creating email folders can help you organize your email and move them out of your Inbox, so you don't have to view them each time you check your email.
- Delete: To remove a message from the server. Because this is irreversible, be sure you want to delete the mail before selecting Purge Deleted Messages from the Edit menu item.

Challenge

Challenge exercises expand on or are somewhat related to skills presented in the lessons. Each exercise provides a brief narrative introduction, followed by instructions in a numbered-step format that are not as detailed as those in the Skill Drill section.

1. Sending Out a Group Mailing

One of your objectives is to keep your current customers aware of new releases. You collect email addresses of regular customers and send out a periodic mailing to arouse their interest and keep them coming back.

Sending out unwanted email on the Internet is considered bad form. Make sure that you include only those people on your list who want to be included.

1. Collect email addresses of those who want to be on your list. For the purposes of this exercise, you can use the following addresses:

   rsmith@mtv.com

   jonesm@usc.edu

   david433@aol.com

   oscar@ucab.al.us

   pitts@umaine.maine.edu

These are not real addresses; messages sent to these addresses will bounce back to you. If you want to substitute real addresses, feel free to do so.

2. Open your address book by selecting Address Book from the Tools menu.
3. Select New Group by clicking on the New Icon and holding down the mouse button, as shown in Figure 2.24.

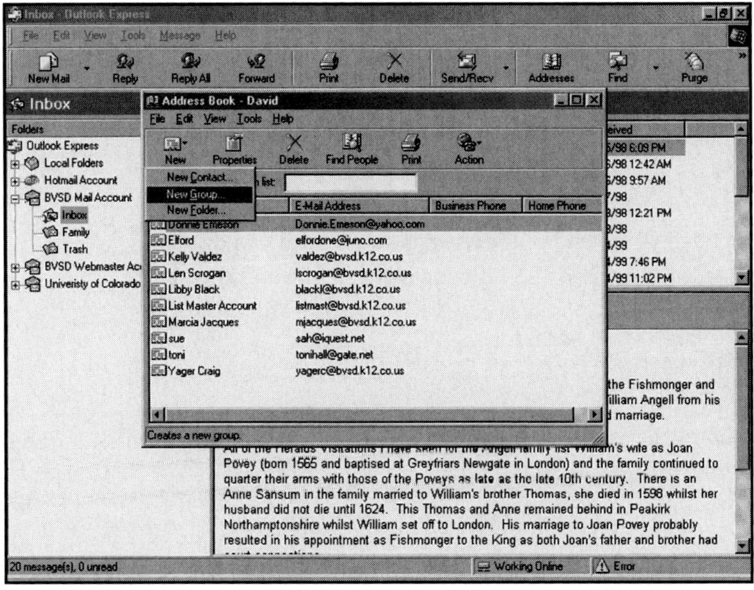

Figure 2.24
Click the New Group option.

4. Type a name for the group. This is the name you put in the To: field when composing an email message.
5. Click Select Members if you want to add contacts who are already listed in your address book. If you want to add a new group member who is not in your address book, click the New Contact Button instead and fill in the information manually. Click OK when you finish.
6. Highlight each name you want to include and click Select. Each is added to the group. Click OK when you finish. Your new email group is now ready to be used.

2. Sending and Receiving Attachments

An email attachment can be anything from a photograph to a document created in your favorite word processing program, to a piece of software. It is handy to be able to include these documents in your email.

1. Create a document in your favorite word processing program and save it as `attachment.doc`.
2. Compose a new message using Outlook Express. Fill in your own email address as the recipient.
3. Select File Attachment from the Insert menu.
4. Navigate to the attachment.doc's location in the window that appears. Click once to select it.
5. Click Attach.

When you send the message, the file will be attached to the email.

To open an attachment, double-click the attachment's icon that appears in your received email message.

Email Viruses

The computing world has recently experienced a rash of computer viruses being spread via email attachments. These attachments can masquerade as emails from a trusted friend.

You cannot get a virus simply by receiving an email that contains an attachment. The virus won't spread until the attachment is opened. Open only attachments that you know you can trust.

It's also a very good idea to maintain virus-protection software on your computer and to update it regularly.

3. Creating a Signature File

A signature file is a file that is appended at the end of every email you send. It can contain information such as your name and email address. Some people like to use these to include a favorite quote or the URL of their own homepage.

1. Select Options from the Tools menu.
2. Click the Signature tab.
3. Click New.
4. Fill out your information in the text box that appears in the window.
5. Make sure that the box next to Add this signature to all outgoing messages is checked.
6. Click OK.

From now on, each message you send will contain your signature file at the bottom of the email message.

Discovery Zone 

Discovery Zone exercises require an advanced knowledge of topics presented in *Essentials* lessons, the application of skills from multiple lessons, or self-directed learning of new skills.

1. Replying to All

Notice there are two reply buttons on the Outlook Express Toolbar. There are two options for replying, and understanding the difference can save you a fair amount of trouble.

Reply is used to reply to a single person, the author of the email message.

Reply to all is used for situations when you are part of a mailing list and want to reply to all members of that group. This is especially handy when an online discussion is being handled via email.

Use the Address Book to create a group, as described in Lesson 5. Include your email in that group, and then send out a mailing. Practice using the reply and reply to all functions. Using the Reply to all function to send a personal response to an individual is considered very bad form. Make sure that you know who the mail will be delivered to before you click that Send button.

2. Spell-checking

Most email programs have a built-in spell-checker. Outlook Express is no different. Sending out an email message with multiple words misspelled is the virtual equivalent of going into work while having a "bad hair day." You don't make a very good impression. We can't do anything about your hair, but Outlook Express can make suggestions about your spelling.

Select Options from the Tools menu and click the Spelling tab. There are several options that you can set. Take some time to explore these options and decide what works best for you.

3. Expressing Yourself Online

It is not always easy to express yourself correctly when using email. During a phone conversation, voice inflection and tone can tell you a lot about how the other person feels about what they are saying. In a face-to face-conversation, you can add body language to your list of indicators. However, all of that has been stripped away in email, and you have to choose your words very carefully. Luckily, there are now online conventions to assist you.

Practice using some of these conventions in your email:

- DON'T WRITE EMAIL IN ALL CAPS!

  This is the equivalent of shouting. Use it only when you want to get someone's attention and use it sparingly.

- Use smileys, or emoticons, to convey how you feel about a particular comment you made. Smileys are textual representations of the human face in a variety poses. Your basic smiley looks like this:

  :-)

  This symbol may look like garbage until you look at it sideways and see the smile. You would use this symbol to express happiness about something you said. Another frequently used smiley is used to express sadness or disapproval:

  :-(

  Notice the following smiley, in which the wink is used as a sarcastic situation or to let the recipient know that you're not entirely serious about a remark you've just made.

  ;-)

4. Using Formatting

You want to add a little bit of class to your email by altering font color and size. Be aware that the recipient can only view these changes to your message if they use Outlook Express or a compatible program to read their email.

Click on New Mail to bring up a window in which to type new mail. Select Rich Text (HTML) from the Format menu item. Tools appear above the message window that enable you to change the font attributes like those used in most word processing programs. Experiment with these options to create some interesting effects and friendlier email messages.

Project 3

Searching the World Wide Web

Objectives

In this project, you learn how to

- **Access and Search a World Wide Web Subject Index**
- **Access the World Wide Web Search Engines**
- **Search the World Wide Web Using a Variety of Search Engines**
- **Define Your Search Parameters**
- **Refine Your Search**
- **Save, Print, or Email the Information You Found**
- **Save Your Site in Your Favorites File**

Key terms introduced in the project include

- search engine
- subject directory
- subject index
- text box

Source: Essentials: Internet, 4/e, Clark

Why Would I Do This?

Being able to search the World Wide Web for a topic of interest has, more than anything else, made the Internet an accessible and useful tool for the millions of people who use it. Many good search engines have been created in the past couple of years. A ***search engine*** is an online utility that allows you to search the vast contents of the World Wide Web, or WWW, for short. You can type a keyword of interest and press ↵Enter. Within seconds, dozens, hundreds, or even thousands of links are presented on the screen for you to follow to explore your area of interest. Want to learn to play baccarat? Thinking about taking up sky diving? Use those terms as keywords and it's a sure thing that a World Wide Web search engine will find more links for you to follow than you'll have time to explore between now and the start of the next millenium.

Another popular method of navigating the World Wide Web is to use a subject directory. A ***subject directory*** presents itself as a hierarchical series of menus, each more specific than the one above it. You can move from Science to Astronomy to Telescopes, and view images from deep space with just a few clicks of your mouse.

This Project shows you how to access these searching tools and how to formulate a query to help you efficiently find what you are looking for.

Visual Summary

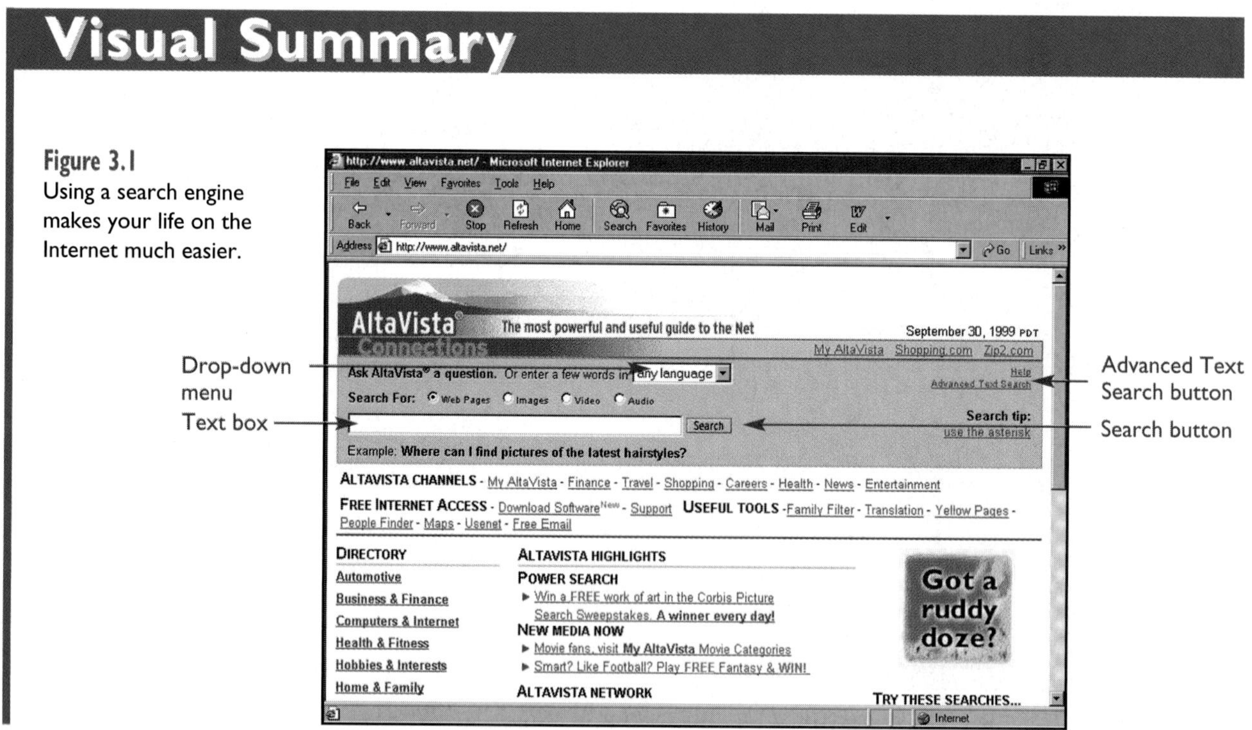

Figure 3.1
Using a search engine makes your life on the Internet much easier.

Lesson 1: Accessing and Searching a WWW Subject Index

Using a subject index on the World Wide Web can be an effective and easy way to find the information you need. A ***subject index*** is a system of hierarchical menus on a Web page, each more specific than the last. When you know exactly what you are looking for, navigating through a subject index can take you directly to the information you're seeking.

To Access and Search a WWW Subject Index

1 Start Internet Explorer.

2 Type `http://www.yahoo.com` in the address box and press Enter.

This connects you to the Yahoo! Web site. Yahoo! has a search engine associated with it that will search the massive holdings at the Yahoo! site. You won't be using Yahoo! to perform a keyword search in this lesson. Instead, you'll navigate through the menus in a hierarchical fashion to find the information you're looking for.

Yahoo! Is an Original

Yahoo! was one of the first attempts to organize the World Wide Web. It was created by two Stanford University students who saw the potential of creating an online directory. Besides having a catchy name, Yahoo! has succeeded in becoming one of the top starting points on the Internet for millions. Those two students are rich men today. Yahoo! also expanded to offer online games, chat rooms, online auctions, and a whole lot more.

Notice that the Yahoo! site is organized into subject category links, as shown in Figure 3.2. You'll look for current movie showing times in your area.

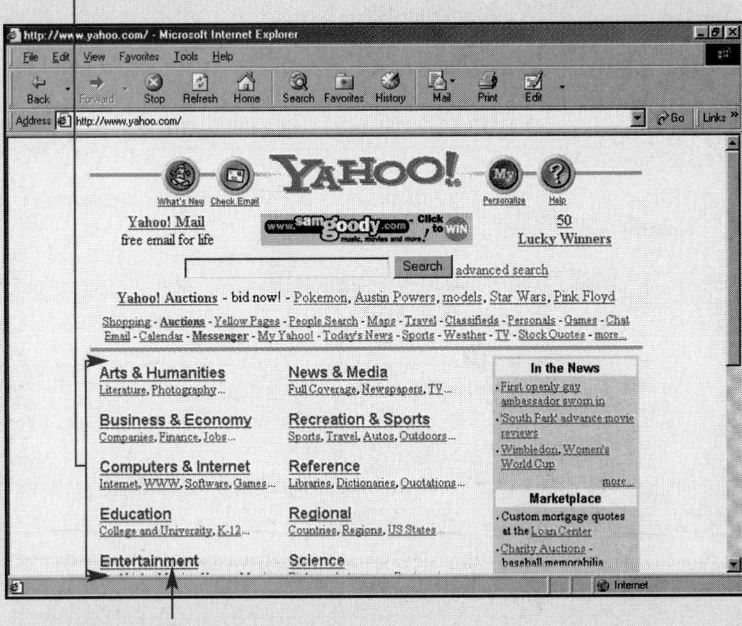

Figure 3.2
The Yahoo! home page offers many topics of interest that are just a click away.

3 Click the Entertainment link.

This seems logical because you probably wouldn't look for movie information under the science category! The Yahoo! Entertainment page appears on your screen, as shown in Figure 3.3.

continues ▶

To Access and Search a WWW Subject Index (continued)

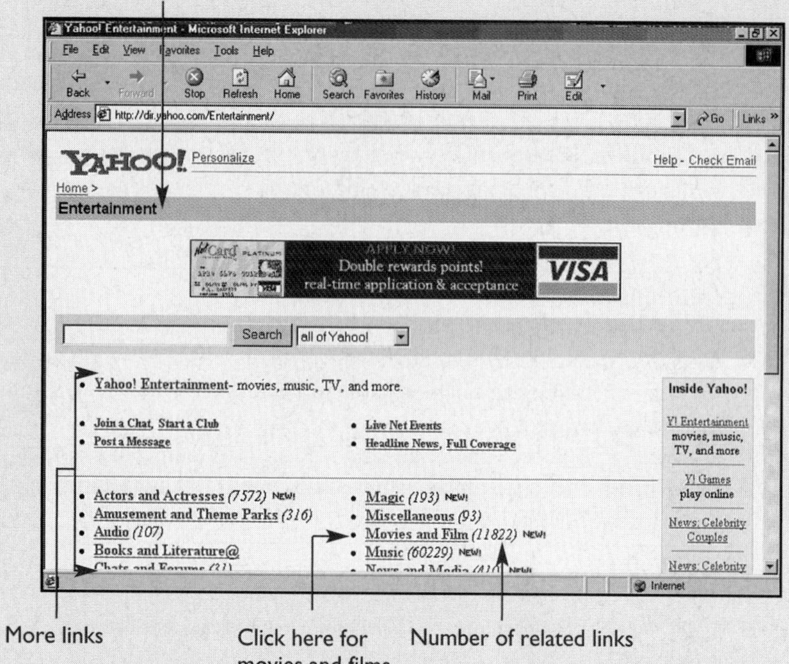

Figure 3.3
Click the Movies and Film link.

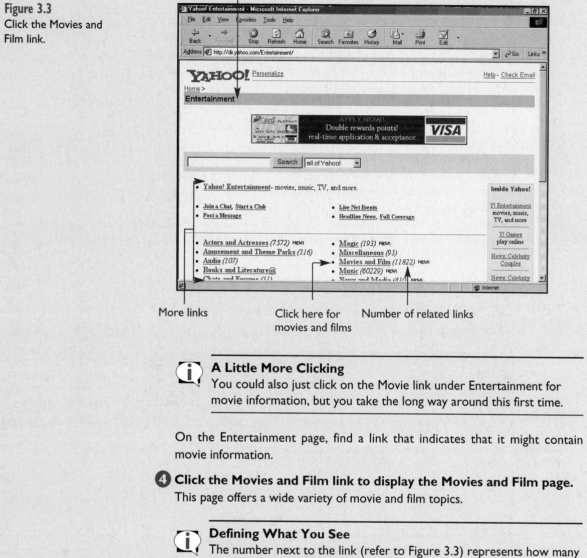

A Little More Clicking
You could also just click on the Movie link under Entertainment for movie information, but you take the long way around this first time.

On the Entertainment page, find a link that indicates that it might contain movie information.

4 **Click the Movies and Film link to display the Movies and Film page.**
This page offers a wide variety of movie and film topics.

Defining What You See
The number next to the link (refer to Figure 3.3) represents how many movie-related links you'll find on Yahoo! (In this case, more than 11,000!) Don't be alarmed—you keep narrowing your search until you find what you need. It's easier and faster than you think.

The New! icon, highlighted in yellow, tells you that there is new and current information at these Web sites.

5 **Search the Movies and Film page for a link that indicates movie times.**
The language can change from one subject index to the next, so you may have to search a bit. In Yahoo!'s case, though, there is a link called `Showtimes`. This could be what you're looking for!

6 **Click the Showtimes link.**
The Showtimes page appears, as shown in Figure 3.4.

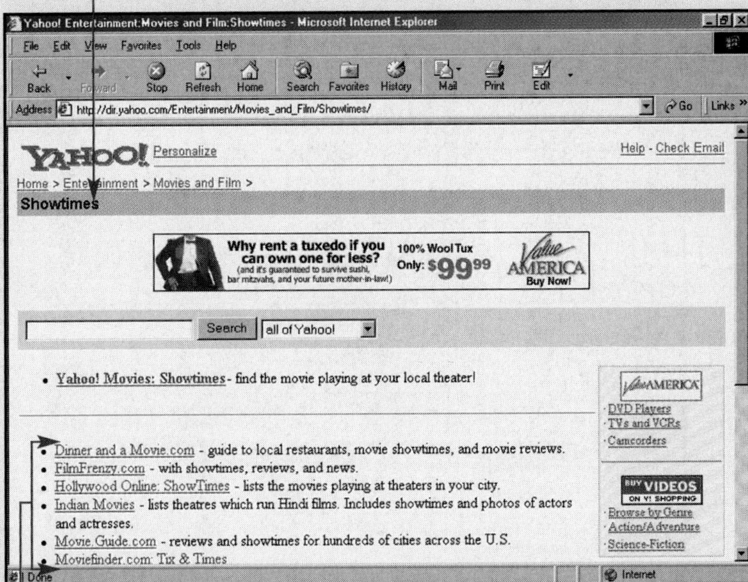

Figure 3.4
Your search for movie showing times is narrowing.

7 **Click the Yahoo! Movies: Showtimes link to go to the Yahoo! Movies: Showtime page, as shown in Figure 3.5.**

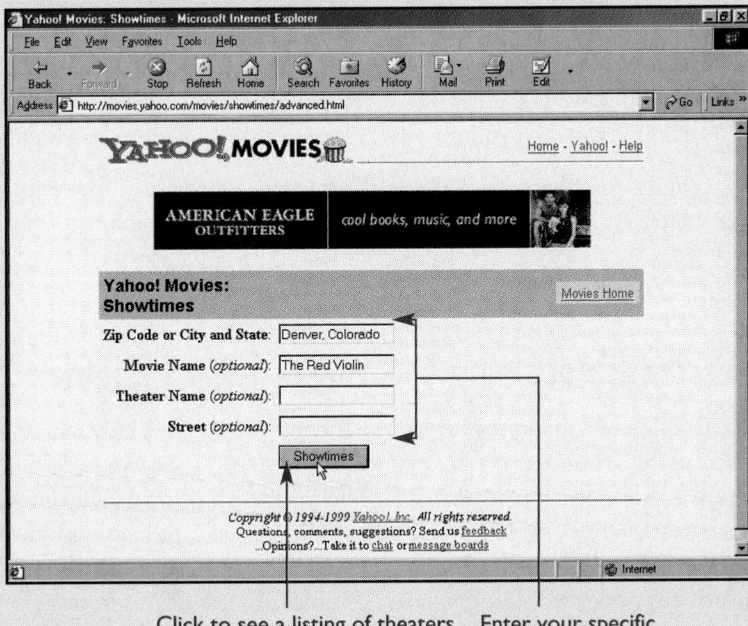

Figure 3.5
It's show time! Just type in your information and you'll see movie showing times in your area.

You're almost there. The next page asks you specific information about your location and the movie you want to see. The only required information is where you want to view the movie.

continues ▶

To Access and Search a WWW Subject Index (continued)

8 Type in the location and any of the optional information and click Showtimes.

Yahoo! returns a page that shows you the movie theaters in your area that are showing the movie you want to see (see Figure 3.6).

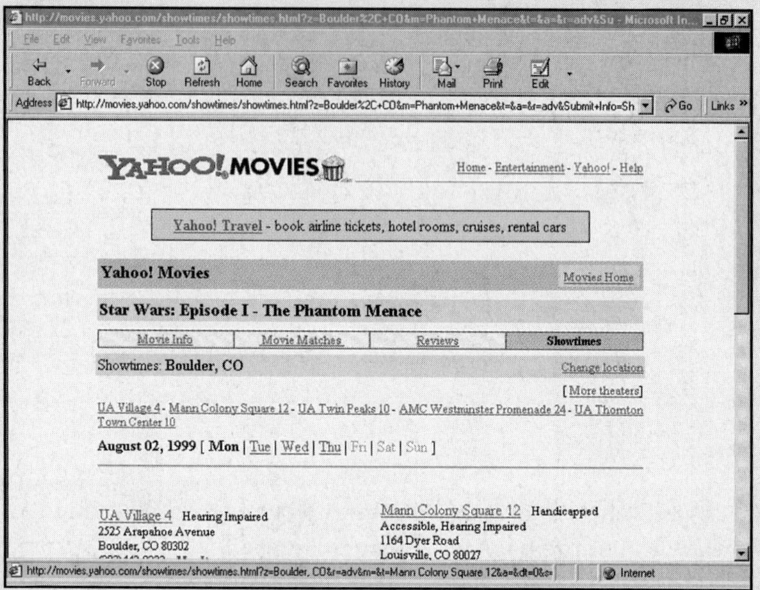

Figure 3.6
You can use the World Wide Web to plan your evening's entertainment.

You can use a subject index to find a good deal of specific information. Learning to use a subject index can save you some time. Why search for something when you can navigate right to the information you need!

In the next Lesson, you'll look at using keywords to search the Internet. Leave Internet Explorer open and proceed to the next lesson.

Lesson 2: Accessing the WWW Search Engines

For times when the location of your information is not quite clear, and that will be often, a good search engine is the answer to your prayers. A search engine is a utility on the Internet that allows you to search for information based on a keyword that you supply. A good search engine can save you hours of searching time, and turn an incomprehensible jumble of links and information into something manageable. Fortunately, several good search engines exist. These provide the results as a page of hyperlinks for you to follow. In this lesson, you learn how to access these search tools using the AltaVista search engine.

To Access the WWW Search Engines

1 Start Internet Explorer and connect to http://www.altavista.net.

This connects you to the AltaVista search engine home page, as shown in Figure 3.7.

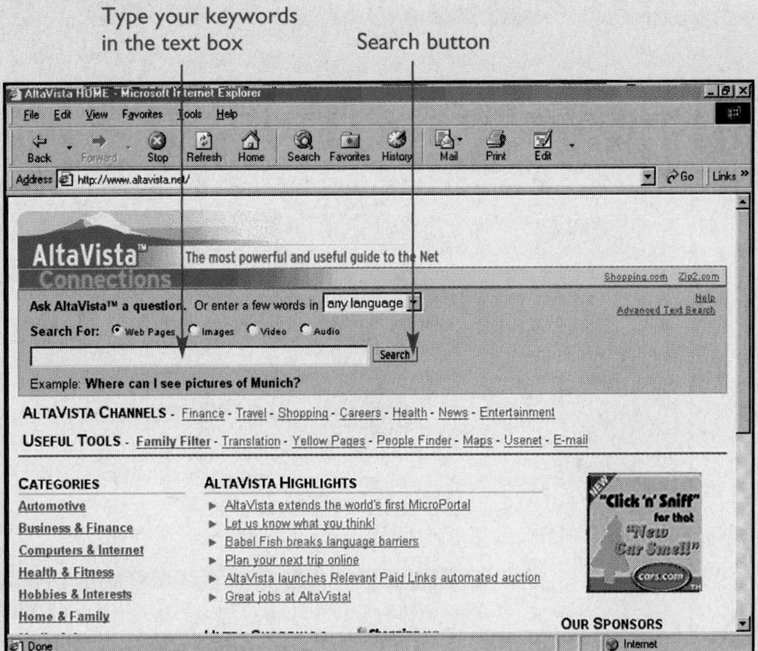

Figure 3.7
AltaVista is one of several powerful search engines.

Searching with the Search button

There is a Search button on the Internet Explorer toolbar. You can press this button to perform a search as well. Clicking it brings up a different search engine. This can be a handy tool to use when you forget the URL of your favorite search engine.

The AltaVista Home Page contains a ***text box***, in which you type your keywords or the subject of your search. A text box is a box on a Web page in which you can enter text. In this case, enter your keywords to perform your search. Do a search for a killer cheesecake recipe.

2 Type the word `recipe` in the text box, and then click the Search button.

`Recipe` is a broad category and will return a lot of results—in fact, more than you'll have time to go through in this lifetime, as shown in Figure 3.8.

Be sure to use `recipe`, not `recipes`, as your keyword for this exercise. AltaVista treats these words differently and you'll get results that may differ from this exercise.

A search for `recipe` turned up 2,110,050 results. It's unlikely that you'll have to go through that many to find what you need. Frequently, the best links are on the first couple of pages. If they aren't there, modifying your search parameters a bit may be your best course of action. We'll look at that later. For now, you have two options:

- You can scroll down the page looking for a link that may contain what you need.
- You can add another keyword to your search.

continues ▶

To Access the WWW Search Engines (continued)

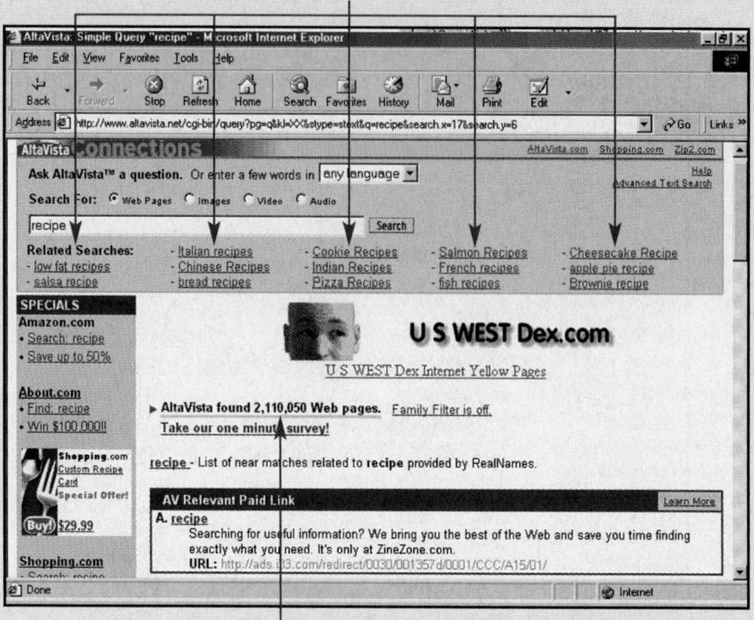

Figure 3.8
So many recipes, so little time!

Certainly, scrolling through a number of links can be an interesting way to stumble onto new sites, but you're looking for specific information.

5 Add the word `cheesecake` in the text box (be sure to leave a space between the words `recipe` and `cheesecake`). Click the Search button, as shown in Figure 3.9.

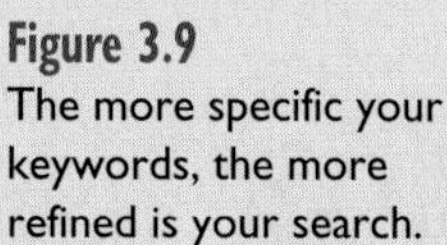

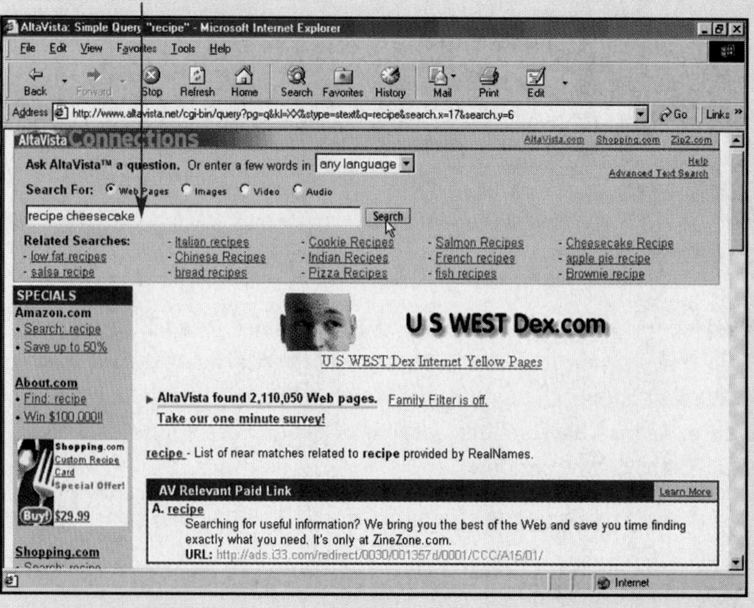

Figure 3.9
The more specific your keywords, the more refined is your search.

AltaVista now has a better idea of what you're looking for and returns considerably fewer links for you to go through. And it's unlikely that you'll need to go through even that many.

6. **Click one of the hyperlinks that was returned by the latest search.**
   You're only a click away from a great dessert!

   Recipes aren't the only things you'll find by searching the Internet. In Lesson 3, you'll use the HotBot search engine to attempt a more challenging search. Leave Internet Explorer open and proceed to the next Lesson.

Lesson 3: Defining Your Search Parameters

Sometimes, you want to perform a refined and specific search. With many of the search engines, you can get very specific on the topic for which you are searching. Suppose that you want to do a specific search for raptors that are on the endangered species list, specifically the peregrine falcon. Here is one way to do it.

To Define Your Search Parameters

1. **Connect to http://www.hotbot.com.**
   This connects you to the HotBot search engine, as shown in Figure 3.10.

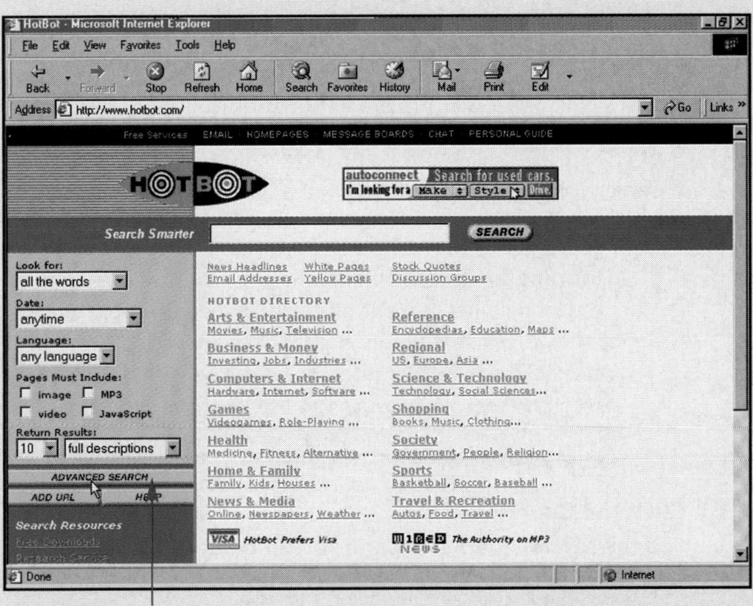

Figure 3.10
Connect to the HotBot search engine.

Advanced Search button

2. **Click on the Advanced Search button.**
   This brings up a page in which you can get very specific about what you are searching for. HotBot enables you to perform an advanced search by using a variety of keywords. You use a series of drop-down menus to help you customize your search parameters.

continues ▶

To Define Your Search Parameters (continued)

3 Type the keywords `endangered species` in the text box at the top. Use the drop-down menus, as shown in Figure 3.11, to narrow your search parameters.

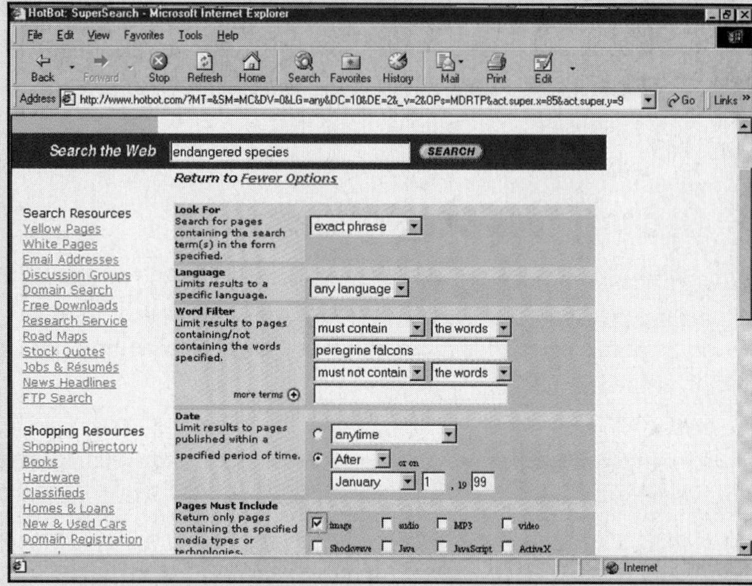

Figure 3.11
Narrowing your search parameters can result in fewer hits returned.

The parameters you set for this search are the following:

- Search by using the exact phrase `endangered species`
- Search for pages that include information about peregrine falcons
- Search for pages that have been updated since January 1, 1999
- Search for pages that include images

Defining an Exact Phrase
HotBot includes the option to treat the keywords as an exact phrase; that is, it will search for those words appearing together. Not all engines have this helpful feature. To define an exact phrase in one of these engines, place quotation marks around to phrase to bind the words together as a phrase for searching purposes.

4 Click the Search button.
You see several options of pages to visit that provide you with information on your topic.

5 Select a few links to explore.
If the page doesn't contain the information you're looking for, you can click the Back button in the Internet Explorer toolbar to return to the search results page. You can then try another link.

There are many other features you can use on the HotBot home page. If, for example, you want more general information about raptors, but want to exclude information about peregrine falcons, you can fashion a query similar to the one shown in Figure 3.12.

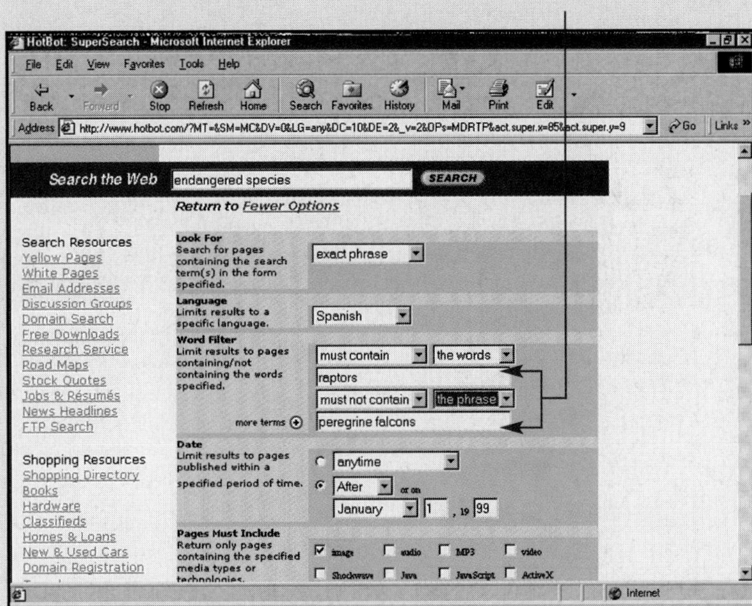

Figure 3.12
You can refine your search for raptors that aren't peregrine falcons.

According to this criterion, the page results must contain the word `raptors`, but not the phrase `peregrine falcons`.

Explore the HotBot search engine options, if you choose. When you're ready, proceed to Lesson 4, in which you learn another way to narrow your searches.

Lesson 4: Refining Your Search

With some search engines, you can refine your search parameters even further. You can even search the search results themselves. For instance, if you want information relating specifically to peregrine falcons, you can first perform the search for raptors, and then search those results for information on peregrine falcons by using those words as your keywords. In this lesson, you perform this search using the Infoseek search engine.

To Refine Your Search

1. **Connect to http://infoseek.go.com.**
   Infoseek maintains a large database of Web pages, and delivers a very comprehensive list of results.

2. **Type the keywords `endangered species` in the search text box, separating the words by a space (see Figure 3.13).**
   To ensure that `endangered species` is searched as a phrase rather than as two separate keywords, place quotation marks around the words.

continues ▶

To Refine Your Search (continued)

Adding quotation marks around keywords tells the search engine to search for a whole phrase, not two separate words

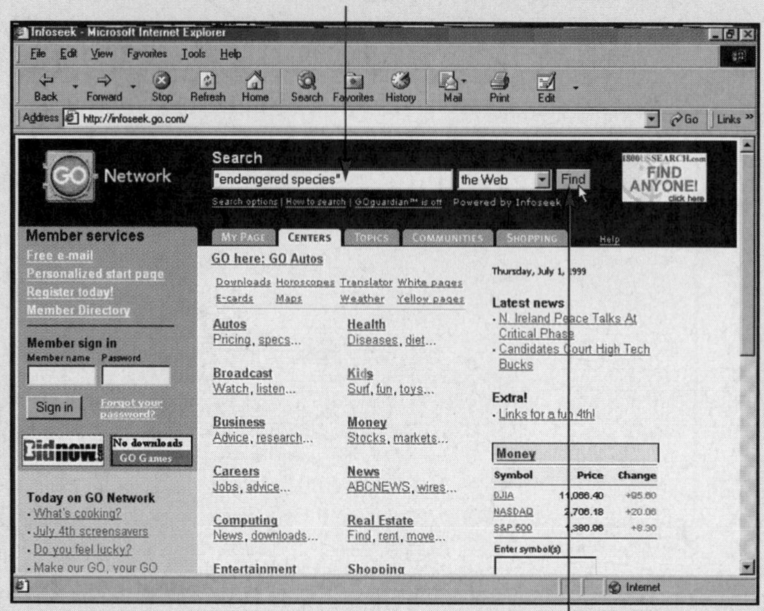

Click Find to start your search

Figure 3.13
Using Infoseek, you can refine and narrow your search.

3 Click Find.

Infoseek returns a large number of pages for your perusal—possibly more that you want.

Next, add another keyword to pull in information relating only to peregrine falcons.

4 Click the option button next to Search Within Results.

This tells Infoseek to search only in the results of your original search.

5 Type the words `peregrine falcon` in the text box (see Figure 3.14).

6 Click the Find button.

Infoseek presents a variety of links, and gives you the option to add more keywords if you want even more specific search results.

7 Select one of these links to go to (see Figure 3.15).

You use this link in the next Lesson 5, in which you learn how to save, print, or send the information you find on the Web.

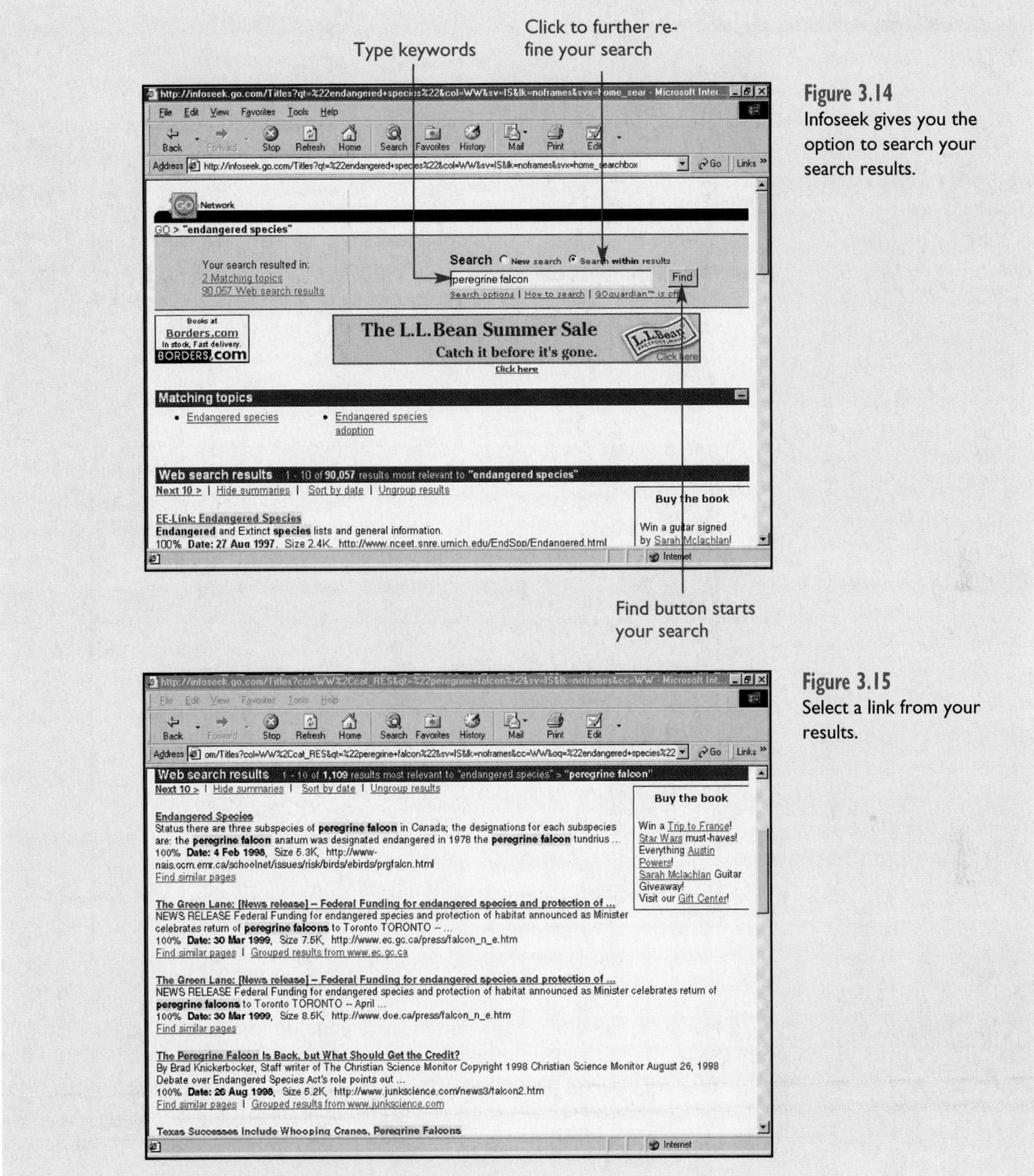

Figure 3.14
Infoseek gives you the option to search your search results.

Figure 3.15
Select a link from your results.

Lesson 5: Saving, Printing, or Emailing the Information You Find

When you find information that you consider pertinent to your research, you need to be able to access it at a later date. As tempting as it is, you can't stay on the Internet forever! You have several options for keeping the information you find—you can save it as a document, print it, or email it to yourself or to someone else. You can also save the Web site on your personal list for future reference.

To Save the Information as a Document

1 With the page that you want to save displayed onscreen, choose Save As from the File menu.

The Save As dialog box displays, requesting a location where you want to save your document, such as a folder on your hard drive or a floppy disk.

2 In the Save as type drop-down list box, select Text File if you want to be able to view your document through your word processing program (see Figure 3.16). Only the text will be saved; you won't be able to view any graphics. If you want to view the document through Internet Explorer, select Web Page, complete.

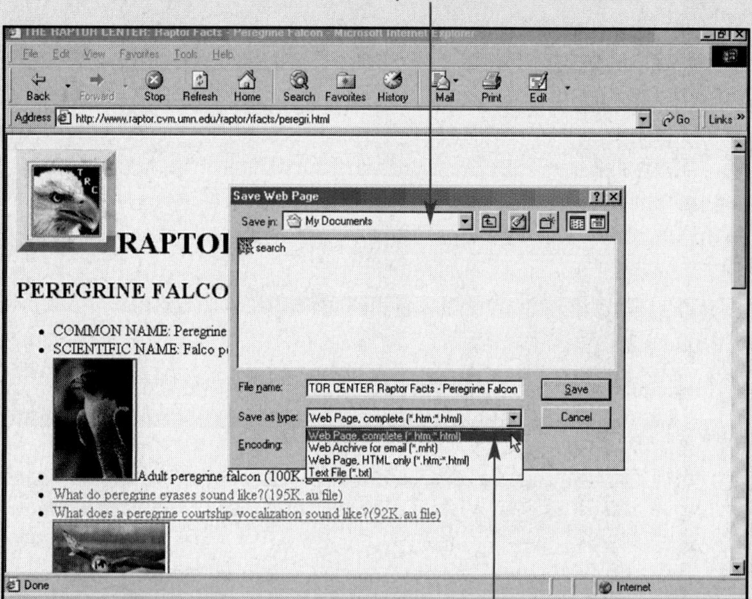

Figure 3.16
You can save your document for future reference.

3 Navigate to where you want to save your document, and then click Save.

Your document is now saved, and you can access it when you need it.

Using the Plain Text Option

Selecting Plain Text as your Save as type option allows you to view the contents of the page later in any word processing program, although some of the newer word processing programs are developing the ability to view Web pages. Leave the Save as type option as Web Page, complete if you want to view the page later by using Internet Explorer. To do this, open Internet Explorer, Select Open from the File menu, and navigate to your saved page.

To Print the Document

1 With the page that you want to print displayed onscreen, choose Print from the File menu.

The Print dialog box displays, asking you to confirm your print settings.

Alternatively, you can click the Print button on the Internet Explorer toolbar. Doing this prints the page without first displaying the Print dialog box.

2 Click OK or Print.

Your document is then sent to the printer.

To Email the Document to Yourself

Emailing to Yourself

Emailing a document to yourself can be one of the best ways to save a document for later viewing. No disk drives to deal with, and it always accessible from any machine with an Internet connection. After it is emailed, it can be viewed at any computer where you can check your email.

1 With the page that you want to mail displayed onscreen, choose Send from the File menu.

You have two options for sending your page via email.

Choosing Page or Link

Selecting Page by E-mail sends the contents of the Web page to a specified email address. You select this option in this lesson.

Selecting Link by E-mail sends the URL of the Web page to the email address you specify.

2 Select Page by Email in the pop-up menu that appears (See Figure 3.17).

An Outlook Express window appears, in which you can enter an email address.

3 Enter an email address in the To: text box, as shown in Figure 3.18.

For this exercise, use your own email address.

4 Click Send.

The email is sent on its way. The next time you check your email, your message will be waiting for you.

continues ▶

To Email the Document to Yourself (continued)

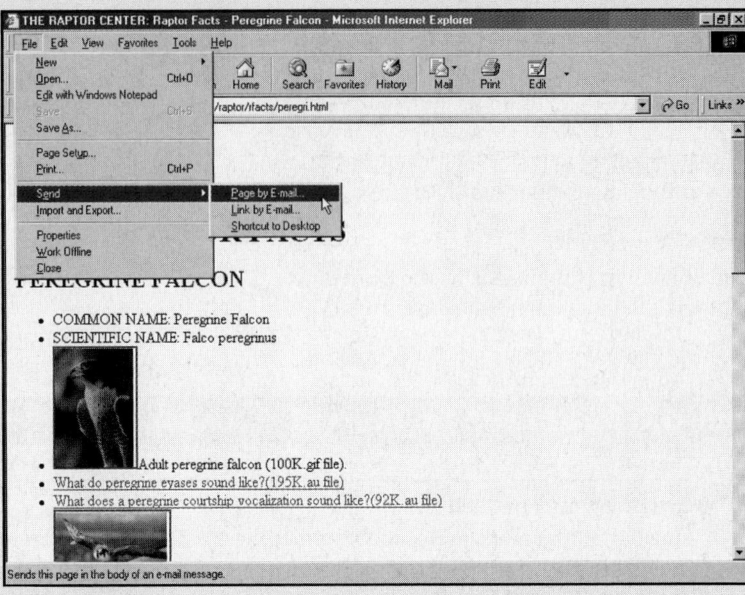

Figure 3.17
Select Page by E-mail if you want to send the page contents via email.

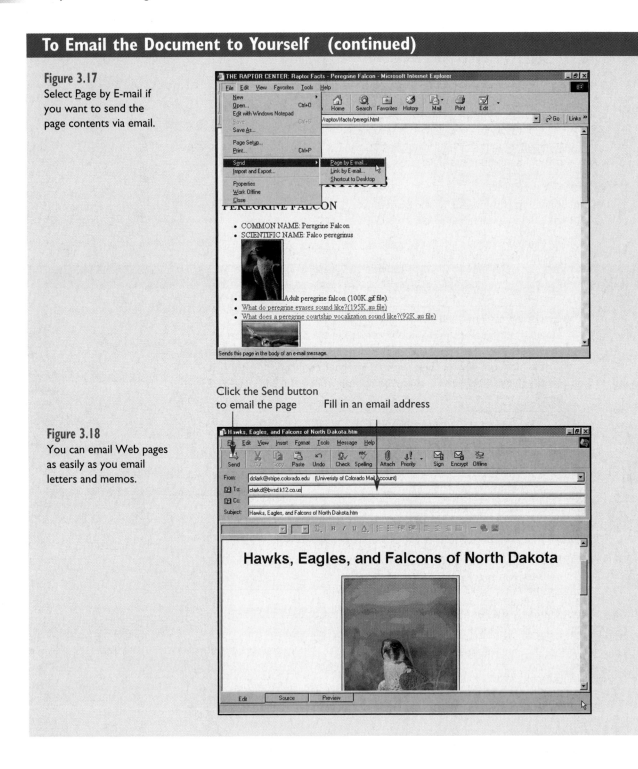

Click the Send button to email the page

Fill in an email address

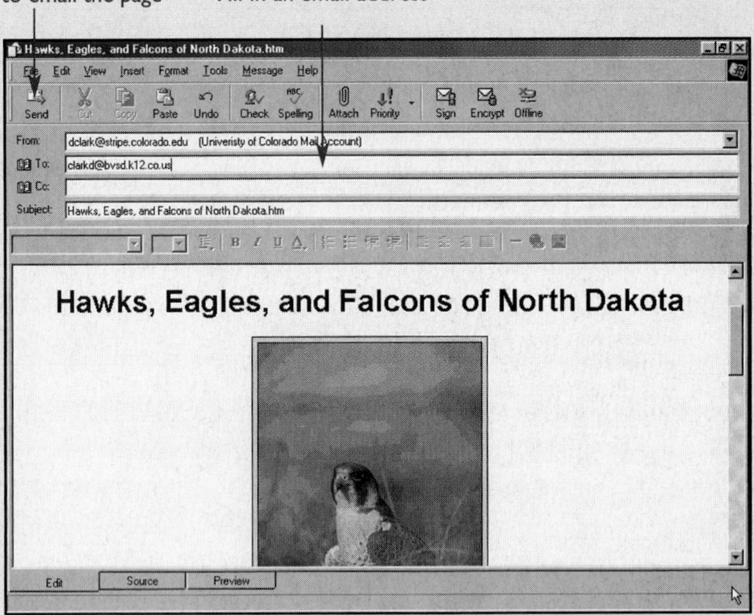

Figure 3.18
You can email Web pages as easily as you email letters and memos.

To Add a Web Site to Your Favorites List

Internet Explorer enables you to add Web pages that you want to return to later to your Favorites list. Add a link that you found in the preceding lesson to your Favorites list.

1 With the page that you want to add to your favorites list displayed onscreen, choose Favorites, and then Add To Favorites.

2 Click OK in the window that appears.

The Web page is now added to your Favorites list (see Figure 3.19).

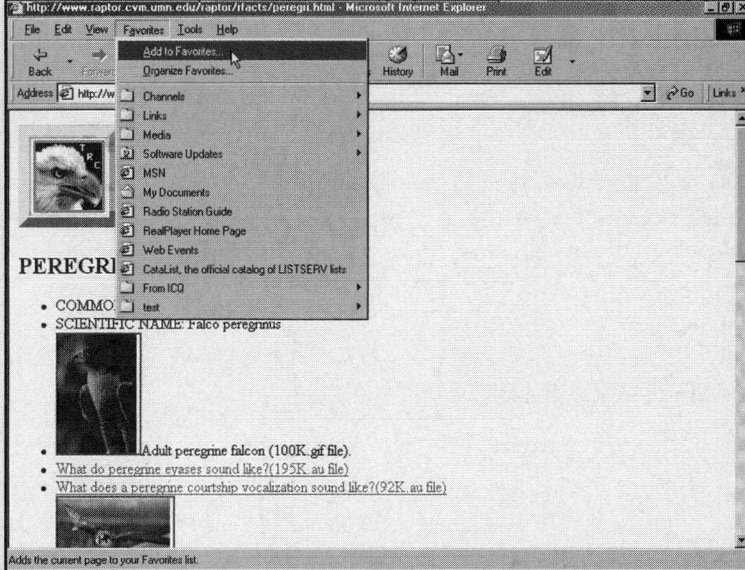

Figure 3.19
When you add a Web site to your Favorites list, you can find and access it easily.

3 To access your page, choose the appropriate link from the Favorites menu.

Internet Explorer automatically connects to that site.

Web addresses can and will change frequently. If a Web page's address changes, the link in your Favorite's file will no longer work.

If you have completed your session on the computer, exit Internet Explorer and check with your instructor for further instructions. Otherwise, continue with Skill Drills at the end of this project.

Summary

In this lesson, you learned the most important tools for finding information on the Internet—subject indexes and search engines. Using a subject index, you can now move through a series of menus, each more specific than the last. This is a great tool to know how to use if you know exactly what you're looking for.

Using a search engine, you can search the World Wide Web by using keywords. You can perform a simple search or employ advanced techniques to hone your search so it returns exactly the results you're looking for.

You also learned what do with those results. You can save and print the document, email it to yourself or others, or add the site to your Favorites list so you can access it easily later.

Checking Concepts and Terms ✓

True/False

For each of the following, check *T* or *F* to indicate whether the statement is true or false.

__T __F **1.** The most pertinent links to your search will usually appear on the first couple of pages of returned links. [L2]

__T __F **2.** It is possible to conduct a search by using an Internet subject index. [L1]

__T __F **3.** Selecting Text File as your option when saving a Web page does not save the graphics. [L5]

__T __F **4.** Many search engines allow you to search the results from a previous search. [L4]

__T __F **5.** When saving a Web page document, select Plain Text as the Save as type option in the Save As dialog box if you want to view the document with your word processing program. [L5]

Multiple Choice

Circle the letter of the correct answer for each of the following.

1. Which of the following is *not* a Web search engine? [L2–4]

a. AltaVista

b. Outlook

c. Lycos

d. all of above are Web search engines

2. If, at a later time, you want to access the information you found in a document on the Web, which of the following methods can you use? [L5]

a. Save the document as a text or as a Web page.

b. Mail the document to yourself.

c. Add the site to your list of favorites.

d. all of the above

3. If you want to email a Web page to yourself, you can do which of the following? [L5]

a. Send the whole page to yourself.

b. It isn't possible to send Web pages via email.

c. Send the URL only.

d. either a or c

4. You can refine your searches using the HotBot search engine to do which of the following? [L3]

a. include only recently updated documents

b. include certain words and exclude others

c. look for image and sound files

d. all of the above

5. It is possible to specifically include which file types in your search results? [L3]

a. text

b. audio

c. images

d. all of the above

Screen ID

Identify each of the items shown in Figure 3.20.

Figure 3.20

A Print button

B Text box

C Subject index

D Search button

E Web address

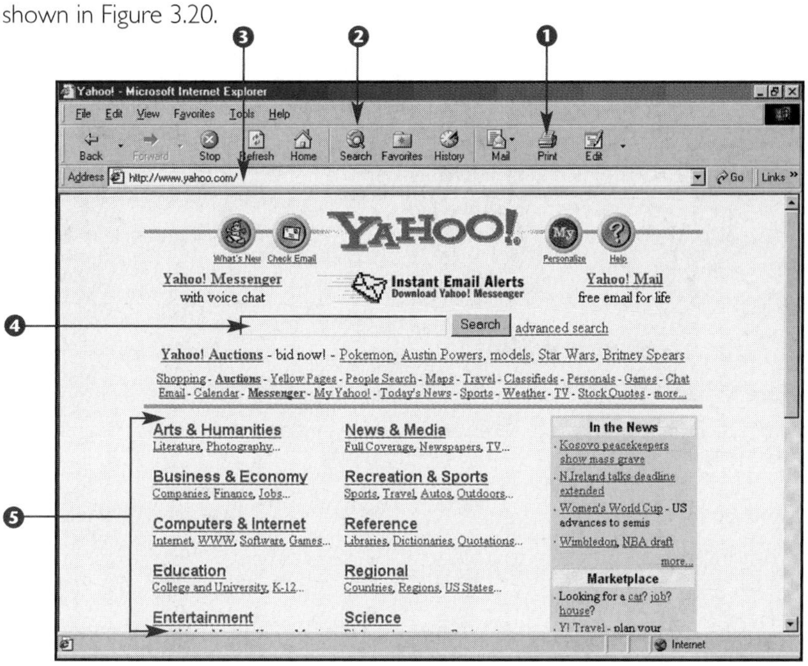

1. ____________________ **3.** ____________________ **5.** ____________________

2. ____________________ **4.** ____________________

Discussion Questions

1. Discuss the differences between using a search utility and a subject index. When would it be to your advantage to use one over the other? [L1–2]
2. After spending some time exploring the different search engines available, discuss which one best meets your needs and why. [L1–L4]
3. If you were to design a new World Wide Web search engine, what types of features would you include in your design? What would make searching the Web an easier experience for users? [L1–4]

Skill Drill

Skill Drill exercises reinforce project skills. Each skill that is reinforced is the same, or nearly the same, as a skill presented in the project. Detailed instructions are provided in a step-by-step format.

1. Using the Subject Index

Yahoo! isn't the only subject index around—there are several others. In this exercise, you take a look at another one.

1. Start Internet Explorer if isn't already running.
2. Connect to `www.excite.com`. Try to find the same information on Excite that you searched for using Yahoo!—the current showtimes for movies in your area.
3. Click Entertainment.
4. Click Excite Movies in the page that appears. Fill out the information in the next page to search for the local showing time of a movie that interests you.

2. Exploring the Search Engine Window

Many of the search engine pages have a good deal of pertinent information right on their home page. You don't even have to search for it. Spend some time exploring the offerings of a page such as AltaVista.

1. Connect to `www.altavista.net.`
2. Scroll through the page, looking for links that might interest you. When you find something interesting, click that link to go to the site.
3. Click the Back button to return to the AltaVista home page when you're done exploring a page. From there, you can click more links to go to more interesting pages.

3. Using Search Parameters with HotBot

As you saw in Lesson 3, the HotBot advanced search engine has a number of different options that you can set. Practice creating search parameters by using the HotBot search engine.

1. Connect to `www.hotbot.com`.
2. Click on the Advanced search button to access the Advanced Search utility.
3. Type in a keyword(s) in the text box and set the parameters of your search. Click Search.
4. Change the parameters of your search, except for the keyword—such as pages that have video or audio files or that were created only in the past few months.

Challenge

1. Organizing your Favorites

As you add more and more sites to your Favorites list, it can get pretty large and unwieldy. Internet Explorer lets you organize your favorite sites into folders for quicker and easier access. Using this method, you can create folders to contain links related to your hobbies, your job, finances, tomorrow's weather, and so on.

1. Select Organize Favorites from the Favorites menu item. The Organize Favorites dialog box appears, as shown in Figure 3.21.

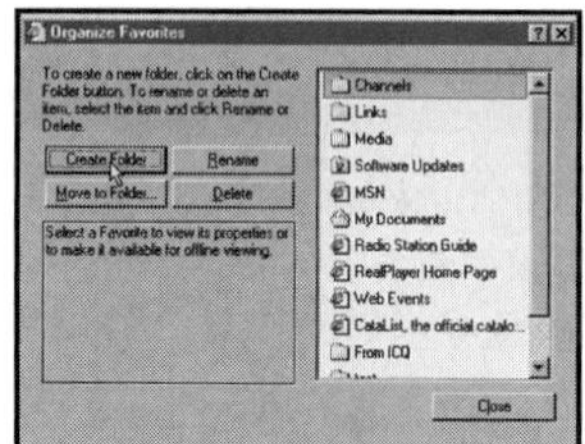

Figure 3.21
Organize your bookmark to make returning to sites a simple process.

2. Create a new folder by clicking Create Folder. A new folder appears. Type a name for the folder.
3. Place a favorite site into the new folder by clicking it once and dragging it on top of the folder you just created.

2. Searching Newsgroups

Deja.com is a search engine that allows you to search the contents of newsgroups. Because Internet discussion groups can hold a good deal of pertinent information, this is an important tool to know about.

1. Connect to deja.com at `http://www.deja.com` (see Figure 3.22).

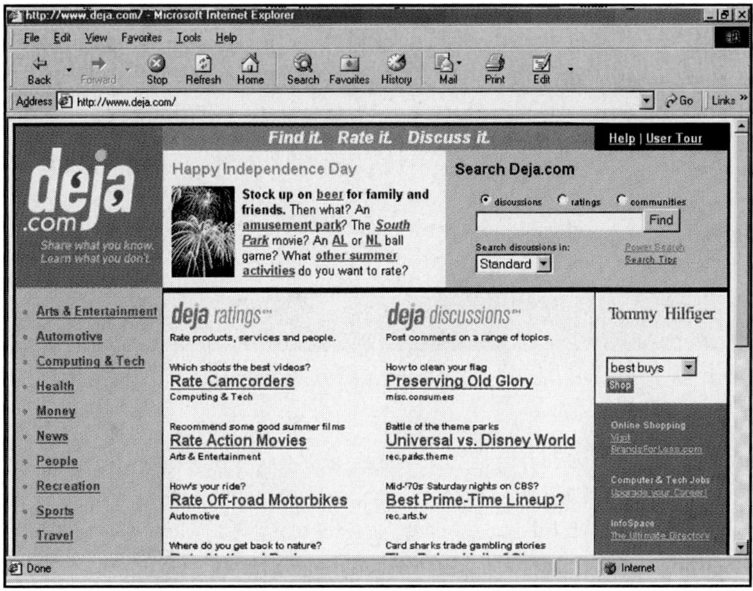

Figure 3.22
Deja.com enables you to search newsgroups.

2. Type a keyword in the text box.
3. Click Find.
4. As with many of the other search engines, deja.com has an advanced search utility. Click the Power Search button to use it.

3. Searching for Yourself

You might be surprised to learn that information about you already exists on the World Wide Web. If you've done anything slightly of note, it might exist on the Web.

1. Connect to your favorite search engine.
2. Type in your name as the keywords. Put quotation marks around your name so the search engine knows to treat your name as a complete phrase.
3. Click the Search button. If you have a fairly common name, you might want to narrow your search parameters a bit.

4. Comparing Search Engines

1. Choose a topic of personal interest and define a keyword that you can use to search the Net.

2. Select four search engines and, one at a time, make a connection. Use the search engines you used previously. Here are a couple of new search engines for you to try as well:
   - www.lycos.com
   - www.goto.com
3. Compare your results. How many links did each search engine find? Did one engine seem to bring back more pertinent information on your topic?
4. Compare the results with those of other people you know. Is it possible to agree on which search engine is the best for everybody? Performing this kind of exercise can help you decide which search engine to use first when you are starting to research a topic.

Discovery Zone

1. Searching for People on the Net

You can search for names, addresses, telephone numbers, businesses, and so on by using the World Wide Web. Connect to Yahoo! Click the Yellow Pages link and follow the steps to look for a business in your area. Click the People Search link to search for other people. Try to look up your own address and phone number, and see if you can find it.

2. Sharing Your Favorites File

After you've spent some time creating and organizing your Favorites file, you might want to make it available for other people to use. You can place your Favorites file on a disk for other people to use. Open Internet Explorer and select Import and Export from the File menu. The Import/Export Wizard appears onscreen and assists you through the rest of the steps. You have the option of of exporting all of your favorites or just those contained in a folder specified by you. You can save your favorites onto a floppy disk or onto a file that can be transmitted via email to a friend.

3. Using Specialized Search Engines

The search engines used in this project are comprehensive—that is, they search a wide range of informational sources. There are also several specialized search engines that let you search in a specific subject area. Connect to `http://dir.yahoo.com/Computers and Internet/Internet/World Wide Web/Searching the Web/Search Engines`.

You see a large listing of search engines that search just about anything under the sun.

4. Using the Internet Explorer Help Function

Internet Explorer has many more functions that can be covered here. If you have a question about how to manage your favorites, you can use the Internet Explorer help utility to help you find the answers to your questions. Select Contents and Index from the Help menu. You see three tabs that can help you find answers. The Contents tab lists broad topics, the Index tab contains an alphabetical list of topics, and Search allows you to perform a keyword search. Spend some time to familiarize yourself with this important utility.

Part II Word

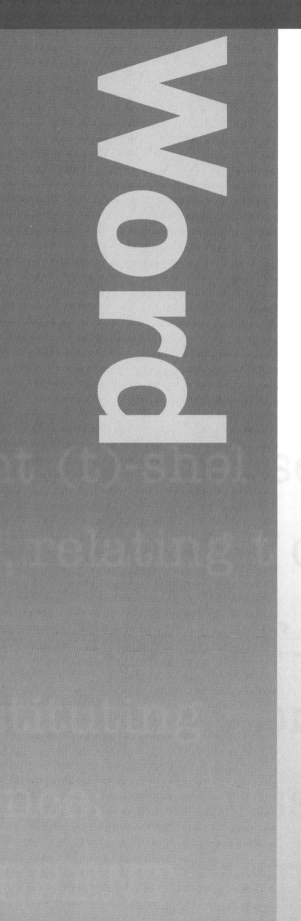

1 Getting Started with Word

2 Editing a Document

3 Formatting Text

4 Formatting a Document

5 Working with Tables

Introduction to Microsoft Word 2000

Modern word processing enables the average person to produce and edit typewritten documents more quickly and more accurately than ever before. The development of written language, paper, ink, and the printing press all had a role in the steps that eventually lead to the use of a personal computer to write a letter. Typewritten documents can be traced to Johann Gutenberg, who is traditionally credited with inventing the type mold printing press in Germany in 1450. This invention also made the mass distribution of written materials possible, which has grown exponentially with the use of the personal computer. As printing developed in the 17th and 18th centuries, many beautiful typefaces were created. Many of these have survived and can be seen in the list of fonts that are available in a word processing program.

The typewriter was another key development along the way. Typewriters came into use in the 1870s and made it possible for individuals to write documents using typeface. It also resulted in the widespread use of the QWERTY keyboard layout (the name refers to the sequence of letters on the left side of the keyboard), which is still in use today with the personal computer. Typewriters were an integral part of the modern office until the 1980s, when personal computers (PCs) began to infiltrate the office and replaced (or at least displaced) the typewriter. In an office environment, the PC is most commonly used as a word processor.

Microsoft Word is a word processing application program. Unlike a typewriter, a word processing program running on a PC allows you to enter text and then change it by editing existing text, moving blocks of text, or changing the appearance of the letters. The document is stored electronically, so it can be duplicated, printed, copied, and conveniently shared with others. Stored documents can be modified and saved with a new name. Documents can be sent from your computer to another computer by using an online fax connection, by email, or by publishing the document as a Web page. Gutenberg's press made it possible for a person's thoughts to be shared with thousands of people in a matter of days; word processing, combined with email or the Internet, makes it possible for a person to share his or her thoughts instantly with the world.

The computer screen is used to represent a page of paper. In Word, you can choose to work in a simulated page, called Print Layout view, that shows the page with its edges, margins, headers, footers, automatic page numbers, and graphics objects. This view uses an inch or so on each side to display the margins, so the available space for viewing each line of text is reduced. For this reason, most people work in Normal view when they are working with text; it utilizes the full width of the screen for displaying each line.

When you type on the keyboard, your text appears on the screen. A vertical flashing line indicates the insertion point, so you can tell where your text will go when you start to type. A short horizontal line marks the end of the existing text. When you are typing and reach the end of a line, just continue to type—the program decides whether the next word fits. If the word does not fit, it moves down to the next line. This feature, known as word wrap, is common to all word processing programs. You press ↵Enter only when you get to the end of a paragraph or when you want to create empty lines to add extra space between paragraphs.

Word has many features that you can use for special purposes. It is not necessary for you to learn them all. After you have mastered the basics, you can add the skills that are most useful in your pursuits.

In this section, you learn how to create a simple word document. You add, replace, move, and copy text. You learn how to format the text in a document, format individual paragraphs, create bullet lists, change margins, and set line spacing. Finally, you learn how to use clip art and work with tables. Microsoft Word 2000 is an easy program to use and is a convenient way to write at the office, at school, or at home.

Project 1

Getting Started with Word

Objectives

In this project, you learn how to

- **Open a New Document and Enter Text**
- **Move Around in a Document**
- **Correct Errors Using the Backspace and Delete Keys**
- **Correct Spelling and Grammar Errors**
- **Save, Print, and Close a Document, and Exit from Word**

Key terms introduced in this project include

- word wrap

SOURCE: *Essentials: Office 2000,* Ferrett-Preston-Preston

Why Would I Do This?

Word processing is the most common application found on personal computers and one that almost everyone has a reason to use. When you learn word processing, you also learn about many fundamental tools and techniques that you need to work efficiently on a personal computer. You can use Microsoft Word to perform basic word-processing tasks, such as writing a memo, an essay, or a letter. Word is a robust program that also enables you to perform complex word-processing tasks, such as design sophisticated tables, embed graphics, and link to other documents and the Internet. It is a program you can learn gradually over time. After you master the fundamental skills necessary to produce a basic document, you can build your word-processing repertoire by adding advanced skills one at a time.

In this project, you write a simple letter. In the process of writing the letter, you learn how to enter and edit text, correct simple errors, correct spelling and grammar mistakes, and save and print your document. You then learn how to close the file and exit the program. When you have completed the project, you will have created a letter that looks like the one in Figure 1.1.

Visual Summary

When you have completed this project, you will have created a document that looks like Figure 1.1:

Figure 1.1
A letter created using Microsoft Word.

Spelling and grammar errors have been corrected

July 5, 2000

The Lewis Family
1849 Hawken Blvd.
Ann Arbor, MI 48104

Dear Lewis Family:

Thank you for purchasing your swimming pool from Armstrong Pool, Spa, and Sauna. Your new pool is our top-of-the-line model, and should last thirty or forty years if properly maintained.

We hope you were completely satisfied with the installation. Dick and his crew have been installing swimming pools, spas, and saunas for us for a number of years, and no one does a better job!

Thanks again for choosing Armstrong Pool, Spa, and Sauna for your purchase. To show our appreciation, we will give you 10% off all pool chemicals and accessories for one full year from the date of purchase of your pool!

Sincerely,

<your name>
Ann Arbor Manager
Armstrong Pool, Spa, and Sauna

Words have been replaced

Lesson 1: Opening a New Document and Entering Text

You can use word processing programs to create written documents such as letters, memos, research papers, and so on. When you launch Word, you automatically create a blank document where you can begin entering text. It is just like taking a blank piece of paper and writing with a pen or pencil, except that you write using a computer keyboard.

In this lesson, you create a new document. Don't worry if you make mistakes; you learn to correct them in Lesson 3.

To Open a New Document and Enter Text

1. **Launch Microsoft Word. If you need assistance launching Word, refer to the project on Office Basics at the beginning of this book.**
   A new document displays. The default name is `Document` followed by a number. The insertion point is a blinking line that indicates where text will be inserted when you begin typing. It appears in the upper-left corner of the work area. The insertion point is sometimes referred to as the cursor. The end-of-document marker appears just below the insertion point. The ***pointer*** shows the location of the mouse indicator on the screen. The pointer may appear in the shape of an arrow, I-beam, or other symbol depending on its location on your screen. Figure 1.2 shows the different parts of the Word screen. (*Note*: Your screen may look somewhat different.)

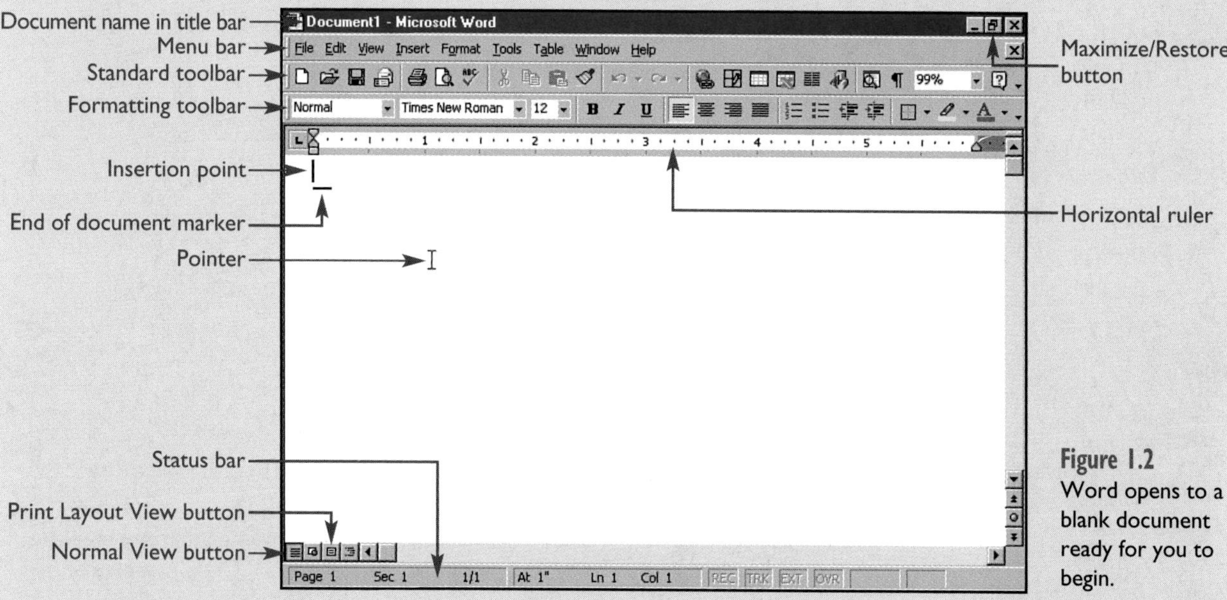

Figure 1.2
Word opens to a blank document ready for you to begin.

Word assigns a default name to new documents consisting of the word Document, followed by a number. The first time Word launches, the default document name is `Document1`. The number that displays depends on how many other documents are open or have been created since Word was launched; therefore, the number of the document on your screen may differ from the example shown.

2. **If necessary, click the Normal View button and click the Maximize button to maximize the window.**
   Refer to Figure 1.2 to identify these buttons. Use the view buttons located on the status bar to change the way the document appears on your screen. Normal view shows document formatting with a simplified page layout for quick and easy typing. Print Layout view enables you to see how the text looks on the page, so that you can edit margins, breaks between pages, and other print layout features.

3. **Type the following date: `July 5, 2000`.**
   Notice that the text displays at the top of the new document.

continues ▶

To Open a New Document and Enter Text (continued)

4 Press ↵Enter.

The insertion point and the end of document marker move down a line.

5 Press ↵Enter again to create a blank line, type `The Lewis Family`, and then press ↵Enter.

The beginning of the document should look like the one in Figure 1.3.

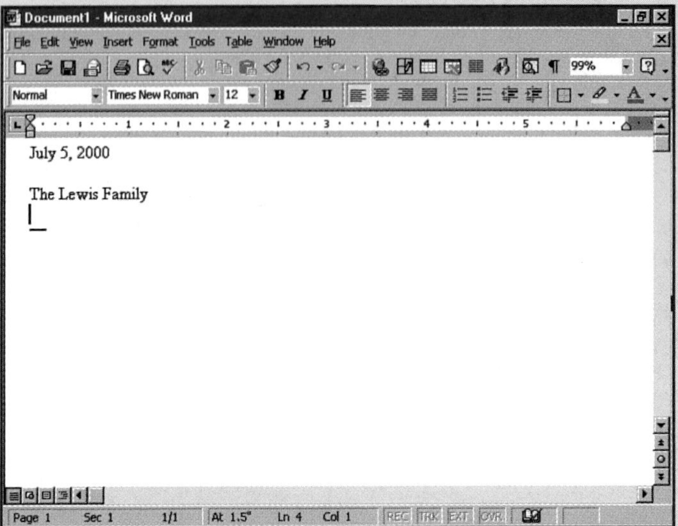

Figure 1.3
The date and the first line of the address for your letter are shown.

6 Finish the address with the following text:

`1849 Hawken Blvd.`
`Ann Arbor, MI 48104`

Press ↵Enter to create a blank line after the address.
Type the salutation:

`Dear Lewis Family:`

Press ↵Enter twice to create a blank line after the salutation.
Press ↵Enter to create a blank line between the address and the salutation.

The Office Assistant might open on your screen and ask whether you need assistance writing a letter. Click the Cancel button to close the Office Assistant. The Office Assistant is part of the Help program covered in the Office Basics project at the beginning of this book.

Jagged underlines might appear below some of the text you entered. A red jagged underline means that the word is not in the dictionary, and a green jagged underline means that the program thinks there may be a grammatical mistake. To verify that these options are turned on, click Tools, Options on the menu bar. Click the Spelling & Grammar tab and make sure a check mark is in the box next to Check spelling as you type and in the box next to Check grammar as you type. Then click OK to close the Options dialog box.

7 Type the following text. Press ↵Enter only after you type the entire paragraph. (Note: Misspell purchaseing in the first sentence, as shown in the following passage. You learn how to fix this type of error in a subsequent lesson.)

`Thank you for purchaseing your swimming pool from Armstrong Pool, Spa, and Sauna. Your new pool is our top-of-the-line model, and should last thirty or forty years if properly maintained.`

Your letter should look like the one in Figure 1.4.

Using Word Wrap

The insertion point for the text moves from one line to the next because of a feature called ***word wrap***. Word wrap is a word-processing function that automatically moves the first word that reaches the right margin to the next line. You do not press ↵Enter until you get to the end of a paragraph. Pressing ↵Enter marks the end of the paragraph with a special character (¶) that also includes information about the formatting of the entire paragraph.

The words on your screen might not wrap the same way as they do in the figure due to a difference in the document width or font size setting. A difference might also be due to the number of spaces between sentences—this text has one space between sentences. Do not be concerned if the words wrap at a different place in the paragraph.

If you accidentally press ↵Enter before you reach the end of the paragraph, press ←Backspace to remove the paragraph marker (which is probably hidden on your screen, but is there nonetheless).

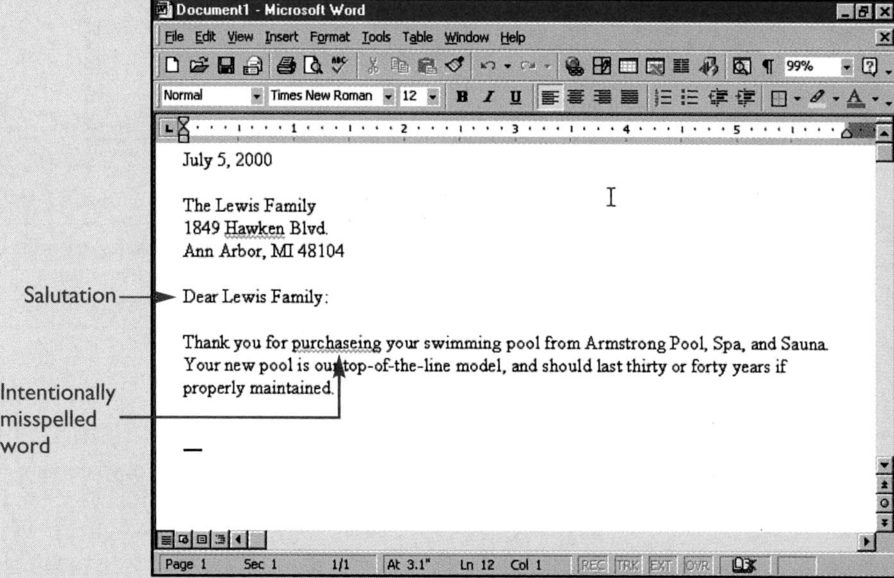

Figure 1.4
The opening paragraph of the letter is typed.

8. **Press ↵Enter again to create a blank line between the paragraphs. Then finish the letter by typing the following text, complete with grammatical errors.**

```
We hope you was completely satisfied with the installation. Dick and
his crew have been installing swimming pools, spas, and saunas for us
for a number of years, and no one does a better job!

Thanks again for choosing Armstrong Pool, Spa, and Sauna for your purchase.
To show our appreciation, we will give you 10% off all pool chemicals and
pool toys for one full year from the date of purchase of your pool!

Sincerely,




<your name>
Ann Arbor Manager
Armstrong Pool, Spa, and Sauna
```

Leave four blank lines between the closing and your name.

continues ▶

To Open a New Document and Enter Text (continued)

Make sure you type your name in the third-to-last line. The completed letter should look like the one in Figure 1.5. Leave the file open for use in the next lesson.

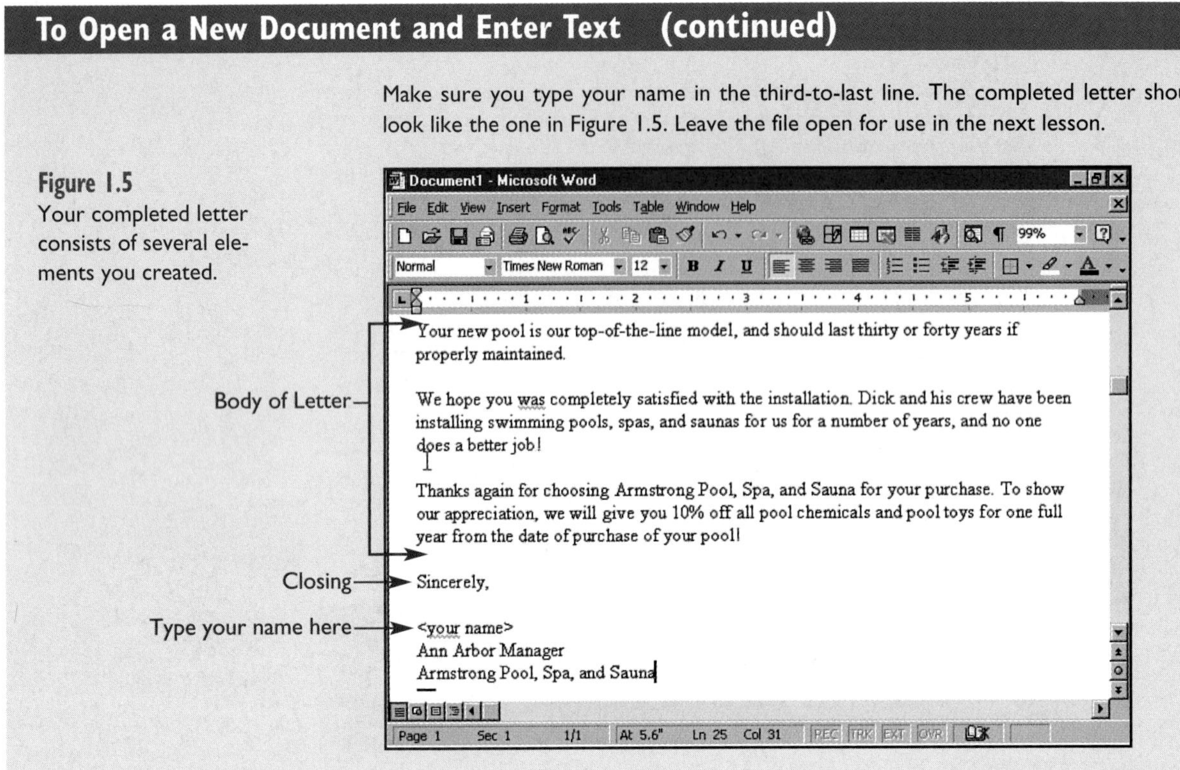

Figure 1.5
Your completed letter consists of several elements you created.

Depending on how your monitor is set up, the entire letter might not be displayed on the screen. If the top of the letter scrolls out of sight when you type your name and title, don't be concerned. In the next lesson, you learn how to move around in your document.

Lesson 2: Moving Around in a Document

When you typed the letter in the first lesson, the insertion point moved automatically as you typed or when you pressed ↵Enter. When you reached the end of the letter, the screen automatically scrolled the text up and out of view so that you could see the new lines as you typed. In the next lesson, you learn how to move around in the document so that you can select text, enter new text, edit existing text, or see different parts of your document. You can move around in a document in many different ways. You can use the pointer to move the insertion point to a new location. You can use arrow keys to move up, down, left, or right in the text. You can use the scrollbars or use combinations of keys to move the document up or down one screen at a time. The scrollbars are located on the right side and bottom of the screen and enable you to move a document up and down or side to side on the screen. Knowing how to move around in your document enables you to enter and edit text quickly.

In this lesson, you use different techniques to navigate in your document.

To Move Around in a Document

1. **Click the arrow at the top of the vertical scrollbar several times to scroll to the top of your letter (see Figure 1.6).**
   Notice that the screen scrolls up one line at a time. If you click the arrow and hold down the left mouse button, your screen scrolls rapidly.

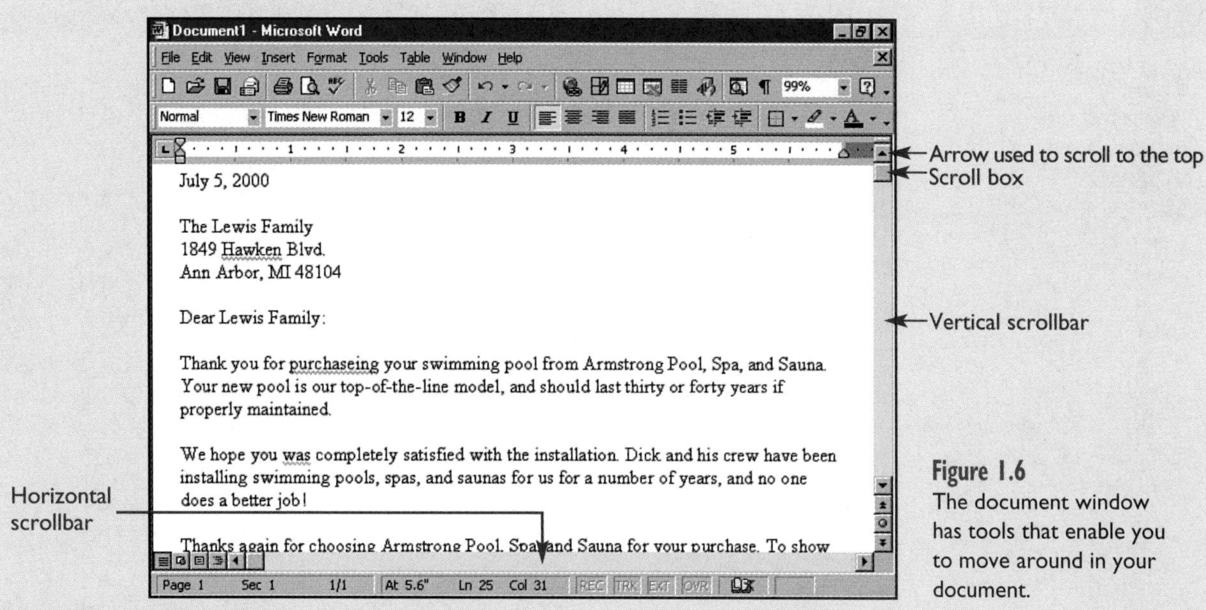

Figure 1.6
The document window has tools that enable you to move around in your document.

2. **Position the pointer on the blank line between the first and second full paragraphs, and click.**
   The insertion point moves to the beginning of the blank line. If you begin typing, the words appear at the insertion point location, not at the pointer location.

> When you first use Word, you might have a little trouble distinguishing between the pointer, which shows the movement or location of the mouse, and the blinking insertion point, which is the point at which you begin to type. Any text that you type always appears at the insertion point location, never at the pointer location. The mouse pointer appears as an I-beam on the document and as a white arrow when you place it on the toolbars, scrollbars, status bar, or at the left edge of a document.

3. **Press ↑ on your keyboard until the insertion point is just below the salutation.**
   Using an arrow key changes the location of the insertion point in your document. If necessary, the text on your screen scrolls up or down, so that you can continue to see the insertion point.

4. **Press PgDn to move down one screen.**
   Notice that the insertion point moves and only the bottom of the document displays.

5. **Press the PgUp key to move up one screen.**
   Notice that the top of the letter displays and that the insertion point is near the top of the letter. This feature is very helpful for longer documents. You should be aware, however, that the PgDn and PgUp keys move the view one screen at a time, not one page of the document. Your screen should look like the one in Figure 1.7. Table 1.1 shows additional key combinations you can use to navigate in the document.

   Leave the document open for use in the next lesson.

continues ▶

To Move Around in a Document (continued)

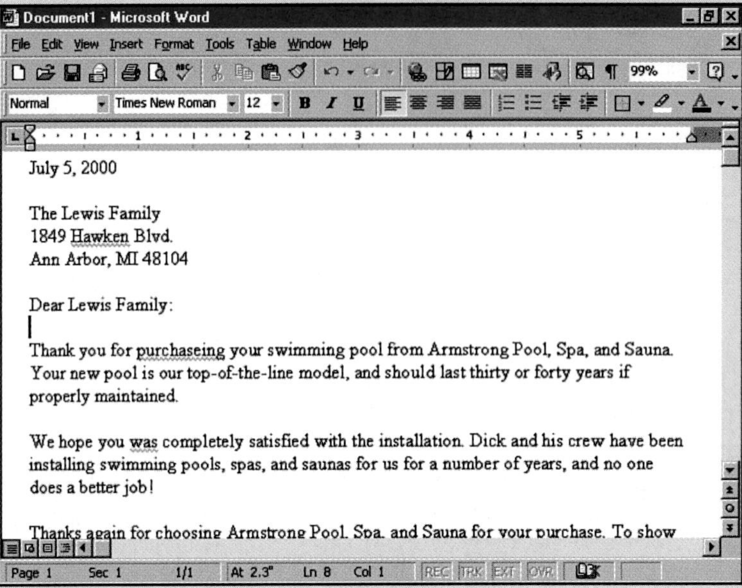

Figure 1.7
The top of the letter displays at the top of the screen.

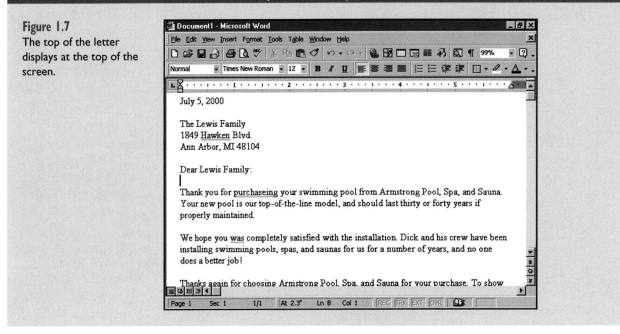

Table 1.1 Keyboard Shortcuts for Moving Around in a Document

Key(s)	Moves the Insertion Point
←	One character to the left
→	One character to the right
↓	Down one line
↑	Up one line
Home	To the beginning of the line
End	To the end of the line
PgUp	Up one screen
PgDn	Down one screen
Ctrl+Home	To the beginning of the document
Ctrl+End	To the end of the document
Ctrl+←	One word to the left
Ctrl+→	One word to the right

Scrolling Through a Document

Notice the box in the vertical scrollbar. This box lets you know your location in the document—it is at the top of the scrollbar when you are at the top of the document and at the bottom of the scrollbar when you are at the end of the document. You can point to the box, click and hold the left mouse button, and then drag the box up or down the scrollbar to move quickly to a new location in your document. A ScreenTip displays the current page number as you scroll through a multipage document. This action moves the text displayed on your screen, but it does not change the location of the insertion point. You need to click at the point where you want to begin to type to move the insertion point to that location.

Lesson 3: Correcting Errors Using the Backspace and Delete Keys

While you are creating a document, you might make typographical errors that you want to correct immediately. You might also find changes that you want to make when you proofread what you've written. You can correct errors in several ways. The two most common methods are to use the Backspace and Delete keys.

Pressing ←Backspace deletes text to the left of the insertion point, and pressing Del deletes text to the right of the insertion point. These keys are good for removing single characters or short words. In Project 2, "Editing a Document," you see how they can also be used to remove selected words, sentences, or paragraphs.

In this lesson, you edit text using ←Backspace and Del.

To Correct Errors Using the Backspace and Delete Keys

1 Use the skills you just learned to place the insertion point immediately to the left of the word toys in the last full paragraph.

2 Press ←Backspace once.

Notice that the insertion point moves to the left and removes the space between the words `pool` and `toys` as shown in Figure 1.8.

We hope you was completely satisfied with the installation. Dick and his crew have been installing swimming pools, spas, and saunas for us for a number of years, and no one does a better job!

Thanks again for choosing Armstrong Pool, Spa, and Sauna for your purchase. To show our appreciation, we will give you 10% off all pool chemicals and pooltoys for one full year from the date of purchase of your pool!

The space is removed

Figure 1.8
Pressing the Backspace key removes characters to the left of the insertion point.

3 Press ←Backspace four more times.

Notice that the word `pool` is deleted.

4 Press Del once.

Notice that the first letter of the word `toys` to the right of the insertion point is removed, even though the insertion point didn't move.

5 Press Del three more times.

The word `toys` is removed. Do not remove the space to the right of the word.

6 Type the word `accessories` at the insertion point.

The new word is inserted at the insertion point and the existing text moves to the right as shown in Figure 1.9. Leave the document open for use in the next lesson.

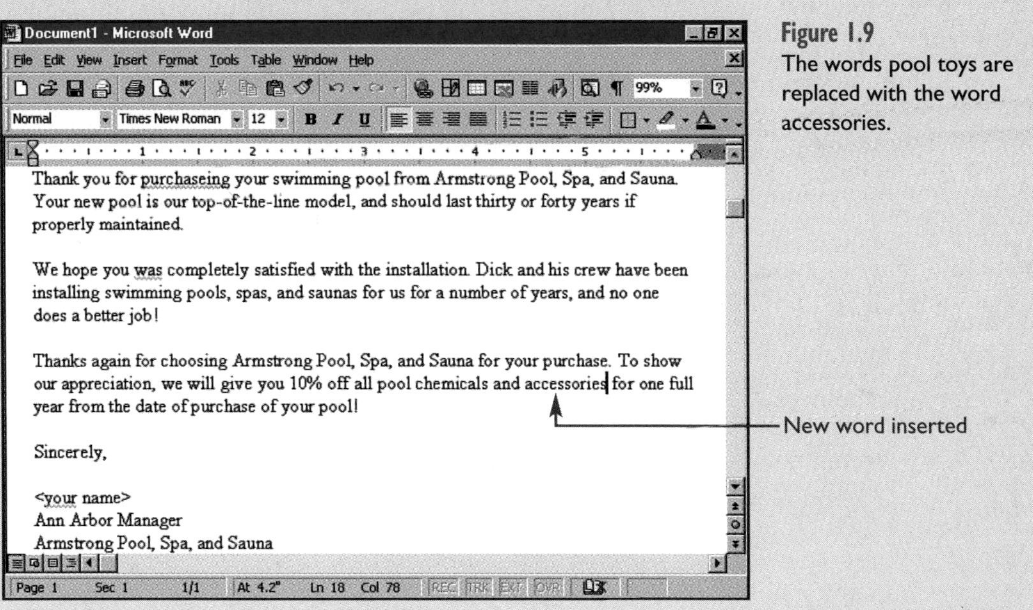

Thank you for purchaseing your swimming pool from Armstrong Pool, Spa, and Sauna. Your new pool is our top-of-the-line model, and should last thirty or forty years if properly maintained.

We hope you was completely satisfied with the installation. Dick and his crew have been installing swimming pools, spas, and saunas for us for a number of years, and no one does a better job!

Thanks again for choosing Armstrong Pool, Spa, and Sauna for your purchase. To show our appreciation, we will give you 10% off all pool chemicals and accessories for one full year from the date of purchase of your pool!

Sincerely,

<your name>
Ann Arbor Manager
Armstrong Pool, Spa, and Sauna

Figure 1.9
The words pool toys are replaced with the word accessories.

Lesson 4: Correcting Spelling and Grammar Errors

Spelling and grammar errors in a document tend to reduce the credibility and effectiveness of the message. Microsoft Word gives you two ways to check spelling and grammar. The first is a program that gives you a great deal of flexibility in checking and correcting the errors. The second is a shortcut that can save a considerable amount of time in a long document.

In this lesson, you use a shortcut menu to correct spelling and grammar errors.

To Correct Spelling and Grammar Errors

1. **Locate the misspelled word `purchaseing` in the first paragraph. Move the pointer onto the word and right-click.**
   A shortcut menu opens and suggests the correct spelling. The top section of the shortcut menu contains suggestions for replacing the misspelled word, as shown in Figure 1.10.

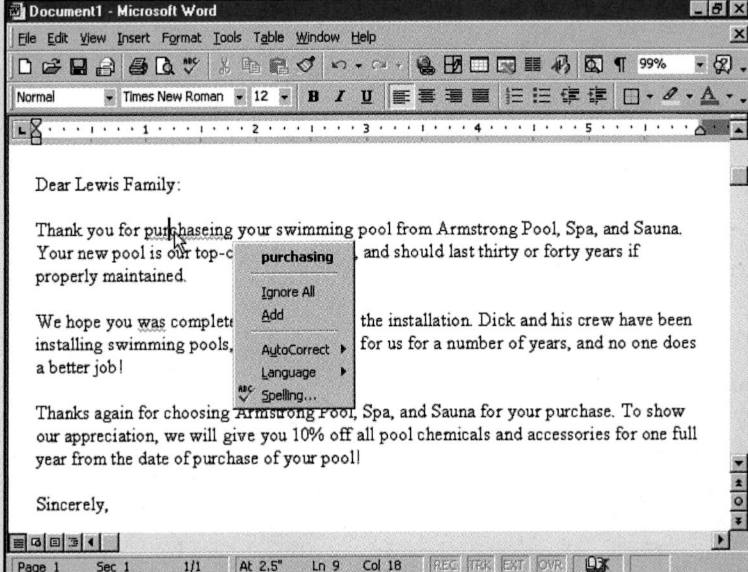

Figure 1.10
You can use the shortcut menu to correct spelling errors quickly.

2. **The suggestion is correct. Move the pointer to the word `purchasing` in the shortcut menu to select it. Click the selected text.**
   The correctly spelled word replaces the misspelled word, and the shortcut menu closes.

3. **Right-click the word `Hawken` in the address line.**
   The shortcut menu opens with suggestions, but none of the suggestions are correct (see Figure 1.11).

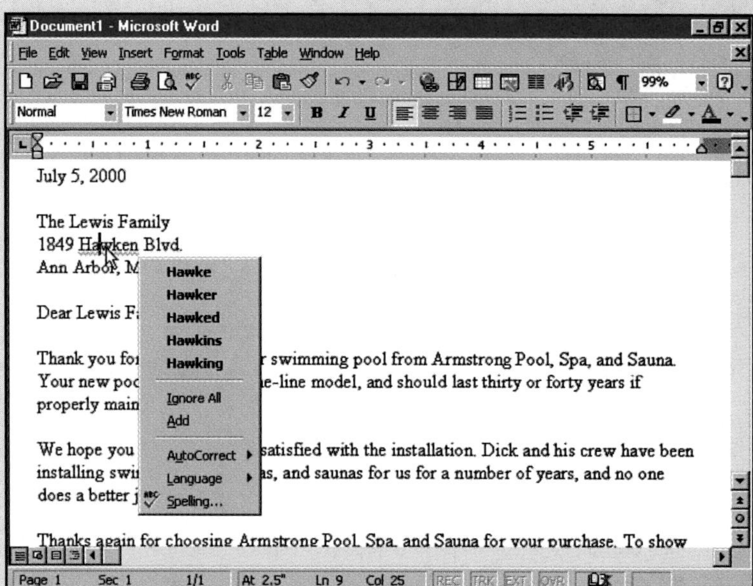

Figure 1.11
Sometimes the dictionary doesn't recognize a word.

4 Click the Ignore All button to ignore all further occurrences of the word in this document.
The red jagged line disappears.

5 Right-click the word was **in the second full paragraph.**
A shortcut menu displays, as shown in Figure 1.12. The green jagged underline indicates a grammar error. To correct grammar errors, you use the same technique you used to correct spelling errors.

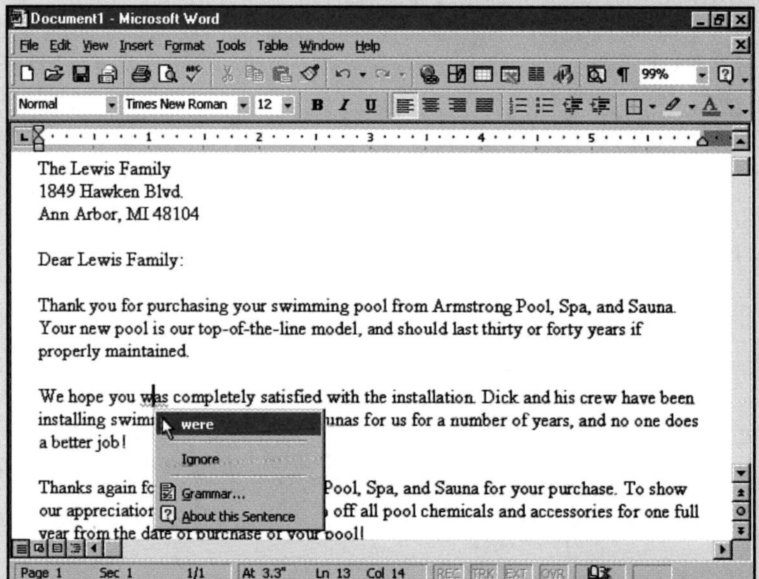

Figure 1.12
Grammar errors are identified with a green jagged underline.

6 Click were **in the shortcut menu to select it.**
This action replaces was in the sentence and the green jagged underline disappears. Leave the document open for use in the next lesson.

Accessing the Spelling and Grammar Checking Programs

To access the full spelling and grammar checking programs, click the Spelling and Grammar button on the Standard toolbar. The Spelling and Grammar dialog box opens and gives you additional options. For example, you can ignore single occurrences of words that the checker thinks are misspelled. The Spelling and Grammar dialog box also gives you information about the type of grammar error it highlighted.

The Spelling checker uses a dictionary that has thousands of words in it. When you type a word that is not in its dictionary, the Spelling checker highlights the word with a red jagged line. Just because the word is not in the program's dictionary does not mean that it is misspelled; it could be a proper noun, a technical term, or an unusual word.

When the Spelling checker identifies a word that is not in the dictionary, you have the option to add the word to the dictionary. Be very careful! If you add a misspelled word to the dictionary, it accepts the word in the future without warning. In general, do not add words to the dictionary if you are using someone else's computer or are working in a computer laboratory.

Extra Word Spaces

The Grammar checker also detects extra spaces between words and marks it as a grammar error. If you see an error marked and it appears as though nothing is wrong, it might be an extra space. Use the shortcut menu to correct this type of error.

Lesson 5: Saving, Printing, and Closing a Document, and Exiting from Word

When you write a letter, memo, or other type of document, you often want to save a permanent record of it for future reference. To create a permanent record of your document, you need to save it on your hard drive or on a floppy disk. You might also need a printed copy of your document, as in this case to send to the client. When you are finished using the file, it is important to close it before you exit from the application.

In this lesson, you save the Lewis letter, print a copy of it, and then close the file and exit Word.

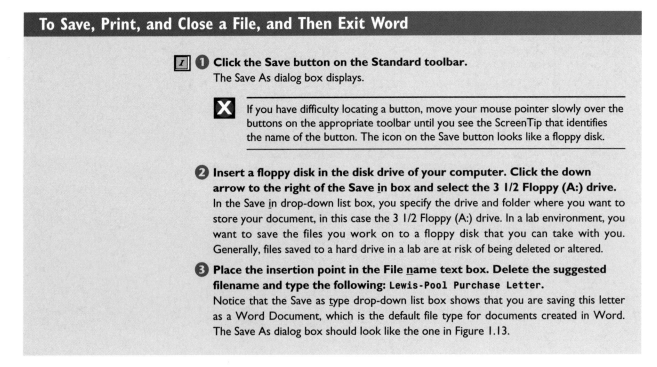

To Save, Print, and Close a File, and Then Exit Word

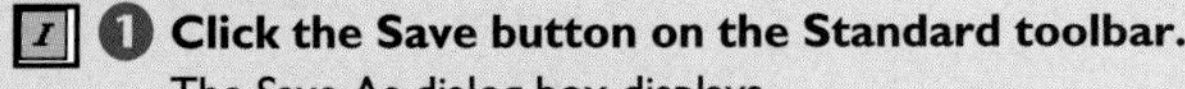

1. **Click the Save button on the Standard toolbar.**
   The Save As dialog box displays.

   If you have difficulty locating a button, move your mouse pointer slowly over the buttons on the appropriate toolbar until you see the ScreenTip that identifies the name of the button. The icon on the Save button looks like a floppy disk.

2. **Insert a floppy disk in the disk drive of your computer. Click the down arrow to the right of the Save in box and select the 3 1/2 Floppy (A:) drive.**
   In the Save in drop-down list box, you specify the drive and folder where you want to store your document, in this case the 3 1/2 Floppy (A:) drive. In a lab environment, you want to save the files you work on to a floppy disk that you can take with you. Generally, files saved to a hard drive in a lab are at risk of being deleted or altered.

3. **Place the insertion point in the File name text box. Delete the suggested filename and type the following: `Lewis-Pool Purchase Letter`.**
   Notice that the Save as type drop-down list box shows that you are saving this letter as a Word Document, which is the default file type for documents created in Word. The Save As dialog box should look like the one in Figure 1.13.

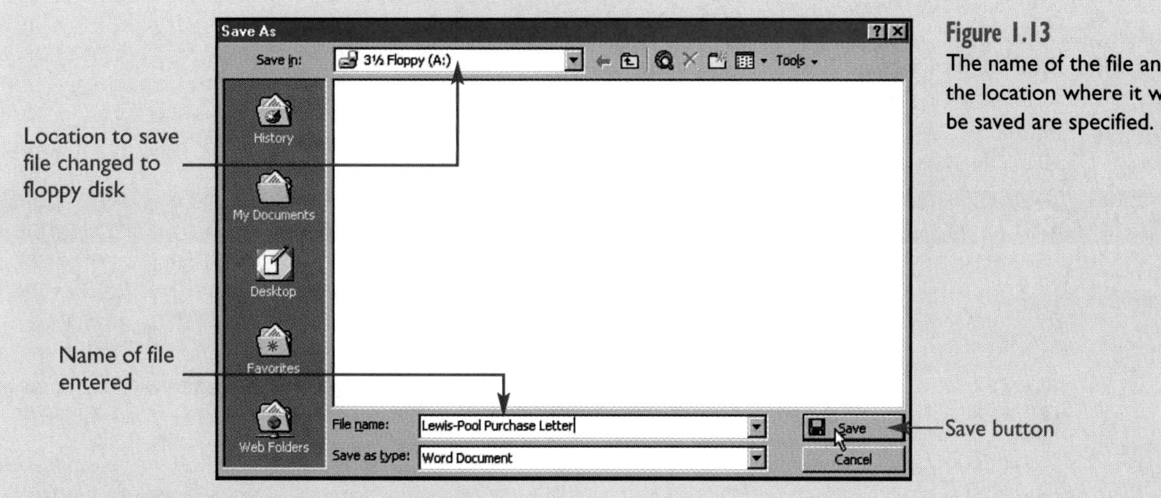

Figure 1.13
The name of the file and the location where it will be saved are specified.

4. **Click the Save button in the dialog box.**
   The document is saved to your disk and the name of the file displays in the title bar.

5. **Make sure your printer is turned on. Then click the Print button on the Standard toolbar.**
   The document goes to the printer.

6. **Click the Save button on the Standard toolbar again to save your work if you made any changes.**
   Because the file has already been saved once, the Save As dialog box does not reopen. After you save a file, you can save any changes quickly by clicking the Save button.

7. **Click the Close Window button at the right end of the menu bar.**
   The Lewis letter closes, but Word remains open.

8. **Click the Close button in the upper-right corner of the title bar.**
   Word closes and the screen returns to the Desktop.

Closing a Document

If you have not saved your changes when you click the Close button, the program asks you whether you want to save them.

More than one document can be open at a time. Each document has a button on the Windows taskbar, and you can switch between open documents by clicking the taskbar button. When more than one document is open, the active document has a Close button in the title bar. Clicking it closes the document and displays the next open document. When only one document is open, Word 2000 displays a Close Window button in the menu bar and a Close button in the title bar. The Close Window button closes the document, whereas the Close button in the title bar closes both the document and the application.

Creating a New Document

After you close a document, Word is still open but the window is empty and there is no document showing. To start working on a new document, click the New Blank Document button located at the left end of the Standard toolbar. A new empty document opens and you can begin to write something new.

Summary

In this project, you learned how to create a document after you opened Word. You entered text and learned how to correct simple errors by using ←Backspace and Del. You also practiced using the shortcut menu to correct spelling and grammar errors. Finally, you saved and printed the letter you wrote, and then closed the file and exited from Word.

Throughout this book, you will be referred to Help as a source of additional information concerning various topics. To expand your knowledge about the Word window, use the What's This? Help command to identify different parts of the screen. You practice entering and editing text in the exercises at the end of this chapter.

Checking Concepts and Terms

True/False

For each of the following, check *T* or *F* to indicate whether the statement is true or false.

__T __F 1. When you launch Word, it automatically opens a blank document called Document1. [L1]

__T __F 2. To create a blank line between lines of text, you press the Insert Blank Line button. [L1]

__T __F 3. To move the insertion point in your document, you can use the arrow keys on your keyboard. [L2]

__T __F 4. If you are typing a paragraph that does not fit on a single line, you press Enter at the end of each line of text. [L1]

__T __F 5. The Spelling checker identifies any words not found in its dictionary, even if the words are proper names or technical terms. [L4]

__T __F 6. When you type, the new characters go where the pointer happens to be when you start typing. [L2]

__T __F 7. Pressing Del deletes the character to the right of the insertion point's current position. [L3]

__T __F 8. Pressing Backspace causes all the text to the left of the insertion point to move to the left by one space each time Backspace is pressed. [L3]

__T __F 9. Spelling errors are indicated by a red jagged underline, and grammar errors are indicated by a green jagged underline. [L4]

__T __F 10. The first time you try to save a new document by pressing the Save button, the Save As dialog box opens to give you the opportunity to change the name and location of the file. [L5]

Multiple Choice

Circle the letter of the correct answer for each of the following.

1. When you find a spelling error, you can use the shortcut menu to _______________. [L4]
   a. replace the word
   b. ignore all occurrences of the word
   c. add the word to the dictionary
   d. all of the above

2. A word-processing function where the first word to reach the right margin automatically moves to the next line is known as _______________. [L1]
   a. text wrapping
   b. word wrap
   c. automatic paragraphs
   d. none of the above

3. When you type, the text is always entered at the _______________. [L1]
   a. insertion point
   b. pointer location
   c. I-beam
   d. end of the document

4. The box in the vertical scrollbar can be used to _______________. [L2]
   a. click and drag to move up or down through a document
   b. tell the relative size of the document
   c. identify page numbers when you scroll
   d. do all of the above

5. What is used to move the view of the document down one screen at a time? [L2]
   a. ↓ on keyboard
   b. ↓ at the end of the vertical scrollbar
   c. PgDn
   d. End

Screen ID

Refer to Figure 1.14 and identify the numbered parts of the screen. Write the letter of the correct label in the space next to the number.

Figure 1.14

A. Print button
B. Vertical scrollbar
C. Close Window button
D. Horizontal scrollbar
E. Pointer
F. Save button
G. End of document marker
H. Insertion point
I. Normal View button
J. Maximize/Restore button

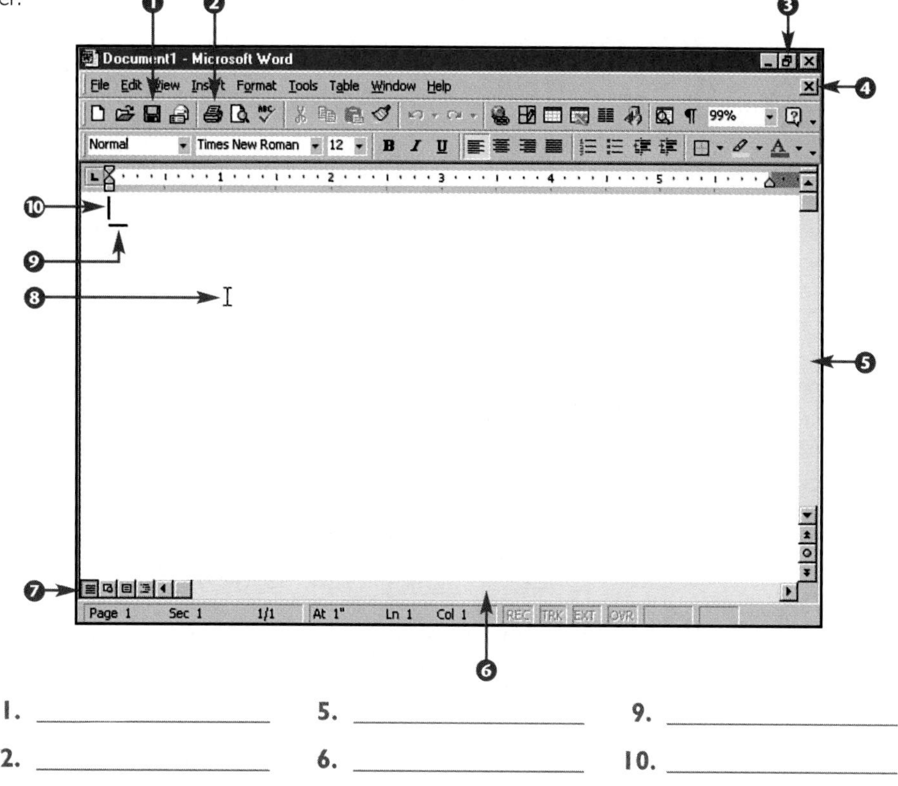

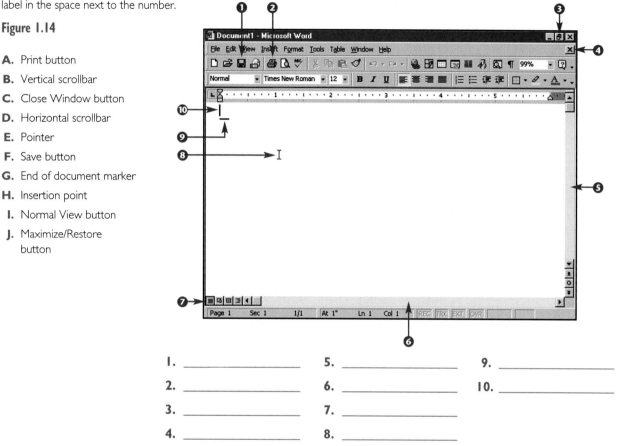

1. ______ **5.** ______ **9.** ______
2. ______ **6.** ______ **10.** ______
3. ______ **7.** ______
4. ______ **8.** ______

Discussion Questions

1. Have you used a typewriter? Have you used a word-processing program before? What program have you used? What have you used it for? What did you like or dislike about the program?
2. What needs do you have for using a word processor?
3. How does word processing differ from using a typewriter? How are they similar? What are the advantages or disadvantages of one over the other?

Skill Drill

Skill Drill exercises reinforce project skills. Each skill reinforced is the same, or nearly the same, as a skill presented in the project. Detailed instructions are provided in a step-by-step format.

In these exercises, you launch Word and type a business letter from a bank executive to a customer. Refer to Figure 1.15 to see the body of the letter. Two intentional spelling mistakes and two intentional grammar errors are included in this text. These mistakes (as well as any additional typing errors you make) are corrected. The letter is then printed and saved.

The following exercises produce and use a single document. They should be performed in sequence.

1. Launching Word and Entering a Date, Name, and Salutation

1. Launch Word.
2. Type today's date—for example, August 27, 2002.
3. Press ↵Enter to end the first line and move to the next line. Press ↵Enter again to create a blank line between the date and the name and address lines.
4. Type the following name and address. Press ↵Enter at the end of each line. If the Office Assistant appears, do not use it at this time.

```
Bill Williams
1835 Long Lake Road
Ann Arbor, MI 48104
```

5. Press ↵Enter again after the zip code to leave a blank line. Type the salutation:

   `Dear Mr. Williams:`

6. Leave the document open for use in the next exercise. [L1]

2. Entering the Body of the Letter

1. Place the insertion point to the right of the last (salutation) paragraph in your letter; then press ↵Enter twice and type the first full paragraph of the letter:

   `Thank you for your letter concerning the rate on the Gold Card you hold with our bank.`

2. Press ↵Enter twice, and then type the next paragraph exactly as shown, including any typing and grammatical errors:

   `The account you have is a variable rate account. The rate are tied to the prime rate, as quated in the Wall Street Journal. It is going down to 11.8%, effective today, based on the recent decline in the prime rate. If you pay your credit card account in full each month, you can take advantage of the 25-day grace period before interest is assessed. The benefit is that accounts that are paid in full each month do not acummulate interest charges. This feature are not available on all variable rate accounts.`

   Compare your results to Figure 1.15

Figure 1.15

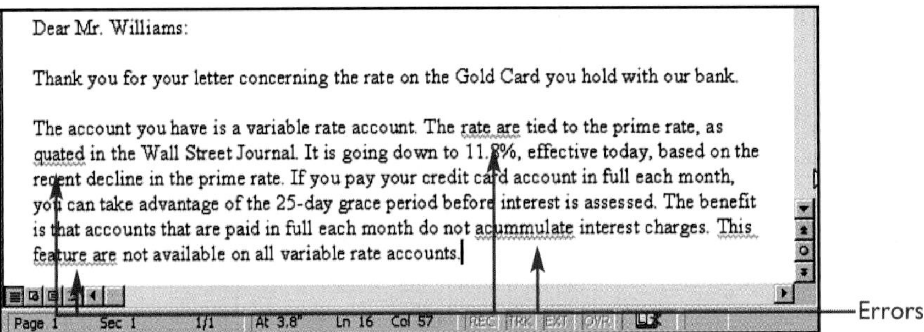

3. Press ↵Enter twice and then type the next paragraph:

   `Thank you for taking the time to write to us to share your thoughts. If you have further questions, please call me at (734) 555-1234.`

4. Press ↵Enter twice and then type the following:

   `Sincerely,`

5. Press ↵Enter three times to make room for the signature, and then type the following. (Press ↵Enter at the end of each line.)

   ```
   Mary Nelson
   Vice president
   Branch Administration
   ```

6. Press ↵Enter twice, and then type the following:

   `cc: Revolving Credit`

7. Leave the document open for use in the next exercise. [L1]

3. Moving the View and the Insertion Point and Correcting Spelling and Grammar Errors

1. Use the vertical scrollbar, ↑, or PgUp to move the view to display the top half of the letter.
2. Right-click the words `rate are` and choose `rate is`.
3. Right-click the misspelled word **`quated`** and replace it with the first choice, **`quoted`**.
4. Right-click the misspelled word **`acummulate`** and select **`accumulate`**.
5. Right-click the phrase `This feature are` and replace it with the first choice, `This feature is`.
6. Use the vertical scrollbar, ↓, or PgDn to move the view to display the bottom half of the letter.
7. Use this method to find and fix any other spelling or grammar errors that you may have made while typing the document. After you correct all the errors, the red and green jagged lines disappear.
8. Leave the document open for use in the next exercise. [L2, 4]

4. Editing and Saving the Document

1. Move the insertion point to Mary Nelson's name at the end of the document. Use Del or Backspace to delete her name and type your name.
2. Click the Save button on the toolbar.
3. In the Save As dialog box, locate the File name box and type `Letter to a Bank Customer`.
4. Select your floppy-disk drive or the folder where you want to save the document.
5. Click the Save button.
6. Leave the document open for use in the next exercise. [L3, 5]

5. Printing and Closing the Document

1. Make sure the printer that is connected to your computer is turned on.
2. Click the Print button on the toolbar. Print one copy of your letter.
3. Click the Close Window button at the upper-right corner of the menu bar to close the document.
4. Click the Close button on the upper-right corner of the Word title bar to exit Word. [L5]

Challenge

Challenge exercises expand on or are somewhat related to skills presented in the lessons. Each exercise provides a brief narrative introduction followed by instructions in a numbered step or bulleted list format that are not as detailed as those in the Skill Drill section.

In these exercises, you use the Print Layout view to create a title page. Then you use the Show/Hide button to help you eliminate extra lines in the document. Lastly, you save the file in a different format. The exercises should be done in order as presented.

1. Creating a Title Page in the Print Layout View

Some people prefer to work entirely in Print Layout view rather than Normal view. In Print Layout view, the text is slightly smaller to display the page margins. The advantage to Print Layout view is that you can see how to place illustrations, how the text looks relative to the margins, and you can see the headers and footers. [L1]

In this exercise, you create a title page by using the Print Layout view.

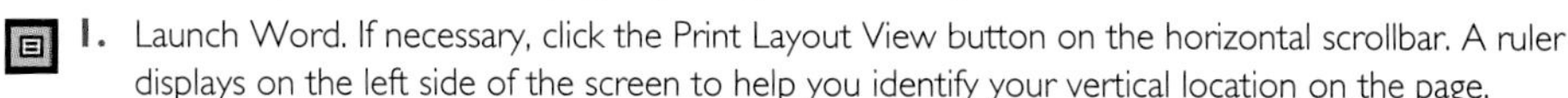

1. Launch Word. If necessary, click the Print Layout View button on the horizontal scrollbar. A ruler displays on the left side of the screen to help you identify your vertical location on the page.

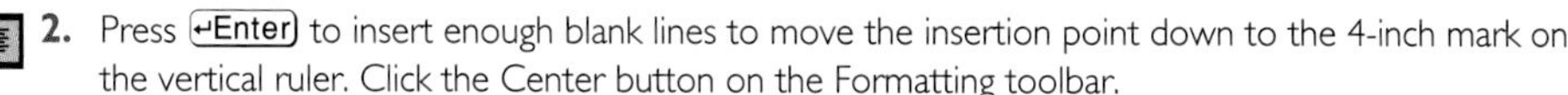

2. Press Enter to insert enough blank lines to move the insertion point down to the 4-inch mark on the vertical ruler. Click the Center button on the Formatting toolbar.
3. Type the name of the class you are taking. Press Enter and type your name.
4. Press Enter twice and type today's date.
5. Leave the file open for use in the next Challenge exercise.

2. Using the Show/Hide Feature to Delete Blank Lines in a Document

Sometimes a document has blank lines that you want to remove. In this Challenge exercise, you use the Show/Hide button to display the end-of-paragraph marks and delete some of the blank lines in your title page document.

To delete blank lines from the title page document, do the following:

1. Use the file you created in the first Challenge exercise.
2. Click the Show/Hide button near the right end of the Standard toolbar. The spaces between words show as dots and the end of paragraph ¶ mark shows each time the Enter key was used.
3. Position your mouse on the first empty line above the first line of text, and click.
4. Press Backspace five times. Notice that the text moves up on the page. You removed the five empty lines.
5. Move the insertion point to the top of the page and press Del three times. Three more lines are removed. You can use either Backspace or Del to remove blank lines.
6. Keep the file open for use in the next Challenge exercise.

3. Saving a Document Using a Different File Format

When you save a file in Word, it is saved as a Word Document with a .doc file extension, which tells the computer the type of file and the software that you used to create the file. Sometimes you need to save a file in a different file format, so that someone with a different word-processing program can open and read the file. In this Challenge exercise, you save the title page document you created previously as a Text Format (.txt) document.

To save a file using the Text file format and open it in Notepad or WordPad, do the following:

1. Click File, Save.
2. Change the Save in box to the 3 1/2 floppy (A:) disk.
3. Type `Title Page` in the File name box.
4. Click the down arrow at the end of the Save as type box.
5. Select Text Only, then click Save. A warning displays saying that you might lose some formatting. Click Yes. Close the document.
6. Launch a simple word-processing program that comes with Windows called Notepad. Use WordPad if you do not have Notepad. (Use the Start button on the taskbar, choose Programs, Accessories to locate the program.)
7. Choose File, Open. Change the Look in box to your floppy disk; click the file to select it, and click the Open button to open the file.
8. Choose File, Print to print the document. Close the document and exit the program.

Discovery Zone

Discovery Zone exercises require advanced knowledge of topics presented in *Essentials* lessons, application of skills from multiple lessons, or self-directed learning of new skills.

In these exercises, you use Help to print a list of keys used to move around in a document. Then you use the Letter Wizard to assist you in creating a letter. Finally, you explore changing the page orientation for a document.

1. Using Help to Find a List of Keys Used for Editing

Table 1.1 shows a brief list of keys that you can use to move the insertion point around in your document. Sometimes it is useful to have such a list printed for easy reference. Use the Office Assistant to find the topic entitled Keys for editing and moving text and graphics. Select the topic Move the insertion point, which shows an expanded list of keys you can use to move the insertion point around in the document. Look at the other lists of keys and their functions. Click the printer icon to print the topic. The entire list prints.

2. Using the Letter Wizard to Create a Letter Layout

If you are uncertain about the proper format for a letter, Word includes a Letter Wizard that can assist you. You can ask for help and get instructions to create a letter in the style you want. The wizard guides you through the process, during which you answer a series of questions that enable Word to create the basic layout for your letter.

In this exercise, you use the assistance provided by the Letter Wizard to create a letter.

Click the Office Assistant, or open it from the Help menu, and type `How do I write a letter?` Choose `Create a letter` from the list of options (you might have to click the See More button in the options list to find the Create a letter option). Click the Assistant and drag it out of the way, if necessary. Read the instructions on how to launch the Letter Wizard. Launch the Letter Wizard and do the following:

- Select the Letter Format tab. Click the Date line box to include the current date.
- Click the down arrow at the end of the box under Choose a page design. Select one of the options.
- Click the down arrow at the end of the box under Choose a letter style. Select one of the options.
- Click Next to move to the next wizard page, where you type the recipient information. Type the name and address in the labeled boxes for your mom or dad, or for a friend.
- In the Salutation area, select a greeting from the list or type one in the box. Try the option buttons to the right to see different greetings.

- Click the Next button to move to the Other Elements page. (You can also click the Other Elements tab at the top of the dialog box.) Review the options available on this page. Use one of the check boxes if you want to, and fill in the appropriate information. You can use more than one of the choices available on this page.
- Click the Next button to move to the Sender Info page. Type your name and address in the appropriate boxes. In the Closing area, select a closing and any other options you want to include.
- Click the Finish button. A letter layout is created based on the choices you made. If you made an error, you can choose Rerun Letter Wizard to change the selections you made for this letter. Notice that you can also make an envelope or a mailing label.
- Click after the salutation and press ↵Enter. Add a line or two of text to your letter and print it.
- Close Help, and then save the letter on your floppy disk with the name **`Letter Wizard`**. Close the letter.

3. Changing a Document to a Landscape Layout

Most documents are printed on a standard 8 1/2 by 11 sheet of paper using the portrait orientation with the length held vertically. Sometimes, however, you need documents to print using the landscape orientation (with the length held horizontally). When this is the case, it is best to create the document using the landscape orientation, so that you can see on the screen how text wraps.

In this Discovery exercise, you use Help to find information about how to set the page so that it utilizes a landscape orientation while you write.

Launch Word if necessary, or click the New Blank Document button to open a new blank document. Open Help and select the Office Assistant. Type **`landscape orientation`**. Choose the topic Select the page orientation. Click the Office Assistant icon to close the yellow topic list. Follow the instructions and change the orientation to landscape. (To see the change in orientation more clearly, click the down arrow next to the Zoom drop-down list box and select Page Width.) You see the orientation of the page in the Word window change. Repeat the procedure to change it back to portrait orientation. Print the topic to hand in to your instructor, and then close the Help window and close Word.

Project 2

Editing a Document

Objectives

In this project, you learn how to

- **Open an Existing Document and Save It with a Different Name**
- **Insert Text**
- **Use the Click and Type Feature**
- **Select Text to Delete or Replace**
- **Move Text Using Cut-and-Paste**
- **Use Undo and Redo**
- **Move Text Using Drag-and-Drop**
- **Print a Document Using the Menu**

Key terms introduced in this project include

- Click and Type
- Copy
- Cut
- cut-and-paste
- drag-and-drop
- Office Clipboard
- Paste

SOURCE: *Essentials: Office 2000,* Ferrett-Preston-Preston

Why Would I Do This?

You will probably need to alter nearly every document you create to make it appear more readable, professional, or just look better. Some alterations are necessary because you made typographical errors or you want to delete, change, or add to your text. Word gives you many ways to edit a document. The most basic of these methods is the insertion, selection, deletion, and replacement of text. Word also provides ways to copy and paste, or move text.

In this project, you learn how to use several techniques to edit text in a document.

Visual Summary

When you complete this project, your document should look like Figure 2.1:

Figure 2.1
Word gives you many tools that enable you to work with text in a document.

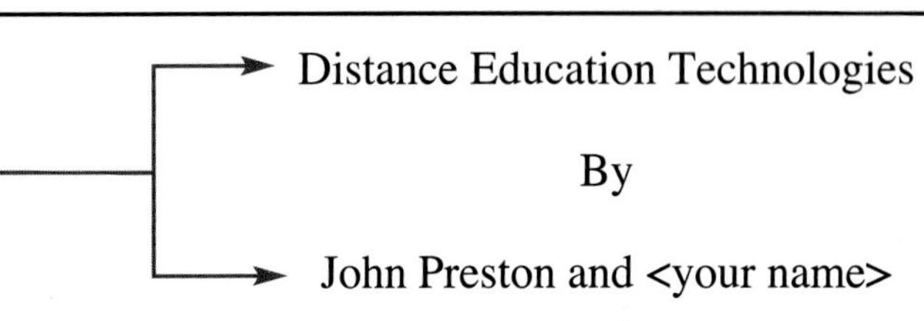
Distance Education Technologies

By

John Preston and <your name>

Titles are added using the Click and Type feature

New Technologies Affect Distance Education
The rapidly increasing capability of computers is affecting the way we communicate with each other. This year the Internet carried more personal mail than the US Postal Service ~~and this article was dictated directly to a computer using voice dictation software.~~ In this article we will look at how new technologies affect our ability to provide training when the instructor and the trainee are separated by distance or by incompatible time schedules.

This sentence has been moved

Classroom Instruction
The most common format for training is an instructor standing in front of a class of trainees. This method is popular because it allows the instructor to adapt content and the pace of instruction to each individual group based on the verbal and nonverbal cues picked up from the audience. If a class is to be conducted at a distance, it needs to be done in such a way that the instructor can get feedback from the students in order to make necessary adjustments and students need to be able to interact with the instructor and their peers.
Some classes are now being taught using digital video conferencing. However, there are still significant limitations. The biggest limitation that must be addressed is that of transmission speed. One full color screen image can take over seven million bits of data to transmit. A video needs 30 frames per second to simulate smooth motion, which could require a data transfer rate of up to 220 Megabits per second. This is four thousand times faster than the fastest modems that are used to connect home computers to the Internet, and it is approximately twice as fast as the entire capacity of most local are a networks. Consequently, video conferencing systems that rely on telephone or local area networks must make compromises. These compromises are some combination of using smaller than full-screen images, fewer than 30 frames per second, and special compression algorithms that do not transmit redundant data, such as backgrounds that do not move. Given these limitations, no one argues that videoconferencing in its present form is better than a live presentation. However, it is better than a presentation with no feedback or no presentation at all.
One option for distance courses is to provide video from the instructor, and use a response system that does not involve video but can provide specific feedback to the instructor. These systems consist of a keypad for each individual that is connected to a computer and a phone line. The learner can respond to an instructor's questions by pressing keys on the keypad or even signal the desire to ask a question. Some brands of student response systems include a microphone so that the individual student can ask a question and also have an archive of student pictures that can be displayed to the rest of the class while the student is talking. One of the advantages of this type of system is that the computer can analyze student responses immediately and display them to the instructor. In this way the instructor has a much better idea of how well the students understand what is being said. Student response systems can be used during a live presentation or at a distance. If the class is being offered locally and remotely at the same time, this type of system can be used to quantify and compare the two types of classes.

A sentence has been inserted

A phrase has been inserted

Text has been replaced

Lesson 1: Opening an Existing Document and Saving It with a Different Name

Creating a document involves writing, proofreading, and editing. Although writing is an important step, it is also important to check your document carefully and then make the necessary changes. Often, you create a draft of a document, save it, and close it and edit it later. In some instances, you might want to open an existing document and use it as the basis for a new document. You can open an existing document, make changes to it, and save it with a new name. This retains the original document without any changes, and creates a second document with a different name.

In this lesson, you open an existing file and save it with a new name.

To Open an Existing Document and Save It with a Different Name

1. **Launch Word.**
   Word opens and a blank document called Document1 displays.

2. **Place the CD-ROM that is included with the book in your computer and click the Open button.**
   The Open dialog box displays.

3. **Click the arrow to the right of the Look in drop-down list box and click the drive where you have placed your CD-ROM. Locate the Student folder and double-click it.**
   The program displays all the Word files on the disc. The CD-ROM drive is usually identified with the letter D or E. If you are not certain of its designation, ask your instructor.

4. **Locate the WO-0201 file in the Student folder on the CD-ROM and click to select it.**
   The Open dialog box should look similar to the one in Figure 2.2. Some of the filenames and locations are different from the ones on your screen, and your screen layout might be different.

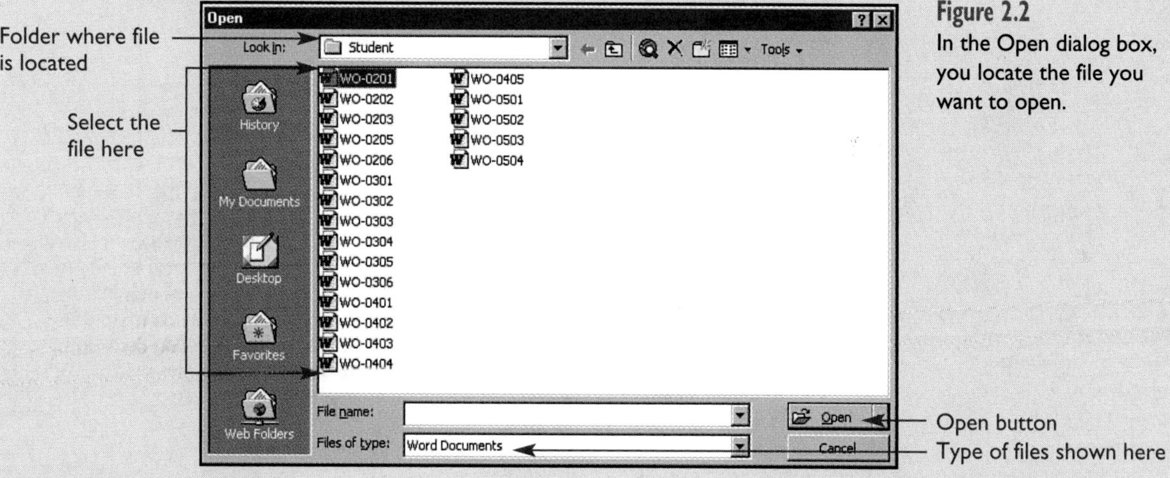

Figure 2.2
In the Open dialog box, you locate the file you want to open.

5. **Click the Open button in the Open dialog box.**
   Word opens the file. The name of the file is shown on the title bar (see Figure 2.3). Most compact discs are CD-ROM, which means compact disc–read-only memory. You must save files that you open from the CD-ROM elsewhere before you can make changes to them. This may also be true of files that are stored on a network where many people can access a file, but cannot change it until it is saved on a floppy disk or hard drive.

continues ►

To Open an Existing Document and Save It with a Different Name (continued)

Figure 2.3
If you open a document directly from a CD-ROM, you cannot make changes to it without saving it under another name.

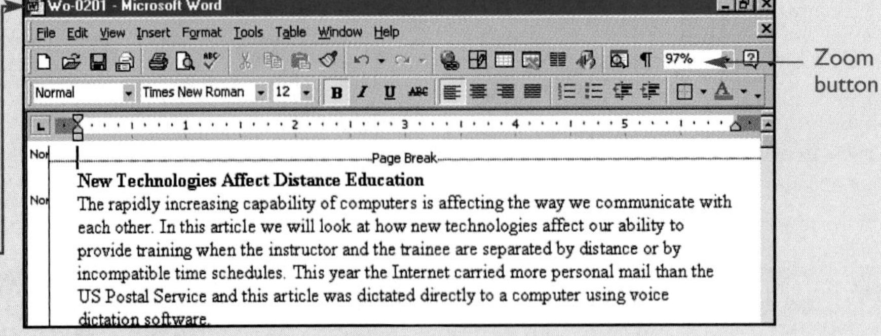

Filename displayed in title bar

Zoom button

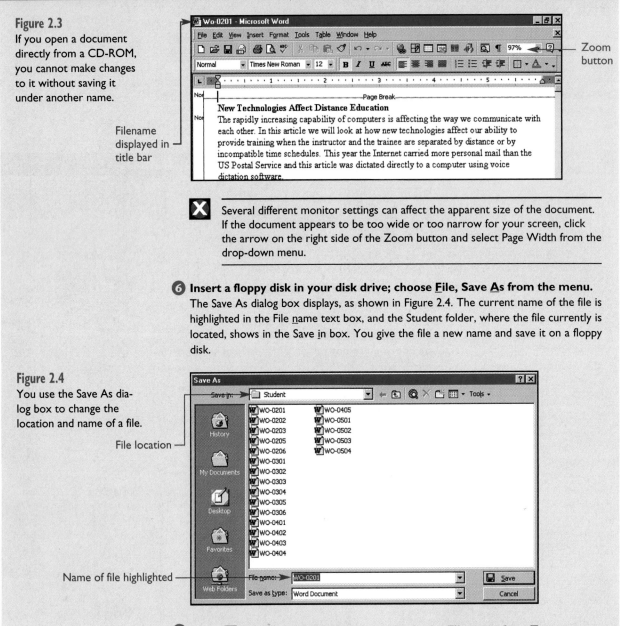

Several different monitor settings can affect the apparent size of the document. If the document appears to be too wide or too narrow for your screen, click the arrow on the right side of the Zoom button and select Page Width from the drop-down menu.

6. **Insert a floppy disk in your disk drive; choose File, Save As from the menu.**
The Save As dialog box displays, as shown in Figure 2.4. The current name of the file is highlighted in the File name text box, and the Student folder, where the file currently is located, shows in the Save in box. You give the file a new name and save it on a floppy disk.

Figure 2.4

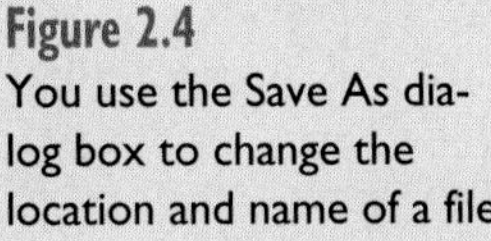

You use the Save As dialog box to change the location and name of a file.

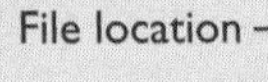

File location

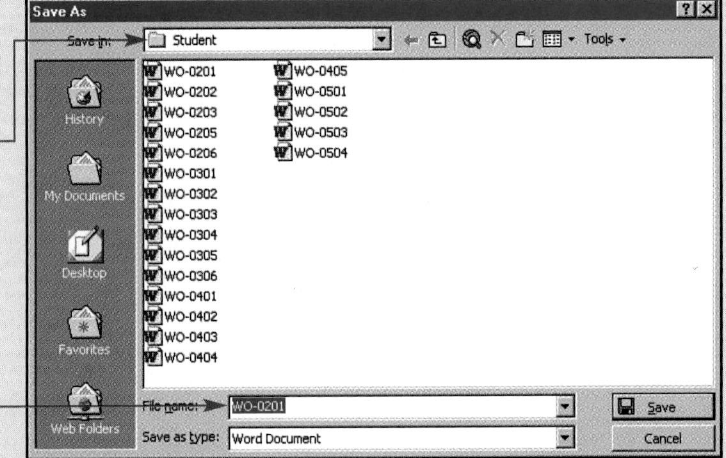

Name of file highlighted

7. **Press Del to delete the highlighted name in the File name box. Type `New Technologies 1`. Click the down arrow at the end of the Save in box and select 3 1/2 Floppy (A:) from the list.**
Make sure your changes look like the dialog box in Figure 2.5.

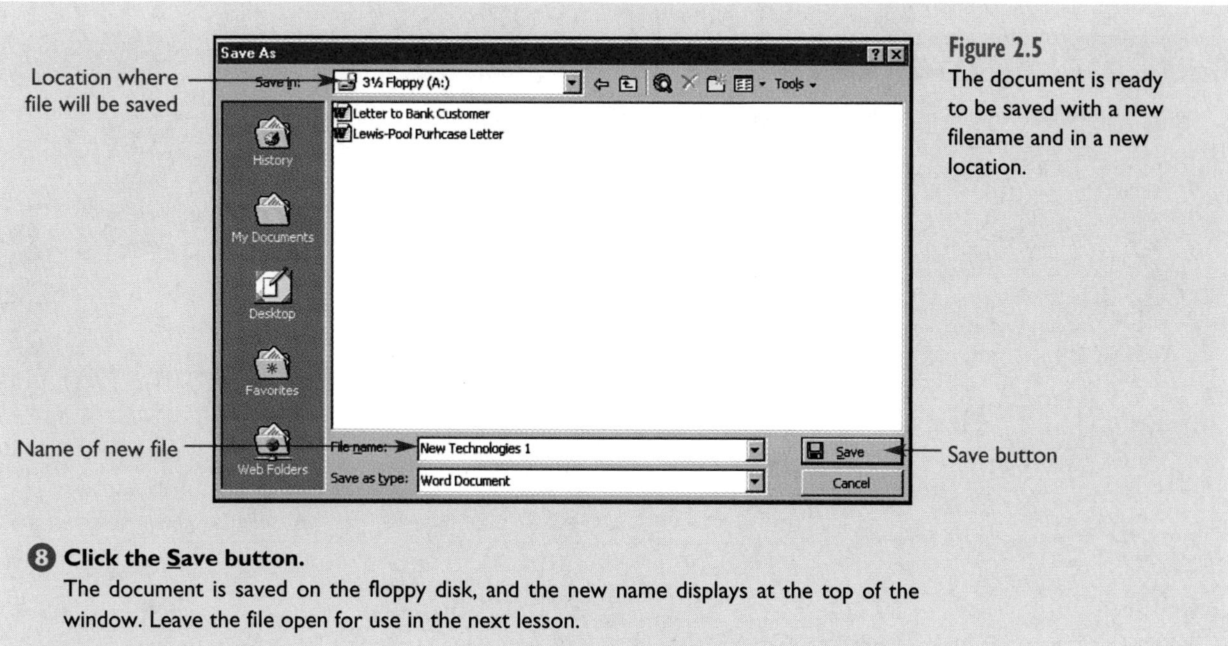

Figure 2.5
The document is ready to be saved with a new filename and in a new location.

8. **Click the Save button.**
The document is saved on the floppy disk, and the new name displays at the top of the window. Leave the file open for use in the next lesson.

Hiding File Extensions
Windows may be set to display or hide the file extensions. Word documents all have the extension .doc to identify them. If you do not see the file extensions on your files, do not be concerned: Your computer is set to hide the extensions. You can change the setting in Windows 98 by using My Computer's menu options: View, Folder Options, View, Hide file extensions for known file types. For Windows 95 and Windows NT, select View, Options, View, and select the option that turns off file extensions.

Lesson 2: Inserting Text

In most cases, you write the first draft of a document quickly to record your initial thoughts. During the proofreading and editing process, you may want to expand on the existing text and add new ideas to your document. If you allow the computer to wrap the text at the end of each line when you create the document, the program automatically adjusts the existing text to make room for any new text you insert. This freedom to express your thoughts quickly and to then make extensive additions and changes is a major advantage of using a word processor over a typewriter.

In this lesson, you insert text into an existing document.

To Insert Text

1. **Click the down arrow on the vertical scrollbar to scroll down in the New Technologies 1 file. Stop when the last paragraph and the end of document marker are displayed.**
2. **Place the insertion point in front of the word `is` in the first line of the last paragraph.**
3. **Type the words `for distance courses` at the insertion point. Make sure you add a space at the end of the inserted text.**
The words to the right of the insertion point move to the right as you type and the new text is inserted as shown in Figure 2.6.

continues ▶

To Insert Text (continued)

Figure 2.6
You can insert text wherever you place the insertion point.

Inserted text

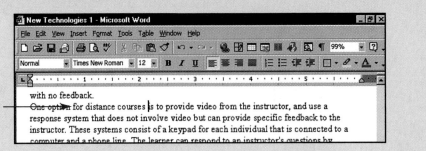

When you are first learning to use the mouse, you may sometimes place the insertion point in the wrong location. You can use → and ← to move the insertion point one character at a time to the right or left. You can also insert spaces by pressing the spacebar when needed.

4. **Use the up arrow on the vertical scrollbar to display the paragraph that begins `Some classes are now being taught`.**

5. **Place the insertion point before the word `Consequently` in the sixth sentence of this paragraph.**

6. **Type the following sentence to help expand on the previous sentence:** `This is four thousand times faster than the fastest modems that are used to connect home computers to the Internet, and it is approximately twice as fast as the entire capacity of most local area networks.`

   After you insert the text, the paragraph should look like the one in Figure 2.7.

Figure 2.7
A new sentence is inserted in a paragraph.

Inserted text

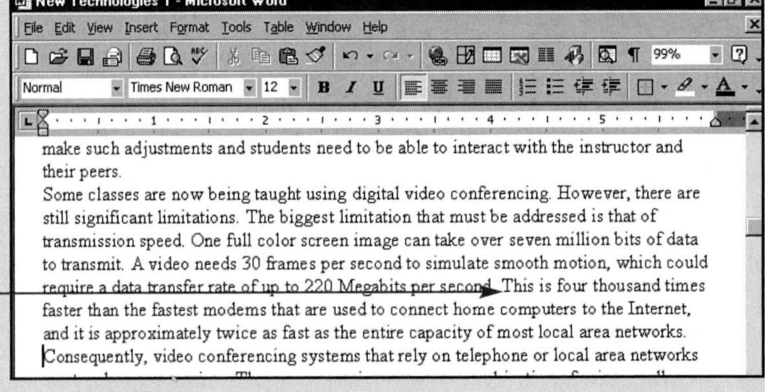

7. **Click the Save button on the Standard toolbar to save your changes.**
   The status bar indicates that the file is being saved. Leave the document open for use in the next lesson.

Overwriting Text

If you want to write over text that appears in a document, you can turn on Word's Overtype feature by double-clicking the OVR button on the status bar at the bottom of the screen. New text you type overwrites and replaces the text to the right of the insertion point. To deactivate this feature, double-click the OVR button and it is dimmed again.

Lesson 3: Using the Click and Type Feature

If you want to type something in the middle of a blank page or beyond the end-of-document marker, you do not have to enter a series of empty lines. The ***Click and Type*** feature enables you to insert text, graphics, tables, or other items outside the current text areas in a single step. To use Click and Type, you must be in Print Layout view; the feature is not available in Normal view, Outline view, or Print Preview.

In this lesson, you use the Click and Type feature to add a title to the first page of the document.

To Use the Click and Type Feature

1. **Click the Print Layout View button on the horizontal scrollbar.**
   The pages display as they will appear when printed. The first page is blank. You use this page to create a title page for this document.

2. **Click the arrow on the right side of the Zoom button and select Two Pages. The page on the left is blank. Move the pointer to the position shown in Figure 2.8.**
   Notice the centering icon that appears near the pointer. When the pointer is on the left side of the page, the icon is a left-alignment icon, and on the right side it changes to a right-alignment icon. When you center the pointer, the icon becomes a centering icon.

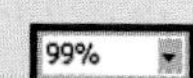

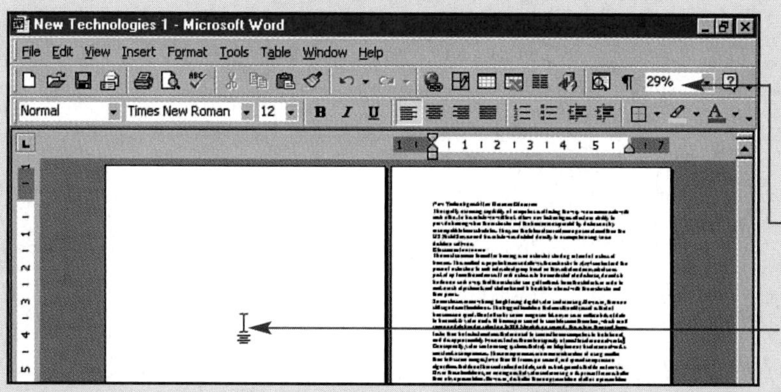

Figure 2.8
When you move the pointer across an open space in a document, it displays an alignment icon.

> If your pointer does not change after a second or so, move it a little bit. If you cannot get it to change at all, it usually means one of two things: you do not have the Click and Type feature turned on, or you are not in the Print Layout view. The Click and Type feature does not work in Normal view. To turn the feature on, select Tools, Options from the menu and click the Edit tab. Click the check box next to Enable click and type and click OK.

3. **Double-click the left mouse button.**
   The insertion point appears in the middle of the line at the position you have chosen.

4. **Change the Zoom to Page Width and type `Distance Education Technologies` as the title of the document.**
   The title displays in the center of the first page of the document.

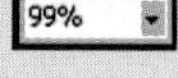

5. **Press ↵Enter twice and type `By`. Press ↵Enter twice and type `John Preston and <your name>`.**
   The author's name and your name are added to a title page as shown in Figure 2.9.

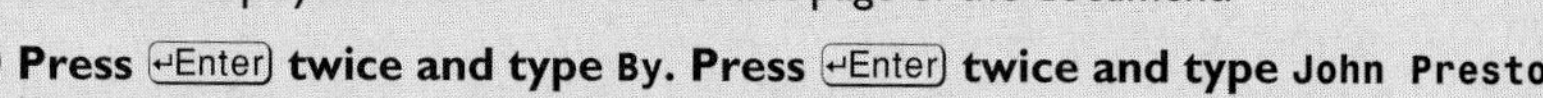

continues ▶

To Use the Click and Type Feature (continued)

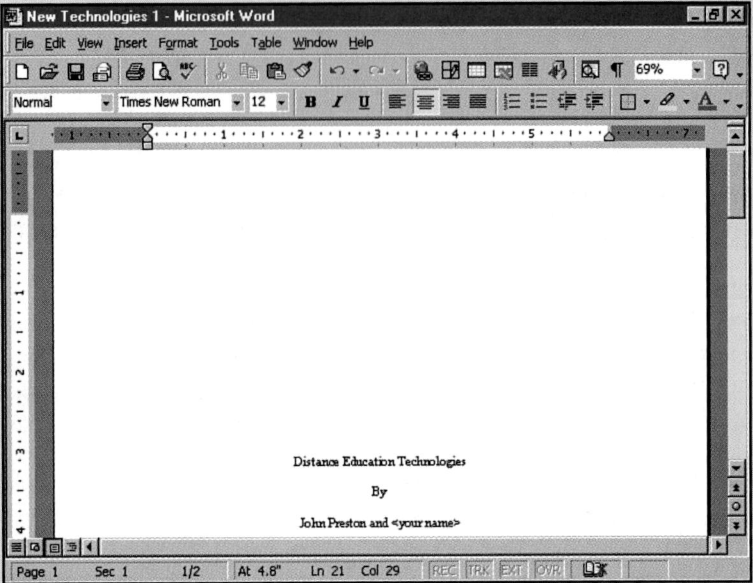

Figure 2.9
The title and author appear centered on the opening page of the document.

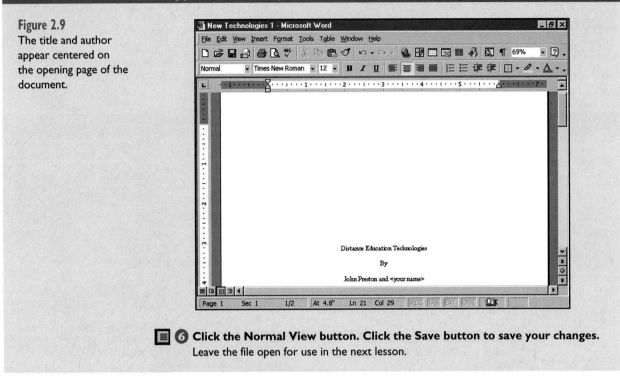

 **6 Click the Normal View button. Click the Save button to save your changes.**
Leave the file open for use in the next lesson.

Page Break Option
The dotted line labeled `Page Break` represents a special command that forces a break between two pages. It can be inserted or deleted like other characters and has been used in Figure 2.9 to create a title page. You learn more about inserting breaks in later lessons.

Lesson 4: Selecting Text to Delete or Replace

In Project 1, you used ←Backspace and Del to delete one character at a time. If you want to remove words, phrases, sentences, or even whole paragraphs, using these two procedures would be tedious. You can select and delete multiple characters in a way that saves you a great deal of time.

You might also want to replace text because you think of a better word or phrase. You could select and delete the existing word or phrase and then insert its replacement, but it is faster to combine these two steps and simply select the old word or phrase and type a new one.

In this lesson, you use new techniques to select and delete text. Then you use these same techniques to select and replace text.

To Select and Delete Text

1 Use the vertical scrollbar, if necessary, to display the first two paragraphs following the heading, `Classroom Instruction`.

2 Double-click the word such in the third sentence of the first full paragraph.
The word, along with the following space, is selected as shown in Figure 2.10.

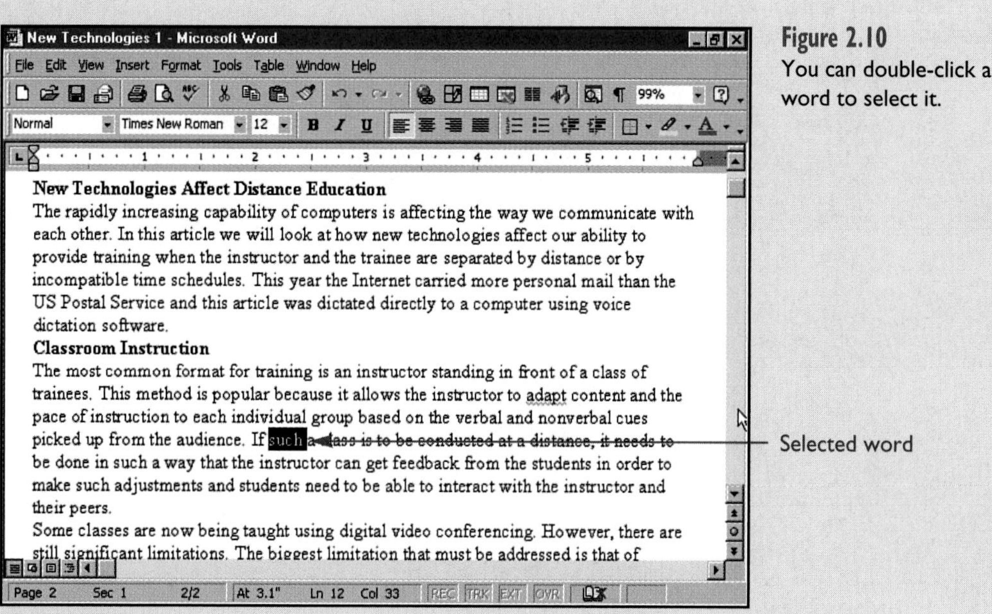

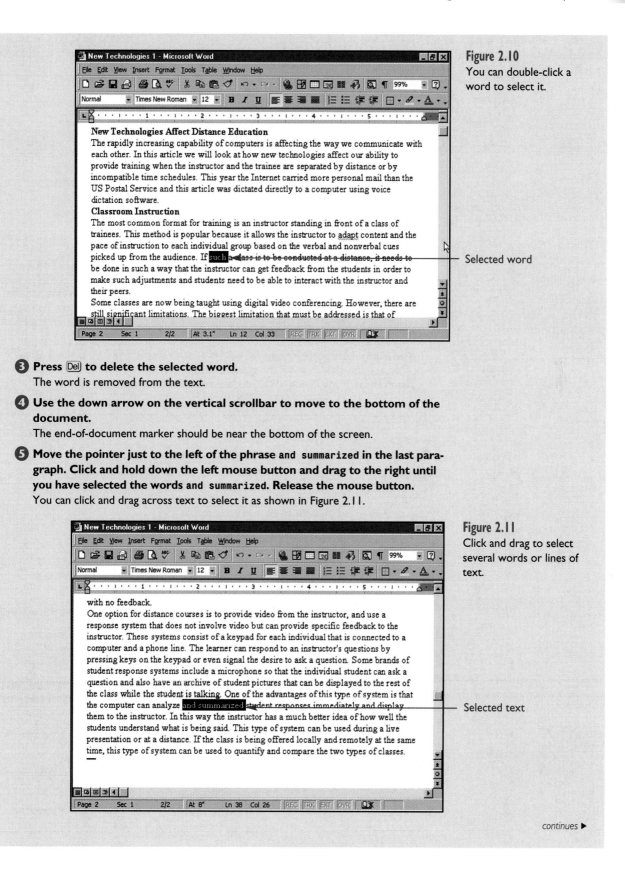

Figure 2.10
You can double-click a word to select it.

3. **Press Del to delete the selected word.**
   The word is removed from the text.
4. **Use the down arrow on the vertical scrollbar to move to the bottom of the document.**
   The end-of-document marker should be near the bottom of the screen.
5. **Move the pointer just to the left of the phrase `and summarized` in the last paragraph. Click and hold down the left mouse button and drag to the right until you have selected the words `and summarized`. Release the mouse button.**
   You can click and drag across text to select it as shown in Figure 2.11.

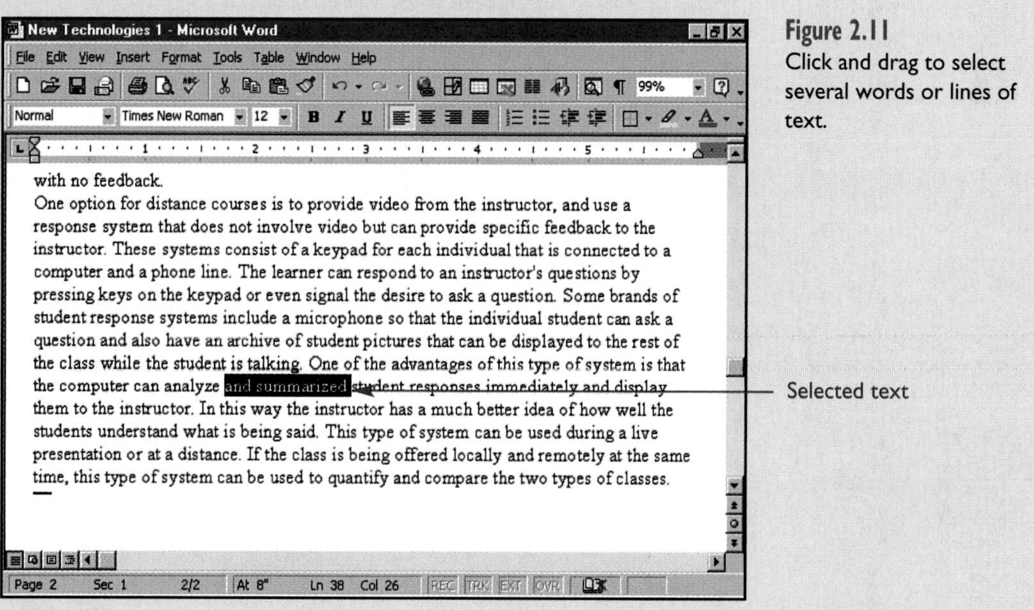

Figure 2.11
Click and drag to select several words or lines of text.

continues ▶

To Select and Delete Text (continued)

If the words you want to select are located on two lines, you need to click at the beginning of the first word and drag down and to the left until the words you want to edit are selected. You might have to try this procedure several times until you feel comfortable selecting text.

6 Press Del.

The selected words are deleted and one space is left in their place. Leave the document open for use in the next lesson.

Text Selection Shortcuts

Word offers several keyboard shortcuts that you can use to select text in a document. After you learn the commands, using keys can be more convenient if you prefer to keep your hands on the keyboard rather than move one hand to the mouse to click and drag across text. Place the insertion point where you want to start selecting text. To select one character at a time, hold down Shift and press the left or right arrow to select text.

You can also use the left margin to select a single line, multiple lines, or a paragraph. Move the mouse pointer to the left margin until it changes to a right-pointing arrow. Then you can click to select the adjacent line, or click and drag down the margin to select several lines. If you double-click, you select the entire paragraph.

Table 2.1 is a partial listing of keyboard and mouse shortcuts you can use to select text.

Table 2.1 Shortcuts to Select Text

To Select	Using the Keyboard	Using the Mouse
A word	Press Shift+Ctrl+→ to select a word to the right of the insertion point or press Shift+Ctrl+← to select a word to the left	Double-click the word.
A line	Place the insertion point at the beginning of the line and press Shift+End	Move the pointer to the left margin until it turns into a white arrow and click once.
A sentence	Press Ctrl and click in the sentence	Click and drag across the sentence.
A paragraph	Place the insertion point at the beginning of the paragraph and press Shift+Ctrl+↓	Triple-click anywhere in the paragraph, or double-click in the left margin next to the paragraph.
A block of text	Place the insertion point at the beginning of the block and press Shift+→ or Shift+↓	Click at the beginning of the block, and Shift+click at the end of the block.
A vertical block of text	None	Press Alt while dragging through the text.
The whole document	Place the insertion point at the beginning of the document and press Ctrl+A or press Shift+Ctrl+End	Press Ctrl and click anywhere in the left margin.

In the next part of this lesson, you combine the process of selecting and replacing existing text in the document.

To Select and Replace Text

1. **Click and drag the scroll box on the vertical scrollbar to move to the top of the text of the New Technologies 1 document. Double-click the second instance of the word `such` in the last full sentence of the second paragraph.**
   The word is selected. Now you type over the word to replace it.

2. **Do not delete the selected word. Type `necessary`.**
   The new word replaces the selected word as shown in Figure 2.12.

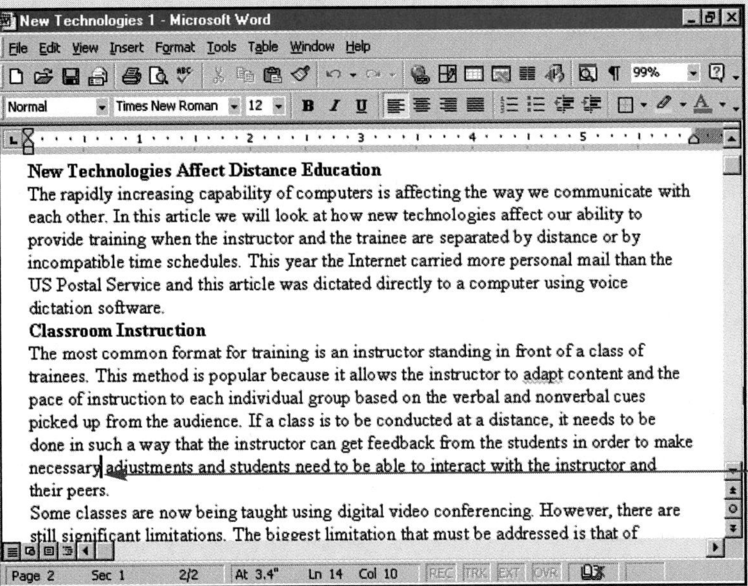

Figure 2.12
You can select a word or phrase and type over it to replace it rather than first deleting the text you intend to replace.

3. **Scroll to the bottom of the document. The end-of-document marker should be near the bottom of the screen. Locate the second-to-last sentence in the last paragraph. Click and drag across the words `This type of system` to select them.**
   Figure 2.13 shows the selected text that will be replaced.

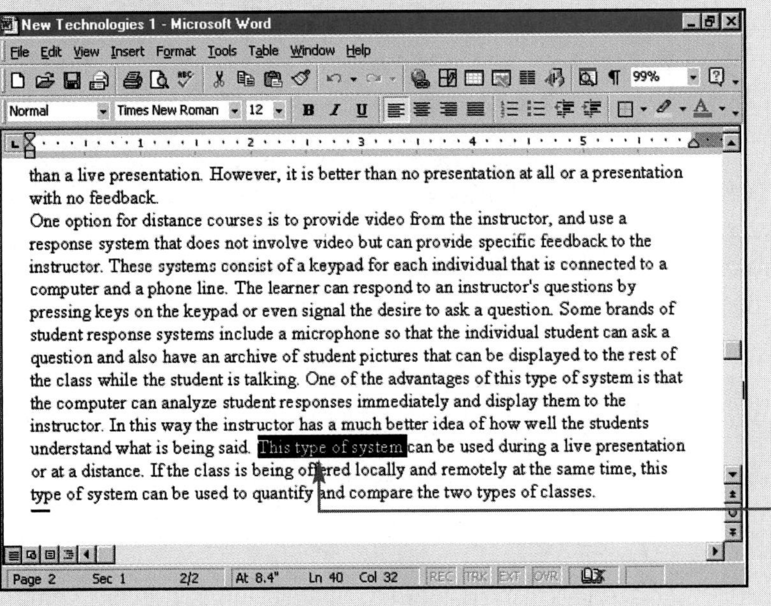

Figure 2.13
To replace existing text with new text, first select the text you want to replace.

continues ▶

To Select and Replace Text (continued)

4. **Type `Student response systems` to replace the words you selected. Click the Save button on the Standard toolbar to save your work.**
   The changes are saved. Leave the file open for use in the next lesson.

Lesson 5: Moving Text Using Cut-and-Paste

If you want to relocate text in a document, you could use the skills you learned earlier in this lesson; that is, you could delete the text in its original location, move the insertion point to the new location, and retype the text. Moving the text using the ***cut-and-paste*** method is a quicker, easier way to relocate text without having to do any additional typing. This method uses the Cut and Paste commands to move text from one location to another. During this process the selected text is removed from one location using the ***Cut*** command. The text is stored temporarily in a location known as the ***Office Clipboard***. Then you position the mouse pointer where you want to place the text and use the ***Paste*** command to insert the text that is stored in the Office Clipboard. The Office Clipboard**,** Clipboard for short, also stores items that you want to copy from one location to another. You use the ***Copy*** command to duplicate text from one part of a document and place it in a second location.

In this lesson, you move text by cutting text from one location and pasting it into a new location.

To Move Text Using the Cut and Paste Commands

1. **Click and drag the scroll box on the vertical scrollbar to move to the top of the text.**
2. **Click just to the left of the second sentence in the first full paragraph, beginning with `In this article`, and select the text to the period at the end of the sentence, as shown in Figure 2.14.**
   Make sure you highlight the period at the end of the sentence.

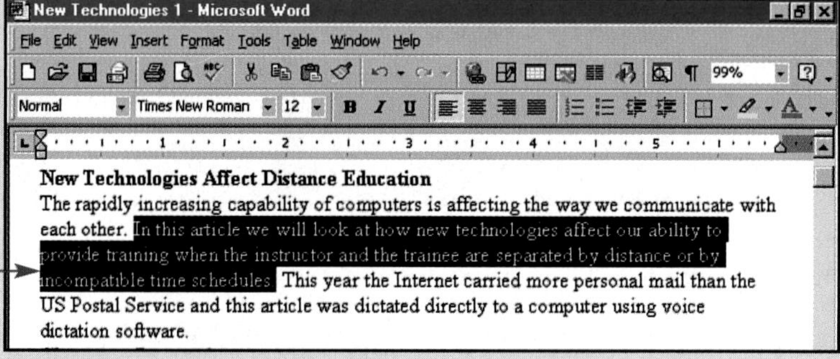

Figure 2.14
To move text, you must first select it.

3. **Click the Cut button on the Standard toolbar.**
   The sentence is removed and placed in the Office Clipboard, where it is stored temporarily.
4. **Place the insertion point to the right of the period at the end of the last sentence in the first paragraph.**

5. **Click the Paste button on the Standard toolbar.**
   The sentence you cut is now pasted at the insertion point (see Figure 2.15). Do not save your document at this time, but leave it open for use in the next lesson.

Word should automatically add a space before the text you just pasted. If it does not, add a space by pressing Spacebar. To have the program automatically adjust spaces before and after text pastes, choose Tools, Options from the menu, and click the Edit tab. Click the Use smart cut and paste check box.

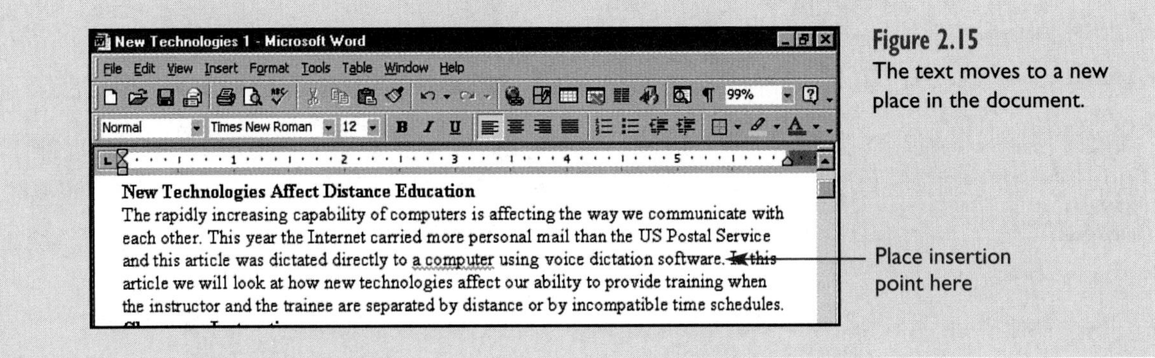

Figure 2.15
The text moves to a new place in the document.

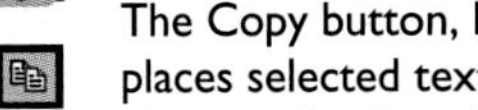

Copying and Pasting Text

The Copy button, located to the right of the Cut button on the Standard toolbar, also places selected text in the Clipboard, but it leaves the text in its original location as well. You use the Copy button to duplicate text, which you can then paste into another location in the same or a new document without any of the original text being moved. Notice that the Copy and Cut buttons are currently dimmed and are not available for use. You must select text before you can use these buttons.

The Office Clipboard can store up to twelve items. This is useful if you need to cut or copy multiple items from one document and place them in a different document. You can use the Clipboard toolbar to select the item you want to paste. If you want to see the contents of the Clipboard toolbar, choose View, Toolbars, Clipboard from the menu.

Cut, Copy, and Paste Shortcuts

You can also use keyboard shortcuts to activate the Cut, Copy, or Paste commands, rather than move your hand to the mouse to use the buttons. The keyboard command to cut text is Ctrl+X; to copy text, use Ctrl+C; and to paste text, use Ctrl+V. The three keys used for these commands are next to each other on the keyboard and are widely used in Windows applications.

Lesson 6: Using Undo and Redo

Sometimes you might accidentally delete text or paste something in the wrong location. You also, on occasion, might make several changes in a document and then decide that you would rather not use the changes you made. Word gives you the option of undoing and redoing changes you made. This capability saves you from having to retype text. It also helps you when you can't quite remember the changes you have made; the computer remembers for you.

In this lesson, you undo and redo the changes you made in the previous lesson.

To Undo and Redo Changes

1. **With the top of the New Technologies 1 document onscreen, move the pointer to the Undo button on the Standard toolbar.**

   A ScreenTip that says `Undo Paste` displays (see Figure 2.16) because the last action you performed was to paste text into a new location.

continues ▶

To Undo and Redo Changes (continued)

Figure 2.16
When you move your mouse pointer on the Undo button you can see the last action you performed.

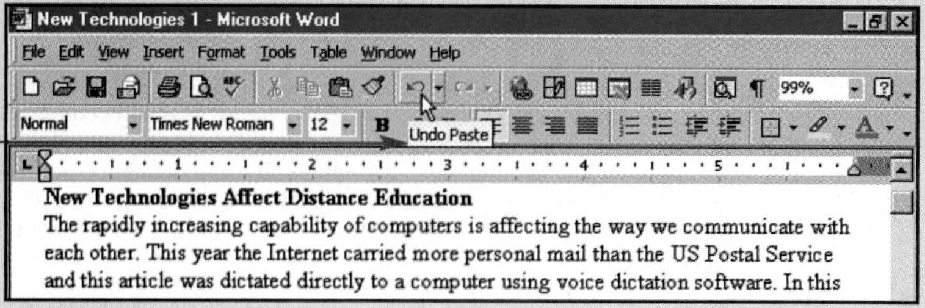

ScreenTip

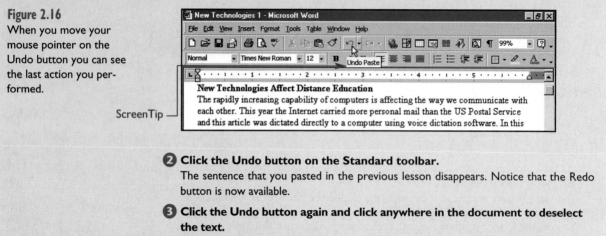

2 **Click the Undo button on the Standard toolbar.**
The sentence that you pasted in the previous lesson disappears. Notice that the Redo button is now available.

3 **Click the Undo button again and click anywhere in the document to deselect the text.**
The sentence you cut returns to its original location. You have undone the last two edits you made to the document (see Figure 2.17).

Figure 2.17
The sentence appears in its original location.

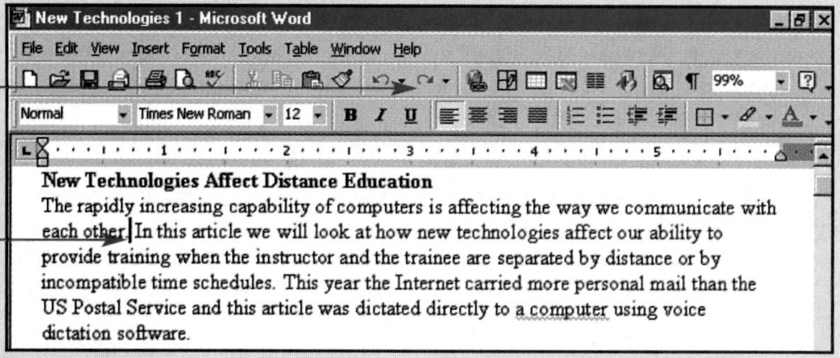

Redo button is activated

Sentence returned to original location

4 **Click the Redo button twice to redo the last two steps.**
The cut and paste are redone. The Redo button turns light gray, indicating that no more steps can be redone. Leave the file open for use in the next lesson.

Using Undo and Redo
You can undo or redo many steps by clicking the Undo or Redo button repeatedly. A faster way to undo or redo several steps is to click the list arrow next to the Undo or Redo button to display a list of recent actions. If you click one of the items on the list, all the actions from the top of the list down to that point are undone or redone.

Lesson 7: Moving Text Using Drag-and-Drop

The cut-and-paste method of moving text is faster than deleting and retyping. An even quicker way to move text around, particularly if the text to be moved and the destination are on the same screen, is called the ***drag-and-drop*** method. You use this method to move text from one location to another by dragging it from the original location and dropping it at the desired location on your screen; hence the name drag-and-drop.

In this lesson, you move text by using drag-and-drop.

To Move Text Using Drag-and-Drop

1 Use the vertical scrollbar to move near the bottom of the New Technologies 1 document.

The sentence ending with the word `feedback` in the last sentence of the second-to-last paragraph should be visible. Next, you rearrange this sentence.

If the drag-and-drop method covered in this task does not work, choose Tools, Options from the menu and select the Edit tab. Click the Drag-and-drop text editing option box to turn this feature on.

2 Select the words `a presentation with no feedback`, but do not select the period at the end of the sentence (see Figure 2.18).

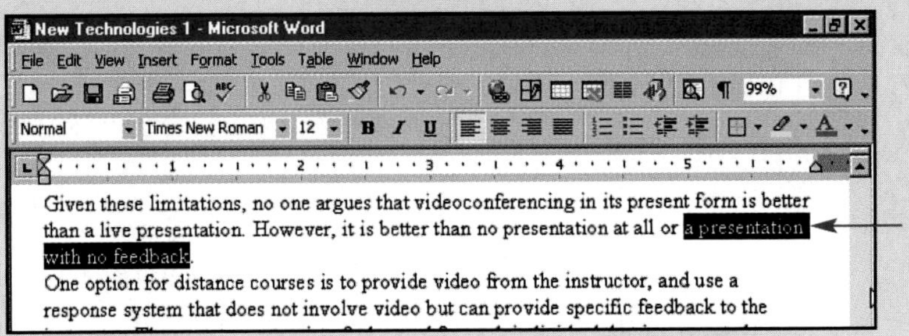
New Technologies 1 - Microsoft Word
File Edit View Insert Format Tools Table Window Help
Normal
Times New Roman
12
99%
Given these limitations, no one argues that videoconferencing in its present form is better
than a live presentation. However, it is better than no presentation at all or a presentation
with no feedback.
One option for distance courses is to provide video from the instructor, and use a
response system that does not involve video but can provide specific feedback to the

Selected text

Figure 2.18
Locate the sentence to be changed and select the text as shown.

3 Move the pointer on top of the selected text.

The pointer changes to an arrow (see Figure 2.19).

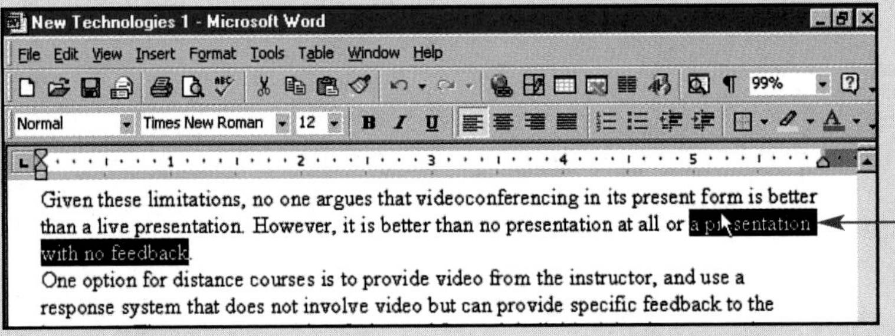
New Technologies 1 - Microsoft Word
File Edit View Insert Format Tools Table Window Help
Normal
Times New Roman
12
99%
Given these limitations, no one argues that videoconferencing in its present form is better
than a live presentation. However, it is better than no presentation at all or a presentation
with no feedback.
One option for distance courses is to provide video from the instructor, and use a
response system that does not involve video but can provide specific feedback to the

Mouse pointer changes to an arrow

Figure 2.19
When the mouse pointer changes to an arrow, you can click and drag the selected text to move it.

4 Click the selected text and hold down the left mouse button while you move the pointer to the left of the phrase `no presentation at all` in the same sentence.

As you drag, the pointer is shaped like an arrow with a small box attached to the bottom. Move the text to the location shown in Figure 2.20.

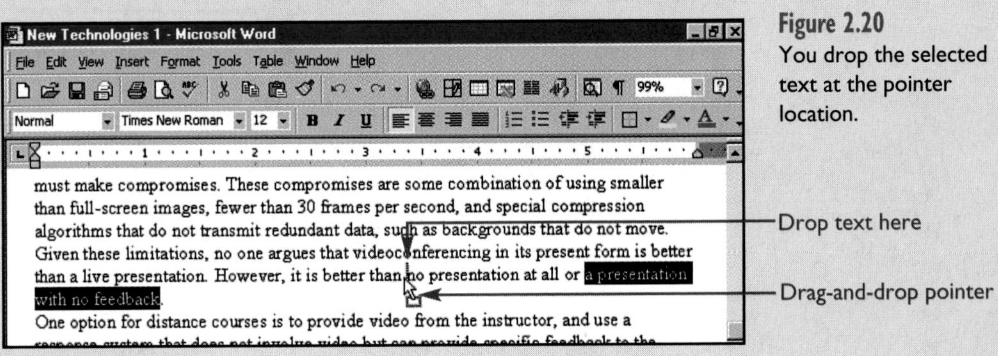
New Technologies 1 - Microsoft Word
File Edit View Insert Format Tools Table Window Help
Normal
Times New Roman
12
99%
must make compromises. These compromises are some combination of using smaller
than full-screen images, fewer than 30 frames per second, and special compression
algorithms that do not transmit redundant data, such as backgrounds that do not move.
Given these limitations, no one argues that videoconferencing in its present form is better
than a live presentation. However, it is better than no presentation at all or a presentation
with no feedback.
One option for distance courses is to provide video from the instructor, and use a
Drop text here
Drag-and-drop pointer

Figure 2.20
You drop the selected text at the pointer location.

continues ▶

To Move Text Using Drag-and-Drop (continued)

5. **Release the mouse button.**
   The highlighted text drops at the new location. Notice that the program placed one space before and after the phrase you moved.

   If you accidentally drop the text too soon or miss the drop location, click the Undo button and try again.

6. **Select the phrase `no presentation at all` and drag and drop it to the right of the word or before the period at the end of the same sentence.**
   The program corrects the spacing between words. The rearranged sentence should look like the one in Figure 2.21.

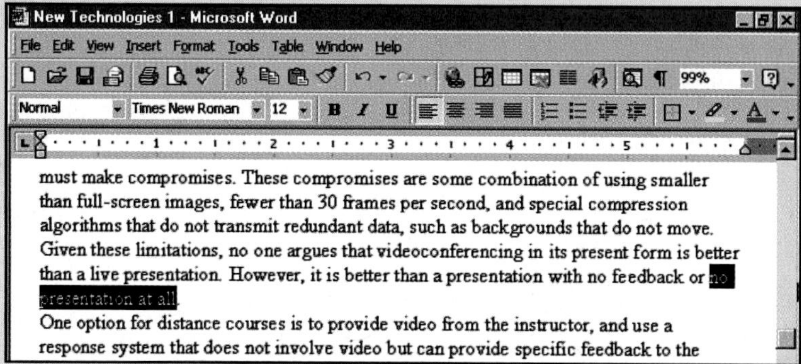
New Technologies 1 - Microsoft Word
File Edit View Insert Format Tools Table Window Help
Normal
Times New Roman
12
99%
must make compromises. These compromises are some combination of using smaller
than full-screen images, fewer than 30 frames per second, and special compression
algorithms that do not transmit redundant data, such as backgrounds that do not move.
Given these limitations, no one argues that videoconferencing in its present form is better
than a live presentation. However, it is better than a presentation with no feedback or no
presentation at all.
One option for distance courses is to provide video from the instructor, and use a
response system that does not involve video but can provide specific feedback to the

Figure 2.21
The sentence is modified using the drag-and-drop method.

7. **Click the Save button to save your changes.**
   Leave the file open for the next lesson.

Lesson 8: Printing a Document Using the Menu

The easiest way to print a document is to click the Print button on the Standard toolbar, as you did in Project 1. Sometimes, though, you might need to print more than one copy of a document, or only one specific page of a multiple-page report. In that case, use the menu option, which displays a dialog box offering many printing choices.

In this lesson, you print a document using the menu.

To Print a Document Using the Menu

1. **Choose File, Print from the menu.**
   The Print dialog box displays (see Figure 2.22).
2. **Make sure your printer is turned on and click OK to send your document to the printer.**
3. **Click the Save button to save your document. Click the document Close Window button to close the document.**
   Leave Word open if you are going to continue with the exercises. If not, close the program.

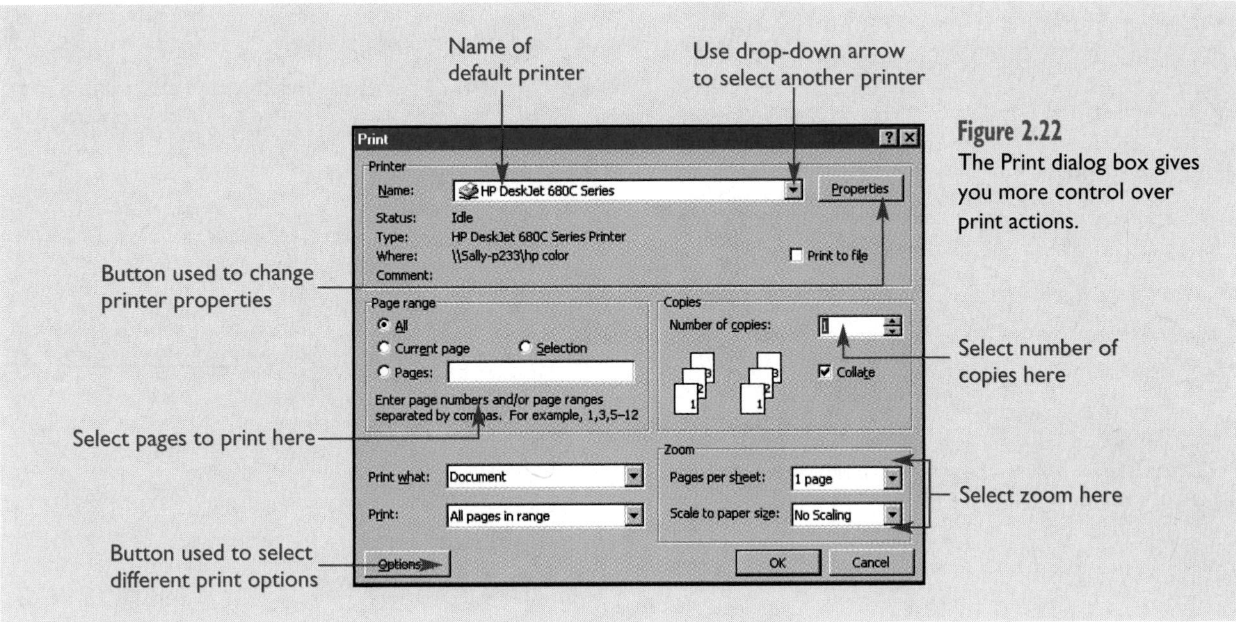

Figure 2.22
The Print dialog box gives you more control over print actions.

Quick Saving
To save a document quickly, press Ctrl+S.

Summary

In this project, you learned techniques to edit an existing document. You opened a document and saved it with a new name. You inserted text in a paragraph, selected and deleted text, and selected and replaced text. You used the Click and Type feature to add a title page to the document. You then edited the document by moving text, first using the cut-and-paste method and then the drag-and-drop method. Finally you used the Print dialog box to print the revised document.

You can expand your learning by using Help to learn more about the Cut, Copy, and Paste procedures and the use of the Clipboard. This process is used in all the Office applications and is one you should master. You can also learn more about the drag-and-drop method by looking for this topic in Help. Although you might find that you prefer to use the Cut, Copy, and Paste commands to move or copy text, the concept of drag-and-drop is also widely used in a Windows environment. It enables you to drag toolbars, graphics, tables, charts, and so on and then drop the selected object in a new location. This helps you manage what is on your screen.

Checking Concepts and Terms

True/False

For each of the following, check *T* or *F* to indicate whether the statement is true or false.

__T __F **1.** To open a document that is stored on a floppy disk, you click the button on the Standard toolbar that looks like a small floppy disk. [L1]

__T __F **2.** When you use the Save As command and type a new filename for a document, the original document is erased and replaced with a new file. [L1]

__T __F **3.** The Click and Type feature works in the Print Layout view but does not work in the Normal view. [L3]

__T __F **4.** When you make a mistake, you can reverse your error by clicking the Undo button. [L6]

__T __F **5.** If you want to undo a mistake, you must do so before you type anything else. The program can undo only one previous action. [L6]

__T __F **6.** The Redo button is the opposite of the Undo button. It enables you to change your mind and restore the actions that you chose to undo. [L6]

__T __F **7.** If you have made 10 changes to the text and notice that the change you made six steps ago is wrong, you may click the drop-down list arrow next to the Undo button, pick that one action from the list, and undo it. The other actions are not affected. [L6]

__T __F **8.** Drag-and-drop refers to a method of erasing blocks of text in which you drag the selected text to the trash. [L7]

__T __F **9.** Using the Print option on the File menu gives you more options for printing than simply clicking the Print button on the toolbar. [L8]

__T __F **10.** When you cut selected text, that text is stored in a memory area called the Office Clipboard. [L4]

Multiple Choice

Circle the letter of the correct answer for each of the following.

1. Which of the following are true for the Office Clipboard? [L5]

a. It stores items that are copied.

b. It stores items that are cut from a document.

c. It can store multiple items.

d. all of the above

2. This button reverses the undo action and returns the text to its condition prior to the undo. [L6]

a. Redo

b. Reverse

c. Restore

d. none of the above

3. What happens when you double-click a word in a sentence? [L4]

a. The word is removed.

b. The word is selected.

c. The sentence is selected.

d. The sentence is copied.

4. To copy using the keyboard, press ______________ + C. [L5]

a. Alt

b. Ctrl

c. Shift

d. Alt+Ctrl

5. The method used to move text from one location to another by dragging it with the mouse to a new location is known as ______________. [L7]

a. cut-and-paste

b. Click and Type

c. drag-and-drop

d. none of the above

Screen ID

Refer to the figure and identify the numbered parts of the screen. Write the letter of the correct label in the space next to the number.

Figure 2.23

A. Insertion point

B. Copy selected item

C. Drag-and-drop pointer

D. Selected text

E. Undo previous step

F. Cut selected item

G. List of actions to undo

H. Redo previous undo

I. Paste contents of Clipboard at insertion point

J. List of actions to redo

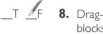

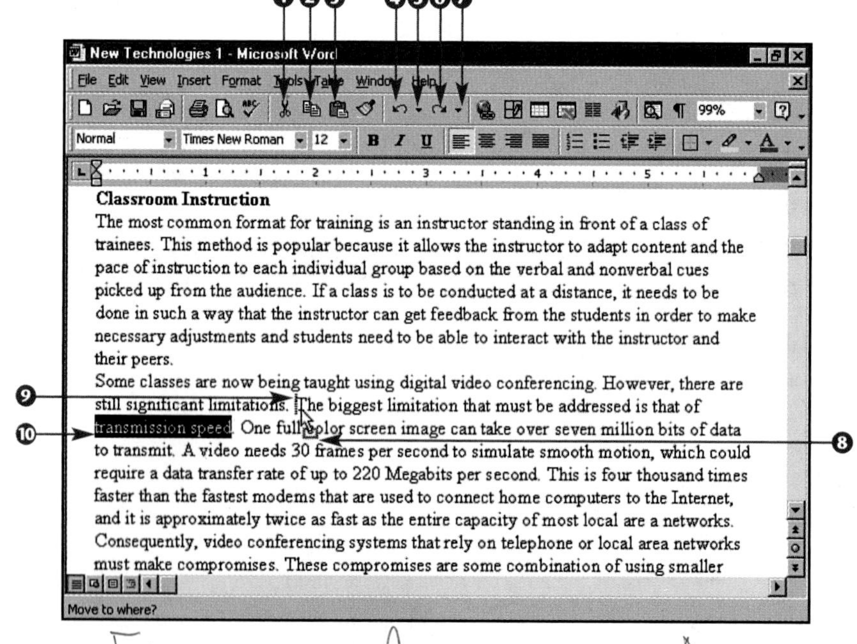

1. ______________
2. ______________
3. ______________
4. ______________
5. ______________
6. ______________
7. ______________
8. ______________
9. ______________
10. ______________

Discussion Questions

1. Are you most likely to use pen and paper, a typewriter, or a word processor when you write? When do you edit using each? After completing a first draft? As you write?
2. Several years ago, experts were predicting that technology would lead to a "paperless society." Now that nearly all text is generated on computers, do you feel that this prediction will come true? Does the ease of making corrections lead to more or less paper use?
3. Prior to the advent of word processing, what was done when a mistake was found in a long legal document? How would it be handled using a word processing environment?

Skill Drill

Skill Drill exercises reinforce project skills. Each skill reinforced is the same, or nearly the same, as a skill presented in the project. Detailed instructions are provided in a step-by-step format.

In this set of Skill Drill exercises, you open a file and save it with a new name. Then you practice the techniques used in the project to edit the paper. Leave the file open from one Skill Drill to the next until you have completed all the exercises.

This set of Skill Drill exercises uses file `WO-0202`.

1. Opening an Existing File and Saving It Under a Different Name

In the first exercise, you locate and open a file, and save it with a new name. The original file is preserved and a new file is created. [L1]

1. Open file `WO-0202` in the Student folder on the CD-ROM.
2. If necessary, use the Zoom button to change the document to Page Width.
3. Use the File, Save As menu option to save the file on a floppy disk in drive A: with the name `New Technologies 2`.

2. Inserting Text into an Existing Document

You can insert text any place in a document simply by moving the insertion point to a new position and typing the text. [L2]

To insert text into a document, follow these steps:

1. Scroll to the beginning of the document.
2. Place the insertion point in front of the first word.
3. Type `Edited by:`, followed by your name. The existing title is forced to the right.
4. Press Enter.
5. Click the Save button to save your changes.

3. Selecting, Deleting, and Replacing Text

You can use many methods to select text (refer to Table 2.1). Try using a different technique when you select the text that is deleted and replaced in the following steps. [L4]

1. Select the second full paragraph in the section on self study. (This paragraph starts with the phrase `There are several`.)
2. Press Del to delete the paragraph.
3. Scroll down to the `Future Technologies` section.
4. Select the title `Future Technologies` and replace it by typing `Anticipated Increases in Transmission Speed`.
5. Click the Save button to save your work.

4. Moving Text Using Cut-and-Paste and Drag-and-Drop, Then Printing the Page

One of the greatest advantages of using a word processor is the capability to move things around and rearrange text, then change your mind and undo the changes you have made. The cut-and-paste and drag-and-drop techniques are used throughout Windows applications. [L5, L7–L8]

To rearrange text, follow these steps:

1. Locate the sentence in the first paragraph that begins with `Many people try`.
2. Move this sentence to the beginning of the paragraph by using the cut-and-paste method. Try using the keyboard combinations (Ctrl+X to cut and Ctrl+V to paste) when you cut and paste the text.
3. Click Undo twice.
4. Select the same sentence and move it to the beginning of the paragraph using the drag-and-drop method.
5. Check the spacing between the sentence you just moved and the following sentence. Insert a space if necessary to provide at least one space between them.
6. Click anywhere to deselect the text, if necessary. Compare your document to the example in Figure 2.24.

Figure 2.24

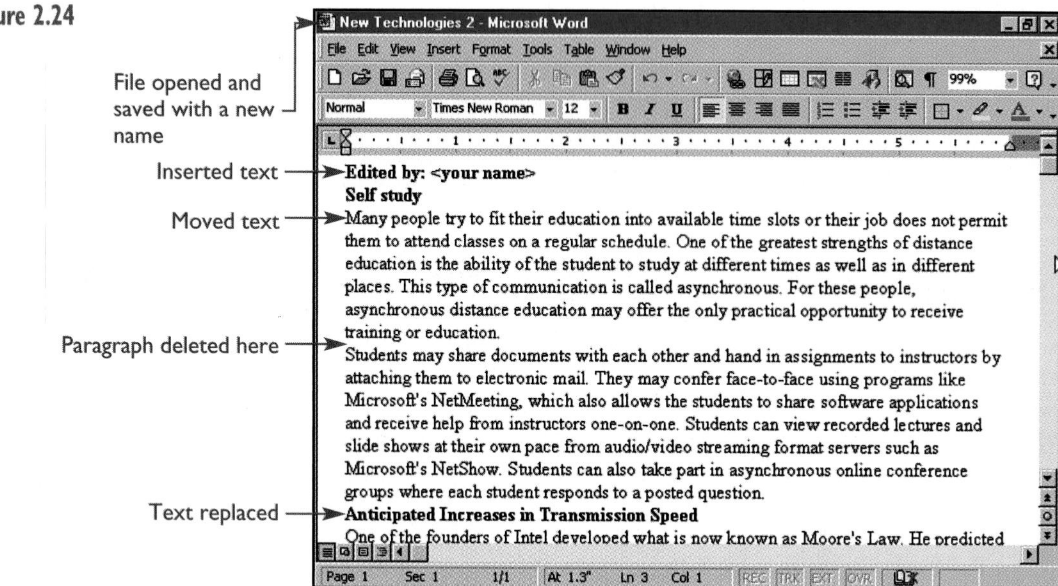

7. Select File, Print, and OK to print the page.
8. Click Save to save your changes.
9. Close the document and exit Word.

Challenge

Challenge exercises expand on or are somewhat related to skills presented in the lessons. Each exercise provides a brief narrative introduction followed by instructions in a numbered step or bulleted list format that are not as detailed as those in the Skill Drill section.

In these Challenge exercises, you use the Copy and Paste commands to copy text from one location and paste to multiple locations. Then you learn how to undo multiple changes. Lastly, you print multiple copies of your document. These exercises all use file `W0-0203`. Leave the file open from one exercise to the next.

1. Copying and Pasting the Same Text to Two Locations

At some point, you might want to cut or copy text from one part of a document and place it in several locations. You can use the skills that you learned in this lesson to copy the text and paste it in multiple locations. [L5]

To copy text from one part of a document and paste it in two other locations, follow these steps:

1. Launch Word. Locate and open the `WO-0203` file in the Student folder on the CD-ROM. Save the file as `Business Organizations` on your floppy disk.
2. Highlight the first use of the word `Advantages` and type `Benefits`.
3. Highlight the word `Benefits` you just typed. Click the Copy button.
4. Highlight `Advantages` under `2. Partnership` and click the Paste button. Highlight the word `Advantages` under `3. Corporation` and click the Paste button again. The word Benefits replaces the text in both sections.
5. Repeat this process to replace the word `Disadvantages` with the word `Risks` under each topic.
6. Print the document and save your changes. Leave the document open for use in the next Challenge exercise.

2. Undoing Multiple Changes

In this project, you learned how to use the Undo button to reverse a change you just made. You can also undo the last several changes by using the drop-down arrow next to the Undo button. In this exercise, you undo the changes you made to the Business Organizations document used in the previous exercise. If you did not do the previous exercise, do it now. [L6]

To undo multiple changes in a document, follow these steps:

1. With the `Business Organizations` document still open, click the down arrow next to the Undo button.
2. Select the last six actions to undo the changes made to the document.
3. Use the Click and Type feature to add your name at the bottom of the document on the right side.
4. Save the document on your floppy disk with the name `Business Org2` and leave it open for use in the next exercise.

3. Printing Multiple Copies of a Document

You now need to print more than one copy of this document. Using what you learned in this project about the Print dialog box, complete the following exercise. [L8]

To print two copies of the **Business Org2** document, follow these steps:

1. With the **Business Org2** document still open, choose File, Print.
2. In the Print dialog box, change the Number of copies to 2.
3. Press Enter or click OK.
4. Close the document. Close Word if you are not going to complete the Discovery Zone exercises.

Discovery Zone

Discovery Zone exercises, require advanced knowledge of topics presented in *Essentials* lessons, application of skills from multiple lessons, or self-directed learning of new skills.

These Discovery Zone exercises are independent of each other and can be completed in any order. In the first exercise, you open a file that has been saved with a different file format. In the second exercise, you select a vertical column of text and delete it. In the third exercise, you use the Print dialog box to print thumbnails of a document. In the last exercise, you use Help to learn more about the Office Clipboard.

1. Opening a Document That Has a Different File Format

Files from other programs are saved with a different file format. If someone gives you a file created using a different word processing program, you need to know how to open it so you can work on it in Word. Files containing explanations about installing new software, called Read Me files, are usually saved as a text file with a .txt extension.

In this exercise, you open files that are in a different file format.

Launch Word and click the Open button. Locate the Word files in the Student folder on the CD-ROM. Click the drop-down arrow next to the Files of type drop-down list box and scroll through the list to see the different file formats that you can select.

First, select Text files and see how the list of available files changes. Next, try Encoded Text Files, and then try MS-DOS Text with Layout. Finally, change the Files of type drop-down list box to All Files. Select the **WO-0204** file, which shows the type as Text Document. If the Open dialog box does not show the Type column, use the View button on the dialog box toolbar to change the view to Details. Open this file. Add your name to the top of the document after the words **Alaska Journal**. Now save the file as a Word document and name it **My Alaska Journal**. Close the document.

2. Deleting a Column of Text Using the Alt Key

When you are editing a document, you may need to remove a column of text. Rather than removing each item one by one, you can use Alt to select a column of text which can then be removed all at the same time. You can also use this same selection technique to apply a format or some other feature to a column of text. This process can be useful for files that are downloaded from the Internet or are in some other file format.

In this exercise, you remove a column of days from the Alaska Itinerary document.

Locate and open the **WO-0205** file in the Student folder on the CD-ROM. Save the file on your floppy disk with the name **Alaska Itinerary**. Hold down the Alt key, and click and drag across the word **Monday**. Continue dragging downward to select the rest of the days of the week displayed on the left side of the page. You must press Alt continuously to select the column of text. Make sure all of the word **Wednesday** is selected; this is the widest point in the column. The last date is Sunday, July 7.

When all the text is selected, press Del. The text is removed, and everything moves to the left. The July dates should be lined up on the left margin. If this is not the case, click Undo and try again. Change the title at the top of the page to **Alaska Itinerary for <your name>**. Save the document and close the file.

3. Printing Thumbnails

You may want to print several pages of a document on one or two sheets of paper to get an overview of how the document flows on the page or to use as a handout. This can be useful for outlines or other formats that contain a lot of white space. The Print dialog box contains an option that enables you to select the number of pages per sheet. In this exercise, you use this option to print "thumbnails" of an outline.

Locate and open the **`WO-0206`** file in the Student folder on the CD-ROM. Save it on your floppy disk with the name **`Computer Upgrade`**. Use the Click and Type feature to add your name at the center of the bottom of the last page of the document. (*Hint*: Change to Print Layout view.) Open the Print dialog box and choose 4 pages in the Pages per sheet box in the Zoom area. In the Scale to paper size box, select Letter (8.5x11). Print the document. Save and close the file and exit Word.

4. Learning More About the Office Clipboard

The Office Clipboard can be used to temporarily store multiple items. Use the Office Assistant to find out how to use this feature. Answer the following questions: If you have cut or copied six items, how do you select the third item to place in a new location? What are the differences between the Office Clipboard and the Windows Clipboard?

Project 3

Formatting Text

Objectives

In this project, you learn how to

- ➤ **Change the Font Type, Size, and Emphasis**
- ➤ **Align Text in a Paragraph**
- ➤ **Change Line Spacing**
- ➤ **Create a Bulleted List**
- ➤ **Indent the First Line of a Paragraph**
- ➤ **Use the Format Painter**
- ➤ **Create a Hanging Indent**
- ➤ **Add Spaces After Paragraphs**
- ➤ **Work with Tabs**

Key terms introduced in this project include

- centered
- font
- Format Painter
- hanging indent
- justified
- leaders
- left aligned
- points
- right aligned
- sans serif
- serif

SOURCE: *Essentials: Office 2000*, Ferrett-Preston-Preston

Why Would I Do This?

When you write letters, memos, or other papers, you want to make the document easy to read and understand. One way to help a reader absorb printed information is to use headings to separate one topic from the next. Emphasizing text makes a heading standout from the rest of the text. To do this you can change the font size or style, or make the text bold, italic, or underlined. Documents that are densely packed with text are often more difficult to read, and certainly have less visual appeal. Adding spacing between paragraphs, indenting text, using bulleted lists and other techniques adds white space to a document and makes it easier to follow and absorb. Using these techniques gives a document a clean, professional appearance and helps to convey information clearly and quickly.

In this project, you learn how to use the most important Word formatting tools.

Visual Summary

When you have completed this project, you will have a document that looks like the one in Figure 3.1.

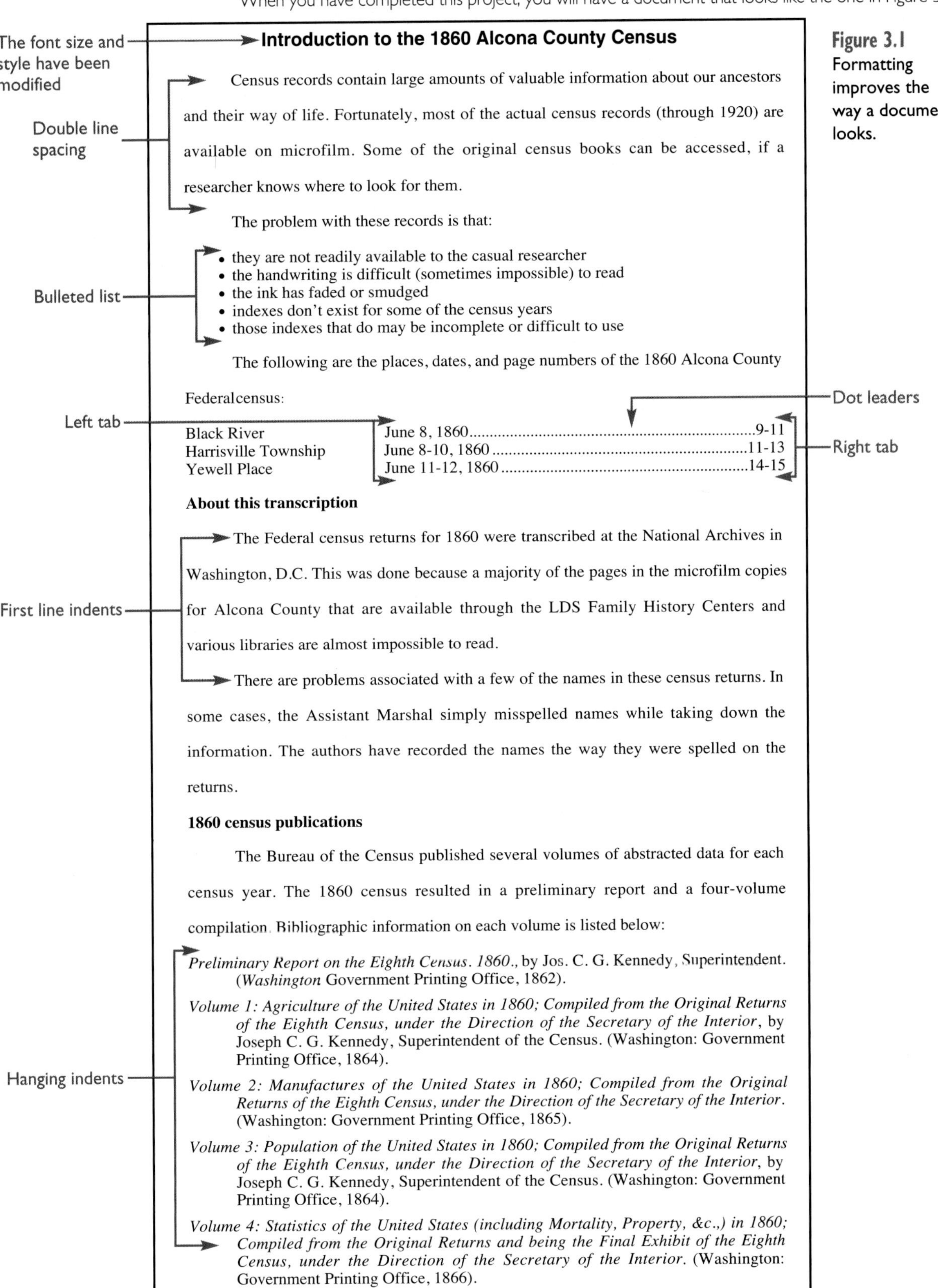

Introduction to the 1860 Alcona County Census

Census records contain large amounts of valuable information about our ancestors and their way of life. Fortunately, most of the actual census records (through 1920) are available on microfilm. Some of the original census books can be accessed, if a researcher knows where to look for them.

The problem with these records is that:

- they are not readily available to the casual researcher
- the handwriting is difficult (sometimes impossible) to read
- the ink has faded or smudged
- indexes don't exist for some of the census years
- those indexes that do may be incomplete or difficult to use

The following are the places, dates, and page numbers of the 1860 Alcona County Federalcensus:

Black River	June 8, 1860........9-11
Harrisville Township	June 8-10, 1860........11-13
Yewell Place	June 11-12, 1860........14-15

About this transcription

The Federal census returns for 1860 were transcribed at the National Archives in Washington, D.C. This was done because a majority of the pages in the microfilm copies for Alcona County that are available through the LDS Family History Centers and various libraries are almost impossible to read.

There are problems associated with a few of the names in these census returns. In some cases, the Assistant Marshal simply misspelled names while taking down the information. The authors have recorded the names the way they were spelled on the returns.

1860 census publications

The Bureau of the Census published several volumes of abstracted data for each census year. The 1860 census resulted in a preliminary report and a four-volume compilation. Bibliographic information on each volume is listed below:

Preliminary Report on the Eighth Census. 1860., by Jos. C. G. Kennedy, Superintendent. (*Washington* Government Printing Office, 1862).

Volume 1: Agriculture of the United States in 1860; Compiled from the Original Returns of the Eighth Census, under the Direction of the Secretary of the Interior, by Joseph C. G. Kennedy, Superintendent of the Census. (Washington: Government Printing Office, 1864).

Volume 2: Manufactures of the United States in 1860; Compiled from the Original Returns of the Eighth Census, under the Direction of the Secretary of the Interior. (Washington: Government Printing Office, 1865).

Volume 3: Population of the United States in 1860; Compiled from the Original Returns of the Eighth Census, under the Direction of the Secretary of the Interior, by Joseph C. G. Kennedy, Superintendent of the Census. (Washington: Government Printing Office, 1864).

Volume 4: Statistics of the United States (including Mortality, Property, &c.,) in 1860; Compiled from the Original Returns and being the Final Exhibit of the Eighth Census, under the Direction of the Secretary of the Interior. (Washington: Government Printing Office, 1866).

Figure 3.1 Formatting improves the way a document looks.

Lesson 1: Changing the Font Type, Size, and Emphasis

Text formatting is used to emphasize important elements of a document. It helps you create effective, readable text. When you open the document used in this project, notice that it is difficult to read. At first glance, all the text looks similar, even though it contains titles and subtitles. Changing size and style of the typeface and adding emphasis by applying bold, italic, or underline characteristics to text help lead the reader through a document and aid in its overall organization.

In this lesson, you format titles and subtitles by altering the look of the font.

To Change the Font Type, Size, and Emphasis

1. **Launch Word and click the Open button. Find `WO-0301` in the Student folder on the CD-ROM and save it as `Book Introduction` on your floppy disk. Select Page Width from the Zoom button drop-down list box, if necessary.**
   The file opens and is saved on your floppy disk under a new name.

2. **Select the first line of text, which is a title (see Figure 3.2).**
   Notice that the text is on a separate line at the beginning of the document and that the line is not followed by a period. This is the title of this document.

Figure 3.2
To add emphasis to text you must first select it.

Selected paragraph

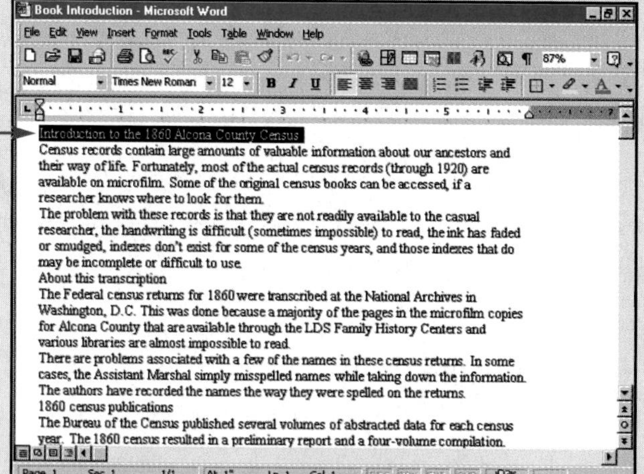

3. **Click the Bold button on the Formatting toolbar.**
   The selected text is now in boldface, which makes it stand out from the rest of the text.

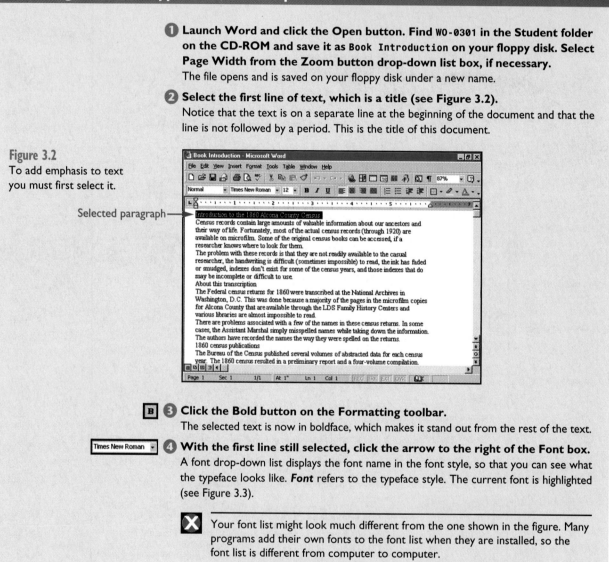

4. **With the first line still selected, click the arrow to the right of the Font box.**
   A font drop-down list displays the font name in the font style, so that you can see what the typeface looks like. ***Font*** refers to the typeface style. The current font is highlighted (see Figure 3.3).

> Your font list might look much different from the one shown in the figure. Many programs add their own fonts to the font list when they are installed, so the font list is different from computer to computer.

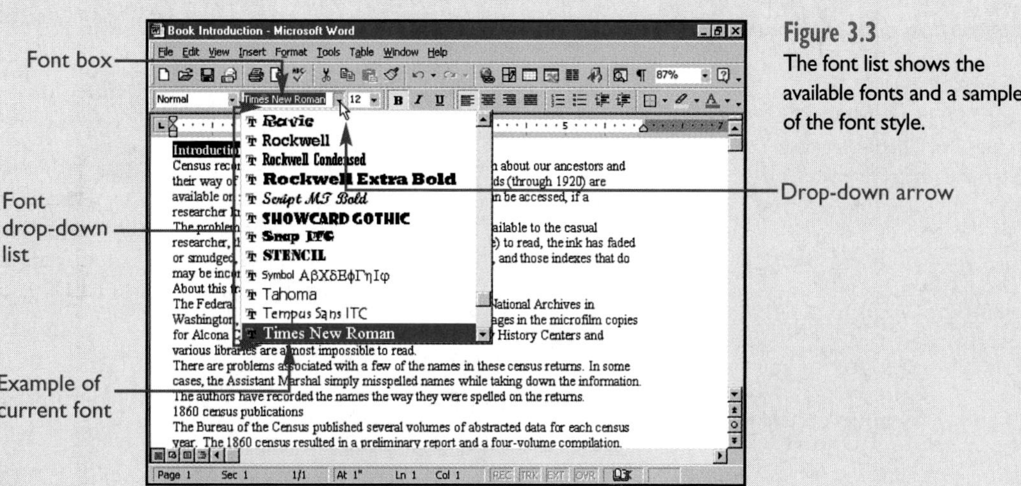

Figure 3.3
The font list shows the available fonts and a sample of the font style.

5 **Scroll to the top of the list and choose Arial.**
The font changes.

6 **Click the arrow to the right of the Font Size drop-down list box. Choose** `12` **from the font size drop-down list. Click anywhere in the document to deselect the text.**
The size of the text increases. The title font and font size change and the bold emphasis is added (see Figure 3.4).

12

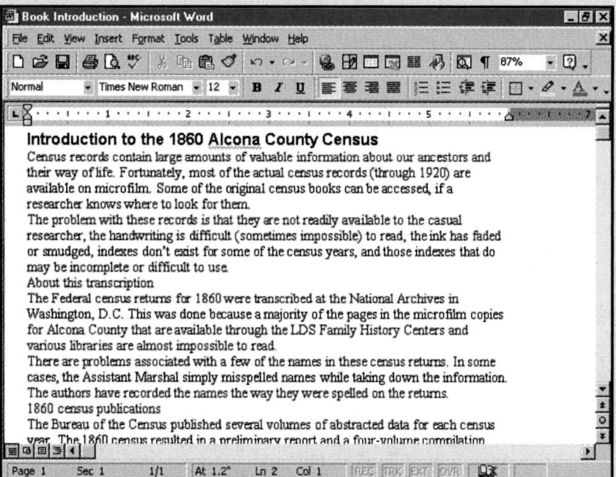

Figure 3.4
The title now has a more distinct appearance that makes it stand out from the rest of the text.

7 **Highlight the first subtitle** `About this transcription` **and click the Bold button to boldface the text. Deselect the text by clicking anywhere else in the document.**
Notice that this one step enables you to recognize the subtitle quickly.

8 **Highlight the second subtitle,** `1860 census publications`**, and click the Bold button to boldface the text. Deselect the text by clicking anywhere else in the document.**
Both subtitles are now emphasized (see Figure 3.5). Leave the file open for the next lesson.

continues ▶

To Change the Font Type, Size, and Emphasis (continued)

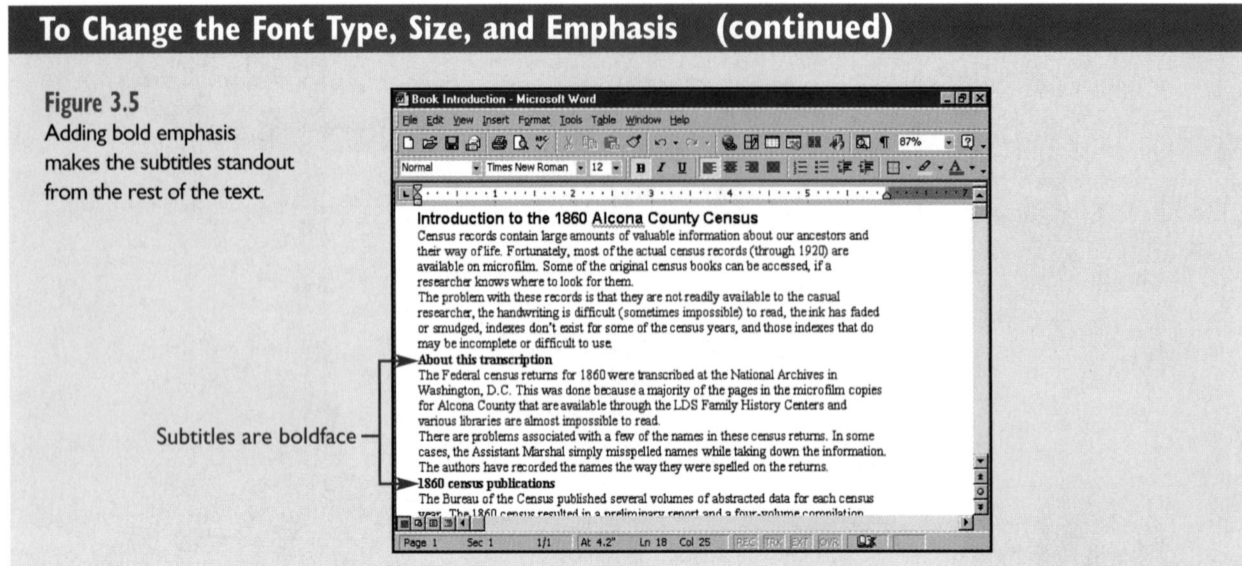

Figure 3.5
Adding bold emphasis makes the subtitles standout from the rest of the text.

Font Sizes and Styles

Font size is measured in ***points,*** which is a measurement of the font height. One inch has 72 points. The larger the font size, the larger the text looks when you print the document. A 12-point font is standard for most documents and is the default font size that is used in Word 2000. A font style can be either a serif font or a sans serif font. ***Serif*** refers to the lines at the top and bottom of a letter that help the reader's eyes move across a line of text. Times New Roman, the default style for Word 2000, is a serif font. Arial is a ***sans serif*** font, a typeface without the guiding lines. A sans serif font has a cleaner look and generally is used for headings and other short blocks of text, whereas a serif font is used for the body of the text.

Formatting Shortcuts

Word offers keyboard shortcuts for the major text formatting options. To boldface text, press Ctrl+B. You can use this shortcut to turn boldfacing on, and use the shortcut again to turn it off. This way, you do not have to take your hands off the keyboard. The shortcut for italic is Ctrl+I, and the shortcut for underline is Ctrl+U.

Lesson 2: Aligning Text in a Paragraph

Most text is arranged on the page so that there is a uniform margin between the left edge of the paper and the beginning of each line. Because the words in each line are of different lengths, the right edge of the paragraph is usually uneven. This type of alignment is called ***left aligned***. You can also ***right align*** text, with the right margin straight and the left margin uneven.

The computer calculates the length of a line and the available space between margins. If you want to center a line of text, the computer uses this information to position the line in the center of the available space. ***Centering*** is a type of alignment used to make titles distinct from other parts of the document and to draw the reader's attention.

If you are creating a newsletter or prefer to have the text line up on both sides, you can specify an alignment that is called ***justified***. To accomplish this, the computer adjusts the size of the spaces between the words in each line. When you are trying to align text, it is important to remember that the computer does not consider a space to be a consistent size.

In this lesson, you center titles and justify text.

To Align Text in a Paragraph

1. **With your Book Introduction file still active, select the first line, which is the title of the document.**

2 Click the Center button on the Formatting toolbar.

The title is now centered in the document (see Figure 3.6).

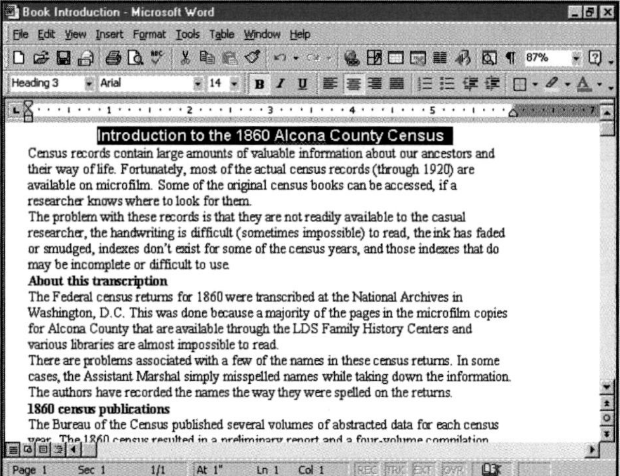

Figure 3.6
The title of the document is centered on the page.

3 Click in the margin to the left of the second line of the document and hold the mouse button down. Drag down to the end of the document to select all but the first line.

All the text is highlighted, so you can justify the body of the document all at the same time.

> Make sure you go to the end of the document, not just to the end of the screen. When you go below the bottom of the text, the screen scrolls down. Don't stop until you see the end-of-document marker and select the period at the end of the last line.

4 Click the Justify button on the Formatting toolbar; scroll to the top of the document, and click anywhere on the text to deselect it.

All the selected text is now justified. Examine the document on your screen and in Figure 3.7. Notice how the spacing between words varies to ensure that the text on both the left and right margin is evenly aligned.

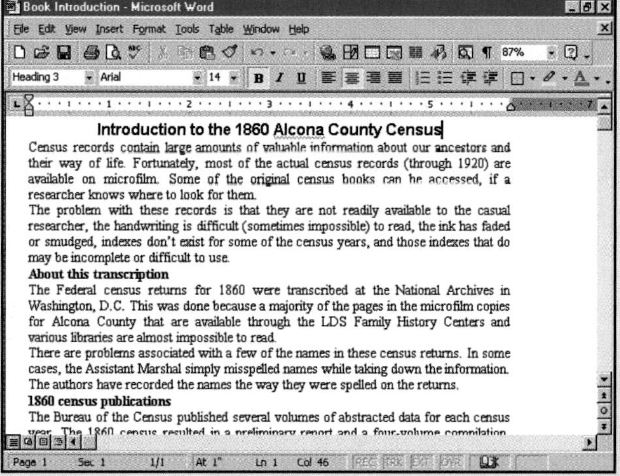

Figure 3.7
When you use justified alignment, the text on both margins is evenly aligned.

5 Click the Save button on the Standard toolbar to save your work up to this point.

Leave the file open for the next lesson.

Formatting Shortcuts

On very long documents, scrolling to select a large portion of text can be cumbersome. A quicker method is to click at the beginning of the text that is to be selected. Position the pointer at the end of the text you want highlighted and hold down Shift and click. All the text from the insertion point to the location of the second click is selected. Then you can apply the desired formatting to the selected text.

Text Alignment Shortcuts

Word provides keyboard shortcuts for text alignment options. To center a paragraph, press Ctrl+E. The shortcut for left aligning text is Ctrl+L; to right align text use Ctrl+R, and to justify text use Ctrl+J.

Lesson 3: Changing Line Spacing

In many cases, you type a document using single-spacing, but change the spacing to double-spacing at a later time. Composing the document with single-spacing enables you to see twice as much text onscreen as you would with double-spacing. However, if you change to double-spacing before you print a copy of the document, the document is easier to edit. Double-spacing allows room for editing notations between the lines.

In this lesson, you change the line spacing in a document.

To Change Line Spacing

1. **With your Book Introduction file still active, choose Edit, Select All from the menu.**
   The entire document is now selected. You can also use the Ctrl+A keyboard shortcut to select all the text in a document.

2. **Choose Format, Paragraph from the menu.**
   The Paragraph dialog box opens (see Figure 3.8). You use the Paragraph dialog box to control alignment, indents, line spacing, tab settings, and other paragraph formatting options.

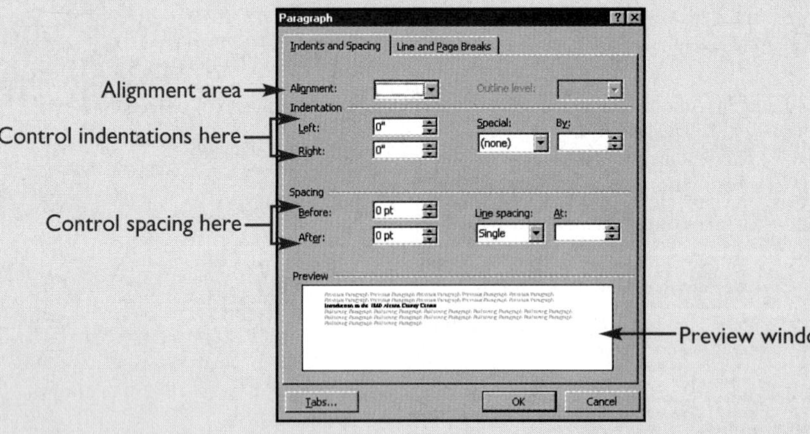

Figure 3.8
The Paragraph dialog box contains options for controlling paragraph formatting.

3. **Select Double from the Line spacing drop-down list.**
   The preview window displays the text as double-spaced.

4. **Click OK, and then click anywhere in the document to deselect the text.**
   Notice that the document is now double-spaced (see Figure 3.9).

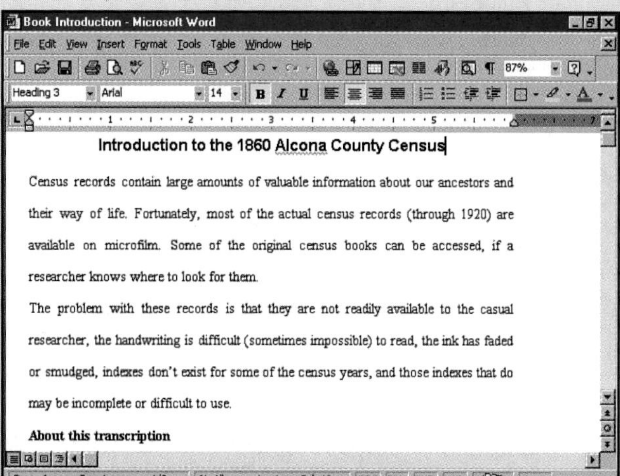

Figure 3.9
The text is double-spaced.

❺ **The bibliography at the end of the document should be single-spaced. Scroll down if necessary, and select the text that extends from the first bibliography entry (the paragraph that begins `Preliminary Report`) to the end of the document.**
To format line spacing, you must first select the paragraphs you want to change.

❻ **Choose Format, Paragraph from the menu.**
The Paragraph dialog box opens.

❼ **Select Single from the Line spacing drop-down list. Click OK and click anywhere in the text to deselect the text.**
The bibliographic entries are again single-spaced (see Figure 3.10).

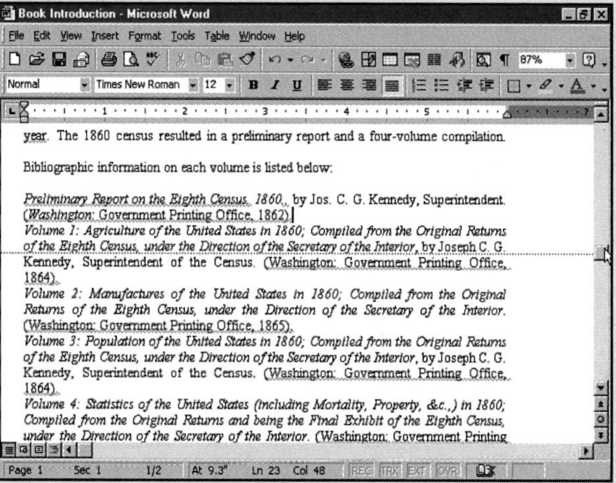

Figure 3.10
The bibliography is single-spaced.

❽ **Click the Save button to save your work. Leave the file open for the next lesson.**

Opening the Paragraph Dialog Box

You can also open the Paragraph dialog box by right-clicking the selected paragraph. A short-cut menu opens. One of the options is Paragraph. Click the Paragraph option to open the Paragraph dialog box.

Line Spacing Keyboard Combinations
You can also change line spacing using keyboard combinations. To choose single-space use Ctrl+1, for double-space use Ctrl+2, to set 1.5-line spacing use Ctrl+5.

Lesson 4: Creating a Bulleted List

A bulleted or numbered list helps draw the reader's attention to key points. Many people are busy and only glance at memos or letters they receive. The use of bulleted lists helps to ensure that the reader sees the most important points in a document. Word gives you the option of quickly creating effective, professional-looking lists.

In this lesson, you create a bulleted list.

To Create a Bulleted List

1. **With your Book Introduction file still active, scroll to the top of the document and place the insertion point just to the right of the word `that` in the first line of the second full paragraph. Press Del to remove the space; then type a colon (:).**
The insertion point should be to the right of the colon (see Figure 3.11).

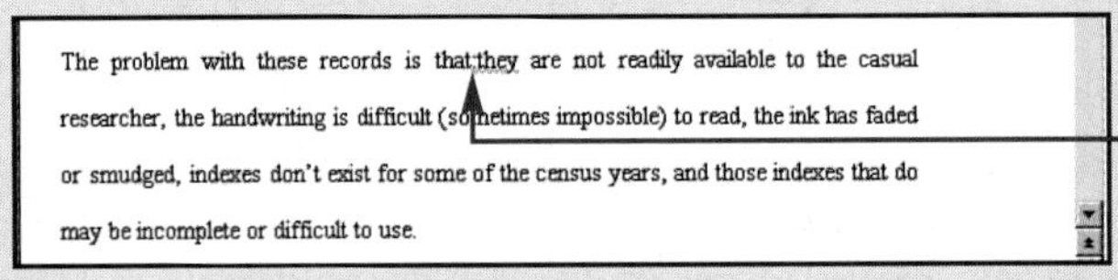

The problem with these records is that they are not readily available to the casual researcher, the handwriting is difficult (sometimes impossible) to read, the ink has faded or smudged, indexes don't exist for some of the census years, and those indexes that do may be incomplete or difficult to use.

Type colon here

Figure 3.11
A colon added to the text signals the beginning of a list.

2. **Press ↵Enter.**
A new paragraph is created, which begins with the phrase `they are not readily available`. This paragraph is the first item in a list of five items.

3. **Select the comma and space after the word `researcher` in the same line and press ↵Enter.**
The comma and space are deleted, and a new paragraph is created (see Figure 3.12). Pressing ↵Enter inserts the paragraph mark, which replaces the selected characters, in this case a comma and a space.

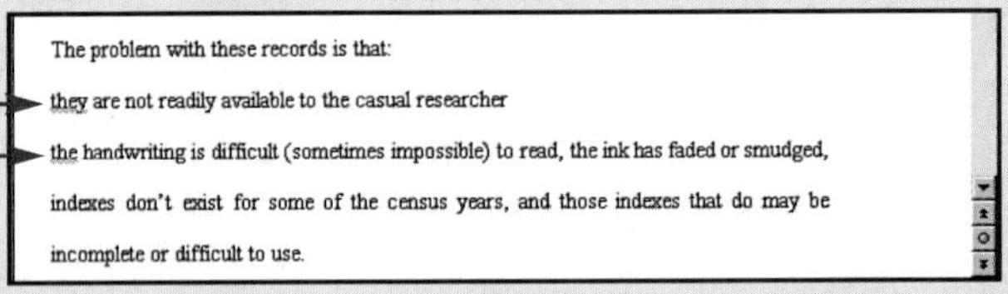

The problem with these records is that:
they are not readily available to the casual researcher
the handwriting is difficult (sometimes impossible) to read, the ink has faded or smudged, indexes don't exist for some of the census years, and those indexes that do may be incomplete or difficult to use.

First item in list
Beginning of second item

Figure 3.12
The first line in the bulleted list is separated from the rest of the text and a second paragraph is started.

4. **Select the comma and space after the words `to read` and press ↵Enter.**
Another new paragraph is created and the second bulleted point is separated from the rest of the text.

5. **Select the comma and space after the word `smudged` and press ↵Enter.**
The fourth new paragraph is created.

6. **Select the comma and space after the words `census years` and press ↵Enter.**
The last new paragraph is created.

7. **Press Del four times to delete the word `and` as well as the following space in the paragraph. Delete the period following the word `use` at the end of the same line.**
The five points that make up the list appear on separate lines of text (see Figure 3.13).

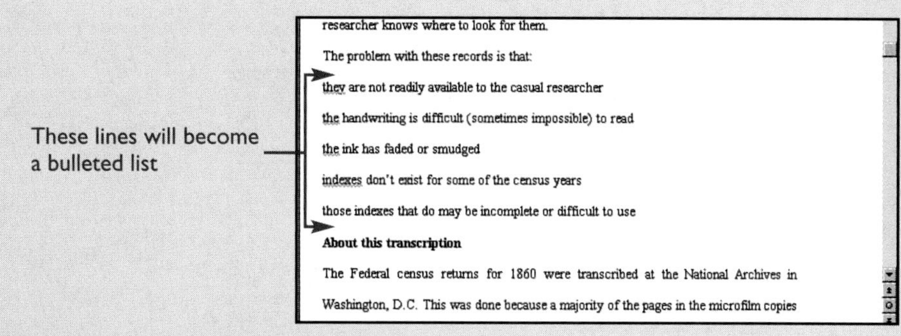

Figure 3.13
The points that you want to make a bulleted list are identified.

8 **Select all five items that make your new list.**

9 **Click the Bullets button on the Formatting toolbar.**

Bullets appear in front of the list items, and the list is indented 0.25 inches to the bullets and 0.5 inches to the text (see Figure 3.14).

Formatting Bulleted Lists

You can change the look of your bulleted lists by choosing Format, Bullets and Numbering from the menu. Select the Bulleted tab, if necessary, and click the Customize button. You can change the shape of the bullet, the bullet position, and the text indent.

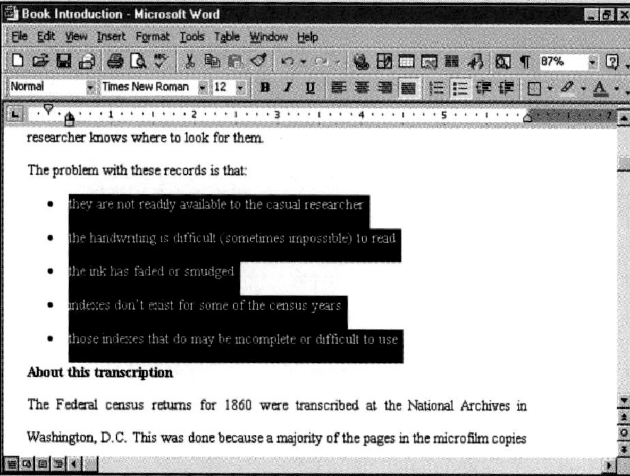

Figure 3.14
The bullets appear at the beginning of each paragraph of text.

10 **With the list still selected, choose Format, Paragraph from the menu. Select the Indents and Spacing tab in the Paragraph dialog box, if necessary, and select Single from the Line spacing drop-down list. Click OK, and click anywhere in the document to deselect the text.**

The bulleted list is now single-spaced (see Figure 3.15). Save your work and leave the file open for the next lesson.

continues ▶

To Create a Bulleted List (continued)

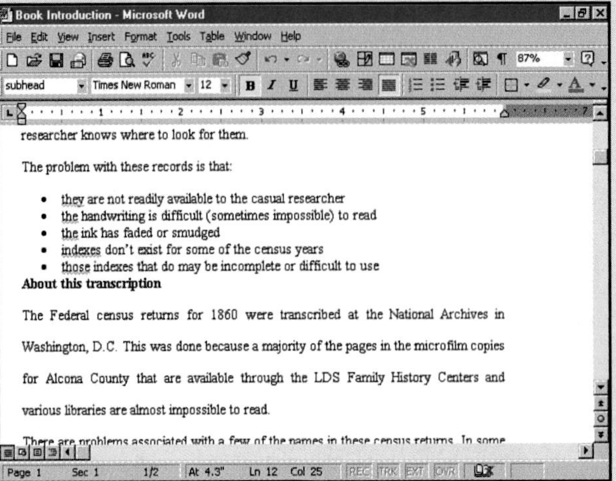

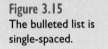

Figure 3.15
The bulleted list is single-spaced.

Creating Lists

If the information in a list is in some kind of sequential order, you might consider using the Numbering button, which is to the left of the Bullets button. If the information is in no particular order, it is best to use a bulleted list. To create a list from scratch, you can click the Bullets or Numbering button first, type the list, and click the Bullets or Numbering button again to turn it off.

Indenting a Bulleted List

If you want to move the bulleted (or numbered) list to the right or left, click the Increase Indent button or the Decrease Indent button on the Formatting toolbar. Each click of one of these buttons moves the highlighted list a half-inch.

Lesson 5: Indenting the First Line of a Paragraph

Some writing styles call for the first line of each paragraph to be aligned with the rest of the paragraph; others require that you indent the first line a certain amount of space. Many people indent the first line by typing five or six spaces. This method works well on typewriters that always use the same size spaces, but it does not work well on computers that vary the size of spaces depending on the size of the paragraph's font.

Another method commonly used to indent the first line of a paragraph is to press Tab. This method works well, but it has two drawbacks. If no tabs have been set, Word assumes that you want to move 0.5 inches to the right each time you press Tab. If you try to edit this paragraph and set a tab for some other purpose, the indent lines up with the new tab. The real problem with using a tab to indent is evident when you try to use it to create ***hanging indents*** (paragraphs with all but the first line indented). Pressing Tab at the beginning of each subsequent line introduces tab characters that cause problems if you try to change the length of the line by editing the text or changing the font size.

If you use the Format, Paragraph menu options, you can specify the size of the indent in inches, set a standard that can be applied to more than one paragraph, and avoid later editing problems.

In this lesson, you indent the first line of a paragraph.

To Indent the First Line of a Paragraph

1. **With your Book Introduction file still active, select the first two paragraphs, but not the title (see Figure 3.16).**
   This text includes the introduction to the bulleted list you created in the previous lesson, but not the list itself.

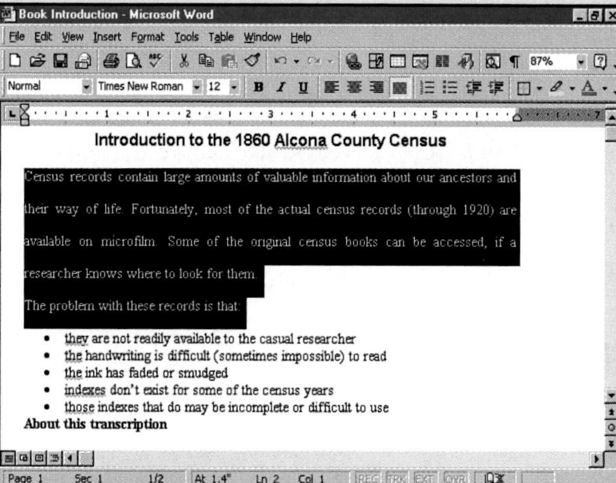

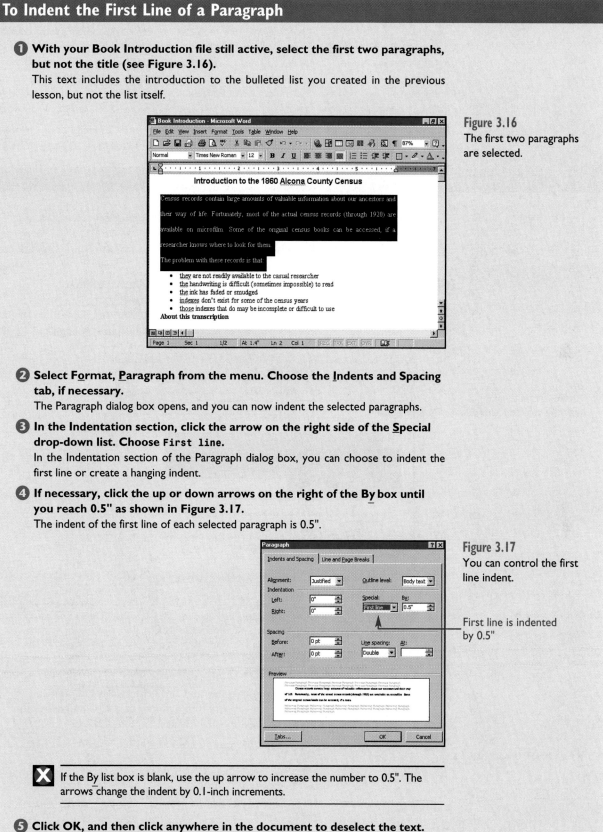

Figure 3.16
The first two paragraphs are selected.

2. **Select Format, Paragraph from the menu. Choose the Indents and Spacing tab, if necessary.**
   The Paragraph dialog box opens, and you can now indent the selected paragraphs.
3. **In the Indentation section, click the arrow on the right side of the Special drop-down list. Choose `First line`.**
   In the Indentation section of the Paragraph dialog box, you can choose to indent the first line or create a hanging indent.
4. **If necessary, click the up or down arrows on the right of the By box until you reach 0.5" as shown in Figure 3.17.**
   The indent of the first line of each selected paragraph is 0.5".

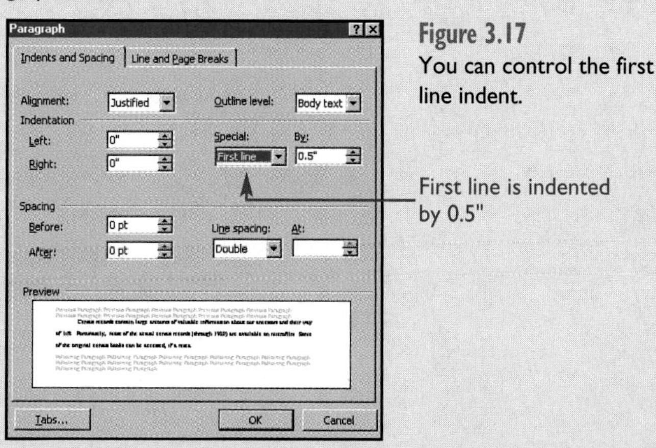

Figure 3.17
You can control the first line indent.

First line is indented by 0.5"

If the By list box is blank, use the up arrow to increase the number to 0.5". The arrows change the indent by 0.1-inch increments.

5. **Click OK, and then click anywhere in the document to deselect the text.**
   The selected paragraphs are now indented half an inch. Save your work and leave the file open for the next lesson.

Lesson 6: Using the Format Painter

To apply a consistent look to your document, it is a good idea to have all the paragraphs in the document formatted the same way. When you change the format of a paragraph, you usually change the format of other paragraphs to match. If they are continuous, you can simply highlight all the paragraphs and then do the formatting one time. If lists, subtitles, tables, or other text that requires different formatting separates the paragraphs, you can use a different formatting technique. The ***Format Painter*** is a tool that enables you to copy the formatting of one paragraph and paint it onto another paragraph. This tool can help you apply formatting characteristics quickly and easily.

In this lesson, you use the Format Painter to copy the indentation formatting to other paragraphs.

To Use the Format Painter

1 With your Book Introduction file still active, select the first full paragraph (but not the title).

The first line in this paragraph is indented. You apply the format of this paragraph to several other paragraphs in the document.

2 Double-click the Format Painter button on the Standard toolbar.

The format of the first paragraph attaches to the Format Painter. The pointer now includes a paintbrush (see Figure 3.18). You can apply the format of the first paragraph to multiple paragraphs without having to click the Format Painter button again.

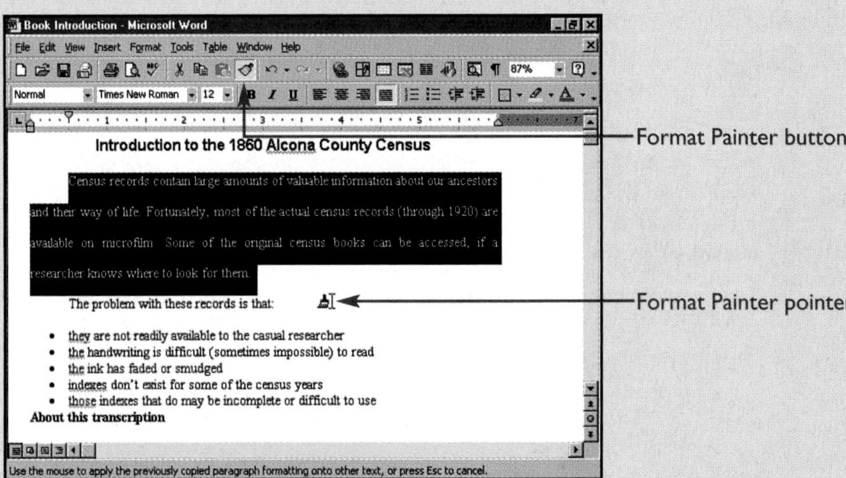

Figure 3.18
Use the Format Painter to apply the selected format to other paragraphs in your document.

If you click the Format Painter button once, you can change only one paragraph before the painter is turned off. By double-clicking, you activate the Format Painter for as many uses as you want. It does not turn off until you click the Format Painter button again.

3 Use the vertical scrollbar to move the text until the two paragraphs after the `About this transcription` subtitle display onscreen. Click anywhere in the first paragraph after the `About this transcription` subtitle.

4 Click anywhere in the second paragraph after the `About this transcription` subtitle.

This paragraph now exhibits the same formatting as the original paragraph (see Figure 3.19).

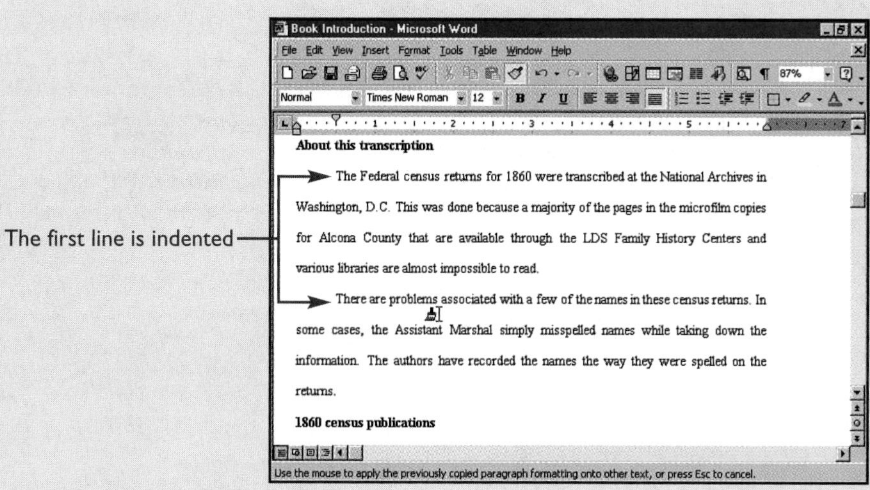

Figure 3.19
Using the Format Painter you can quickly copy a formatting style to another paragraph.

5. **Scroll down and click anywhere in the first paragraph after the `1860 census publications` subtitle.**
   This paragraph's first line is now indented. This is the last paragraph that needs a format change.
6. **Click the Format Painter button to turn it off.**
   The pointer returns to its normal I-beam shape. Click the Save button to save your changes. Leave the file open for the next lesson.

Hidden Characters

When you press ↵Enter to mark the end of a paragraph, Word places a hidden character in the text. That character does more than just mark the end of the paragraph; it also stores the paragraph's formatting information. If you use the Format Painter to copy the format of a paragraph, the hidden paragraph mark must be included in the original selection. To see hidden characters, such as the paragraph mark, spaces, and tabs, click the Show/Hide button on the Standard toolbar.

Using the Format Painter

Depending on the type of format that is being copied, you may need to select the entire line or paragraph to apply the format. In this lesson, just clicking anywhere on the paragraph applies the indent to the paragraph.

Lesson 7: Creating a Hanging Indent

Some styles use a hanging indent, which means that the first line of the text is to the left of the rest of the text in the paragraph. For example, it is common for bibliographic references to call for the first line of a bibliographic entry to be a half-inch to the left of the rest of the entry. This is another formatting style you can apply using the options available in the Format, Paragraph menu.

In this lesson, you apply the hanging indent format to the bibliography.

To Create a Hanging Indent

1. **With your Book Introduction file still active, select the last five paragraphs in the document, starting with the paragraph beginning `Preliminary Report`.**
   These are the bibliographic references.
2. **Select Format, Paragraph from the menu.**
   The Paragraph dialog box opens.

continues ▶

To Create a Hanging Indent (continued)

3 Select the Indents and Spacing tab, if necessary. In the Indentation section, click the arrow on the right side of the Special drop-down list. Choose Hanging. The By box should read 0.5".

In this hanging indent, the first line is a half-inch to the left of the rest of the paragraph. This structure is accomplished by indenting the rest of the text in each paragraph. The preview window displays the hanging indent (see Figure 3.20).

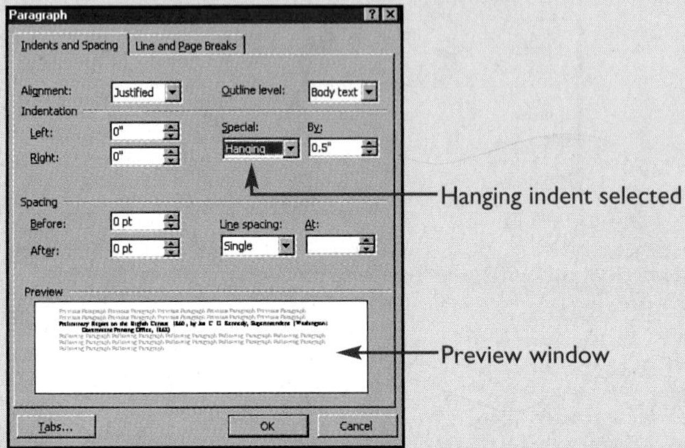

Figure 3.20
The hanging indent style is applied to the selected text.

If the By list box is not set at 0.5", use the up or down arrows to adjust the number to that measurement. In each paragraph selected, all the lines after the first line are indented by 0.5 inches when the hanging indent is applied.

4 Click OK.

The five bibliographic entries are formatted with hanging indents. Click anywhere in the document to deselect the text. Notice how much easier the entries are to read (see Figure 3.21).

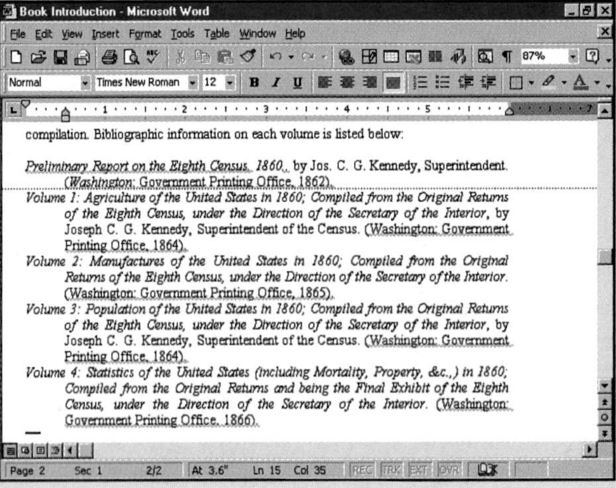

Figure 3.21
The paragraphs of the bibliography are formatted with hanging indents.

5 Click the Save button to save your work. Leave the file open for the next lesson.

Lesson 8: Adding Spaces After Paragraphs

In many cases, extra space between paragraphs makes the document easier to read because it adds white space and creates a visual separation. This is particularly true if the text is single-spaced. You can set up your paragraphs to add extra space automatically before or after a paragraph. Adding this type of paragraph formatting means that you do not have to press ↵Enter a second time to have an empty line between paragraphs. It also enables you to control how much space there is between paragraphs. For example, you may want to have more empty space after a heading or after the end of a section of a document. This visual separation helps the reader see that you are moving to a new topic.

In this lesson, you add spaces of different heights after paragraphs.

To Add Spaces After Paragraphs

1. **With your Book Introduction file still active, select the last five paragraphs in the document.**
   These paragraphs are the bibliographic entries you added hanging indents to in the previous lesson. These references would be easier to read if each one is separate from the next. This is not the same as double-spacing. Each paragraph, or reference, needs to be single-spaced and separated from the next entry by white space.

2. **Select Format, Paragraph from the menu.**
   The Paragraph dialog box opens.

3. **Select the Indents and Spacing tab, if necessary. In the Spacing area of the dialog box, click the up arrow in the After box, which changes the number to 6 pt.**
   A preview of the new look of the text appears in the preview area (see Figure 3.22).

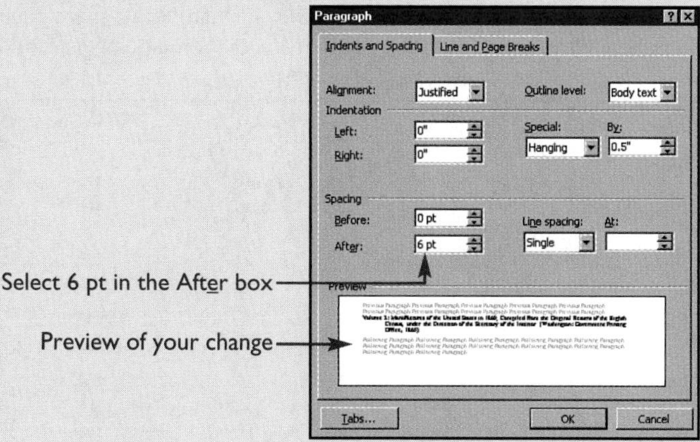

Figure 3.22
You use the Spacing area of the Paragraph dialog box to add spacing before or after a paragraph.

4. **Click OK, and then click anywhere in the document to deselect the text.**
   A 6-point space separates each selected paragraph, making the bibliographic entries easier to read.

5. **Scroll to the top of the document and select the last item in the bulleted list.**

6. **Select Format, Paragraph from the menu. Select the Indents and Spacing tab, if necessary. In the Paragraph dialog box click the up arrow in the After box twice to add a 12-pt space.**

7. **Click OK, and click anywhere in the document to deselect the text.**
   A 12-point space appears after the bulleted list (see Figure 3.23). This spacing matches the other between-paragraph spaces in the surrounding area of the document.

continues ▶

To Add Spaces After Paragraphs (continued)

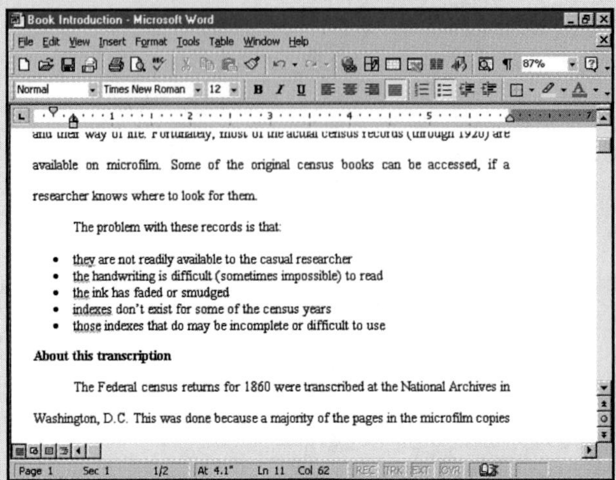

Figure 3.23
A 12-point space appears after the last bulleted list item.

8 **Save your work and leave the file open for the next lesson.**

Adding Spacing Before or After the Paragraph

You can also add additional space before the paragraph using the Before spacing option from the Paragraph dialog box. It is a good idea, however, to be consistent and use either before or after spacing to avoid unintended extra spacing.

When you see 6 pt in the After box, it means that a space equivalent to a line of 6-point text is added after each selected paragraph. A 6-point space is about the height of half a line when you are using 12-point type.

Lesson 9: Working with Tabs

Tabs have become less and less important in word processing documents in favor of other indenting techniques and tables. It is necessary, however, to know how to use tabs. For example, it is often helpful to use a tab to line up the decimals in a column of numbers with decimal points. Tabs are also the only way to put regular dots or dashes, called ***leaders***, between columns. Leaders often connect chapter titles with page numbers in a table of contents. If you have a line of text with some words left aligned, other words centered, and still other words right aligned, you might want to use tabs.

The default for tabs in Word is a tab stop at every half-inch. Rather than pressing Tab several times to reach the desired stop, you should set the tabs to the needed location before entering text. Doing so ensures that the text entered aligns properly regardless of differences in the length. Knowing how to use tabs increases your ability to create professional-looking documents.

In this lesson, you use different kinds of tabs in a short table of information.

To Use Tabs

1 **Place the insertion point at the end of the last item in the bulleted list of the Book Introduction document. Press Enter.**

A new bullet point is added below the last one.

2 **Click the Bullets button to turn off the Bullet feature.**

The new bullet is removed and the insertion point moves back to the left margin.

3 **Type `The following are the places, dates, and page numbers of the 1860 Alcona County Federal census:` and press Enter.**

Text is added just below the bulleted list (see Figure 3.24).

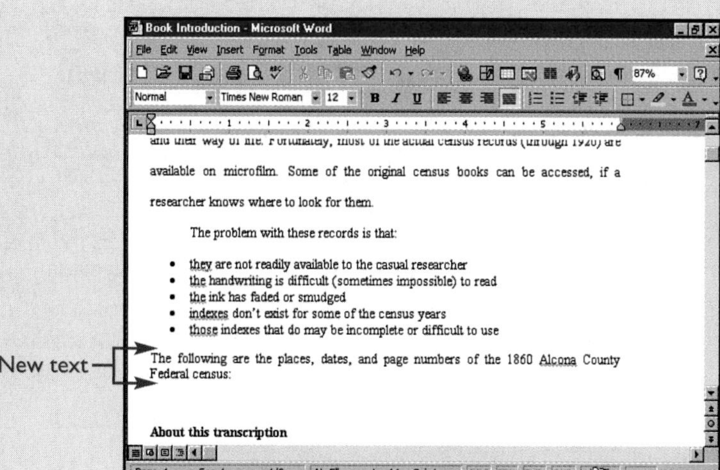

Figure 3.24
A new line of text is added.

4 Select Format, Tabs from the menu.
The Tabs dialog box opens (see Figure 3.25). If the Tabs menu option is not visible when you choose the Format menu option, click the double down arrow at the bottom of the Format drop-down menu to display the rest of the formatting options.

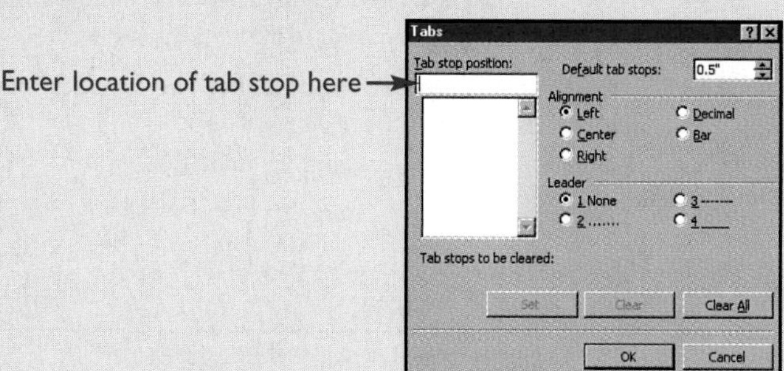

Figure 3.25
In the Tab dialog box, you set the type of tab and the spacing between tabs.

5 Type 2 in the Tab stop position; select Left in the Alignment area, and make sure 1 None is selected in the Leader area. Click Set to enter the tab at the 2-inch mark.
The first tab is defined as shown in Figure 3.26.

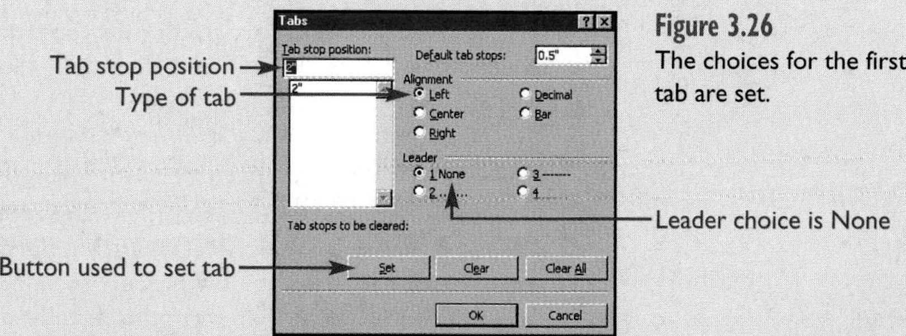

Figure 3.26
The choices for the first tab are set.

6 Type 6 over the measurement 2" in the Tab stop position text box; select Right in the Alignment area, and select 2...... from the Leader area. Click Set to enter the tab at the 6-inch mark.
The second tab is set as a right-aligned tab at the 6-inch mark, which means the text lines up on the right edge. A dot leader precedes the text.

7 Click OK.
The tabs you added appear in the ruler at the top of the work area (see Figure 3.27). If the ruler is not showing on your screen, select View, Ruler from the menu.

continues ▶

To Use Tabs (continued)

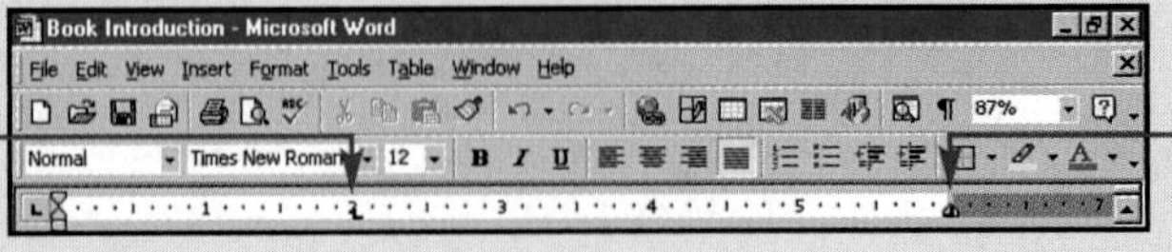

Figure 3.27
The two tabs that have been set appear on the horizontal ruler at the top of the document.

❽ **Type `Black River` and press Tab.**
This moves the insertion point to the left tab at the 2-inch mark.

❾ **Type `June 8, 1860` and press Tab.**
When you type the date, it moves to the right of the tab. The left tab you set lines up the left edges of the dates. The dot leader appears when you press Tab (see Figure 3.28).

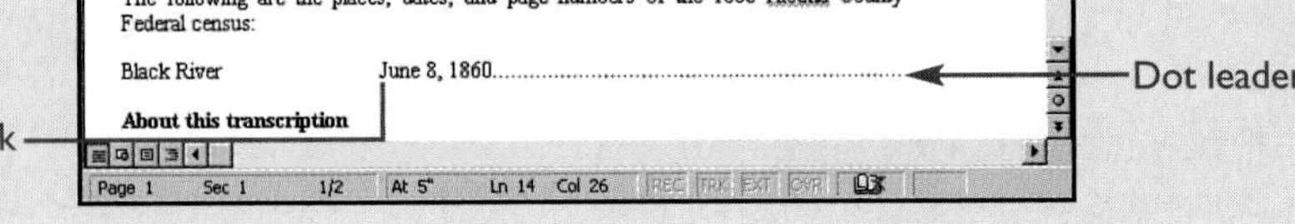

Figure 3.28
A dot leader is added after the date.

❿ **Type `9-11` for the page numbers and press Enter.**
Notice that because the right tab is used, the numbers move to the left as they are typed, ensuring that the numbers line up on the right side.

⓫ **Enter the following information using the same procedure. (Don't press Enter after the `Yewell Place` line.)**

```
Harrisville Township    June 8-10, 1860     11-13
Yewell Place            June 11-12, 1860    14-15
```

Figure 3.29 shows the completed list of information.

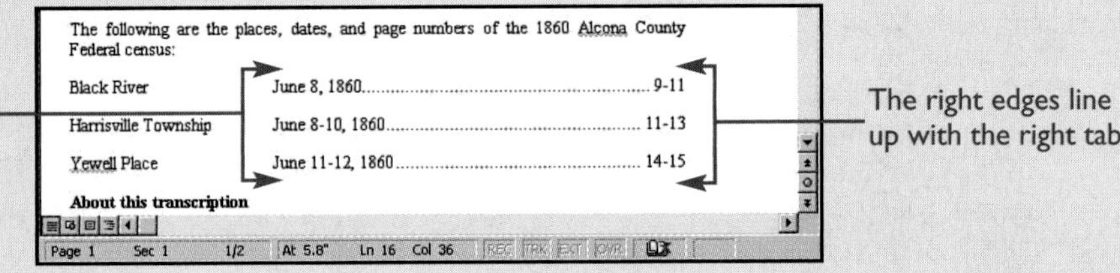

Figure 3.29
Data lines up into columns of information when you set tabs to align text on the left or right edge.

⓬ **Highlight the first full paragraph (not the title) of the document; then click the Format Painter button and click the paragraph beginning with `The following are the places`.**
The format of the first paragraph is applied to the paragraph that provides the lead-in to the table of data.

⓭ **Select the two new lines beginning with `Black River` and `Harrisville Township`; then choose Format, Paragraph from the menu. In the Indents and Spacing tab, use the down arrow to select 0 pt in the After box. Click OK, and then click anywhere in the document to deselect the text.**
The spacing between each item in the list is removed. After you change the formatting, the list of dates, locations, and pages should look like Figure 3.30.

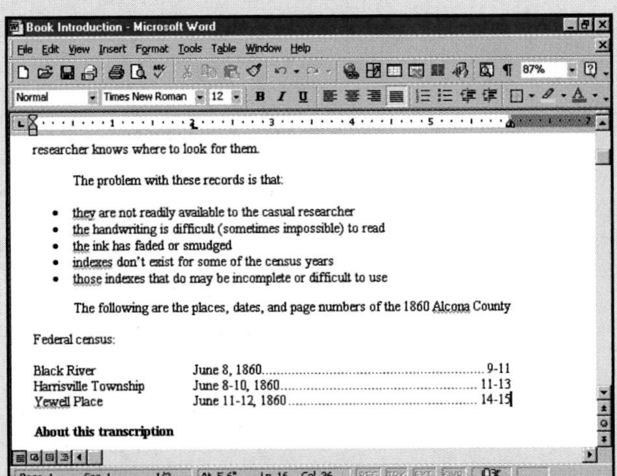

Figure 3.30
Removing the spacing between items creates a concise, cohesive appearance.

⑭ **Click the Save button to save your work. Print the document and close the file.**

Working with Tabs

You can select different types of tabs by clicking the tab marker at the left end of the horizontal ruler. When the tab you want to use displays, add it to the horizontal ruler by clicking the ruler at the position where you want the tab. A tab marker is added to the ruler. To remove a tab, click the paragraph where you want the tab deleted. Click the tab marker on the ruler and drag it down and off of the ruler. The tab is deleted from the selected paragraph.

Adding Center and Decimal Tabs

You can also add a center tab to the ruler. When you press Tab to go to a center tab, the text you type is centered on that tab. Another useful type of tab is the decimal tab. When you use this tab, the numbers move to the left until you press the decimal point, at which point the numbers move to the right of the decimal as you type them. This ensures that the numbers line up on the decimal point.

Summary

In this project, you learned different techniques for formatting text in a document. The elements that were demonstrated included font style, size and emphasis, paragraph alignment, and line spacing. You copied formats from one paragraph to others by using the Format Painter. You created a bulleted list, a table using tabs, and different indentation styles for a paragraph. You also learned how to add extra white space between paragraphs as part of the paragraph format. Many of the features you used are controlled in the Paragraph dialog box.

[?] You can expand your learning by using Help to learn more about formatting paragraphs. Explore the topics: `View format settings for a paragraph`, and `Troubleshooting paragraph formatting`. Open the Paragraph dialog box and look at the other options that are available, including options available on the Line and Page Breaks tab. Test other options to see how they affect text. To learn more about working with tabs explore this topic in Help. Click the tab button at the left end of the horizontal ruler to see the different tab styles. Try dragging a tab symbol on the ruler to move it or drag it off the ruler to delete it.

Checking Concepts and Terms

True/False

For each of the following, check *T* or *F* to indicate whether the statement is true or false.

__T __F **1.** When you select text and change the font, the shape of the letters changes. [L1]

__T __F **2.** If you change the size of the selected text to 36-point type, the text is about an inch high when it prints. [L1]

__T __F **3.** If you format a paragraph with a hanging indent, the first line begins further to the right than the rest of the lines in the paragraph. [L7]

__T __F **4.** To make the letters thicker and appear more important, you can select the text and click the button on the toolbar that has a capital letter B on it. [L1]

__T __F **5.** Creating a first-line indent by pressing Spacebar five times is the same as setting the first-line indent to 0.5 inches. [L5]

__T __F **6.** There is a certain type of tab that can be used to align a column of dollar figures so that the decimal points line up. [L9]

__T __F **7.** If you want to apply the formatting of one paragraph to another, select Edit, Copy, Paste Special from the menu. [L6]

__T __F **8.** If you set up a tab with a dot leader, pressing Tab produces a series of dots between the previous text and the text at that tab. [L9]

__T __F **9.** The only way to place extra space between paragraphs is to press Enter one or two extra times. [L8]

__T __F **10.** If you want to insert a bulleted list, you can click the Bullets button and type the list. [L4]

Multiple Choice

Circle the letter of the correct answer for each of the following.

1. What is the correct way to create a paragraph whose first line begins to the right of the rest of the lines of text? [L5]

a. Select the paragraph and choose Format, Paragraph, and select `Hanging` in the Special box.

b. Position the pointer at the beginning of the paragraph and click the increase indent button.

c. Position the pointer at the beginning of the paragraph and press Spacebar five times.

d. Select the paragraph and choose Format, Paragraph, and select First Line in the Special box.

2. What is the correct way to create a paragraph whose first line of text is further to the left than the rest of the lines? [L7]

a. Select the paragraph and choose Format, Paragraph, and select Hanging in the Special box.

b. Position the pointer at the beginning of the paragraph and click the increase indent button.

c. Position the pointer at the beginning of the paragraph and press Tab.

d. Select the paragraph and choose Format, Paragraph, and select Indent in the Special box.

3. Which tab moves inserted text to the left as you type to ensure that the right side of the text stays aligned with the position of the tab? [L9]

a. Left tab

b. Center tab

c. Right tab

d. Decimal tab

4. A line of text that has the same amount of space between its first word and the left margin and its last word and the right margin uses which kind of alignment? [L2]

a. right

b. center

c. left

d. justified

5. When all the lines of a paragraph line up at both the left and right margins, the paragraph is ______________. [L2]

a. right aligned

b. centered

c. left aligned

d. justified

Screen ID

Refer to Figure 3.31 and identify the numbered parts of the screen. Write the letter of the correct label in the space next to the number.

Figure 3.31

- **A.** Bulleted list
- **B.** Buttons used for adding emphasis
- **C.** Buttons used for aligning text
- **D.** Centered text emphasized with boldface
- **E.** Dot leader
- **F.** Double-spaced paragraph with the first line indented
- **G.** Font size
- **H.** Format Painter
- **I.** Name of font
- **J.** Ruler displaying tabs for currently selected line
- **K.** Left tab stop
- **L.** Right tab stop

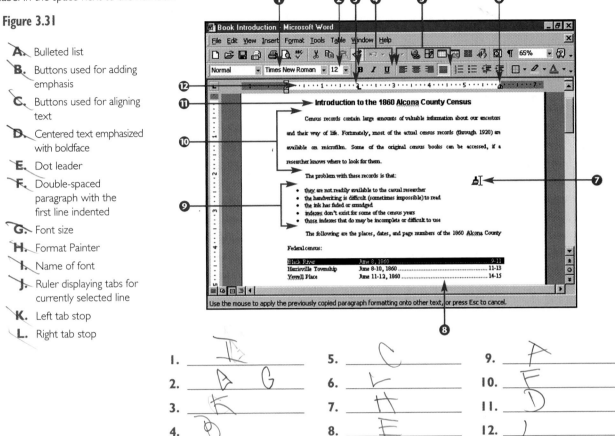

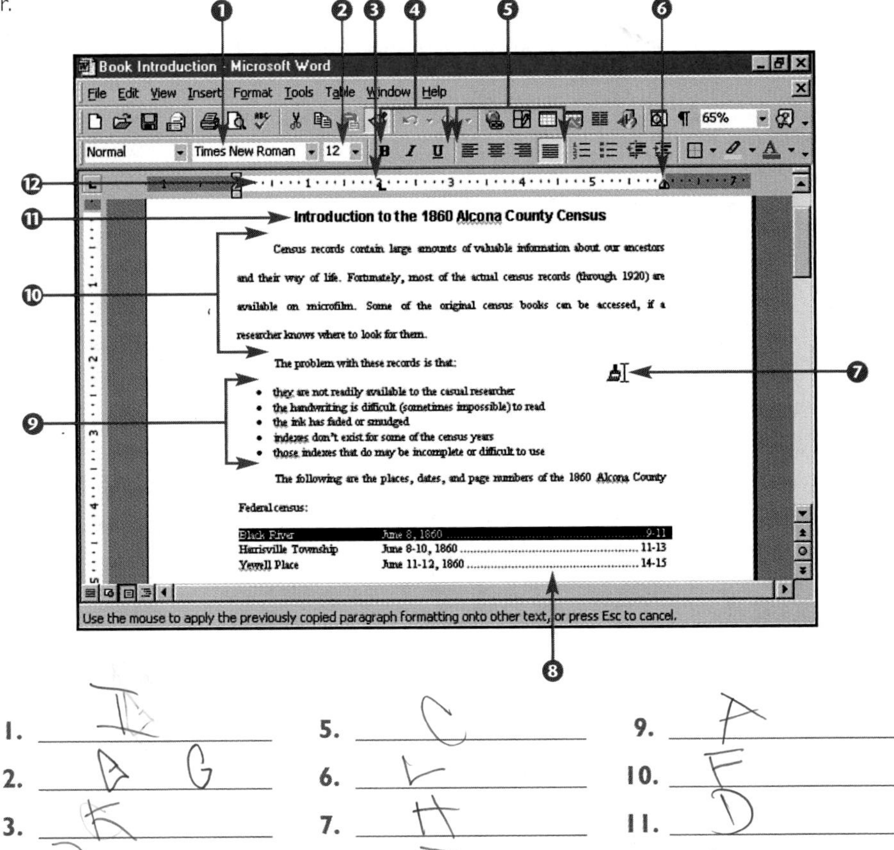

1. ______
2. ______
3. ______
4. ______
5. ______
6. ______
7. ______
8. ______
9. ______
10. ______
11. ______
12. ______

Discussion Questions

1. Which formatting tools demonstrated in this chapter would be most useful to you? When would you use them?
2. In the documents you write, which alignment, font style, and size do you prefer to use? Is there a standard that your employer or teachers require? What is the standard? Is there a value in establishing a standard?
3. If you were responsible for establishing a letter or memo standard for your company, what would that standard be? Consider each of the formatting elements demonstrated in this project.

Skill Drill

Skill Drill exercises reinforce project skills. Each skill reinforced is the same, or nearly the same, as a skill presented in the project. Detailed instructions are provided in a step-by-step format.

In this set of Skill Drill exercises, you work with a document about distance education technologies. You change font characteristics, use the Format Painter, format paragraphs, create a bulleted list, indent paragraphs using the hanging indent, and add an extra line at the end of the paragraph.

This set of Skill Drill exercises uses file WO-0302. Leave the file open from one Skill Drill exercise to the next.

1. Changing the Font Type, Size, Alignment, and Emphasis

Titles identify the subject of a paper and its author. In this exercise, you format the title and author information so that it stands out from the body of the document. [L1]

1. Launch Word. Open the document `WO-0302` from the Student folder on the CD-ROM. Save it to your floppy disk as `Distance Education Technologies`.
2. Select the first two lines of the document, which make up the title.
3. Change the font to Arial.
4. Change the font size to 14 point.
5. Change the emphasis to bold.
6. Change the alignment to centered.
7. Select the three lines that identify the author and date.
8. Change their alignment to centered.
9. Select the line following the date. Type `Edited by: <Your Name>` (use your own name) and press Enter. Center this line.
10. Leave the document open for use in the next exercise.

2. Using the Format Painter to Format Several Other Lines of Text

In this exercise, you format some subheadings and then use the Format Painter to apply the same formatting characteristics to other subheadings. This tool can be a very efficient tool for ensuring that the same format is applied to multiple locations. [L6]

1. Click the Show/Hide button to reveal the hidden paragraph marks.
2. Select the subheading `Interactive Technologies`, which follows the first long paragraph. Make sure to include the paragraph mark at the end of the line.
3. Make it bold and change its alignment to centered.
4. Choose Format, Paragraph to open the Paragraph dialog box.
5. Change the After spacing box to 6 pt and click OK.
6. Double-click the Format Painter button on the toolbar.
7. Scroll to the bottom of page two to find the next subheading, `Conclusion`.
8. Click the word `Conclusion` to center it. If you double-click the Format Painter button, it remains depressed to indicate that you can use it again.
9. Scroll down and find the subheading `Reference List`. Click it to center it.
10. Click the Format Painter button to deselect it.
11. Leave the document open for use in the next exercise.

3. Formatting Paragraphs

In this exercise, you format a paragraph to be double-spaced with the first line indented. You use the Format Painter to copy this format to other paragraphs. [L6]

1. Scroll to the top of the document and double-click in the left margin next to the paragraph that starts with `Distance education is`. The paragraph is selected.
2. Choose Format, Paragraph to open the Paragraph dialog box.
3. Set the line spacing to Double.
4. Set the special indent to First line and click OK.
5. Double-click the Format Painter button on the toolbar.
6. Use the Format Painter to apply formats to all the paragraphs that follow except the underlined subheadings, the centered subheadings or titles, and the references at the end of the document.
7. Click the Format Painter button to turn it off.
8. Leave the document open for use in the next exercise.

4. Creating a Bulleted List

Next, convert part of the text into a bulleted list. This helps to highlight the conclusions of the document so someone who just wants to scan it can move to the conclusion and read the key points. [L4]

1. Locate the `Conclusion` section.
2. Select the four paragraphs that follow the phrase `Consider the following`. Because it is difficult to drag across text and scroll at the same time, click once to place the insertion point at the beginning of the first of the four paragraphs; scroll to the end of the fourth paragraph; hold Shift and click at the end of the paragraph. This is a good method for selecting large blocks of text.
3. Click the Bullets button on the toolbar.
4. Click the Decrease Indent button twice on the formatting toolbar to move the bulleted list to the left.
5. Deselect the text and see how these changes set off the concluding points.
6. Leave the document open for use in the next exercise.

5. Formatting a Hanging Indent and Following Spaces

In the final Skill Drill exercise, you format the references with a hanging indent and add an extra space between each reference to separate one from the next. [L5]

1. Select all the references at the end of the document.
2. Choose Format, Paragraph to open the Paragraph dialog box.
3. Set the special indent to Hanging.
4. Set the line spacing to Single, if necessary.
5. Set the spacing after the paragraph to 6 pt and click OK.
6. Save the file and print the document.
7. Close the file.

Challenge

Challenge exercises expand on or are somewhat related to skills presented in the lessons. Each exercise provides a brief narrative introduction followed by instructions, in a numbered step or bulleted list format, that are not as detailed as those in the Skill Drill section.

In these Challenge exercises, you explore some other text and paragraph formatting options. First, you create a table of data using tabs, this time using the center and decimal tabs. In the second exercise, you create a numbered list in a paper about nuclear energy. In the last exercise, you apply subscript and superscript formats to notations in the nuclear energy paper. The first exercise does not use an existing file; you create it as a new file. The last two exercises use file WO-0303.

1. Using the Center and Decimal Tabs and Underlining Words in a Title

In Lesson 9, you created a list of data that used a left-aligned and right-aligned tab. The decimal tab is another specialized tab that is useful for aligning numbers on a decimal point. The center tab enables you to center the title over the data. [L9]

To create a chart that uses the center tab, decimal tabs, and underlining, follow these steps:

1. Start a new document and examine the data shown in Figure 3.32. You complete a similar data chart in this exercise.

Figure 3.32

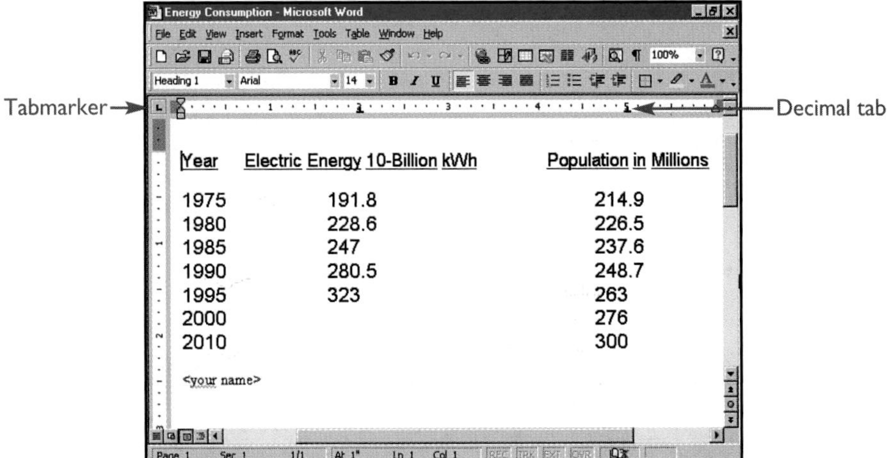

2. For the first line of text, use center tabs at the 2-inch and 5-inch marks. Click the tab marker at the left end of the horizontal ruler to change the tab selection to the center tab mark. Click the ruler at the 2-inch mark and the 5-inch mark to set the tab locations. Now you are ready to type the first line of the chart. (*Hint*: Use the ScreenTip to help you identify the center tab notation.)
3. For the remaining data, use decimal tabs at the 2-inch and 5-inch marks. One way to do this is to remove the old tab markers first and add the decimal tabs.
4. Select the first line of the chart and choose Format, Font. Change the Underline style to Words only.
5. Change the font of the heading line to Arial, 14 point.
6. Change the font of the data to Arial, 16 point.
7. Add your name after the end of the chart.
8. Save the document on your floppy disk as `Energy Consumption`. Print the document, and close it.

2. Using a Numbered List

Instead of a bulleted list, you might want to create a numbered list and choose the style of the numbers you use. In this exercise, you add numbers to paragraphs in a paper about nuclear energy and select the number style. [L4]

To change paragraphs in a paper to a numbered list, follow these steps:

1. Open the `WO-0303` file in the Student folder on the CD-ROM. Save it on your floppy disk with the name `Nuclear Energy`.

2. At the top of the page, under the By line, type **Edited by** and your name.
3. Select the first full paragraph and all of the following paragraphs except the last one. Click the Numbering button on the Formatting toolbar.
4. With the text still selected, choose Format, Bullets and Numbering from the menu. In the Bullets and Numbering dialog box, format the numbers using the fourth option in the first row. This applies Roman numerals to the list.
5. Save the document and leave it open for use in the next exercise.

3. Formatting Text to Subscripts and Superscripts

It is customary to use subscripts and superscripts in scientific papers and mathematical formulas. The Format, Font command enables you to select this type of format so you can properly represent scientific and mathematical notations. In this exercise, you apply these formatting options to notations in the Nuclear Energy paper.

To change characters to subscript and superscript formats, follow these steps:

1. Use the Nuclear Energy document from the previous Challenge exercise, or locate and open **WO-0303** from the Student folder on the CD-ROM and save it on your floppy disk with the name **Nuclear Energy**.
2. If necessary, add **Edited by** and your name at the top of the page, under the By line.
3. Scroll to the bottom of the first page. Notice the subscript and superscript formats that have been used in the paragraph about chain reaction. These are notations identifying uranium and plutonium isotopes.
4. Go to the bottom of the document. Change the notations in the paragraph about breeder reactors so they match the format you just examined. Select 92 in the first notation and choose Format, Font, and click Subscript in the Effects area. Select 238; open the Font dialog box again, and click Superscript.
5. Repeat this process for the remaining five notations in this paragraph. You might try using the Format Painter. (*Hint:* You cannot do it in one step. The subscript and superscript are two different formats and have to be selected and applied or "painted" separately.)
6. Save your changes and print the document before you close it.

Discovery Zone

Discovery Zone exercises require advanced knowledge of topics presented in *Essentials* lessons, application of skills from multiple lessons, or self-directed learning of new skills.

These Discovery Zone exercises are independent of each other and can be completed in any order. Each exercise uses a different file. In the first exercise, you change the size and shape of bullets in a bulleted list. In the second exercise, you create a multilevel numbered list. In the last exercise, you sort a bulleted list.

1. Changing the Size and Shape of Bullets

When you use a bulleted list, you might want to change the size or shape of the bullet to something that is more relevant to the topic or something that provides greater visual appeal.

In this exercise, you learn how to change the size and shape of the bullets in a bulleted list.

Open the **WO-0304** file in the Student folder on the CD-ROM. Save the file on your floppy disk with the name **Case Study**. This is a list of topics about the implementation of a computer system. Select the bulleted list and choose Format, Bullets and Numbering to open the Bullets and Numbering dialog box. Try one of the other bullet options.

Make sure the bulleted list is still selected, and open the Bullets and Numbering dialog box. Use the Office Assistant to help you figure out how to do the following. Change the indent for the bullet position to 1" and the indent for the text position to 1.25". Notice how these changes are shown in the Preview box. Change the bullet type to one of the Wingdings options. In the top row, the second icon from the right is a computer. Try this as a bullet for this list, or pick one of your own. When you are satisfied with your results, add your name to the page, and print and save the document. Close the file.

2. Creating a Multilevel Numbered List

There might be a time when you want to create a numbered list that has more than one level, similar to an outline.

In this exercise, you change a rough draft about a computer system implementation project into a multilevel numbered list.

Open the **WO-0305** file in the Student folder on the CD-ROM. Save the file on your floppy disk with the name **Computer Implementation**. Select the body of the text. Open the Bullets and Numbering dialog box, and click the Outline Numbered tab. Select the second option to show a multilevel outline format. When you click OK, the document is reformatted as an outline. Review the document to make sure it was all converted to the outline. On the second title line, add **Formatted by: *<your name>***. Print and save the document. Close the file.

3. Sorting a Bulleted List

Information you include in a document may need to be sorted alphabetically, by date, or by number. You can use the Sort command found in the Table menu to sort information in a bulleted list. In this exercise, you sort data in a bulleted list, first alphabetically by name, and then by date.

Open the **WO-0306** file in the Student folder on the CD-ROM and save it on your floppy disk with the name **Birthdays**. This is a listing of names and birthdays. Add your name and birthday to the bottom of the list. Select the bulleted list and choose Table, Sort from the menu to open the Sort Text dialog box. Sort by Paragraphs and Text. Do a second sort, this time sorting by Field 2 and Date. The list is sorted in date order. Print the document; save your changes, and close the file. Exit Word.

Project 4

Word

Formatting a Document

Objectives

In this project, you learn how to

- ➤ **Set Margins**
- ➤ **Insert Page Numbers**
- ➤ **Create a Header or Footer**
- ➤ **Insert Page Breaks**
- ➤ **Work with Clip Art**
- ➤ **Use Print Preview**

Key terms introduced in this project include

- clip art
- default
- footer
- header
- layout
- margins
- page breaks
- Print Preview
- sizing handles

SOURCE: *Essentials: Office 2000,* Ferrett-Preston-Preston

Why Would I Do This?

In Project 3, "Formatting Text," you used many important Microsoft Word text and paragraph formatting tools. Word also offers a wide range of formatting options that affect the ***layout*** of the document, or the way the text flows on a page and from one page to the next.

Margins are the spaces between the edge of your paper and the main text of the document—on the top and bottom, and on the sides. Word enables you to set the left, right, top, and bottom margins independently. The top and bottom margins are also used for information that can be displayed on each page of a document. This area on a page is known as the ***header*** or ***footer*** and can contain page numbers, dates, company logos, or general text. The top and bottom margins must be large enough to contain text you place in the header or footer.

When formatting your document, you can also insert ***page breaks***. If there is space at the bottom of a page for the first few lines of the next topic, but you want those lines to be at the top of the next page, you can insert a page break. This creates an artificial break and moves the text following the page break to a new page. This feature enables you to control your document, so that lines of text, images, or figures that should be displayed together appear on the same page.

You can add visual interest to a document by inserting ***clip art***, which is a graphics image used to convey an idea. In this project, you insert and move a clip art image.

Finally, Word offers a ***Print Preview*** option, which displays the layout of the document the way it appears when it is printed. This enables you to verify that the text of your document is placed on the pages exactly the way you desire.

In this lesson, you learn how to set margins, work with headers and footers, insert page breaks, insert clip art, and use the Print Preview feature. When you have completed this project, you will have a document that looks like the one in Figure 4.1.

Visual Summary

When you have completed this project, you will have created a document that looks like this:

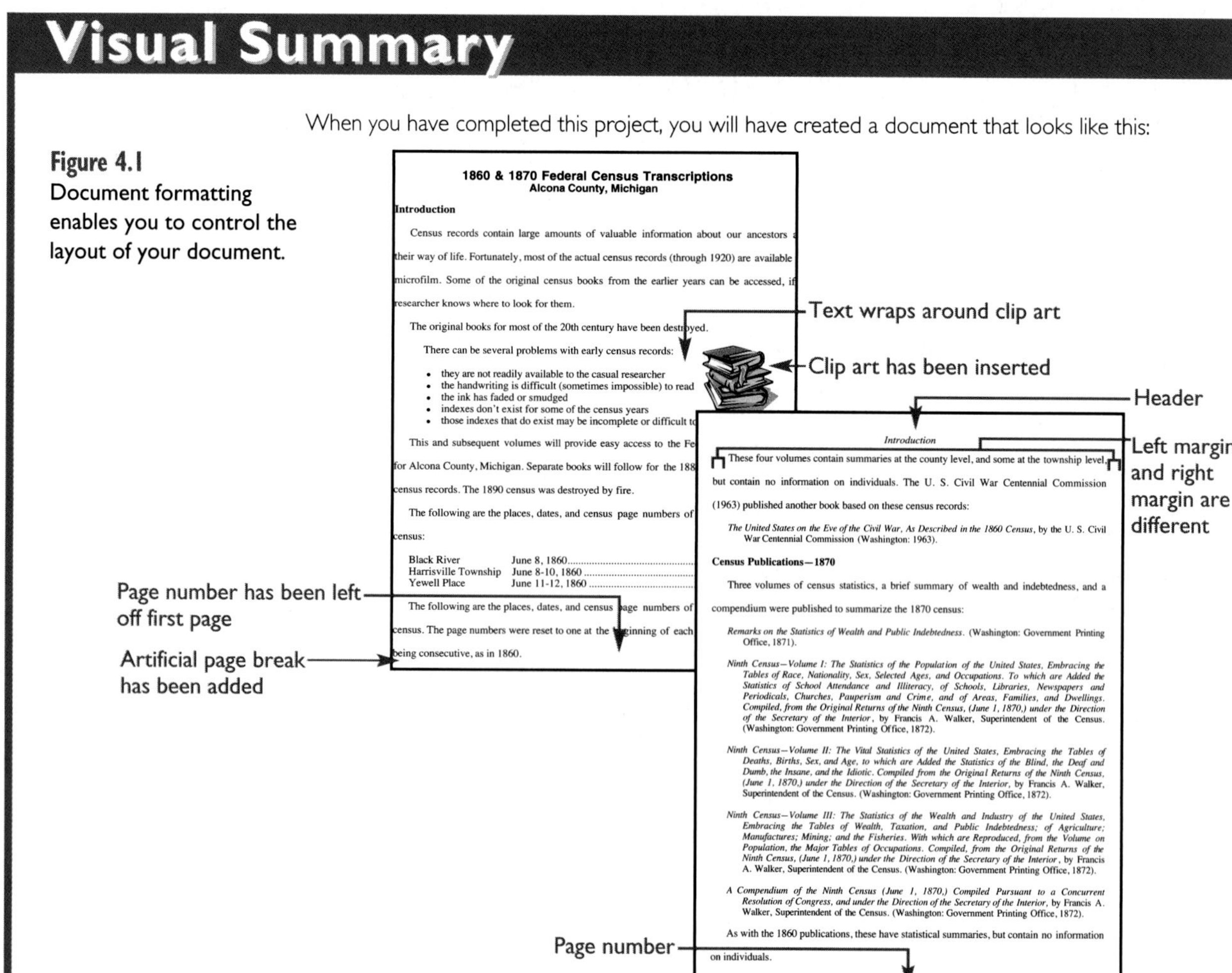

1860 & 1870 Federal Census Transcriptions
Alcona County, Michigan

Introduction

Census records contain large amounts of valuable information about our ancestors their way of life. Fortunately, most of the actual census records (through 1920) are available microfilm. Some of the original census books from the earlier years can be accessed, if researcher knows where to look for them.

The original books for most of the 20th century have been destroyed.

There can be several problems with early census records:

- they are not readily available to the casual researcher
- the handwriting is difficult (sometimes impossible) to read
- the ink has faded or smudged
- indexes don't exist for some of the census years
- those indexes that do exist may be incomplete or difficult to

This and subsequent volumes will provide easy access to the Fe for Alcona County, Michigan. Separate books will follow for the 188 census records. The 1890 census was destroyed by fire.

The following are the places, dates, and census page numbers of census:

Black River June 8, 1860..........
Harrisville Township June 8-10, 1860..........
Yewell Place June 11-12, 1860..........

The following are the places, dates, and census page numbers of census. The page numbers were reset to one at the beginning of each being consecutive, as in 1860.

Introduction

These four volumes contain summaries at the county level, and some at the township level, but contain no information on individuals. The U. S. Civil War Centennial Commission (1963) published another book based on these census records:

The United States on the Eve of the Civil War, As Described in the 1860 Census, by the U. S. Civil War Centennial Commission (Washington: 1963).

Census Publications—1870

Three volumes of census statistics, a brief summary of wealth and indebtedness, and a compendium were published to summarize the 1870 census:

Remarks on the Statistics of Wealth and Public Indebtedness. (Washington: Government Printing Office, 1871).

Ninth Census—Volume I: The Statistics of the Population of the United States, Embracing the Tables of Race, Nationality, Sex, Selected Ages, and Occupations. To which are Added the Statistics of School Attendance and Illiteracy, of Schools, Libraries, Newspapers and Periodicals, Churches, Pauperism and Crime, and of Areas, Families, and Dwellings. Compiled, from the Original Returns of the Ninth Census, (June 1, 1870,) under the Direction of the Secretary of the Interior, by Francis A. Walker, Superintendent of the Census. (Washington: Government Printing Office, 1872).

Ninth Census—Volume II: The Vital Statistics of the United States, Embracing the Tables of Deaths, Births, Sex, and Age, to which are Added the Statistics of the Blind, the Deaf and Dumb, the Insane, and the Idiotic. Compiled from the Original Returns of the Ninth Census, (June 1, 1870,) under the Direction of the Secretary of the Interior, by Francis A. Walker, Superintendent of the Census. (Washington: Government Printing Office, 1872).

Ninth Census—Volume III: The Statistics of the Wealth and Industry of the United States, Embracing the Tables of Wealth, Taxation, and Public Indebtedness; of Agriculture; Manufactures; Mining; and the Fisheries. With which are Reproduced, from the Volume on Population, the Major Tables of Occupations. Compiled, from the Original Returns of the Ninth Census, (June 1, 1870,) under the Direction of the Secretary of the Interior, by Francis A. Walker, Superintendent of the Census. (Washington: Government Printing Office, 1872).

A Compendium of the Ninth Census (June 1, 1870,) Compiled Pursuant to a Concurrent Resolution of Congress, and under the Direction of the Secretary of the Interior, by Francis A. Walker, Superintendent of the Census. (Washington: Government Printing Office, 1872).

As with the 1860 publications, these have statistical summaries, but contain no information on individuals.

Alcona Transportation 4 DRAFT-12/16/98 3:31 PM

Figure 4.1
Document formatting enables you to control the layout of your document.

Lesson 1: Setting Margins

In Word, you can control the four margin settings individually. Specific margin settings are required for particular writing styles, such as research papers that use the APA or MLA style. Increasing or decreasing one or more of the margins can also make a document look better on a page or fit on fewer pages, depending on your need. Additionally, you might want to increase the left margin, so that you can bind the document or punch holes in it. Knowing how to work with margins helps you design the layout of your document to fit a specific purpose.

In this lesson, you change the margins of a document.

To Change the Margins

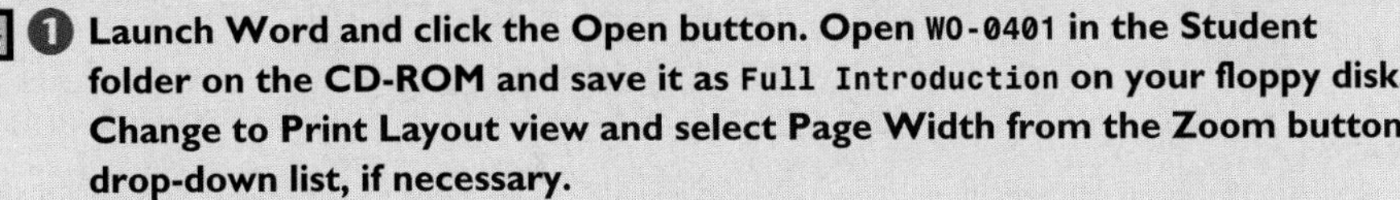

1 Launch Word and click the Open button. Open `WO-0401` in the Student folder on the CD-ROM and save it as `Full Introduction` on your floppy disk. Change to Print Layout view and select Page Width from the Zoom button drop-down list, if necessary.

Look at the right end of the ruler and notice that the document is six inches wide.

The ruler should be visible at the top of the screen. If not, choose View, Ruler from the menu bar. The width of the page on the ruler shows in white. The margin area on the right is dark gray. Although 6 is not shown on the ruler, you can see that the measurement from 5 to the right margin is a full inch when you compare it to the measurements showing on the ruler.

2 Select File, Page Setup from the menu.

The Page Setup dialog box opens (see Figure 4.2).

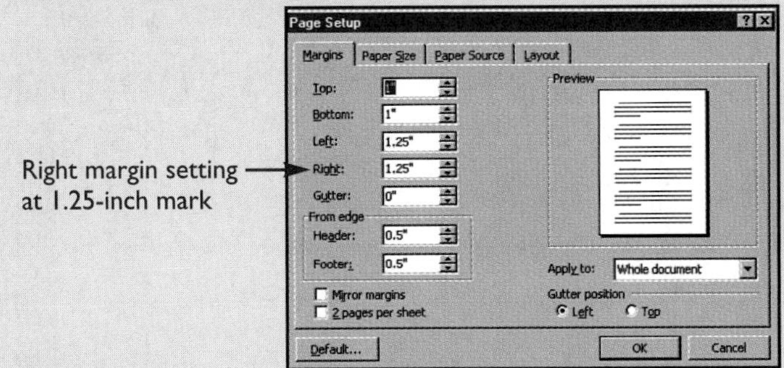

Figure 4.2
In the Page Setup dialog box, you can change margin settings.

3 Make sure that the Margins tab is selected, and highlight the Top box, if necessary.

The number in the Top box controls the distance, in inches, from the top of the page to the top of the text on the page (excluding the header text).

4 Leave the top margin at 1 inch, and then press Tab to move to the Bottom box. Type `.75`.

This leaves a three-quarter inch margin at the bottom of the document.

5 Press Tab to move to the Left box. Type `1.5`, which leaves enough room to bind the final document.

You can use the up or down arrows, or spinners, on the right side of the margin boxes to increase or decrease the margins 0.1" at a time.

continues ▶

To Change the Margins (continued)

6 Press Tab to move to the Right box. Type .75 to make the right margin .75 inches.

Make sure that the Apply to drop-down list says Whole document. Compare the changes you made to the ones shown in Figure 4.3.

Figure 4.3
The new margins are selected for the document.

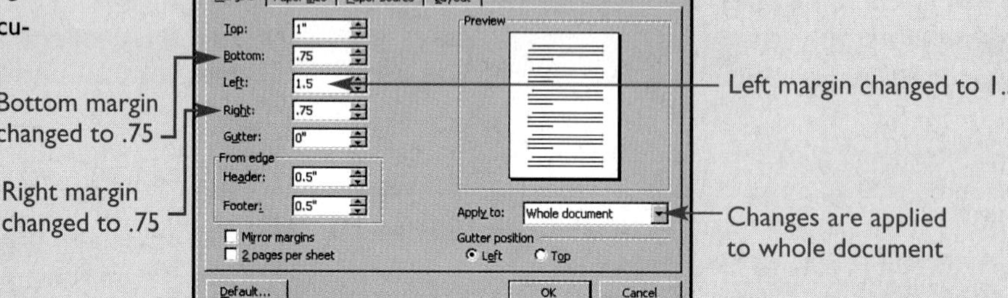

7 Click OK.

Notice that the document is now 6.25 inches wide. The dark gray section at either end of the ruler displays how wide each margin is, measured in inches. The white area on the ruler starts at zero (although no number displays) for the left margin and measures the inches across to the right margin. Figure 4.4 shows the result of the change in margins. Leave the file open for the next lesson.

Figure 4.4
The margins change for the entire document.

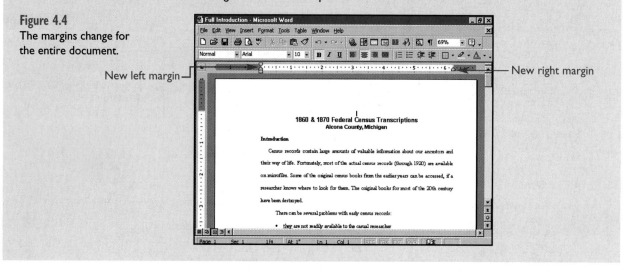

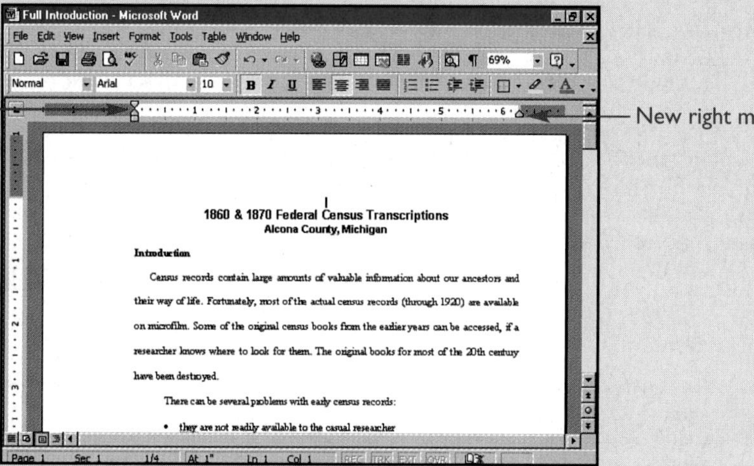

Default Margin Settings

The margin settings are saved with the document. When you create a new document, the ***default*** margin settings are applied. The program uses default settings unless someone changes the settings with a specific action. The most common default margin settings are either an inch for all four sides; or an inch at the top and bottom, and an inch and a quarter on the left and right (see Figure 4.2). You can change the default margin settings by setting new ones and clicking the Default button in the Page Setup dialog box. You should only do this on your own computer.

Opening the Page Setup Dialog Box

You can open the Page Setup dialog box by double-clicking the gray portion of the ruler.

Lesson 2: Inserting Page Numbers

Documents of more than two pages usually need page numbers. Page numbers help keep loose pages in order and provide easy reference for long documents. Word gives you a way to automatically insert page numbers at the top or bottom of a document. These numbers adjust themselves as necessary when you add or delete text.

In this lesson, you add page numbers to the document footer.

To Insert Page Numbers

1. **With your Full Introduction file open from the last lesson, choose Insert, Page Numbers from the menu.**
   The Page Numbers dialog box opens (see Figure 4.5).

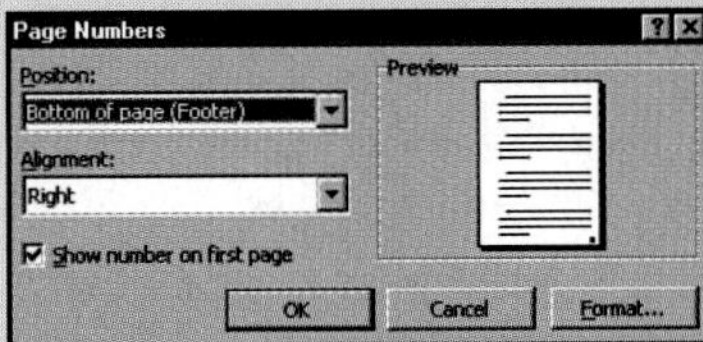

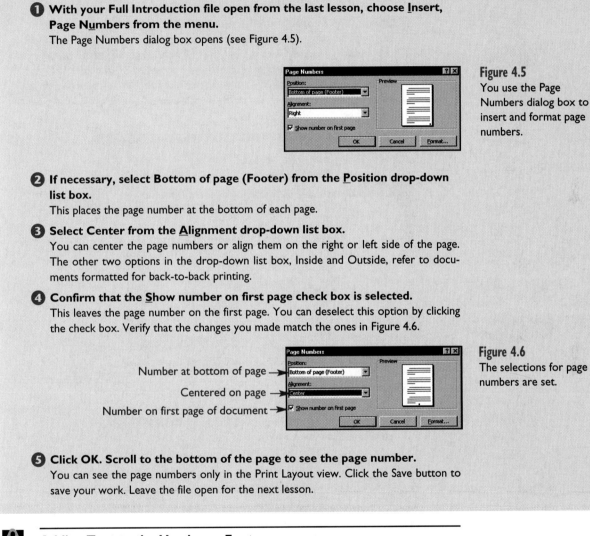

Figure 4.5 You use the Page Numbers dialog box to insert and format page numbers.

2. **If necessary, select Bottom of page (Footer) from the Position drop-down list box.**
   This places the page number at the bottom of each page.
3. **Select Center from the Alignment drop-down list box.**
   You can center the page numbers or align them on the right or left side of the page. The other two options in the drop-down list box, Inside and Outside, refer to documents formatted for back-to-back printing.
4. **Confirm that the Show number on first page check box is selected.**
   This leaves the page number on the first page. You can deselect this option by clicking the check box. Verify that the changes you made match the ones in Figure 4.6.

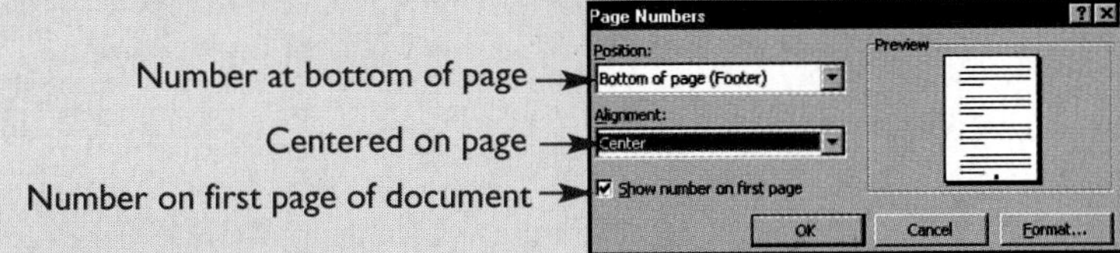

Figure 4.6 The selections for page numbers are set.

5. **Click OK. Scroll to the bottom of the page to see the page number.**
   You can see the page numbers only in the Print Layout view. Click the Save button to save your work. Leave the file open for the next lesson.

Adding Text to the Header or Footer

If you plan to add other text to the header or footer, add that text before you elect to turn off the page number on the first page. Otherwise, you end up with the header or footer text on the first page only and the page numbers on every page but the first. Therefore, make certain a check mark is in the Show number on first page check box in the Page number dialog box. Later, you can elect to turn off the header and footer on the first page, and the page number and other text do not show.

Using Print Layout View

The Print Layout view shows you the position of the document elements on the page. The edges of the page display if you scroll to either side or if you set the zoom to display a wide view of the page. The document looks like it will when it is printed, but you can edit text in this view. It is more than a preview window.

Lesson 3: Creating a Header or Footer

You use headers and footers to display information that needs to appear on every page of a document, with the possible exception of the first page. You can add text to the header and footer to identify your document, its author, the current version, and other relevant information.

In the first part of this lesson, you add text to the header and footer of the Full Introduction document.

To Enter Text in a Header or Footer

1 With your Full Introduction file open from the previous lesson, choose View, Header and Footer from the menu.
The page header displays with the document text shown in light gray in the background. The insertion point is automatically placed at the beginning of the header area. The Header and Footer toolbar also displays (see Figure 4.7). (If your toolbar is in the middle of the screen, click the title bar and drag it to the bottom of the screen to dock it.) Notice that there is a center tab at the 3-inch mark and a right tab at the 6-inch mark on the ruler.

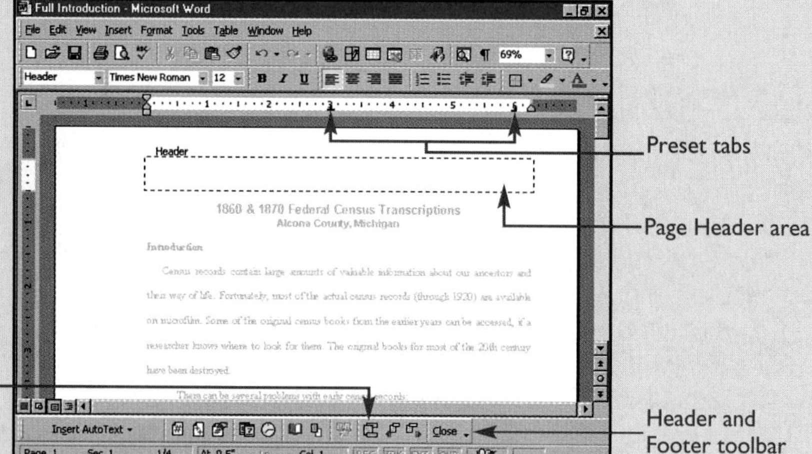

Figure 4.7
Text in the header repeats on each page.

Moving to and from the Header or Footer
After you create a header or footer, you can move back into the document by double-clicking anywhere in the document text. When you are editing the document, you can quickly move into a header or footer by double-clicking it. This works only in Print Layout view.

2 Type `Introduction` at the left edge of the header.

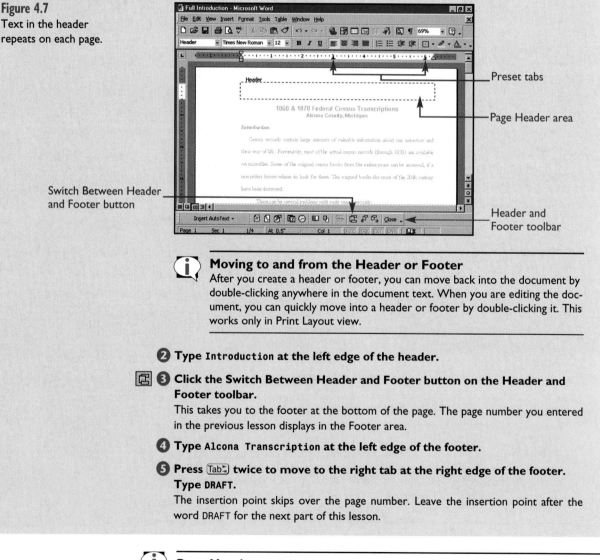

3 Click the Switch Between Header and Footer button on the Header and Footer toolbar.
This takes you to the footer at the bottom of the page. The page number you entered in the previous lesson displays in the Footer area.

4 Type `Alcona Transcription` at the left edge of the footer.

5 Press Tab twice to move to the right tab at the right edge of the footer. Type `DRAFT`.
The insertion point skips over the page number. Leave the insertion point after the word DRAFT for the next part of this lesson.

Page Numbers
Notice that the page number you added earlier shows in the page footer. You could also add this page number by using the page footer options on the toolbar.

In many cases, documents you work on go through several revisions, often by more than one person. More than one version of a document might be circulating at the same time. It is easy to tell when a document was revised if you add the Current Date feature to the header or footer. With this feature, the current date appears on every page of the document whenever you make a revision and print the document.

Next you add a current date to the footer of the document.

To Add a Date to a Footer

1. **With the insertion point at the right of the word DRAFT in the page footer of your Full Introduction file, add a dash (—).**
   You add a date to show when the draft copy of your document is printed.

2. **Select Insert, Date and Time from the menu.**
   The Date and Time dialog box opens and lists formats for adding the current date, the current time, or both (see Figure 4.8).

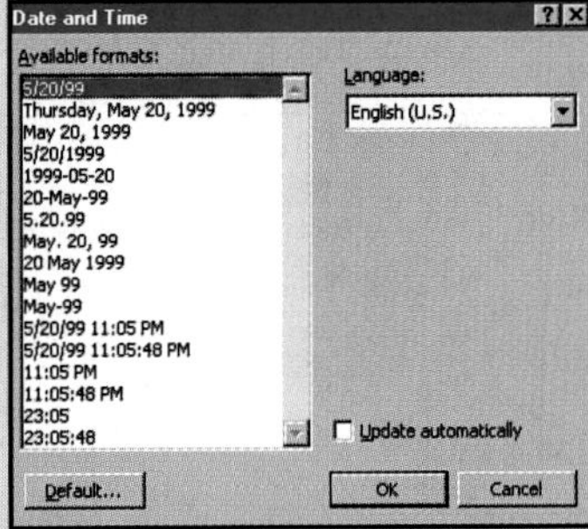

Figure 4.8
The Date and Time dialog box displays samples of date and time formats using current values.

3. **Select the MM/DD/YY 11:05 PM format.**
   The actual date shown in your dialog box is the date on which you are working on this task.

4. **Click the Update automatically box to select it, if necessary.**
   This inserts the current date and time every time you open the document.

5. **Click OK.**
   The date and time appear after the word DRAFT in the footer (see Figure 4.9).

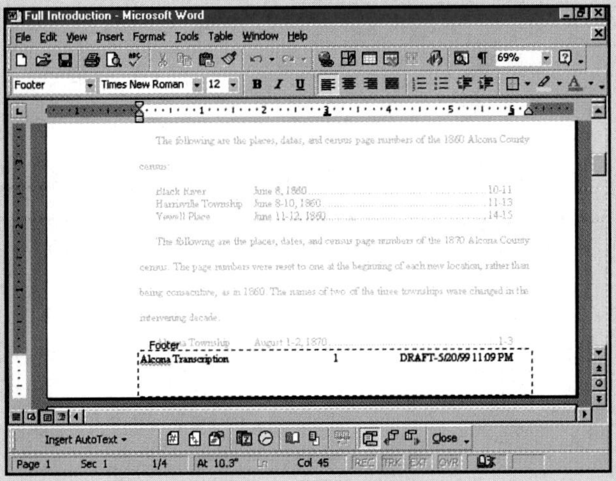

Figure 4.9
The current date and time appear in the Footer area.

6. **Click the Save button to save the changes to your document.**
   Stay in the footer for the next part of this lesson.

Adding a Date
You can also add a date by clicking the Insert Date button on the Header and Footer toolbar. Using the Insert, Date and Time option from the menu enables you to select the formatting you prefer for your date.

You might want to use a different format for the information in the header and footer than you used in the text. Many of the same formatting tools that work on the regular text in your document also work in the header and footer. For example, you can change the font, font size, emphasis, or alignment of selected text. You can even use page setup tools. Therefore, you have a great deal of flexibility when you are working with header and footer text.

In this part of the lesson, you center and emphasize text and adjust the tabs in the header and footer.

Formatting Text in a Header or Footer

1 Make sure the insertion point is to the right of the date in the footer.
Notice that the right tab is still at the 6-inch mark, and the right indent and right margin are at 6.25 inches (see Figure 4.10).

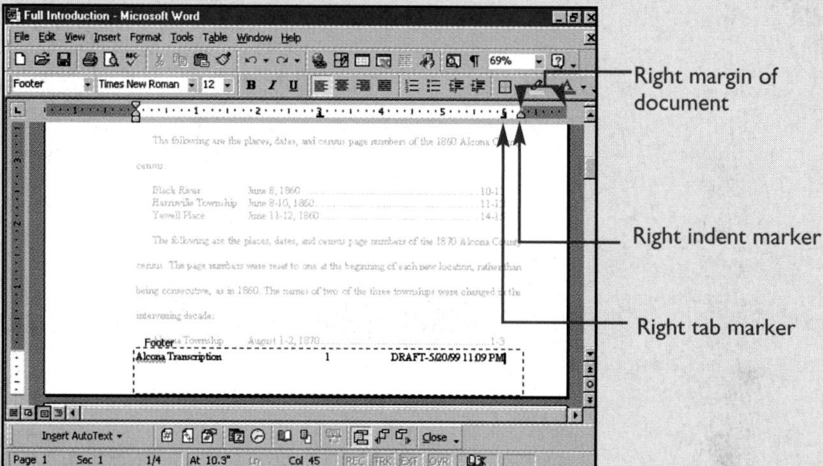

Figure 4.10
You can change the footer margins to match those in the document.

2 Click the right tab at the 6-inch mark; drag the tab to the 6.25-inch mark and release the mouse button.
A vertical dotted line appears as you drag the tab, indicating the new tab location. The date now lines up with the right margin of the document (see Figure 4.11).

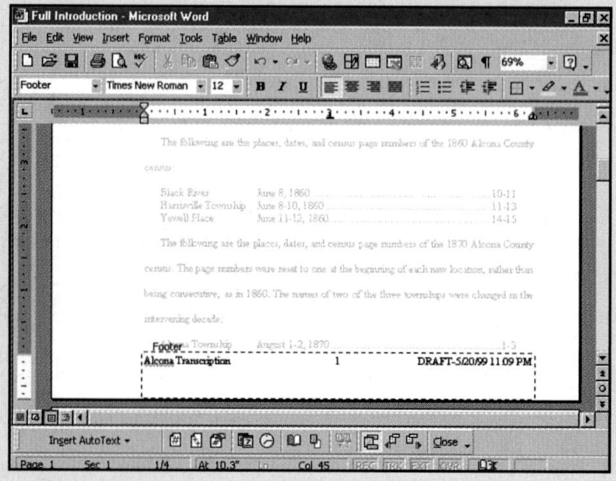

Figure 4.11
The date lines up with the text in the rest of the document.

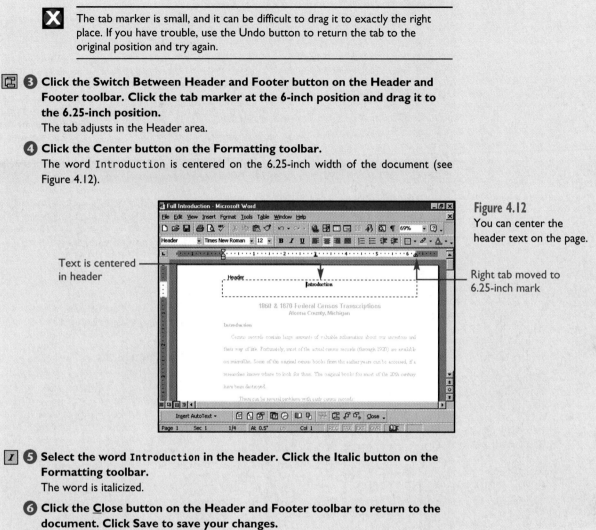

The tab marker is small, and it can be difficult to drag it to exactly the right place. If you have trouble, use the Undo button to return the tab to the original position and try again.

3. **Click the Switch Between Header and Footer button on the Header and Footer toolbar. Click the tab marker at the 6-inch position and drag it to the 6.25-inch position.**
   The tab adjusts in the Header area.

4. **Click the Center button on the Formatting toolbar.**
   The word `Introduction` is centered on the 6.25-inch width of the document (see Figure 4.12).

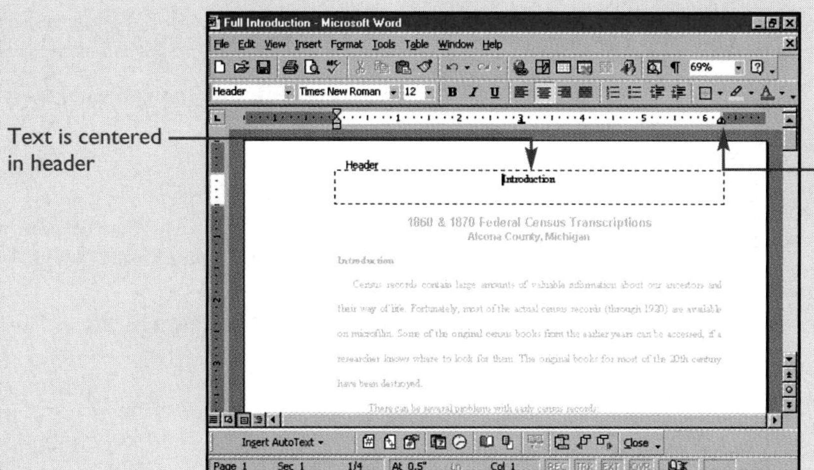

Figure 4.12
You can center the header text on the page.

5. **Select the word `Introduction` in the header. Click the Italic button on the Formatting toolbar.**
   The word is italicized.

6. **Click the Close button on the Header and Footer toolbar to return to the document. Click Save to save your changes.**
   Leave the file open for the next lesson.

Centering Text

You can also insert a tab and use the centering tab that is inserted by default into the header. This centering tab does not move when you change the document margins. If you have only one word or phrase in the header, use the centering button to center it between the margins.

Placing and Adjusting Tab Stops

To display the distance from either side of the document, point at the tab on the toolbar and hold down both buttons on the mouse. You can drag the tab using this method.

An alternative way to place and adjust tab stops is to use the Format, Tabs option from the menu.

Lesson 4: Inserting Page Breaks

You often find that elements which should be kept together, such as a list of related data, begin on one page and finish on the next. You may be tempted to insert several blank lines to force the text onto the next page. This practice can cause problems when you make changes to the text. If you insert several blank lines and then add or remove text, you can end up with blank lines in the middle of a page. Inserting a page break is an effective way to resolve this problem. A page break enables you to edit the previous page without changing the placement of the text on the page following the break. Careful use of page breaks can help you control the layout of your document when it prints.

In this lesson, you insert a page break into a document.

To Insert Page Breaks

1. **With your Full Introduction file active, click the Normal View button to change to the Normal view.**

2. **Scroll down until you can see the dotted line that indicates the bottom of page 1 and the top of page 2.**
   Notice that an automatic page break divides the list of items (see Figure 4.13). This list and its introductory sentence should be together on the same page.

3. **Place the insertion point to the left of the last sentence in the preceding paragraph that begins `The names of two of the` (see Figure 4.13).**

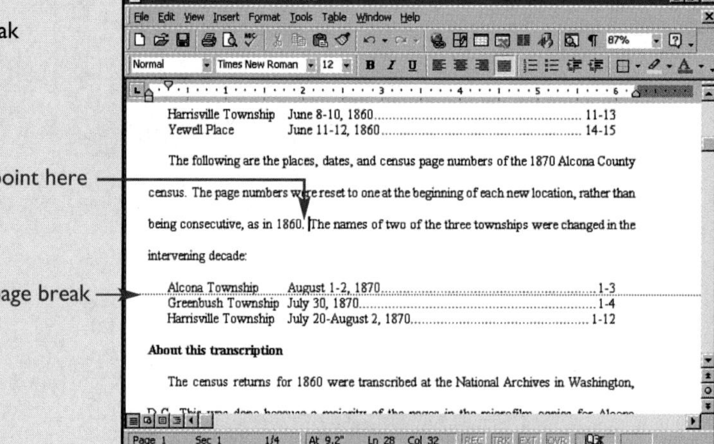

Figure 4.13
The automatic page break interrupts a list of data.

4. **Select Insert, Break from the menu.**
   The Break dialog box opens (see Figure 4.14). The dialog box has two areas. In the first, you select the type of break. In the second, you can select the type of section break.

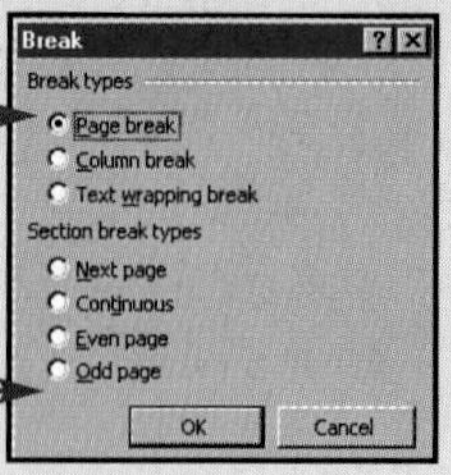

Figure 4.14
From the Break dialog box, you can insert a page break, column break, or text-wrapping break.

Break options

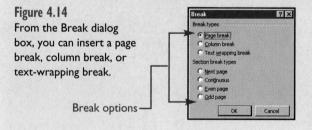

5 Select Page break from the Break types area of the dialog box, if necessary, and click OK.

The new, artificial page break appears as a dotted line that has the words `Page Break` in the middle (see Figure 4.15).

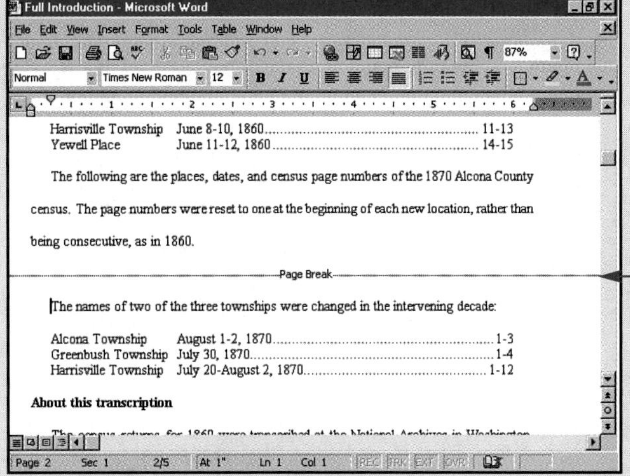

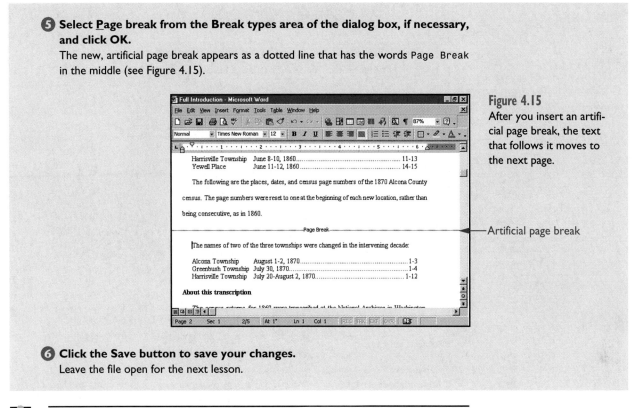

Figure 4.15
After you insert an artificial page break, the text that follows it moves to the next page.

6 Click the Save button to save your changes.

Leave the file open for the next lesson.

Adding or Deleting a Page Break

You can also add a page break at the insertion point by holding down Ctrl+Enter. To delete a page break, click it, and press Del.

Lesson 5: Working with Clip Art

Microsoft Word includes many clip art images. These images cover a wide range of topics and styles, from black-and-white line art to detailed color drawings. Clip art adds visual interest to a flyer, poster, brochure, or paper. You can usually find an appropriate image to illustrate a point or appeal to your audience. After you add an image, it usually needs to be resized and moved to the appropriate location on your document. You might also need to change the way the text wraps around the image, so that it does not create empty space in a document.

In the first part of this lesson, you insert a clip art image into the Full Introduction document.

To Add Clip Art

1 With your Full Introduction file still open, scroll to the top of the document. Click the end of the sentence that introduces the bulleted list.

This sentence ends with `early census records:`

2 Select Insert, Picture, Clip Art from the menu.

The Insert ClipArt dialog box opens (see Figure 4.16). You can search for a clip art image by typing one or more words in the Search for clips text box, or by selecting a category and scrolling through the images.

continues ▶

To Add Clip Art (continued)

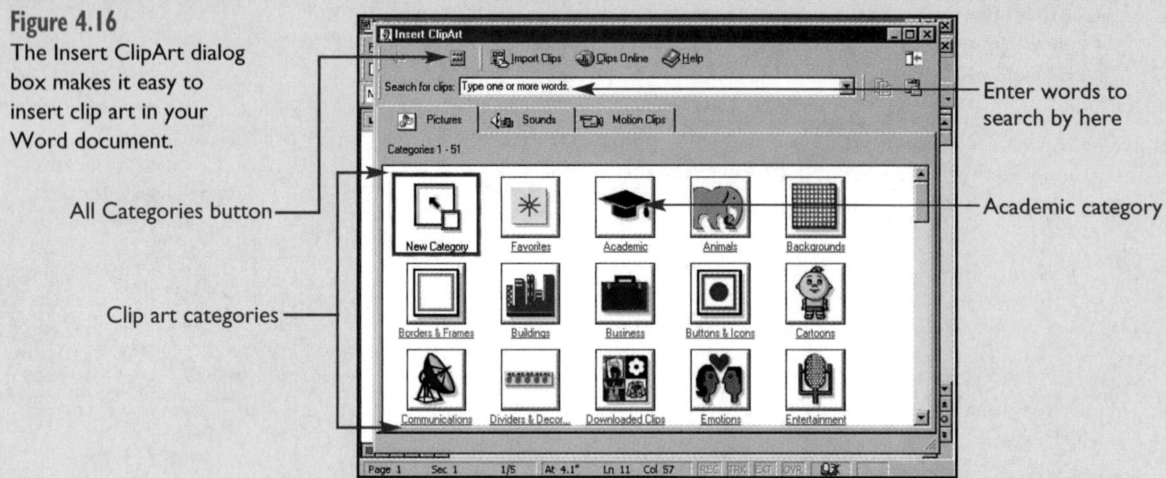

Figure 4.16
The Insert ClipArt dialog box makes it easy to insert clip art in your Word document.

3. **Click the Academic category.**
The first page of academic-related images displays. When you move the mouse pointer over an image, a keyword description, which might include several categories, displays. It also shows how large the image is in terms of computer memory.

4. **Click the books image in the top row.**
The image is selected and a pop-up toolbox that gives you four options displays (see Figure 4.17). The first option is to insert the image. The other three options enable you to preview the clip, add the clip to the Favorites category, or find similar clips. When you move the mouse pointer over each of the icons in the toolbox, a ScreenTip displays.

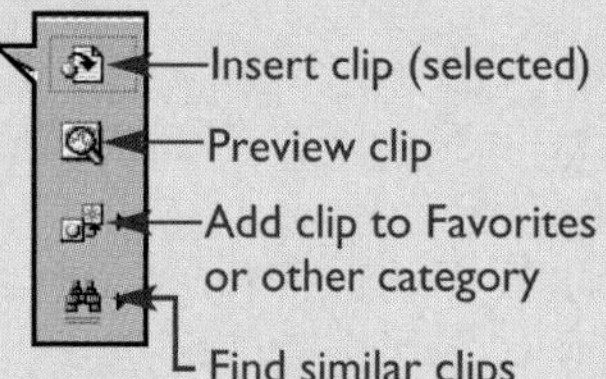

Figure 4.17
You can scroll through images to find one that suits your needs.

5. **Click the Insert Clip button on the toolbar. Click the Close button in the corner of the Insert ClipArt dialog box.**
An image of a huge stack of books appears in the middle of your page. Obviously, this image is too big in its present state and needs to be reduced in size. Leave the file open for the next part of this lesson.

When you click the Insert Clip button, it seems like nothing happens, and you might be tempted to click the button a second time. If you do, two images appear on your screen. Click one of them and press Del. The Insert ClipArt dialog box stays open, so that you can insert multiple images at one time. You have to close the dialog box to see the inserted image. If Word cannot find the image you selected, a warning box displays informing you that it could not locate the image. Choose Cancel, and select another image.

Returning to the Previous Page
If you search a category and do not find anything you like, click the All Categories button to return to the Category list. You can also click the Back button on the toolbar to return to a previous page of clip art.

Images that you use are rarely the right size, or inserted in exactly the right place. To make the clip art image effective, you need to resize it and move it to the correct location in your document. The techniques used here are used throughout Office applications to resize images.

In the next part of this lesson, you reduce the size of the clip art image and place it in the best location on the document.

To Resize and Move Clip Art

1. **Click the clip art image.**
The image is selected. A border with ***sizing handles*** on the sides and in each corner displays around the image. Sizing handles are small square boxes that you use to resize an image. Sometimes they are referred to simply as handles. You can tell an image is selected when you see these sizing handles.

2. **Move the mouse pointer to the lower-left sizing handle (see Figure 4.18).**
To resize an image, you position the mouse over a sizing handle. When the mouse pointer changes to a double-headed arrow, you can click and drag to resize the image. To make it smaller, you drag toward the center of the image. To make it bigger, drag away from the center.

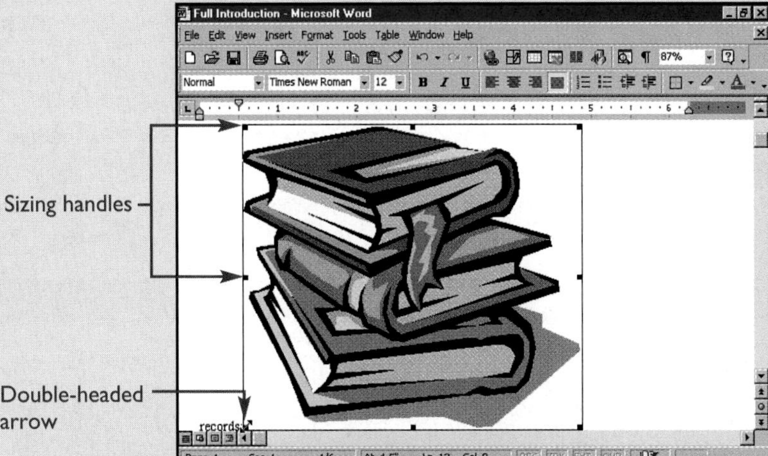

Figure 4.18
Clicking the image selects it.

3. **Click and drag from the lower-left corner toward the upper-right corner. Reduce the image until it is about one-sixteenth of its former size, and release the mouse (see Figure 4.19).**
As you click and drag, an outline of the new reduced size displays. The image is now smaller, but it has created a gap in the text that looks awkward. Leave the file open and move to the last part of this lesson where you wrap the text around the image.

continues ▶

To Resize and Move Clip Art (continued)

Figure 4.19
Click and drag a sizing handle to reduce the size of an image.

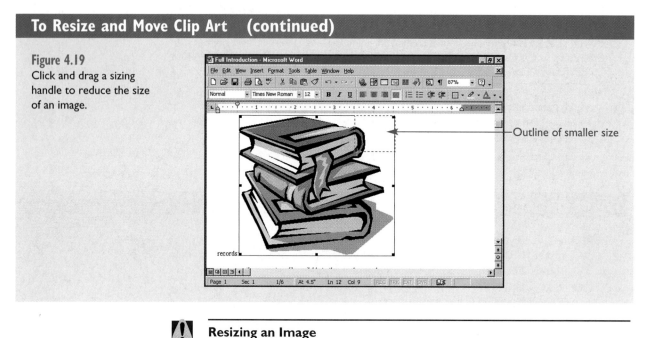

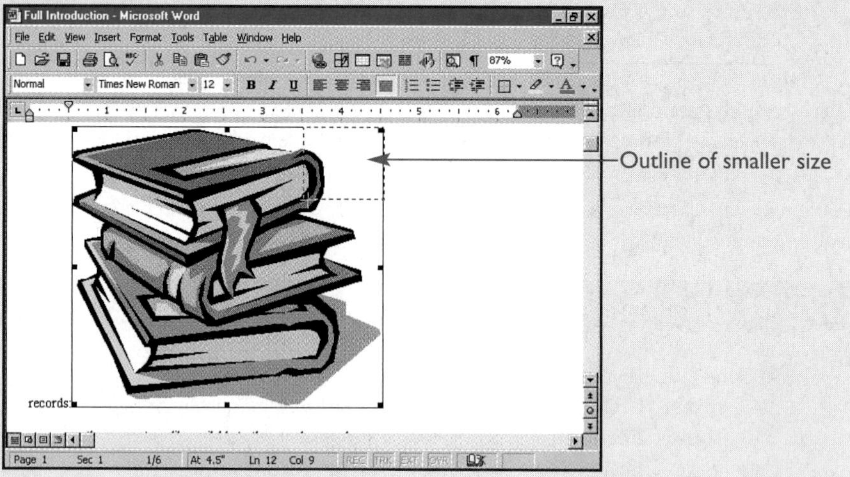

Resizing an Image

When you resize an image, it is generally best to use a handle in one of the corners to keep the image proportional. If you use the handles on the sides, the image is reproportioned vertically or horizontally, resulting in a distorted image. Sometimes this is the effect that you want, but not usually.

When you first insert a clip art image, the image is placed at the insertion point. It acts like any other character in a sentence. To accommodate the image, the text moves to locations above or below the image. This is known as the wrapping style, and the default wrapping style is called In line with text. This style tends to displace text and create an empty space on the page. You can change this easily to a style that is better suited to your document.

In the last part of this lesson, you change the wrapping style for the clip art image in the Full Introduction document.

To Wrap Text Around Clip Art

1. **Make sure the books clip art image is selected.**
   The sizing handles should display around the edge of the picture (see Figure 4.20).

Figure 4.20
The resized image appears at the end of the sentence that introduces the bulleted list.

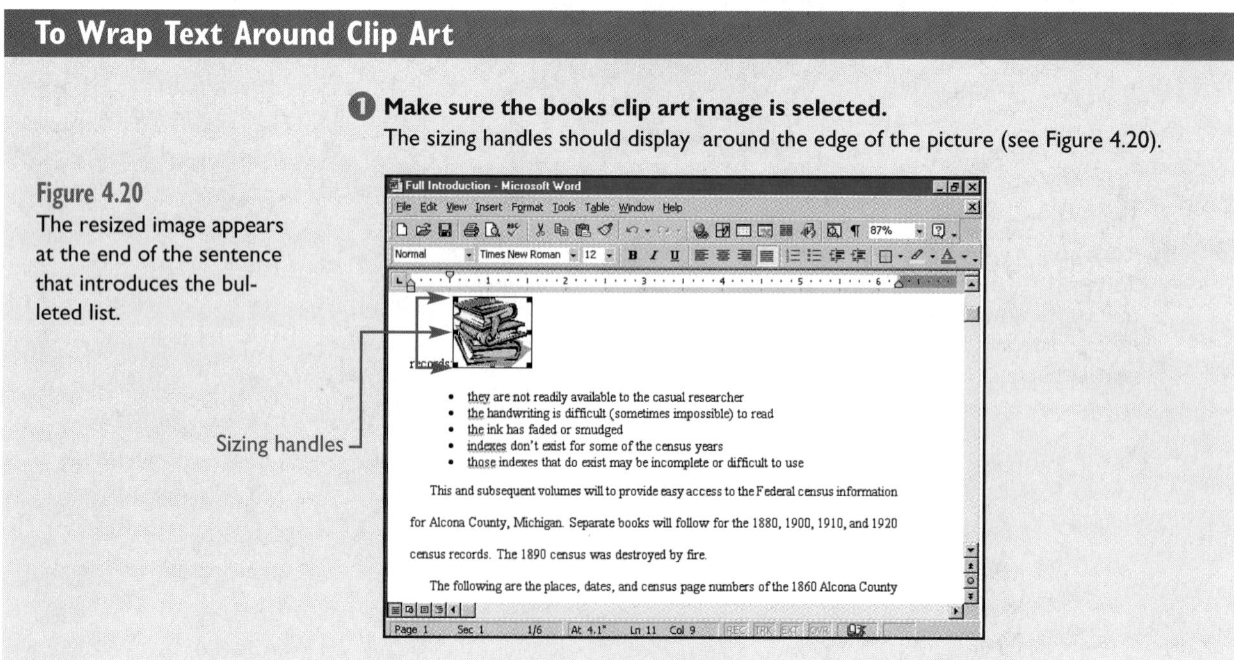

2 Choose Format, Picture from the menu.
The Format Picture dialog box opens.

3 Click the Layout tab.
The default setting called In line with text is selected. Notice the dark blue border around the image for this option.

4 Click the Tight image to select it, and click Right under Horizontal alignment.
The Format Picture dialog box on your screen should look like the one shown in Figure 4.21.

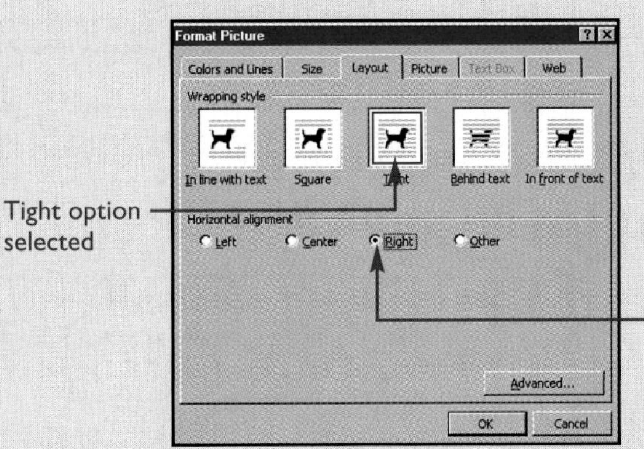

Figure 4.21
Use the Format Picture dialog box to change the text wrapping style.

5 Click OK. Scroll down, if necessary, to see the placement of the clip art in relationship to the text.

The image moves to the right of the text and you can now move it to finalize the image placement. Notice that the sizing handles around the image are now white boxes. When you move your mouse pointer onto the image, the pointer changes to a four-headed arrow. When the mouse pointer is in this shape you can click and drag the image to a new location on your document.

When you choose to have the text wrap around the image, the image sometimes appears in odd locations on the screen. If this happens, click and drag the image to the proper position.

6 If necessary, click and drag the image so that it is positioned as shown in Figure 4.22. When it is positioned to your satisfaction, click outside of the image to deselect it.
Your final image should look like the one shown in Figure 4.22.

continues ▶

To Wrap Text Around Clip Art (continued)

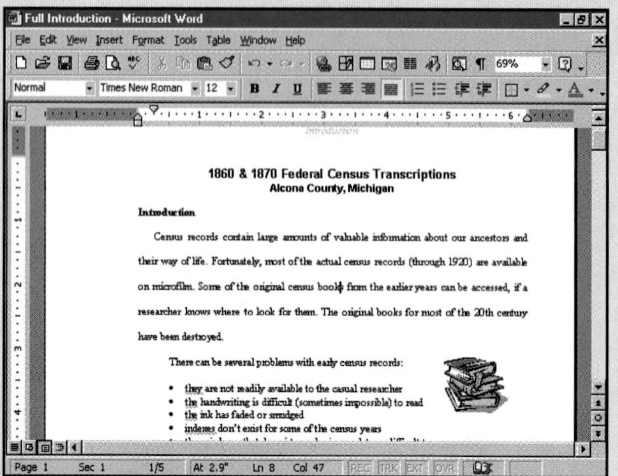

Figure 4.22
The image appears to the right of the list of reasons why records in old census books are difficult to use.

Sometimes the process of inserting a clip art image can result in an extra line or hard return being inserted as well. If the spacing does not seem to adjust correctly, click the Show/Hide button and look for an extra paragraph mark. If an extra paragraph mark displays, select and delete it.

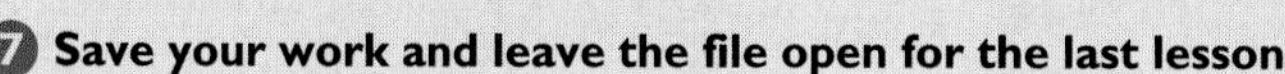

7 Save your work and leave the file open for the last lesson.

Inserting Other Images
You can use the same basic procedure to insert images from other sources. These could be images that you have saved on your computer or images that you can download from a Web site. Many graphic software collections are available and you can use them to add images. You are not limited to the ones provided with the software.

Modifying Pictures or Clip Art
You can also open the Format Picture dialog box by right-clicking the image and selecting Format Picture from the shortcut menu. You can open the Picture toolbar from the shortcut menu and use it to make changes to clip art or pictures.

Lesson 6: Using Print Preview

Inserting or removing text can have unexpected consequences, especially if you inserted page breaks. Word gives you an easy way to look at one or more pages of your document at the same time to see how the text flows from one page to the next. Print Preview shows you how each page looks when it prints.

In this lesson, you use Print Preview to examine the way your document will look when printed. You also learn how to turn off the header and footer information on the first page.

To Use Print Preview

1. **With your Full Introduction file active, scroll to the top of the document.**

2. **Click the Print Preview button.**
   The first page of the document displays. The text might be difficult or impossible to read depending on your monitor, but the layout of the page displays clearly (see Figure 4.23).

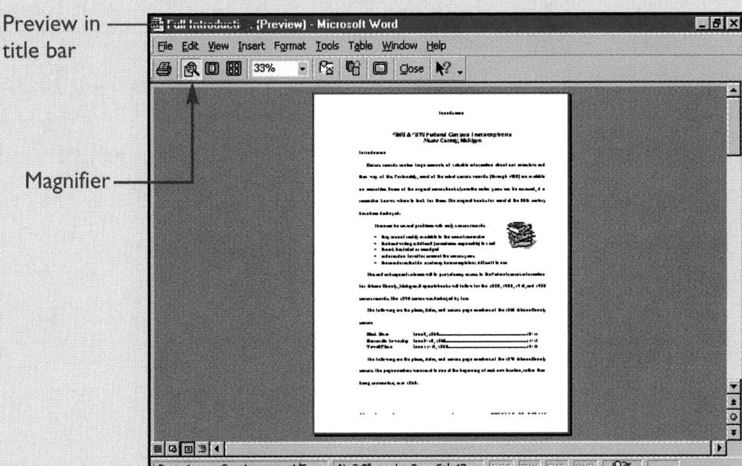

Figure 4.23
The Print Preview window enables you to see how the document will look on the page when it is printed.

3. **Position the pointer anywhere in the document.**
   The pointer changes to a magnifying glass with a plus sign (+) in the middle.

4. **Click the page number at the bottom of page 1.**
   The page enlarges and you can now read the text at the bottom of the page and the footer information (see Figure 4.24). This footer information should not appear on the first page. Notice that the magnifying glass now has a minus sign (–) in it. If you click again, the size of the page is reduced. By clicking the page in Print Preview, you can toggle between the whole page or part of the page.

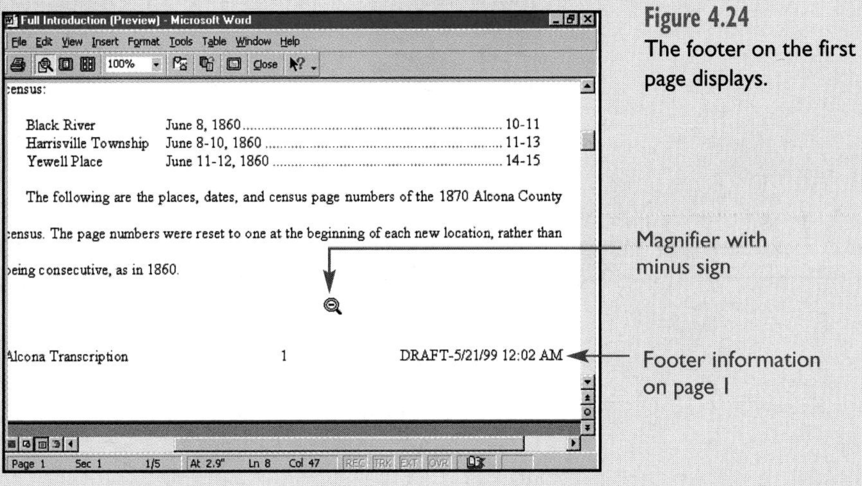

Figure 4.24
The footer on the first page displays.

continues ▶

To Use Print Preview (continued)

5 **Choose File, Page Setup, and click the Layout tab in the Page Setup dialog box.**

6 **Click the Different first page check box in the Headers and footers area.**
This creates a separate header and footer for the first page, which has the effect of turning off the header and footer information on the first page of the document (see Figure 4.25).

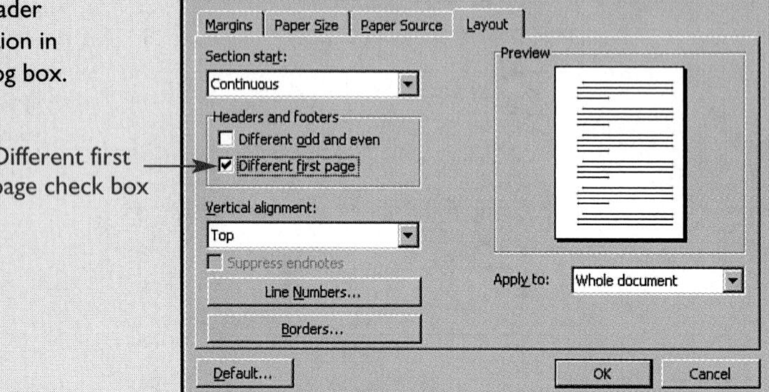

Figure 4.25
You turn off the header and footer information in the Page Setup dialog box.

7 **Click OK. Click the magnifying glass to fit the whole page on the screen.**
Notice that no header or footer information displays on the first page (see Figure 4.26).

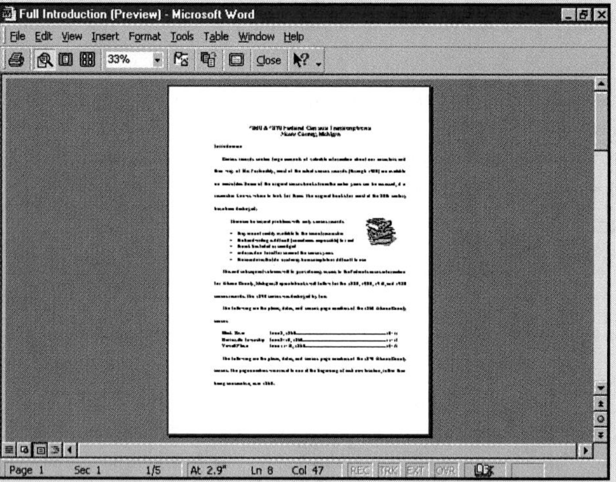

Figure 4.26
Header and footer information does not display on the first page.

8 **Click the Multiple Pages button on the Print Preview toolbar. Drag the pointer across the first three page icons in the first row of the menu to indicate that you want to see three pages in the same row and click.**
Three full pages (pages 1, 2, and 3) display. You cannot read the text with this view, but you can detect the major sections in the document and see how the text flows across pages. Notice that the heading at the bottom of page two is completely separated from the following text (see Figure 4.27). You can correct this by inserting a page break.

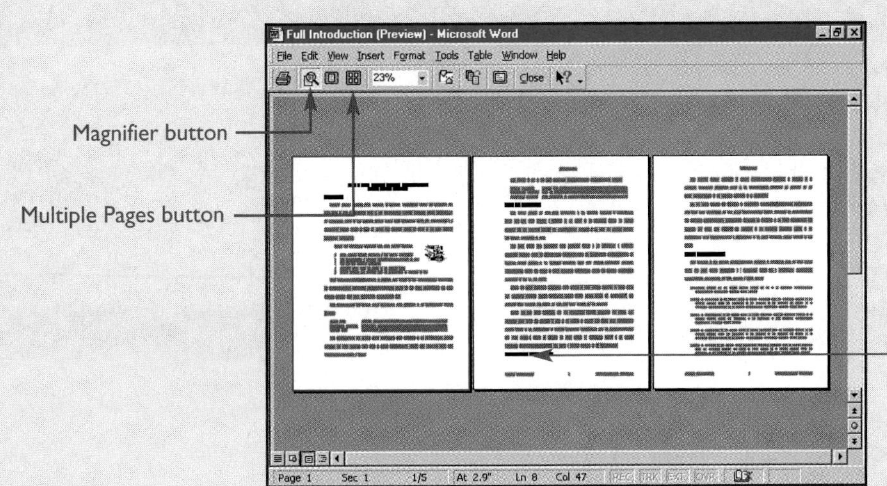

Figure 4.27
Print Preview enables you to see where adjustments in the page layout are needed.

Heading separated from its text

9. **Click the Magnifier button on the toolbar.**
   This turns off the Magnifier function and returns the mouse pointer to its normal shape, which enables you to place the insertion point to the left of the heading at the bottom of page 2.

10. **Click to place the insertion point to the left of the heading at the bottom of page 2. Press Ctrl+↵Enter to insert a page break.**
    The heading moves to the top of the third page (see Figure 4.28).

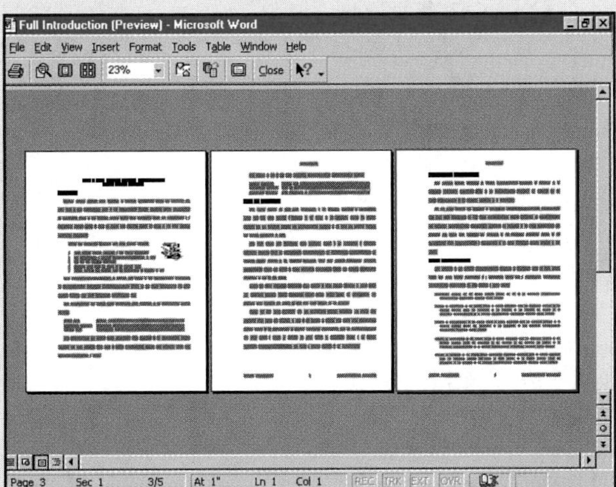

Figure 4.28
You can make minor adjustments to a document in Print Preview.

11. **Scroll to the bottom of the page using the vertical scrollbar.**
    Pages 4 and 5 display. No other odd breaks between headings and text exist.

12. **Click the Print button on the Print Preview toolbar, and click the Close button on the Print Preview toolbar.**
    The document prints, and the screen returns to the Print Layout view.

13. **Save your work and close the file.**

Print Layout View or Normal View?
It is a matter of personal preference whether you work in Print Layout view or Normal view. You can use either view to enter and edit text. Working in some areas, such as headers and footers, or graphics, automatically changes your document to the Print Layout view. You can change views to suit your personal preference.

Summary

In this project, you worked with elements that affect the layout of a document on the printed page. You changed margin settings, inserted page numbers, created a header and footer, inserted page breaks, inserted clip art, and used Print Preview.

You can expand your learning by using Help to learn more about setting margins or creating headers and footers. Look for the topics `Overview of page margins`, and `Overview of Headers`. Open the Insert ClipArt dialog box and explore the wide selection of clip art that is available. Try locating clip art by typing keywords in the Search for text box.

Checking Concepts and Terms

True/False

For each of the following, check *T* or *F* to indicate whether the statement is true or false.

__T __F **1.** The margins are set by using the Format option on the menu bar. [L1]

__T __F **2.** The header is placed in the top margin. [L3]

__T __F **3.** The text in the footer must be the same font as the text in the body of the document. [L3]

__T __F **4.** It is possible to enter a special date field into the header that automatically updates to the current date every time the document is used or printed. [L3]

__T __F **5.** If a new topic starts near the bottom of a page, it is best to insert several blank lines in front of it to force it to the top of the next page. [L4]

__T __F **6.** Print Preview enables you to see several pages at a time so that you can see how the text flows from one page to the next. [L8]

__T __F **7.** When you first place a clip art image in a document, it is treated as a large character in a line of text. [L5]

__T __F **8.** If you use automatic page numbering, you have to use the Recalculate Page Numbers command when you delete or add enough text to change the previous page numbers. [L2]

__T __F **9.** Headers and footers are used for information you want to appear at the top and bottom of every page (with the possible exception of the title page). [L3]

__T __F **10.** Only one format is available for the automatic date in a header or footer. Dates must be in the dd/mm/yy format. [L3]

Multiple Choice

Circle the letter of the correct answer for each of the following.

1. Which dialog box do you use to change the margins in a document? [L1]

a. Margin Settings

b. Paragraph

c. Page Setup

d. Print Layout

2. To create a header or footer, which of the following options would you choose? [L3]

a. Edit, Header or Footer

b. View, Header or Footer

c. Insert, Header or Footer

d. Format, Header or Footer

3. What can the Print Preview window be used to do? ______________. [L8]

a. see multiple pages at one time

b. see how text flows from one page to the next

c. insert page breaks where needed

d. all of the above

4. When you click a clip art image in the Insert ClipArt dialog box, what are the options available in the pop-up menu? [L5]

a. Insert clip, Add clips to Favorite or other category, Preview clip, Find similar clips

b. Insert clip, Delete clip, Modify image, Preview clip

c. Insert clip, Preview clip, Crop image, Change colors

d. Insert clip, Delete clip, Move clip, Resize clip

5. To add a Microsoft clip art image to a document, click where you want the image to be placed and choose ______________ from the menu. [L5]

a. View, Clip Art

b. Insert, Picture, Clip Art

c. Add, Clip Art

d. none of the above

Screen ID

Refer to figure 4.29 and identify the numbered parts of the screen. Write the letter of the correct label in the space next to the number.

Figure 4.29

A. Text in footer

B. Clip art image

C. Changes whenever file is opened

D. Right margin

E. Button that closes the Print Preview view

F. Right align tab marker at 6-inch mark

G. Text in header, centered

H. Print Preview button

I. Switch Between Header and Footer button

J. Used to change Magnifier so you can edit the document

K. Multiple Pages button

L. Header and Footer toolbar

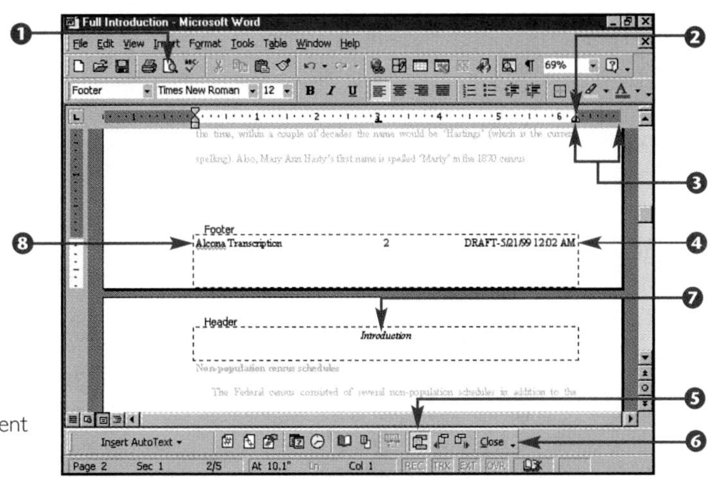

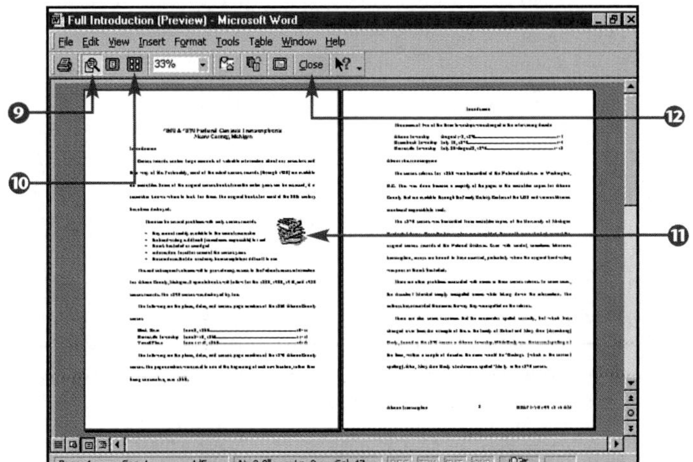

1. ______________	**5.** ______________	**9.** ______________
2. ______________	**6.** ______________	**10.** ______________
3. ______________	**7.** ______________	**11.** ______________
4. ______________	**8.** ______________	**12.** ______________

Discussion Questions

1. Examine your textbook, and note the many page layout options that have been used in the book. Where are the page numbers placed? Are they in the same place on the odd and even pages? Are headers or footers used? Where have obvious page breaks been used?
2. Examine your textbook, and identify the graphical elements that have been used. Are these useful? How do they help you as a student? Are they good learning tools?
3. What skills have you learned that you will want to use when you write papers for other classes? What benefits do you expect to realize from using these document formatting tools?

Skill Drill

Skill Drill exercises reinforce project skills. Each skill reinforced is the same, or nearly the same, as a skill presented in the project. Detailed instructions are provided in a step-by-step format.

In this set of Skill Drill exercises, you work with the paper about distance education. You work with page layout elements, such as margins, headers and footers, page numbers, page breaks, and clip art. Finally, you use the Print Preview window to view how the information will print.

This set of Skill Drill exercises uses file WO-0402. Leave the file open from one Skill Drill exercise to the next.

1. Changing the Margins in a Document

In the first exercise, you open the file, save it on your floppy disk with a new name, and change the margins in the document. [L1]

1. Launch Word. Open the document `WO-0402` from the Student folder on the CD-ROM. Save it on your floppy disk as `Distance Education 2`.
2. Switch to the Print Layout view, if necessary.
3. Select File, Page Setup.
4. Change the top and bottom margins to 1.0 inch. (*Hint*: Try clicking the up or down arrow at the end of each box to decrease the margin.)
5. Change the left margin to 1.50 inches and the right margin to .75 inches.
6. Leave the document open for use in the next exercise.

2. Adding a Header and Footer and Inserting Page Numbers

In this exercise, you create a header and footer and insert page numbers in the header. [L2–3]

1. Select View, Header and Footer from the menu.
2. In the header at the left side, type `Affordable New Technologies`.
3. Tab twice to move to the right edge of the header, and click the Insert Page Number button on the Header and Footer toolbar to insert the page number. Drag the right tab to the 6.25-inch mark, so that the page number is even with the margin.
4. Switch to the footer. Use the Insert, Date and Time option from the menu to insert the date at the left side of the footer. Select the `December 18, 1999` format. Make sure that the Update Automatically option is deselected.
5. On the right side of the Footer area, type your name. (Use the tab, not spaces, to align your name.) Move the right tab to the 6.25-inch mark, if necessary.
6. Select your name and change the font to a style of your choice. Make it bold to add emphasis.
7. Click the Page Setup button on the Header and Footer toolbar and select Different First Page. Leave the header and footer on the first page empty.
8. Save your work, and leave the document open for use in the next exercise.

3. Inserting Clip Art in a Document

In this exercise, you add a clip art image to enhance the paper with a graphics illustration. [L5]

1. With the Distance Education 2 document open, scroll to the beginning of the `Interactive Technologies` heading. Click at the end of the heading to move the insertion point.
2. Choose Insert, Picture, Clip Art from the menu. Scroll down and select the Communications category.
3. Insert an image that you think conveys the idea of telecommunications, or video-conferencing. If you don't see anything you like in the first page of images, click the Keep looking button at the end of the page to view more clip art.
4. Resize the image, so that it is 1.5 to 2 inches square.
5. Choose Format, Picture, and click the layout tab. Change the wrapping style to Tight and the horizontal alignment to Right.
6. Click and drag the image to the right edge of the first paragraph under the Interactive Technologies heading (see Figure 4.31).
7. If necessary, resize the image to make it fit in this space, as shown in the figure. Save your work and leave the file open for the next exercise.

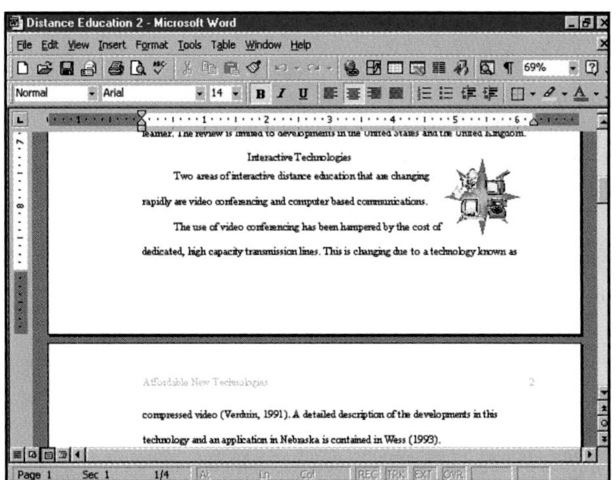

Figure 4.31

4. Inserting Page Breaks in a Document

You might want each section in a document to start on a separate page. Next you insert page breaks at the beginning of each section in the Distance Education 2 document. [L4]

1. Position the insertion point in front of the title `Interactive Technologies`, and press Ctrl+Enter to insert a page break.
2. Add a page break before the subtitle `Computer based conferencing`, so that it is on the same page as the rest of the text that follows that topic.
3. If necessary, add a page break in front of the `Conclusion` and `Reference List` sections of the paper. The paper should now have five pages.
4. Leave the document open for use in the next lesson.

5. Using Print Preview

Click the Print Preview button to see how the document looks. [L6]

1. Switch to multiple pages, if necessary.
2. Verify that the Header and Footer areas on the first page are empty and that the remaining four pages each show information in their headers and footers.
3. Go to the Print dialog box. In the page range section, click the Pages option button and type **1-2** to print the first two pages of the document.
4. Save your work, and close the document.

Challenge

Challenge exercises expand on or are somewhat related to skills presented in the lessons. Each exercise provides a brief narrative introduction followed by instructions, in a numbered step or bulleted list format, that are not as detailed as those in the Skill Drill section.

In these Challenge exercises, you explore other options for headers and footers. First you use a multiple-line header. In the second exercise, you add a line as a visual separator from the body of the text. In the third exercise, you add a graphic to the header and choose the Behind Text option. These exercises use file WO-0403 and should be done in sequence. Leave the file open from one exercise to the next.

1. Using a Multiple-Line Header

You may want to include more than one line of information in a header or footer. In this Challenge exercise, you create a two-line header for a document written for a training proposal. [L3]

To create a multiple-line header in a document, follow these steps:

1. Open the **WO-0403** file in the Student folder on the CD-ROM. Save it on your floppy disk as `Training Proposal`.
2. View the header and footer. In the header, tab to the center and type `Joseph A. Schwartz & Associates`.

3. Press ↵Enter to move to a second line in the Header. Press Tab and type **A Computer Training Company**.
4. Move to the footer and enter the date at the left side. Add your name at the right side. Make sure the right tab lines up with the right margin.
5. Save the changes, and leave the document open for use in the next Challenge exercise.

2. Changing the Formatting of a Header and Adding a Line Separator

If you use the header to identify your company, as you did in the previous exercise, you might also want to change the formatting of the font to make the header stand out. Adding a line is a nice finishing touch to a header or footer. This sets off the Header or Footer area and adds a professional look to your document. In this Challenge exercise, you change the header font style, size, and color and add a border to create a line at the bottom of your header.

To format a header and add a separating line, follow these steps:

1. Use the Training Proposal document from the previous Challenge exercise.
2. Select the two lines of text in the header and change the font to a style of your choice. Change the size of the font to 14. If you want, use the Font Color button to change the color of the font.
3. Move the insertion point to the end of the second line in the header. Click the drop-down arrow next to the Border button. (*Hint*: The Border button is toward the right end of the Formatting toolbar. The ScreenTip displays the name of the currently selected option followed by the word **Border**.) Select Bottom Border from the options. It appears as though nothing has happened. Close the Header and Footer toolbar to see the results.
4. Increase the spacing between the header and the beginning of the document by adding an empty line where necessary.
5. Save the changes and leave the document open for the next exercise.

3. Inserting Clip Art and Placing It Behind Text

If you want to create your own logo for your company, you can insert it into a header and create the equivalent of letterhead paper. In this exercise, you add a graphics image to the Training Proposal document and choose the Behind Text wrapping option. [L5]

To insert clip art in a header, follow these steps:

1. Open the header in the Training Proposal document, and move the insertion point to the end of the second line of text in the header.
2. Open the Insert ClipArt dialog box, and type **training** in the Search for text box. Press ↵Enter.
3. Insert one of the suggested images, or search through the categories until you find one you like.
4. Resize the image, if necessary.
5. With the image selected, open the Format Picture dialog box; click the Format tab, and choose Behind Text as the wrapping style.
6. Move the clip art to the right side of the header (see Figure 4.32).
7. Scroll to page 3 of the document to see how the image looks and make adjustments if necessary.
8. When you are satisfied with the results, preview it in the Print Preview window. Print the document.

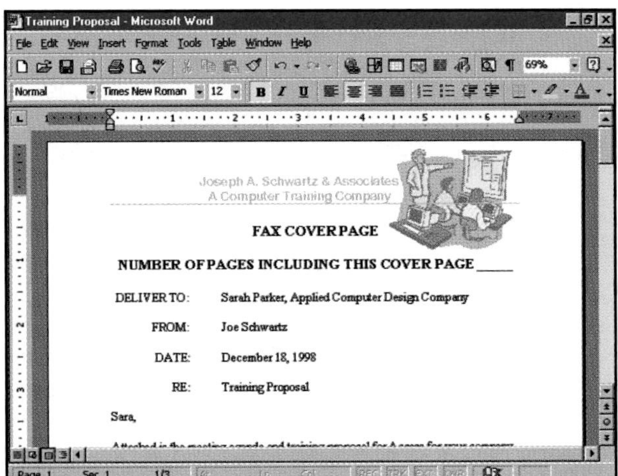

Figure 4.32

Discovery Zone

Discovery Zone exercises require advanced knowledge of topics presented in *Essentials* lessons, application of skills from multiple lessons, or self-directed learning of new skills.

In the first Discovery Zone exercise, you use Help to learn about other margin options, set mirror and gutter margins, and set outside-margin page numbers for a document, so that it can be printed on two sides and bound. In the second exercise, you create a different first page header for the document. In the last exercise, you change the document so that part of it prints in two columns. Because all of these exercises use the file Stockton Story, leave the file open from one exercise to the next.

1. Setting Mirror and Gutter Margins, and Inserting Outside-Margin Page Numbers

If you need to create a document that is going to be printed on both sides and bound in the middle, you should use the Mirror Margins feature. This ensures that the inside margin of each page is wide enough to accommodate the binding. When you format a document with different inside and outside margins, you usually place the page number for the document on the outside edge. When you use mirror margins, the location of the outside edge alternates every other page.

In this Discovery Zone exercise, you use Help to learn about the different margin options. Then you set mirror margins with a gutter for a short story and insert page numbers in the outside margin.

Locate the **WO-0404** file that is in the Student folder on the CD-ROM that came with your book, and open it. Save the document on your floppy disk as **Stockton Story**. Open Help and look for information about page margins. In the Page Margin Help window, click each of the linked topics to find out about changing margins, setting mirror margins, and creating a gutter margin. In the open document, select Mirror margins on the Page Setup dialog box. Set the margins as follows: Top .75", Bottom 1", Inside 1", Outside 0.8", and Gutter 0.25". Use Print Preview to see how the margins look. Save your changes, and leave the document open for use in the next Discovery Zone exercise.

2. Creating a Different First Page Header

Documents that have several sections often require a different header or footer for each section. You use the Header and Footer toolbar to control the information in that area for each section of a document. In this Discovery Zone exercise, you move the title and first paragraph about the author to the header on the first page. Because you do not want this to repeat on subsequent pages, you create a different header for the first page of this document.

Use the file from the previous exercise, or locate and open **WO-0404** in the Student folder on the CD-ROM that came with your book. Save the document on your floppy disk as **Stockton Story**. Use the Page Setup dialog box to choose Different first page for the headers and footers. Select the title, author, and first paragraph. Cut and paste them into the header on the first page. Indent this paragraph .5-inch from both the left and right margins. Notice that the header box is titled First Page Header. Now use the Insert, Page Numbers command to add page numbers to the outside margin. Make sure the Show number on first page check box is not checked. Go to Print Preview to see how the document looks. Save your changes, and leave the file open for use in the next Discovery exercise.

3. Changing Part of a Document to Two Columns

Columns are used for newsletters and other documents to make reading easier. Sometimes, you want part of the document to be in two columns and the rest to be in one column. When you change text that is already written to a two-column format, Word automatically puts in a section break. To change it back to one column, you need to put in a section break and change the layout. In this Discovery Zone exercise, you change the body of the Stockton Story to a two-column layout. You add a section break at the end of the story and change the layout back to one column. First, you use Help to learn more about columns.

Use the file from the previous exercise, or locate and open **WO-0404** that is in the Student folder on the CD-ROM. Save the document on your floppy disk as **Stockton Story**. Open Help and look for information on newspaper columns. Review the page about removing columns. Be sure to look at the definition for Sections.

When you begin, make sure you are in Print Layout view. Select the body of the story (everything but the header). Use the Columns button to select a two-column format. Use the Show/Hide button to view the section break that has been inserted at the beginning of the story. Move to the end of the document. Insert a continuous section break. Use the Column button again to change the format back to one column. At the end of the document in this new section, change the font size to 20 and type **This is the conclusion of Captain Eli's Best Ear story, written by Frank Stockton, and formatted by <your name>**. This sentence should be displayed across the entire width of the page.

Check to make sure the page numbers are turned on for all pages except the first page. Save your changes. Print the first and last page of the document, and close the file.

Project 5

Working with Tables

Objectives

In this project, you learn how to

- ➤ **Insert a Table**
- ➤ **Enter Information into a Table**
- ➤ **Add Rows and Columns to a Table**
- ➤ **Use AutoFormat**
- ➤ **Align Text and Align a Table**

Key terms introduced in this project include

- AutoFit
- AutoFormat
- cell
- table

SOURCE: *Essentials: Office 2000,* Ferrett-Preston-Preston

Why Would I Do This?

Sometimes information is best displayed in parallel columns with related information in side-by-side paragraphs. In Word, you can use tables for this purpose. A ***table*** contains lists of information set up in a row-and-column format, somewhat like the layout of a spreadsheet. Each intersection of an individual row and column in a table is called a ***cell***. The cells can contain text, numbers, or graphics.

Tables can be used for many purposes. They are excellent for two-column tasks, such as creating a résumé, in which the topic is on the left and the details are on the right. You can also use tables to display financial data, information summaries, or even help guidelines.

In this lesson, you learn how to set up and edit a table. You also learn how to use a very powerful automatic formatting tool.

Visual Summary

When you have completed this project, you will have created a document that looks like Figure 5.1.

Figure 5.1
Tables display information in a row-and-column format.

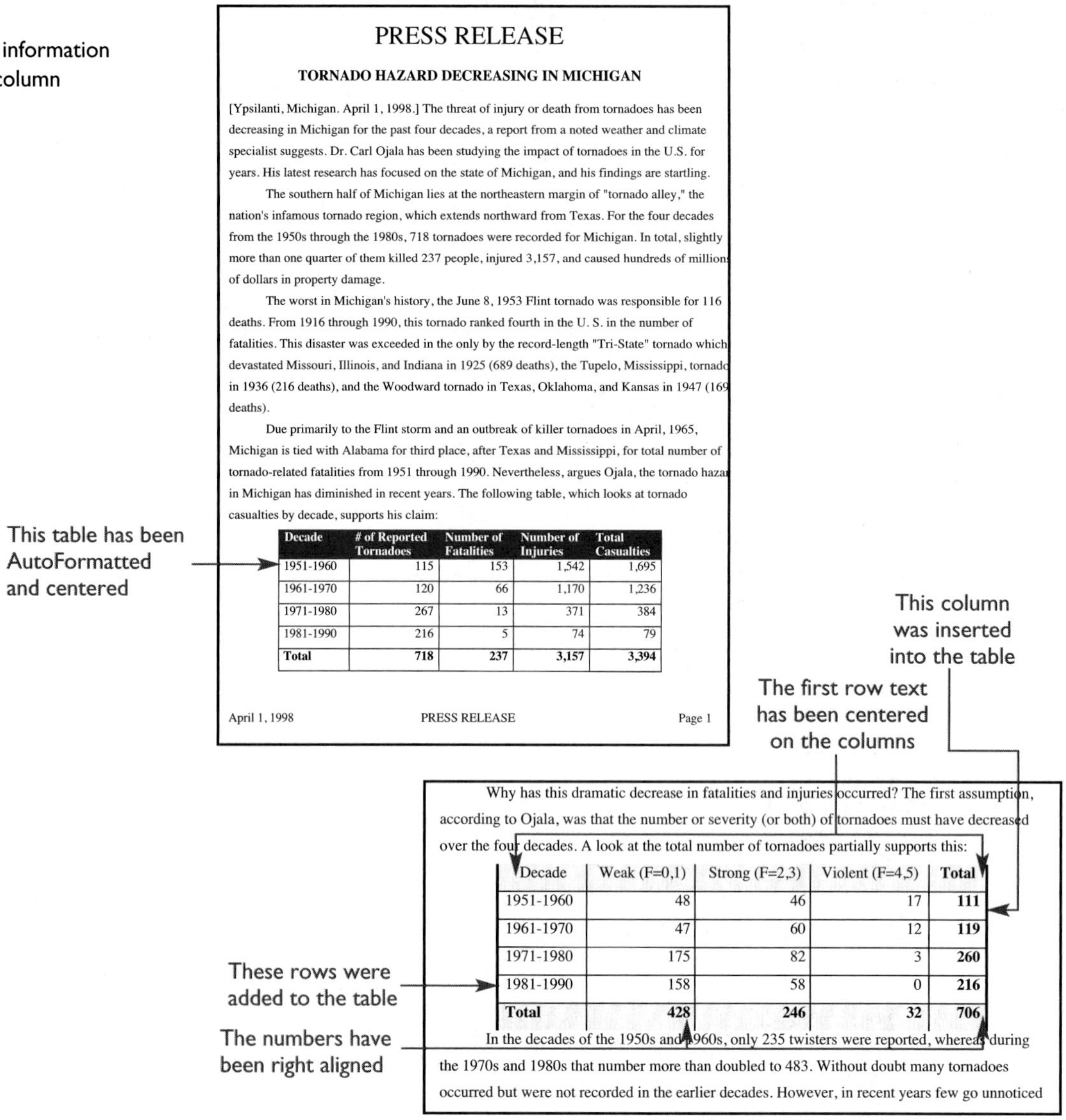

PRESS RELEASE

TORNADO HAZARD DECREASING IN MICHIGAN

[Ypsilanti, Michigan. April 1, 1998.] The threat of injury or death from tornadoes has been decreasing in Michigan for the past four decades, a report from a noted weather and climate specialist suggests. Dr. Carl Ojala has been studying the impact of tornadoes in the U.S. for years. His latest research has focused on the state of Michigan, and his findings are startling.

The southern half of Michigan lies at the northeastern margin of "tornado alley," the nation's infamous tornado region, which extends northward from Texas. For the four decades from the 1950s through the 1980s, 718 tornadoes were recorded for Michigan. In total, slightly more than one quarter of them killed 237 people, injured 3,157, and caused hundreds of million of dollars in property damage.

The worst in Michigan's history, the June 8, 1953 Flint tornado was responsible for 116 deaths. From 1916 through 1990, this tornado ranked fourth in the U. S. in the number of fatalities. This disaster was exceeded in the only by the record-length "Tri-State" tornado which devastated Missouri, Illinois, and Indiana in 1925 (689 deaths), the Tupelo, Mississippi, tornado in 1936 (216 deaths), and the Woodward tornado in Texas, Oklahoma, and Kansas in 1947 (169 deaths).

Due primarily to the Flint storm and an outbreak of killer tornadoes in April, 1965, Michigan is tied with Alabama for third place, after Texas and Mississippi, for total number of tornado-related fatalities from 1951 through 1990. Nevertheless, argues Ojala, the tornado hazard in Michigan has diminished in recent years. The following table, which looks at tornado casualties by decade, supports his claim:

This table has been AutoFormatted and centered

Decade	# of Reported Tornadoes	Number of Fatalities	Number of Injuries	Total Casualties
1951-1960	115	153	1,542	1,695
1961-1970	120	66	1,170	1,236
1971-1980	267	13	371	384
1981-1990	216	5	74	79
Total	**718**	**237**	**3,157**	**3,394**

April 1, 1998 PRESS RELEASE Page 1

This column was inserted into the table

The first row text has been centered on the columns

Why has this dramatic decrease in fatalities and injuries occurred? The first assumption, according to Ojala, was that the number or severity (or both) of tornadoes must have decreased over the four decades. A look at the total number of tornadoes partially supports this:

Decade	Weak (F=0,1)	Strong (F=2,3)	Violent (F=4,5)	Total
1951-1960	48	46	17	**111**
1961-1970	47	60	12	**119**
1971-1980	175	82	3	**260**
1981-1990	158	58	0	**216**
Total	**428**	**246**	**32**	**706**

These rows were added to the table

The numbers have been right aligned

In the decades of the 1950s and 1960s, only 235 twisters were reported, whereas during the 1970s and 1980s that number more than doubled to 483. Without doubt many tornadoes occurred but were not recorded in the earlier decades. However, in recent years few go unnoticed

Lesson 1: Inserting a Table

Adding a table to a document is only one way to display lists of information in columns and rows. You can use tabs for many of the same functions. Tables are much easier to use than tabs, however, and they are far more powerful and flexible. After you master the use of tables, you will find that you save a great deal of time and end up with a better-looking finished product.

In this lesson, you insert a table into a document using the Insert Table button.

To Insert a Table

1. **Launch Word and click the Open button. Find WO-0501 in the Student folder on the CD-ROM and save it as `Michigan Tornadoes` on your floppy disk.**
   This paper is about the decline in hazardous tornadoes in Michigan.

2. **Select Page Width from the Zoom button drop-down list box. Scroll to the second page until you can see the paragraph that begins with the words `In the decades`. Place the insertion point at the beginning of that paragraph.**
   You insert a table at the insertion point. The table will display information to support the preceding paragraph, which ends in a colon (see Figure 5.2)

99%

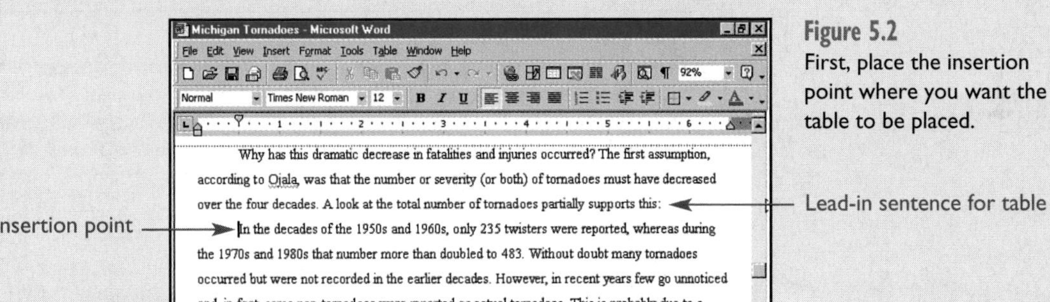

Figure 5.2
First, place the insertion point where you want the table to be placed.

3. **Click the Insert Table button on the Standard toolbar.**
   A matrix that enables you to choose the number of rows and columns for your new table displays (see Figure 5.3).

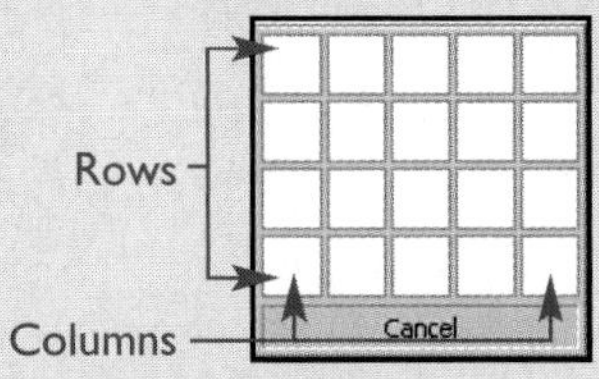

Figure 5.3
Use the Insert Table button to select the number of columns and rows for your table.

4. **Move the pointer down and to the right until you highlight four rows and four columns.**
   The table size appears at the bottom of the matrix (see Figure 5.4). The first number is the number of rows; the second number is the number of columns.

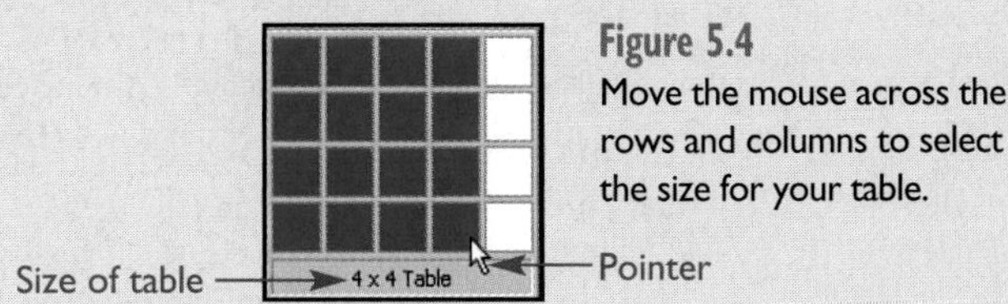

Figure 5.4
Move the mouse across the rows and columns to select the size for your table.

5. **Click to insert a 4 × 4 table.**
   The outlines of the columns and rows for the table display at the insertion point (see Figure 5.5).

continues ▶

To Insert a Table (continued)

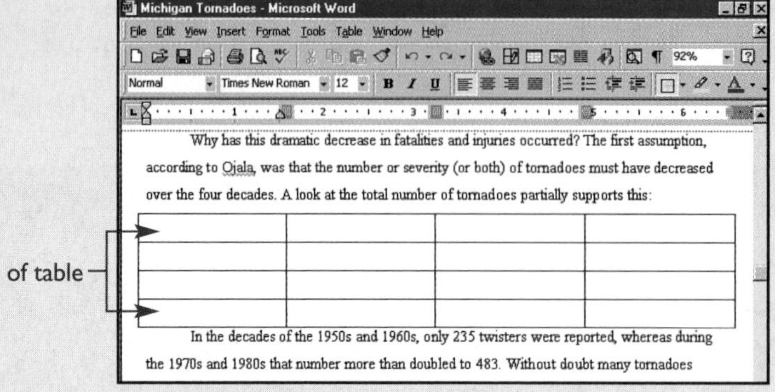

Figure 5.5
After you select the table size, click to insert the table.

6. **Click the Save button to save your changes.**
   Leave the file open for the next lesson.

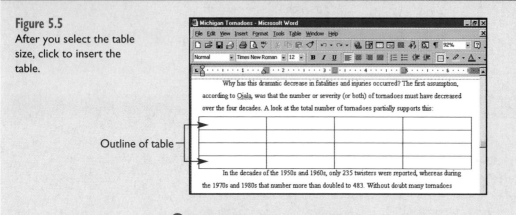

Enlarging the Table
If you want a larger table, move the pointer to the right or bottom edge of the grid; click and hold the mouse button down, and drag down or to the right. You can also use the Table, Insert, Table command from the menu. When the Insert Table dialog box opens, type the number of columns and rows in the appropriate text boxes.

Lesson 2: Entering Information into a Table

After you set up the rows and columns of your table, you enter information into the table cells. You can enter any kind of information you want. The most common table entries are text and numbers, but you can also enter graphics or Internet locations.

In this lesson, you enter text and numbers into a table.

To Enter Information into a Table

1. **With the new table in the Michigan Tornadoes document on the screen, place the insertion point in the first cell, if necessary.**
2. **Type `Decade`.**
   This is the column heading for the first column of the table. Notice that the text is left-aligned by default.
3. **Press Tab.**
   The insertion point moves to the second cell of the first row.

Many people automatically press Enter when they finish typing a cell entry in a table. If you do so, the insertion point does not move to the next cell but instead creates a new line in the current cell. To recover from this error, press Backspace to remove the extra paragraph marker in the cell, and then press Tab to move to the next cell.

4. **Type `Weak (F=0,1)` in the second cell in the top row, and then press Tab. Type `Strong (F=2,3)` in the third cell in the top row. Finish the column headers by typing `Violent (F=4,5)` in the last cell of the first row.**
   Remember to use Tab to move from one cell to the next. The first row of information should look like the one in Figure 5.6.

To Enter Information into a Table (continued)

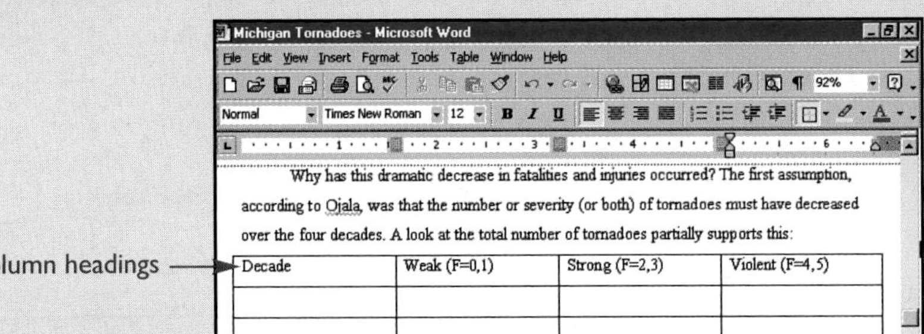

Figure 5.6
The first row of information usually contains column headings.

❺ **Press Tab to move to the beginning of the next row. Fill in the next three rows with the following information:**

Decade	Weak (F=0,1)	Strong (F=2,3)	Violent (F=4,5)
1951-1960	48	46	17
1961-1970	47	60	12
1971-1980	175	82	3

After you enter all the data in the table, your table should look like the one in Figure 5.7.

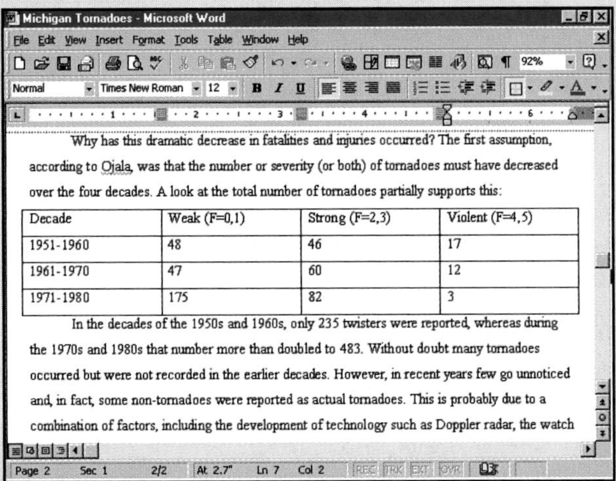

Figure 5.7
The information you entered appears in the table.

❻ **Click the Save button to save your changes.**
Leave the file open for the next lesson.

Moving Around in a Table
If you need to change information in a cell, Word offers faster ways of moving around in the table than going across each row using Tab. You can use the mouse to click the desired cell, or you can use the arrow keys to move up or down one cell at a time. To move back one cell, press Shift+Tab.

Lesson 3: Adding Rows and Columns to a Table

When you create a table, you might not always know ahead of time how many rows or columns you need. After you create a table, you can easily add more rows or columns to it.

In this lesson, you add two rows to the bottom of the table and enter more information. Then you add a column at the right end of the table.

To Add Rows to a Table

1 Place the insertion point to the right of the entry in the last cell in the table, if necessary.

2 Press Tab.

A new row is automatically added to the end of the table.

3 Add the following information to the last row of your table:

Decade	Weak (F=0,1)	Strong (F=2,3)	Violent (F=4,5)
1981-1990	158	58	0

4 With the cursor at the end of the new row, press Tab again and enter the following information in the last row.

Decade	Weak (F=0,1)	Strong (F=2,3)	Violent (F=4,5)
Total	428	246	32

After you add the two rows of information, your table should look like the one in Figure 5.8.

over the four decades. A look at the total number of tornadoes partially supports this:

Decade	Weak (F=0,1)	Strong (F=2,3)	Violent (F=4,5)
1951-1960	48	46	17
1961-1970	47	60	12
1971-1980	175	82	3
1981-1990	158	58	0
Total	428	246	32

In the decades of the 1950s and 1960s, only 235 twisters were reported, whereas during

Rows added

Figure 5.8
To add a row at the end of a table, simply press Tab.

You may find that you also need to add columns to a table. To do this, you use a menu command. In the next part of the lesson, you add a column to the right of the data, so that you can include the totals for each decade.

To Add Columns to a Table

1 Click a cell in the last column of the table.

To insert a new column, you must first move the insertion point to the column that you want it adjacent to.

2 Choose Table, Insert, Columns to the Right from the menu.

A new column is inserted to the right of the column in which you placed your insertion point. The new column is all black, which indicates that the entire column is selected.

3 Click the first cell of the new column and type `Total`. Press ↓ to move to the next empty cell.

4 Type the following numbers in the next five cells in this column, using the ↓ to move from one cell to the next.

111 119 260 216 706

After you add the data, your table should look like the one in Figure 5.9.

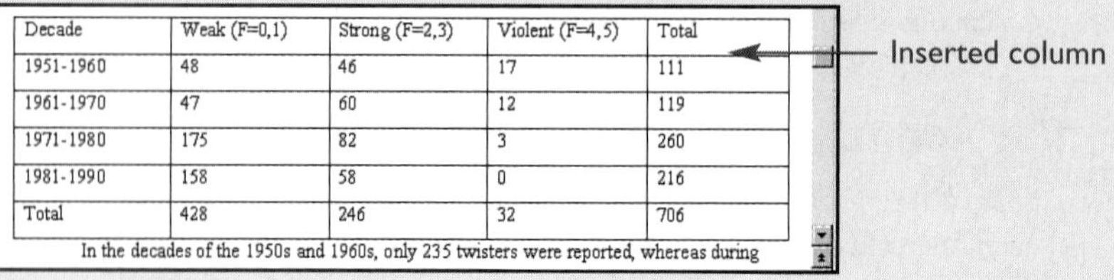

Decade	Weak (F=0,1)	Strong (F=2,3)	Violent (F=4,5)	Total
1951-1960	48	46	17	111
1961-1970	47	60	12	119
1971-1980	175	82	3	260
1981-1990	158	58	0	216
Total	428	246	32	706

In the decades of the 1950s and 1960s, only 235 twisters were reported, whereas during

Inserted column

Figure 5.9
To insert a column, use the Table menu.

5 Click the Save button to save your changes.
Leave the file open for the next lesson.

Adding Rows to the Middle of a Table

If you want to add rows to the middle of a table, click above or below where you want the new row to appear. Choose Table, Insert, Rows Above (or Rows Below) from the menu. Also, when you select a row or column, the appropriate Insert button (Insert Rows or Insert Columns) displays on the Standard toolbar in place of the Insert Table button.

Lesson 4: Using AutoFormat

The *AutoFormat* option, which enables you to choose from many different table styles, saves you a great deal of time in formatting a table. After you select a table style, you can make additional formatting and style changes to suit your needs.

In this lesson, you change the format of a table using the AutoFormat command.

To Use AutoFormat

1 Make sure the insertion point is somewhere in the table.

2 Choose Table, Table AutoFormat from the menu.
The Table AutoFormat dialog box opens (see Figure 5.10). Scroll down the list of table types in the Formats area and click several to see their appearance in the Preview box.

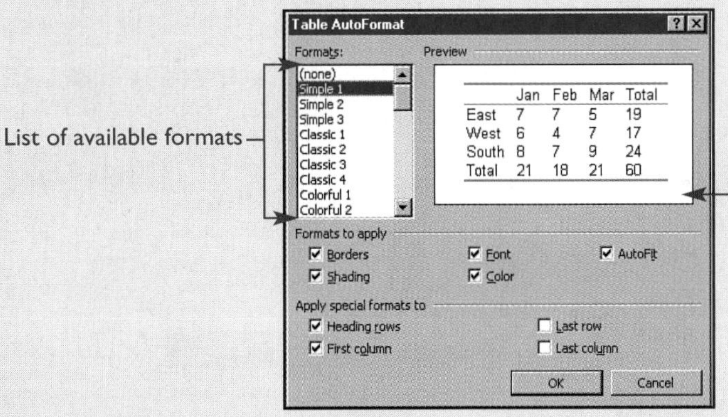

Figure 5.10
In the Table AutoFormat dialog box, you can select from preset formatting styles for a table.

Table Formatting

If you prefer, you can format a table without using the AutoFormat feature. First, select the cell, column, or row, and choose the formats that you want to apply. You can change font, font size, emphasis, or color. You can add borders or remove gridlines. You can even add background colors or shading. Using the AutoFormat feature is simply the quickest way to format a table.

3 Scroll down and select Grid 4 from the Formats list box. Click the check boxes to select Last row and Last column in the Apply special formats to area.
Look at the preview to verify that the last column and row are now boldfaced and a background color is applied to the first and last rows.

4 Click OK.
The table in the document now looks like the sample you saw in the Preview area (see Figure 5.11).

continues ▶

To Use AutoFormat (continued)

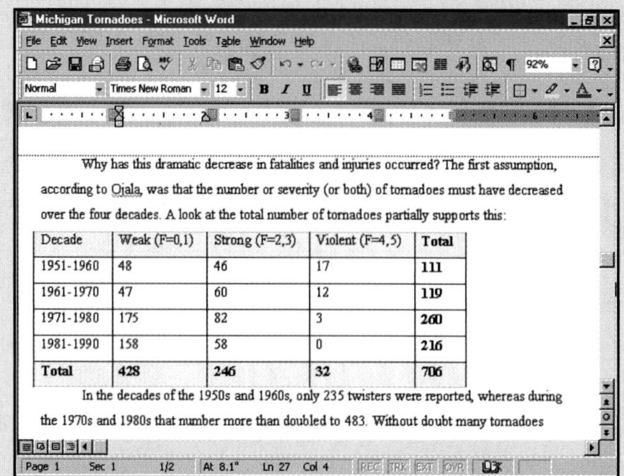

Why has this dramatic decrease in fatalities and injuries occurred? The first assumption, according to Ojala, was that the number or severity (or both) of tornadoes must have decreased over the four decades. A look at the total number of tornadoes partially supports this:

Decade	Weak (F=0,1)	Strong (F=2,3)	Violent (F=4,5)	**Total**
1951-1960	48	46	17	**111**
1961-1970	47	60	12	**119**
1971-1980	175	82	3	**260**
1981-1990	158	58	0	**216**
Total	**428**	**246**	**32**	**706**

In the decades of the 1950s and 1960s, only 235 twisters were reported, whereas during the 1970s and 1980s that number more than doubled to 483. Without doubt many tornadoes

Figure 5.11
The formatting style emphasizes the heading and Total rows.

5. **Scroll up the document until you see the table at the end of the first page.**
Now you format another table using the same technique.

6. **Click the table at the bottom of the first page and choose Table, Table AutoFormat from the menu.**
The Table AutoFormat dialog box opens.

7. **Select Grid 8. Click the Last row check box, and click OK to apply the style.**
A different AutoFormat style is applied to this table (see Figure 5.12).

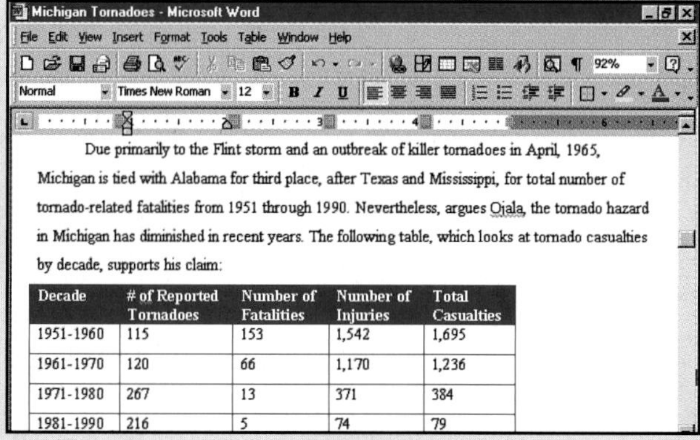

Due primarily to the Flint storm and an outbreak of killer tornadoes in April, 1965, Michigan is tied with Alabama for third place, after Texas and Mississippi, for total number of tornado-related fatalities from 1951 through 1990. Nevertheless, argues Ojala, the tornado hazard in Michigan has diminished in recent years. The following table, which looks at tornado casualties by decade, supports his claim:

Decade	# of Reported Tornadoes	Number of Fatalities	Number of Injuries	Total Casualties
1951-1960	115	153	1,542	1,695
1961-1970	120	66	1,170	1,236
1971-1980	267	13	371	384
1981-1990	216	5	74	79

Figure 5.12
This formatting style places primary emphasis on the heading row.

8. **Click the Save button to save your changes.**
Leave the file open for the next lesson.

Using AutoFit

If you format a table on your own, you can use the ***AutoFit*** feature. AutoFit is a tool in the Table menu that changes the width of the columns to best fit the data that you enter. The AutoFormat dialog box contains an AutoFit check box, and Word applies the AutoFit feature by default when you apply an automatic formatting style.

Lesson 5: Aligning Text and Aligning a Table

Another way to make your table look more professional is to align the items in an attractive manner. Notice that your numbers do not line up on the right side of the table you created. Generally, you line up text on the left and numbers on the right. One exception to that rule is column headings, which should generally be right aligned or centered if they are above numbers. To improve the appearance of this table, the numbers and text need to be properly aligned.

In this lesson, you right align numbers and center the column headings.

To Align Text in a Table

1. **Scroll down the screen and click any cell of the second column of the tornado severity table you created (the second table in the document).**
   To align a column of data, place the insertion point anywhere in the column.

2. **Choose Table, Select, Column from the menu.**
   The column is selected (see Figure 5.13).

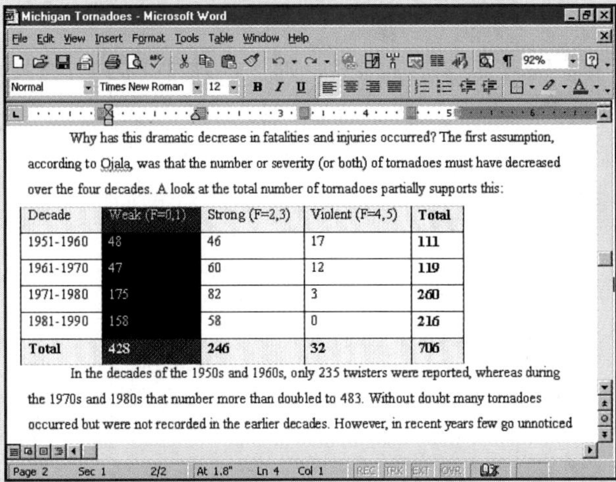

Figure 5.13
You must highlight the data before you can set the alignment.

Selecting Columns with the Pointer
To select a column, you can also position the pointer at the very top of the column. The pointer changes into a small, black, downward-pointing arrow. When you see this pointer shape, you can click to select the column. You can select multiple columns with this pointer by clicking and dragging the pointer to the right or left.

3. **Click the Align Right button on the Formatting toolbar, and then click somewhere else to deselect the column.**
   The data in the column is aligned on the right side of the cell (see Figure 5.14). You can also select groups of cells to align at one time.

4. **Move the pointer, so that it points at the number 46 in the cell under the column heading `Strong (F=2,3)`.**
   The pointer changes to a selection arrow (see Figure 5.14). Use this small black arrow to select a group of cells.

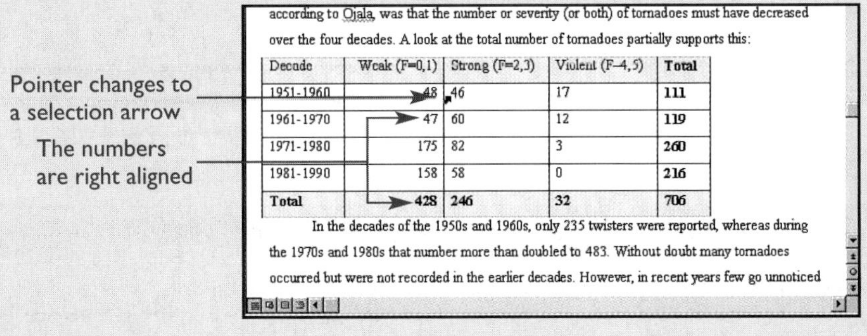

Figure 5.14
The pointer changes to a selection arrow that you can use to select a group of cells.

5. **Click and drag down and to the right to select the last three columns of numbers. Click the Align Right button.**
   The numbers align on the right side of the columns (see Figure 5.15).

continues ▶

To Align Text in a Table (continued)

Figure 5.15
You can select a group of cells to align.

The numbers are right aligned

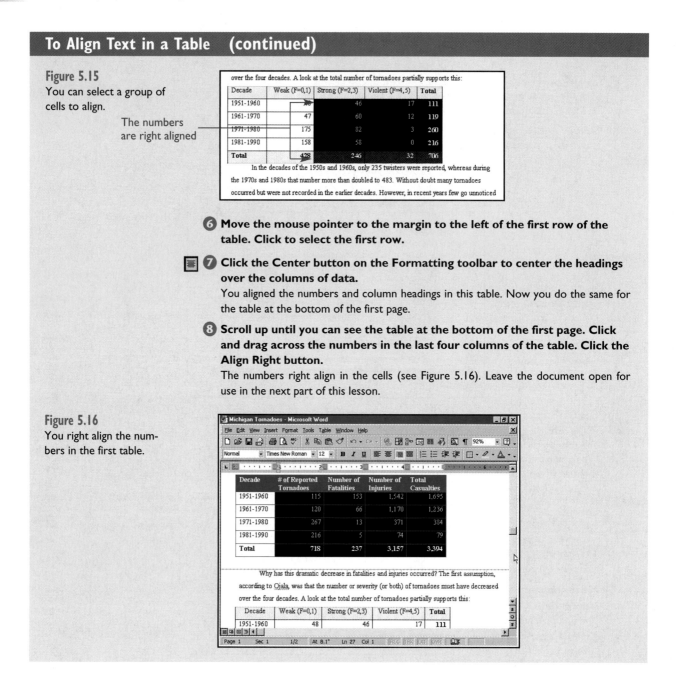

over the four decades. A look at the total number of tornadoes partially supports this:

Decade	Weak (F=0,1)	Strong (F=2,3)	Violent (F=4,5)	Total
1951-1960	48	46	17	111
1961-1970	47	60	12	119
1971-1980	175	82	3	260
1981-1990	158	58	0	216
Total	428	246	32	706

In the decades of the 1950s and 1960s, only 235 twisters were reported, whereas during the 1970s and 1980s that number more than doubled to 483. Without doubt many tornadoes occurred but were not recorded in the earlier decades. However, in recent years few go unnoticed

6. **Move the mouse pointer to the margin to the left of the first row of the table. Click to select the first row.**

7. **Click the Center button on the Formatting toolbar to center the headings over the columns of data.**
   You aligned the numbers and column headings in this table. Now you do the same for the table at the bottom of the first page.

8. **Scroll up until you can see the table at the bottom of the first page. Click and drag across the numbers in the last four columns of the table. Click the Align Right button.**
   The numbers right align in the cells (see Figure 5.16). Leave the document open for use in the next part of this lesson.

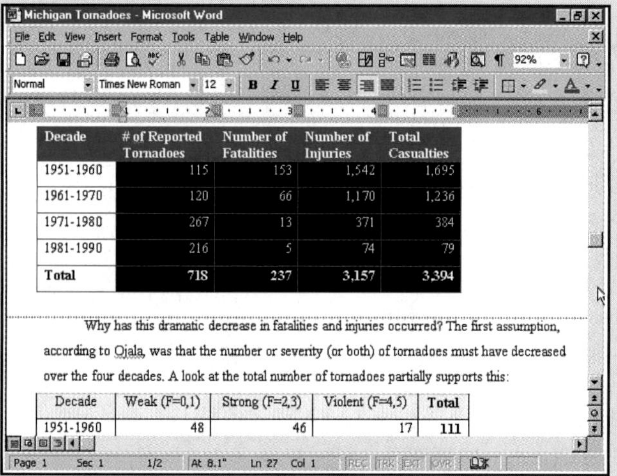

Decade	# of Reported Tornadoes	Number of Fatalities	Number of Injuries	Total Casualties
1951-1960	115	153	1,542	1,695
1961-1970	120	66	1,170	1,236
1971-1980	267	13	371	384
1981-1990	216	5	74	79
Total	718	237	3,157	3,394

Why has this dramatic decrease in fatalities and injuries occurred? The first assumption, according to Ojala, was that the number or severity (or both) of tornadoes must have decreased over the four decades. A look at the total number of tornadoes partially supports this:

Decade	Weak (F=0,1)	Strong (F=2,3)	Violent (F=4,5)	Total
1951-1960	48	46	17	111

Figure 5.16
You right align the numbers in the first table.

Not only can you align text in a cell, the table looks better if you align it on the page. With a wide table it is best to center it on the page. If you have a small table that takes up half a page or less, you might want to wrap related text on one side of the table. In the last part of the lesson, you center both tables on the page.

To Align a Table in a Document

1. **With the four columns of data still selected, choose Table, Select, Table from the menu.**
   The entire table is selected.

2. **Click the Center button on the Formatting toolbar.**
   The table moves to the right and centers on the page (see Figure 5.17).

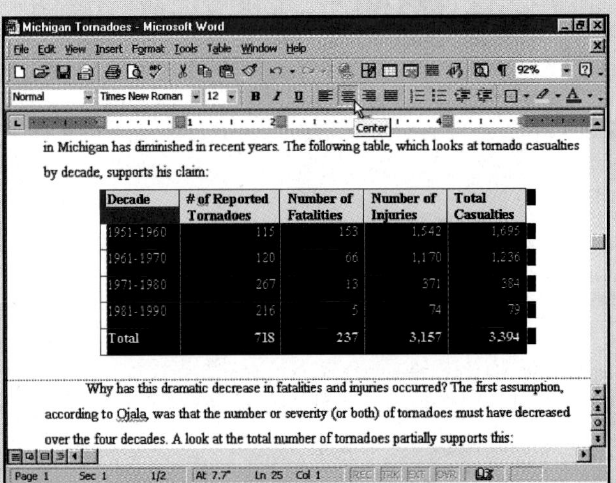

in Michigan has diminished in recent years. The following table, which looks at tornado casualties by decade, supports his claim:

Decade	# of Reported Tornadoes	Number of Fatalities	Number of Injuries	Total Casualties
1951-1960	115	153	1,542	1,695
1961-1970	120	66	1,170	1,236
1971-1980	267	13	371	384
1981-1990	216	5	74	79
Total	718	237	3,157	3,394

Why has this dramatic decrease in fatalities and injuries occurred? The first assumption, according to Ojala, was that the number or severity (or both) of tornadoes must have decreased over the four decades. A look at the total number of tornadoes partially supports this:

Figure 5.17
The table appears centered between the margins.

3 **Scroll down and place the insertion point in the tornado severity table you created at the top of the second page.**

4 **Choose Table, Select, Table from the menu, and click the Center button. Click elsewhere to deselect the table.**
The second table centers on the page (see Figure 5.18).

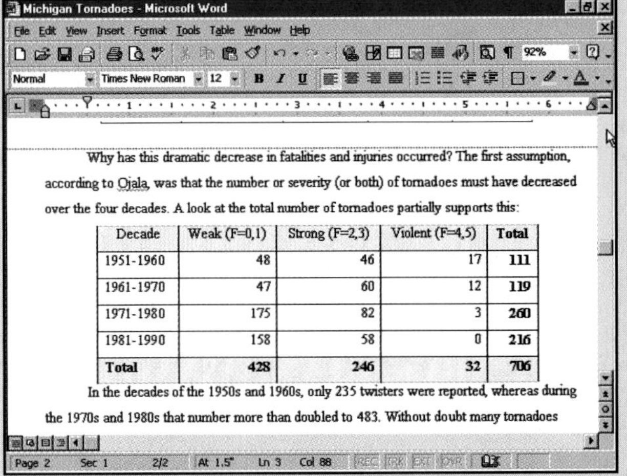

Why has this dramatic decrease in fatalities and injuries occurred? The first assumption, according to Ojala, was that the number or severity (or both) of tornadoes must have decreased over the four decades. A look at the total number of tornadoes partially supports this:

Decade	Weak (F=0,1)	Strong (F=2,3)	Violent (F=4,5)	Total
1951-1960	48	46	17	111
1961-1970	47	60	12	119
1971-1980	175	82	3	260
1981-1990	158	58	0	216
Total	428	246	32	706

In the decades of the 1950s and 1960s, only 235 twisters were reported, whereas during the 1970s and 1980s that number more than doubled to 483. Without doubt many tornadoes

Figure 5.18
The tornado severity table appears centered between the margins.

5 **Click the Save button to save your work. Print the document and close the file.**

Embedding a Table in Text

If your table is small, you might want to embed it in the text. You can wrap the text around the table by selecting the table, and choosing Table, Table Properties from the menu. Select Around from the Text wrapping area, and click OK.

Summary

In this project, you inserted a table into a document, entered data in the table, added rows and columns, and used AutoFormat to format the table. You also aligned data in the cells of the table and centered the table on the page.

Tables are flexible tools that are useful for displaying information in a side-by-side format. You can expand your knowledge by using Help to learn more about tables. Specifically under the topic `About Tables`, look at the subtopics entitled `Overview of tables`, `Parts of a Table`, `Creating Tables`, and `Formatting Tables`.

Checking Concepts and Terms

True/False

For each of the following, check *T* or *F* to indicate whether the statement is true or false.

__T __F **1.** Tables consist of rows and columns of cells that resemble a spreadsheet. [L1]

__T __F **2.** To create a table in a document, you enter the data, using tabs to separate the columns; select the data, and choose Format, Table from the menu. [L1]

__T __F **3.** When you enter text in a table, the text is aligned to the left by default. [L2]

__T __F **4.** To add an extra row when you reach the last cell at the bottom of a table, press Tab. [L3]

__T __F **5.** When you enter data into the cells of a table, you press Enter to move from one cell to the next. [L2]

__T __F **6.** To center a table on the page, select the table and click the Center button. [L5]

__T __F **7.** When you enter numbers in a table, they automatically align to the right side of each cell. [L2]

__T __F **8.** A row or column of data can be aligned separately from the rest of the table. [L5]

__T __F **9.** When you use an AutoFormat style, you cannot make changes to the formatting or alignment. [L4]

__T __F **10.** AutoFormat provides a quick way to format a table. [L4]

Multiple Choice

Circle the letter of the correct answer for each of the following.

1. Which key(s) do you press to add another row to the table if the pointer is in the lower-right cell (the last cell in the table)? [L3]

a. Enter

b. Shift+Enter

c. Tab

d. Shift+Tab

2. To wrap text around a table, ______________. [L5]

a. click the Wrap button on the toolbar

b. select the table, choose Table, Table Properties from the menu, and select Around

c. choose Table, Around from the menu

d. none of the above

3. Which of the following is the method you use to select a column? [L5]

a. Click and drag down the cells in the column.

b. Click the column, and choose Table, Select, Column from the menu.

c. Position the mouse pointer at the top end of the column and click.

d. all of the above

4. What is the name of the intersection of a row and column in a table? [Intro]

a. connection

b. cell

c. junction

d. union

5. Which of the following types of information can be placed in a table? [Intro]

a. text

b. numbers

c. graphics

d. all of the above

Screen ID

Refer to figure 5.19 and identify the numbered parts of the screens. Write the letter of the correct label in the space next to the number.

Figure 5.19

A. Left-aligned (boldfaced) text

B. Selected column

C. Right-aligned column of numbers

D. Selection pointer

E. Used to center a table between the left and right margins

F. Column headings

G. Insert Columns button

H. Align Right button

I. Table centered left to right

J. Insert Table button

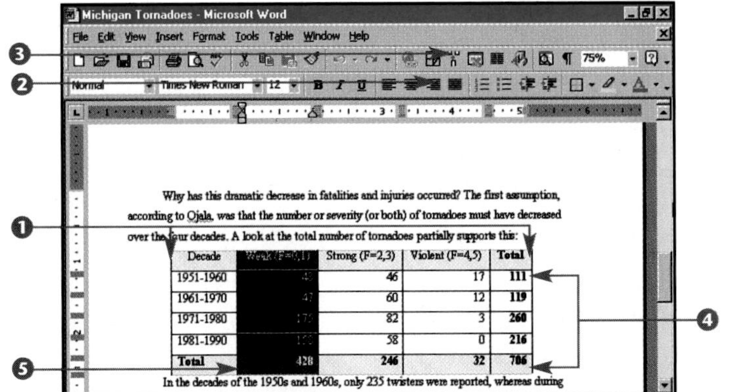

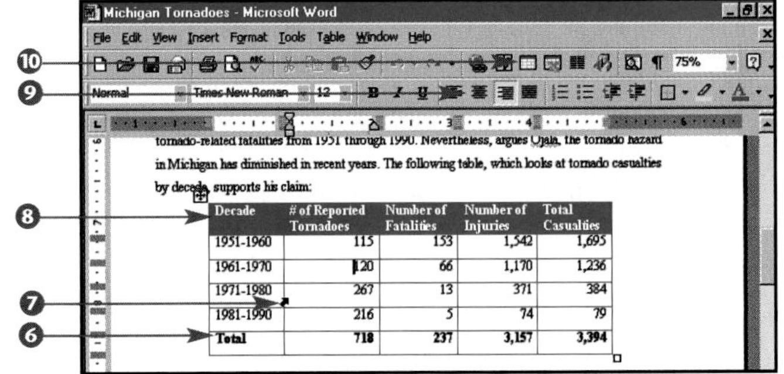

1. ____________________ **5.** ____________________ **9.** ____________________

2. ____________________ **6.** ____________________ **10.** ____________________

3. ____________________ **7.** ____________________

4. ____________________ **8.** ____________________

Discussion Questions

1. In papers you write for other classes, how can the use of tables help you present information? Give some examples of information that would be better presented in a table format.
2. Examine a textbook from another class. Locate tables that have been used in the book. How do they help you as a student? Are they good learning tools?
3. Tables are often good tools for a résumé. If you had to prepare a résumé, how many columns would you include? What kinds of information would go in each column?

Skill Drill

Skill Drill exercises reinforce project skills. Each skill reinforced is the same, or nearly the same, as a skill presented in the project. Detailed instructions are provided in a step-by-step format.

In this set of Skill Drill exercises, you continue with the severe weather theme by working with a paper about Lightning Strikes. You insert a table, enter data into the table, and add a new row and a new column. Then you format the table, align numbers in the table, and center the table on the page.

This set of Skill Drill exercises uses file WO-0502, renamed Lightning Strikes. Leave the file open from one Skill Drill exercise to the next.

1. Inserting a Table into a Document

First, you select the size table you need, and then you enter the data in the cells of the table. [L1]

1. Launch Word and click the Open button. Find `WO-0502` in the Student folder on the CD-ROM and save it as `Lightning Strikes` on your floppy disk.
2. Type your name below the title in the space provided.
3. Scroll to the bottom of the second paragraph. Click in the blank space below the second paragraph.
4. Choose Table, Insert, Table from the menu.
5. Choose a table that has two columns and nine rows. Do not use the AutoFormat feature. Click OK.
6. Start at the upper-left cell and enter the following data:

Location	Number
Playground/Ballpark	23
Under trees	19
Golfing	10
Water-related	8
Farm equipment	2
Telephone	2
Radio equipment	1
Other locations	16

7. Leave the document open for use in the next exercise.

2. Adding a Row and a Column to a Table

If you did not include enough rows or columns, you can easily add them and enter the additional information. [L3]

1. Make sure the cursor is located in the last cell in the bottom row of the table that you inserted in the previous exercise.
2. Press Tab to insert another row at the bottom of the table.
3. Add the following summary data to the two cells in the newly created row: **`Totals, 81`**.
4. Choose Table, Insert, Columns to the Right from the menu to add a new column to the right side of the table.
5. Enter the following data in this third column:

```
Percent of Total
28.4
23.4
12.3
9.9
2.5
2.5
1.2
19.8
100.0
```

6. Leave the document open for use in the next exercise.

3. Formatting the Table

After you enter the data, you can improve the appearance of a table by applying formatting to the table. You can do this by selecting the formatting you want for each row or column of data, or you can use the AutoFormat feature. [L4]

1. Choose Table, Table AutoFormat from the menu.
2. Select the Simple 1 style.
3. Do not change the default settings. Click OK.
4. Scroll down the page and place the insertion point in the next table.
5. Choose Table, Table AutoFormat from the menu.
6. Select Simple 2 from the list of formatting designs.
7. Do not change any of the default settings. Click OK.
8. Save the changes and leave the file open for the next exercise.

4. Aligning Numbers in a Table and Aligning the Table

If the table contains numerical information, you generally need to change the alignment of the cells, so the numbers are right aligned. You also need to position the table on the page to center it between the margins. [L5]

1. In the table you just formatted, select all the cells that contain numbers.
2. Change their alignment to the right side of their respective cells.
3. Select the table and center it on the page.
4. Return to the table you inserted on the first page.
5. Select all the cells that contain numbers and change their alignment to the right side of their respective cells.
6. Select the table and center it on the page.
7. Save the document.
8. Print the document and close it.

Challenge

Challenge exercises expand on or are somewhat related to skills presented in the lessons. Each exercise provides a brief narrative introduction followed by instructions, in a numbered step or bulleted list format, that are not as detailed as those in the Skill Drill section.

This project demonstrated the basics in creating a table. Word contains many other table-formatting options that you can explore. In these Challenge exercises, you use some additional alignment options. First, you merge cells to create a heading that covers multiple columns. In the second exercise, you explore some of the other cell alignment options that are available in a table. In the last exercise, you use a vertical cell alignment. As stated previously, you can apply formatting options to individual cells, columns, or rows. You apply some formats to parts of the table as you work through these three exercises. The exercises use file WO-0503, renamed Business Forms, and should be done in sequence. Leave the file open from one exercise to the next.

1. Merging Cells in a Table

Some table designs have several topics you can group together under one heading. To create a heading that covers multiple columns, you merge selected cells into one cell. In this Challenge exercise, you add a row at the top of a table, merge cells, and add headings to individual columns.

To create headings for a table by merging cells, follow these steps:

1. Open the WO-0503 file in the Student folder on the CD-ROM. Save it on your floppy disk as **`Business Forms`**. This table is set up to print in a landscape layout and displays at 50 percent so that you can see all the rows and columns.
2. Click the first row of the table and select Table, Insert, Rows Above.
3. Select the second, third, and fourth cells of the new empty row. Right-click, and select Merge Cells from the shortcut menu.
4. Repeat this process to merge the next three cells and then again to merge the last two cells. (The third-from-last cell contains its own heading.) Not counting the first column, you should now have four cells for a group heading in the first row.
5. Starting in the first merged cell and continuing across the row, type the following four headings: **`Human Resources, Initial Funding, Government Regulations, Revenue`**. (Change the zoom, if necessary, to see what you are typing.)
6. Save your changes, and leave this file open for use in the next Challenge exercise.

2. Using Other Cell Alignment Options

You can align text horizontally at the top, center, or bottom of a cell. In this exercise, you explore some of these options and change the alignment on the first row and column of the Business Forms table.

To use other cell alignment options in a table, follow these steps:

1. Use the Business Forms document from the previous Challenge exercise.
2. Select the first row of headings, if necessary, and change the font to Arial, 12 point, bold.
3. Position the pointer on the Move Table Column indicator on the Ruler that lines up with the right side of the **`Government Regulations`** column. When the two-headed arrow displays, click and drag to the right to adjust the column width. Adjust it just enough to enable the words **`Government Regulations`** to display on two lines.
4. Select the four group headings; point to one of the headings, and right-click. A shortcut menu displays. From the shortcut menu, point to Cell Alignment, and select the option in the middle of the bottom row.
5. Select the three cell headings (**`Corporation`**, **`Partnership`**, and **`Proprietorship`**) on the left side of the table. Point to one of the headings, and right-click. A shortcut menu displays. From the shortcut menu, point to Cell Alignment and select the middle option in the middle row. The headings line up in the middle of the cells.
6. Save your changes, and leave this file open for use in the next Challenge exercise.

3. Aligning Text Vertically Within a Cell

In addition to changing the horizontal alignment of text within a cell, you can also display text vertically. This is useful to save space or to create a group heading similar to the one used at the top of the Business Forms table. In this exercise, you change the alignment of the headings on the side of the table to display vertically.

To display text vertically in a cell, follow these steps:

1. Use the Business Forms document from the previous Challenge exercise.
2. Select the three row headings at the left of the table.
3. Point to one of the selected headings and right-click. Select Text Direction from the shortcut menu. Select the vertical orientation that is displayed on the left. Notice that the option is displayed in the Preview area of the dialog box. Click OK.

4. Position the pointer over the Adjust Table Row indicator near the 2-inch mark on the vertical Ruler on the left edge of the screen. When the double-headed arrow appears, click and drag down to adjust the row height between **Partnership** and **Proprietorship** to enable the first heading to display on one line.
5. Choose Table, AutoFit, AutoFit to Contents to readjust the column and row sizes.
6. At the end of the document, outside of the table type **Formatted by <your name>**.
7. Save your changes, print the document, and close the file.

Discovery Zone 

Discovery Zone exercises require advanced knowledge of topics presented in *Essentials* lessons, application of skills from multiple lessons, or self-directed learning of new skills.

In the first Discovery Zone exercise, you change existing text to a table format. In the second exercise, you sort the data. In the last exercise, you use Help to learn about using formulas in a table; you then sum two columns in the table you created. All these exercises use the file WO-0504, renamed January Sales, so leave the file open from one exercise to the next.

1. Changing Text to a Table

You might find that text already entered in a document would work better if it were in a table. Word provides a table command that converts text to a table, or a table to text.

In this exercise, you convert a text file to a table.

Locate and open the **WO-0504** file in the Student folder on the CD-ROM. Save the document on your floppy disk as **January Sales**. Select everything but the main title. This includes all the text from the Date heading through the end of the data. Choose Table, Convert, Text to Table. The Convert Text to Table dialog box opens and displays the number of columns it detects. This number may or may not agree with the number you see in the data. It is best to accept the suggested number and modify the table as needed. If this does not work, you can always click Undo and start over again. Notice that you can convert data that is separated by tabs, paragraph marks, commas, or some other notation. The program has correctly identified the delimiter in this data to be tabs. Click OK to convert the text to a table. Format the table, so that numbers and dates right-align; center the headings, and make columns wide enough for the data without wrapping the words. Select the extra column and choose Table, Delete, Columns from the menu. Save your changes, and leave the document open for use in the next exercise.

2. Sorting Multiple Columns in a Table

Another useful table feature is sorting. In a table, you can sort more than one column of data at the same time. In this exercise, you sort the data in the January Sales table first by product, and then by date.

Use the January Sales document from the previous exercise. If you have not completed that exercise, do so now. Click the first cell of the table and choose Table, Sort. In the Sort by list box, select Product; in the first Then by list box, select Date. Make sure the Header row option is selected before you click OK. Word sorts the table according to the criteria you select. If you wanted to go back to the previous sort order, use the Undo button to reverse this action. Save your changes, and leave the file open for use in the next exercise.

[?] 3. Using a Formula in a Table

When you have a table of data that includes a column of numbers, you might need to use the Table, Formula command to calculate a total. Although using formulas in a table of data in Word is not as foolproof as using formulas in Excel, it is a handy tool and is better than adding the figures separately on a calculator. In this Discovery Zone exercise, you use Help to learn about using formulas in a table, and then you sum the Amount and Points columns in the January Sales document.

Open Help and locate the topic **Perform Calculations in a Table**. Review the procedure, and use the information as a guide to help you with the rest of the exercise.

Use the January Sales document from the previous exercise. Add a row to the end of the table. Click the empty cell at the bottom of the Amount column. Choose Table, Formula. The Formula dialog box opens and displays **=SUM(ABOVE)** in the Formula box. Use the drop-down arrow at the end of the Number format box to select the format for dollars (the third option listed). A total of **$983,600.00** displays. Repeat this procedure to add a total at the bottom of the Points column. (Do not format this as dollars.) The total should be **9303.3**. Add your name after the end of the table. Save your changes, print the document, and close the file.

Part III Excel

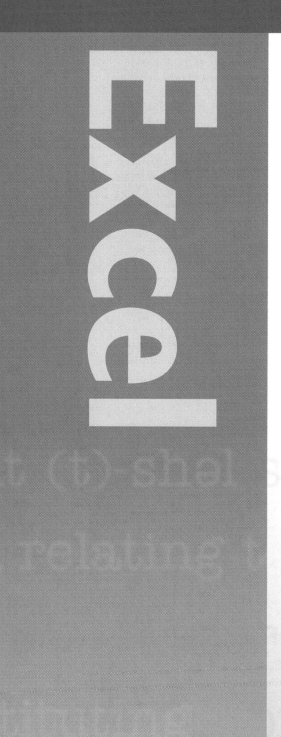

1 Introduction to Excel

2 Enhancing the Appearance of the Worksheet

3 Techniques for Working Efficiently in Excel

4 Making the Computer Do the Math

5 Understanding the Numbers by Using a Chart

6 Using Excel's Interactive Features

Introduction to Microsoft Excel 2000

Computers were first designed for calculating large quantities of numerical information. In fact, people who had the job of summing columns of numbers for statistical charts were known as computers. The form they used to record the numbers was called a spreadsheet, which is a tabular form that is divided into vertical columns and horizontal rows. Accountants use spreadsheets to manually keep track of financial data. The first electronic spreadsheet program written for the personal computer was called VisiCalc. It was introduced in 1979 by Bob Frankston and Dan Bricklin, and is considered by many in the computer industry to be the single most important reason why personal computers gained acceptance in the business world.

Microsoft Excel is a popular electronic spreadsheet program designed for the purpose of recording, calculating, and graphing numerical data. In Excel, a book of spreadsheets is referred to as a workbook and can be compared to an accounting ledger book that is bound and has many pages. When you open Excel, you open a workbook that can consist of up to 255 worksheets. A tab at the bottom of the window identifies each worksheet, which is also referred to as a sheet. The tab for each sheet is labeled with the word **Sheet** and the number of the sheet. Only three sheets show when you open Excel, but you can easily add sheets when you need to. Each worksheet consists of 256 columns and 16,384 rows. You see only a fraction of the available columns and rows on the screen and must use the scrollbar, scroll arrows, and keyboard to move around on a worksheet.

The value of an electronic spreadsheet program, such as Excel, is its capability to perform calculations rapidly and to recalculate formulas when the data changes. This saves an enormous amount of time, reduces the risk of errors, and provides the opportunity to examine scenarios for the future. The capability to consider the impact of changes in numerical assumptions helps decision makers examine numerous options to find the best plan for the future.

Spreadsheet programs are widely used in a variety of formats throughout business and industry. To use a spreadsheet program successfully, you need to understand the basic concepts of how the program works. You need to know the features that are available and the methods to use to enter data, write formulas, and create charts. These tools assist you in your career development and in tracking personal information. They can help you make purchase decisions for a car or a home. You can record information for taxes, investments, or retirement. Knowing how to use a spreadsheet program is a valuable skill to have.

Project 1

Introduction to Excel

Objectives

In this project, you learn how to

- **Navigate a Workbook**
- **Select Individual Cells**
- **Enter Text and Numbers into Cells**
- **Edit the Contents of a Cell**
- **Insert and Delete Rows or Columns**
- **Sum a Column of Numbers**
- **Save a Workbook, Print the Worksheet, and Exit Excel**

Key terms introduced in this project include

- active cell
- calculations
- cell
- cell address
- column heading
- display settings
- Formula bar
- marquee
- row heading
- select
- sheet
- workbook
- worksheets
- zoom

SOURCE: *Essentials: Office 2000*, Ferrett-Preston-Preston

Why Would I Do This?

To get started with Excel, you need to be able to identify the basic components of the program and to learn how to move around in the Excel window. The most widely used application for Excel is a recording of columns of numbers that are classified into categories. The columns and rows are usually labeled to identify the meaning of the numbers. An example would be tracking inventory by location. The labels for the inventory would appear across the top of the worksheet, and the rows would contain labels for the store locations. The total quantity for each category of inventory can then be calculated for all locations. This basic layout is the cornerstone for using a worksheet.

In this project, you create a simple worksheet, edit the text, insert a column and a row, sum a column of numbers, and print and save the worksheet. The completed worksheet will look like Figure 1.1.

Visual Summary

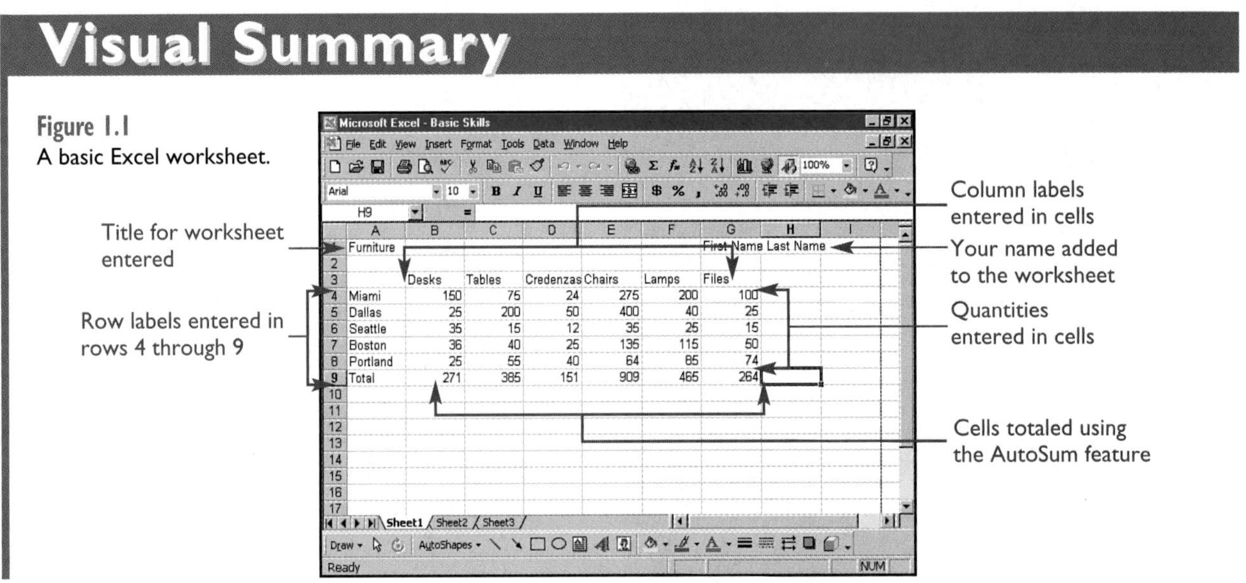

Figure 1.1
A basic Excel worksheet.

Lesson 1: Navigating a Workbook

To understand how to use Excel, you first need to have a basic understanding of how Excel is structured. An Excel file is a ***workbook*** that consists of several ***worksheets*** identified by tabs at the bottom of the window. A workbook is a collection of worksheets saved under one filename. A worksheet or ***sheet*** is a page in a workbook consisting of a set of ***cells*** that are identified by ***row and column headings***. The column heading is the letter at the top of each column that identifies the column. The row heading is the number to the left of each row that identifies the row. The intersections of the rows and columns of a sheet form a grid of cells. A cell is identified by its ***cell address***, the column letter and row number that designate the location of the cell. Many more rows and columns are available than those that show in the window; therefore, to work in Excel, you need to know how to navigate in a worksheet to see different rows and columns.

In this lesson, you select a sheet and scroll the window to display additional rows and columns.

To Navigate a Workbook

1. **Click the Start button on the taskbar; choose Programs, Microsoft Excel.**
   Excel opens and a workbook displays the title Book1. See Figure 1.2 to identify the different parts of the Excel window.

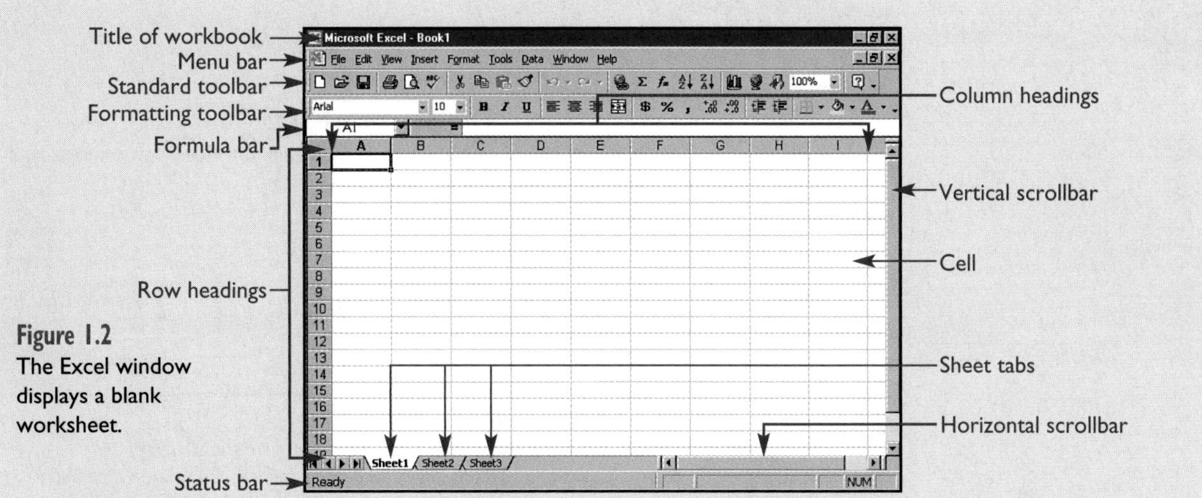

Figure 1.2
The Excel window displays a blank worksheet.

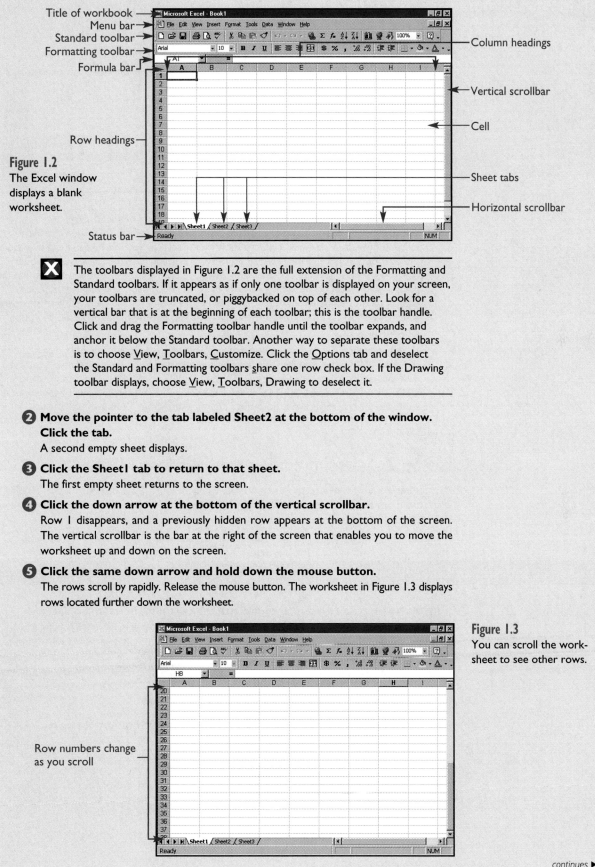

The toolbars displayed in Figure 1.2 are the full extension of the Formatting and Standard toolbars. If it appears as if only one toolbar is displayed on your screen, your toolbars are truncated, or piggybacked on top of each other. Look for a vertical bar that is at the beginning of each toolbar; this is the toolbar handle. Click and drag the Formatting toolbar handle until the toolbar expands, and anchor it below the Standard toolbar. Another way to separate these toolbars is to choose View, Toolbars, Customize. Click the Options tab and deselect the Standard and Formatting toolbars share one row check box. If the Drawing toolbar displays, choose View, Toolbars, Drawing to deselect it.

2. **Move the pointer to the tab labeled Sheet2 at the bottom of the window. Click the tab.**
   A second empty sheet displays.
3. **Click the Sheet1 tab to return to that sheet.**
   The first empty sheet returns to the screen.
4. **Click the down arrow at the bottom of the vertical scrollbar.**
   Row 1 disappears, and a previously hidden row appears at the bottom of the screen. The vertical scrollbar is the bar at the right of the screen that enables you to move the worksheet up and down on the screen.
5. **Click the same down arrow and hold down the mouse button.**
   The rows scroll by rapidly. Release the mouse button. The worksheet in Figure 1.3 displays rows located further down the worksheet.

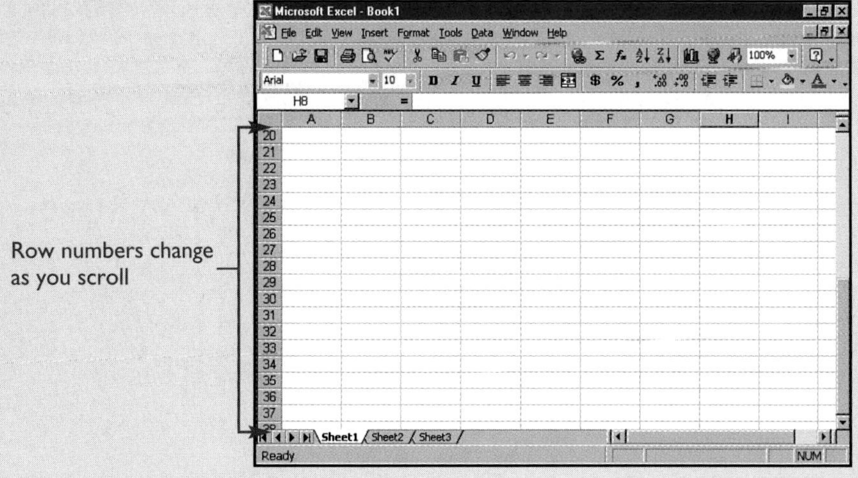

Figure 1.3
You can scroll the worksheet to see other rows.

continues ▶

To Navigate a Workbook (continued)

6. **Click the right arrow on the horizontal scrollbar.**
Column A scrolls off the screen, and the next column to the right displays. The horizontal scrollbar is the bar at the bottom of the screen that enables you to move the worksheet left and right on the screen.

7. **Click the left arrow on the horizontal scrollbar.**
The view scrolls to the left, and column A displays again.

8. **Leave the worksheet open for use in the next lesson.**

Changing Display and Zoom Settings

The number of columns and rows shown on a screen depend on the ***display settings*** and the ***zoom***. The display settings are the default choices that determine such things as how many rows and columns show on the screen. You can change them by clicking the Start button and choosing Settings. It is not proper etiquette to change them if you do not have the permission of the computer's owner. Zoom is the magnification setting that can be used to increase or decrease the size of the active document. You can use the Zoom control on the Standard toolbar to change the zoom setting for the displayed worksheet. If your screen displays more rows and columns than the illustrations in this book, do not be concerned.

When you use the scrollbars to move around in a worksheet, you can also click and drag the small box on the scrollbar. The box on the scrollbar indicates the relative size of the data that displays compared to the size of the whole amount contained on the worksheet. It also shows the relative position of the displayed information compared to the entire worksheet. This works like it does with Word or any other Windows application.

Lesson 2: Selecting Individual Cells

You must ***select*** a cell before you can enter text, numbers, or formulas. When you click a cell, it is selected and outlined with a dark border. When it is selected, it is ready for you to edit by entering or changing the data in the cell.

In this lesson, you move the selection from one cell to another on a worksheet.

To Select Individual Cells

1. **Use the mouse to move the pointer to the cell that is in column B and row 2.**
This cell is referred to as cell B2, which is known as the cell address. The mouse pointer is in the shape of a wide, white plus sign. Notice that the cell selection does not move with the pointer. The Name box, located at the left end of the Formula bar, identifies the selected cell, chart item, or drawing object. In Figure 1.4, cell A1 is selected and displays in the Name box.

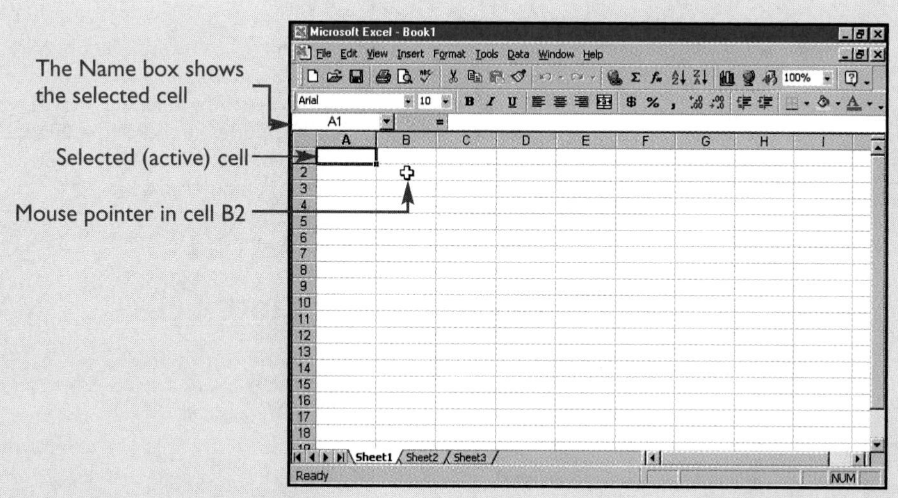

Figure 1.4
Just moving the mouse pointer does not select a cell.

If you start typing without clicking the cell to select it, your text or number is placed in the cell that is currently selected.

2. **Click the cell.**
   Cell B2 is selected and is referred to as the ***active cell***. Notice that the border of cell B2 changes to a darker line; the column heading and row heading become bold, and the address of the cell (B2) shows in the Name box. The column headings are the letters at the top of each column. The row headings are the numbers at the left of each row.
3. **Press ↑ on your keyboard once.**
   Notice that the selection moves to cell B1. You can use the arrow keys on the keyboard to move around cells.
4. **Press Tab three times.**
   The selection moves one cell to the right each time you press this key. Cell E1 is now selected.
5. **Press ↵Enter.**
   The selection drops to the next row and returns to B2, the cell below B1.
6. **Leave the worksheet open for the next lesson.**

Navigating a Worksheet with the Keyboard

You can use the arrow keys on your keyboard to move from one cell to the next. Table 1.1 is a list of keys that you can use to move around in a worksheet.

Table 1.1 Key Combinations Used to Navigate a Worksheet

Keys	Results
Tab or →	Active cell moves to the right
⇧Shift+Tab or ←	Active cell moves to the left
↓	Active cell moves down
↑	Active cell moves up
Ctrl+Home	Cell A1 becomes active, and the window moves if needed
Ctrl+End	Cell in the lower-right corner of the active worksheet becomes active, and the window moves if needed
PgUp	Active cell moves up one screen
PgDn	Active cell moves down one screen
Alt+PgDn	Active cell moves one screen to the right
Alt+PgUp	Active cell moves one screen to the left

Changing Direction with ↵Enter and Tab

If you use Tab to move the selection to the right and ↵Enter to return, the program drops down a row and returns to the original column. This method makes it easier to enter multiple rows of data. You can change the direction that the selection moves when you press ↵Enter. To change the setting, choose Tools, Options, and click the Edit tab. In the Move selection after Enter box, change the direction to the one you prefer. Do not make this type of change on another's computer or on a computer in a lab.

Lesson 3: Entering Text and Numbers into Cells

You can enter three types of data into a cell: text, a value, or a calculation. You enter text into cells to provide labels and other information for users of the sheet. Numbers are values that you enter to represent dollars, quantities, or dates. Values are used in calculations and formulas. A cell can contain text or numbers, but generally not both. After the numbers have been entered into the cells, you can manipulate the numbers, perform calculations, and use the numbers to visually portray a trend by creating a chart.

In this lesson, you enter text and numbers into cells.

To Enter Text and Numbers into Cells

1. **Move the pointer to cell A1, and click to select the cell.**
   A dark border appears around the cell to indicate that it is selected.
2. **Type the word `Stock`, and press ↵Enter.**
   A label is entered in cell A1, and the insertion point moves to cell A2.
3. **Select cell A3.**
   Cell A3 is in the upper-left corner of the table of data. It is blank.
4. **Press Tab.**
   This moves the selection to cell B3. (If you accidentally pressed the wrong key, click cell A3 and start over.) Now you enter labels for the columns of data.
5. **Type `Desks`, and press Tab.**
   The text is entered, and the selection moves to cell C3.
6. **Type `Tables`, and press Tab.**
   Repeat this process to enter `Chairs` and `Lamps` in cells D3 and E3.
7. **Type `Files` in F3, but press ↵Enter instead of Tab.**
   The selection automatically returns to cell A4 to start the next row. When you are done, your worksheet should look like the one in Figure 1.5.

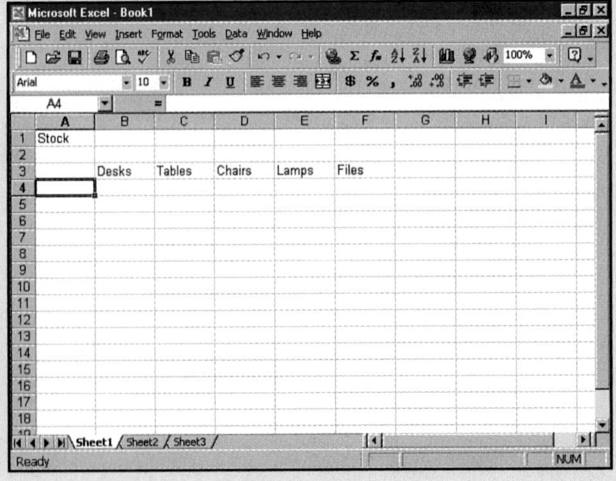

Figure 1.5
Labels are entered for the columns of the worksheet.

8 Type `Miami` in cell A4, and press Tab.

The label for the first row is entered. Now you fill in the rest of the data.

9 Enter the rest of the data for the table, as follows (see Figure 1.6).

If you make mistakes entering the text or the numbers, leave them for now. You learn how to fix mistakes in the next lesson.

	Desks	Tables	Chairs	Lamps	Files
Miami	150	75	275	200	100
Chicago	85	23	97	50	200
Dallas	25	200	400	40	25
Seattle	35	15	35	25	15
Portland	25	55	64	85	74

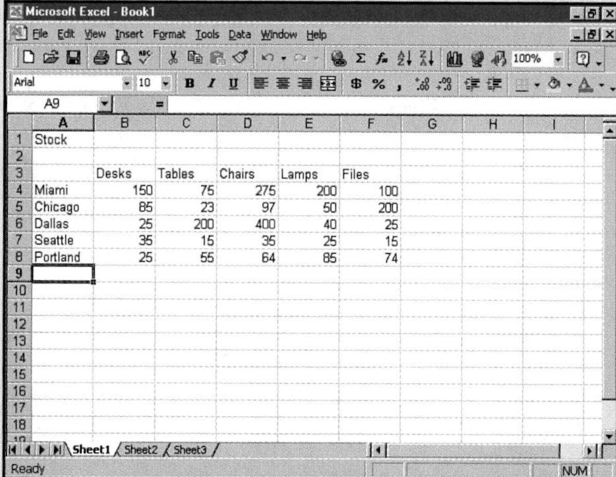

Figure 1.6
The data is entered in the worksheet.

10 Select cell F1, and type your last name. Press Enter.

If your name is too long to fit in the cell, enter it anyway. You learn how to deal with this in the next project.

Lesson 4: Editing the Contents of a Cell

Using an electronic spreadsheet enables you to change information easily and have formulas recalculated. It is possible to make mistakes when you enter data. Also, information can change and may need to be adjusted. You can change information directly in the cell, or you can use the Formula bar to edit a cell.

In this lesson, you fix simple typing errors and edit the contents of the cells.

To Fix Errors and Edit the Contents of a Cell

1 Select cell A9, and type `Totle` in the cell. Do not press Enter or Tab yet.

Notice that a vertical line marks the position where text is entered. This line is called the insertion point.

2 Press Backspace twice.

The insertion point moves to the left, erasing the last two letters.

continues ▶

To Fix Errors and Edit the Contents of a Cell (continued)

3. **Type al, and press Tab.**
The error is corrected and the word Total appears in the cell.

4. **To replace an entire entry, you type over it. Select cell A1; type Furniture, and press Enter.**
The word Furniture replaces the word Stock.

5. **If you change your mind and want to undo your action, you can click the Undo button on the Standard toolbar.**
The previous word, Stock, returns.

6. **Click the Redo button to change the cell back to Furniture.**
The Redo button reverses the previous undo action and returns the word Furniture to the cell, as shown in Figure 1.7.

Figure 1.7
The Undo button reverses a change to a cell, and the Redo button reverses the previous undo action.

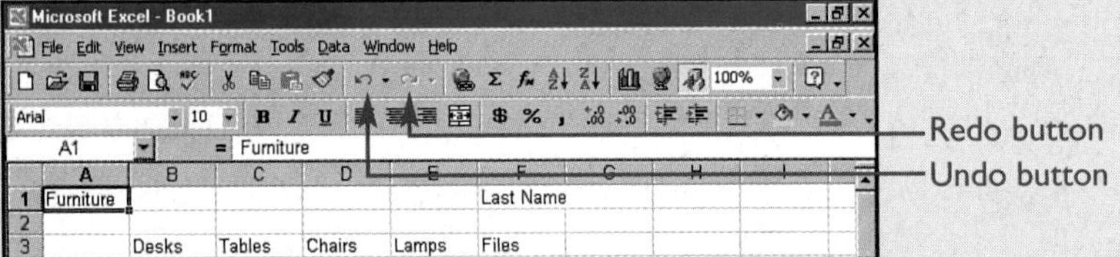

If you have not expanded your toolbars, you might not see the Redo button. If your toolbars are still truncated, you can access the Redo button by clicking the More Buttons button.

7. **You can also edit the contents of a cell. Move the pointer to cell F1. Double-click to place the insertion point in the text within the cell.**
Double-clicking places the insertion point in a cell, so that you can edit it.

You might have trouble double-clicking. Rolling the mouse slightly between clicks is the most common problem. Rest the heel of your hand on the table so the mouse is less likely to roll. It may take a little practice. If this is frustrating you, click the cell once and the contents appear in the ***Formula bar***, the bar near the top of the window that displays the address of the active cell and any data in the cell. Click the text in the Formula bar and edit it there.

8. **Use the left arrow on the keyboard to position the insertion point to the left of your last name and type in your first name. Press Enter.**

9. **Leave the file open for use in the next lesson.**

Using Backspace and Del

You can move the insertion point within the text by using the right and left arrow keys on the keyboard. You can then delete letters by using Backspace or Del. Backspace deletes letters to the left of the insertion point, and Del deletes letters to the right of the insertion point.

Lesson 5: Inserting and Deleting Rows or Columns

If your worksheet lists items in a particular order, it would not be satisfactory to add a new item at the bottom of the list if it did not belong there. Similarly, if you delete information in a row or column, it would not look right to leave the row or column empty. Excel can insert or delete rows or columns in a worksheet and automatically move the rest of the data. It also revises any formulas that are affected by the change. This feature enables you to expand a worksheet by inserting columns or rows of information in a logical order. Likewise, you can remove information that is no longer relevant to the worksheet. You insert rows and columns using the Insert menu option, but you delete them using the Edit menu option.

In this lesson, you delete and add a row, and then add a column in your worksheet.

To Insert or Delete Rows or Columns

1 Click the row heading for row 5 to select the entire row.
The row is highlighted and outlined to indicate that it is selected (see Figure 1.8).

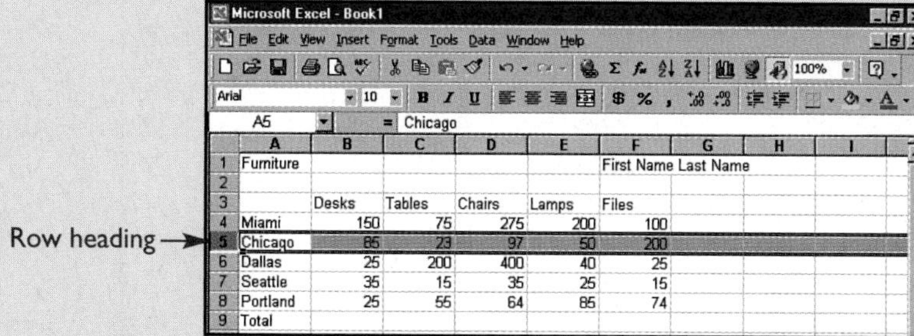

Figure 1.8
To delete a row or column, first select the one you want to delete.

2 Choose Edit, Delete.
The entry for `Chicago` disappears, and the entry for `Dallas` moves up to row 5.

3 Select any cell in row 7; choose Insert, Rows.
All rows from row 7 on are moved down one row, as shown in Figure 1.9.

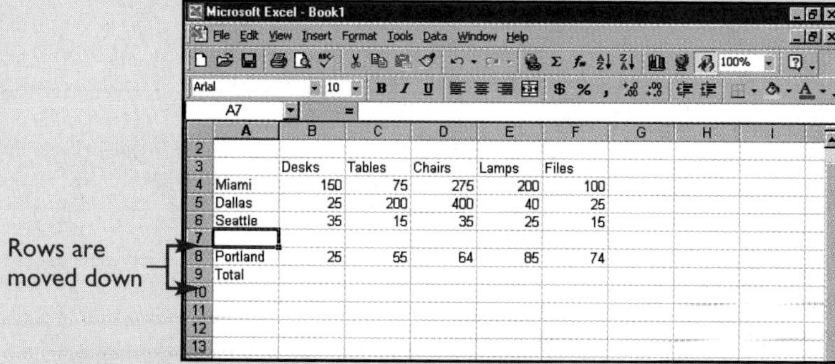

Figure 1.9
To insert a row, select any cell in a row where you want to add a new row.

4 Enter the following information in the new, empty row:
`Boston 36 40 135 115 50`
Next, you add a new column.

5 Select any cell in column D; choose Insert, Columns.
All columns from column D on move to the right, as shown in Figure 1.10.

continues ▶

To Insert or Delete Rows or Columns (continued)

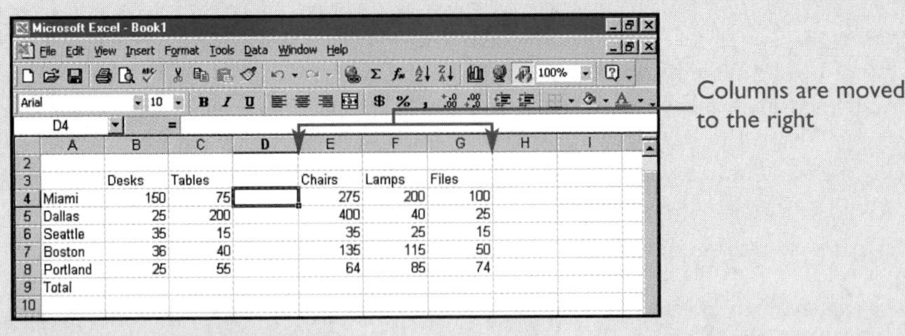

	A	B	C	D	E	F	G
3		Desks	Tables		Chairs	Lamps	Files
4	Miami	150	75		275	200	100
5	Dallas	25	200		400	40	25
6	Seattle	35	15		35	25	15
7	Boston	36	40		135	115	50
8	Portland	25	55		64	85	74
9	Total						

Figure 1.10
To insert a column, select any cell in the place where you want to add the new column.

6 Add the following information in the new empty column:

`Credenzas 24 50 12 25 40`

When you are done, your worksheet should look like the one in Figure 1.11. Leave the file open for use in the next lesson.

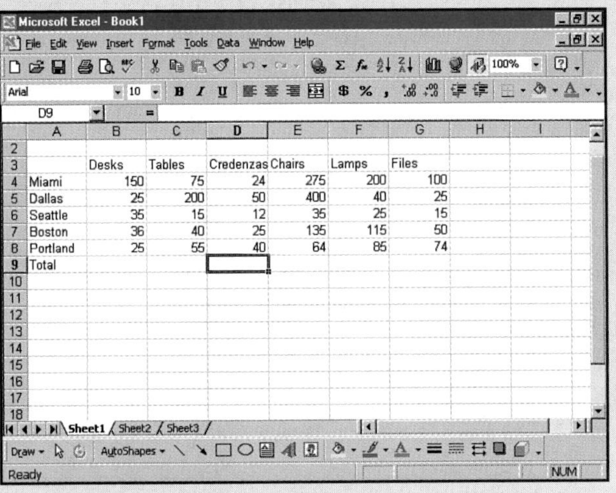

	A	B	C	D	E	F	G
3		Desks	Tables	Credenzas	Chairs	Lamps	Files
4	Miami	150	75	24	275	200	100
5	Dallas	25	200	50	400	40	25
6	Seattle	35	15	12	35	25	15
7	Boston	36	40	25	135	115	50
8	Portland	25	55	40	64	85	74
9	Total						

Figure 1.11
The new column of data has been included.

Deleting a Row

It would seem that you should be able to delete a row by highlighting it and pressing Del. This removes the contents of the cells, but does not delete the row.

Inserting Rows and Columns

To insert more than one row at a time, select more than one cell in a column and choose Insert, Rows. The number of new rows equals the number of cells selected. To insert more than one column at a time, select more than one cell horizontally and choose Insert, Columns.

Lesson 6: Summing a Column of Numbers

The purpose of most worksheets is to make ***calculations*** based on the data you enter. Simply stated, a calculation is any mathematical operation involving data in the worksheet cells. The simplest and most commonly used calculation is the sum calculation. It is used so often, in fact, that Excel has a built-in AutoSum button. You can use this button with a single column or row.

In this lesson, you sum columns of numbers using AutoSum.

To Sum Columns of Numbers

1 Select cell B9.

2 Click the AutoSum button located on the Standard toolbar.

Several things happen. The program guesses the cells you want to sum and a formula, `=SUM(B4:B8)`, displays in cell B9 and in the Formula bar. Also, a moving dashed line called a ***marquee*** surrounds the group of cells you want to sum (see Figure 1.12).

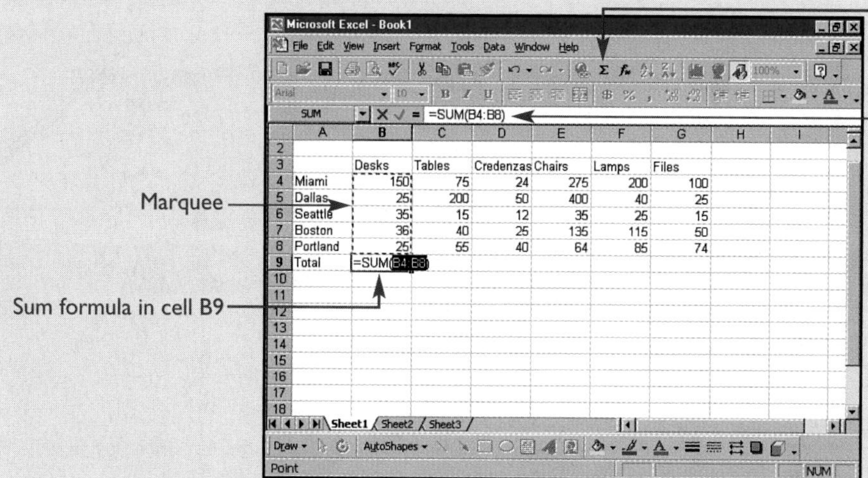

	A	B	C	D	E	F	G
3		Desks	Tables	Credenzas	Chairs	Lamps	Files
4	Miami	150	75	24	275	200	100
5	Dallas	25	200	50	400	40	25
6	Seattle	35	15	12	35	25	15
7	Boston	36	40	25	135	115	50
8	Portland	25	55	40	64	85	74
9	Total	=SUM(B4:B8)					

Figure 1.12
The AutoSum button sums columns or rows of numbers.

3 Press Tab to activate the formula.

The sum for the total number of desks on-hand in the various locations is added to the worksheet. The insertion point moves to cell C9.

4 Repeat this process for each of the remaining columns.

Each column is totaled, and the worksheet looks like the one in Figure 1.13.

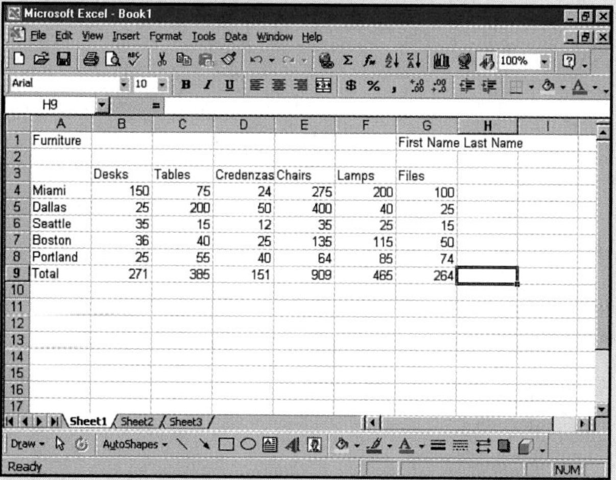

	A	B	C	D	E	F	G	H
1	Furniture						First Name	Last Name
3		Desks	Tables	Credenzas	Chairs	Lamps	Files	
4	Miami	150	75	24	275	200	100	
5	Dallas	25	200	50	400	40	25	
6	Seattle	35	15	12	35	25	15	
7	Boston	36	40	25	135	115	50	
8	Portland	25	55	40	64	85	74	
9	Total	271	385	151	909	465	264	

Figure 1.13
The columns are totaled.

Editing the Formula

Excel guesses which group of numbers you want to sum. If the correct group is not selected, you can edit the formula just as you edit text. In the formula in step 2, B4:B8 refers to all the cells in a rectangle that starts with B4 and ends with B8. If you wanted to add a different range of cells, you would edit the formula and put in different cell addresses.

Lesson 7: Saving a Workbook, Printing the Worksheet, and Exiting Excel

A computer has a short-term memory that forgets when the power is turned off or interrupted. To record your worksheet for later use, you need to make a more permanent copy of it. One way to do this is to save a copy magnetically on a disk.

Even in an age of digital communications, there are still advantages to recording data on paper. A paper copy is lightweight, portable, and compatible with older storage systems. It is often easier to scan several pages of data simultaneously and share the information with others who do not have a computer. Or you may need a paper copy to fax information to someone at another location.

Finally, you need to properly close and exit the program. The program creates temporary files on your computer's hard disk that are used to protect your work in case of unexpected power failure and loss of memory. If you simply turn off the power to the computer, these temporary files are not erased and can cause a problem the next time the computer is turned on.

In this lesson, you print a worksheet, save the workbook on disk, close the file, and exit Excel.

To Save a Workbook on Disk, Print the Worksheet, and Exit Excel

1 Click the Save button on the Standard toolbar.

The Save As dialog box opens and displays a suggested filename, highlighted in the File name box.

2 Type `Basic Skills`; it replaces the highlighted text in the File name box. Do not press Enter yet.

Next, you select the floppy drive as the location for saving this file.

A dialog box has buttons in it that you can click to produce certain actions. Often, one of the buttons is indicated as the default choice; its border appears darker and thicker. In this case, the Save button is the default. If you press Enter after typing in the name of the file, Excel saves the file in whatever folder or disk is currently selected. If you do this by mistake, click File and Save As to open the Save As dialog box and select the folder where you want to save the file.

3 Click the down arrow at the right side of the Save in box.

A diagram of your computer's disk drives appears.

4 Click the 3 1/2 Floppy (A:) drive.

This saves the file to a floppy disk in drive A: (see Figure 1.14). If your class is using another disk drive, follow your instructor's directions.

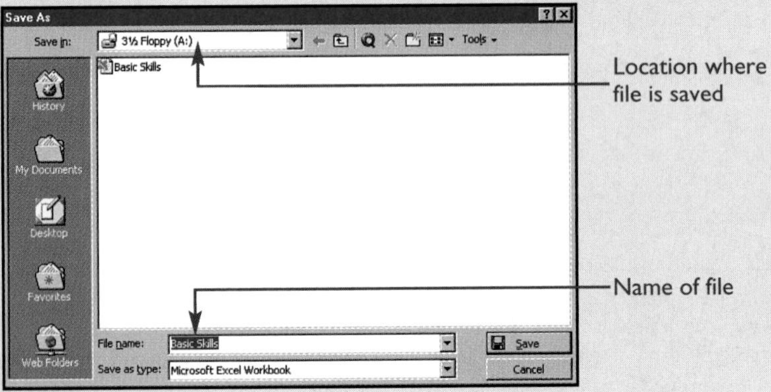

Figure 1.14
The file is saved on a floppy disk.

5 Click Save.
A copy of the workbook is saved on your floppy disk. Next, you print your file.

6 Check to make sure that your printer is connected and turned on; click the Print button on the Standard toolbar.
The current worksheet goes to the printer.

7 Click the Close Window button on the menu bar.
The file closes. If Excel asks you to save changes again, choose Yes.

8 Click the Close (X) button on the title bar to close Excel.
Excel closes, and the desktop returns to your screen.

File Extensions
When you install a program, Windows records this fact. Most Windows programs, sometimes called registered programs, use unique extensions to identify the files that they create. The conventions of this book assume that the file extensions for registered programs are hidden. If this is not the case in your computer setup, you see an .xls extension added to your Excel filenames. You can turn file extensions on or off in the Windows Explorer under View, Options.

Summary

In this project, you learned to move around in Excel by selecting different sheets in a workbook, using the scrollbars to move around on a worksheet, and selecting individual cells in a worksheet. You created a basic worksheet by entering data into cells and editing cells. You learned to insert and delete rows and columns. You learned how to use the AutoSum function in Excel. Finally, you learned to save a workbook, print a worksheet, close the file, and exit Excel.

You can extend your knowledge by using Help and reviewing the following topics: `Enter data in worksheet cells`; `Insert cells, rows, or columns`; and `Quick calculations on a worksheet`.

Checking Concepts and Terms

True/False

For each of the following, check *T* or *F* to indicate whether the statement is true or false.

__T__F **1.** The scrollbar at the right of the screen is the vertical scrollbar. [L1]

__T__F **2.** Workbook and worksheet are the same thing. The words may be used interchangeably. [L1]

__T__F **3.** The cells that are visible on the screen when you first open Excel are the only ones available. [L1]

__T__F **4.** The vertical scrollbar and its arrows can be used to rapidly scroll through the sheet or scroll one row at a time. [L1]

__T__F **5.** A cell that was in column C and row 2 would be referred to as cell 2C. [L2]

__T__F **6.** The active cell has a darker border than the other cells. [L2]

__T__F **7.** When you press Enter, the selection always moves to the cell below it. This is a basic feature of Excel that cannot be changed. [L2]

__T__F **8.** Text and numbers should be placed in the same cell together to save space. [L3]

__T__F **9.** Clicking the AutoSum button places a formula in the currently selected cell that automatically adds up the nearest row or column of numbers. [L6]

__T__F **10.** Pressing Del deletes the character to the right of the insertion point. [L4]

Multiple Choice

Circle the letter of the correct answer for each of the following.

1. To move from one cell to the next across the worksheet, press ______________. [L1]

a. ↓

b. ↵Enter

c. Tab

d. any of the above

2. You can edit a cell by ______________. [L4]

a. double-clicking the cell and changing the contents in the cell

b. clicking the cell and then making the changes in the Formula bar

c. using the arrow keys to move to the cell and then using the Formula bar to edit the contents

d. all of the above

3. To insert a row in a worksheet, click in a cell in the row where you want to insert a new row and ______________. [L5]

a. choose Insert, Row

b. choose Edit, Row

c. click the Insert Row button on the Standard toolbar

d. press Ctrl+Insert

4. When you use the AutoSum button, you know which cells will be added because ______________. [L6]

a. the formula showing the cell addresses displays in the active cell

b. the formula showing the cell addresses displays in the Formula bar

c. a marquee outlines the cells that are included in the sum

d. all of the above

5. To delete a column on a worksheet, ______________. [L5]

a. click in a cell in the column and press Del

b. click the column heading and choose Edit, Delete from the menu

c. click the column heading and press Del

d. any of the above

Screen ID

Refer to Figure 1.15 and identify the numbered parts of the screen. Write the letter of the correct label in the space next to the number.

Figure 1.15

A. Tabs to identify sheets

B. Column heading

C. Row heading

D. Vertical scrollbar

E. Horizontal scrollbar

F. Save button

G. Print button

H. Active cell

I. Close Window button

J. AutoSum button

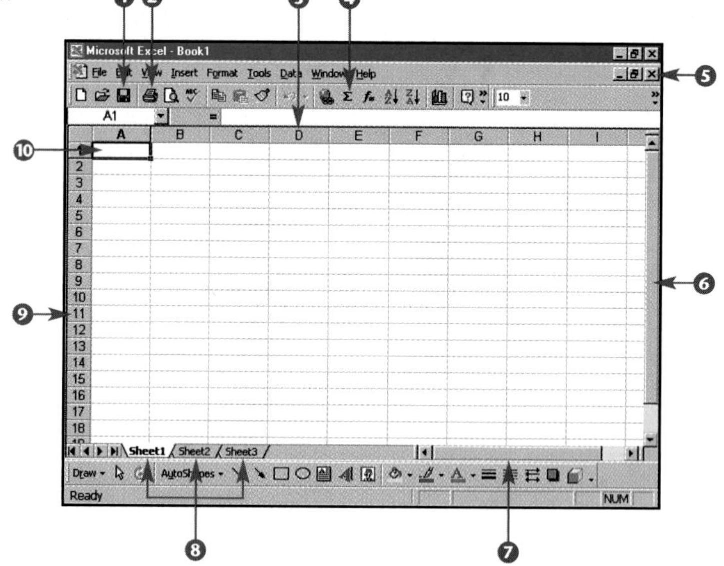

1. ______________

2. ______________

3. ______________

4. ______________

5. ______________

6. ______________

7. ______________

8. ______________

9. ______________

10. ______________

Discussion Questions

1. When have you needed to add a column of numbers? What kind of information was it? What method did you use? (For example, calculator, paper and pencil, in your head, adding machine, and so on.)
2. What types of job functions would require adding columns of numbers or keeping track of financial information?
3. If you were to itemize your deductions for income tax purposes, what kinds of deductions would you need to record? How could you use a worksheet to accomplish that goal?
4. Assume you are a sales representative for a company and your boss requires a detailed accounting of your expenses each month by category. What kinds of expenses would you need to record? How could a worksheet help you track your expenses? What layout would you use to record the expenses using a worksheet?

Skill Drill

Skill Drill exercises reinforce project skills. Each skill reinforced is the same, or nearly the same, as a skill presented in the project. Detailed instructions are provided in a step-by-step format.

In this set of Skill Drill exercises, you create a worksheet to record utility expenses for store locations for January and February. You use multiple sheets and print each with your name. Leave the file open from one Skill Drill to the next until you have completed all five exercises.

1. Creating a Worksheet to Show Income for January

In the first Skill Drill exercise, you create a simple worksheet and enter the utility expenses for January for a company that has a store with four locations. You total the utilities by category and print the worksheet. To create the worksheet follow these steps: [L1–7]

1. Launch Excel, and display Sheet1 in a new, blank workbook.
2. Type `January` in cell A1.
3. Enter the following column headings in cells B3 through E3:

```
Gas    Water    Electric    Phone
```

4. Type the following data in the table beginning in cell A4:

```
East Side    200    55    550    120
West Side    100    35    450     67
Downtown     384   120    980    520
North Side   200    85    350    250
Total
```

5. Use the AutoSum button to add up the columns and place the sum in the total cell for each column.
6. Enter your name in Cell F1.
7. Save the workbook on your disk. Name it `Utilities`. (Do not include the period at the end of the previous sentence in the name of the file.)
8. Print Sheet1.
9. Leave the workbook open for use in the next exercise.

2. Using Another Sheet

In this exercise, you use Sheet2 to record the utilities for this company for the month of February. To use a second sheet, follow these steps: [L3, 6]

1. Click the Sheet2 tab to select the second sheet of the Utilities workbook.
2. Enter the text and numbers as shown in Figure 1.16. Use the AutoSum button to calculate the sum of the column of numbers.

Figure 1.16

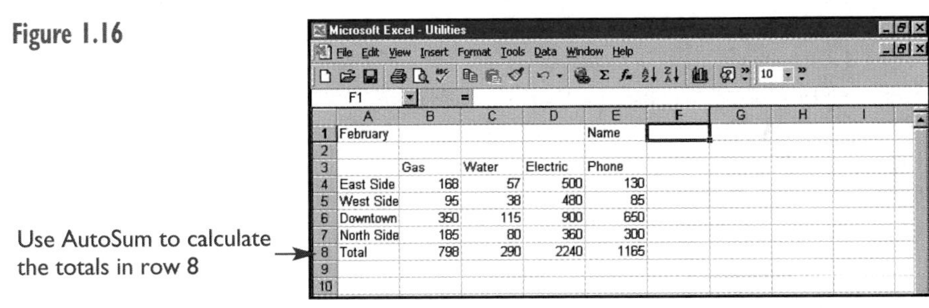

	A	B	C	D	E	F
1	February				Name	
2						
3		Gas	Water	Electric	Phone	
4	East Side	168	57	500	130	
5	West Side	95	38	480	85	
6	Downtown	350	115	900	650	
7	North Side	185	80	360	300	
8	Total	798	290	2240	1165	
9						
10						

3. Place your name in cell E1.
4. Click the Save button on the Standard toolbar to save your changes. (You do not need to give it a name again. Saving automatically updates the existing file on your disk.)
5. Click the Print button to print this sheet.
6. Leave the workbook open for use in the next exercise.

3. Editing a Worksheet

You have just learned that one of the figures entered for January was incorrect. You need to return to the first worksheet and correct the gas bill for the East Side Store. [L4, 7]

To edit the worksheet, follow these steps:

1. Click the Sheet1 tab to select Sheet1.
2. Edit cell B4 to read **240**. (If you have used the AutoSum button correctly, the sum of the January gas bills in column B is automatically updated to **924**.)
3. Click the Save button to save the change.
4. Print Sheet1.
5. Leave the workbook open for use in the next exercise.

4. Inserting a Column and a Row into a Worksheet

The company has recently been connected to a local cable provider for an Internet connection. The service began in February. You need to return to Sheet2 and insert a new column for the cable expenses. The company also opened a new store this month, and it needs to be entered on the February worksheet. To insert categories of information, follow these steps: [L5, 6]

1. Click the Sheet2 tab to select Sheet2.
2. Insert a column between Electric and Phone.
3. Starting in cell E3, in the new blank column between Electric and Phone, add the following data about cable expenses:

   `Cable 67 145 290 94`

4. Use AutoSum to sum the column.
5. Insert a new row above the Total line, and enter the following information for a new store.

   `South Side 142 0 285 0 176`

6. Do not click the Save button at this time.
7. Print the sheet.
8. Leave the workbook open for use in the next exercise.

5. Closing and Exiting Excel

In this last Skill Drill exercise, you close your file and exit the program. Because you did not save the changes made in the last exercise, the program asks you whether you want to save your changes. [L7]

To close and exit Excel, follow these steps:

1. Click the Close button for the Excel program.
2. Confirm that you want to save the most recent changes to the workbook. (If you have forgotten to save your work, the program always asks before it closes.)

Challenge

Challenge exercises expand on or are somewhat related to skills presented in the lessons. Each exercise provides a brief narrative introduction followed by instructions, in a numbered step or bulleted list format, that are not as detailed as those in the Skill Drill section.

1. Creating a Monthly Income and Expense Sheet

Sometimes it is not obvious where your money is going. You can use Excel to take a look at the amount of money coming in and compare it to your expenses. Because many expenses occur on a monthly basis, it is useful to compare them to monthly income. [L1–7]

In this exercise, you create a worksheet (see Figure 1.17) to compare your income and expenses, use the AutoSum feature to add the incomes and expenses, and print the worksheet.

Figure 1.17

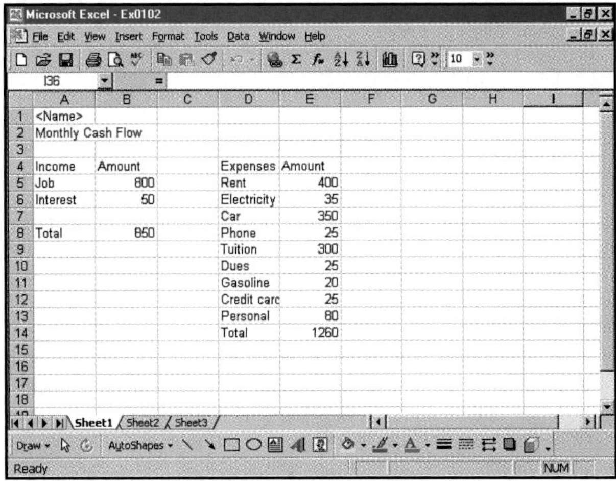

Microsoft Excel - Ex0102

I36 =

	A	B	C	D	E
1	<Name>				
2	Monthly Cash Flow				
3					
4	Income	Amount		Expenses	Amount
5	Job	800		Rent	400
6	Interest	50		Electricity	35
7				Car	350
8	Total	850		Phone	25
9				Tuition	300
10				Dues	25
11				Gasoline	20
12				Credit carc	25
13				Personal	80
14				Total	1260

Follow these steps to complete the worksheet:

1. Click the New button on the Standard toolbar to open a new workbook. Place your name in cell A1.
2. Refer to the figure, and set up two columns to list the type and amount of monthly income you have and two more columns to list the type and amount of monthly expenses. (It is not necessary to use your actual data—you can make up these numbers.) Fill in all four columns with types and amounts of income and expenses. Use your own numbers. Change the types of incomes or expenses as needed to match your incomes and expenses.
3. Use AutoSum to sum the amount of income in the cell at the bottom of the column of income amounts and the amount of expenses at the bottom of the column of expenses.
4. Save the workbook on your disk as `Expenses`.
5. Print the worksheet. Leave the workbook open for use in the next exercise.

2. Finding the Present Balance of a Checkbook

If the total income exceeds or matches the total expenses for a month, you might still run out of money in your checking account depending on when you make the deposits and when you write the checks. [L6]

In this exercise, you create a worksheet that resembles a check register (see Figure 1.18). Enter the deposits as positive numbers and check amounts as negative numbers. Sum the starting balance, deposits, and check amounts using the AutoSum feature.

Figure 1.18

Microsoft Excel - Ex0102

C14 = =SUM(C3:C13)

	A	B	C
1	<Student Name>		
2			
3	Date	CH/DEP	300
4	2/1/99	101	-27.5
5	2/5/99	Deposit	100
6	2/6/99	102	-53.45
7	2/9/99	103	-42.6
8	2/12/99	104	-200.34
9	2/15/99	Deposit	300
10	2/17/99	105	-34.59
11	2/19/99	106	-193.23
12	2/21/99	107	-82.19
13	27-Feb	108	-14.29
14		Balance	51.81

1. Select Sheet2. Set up a three-column system for calculating a checkbook balance, as shown in Figure 1.18.

2. Enter a starting balance, deposit, and check amounts. The starting balance and the deposits should be positive numbers, and the checks should be negative numbers (Most keyboards have two negative signs: one at the upper-right corner of the number keypad, and the other two keys to the left of ←Backspace.)
3. Use the AutoSum feature to display the balance at the bottom of the column.
4. Look at the starting balance, the deposits, and the check amounts. Estimate what the balance should be to within ten dollars. Does the final balance agree with your estimate? If so, it is probably right. Always do a quick check of your worksheet to make sure that it makes sense.
5. Save the workbook. Print Sheet2.

3. Inserting Multiple Rows or Columns

Sometimes you need to add multiple rows or columns at one time to your worksheets. You can do this by selecting several cells, either horizontally to add multiple columns, or vertically to add multiple rows. [L5]

In this exercise, you add two columns, to the checkbook register: One to record the payees for the check and one to record the date the check was paid. You also add three rows to record transactions you forgot, such as ATM withdrawals.

To add multiple rows and columns, follow these steps:

1. In Sheet2 of the Expenses workbook, click and drag across cells C2 and D2 to select them.
2. Choose Insert, Columns from the menu.
3. Enter **Payee** in cell C3 and **Date Paid** in Cell D3.
4. Enter the names of the payees or the purpose of each check, and the date the check was paid. (Do not worry if the names in the payee column appear to be cut off. What you entered shows in the Formula bar. You learn how to adjust column widths in Project 2, "Enhancing the Appearance of the Worksheet.")
5. Click and drag from cell A14 to A16 to select cells in rows 14 to 16.
6. Chose Insert, Rows from the menu. Three rows are inserted above the word Balance.
7. Record three more transactions in your register.
8. Save the file. Print Sheet2, and close and exit Excel.

Discovery Zone

Discovery Zone exercises require advanced knowledge of topics presented in *Essentials* lessons, application of skills from multiple lessons, or self-directed learning of new skills.

In these Discovery Zone exercises, you use Help to learn more about entering text and numbers in a worksheet. You learn how to enter the same data in multiple worksheets and apply what you have read by entering information into multiple worksheets. In exercise 3, you learn another technique for adding and deleting columns and rows. Finally, you learn how to hide or unhide columns or rows. Exercises 2–4 should be done in sequence, and you should leave the file you create in exercise 2 open until you have completed exercises 3 and 4.

1. Using Help to Learn More About Entering Text and Numbers in a Worksheet

It is helpful to know how Excel treats numbers, letters, and other characters that you enter into a worksheet. In this exercise, you use Help to learn how the program treats data that is entered. When you are finished, you should understand what cues Excel uses to determine whether something should be treated as a number, text, date, or time, as well as how different kinds of data are aligned in a cell.

Launch Excel and search on the topic **data entry**. Select the topic **Enter data in worksheet cells**; select the topic **Enter numbers, text, a date, or a time**. Read the contents, and go to each of the three additional information pages about entering numbers, entering text, and entering a date or time. Print the pages that provide detailed information about entering numbers, text, and date or time.

2. Entering Information on Multiple Sheets

In this project, you learned how to move from one sheet to the next and enter data in separate worksheets. Sometimes you need to enter the same basic layout, or column and row headings, for multiple worksheets, but the detail information will be different for each sheet. For instance, you might need to create an expense sheet for each store in a company. Each store has the same expense categories, but the amounts will be different. In this exercise, you use Help to learn how to enter the same data on multiple sheets; then you apply what you have learned by creating a worksheet that uses this technique.

Open the Office Assistant and type **Enter the same data on multiple worksheets**. Go to this topic and read the information. Click the word **How?** that is in blue. This is a hyperlink to another topic that tells you how to select multiple sheets in a workbook. If necessary, print the topic, or leave it on your screen while you enter data on multiple worksheets.

Use what you have learned to select Sheet1 and Sheet2 in a new, blank workbook, and enter the data, as shown in Figure 1.19. Use the Help information and deselect both sheets; look at Sheet2 to verify that the data is entered on that sheet as well as on Sheet1. Save the file as **Expenses2**. Add your name to cell A14. Leave the file open if you are completing the next Discovery Zone exercise; otherwise, print the worksheet and close the file.

Figure 1.19

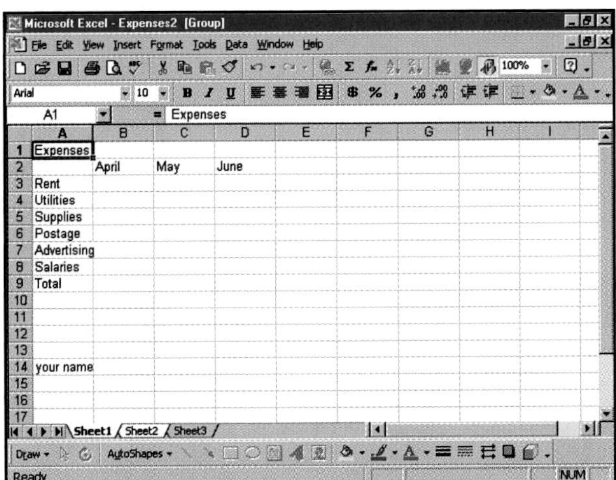

3. Using the Keyboard to Add or Delete Rows and Columns

In this project, you used the Insert menu to add rows and columns and the Edit menu to delete rows and columns. You can use a keyboard combination to add and delete rows and columns, and it enables you to add or delete as many as you need.

If necessary, open the worksheet that you created in the previous Discovery Zone exercise. Select Sheet1. Hold down the Shift key and click Sheet2 to select both sheets so your changes are made on both sheets. Click the B column heading to select the entire column. Hold down Ctrl and press +. Each time you press +, a new column is inserted. Press +, three more times. Four columns are added. (*Hint*: If you use the + on the alpha-numeric keyboard, remember to also use Shift.) Now hold down Ctrl and press -. One of the columns is deleted. Type **January**, **February**, **March** as the headings for the three new columns. This same technique works for rows. Try inserting and deleting rows using this method. Verify that the changes were made to both Sheet1 and Sheet2. Save the workbook.

4. Hiding and Unhiding Columns

Sometimes you want to display only certain columns. For example, in the Expenses2 worksheet you just created, you might want to view only the first quarter or the second quarter information. Sometimes your worksheet has numerous columns, and it is difficult to manage the display and printouts. In these situations, it is often useful to hide certain columns, so you view only the data you want or so printouts display only the columns you need. In this exercise, you learn how to hide and unhide columns.

If necessary, open the Expenses2 worksheet used in the previous exercise. First select Sheet1; click and drag across the column headings for columns B, C, and D. Choose Format, Column, Hide on the menu. The three columns you selected are hidden. Notice that the letters for the columns go from A to E, and a dark line appears between columns A and E. This is how you can tell that columns are hidden. To unhide the columns, you must first select the columns on either side of the ones that are hidden; in this case, columns A and E. Choose Format, Column, Unhide, and the hidden columns are restored. If you print a worksheet while columns are hidden, the hidden columns do not print. Save your workbook; close the file, and exit Excel.

Project 2

Enhancing the Appearance of the Worksheet

Objectives

In this project, you learn how to

- **Open a File and Select a Group of Cells**
- **Format Large Numbers, Currency, Decimal Places, and Dates**
- **Adjust Columns and Cells for Long Text or Numbers**
- **Align Text in the Cell**
- **Change the Font, Size, Emphasis, and Color of Text**
- **Add Lines, Borders, and Shading**
- **Rename a Worksheet**

Key terms introduced in this project include

- Arial
- font size
- Times New Roman

SOURCE: *Essentials: Office 2000,* Ferrett-Preston-Preston

Why Would I Do This?

You can use a variety of formatting techniques to improve the appearance of a worksheet. Formatting your worksheet can also make it easier to read and understand. This is especially important for worksheets that others will use.

In this project, you learn how to work with existing worksheets to improve their appearance, make them easier to read, and give them a professional look. When you have completed the project, you will have created a worksheet that looks like the one in Figure 2.1.

Visual Summary

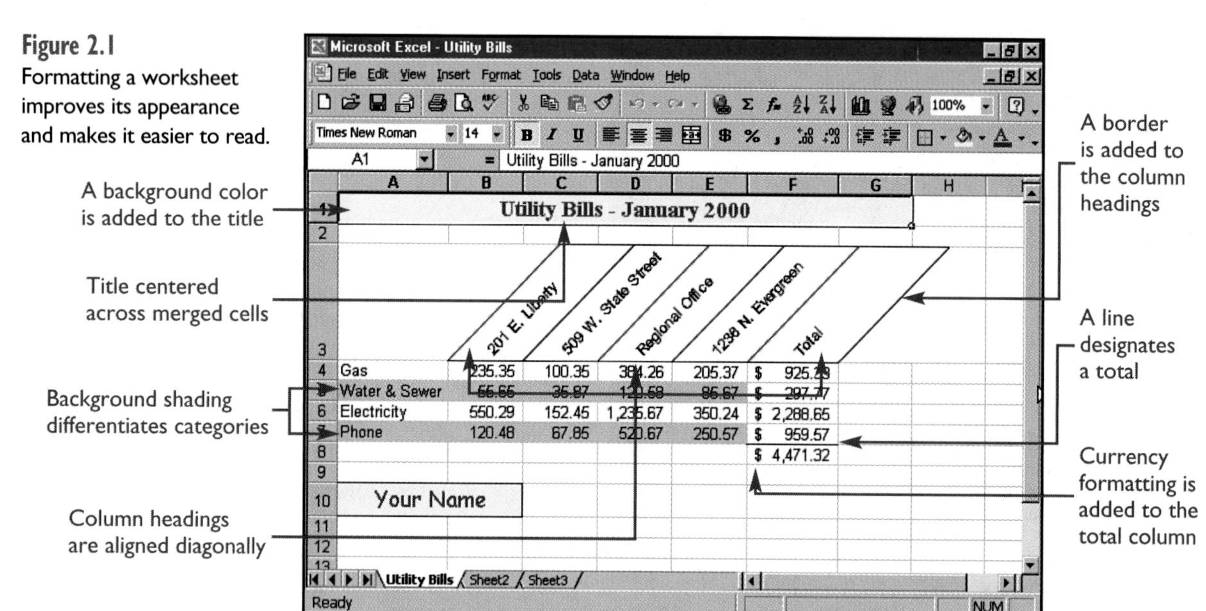

Figure 2.1
Formatting a worksheet improves its appearance and makes it easier to read.

Lesson 1: Opening a File and Selecting a Group of Cells

Launching Excel opens a blank workbook. At times, however, you might like to use a workbook that you previously created. Just like opening a Word document, you must first locate the file. After you open the file, you rename it and save it on your floppy disk, so you can edit the file.

To change the formatting of a cell, you must select the cell. It is common to want to change the formatting of groups of cells, so it is preferable to select the entire group and format them all at the same time. You can select the entire sheet, an entire row or column, a rectangle of cells, or unconnected groups of cells. By formatting the entire group of cells, you help ensure that the same formatting is applied.

In this lesson, you open a file, save it on your student disk, and learn the different techniques for selecting groups of cells.

To Open an Existing File and Save It with a New Name

1. **Launch Excel, and choose File, Open from the Menu.**
   Excel opens to a blank workbook, and the Open dialog box displays. Make sure the CD that came with your book is in your computer's CD-ROM drive.
2. **Click the down arrow on the right of the Look in list, and click the CD-ROM drive where you placed your book's disc.**
   The program displays the folders that are on that disc.

3 **Double-click the Student folder. Select file `EO-0201` (see Figure 2.2), and click the Open button.**

The file opens on your screen. The name of the file is shown in the title bar, and the selected cell is wherever the cursor was when the file was last saved.

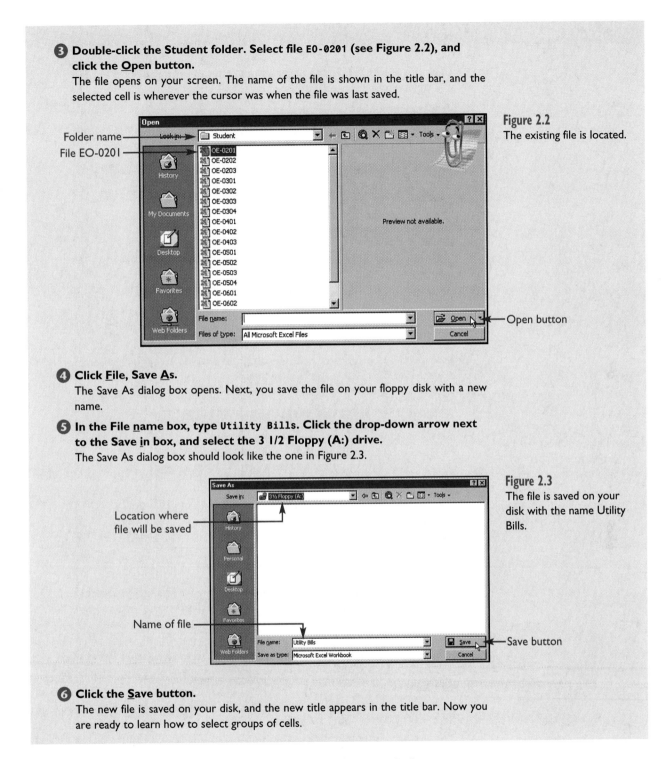

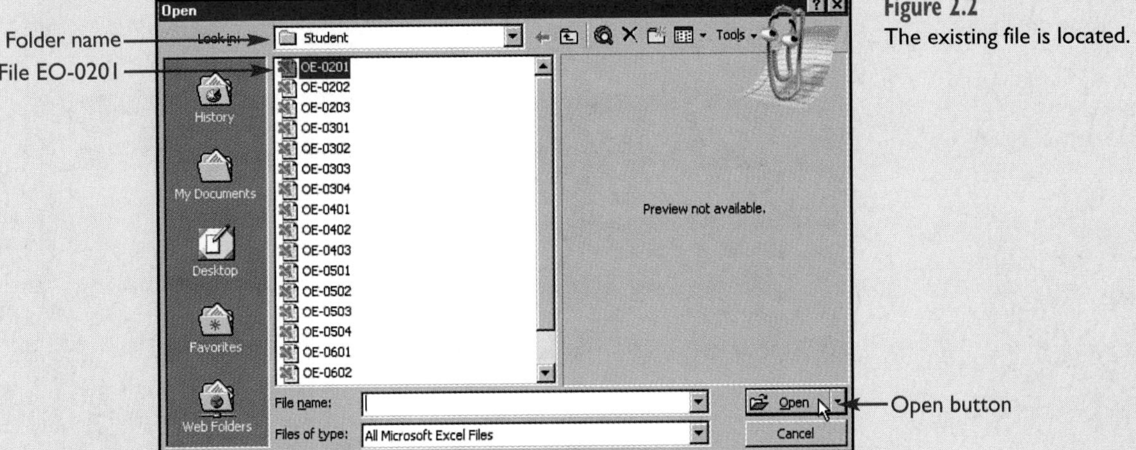

Figure 2.2
The existing file is located.

4 **Click File, Save As.**

The Save As dialog box opens. Next, you save the file on your floppy disk with a new name.

5 **In the File name box, type `Utility Bills`. Click the drop-down arrow next to the Save in box, and select the 3 1/2 Floppy (A:) drive.**

The Save As dialog box should look like the one in Figure 2.3.

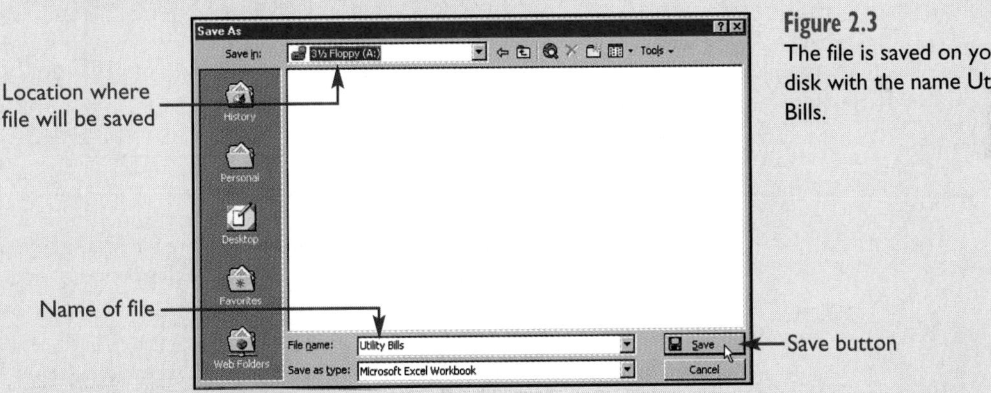

Figure 2.3
The file is saved on your disk with the name Utility Bills.

6 **Click the Save button.**

The new file is saved on your disk, and the new title appears in the title bar. Now you are ready to learn how to select groups of cells.

In the next part of this lesson, you learn various methods for selecting groups of cells.

To Select Groups of Cells

1 Click the Select All button in the upper-left corner of the sheet.
The entire worksheet is selected (see Figure 2.4).

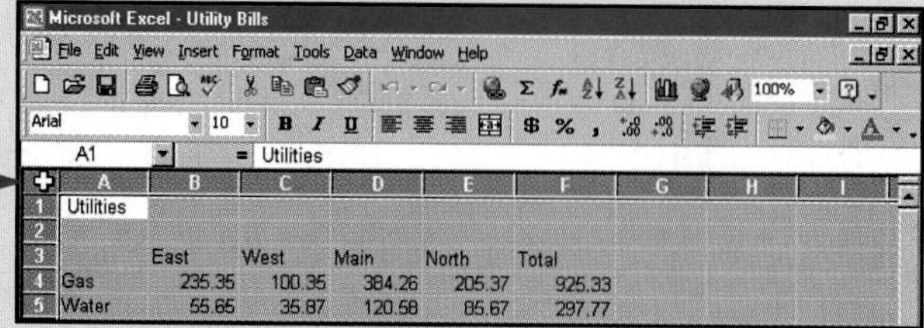

Figure 2.4
You can use the button in the upper-left corner of the worksheet to select the entire worksheet quickly.

Select All button

2 Click the heading for column F.
The entire column of totals is selected. You can use any column heading to select the entire column.

3 Click the heading for row 5.
The entire row pertaining to water bills is selected. Notice that the first cell of the group is always the opposite highlight of the rest of the selected cells. It is still one of the selected group.

4 Position the pointer over cell B4. Click and drag a rectangular selection area to cell E7; release the mouse button.
This selects the actual bills listed on the worksheet (see Figure 2.5).

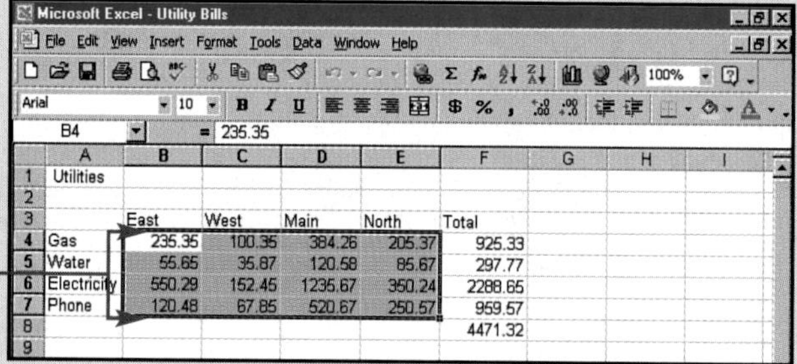

Figure 2.5
You can click and drag over a group of cells to select adjacent cells.

Cells from B4 to E7 are selected

To select a group of cells, click and hold down the mouse button. While holding the button down, move the mouse to cover the area that you want to select; then release the mouse button. This technique is known as ***clicking and dragging***.

5 Selecting two groups of cells that are not next to each other is a two step-process. First, click and drag to select cells B4 through B7, and release the mouse button.
The first group of cells is selected (see Figure 2.6). Next, select a second group of cells that is not adjacent to the first group.

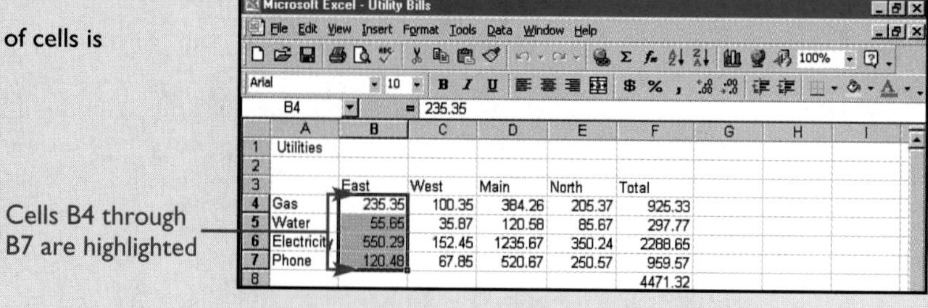

Figure 2.6
The first group of cells is selected.

Cells B4 through B7 are highlighted

6 Hold down Ctrl and select cells E4 through E7. Release the mouse button and Ctrl.

Both sets of cells are selected (see Figure 2.7). This is a useful skill that you need in a later lesson to chart sets of numbers that are not next to each other.

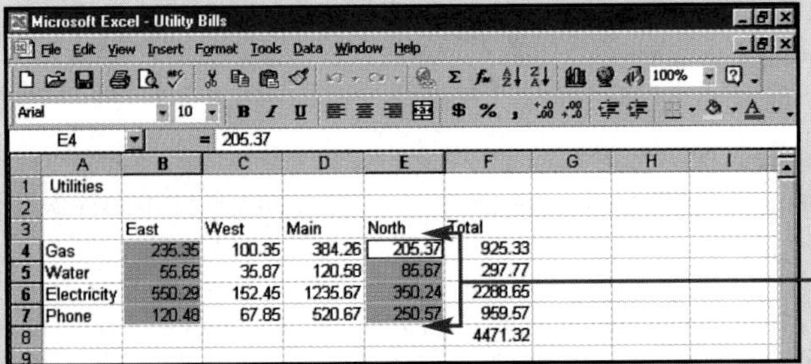

Cells E4 through E7 are also highlighted

Figure 2.7
Use Ctrl to select nonadjacent groups of cells.

7 Click cell B1 to select it. Click the arrow at the bottom of the vertical scrollbar to scroll down to see cell B30.

8 Hold down ⇧Shift, and click cell B30.

This selects all the cells between B1 and B30, as shown in Figure 2.8. This method is useful when you are selecting a group of cells that are so far apart that you have to use the scrollbar to find the other end of the group.

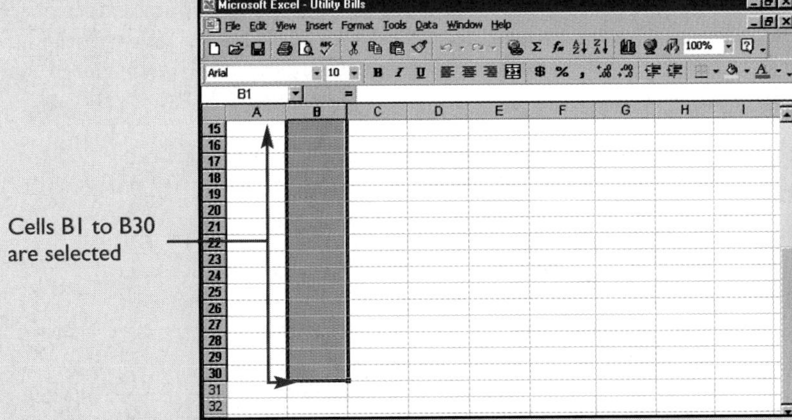

Figure 2.8
Use ⇧Shift to select large groups of adjacent cells that are far apart.

If you try to select a large group of cells that extends beyond the edge of the screen by using the click-and-drag method, you might find that the screen scrolls by so fast that you are hundreds of rows or columns beyond your intended destination. Scroll back to the beginning of the group and try it again using ⇧Shift, as described in steps 7 and 8.

9 Scroll to the top of the sheet, and leave the file open for use in the next lesson.

Selecting Cells

When you use the column heading or row heading to select cells, all the cells in the column or row are selected, including those that are not visible. Be careful when you select an entire sheet, row, or column. You might unintentionally make changes to cells that are not on the screen.

Lesson 2: Formatting Large Numbers, Currency, Decimal Places, and Dates

Numbers greater than 999 should have commas inserted to make them easier to read. In some cases, numbers represent money and should have commas and dollar signs. Many numbers have decimal components, and you have to decide how many places to display. Excel enables you to format numbers the way you want them to be displayed. You also need to know how to handle dates.

In this lesson, you apply different types of numerical formats to the Utilities workbook.

To Format Large Numbers, Currency, Decimal Places, and Dates

1 Select the cells from B4 through E7, and click the Comma Style button.
Notice the electricity bill for the Main office now displays with a comma.

> If your toolbars are still truncated, click the More Buttons button at the end of the Formatting toolbar to use the Comma Style button.

2 Select the cells from F4 through F8, and click the Currency Style button.
A dollar sign is added to the left side of the cells. Leave this range selected for the next step.

3 Click the Decrease Decimal button.
Notice that the numbers display with one less decimal place. Examine Figure 2.9 and compare it with Figure 2.7 to determine which numbers were rounded up and which ones were rounded down. (See the Need to Know box at the end of this lesson for more information about how Excel rounds numbers.)

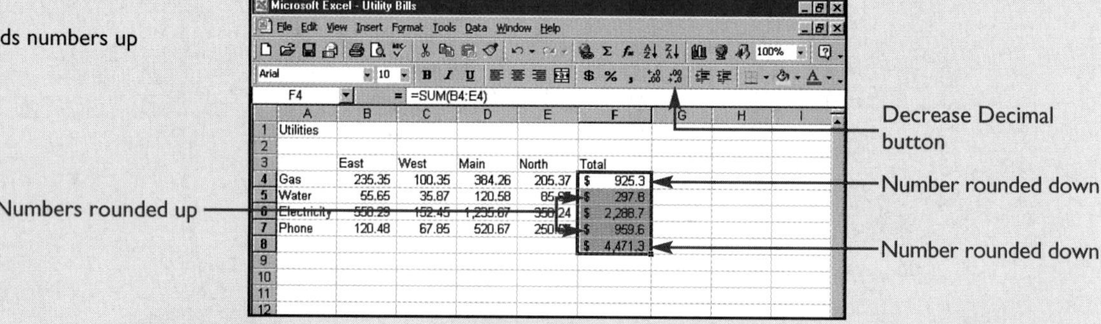

Figure 2.9
Excel rounds numbers up and down.

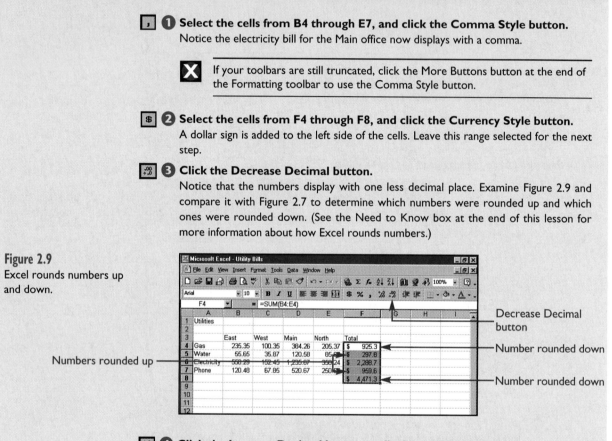

4 Click the Increase Decimal button to display two decimal places.

> Rounding the display does not change the actual number in the cell or any cell that depends upon it. If you use the Decrease Decimal button to change the display so that it does not show any of the decimal places in cells F4 through F8, the rounded numbers do not appear to add correctly to the sum in cell F8.

5 Select cell C1, type `1/30/00`, and press Enter.
A date is entered on the worksheet.

6 **Select cell C1 again. Choose Format from the menu, and choose Cells.**
The Format Cells dialog box appears. Click the Number tab, if necessary. The Format Cells dialog box, as shown in Figure 2.10, gives you more options for applying different formats to cells. The format is applied to the cells that you selected, in this case, cell C1.

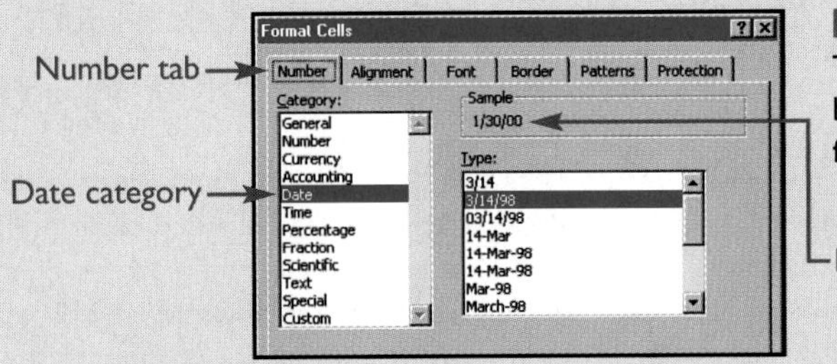

Figure 2.10
The Format Cells dialog box shows options for formatting.

7 **Click Date, if necessary, to select it. Click the example, Mar-98, in the Type box. Click OK.**
The date displays showing only the month and year. Notice the actual content of the cell displays in the Formula bar (see Figure 2.11).

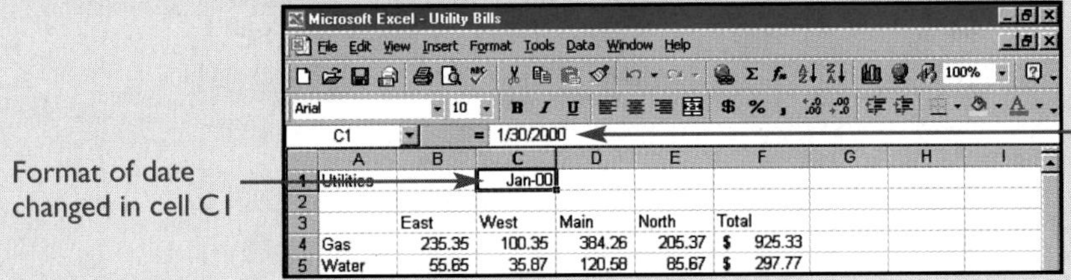

Figure 2.11
Excel offers several different formats that you can apply to a date.

8 **With cell C1 still selected, choose Edit, Clear, and Formats.**
The number 36555 displays. Excel values dates by calculating the number of days from a fixed date in the past. When you remove the formatting from the cell, it displays the number that it actually is using. This makes it possible to subtract one date from another to determine the number of days between two dates.

9 **Choose Edit, Clear, All (or press Del).**
The date is removed.

10 **Save your changes, and leave the file open for use in the next lesson.**

Rounding Off Numbers in Cells
The display of a number in a cell might be rounded off; however, Excel shows the full number in the Formula bar and uses it in calculations. If the number that needs to be rounded ends in a 5, Excel rounds up. Excel rounds numbers 0 through 4 down and rounds up numbers 5 through 9.

Lesson 3: Adjusting Columns and Cells for Long Text or Numbers

Text and numbers entered into a cell are often longer than the cell width. If the cell to the right contains an entry, the text in the left cell is cut off. If a number is too large, Excel displays a string of pound (#) signs.

In this lesson, you change column widths to accommodate entries and center titles across several columns.

To Adjust Columns and Cells for Long Text or Numbers

1. **Select cell A5, and edit the entry to read `Water & Sewer`. Press Enter.**
   Notice that words are cut off. The text is too long for the width of the cell, and the cell immediately to its right is not empty. If the cell next to it were empty, the word would spill over into the next cell, until the adjacent cell (in this case B5) had its own content.

2. **Move the pointer to the line that separates the headings for columns A and B.**
   The mouse pointer turns into a double-headed black arrow.

3. **Double-click the line dividing the columns, and the column width automatically adjusts to fit the longest word in any of the cells in column A.**
   You can quickly adjust the column width by double-clicking the line that divides the column headings. You can also adjust the width of the column by clicking and dragging this line; drag to the left to make a column narrower or to the right to make the column wider.

4. **Select cell A1 and type `Utility Bills – January 2000`. Press Enter.**
   Notice that the text overlaps the cells to the right and displays because the cell is empty (see Figure 2.12).

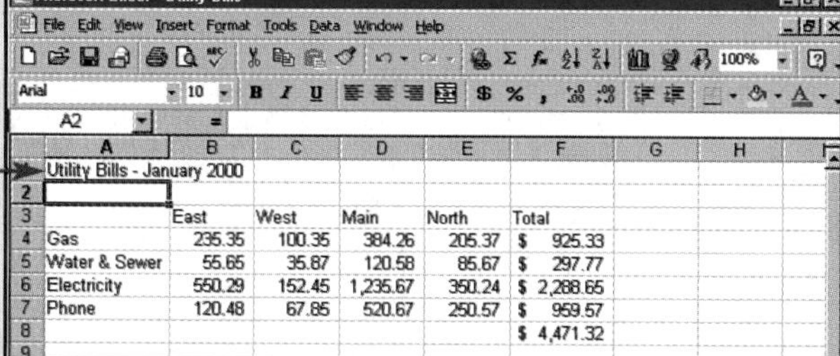

Figure 2.12
Text appears to overlap into adjacent cells if those cells are empty.

5. **Select cells A1 through G1. Click the Merge and Center button.**
   The selected cells merge, and the text displays as though it were in one cell. The long title centers in the selected cells over the body of the worksheet (see Figure 2.13).

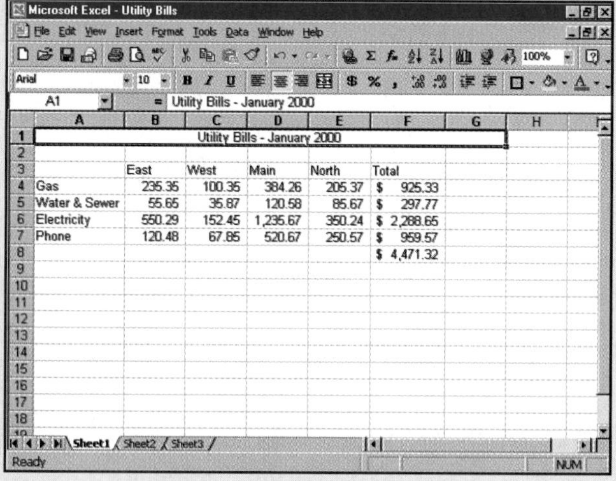

Figure 2.13
The title is centered in cells A1 to G1 over the body of the worksheet.

6. **Select cell D6; type `7000`, and press Enter.**
   Notice that a series of pound signs displays in cell F8 (see Figure 2.14). The size of the total exceeded the available cell space. Anytime you see a series of pound signs in a cell, it means the cell is too small for the size of the number. Unlike text, a number does not spill over into the next cell, even if it is empty.

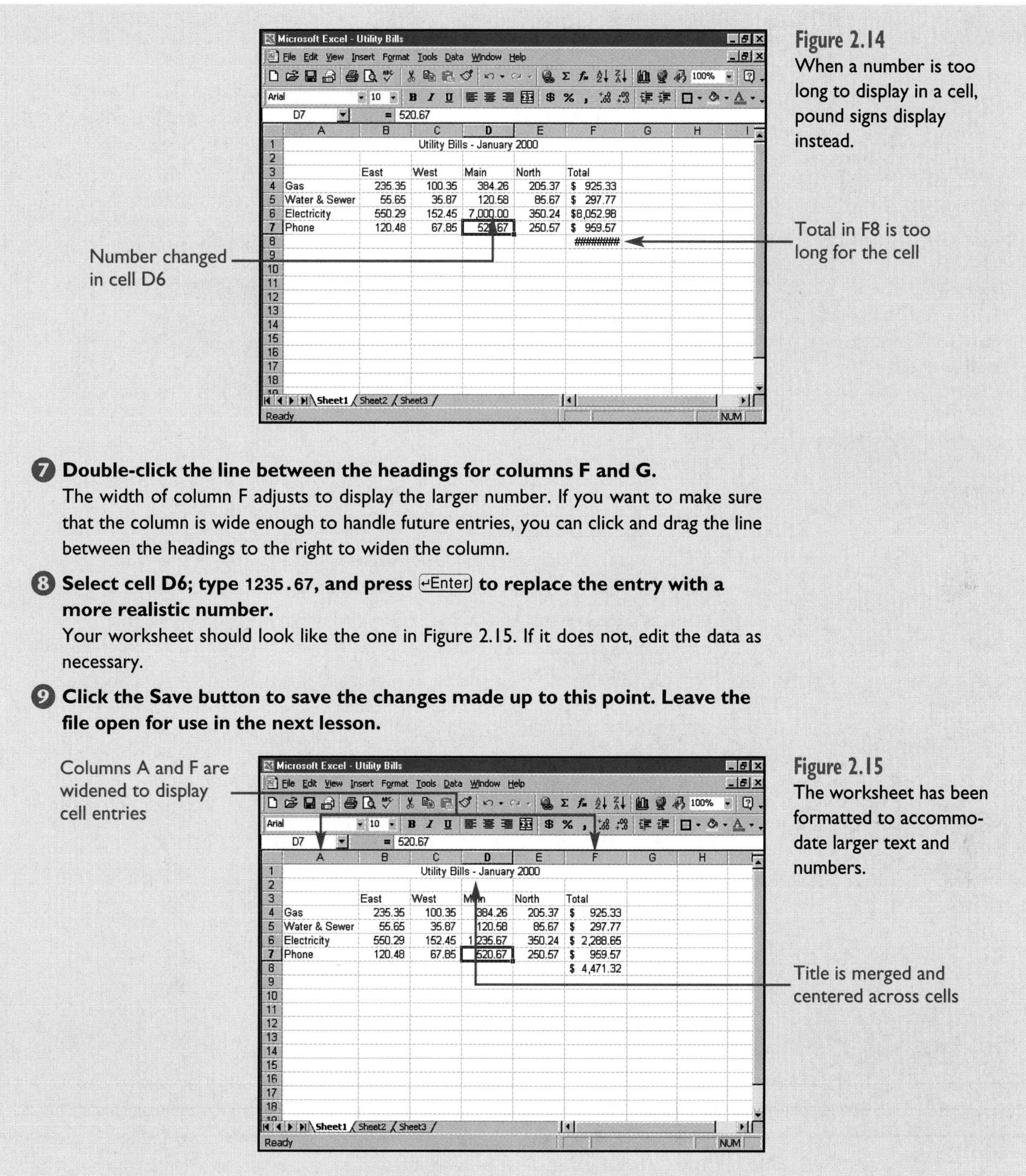

Figure 2.14
When a number is too long to display in a cell, pound signs display instead.

7. **Double-click the line between the headings for columns F and G.**
   The width of column F adjusts to display the larger number. If you want to make sure that the column is wide enough to handle future entries, you can click and drag the line between the headings to the right to widen the column.

8. **Select cell D6; type `1235.67`, and press Enter to replace the entry with a more realistic number.**
   Your worksheet should look like the one in Figure 2.15. If it does not, edit the data as necessary.

9. **Click the Save button to save the changes made up to this point. Leave the file open for use in the next lesson.**

Figure 2.15
The worksheet has been formatted to accommodate larger text and numbers.

Lesson 4: Aligning Text in the Cell

If text is used to label a row or column, you might find that it looks better if the text is centered in the cell or aligned with the right side of the cell. If the text used as a column label is much longer than the numbers in the column, you might want to increase the height of the row and wrap the text in the cell. This is similar to the word wrap feature in Word, with which the program senses the margin and automatically moves text down to the next line in a paragraph. In Excel, the cell size defines the space in which the text is wrapped. Another way to handle long column labels is to slant the contents of cells at an angle.

In this lesson, you align long text labels in the Utilities workbook.

To Align Text in Cells

1 Select the text in cell B3 and type `201 E. Liberty`. Press Tab, and type `509 W. State Street`. Press Tab, and type `Regional Office`. Press Tab, and type `1236 N. Evergreen`. Press Enter.

Labels are entered for the columns of numbers, but the text does not show completely in each cell because the cell is not wide enough (see Figure 2.16). You could simply increase the width of each column to accommodate the column label, but then the column would be much wider than it needs to be for the amounts that are listed.

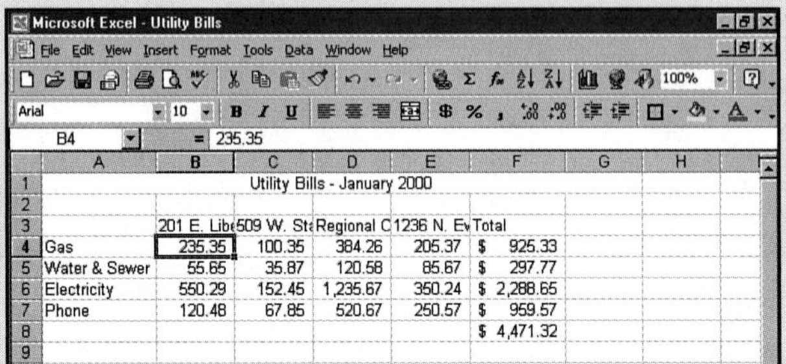

Figure 2.16
The column labels in the range B3:E3 are too large for the cells.

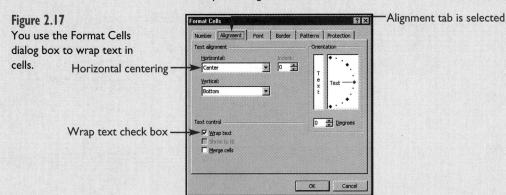

2 Select cells B3 through F3. Click Format, Cells from the menu. In the Format Cells dialog box, click the Alignment tab if it is not already selected.

3 Click the Wrap text check box. Click the down arrow next to the Horizontal box, and select Center. Make sure the dialog box looks like the one in Figure 2.17.

The height of the row increases and the text wraps within the cells as if it were a word-processing document.

Alignment tab is selected

Horizontal centering

Wrap text check box

Figure 2.17
You use the Format Cells dialog box to wrap text in cells.

4 Click OK.

The height of the row increases, and the text moves to the next line within the cells, as shown in Figure 2.18. This is similar to the word wrap feature in a word-processing program.

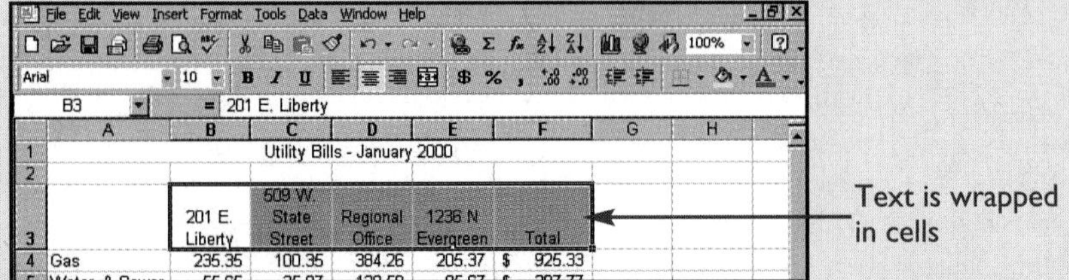

Figure 2.18
You can use the Wrap text feature to expand cells and move text to the new line within the cell.

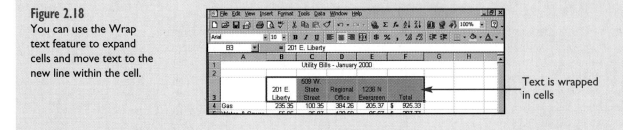

Excel's word wrapping feature does not have an automatic hyphenation feature and is not as smart as a word processor when it comes to estimating where to break words. Check your work when you use the Wrap text feature.

5 **Click the Undo button to remove the Wrap text feature.**
You can handle this type of column label in another way.

6 **Make sure that cells B3 to F3 are still selected, and click Format, Cells.**
The Format Cells dialog box opens.

7 **Click and drag the small red diamond in the Orientation window up until the Degrees box reads 45.**
The text displays at a 45-degree angle.

8 **Click the down arrow next to the Horizontal box. Click Center.**
The text centers in the cell. Make sure the Format Cells dialog box looks like the one in Figure 2.19.

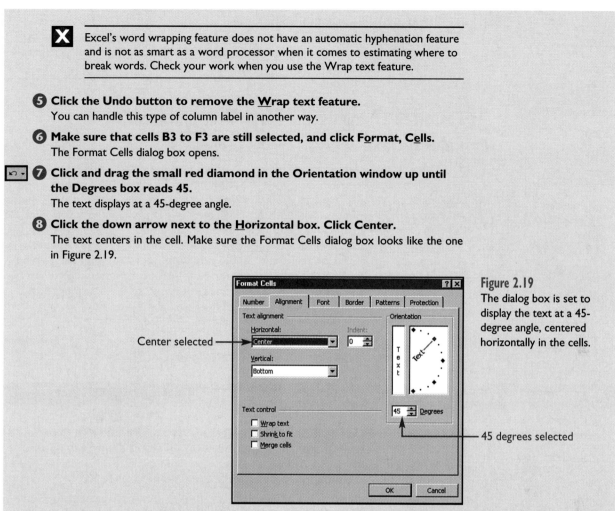

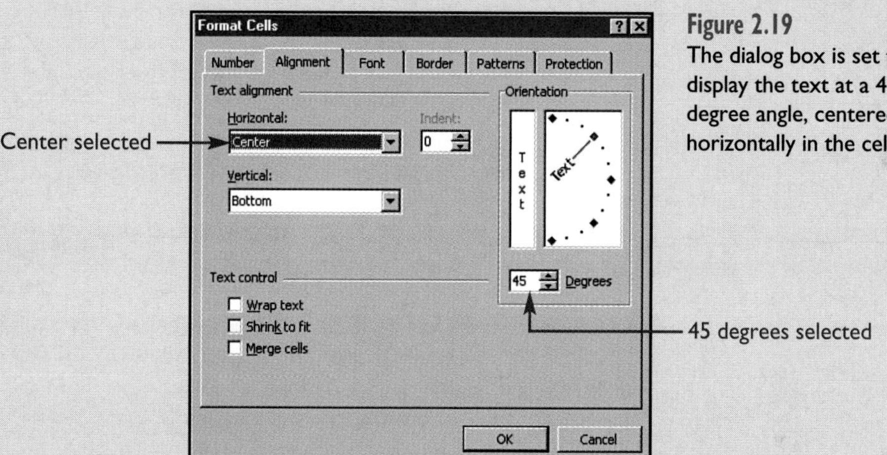

Figure 2.19
The dialog box is set to display the text at a 45-degree angle, centered horizontally in the cells.

9 **Click OK.**
The text in cells B3 to F3 displays at an angle (see Figure 2.20).

10 **Click a cell outside the highlighted range to deselect the range, and click the Save button to save your changes. Leave the file open for use in the next lesson.**

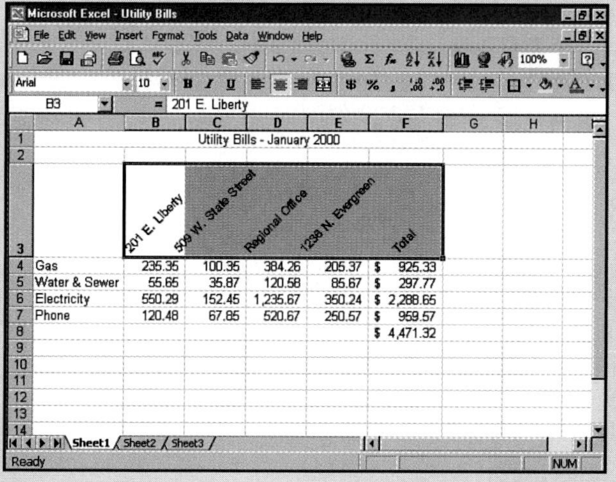

Microsoft Excel - Utility Bills

Utility Bills - January 2000

	201 E. Liberty	509 W. State Street	Regional Office	1236 N. Evergreen	Total
Gas	235.35	100.35	384.26	205.37	$ 925.33
Water & Sewer	55.65	35.87	120.58	85.67	$ 297.77
Electricity	550.29	152.45	1,235.67	350.24	$ 2,288.65
Phone	120.48	67.85	520.67	250.57	$ 959.57
					$ 4,471.32

Figure 2.20
The labels for the columns display at an angle, and the size of the cells adjusts automatically.

Changing Horizontal Alignment

A faster way to change horizontal alignment is to use one of the three buttons on the Formatting toolbar: Align Left, Center, or Align Right. These three buttons should show if your Formatting toolbar is fully expanded.

Lesson 5: Changing the Font, Size, Emphasis, and Color of Text

You might want to emphasize titles and important words by making them larger and by using a different font, which is a typeface style that determines the appearance of text. The default font used in Excel is ***Arial***, which is a Microsoft True Type font that does not have horizontal lines at the end of each vertical letter stroke. This is known as a sans serif font, which is often used for word groups, such as labels and titles. An example of a serif font is ***Times New Roman***, which is another Microsoft True Type font. This font type has horizontal lines at the end of each letter, which help the reader to track words across a page. You can also increase the size of the numbers and letters, known as the ***font size***. Font size is measured in points, with 72 points equal to one inch. The font size increases as the point size increases. In Excel, 10-point is the default font size. You can also add emphasis to the text by using the bold, italic, or underline options. Additionally, you can use color to enhance the appearance of your text. Using these tools can help to improve the overall appearance of your worksheet.

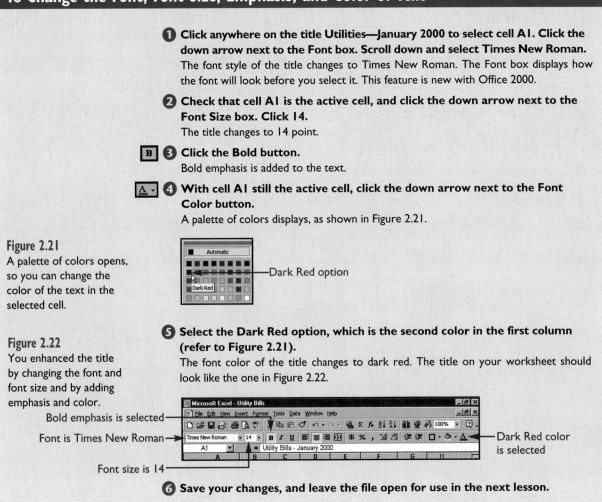

In this lesson, you learn how to change the point size of a title and change a font from Arial to Times New Roman. You add emphasis with boldface and color.

To Change the Font, Font Size, Emphasis, and Color of Text

1. **Click anywhere on the title Utilities—January 2000 to select cell A1. Click the down arrow next to the Font box. Scroll down and select Times New Roman.**
   The font style of the title changes to Times New Roman. The Font box displays how the font will look before you select it. This feature is new with Office 2000.

2. **Check that cell A1 is the active cell, and click the down arrow next to the Font Size box. Click 14.**
   The title changes to 14 point.

3. **Click the Bold button.**
   Bold emphasis is added to the text.

4. **With cell A1 still the active cell, click the down arrow next to the Font Color button.**
   A palette of colors displays, as shown in Figure 2.21.

Figure 2.21
A palette of colors opens, so you can change the color of the text in the selected cell.

5. **Select the Dark Red option, which is the second color in the first column (refer to Figure 2.21).**
   The font color of the title changes to dark red. The title on your worksheet should look like the one in Figure 2.22.

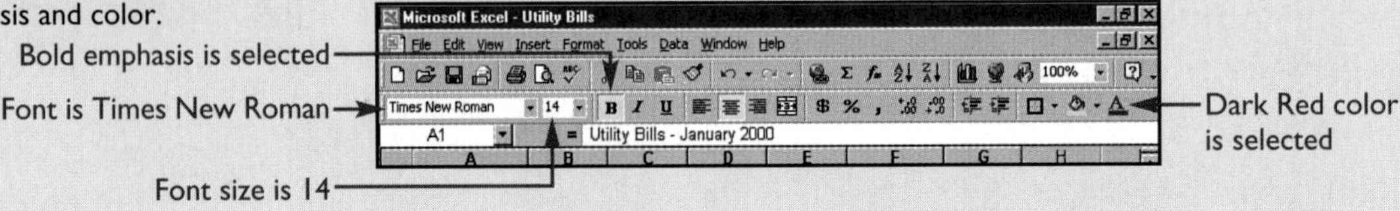

Figure 2.22
You enhanced the title by changing the font and font size and by adding emphasis and color.

6. **Save your changes, and leave the file open for use in the next lesson.**

Deleting Formatting

When you use Del to delete the contents of a cell, only the contents are removed. Any formatting that you added, such as decimal places, currency, and character formatting, remains. This formatting is applied to anything new that you enter in that cell. To ensure that the formatting is removed, choose Edit, Clear, Formats from the menu.

Formatting with Underline and Italic

In addition to **Bold**, you can use the Underline or *Italic* buttons to change the emphasis of text or numbers. Simply select the cells you want to change and click the appropriate button on the Formatting toolbar. You can find numerous other options by using Format, Cells, and selecting the Font tab.

Lesson 6: Adding Lines, Borders, and Shading

You might want to separate a column's total from the preceding numbers, or add shading or background color and borders to assist the reader in following a row of numbers across a complex page. Color, if used carefully, can add a special emphasis. Unless you have a color printer, use of colors on printed documents can hinder rather than help. It is important to use colors judiciously.

In this lesson, you add borders and shading to various parts of the worksheet.

To Add Lines, Borders, and Shading

1. **Make sure that the title in cell A1 is still selected. Click the down arrow next to the Borders button.**
   A selection of border options displays, as shown in Figure 2.23.

Figure 2.23
The common border options display.

The Border button displays the last selection that was used and may appear different from the icon shown next to this step. The Border button is located toward the right end of each Formatting toolbar. Rest your mouse pointer over the button until you see the ScreenTip that displays the word `Borders`.

2. **Click the Thick Box Border style located in the lower-right corner.**
   A heavy box is added as a border around the title.

3. **Select cells B3 to F3. Click the down arrow next to the Borders button, and select the All Borders style, which is the second option from the left in the bottom row.**
   A border outlines each cell that contains column labels.

4. **Select cell F7. Click the down arrow next to the Borders button and select the Bottom Border style, which is the second option from the left in the top row.**
   This step adds a line to the bottom of the cell, which is commonly used in accounting to indicate a sum.

continues ▶

To Add Lines, Borders, and Shading (continued)

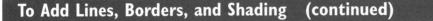

5 Select cells A5 through E5. Hold down Ctrl and select cells A7 through E7. Click the down arrow next to the Fill Color button, and select the Gray-25% button, as shown in Figure 2.24.

The selected cells are shaded. To see the gray, deselect the shaded cells by clicking in any other cell.

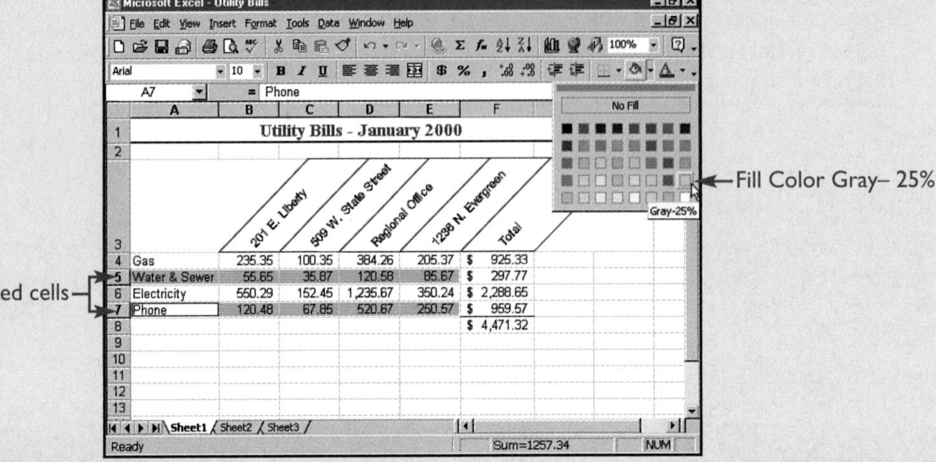

Figure 2.24
A background color is added to the selected cells.

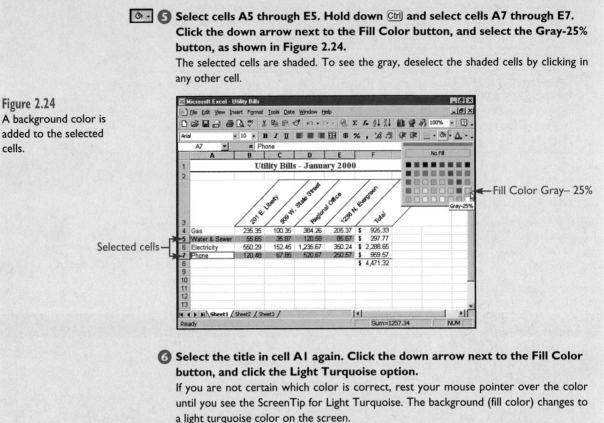

6 Select the title in cell A1 again. Click the down arrow next to the Fill Color button, and click the Light Turquoise option.

If you are not certain which color is correct, rest your mouse pointer over the color until you see the ScreenTip for Light Turquoise. The background (fill color) changes to a light turquoise color on the screen.

7 Select cell A10, and type your name. Change the font, font size, border, background color, and font color to something that you like. Merge across two or more cells if your name exceeds the current column width.

After you add the borders and shading, your worksheet should look like the one in Figure 2.25.

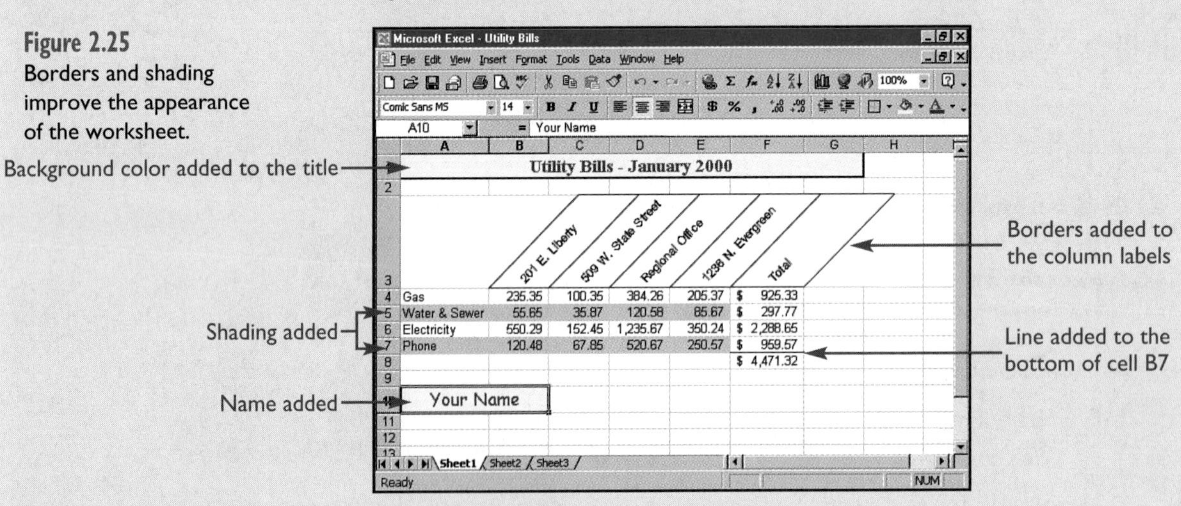

Figure 2.25
Borders and shading improve the appearance of the worksheet.

8 Save your work, and leave the file open for use in the next lesson.

Watch Out for Gray
If you do not have a color printer, the program assigns different shades of gray to different colors. If you pick two colors for your text and background that are assigned to the same shade of gray, the printout is unreadable.

Use Formatting Buttons to Apply Emphasis
The Font Color, Fill Color, and Borders buttons on the Formatting toolbar display the most recent choices. If you want to use the type of emphasis displayed on the button, you can apply it by clicking the button without using the drop-down menu.

Lesson 7: Renaming a Worksheet

If you are using multiple worksheets in a workbook, it is helpful to rename each worksheet to reflect the type of information it contains, such as income, expenses, or cash flow. In this lesson, you change the name of the worksheet and print it.

To Rename a Worksheet

1. **Double-click the Sheet1 tab.**
   Sheet1 is highlighted. You can now simply type to change the name of the sheet.
2. **Type `January`.**
   The sheet is renamed.
3. **Click in any cell to deselect the worksheet name.**
4. **Click the Save button to save the changes you made.**
5. **Make sure your printer is connected and turned on. Click the Print button to print a copy of the worksheet.**
6. **Click the Close Window button to close the workbook.**
   Your file is saved and closed and you have a printout of your worksheet that you can hand in to your instructor, if requested.

Summary

In this project, you learned how to format a worksheet. First, you learned different techniques for selecting groups of cells. You applied comma, decimal, and currency formats to numbers on the worksheet. You adjusted the column width to accommodate long text and numbers. You aligned text in a cell; you changed the font and font size and added emphasis and color. Then you added lines, borders, colors, and shading to the worksheet. Finally, you renamed the worksheet.

To learn more about formatting options, look at the Format menu. In particular, open the Format Cells dialog box and examine each of the tabs and the types of cell formatting available. Look at the Format, Row, Column and Sheet submenus to see the commands you can use to format these parts of a worksheet. Try formatting a worksheet using the Format, AutoFormat menu command. This opens the AutoFormat dialog box, which is similar to the Table AutoFormat dialog box you worked with in Word. You can choose a preformatted style from a variety of options.

Checking Concepts and Terms

True/False

For each of the following, check *T* or *F* to indicate whether the statement is true or false.

__T __F **1.** To open an existing workbook, use the Insert, File options from the menu. [L1]

__T __F **2.** You can select all the cells in a row by clicking the row heading. [L1]

__T __F **3.** All the cells in a selection must be touching each other; separate groups of cells cannot be selected at the same time. [L1]

__T __F **4.** If you select a group of cells and click the Comma Style button, all the numbers in those cells have a comma placed between every two numbers. [L2]

__T __F **5.** If a selected cell contains the number 5.25 and you click the Decrease Decimal button, the number 5.2 displays. [L2]

__T __F **6.** If a cell displays a row of # signs, it means that you made a mistake in writing a formula. [L3]

__T __F **7.** One way to handle long labels is to use the Wrap text option. [L4]

__T __F **8.** A 16-point character is larger than an 8-point character. [L6]

__T __F **9.** If you have a printer with only one color of ink, it does not matter which colors you choose for text and background. [L6]

__T __F **10.** It is possible to print long column labels at an angle. [L4]

Multiple Choice

Circle the letter of the correct answer for each of the following.

1. What is the method used to automatically adjust the width of a column to accommodate the widest cell entry? [L3]

a. Choose Edit, Adjust Column, Width.

b. Choose Format, Column, Width.

c. Double-click the line dividing the column headings.

d. Click and drag the column heading until it appears to be wide enough.

2. What is the symbol used to indicate that a number is too big to fit in a cell? [L3]

a. Pound sign

b. Question mark

c. Asterisk

d. Dollar sign

3. What is the setting that forces long text entries to fit within the available column width by increasing the row height and displaying the text on several lines within the cell? [L4]

a. Word wrap

b. Wrap text

c. Grow cell

d. Expand cell

4. How would you add underlining to a cell? [L6]

a. Click the Underline button.

b. Click the Line button.

c. Click the Borders button.

d. Click the down arrow on the Borders button, and select the single underline option.

5. Which key is used to help select nonadjacent groups of cells? [L1]

a. Alt

b. Ctrl

c. Tab

d. Shift

Screen ID

Identify each of the items in Figure 2.26.

Figure 2.26

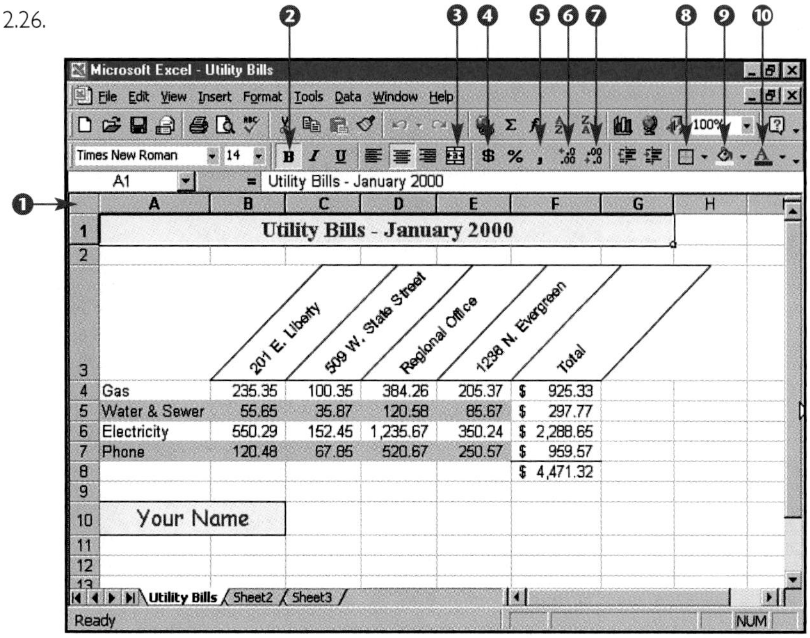

A. Font Color button

B. Borders button

C. Select All button

D. Comma Style button

E. Currency Style button

F. Decrease Decimal button

G. Increase Decimal button

H. Merge and Center button

I. Fill Color button

J. Bold button

1. ______________ **5.** ______________ **9.** ______________

2. ______________ **6.** ______________ **10.** ______________

3. ______________ **7.** ______________

4. ______________ **8.** ______________

Discussion Questions

1. What kinds of formatting have you seen applied to a worksheet that you liked? That you disliked?
2. When do you think it is appropriate to use formatting? For what kinds of information? When would you not use formatting?
3. What other formatting techniques have you seen that you would like to learn?
4. Do you think it is worth the time and effort to format a worksheet? Does it improve the appearance sufficiently to be worth the effort?
5. What kinds of formatting do you think you would be most likely to use?

Skill Drill

Skill Drill exercises reinforce project skills. Each skill reinforced is the same, or nearly the same, as a skill presented in the project. Each exercise includes a brief narrative introduction, followed by detailed instructions in a step-by-step format.

These exercises all use the same workbook. Leave the workbook open at the end of each exercise for use in the next exercise. You use three worksheets in the workbook, and you apply different formats to each. The first is a worksheet that compares the costs of office dividers. The second is the same data, but you apply different formats. The third sheet is a cash flow of income and expenses. Locate and open file `EO-0202` in the Student folder that is on the CD that came with your book. Save the file as `Formats` on your floppy disk for use in the following exercises.

1. Applying Formats to an Existing Worksheet

In the first worksheet, you use the Merge and Center function, wrap the text in the title cells, and apply various formatting changes. [L1-7]

To change the formats on the first worksheet, follow these steps:

1. Select Sheet1 in the Formats workbook.
2. Enter your name in cell A18.
3. Use the Merge and Center button to center the main title across columns A through F. Center the subtitle **All Metal** across cells C2 and D2 and the subtitle **Glass and Metal** across cells E2 and F2.
4. Center and wrap the text in cells B3 through F3.
5. Center data in all cells from B4 through F13.
6. Refer to Figure 2.27, select both groups of shaded cells, and choose a background of Gray-25%.

Figure 2.27

Microsoft Excel - Formats

E15 =

	A	B	C	D	E	F
1		Comparison of Office Dividers				
2			All Metal		Glass and Metal	
3	Characteristics	Weight For Relative Importance	Rating On Individual Characteristics	Weighted Rating	Rating On Individual Characteristics	Weighted Rating
4	**Cost-Related**					
5	Initial Cost	9	5	45	7	63
6	Maintenance Cost	8	1	8	6	48
7	**Physical Attributes**					
8	Sound Transmission	3	1	3	10	30
9	Durability	10	3	30	3	30
10	Movability	5	4	20	6	30
11	**Other Benefits**					
12	Appearance	10	6	60	9	90
13	Privacy	2	6	12	4	8
14	**Total (Weighted Values)**			178		299
15	**Actual cost**			$ 17,000		$ 20,000
16	**Ratio of Value Points to Cost**			0.010		0.015

Office Dividers / Sheet2 / Sheet3 / Sheet4 / Sheet5

Ready NUM

7. Select cells A1, A4, A7, A11, A14, A15, and A16. Make them bold.
8. Select D15 and F15; format the numbers to display currency with no decimals.
9. Select D16 and F16; format the numbers to display only three decimal places.
10. Adjust the column widths where necessary.
11. Rename Sheet1 **Office Dividers**; save the workbook and print the sheet.

2. Adding Border Lines and Colors

In the second worksheet, you apply borders and colors to a worksheet that has been partially formatted. [L3, 5-7]

1. Select Sheet2 in the Formats workbook. Enter your name in cell A17.
2. Add borders and colors to match Figure 2.28. (The status bar has been turned off to display the entire sheet in the figure; you might have to scroll to see the last line on your screen.) See the following steps for more information.

Figure 2.28

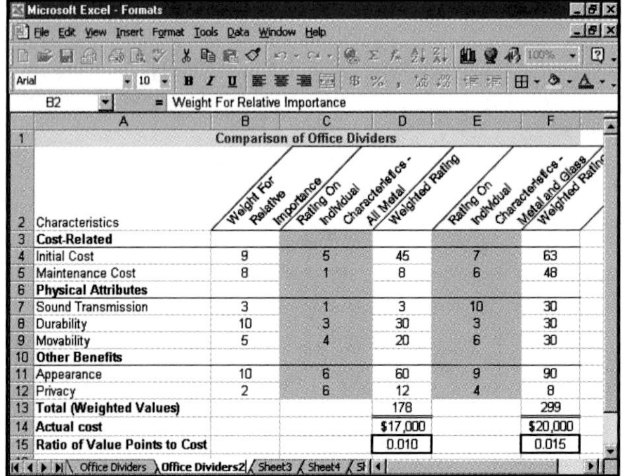

Microsoft Excel - Formats

B2 = Weight For Relative Importance

	A	B	C	D	E	F
1		Comparison of Office Dividers				
2	Characteristics	Weight For Relative Importance	Rating On Individual Characteristics - All Metal	Weighted Rating	Rating On Individual Characteristics - Metal and Glass	Weighted Rating
3	**Cost-Related**					
4	Initial Cost	9	5	45	7	63
5	Maintenance Cost	8	1	8	6	48
6	**Physical Attributes**					
7	Sound Transmission	3	1	3	10	30
8	Durability	10	3	30	3	30
9	Movability	5	4	20	6	30
10	**Other Benefits**					
11	Appearance	10	6	60	9	90
12	Privacy	2	6	12	4	8
13	**Total (Weighted Values)**			178		299
14	**Actual cost**			$17,000		$20,000
15	**Ratio of Value Points to Cost**			0.010		0.015

Office Dividers / Office Dividers2 / Sheet3 / Sheet4

3. Place a solid dark border around the two ratio numbers in cells D15 and F15.
4. Add a single lightweight line to the bottom of the cells in rows 3, 6, and 10 columns A through F only. (Do not use the row header to select the row.)
5. Add a double line border to the bottom of cells D13 and F13.
6. Change the Fill Color of the title to Turquoise, and change the Font Color to Dark Red.
7. Change the orientation of the column labels to a 45-degree angle. Select the border that shows all lines. (Your text wrap might be different from that shown in the figure.)
8. Adjust the column widths, if necessary.
9. Change the name of Sheet2 to `Office Dividers2`; save the workbook, and print the sheet.

3. Editing a Worksheet

In this exercise, you add some formatting to a different worksheet with less specific instructions. Use the figure provided to add the formatting. [L3-6]

1. Select Sheet3 in the Formats workbook and rename it `Cash Flow`.
2. Enter your name in cell A17.
3. Format the sheet to match Figure 2.29. Make sure you change font, font size, and emphasis, merge and center the title, add fill color to the columns shown, change text alignment, center text, and add borders and emphasis to the subtitles. Remember to adjust the columns to fit the data. Use Figure 2.29 as a guide. (*Hint*: It is easiest to select long columns and rows of cells if you change the zoom to 75 percent, so you can see more of the worksheet.)

Figure 2.29

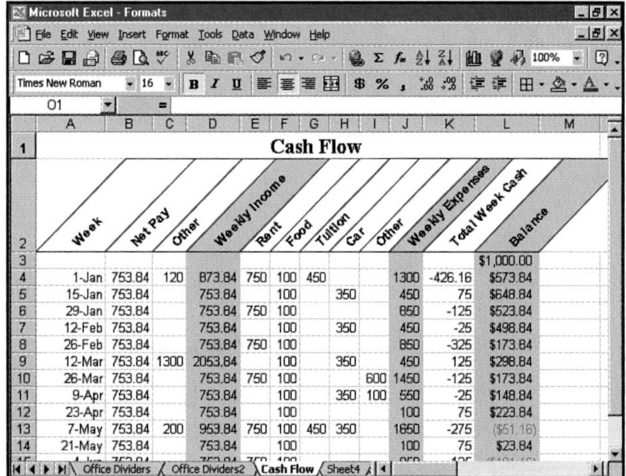

4. Save the workbook and print the sheet.
5. Close the file and exit Excel.

Challenge

Challenge exercises expand on or are somewhat related to skills presented in the lessons. Each exercise provides a brief narrative introduction followed by instructions, in a numbered step or bulleted list format, that are not as detailed as those in the Skill Drill section.

In these Challenge exercises, you use file `EO-0203` and save it on your student floppy disk as `Compare`. In the first exercise, you format a worksheet for distribution to different functional groups in an organization. In the second exercise, you learn more about using angled formats for cells. In the third exercise, you use Help to learn how Excel handles dates and numbers. You use one file for all three exercises. The first and second exercises need to be done in order.

1. Using Borders, Text Wrap, and Merge Cells to Format a Table

If a table of data is to be distributed to several people, it is useful to use formatting tools to organize the cells into functional groups. In this example, several people in the office have been asked to evaluate and compare two room divider systems using a weighted scale. [L3-6]

Format Sheet1 in the Compare workbook to look like the example in Figure 2.30. Use the following steps as a guide:

Figure 2.30

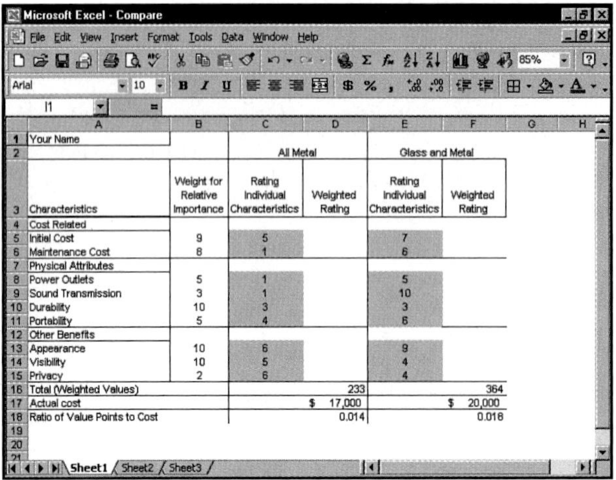

	A	B	C	D	E	F
1	Your Name					
2			All Metal		Glass and Metal	
3	Characteristics	Weight for Relative Importance	Rating Individual Characteristics	Weighted Rating	Rating Individual Characteristics	Weighted Rating
4	Cost Related					
5	Initial Cost	9	5		7	
6	Maintenance Cost	8	1		6	
7	Physical Attributes					
8	Power Outlets	5	1		5	
9	Sound Transmission	3	1		10	
10	Durability	10	3		3	
11	Portability	5	4		6	
12	Other Benefits					
13	Appearance	10	6		9	
14	Visibility	10	5		4	
15	Privacy	2	6		4	
16	Total (Weighted Values)			233		364
17	Actual cost			$ 17,000		$ 20,000
18	Ratio of Value Points to Cost			0.014		0.018

1. Place your name in cell A1.
2. Merge the titles for the two types of room dividers across columns C and D and columns E and F, respectively.
3. Widen column A. Wrap and center the text in row 3 and adjust the column widths and row height as shown.
4. Center the text and numbers in cells B3 through F15.
5. Format the numbers at the bottom of columns D and F, as shown.
6. Use Tools, Options, Gridlines to turn off the gridlines on the screen. (It's on the View tab.)
7. Use borders to add the lines shown.
8. Shade the cells shown with a 25 percent gray fill.
9. Save and print the worksheet. Leave the workbook open for use in the next exercise.

2. Learning About Alignment of Text That Is Displayed at an Angle

When you display a column heading at a 45-degree angle, it is unclear which direction is indicated by the horizontal or vertical controls. [L4, 6]

In this exercise, use the worksheet formatted in the previous exercise and change the column headings to display at a 45-degree angle, adjust the height of the row so that the text wraps, add borders, and set the vertical and horizontal alignments to match Figure 2.31. Use the figure and the following steps as a guide.

Figure 2.31

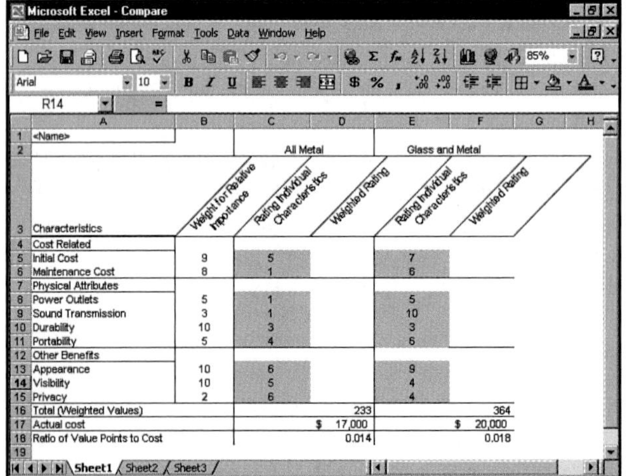

	A	B	C	D	E	F
1	<Name>					
2			All Metal		Glass and Metal	
3	Characteristics	Weight for Relative Importance	Rating Individual Characteristics	Weighted Rating	Rating Individual Characteristics	Weighted Rating
4	Cost Related					
5	Initial Cost	9	5		7	
6	Maintenance Cost	8	1		6	
7	Physical Attributes					
8	Power Outlets	5	1		5	
9	Sound Transmission	3	1		10	
10	Durability	10	3		3	
11	Portability	5	4		6	
12	Other Benefits					
13	Appearance	10	6		9	
14	Visibility	10	5		4	
15	Privacy	2	6		4	
16	Total (Weighted Values)			233		364
17	Actual cost			$ 17,000		$ 20,000
18	Ratio of Value Points to Cost			0.014		0.018

1. Select cells B3 through F3, and align the text at 45 degrees.
2. Use the border option that looks like a window with four panes.
3. If necessary, click and drag the line that divides row 3 and 4 to expand the height of the row, so the text does not split in the middle of a word.
4. Experiment with the Horizontal and Vertical alignment options to find the combination that matches the figure. Observe what the effect of each option is on the placement of the text in the cell.
5. Save the workbook. Print the sheet.

3. Learning How Excel Works with Dates

Computers work with dates and times as if they were numbers, which enables you to subtract one date (or time) from another.

In this exercise, you use the Office Assistant to find out how Excel works with dates.

1. Click the Office Assistant or click the Microsoft Excel Help button to open the Office Assistant dialog box.
2. Type the following question: `How does Excel subtract one date from another?` Click the Search button.
3. Click How Microsoft Excel stores dates and times. The Microsoft Excel Help window displays.
4. Read the topic; and print a copy.
5. Close the workbook.

Discovery Zone

Discovery Zone exercises require advanced knowledge of topics presented in *Essentials* lessons, application of skills from multiple lessons, or self-directed learning of new skills.

In these Discovery Zone exercises, you learn about the Year 2000 issues and how to work with them in Excel. Then, you learn how to apply conditional formatting to a cell. Finally, you learn how to protect a worksheet, so that unintentional entries cannot be made. The exercises are independent of each other, but the third exercise that protects the worksheet should be completed last. All three exercises use the same file.

1. Exploring Some Effects of the Year 2000 Problem

Representing the year in a date with only two digits creates problems because the computer is forced to guess the century in which it belongs.

In this exercise, you determine how to work with the century assumptions built into Excel 2000, so that you know when you must use four digits to represent the year in a date.

- Locate and open file `EO-0204` found in the Student folder on the CD-ROM that came with your book. Save it on your floppy disk as `Year2000`. Place your name in cell A1.
- In cell B3, type a date of birth from the twenties, such as 5/20/28. Notice the calculation in cell D3 displays a negative number because it assumed you meant 2028 rather than 1928. Click the cell again, and look in the Formula bar to see how the date was interpreted.
- Type the date in again but specify the year using four digits.
- Refer to Excel's Help on this matter, and write a directive that you might send out to your staff telling them when to use four digits for the year in Excel worksheets. Enter the message in cell A6.
- Widen column A to about four times its current width, and format the text in Cell A6 to wrap.
- Leave the page open for use in the next exercise.

2. Learning How to Use Conditional Formatting

You can use formatting to draw attention to errors or unusual results. Use the Year2000 file that you created in the previous exercise or open **EO-0204** and save it as **Year2000** on your disk.

In this exercise, you use Help to learn about Conditional Formatting. Format cell D3 in the Year2000 worksheet so that the number displays in red, bold face type whenever the number is negative.

- Search Help for information about Conditional Formatting.
- Format cell D3 as described previously.
- Under date of birth, enter a date from the year 2000. The value in cell D3 should display as described.
- Print the page.
- Leave the file open for use in the next exercise.

3. Protecting Cells from Unintentional Change

The formula in cell D3 will be lost if someone accidentally enters a value in the cell. Similarly, you do not want others to change the column headers or message you have chosen. To prevent users from overwriting formulas or making unauthorized changes, you can choose the cells in which they can write by unlocking those cells and protecting the rest of the sheet.

In this exercise, you unlock cells A3, B3, and C3 and protect the rest of the sheet so users can change only the values in cells B3 and C3. Before you begin, you can use Help to search on **Protection**. Read the available information, and close the Help window.

- In the Year 2000 workbook, select cells A3, B3, and C3. Choose Format, Cells and Protection. Unlock the cells.
- Use the Tools menu to protect the sheet. Do not use a password.
- Try to make changes to any other part of the sheet, and observe the error message. Enter a new birth date to make sure you can change it.
- Save the changes you have made. Close the workbook, and close Excel.

Project 3

Techniques for Working Efficiently in Excel

Objectives

In this project, you learn how to

- ➤ **Create Sequential Text Headings**
- ➤ **Create a Series of Numbers**
- ➤ **Change Zoom and Freeze Panes**
- ➤ **Copy Cell Contents**
- ➤ **Improve the Printed Worksheet**
- ➤ **Preview Print Settings and Print a Range**

Key terms introduced in this project include

- fill
- fill handle
- gridlines

SOURCE: *Essentials: Office 2000*, Ferrett-Preston-Preston

Why Would I Do This?

Often information that is entered in a worksheet is repetitive or sequential. For example, you might need to enter a series of dates or times as row or column labels. You can ***fill*** the cells with data, using a technique that is used to enter a group of adjacent cells with the same values, formulas, or a series. Examples of series include dates, numbers, days of the week, and months of the year. You will also find occasions where the same text must be entered into numerous cells. Excel has powerful tools that help you with these tasks and which can help improve your efficiency. Finally, you might want to print only part of a worksheet, or have certain rows or columns show on multiple pages of a printout. The Page Setup dialog box gives you access to the layout of the printed worksheet.

Visual Summary

In this project, you fill sequences of labels and copy cell contents to produce a work schedule for several part-time employees. When you are done with the project, you will have created a worksheet that looks like the one in Figure 3.1.

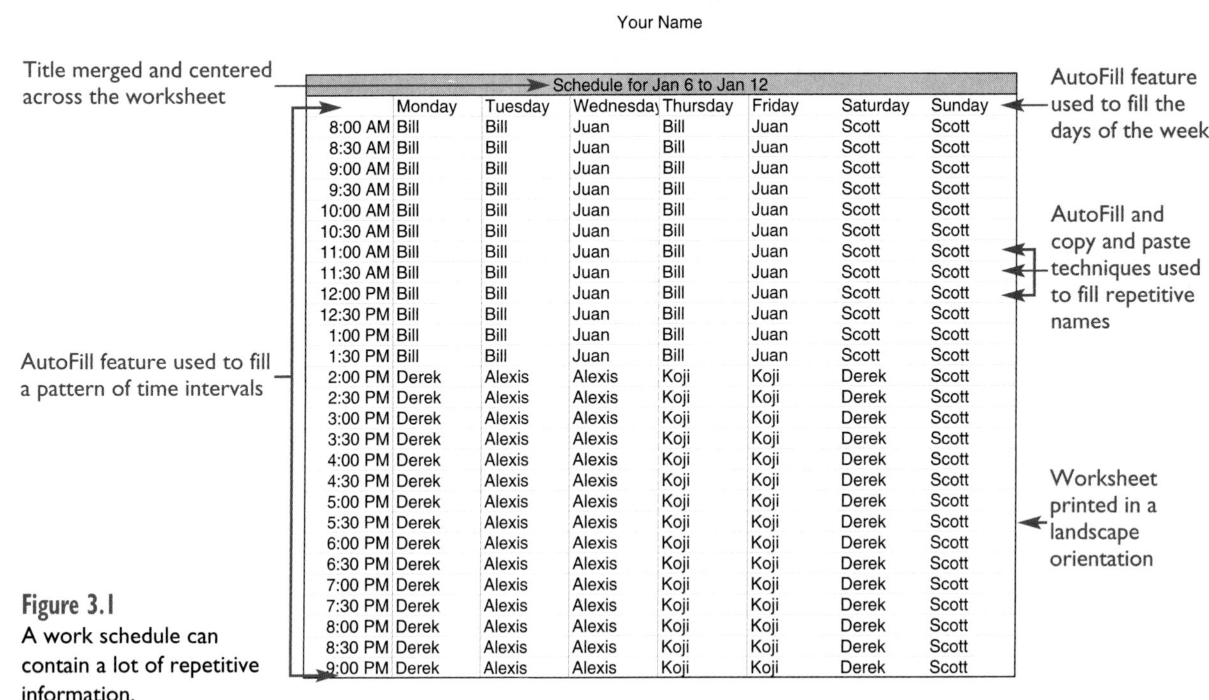

Your Name

Schedule for Jan 6 to Jan 12							
	Monday	Tuesday	Wednesday	Thursday	Friday	Saturday	Sunday
8:00 AM	Bill	Bill	Juan	Bill	Juan	Scott	Scott
8:30 AM	Bill	Bill	Juan	Bill	Juan	Scott	Scott
9:00 AM	Bill	Bill	Juan	Bill	Juan	Scott	Scott
9:30 AM	Bill	Bill	Juan	Bill	Juan	Scott	Scott
10:00 AM	Bill	Bill	Juan	Bill	Juan	Scott	Scott
10:30 AM	Bill	Bill	Juan	Bill	Juan	Scott	Scott
11:00 AM	Bill	Bill	Juan	Bill	Juan	Scott	Scott
11:30 AM	Bill	Bill	Juan	Bill	Juan	Scott	Scott
12:00 PM	Bill	Bill	Juan	Bill	Juan	Scott	Scott
12:30 PM	Bill	Bill	Juan	Bill	Juan	Scott	Scott
1:00 PM	Bill	Bill	Juan	Bill	Juan	Scott	Scott
1:30 PM	Bill	Bill	Juan	Bill	Juan	Scott	Scott
2:00 PM	Derek	Alexis	Alexis	Koji	Koji	Derek	Scott
2:30 PM	Derek	Alexis	Alexis	Koji	Koji	Derek	Scott
3:00 PM	Derek	Alexis	Alexis	Koji	Koji	Derek	Scott
3:30 PM	Derek	Alexis	Alexis	Koji	Koji	Derek	Scott
4:00 PM	Derek	Alexis	Alexis	Koji	Koji	Derek	Scott
4:30 PM	Derek	Alexis	Alexis	Koji	Koji	Derek	Scott
5:00 PM	Derek	Alexis	Alexis	Koji	Koji	Derek	Scott
5:30 PM	Derek	Alexis	Alexis	Koji	Koji	Derek	Scott
6:00 PM	Derek	Alexis	Alexis	Koji	Koji	Derek	Scott
6:30 PM	Derek	Alexis	Alexis	Koji	Koji	Derek	Scott
7:00 PM	Derek	Alexis	Alexis	Koji	Koji	Derek	Scott
7:30 PM	Derek	Alexis	Alexis	Koji	Koji	Derek	Scott
8:00 PM	Derek	Alexis	Alexis	Koji	Koji	Derek	Scott
8:30 PM	Derek	Alexis	Alexis	Koji	Koji	Derek	Scott
9:00 PM	Derek	Alexis	Alexis	Koji	Koji	Derek	Scott

Figure 3.1
A work schedule can contain a lot of repetitive information.

Lesson 1: Creating Sequential Text Headings

Many spreadsheet applications use days of the week, months of the year, fiscal quarters, or other sequences of labels as column or row labels. Excel recognizes text that begins such sequences and assists you in entering them. Using this feature of Excel improves your efficiency in creating your worksheet.

In this lesson, you create sequential labels.

To Create Sequential Text Headings

1. **Launch Excel. Locate and open EO-0301 from the Student\Excel\Project03 folder on the CD that came with your book, and save it on your floppy disk as `Work Schedule`.**
   The file opens, and the new workbook name displays in the title bar.
2. **Select cell B2; type `Monday`, and press Tab.**

3 Select cell B2 again. Move the pointer to the small black square at the lower-right corner of the cell.

The small black square in the lower-right corner of the cell is called the ***fill handle***. This handle is used to fill adjacent cells with a series of entries that are based on the contents of the current cell. When the pointer rests on the fill handle, the pointer turns into a black plus sign (see Figure 3.2).

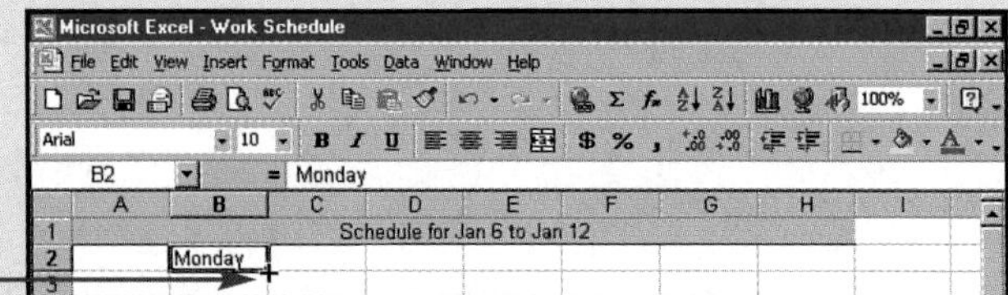

Pointer on the fill handle

Figure 3.2
Use the fill handle to complete a series or sequence.

4 Click and drag the fill handle to the right to cell H2.

Notice that the name of the next day in the sequence displays in a ScreenTip as you drag.

5 Release the mouse button.

The sequence of days is filled in, as shown in Figure 3.3.

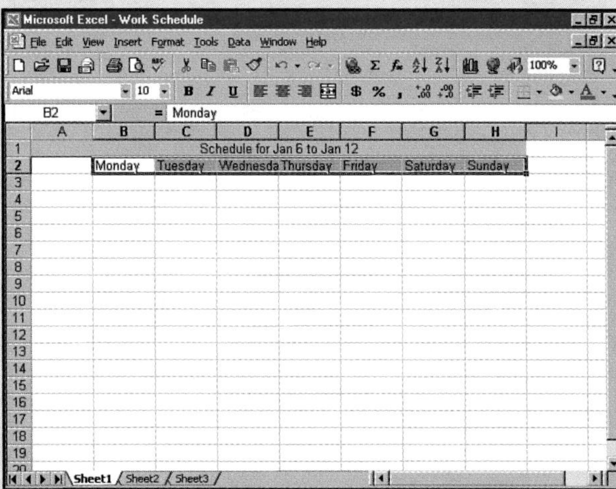

Figure 3.3
With one quick stroke, a whole series of week names is filled in.

6 Click the Save button. Leave the file open for use in the next lesson.

The workbook is saved on your floppy disk.

Filling with Dates and Numbers

Several interesting options are available when you fill with dates or numbers. Hold down the right mouse button rather than the left button when you drag the fill handle, and you get a shortcut menu of options. One option is to fill weekdays, excluding weekend days. Other choices include filling months or years, and numeric series using growth, linear, or specific trends. You explore these options in the end-of-project exercises.

Lesson 2: Creating a Series of Numbers

Normally in a worksheet, numbers are entered to make calculations, which is why they are entered in separate cells. Sometimes you use numbers to represent dates or times as the labels for rows or columns. Excel can recognize date formats, such as 9/5 or 9-5-99, entered in a cell. You can choose how to format dates or times.

In this lesson, you create a series of times as row labels and set both common and custom intervals.

To Create a Series of Times as Row Labels

1. **Select cell A3; type `8:00`, and press ⏎Enter.**
   This is the first time in the series of time values.
2. **Select cell A3 again. Click and drag the fill handle to cell A10. Release the mouse button.**
   Notice that the sequence of times increases by one hour and that they display using a 24-hour format, as shown in Figure 3.4. As you click and drag the series, a ScreenTip displays to show the time that is being entered in each cell.

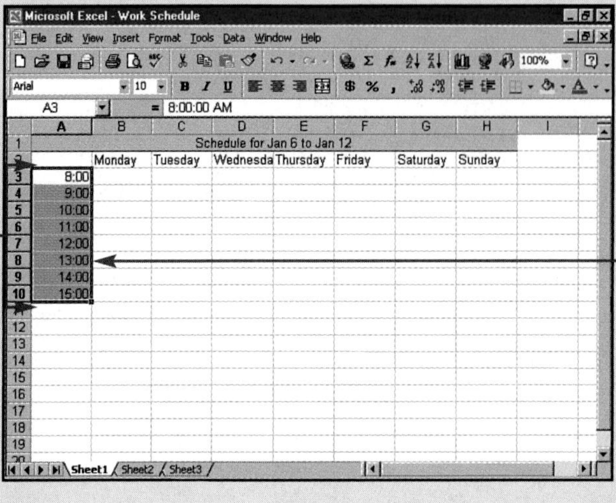

Figure 3.4
A series of times is completed.

Results of filling a range based on the data in cell A3

1:00 PM displays as 13:00 in a 24-hour time format

3. **Click the Undo button.**
   The fill is undone. This company schedules its part-time workers on the half-hour. To establish this half-hour pattern, you need to enter data in at least two cells before applying the fill.
4. **Select cell A4, type `8:30`, and press ⏎Enter.**
   The second time in the series is entered into cell A4.
5. **Select cells A3 and A4, and release the mouse.**
   Remember, because the first cell of a selected group does not change color, it might not look like cell A3 is selected. The thick line encloses both cells if they are both selected. It is important to select both cells to create the pattern for the series.
6. **Click and drag the fill handle down to cell A18. Release the mouse button.**
   The sequence is filled in half-hour increments, as shown in Figure 3.5.

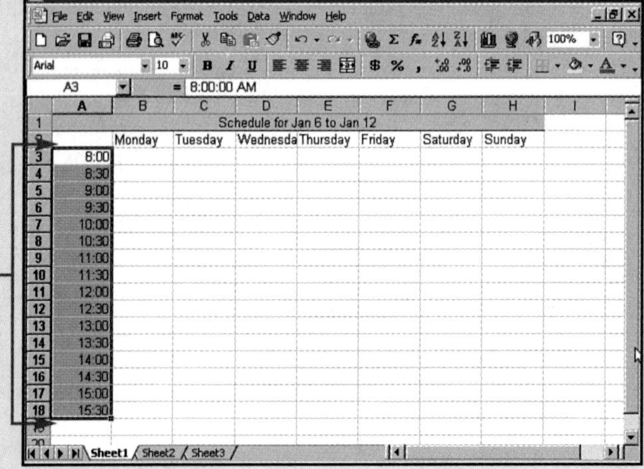

Figure 3.5
The first two cells establish the series that Excel uses to complete the column of times.

Results of filling a range based on the two-cell pattern entered in cells A3 and A4

7. **Use the vertical scrollbar to scroll and display rows 18 through 30.**
8. **Click and drag the fill handle to cell A29. Release the mouse.**
   The sequence of half-hour time increments is extended. Cells A3 through A29 are still selected.
9. **Choose Format, Cells, and select the Number tab in the Format Cells dialog box.**
   On the Number tab, the Time category is selected.
10. **Click the 1:30 PM sample format, and click OK.**
    The column of times is formatted to display AM and PM, as shown in Figure 3.6.

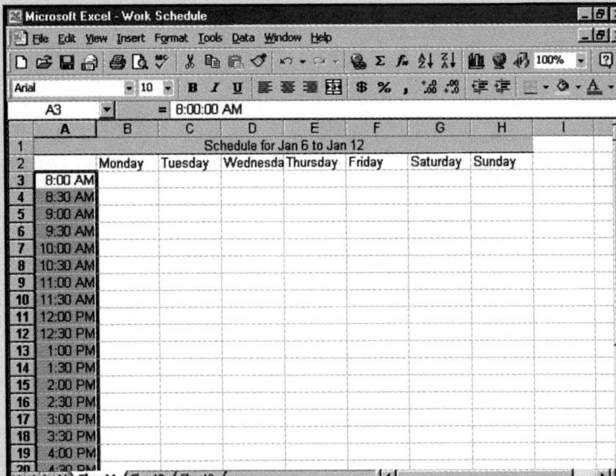

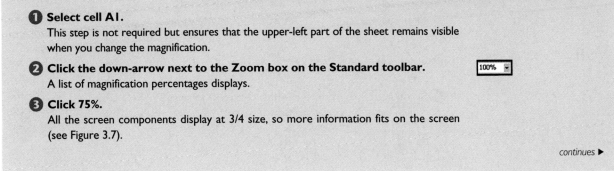

Figure 3.6
The times display with AM or PM designations.

11. **Save the file, and leave it open for use in the next lesson.**

Lesson 3: Changing Zoom and Freezing Panes

When rows and columns are too long to be viewed on the screen in their entirety, you have to scroll the window to see cells at the end of the row or column. Unfortunately, when you get to the cell, the row or column label is no longer visible, so you can easily mistake one row or column for another.

In this lesson, you change the magnification of the view so that you can see larger areas of the worksheet. You also freeze the row and/or column labels, so they stay visible while you scroll.

To Change the Zoom and Freeze Panes

1. **Select cell A1.**
   This step is not required but ensures that the upper-left part of the sheet remains visible when you change the magnification.
2. **Click the down-arrow next to the Zoom box on the Standard toolbar.**
   A list of magnification percentages displays.
3. **Click 75%.**
   All the screen components display at 3/4 size, so more information fits on the screen (see Figure 3.7).

continues ▶

To Change the Zoom and Freeze Panes (continued)

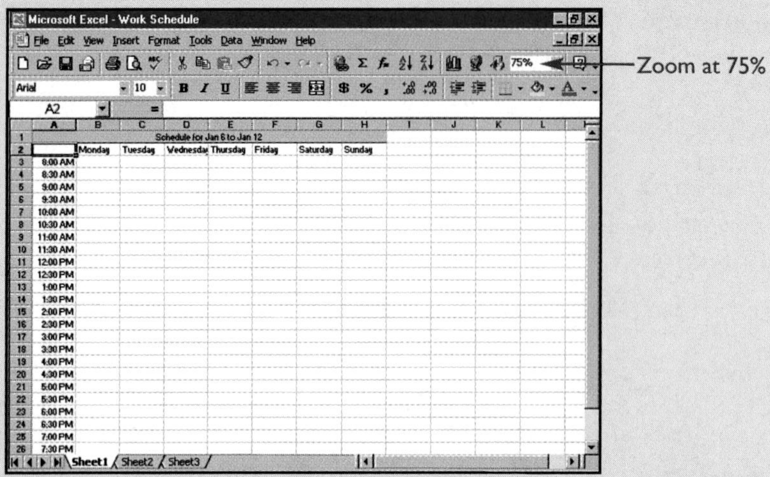

Figure 3.7
Use the Zoom button to help you see more of your worksheet on the screen.

4. **Click the down-arrow next to the Zoom box, and click 100% to return to normal magnification.**

5. **Click cell B3.**
   This cell is below rows 1 and 2 and to the right of column A.

6. **Choose Window, Freeze Panes from the menu.**
   The rows above the selected cell and the columns to the left of the selected cell remain on the screen regardless of how far to the right or bottom you scroll. Look at Figure 3.8 and notice the horizontal and vertical lines that mark the edges of the panes above and to the left of cell B3.

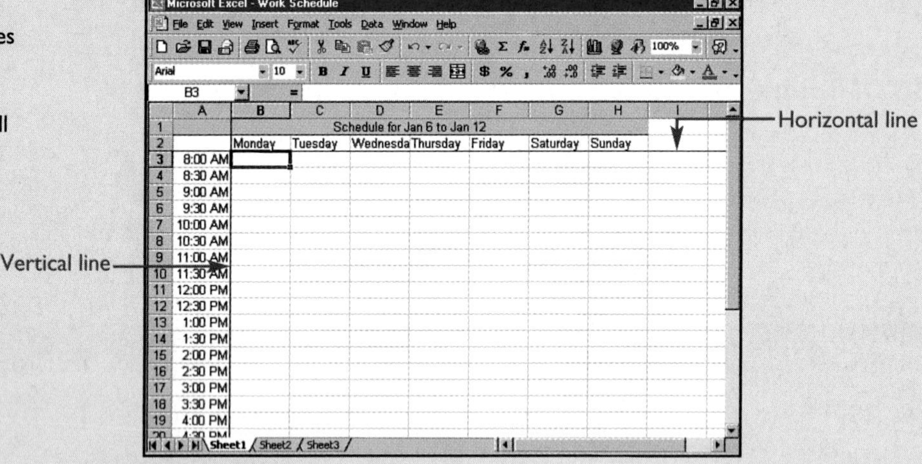

Figure 3.8
Using the Freeze Panes command keeps row and column labels visible while you scroll the worksheet.

7. **Scroll down until row 14 follows row 2.**
   Notice that rows 1 and 2 remain on the screen.

8. **Scroll to the right until column D is next to column A.**
   Notice that column A remains on the screen (see Figure 3.9).

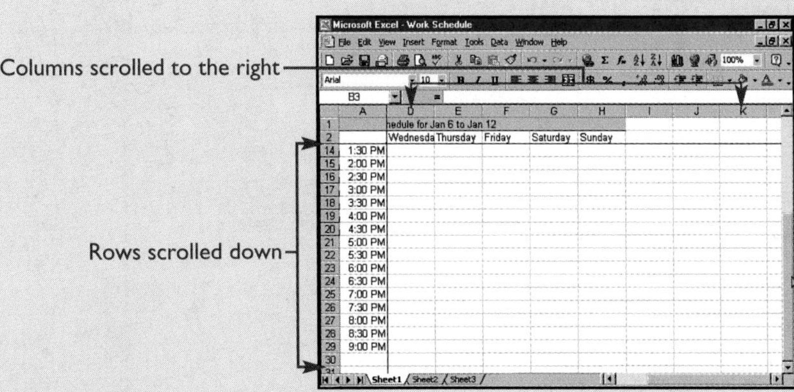

Figure 3.9
Column and row labels remain stationary while you view other parts of the worksheet.

9. **Choose Window, Unfreeze Panes.**
   Columns B and C and rows 3 through 13 return to view.

10. **Leave the file open for use in the next lesson.**

Using the Zoom Feature
When you use the Zoom button, the cells look smaller on the screen, but this setting doesn't alter the size of printed output. You can choose any screen magnification you desire by typing the percentage directly into the Zoom box.

Lesson 4: Copying Cell Contents

Some worksheets require the display of the same data in many cells. You can use the Copy and Paste commands to copy existing data to other locations in the worksheet, saving you the time of re-entering the duplicate data. You also can fill a range of cells with data based on a pattern established in one cell or multiple adjacent cells.

In this lesson, you use the Fill, Copy, and Paste commands to fill a form with repetitive data.

To Copy Cell Contents

1. **Select cell B3; type `Bill`, and press ↵Enter. Select cell B3 again. Click and drag the fill handle to cell B14. Release the mouse button.**
   Bill's name is filled into the cells from B4 to B14.

2. **With cells B4 to B14 still highlighted, click the fill handle on the corner of B14 and drag it to the right to cell C14. Release the mouse button.**
   Cells C4 to C14 are filled with Bill's name (see Figure 3.10). You can use the fill handle to fill repetitive data into adjacent columns.

continues ▶

To Copy Cell Contents (continued)

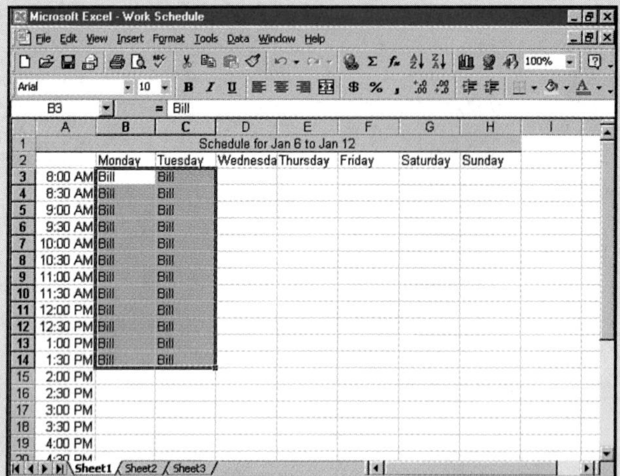

Figure 3.10
Use the fill handle to copy the contents of a cell to adjacent cells.

3 Click cell B3 again to select a cell that contains Bill's name. Click the Copy button on the Standard toolbar.

Bill's name is copied and is stored in the clipboard, which is a temporary storage area used for holding information that has been copied or cut from an application file. Notice that a marquee shows around the cell that has been copied.

4 Select cells E3 through E14. Click the Paste button on the Standard toolbar.

Bill's name is filled into the entire cell range, as shown in Figure 3.11.

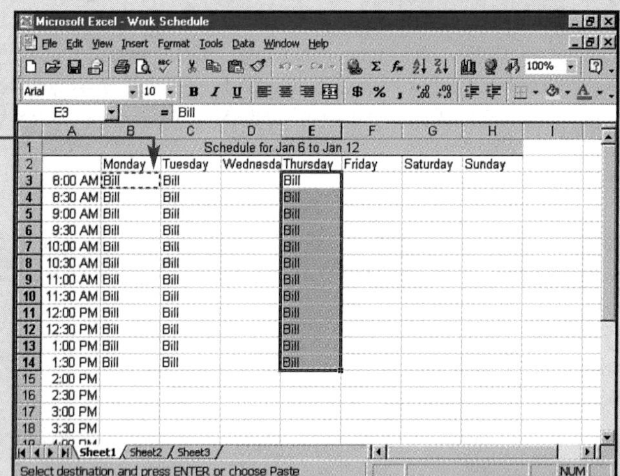

Figure 3.11
You can fill a range of cells with one click of the Paste button.

5 Use the Fill and Copy techniques described in the previous steps to fill out the rest of the schedule, as shown in Figure 3.12.

Figure 3.12 is shown at 75% zoom with two toolbars, scrollbars, and the status bar turned off to show the whole work schedule. You do not have to make these changes.

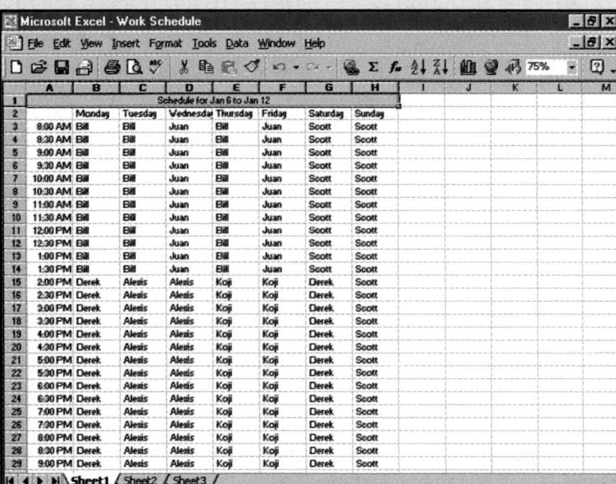

	A	B	C	D	E	F	G	H
1	Schedule for Jan 6 to Jan 12							
2		Monday	Tuesday	Wednesda	Thursday	Friday	Saturday	Sunday
3	8:00 AM	Bill	Bill	Juan	Bill	Juan	Scott	Scott
4	8:30 AM	Bill	Bill	Juan	Bill	Juan	Scott	Scott
5	9:00 AM	Bill	Bill	Juan	Bill	Juan	Scott	Scott
6	9:30 AM	Bill	Bill	Juan	Bill	Juan	Scott	Scott
7	10:00 AM	Bill	Bill	Juan	Bill	Juan	Scott	Scott
8	10:30 AM	Bill	Bill	Juan	Bill	Juan	Scott	Scott
9	11:00 AM	Bill	Bill	Juan	Bill	Juan	Scott	Scott
10	11:30 AM	Bill	Bill	Juan	Bill	Juan	Scott	Scott
11	12:00 PM	Bill	Bill	Juan	Bill	Juan	Scott	Scott
12	12:30 PM	Bill	Bill	Juan	Bill	Juan	Scott	Scott
13	1:00 PM	Bill	Bill	Juan	Bill	Juan	Scott	Scott
14	1:30 PM	Bill	Bill	Juan	Bill	Juan	Scott	Scott
15	2:00 PM	Derek	Alexis	Alexis	Koji	Koji	Derek	Scott
16	2:30 PM	Derek	Alexis	Alexis	Koji	Koji	Derek	Scott
17	3:00 PM	Derek	Alexis	Alexis	Koji	Koji	Derek	Scott
18	3:30 PM	Derek	Alexis	Alexis	Koji	Koji	Derek	Scott
19	4:00 PM	Derek	Alexis	Alexis	Koji	Koji	Derek	Scott
20	4:30 PM	Derek	Alexis	Alexis	Koji	Koji	Derek	Scott
21	5:00 PM	Derek	Alexis	Alexis	Koji	Koji	Derek	Scott
22	5:30 PM	Derek	Alexis	Alexis	Koji	Koji	Derek	Scott
23	6:00 PM	Derek	Alexis	Alexis	Koji	Koji	Derek	Scott
24	6:30 PM	Derek	Alexis	Alexis	Koji	Koji	Derek	Scott
25	7:00 PM	Derek	Alexis	Alexis	Koji	Koji	Derek	Scott
26	7:30 PM	Derek	Alexis	Alexis	Koji	Koji	Derek	Scott
27	8:00 PM	Derek	Alexis	Alexis	Koji	Koji	Derek	Scott
28	8:30 PM	Derek	Alexis	Alexis	Koji	Koji	Derek	Scott
29	9:00 PM	Derek	Alexis	Alexis	Koji	Koji	Derek	Scott

Figure 3.12
Complete the worksheet as shown.

6 Click the Save button to save your work. Leave the file open for use in the next lesson.

Key Combinations for Copying, Cutting, and Pasting

Sometimes when you are copying information, it is quicker to use key combinations instead of buttons on the toolbar. To copy, use Ctrl+C; to cut, use Ctrl+X; to paste, use Ctrl+V. These key combinations are used in all Microsoft applications and in most other Windows-compatible applications.

Pasting into Selected Cells

When you use the copy and paste techniques, after you select the destination cells, you can press ↵Enter. Excel pastes the contents you copied into the selected cells.

Lesson 5: Improving the Printed Worksheet

Excel provides several options that you can use to make your printed worksheets look better and make them easier to identify and read. Sometimes a worksheet has many columns and the page orientation (landscape or portrait) needs to be changed to accommodate all the information. It is also useful to add information that you will want repeated in each page of the printed worksheet in a header. This information can include the current date, the name of the file, or your name. Finally, to give your work a professional appearance, the columns of data should be centered on the page.

In this lesson, you change the orientation of the page to handle wider worksheets, center data on the page, and add your name and an automatic date to a header.

To Improve the Printed Worksheet

1 Choose File, Page Setup, and click the Page tab, if it is not already selected.
The Page Setup dialog box displays, as shown in Figure 3.13.

continues ▶

To Improve the Printed Worksheet (continued)

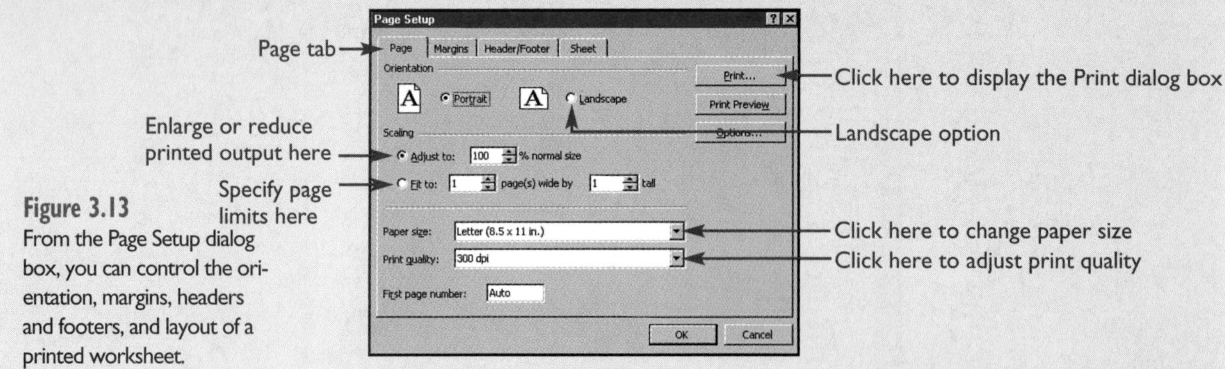

Figure 3.13
From the Page Setup dialog box, you can control the orientation, margins, headers and footers, and layout of a printed worksheet.

2 **Click the Landscape option.**

3 **Click the Margins tab.**

The Margins sheet displays, as shown in Figure 3.14. Here you can change the top, left, right, and bottom margins, and the margin from the edge of the page to the header or footer. You also use this window to center the worksheet on a page horizontally and vertically.

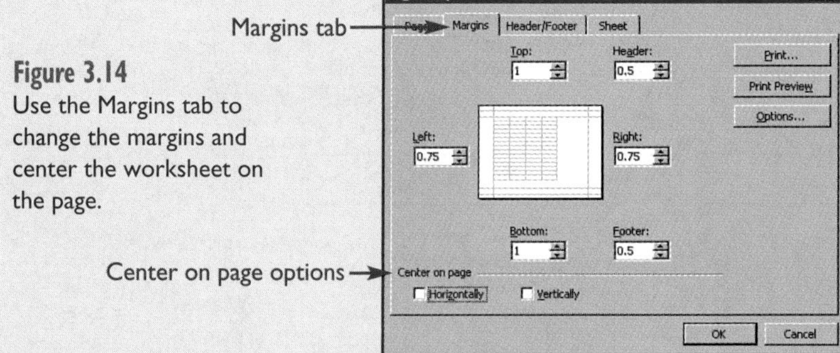

Figure 3.14
Use the Margins tab to change the margins and center the worksheet on the page.

4 **Click the Horizontally option in the Center on page section at the lower-left of the dialog box.**

The sample layout in the middle of the window shows how the data will be centered left-and-right on the page.

5 **Click the Header/Footer tab.**

The Header/Footer sheet displays, as shown in Figure 3.15. To change the header or footer, you need to click Custom Header or Custom Footer. The header or footer is the area at the top or bottom of the worksheet, respectively. Use a header or footer for information that you want to appear on each page of the printout, but not as part of the worksheet itself. Usually information such as date, time, page number, file location, or author is included in the header or footer area.

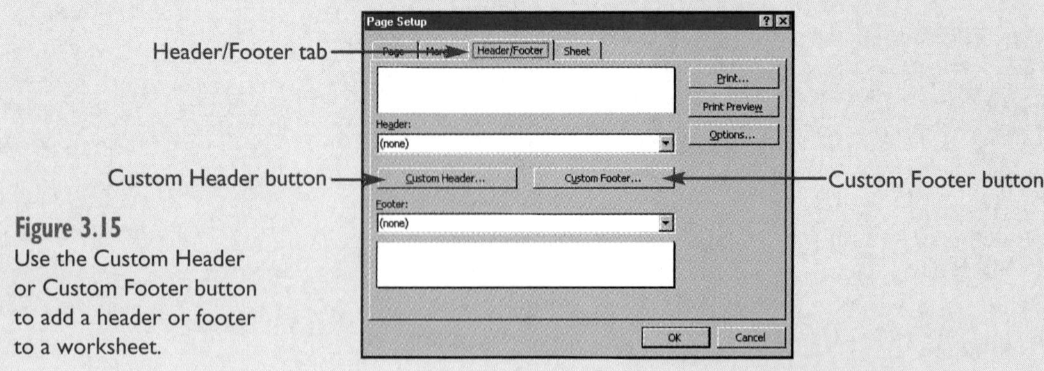

Figure 3.15
Use the Custom Header or Custom Footer button to add a header or footer to a worksheet.

6 Click the Custom Header button.

The Header page displays, as shown in Figure 3.16. The header is divided into three sections: Left, Center, and Right. Several buttons, which you use to format the font, add the time or date, or include page numbers, display.

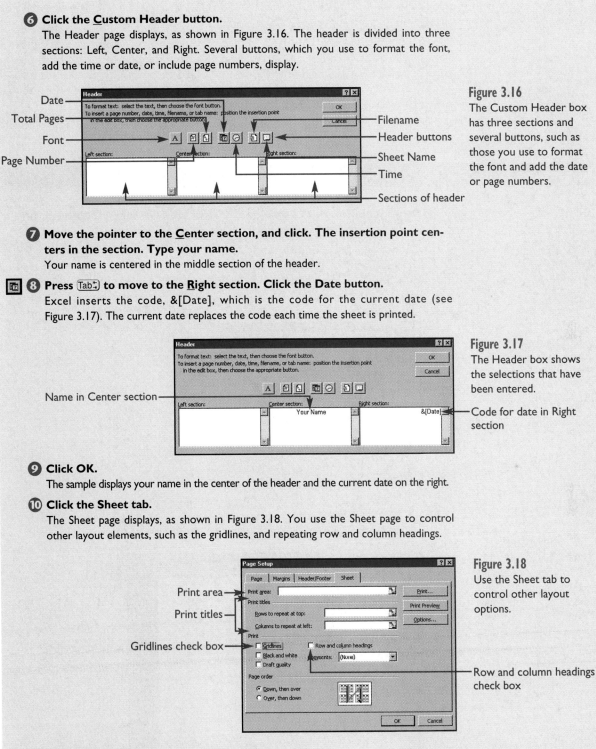

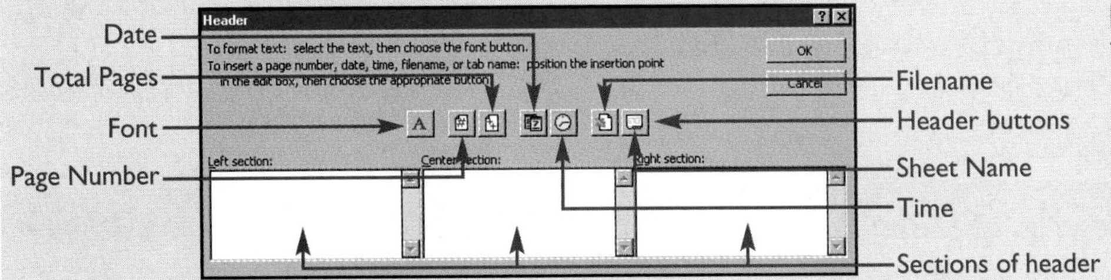

Figure 3.16
The Custom Header box has three sections and several buttons, such as those you use to format the font and add the date or page numbers.

7 Move the pointer to the Center section, and click. The insertion point centers in the section. Type your name.

Your name is centered in the middle section of the header.

8 Press Tab to move to the Right section. Click the Date button.

Excel inserts the code, &[Date], which is the code for the current date (see Figure 3.17). The current date replaces the code each time the sheet is printed.

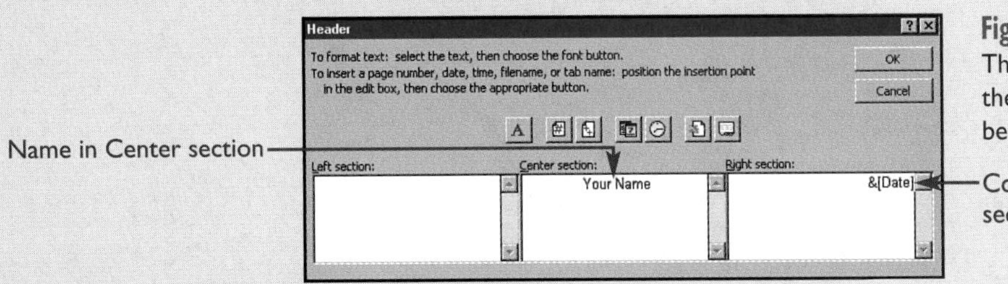

Figure 3.17
The Header box shows the selections that have been entered.

9 Click OK.

The sample displays your name in the center of the header and the current date on the right.

10 Click the Sheet tab.

The Sheet page displays, as shown in Figure 3.18. You use the Sheet page to control other layout elements, such as the gridlines, and repeating row and column headings.

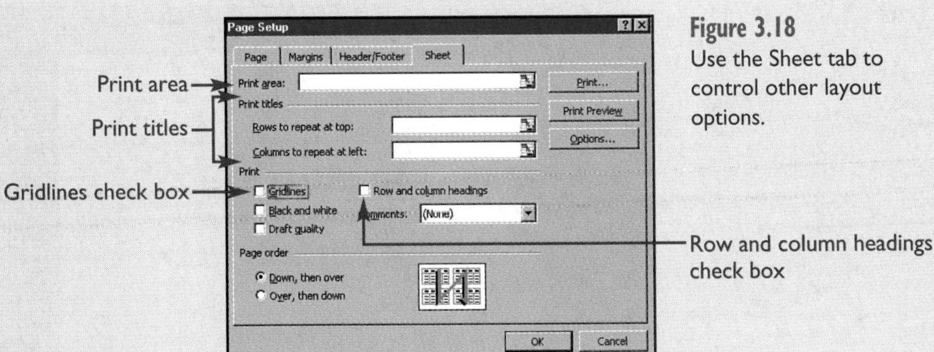

Figure 3.18
Use the Sheet tab to control other layout options.

11 Click the Gridlines check box to print the gridlines.

The ***gridlines*** outline the cells and make it easier to follow rows or columns. The default setting is to omit gridlines when the worksheet prints. If you want the gridlines to show, you need to select it on the Sheet tab of the Page Setup dialog box.

12 Click OK, and save the file.

The Page Setup window closes. Leave the file open for use in the next lesson.

Lesson 6: Previewing Print Settings and Printing a Range

If a worksheet is too large to fit on one page, or you do not want to print an entire sheet, you can select a portion of the sheet to print. If your worksheet will print on several pages, it is useful to have the title of the worksheet and the column labels appear on each page so that information on pages beyond the first page is properly labeled. It is useful to first preview the printout on the screen to catch errors in layout and formatting, such as one column printing on a page by itself. You can make the necessary adjustments and save time and paper by not printing mistakes.

In this lesson, you select part of the schedule to print, select column labels to print, and preview the page before you print it.

To Preview Print Settings and Print a Range

1. **Scroll to display rows 15 through 29. Select the cells from A15 through H29.**
   This includes the row labels and all the work scheduled after 2 p.m.

2. **Choose File, Print, and Selection.**
   The Print dialog box opens (see Figure 3.19) and you can choose what you want to print. In this case, you have chosen to print the selected cells, but first you use the preview option to view the results.

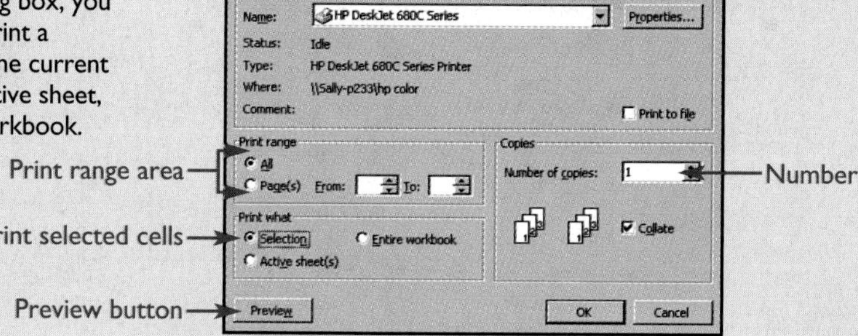

Figure 3.19
In the Print dialog box, you can choose to print a range of pages, the current selection, the active sheet, or the entire workbook.

3. **Click the Preview button.**
   The page displays as it will look when you print it (see Figure 3.20).

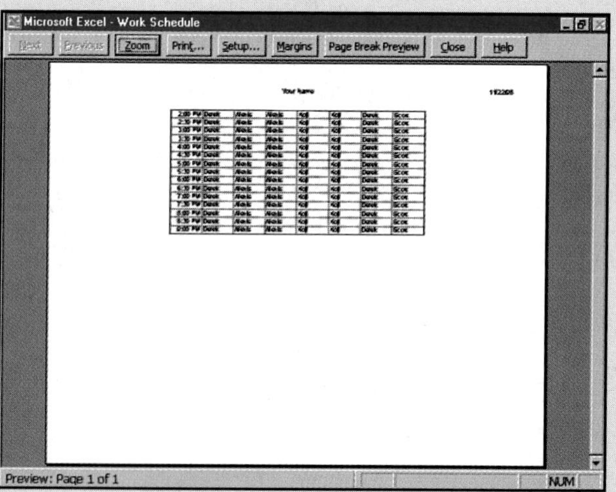

Figure 3.20
The Print Preview enables you to examine how the worksheet will look when it is printed.

4. **Click the Zoom button to switch the magnification.**
   Notice that the column labels in rows 1 and 2 of the worksheet do not display, because they were not part of the print area you selected. This problem is addressed in the next part of this lesson. To change magnification, you can also click the preview. Click again to change it back.

5 Click the Close button on the toolbar. Change the zoom setting to 50%.
The worksheet displays dotted lines to indicate how many columns and rows will fit on the page (see Figure 3.21).

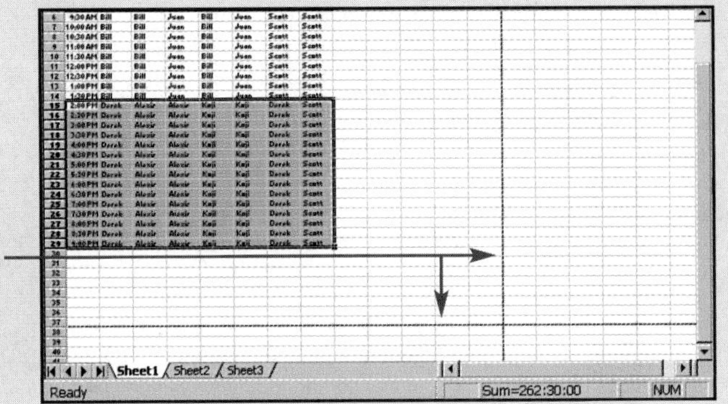

Dotted lines mark the boundaries of a printed page

Figure 3.21
The dotted line indicates how many columns and rows will fit on a printed page.

6 Change the zoom back to 100%.

In the next section, you add the column labels to the page setup, so the labels for the columns of the worksheet print above the selection.

To Select a Column or Row to Print as a Label

1 Choose File, Page Setup, and click the Sheet tab, if necessary.
The Page Setup dialog box opens, and the Sheet tab displays.

2 Click the Collapse Dialog button at the right end of the Rows to repeat at top box.
The dialog box shrinks to a single item so that you can see the sheet and select the rows to repeat (see Figure 3.22). If the collapsed dialog box is in the way, click the blue title bar and drag it to another location.

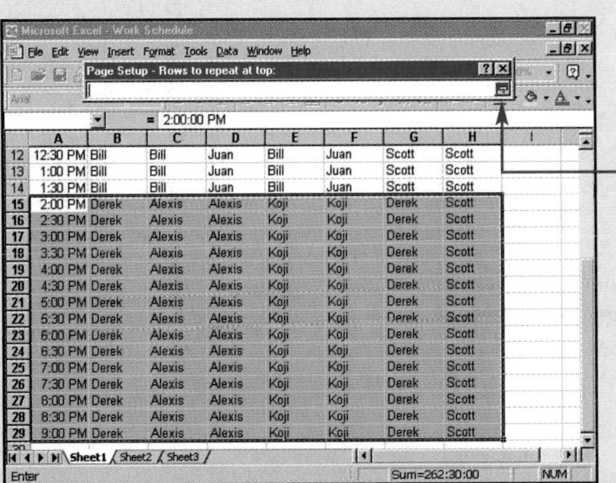

Figure 3.22
The Page Setup dialog box collapses so you can see the worksheet.

Button used to expand and collapse the dialog box

3 Scroll to the top; click and drag to select row headings 1 and 2.
The code for rows 1 and 2 ($1:$2) displays in the Page Setup—Rows to repeat at top box. By selecting rows 1 and 2, you are selecting the cells that contain the label for the worksheet title and the labels for the columns of data.

4 Click the Expand Dialog button at the right end of the collapsed Page Setup box.
The Page Setup window expands.

continues ▶

To Select a Column or Row to Print as a Label (continued)

5 Click OK to close the dialog box. Choose File, Print; click Selection in the Print what area, and click the Preview button.

Notice that the labels are now included (see Figure 3.23). Also, the information in the Header area, which you entered in the previous lesson, shows in the preview.

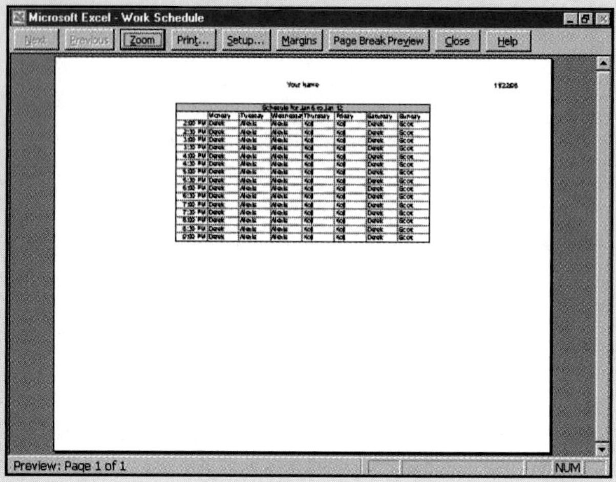

Figure 3.23
The column labels show above the selection.

6 Click the Print button to print the selected cells with the labels from rows 1 and 2.

Your printout should look like the one shown in Figure 3.24.

Figure 3.24
The printout should look like this (the date in the upper-right corner is not shown in the figure).

Your Name

Schedule for Jan 6 to Jan 12							
	Monday	Tuesday	Wednesday	Thursday	Friday	Saturday	Sunday
2:00 PM	Derek	Alexis	Alexis	Koji	Koji	Derek	Scott
2:30 PM	Derek	Alexis	Alexis	Koji	Koji	Derek	Scott
3:00 PM	Derek	Alexis	Alexis	Koji	Koji	Derek	Scott
3:30 PM	Derek	Alexis	Alexis	Koji	Koji	Derek	Scott
4:00 PM	Derek	Alexis	Alexis	Koji	Koji	Derek	Scott
4:30 PM	Derek	Alexis	Alexis	Koji	Koji	Derek	Scott
5:00 PM	Derek	Alexis	Alexis	Koji	Koji	Derek	Scott
5:30 PM	Derek	Alexis	Alexis	Koji	Koji	Derek	Scott
6:00 PM	Derek	Alexis	Alexis	Koji	Koji	Derek	Scott
6:30 PM	Derek	Alexis	Alexis	Koji	Koji	Derek	Scott
7:00 PM	Derek	Alexis	Alexis	Koji	Koji	Derek	Scott
7:30 PM	Derek	Alexis	Alexis	Koji	Koji	Derek	Scott
8:00 PM	Derek	Alexis	Alexis	Koji	Koji	Derek	Scott
8:30 PM	Derek	Alexis	Alexis	Koji	Koji	Derek	Scott
9:00 PM	Derek	Alexis	Alexis	Koji	Koji	Derek	Scott

7 Save your changes, and close the workbook.

Summary

This project showed you how to use tools that can help you work more efficiently with a worksheet. Specifically, you used the fill handle to fill in sequential lists of days of the week, times of the day, and text. You created a custom list by creating a pattern and using the fill handle to repeat the series. You copied data to adjacent cells and columns and copied and pasted data from one cell to a group of nonadjacent cells. You also learned how to freeze panes and use the Zoom feature to help with scrolling a large worksheet. Finally, you used some tools for managing the printed worksheet.

To learn more about using the fill handle, try experimenting with a sequence that you might find useful. Create a series and then see if it repeats. Use Excel Help to learn more about sequences and series, as well as additional printing options.

Checking Concepts and Terms

True/False

For each of the following, check *T* or *F* to indicate whether the statement is true or false.

__T __F **1.** If you select cell B4 and freeze the panes, rows 1 through 3 would be frozen as well as column A. [L4]

__T __F **2.** The fill handle is located in the lower-left corner of the selected cell. [L4]

__T __F **3.** If you select a cell that contains the word "Jane" and drag the fill handle to an adjacent cell, the adjacent cell would contain the word "Jane". [L4]

__T __F **4.** To print a range of cells, select the range and click the Print button on the toolbar. [L6]

__T __F **5.** If Zoom is currently set at 100% and you change the Zoom percentage to 75%, you can see more cells on the screen. [L6]

__T __F **6.** The Copy button on the Standard toolbar looks like a small Clipboard with a page in front of it. [L4]

__T __F **7.** The Preview window has a Zoom button but it only toggles back and forth between two sizes. [L6]

__T __F **8.** If you had a worksheet that was wider (columns) than it was long (rows), you would use the Portrait page orientation. [L5]

__T __F **9.** The Collapse Dialog Box button is used to shrink the dialog box to make it easier to make a selection from the worksheet. [L6]

__T __F **10.** It is better to print several copies of the worksheet as you create it to make sure the final copy is error-free. [L6]

Multiple Choice

Circle the letter of the correct answer for each of the following.

1. The Page Setup dialog box is used to do which of the following? [L6]

a. change the orientation of the page to landscape

b. add information to a header or a footer

c. select rows to repeat at the top of the worksheet

d. all of the above

2. How would you print part of a worksheet? [L6]

a. Select the range and use File, Print, Selection.

b. Open the Print dialog box, and choose Print selection.

c. Select the range, and click the Print button.

d. You can't print only part of a worksheet.

3. If you wanted to freeze rows 1 through 3 and columns A and B, what cell would you select before choosing Windows, Freeze Panes? [L4]

a. A2

b. B3

c. C4

d. none of the above

4. What method would you use to put the same word into 20 cells in a nonadjacent column? [L4]

a. click and drag

b. copy and paste

c. fill handle

d. click and fill

5. Which of the following could be used as the first label in a sequence? [L1]

a. Tuesday

b. September

c. 1st Quarter

d. all of the above

Screen ID

Identify each of the items shown in Figure 3.25.

Figure 3.25

A. Pointer on the fill handle
B. Copy button
C. Paste button
D. Zoom button
E. Freeze Panes option found here
F. Indicates the last column that will fit on the page
G. Selected Area

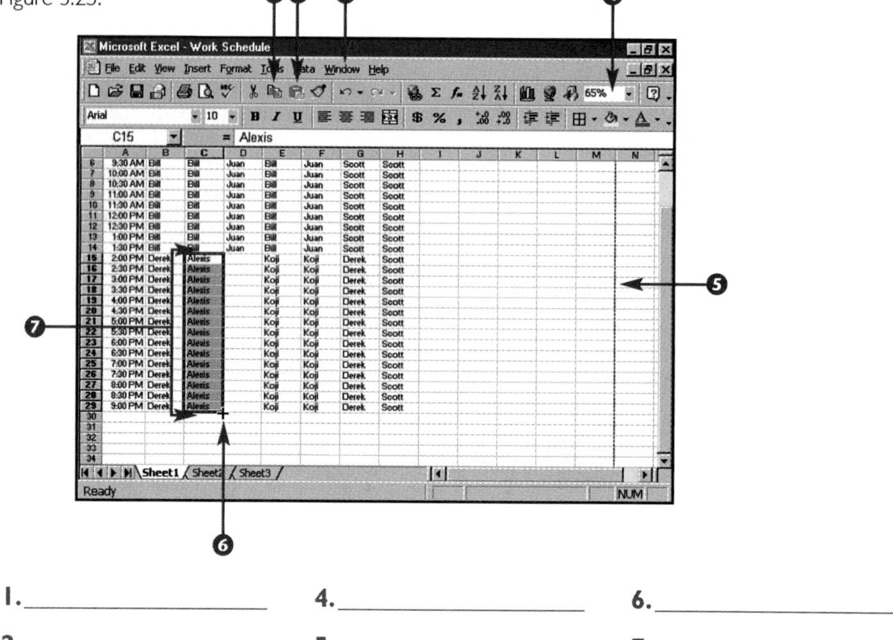

1.__________________ 4.__________________ 6.__________________

2.__________________ 5.__________________ 7.__________________

3.__________________

Discussion Questions

1. What are some sequences that you might use on a worksheet? What series would you want to be able to create?
2. When would you use the Zoom feature instead of freezing panes? When would you freeze the panes in a worksheet instead of changing the magnification?
3. Do you prefer to have gridlines displayed or omitted when you print a worksheet? Why? When would you be more likely to print gridlines?

Skill Drill

Skill Drill exercises reinforce project skills. Each skill reinforced is the same, or nearly the same, as a skill presented in the project. Each exercise includes a brief narrative introduction, followed by detailed instructions in a step-by-step format.

In these exercises, you create four different worksheets that use the special fill capabilities of Excel. First, you create a worksheet that tracks leases for offices in a small office building. In the second exercise, you create a worksheet to keep track of time spent on various accounts during the workweek. Then, you create a worksheet to keep track of an activity that occurs once a week. In the last exercise, you use the Fill function to project population growth.

All these exercises use the file EO-0302 found in the Student folder on the CD-ROM that came with your book. Open the file and save it your floppy disk with the name `Sequences`.

1. Creating a Sheet to Track Leases

In this exercise, you create a lease report worksheet for a small office building. [L1–6]

1. Select Sheet1. Rename the tab at the bottom `Leases`.
2. Fill in the months in column A.
3. Select the first two office numbers in cells B3 and C3, and fill in the column labels up to 120 in cell L3.
4. Type `Armstrong` in cell B4. Copy the name into the cells as shown for offices 100, 102, and 104. (Try the Fill method, just to see what happens.)
5. Use Fill and/or Copy to put `Tax` (a tax accounting firm) in office 104 from July to December, and for the entire year in offices 108 through 118. Place `Arch` (an architectural firm) in 106 and `Admin` (administrative staff) in 120.
6. Adjust column widths, if necessary, to show all cell data.
7. Center the column labels in row 3. The finished worksheet should look like the one in Figure 3.26.

8. Change the page orientation to Landscape.
9. Choose File, Page Setup, and create a header that contains your name, centered.
10. Save the workbook; preview and print the sheet.

Figure 3.26

Microsoft Excel - Sequences

Month	100	102	104	106	108	110	112	114	116	118	120
January	Armstrong	Armstrong	Armstrong	Arch	Tax	Arch	Tax	Tax	Tax	Tax	Admin
February	Armstrong	Armstrong	Armstrong	Arch	Tax	Arch	Tax	Tax	Tax	Tax	Admin
March	Armstrong	Armstrong	Armstrong	Arch	Tax	Arch	Tax	Tax	Tax	Tax	Admin
April	Armstrong	Armstrong	Armstrong	Arch	Tax	Arch	Tax	Tax	Tax	Tax	Admin
May	Armstrong	Armstrong	Armstrong	Arch	Tax	Arch	Tax	Tax	Tax	Tax	Admin
June	Armstrong	Armstrong	Armstrong	Arch	Tax	Arch	Tax	Tax	Tax	Tax	Admin
July	Armstrong	Armstrong	Tax	Arch	Tax	Arch	Tax	Tax	Tax	Tax	Admin
August	Armstrong	Armstrong	Tax	Arch	Tax	Arch	Tax	Tax	Tax	Tax	Admin
September	Armstrong	Armstrong	Tax	Arch	Tax	Arch	Tax	Tax	Tax	Tax	Admin
October	Armstrong	Armstrong	Tax	Arch	Tax	Arch	Tax	Tax	Tax	Tax	Admin
November	Armstrong	Armstrong	Tax	Arch	Tax	Arch	Tax	Tax	Tax	Tax	Admin
December	Armstrong	Armstrong	Tax	Arch	Tax	Arch	Tax	Tax	Tax	Tax	Admin

2. Creating a Sheet to Track Time

In a work environment, you might need to track the time you spend for different clients for billing purposes. In this exercise, you create a worksheet to track the time spent on several different accounts during the workweek. To do this you use the fill handle to fill in the days of the workweek only, excluding weekends. [L1, 3, 6]

1. Select Sheet2. Rename the Sheet tab at the bottom, `Timesheet`. Change the Zoom to 75%.
2. Select cell A4.
3. Right-click the fill handle and drag to cell A23. Release the mouse button.
4. Select Fill Weekdays from the shortcut menu. Make sure that there are no Saturdays or Sundays.
5. Select cell B4. Repeat the same process to fill in the dates for the weekdays. Notice how the program displays the year 1998. Your timesheet should look like the one in Figure 3.27.
6. Choose File, Page Setup, and create a footer that contains your name left-aligned.
7. Save the workbook. Preview and print the sheet.

Figure 3.27

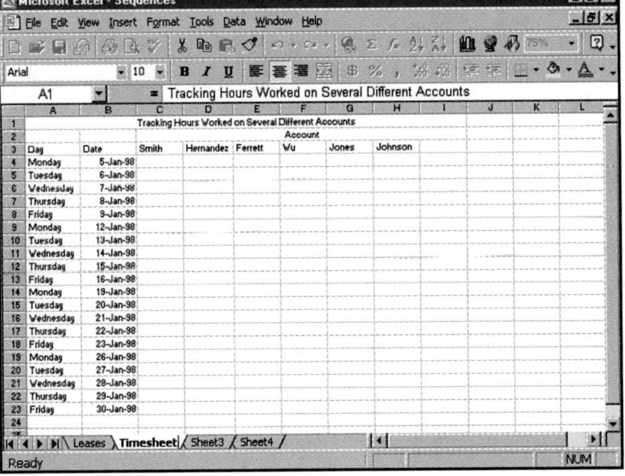

Tracking Hours Worked on Several Different Accounts

Day	Date	Smith	Hernandez	Ferrett	Wu	Jones	Johnson
Monday	5-Jan-98						
Tuesday	6-Jan-98						
Wednesday	7-Jan-98						
Thursday	8-Jan-98						
Friday	9-Jan-98						
Monday	12-Jan-98						
Tuesday	13-Jan-98						
Wednesday	14-Jan-98						
Thursday	15-Jan-98						
Friday	16-Jan-98						
Monday	19-Jan-98						
Tuesday	20-Jan-98						
Wednesday	21-Jan-98						
Thursday	22-Jan-98						
Friday	23-Jan-98						
Monday	26-Jan-98						
Tuesday	27-Jan-98						
Wednesday	28-Jan-98						
Thursday	29-Jan-98						
Friday	30-Jan-98						

3. Creating a Schedule for a Once-a-Week Activity

You might have an activity that occurs once a week for which you need to create a schedule. This could be a bowling league, church meeting, or sporting event. In this exercise, you fill in the dates for the football schedule for the local university. [L1, 6]

1. Select Sheet3 and rename it `Football`.
2. Select the dates in cells A3 and A4. Drag the fill handle down to cell A16.

3. Repeat this process in columns C and E to fill in the dates associated with the schools listed in columns D and F, respectively. The Football worksheet should look like the one in Figure 3.28.

4. Choose File, Page Setup, and create a header that contains your name left-aligned.

5. Save the workbook. Preview and print the sheet.

Figure 3.28

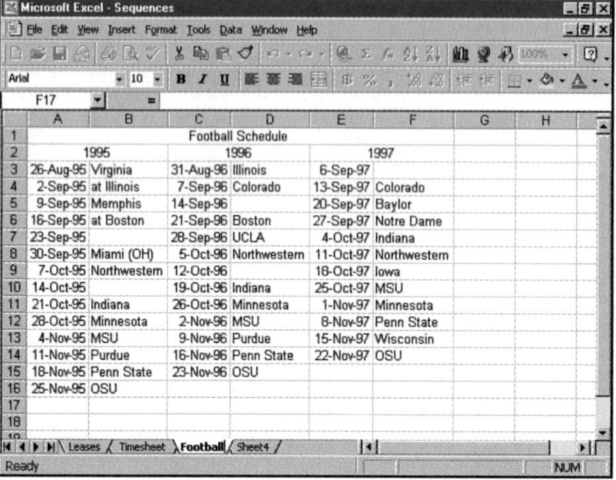

	A	B	C	D	E	F
1			Football Schedule			
2	1995		1996		1997	
3	26-Aug-95	Virginia	31-Aug-96	Illinois	6-Sep-97	
4	2-Sep-95	at Illinois	7-Sep-96	Colorado	13-Sep-97	Colorado
5	9-Sep-95	Memphis	14-Sep-96		20-Sep-97	Baylor
6	16-Sep-95	at Boston	21-Sep-96	Boston	27-Sep-97	Notre Dame
7	23-Sep-95		28-Sep-96	UCLA	4-Oct-97	Indiana
8	30-Sep-95	Miami (OH)	5-Oct-96	Northwestern	11-Oct-97	Northwestern
9	7-Oct-95	Northwestern	12-Oct-96		18-Oct-97	Iowa
10	14-Oct-95		19-Oct-96	Indiana	25-Oct-97	MSU
11	21-Oct-95	Indiana	26-Oct-96	Minnesota	1-Nov-97	Minnesota
12	28-Oct-95	Minnesota	2-Nov-96	MSU	8-Nov-97	Penn State
13	4-Nov-95	MSU	9-Nov-96	Purdue	15-Nov-97	Wisconsin
14	11-Nov-95	Purdue	16-Nov-96	Penn State	22-Nov-97	OSU
15	18-Nov-95	Penn State	23-Nov-96	OSU		
16	25-Nov-95	OSU				

4. Projecting Population Growth

The fill options also include a growth rate, either a specific linear rate of growth, or an exponential growth rate. In this exercise, you complete a worksheet to project United States population growth at a rate of 1% per year for the next 20 years. [L1–2, 5–6]

1. Select Sheet4 and rename it `Population`.

2. Fill in a sequence of years from 1997 to 2017 in column A. Refer to Figure 3.29 for guidance. All the years do not show in the figure, but it provides a general idea of the layout of the worksheet.

3. Select cell B3, which shows the 1997 population of the United States in millions of people.

4. Right-click and drag the fill handle to cell B23. Release the mouse button.

5. When the shortcut menu appears, choose Series (not Fill Series).

6. In the Series window, choose Growth and set the Step Value to `1.01`. This causes the value in each cell to be 1 percent larger than the preceding value. Click OK. (The value in the year 2017 will exceed 300 million.)

7. Format the population cells to show two decimal places. The Population worksheet should look like the one in Figure 3.29.

8. Choose File, Page Setup, and create a header that contains your name left-aligned.

9. Save the workbook. Preview and print the sheet.

10. Close the workbook.

Figure 3.29

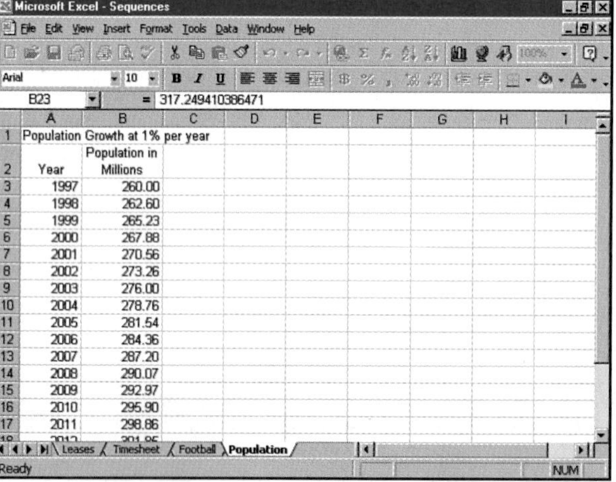

	A	B
1	Population Growth at 1% per year	
2	Year	Population in Millions
3	1997	260.00
4	1998	262.60
5	1999	265.23
6	2000	267.88
7	2001	270.56
8	2002	273.26
9	2003	276.00
10	2004	278.76
11	2005	281.54
12	2006	284.36
13	2007	287.20
14	2008	290.07
15	2009	292.97
16	2010	295.90
17	2011	298.86

Challenge

Challenge exercises expand on or are somewhat related to skills presented in the lessons. Each exercise provides a brief narrative introduction followed by instructions, in a numbered step or bulleted list format, that are not as detailed as those in the Skill Drill section.

In these Challenge exercises, you complete a worksheet that was created for a car payment. In the first exercise, you create a customized fill list. In the second exercise, you select among predefined header and footer options. In the third exercise, you select rows to repeat at the top of a worksheet when it is printed.

The following exercises use the file EO-0303. Locate the file in the Student folder on the CD that came with your book. Open the file and save it on your floppy disk as `Car Payment`.

1. Customizing a Fill List

Excel recognizes several common sequences of names. You might want to create your own. For example, if your company works six days a week (closed Sunday) you might want to fill in a sequence of days that does not include Sundays. In this example, three friends decide to buy a car together and take turns paying the car payment. [L2]

In this exercise, you create a custom list of three names that can be used to fill in the column that shows whose turn it is to pay the loan.

This worksheet contains formulas that you learn about in later projects. It has also been protected, so that you don't accidentally overwrite those formulas.

To create a customized list, follow these guidelines:

1. Select the Car Payment sheet.
2. Enter the names `Jack`, `Bill`, and `Mary` in cells E4, E5, and E6 respectively. Select these three cells.
3. To create a custom list of the three selected names, choose Tools, Options; click the Custom Lists tab, and click the Import button. Your list of entries displays. Click OK.
4. Fill in the rest of the names in column E. The three names should repeat so that each person is responsible for a payment every third month.
5. Save the workbook. Leave the workbook open for use in the next exercise.

2. Using Header and Footer Options

Excel has several default options for headers and footers. In this exercise, you print the Car Payment sheets using a built-in header and footer. [L5]

To print a two-page worksheet using one of the built-in headers and footers, follow these guidelines:

1. Use the Car Payment workbook that you created in the previous exercise. If you do not have this file, open EO-0303, and save it as `Car Payment`.
2. Choose File, Page Setup, Header/Footer.
3. Click the list arrow at the right end of the Header box. Select the built-in header that begins `Prepared by`....
4. Use a similar method to select a built-in footer.
5. Save the workbook, and preview the printout. Use the Print dialog box to print the first page only. Leave the workbook open for use in the next exercise.

3. Including Row and Column Labels for Multiple Sheet Printouts

If a worksheet is too large to print on one sheet, the data prints on additional sheets but the column labels do not. You can end up with sheets of data that have no labels and are hard to identify. It is possible to specify rows or columns that print on every page to provide column labels for pages beyond the first page.

To specify that the first three rows of the Car Payment sheet print on all pages, follow these steps:

1. Use the Car Payment workbook that you created in the first Challenge exercise. If you do not have this file, open EO-0303 and save it as `Car Payment`.
2. Select File, Page Setup, Sheet.
3. Click the Rows to repeat at top box.
4. Click the Collapse button at the right of the Rows to repeat at top box and drag down the first three rows. Click the Expand button. The Rows to repeat at top box should indicate the first three rows with the code **$1:$3**.
5. Save the workbook, and preview the second page of the printout to confirm that the first three rows will print there as well.

6. Print both pages of the sheet.
7. Close the workbook.

Discovery Zone

Discovery Zone exercises require advanced knowledge of topics presented in *Essentials* lessons, application of skills from multiple lessons, or self-directed learning of new skills.

In the first exercise, you experiment with using the linear and growth fill options. The second exercise assumes that you completed Exercise 1. You select an area to print and learn how to force a page break where you want it on the page. The exercises use the same file.

1. Using Advanced Fill Options

The right mouse button can be used with the fill handle to provide several useful options. In this exercise, use the fill handle with the right mouse button to fill in the columns, as shown in Figure 3.30. Use the Series option for the last two and experiment with the Step feature to determine how to produce a linear and a growth series.

Figure 3.30

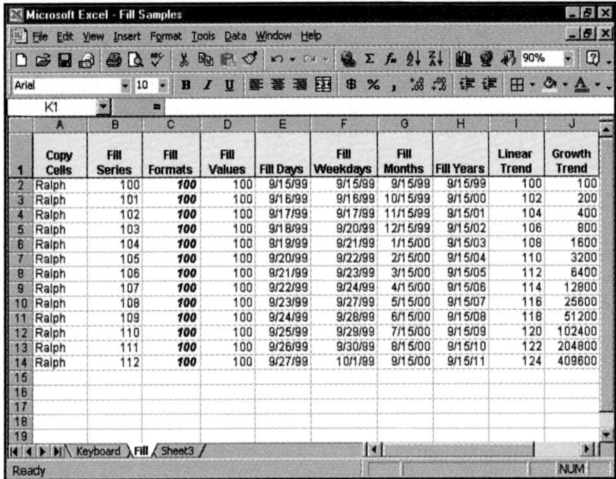

	Copy Cells	Fill Series	Fill Formats	Fill Values	Fill Days	Fill Weekdays	Fill Months	Fill Years	Linear Trend	Growth Trend
2	Ralph	100	100	100	9/15/99	9/15/99	9/15/99	9/15/99	100	100
3	Ralph	101	100	100	9/16/99	9/16/99	10/15/99	9/15/00	102	200
4	Ralph	102	100	100	9/17/99	9/17/99	11/15/99	9/15/01	104	400
5	Ralph	103	100	100	9/18/99	9/20/99	12/15/99	9/15/02	106	800
6	Ralph	104	100	100	9/19/99	9/21/99	1/15/00	9/15/03	108	1600
7	Ralph	105	100	100	9/20/99	9/22/99	2/15/00	9/15/04	110	3200
8	Ralph	106	100	100	9/21/99	9/23/99	3/15/00	9/15/05	112	6400
9	Ralph	107	100	100	9/22/99	9/24/99	4/15/00	9/15/06	114	12800
10	Ralph	108	100	100	9/23/99	9/27/99	5/15/00	9/15/07	116	25600
11	Ralph	109	100	100	9/24/99	9/28/99	6/15/00	9/15/08	118	51200
12	Ralph	110	100	100	9/25/99	9/29/99	7/15/00	9/15/09	120	102400
13	Ralph	111	100	100	9/26/99	9/30/99	8/15/00	9/15/10	122	204800
14	Ralph	112	100	100	9/27/99	10/1/99	9/15/00	9/15/11	124	409600

- Open OE-0304 from the CD, and save it as `Fill Samples`. Select the Fill sheet.
- Fill in the columns as shown.
- Save the workbook. Leave it open for use in the next exercise.

2. Setting Print Area and Print Preview

If you click the Print button on the toolbar, the entire sheet prints. You can specify a different default range to print automatically. The range is called the Print area. If you want to print a small range within a single sheet, use File, Print Area, Set Print Area option. If you want to control the areas printed together in a multipage printout, you need to know how to use the Page Break Preview option.

- Use the file from the previous exercise. If you did not do that exercise, open EO-0304 from the CD, and save it as `Fill Samples`. Select the Fill sheet.
- Use the method mentioned above to set the print area to cells C1 through C14. Click the Print button on the toolbar and print that range automatically. After you print the column, reverse the steps and clear the Print area.
- Use Help to learn about setting the Print area with the Page Break Preview option. Print the sheet on two pages where the second page has the Linear Growth and Growth Trend columns and the other columns are on the first page.
- Save the workbook and close it.

Project 4

Making the Computer Do the Math

Objectives

In this project, you learn how to

- **Add, Subtract, Multiply, and Divide Using Cell References and Numbers**
- **Create Formulas with More Than One Cell Reference**
- **Combine Operations and Fill Cells with Formulas**
- **Fill Cells with Relative and Absolute Formulas**
- **Apply Basic Formulas to a Loan Repayment**
- **Use Built-in Financial Formulas**
- **Use Counting and Conditional Formulas**
- **Use Excel to Explore Different Possibilities**

Key terms introduced in this project include

- absolute reference
- APR
- arguments
- COUNTIF function
- formula palette
- function
- Paste function
- Payment (PMT) function
- relative reference

Source: Essentials: Office 2000, Ferrett-Preston-Preston

Why Would I Do This?

One of the primary advantages of using a computer spreadsheet program is the computer's capability to perform complex calculations quickly. Excel is at your command, whether you need to do basic arithmetic or advanced statistics. After you set up an Excel worksheet, you can change the numbers many times to see how those changes affect the bottom line. In this project, you work on four worksheets. You use the first worksheet to perform basic math calculations using Excel. In the next worksheet, you use the Fill function with a formula and learn about absolute and relative cell references. In the third worksheet, you learn how to use the Paste function to calculate a monthly payment on a car or house loan. You also calculate the total amount you will pay for the loan. In the last worksheet, you use the COUNTIF function to complete an employee's work schedule and to determine total hours worked and wages due.

After you have worked with these four worksheets, you make changes to various numbers and see how Excel quickly recalculates the numbers and gives you the results of these changes. The power to quickly recalculate enables you to see the impact of changes that you may want to consider.

When you are done with this project, you will have created four worksheets that look like the ones in Figure 4.1–4.4.

Visual Summary

Sample Numbers:	
200	6
3	12

Cell and number:	Two cells	Combinations	
Addition:	Addition:	Grouping - example one:	
17	9		68.66666667
Subtraction:	Subtraction:	Grouping - example two:	
7	197		1.333333333
Multiplication:	Multiplication:	Filling:	
600	600	Relative	200
			3
Division:	Division:		
50	2	Absolute	200
			200

Figure 4.1
You can write formulas using cell references and numbers.

Figure 4.2
You can calculate commissions using an absolute reference to a cell.

Your Name

Calculation of Sales Commission

Commission rate: 7%

Weekly Sales	Dave	Eric	Sally	Natasha	Siri	Totals
Monday	2,500	2,000	600	800	1,900	7,800
Tuesday	1,500	1,800	3,000	700	2,500	9,500
Wednesday	600	1,400	2,000	550	2,000	6,550
Thursday	1,900	1,500	1,900	3,000	900	9,200
Friday	1,000	1,900	1,400	700	800	5,800
Saturday	1,000	500	900	2,000	2,000	6,400
Totals	8,500	9,100	9,800	7,750	10,100	$ 45,250
Commission Earned	$ 595.00	$ 637.00	$ 686.00	$ 542.50	$ 707.00	$ 3,168

Figure 4.3
You can calculate a loan payment using the PMT function.

Your Name

Loan Amount (pv):	$ 10,000
Annual Interest	7.50%
Monthly Interest (rate)	0.625%
Years to Pay Back	4
Number of Payments (nper)	48
Monthly Payment	($241.79)
Total of All Payments	$ (11,605.87)

Figure 4.4
Half-hour intervals, hours, and wages are calculated.

Your Name

Schedule for Jan 6 to Jan 12							
	Monday	Tuesday	Wednesday	Thursday	Friday	Saturday	Sunday
8:00 AM	Bill	Bill	Juan	Bill	Juan	Scott	Scott
8:30 AM	Bill	Bill	Juan	Bill	Juan	Scott	Scott
9:00 AM	Bill	Bill	Juan	Bill	Juan	Scott	Scott
9:30 AM	Bill	Bill	Juan	Bill	Juan	Scott	Scott
10:00 AM	Bill	Bill	Juan	Bill	Juan	Scott	Scott
10:30 AM	Bill	Bill	Juan	Bill	Juan	Scott	Scott
11:00 AM	Bill	Bill	Juan	Bill	Juan	Scott	Scott
11:30 AM	Bill	Bill	Juan	Bill	Juan	Scott	Scott
12:00 PM	Bill	Juan	Juan	Bill	Juan	Scott	Scott
12:30 PM	Bill	Juan	Juan	Bill	Juan	Scott	Scott
1:00 PM	Bill	Juan	Juan	Bill	Juan	Scott	Scott
1:30 PM	Bill	Juan	Juan	Bill	Juan	Scott	Scott

Employee	Bill	Juan	Scott
Hourly Wage	$ 6.25	$ 6.50	$ 6.20
Time Blocks Worked	32	28	24
Hours Worked	16	14	12
Pay	$ 100.00	$ 91.00	$ 74.40

Lesson 1: Adding, Subtracting, Multiplying, and Dividing Using Cell References and Numbers

Spreadsheets have been used in a paper form for years as a means of keeping track of financial data. The value of using an electronic spreadsheet program, such as Excel, is its capability to make mathematical calculations quickly. Before the era of computers, people were employed to calculate rows and columns of numbers for use in navigational charts or other types of computational charts.

The job title for the people who performed these calculations was Computer. In today's world, electronic computers keep track of financial data and perform mathematical computations. Computers are faster and more accurate for these kinds of tasks than people are.

When you use Excel to perform a mathematical operation, it needs to be done in a way that is similar to ordinary math but with a few special rules. For example, all formulas must begin with an equal sign (=), and you use cell names in the formulas. In this lesson, you practice applying the basic formula rules in Excel. The sheet that you produce will serve as a convenient reference for later use.

To Add, Subtract, Multiply and Divide Using Cell References and Numbers

1. **Launch Excel. Locate and open `E0-0401` from the CD that came with your book, and save it on your floppy disk as `Math`.**
   The file opens and the new workbook name displays in the title bar.

2. **If necessary, click the Basic Operations sheet; select cell B7, and type `=B3+5` in the cell.**
   This formula adds the contents of cell B3 and the number 5. Notice that the formula appears in the Formula bar and in cell B7 (see Figures 4.5 and 4.6).

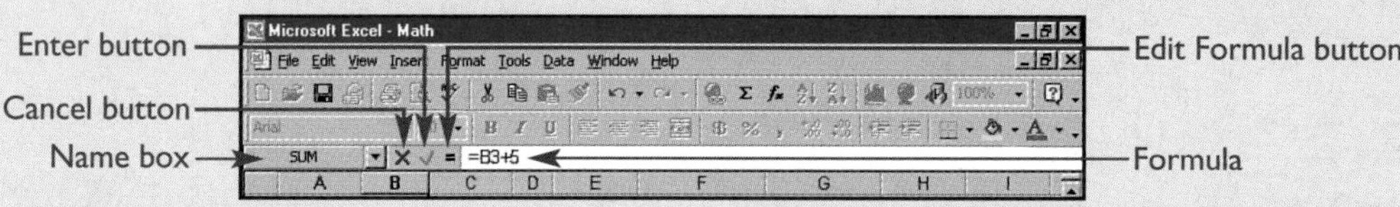

Figure 4.5 The formula appears in the Formula bar and in the cell where it is written.

You might have a different function showing in the Name box on the Formula bar on your computer than the name in the figure. The most recently used function displays in this area. This is nothing to be concerned about. It does not affect the formula you have just entered.

3. **Click the green √ (Enter) button on the Formula bar.**
   Notice that cell B3 contains the number 12 and cell B7 displays the result of adding 5 to the contents of B3.

4. **Select cell B10, and type `=B3-5`.**
   Determine what you think the answer should be before you proceed. In this case, you subtract 5 from the contents of cell B3.

5. **Click the green √ (Enter) button on the Formula bar.**
   If you anticipated a different answer, take the time to figure out why.

6. **Select cell B13, and type `=A2*3`.**
   Excel uses the asterisk (*) to indicate multiplication. Determine what you think the answer should be before you proceed. In this case, you multiply the contents of cell A2 by 3.

7. **Click the green √ (Enter) button on the Formula bar.**
   If you anticipated an answer other than 24, take the time to figure out why.

8. **Select cell B16, and type `=A2/4`.**
   Excel uses the slash to indicate division. Determine what you think the answer should be before you proceed. In this case, you divide the contents of cell A2 by 4.

9. **Click the green √ (Enter) button on the Formula bar.**
   If you anticipated an answer other than 2, take the time to figure out why.

Notice the two slash keys on your keyboard. The forward slash (/) indicates division in Excel formulas. If you use the backslash (\) by mistake, Excel displays #NAME? to indicate that it does not recognize your entry as a formula, but thinks it is a misspelled cell name.

⑩ Check that your results match those shown in Figure 4.6 and make changes as necessary.

You now have one example each of adding, subtracting, multiplying, and dividing a cell reference and a number.

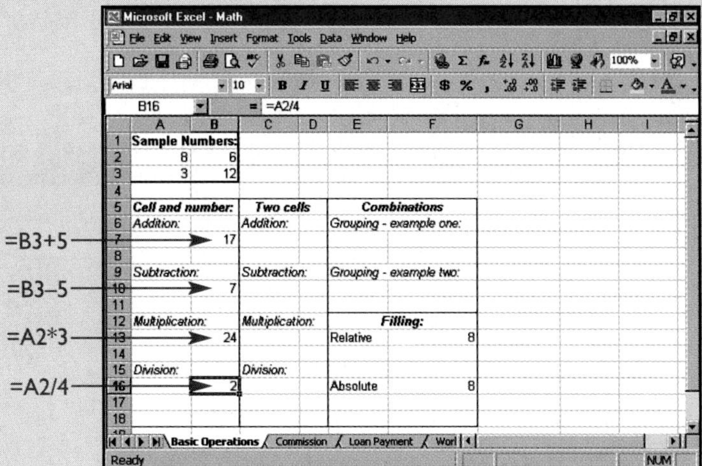

Figure 4.6
Examples of cell references and numbers used to add, subtract, multiply, or divide.

⑪ Save your changes to the Math workbook.

Leave the file open for use in the next lesson.

Entering Formulas

You can enter a formula by pressing Enter or Tab but the selection moves to another cell and you have to move the selection back if you want to see what the formula is in the Formula bar. If you click the √ button on the Formula bar, the selection does not move to another cell.

Lesson 2: Creating Formulas with More Than One Cell Reference

When writing a formula or equation used to calculate values in a cell, it is common to refer to numbers entered in more than one cell on your worksheet. For example, if you want to know the profit for your business, you subtract expenses from income. If you want to know the percentage increase in sales, you use numbers entered for two different sales periods to make that calculation.

In this lesson, you use numbers from more than one cell to make calculations. You also learn how to trace cell dependants using the Tools, Auditing command.

To Create Formulas with More Than One Cell Reference

① Select cell D7 on the Basic Operations sheet in the Math workbook; type =A2+A3; estimate the answer, and click the √ (Enter) button.

In this case, the formula adds the numbers in cells A2 and A3.

② Select cell D10; type =A2–A3; determine what the answer should be, and click the √ (Enter) button.

This formula tells the program to take the number in cell A2 and subtract the number in cell A3.

continues ▶

To Create Formulas with More Than One Cell Reference (continued)

3 Select cell D13; type `=A2*A3`; determine what the answer should be if the numbers in these cells were multiplied together, and click the √ (Enter) button.

In this case, you told the program to multiply the number in cell A2 by the number in cell A3.

4 Select cell D16; type `=B3/B2`; determine what the answer should be, and click the √ (Enter) button.

In this case, you told the program to take the number in cell B3 and divide by the number in cell B2. You now have one example each for adding, subtracting, multiplying or dividing by using two cell references (see Figure 4.7).

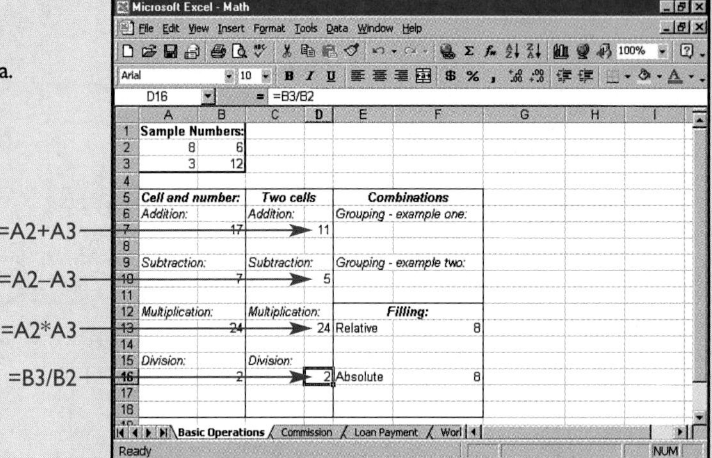

Figure 4.7
You can use two or more cell references in a formula.

5 Select cell A2; choose Tools, Auditing, and Trace Dependants.

Arrows appear on the screen to show which cells contain formulas that depend on cell A2 (see Figure 4.8). The Trace Dependants tool is helpful when you are analyzing a worksheet and want to review formulas or see the relationship between cells.

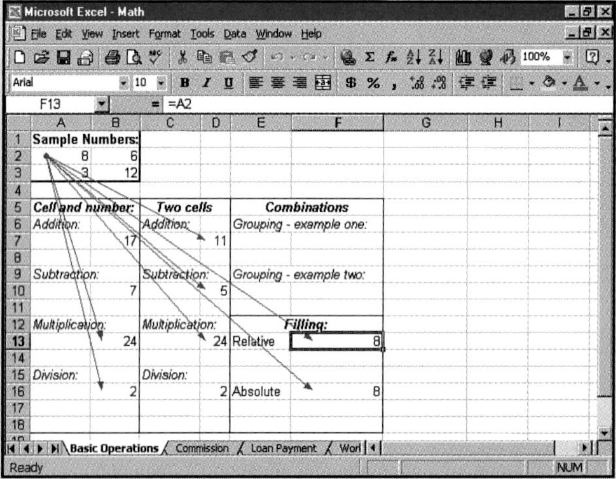

Figure 4.8
The Auditing tools can help you understand the relationship between cells in a worksheet.

When you first click the Tools menu, the Auditing submenu might not appear. Wait a moment for the menu to expand, or go to the bottom of the menu and click the double arrow to expand the menu.

6 Choose Tools, Auditing, and Remove All Arrows.

The arrows are erased.

7 Double-click cell D7.

The formula displays in the cell and in the Formula bar. Look at Figure 4.9 and examine your screen. Notice that the cell references in the formula and the cells to which they refer change to matching colors. Also check to see whether an insertion mark is placed in the formula. You could edit the formula in the cell or by selecting the cell and clicking the Formula bar.

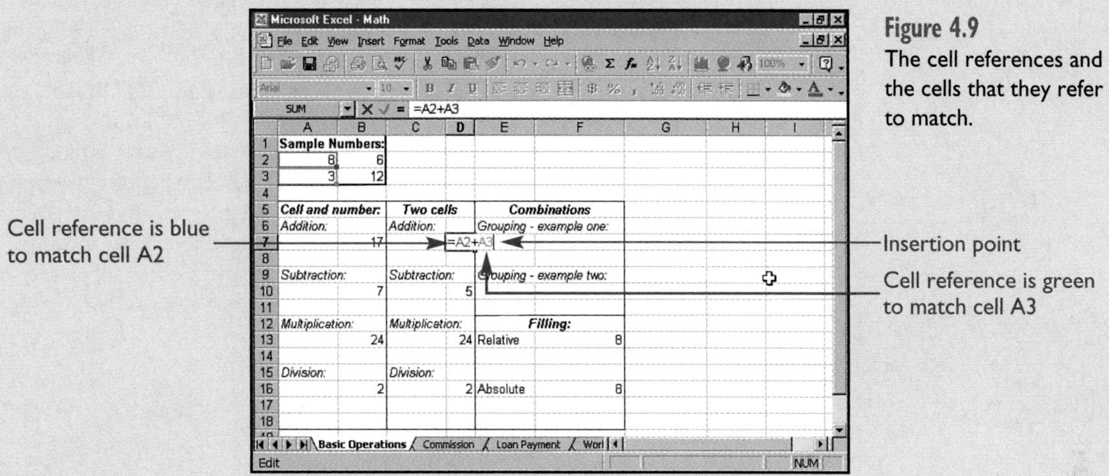

Figure 4.9 The cell references and the cells that they refer to match.

8 Edit the formula the way you would ordinary text. Change it to =B2+A3. Click the √ (Enter) button to finish the change.

The number 9 displays in cell D7, and =B2+A3 displays in the Formula bar.

9 Save your changes to the Math workbook.

Leave the file open for use in the next lesson.

Undoing Mistakes

If you make a mistake and want to start over, click the Cancel button (the X next to the √ Enter button) on the Formula bar or press Esc on the keyboard.

Cell names are not case sensitive. Excel interprets A2 the same way as it interprets a2. When entering cell names, it is not necessary to capitalize the column reference letter.

Clicking to Enter Names in Formulas

After typing an equal sign to begin the formula, you can point to a cell and click to enter its name in the formula. You can then type the math symbol you want to use before you point and click the next cell that you want in the formula. When you use this method, a marquee outlines the cell that you selected. This method is preferable if you are writing a formula and the cell you want is off the screen where you cannot see the cell reference.

Lesson 3: Combining Operations and Filling Cells with Formulas

You might want to add the contents of several cells together and then divide by the contents of another cell. Excel uses the same order of operation rules that you use in algebra. As with algebra, you can use parentheses to group operations together to make sure they are done first. Without parentheses, Excel calculates formulas using the order of operation shown in Table 4.1.

Table 4.1 The Order of Operation Used by Excel

Action	Symbol Used
Negation (negative numbers)	–
Percentages	%
Exponents	^
Multiplication and Division	* /
Addition and Subtraction	+/–

If you use the same formula in several cells, you can fill it into those cells by using the fill handle. Sometimes you want cell references to change to adapt to the new position they are in; for example, you might have a formula that totals the cells above it and want to copy this formula across several cells. In each case, you want the formula to add the column of cells directly above the formula. This is known as a ***relative reference,*** which is a cell reference that changes when the formula is copied, moved, or filled into other cells. In other cases, you want the cell reference to always refer to a specific cell. This type of reference is known as an ***absolute reference,*** which is a cell reference that does not change when copied or filled into other cells.

In this lesson, you group operations in a formula and fill formulas using relative and absolute cell references. You also learn how to display formulas in the worksheet.

To Combine Operations and Fill Cells with Formulas

1. **Select cell F7 on the Basic Operations sheet in the Math workbook, and type `=(A2+B2)/A3`.**
   Estimate what the result should be if you add the contents of cells A2 and B2 and then divide by the number in cell A3 (it will not be a whole number).
2. **Click the √ (Enter) button to confirm your estimate.**
   Notice that the numbers in cells A2 and B2 (8 and 6) are added first and then divided by the number in cell A3 (3).
3. **Select cell F10 and type `=B3/(A3+B2)`.**
   Estimate what the answer will be if the number in cell B3 is divided by the sum of the numbers in cells A3 and B2.
4. **Click the √ (Enter) button to confirm your estimate.**
   Compare your answers for cell F7 and F10 with the ones in Figure 4.10.

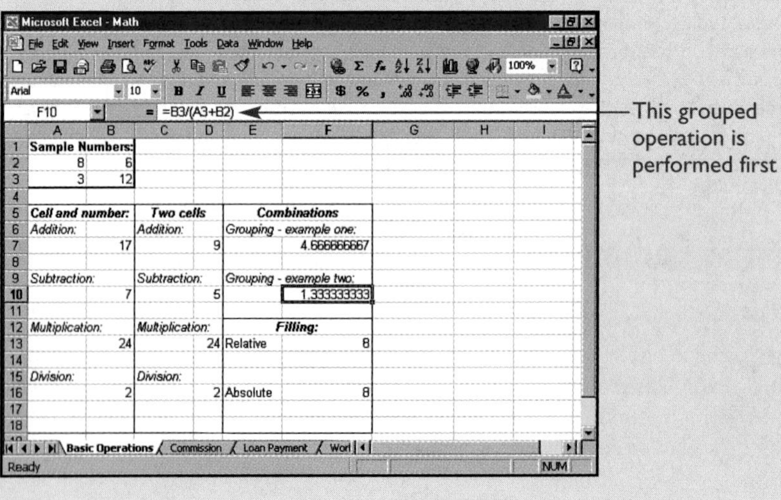
This grouped operation is performed first

Figure 4.10
You can group cells using parentheses.

5 Select cell F13.
Look at the formula in the Formula bar. It shows that the formula simply equals the value of cell A2.

6 Click, and drag the fill handle from cell F13 down to cell F14. Release the mouse button.
Notice that cell F14 displays the number 3, which is the value in cell A3.

7 Select cell F14.
Notice that the formula changes to equal the value in cell A3 (see Figure 4.11). The formulas in cells F13 and F14 refer to a cell that is eleven rows up and five columns to the left. This is an example of a relative reference. A formula entered with only an equal sign can be copied to another cell to produce a relative reference. A relative reference points to the cell that is in the same relative position to the new cell that the original formula is to the old cell. You learn more about this concept in the next lesson.

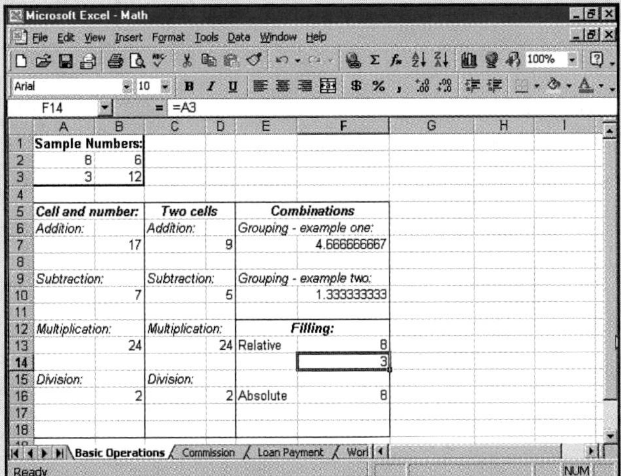

Figure 4.11
The values in cells F13 and F14 are the same values as in cells A2 and A3 because they contain formulas for a relative reference to cells A2 and A3.

8 Select cell F16.
Look at the formula in the Formula bar (see Figure 4.12). In this case, a $ has been placed to the left of the column and row identifiers to indicate that the cell reference will not change when it is copied.

9 Use the fill handle to fill this formula into cell F17.
Notice that F17 also displays the contents of cell A2.

10 Select cell F17.
Look at the formula in the Formula bar. Notice that it did not change when the formula was filled into the cell. This type of cell reference (with the $ signs) is called an absolute reference. Use an absolute reference when you want to ensure that the formula will always refer to a specific cell.

continues ▶

To Combine Operations and Fill Cells with Formulas (continued)

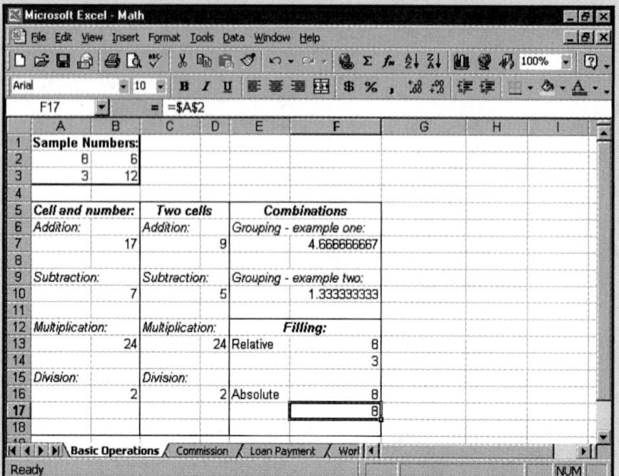

Figure 4.12
An absolute reference always refers to the same cell.

11 Press Ctrl+` (the accent grave found on the key to the left of the 1 key).
The formulas for each cell display as shown in Figure 4.13. You can also display formulas by choosing Tools, Options, selecting the View tab in the Options dialog box, and clicking the Formulas check box in the Window options area.

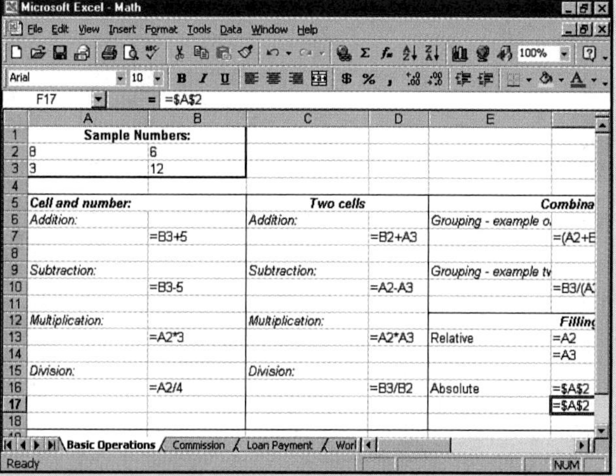

Figure 4.13
You can display the formulas in your worksheet at any time.

12 Add your name to the header, center section, using the Page Setup dialog box. Print the worksheet.

13 Press Ctrl+` to return the worksheet to Normal view showing formula results.
You can also restore a display of formula results by choosing Tools, Options, selecting the View tab in the Options dialog box, and clicking the Formulas check box to remove the check marks.

14 Save your changes to the Math workbook.
Leave the file open for use in the next lesson.

Using a Relative Cell Reference

When you fill a formula from one cell to another, Excel uses a relative cell reference. In the example used in this lesson, when you used the fill handle to copy the formula from F13 to F14, Excel used A3 to fill cell F14. Cell F14 is one position below F13, and cell A3 is one position below A2. Excel uses the relative position of the cell that is being referenced to determine the location of the next value to place in the new cell. This is called a relative reference, and it is the default method that Excel uses to fill a formula from one cell to another.

What Does the Dollar Sign Mean?

The dollar sign ($) that you use as a code to prevent the reference from changing has nothing to do with currency. It is a symbol that was used in the earliest spreadsheets for this purpose and has been used ever since.

Lesson 4: Filling Cells with Relative and Absolute Formulas

In Excel Project 3, "Techniques for Working Efficiently in Excel," you learned how to fill in a worksheet by using the fill handle and by using the copy-and-paste method. These techniques enable you to complete a worksheet quickly. You can use these same techniques to copy formulas from one cell to the next. Most formulas and functions that you copy use a relative reference. A ***function*** is a predefined formula, such as =SUM(B5:B10), that adds the values in cells B5 through 10. If you were to enter the sample function in cell B11 and copy it to the range C11:F11, Excel would create formulas with relative references including =SUM(C5:C10) in cell C11, =SUM(D5:D10) in cell D11, =SUM(E5:E10) in cell E11, and =SUM(F5:F10) in cell F11. When you want to refer to a specific cell on a constant basis in a formula that you need to copy, you use the absolute reference symbol ($). This ability to fill formulas into adjacent cells greatly increases the power of a worksheet to do the calculations that you need.

In this lesson, you use the techniques you learned in the previous lessons and apply them to a worksheet that uses both relative and absolute cell references in formulas.

To Fill Cells with Relative and Absolute Formulas

1 Click cell B11 on the Commission sheet in the Math workbook.

Notice that it contains a formula that adds the contents of cells B5 through B10, which are directly above B11 (see Figure 4.14).

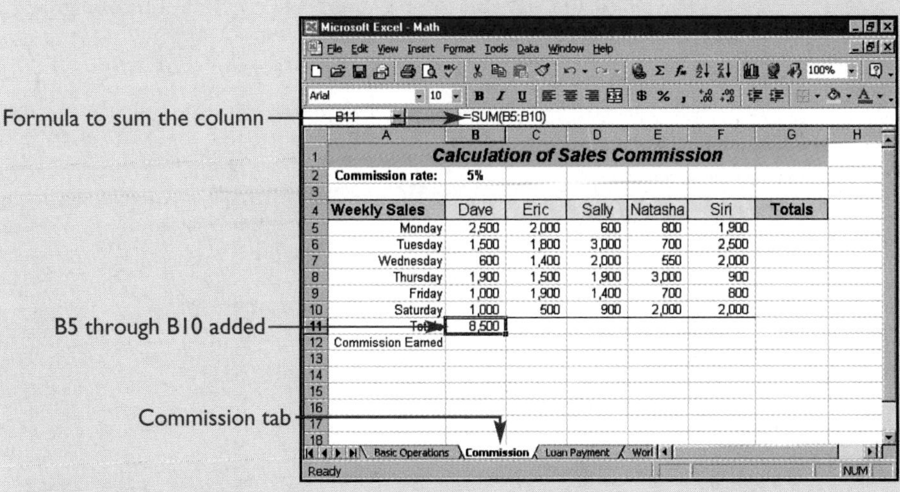

Figure 4.14
A SUM function added the column of numbers in cells B5 through B10.

2 Drag the fill handle to cell F11 and release the mouse.

The formula fills into cells C11 through F11.

continues ▶

To Fill Cells with Relative and Absolute Formulas (continued)

3 Click cell D11, and you see that the formula changed to add the six cells in the column above cell D11 (see Figure 4.15).

This step shows how the absence of dollar signs ($) in a formula results in relative cell references when the formula is copied.

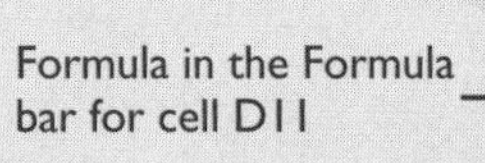

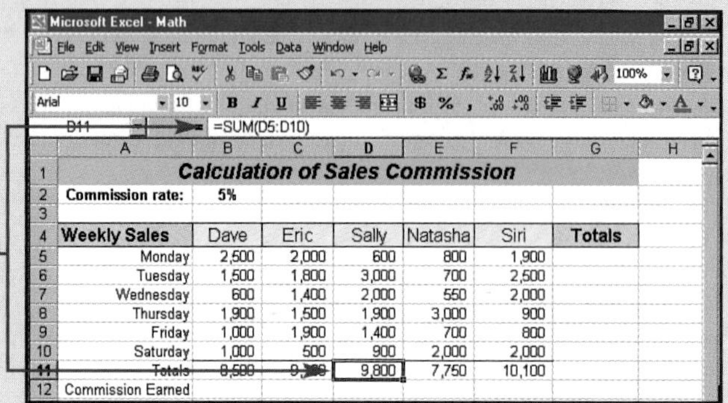

Figure 4.15
Each copied formula in row 11 contains references to cells above the formula.

4 Type =B11*$B$2 in cell B12, and click the √ (Enter) button.

This formula multiplies the sum of Dave's sales in cell B11 by the commission rate in cell B2 (see Figure 4.16). The reference to B11 is relative, and the reference to B2 is absolute.

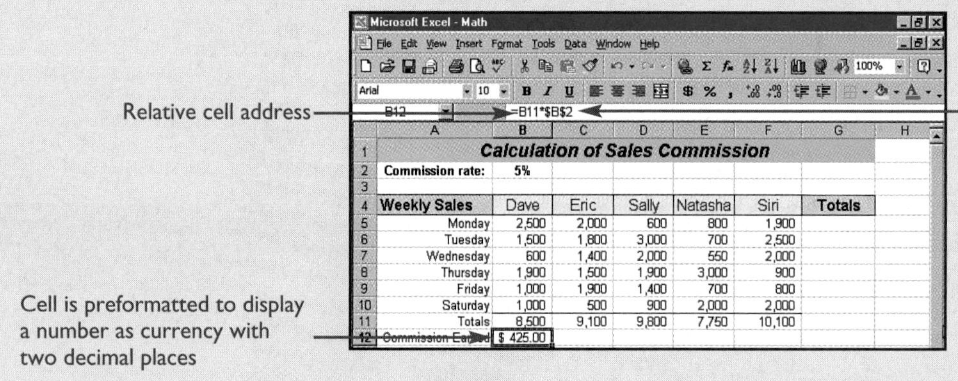

Figure 4.16
You enter a formula that contains an absolute reference to the cell containing the sales commission rate.

5 Drag the fill handle to the right to cell F12, and release the mouse button.

The formula is filled in for all of the sales staff.

6 Click cell D12, and look at the Formula bar.

The relative reference changes to refer to the sum of Sally's sales in cell D11, but the absolute reference to the commission rate in cell B2 doesn't change (see Figure 4.17).

Figure 4.17
This is an example of a formula that uses both an absolute and a relative cell reference to compute sales commissions.

Formula in the Formula bar for cell D12

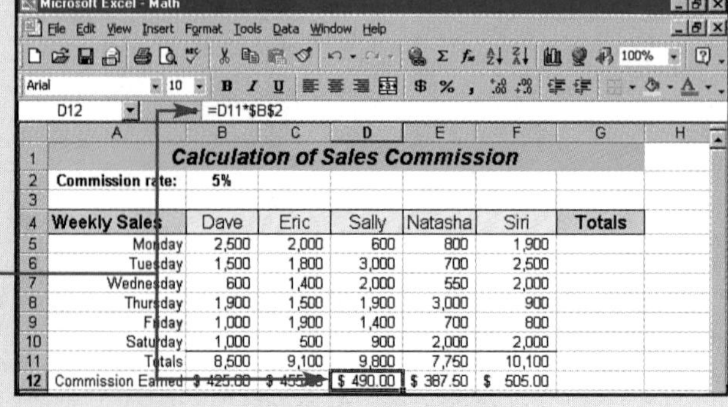

7 Select cell G5, and click the AutoSum button.
Excel displays the function `=SUM(B5:F5)` in cell G5 and in the Formula bar. A marquee surrounds the range `(B5:F5)`.

8 Press ↵Enter to accept the suggested formula.
The 7,800 total for sales on Monday displays in cell G5.

9 Use the fill handle to copy this formula from cell G5 through cell G12.
Excel calculates the total sales for each day, total sales for the week, and total commissions for the week.

10 Format cell G11 to currency with no decimals. Format cell G12 to currency with two decimals. Add a line at the bottom of cell G11 and a heavy border around cell G12.
The completed worksheet should look like Figure 4.18.

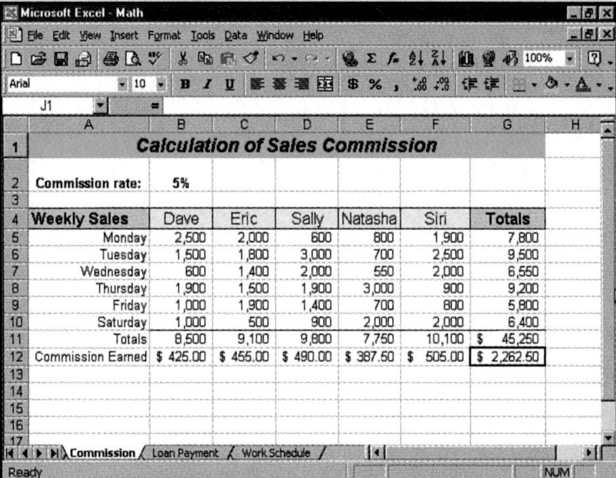

	A	B	C	D	E	F	G
1	Calculation of Sales Commission						
2	Commission rate:	5%					
3							
4	Weekly Sales	Dave	Eric	Sally	Natasha	Siri	Totals
5	Monday	2,500	2,000	600	800	1,900	7,800
6	Tuesday	1,500	1,800	3,000	700	2,500	9,500
7	Wednesday	600	1,400	2,000	550	2,000	6,550
8	Thursday	1,900	1,500	1,900	3,000	900	9,200
9	Friday	1,000	1,900	1,400	700	800	5,800
10	Saturday	1,000	500	900	2,000	2,000	6,400
11	Totals	8,500	9,100	9,800	7,750	10,100	$ 45,250
12	Commission Earned	$ 425.00	$ 455.00	$ 490.00	$ 387.50	$ 505.00	$ 2,262.50

Figure 4.18
The daily, weekly, and commission figures are totaled.

11 Add your name to the sheet header. Save your work and print the worksheet.
Leave the file open for use in the next lesson.

Using AutoSum

When you use the AutoSum button, it guesses which range of numbers you want to add, and under certain circumstances, it guesses incorrectly. When you use the AutoSum button, Excel first looks to the column above the destination cell for numbers to add. Finding none, it then looks to the left. The problem occurs when there are numbers both above and to the left of the destination cell. Excel assumes you want to add the numbers in the column rather than the row. If you want to add numbers in a row rather than a column, simply change the range by clicking and dragging over the cells you want to sum.

Using F4 for Dollar Signs

Instead of typing the dollar signs to create an absolute reference, you can use F4. Enter the cell reference in your formula and press F4 before continuing with the rest of your formula. If you want to add an absolute reference after the formula is typed, select the cell reference you want to be absolute and press F4.

Lesson 5: Applying Basic Formulas to a Loan Repayment

When you borrow money for a car or a house, the loan repayment is based on several factors, such as interest rate, time to repay, and the loan amount. With Excel, you can set up a worksheet to calculate your monthly payments based on these factors. Then you can use the basic formula created in the worksheet and change the values referenced in the formula to match the loan terms quoted to you by a bank or other lender.

In this lesson, you set up a worksheet to calculate the amount of a monthly payment on a loan and the total monthly payments on the loan. You also enter the formula to calculate the total monthly payments.

To Apply Basic Formulas to a Loan Repayment

1. **Click the Loan Payment tab to switch to the Loan Payment sheet.**
This worksheet has labels in column A and a place for values and formulas in column B (see Figure 4.19).

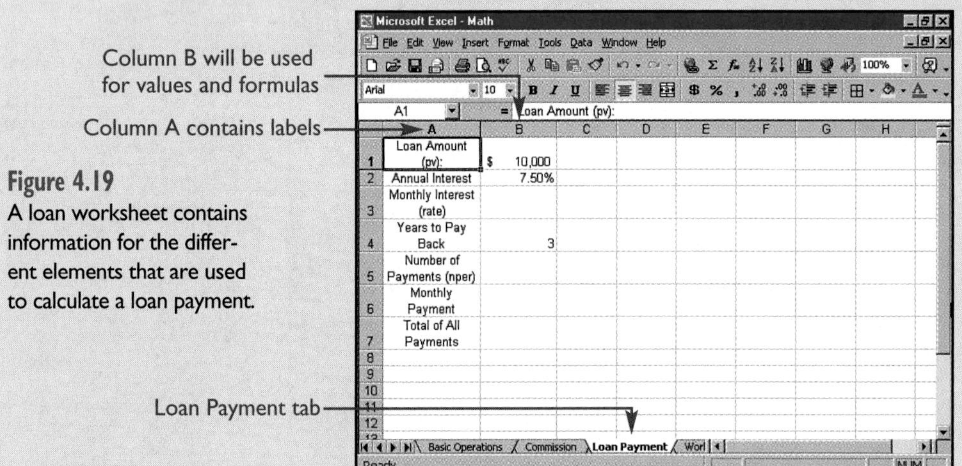

Figure 4.19
A loan worksheet contains information for the different elements that are used to calculate a loan payment.

2. **Select cell B3; type =B2/12, and click the Enter button.**
This formula calculates the monthly interest rate by dividing the annual interest rate in cell B2 by 12 months.

3. **Select cell B5; type =B4*12, and click the Enter button.**
This formula calculates the number of months over which the loan will be repaid.

4. **Select cell B7; type =B5*B6, and click the Enter button.**
Your screen should look like Figure 4.20. The formula in cell B7 multiplies the number of payments in cell B5 by the amount of the payment in B6 to calculate the total of all payments. In this case, no number will be displayed in the cell because cell B6 is still empty. However, B7 has been formatted to show a dollar sign and a dash when the value is zero. Leave the file open for use in the next lesson.

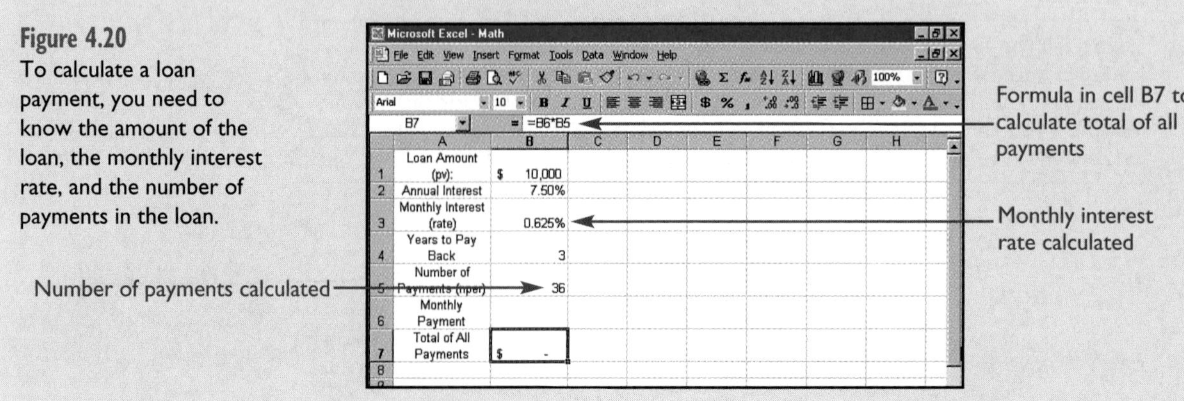

Figure 4.20
To calculate a loan payment, you need to know the amount of the loan, the monthly interest rate, and the number of payments in the loan.

Calculating Interest Costs
To calculate the monthly payment, the formula requires the number of months and the interest rate per month. Most loan interest rates are given as Annual Percentage Rate, or ***APR***. If the payment is made every month, the formula needs to use one twelfth of the annual interest rate to calculate the interest cost per month.

Lesson 6: Using Built-in Financial Formulas

When you take out a loan, you usually rely on someone else to tell you how much the payment will be. To shop around for the best rate or terms, it is helpful to be able to see the effect of different loan terms that may be quoted to you. The previous lesson outlined the factors used to calculate a loan. In this lesson, you use the ***Paste function*** to help you write the payment formula. The Paste function is a button on the toolbar that enables you to select from a library of preprogrammed calculations.

In this lesson, you use one of the built-in financial formulas named PMT. The ***PMT function*** is a formula used to calculate the periodic payment due based on amount borrowed, interest rate, and number of payments.

To Use Built-in Financial Formulas

1. **Click cell B6 on the Loan Payment sheet in the Math workbook. Click the Paste Function button on the Standard toolbar.**
The Paste Function dialog box opens, and the Office Assistant might open as well, unless you have it turned off. Click No, don't provide help now to close the Office Assistant. In the Paste Function dialog box the first choice, Most Recently Used, displays a list of recently used functions in the box to the right. This list differs for each computer because it is based on personal use (see Figure 4.21).

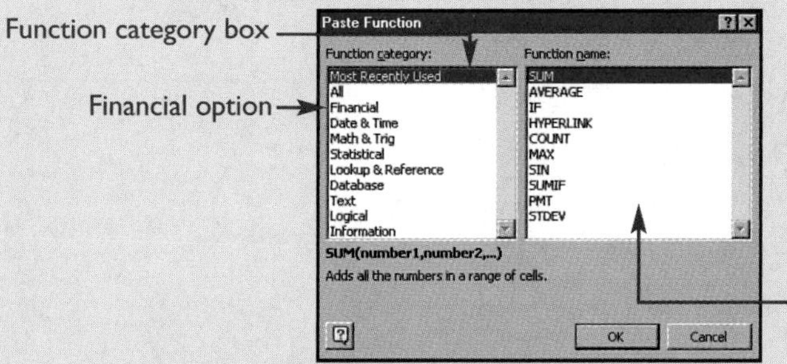

Figure 4.21
The Paste Function dialog box displays function categories on the left, and the names of functions within the selected category on the right.

2. **Click the Financial option in the Function category box.**
A list of built-in financial formulas appears in the Function name box.
3. **Click the PMT function in the Function name box.**
The name of the function and the values it requires display, as shown in Figure 4.22. The words or values required for a function to perform a calculation are called ***arguments***.

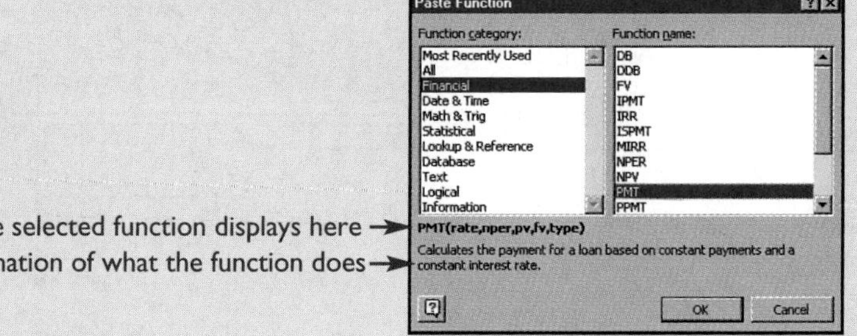

Figure 4.22
You can use the payment function (PMT) to calculate the monthly payment for a car loan.

continues ▶

To Use Built-in Financial Formulas (continued)

4. **Click OK.**
A formula palette displays. A ***formula palette*** guides entry of worksheet functions by displaying and explaining each of its arguments. You enter specifications for arguments in windows to the right of each argument's name. In this case, the first three arguments are required and their names are in boldface type. The last two arguments are not needed in all cases, and they display in normal type. An explanation of the first argument is shown at the bottom of the formula palette (see Figure 4.23).

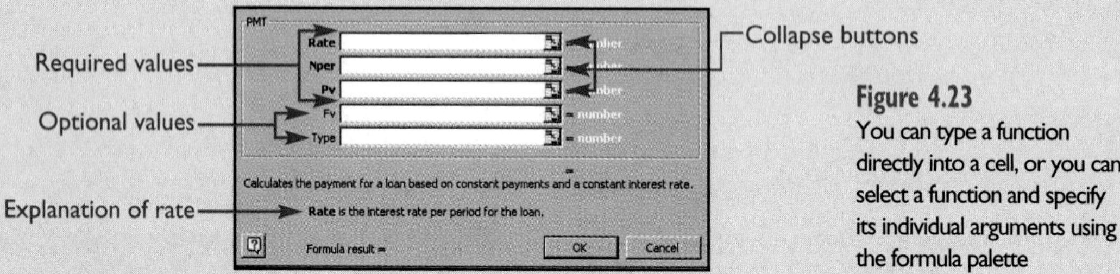

Figure 4.23
You can type a function directly into a cell, or you can select a function and specify its individual arguments using the formula palette

5. **Click the Collapse button at the right end of the Rate box.**
The formula palette collapses and displays as a single line beneath the Formula bar (see Figure 4.24).

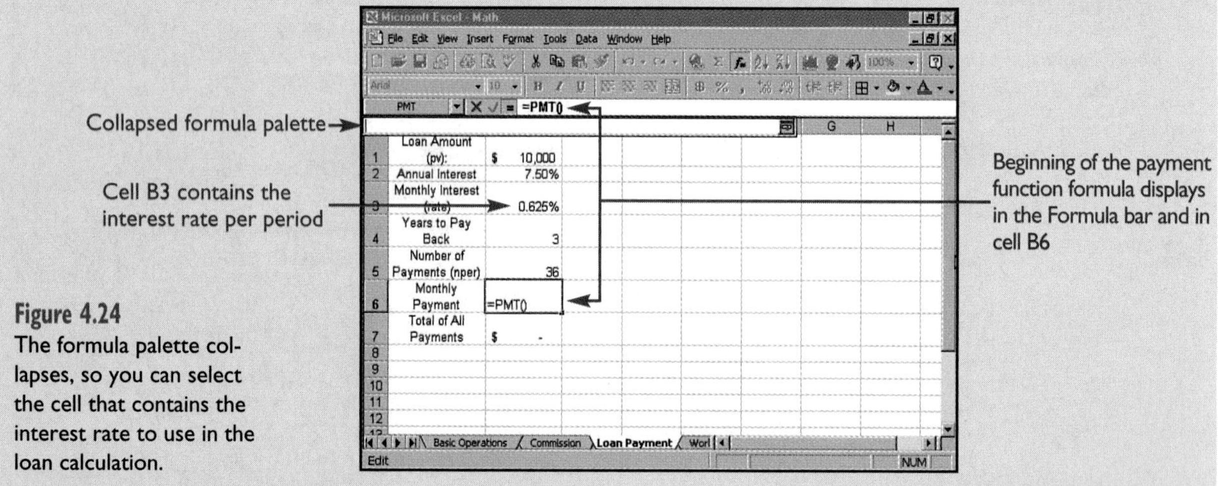

Figure 4.24
The formula palette collapses, so you can select the cell that contains the interest rate to use in the loan calculation.

6. **Click cell B3.**
Excel enters this cell reference in the rate line of the collapsed formula palette and in the Formula bar as the first argument. A marquee displays around the selected cell (see Figure 4.25).

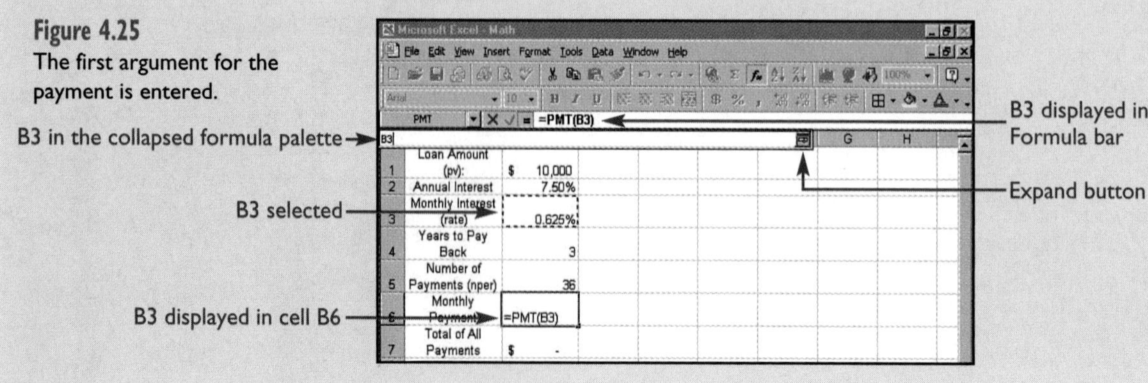

Figure 4.25
The first argument for the payment is entered.

7 Click the Expand button to restore the formula palette.
The cell reference displays in the Rate box, and the number in the cell displays to the right of the box (see Figure 4.26).

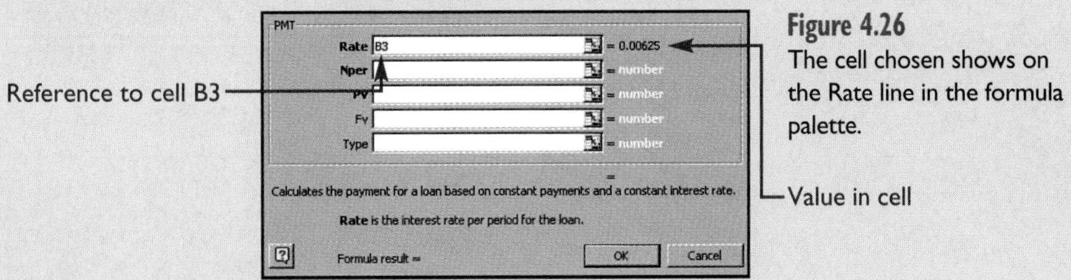

Figure 4.26
The cell chosen shows on the Rate line in the formula palette.

8 Press Tab to move to the Nper box.
The message at the bottom of the box explains that this is the total number of loan payments. In the previous lesson, you calculated this by multiplying the number of years for the loan by 12 to arrive at the total number of payments needed for the payment function.

9 Click the Collapse button at the right side of the Nper box; click cell B5, and click the Expand button.
The reference to cell B5 is added as the second argument to the formula.

10 Press Tab to move to the Pv box.
This argument identifies the present value of the loan, or the amount you want to borrow.

11 Click the Collapse button; click cell B1, and click the Expand button.
The reference to cell B1 is added as the third argument to the formula. The formula now has enough information to calculate the payment. The result displays at the bottom of the formula palette (see Figure 4.27).

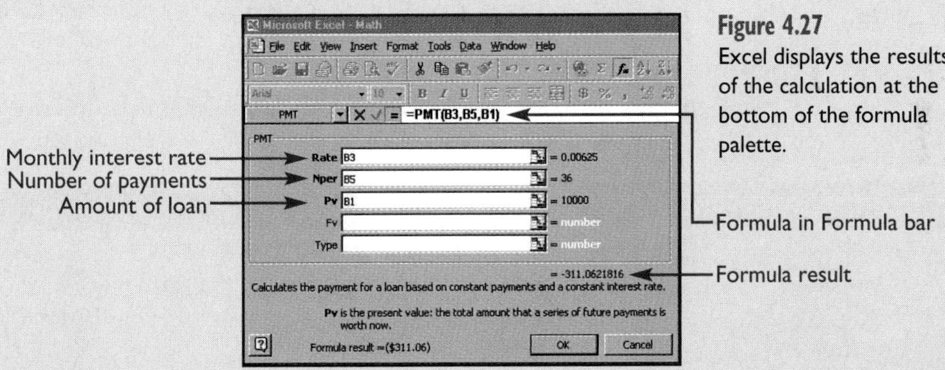

Figure 4.27
Excel displays the results of the calculation at the bottom of the formula palette.

12 Click OK.
The calculated payment displays (see Figure 4.28). The currency format that has been chosen for this cell displays negative numbers in red, enclosed by parentheses. (If the loan amount is entered as a positive number, the payment will be negative.) Notice that cell B7 now shows the total amount of all payments.

continues ▶

To Use Built-in Financial Formulas (continued)

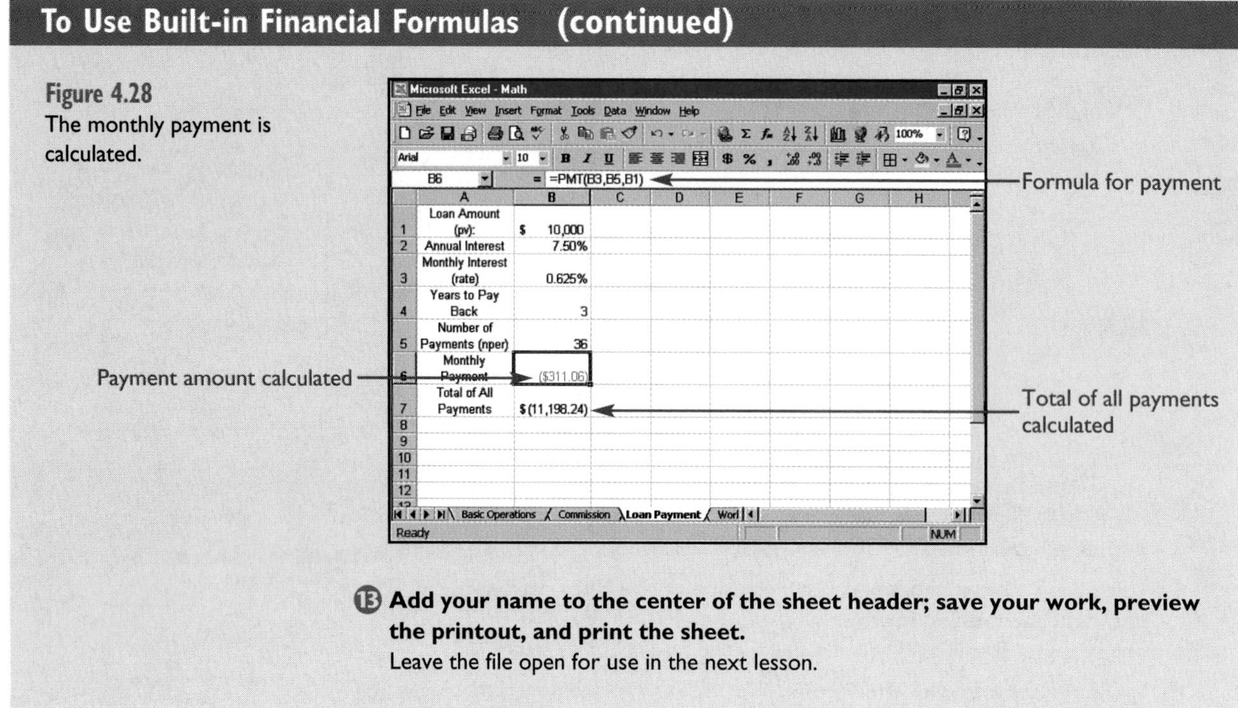

Figure 4.28
The monthly payment is calculated.

⓭ **Add your name to the center of the sheet header; save your work, preview the printout, and print the sheet.**
Leave the file open for use in the next lesson.

Lesson 7: Using Counting and Conditional Formulas

The employee time sheet that you filled out in an earlier lesson is useful for posting on a bulletin board to inform workers when they are scheduled to work. When it comes time to calculate wages, you might need help translating the schedule into dollars earned. Excel has a built-in function, called the ***COUNTIF function***. The COUNTIF function counts the number of cells within a range that meet the given criteria. You use this function to count the number of cells that contain the words you specify.

In this lesson, you count the number of cells assigned to each worker and calculate the week's wages based on the individual salaries and the amount of time worked.

To Use Counting and Conditional Formulas

❶ **Select the Work Schedule sheet in the Math workbook.**
The Work Schedule sheet displays (see Figure 4.29). This is part of the worksheet that you worked on in an earlier lesson.

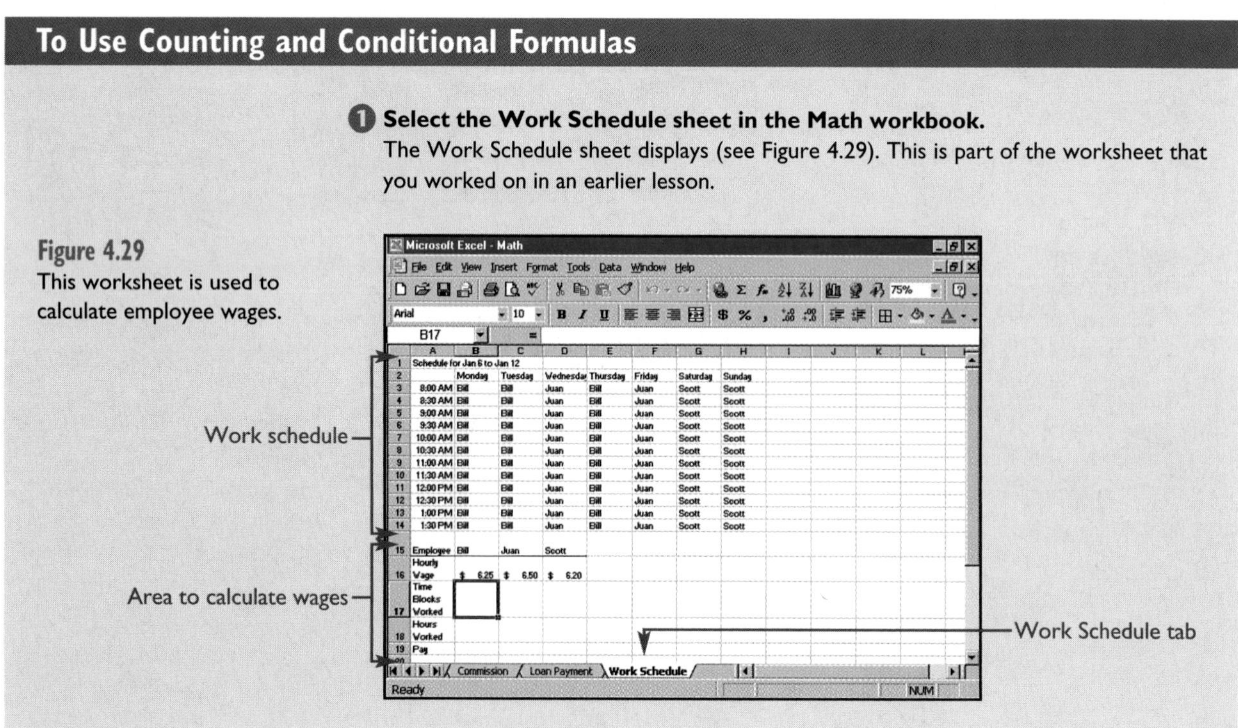

Figure 4.29
This worksheet is used to calculate employee wages.

2 Select cell B17, and click the Paste Function button.

3 Click Statistical in the Function category box. Scroll down the list in the Function name box and select COUNTIF.

A message explains that this function counts the number of cells that meet a condition (see Figure 4.30).

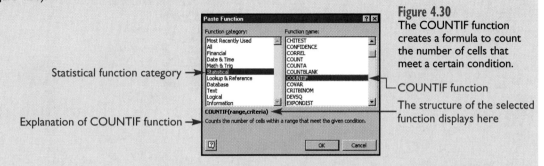

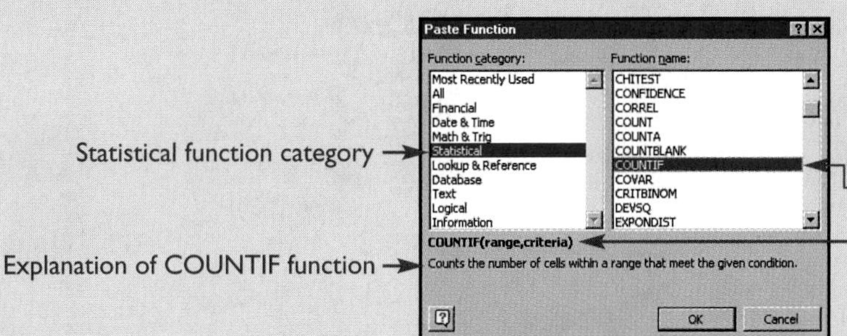

Figure 4.30
The COUNTIF function creates a formula to count the number of cells that meet a certain condition.

4 Click OK.

The COUNTIF formula palette opens. This function has two required arguments. First, you define the range; then, you state the criteria.

5 Click the Collapse button next to the Range box.

You may notice that the complete COUNTIF( ) does not show in cell B17, due to a lack of space in the cell. The Formula bar and the name box show the complete name of this function.

6 Select the range of cells from B3 through H14, and press F4.

A marquee outlines the area you selected and the absolute range $B$3:$H$14 shows in the Formula bar and in the collapsed formula palette (see Figure 4.31). Pressing F4 inserted the dollar signs that made cell references absolute.

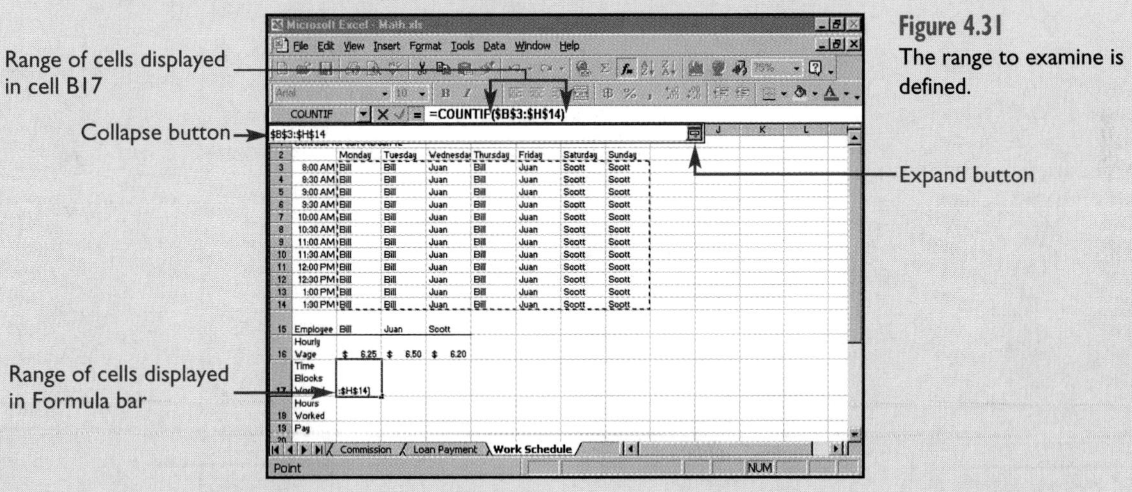

Figure 4.31
The range to examine is defined.

7 Click the Expand button.

The formula palette reappears with the range filled in.

8 Press Tab to move to the Criteria box; click cell B15 (the cell containing the name `Bill` in the employee row). Click OK.

The number 36 displays in cell B17 (see Figure 4.32).

continues ▶

To Use Counting and Conditional Formulas (continued)

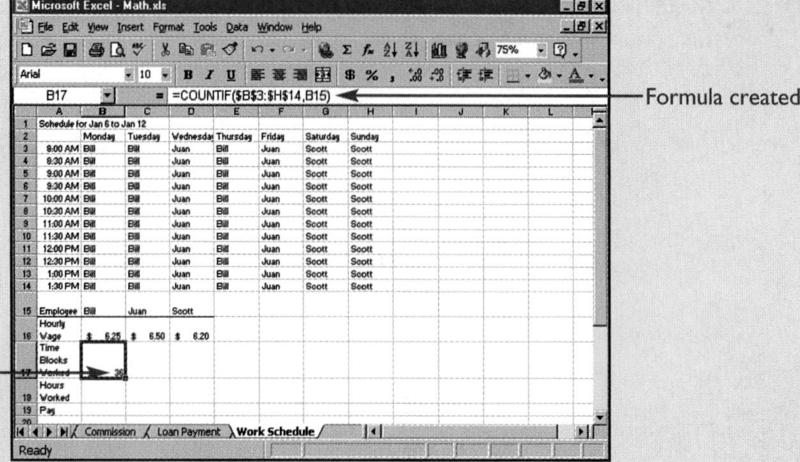

Figure 4.32
The COUNTIF function counts the number of times Bill appears in the range of cells selected.

9. **Select cell B18; type `=B17/2`, and click the Enter button.**
   Each cell represents a half-hour of work. Therefore, to calculate how many hours the person has worked, you must divide by 2.

10. **Select cell B19; type `=B16*B18`, and click the Enter button on the Formula bar.**
    Notice that the Hourly Wage in cell B16 was multiplied by the Hours Worked in cell B18.

11. **Select cells B17 through B19. Drag the fill handle to cell D19.**
    The finished worksheet should look like the one in Figure 4.33.

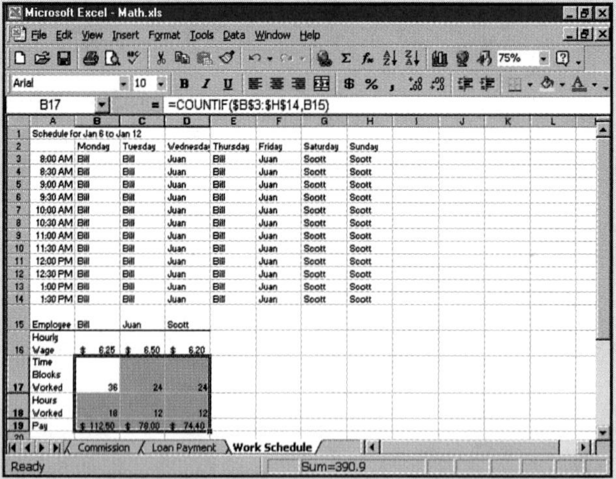

Figure 4.33
The formulas for time blocks worked, hours worked, and wages earned are copied to the rest of the worksheet.

12. **Add your name to the center of the sheet header. Turn on the gridlines. (Use Sheet in Page Setup.) Save your work, and preview and print the sheet.**

Lesson 8: Using Excel to Explore Different Possibilities

One of the rewards of designing a worksheet using formulas is that the computer does all of the recalculations any time you change any of the data. This means you can easily see the effects of your changes and rapidly try out different possibilities.

In this lesson, you recalculate formulas that you created in the previous lessons.

To Use Excel to Explore Different Possibilities

1. **Select the Basic Operations sheet in the Math workbook.**
2. **Select cell A2. Choose Tools, Auditing, and Trace Dependents.**
   The arrows quickly identify which cells contain formulas that depend upon the value in this cell.
3. **Type `200`, and click the Enter button on the Formula bar.**
   All the cells that depend on cell A2 are recalculated with the new number (see Figure 4.34).

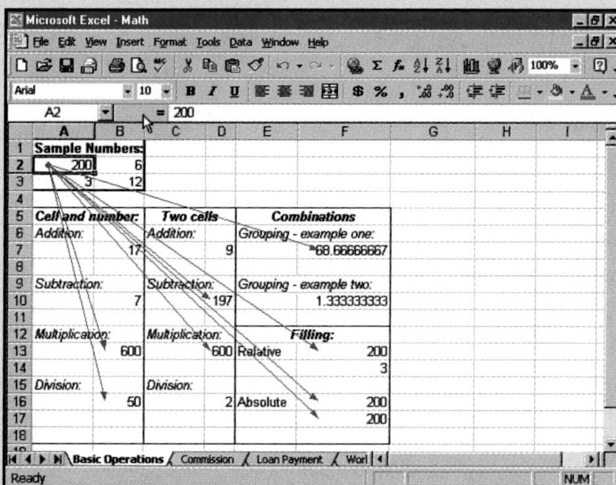

Figure 4.34
Excel recalculates the formulas that depend on cell A2 when the value in that cell changes.

4. **Click the Commission tab to switch to that sheet and select cell B2.**
5. **Type `7`, and click the Enter button on the Formula bar.**
   Notice that all of the commissions have been recalculated (see Figure 4.35).

If typing 7 results in 700%, re-enter the figure as .07. Excel has an option called Enable automatic percent entry. If this option has been deselected on your computer, numbers you enter in cells that are formatted as a percent first need to be converted to a decimal. To turn this option on or off, choose Tools, Options, and click the Edit tab. Click the Enable automatic percent entry check box to activate or deactivate this feature.

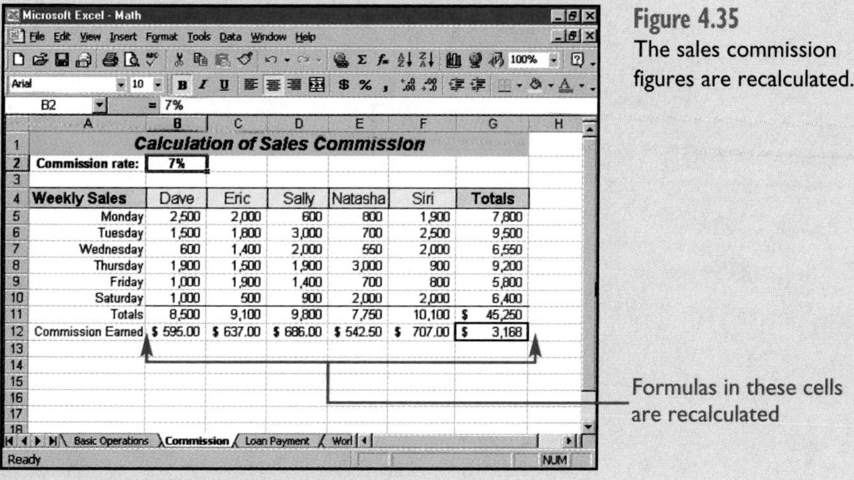
Formulas in these cells are recalculated

Figure 4.35
The sales commission figures are recalculated.

continues ▶

To Use Excel to Explore Different Possibilities (continued)

6. **Click the Loan Payment tab to switch to that sheet.**

7. **Select cell B4; type 4, and click the Enter button on the Formula bar.**
Notice that the new payment ($241.79) is less, but the total paid for the loan is more (see Figure 4.36).

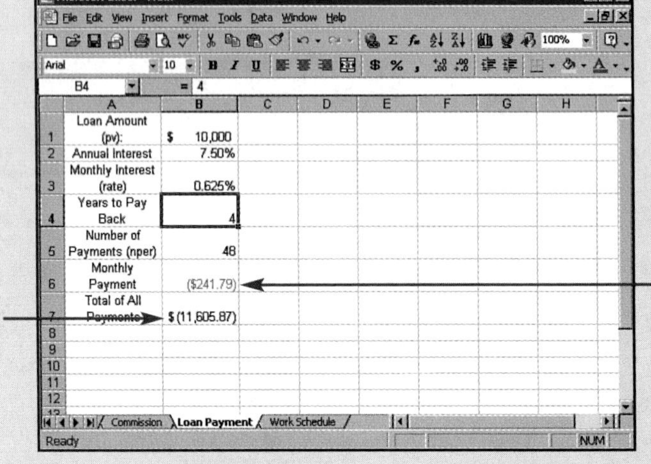

Total of payments was $11,198.24 on a 36-month loan
Payment was $311.06 on a 36-month loan

Figure 4.36
The payment amount reduces when you pay over a longer time period, but the total paid increases.

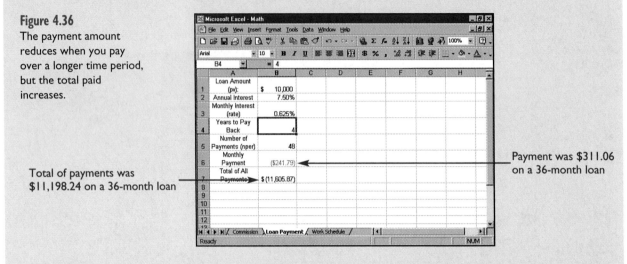

8. **Click the Undo button to see the previous values.**

9. **Click the Redo button to go back to the four-year payment plan.**

10. **Click the Work Schedule tab.**

11. **Assume that Bill asked Juan to take his Tuesday lunch shift from 12 to 2. Enter Juan's name in cells C11 through C14.**
Notice that the hours worked and pay automatically recalculate for both employees (see Figure 4.37).

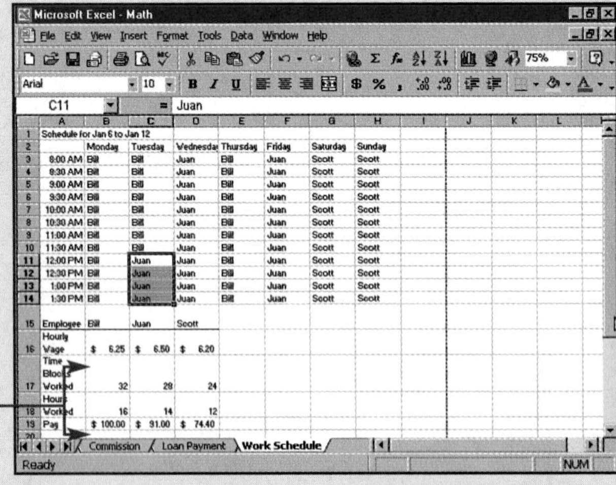

Formulas in these cells are recalculated

Figure 4.37
The wages and hours automatically adjust to reflect the change.

12. **Save the changes, and close the workbook.**

Summary

This project showed you how to create formulas in Excel. It started with simple examples that used cells and numbers, two cells, and more than two cells. It showed you the difference between an absolute cell reference and a relative cell reference. Then it applied these basic concepts to worksheets; the first one calculated sales commissions. Then the Paste Function was introduced with its library of preprogrammed calculations. You used the payment function to calculate a payment for a car loan. Then you used the COUNTIF function to count names in a list and calculate wages.

To learn more about writing formulas, try creating some that you might use in your work or personal life. Open the Paste Function dialog box and examine the different categories and functions listed. If you are uncertain what a function abbreviation might mean, click it and read the explanation. If you find ones you are interested in using, open the formula palette and examine the argument statements that are required.

Checking Concepts and Terms

True/False

For each of the following, check *T* or *F* to indicate whether the statement is true or false.

__T __F **1.** You can use only one cell reference in a formula. [L1]

__T __F **2.** Math operations that are grouped inside parentheses are calculated first in a formula. [L3]

__T __F **3.** When you use the fill handle to copy a formula that sums a column, Excel assumes an absolute reference to the numbers in the original column. [L4]

__T __F **4.** To designate a cell reference as absolute, place a $ to the left of both the column and row identifiers. [L4]

__T __F **5.** To view the formulas used in an Excel worksheet, press Ctrl+`, which is found on the key to the left of the 1 key. [L3]

__T __F **6.** The loan payment formula uses an annual interest rate and the number of years of the loan to calculate the monthly payment amount. [L6]

__T __F **7.** The Paste Function button on the Standard toolbar opens a formula palette that you can use to enter formulas for making a variety of financial calculations. [L6]

__T __F **8.** Relative reference is a cell reference that changes when the formula is copied, moved, or filled. [L3]

__T __F **9.** The COUNTIF function in Excel can be used to count the number of cells that contain a selected word or number. [L7]

__T __F **10.** When you change a number in a cell, it automatically changes the results of every formula that uses that cell. [L8]

Multiple Choice

Circle the letter of the correct answer for each of the following.

1. What is the term for numbers or words that are used by a function to perform a calculation or operation? [L6]

a. collateral

b. attribute

c. function

d. argument

2. What would you use the COUNTIF function for? [L7]

a. to count the number of occurrences of a word or a number in a range of cells

b. to count the number of apples sold in a column of numbers that recorded the quantity of sales daily

c. to count the number of payments in a worksheet that calculates a loan payment

d. none of the above

3. Assume you have a worksheet that calculates wages and it includes a cell for the fixed state tax rate and cells for each employee's total wages. If you wanted to calculate the amount of state tax to deduct for each employee, which approach would work best? [L8]

a. an absolute reference to the tax rate and to each employee's total wage

b. a relative reference to the tax rate and to each employee's total wage

c. an absolute reference to the tax rate and relative reference to the employee's total wage

d. a relative reference to the tax rate and an absolute reference to the employee's total wage

4. What arguments are required by the PMT (payment) function to calculate a new car loan payment? [L6]
   a. APR, number of years, cost of new car
   b. number of payments, interest rate per payment period, and the amount loaned
   c. the total of the payments, the first due date, and the interest rate
   d. the make, model, and year of the car being purchased

5. A cell reference that changes when copied or filled is known as a(n) ______________. [L4]
   a. variable reference
   b. absolute reference
   c. relative reference
   d. certain reference

Screen ID

Identify each of the items shown in Figure 4.38.

Figure 4.38

A. Paste Function button
B. Enter button
C. Projected payment amount
D. Interest rate per loan period
E. Amount of money that is borrowed
F. Number of payments in a loan
G. Collapse button
H. Formula with arguments
I. Edit Formula button
J. Cancel button

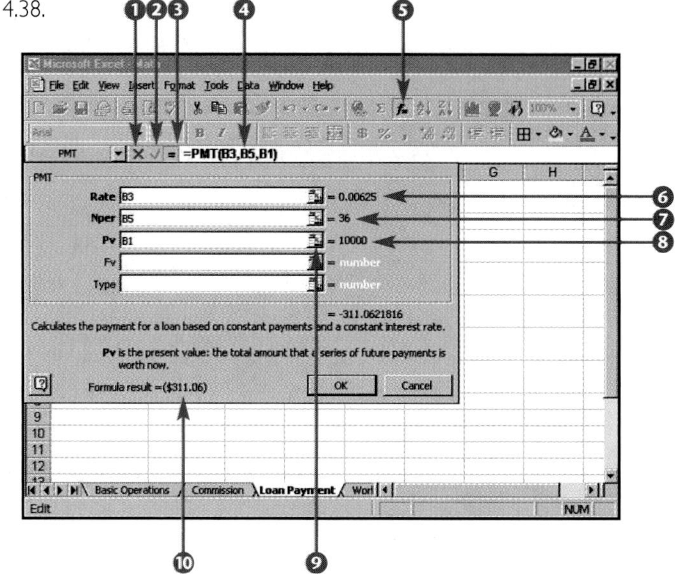

1. ______________
2. ______________
3. ______________
4. ______________
5. ______________

6. ______________
7. ______________
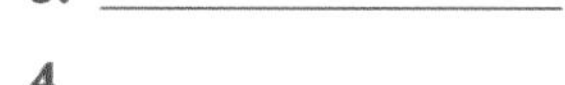
8. ______________
9. ______________
10. ______________

Discussion Questions

1. Look at the categories in the Paste Function formula palette. What are some math functions that you want to know how to use in Excel?
2. Why do you enter cell references in formulas instead of just putting in the number?
3. Why is an asterisk used in formulas for multiplication rather than an X or a dot?
4. What are some examples of when you would use an absolute reference?
5. Open the Paste Function formula palette and examine the three other count functions listed under the statistical category. Think of an example for when you would use each of these counting functions.

Skill Drill

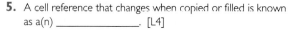

Skill Drill exercises reinforce project skills. Each skill reinforced is the same, or nearly the same, as a skill presented in the project. Each exercise includes a brief narrative introduction, followed by detailed instructions in a step-by-step format.

In these exercises, you work with four different worksheets to practice the math skills you have just learned. In the first exercise, you use basic Excel math formulas and the fill function to complete an inventory worksheet. In the second exercise, you use absolute and relative cell references to complete a worksheet that calculates net salaries. The third worksheet uses the payment function to calculate a mortgage payment and an amortization schedule for the first five years of the loan. In the last worksheet, you use the COUNTIF function to calculate the wages earned for a hospital work schedule. All of these exercises use the file `EO-0402` found in the Student folder on the CD-ROM that came with your book. Open the file and save it to your floppy disk with the name `Math2`.

1. Using Basic Excel Formulas

In this exercise, you complete an inventory worksheet for the Patio Furniture Division of Armstrong Pool, Spa, and Sauna Co. You calculate the total cost, retail value, percent mark up, and percent contribution for the inventory. The quantity, average cost, and retail price columns are already complete when you open the worksheet. [L1–3]

1. Select Sheet1, and change the sheet tab name to `Patio Division`.
2. Modify the Patio Furniture Division worksheet to match Figure 4.39. See the following steps for more details. (The sheet zoom is set at 80% to provide a full view of the worksheet.)

Figure 4.39

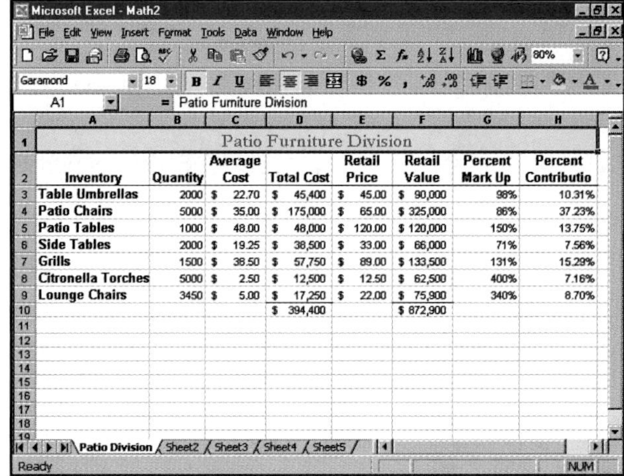

Microsoft Excel - Math2

A1 = Patio Furniture Division

	A	B	C	D	E	F	G	H
1	Patio Furniture Division							
2	Inventory	Quantity	Average Cost	Total Cost	Retail Price	Retail Value	Percent Mark Up	Percent Contributio
3	Table Umbrellas	2000	$ 22.70	$ 45,400	$ 45.00	$ 90,000	98%	10.31%
4	Patio Chairs	5000	$ 35.00	$ 175,000	$ 65.00	$ 325,000	86%	37.23%
5	Patio Tables	1000	$ 48.00	$ 48,000	$ 120.00	$ 120,000	150%	13.75%
6	Side Tables	2000	$ 19.25	$ 38,500	$ 33.00	$ 66,000	71%	7.56%
7	Grills	1500	$ 38.50	$ 57,750	$ 89.00	$ 133,500	131%	15.29%
8	Citronella Torches	5000	$ 2.50	$ 12,500	$ 12.50	$ 62,500	400%	7.16%
9	Lounge Chairs	3450	$ 5.00	$ 17,250	$ 22.00	$ 75,900	340%	8.70%
10				$ 394,400		$ 872,900		

Patio Division / Sheet2 / Sheet3 / Sheet4 / Sheet5

3. To calculate the Total Cost of each item, select cell D3 and enter `=B3*C3`. Adjust the column width as necessary.
4. Use the fill handle to copy the formula in D3 to cells D4 through D9. Format the values in this column as currency with no decimals. Adjust the column width.
5. To calculate the Retail Value, select cell F3 and enter `=B3*E3`.
6. Use the fill handle to copy the formula in F3 to cells F4 through F9. Format the values in this column as currency with no decimals.
7. Apply a bottom border to cells D9 and F9. Use the AutoSum button to place a Sum function in cells D10 and F10 to add the numbers in the column above.
8. To calculate the Percent Mark-up, select cell G3 and enter `=(E3-C3)/C3`. Fill the formula to the other cells in the column. Format the values in this column as percentages with no decimals.
9. To calculate the Percent Contribution, select cell H3 and type `=F3/$F$10`. Fill the formula to the other cells in the column. Format the values in this column as percentages with two decimals. (Use the % button on the Formatting toolbar.)
10. Add your name to the sheet header, and choose Landscape orientation.
11. Preview and print the sheet.
12. Change the worksheet to show the formulas. Adjust the columns, and wrap the column headings so the worksheet prints on one page. Select Sheet in the Page Setup dialog box, and choose Gridlines and Row and column headings, so that these print with the formulas. Print the sheet showing the formulas. The printed sheet should look like the one in Figure 4.40.
13. Change the worksheet to show the values rather than the formulas and restore the previous column widths. Save your work.

Figure 4.40

Your Name

Patio Furniture Division

Inventory	Quantity	Average Cost	Total Cost	Retail Price	Retail Value	Percent Mark Up
Table Umbrellas	2000	22.7	=B3*C3	45	=B3*E3	=(E3-C3)/C3
Patio Chairs	5000	35	=B4*C4	65	=B4*E4	=(E4-C4)/C4
Patio Tables	1000	48	=B5*C5	120	=B5*E5	=(E5-C5)/C5
Side Tables	2000	19.25	=B6*C6	33	=B6*E6	=(E6-C6)/C6
Grills	1500	38.5	=B7*C7	89	=B7*E7	=(E7-C7)/C7
Citronella Torches	5000	2.5	=B8*C8	12.5	=B8*E8	=(E8-C8)/C8
Lounge Chairs	3450	5	=B9*C9	22	=B9*E9	=(E9-C9)/C9
			=SUM(D3:D9)		=SUM(F3:F9)	

2. Using Absolute and Relative References

In this exercise, you use absolute and relative cell references to complete a payroll worksheet. You calculate typical deductions and then compute the net pay for the first six months of the year for Computer Technical Support Inc. [L4]

1. Select Sheet2 and change the sheet tab name to `Tech Support`.
2. Modify the Computer Technical Support Inc. worksheet to match Figure 4.41. See the following steps for more details.

Figure 4.41

B11 = =B3-B9

	A	B	C	D	E	F	G
1	Computer Technical Support Inc.						
2		January	February	March	April	May	June
3	Salaries	$2,584,625	$2,001,489	$2,657,881	$2,600,579	$2,701,544	$2,675,255
4	Deductibles:						
5	Social Security Tax	160,247	124,092	164,789	161,236	167,496	165,866
6	Federal Income Tax	516,925	400,298	531,576	520,116	540,309	535,051
7	State Income Tax	118,893	92,068	122,263	119,627	124,271	123,062
8	Medicare Tax	38,769	30,022	39,868	39,009	40,523	40,129
9	Total Deductibles	834,834	646,481	858,496	839,987	872,599	864,107
10							
11	Net Salaries	$1,749,791	$1,355,008	$1,799,385	$1,760,592	$1,828,945	$1,811,148
12							
13	Fixed Percentages						
14	Medicare Tax	1.50%					
15	Social Security Tax	6.20%					
16	State Tax	4.60%					
17							

Patio Division / Tech Support / Sheet3 / Sheet4 / Sheet

Ready Sum= $ 10,304,870 NUM

3. Select cell B5 and enter **=B3*$B$15**. Use the fill handle to copy the formula to cell G5. With the cells still selected, use the Comma Style button to format the cells, if needed, and then decrease the decimals to show no decimals.
4. Select cell B6 and type **=B3*.20**. Use the fill handle to copy the formula to cell G6. Format row 6 the same way as you formatted row 5.
5. Select cell B7, and type **=B3*$B$16**. Use the fill handle to copy the formula to cell G7. Format row 7 the same way as you formatted rows 5 and 6.
6. Select cell B8. Write a formula that multiplies the salaries by an absolute reference to the Medicare Tax percent (refer to the Fixed Percentages table). Use the same format for these cells.
7. Add a bottom border to the figures in row 8 and sum the deductibles in each column in row 9. Notice that the empty cell in row 4 prevents the AutoSum function from accidentally selecting the salaries in row 3.
8. Calculate the net salary figures by writing a formula in cell B11 that takes the salaries for the month and subtracts the deductibles for the month. Copy the formula to cell G11.
9. Check the results of your formulas against the figure to be sure that they are working properly. Change the State tax to **6%**.
10. Add your name to the sheet header. Change the orientation to Landscape, and print a copy of the worksheet. Save your work.

3. Calculating a House Payment and Amortization Schedule for a Five-Year Balloon Mortgage

In this exercise, you calculate a payment and amortization schedule for a house's five-year balloon mortgage. [L5]

1. Select Sheet3, and change the sheet tab name to `Mortgage`.
2. Modify the Mortgage worksheet to match Figure 4.42. See the following steps for more details.

Figure 4.42

B8 = =PMT(B5,B7,B3)

	A	B	C	D	E	F	G
1	Mortgage for 1602 Stoney Creek Drive						
2							
3	Loan Amount	$ 125,000		Amortization Schedule of Payments			
4	Annual Percentage Rate (APR)	7.75%		Date	Payment	Interest Paid	Balance
5	Monthly Interest Rate	0.646%		8/1/99	-895.52	$ 807.29	$ 125,000.00
6	Number of Years	30		9/1/99	-895.52	$ 806.72	$ 124,911.78
7	No. of Monthly Payments	360		10/1/99	-895.52	$ 806.15	$ 124,822.98
8	Payment	($895.52)		11/1/99	-895.52	$ 805.57	$ 124,733.62
9				12/1/99	-895.52	$ 804.99	$ 124,643.67
10				1/1/00	-895.52	$ 804.41	$ 124,553.15
11				2/1/00	-895.52	$ 803.82	$ 124,462.04
12				3/1/00	-895.52	$ 803.23	$ 124,370.34
13				4/1/00	-895.52	$ 802.63	$ 124,278.05

Patio Division / Tech Support / Mortgage / Sheet4 / Sh

Ready NUM

3. Select cell B5, and write a formula to determine the monthly interest rate. Format it as a percent showing three decimal places.
4. Select cell B7, and write a formula to determine the number of monthly payments there will be over the term of the loan.
5. Select cell B8, and use the Paste function to insert the payment formula for the mortgage.
6. Select cells D5 and D6, and fill the date column for 5 years. The last date should be **1/1/03** in row 64.
7. Select cells E6 through G6. Drag these three cells to the bottom of the date column to complete the amortization schedule. Look in cell G64. If you have to refinance the home loan in five years, you have to borrow $118,688.66 (and pay closing costs again).
8. Change the Annual Percentage Rate (APR) to **8%**.
9. Add your name to the sheet header; set the first four rows to repeat on the second page, and print a copy of the worksheet (two pages).
10. Save your work.

4. Using the COUNTIF Function to Calculate Wages

In this exercise, you use the COUNTIF function to calculate wages at Metro Hospital. [L6]

1. Select Sheet4 and change the sheet tab name to **Metro Hospital**.
2. Modify the Metro Hospital worksheet to match Figure 4.43. See the following steps for more details.

Figure 4.43

Your Name

Metro Hospital Nursing Schedule

Floor Name							
Nine North	Sun 6-Jul	Mon 7-Jul	Tue 8-Jul	Wed 9-Jul	Thu 10-Jul	Fri 11-Jul	Sat 12-Jul
First Shift:							
Head Nurse	Mary	Mary	Mary	Sue	Sue	Sue	Mary
Nurse	Jo	Pam	Pam	Pam	Kelly	Kelly	Mary Alice
Nurse	Mary Alice	Tom	Tom	Tom	Bertha	Bertha	Bertha
Aide	Tracy	Tracy	Tracy	Matt	Matt	Matt	Tracy
Second Shift:							
Head Nurse	Martha	Robert	Robert	Robert	Kathy	Kathy	Martha
Nurse	Bridgett	Bridgett	Bridgett	Jo	Jo	Jo	Bridgett
Aide	Matt	Kelly	Kelly	Kelly	Chris	Chris	Chris

	Hourly Wage	Number of Shifts	Hours Worked	Wages Earned
Bertha	$ 15.75	3	36	$ 567.00
Bridgett	$ 13.60	4	48	$ 652.80
Chris	$ 12.20	3	36	$ 439.20
Jo	$ 18.00	4	48	$ 864.00
Kathy	$ 19.50	2	24	$ 468.00
Kelly	$ 12.90	5	60	$ 774.00
Martha	$ 18.75	2	24	$ 450.00
Mary	$ 22.00	3	36	$ 792.00
Mary Alice	$ 16.40	2	24	$ 393.60
Matt	$ 14.80	4	48	$ 710.40
Pam	$ 16.00	3	36	$ 576.00
Robert	$ 21.50	3	36	$ 774.00
Sue	$ 22.00	3	36	$ 792.00
Tom	$ 17.90	3	36	$ 644.40
Tracy	$ 13.60	4	48	$ 652.80
				$9,550.20

3. Select cell C16, and use the COUNTIF function to calculate the number of shifts that Bertha worked.

   Be sure to make references to the range B6:H13 absolute. Also use a cell reference instead of the word "Bertha" to specify the criteria.
4. Each shift is 12 hours. Select cell D16 and write a formula that multiplies the number of shifts by 12 to arrive at the number of hours worked.
5. Select cell E16, and write a formula to multiply the Hourly Wage by the Hours Worked for Bertha.
6. Select cell C16 and check that your formula is **=COUNTIF($B$6:$H$13,A16)**. Make changes as necessary.
7. Select the range C16:E16; use the fill handle to copy the three formulas down to complete the chart of hours and wages.
8. Use the AutoSum function to sum the Wages Earned column. If your work is correct, the sum of wages is $9,550.20. Fix any problems.
9. Save the workbook. Add your name to the sheet header, and print a copy of the worksheet.

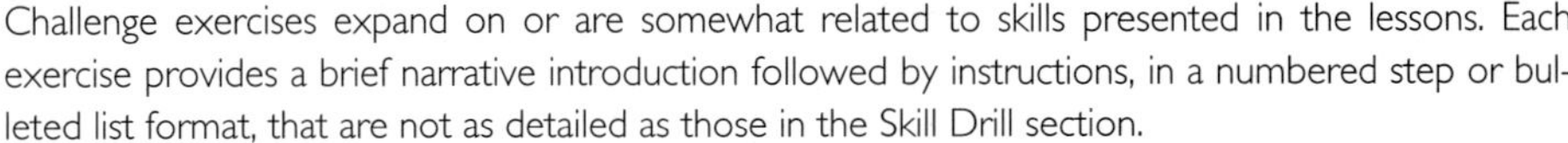

Challenge

Challenge exercises expand on or are somewhat related to skills presented in the lessons. Each exercise provides a brief narrative introduction followed by instructions, in a numbered step or bulleted list format, that are not as detailed as those in the Skill Drill section.

In the first Challenge exercise, you use a tool called Goal Seek to help you find the answer to a question. In the second exercise, you change the price for goods sold based on a percentage increase or decrease in the price. The third exercise uses some common statistical calculations. The following exercises use the file **EO-0403**. Locate the file in the Student folder on the disc that came with your book. Open the file and save it on your floppy disk as **Math3**.

1. Using Goal Seek

Sometimes you know what the answer needs to be but you do not know what the other factors have to be to compute that answer. If you have a worksheet set up to calculate an answer based on one or more cells, you can use an Excel tool named Goal Seek that tries different numbers in the cell you select until the answer in another cell matches the value you set. [L5]

To use Goal Seek to determine the value in one cell that produces the desired result in another cell, follow these steps:

1. With the Math3 file open, make sure the Goal Seek sheet is selected.
2. Select Tools, Goal Seek from the menu.
3. Use the Goal Seek dialog box to set cell B6 to a value of 600 by changing the annual interest rate in cell B2. The resulting Annual Interest Rate is 7.02%.
4. Use this method and this sheet to determine how big a loan you can afford (Loan Amount) on a five-year car loan at an Annual Interest Rate of 8.5% if the most you can afford for a monthly car payment is $350. The result shows the calculated loan amount in cell B1, 8.5% in cell B2, 5 in cell B4, and $350.00 in cell B6. (The sheet is protected, so that you do not accidentally overwrite the formulas.)
5. Save the workbook. Leave the workbook open for use in the next exercise.

2. Changing Prices by Increasing or Decreasing Percentages

Prices are often determined by marking up a wholesale price by a certain percentage. When those items go on sale, the price is reduced by a certain percentage. [L2]

In this exercise, you see how formulas are used to increase or decrease a price by a given percentage. In general, if you want to increase a value by 40% you multiply the value by (1+40%). If you want to decrease the price by 20%, you multiply by (1-20%). An example is provided to show how a merchant starts with a wholesale price for a pair of boots, increases the price by 40% to get the retail price, decreases the retail price by 20% for a sale, and figures out the gross profit and percent profit.

To calculate percentage increases and decreases, follow these steps:

1. Open the Math3 file, and select the Percent sheet.
2. Look at the formula in cell C2. Notice how the retail price for the boots was calculated by multiplying the wholesale price in cell B2 by (1+40%).
3. Enter a similar formula in cell C3 that calculates a retail price for gloves at a 50% increase over the wholesale price.
4. Observe the formula in cell D2 to see how the sale price for boots was determined by multiplying the Retail price by (1-20%).
5. Enter a similar formula in cell D3 to calculate the sale price for gloves if their price is reduced by 30%.
6. Fill the formulas in cells E2 and F2 into cells E3 and F3, respectively. The percent profit on the gloves will be 5% if you have written the formulas correctly.
7. Enter two similar formulas for the hats. Use an increase of 120% to determine the retail price and determine the sale price for a 50% off sale. Fill the Gross Profit and Percent Profit formulas into cells E4 and F4.
8. Save the workbook. Leave the workbook open for use in the next exercise.

3. Calculating Statistics—Average, Median, and Standard Deviation

When we describe a set of numbers, such as the income of a certain group, we often use terms such as average or median. We can use Excel to compute these numbers and see how they describe a set of numbers. Average and median are two ways of describing where the center of a set of numbers is. They do not describe whether the numbers are all close to that central number or if they vary greatly. The statistic that describes this type of variation is the standard deviation. [L6]

In this exercise, you look at the monthly rainfall in Buffalo and Seattle.

To use Excel's statistical functions to compare the average, median, and standard deviation of rainfall, follow these steps:

1. Open the Math3 file, and select the Stats sheet. Notice that both cities have almost the same total annual rainfall. Look at the rainfall for each month of the year—it is apparent that the rainfall in Seattle varies much more from month to month.

2. Paste the Average function in cells B16. (It is one of the Statistics functions.) Use cells B3:B14; do not include the total in cell B15. Use the same method to find the average rainfall in Seattle.
3. The median of a set of numbers is the value that has as many values above it as below it. Find the median rainfall for both cities and place them in the table.
4. To see how much the numbers vary from the average, find the standard deviation of the rainfall for both cities. Use the STDEVP function. About two-thirds of the values will be within this range of the average. A small standard deviation means that the numbers are closely grouped around the average. Does the city with the smaller standard deviation have about the same amount of rain each month? If so, you have done the assignment correctly.
5. Save the workbook and close it.

Discovery Zone

Discovery Zone exercises require advanced knowledge of topics presented in *Essentials* lessons, application of skills from multiple lessons, or self-directed learning of new skills.

These Discovery Zone exercises use three advanced Excel tools. In the first exercise, you use the VLOOKUP function to look up values in a column to complete a calculation. In the second exercise, you learn how to do a frequency distribution using Excel. The last exercise uses the Solver tool, which is similar to Goal Seek used in the first Challenge exercise. These exercises are independent of each other. They each use a separate worksheet in file **EO-0404**. Open this file from your CD and save it on your floppy disk as **Math4**.

1. Using VLOOKUP

If you are providing a quotation for a job, the price often depends on the cost of parts and labor. These costs vary depending on the item and the quantity purchased. It can be very time-consuming to look up information in tables to include in your calculations. Excel has two functions designed to look up values in a table, column or array. These are called VLOOKUP and HLOOKUP. You use VLOOKUP to look up values in a vertical column and HLOOKUP to look up values in a horizontal row. In this exercise, you learn how to use the VLOOKUP function. [L8]

To use the VLOOKUP function to find the correct value in a table and use it in a calculation, follow these steps:

- Select the Lookup sheet in the Math4 file.
- Use Help to find the description of the VLOOKUP function. Read the description and examine the example in cell C4. This formula includes three arguments. The first argument defines the value that is looked up in a table. The second argument defines the table, or range of cells, that should be examined. The third is the column that should be used to locate the matching value. Each column in the defined table is identified with a number, 1, 2, 3, and so on. (*Note*: The values in the first column of a table that is used with this function must be sorted in incrementing order.)
- Test the function by changing values in cells A4 and B4. Use one of the codes from Column 1 of the Quantity Charge table for cell A4, and either a 2 or 3 for cell B4. The number in cell B4 indicates whether column 2 or 3 of the Quantity Charge table should be used to look up the value that matches the code in cell A4.
- Find the Multi-Color Charge table. Paste the VLOOKUP function into cell C18, and select the arguments, so that it finds the correct charge for additional shirt colors and displays it in cell C18.
- Test the function by trying different numbers in cells A18 and B18.
- Save the workbook, and leave it open for use in the next Discovery Zone exercise.

2. Using Frequency Distribution

This exercise requires the Analysis ToolPak Add-in. Look under the Tools menu to determine whether you have the Data Analysis option. If not, select Tools, Add-Ins, Analysis ToolPak. If you plan to do Discovery Zone Exercise 3, select the Solver Add-in, too. You might need your Office 2000 CD or to ask your lab administrator to install these features. [L8]

If you are trying to determine how many of each number you have in a group, you want to know the frequency distribution. For example, 25 people have answered a question that has five possible answers numbered 1 through 5 and you would like to know how many people chose each answer.

Excel provides two options for determining the frequency distribution. There is a Frequency Distribution function that you can find by using the Paste Function button. The other is part of the Histogram tool in the Analysis ToolPak. The Histogram tool is much easier to use and can also produce a chart that is used in the next lesson.

To use the Histogram tool to determine the number of people answering each option for a question, follow these steps:

- If necessary, open the `Math4` file, and select the Frequency sheet.
- Locate and read the information in Help on the Histogram analysis tool.
- Look at the example analysis that was done on the first question.
- Use the Histogram analysis tool to produce a similar analysis of the second question. Select cell Y14 as the output cell that will be used as the upper-left corner of the output range.
- Save the workbook, and leave it open for use in the next exercise.

3. Using Solver

Solver is similar to Goal Seek, but it has more options. It can change more than one input cell, and you can specify constraints on several cells. You can have it determine the inputs to produce a match, a maximum value, or a minimum value. [L8]

A classic physics problem is to determine how high a projectile will go if it is shot straight up at a given initial speed. The formula is $H=-16T^2 + ST$, where H stands for height, T for time, and S for speed. This formula can be written in Excel as =–16*(cell reference for time)^2+(cell reference for speed)*(cell reference for time). In the example sheet used for this exercise, the formula is `=-16*B3^2+B4*B3`. You can solve this problem in two ways. You could use differential calculus to find the derivative; set it equal to zero; solve for T, and plug the value of T into the original formula. A second way would be to try increasing values of time in the formula until the value of the height stopped increasing and started decreasing. To solve for the time down to the nearest tenth of a second, you would have to do the formula many times.

The Solver works by trying different values in the formula, subject to the constraints you have imposed, until the target cell matches the value you have chosen or is a maximum or minimum if you have selected either of those options.

To use the Solver tool to find the maximum height to which a projectile will rise given an initial speed, follow these steps:

- Open the `Math4` file and select the Solver sheet.
- Search Help for guidelines on using the Solver.
- Use the Solver to determine the maximum value for the formula in cell B5 by changing the time values in cell B3.
- Keep the Solver solution.
- Save the workbook, and close it.

Project 5

Understanding the Numbers by Using a Chart

Objectives

In this project, you learn how to

- Create a Chart to Show a Trend
- Create a Chart to Make Comparisons
- Create a Chart to Show Contributions to a Whole
- Edit Chart Elements
- Print a Chart

Key terms introduced in this project include

- bar chart
- Category (X) axis
- chart
- chart sub-type
- Chart Wizard
- column chart
- data series
- legend
- line chart
- pie chart
- x-axis
- y-axis
- Value (Y) axis
- Value (Z) axis

Source: Essentials: Office 2000, Ferrett-Preston-Preston

Why Would I Do This?

It is sometimes easier to analyze numbers when looking at a visual representation. A ***chart*** is a graphic representation of a series of numbers, sometimes referred to as a graph. A chart, or graph, helps you see the relationship between numbers. Some types of graphs are better for specific purposes than other types. For instance, when you want to show a trend (change over time), a ***line chart*** is usually most effective. A line chart is a graph that shows a line running through each data point. But if you need to show the contribution of each part to the whole, a ***pie chart*** is best. It is a round graph, divided into pie-shaped pieces, or wedges, where the size of each piece indicates its relative contribution to the total.

Visual Summary

This project is designed to provide you with the basic skills you need to create a variety of charts to include with your worksheets. You use Excel's ***Chart Wizard***, which is a miniprogram that guides you through the steps necessary to create a chart. When you have completed this project, you will have created charts that look like the ones in Figures 5.1–5.3.

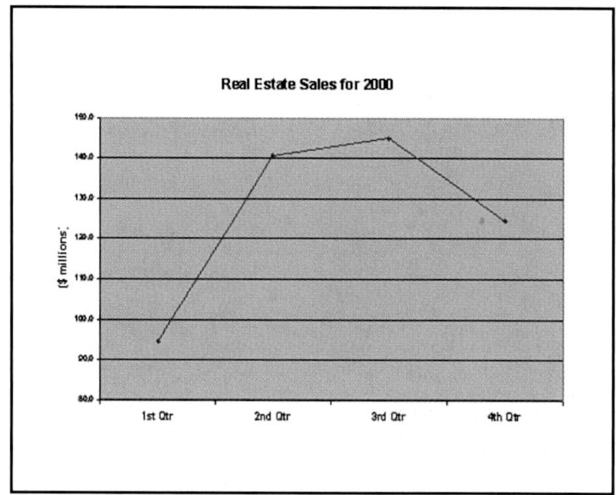

Figure 5.1
A line chart shows change over time.

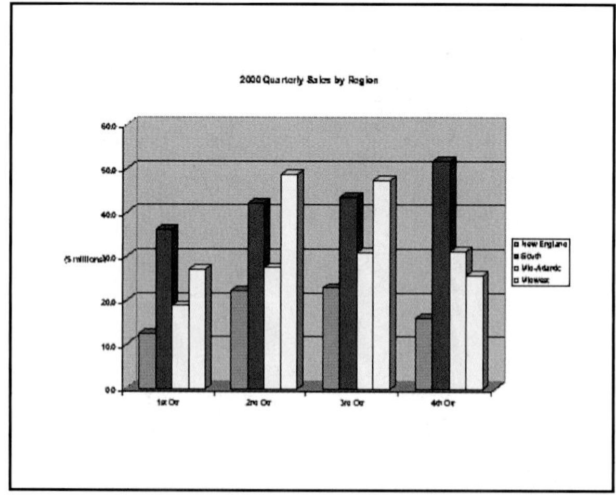

Figure 5.2
A column chart shows comparisons between categories.

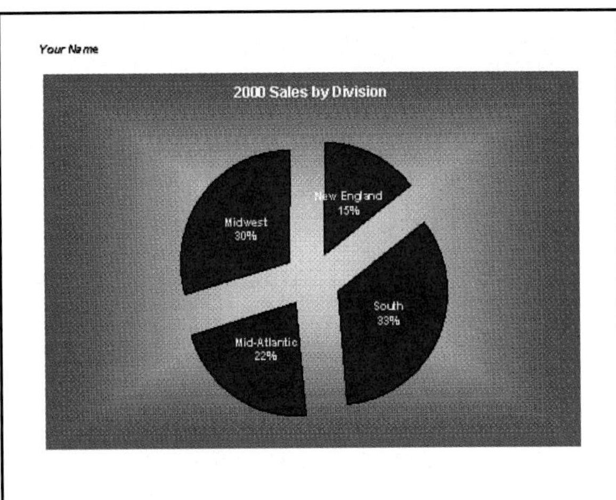

Figure 5.3
A pie chart shows the contribution of each unit to the whole.

Lesson 1: Creating a Chart to Show a Trend

A line chart is an effective tool for showing a trend. It is easy to see how an item has changed over time and whether the general direction is up or down. You can place several lines for different values on a single line chart, which helps you to see how one item compares to the next. This type of graph is used to show trends in the financial world, such as fluctuations in the stock market, or the price of gold or commodities.

In this lesson, you create a line chart to show the sales trend for a real estate firm. You chart one ***data series***—a group of related data points plotted in a chart—showing total sales in millions of dollars for each quarter during the year 2000.

To Create a Line Chart

1 Launch Excel. Locate and open EO-0501 from the CD that came with your book and save it on your floppy disk as `Sales`.

The file opens and the new workbook name displays in the title bar, as shown in Figure 5.4. The worksheet shows the sales for each division in the company by calendar quarter and for the year as a total.

Microsoft Excel - Sales.xls

File Edit View Insert Format Tools Data Window Help

A3 = Division

	A	B	C	D	E	F
1	The Real Estate Brokers					
2	Sales ($million) for 2000					
3	Division	1st Qtr	2nd Qtr	3rd Qtr	4th Qtr	Year
4	New England	12.4	22.3	23.0	15.9	73.6
5	South	36.2	42.1	43.6	51.7	173.6
6	Mid Atlantic	18.9	27.6	31.1	31.2	108.8
7	Midwest	27.1	48.7	47.3	25.9	149.0
8	Total Sales	94.6	140.7	145.0	124.7	505.0

2000 Sales / 2001 Sales / 2002 Sales

Ready

Figure 5.4
The Real Estate Brokers worksheet shows sales by region for each quarter.

continues ▶

To Create a Line Chart (continued)

2 Move the pointer to cell A3, if necessary, and click and drag to select cells A3 through E3. Hold down Ctrl and select cells A8 through E8.

This selects the labels of the columns and the total sales figures for the year to use in the chart (see Figure 5.5).

Figure 5.5
Select the cells to use in the chart first.

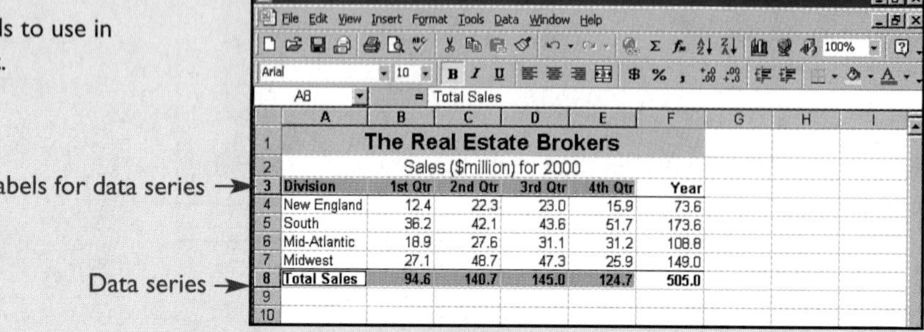

	A	B	C	D	E	F
1	The Real Estate Brokers					
2	Sales ($million) for 2000					
3	Division	1st Qtr	2nd Qtr	3rd Qtr	4th Qtr	Year
4	New England	12.4	22.3	23.0	15.9	73.6
5	South	36.2	42.1	43.6	51.7	173.6
6	Mid-Atlantic	18.9	27.6	31.1	31.2	108.8
7	Midwest	27.1	48.7	47.3	25.9	149.0
8	Total Sales	94.6	140.7	145.0	124.7	505.0

3 Click the Chart Wizard button.

The first Chart Wizard dialog box displays. (If the Office Assistant opens, close it.)

4 Click Line in the Chart type area.

Notice that the default ***chart sub-type*** is a line with data markers (see Figure 5.6). Each chart type has several chart sub-types, which are variations on the basic chart that you can use to display the data using different emphases and views of the chart.

Figure 5.6
The first step in the Chart Wizard is to select the type of chart you want to use.

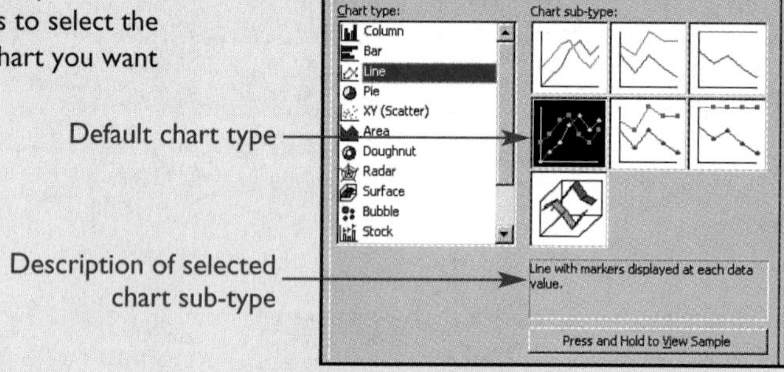

5 Click Next.

The second Chart Wizard dialog box displays. Make sure Rows is selected from the Series in area (see Figure 5.7).

Figure 5.7
The series of data displays in rows.

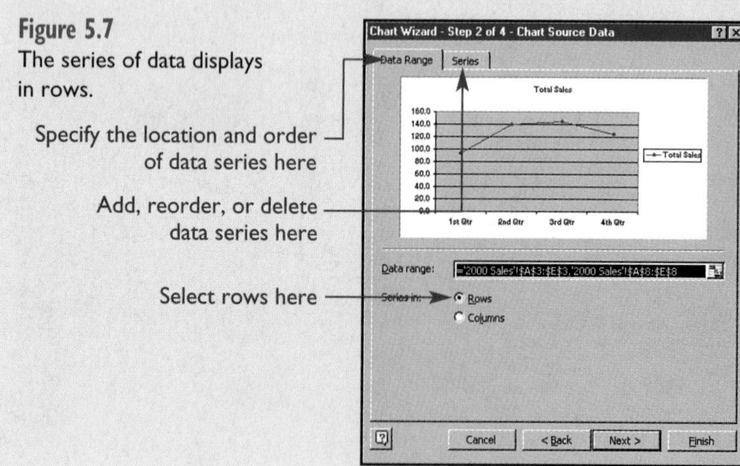

6 **Click Next. In the third Chart Wizard dialog box, select the Titles tab, if necessary. Type `Real Estate Sales for 2000` in the Chart title box. Type `($ million)` in the Value (Y) axis title box.**
Marks along the left side of the chart area are used to measure the value of the data. This side is called the Y-axis by mathematicians. In Excel, the left side of the chart is referred to by both names and may be called the Value axis, the y-axis, or the ***Value (Y) axis***. The bottom of the chart is used to locate the category of the data and is called the x-axis by mathematicians. The bottom of the chart may be called Category axis, the x-axis, or the ***Category (X) axis***.

After you enter the labels, the change is reflected in the Preview area, as shown in Figure 5.8.

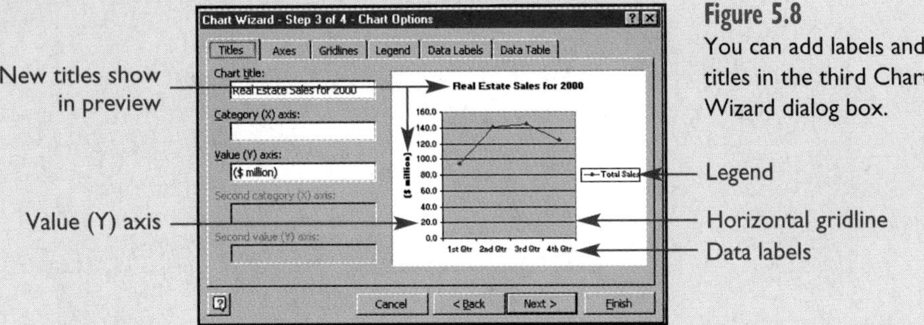

Figure 5.8
You can add labels and titles in the third Chart Wizard dialog box.

7 **Click the Legend tab.**
Just like a key or legend on a map, a ***legend*** in Excel is a list that identifies a pattern or color used in a chart. Excel adds a legend automatically, so you have to make a point to turn this feature off if you do not want a legend. In this example, a legend is unnecessary. This page in the dialog box is used to turn the legend off, or to change its location in the chart.

8 **Click the Show legend box to turn the legend off.**
The legend is removed, and the chart expands to fill the extra space (see Figure 5.9).

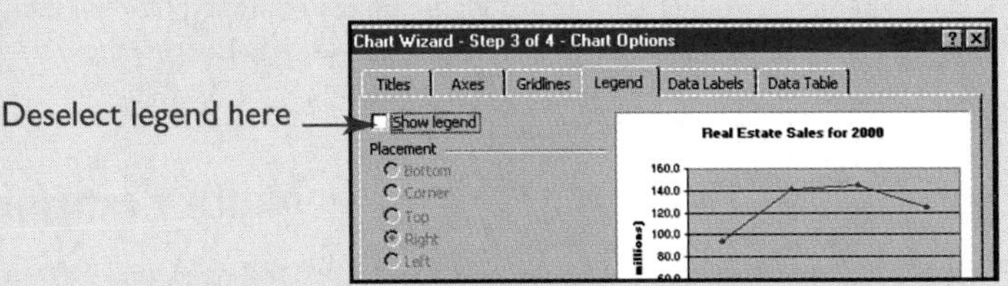

Figure 5.9
The legend is turned off.

9 **Click Next. In the fourth Chart Wizard dialog box, click As new sheet to select it, and type `2000 Sales Chart` in the adjacent box (see Figure 5.10).**
This action names the sheet and saves it on a separate sheet by itself. You can also save a chart on the same sheet as the worksheet data. In either case, Excel links the chart to the data in the worksheet and changes it to reflect any changes in the data.

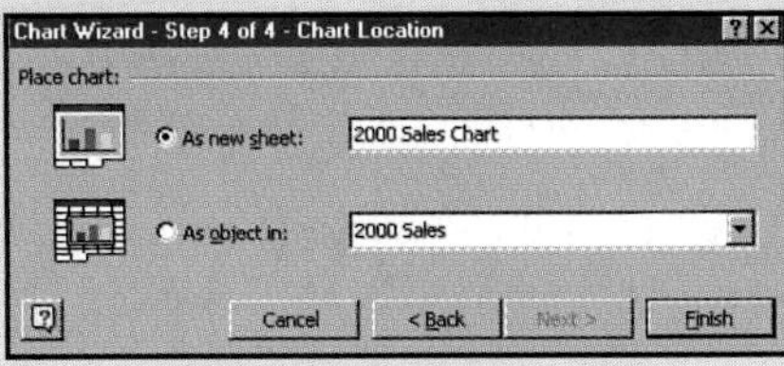

Figure 5.10
Save the chart on a new sheet in the fourth step of the Chart Wizard.

continues ▶

To Create a Line Chart (continued)

10. **Click Finish.**
The chart displays full-size on its own sheet named 2000 Sales Chart (see Figure 5.11).

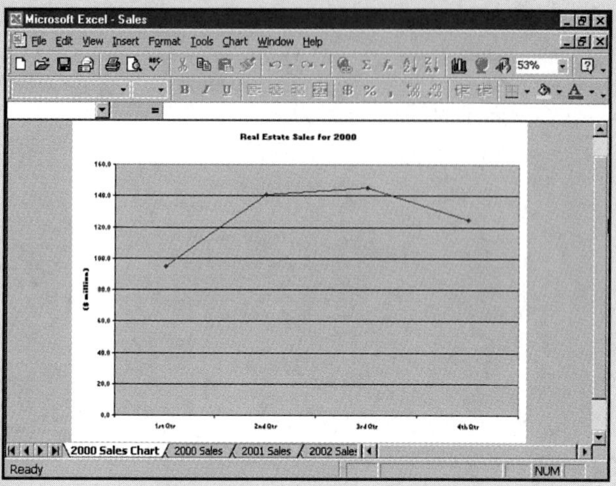

Figure 5.11
The completed line chart for Real Estate Sales for 2000 displays.

11. **Save your work.**
Leave the file open for use in the next lesson.

The Chart toolbar may open automatically when you finish creating the chart. You do not need this toolbar at this time, so click the Close button on the toolbar to close it.

Controlling Chart Elements
The first three Chart Wizard dialog boxes contain multiple tabs. These tabs let you control chart elements, such as the chart scale, whether to show vertical or horizontal gridlines, and how to label the data points.

Lesson 2: Creating a Chart to Make Comparisons

Perhaps the most common use for a chart is to make comparisons. For example, you might want to compare oil production by country over a series of years. To illustrate this type of comparison, a column chart or bar chart is most often used. A ***column chart*** is a chart that compares values across categories using vertical data columns. A ***bar chart*** compares values across categories using horizontal data bars.

In this lesson, you create a column chart that compares a company's regional sales for each quarter in the year 2000.

To Create a Column Chart

1. **Click the 2000 Sales sheet tab. Select cells A3 through E7.**
This selects the regions and their sales figures for each quarter of 2000.

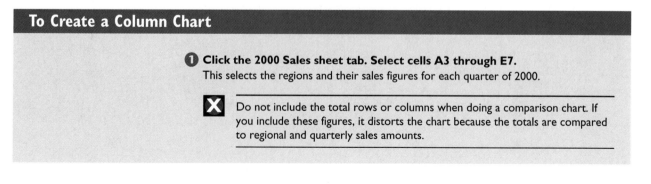

Do not include the total rows or columns when doing a comparison chart. If you include these figures, it distorts the chart because the totals are compared to regional and quarterly sales amounts.

2. **Click the Chart Wizard button. In the first Chart Wizard dialog box, click Column in the Chart type area and select the clustered column chart with 3-D visual effect.**

   The clustered column sub-type is the default style for the column chart. The clustered chart with 3-D visual effect is the first sample in the second row. Be sure to read the description to ensure that you select this style.

3. **Click Next. In the second Chart Wizard dialog box, make sure Rows is selected from the Series in area.**

   This keeps all the sales figures from each quarter together.

4. **Click Next. In the third Chart Wizard dialog box, select the Titles tab, and type `2000 Quarterly Sales by Region` in the Chart title box. Type `($ million)` in the Value (Z) axis box.**

   This action adds a title to the chart and to the figures along the vertical axis. In a 3-D chart, mathematicians label the three axes x, y, and z. The left side of the chart can be called the z-axis. Since it is still used to measure the values of the columns it is called the ***Value (Z) axis***.

5. **Click Next. Select As new sheet, and type `Quarterly Sales` in the adjacent box.**

   The chart displays on a separate sheet, with the name Quarterly Sales.

6. **Click Finish.**

   The chart displays on its own sheet (see Figure 5.12).

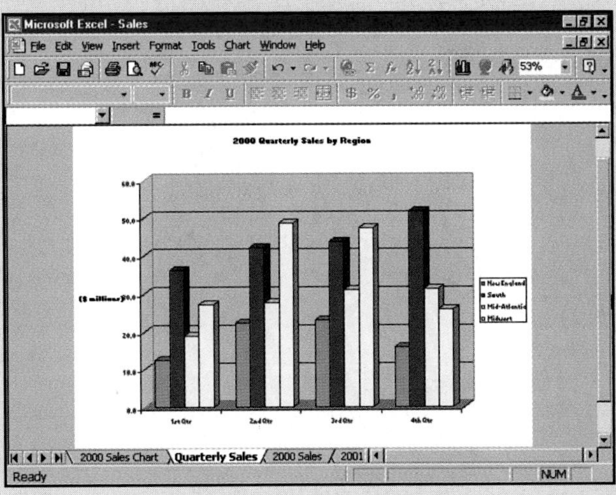

Figure 5.12
The completed column chart shows regional sales by quarter in 2000.

7. **Save your work.**

   Leave the file open for use in the next lesson.

Lesson 3: Creating a Chart to Show Contributions to a Whole

In the first lesson, you created a line chart to show a trend over time. In the second lesson, you created a column chart to show comparisons across categories. Sometimes you need to graphically represent the contribution of various elements to the whole. The best way to illustrate parts of a whole is to use a pie chart. You can chart only one data series in a pie chart.

In this lesson, you create a pie chart that shows the contribution each region made to total sales for the year.

To Create a Pie Chart

1. **Click the 2000 Sales sheet tab. Select cells A3 through A7. Hold down Ctrl and select cells F3 through F7.**
   To create a pie chart, you need to select the labels for the parts and the values for the parts that make up the whole pie.
2. **Click the Chart Wizard button. In the first Chart Wizard dialog box, click Pie in the Chart type area, and select the default chart sub-type.**
   The default chart sub-type is a simple flat pie shape.
3. **Click Next. In the second Chart Wizard dialog box, make sure Columns is selected from the Series in area, because the data you are charting is in a column.**
4. **Click Next. In the third Chart Wizard dialog box, click the Titles tab, if it is not already selected. Type `2000 Sales by Region` in the Chart title box.**
5. **Click Next. In the fourth Chart Wizard dialog box, select As new sheet, and type `2000 Sales by Division` in the adjacent box.**
6. **Click Finish.**
   The chart displays on its own worksheet (see Figure 5.13). In the next lesson, you change the size of the title and legend.

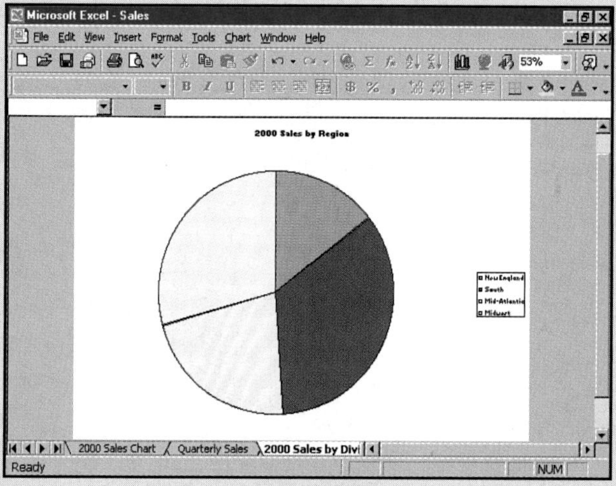

Figure 5.13
The completed pie chart shows the contribution of each division to total sales for 2000.

7. **Save your work.**
   Leave the file open for use in the next lesson.

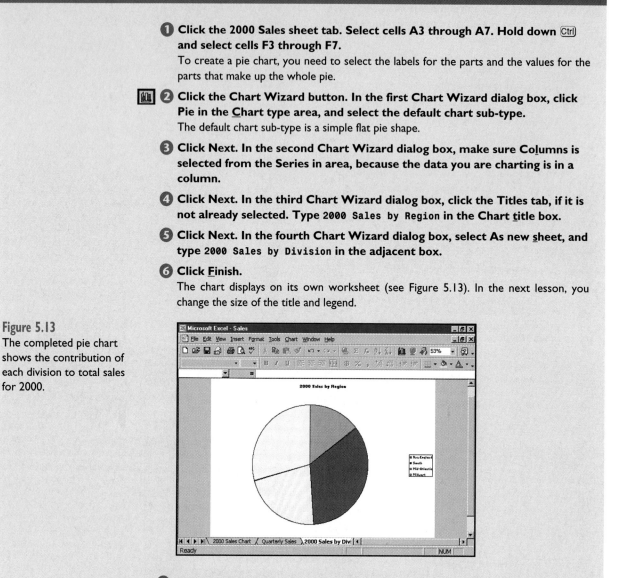

Creating an Effective Pie Chart
When you create a pie chart, you want to show the contribution each part makes to the whole. A common mistake when building a chart from a worksheet that contains totals is to include the totals with the data. Doing this defeats the purpose of a pie chart because the total figure appears to be a piece of the pie rather than the sum of the parts.

Lesson 4: Editing Chart Elements

When you create a chart in Excel, you often need to adjust the proportions of the various elements. For example, the text on the axes, titles, and legends on the charts you just created are too small. You can change the elements in your charts to make them more readable and visually appealing. You might decide that you want to try a different style of chart, but it is difficult to imagine how data will look using a different type of chart. Fortunately, it is easy to preview chart types, or to change chart types until you find the one that is most effective for the data you want to display. You can change the chart type or chart sub-type in several ways.

In this lesson, you make changes to the line chart entitled 2000 Sales Chart. You format the titles and the axes to make it easier to read and to emphasize the variation from one quarter to the next. Then you examine different chart sub-types for the pie chart and change the chart sub-type.

To Format Elements in a Chart

1 Select the 2000 Sales Chart sheet. Right-click the title `Real Estate Sales for 2000`.

A shortcut menu displays (see Figure 5.14). You can select each element on a chart to change by right-clicking to bring up a shortcut menu.

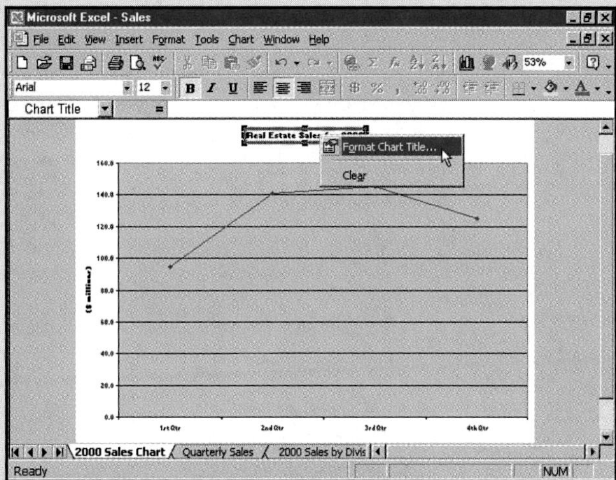

Figure 5.14
You can use a shortcut menu to open dialog boxes, so you can make changes to chart elements.

2 Select Format Chart Title from the shortcut menu, and click the Font tab in the Format Chart Title dialog box. Scroll down the list of available font sizes and select 18.

You can change the font size, style, or emphasis for the chart title using the Format Chart Title dialog box. Notice that there is also a tab for alignment and for patterns that you can use to change the chart title.

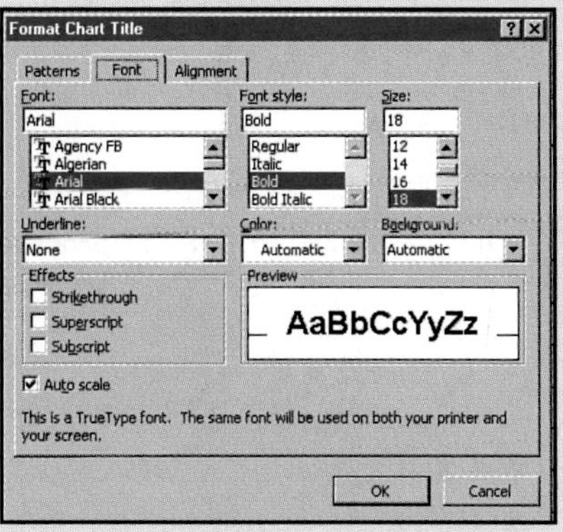

Figure 5.15
The Format Chart Title dialog box can be used to change the chart title.

3 Click OK.

The font size increases, and the title is much easier to read now.

4 Right-click the Value (Y) axis title ($ millions), and choose Format Axis Title from the shortcut menu. Change the size of the font to 14 point.

continues ▶

To Format Elements in a Chart (continued)

Each title or label has its own dialog box that you use to change the appearance of the font.

Each element on a chart has a name that Excel uses to identify that part of the chart. To find the name for any part of a chart, rest your mouse pointer on an area and wait a moment until the ScreenTip displays. The ScreenTip identifies the name of the element. Sometimes a very slight movement changes the selected element. Make sure that when you right-click, you are pointing to the element that you want to change to ensure that the correct shortcut menu displays. If you get the wrong menu or open the wrong dialog box, simply cancel the dialog box, or press Esc to close the shortcut menu.

5 Use this procedure to change the size of the category labels to 14 point.

These are the labels for the quarters along the x-axis, the horizontal line at the bottom of the chart. The ***x-axis*** is referred to as the Category Axis in an Excel chart. You can tell that the axis is selected when you see its name displayed in the Name box and small black sizing handles on either end of the axis, as shown in Figure 5.16. Sizing handles are small black squares in the corners, middle, and outside border of a chart or graphic object that you use to resize the chart or object.

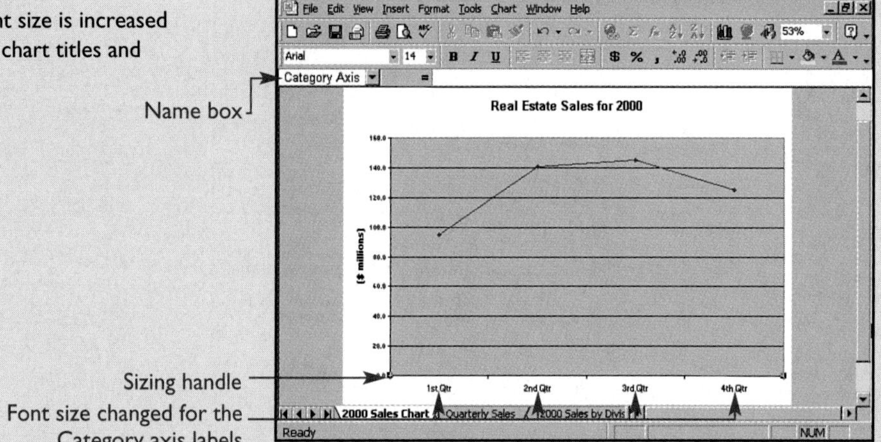

Figure 5.16
The font size is increased for the chart titles and labels.

6 Position the pointer on the numbers on the y-axis.

The ***y-axis*** is the vertical line at the left edge of the chart. Excel refers to this as the Value Axis in the chart. You have correctly identified this axis when the ScreenTip displays the term Value Axis.

7 Right-click and select Format Axis from the shortcut menu. Click the Scale tab. Change the Minimum value to 80 as shown in Figure 5.17.

You can use the Format Axis dialog box to change the scale on the graph, format the font, change the alignment of the numbers, select a numerical style—such as currency or percentages—or add color or other patterns.

8 Click OK.

By having the minimum value start at 80, rather than 0, the scale emphasizes the difference in the values (see Figure 5.18).

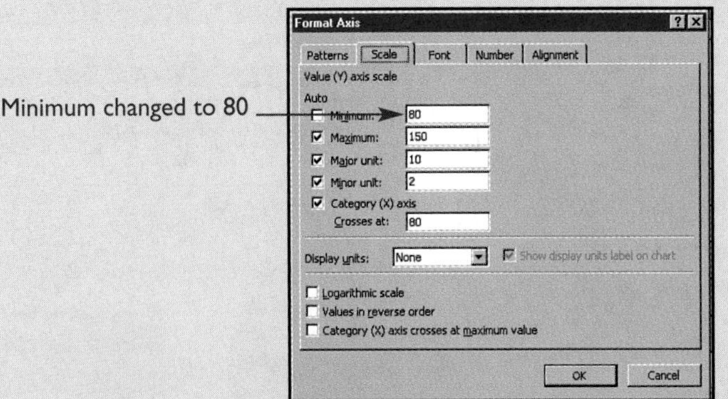

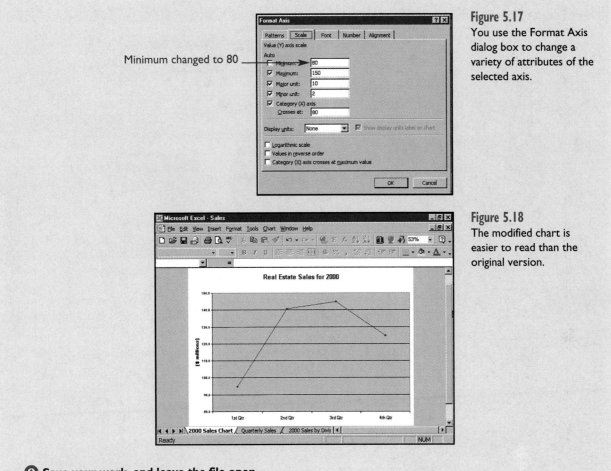

Figure 5.17
You use the Format Axis dialog box to change a variety of attributes of the selected axis.

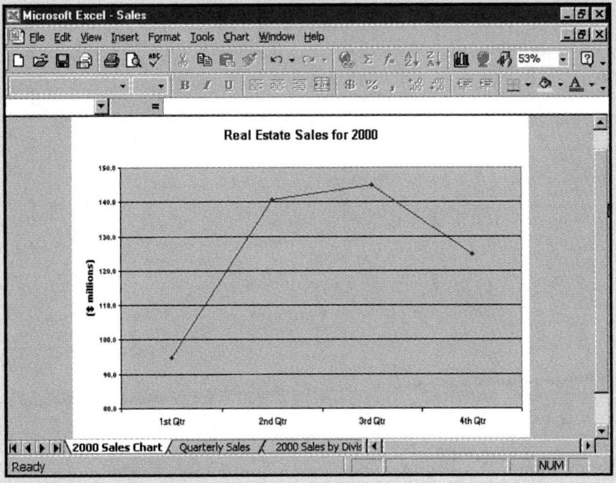

Figure 5.18
The modified chart is easier to read than the original version.

9 Save your work, and leave the file open.

Identifying Chart Elements
You can also use the Name box on the Formula bar to identify the name of any element in the chart. Simply click part of the chart, and the name displays in the Name box. (Refer to Figure 5.16 to see how the Category Axis has been identified in the Name box.)

Next, you change the chart sub-type for the pie chart you created in Lesson 3 for a more effective display of the data.

To Change a Chart Type

1 Scroll the sheet tabs to the right, and click the 2000 Sales by Division sheet tab. Right-click an empty area of the chart.

A shortcut menu displays, as shown in Figure 5.19. This shortcut menu enables you to change the chart type, the data that is graphed, where the chart is saved, or the title for the chart.

continues ▶

To Change a Chart Type (continued)

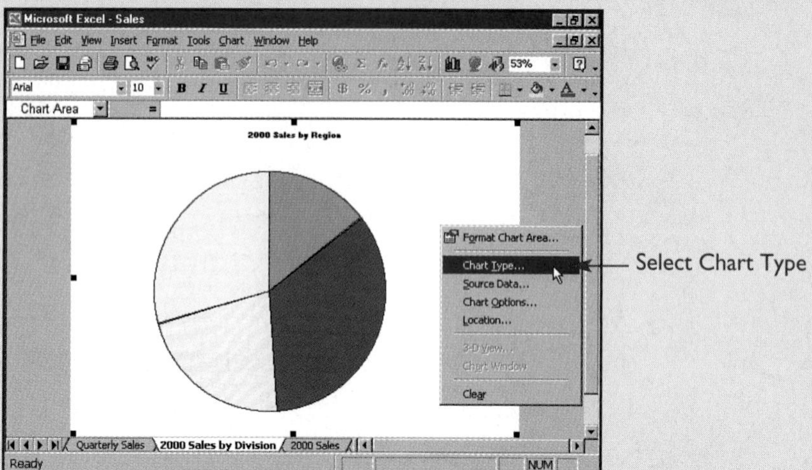

Figure 5.19
Select Chart Type from the shortcut menu to change the chart sub-type.

2. **Click Chart Type to display the Chart Type dialog box. Confirm that the Chart type is Pie, and click the Pie with a 3-D visual effect chart sub-type.**
   The 3-D sub-type is the middle sample in the top row.

3. **Move the pointer to the Press and Hold to View Sample button. Click and hold the left mouse button.**
   An example of how the chart would look displays (see Figure 5.20).

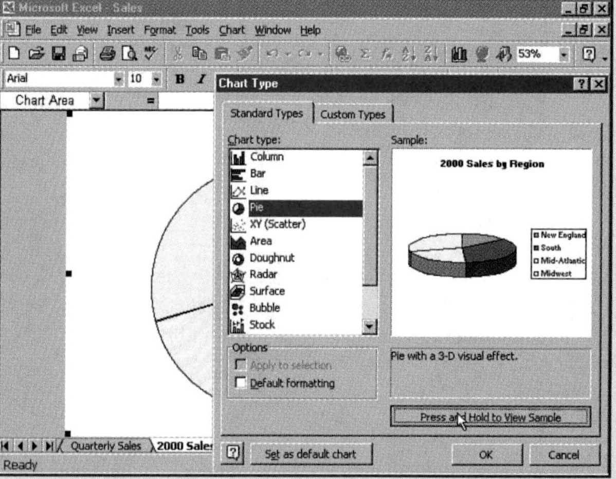

Figure 5.20
A sample of a 3-D chart displays.

4. **Release the mouse button. Select the Exploded pie with a 3-D visual effect sub-type. Click and hold the Press and Hold to View Sample button.**

5. **Click the Custom Types tab, and select the Blue Pie option.**
   This is an example of one of the many custom designs.

6. **Click OK to select this custom sub-type.**
   Examine your screen and Figure 5.21. Notice that the wording of the title needs to be changed; it should be larger, and it would be easier to read if it were white instead of black. Also, the labels should be larger.

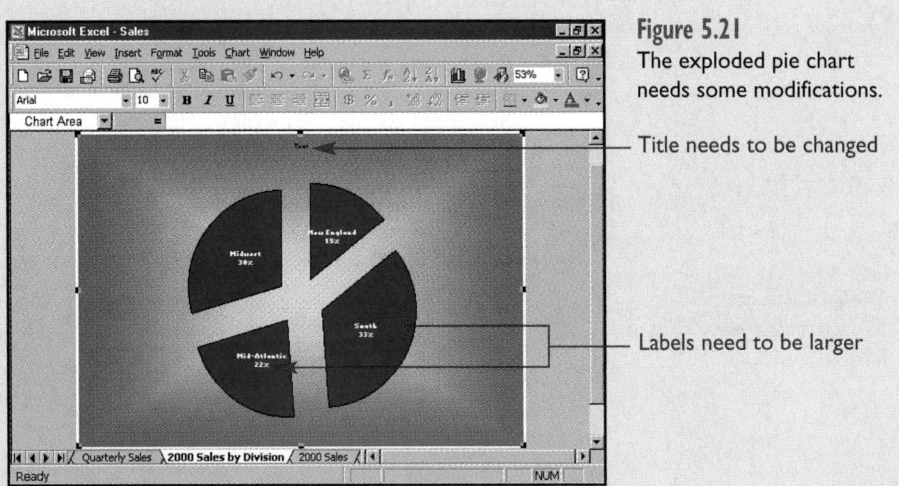
Title needs to be changed
Labels need to be larger

Figure 5.21
The exploded pie chart needs some modifications.

7. **Right-click the title, and select Format Chart Title from the shortcut menu. Select the Font tab if necessary. Change the font size to 18 and select Bold under Font style.**

8. **Click the down arrow next to the Color box to display a list of available colors.**
   A palette of colors that you can use to change the color of the font for the title displays (see Figure 5.22).

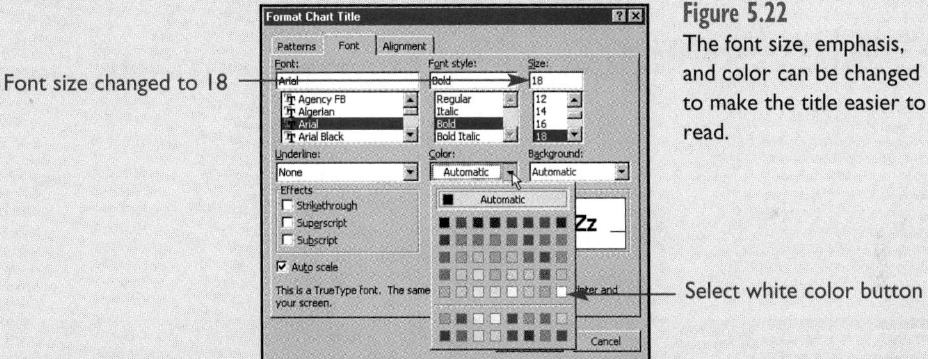
Font size changed to 18
Select white color button

Figure 5.22
The font size, emphasis, and color can be changed to make the title easier to read.

9. **Click the white box, and click OK. Notice that the title is still selected. Type `2000 Sales by Division`.**
   The new title appears in the Formula bar, as shown in Figure 5.23.

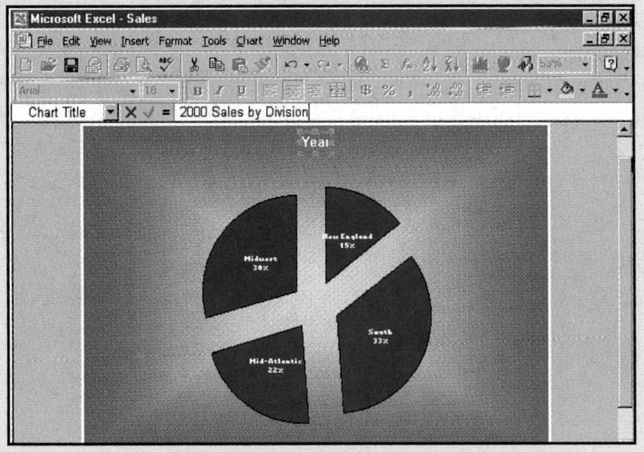

Figure 5.23
The title appears in the Formula bar.

continues ▶

To Change a Chart Type (continued)

⑩ **Press ↵Enter. Right-click one of the four labels, and select Format Data Labels from the shortcut menu. Change the size of the font to 14 point. Click OK.**

The title changes, and the labels for each section of the pie enlarge. Figure 5.24 shows the final modifications to the pie chart.

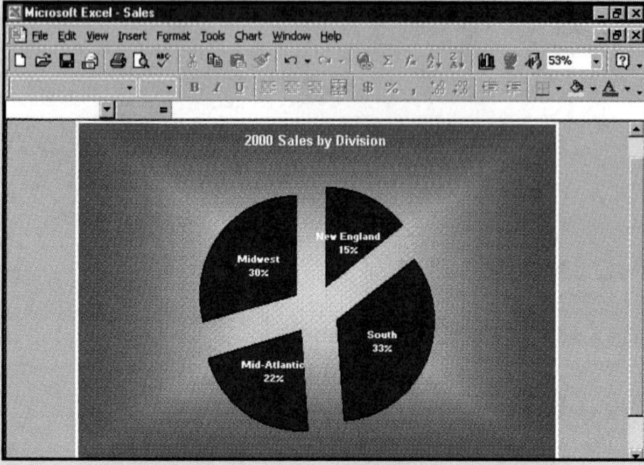

Figure 5.24
The final pie chart shows the contributions to sales for each division.

⑪ **Save your work.**

Leave the file open for use in the next lesson.

Lesson 5: Printing a Chart

Many worksheets are created for the sole purpose of generating one or more charts. You might print these charts on paper to include them in a report or on overhead transparencies to use as part of a presentation.

In this lesson, you print a chart.

To Print a Chart

1. **Click the 2000 Sales by Division sheet tab. Click the Print Preview button.**
   If your computer is connected to a color printer, the preview is in color and the chart prints in color.
2. **Click Setup, Header/Footer tab and Custom Header. Type your name in the Left section of the header.**
3. **Select your name in the left section of the Header dialog box, click the Font button, and change the size of the font to 14 point and the Font style to Bold Italic.**
   The font size increases, and the style changes (see Figure 5.25).
4. **Click OK to return to the Header dialog box. Click OK twice more to return to the Print Preview.**
5. **Click the Print button to print the chart. Click the Close button to close the Print Preview.**
6. **Save your changes and close the workbook.**

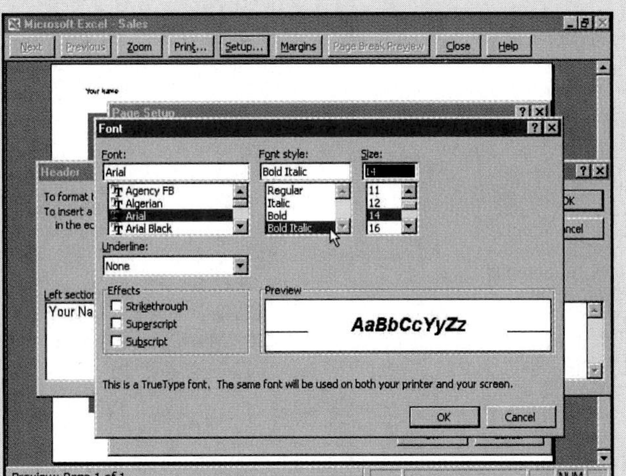

Figure 5.25
You use the Font button in the Header dialog box to open the Font dialog box, so you can change the font.

Creating Transparencies
If you plan to create transparencies from your charts, you should know about several issues. If you plan to print the transparency directly in your printer, you must use a transparency designed for your type of printer. Colors seldom look dark or saturated enough. If your office has transparencies that work with your copier, you would be wise to print the charts on regular paper and then use the copier. Transparency material is expensive, and you usually have to buy an entire box. Preview your work, and print samples on paper to avoid costly reprints. Transparencies often jam when you try to feed several through the printer or copier.

Summary

This project introduced using charts in Excel where you created charts for three different purposes. You created a line chart to show a trend over time, a column chart to show differences across categories, and a pie chart to show contributions to the whole. You also learned how to modify a chart and to identify the names for different parts of a chart.

Many chart styles are available in Excel. To learn about different chart options, open the Chart Wizard and click the different chart types to see a general description of each chart type and the available sub-types. Open Help and read information about creating a chart, embedding a chart in the worksheet, and copying a chart to another application, such as Word or PowerPoint. Use the example for this project and try creating a chart in one step, following the directions in Help.

Checking Concepts and Terms 

True/False

For each of the following, check *T* or *F* to indicate whether the statement is true or false.

__T__F **1.** The Chart Wizard walks you through the creation of a chart. [L1]

__T__F **2.** Pie charts are used to show trends. [L3]

__T__F **3.** A 3-D chart requires at least three columns (or rows) of selected data. [L3]

__T__F **4.** When selecting data to chart, always include the row and column totals. [L3]

__T__F **5.** When you right-click a chart title, it automatically sizes the font to produce a title that spans three-quarters of the printed page. [L4]

__T__F **6.** Column charts and bar charts are both used to illustrate data that shows comparisons. [L2]

__T__F **7.** When you increase the font size of the y-axis, the size of the plot area remains the same. [L4]

__T__F **8.** One of the choices you can make in the Chart Wizard is whether you want your chart to be on the same worksheet as the data or on its own sheet. [L1]

__T__F **9.** After a line chart is created, the y-axis scale must always start at zero. [L4]

__T__F **10.** Right-clicking a chart element calls up a shortcut menu that enables you to make changes. [L4]

Multiple Choice

Circle the letter of the correct answer for each of the following.

1. If you needed to show how much each division contributed to the profits of your company, which type of chart would you use? [L3]

a. line chart

b. bar chart

c. column chart

d. pie chart

2. If you wanted to show the growth of income over the past ten years and compare it to profits over the same period, which type of chart would not be a good choice? [L1]

a. line chart

b. bar chart

c. column chart

d. pie chart

3. If you wanted to show a comparison of your company's income and expenses to a group of peers, which type of chart would you use? [L2]

a. line chart

b. column chart

c. pie chart

d. none of the above

4. A list that identifies a pattern or color used in an Excel worksheet chart is called the ______________. [L1]

a. ScreenTip

b. Key

c. Legend

d. Name box

5. In Excel, the x-axis is called the category axis, and the y-axis is known as the ______________ axis. [L4]

a. vertical

b. value

c. horizontal

d. none of the above

Screen ID

Identify each of the items shown in Figure 5.26.

Figure 5.26

A. Category axis (x-axis)

B. Name box

C. Print Preview button

D. Value axis (y-axis)

E. Y-axis title

F. Chart Wizard button

G. Sheet tab

H. Chart title

I. Minimum scale value

J. Line connecting data points

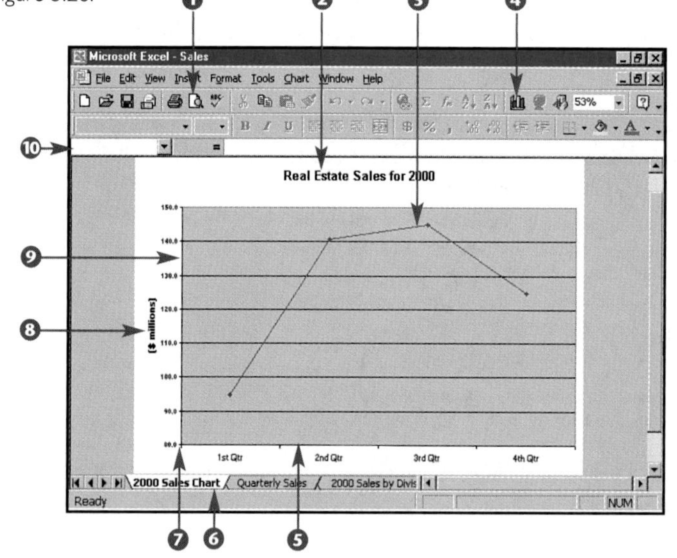

1. ______________

2. ______________

3. ______________

4. ______________

5. ______________

6. ______________

7. ______________

8. ______________

9. ______________

10. ______________

Discussion Questions

1. Generally, it is best to use a bar or column chart to show comparisons across categories. When would you use a line chart to show comparisons rather than a bar or column chart?

2. When you create a pie chart, you can explode the pie, (have each piece separated from the next) or keep the pie whole, or pull out one individual piece. When would you use each of these options and why?

3. What are some of the design considerations in creating a worksheet that would affect your ability to create a chart?

Skill Drill

Skill Drill exercises reinforce project skills. Each skill reinforced is the same, or nearly the same, as a skill presented in the project. Each exercise includes a brief narrative introduction, followed by detailed instructions in a step-by-step format.

These exercises all use a worksheet containing data about tornadoes in Michigan for the decades from the fifties through the eighties. You use this data to create a pie chart to show the number of casualties each decade compared to the whole, a column chart to show the number of tornadoes that occurred in each decade, and a line chart to show the decline of casualties over time. Then you change the column chart to a bar chart. In the last Skill Drill exercise, you create a combination line/column chart to show the decline in casualties compared to the increase in number of tornadoes.

All these exercises use the file `EO-0502` found in the Student folder on the CD-ROM that came with your book. Open the file and save it your floppy disk with the name `Tornadoes`.

1. Creating and Printing a Pie Chart

In this exercise, you create a 3-D pie chart showing how each decade has contributed to the total number of casualties caused by tornadoes during four decades. [L1–5]

1. Change the Sheet1 tab name to `Casualties`.
2. Select cells A2 through A6 and cells E2 through E6.
3. Click the Chart Wizard button. Choose the Pie chart type, and choose the 3-D chart sub-type (the middle choice on the top row).
4. In the third dialog box, change the title to `Michigan Tornado Casualties by Decade`.
5. In the fourth dialog box, choose to save the chart as a new sheet named `Pie Chart`.
6. Change size of the font in the title and the legend to 18 point.
7. Add your name to the header using Bold, Italic, 12-point font. Preview and print the chart. The finished chart should look like the one in Figure 5.27.
8. Move your mouse pointer over each piece and notice that a ScreenTip displays the value and percentage of the whole.
9. Save your work, and leave the file open for use in the next exercise.

Figure 5.27

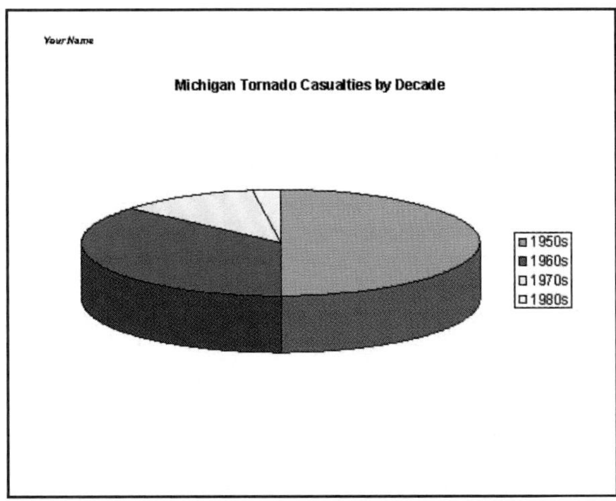

2. Creating and Printing a Column Chart

In this exercise, you create a column chart to compare the number of tornadoes to the number of casualties in each decade. [L2, 5]

1. With the Tornadoes file open, select the Casualties sheet.
2. Select cells A2 through B6.
3. Click the Chart Wizard button. Choose the Column chart type, and choose the Clustered column with a 3-D visual effect chart sub-type (the first choice in the second row).
4. View a sample of the chart and compare it to Figure 5.28.
5. Change the title to `Michigan Tornadoes by Decade`.
6. In the fourth dialog box, place the chart on a new sheet named `Column Chart`.
7. Change the size of the title font to 18 point. Remove (clear) the legend. Change the size of the x- and y-axis labels to 12 point.
8. Add your name to the footer in the lower-left corner. Save and print the chart.

Figure 5.28

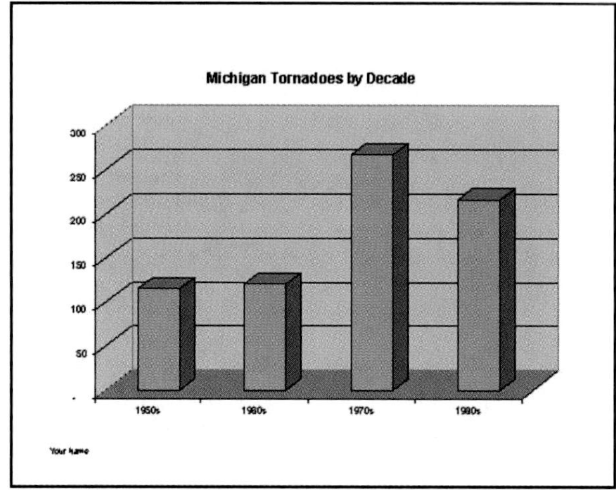

3. Showing a Trend with a Line Chart

In this exercise, you create a chart that shows the trend in total casualties over the forty-year span. [L1]

1. With the Tornadoes file open, select the Casualties tab.
2. Select cells A2 through A6 and cells E2 through E6.
3. Click the Chart Wizard button, and select the Line chart type and 3-D Line as the chart sub-type.
4. Change the title to `Tornado Casualties in Michigan`.
5. Save as a new sheet with the name `Line Chart`.
6. Clear the legend and the axis title. Change the size of the font in the title to 18 point.
7. Add your name to the header in the upper-left corner. Change the font to 12-point bold italic. Save the chart; preview and print the chart. The finished chart should look like the one in Figure 5.29. Leave the file open for the next exercise.

Figure 5.29

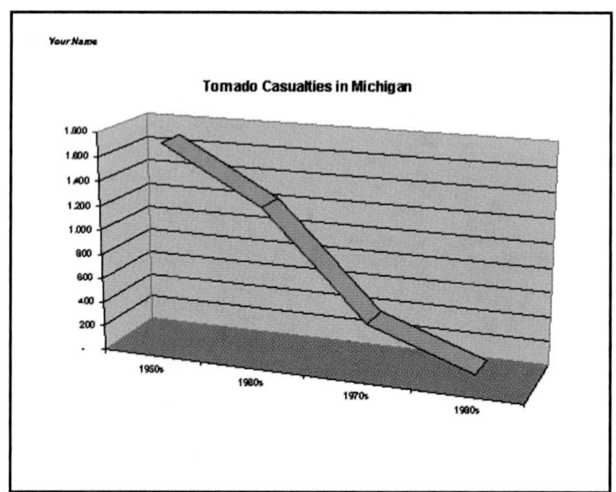

4. Changing the Chart Type

In this exercise, you change the column chart to a bar chart. [L1, 5]

1. With the Tornadoes file open, select the Column Chart worksheet.
2. Right-click an unused part of the chart, such as the white background, and select Chart Type from the shortcut menu.
3. Select Bar chart type and Clustered bar with 3-D visual effect sub-type.
4. Preview the printout and confirm that your name appears in the lower-left corner.
5. Print the chart.
6. Change the sheet tab name to `Column-Bar Chart`. Save the changes you made. The modified chart should look like the one in Figure 5.30.

Figure 5.30

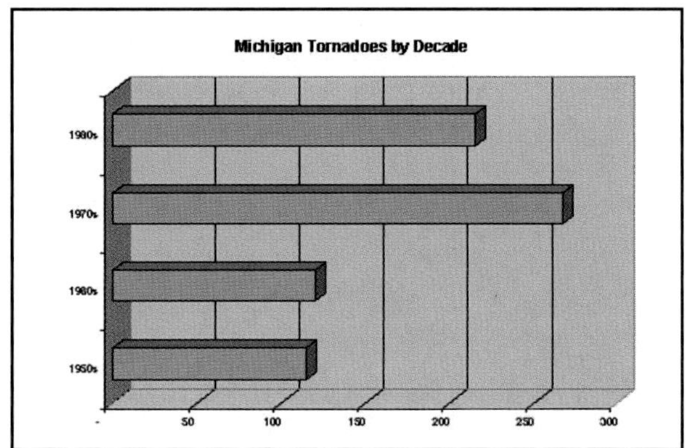

5. Creating a Combination Line and Column Chart

In reviewing the charts you have created, it might be apparent that the number of tornadoes over this 40-year span has increased somewhat, whereas the number of casualties has declined dramatically. These two figures, however, are on widely different scales. The number of tornadoes is in the hundreds, but the number of casualties drops from 1695 to 79 over forty years. To accurately display this data on the same chart, it is best to use a combination line and column chart with two different scales: one on the left and one on the right. [L3–5]

To create this combination chart, follow these steps:

1. With the Tornadoes file open, select the Casualties worksheet.
2. Select cells A2 through B6 and cells E2 through E6. Click the Chart Wizard button.
3. Click the Custom Types tab; scroll down and select Line-Column on 2 Axes as the chart type.
4. Title the chart `Casualties Decrease Compared to the Number of Tornadoes`.
5. Save this on a separate sheet with the name `Combo Chart`.
6. Move the Legend to the bottom of the chart, and increase the font size to 12-point.
7. Increase the title font to 18-point, and increase the font for all three axes labels to 12-point.
8. Right-click any part of the charted line, and select Format Data Series from the shortcut menu. Click the Data Labels tab, and choose the Show value option.
9. Right-click one of these new data labels, and select Format Data Labels. Change the font to 12-point bold.
10. Add your name to the lower-right corner of the chart, and remove the page number coding from the center footer section. Also remove the coding to print the sheet name from the center section of the header. The completed chart should look like Figure 5.31.
11. Save and print the chart and close the file.

Figure 5.31

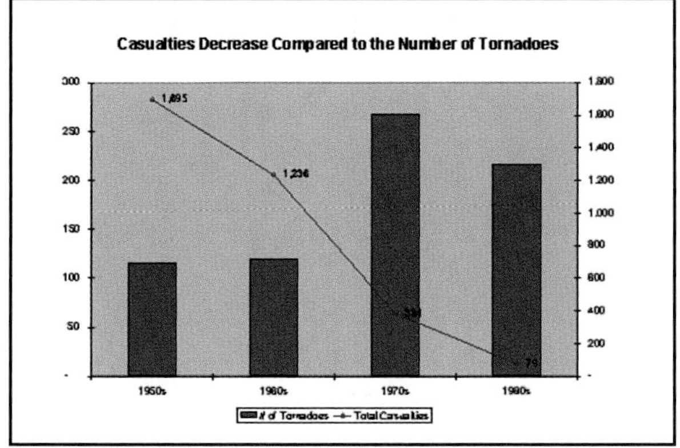

Challenge

Challenge exercises expand on or are somewhat related to skills presented in the lessons. Each exercise provides a brief narrative introduction followed by instructions, in a numbered step or bulleted list format, that are not as detailed as those in the Skill Drill section.

In these Challenge exercises, you work with data concerning the consumption of energy compared to gross national product (GNP) for 16 countries around the world. You use Excel's charting capability to determine whether the amount of energy that people use is proportional to the amount of goods they produce. In other words, if a person in an affluent country consumes ten times as much energy as a person in a poor country, does that person produce ten times as much? If the amount of goods produced is directly proportional to the energy consumed, a line chart of the data should be a fairly straight line.

In these exercises, you examine this data to see whether such a relationship exists using some of the advanced Excel charting tools. First, you create a simple chart that displays the energy used per person for each country and save it as an object in the worksheet. Then you create a line chart of the energy consumption and GNP as a first attempt to show data with unequal intervals. Finally, you create a chart of the data to show the relationship between energy consumption and GNP using an X-Y scatter chart.

Both the Challenge and Discovery Zone exercises use the same file. Locate file EO-0503 in the Student folder on the disc that came with your book. Open the file and save it on your floppy disk as **Energy Charts**.

1. Placing a Chart on the Same Sheet as the Data

In this example, you chart the energy used per person by country and save it on the same sheet as the data. [L1, 4–5]

To create a column chart that displays the country and the energy used per capita and place it on the worksheet, follow these steps:

1. With the Energy Charts file open, select the data (and headings) in the Country and Energy columns.
2. Create a Clustered Column chart. On the third Chart Wizard page deselect Show legend. Save the chart as an object in the Energy worksheet.
3. Deselect the chart, and change the Zoom to 50%.
4. Move the chart to a place below the data and drag one of its handles to stretch the chart to column H.
5. Return the Zoom to 100%, and examine the chart to see whether the names of the countries are all displayed. Chances are that every other name is showing. Double-click one of the country names on the chart and change the font size to 10-point. The font size reduces, and Excel automatically changes the names to display at an angle. If all the names are not yet fully displayed, try stretching the chart down to increase its depth.
6. Work with the Print Preview option to make sure the chart and the worksheet data print on the same page. The printed worksheet and chart should look like Figure 5.32. (*Hint:* if you have difficulty displaying this in a portrait layout, you might want to change the Page Setup to Landscape and widen the chart.)
7. Add your name to the footer and print the worksheet. Save the workbook, and leave it open for use in the next exercise.

Figure 5.32

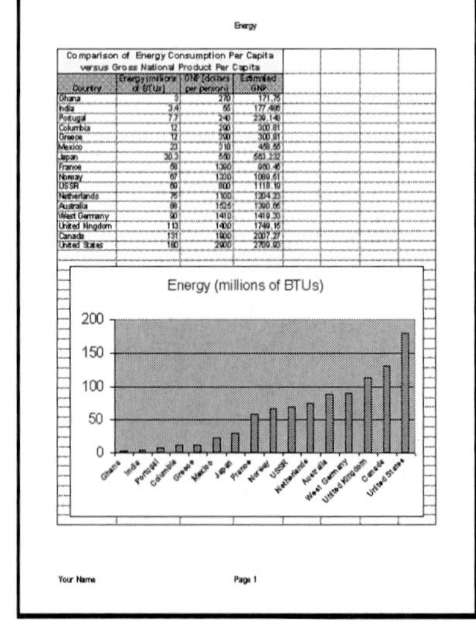
Energy

Comparison of Energy Consumption Per Capita versus Gross National Product Per Capita

Country	Energy (millions of BTUs)	GNP (dollars per person)	Estimated GNP
Ghana	3	270	171.75
India	3.4	55	177.488
Portugal	7.7	240	239.148
Columbia	12	290	300.81
Greece	12	390	300.81
Mexico	23	310	458.55
Japan	30.3	550	563.232
France	58	1390	960.46
Norway	67	1330	1089.61
USSR	69	800	1118.19
Netherlands	75	1100	1204.23
Australia	88	1525	1390.66
West Germany	90	1410	1419.33
United Kingdom	113	1400	1749.15
Canada	131	1900	2007.27
United States	180	2900	2709.93

2. Charting Data with Unequally Spaced Category Values Using a Line Chart

If the value on the y-axis is supposed to depend on its corresponding value on the x-axis, it is important that the numeric intervals between the values on the x-axis are equal. If you use a line chart, the data in the leftmost column is automatically placed along the x-axis, spaced at even intervals, even if the values between the data points are not equal. The result is a chart where it is not easy to determine whether a proportional, or straight-line, relationship exists. In this exercise, you chart the energy used per capita compared to the GNP per capita using a line chart, so you can see what the problem looks like. In the next exercise, you use an X-Y chart so you can compare the two types of graphs. [L1]

To chart related data using a line chart, follow these steps:

1. Select the Energy sheet in the Energy Charts workbook; select the Energy and GNP data, including the column headings; activate Chart Wizard and select Line with markers as the chart type.

   Two data series display—GNP values and Energy values. In this case, however, you want the Energy values to be the x-axis labels instead of a charted line.

2. In the Step 2 of 4 Chart Wizard dialog box, select the Series tab and remove the Energy series.
3. Continue to work in the Step 2 of 4 Chart Wizard dialog box, and click the Collapse button on the Category (X) axis labels box.
4. Select the data in the Energy column. Do not include the column label.
5. Add GNP Per Energy Used for the chart title, BTUs Per Person for the x-axis, and Dollars for the y-axis
6. Create the chart on its own sheet named **`Line Chart`**. Your completed chart should look like Figure 5.33.

Figure 5.33

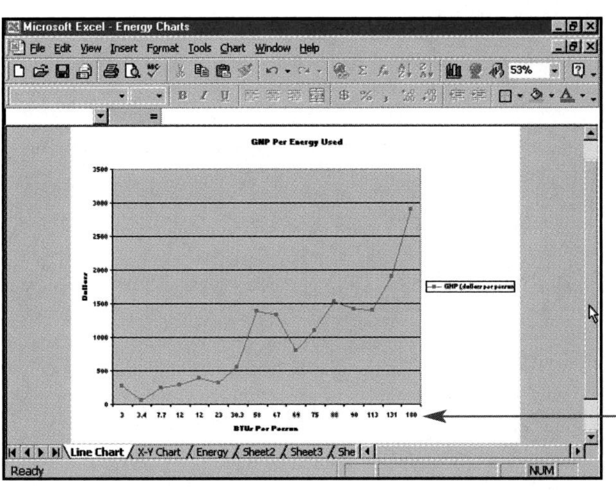

Use the Energy data in the range B3:B18 as labels for the x-axis

7. Save the workbook.

Examine the chart. The values along the x-axis are evenly spaced even though they do not represent equal intervals. For example, two data points use 12 BTUs per person; these two points display at different locations along the horizontal or x-axis. Obviously, a graph with two data points of the same value in two different locations creates a misleading picture. It is not a good idea to represent data where the value of the y-axis depends on the value shown on the x-axis using a line chart unless the intervals between the values on the x-axis are already equally spaced. Do the next exercise to see how this example data should be charted.

3. Charting Related Data Using the X-Y Chart

If you are charting two columns of numbers where the second column is dependant (or related) to the first column, you should use an X-Y chart (sometimes called a scatter chart). The data points are scattered on the chart to indicate each intersection of the X and Y coordinates. When plotting real-life data, you seldom get an exact relationship. You look to see whether the points represent a general trend, such as a straight line or a curve. In our example, the Energy used per person is the X coordinate and the GNP per person is the Y coordinate. [L1]

To chart the GNP per person as it relates to the amount of energy used per person, follow these steps:

1. Select the Energy sheet in the Energy Charts workbook; select the Energy and GNP data, including the column headings; activate the Chart Wizard and select XY (Scatter) as the chart sub-type (see Figure 5.34).
2. Use **GNP per Energy Used** for the chart title, **BTUs per Person** for the x-axis title, and **Dollars** for the y-axis title.
3. Do not show the legend.
4. Save the chart on its own sheet named **X-Y Chart.**

Notice in Figure 5.34 that the values on the x-axis have evenly spaced intervals so that the relationship between the two factors appears to be more linear. The two data points with 12 BTUs are at the same value on the x-axis (horizontal axis) and vary slightly on the y-axis (vertical axis) because of a difference in GNP.

Figure 5.34

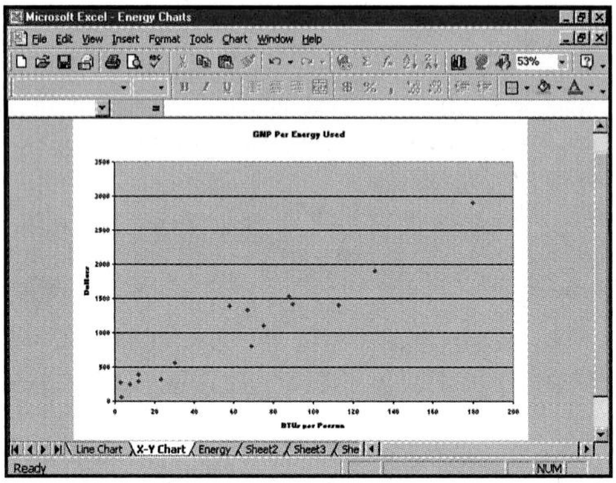

If you are done with the exercises, close the workbook. If you want to continue to the Discovery Zone exercises, leave the workbook open.

Discovery Zone

Discovery Zone exercises require advanced knowledge of topics presented in *Essentials* lessons, application of skills from multiple lessons, or self-directed learning of new skills.

These Discovery Zone exercises continue the exploration of using advanced Excel charting concepts and statistical analysis. These exercises use the X-Y Chart that you created in Challenge Exercise 3. These exercises should be completed in order as presented. In the first exercise, you add data labels to the X-Y Chart. In the second exercise, you add a trend line to the chart and determine how much the GNP per person depends on the Energy consumed per person. In the last exercise, you use the trend line formula to estimate the future GNP for the countries listed in the worksheet.

1. Adding Data Labels to an X-Y Chart

You can add information to a chart using the shortcut menu that displays when you right-click a data point on the chart. In this exercise, you add the value for the y-axis next to each data point on the X-Y Chart. [L4]

The finished chart should look like Figure 5.35.

Figure 5.35

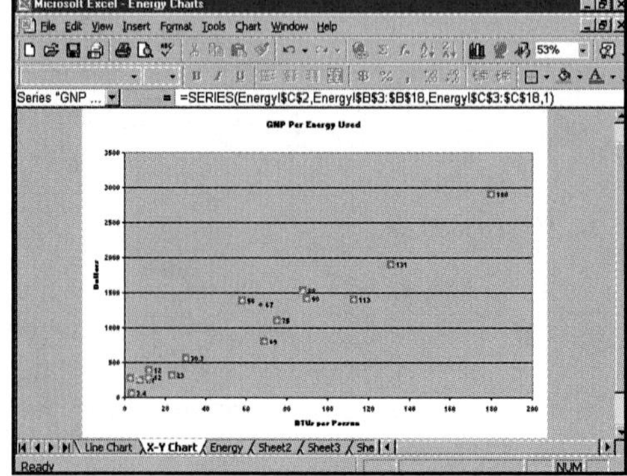

- Make sure the Energy Chart file is open. Select the X-Y Chart sheet that you created and right-click one of the chart's data points.
- Format the Data Series so that the data labels display, as shown in Figure 5.35.
- Leave the workbook open for use in the next Discovery Zone exercise.

2. Adding a Trend Line to an X-Y Chart

If there is a linear relationship between the values displayed on the x-axis and those displayed on the y-axis of an X-Y chart, the data points are close to a straight line. Excel can calculate the formula for the straight line that is the best fit to the data points and add it to the chart. [L1]

The method of determining the formula for the best fitting straight line is called a linear regression analysis. The degree of fit is represented by the R^2 value. A perfect fit would have an R^2 value equal to 1.

In this exercise, you add the trend line to the X-Y chart that is the best fit to the data. Use the R^2 value to determine whether the best fit is a straight line or one of the other shapes.

- Select the X-Y Chart sheet.
- Right-click one of the data points, and choose Add Trendline.
- Choose one of the six types of trend lines. Click the Option tab, and choose to display the R-squared value.
- Look at the trend line and its R-squared value; delete the trend line.
- Try each of the trend lines and decide which one is the best fit (has the highest value of R-squared). The R-squared value appears near the top edge of the trend line.
- After you determine which trend line is the best fit, add it to the data and display the R-squared value on the chart. (An R-squared value above .9 means that the two are closely related.)
- Save the workbook and leave it open for use in the next exercise.

3. Using the Trend Line Formula to Estimate Values

Excel displays the formula for a trend line on a chart. You can use this formula to estimate new values or determine how much a given point differs from the trend line. For this example, you use the straight trend line to keep the formula as simple as possible.

In this exercise, you determine the formula for the straight trend line and use it to generate a new column of estimated GNP values.

- Make a copy of the X-Y Chart sheet in the Energy Charts workbook. Name the copy `Estimate`.
- On the Estimate sheet, delete the trend line.
- Use the shortcut menu to add a Linear trend line to the data points. Set the option to display the formula of the line.
- Select the Energy sheet. Rewrite this formula so that you can use it in cell D3 to estimate the GNP based on the value in cell B3. (The estimated value for Ghana will be 171.75. Ghana's GNP per Energy used, 270, is much higher than the estimate.)
- Fill this formula into the cells below (in column D) to create a new column of estimated GNP for each country.
- Print the Energy sheet.
- Save the workbook and close it.

Project 6

Using Excel's Interactive Features

Objectives

In this project, you learn how to

- **Insert and Move a New Sheet**
- **Design a Summary Sheet for Convenient Charting**
- **Link the Results of Several Sheets to a Summary Sheet**
- **Insert a Hyperlink to Another Workbook**
- **Save a Worksheet as a Web Page**
- **Use a Worksheet on the Web**

Key terms introduced in this project include

- browser
- Extensible Markup Language (XML)
- hyperlink
- Internet
- intranet
- local area network (LAN)
- Uniform Resource Locator (URL)
- World Wide Web (WWW or Web)

Source: Essentials: Office 2000, Ferrett-Preston-Preston

Why Would I Do This?

A new phenomenon in the 1990s has been the development and widespread use of the Internet and the World Wide Web. The ***Internet*** is a worldwide communications network of computer connections that enables people to access thousands of online resources. The ***World Wide Web,*** simply called the ***Web*** or ***WWW,*** is a graphical interface that utilizes hyperlinks and makes it much easier to use the Internet. A ***hyperlink*** is a connection between a word or label in one location and a file in another location.

Excel 2000 has several powerful tools that enable you to collaborate with others by using Internet and Web technology. You can connect your worksheet to other worksheets or documents that are on your computer or on other computers anywhere in the world over the Internet. You can share files with co-workers by saving your worksheet as a Web page that can be viewed using a company intranet. An ***intranet*** is a closed network that uses the same technology as the Internet, but restricts access to authorized users. You learn how to use this connectivity to share the results of your work.

Visual Summary

In this project, you create a summary worksheet that creates formulas based on information from other worksheets. You compare your results to a worksheet in another file to determine whether there are any discrepancies. Then you publish your worksheet, so it can be viewed using Web technology. Finally, you learn how to work with the worksheet in an Internet environment. When you are done with this project, you will have created a worksheet that looks like Figure 6.1 and published a worksheet that looks like Figure 6.2.

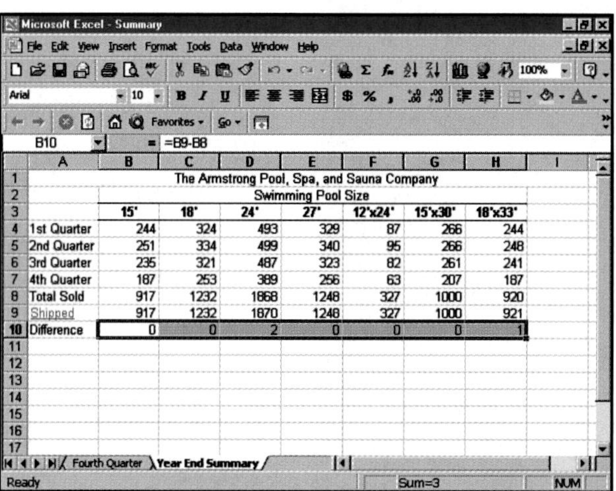

Figure 6.1
You create a summary worksheet.

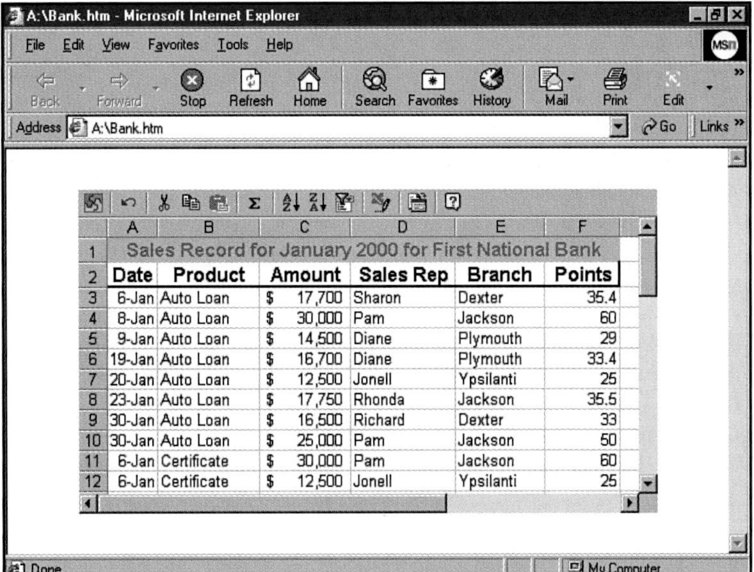

	A	B	C	D	E	F
1	Sales Record for January 2000 for First National Bank					
2	Date	Product	Amount	Sales Rep	Branch	Points
3	6-Jan	Auto Loan	$ 17,700	Sharon	Dexter	35.4
4	8-Jan	Auto Loan	$ 30,000	Pam	Jackson	60
5	9-Jan	Auto Loan	$ 14,500	Diane	Plymouth	29
6	19-Jan	Auto Loan	$ 16,700	Diane	Plymouth	33.4
7	20-Jan	Auto Loan	$ 12,500	Jonell	Ypsilanti	25
8	23-Jan	Auto Loan	$ 17,750	Rhonda	Jackson	35.5
9	30-Jan	Auto Loan	$ 16,500	Richard	Dexter	33
10	30-Jan	Auto Loan	$ 25,000	Pam	Jackson	50
11	6-Jan	Certificate	$ 30,000	Pam	Jackson	60
12	6-Jan	Certificate	$ 12,500	Jonell	Ypsilanti	25

Figure 6.2
This is how a worksheet looks when it is published as a Web page.

Lesson 1: Inserting and Moving a New Sheet

It might make sense to divide your data into several separate sheets when you are working with it to make the data easier to manage and to chart. However, you often need to bring the results of these sheets together in one place, so that they can be compared and summarized. When you are ready to summarize your work, you might need to add a worksheet and place it into your workbook in a particular location, so you can create the summary sheet that you need.

In this lesson, you open a workbook with four sheets, each displaying sales of pools for one quarter. You add a new sheet to use as a year-end summary sheet and move the sheet into position.

To Insert and Move a New Sheet

1. **Launch Excel. Locate and open EO-0601 from the CD that came with your book and save it on your floppy disk as `Summary`.**
   The file opens, and the new workbook name displays in the title bar.

2. **Choose Insert, Worksheet**
   A blank worksheet is added called Sheet1.

3. **Double-click the Sheet1 tab to select it, and type `Year End Summary`. Press Enter.**
   The sheet is renamed. Next you move the worksheet, so it is the last one.

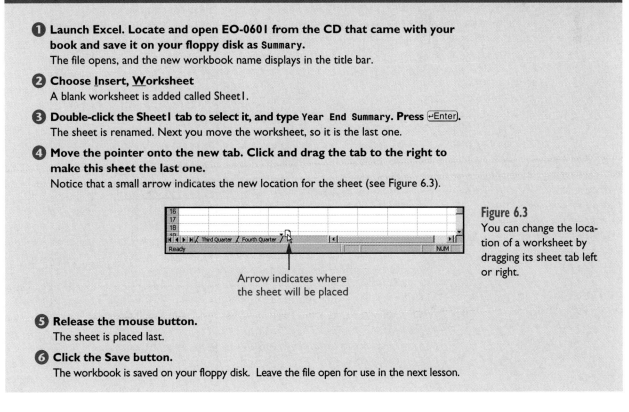

4. **Move the pointer onto the new tab. Click and drag the tab to the right to make this sheet the last one.**
   Notice that a small arrow indicates the new location for the sheet (see Figure 6.3).

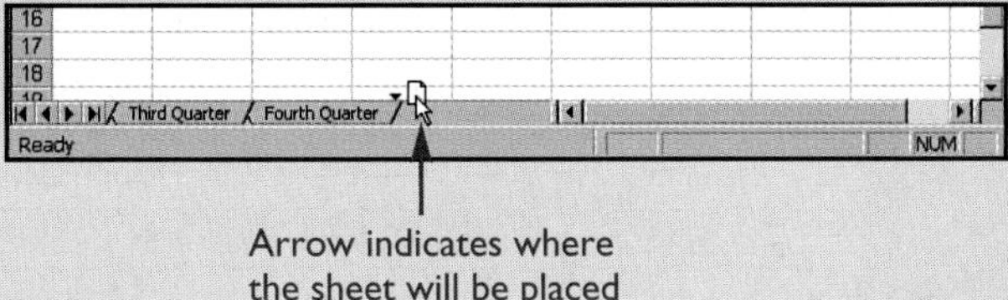

Figure 6.3
You can change the location of a worksheet by dragging its sheet tab left or right.

5. **Release the mouse button.**
   The sheet is placed last.

6. **Click the Save button.**
   The workbook is saved on your floppy disk. Leave the file open for use in the next lesson.

Lesson 2: Designing a Summary Sheet for Convenient Charting

The summary sheet consolidates the data from several other pages. Because this is summary information, it will probably be charted. To create charts, you must arrange data into adjacent cells in rows or columns. Therefore it is important that the design of the worksheet allows for easy comparative charting.

In this lesson, you set up labels for a sheet that summarizes the sales from each of the quarters represented by the other four sheets.

To Design a Summary Sheet for Convenient Charting

1. **Select cell A1 in the Year End Summary worksheet within the Summary workbook. Type `The Armstrong Pool, Spa, and Sauna Company`. Press Enter.**
2. **Select cells A1 through I1. Click the Merge and Center button.**
3. **Select cell B2. Type `Swimming Pool Size`. Press Enter**
4. **Select cells B2 through H2. Click the Merge and Center button.**
   The main title and subtitle are entered and merge across the cells (see Figure 6.4).

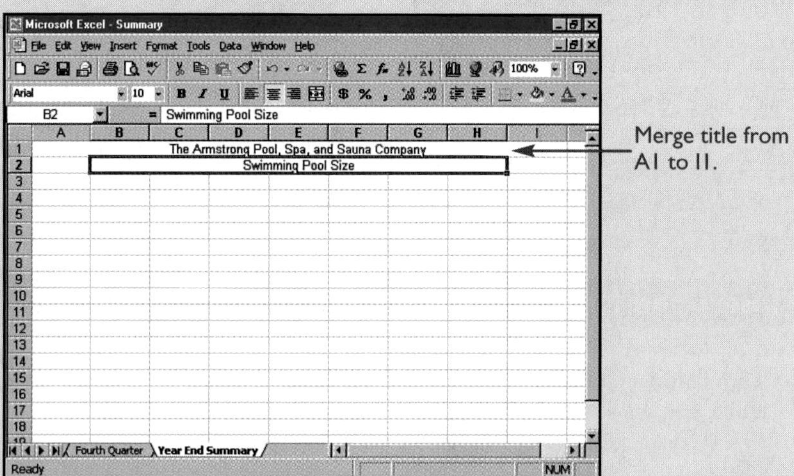

Figure 6.4
The titles for the worksheet are entered.

5. **Click the Fourth Quarter sheet tab, and select cells C3 through I3.**
6. **Click the Copy button.**
   Cells C3 through I3 have a marquee around them to show that they have been copied (see Figure 6.5).

Figure 6.5
You can copy headings from another worksheet to place into a new worksheet.

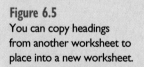

7. **Click the Year End Summary sheet tab, and select cell B3. Click the Paste button.**
   The column headings from the Fourth Quarter sheet are pasted into cells B3 through H3.
8. **Select cell A4; type `1st Quarter`, and press Enter.**

9 **Select cell A4. Drag the fill handle from cell A4 down to cell A7 and release the mouse. Adjust the column width to accommodate the titles in the first column.**
The cells fill with a series from 1st Quarter through 4th Quarter, as shown in Figure 6.6.

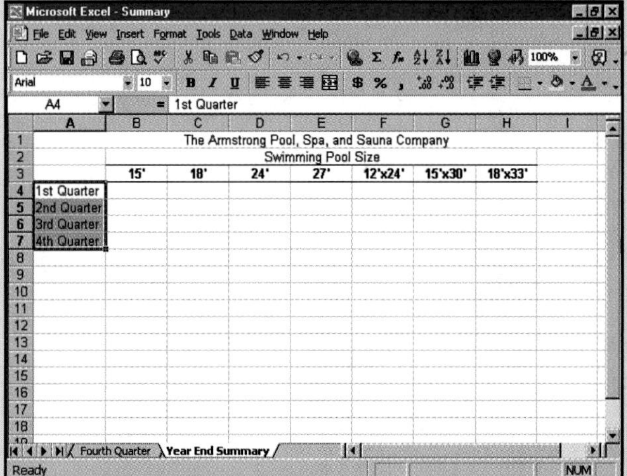

Figure 6.6
The row headings are filled for four quarters of the year.

10 **Save your changes to the file.**
Leave the file open for use in the next lesson.

Lesson 3: Linking the Results of Several Sheets to a Summary Sheet

When you copy information from one sheet to another, there is no link established between the data in the two worksheets. To be able to change data in one sheet and have that change reflected in a summary worksheet, you need to create a link between the worksheets. You do this by using a relative reference technique that points directly to a key cell in the worksheet that contains the original data. Then you only have to enter information in one location and any changes automatically reflect in the summary worksheet. For example, if you copy the data from the First through Fourth Quarter sheets into your Year End Summary sheet, the values do not change whenever you update the data. However, if you place a formula in a cell in the Year End Summary sheet, you can make it refer to specific cells in the quarterly worksheets. When the data in the quarterly sheets changes, the changes reflect in the summary sheet.

In this lesson, you place formulas in the summary sheet. The formulas refer to the totals by category in each of the quarterly sales sheets.

To Link the Results of Several Sheets to a Summary Sheet

1 **Select cell B4 on the Year End Summary sheet in the Summary workbook.**

2 **Type = to indicate that the following entry is a formula.**
After the equal sign (=), you could type the complete formula in cell B4 if you knew the cell references you wanted to select. In this case, as you will see, it is easier to use your mouse to locate the cell references, because the cells to which you want to refer are on another sheet.

3 **Click the left most Tab Scrolling button to find the First Quarter sheet tab. Click the First Quarter tab.**
The First Quarter sheet displays. Notice that the name of the sheet appears in the Formula bar between single quotation marks followed by an exclamation mark (see Figure 6.7).

continues ▶

To Link the Results of Several Sheets to a Summary Sheet (continued)

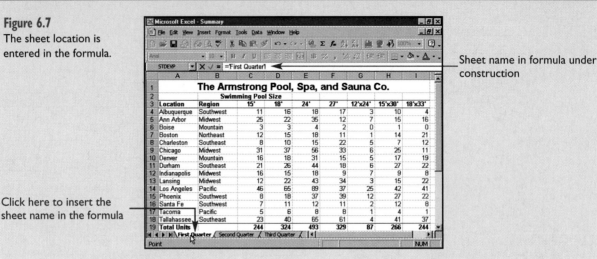

Figure 6.7
The sheet location is entered in the formula.

Sheet name in formula under construction

Click here to insert the sheet name in the formula

4 Click cell C19.

A marquee displays around cell C19. Notice that the formula in the Formula bar now refers to this sheet and the selected cell, as shown in Figure 6.8. (*Note*: This is the formula you would have typed in cell B4 in Step 2, if you had known that the cell reference was C19 and how to state the formula.)

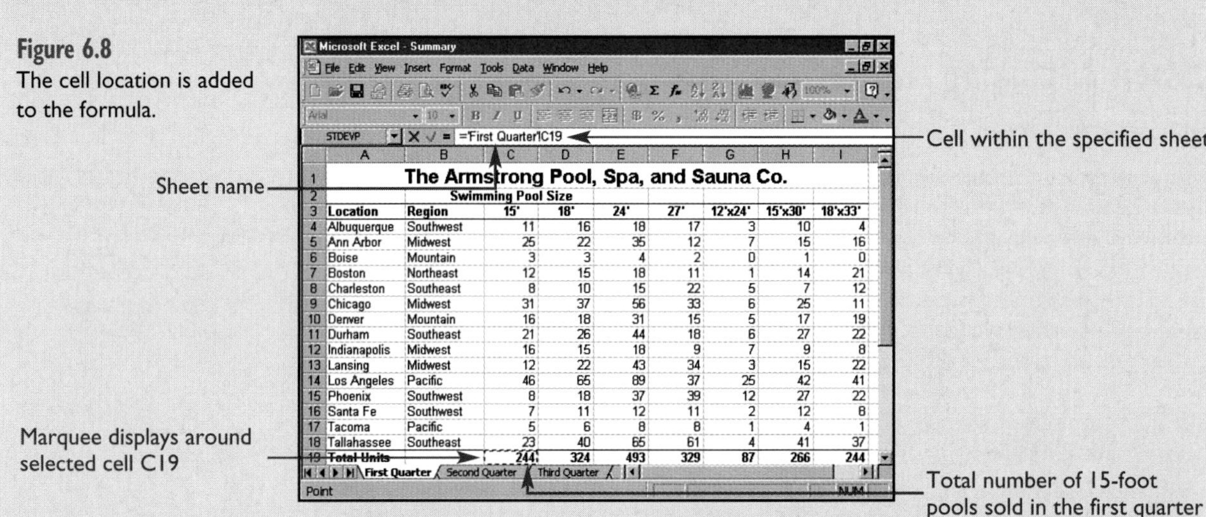

Figure 6.8
The cell location is added to the formula.

5 Click the √ (Enter) button on the Formula bar.

The screen automatically returns to the Year End Summary sheet (see Figure 6.9). The value, 244, from cell C19 on the First Quarter sheet displays in cell B4 where you placed the formula.

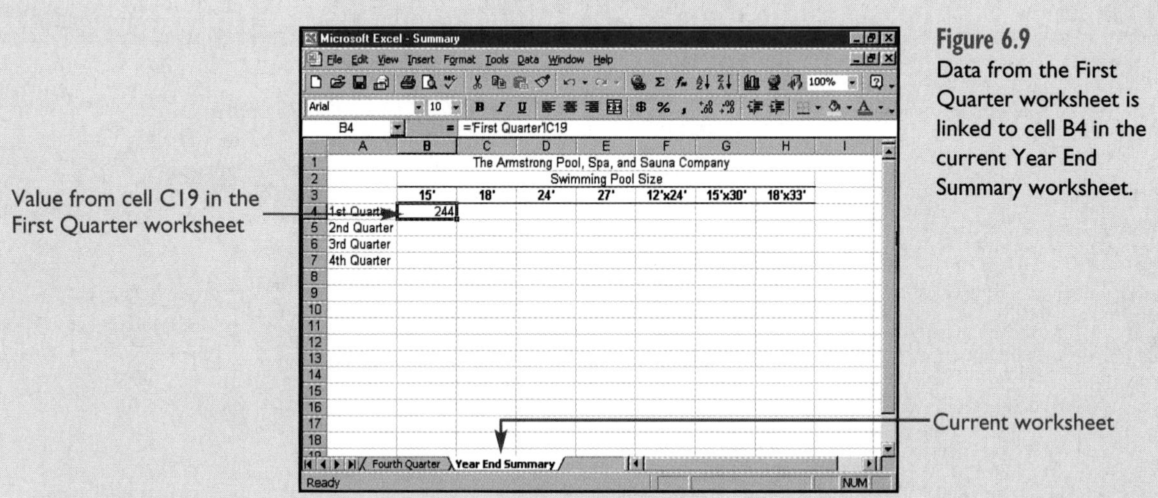

Figure 6.9
Data from the First Quarter worksheet is linked to cell B4 in the current Year End Summary worksheet.

❻ **Drag the fill handle from cell B4 to H4, release the mouse button, and click a cell containing copied data, such as cell D4.**

The cells from C4 through H4 on the Year End Summary sheet fill with relative formulas that refer to cells D9 through I19 on the First Quarter sheet. Click in the other cells to see how the formula is written.

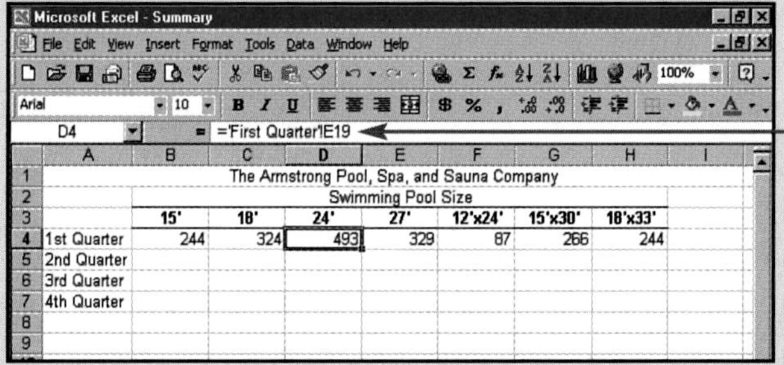

Figure 6.10
The formula with the relative reference to the First Quarter sheet is filled to the other cells.

❼ **Select cell B5, and type =. Switch to the Second Quarter sheet; select cell C19, and click the Enter button on the Formula bar.**

The value for total unit sales of 15-foot pools during Quarter 2 (251) displays in cell B5 on the Year End Summary sheet.

❽ **Drag the fill handle from cell B5 to H5 and release the mouse.**

The values from the second quarter fill in.

❾ **Repeat this process in rows 6 and 7 to display the values from the Third Quarter and Fourth Quarter sheets.**

Compare numbers on your worksheet to the ones in Figure 6.11 to ensure that you created references to the correct cells.

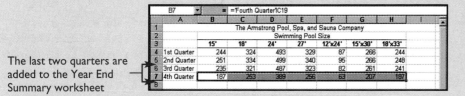

B7 =Fourth Quarter!C19

The Armstrong Pool, Spa, and Sauna Company
Swimming Pool Size

	15'	18'	24'	27'	12'x24'	15'x30'	18'x33'
1st Quarter	244	324	493	329	87	266	244
2nd Quarter	251	334	499	340	95	266	248
3rd Quarter	235	321	487	323	82	261	241
4th Quarter	187	253	389	256	63	207	187

The last two quarters are added to the Year End Summary worksheet

Figure 6.11
Figures from multiple worksheets can be easily linked to a summary worksheet.

❿ **Select cell A8. Type `Total Sold`, and press Tab.**

continues ▶

To Link the Results of Several Sheets to a Summary Sheet (continued)

11 Select cell B8, and double-click the AutoSum button to sum the contents of cells B4 through B7.

12 Drag the fill handle from cell B8 to H8 and release the mouse.
Sales for each size pool are summed, as shown in Figure 6.12.

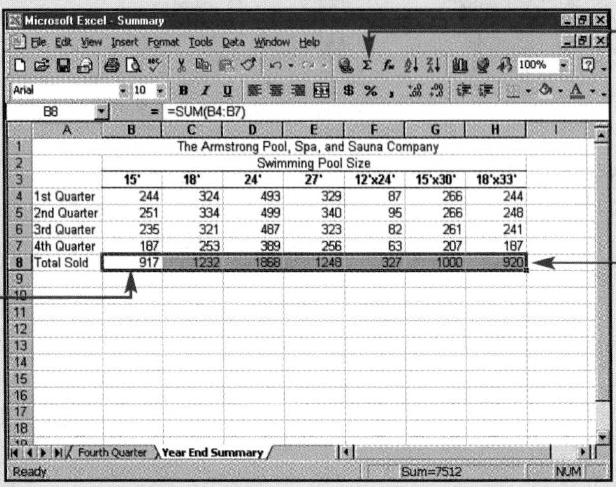

Figure 6.12
The annual sales in units for each pool size are calculated in the Year End Summary worksheet.

	A	B	C	D	E	F	G	H
1		The Armstrong Pool, Spa, and Sauna Company						
2		Swimming Pool Size						
3		15'	18'	24'	27'	12'x24'	15'x30'	18'x33'
4	1st Quarter	244	324	493	329	87	266	244
5	2nd Quarter	251	334	499	340	95	266	248
6	3rd Quarter	235	321	487	323	82	261	241
7	4th Quarter	187	253	389	256	63	207	187
8	Total Sold	917	1232	1868	1248	327	1000	920

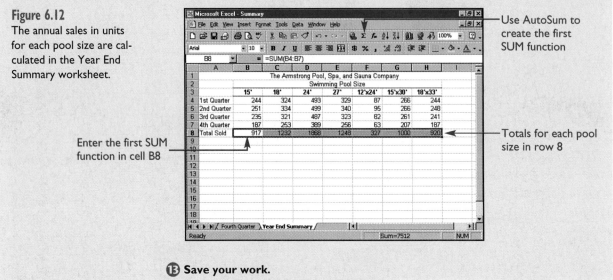

Use AutoSum to create the first SUM function

Totals for each pool size in row 8

Enter the first SUM function in cell B8

13 Save your work.
Leave the file open for use in the next lesson.

Lesson 4: Inserting a Hyperlink to Another Workbook

Sometimes it is important to look at data from someone else's workbook, Word document, or Web page. A convenient way to do this is to insert a hyperlink. When you click a word or label that has been made into a hyperlink, it connects you directly to information in another file.

Using hyperlinks to connect to other files can increase your efficiency by getting you to the information you need quickly. For example, imagine that the manager of the warehouse for The Armstrong Pool, Spa, and Sauna Company keeps a record of the pool inventory. The number of pools shipped should match the number of pools sold.

In this lesson, you insert a hyperlink in the Year End Summary sheet to compare the warehouse inventory records with yours.

To Insert a Hyperlink to Another Workbook

1 Select cell A9 in the Year End Summary sheet of the Summary workbook; type `Shipped`, and press ↵Enter.

2 Select cell A9, and click the Insert Hyperlink button on the Standard toolbar.
The Insert Hyperlink dialog box opens (see Figure 6.13). The Existing File or Web Page button at the top of the Link to: panel on the left should be selected. The files that display on your screen will be different from the ones in the figure because they reflect the files that have been linked to on your computer. Any one of the three buttons under the section Or select from list: might be selected on your machine depending on its last hyperlink use. To locate a file, you can select from existing files by using the File button located under the words Browse for.

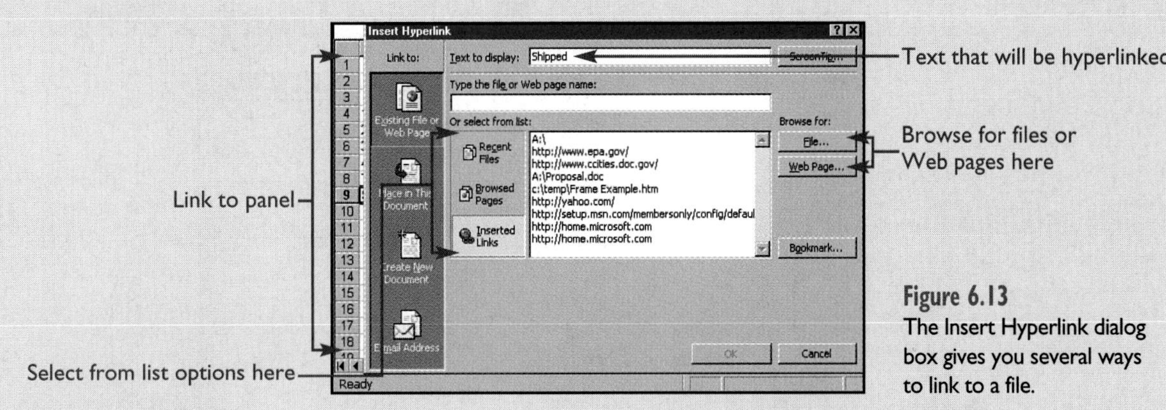

Figure 6.13
The Insert Hyperlink dialog box gives you several ways to link to a file.

3. **Click the File button.**
   The Link to File dialog box opens, as shown in Figure 6.14. (*Note*: It is likely that your dialog box will display files different from those in the figure.) This dialog box works like the Open dialog box and helps you find files in folders.

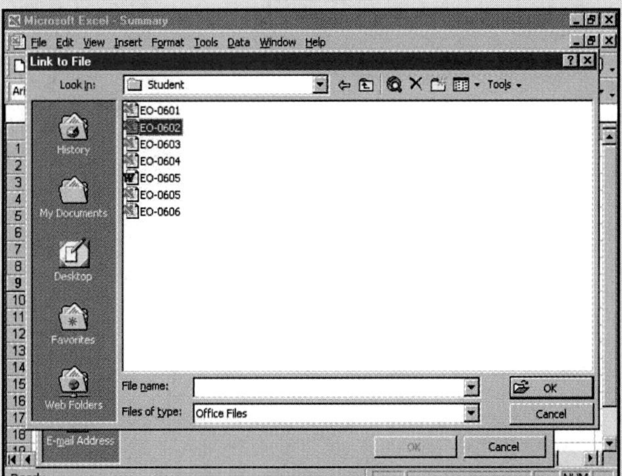

Figure 6.14
Use the Link to File dialog box to locate the file you want to create a link to.

4. **Find the file, EO-0602, in the location where you have stored the student files accompanying this book. Select that file and click OK.**
   The Insert Hyperlink dialog box reappears, and the location of the selected file displays in the Type the file or Web page name box.
5. **Click OK.**
   The text in cell A9 is underlined and changes color.
6. **Move the pointer to cell A9.**
   The pointer changes to a small hand and the location of the file displays in a ScreenTip, as shown in Figure 6.15.

continues ▶

To Insert a Hyperlink to Another Workbook (continued)

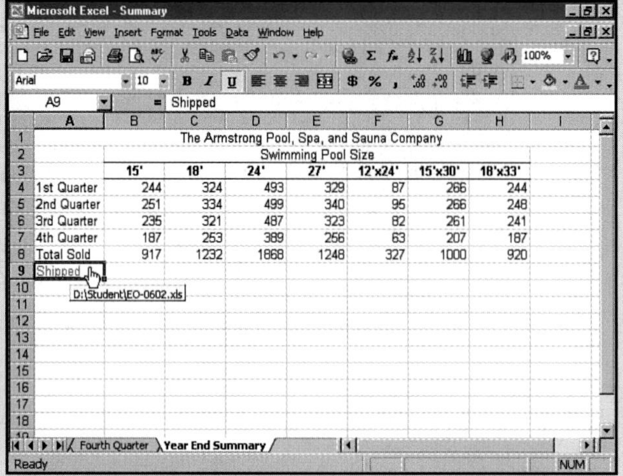

Figure 6.15
The hyperlink location displays in a ScreenTip.

7. **Click cell A9.**
The Inventory sheet opens, as shown in Figure 6.16.

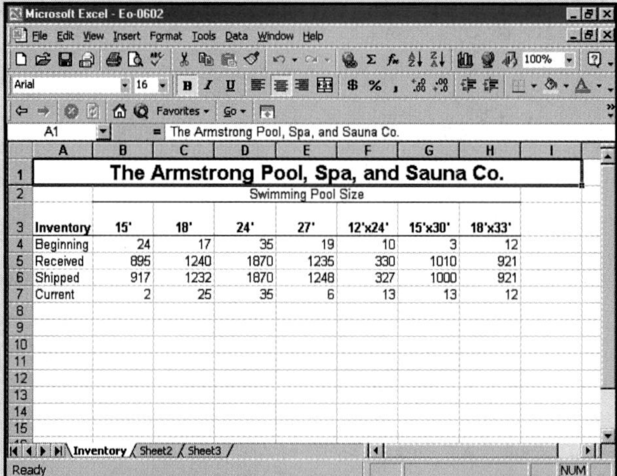

Figure 6.16
Clicking the hyperlink opens the Inventory Sheet in the file to which you linked.

8. **Select cells B6 through H6. Click the Copy button.**

9. **Close the file EO-0602. Click No, if you are prompted to save the changes. Select cell B9, and click the Paste button.**
The number of pools shipped is placed below the total number of pools sold.

10. **Select cell A10; type `Difference`, and press Tab.**

11. **Select cell B10; type `=B9-B8`, and click the Enter button on the Formula bar.**

12. **Drag the fill handle right to cell H10 and release the mouse.**
The formula fills across the worksheet. The cells that have a value other than zero indicate a discrepancy. In this case, three more pools shipped than were sold (see Figure 6.17).

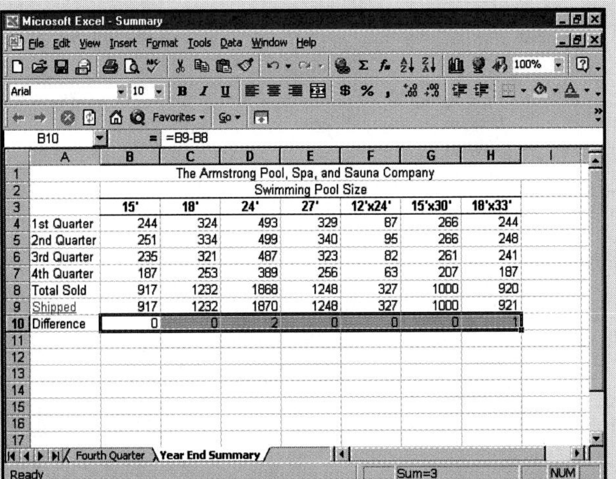

Figure 6.17
Using a hyperlink, you can copy cells from the related worksheet and locate the discrepancies.

⓭ **Save your work. Add your name to the header; preview, and print the Year End Summary sheet. Close the Summary workbook.**

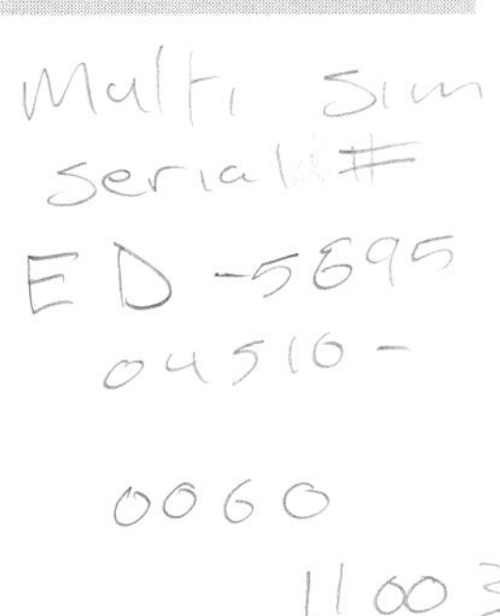

Creating a Hyperlink

When you create a hyperlink, the file that you link to does not have to be located on your computer. The file could be located anywhere on the Internet or on the ***local area network (LAN)*** to which you have access. A LAN is a system that uses telephone lines or cables to join two or more personal computers, enabling them to communicate with each other. The hyperlink creates a reference to the drive and folder where the file resides, or to its ***Uniform Resource Locator (URL)***, which is its address on the Internet. You use the Browse button to find that file location or URL.

Lesson 5: Saving a Worksheet as a Web Page

You can save your worksheet as an interactive Web page that can be used by anyone on the Web who has permission to view your site. You can use this feature to provide information in a searchable form, or you can enable the user to enter new data. Excel 2000 uses a new Web language called ***Extensible Markup Language*** **(XML)**. XML is a Web language that enables the program to attach additional information to data and enables the user to interact with the worksheet using a browser. A ***browser*** is a program, such as Netscape Navigatior or Internet Explorer, that helps you connect to the Internet and view Web pages.

In this lesson, you use a file that contains sales records for bank personnel. You open the file and save it as an interactive Web page.

To Save a Worksheet as a Web Page

➊ **Open EO-0603 from your student disc, and save it on your floppy disk as Bank.**
The file opens and the new workbook name displays in the title bar.

➋ **Choose File, Save as Web Page.**
The Save As dialog box opens, as shown in Figure 6.18.

X If you do not see the Save as Web Page command, point to the arrows at the bottom of the menu list to expand it, and locate Save as Web Page immediately following the Save as command.

continues ▶

To Save a Worksheet as a Web Page (continued)

Figure 6.18
Use the Save As dialog box to save your file as a Web page.

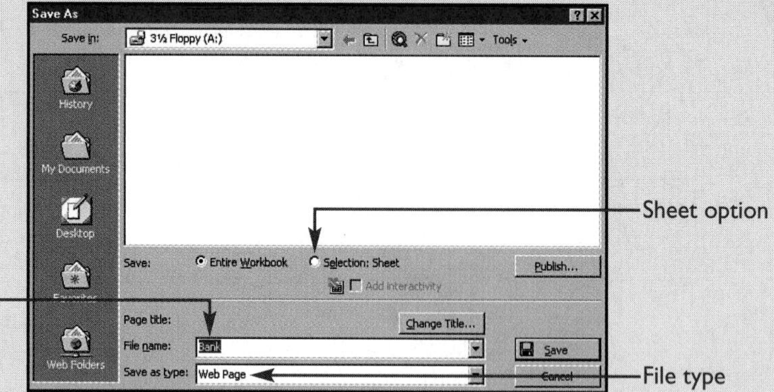

3 **Click the Sheet option. (The Add Interactivity option becomes active.) Change the location specified in the Save in box if necessary, so the file will be saved to your disk.**

4 **If Bank (or Bank.htm) does not already display in the File name box, enter it now.**
The Save As dialog box should look similar to the one in Figure 6.19.

Figure 6.19
The dialog box used to save a file as a Web page is similar to the regular Save As dialog box.

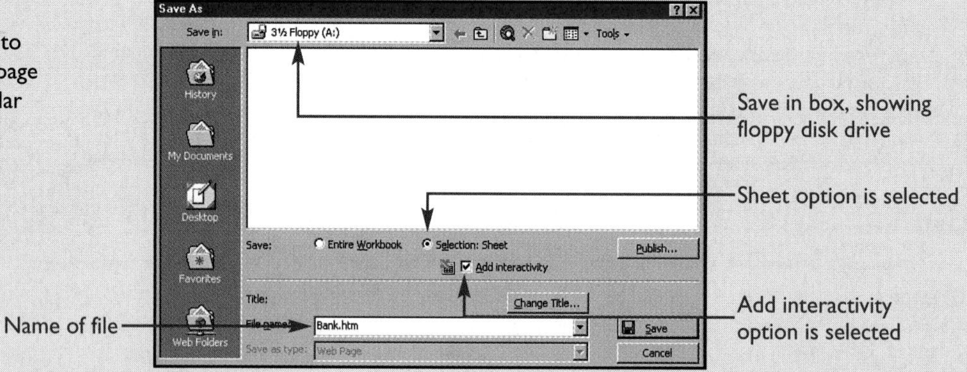

5 **Click Save. The Web page is saved on your disk. Close the workbook, and save the changes. Close Excel.**

Lesson 6: Using a Worksheet on the Web

New Web browsers, such as Microsoft's Internet Explorer 5, can read files that have XML features. Older browsers see only a static page. Using the XML feature, you can interact with a worksheet on the Web in new ways.

In this lesson, you launch Microsoft Internet Explorer 5 and browse the Bank.htm file on your disk as if it were posted to a Web server. You use some of Excel's data sorting tools in a Web environment to learn how you can use an interactive Web page. The figures in this lesson show Microsoft Internet Explorer 5. If you are using a different browser, your screens will look different.

To Use a Worksheet on the Web

1 **Launch Microsoft Internet Explorer 5 or launch another browser that supports XML. Maximize the window.**
The browser opens and displays the home page that it is set to display.

You do not need to be connected to the Internet to practice using this feature. If you are working in a lab setting, it is assumed that your machine will automatically connect to the Internet. If you are not connected to the Internet, the browser displays a dialog box asking you to connect. Choose cancel to bypass connecting to the Internet and work offline.

2 Click the Address box, and enter the location of the Bank.htm file that you created in the previous task. If you saved it on your disk in drive A:, enter `A:\Bank.htm` in the Address box (see Figure 6.20).

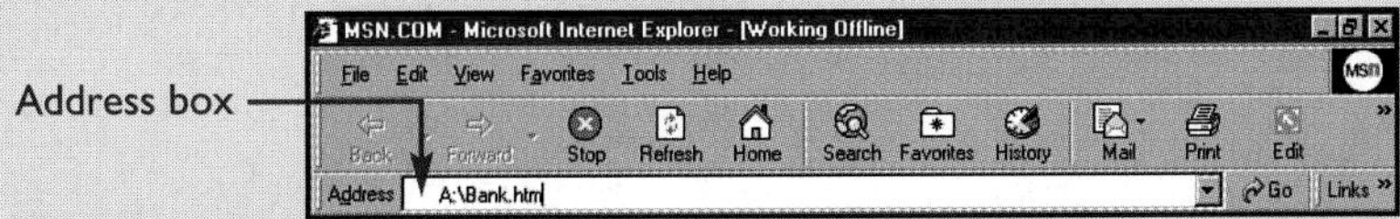

Figure 6.20 The address of the file you want to use is entered in the browser.

3 Press ↵Enter.
The worksheet displays in the browser as an interactive Web page, as shown in Figure 6.21. The worksheet includes an abbreviated toolbar that enables you to sort, filter, and manipulate the file.

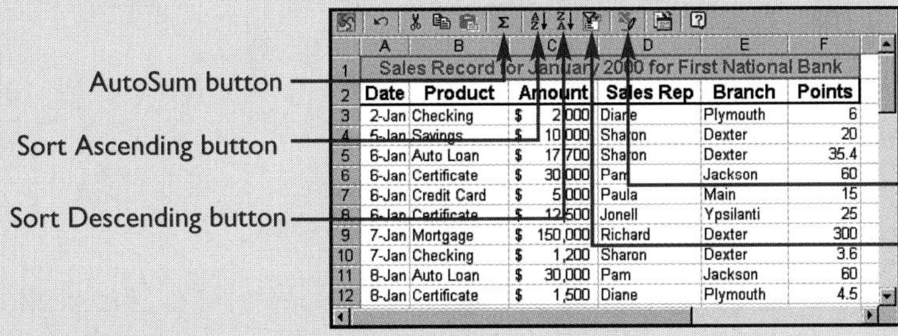

	A	B	C	D	E	F
1	Sales Record for January 2000 for First National Bank					
2	Date	Product	Amount	Sales Rep	Branch	Points
3	2-Jan	Checking	$ 2,000	Diane	Plymouth	6
4	5-Jan	Savings	$ 10,000	Sharon	Dexter	20
5	6-Jan	Auto Loan	$ 17,700	Sharon	Dexter	35.4
6	6-Jan	Certificate	$ 30,000	Pam	Jackson	60
7	6-Jan	Credit Card	$ 5,000	Paula	Main	15
8	6-Jan	Certificate	$ 12,500	Jonell	Ypsilanti	25
9	7-Jan	Mortgage	$ 150,000	Richard	Dexter	300
10	7-Jan	Checking	$ 1,200	Sharon	Dexter	3.6
11	8-Jan	Auto Loan	$ 30,000	Pam	Jackson	60
12	8-Jan	Certificate	$ 1,500	Diane	Plymouth	4.5

Export to Excel button

AutoFilter button

Figure 6.21 The worksheet appears with an abbreviated toolbar at the top.

Depending on the display settings for your computer, some of the columns may not show completely. If necessary, adjust the column width, so you can see the last column entitled `Points`.

4 Click the Sort Ascending button, and choose Product from the pop-up list.
The data in the worksheet sorts in alphabetical order by the product names.

5 Make sure one of the cells in row 2 is selected. Click the AutoFilter button.
AutoFilter arrows are added to the top of each column, as shown in Figure 6.22. You use the AutoFilter arrows to select the data you want to view. You can make selections on one or more categories.

	A	B	C	D	E	F
1	Sales Record for January 2000 for First National Bank					
2	Date	Product	Amount	Sales Rep	Branch	Points
3	6-Jan	Auto Loan	$ 17,700	Sharon	Dexter	35.4
4	8-Jan	Auto Loan	$ 30,000	Pam	Jackson	60
5	9-Jan	Auto Loan	$ 14,500	Diane	Plymouth	29
6	19-Jan	Auto Loan	$ 16,700	Diane	Plymouth	33.4
7	20-Jan	Auto Loan	$ 12,500	Jonell	Ypsilanti	25
8	23-Jan	Auto Loan	$ 17,750	Rhonda	Jackson	35.5
9	30-Jan	Auto Loan	$ 16,500	Richard	Dexter	33
10	30-Jan	Auto Loan	$ 25,000	Pam	Jackson	50
11	6-Jan	Certificate	$ 30,000	Pam	Jackson	60
12	6-Jan	Certificate	$ 12,500	Jonell	Ypsilanti	25

AutoFilter arrows are added to each column

Figure 6.22 The AutoFilter button adds drop-down arrows to each category, so you can filter the data by categories.

continues ▶

To Start PowerPoint (continued)

6. **Click the AutoFilter arrow at the top of the Branch column. Click the check marks to deselect all the branches except Main, as shown in Figure 6.23.**

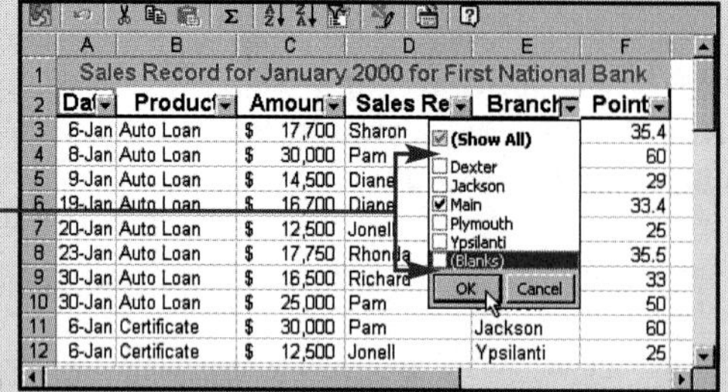

Figure 6.23
Use the drop-down list to select or deselect the data you want to view.

Checks are removed from all boxes except Main

7. **Click OK.**
   The records for the Main branch display, as shown in Figure 6.24.

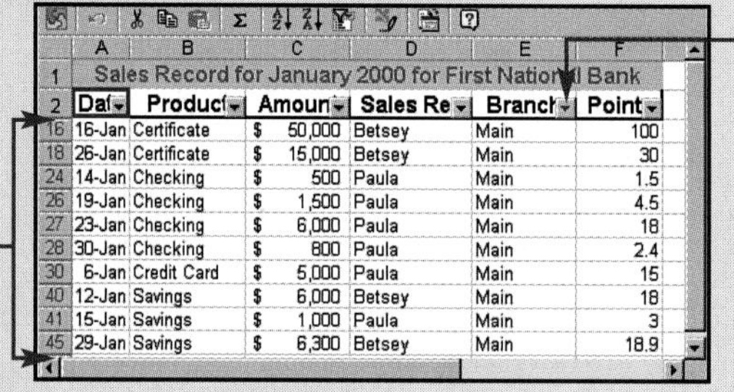

Blue indicates that a filter is active

Figure 6.24
The data is filtered, so you see only the information for the Main branch.

Row numbers of selected records display as blue

8. **Click the AutoFilter button on the Branch column. Select the Show All option, and click OK.**
   All the information displays again.

9. **Scroll to the bottom of the worksheet and select the empty cell below the Amount column C. Double-click the AutoSum button.**
   The cell displays the total of the amounts in the column above it.

10. **Click the Export to Excel button.**
    The Excel program launches and the worksheet displays in Read-Only mode, as shown in Figure 6.25.

Title shows Read-Only

Figure 6.25
When you export an active worksheet from a browser, it displays in Read-Only mode.

11. **Save the open file to your disk as a workbook. Be sure to change the Save as type box to Microsoft Excel Workbook. In the File name box enter** `Bank2`**.**

12. **Close the workbook and Excel. Close the browser.**

Summary

This project showed you how to use some of the tools that enable you to work interactively in Excel. Specifically, you learned how to create a summary worksheet by using references to other pages in a workbook. You added a hyperlink, so you could link to another worksheet in a different file. Then you copied information from that file to help you look for discrepancies. Next, you learned how to save a worksheet as a Web page and how to open that file in a browser and work with the information. In addition, you used the sorting and filtering tools in Excel in the browser environment.

Another way to reference information in cells in another worksheet is to name the cell you want to reference. Look at Help for information about naming cells. To learn more about using Excel on the Web, go to Help and look for information about opening a workbook on the Web. To learn more about using hyperlinks, open the Insert Hyperlink dialog box and use the What's This? icon to learn more about each of the buttons and file search options in this dialog box.

Checking Concepts and Terms

True/False

For each of the following, check *T* or *F* to indicate whether the statement is true or false.

__T __F **1.** To move a worksheet in a workbook, you click and drag the sheet tab to a new position. [L1]

__T __F **2.** If you want cells in one worksheet to reflect changes that are made in another worksheet, you must start with an equal sign in the destination cell. [L3]

__T __F **3.** In a formula, a reference to another worksheet is indicated by an exclamation point at the beginning and the end of the worksheet name. [L3]

__T __F **4.** To copy data in a cell from one worksheet to another, choose Edit, Worksheet. [L2]

__T __F **5.** To copy a row of cells from one worksheet to another, the entire row of cells on the source worksheet must be selected. [L2]

__T __F **6.** To insert a hyperlink in a worksheet, click the Web button. [L4]

__T __F **7.** To save the sheet as an interactive page suitable for publishing on the Internet, choose File, Save as HTML. [L5]

__T __F **8.** You can tell when a worksheet label is a hyperlink because the label appears on the worksheet in a different color. [L4]

__T __F **9.** If a worksheet is saved as an interactive Web page, you can sort the data on the sheet when viewing it with a Web browser. [L5]

__T __F **10.** The Extensible Markup Language that makes interactive worksheets possible is known by the acronym, EML. [L5]

Multiple Choice

Circle the letter of the correct answer for each of the following.

1. What is the worldwide network of computer connections that enables people to have access to thousands of online resources called? [Intro]
   a. intranet
   b. Internet
   c. Microsoft Explorer
   d. Netscape Navigator

2. An address on the Internet is known as a(n) ______________. [L4]
   a. http
   b. file
   c. URL
   d. XML

3. The graphic interface system that makes it easier to access information on the Internet is known as __________. [L4]
   a. WWW
   b. URL
   c. XML
   d. hyperlink

4. A(n) ______________ is a connection between a word or label in one location to a file in another location. [Intro]
   a. URL
   b. handle
   c. intranet
   d. hyperlink

5. Which of the following could be a reference to a cell in another worksheet? [L3]
   a. !Sheet1!B4
   b. =!Sheet1!B4
   c. ='First Quarter'!B4
   d. First Quarter!'B4'

Screen ID

Identify each of the items in Figure 6.26.

Figure 6.26

A. AutoFilter arrows
B. Export to Excel button
C. Horizontal scrollbar
D. AutoSum button
E. Vertical scrollbar
F. Sort Ascending button
G. AutoFilter button
H. Location of active file
I. Sort Descending button

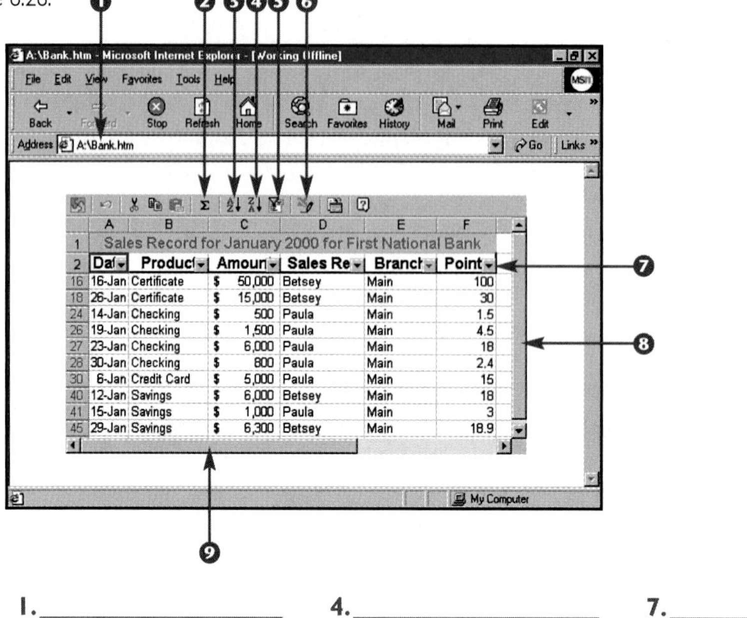

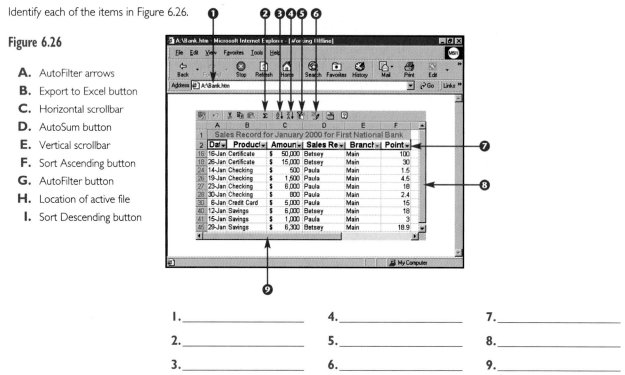

1.__________ 4.__________ 7.__________

2.__________ 5.__________ 8.__________

3.__________ 6.__________ 9.__________

Discussion Questions

1. Have you used the Internet? An intranet? Are you familiar with using a browser? What browser do you usually use? What kinds of activities do you do on the Internet? (For example, do you participate in chat groups, look for information, shop, or use email?) What do you like or dislike about using the Internet?
2. Describe a project (work or school related) that required you to collaborate with others. What were some of the difficulties that arose due to the requirements for collaboration? Would being able to share information and files interactively using Internet and Web technology and tools have changed the process? How?
3. What are some of the concerns and risks in working over the Internet? How would you minimize those risks?

Skill Drill

Skill Drill exercises reinforce project skills. Each skill reinforced is the same, or nearly the same, as a skill presented in the project. Each exercise includes a brief narrative introduction, followed by detailed instructions in a step-by-step format.

In these exercises, you summarize income and expense by quarter for a company worksheet. Then you chart the data that you summarized. Finally, you save the worksheet as an interactive Web page and view it using a browser.

All these exercises use the file EO-0604 found in the Student folder on the CD-ROM that came with your book. Open the file and save it to your floppy disk with the name `Star`.

1. Summarizing Income and Expenses by Quarter

Many companies provide quarterly reports to stockholders. The data that is provided in the first sheet displays the income and expenses by month for the Star Communications Company. You summarize this data on Sheet2 into three-month periods or quarters. [L1]

1. Move to Sheet2, and click in cell B4, where the sum of the incomes for the months of January, February, and March should be displayed.
2. Click the AutoSum button once to place the sum function in cell B4.
3. Click the 2000 sheet tab and drag across cells B9 though D9 to identify the total income for the first three months of the year.
4. Press Enter or click the Enter button on the formula bar. The total income for those three months is 66699; it displays in cell B4 of Sheet2.

5. Repeat this process to represent the total income for April, May, and June in cell C4. The number, 74549, displays in cell C4. Do not use the fill handle for this exercise.
6. Repeat this process to produce the remaining two quarterly summations of income and the four quarterly expenses.
7. Select cell F4, and use the AutoSum function to add the four quarters of income. (The total should be 321668.) Repeat this process for the total expenses in cell F5.
8. Format the numbers to currency with no decimals.
9. Calculate the gross income in row 6 for each quarter and for the year. Add a formatting line at the bottom of the numbers in row 5.
10. Rename Sheet2 as **Quarterly Report**. Save the workbook and leave it open to use in the next exercise.

2. Charting Income and Expense by Quarter

In this exercise, you create two charts. The first chart displays the quarterly income and expenses for the Star Communications Company. The second chart shows the total income and expenses. Use the Star file you worked with in the first exercise. [L2]

1. With the Star file open, select the Quarterly Report sheet if necessary.
2. Create a column chart to compare the income and expense data in these cells by quarter. Add chart titles as shown in the figure. Save the chart as a separate sheet named **Quarterly Chart**. Format the Value-axis to dollars with no decimals. Enlarge the titles and labels to make them more legible. The completed chart should look like the one in Figure 6.27.

Figure 6.27

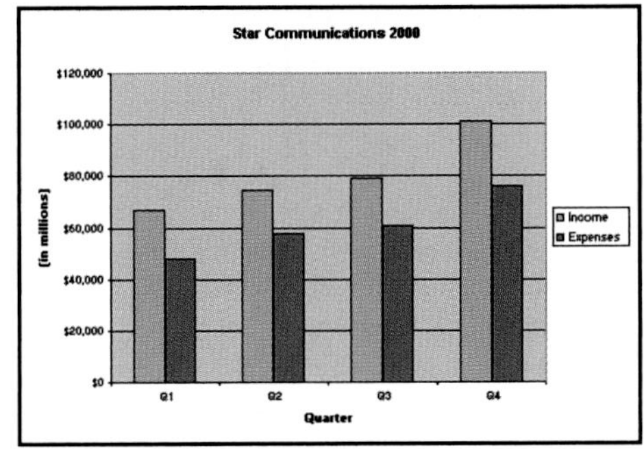

3. Create a second chart that compares the total Income and Expense for the entire year, as shown in Figure 6.28. (Remember to use Ctrl to select columns that are not next to each other.) Save it on its own sheet named **Annual Chart**. Label it as shown.

Figure 6.28

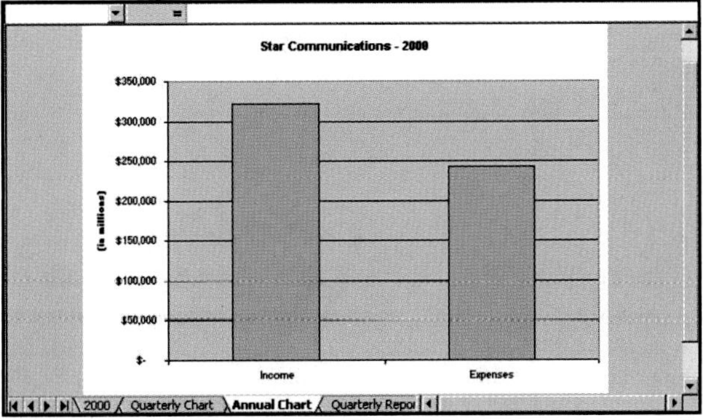

4. Save the workbook, and leave it open to use in the next exercise.

3. Saving a Summary Sheet as an Interactive Web Page

You can share this data with others by saving it as a Web page that can be placed on a Web server or in a folder that is available to others on a local area network. [L5]

1. Select the 2000 sheet. Select cells A1 through M18.
2. Save the selected area as a Web page on your disk. Choose the Add interactive option and name it **Star.htm** in the File name box.
3. Launch your browser, and enter the file's location in the browser's Address box. It should look like Figure 6.29.

Figure 6.29

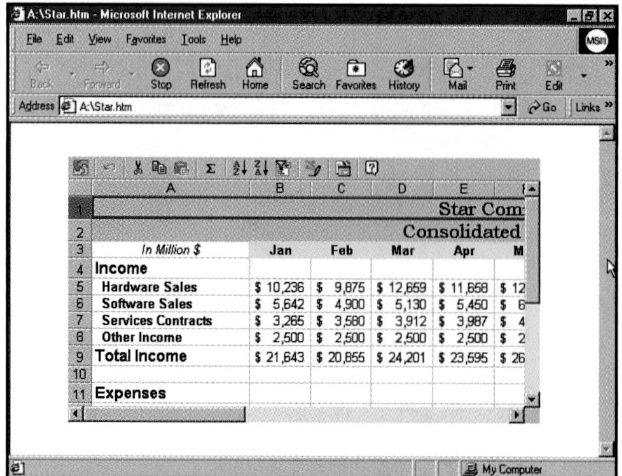

4. Switch back to Excel. Save the workbook and close it.

Challenge

Challenge exercises expand on or are somewhat related to skills presented in the lessons. Each exercise provides a brief narrative introduction followed by instructions, in a numbered step or bulleted list format, that are not as detailed as those in the Skill Drill section.

It is possible to include a worksheet in a Word document in several ways depending on the application. A worksheet can be copied and pasted in such a way that it is converted into a Word table. It is also possible to paste it as an actual worksheet that you can activate and edit. If you paste the worksheet into a Word document as a working worksheet, you also can choose to maintain a link between the document and the parent worksheet so that changes in one are reflected in the other. In the first Challenge exercise, you copy and paste a worksheet to a Word document. In the second exercise, you use the Paste Special function to see how it works differently from the Paste function. In the last exercise, you paste a worksheet and a chart as an object in a Word document.

The following Challenge exercises use Excel file EO-0606 and a Word document file, EO-0605.doc, that you open in Word.

1. Pasting a Worksheet into a Document

In this exercise, you paste an Armstrong Pool, Spa, and Sauna Co. worksheet into a letter to the employees. The results should look like Figure 6.30. [L3]

Use the following guidelines:

1. Launch Microsoft Word. Open EO-0605.doc from the Student folder on the disc that came with your book. Save it on your floppy disk as `Memo.doc`.
2. Launch Excel, and open the file EO-0606 from the Student folder on the disc that came with your book. Save it on your floppy disk as `Sales Volume`.
3. Select the Sales Change sheet. Select the data in cells A2 to D5, and copy it.
4. Use the taskbar to switch to the Memo document in Word and place the insertion point in one of the blank lines between the paragraphs.
5. Choose Edit, Paste.

Figure 6.30

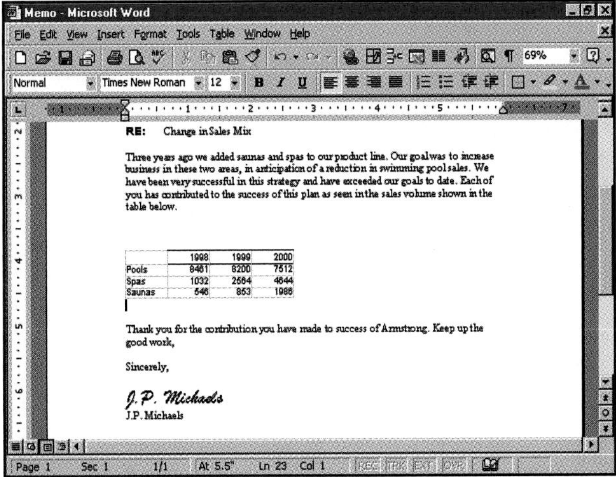

6. Save the document. Leave the document and the workbook open for use in the next exercise.

2. Using Paste Special to Place a Worksheet in a Document

In this exercise, you use the Paste Special option to place the worksheet in the document. Using Paste Special enables you to edit the table using Excel tools rather than the Word Table commands. [L2]

To paste the Sales Volume workbook into the Memo document without linking them together, follow these steps:

1. Switch to the Word document, Memo.doc, if necessary. Save it as `Memo2.doc` on your disk.
2. Delete the table that was pasted into the document in the previous exercise. (Use Table, Delete, Table.)
3. Switch to the Excel workbook Sales Volume, and select the Sales Change sheet. Select the cells that contain data on this sheet and copy them.
4. Switch to the Memo2 document in Word and place the insertion point in one of the blank lines between the paragraphs.
5. Choose Edit, Paste Special. In the As box select Microsoft Excel Worksheet Object (do not link it). Read the description in the Paste Special dialog box. This option enables you to edit the worksheet using Excel.
6. Delete extra blank lines as needed. Double-click the table to activate the worksheet. Your screen should look like the one in Figure 6.31.

   Notice the Excel tools on the toolbar. The table now displays in a worksheet format with cell references and scrollbars. Any changes that you make to this information in the Word document are not reflected in the Sales Volume Excel file. To verify this, change one of the figures, and return to the Excel file; confirm that the change does not show in the original information. Return to the Word file, and click Undo to reverse the change. If you want to make two files interactive, you need to choose Link in the Paste Special dialog box.

Figure 6.31

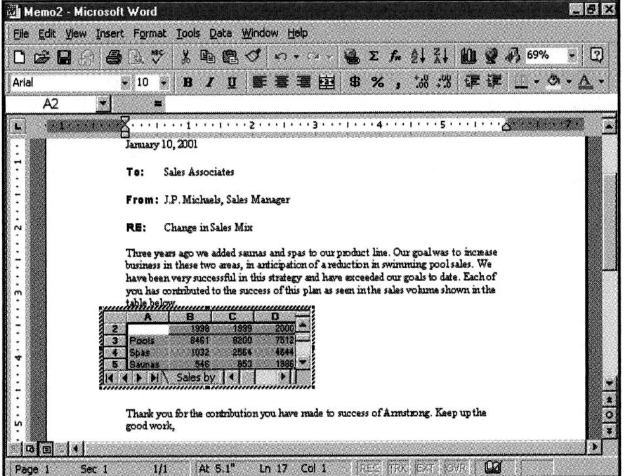

7. To deactivate the worksheet, click another part of the document. Save the document. Leave both files open to use in the next exercise.

3. Pasting a Chart into a Word Document

You can also paste a chart into a Word Document. You can paste the chart by itself, or you can select it along with the data and paste the two together as a Microsoft Excel Object. The completed Word document should look like the one in Figure 6.32. [L2–3]

To paste the worksheet and the chart into the Memo document, follow these steps:

1. Delete the worksheet that you pasted into the document in the previous exercise, and save the file as `Memo3.doc` on your disk.
2. Switch to the Excel workbook Sales Volume. Select cells A2 through F18 of the Sales Change sheet, and click the Copy button in the toolbar.
3. Switch to the Memo3 document in Word, and place the insertion point in one of the blank lines between the paragraphs.
4. Choose Edit, Paste Special. In the As box, select Microsoft Excel Worksheet Object. (Do not link it.)

Figure 6.32

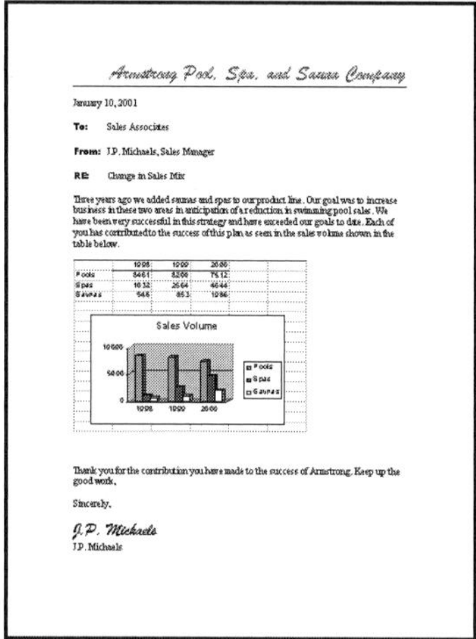

5. Delete extra blank lines as needed. Double-click the table to activate the worksheet.

Notice that both the data and the chart are in a worksheet format together. If you make changes to the data, it is reflected in the chart that is part of this Microsoft Excel object in Word. It does not, however, change the data in the original Excel file. Try it to see how this works. Undo your changes and save the file. Close both files and close Word.

Discovery Zone

Discovery Zone exercises require advanced knowledge of topics presented in *Essentials* lessons, application of skills from multiple lessons, or self-directed learning of new skills.

In the first Discovery Zone exercise, you save a workbook as a Web page and see how you can use the navigation buttons and sheet tabs to move from one sheet to the next. This exercise uses the Summary file that you created in the project. The second exercise inserts a hyperlink to a specific sheet in another workbook. This exercises uses two of the files that have been used for the Armstrong Pool, Spa, and Sauna Company. In the last exercise, you change the properties of a cell in an interactive worksheet. A fourth exercise requires the use of a Web server to complete. If you have this capability, you will want to do the last exercise.

1. Saving a Workbook as a Web Page

If a workbook has several sheets, you can save the entire workbook as a Web page. The workbook then displays as a series of Web pages that you can select using navigation buttons.

Open the Summary workbook you created in this project. To save the Summary workbook as a Web page, follow these steps:

1. Choose File, Save as Web Page to save the entire workbook to your disk. Change the name of the file to **`Summary2.htm`** in the File name box.
2. Launch your Web browser (Internet Explorer 5.0 or another browser capable of reading XML). Enter the location of the file in the browser's Address box. (If your file is on the floppy disk, the address is probably A:\Summary2.htm.)
3. Open the Web page. The workbook displays with sheet tabs, as shown in Figure 6.33.

Figure 6.33

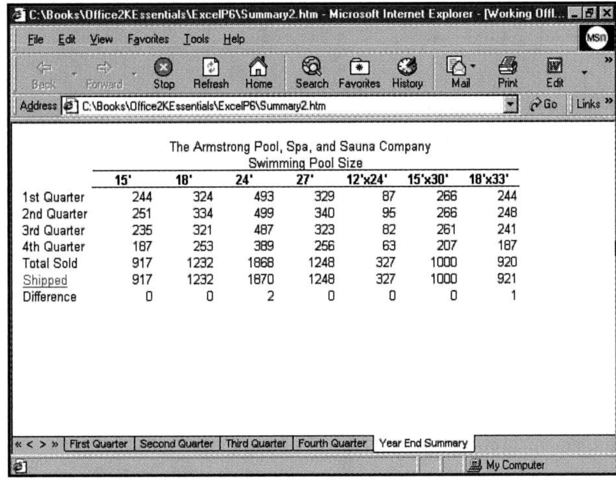

The Armstrong Pool, Spa, and Sauna Company
Swimming Pool Size

	15'	18'	24'	27'	12'x24'	15'x30'	18'x33'
1st Quarter	244	324	493	329	87	266	244
2nd Quarter	251	334	499	340	95	266	248
3rd Quarter	235	321	487	323	82	261	241
4th Quarter	187	253	389	256	63	207	187
Total Sold	917	1232	1868	1248	327	1000	920
Shipped	917	1232	1870	1248	327	1000	921
Difference	0	0	2	0	0	0	1

4. Navigate the different sheets of the workbook using the sheet tabs at the bottom of the page.
5. Close the browser. Close the workbook.

2. Inserting a Hyperlink to a Sheet in another Workbook

If you are linking your worksheet to another workbook, you may want to go to a specific sheet or named range within that workbook. Excel enables you to examine a list of sheet names and range names within the target workbook and select the specific place to link to within the workbook.

Goal: Place a hyperlink in a worksheet that links to a specific sheet within another workbook. The following Discovery Zone exercise uses the Sales Volume file from the Challenge exercises and file EO-0606S.

- Open the Sales Volume file (or open file EO-0606 and save it as **`Sales-Volume`** on your disk). Select cell B3 in the Sales by Product worksheet.
- Click the Insert Hyperlink button. Use the Browse for File button and find the EO-0606S file in the Student folder on the disc that came with your book. (Check the File type box to make sure the dialog box displays the workbooks.)
- After the file EO-0606S is selected, click the Bookmark button. If necessary, click the ⊞ next to Defined Names to expand the list. Select FirstQuarterPools as the defined name. Click OK twice.
- Click the resulting hyperlink to test it. The EO-0606S workbook opens to the total of pools sold for the first quarter.
- Use the Back button on the Web toolbar to return to the Sales Volume worksheet.
- Repeat this process four more times to add hyperlinks to the corresponding cells for the remaining quarters and for the total. (Be careful! The defined names are in alphabetical order, not in numerical order.)
- Test your hyperlinks. Close both files.

3. Changing the Properties of a Cell in an Interactive Worksheet

If you are using an interactive Web page that someone else has posted, you can change some of the cell formatting and you can try different scenarios. In this exercise, you open a Web page on the CD and compare loan balance and resale value of a car. You can change the variables on the left of the screen and examine the columns on the right to determine whether you are ever upside down (loan balance is greater than the resale value) on the loan. To make such a comparison easier, you must reformat the columns so that they both display in currency.

In this exercise, you learn some of the limits and capabilities of the Web version of the worksheet. You also format the cells to make the comparison easier.

- Open EO-0607.htm with an XML enabled browser, such as Internet Explorer 5.
- Select cells or ranges of cells, and right-click them. Use the Properties option to select the appropriate format.
- Scroll down the two columns. Notice that at one point, you owe about $1,200 more on the car than you could get if you sold it (or would get from the insurance company if you totaled it).
- Write a formula in the column at the right to find the difference between the Loan Balance and the Resale Value. See if you can figure out how to copy that formula into the other cells in that column without doing it one cell at a time.
- Try different amounts of down payment in increments of $500 until you find an amount that is sufficient enough to ensure that you can always sell the car for more than the balance on the loan.
- When you have found the down payment that is necessary to prevent a negative or upside down situation, print the sheet (at least the part that shows in the Browser window).
- Save the file to your disk as `Car Loan`. Close the browser.

4. Posting an Interactive Worksheet to a Web Server

To do this exercise, you need to have access to a local area network and a shared folder on that network, or have the permission and software necessary to post a Web page to a Web server. Ask your instructor if either of these is available.

In this exercise, you place an interactive Web page in a location where others can use it.

- If you have access to a public folder on your local area server, copy the file **`EO-0607.htm`** to that location. Use your browser to open the file at that location.
- If you have a user ID and password to post pages to a Web server, transfer the file **`EO-0607.htm`** from the CD to that server. Browse the page on the server.

PowerPoint

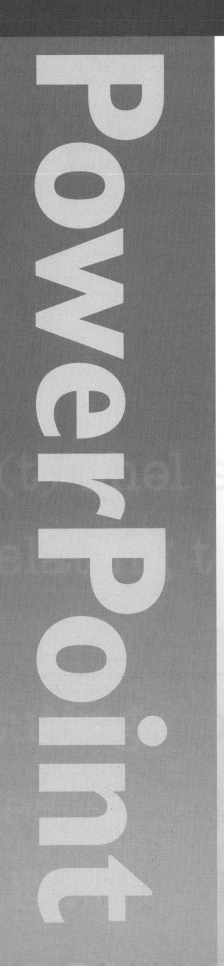

Part IV PowerPoint

1 Getting Started with PowerPoint

2 Improving the Design of the Presentation

3 Charting Numerical Data

4 Adding Animations for the Slide Show

Introduction to Microsoft PowerPoint 2000

Since pre-historic times, mankind has used pictures to communicate ideas. Pictures of bears, horses, mammoths, wooly rhinos, and other Ice Age animals have been found on cave walls in France and Germany. Pictographs have been found throughout North and South America. The tombs of the Pharaohs of ancient Egypt are decorated with elaborate pictures depicting life at the time.

In ancient times, graphics often served as a substitute for written language, or, in some cases, a forerunner to a language that evolved over time. Hieroglyphs are characters that were used in several ancient-writing systems, which included pictorial characters that represented recognizable objects. The term ideogram is used to define a type of sign where a specific object is used to signify that object or something closely related to it, such as using a picture of the sun to mean "sun" or "day".

Fast forward to the world of visual communication in the late twentieth century. We continue to use pictures to help explain ideas and words. We are bombarded by images throughout each day via television, print media, and advertising in a wide variety of forms. Everyone is trying to grab our attention, to make an impression, or to create an image that we will remember.

In the work world, you may be called upon to share your ideas with a group. Most of the time, these will be informal opportunities to share information and ideas. However, there may be times when you need to convince others of your ideas. The use of a visual presentation to reinforce your words and ideas can help to leave a lasting impression with your audience.

PowerPoint is a graphical presentation program that enables you to create handouts, slides, or overheads to use in presenting information. Using PowerPoint, you can include words, pictures, charts, and other graphics elements. It can help you organize your thoughts and create a clear, logical, and impressive presentation. Studies have shown that the more senses that are used in receiving information, the greater the chance that the information will be retained. So, using a visual presentation to reinforce what you say increases the likelihood that your ideas or information will be remembered.

Not all images are good at conveying information, however. The use of pictures and graphs in a presentation should help the viewer to gain a better understanding of the concept that is being presented. Imagine sitting in the back of a room and viewing a projection of a table of numbers that represents the performance of a company. The numbers may be too small to see, or perhaps the data is too detailed to analyze at a distance while someone is talking. Showing you a table of numbers is often not as effective as showing you a chart in which you can see the change in categories from one year to the next. It is important to use images that are related to the content, are visible to the audience, and convey the intended idea.

With PowerPoint, you can create a professional-looking presentation that will impress your colleagues and clients. Whether you need to develop a marketing plan, create a sales presentation, report progress on a project, or simply conduct a meeting, PowerPoint can help you quickly create powerful presentations. You can deliver PowerPoint presentations in various ways: printed handouts, 35mm slides, or overhead transparencies. You can even create an electronic slide show and make your presentation by using a computer-projection device. This is a tool that is being used by an increasing number of sales representatives in the competition for business.

More and more companies are doing business on the Web, and Microsoft PowerPoint 2000 has been updated to be more compatible and interactive with the Web. You can publish your presentation in a Web format and reopen it in PowerPoint without losing the formatting or contents. With presentation broadcasting, you can schedule and present a slide show over the Web. You can collaborate with multiple users by scheduling and conducting meetings online using Microsoft PowerPoint or Microsoft Outlook. Microsoft PowerPoint 2000 is a powerful tool that you can use to work in a global environment and overcome the barriers of time and distance.

In this section, you learn how to create a simple presentation. You insert clip art and other graphics elements, apply designs, and create graphs. Finally, you learn how to animate your slides, make changes to the master slide, and print handouts. PowerPoint 2000 is a fun and exciting program to use that enables you to exhibit your creative talents.

Project 1

Getting Started with PowerPoint

Objectives

In this project, you learn how to

- ➤ **Open a Blank Presentation and Identify Parts of the PowerPoint Window**
- ➤ **Enter Text in Normal View**
- ➤ **Use Slide View and Outline View to Edit Text**
- ➤ **Save a Presentation and Add Speaker Notes**
- ➤ **Preview the Slide Show**
- ➤ **Print an Outline**

Key terms introduced in this project include

- AutoContent Wizard
- demote
- Normal view
- Notes Pages view
- Notes pane
- Outline pane
- Outline view
- placeholder
- presentation graphics
- promote
- Slide pane
- Slide Show view
- Slide Sorter view
- Slide view
- speaker notes

Why Would I Do This?

PowerPoint is a ***presentation graphics*** program that provides features and tools for creating a presentation consisting of a collection of slides, overheads, or handouts. If you need help creating a presentation you can use the ***AutoContent Wizard***, which provides step-by-step assistance to help you organize the content of your presentation. In other cases, you might already know what needs to be included in the presentation, in which case you start with a blank presentation and create the content from scratch.

In this project, you create a simple presentation, make some changes to the text, add speaker notes, save and view the presentation, and print the outline. The completed outline and opening slide look like those shown in Figure 1.1.

Visual Summary

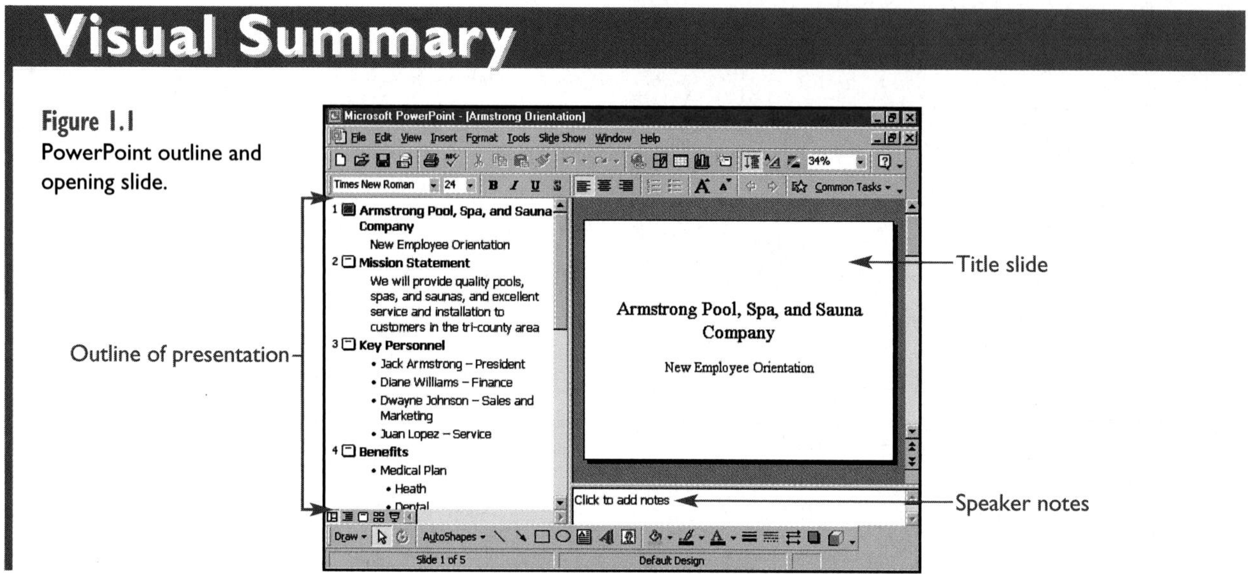

Figure 1.1
PowerPoint outline and opening slide.

Lesson 1: Opening a Blank Presentation and Identifying Parts of the PowerPoint Window

You can create a presentation in several ways. In this example, you create a short presentation to welcome new employees to the Armstrong Pool, Spa, and Sauna Company. You know what you want to say, and you have prepared an outline of your main points. In this case, it is recommended that you start with a blank presentation and enter your points. In this lesson, you open a blank presentation. Then you identify different parts of the PowerPoint window.

To Open a Blank Presentation and Identify Parts of the PowerPoint Window

1. **Click the Start button on the taskbar; choose Programs, Microsoft PowerPoint.**
   The PowerPoint dialog box displays, as shown in Figure 1.2. Four options can be used to work on a PowerPoint presentation: AutoContent Wizard, Design Template, Blank presentation, or Open an existing presentation. In this project, you use the Blank presentation option.

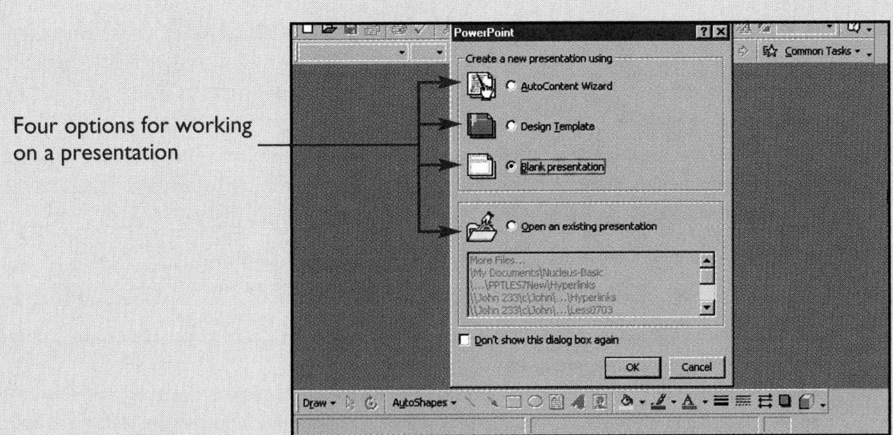

Figure 1.2
In the PowerPoint dialog box, select the way you want to create your presentation.

2 Click Blank presentation; then click OK.

The New Slide dialog box opens, so you can select the layout for your first slide. PowerPoint assumes that you want the first slide in the presentation to be a title slide. The title slide is highlighted with a dark blue border (see Figure 1.3).

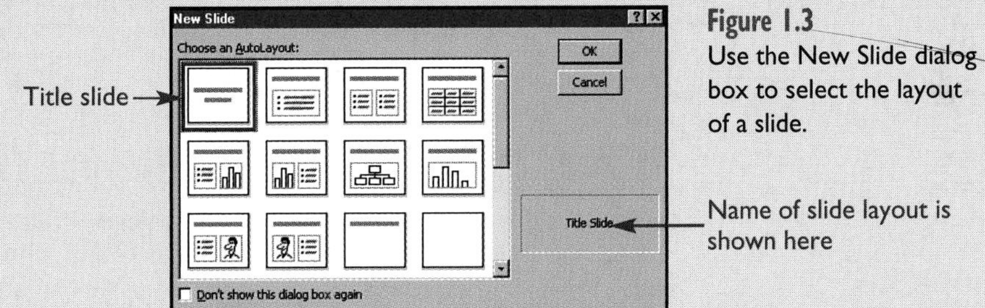

Figure 1.3
Use the New Slide dialog box to select the layout of a slide.

3 Click OK to create a title slide as your first slide.

PowerPoint opens in Normal view. The three panes or work areas in the Normal view are identified in Figure 1.4. The ***Slide pane*** is the area that displays the layout of the slide. The ***Outline pane*** is the area that displays the outline for your presentation. The ***Notes pane*** displays any notes that have been added, which would be printed in a format known as speaker notes. You learn more about speaker notes in Lesson 4 of this project.

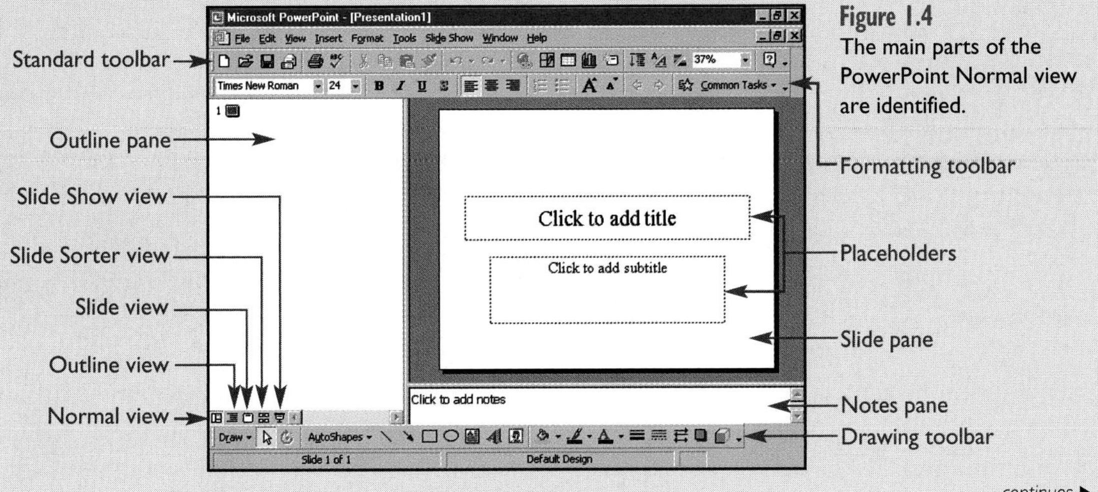

Figure 1.4
The main parts of the PowerPoint Normal view are identified.

continues ▶

To Open a Blank Presentation and Identify Parts of the PowerPoint Window (continued)

4. **Move your mouse pointer slowly over the view buttons at the left end of the horizontal scrollbar.**
   These buttons enable you to change views quickly. As you move the mouse, a ScreenTip that identifies each view displays. Examine Figure 1.4 to see the names of the view buttons and the different parts of the window.
5. **Leave the screen open and continue with the next lesson.**

Viewing Your Presentation
You can view your presentation in one of five ways. ***Normal view*** is the most commonly used option because it is the most flexible. It has three components. You can use it to enter text in an outline or on a slide, or to add speaker notes. The outline shows you how the topics flow from one to another; the slide layout shows you how the topic appears on a slide or an overhead projector, and you can make notes for the speaker as you work along. You can even use this view to add graphics to your slides. Use ***Outline view*** to type the text of a presentation. Its advantage is that it focuses on the flow of ideas. Use ***Slide view*** to view and edit each slide individually. It is the best view for working with graphics. Use ***Slide Sorter view*** to see many slides at one time, to rearrange their order, and to add transitions and animations. ***Slide Show view*** utilizes the full screen, and you can use it to project the slides for viewing by an audience.

Lesson 2: Entering Text in Normal View

Entering text in Normal View has several advantages. You can enter text in the Outline or Slide pane in the Normal view. As you enter text, you can see how it will display on the slide. As you move from one topic to the next, you continue to see the full content of your presentation in the outline while the slide displays the content for the topic you are currently writing. This enables you to see how your ideas flow from one slide to the next while concurrently viewing how the words fit on a slide. In addition, you can make notes for the speaker to use during the presentation.

In this lesson, you enter text in the Normal view, using the Slide pane for the title slide and the Outline pane for the body of the presentation.

To Enter Text in Normal View

1. **Click the slide in the placeholder where it says `Click to add title`. Type `Armstrong Pool, Spa, and Sauna Company`. Click the placeholder for the subtitle and type `New Employee Orientation`. If the Office Assistant opens, right-click it and choose Hide.**
   While you type, the words are added to the slide and to the outline on the left (see Figure 1.5) The ***placeholder*** is a defined area on a slide that has been preformatted by the program to display text using a particular font style, size, and alignment. A placeholder is identified by the dashed line outlining an area. The dashed line changes to diagonal hash marks after you click a placeholder.

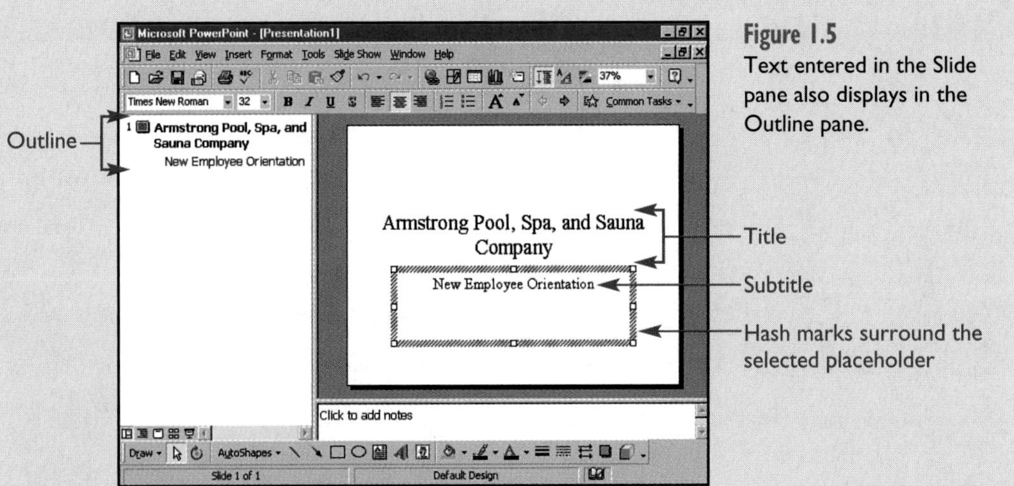

Figure 1.5
Text entered in the Slide pane also displays in the Outline pane.

2. **Click at the end of the text in the subtitle on the Outline pane on the left side of the window.**
   Now you enter the body of the presentation in the outline side of the window where you can focus on the flow of ideas.

3. **Press ↵Enter. The insertion point moves to the next line on the same slide, but you want to create a new slide. Hold down the ⇧Shift key and press Tab⇆.**
   This promotes the insertion point to a title for the new slide. When you ***promote*** a bullet point in a slide, you increase the level of importance of that point to a higher level. A new slide displays in the Slide pane area. The layout of the next slide is a bulleted slide, which is the most common slide used in a presentation.

4. **Type `Mission Statement` and press ↵Enter.**
   The title for the second slide enters in the outline and on the slide. When you press ↵Enter the program starts another line of the outline at the same level of importance, which in this case would be another new slide.

5. **Press Tab⇆. Type `To provide quality pools, spas, and saunas to customers in the tri-county area.`**
   The line is ***demoted*** to a lower level of importance, and the insertion point moves to the first bulleted point where the text is entered.

A lightbulb might appear on the slide as you move to the next level. This is the Help program offering a tip. You can click the lightbulb to see the suggestion. Click OK to close the Tip box. To turn off the tips, choose Help, Microsoft PowerPoint Help, and click Options. Make sure the Options tab is selected, and deselect any check boxes in the Show tips area at the bottom of the dialog box. Click OK and hide the Assistant again.

6. **Make sure your insertion point is at the end of the line of text you just entered. Press ↵Enter, and then ⇧Shift+Tab⇆.**
   This action promotes the next point and moves the insertion point to the title for slide three. A new slide displays in the Slide pane.

7. **Enter the following information for the next three slides. Use Figure 1.6 as a guide to determine the major topics for each slide. Use Tab⇆ to demote points and ⇧Shift+Tab⇆ to promote points. Compare your results for Slides 3 through 5 to Figure 1.6.**

```
Key Personnel
    Jack Armstrong - President
    Diane Williams - Finance
    Dwayne Johnson - Sales
    Juan Lopez - Service
```

continues ▶

To Enter Text in Normal View (continued)

```
Benefits
   Medical Plan
   Retirement
   Day Care

Payroll Options
   Direct Deposit
   Deductions for Charity
```

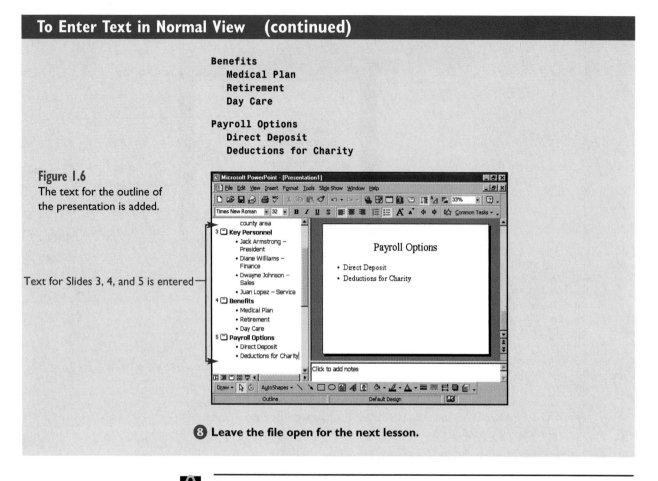

Figure 1.6
The text for the outline of the presentation is added.

Text for Slides 3, 4, and 5 is entered

8 Leave the file open for the next lesson.

Fixing Errors

If you make an error when entering text, you can use the same techniques that are used in a word processor to correct text in PowerPoint. Use ←Backspace to delete letters to the left of the insertion point and Del to delete letters to the right. You can also use the mouse to drag across text and press Del to remove it, or type over the highlighted text to change it.

Lesson 3: Using Slide View and Outline View to Edit Text

So far you have been working in the Normal view, which gives you the most flexibility for working in PowerPoint because you can see the slide, the outline of topics, and create notes all in one window. You can work in other views and you might find these useful when you edit your presentation.

After you complete the first draft of your presentation, you might want to show it to someone else to see whether anything else should be covered. It is likely that you will modify the text of any presentation several times before it is finished. In this lesson, you work in the Outline view and the Slide view to edit your original draft. The Outline view enables you to focus more fully on the content and the flow of ideas. The Slide view is a preview of the final slide. The shape of the letters, numbers, and characters known as the font is best seen using the Slide view as is the font size, which is the height and width of letters, numbers, and characters. Font size is measured in points and there are seventy-two points to one inch. The Slide view is also useful when you are evaluating the overall layout of the slide when graphic elements are added.

In this lesson, you add additional text to some slides using the Outline view and change to the Slide view to change the slide layout for the Mission Statement slide.

To Use Outline View to Edit Text

1. **Click the Outline View button at the bottom of the window.**
   The outline side of the screen expands, the Slide pane is reduced, and the Notes pane expands to fill the vertical space on the right side of the screen.
2. **On the Outline, move the pointer (in the shape of an I-beam) to the right of the word `Sales` on Slide 3 and click. After the insertion point moves, press Spacebar and type `and Marketing`.**
3. **Click to the right of `Medical Plan` on Slide 4. Press ↵Enter and press Tab↹.**
   You are ready to enter a subpoint under `Medical Plan`.
4. **Type `Health`; press ↵Enter and type `Dental`.**
   Two subtopics have been added to this topic.
5. **The mission statement has recently been modified. Change the mission statement on Slide 2 to read as follows:**
   `We will provide quality pools, spas, and saunas, and excellent service and installation to customers in the tri-county area`

   See Figure 1.7 to review the changes made in the preceding five steps.

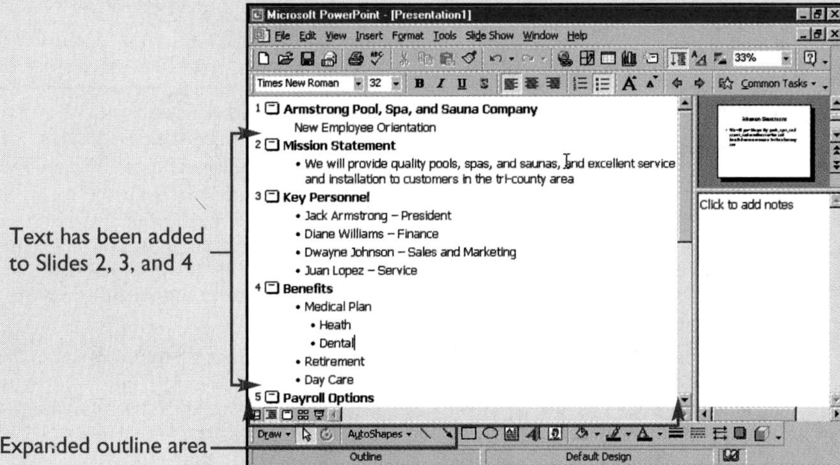

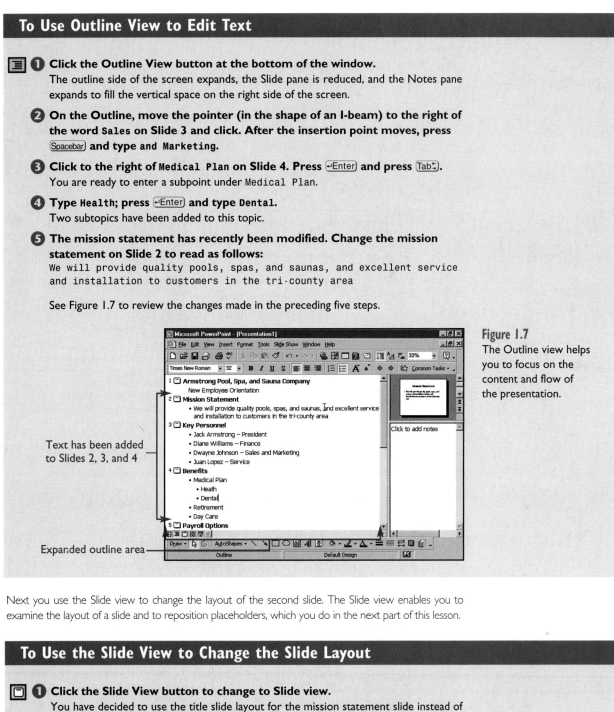

Figure 1.7
The Outline view helps you to focus on the content and flow of the presentation.

Next you use the Slide view to change the layout of the second slide. The Slide view enables you to examine the layout of a slide and to reposition placeholders, which you do in the next part of this lesson.

To Use the Slide View to Change the Slide Layout

1. **Click the Slide View button to change to Slide view.**
   You have decided to use the title slide layout for the mission statement slide instead of a bulleted slide. It is easiest to see the effect of this type of change in the Slide view.
2. **Click the Common Tasks button at the right end of the toolbar at the top of the window.**
   Three menu options display.

3. **Click Slide Layout.**
   The Slide Layout dialog box opens.
4. **Click the Title Slide layout; the first option in the first row, and click Apply.**
   The slide layout changes for Slide 2 to a title slide. Now you reposition the title and subtitle boxes by moving them up on the slide.

continues ▶

To Use the Slide View to Change the Slide Layout (continued)

5. **Click anywhere on the title of the slide.**
The outline of the title placeholder displays. You can use the square sizing handles around the edge of the box to change the size and shape of the placeholder.

6. **Move your mouse pointer to the upper border of the placeholder.**
The mouse changes to a four-headed arrow. You can move a placeholder when the mouse pointer is a four-headed arrow.

7. **Click and drag the box up to the top third of the slide, as shown in Figure 1.8.**
As you drag, you see the new location for the placeholder outlined in a dashed box.

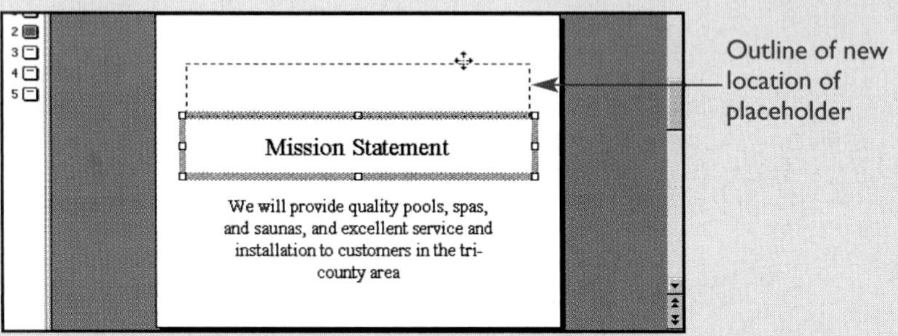

Figure 1.8
The dashed box shows the new location for the title of Slide 2.

If you move your mouse pointer onto one of the square handles, it changes into a two-headed arrow. With this mouse shape you resize the placeholder rather than move it. Be sure the mouse pointer is on the diagonal lines of the border of the placeholder and is in the shape of a four-headed arrow.

8. **Click anywhere on the subtitle of the slide. Move your mouse pointer to the upper-edge of the placeholder. Click and drag it up to the middle of the slide, as shown in Figure 1.9.**
The subtitle placeholder needs to be widened slightly so that the mission statement fits on three lines.

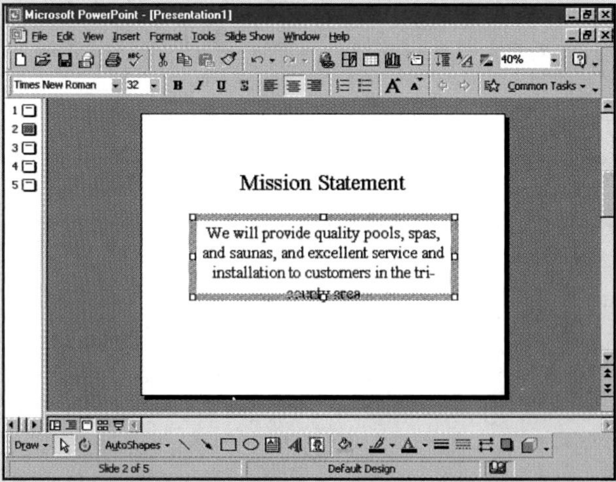

Figure 1.9
The title and subtitle move up on the slide.

9. **Move the mouse pointer to the square sizing handle on the right edge of the placeholder. When the mouse changes to a two-headed arrow, click and drag to the right about 1/2 inch, and then release the mouse.**
As you drag, you see the new shape for the placeholder outlined in a dashed box. If necessary, click the placeholder border and drag the entire box to the left to center it under the title. The results should look like Figure 1.10.

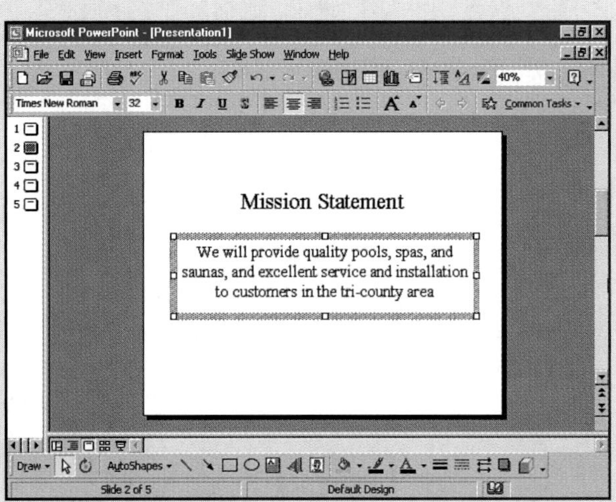

Figure 1.10
The subtitle now fits on three lines.

⑩ **Leave the file open for the next lesson.**

Changing Slides in Slide View
In the Slide view, you can move quickly from one slide to the next by clicking one of the numbered slide icons displayed on the left side of the screen.

Lesson 4: Saving a Presentation and Adding Speaker Notes

PowerPoint creates temporary files on your computer's hard disk. These files are used to protect your work in case of unexpected power failure and loss of memory, but as with all computer files, after you have spent some time creating, it is important to save your work. Similarly, notes used by a speaker during a presentation, known in PowerPoint as ***speaker notes***, helps the speaker ensure that nothing is left out of a presentation. Notes can provide useful reminders about details that need to be mentioned during a presentation. Notes can also help a speaker keep on track. Just like saving a file, having notes in your hand adds a bit of insurance against a temporary memory loss when talking in front of a group. PowerPoint contains a feature that makes it easy to create effective speaker notes.

In this lesson, you save your presentation and create speaker notes.

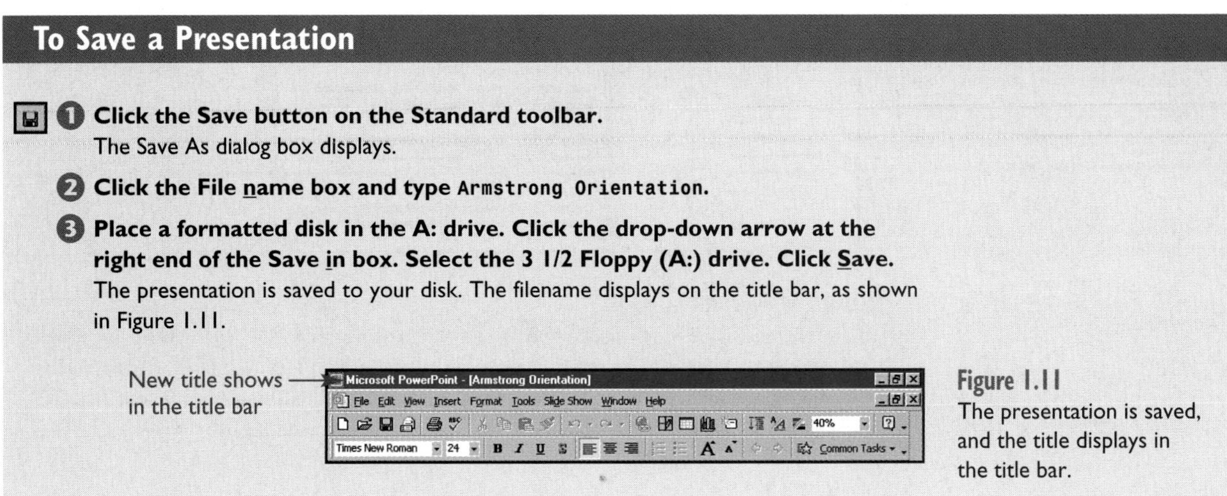

To Save a Presentation

① **Click the Save button on the Standard toolbar.**
The Save As dialog box displays.

② **Click the File name box and type `Armstrong Orientation`.**

③ **Place a formatted disk in the A: drive. Click the drop-down arrow at the right end of the Save in box. Select the 3 1/2 Floppy (A:) drive. Click Save.**
The presentation is saved to your disk. The filename displays on the title bar, as shown in Figure 1.11.

Figure 1.11
The presentation is saved, and the title displays in the title bar.

Next, you create notes for Slide 3. The notes are details about key personnel in the company.

To Add Speaker Notes

1. **Click the Next Slide button at the bottom of the vertical scrollbar (see Figure 1.12).**
   Slide 3 displays.

2. **Click the Outline View button. Move the mouse pointer to the left of the border between the outline and the right side of the window. When the mouse pointer changes to a two-headed arrow, click and drag to the left until the Notes pane expands to a little more than half of the window, as shown in Figure 1.12.**
   The Notes pane expands, so you have more room to add notes for Slide 3.

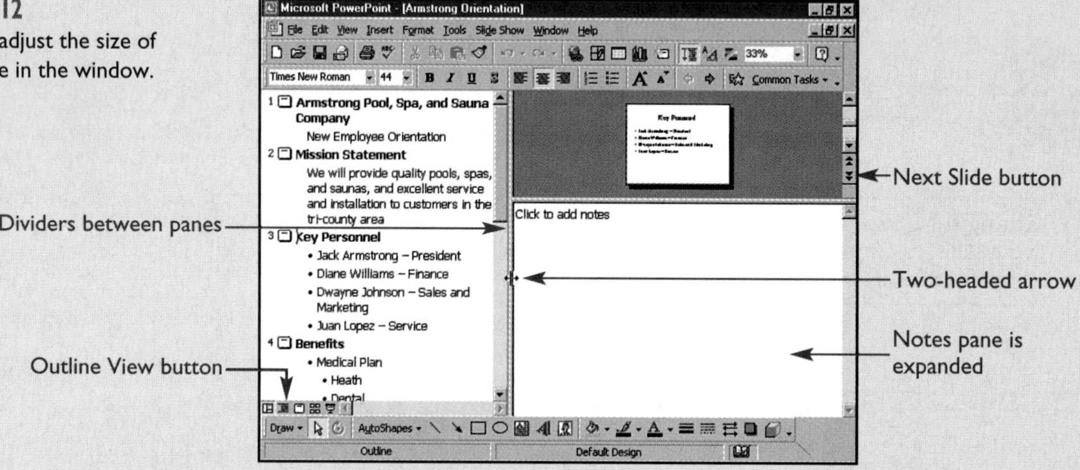

Figure 1.12
You can adjust the size of each pane in the window.

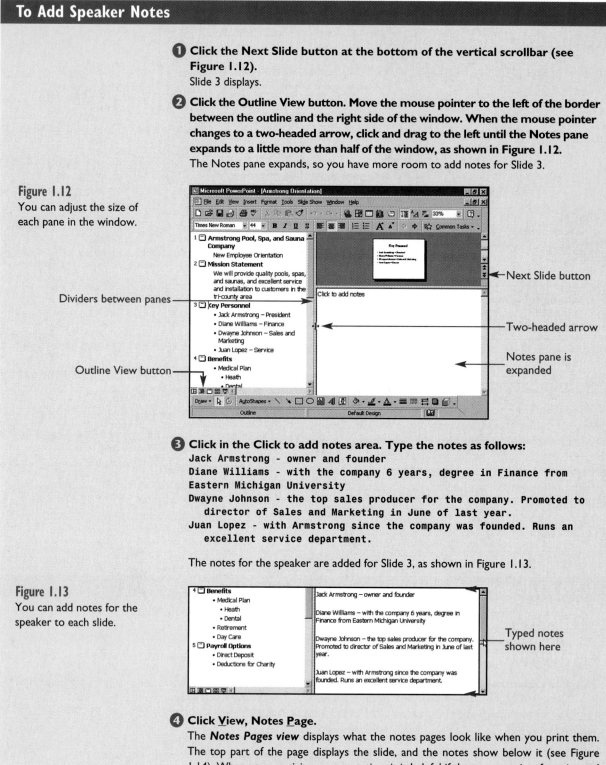

3. **Click in the Click to add notes area. Type the notes as follows:**
   `Jack Armstrong - owner and founder`
   `Diane Williams - with the company 6 years, degree in Finance from Eastern Michigan University`
   `Dwayne Johnson - the top sales producer for the company. Promoted to director of Sales and Marketing in June of last year.`
   `Juan Lopez - with Armstrong since the company was founded. Runs an excellent service department.`

   The notes for the speaker are added for Slide 3, as shown in Figure 1.13.

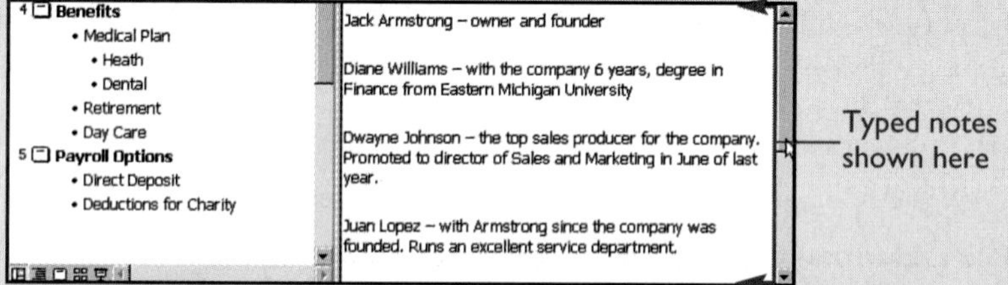

Figure 1.13
You can add notes for the speaker to each slide.

4. **Click View, Notes Page.**
   The ***Notes Pages view*** displays what the notes pages look like when you print them. The top part of the page displays the slide, and the notes show below it (see Figure 1.14). When you are giving a presentation, it is helpful if the notes are in a font size and style that is easy to read at a glance.

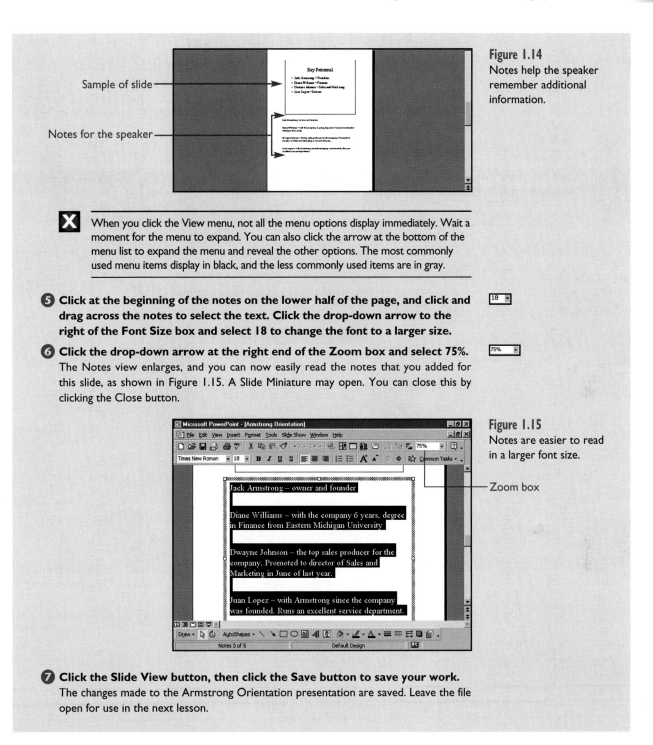

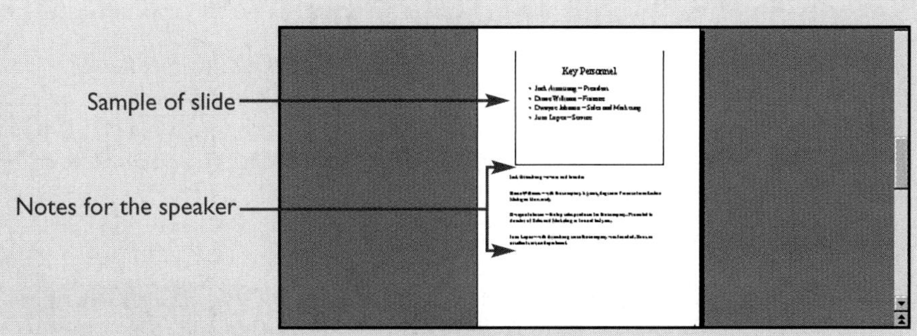

Figure 1.14
Notes help the speaker remember additional information.

When you click the View menu, not all the menu options display immediately. Wait a moment for the menu to expand. You can also click the arrow at the bottom of the menu list to expand the menu and reveal the other options. The most commonly used menu items display in black, and the less commonly used items are in gray.

5. **Click at the beginning of the notes on the lower half of the page, and click and drag across the notes to select the text. Click the drop-down arrow to the right of the Font Size box and select 18 to change the font to a larger size.**

6. **Click the drop-down arrow at the right end of the Zoom box and select 75%.**
   The Notes view enlarges, and you can now easily read the notes that you added for this slide, as shown in Figure 1.15. A Slide Miniature may open. You can close this by clicking the Close button.

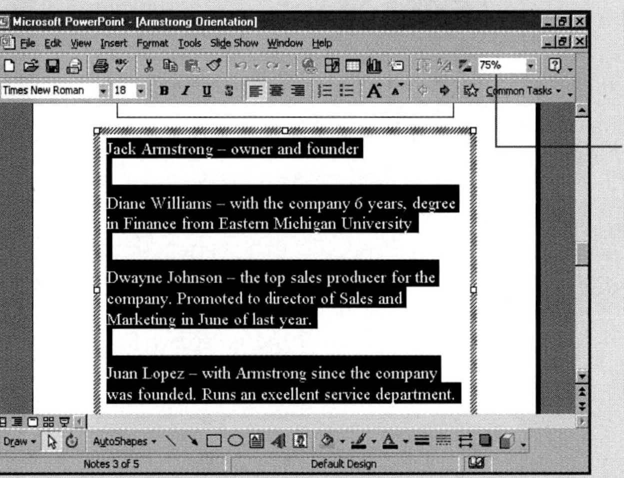

Figure 1.15
Notes are easier to read in a larger font size.

7. **Click the Slide View button, then click the Save button to save your work.**
   The changes made to the Armstrong Orientation presentation are saved. Leave the file open for use in the next lesson.

Moving from Slide to Slide

Slide view has three ways to move from slide to slide. You can use the Next Slide and Previous Slide buttons on the vertical scrollbar; you can click a specific slide icon on the left of the screen; or you can use the vertical scrollbar. If you click the scroll box and drag it up or down the vertical scrollbar, it reveals the slide number and the title as you scroll from one slide to the next. This is useful if you want to go to a specific slide when you know the title but not the slide number.

Lesson 5: Previewing the Slide Show

At any time during the creation process, you might want to see how the slides actually look when they are projected for an audience. The Slide Show view uses the entire screen for each slide. Running the slide show enables you to preview what your audience sees when you give your presentation, whether the presentation is given using a computer screen, a projection device, or overhead transparencies.

In this lesson, you preview your entire series of slides.

To Preview the Slide Show

1. **Click the scroll box and drag it to the top of the scrollbar to scroll to the first slide in the presentation (see Figure 1.16).**
The number of the active slide displays on the status bar at the bottom of the screen, and the icon for that slide is highlighted on the left side of the window.

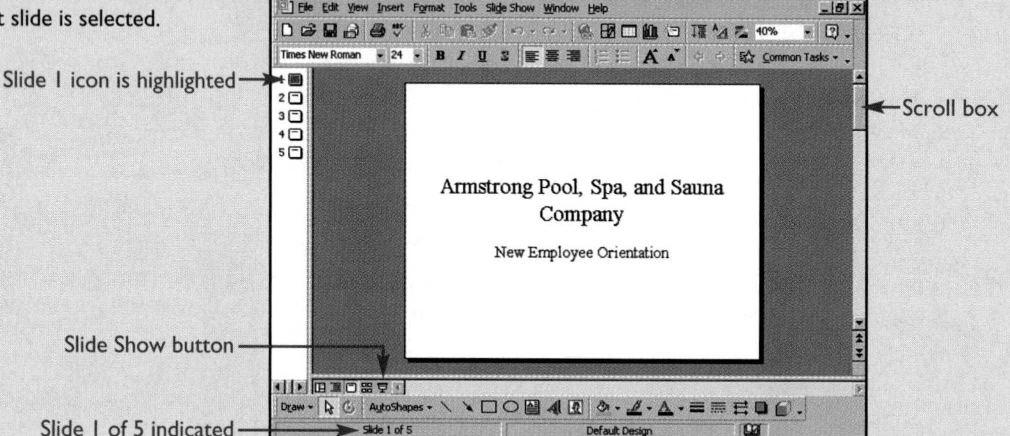

Figure 1.16
The first slide is selected.

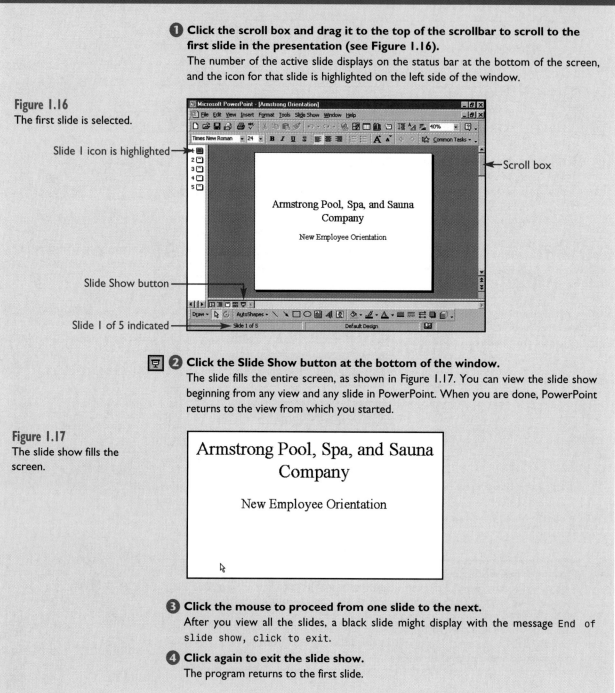

2. **Click the Slide Show button at the bottom of the window.**
The slide fills the entire screen, as shown in Figure 1.17. You can view the slide show beginning from any view and any slide in PowerPoint. When you are done, PowerPoint returns to the view from which you started.

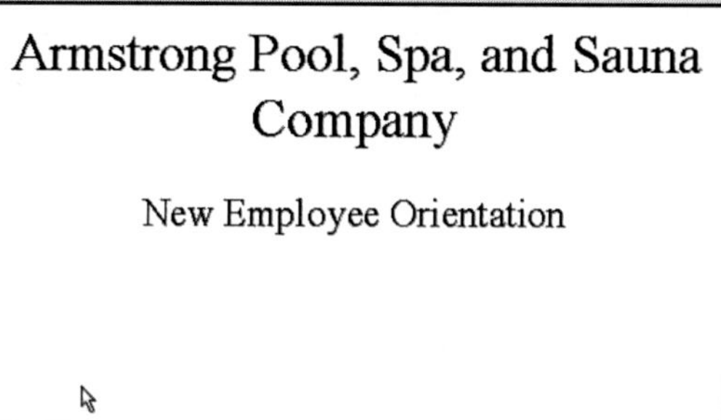

Figure 1.17
The slide show fills the screen.

3. **Click the mouse to proceed from one slide to the next.**
After you view all the slides, a black slide might display with the message `End of slide show, click to exit.`

4. **Click again to exit the slide show.**
The program returns to the first slide.

Displaying the Black Slide
The black slide might not display at the end of the slide show. You can set this option by choosing Tools, Options from the menu. Click the View tab on the Options dialog box, and click the check box next to End with black slide option under the Slide show section. A check mark indicates this feature is selected.

Exiting the Slide Show
Any time you are in the slide show, you can exit by pressing Esc.

Lesson 6: Printing an Outline

It is often useful to print an outline so that you can review the presentation and consider changes when you are away from a computer. Others might want to see your outline too, so they can make changes or respond to your suggested changes.

In this lesson, you print the outline for your Armstrong Orientation presentation.

To Print an Outline of the Presentation

1. **Choose File, Print from the menu.**
   The Print dialog box opens.
2. **Click the down arrow on the Print what box to display a list of options.**
   The Print dialog box gives you several options for controlling what prints (see Figure 1.18). In PowerPoint, you can print slides, handouts, note pages, or the outline. You can print any of these regardless of the view you are using currently.

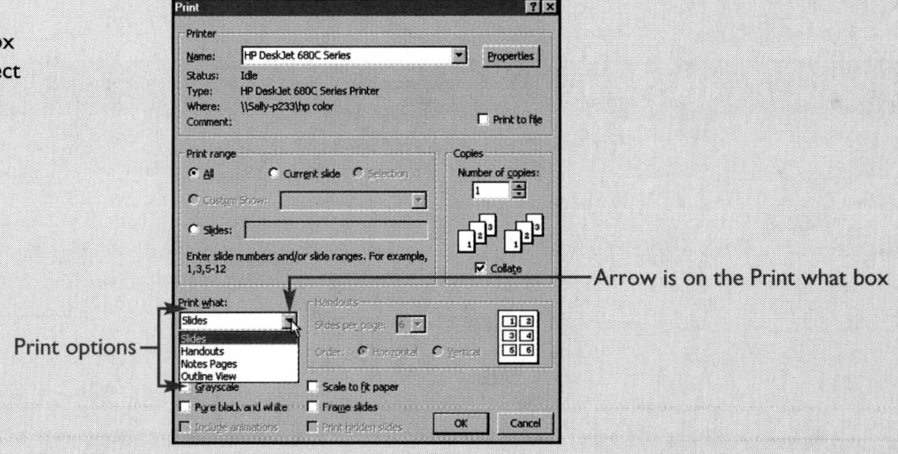

Figure 1.18
The Print dialog box enables you to select what you print.

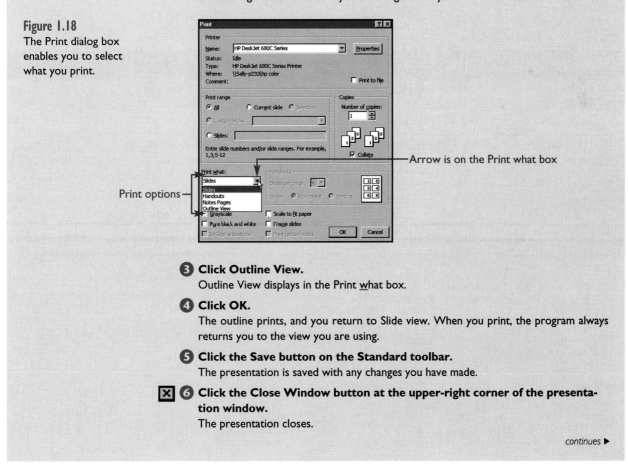

3. **Click Outline View.**
   Outline View displays in the Print what box.
4. **Click OK.**
   The outline prints, and you return to Slide view. When you print, the program always returns you to the view you are using.
5. **Click the Save button on the Standard toolbar.**
   The presentation is saved with any changes you have made.
6. **Click the Close Window button at the upper-right corner of the presentation window.**
   The presentation closes.

continues ▶

To Print an Outline of the Presentation (continued)

The Close Window button for the presentation is directly below the Close button for the PowerPoint program. If you accidentally close the program instead of the presentation, no harm is done. If you have not yet saved the presentation, you will be asked if you want to do so. Choose Yes to save your presentation.

7. **Click the Close button at the upper-right corner of the PowerPoint window to exit PowerPoint.**

Print Menu Option Is Better
In PowerPoint, it is best to use the File, Print menu option rather than the Print button on the Standard toolbar. The default setting for printing is to print all the slides. If you use color designs, pictures, or other art objects, printing slides will consume a lot of paper and ink. It is always best to go to the Print dialog box and select what you want to print.

Summary

In this project, you learned to enter and edit text in the Outline and Slide views of a presentation. You learned how to create speaker notes, print the outline, save the presentation, and view the slide show. You also learned how to move from one view to the next using the view buttons, and how to move from one slide to another.

You can extend your knowledge by using Help to look for the topics: `What can I create with PowerPoint`, or `How do I create a presentation`. Use the Office Assistant and type `Ways to get assistance while you work` to find out about using the Office Assistant for helpful hints in preparing a presentation. Look for the topic: `What's new in PowerPoint 2000` to find out more about the latest features that have been added to PowerPoint.

Checking Concepts and Terms

True/False

For each of the following, check *T* or *F* to indicate whether the statement is true or false.

__T __F **1.** To print an outline, select Outline view in the Print what box. [L6]

__T __F **2.** Each time you press Enter in Outline view, a new line of the outline is started that is the same level as the previous line. [L2]

__T __F **3.** To demote a heading, press Tab. [L2]

__T __F **4.** In Slide view, placeholders designate different preformatted areas on the slide. [L3]

__T __F **5.** You can add notes for the speaker in Slide view. [L4]

__T __F **6.** In Slide view, to move a placeholder, the mouse pointer must be in the shape of a two-headed arrow. [L3]

__T __F **7.** To change a slide's layout from a Bulleted List Slide to a Title Slide, click the Change Outline button on the Standard toolbar. [L3]

__T __F **8.** To move a placeholder on a slide, you first click the border of the placeholder. [L3]

__T __F **9.** To preview or display a slide so that it fills up the entire screen, click the Slide Show button. [L5]

__T __F **10.** If you are viewing the third slide in Slide view and click the Slide Show button, the slide show automatically starts at the first slide. [L5]

Multiple Choice

Circle the letter of the correct answer for each of the following.

1. Which components does PowerPoint's Normal view include? [L1]

a. Slide pane

b. Outline pane

c. Notes pane

d. all of the above

2. Which view is best to use when you want to focus on the flow of ideas from one topic to the next? [L3]

a. Slide view

b. Notes Pages view

c. Outline view

d. Slide Show view

3. How can you develop a presentation in PowerPoint? [Intro]

a. Create a new one completely from scratch.

b. Use the AutoContent Wizard.

c. Use a template.

d. any of the above

4. The main purpose of speaker notes is to _______________. [L4]

a. remind the speaker of additional information related to each particular slide

b. hand out to the audience

c. give the speaker something to hold during a presentation

d. provide an overview of the presentation

5. In Slide view, how do you move from one slide to another? [L4]

a. Click the slide icon displayed on the left side of the window.

b. Click and drag the scroll box to the slide you want.

c. Click the Next Slide or Previous Slide button repeatedly until the slide you want displays.

d. all of the above

Screen ID

Identify each of the items shown in Figure 1.19.

Figure 1.19

A. Normal View button

B. Slide icon

C. Font Size button

D. Outline pane

E. Outline View button

F. Slide View button

G. Slide Show button

H. Notes pane

I. Placeholder border

J. Common Tasks button

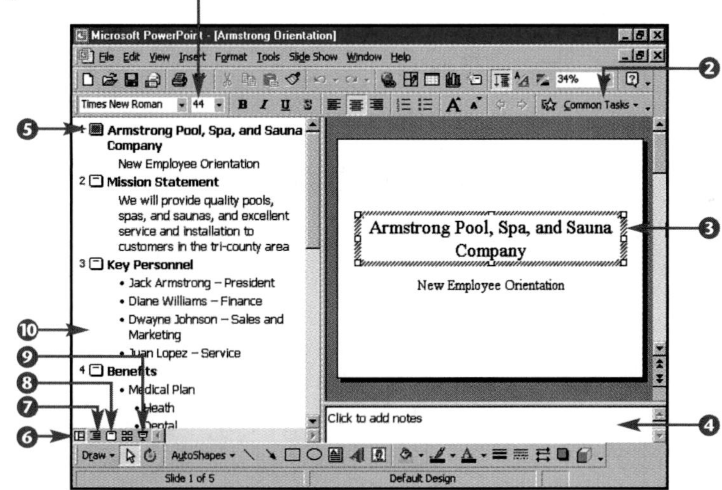

1. _______________
2. _______________
3. _______________
4. _______________
5. _______________
6. _______________
7. _______________
8. _______________
9. _______________
10. _______________

Discussion Questions

1. What presentations have you made to a group? What was the topic? What visual tools did you use to help you deliver your message?
2. When you speak before a group, do you find it useful to have notes? Do you prefer to have a complete speech written or are you comfortable with an outline? How would you use speaker notes?
3. Have you ever seen someone make a presentation facing a screen rather than the audience? What was your impression of that person's speaking style? Did it affect how well you could hear them?
4. What presentations have you seen that used a graphical presentation program? What did you like about it? What did you not like about it?
5. You have been introduced to three views that can be used for entering text in a presentation. When would you use each and why?

Skill Drill

Skill Drill exercises reinforce project skills. Each skill reinforced is the same, or nearly the same, as a skill presented in the project. Detailed instructions are provided in a step-by-step format.

In this set of Skill Drill exercises, you create a presentation from scratch, add speaker notes, save the file, view the slide show, and print the outline. Leave the file open from one Skill Drill to the next until you have completed all five exercises.

1. Launching PowerPoint and Starting a Blank Presentation

The first step in creating a new presentation is to launch PowerPoint and select the method you want to use to create the presentation. [L1]

To start your presentation, follow these steps:

1. Launch PowerPoint.
2. Choose Blank presentation.
3. Click OK to select the Title Slide layout.

2. Entering the Text for a Short Presentation

After you select the method you are going to use to create your presentation, you need to enter the text of the outline. Just like creating an outline for a paper, organize your topics in logical units. Start with the main ideas and add the subpoints under each topic. [L2]

To enter text in your presentation, follow these steps.

1. Click in the title placeholder and type the following title:

   `Sales Meeting`
2. Click the subtitle placeholder and type your name.
3. Click the Outline pane and press Enter, and then press Shift+Tab to move the title for the second slide. Use the Outline pane to enter the following information for the next three slides:

   `New Sales People`
   - `Bill Martin – Adrian`
   - `Mary Jones – Taylor`
   - `Sue Miller – Troy`

   `New Product Promotions`
   - `20% off on the Blue Deluxe Spa Group`
   - `15% rebate on Esther Williams Pools`
   - `10% reduction on all pool chemicals`

   `Monthly Sales Awards`
   - `Mary Shepherd 110% of goal`
   - `Charity Hawken 95% of goal`
   - `Robert Reid 93% of goal`
4. Print the outline.

3. Editing the Text

After you enter the rough draft of your outline, it is a good idea to review it for errors or omissions. You can correct the mistakes and enter any additional information that you want to the outline. [L3]

To edit the text of your outline, follow these steps:

1. Click the Slide View button and click the Slide 2 icon.
2. Change the name of the third person from `Sue` to `Susan`.
3. Click the Next Slide button and change the first item to `25% off on the Blue Deluxe Sauna`.
4. Go to the fourth slide and change the percent for `Charity` to `105%` and for `Robert` to `103%`.
5. Print the outline again.

4. Adding Notes for the Speaker and Saving the Presentation

Next you need to consider additional information that may be needed by the speaker in the form of notes. [L4]

To enter notes for the speaker and save your presentation, follow these steps:

1. Click the Outline View button.
2. Choose Slide 2.
3. Expand the Notes pane and enter the following information:

   `Bill Martin comes to us from Caesar Pools and Spas.`

   `Mary Jones is just out of college and has a degree in Marketing. She has worked in retailing for 5 years.`

   `Sue Miller is new to the area and has worked at several pool and spa related enterprises.`
4. Click View, Notes Page.
5. Select the text in the Notes area. Click the down arrow in the Font Size box and change the size to 18.
6. Save the presentation on your 3 1/2 floppy disk and name it `Sales Meeting`.

5. Previewing and Closing the Show

It is a good idea to review the slides frequently while you are creating them, so you can see how the ideas appear onscreen. This is sometimes a good way to look for errors or additional information that should be included. [L5]

To preview the slide show, follow these steps:

1. Switch to Slide view and scroll to the first slide.
2. Click the Slide Show button.
3. Click the mouse to advance through the slides and click again to return to Slide view.
4. Click the Save button.
5. Close the presentation and exit PowerPoint.

Challenge

Challenge exercises expand on or are somewhat related to skills presented in the lessons. Each exercise provides a brief narrative introduction followed by instructions, in a numbered step or bulleted list format, that are not as detailed as those in the Skill Drill section.

In the Challenge exercises, you create the outline for presentations based on your own experiences, or based on material supplied by the authors. Each exercise is independent of the other; they can be completed in any order. Use the view that you prefer as you work through these exercises. Try using different views to see which ones you like the best.

1. Creating a Presentation Based on a Report

Launch Word and open the Distance Education Technology file located on the CD that came with this book. Click the Print button to print the document. Close the file and close Word. [L1–2, 4]

This paper is about new technologies in distance education. Assume your instructor has to give a presentation on this topic to his or her colleagues and has asked you to create PowerPoint slides covering the presentation's main topics.

Create a PowerPoint presentation based on the Distance Education paper that includes a title slide and four to six slides that cover the following main topics:

- Overview
- Video Conferencing
- Computer-Based Communications
- Conclusion

In addition, make sure you do the following:

- See that each bulleted slide has at least three to five subpoints.
- Include a title slide with your name in the subtitle as `Prepared by:` *<your name>*.
- Print the outline.
- Save the presentation on your disk with the name `New Technologies`.

2. Creating a Presentation with Speaker Notes

In this exercise, you create a short, three- to four-slide presentation, on a procedure with which you are familiar and add notes for another speaker to use. The topic might be registering for classes, applying for a parking permit, changing a flat tire, or any procedure that requires specific steps that need to be followed in a particular order. [L2, 4]

1. Use the Normal view to create this presentation.
2. Add speaker notes to at least two slides, so someone else could deliver the presentation in your absence.
3. Save the presentation on your disk with an appropriate title.

3. Using Help to Learn About Importing an Outline from Word

You might have written an outline in Word and want to use it for a presentation. Rather than re-entering the text in PowerPoint, you can import the outline from Word. The Help program provides instructions on how to import an outline from Word. Locate and print this Help topic.

1. Click Help on the menu and select Microsoft PowerPoint Help.
2. Type `Importing an outline from Word`, and press ↵Enter.
3. Select Create a presentation from an existing outline. Then select Create a presentation by importing an outline from the Help window.
4. Read the explanation about importing an outline from Word.
5. Click the Print button to print the Help topic.
6. Close Help and close the Office Assistant.

4. Using Help to Check Styles

PowerPoint has a feature that automatically checks your presentation for consistency and style. It uses the lightbulb tip symbol to mark problems that it has identified. You might see the lightbulb appear periodically while you work, so it would be helpful to know more about the Style Checker feature.

1. Click Help on the menu and select Microsoft PowerPoint Help.
2. Type `style checker` and press ↵Enter.
3. Select `Check a presentation for style` and read the Help topic.
4. When you are done close Help.

Discovery Zone

Discovery Zone exercises require advanced knowledge of topics presented in *Essentials* lessons, application of skills from multiple lessons, or self-directed learning of new skills.

These Discovery Zone exercises are independent of each other and can be completed in any order. They help you learn how to create presentations using techniques other than the Blank presentation.

1. Using the AutoContent Wizard to Create a Presentation

The AutoContent Wizard can be useful in organizing a presentation for a specific purpose if you are uncertain what topics should be covered.

Launch PowerPoint and choose the AutoContent Wizard option from the PowerPoint dialog box. Follow the steps in the AutoContent Wizard dialog box to select your choice of presentation type, style, and options. Follow the basic content that is suggested for the type of presentation you chose; replace the words with your own words and content. Feel free to make up a product, company, or any other information needed to complete the outline. Print the outline, and save your presentation on your disk with the name `Wizard`.

2. Creating an Outline from a Word Document

If you write an outline in Word and want to use it for a presentation, rather than re-entering the text in PowerPoint, you can import the outline from Word. In the third Challenge exercise, you were directed to look up information about importing a Word document as an outline. If you did not complete that exercise, you might want to go back and do it now.

Launch Word. Locate and open the file named Computer Upgrade on the disc that came with your book. Review the file; close it; and close Word.

Launch PowerPoint. Refer to the information you printed in Challenge exercise 3 to complete this Discovery exercise. Follow the steps listed to import the Computer Upgrade Word file into PowerPoint. The Word document converts to a PowerPoint outline. Change the first slide to a title slide. In the subtitle area of the title slide, add **`Presented by`** ***<your name>***. Print the PowerPoint outline and save it on your disk with the name **`Computer Upgrade`**. Close the file, and close PowerPoint.

3. Creating a Presentation Outline

As you worked with PowerPoint in this project, you may have thought of several presentations that you wanted to create using the program. Use the knowledge you've gained to develop and print the outline for a presentation consisting of a title slide and one to three bulleted slides. Some topics you might consider are

- A presentation you would use in a business setting.
- A presentation you could use to promote an upcoming event.
- A presentation you could use to attract members to a nonprofit organization or club.

Print the outline; save and close the presentation.

Project 2

Improving the Design of the Presentation

Objectives

In this project, you learn how to

- ➤ **Open an Existing Presentation and Apply a Design**
- ➤ **Insert Clip Art**
- ➤ **Add a WordArt Image**
- ➤ **Add Text Objects**
- ➤ **Add Connector Lines Between Objects**
- ➤ **Print Audience Handouts**

Key terms introduced in this project include

- audience handouts
- clip art
- connector handles
- connectors
- design template
- guides
- sizing handles
- text box
- WordArt

Why Would I Do This?

When using PowerPoint to make a presentation, the text you use provides an outline for your topic. It helps to focus your audience on each subject and move them from one idea to the next. Adding a design to your presentation gives it a professional appearance and creates a sense of unity. You can emphasize points in your message by the careful use of images and sound. PowerPoint offers a wide selection of clip art and other graphics sources that you can use to enhance your presentation and increase the interest of your audience. You can also use images from other sources, such as a company logo that has been saved as a computer image. The judicious use of graphics adds to the visual appeal of your presentation and helps to keep the attention of your audience. ***WordArt*** is a special graphics program that turns text into a graphic drawing object. You can use different WordArt styles and effects to give pizzazz to a title on a slide. You can print WordArt horizontally, vertically, or at angle.

You have seen how you can add text to a PowerPoint presentation through the use of bulleted points, titles, and subtitles. At times, however, freeform text is advantageous. You will often want to add text boxes to describe charts, graphs, or illustrations. PowerPoint also enables you to add lines to connect two or more screen objects together, which can help demonstrate a process or flow of ideas.

Visual Summary

Visual Summary

By the time you complete this project, you will have added a design template and clip art to an existing presentation and added a new slide using WordArt, text boxes, and connectors. The results will look like Figures 2.1 and 2.2.

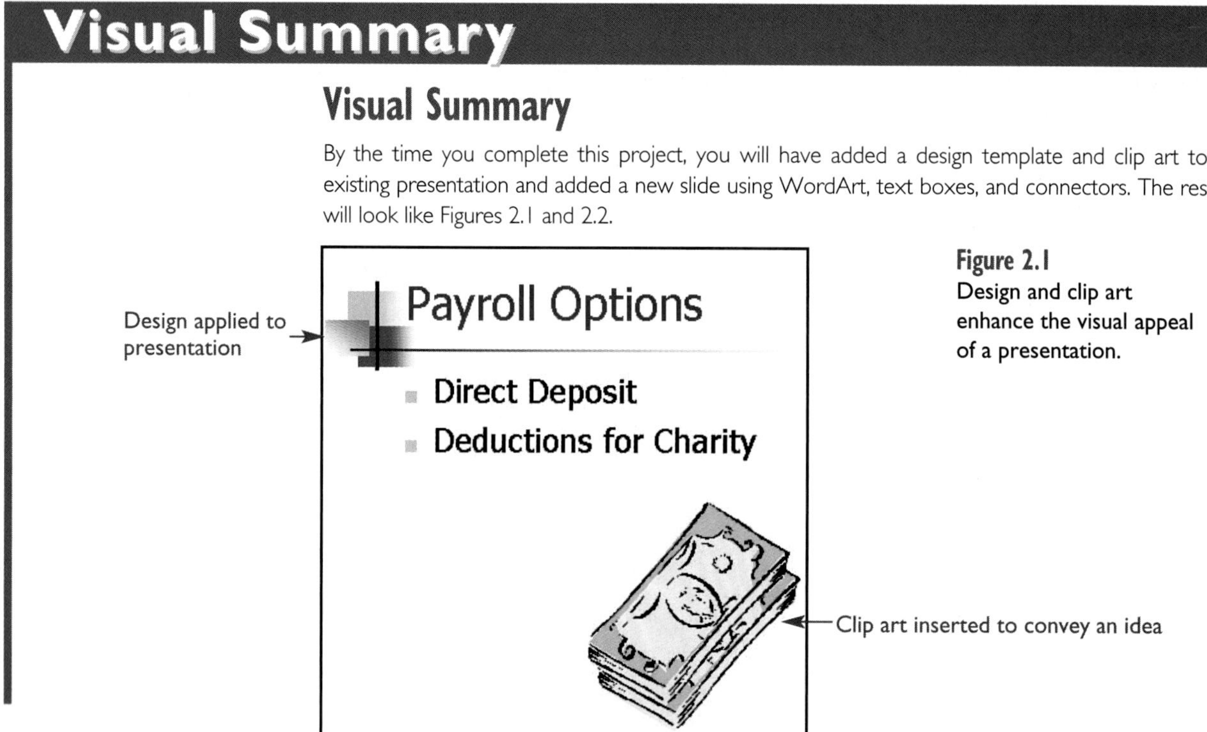

Figure 2.1
Design and clip art enhance the visual appeal of a presentation.

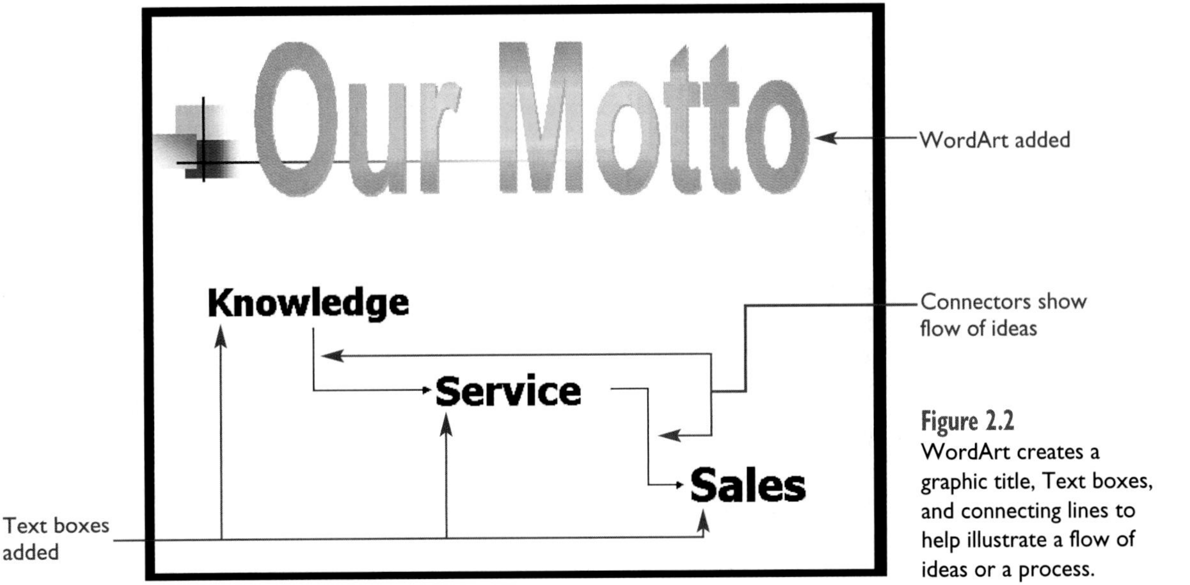

Figure 2.2
WordArt creates a graphic title, Text boxes, and connecting lines to help illustrate a flow of ideas or a process.

Lesson 1: Opening an Existing Presentation and Applying a Design

As with other applications, you will often work on a presentation in stages. After you create the basic outline, you are ready to add graphic elements. First, you need to open an existing presentation and save it with a new name; then you can begin to add various graphics.

PowerPoint offers a variety of design templates that you can use to enhance the overall appearance of your slides. A ***design template*** is a background design with preset graphics, fonts, alignments, bullet symbols, and other elements. Using a design template adds a professional appearance to your presentation. It is possible to design your own background patterns for a presentation, but it is much faster to pick one of the designs that come with the program. Several of the designs available in PowerPoint 2000 are also available to use as graphic elements in Word 2000. If you need to create a proposal to present to a client, documents you create in Word and slides you create in PowerPoint can use the same design to create a uniform appearance for the various components of the presentation.

When you select a design, it is important to know whether you will be using overhead transparencies, an LCD panel connected to a computer, or a high-resolution projection device. It is also useful to know some information about the size of the room and whether you will be able to have the lights on or will need to have the lights dimmed or off during your presentation. Dark backgrounds work well in a lighted room provided you have a high-resolution projection device. If you need to dim the lights, it is better to use a lighter background.

In this lesson, you apply one of PowerPoint's design templates to the Armstrong Orientation presentation. First, you open an existing file.

To Open an Existing Presentation and Apply a Design

1. **Launch PowerPoint.**
   PowerPoint opens and the PowerPoint dialog box displays.

2. **Click Open an existing presentation, and then click OK.**
   The Open dialog box opens, so you can select the file you want to use (see Figure 2.3). If the file you need has been opened recently, it shows in the list at the bottom of the PowerPoint dialog box, and you can select it from that list.

continues ▶

To Open an Existing Presentation and Apply a Design (continued)

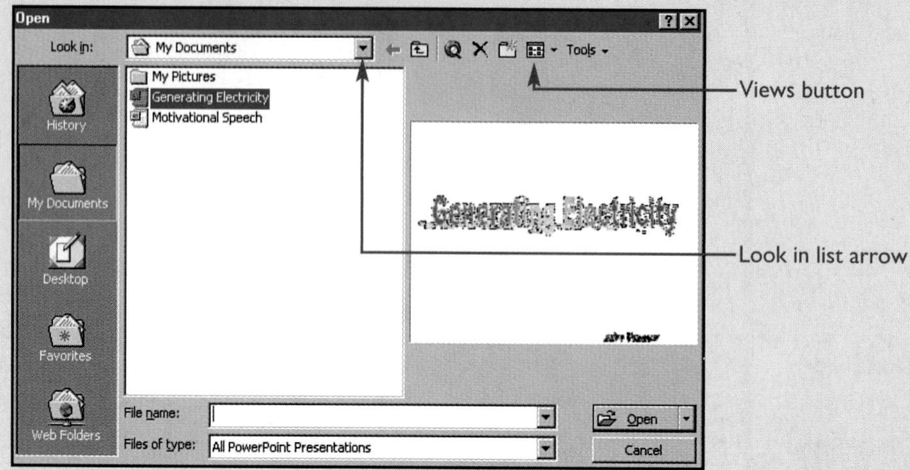

Figure 2.3
Use the Open dialog box to locate the file you want to open.

Files May Be Different

The files you see on your screen will be different from the files listed in the figure. Also, depending on the option selected on your Open dialog box, it might show a list of files on the left side and a preview of the selected presentation on the right side. To see a preview, click the drop-down arrow on the Views button and select Preview.

3. **Insert the CD that came with this book in the CD drive. Click the arrow on the right of the Look in list and select the CD drive. (Ask your instructor for the letter that designates the CD on your computer.) Double-click the PowerPoint folder.**

4. **Navigate to the `PO-0201` file, and then click Open.**
   PowerPoint opens the file in Normal view, the view it was in when it was saved. The name of the file shows in the title bar, and the first slide displays. This presentation is similar to the one you created in PowerPoint Project 1, "Getting Started with PowerPoint," (see Figure 2.4).

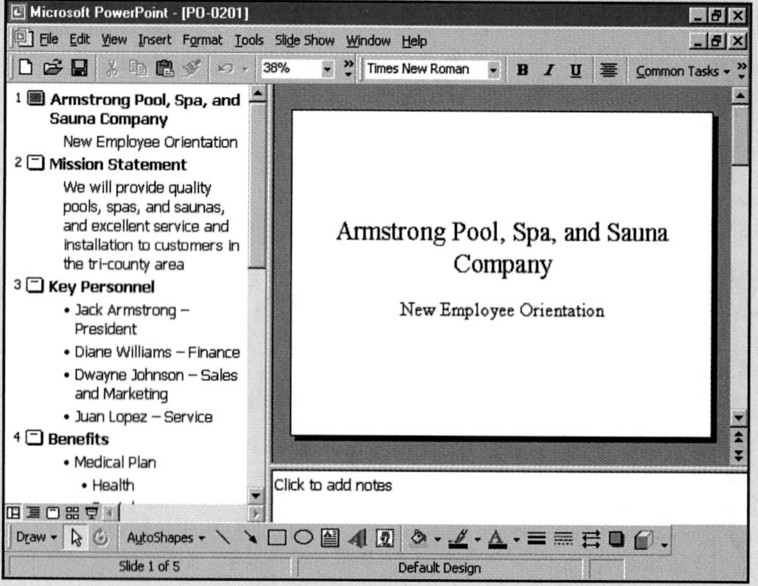

Figure 2.4
The presentation opens in Normal view.

5 Click File and Save As from the menu bar.
The Save As dialog box opens. To preserve the original file in case you need to return to it, save this file with a new name.

6 Type `Armstrong Employee Orientation` in the File name box. Change the Save in box to the 3 1/2 Floppy (A:) drive. (Make sure a disk is inserted in the A: drive.) Click the Save button.
The presentation is saved on the floppy disk, and the new name displays in the title bar at the top of the window.

7 Click the Common Tasks button and select Apply Design Template from the three options.
The Apply Design Template dialog box opens and displays the Artsy design, which is the first one on the list. The left side of the dialog box shows a list of design templates, and the right side shows a preview of the selected design (see Figure 2.5). Take a moment to look at some of the different design options to see what is available.

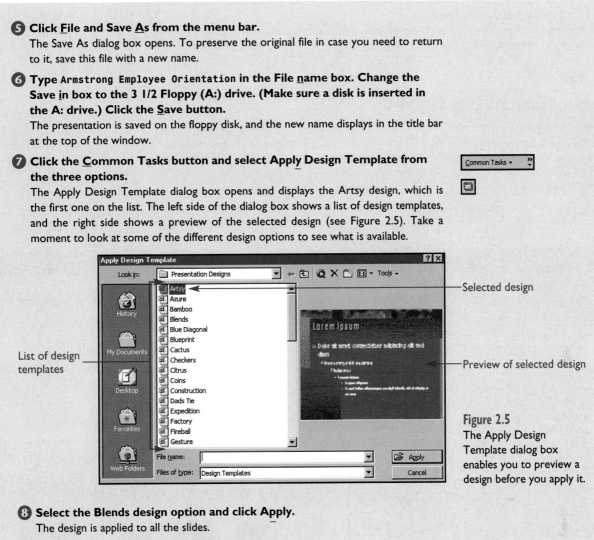

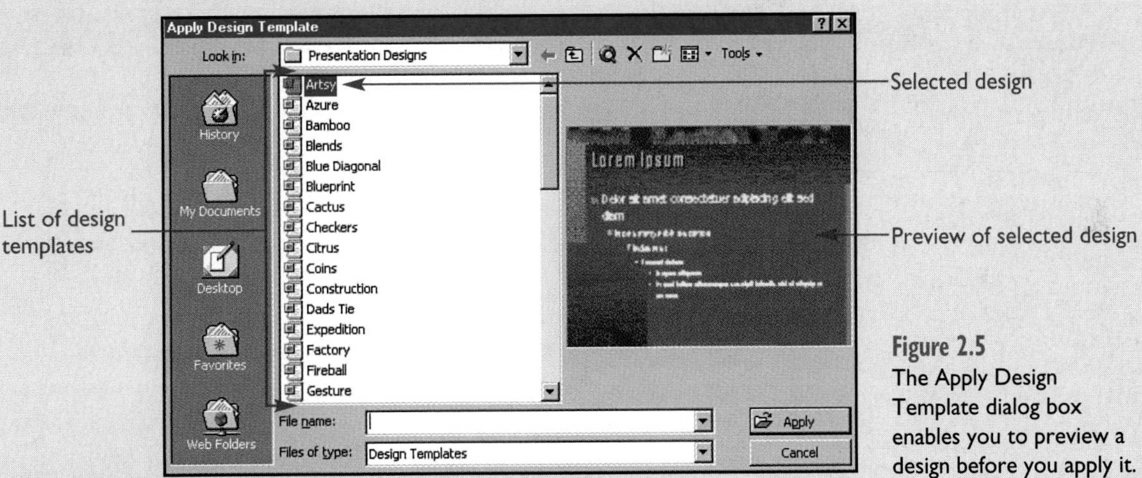

Figure 2.5
The Apply Design Template dialog box enables you to preview a design before you apply it.

8 Select the Blends design option and click Apply.
The design is applied to all the slides.

9 Click the Slide Show button to view the slides.
When you are done, click to end the slide show and return to Normal view (see Figure 2.6). Leave the file open for use in the next lesson.

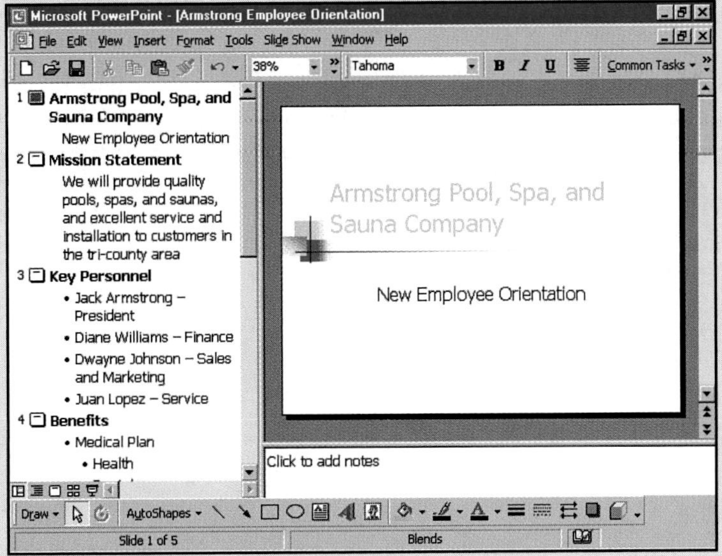

Figure 2.6
The design is applied to all the slides.

Create a Custom Design
You can also create a custom design to use with your presentations. Each design is available in a variety of color combinations and can be customized to your preferences.

Lesson 2: Inserting Clip Art

PowerPoint comes with a wide variety of predefined images. This collection of images includes photographs, drawings, and other types of graphics that you can clip and add to your presentation, hence the name ***clip art***. You can also purchase collections of clip art to use. You might want to insert a clip art image to add visual interest, emphasize an important point, add humor, or add a graphic expression of an idea. Clip art is fun and easy to use.

In this lesson, you add a piece of clip art to the Payroll Options slide; then you move and resize the clip art image.

To Add Clip Art

1. **Click the Slide View button, and then click the icon for Slide 5 on the left side of your window.**
The Payroll Options slide displays in Slide view.

2. **Click Insert, Picture, and Clip Art from the menu bar.**
The Insert ClipArt dialog box opens. The categories of clip art display (see Figure 2.7). You select a category of clip art to peruse and then select the particular clip art you want to include from the images that display.

The All Categories button can be used to return to this screen

Clip art categories

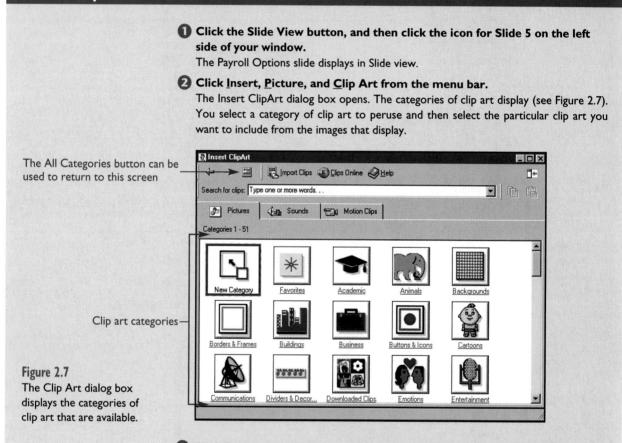

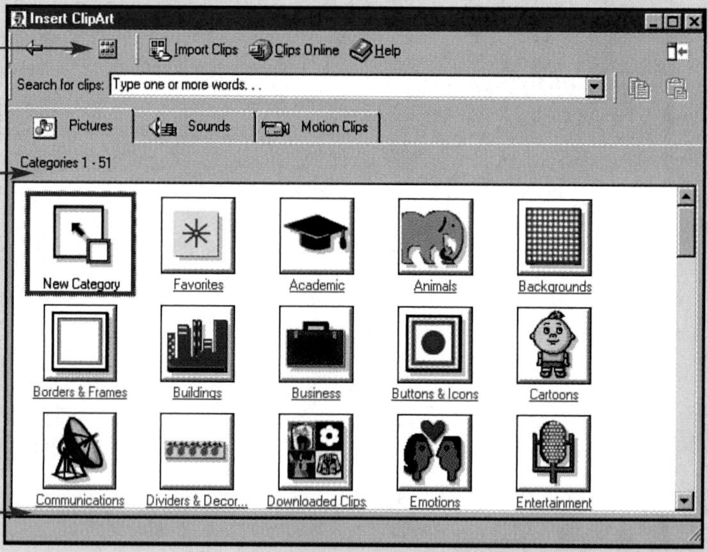

Figure 2.7
The Clip Art dialog box displays the categories of clip art that are available.

3. **Click Business; scroll down one screen and click the image of the stack of money in the middle of the row.**
The image is selected and a pop-up menu with four buttons displays (see Figure 2.8).

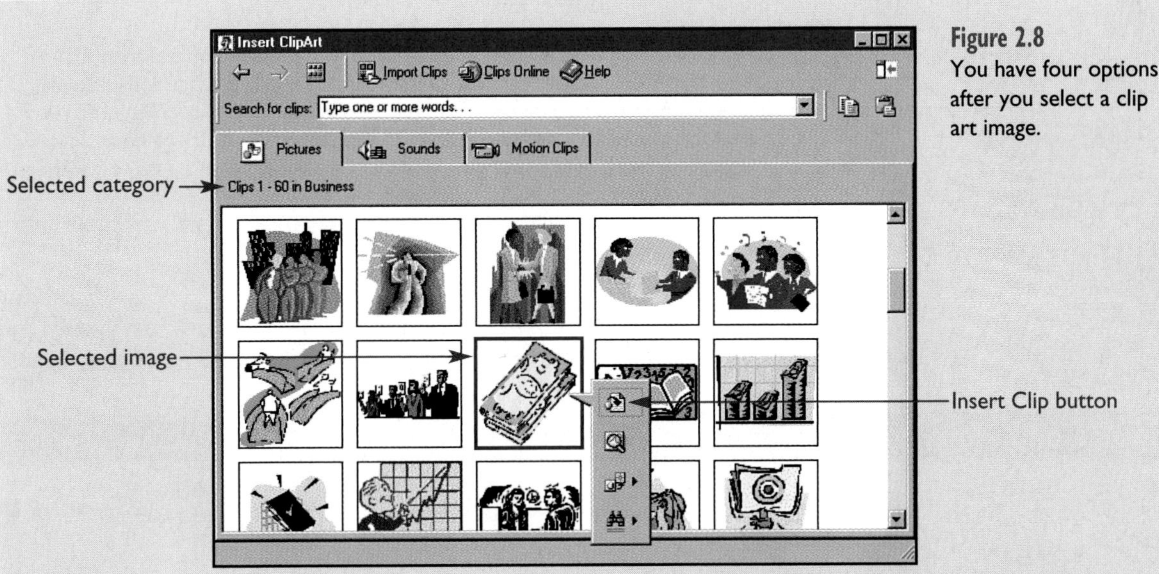

Figure 2.8
You have four options after you select a clip art image.

❹ **Click the first button, Insert Clip, on the pop-up menu. Click the Close button in the Insert Clipart window.**

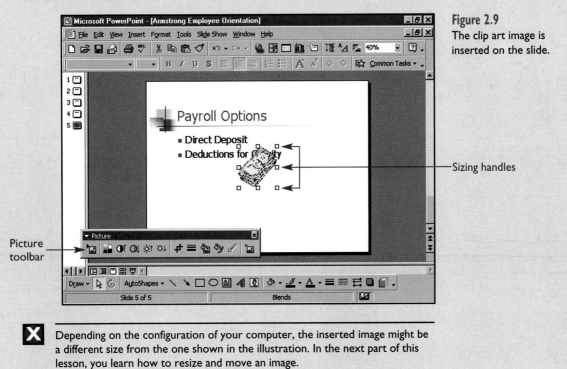

The picture is placed on the slide, as shown in Figure 2.9. ***Sizing handles*** are small square boxes surrounding an object that you use to resize it. You learn more about sizing handles in the next part of this lesson when you resize and move the clip art. The Picture toolbar might also display on your screen. If it does not appear, don't be concerned. The toolbar is not used in this lesson.

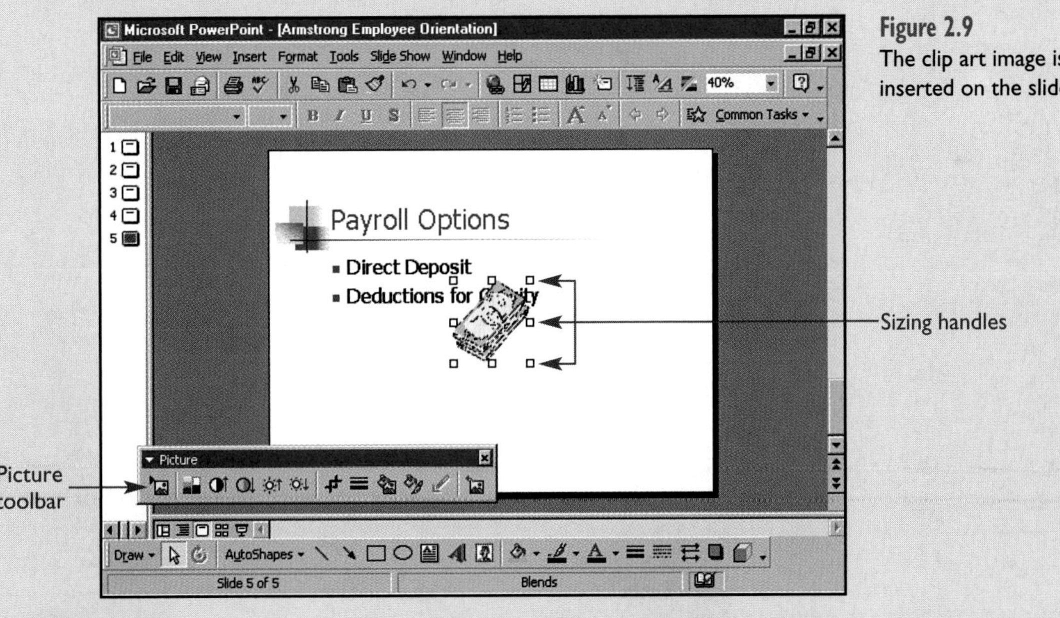

Figure 2.9
The clip art image is inserted on the slide.

Depending on the configuration of your computer, the inserted image might be a different size from the one shown in the illustration. In the next part of this lesson, you learn how to resize and move an image.

Adding Images

If you know you want to include another image, you can insert multiple clip art images before closing the Insert ClipArt window. Simply choose another image and click Insert Clip from the shortcut menu. You can also click the Change to Small Screen button to reduce the size of the Insert ClipArt window. This action positions the window to one side of your screen, so you can see the slide you are working on or change to another slide. When you are done inserting clip art, close the window

When you insert a clip art image, it might not be the size you want or in the location you want. You can increase or decrease the size of a clip art image by using the sizing handles that appear around it when it is selected. You can then move the image to the best location on the slide. In the next part of this lesson, you resize and move the image you inserted on the Payroll Options slide.

To Resize and Move an Image

1. **Close the Picture toolbar. Move the pointer to the lower-right corner sizing handle.**
   The pointer changes into a two-headed arrow.
2. **Click and drag the corner handle down and to the right until the image is about twice its original width and height.**

Using Corner Handles to Resize

You could use any of the corner handles to resize the picture. When resizing a picture, it is best to use one of the corner handles rather than a side handle. Side handles change the proportion of the picture, thereby distorting it.

3. **Move the pointer onto the picture.**
   The pointer turns into a four-headed arrow. You can move the entire picture when the pointer is this shape.
4. **Click and drag the picture to the lower middle of the slide, as shown in Figure 2.10.**
   A dotted outline shows the proposed placement of the image.

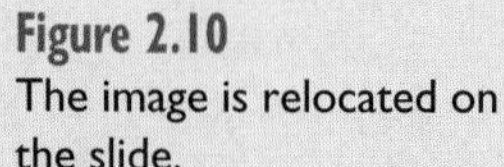

Figure 2.10
The image is relocated on the slide.

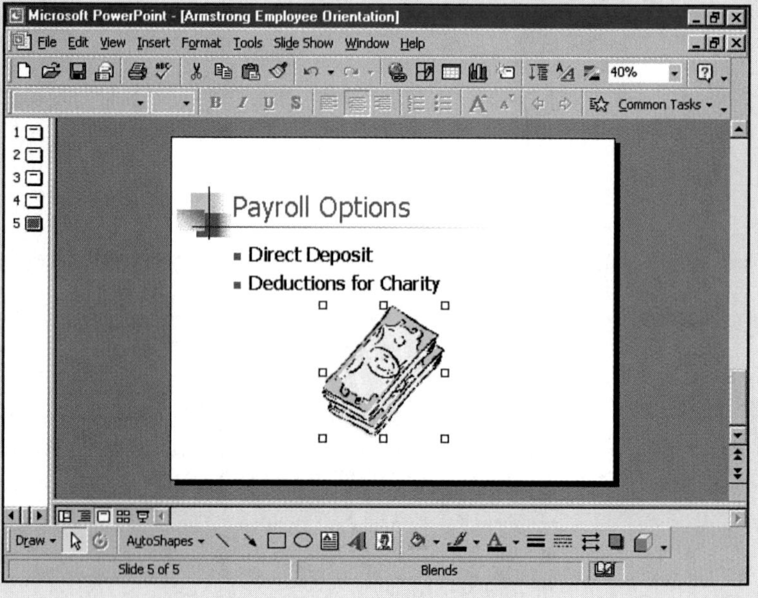

5 **Click outside the image to deselect the clip art.**

6 **Click the Previous Slide button to move to Slide 4. Insert a clip art image of your choice that would be relevant to medical benefits.**
If necessary, refer to Steps 2 through 4 in Lesson 2 to insert the clip art image.

7 **Resize the image as needed and reposition it in the right side of the slide.**
The image shown in Figure 2.11 was found in the Healthcare & Medicine category.

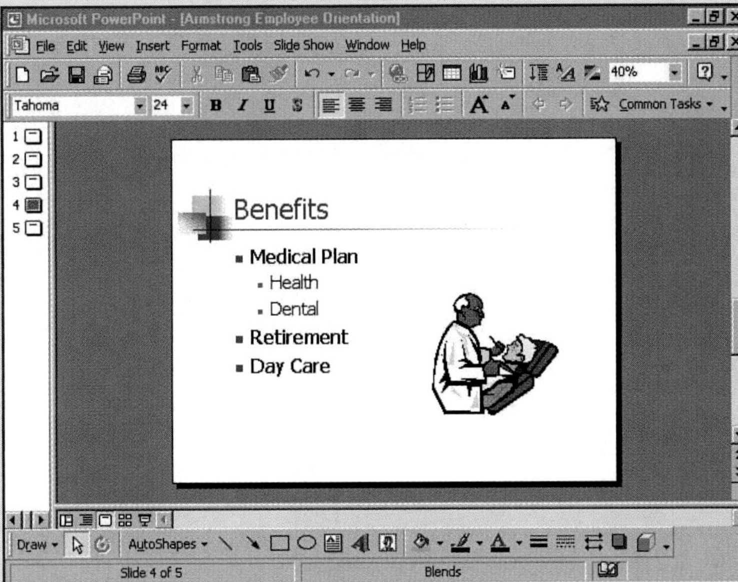

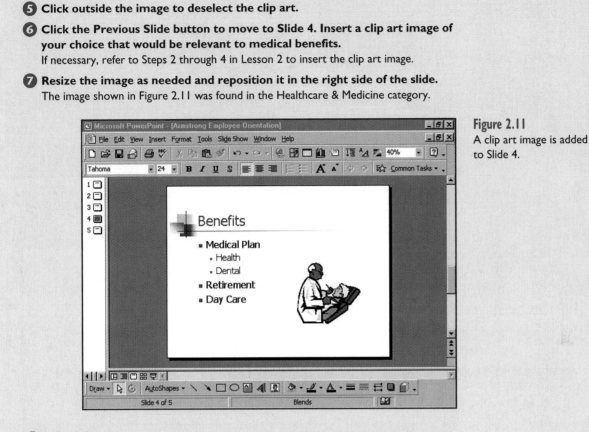

Figure 2.11
A clip art image is added to Slide 4.

8 **Click Save to save your work. Leave the file open for use in the next lesson.**

Lesson 3: Adding a WordArt Image

The title text on a title slide is restricted to standard font shapes and sizes. You can use some highlighting techniques, such as bold and italic. If you want to create customized titles, however, PowerPoint has a very powerful tool called ***WordArt*** that enables you to be very creative with text. WordArt is a program that creates text as a drawing object, enabling you to add special colors, shadows, and 3D effects. WordArt is not restricted to slide titles, but that is where WordArt objects are most often used.

In this lesson, you create a WordArt object for a conclusion slide for the employee orientation. Then you move and resize the image using the same techniques that you learned working with clip art.

To Insert WordArt

1 **Click the Next Slide button on the vertical scrollbar to move to Slide 5.**
Slide 5 displays. Now you add a new slide.

2 **Click the Common Task button, and click the New Slide button.**
The New Slide dialog box displays.

3 **Click the Blank slide option, and click OK.**
A new blank slide displays.

4 **Click the Insert WordArt button on the Drawing toolbar.**
The WordArt Gallery dialog box displays (see Figure 2.12).

continues ▶

To Insert WordArt (continued)

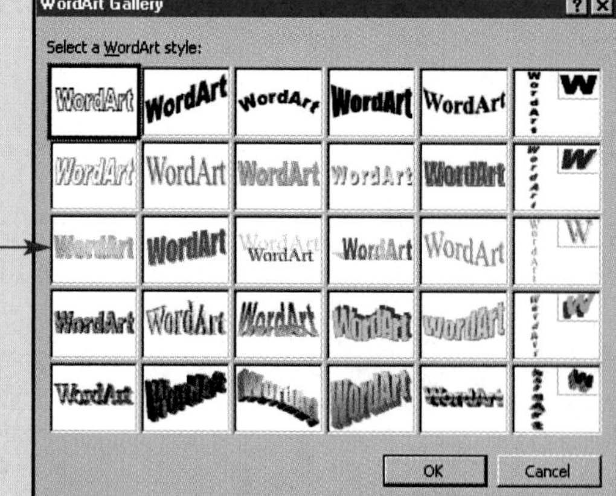

Figure 2.12
Use the WordArt Gallery to select the WordArt style.

5 Select the third option in the first column. Click OK.
The Edit WordArt Text dialog box opens with the phrase `Your Text Here` highlighted (see Figure 2.13).

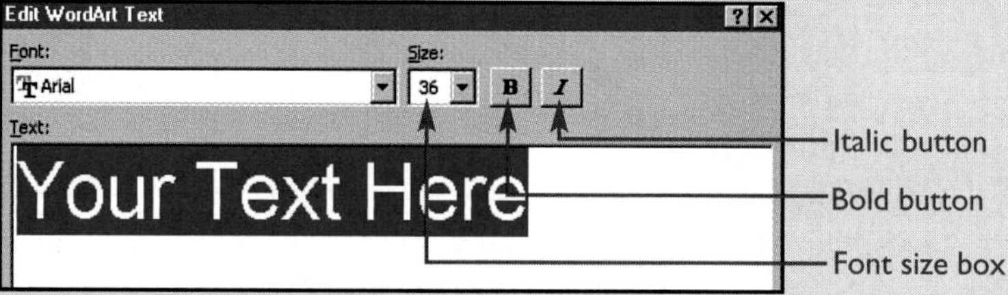

Figure 2.13
Use the Edit WordArt Text dialog box to enter the text for the WordArt image.

6 Type `Our Motto`, and then change the font size to 72 points. Click the Bold button. Click OK.
The WordArt drawing object is placed in the center of the blank slide, and the WordArt toolbar opens (see Figure 2.14).

The WordArt toolbar might display as a floating toolbar on your screen. If you want to dock it, double-click the blue title bar. The toolbar docks near the bottom of the screen. You can also click and drag on the title bar to place the toolbar in a location of your choice on the screen. This toolbar opens and closes automatically, depending on whether the WordArt image is selected or not.

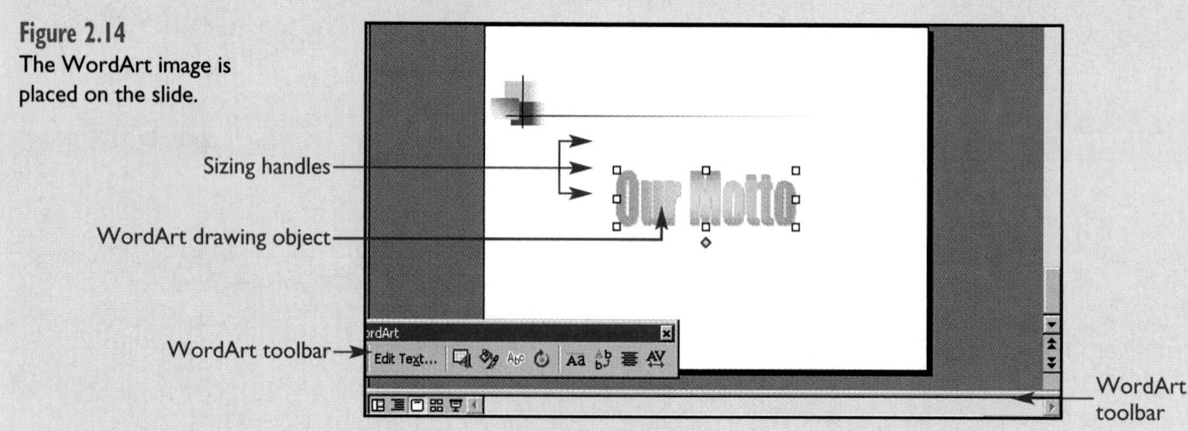

Figure 2.14
The WordArt image is placed on the slide.

You changed the font size from 36 points to 72 points in the preceding lesson, but after looking at the results, you can see that the title is still not large enough. You could go back and change the font size, or you could enlarge the object in the same way you enlarge any drawing object. This way you can make the title the exact size you want it. The same techniques that you used with clip art work with WordArt and with any other drawing or graphic object.

To Move and Resize WordArt

1. **Make sure the WordArt object is selected.**
   The sizing handles surrounding the image indicate that it is selected. If necessary, click the image to select it.
2. **Move the mouse pointer onto the image until the pointer becomes a four-headed arrow. Click and drag the image to center it in the top part of the slide.**
   As you move the image, dotted lines known as ***guides*** display to indicate the boundary and placement of the WordArt object.
3. **Click the sizing handle in the lower-right corner. Click and drag down and to the right. Then click the sizing handle in the upper-left corner and drag up and to the left.**
   The guides display to show the new size of the image.
4. **Use the sizing handles in the middle of the bottom and then in the middle of the side of the image to increase the size of the image until it looks like the one in Figure 2.15. If necessary, move the image again to center it on the slide.**

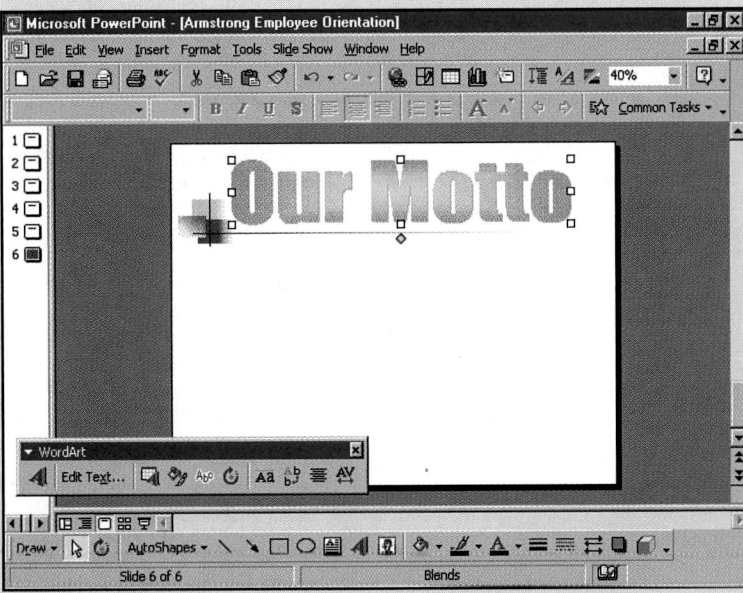

Figure 2.15
The WordArt image is enlarged and centered on the slide.

5. **Click Save to save the changes. Leave the file open for use in the next lesson.**

Lesson 4: Adding Text Objects

In the previous lesson, you used WordArt to create a fancy title for a slide. Oftentimes, however, you will want to add text to a slide in addition to the title. A ***text box*** is a drawing object that you use to add general-purpose free-form text. You use these drawing objects to add text that you can place anywhere on a slide, so you can resize the text just like you can clip art or WordArt.

In this lesson, you add three text boxes to the slide with the WordArt object.

To Add Text Boxes

1 Click the Text Box button on the Drawing toolbar. The pointer changes shape. Position the pointer on the left side of the slide under the WordArt, and click and drag down and to the right until you have a text box similar to the one shown in Figure 2.16. Release the mouse button.

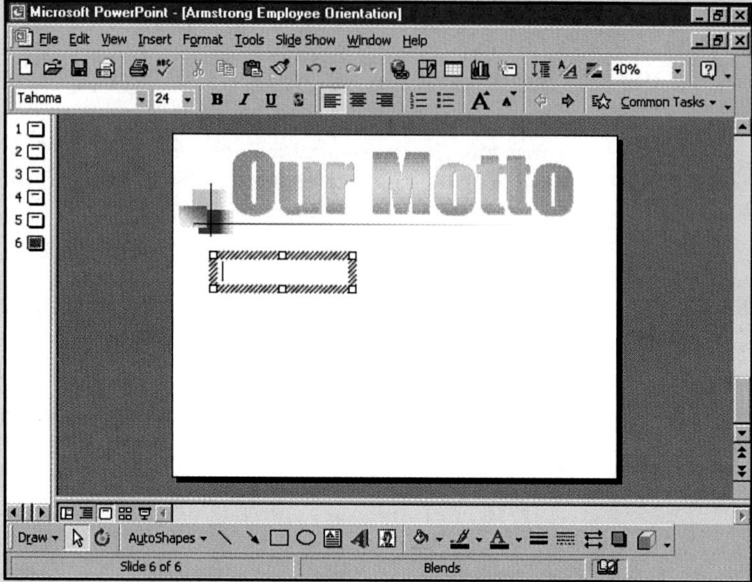

Figure 2.16
A text box is placed on the slide.

Don't worry if your text box is not in exactly the same place or exactly the same shape. You can move and resize it later. If you want to start over, click the edge of the text box and press Del. The text box is removed, so you can try again.

2 Change the font size to 36 point using the Font Size drop-down list. Click the Bold button. Type `Knowledge` in the text box.
The results should look like the text box in Figure 2.17.

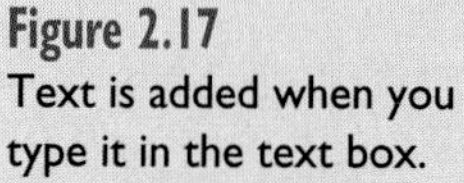

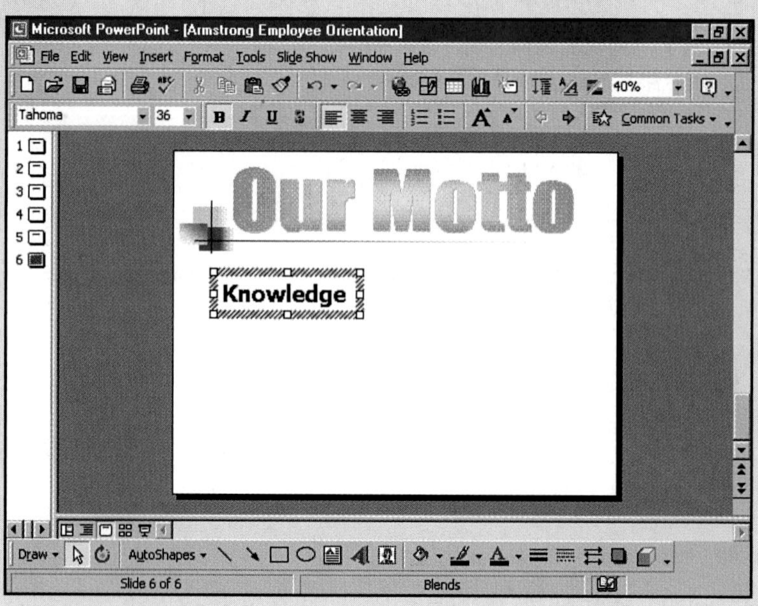

Figure 2.17
Text is added when you type it in the text box.

If you do not make the text box long enough, the word might wrap onto a second line. To fix this, click and drag the middle handle on the right side and enlarge the text box. You can reduce the size of a text box in the same way.

3. **Create a second text box. Change the font to 40 point bold and type `Service`, as shown in Figure 2.18. Adjust the size of the text box as necessary.**
4. **Create a third text box, as shown in Figure 2.18. Change the font to 44 point bold, and type `Sales`. Adjust the size of the text box as necessary.**

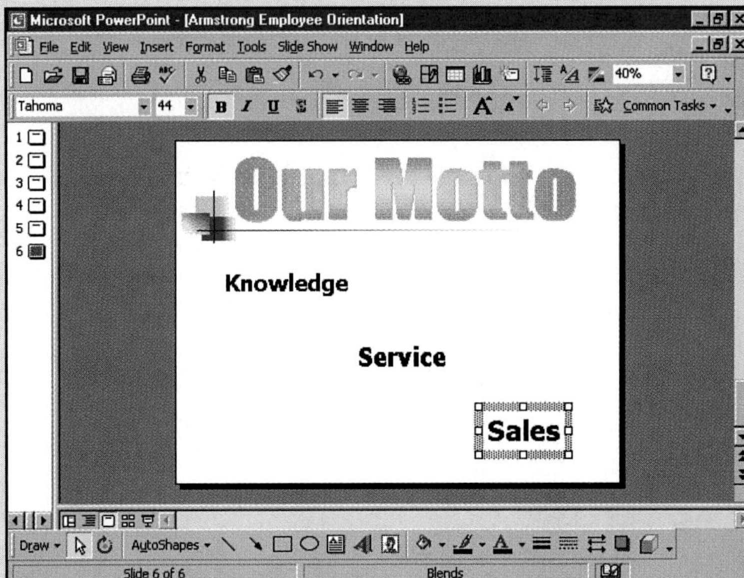

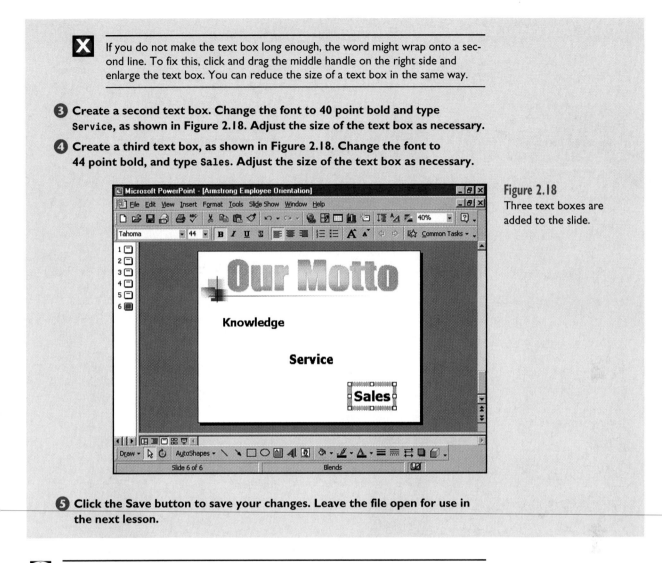

Figure 2.18
Three text boxes are added to the slide.

5. **Click the Save button to save your changes. Leave the file open for use in the next lesson.**

Changing Text in Text Boxes
When using a text box, you can type the text first and change the font characteristics, such as size, style, color, or emphasis, later. To change all the text in a text box, click the border of the box, so the border changes to dots instead of hash marks. To change a specific word, select the word and make the changes.

Lesson 5: Adding Connector Lines Between Objects

You can use some of the drawing tools on the Drawing toolbar to draw lines and arrows on PowerPoint slides. One of the problems with drawing your own arrows is that it is often difficult to get the ends in exactly the right location. ***Connectors*** are lines that link figures together. The ends automatically go from a handle on one object to a handle on another. You also have many more shape and design options with connectors.

In this lesson, you add connectors between the text boxes you added in the previous task.

To Add Connector Lines Between Objects

AutoShapes ▾ **1 Click the AutoShapes button on the Drawing toolbar. Select Connectors.**
The Connectors toolbar displays (see Figure 2.19).

Figure 2.19
The AutoShapes button reveals many different collections of AutoShapes that you can use.

AutoShapes menu

AutoShapes button

Connectors toolbar

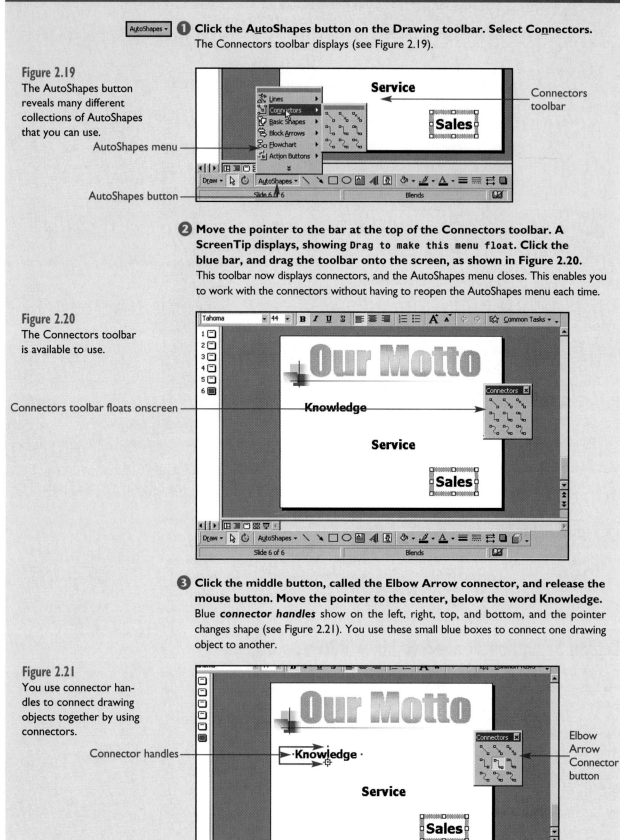

2 Move the pointer to the bar at the top of the Connectors toolbar. A ScreenTip displays, showing `Drag to make this menu float`. Click the blue bar, and drag the toolbar onto the screen, as shown in Figure 2.20.
This toolbar now displays connectors, and the AutoShapes menu closes. This enables you to work with the connectors without having to reopen the AutoShapes menu each time.

Figure 2.20
The Connectors toolbar is available to use.

Connectors toolbar floats onscreen

3 Click the middle button, called the Elbow Arrow connector, and release the mouse button. Move the pointer to the center, below the word Knowledge.
Blue ***connector handles*** show on the left, right, top, and bottom, and the pointer changes shape (see Figure 2.21). You use these small blue boxes to connect one drawing object to another.

Figure 2.21
You use connector handles to connect drawing objects together by using connectors.

Connector handles

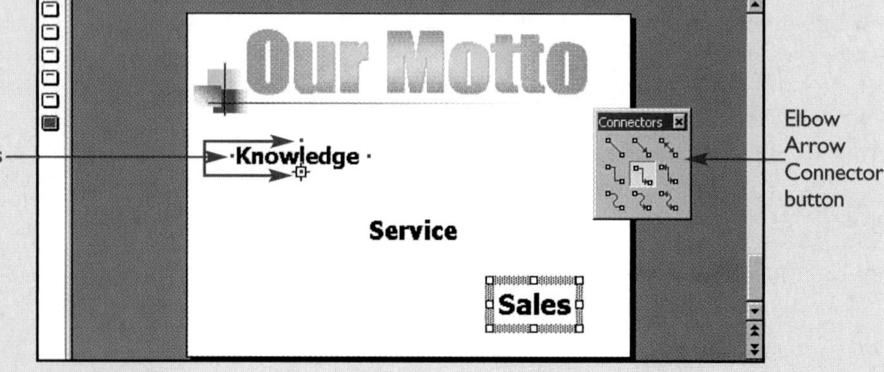

4 **Place the pointer on top of the bottom handle of the word `Knowledge`. Click and drag a connector to the handle that is to the left of the word `Service`. Release the mouse button.**
A connector with handles displays. (*Note*: As you drag the connector, the handles display around the word.)

5 **Click the Elbow Arrow Connector button again. Place the pointer on top of the right handle next to the word `Service`. Drag a connector to the left handle next to the word `Sales` and release the mouse button. The final slide should look like the one shown in Figure 2.22.**

6 **Click the Save button to save your changes. Click the Close button on the Connectors toolbar. Leave the file open for use in the next lesson.**

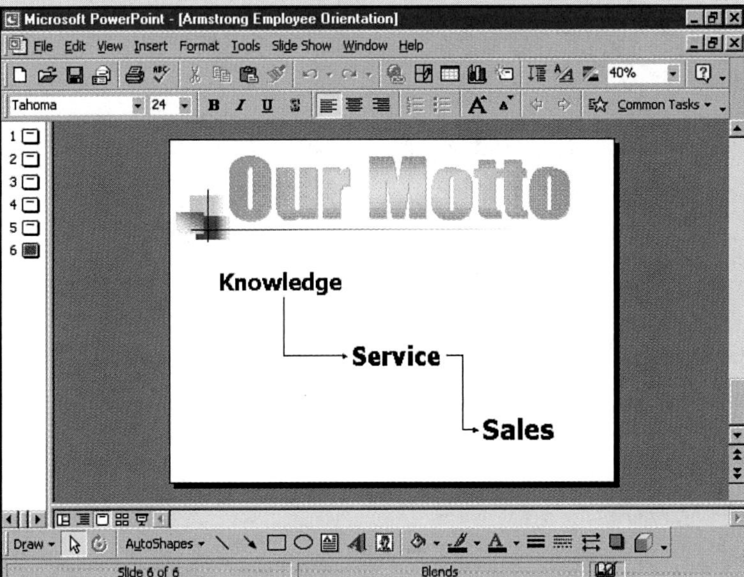

Figure 2.22
The three text boxes are connected.

Learn More About Connectors
To learn more about using connectors, look in Help to learn how connectors can be changed from one object to another.

Lesson 6: Printing Audience Handouts

Audience handouts are printouts that display images of your slides or the outline. When you give your audience handouts, it frees them to concentrate on the presentation and participate in a discussion rather than writing down the bulleted points on your slides. Participants can add clarifying information to the handouts, or jot down questions they might have. Handouts are useful in a teaching or training environment where specific facts are provided.

In this lesson, you print an audience handout that displays all six slides on one page.

To Print Audience Handouts

1 **Choose File, Print from the menu.**
The Print dialog box opens.

2 **Click the down arrow on the Print what box and select Handouts.**

continues ▶

To Print Audience Handouts (continued)

3. **Click the Slides per page box in the Handouts area and select 6.**
4. **Check to make sure the Grayscale and Frame slides check boxes are selected, as shown in Figure 2.23.**
   The frames option adds a border around each slide, which gives it a finished look.

Figure 2.23
The handouts are selected to print.

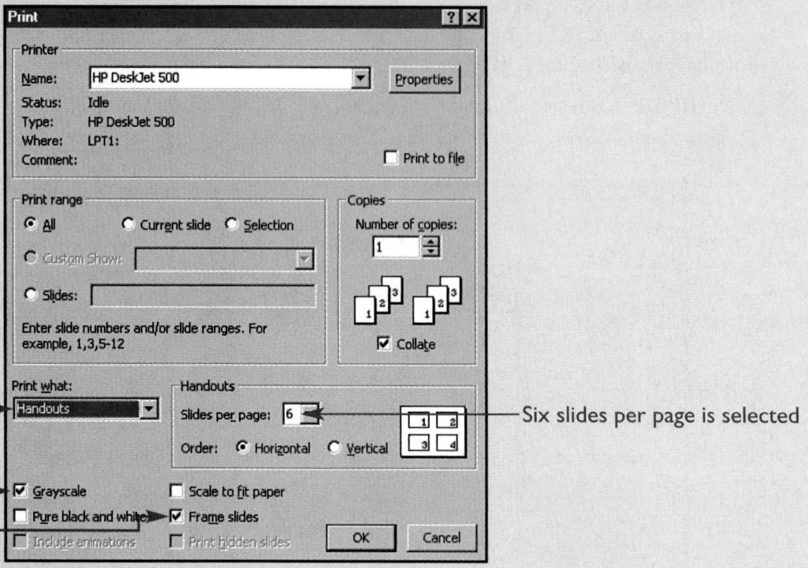

Handouts is selected
Six slides per page is selected
Grayscale is selected
Frame slides is selected

5. **Click OK to print the handouts.**
6. **Click the Save button to save your changes. Click the Close Window button to close the presentation.**

Summary

In this project, you learned how to add and resize clip art; create, move, and resize WordArt; and add text boxes and connectors. You also learned how to open an existing presentation, save it with a new name, and print audience handouts.

You can extend your learning by exploring some of the other AutoShapes and drawing tools. For example, you can add an oval or a rectangle to a presentation and type text in the shape. Try it and see how it is different from a text box. You could also use a Callout shape that is found under AutoShapes. This is a different style drawing object that works like a text box.

Checking Concepts and Terms 

True/False

For each of the following, check *T* or *F* to indicate whether the statement is true or false.

__T __F **1.** If you save a presentation with a new name, the new name displays in the title bar. [L1]

__T __F **2.** When you open an existing presentation, it always displays first in Slide view. [L1]

__T __F **3.** When you insert clip art, the program automatically adjusts the size to the available empty space on the slide, and places the image in that space. [L2]

__T __F **4.** The best way to change the size of a clip art image without distorting it is to click and drag one of the side sizing handles rather than a corner handle. [L2]

__T __F **5.** Clip art is grouped into categories to make it easier to locate the appropriate image. [L2]

__T __F **6.** Text typed in as WordArt is really a drawing object. [L3]

__T __F **7.** Square handles around the outside of a WordArt object indicate that the object has been selected. [L3]

__T __F **8.** Guides display to show you the new size or placement of a WordArt object. [L3]

__T __F **9.** You can increase the length of a text box by dragging one of its sizing handles. [L4]

__T __F **10.** Audience handouts are valuable because your audience does not have to write down what is on the slide and can concentrate on what you are saying. [L6]

Multiple Choice

Circle the letter of the correct answer for each of the following.

1. Connector handles are used to ______________. [L5]

a. attach one text box to another using a connector

b. merge text boxes together into one box

c. connect multiple WordArt objects

d. group clip art together

2. The WordArt Gallery dialog box is used to ______________. [L3]

a. type the text for the WordArt design

b. select the WordArt style

c. display the text you have written as WordArt

d. none of the above

3. Guides are dotted lines that display to indicate ______________. [L3]

a. the margins of the slide in Slide view

b. when you are outside the boundary in a text box

c. the new size or position of a WordArt object

d. the edge of a clip art object

4. Sizing handles ______________. [L2]

a. indicate that an object is selected

b. are used to resize an object

c. are small squares that display when you click an object

d. all of the above

5. You can select audience handouts to display ______________. [L6]

a. 3, 6, or 9 slides to a page

b. 2, 4, or 6 slides to a page

c. a frame around each slide

d. all of the above

Screen ID

Identify each of the items shown in Figure 2.24.

Figure 2.24

A. AutoShapes button

B. Save button

C. WordArt button

D. Connectors toolbar

E. WordArt object

F. Text box

G. Connector

H. Text Box button

I. Clip art

J. Connector handle

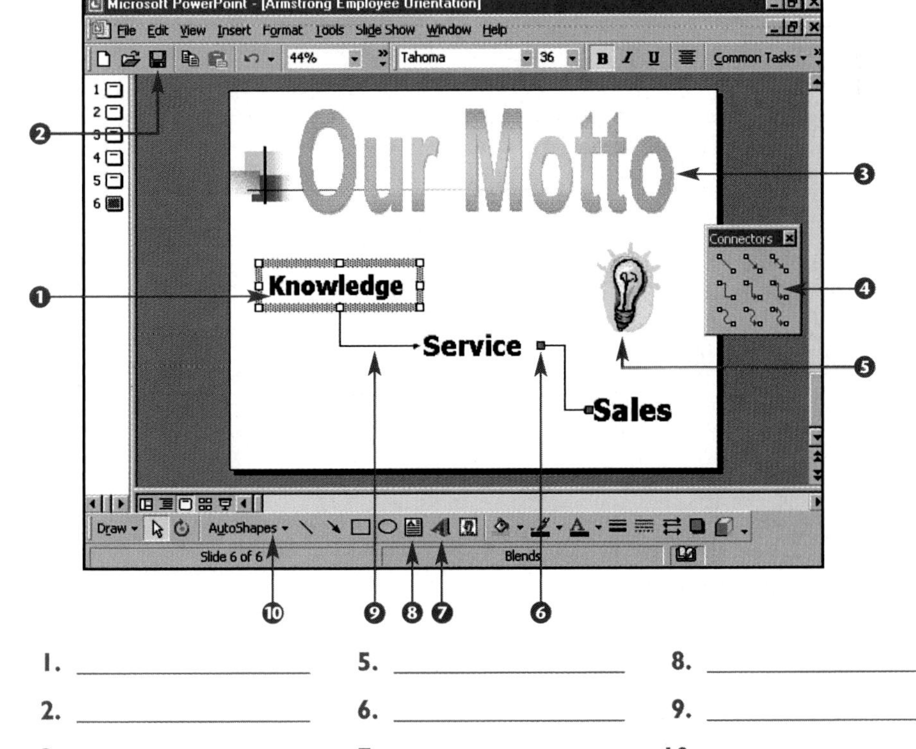

1. ______________

2. ______________

3. ______________

4. ______________

5. ______________

6. ______________

7. ______________

8. ______________

9. ______________

10. ______________

Discussion Questions

1. Describe the difference between WordArt and text boxes. When would you use each in a presentation?
2. What are the advantages and disadvantages of using clip art in a presentation? Based on this discussion, what guidelines should be followed when using clip art?
3. Why would you save an existing presentation with a new name?
4.  Look in Help for information about connector handles. What advantages do these tools have over using regular lines and arrows to connect text boxes? What are some of the issues to be aware of when changing objects that are connected?

Skill Drill

Skill Drill exercises reinforce project skills. Each skill reinforced is the same, or nearly the same, as a skill presented in the project. Detailed instructions are provided in a step-by-step format.

In this set of Skill Drill exercises, you open an existing file and rename it. Then you add a design template, add and resize clip art and WordArt, and add text boxes and connectors. Finally, you print audience handouts. Leave the file open from one Skill Drill to the next until you have completed all five exercises.

These exercises use the file PO-0202.

1. Opening an Existing File, Renaming It, and Applying a Design

First you launch PowerPoint and open and rename an existing presentation. Then you apply a design template to the file. [L1]

1. Launch PowerPoint and choose Open an existing presentation.
2. Locate and open `PO-0202`. Save the file as `Getting Ahead`.
3. Click Common Tasks, Apply Design Template. Review the different options.
4. Select Lock And Key and click Apply.

2. Inserting Clip Art

In this exercise, you add a clip art image to the first slide. To add the image, follow these steps. [L2]

1. Go to Slide view of Slide 1, if necessary.
2. Click Insert, Picture, Clip Art, and select a sailboat. It is in the Transportation category.
3. Move the image, so it does not overlap the text.

3. Inserting, Resizing, and Moving Clip Art

In this exercise, you add another clip art image, and then you resize and move it on the slide. To add, resize, and move clip art, follow these steps. [L2]

1. Use the Next Slide button to advance to Slide 2.
2. Insert the clip art of the owl reading a book. It is in the Animals category and in the Academic category.
3. Enlarge the image without distorting its proportions.
4. Move the image to center it in the available empty space.
5. Add an appropriate clip art image to Slides 3 and 4. Resize and reposition the images you select as needed.

4. Inserting a WordArt Image

In this exercise, you create a Word Art image. [L3]

1. Click the Slide 5 icon to move to Slide 5.
2. Click the Insert WordArt button, and select the fourth option in the first row.
3. Type `We have the course for you!`.
4. Move the WordArt to the top of the slide and increase its size, as shown in Figure 2.25.

Figure 2.25

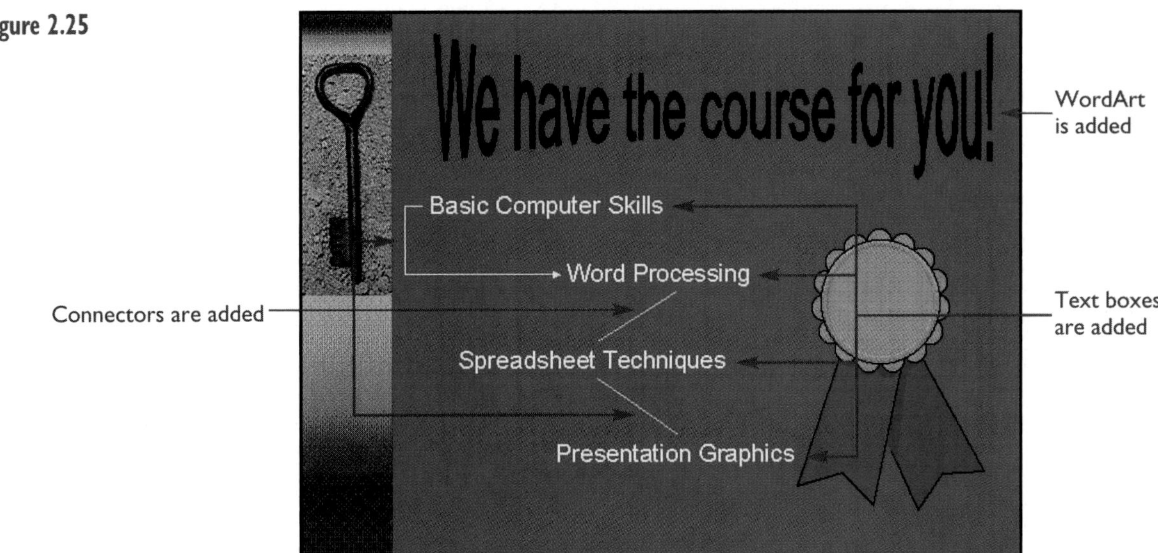

5. Adding Text Boxes and Connectors

In this exercise, you add text boxes and connectors to Slide 5. Use Figure 2.25 as a guide. To add text boxes and connectors, follow these steps. [L4-5]

1. Add four text boxes and type the text shown (refer to Figure 2.25).
2. Add an elbow connector between the first and second box.
3. Add a straight-line connector between the second and third, and third and fourth boxes.
4. Save the presentation.
5. Print the presentation as an audience handout with six slides to a page.

Challenge

Challenge exercises expand on or are somewhat related to skills presented in the lessons. Each exercise provides a brief narrative introduction followed by instructions, in a numbered step or bulleted list format, that are not as detailed as those in the Skill Drill section.

In the Challenge exercises, you work with new techniques and features of using clip art, drawing objects, and WordArt. Each of the five exercises is independent and can be done in any order. In Exercise 3, you use an existing file; in all the others, you create a new file. All files should be saved on your disk and closed at the end of the exercise.

1. Changing a Clip Art Image into a Watermark

Pictures and clip art images can be displayed in four different states: Automatic (the colors as displayed by the image), Black and White, Grayscale, or Watermark. A watermark image is often used as a background for text. [L2, 4]

Create a bulleted slide for a notice about a nature walk, similar to the one shown in Figure 2.26, which includes a watermark image.

Figure 2.26

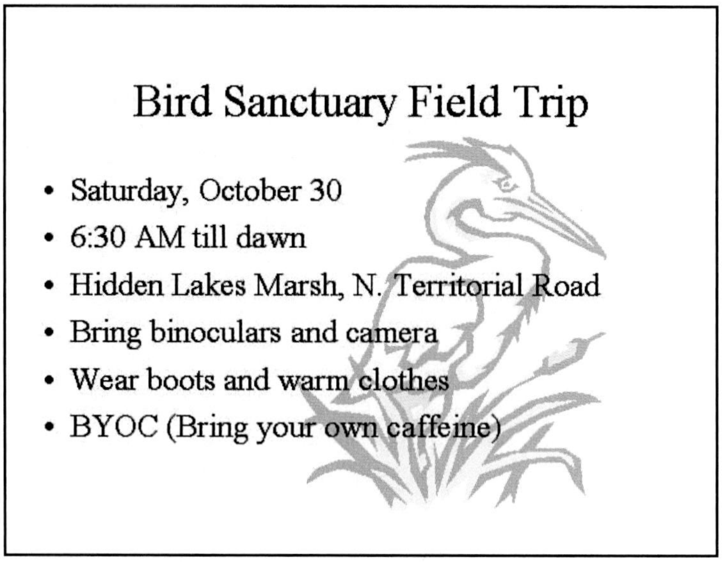

Bird Sanctuary Field Trip
Saturday, October 30
6:30 AM till dawn
Hidden Lakes Marsh, N. Territorial Road
Bring binoculars and camera
Wear boots and warm clothes
BYOC (Bring your own caffeine)

Create a bulleted slide, as shown in Figure 2.26, to announce a field trip to a local bird sanctuary. Add the text and insert the clip art image. The clip art image is found under the Animals category. Follow these steps to change the image to a watermark:

1. Change the image to a watermark by choosing Format, Picture.
2. Click the Picture tab, and then use the drop-down arrow next to Color under the Image Control area to select Watermark.
3. Close the Format Picture dialog box, and then enlarge and reposition the bird as needed.
4. To have the text print on top of the bird, right-click the image and choose Order, Send to Back from the shortcut menu.
5. Click the Print button to print the slide.
6. Save the file on your disk under the name `Watermark` and close it.

2. Adding Colors to Text Boxes, Text Font, and Drawing Objects

You can use many tools with drawing objects to perform tasks, such as changing the background color, font color, size, or style, or changing the border. [L2, 4-5]

To create a slide similar to the one shown in Figure 2.27 that adds colors to text boxes and changes text font color, follow these steps:

Figure 2.27

Achieving Financial Independence
Work
Save
Invest

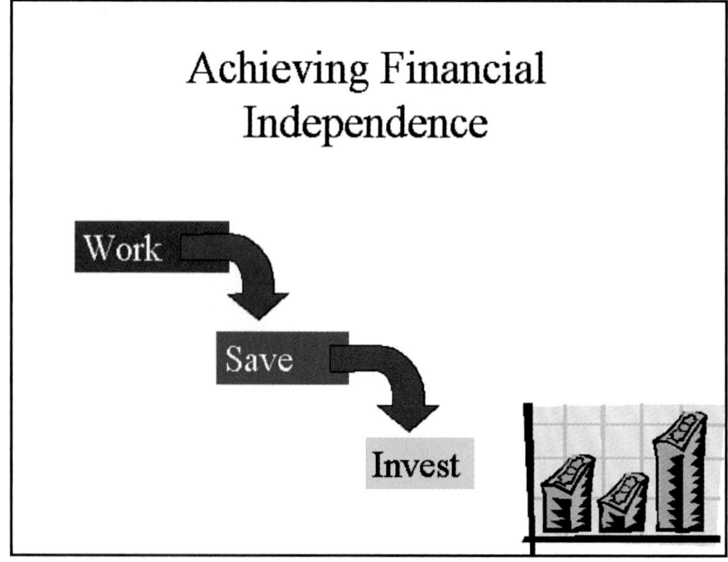

1. Choose the Title only slide layout, and add the title for the slide as shown.
2. Add three text boxes with the words `Work`, `Save`, `Invest`, and position them on the slide as shown. Increase the font size to at least 36 point.
3. Use the AutoShapes button and select Bent Arrow, which is located under the Block Arrows group.
4. Use the Free Rotate button to rotate the arrow 180° and position it between the words `Work` and `Save` as shown.
5. With the arrow still selected, click the Copy button, and then click the Paste button to make a copy of the arrow.
6. Click the new arrow and drag it to a position between the words `Save` and `Invest` as shown.
7. Add a clip art image of your choice having to do with accumulation of wealth and position.
8. Select each text box, and add a color by clicking the drop-down arrow next to the Fill Color button on the Drawing toolbar. Use the More Fill Colors option to increase your color choices.
9. Select each text box, and change the font color to a contrasting color by clicking the drop-down arrow next to the Font Color button on the Drawing toolbar. Choose the colors so that the text shows clearly.
10. Use the Fill Color button to add a color to the two arrows.
11. Save the slide on your disk with the name `Investing`.
12. Print the slide and close the presentation.

3. Adding Connectors and Applying Formats to Text Boxes Using the Format Painter

Processes can be diagrammed using the Flow Chart symbols, which are a group of AutoShapes. In this Challenge exercise, a diagram on how to register for class has been created. You add the connecting arrows and change the format of the flowchart boxes. You then use the Format Painter to apply the format from one box to another. [L4-5]

Add connectors to a Registration diagram slide, as shown in Figure 2.28. To change the format of the text and text boxes by using the Format Painter tool, follow these steps.

Figure 2.28

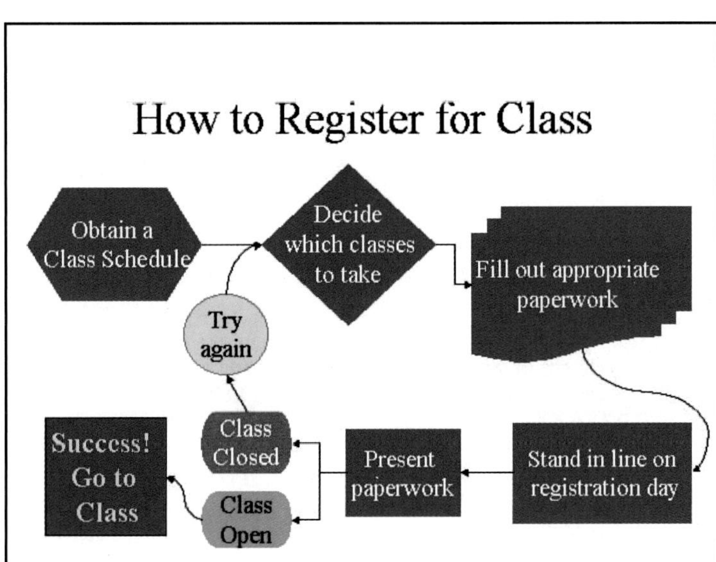

1. Locate and open the `PO-0203` file on the CD that came with your book. Save the file on your disk as `Registration`.
2. Using the diagram as a guide, add the missing text to the chart objects as needed. (*Hint*: Click the text box and type to insert the text. Press ↵Enter to force text to the next line as needed.)
3. Add the connecting arrows. Use the curved arrows where appropriate, as shown.
4. Use the Fill Color button to change the color of the first box to a color of your choice.
5. Use the Line Color button to change the color of the line on this object to match the fill color.
6. Use the Font Color button to change the font color on this object to a contrasting color. (Choose something other than black.)

7. With the first box still selected, double-click the Format Painter button on the Standard toolbar. The mouse pointer has a paintbrush attached to it.
8. Click the next four boxes to copy the format from the first box to the next four boxes, as shown.
9. Save the slide and print it. Close the file.

4. Creating a Vertical WordArt Design for an Orientation Slide

WordArt offers many different styles and formats. One of the unusual styles is vertical WordArt. This can be useful for something that is short, such as a one-word greeting. Anything that is much longer is harder to read in a vertical arrangement. In this Challenge exercise, you create an orientation slide that is an overview to topics to be covered in a presentation. [L3]

Create an orientation slide that includes a vertical WordArt object to the left of a bulleted list like the one shown in Figure 2.29. Follow these steps:

Figure 2.29

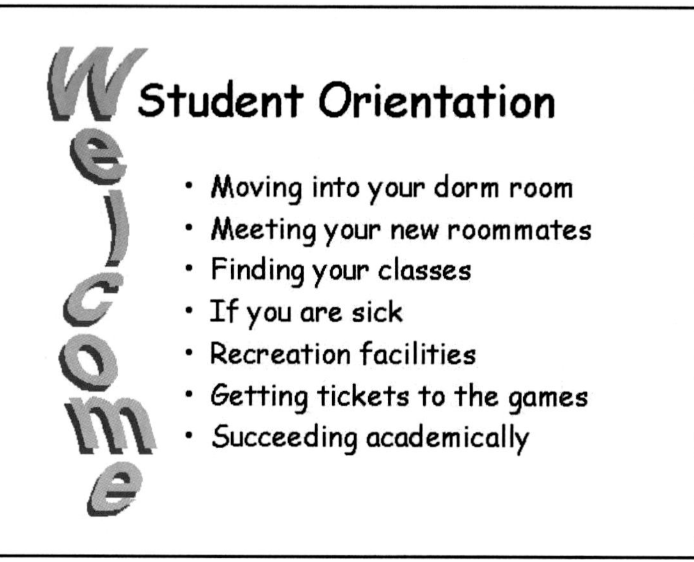

1. Open a blank presentation, and choose the bulleted list slide.
2. Click the title placeholder, and click the drop-down arrow next to the Font box on the Standard toolbar. Change the font to a style of your choice. (The figure shows Comic Sans MS as the font style.)
3. Add the title as shown in the Figure 2.29.
4. Click the bulleted list placeholder; change the font to the same style you selected for the title, and add a list of topics for a student orientation. You can use the ones shown in the figure, or create your own list of six or seven topics.
5. Click the sizing handle on the left side of the bulleted list placeholder, and reduce the size of the bulleted list box as shown, leaving room on the left to add the WordArt object.
6. Add a vertical WordArt object for the word **`Welcome`**. Choose one of the four vertical options available in the WordArt Gallery, and bold the text.
7. Reposition the WordArt, as shown, and expand it to fill the space.
8. Print the slide, and save the presentation as **`Student Orientation`**.

5. Using Parts of a Clip Art Image

Clip art images are composed of smaller objects grouped together to form a larger image. You can break the image down into its component parts and use pieces of the original image for another purpose. [L2]

Use the available Help to guide you through the steps necessary to do the following:

1. Open a blank presentation.
2. Find the clip art image called Question Marks.
3. Ungroup the image.
4. Delete the circle around the question mark.
5. Resize the image so that it is about one-half the height of the page.
6. Group the remaining pieces that make up the question mark back together.
7. Print the slide and save it as **`Question Mark`**.

Discovery Zone

Discovery Zone exercises require advanced knowledge of topics presented in *Essentials* lessons, application of skills from multiple lessons, or self-directed learning of new skills.

These Discovery Zone exercises are independent of each other and can be completed in any order. They help you learn how to use other drawing tools and WordArt designs.

1. Using Other Drawing Tools

In this project, you learned how to use a text box and connectors, which are tools on the Drawing toolbar. The Drawing toolbar has many other tools that you can use. Figure 2.30 shows several shapes and color options that you can use. In this Discovery exercise, you explore different Drawing toolbar options.

Figure 2.30

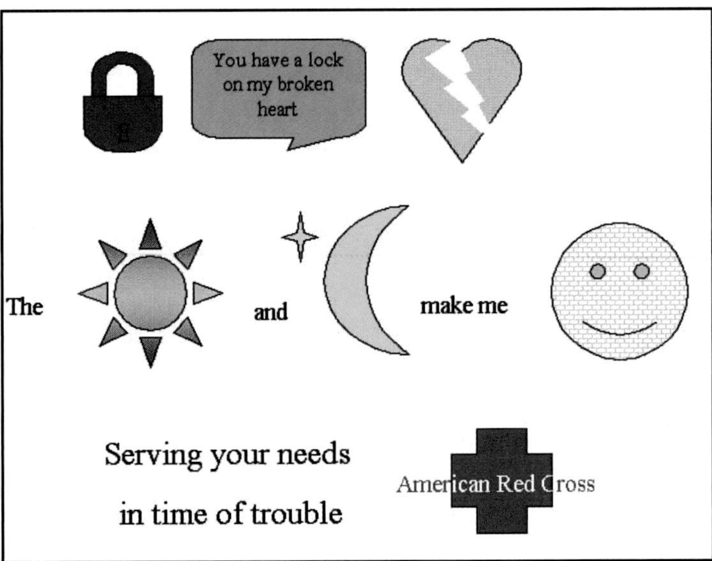

Create a blank slide that utilizes four to six different AutoShapes, add fill colors, add text boxes, and change the color of the text. You use at least one other new option and add a text box that identifies the option you have chosen to use. Save the file on your floppy disk with the name **`Drawing Objects`**.

2. Creating a Circular WordArt Design

One of the more impressive WordArt designs that you can create is a circular design as shown in Figure 2.31. The trick to creating this type of a design is to press ↵Enter between the words, so the first line is at the top of the circle, the middle line is in the middle, and the last line is the bottom part of the circle. It also works best if the text for the top and bottom of the circle is longer and approximately the same length, while the text in the middle is shorter. Use Figure 2.31 as a model for creating this type of WordArt design.

Figure 2.31

In this Discovery exercise, you create a slide that looks like the one shown in Figure 2.31. The figure uses the WordArt style that is in the last row, fourth from the left of the WordArt Gallery window. Enter the text with the returns in the appropriate places to create the three lines of text. The following is a list of other options and changes that need to be made to create this image:

- Impact is the font style used for both the WordArt object and the text box at the bottom.
- The yellow diamond handle needs to be used to straighten the text horizontally.
- The Tilt Right button on the 3-D Settings toolbar needs to be used to straighten the text so that it has a flat perspective.
- The WordArt Shape button on the WordArt toolbar offers a variety of shapes that you can apply to WordArt. The one used for this design is called Button (Pour) and is the last one in the second row.
- 3-D Style 15 was used in this image.
- You need to enlarge the WordArt object and center it before you add the text box at the bottom of the image.
- Save the file as `WordArt Design` and print the slide.

3. Creating a Flowchart Showing Your Family Tree

Use the various shapes found in AutoShapes to create a diagram of your family tree. Start with your grandparents (or great-grandparents if you know the information). Include any siblings, spouses, or children. At a minimum, you should have seven boxes. Add connecting lines to show relationships, and use a symbol of your choice to show marriages, divorces, and so on. Add the names of each family member by typing the name on the appropriate box. (*Hint*: You do not have to use a text box for this; instead, you select the box and type to add the text.) Add a banner at the top of the slide, and add your family name, (for example, Preston Family Tree). Save the file with the name `Family Tree`; print the slide.

Project 3

Charting Numerical Data

Objectives

In this project, you learn how to

- ➤ **Replace Sample Data**
- ➤ **Choose a Chart Type**
- ➤ **Switch Columns and Rows**
- ➤ **Modify a Chart**

Key terms introduced in this project include

- category axis
- datasheet
- legend
- Microsoft Graph
- value axis

Why Would I Do This?

Many presentations include charts. Numerical data is much easier to understand when it is displayed graphically. Charts are good tools for explaining change over time, parts of a whole, trends, or comparisons. This project shows you how to create a chart for the Armstrong Pool, Spa, and Sauna Company. A wide variety of chart types are available to display numerical information. You can modify any of the chart components, change colors of chart elements, font or font size of labels, or even customize a chart.

In this project, you learn how to create a basic column chart like the one in Figure 3.1.

Visual Summary

Figure 3.1
You can use charts to display numerical data.

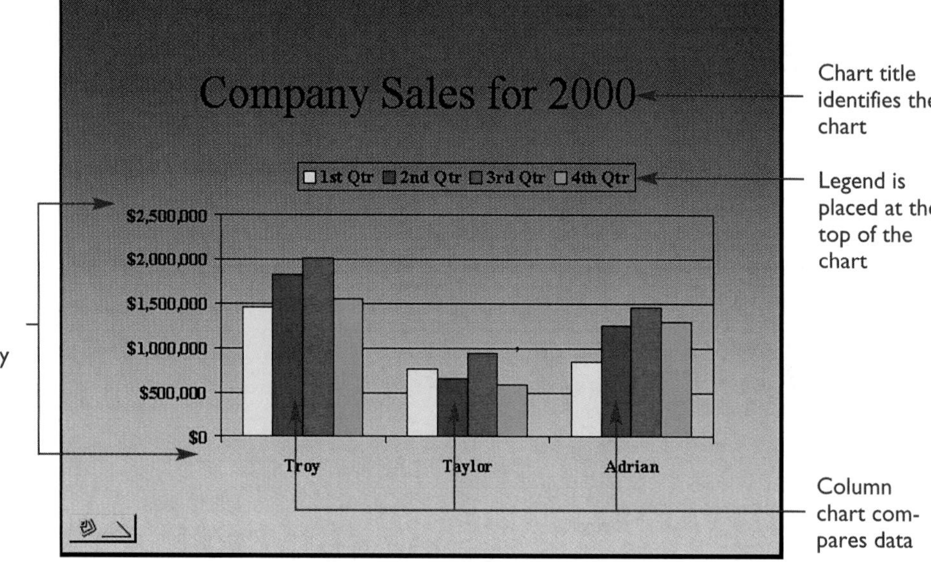

Labels are formatted to currency

Lesson 1: Replacing Sample Data

A PowerPoint chart contains two parts: the chart itself and the datasheet on which the chart is based. A ***datasheet*** is similar to a spreadsheet because it contains the data used to build the chart. When you insert a chart into a PowerPoint presentation, the datasheet includes sample data. To create the chart you change the data, the row and column headings, and add or delete rows or columns as needed. The underlying chart that is displayed changes to reflect the new data as you enter it.

In this lesson, you open an existing file, save it with a new name, add a new slide and replace sample data to create a chart.

To Open an Existing Presentation and Add a New Slide

1. **Launch PowerPoint. Locate and open `PO-0301` from your student CD.**
2. **Save the file on your floppy disk as `Year End Report`.**
3. **If necessary, click the Slide View button to change to the Slide view.**
4. **Click the Common Tasks button in the Formatting toolbar and select New Slide.**
   The New Slide dialog box displays.
5. **Select the Chart option, the fourth option in the second row. Click OK.**
   A new slide displays with placeholders reserving areas for the slide title and for a chart (see Figure 3.2).

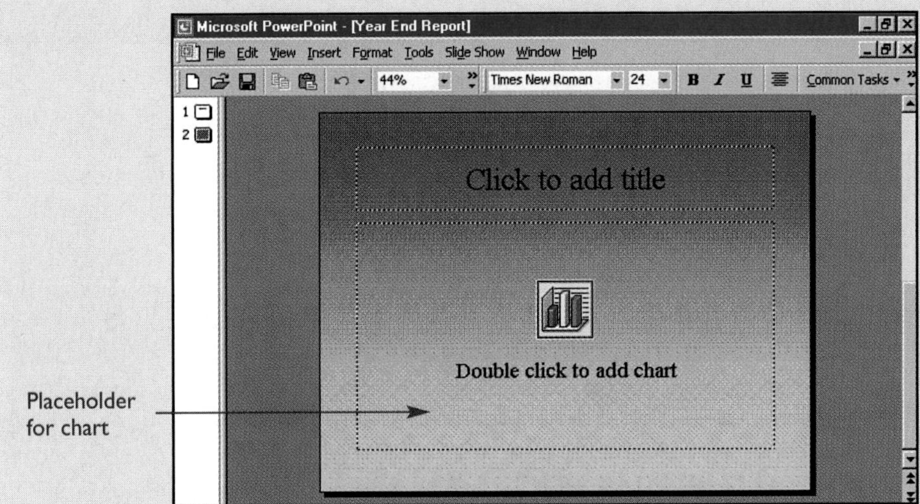

Figure 3.2
You can use the chart type slide to create a new chart.

Adding a Chart to a Slide
You can also add a chart to a plain slide by clicking the Insert Chart button on the Standard toolbar.

After you select the Chart slide, you activate the ***Microsoft Graph*** program, which is a Microsoft subprogram that you use to create or edit a PowerPoint chart. When this program is active, you can enter the data for your chart in the datasheet.

Replacing Sample Data

1. **Double-click anywhere in the box that says Double click to add chart.**
Microsoft Graph, a chart creation and editing program, activates. The chart and datasheet displays with the sample data (see Figure 3.3).

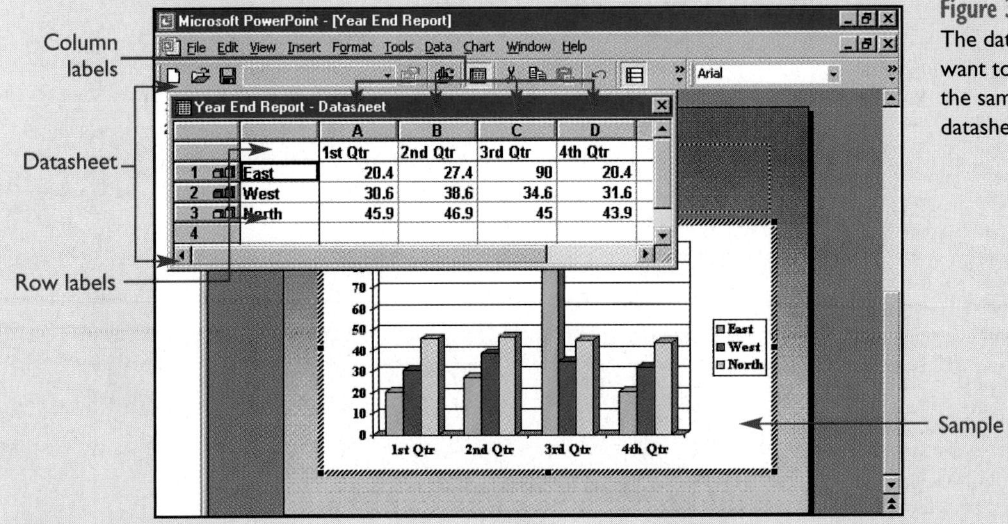

Figure 3.3
The data for the chart you want to create replaces the sample data in the datasheet.

2. **Click the word `East`, the label for the first row of data, and type `Troy`.**
The label for the first row of data changes to `Troy`, one of the store locations for the Armstrong Pool, Spa, and Sauna Company.

3. **Change `West` to `Taylor` and `North` to `Adrian` (see Figure 3.4).**
Use the arrow keys to move from cell to cell. You now have three stores for which to enter data.

continues ▶

Replacing Sample Data (continued)

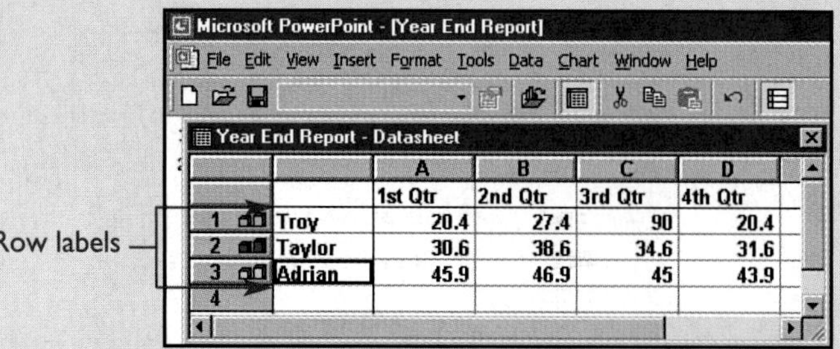

Figure 3.4
The labels for the rows are replaced in the datasheet.

4 Enter the quarterly sales data for each of the stores, as shown in the following table. Use Tab to move across the cells in the datasheet. You can also use the directional arrow keys.

	1st Qtr	2nd Qtr	3rd Qtr	4th Qtr
Troy	1457300	1825000	2012500	1546500
Taylor	764500	654700	943200	584500
Adrian	845600	1263000	1458700	1291100

Watch the chart change in the background chart as you make changes. When you finish, the datasheet should look like the one in Figure 3.5.

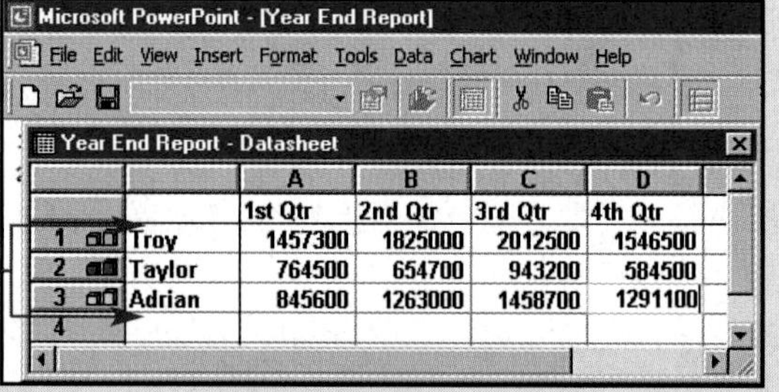

Figure 3.5
The chart changes as you enter data in the datasheet.

Data is entered in the datasheet

5 Click the Close button in the datasheet window.
The datasheet closes, but the chart remains selected, and the Microsoft Graph program remains active (see Figure 3.6). You can tell the Microsoft Graph program is active when the Data and Chart options are available in the menu bar and the chart buttons appear in the Standard toolbar.

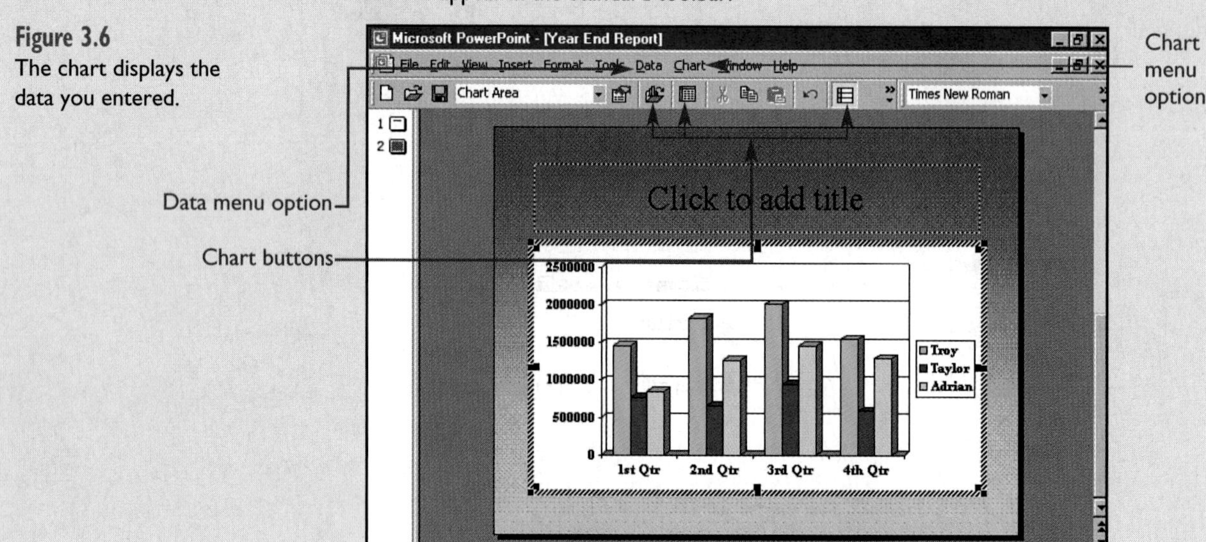

Figure 3.6
The chart displays the data you entered.

6 Click the Save button to save your work. Leave the file open for use in the next lesson.
The chart is saved as part of the Year End Report presentation.

Adding and Deleting Rows or Columns
You can remove or add rows or columns to a datasheet. To add rows or columns, simply type in the new data and labels. To delete a row or column, click the row number or column letter to select the entire row or column; choose Edit, Delete from the menu.

Lesson 2: Choosing a Chart Type

Different chart types give the viewer a different perspective of the same data. Some chart types are more effective with certain types of data. For example, to show parts of a whole, a pie chart works best. To show a sequence over time, a line chart is usually best. PowerPoint gives you an easy way to change the chart type. You might need to try several chart types before you find one that is right.

In this lesson, you change the chart type to see which type works best with your data.

To Change a Chart Type

1 Make sure the chart you created in the previous lesson is active. If the Data and Chart options are not in the menu bar, double-click the chart to activate Microsoft Graph.

2 Click the More Buttons button and point to the Chart Type button.
The Chart Type toolbar opens. If the Chart Type button appears on your toolbar, click the down arrow next to it to display the toolbar.

3 Point to the bar at the top of the Chart Type toolbar, and click and drag it to your screen.
The Chart Type toolbar floats on the screen, so you can use it to select different chart types (see Figure 3.7).

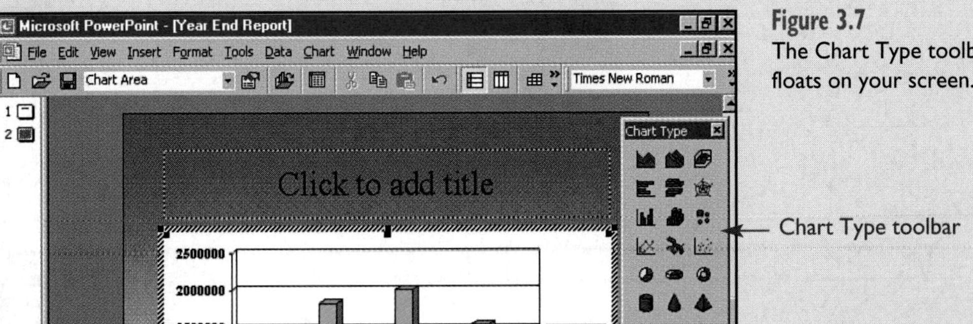

Figure 3.7
The Chart Type toolbar floats on your screen.

4 Click the Area Chart button, the first button in the first column on the Chart Type toolbar.
The area chart provides the same information that is in the column chart you created in the previous lesson, but the area chart is much more difficult to interpret (see Figure 3.8).

continues ▶

To Change a Chart Type (continued)

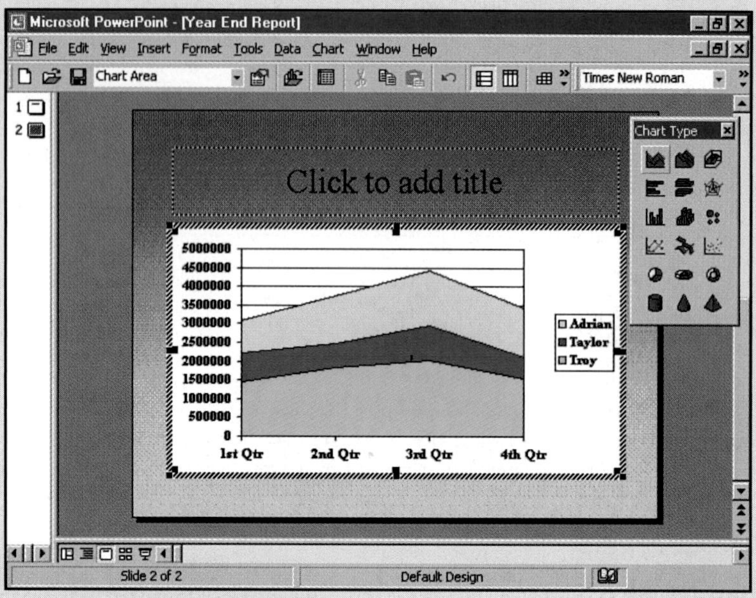

Figure 3.8
The area chart is not appropriate for this type of data.

5 **Click the Line Chart button, the first button in the fourth row of the Chart Type toolbar.**

The line chart is somewhat easier to interpret than the area chart, but is still not very clear (see Figure 3.9).

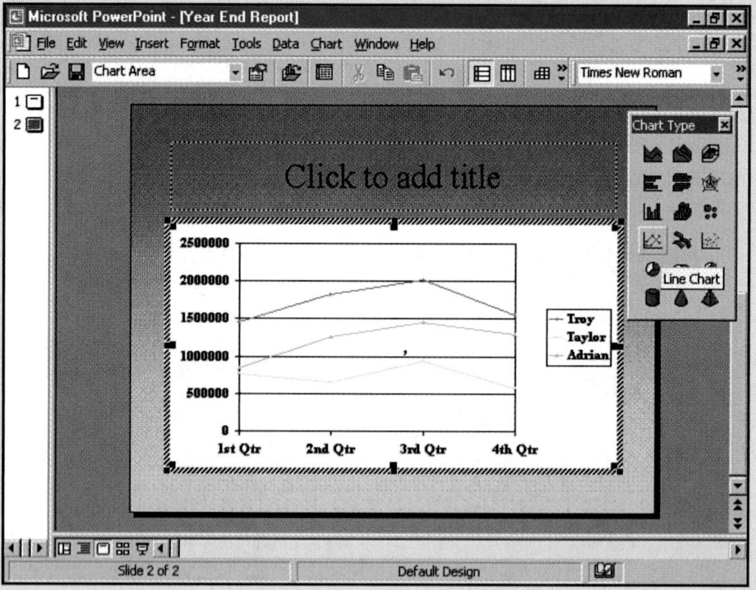

Figure 3.9
The line chart is another type of chart that you can use.

6 **Click the Column Chart button, the first button in the third row of the Chart Type toolbar.**

The column chart, which is the default chart type, is actually best for this type of data (see Figure 3.10).

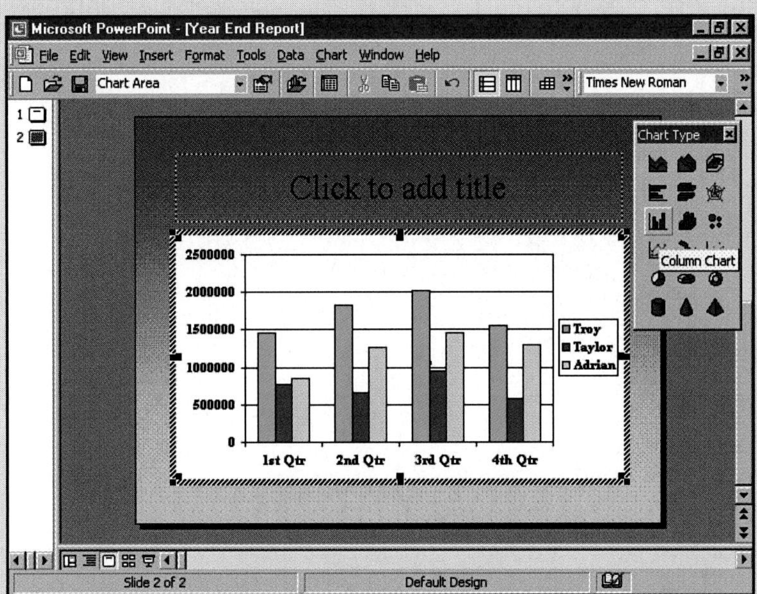

Figure 3.10
The data displays in a column chart.

7 Click the Close button on the Chart Type toolbar. Click the Save button to save your work. Leave the file open for use in the next lesson.

Viewing More Chart Options
You can view a wider assortment of chart types by choosing Chart, Chart Type from the menu. (The Office Assistant opens if you use this method. Right-click Clippit, and click Hide to close it.) The Chart Type dialog box gives you several options under each basic category of chart. You can also use this dialog box to create a custom chart.

Lesson 3: Switching Columns and Rows

The chart you just created displays the four quarters of the year along the category axis for all three stores. If you wanted to display the sales grouped for each store for the whole year, you would need to view the data by column rather than by row. The ***category axis*** is the horizontal line on the chart that displays data labels.

In this lesson, you change the chart format from row format to column format.

To Switch Columns and Rows

1 Make sure the chart is active. If the Data and Chart options are not shown in the menu bar, double-click the chart to activate Microsoft Graph.
Notice that the category axis at the bottom of the chart is divided into quarters.

2 Click the By Column button.
The category axis now shows the data by store, rather than by quarter (see Figure 3.11).

continues ▶

To Switch Columns and Rows (continued)

3. **Click outside the selected chart area to leave Microsoft Graph. Click in the Click to add title area and type in `Company Sales for 2000`.**
Figure 3.11 shows the results of your changes.

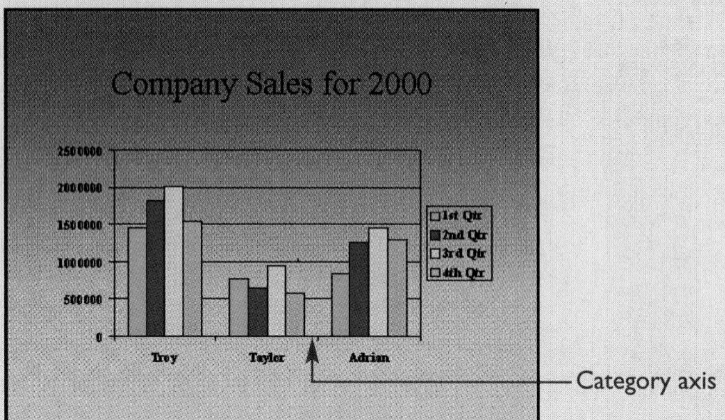

Figure 3.11
The chart displays quarterly data, grouped by stores.

4. **Click outside the title area to see the results of your changes; click the Save button to save your work. Leave the file open for use in the next lesson.**

Identifying Chart Parts With ScreenTips
As you move the mouse pointer around on the chart, ScreenTips display to identify different parts of the chart. Use these ScreenTips when you want to edit a particular part of the chart.

Lesson 4: Modifying a Chart

After you create a chart, you can modify it in a number of ways to better suit your needs. For example, you can change the colors of the bars or lines in the chart to colors you prefer, or to colors that match ones your company might use to designate the quarters of the year, various departments, or product lines. You can change the scale on a chart to create more or less emphasis, or change the format of your numbers. You can move the legend to another location on the chart. You can use two or three approaches to access the dialog boxes that you use to modify a chart. One of the easiest ways is to point to the part of the screen that you want to change; right-click to open the related shortcut menu, and select the appropriate menu option from the list. This is the method that you use in this lesson.

In this lesson, you make some basic modifications to the chart you created.

To Modify a Chart

1. **Double-click the chart to reactivate the Microsoft Graph program. If necessary, click the Close button to close the Year End Report datasheet.**
To modify a chart, you must first be in the graphing program.
2. **Right-click one of the light-blue (3rd Qtr) columns on the chart.**
A shortcut menu displays, and a dark square shows in each of the light-blue columns to indicate that this series has been selected.

3 Click Format Data Series.
The Format Data series dialog box displays.

4 Click the bright red color at the beginning of the third line of the color chart.
The sample color changes to red (see Figure 3.12).

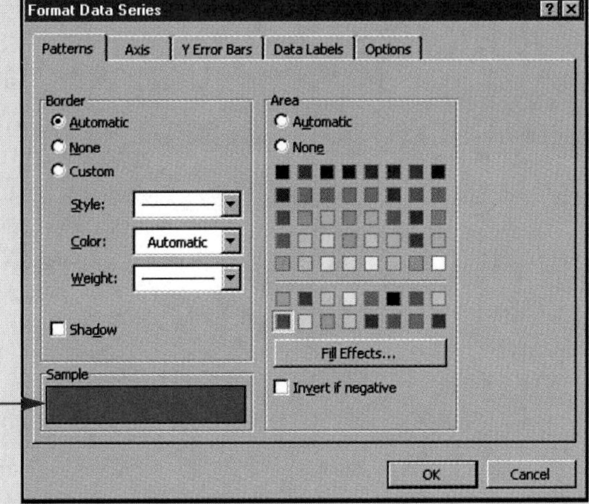

Figure 3.12
Use the Format Data Series dialog box to change different formatting elements.

5 Click OK. Repeat Steps 2 through 4 to change the green column to yellow and the gray column to a dark green.
The color of each data series changes (see Figure 3.13).

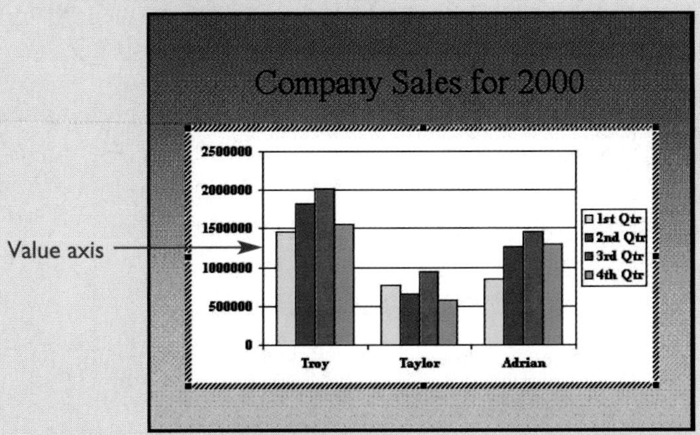

Figure 3.13
The colors of the columns have been changed.

6 Right-click the value axis.
A shortcut menu opens. The ***value axis*** is the vertical line on the left side of the chart where values for the chart display. In this example, the numbers displayed represent sales in dollars.

To ensure that you are selecting the correct part of the chart, hold your mouse pointer over the designated area until the ScreenTip displays. When right-clicking, if you move the mouse slightly, you might slip off the desired area and get a different menu. Click elsewhere to close the menu and try again. Remember, to open a shortcut menu, use the right mouse button; to select a choice on the menu use the left mouse button.

continues ▶

To Modify a Chart (continued)

7. **Select Format Axis to open the Format Axis dialog box. Click the Number tab. Select Currency in the Category box and change the Decimal places to `0` (see Figure 3.14).**

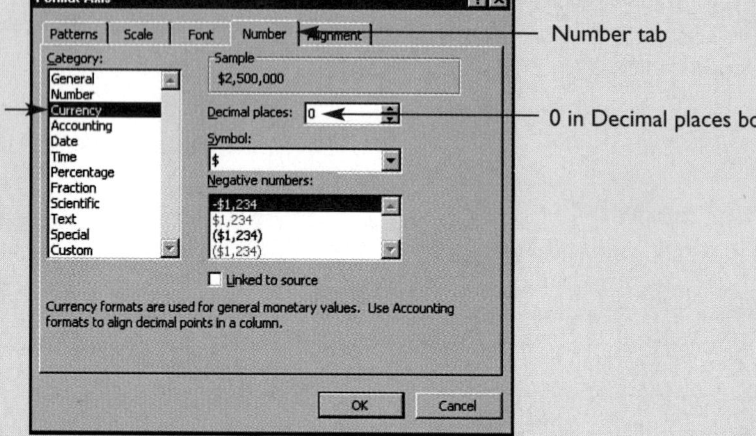

Figure 3.14
Use the Format Axis dialog box to format the value axis.

8. **Click OK.**
The figures are formatted as currency (see Figure 3.15). Next you move the legend to the top of the chart. The ***legend*** in a chart is a key that identifies the color code for each series of data.

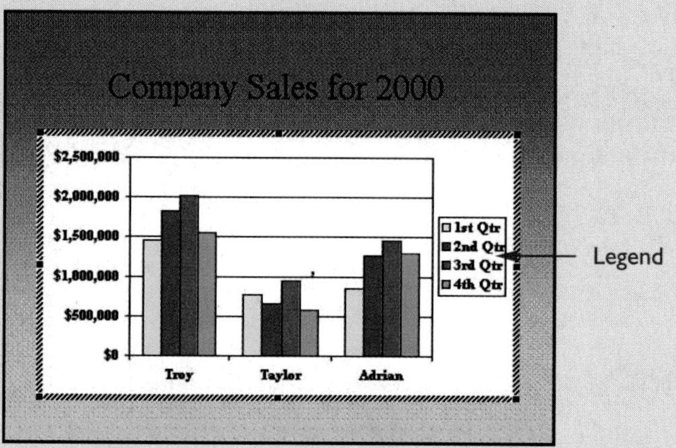

Figure 3.15
The number values change to currency.

9. **Right-click the Legend and select Format Legend. Select the Placement tab; click the Top option button. Click OK.**
The legend moves to the top of the chart (see Figure 3.16).

10. **Click outside the chart to view your changes and exit the Microsoft Graph program. Save your work.**
Your chart should look like the one shown in Figure 3.15.

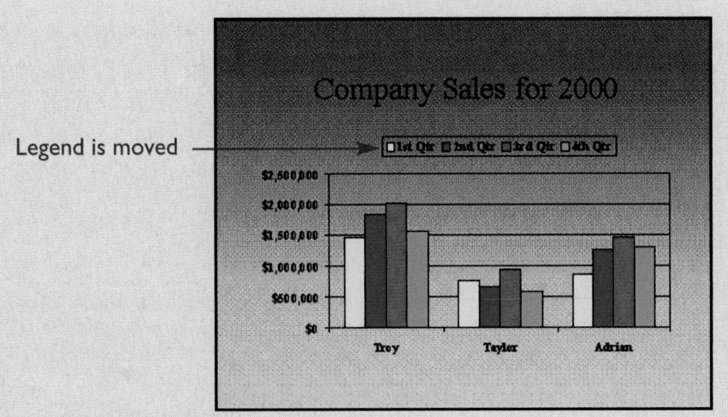

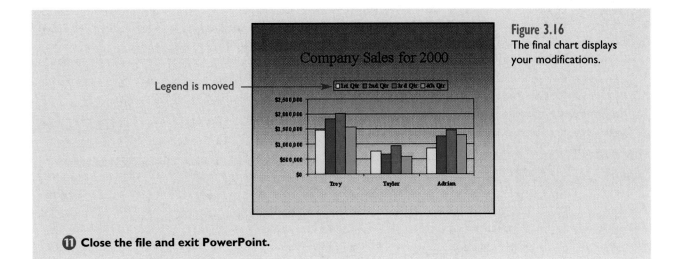

Figure 3.16
The final chart displays your modifications.

⑪ **Close the file and exit PowerPoint.**

Modifying Charts

When you change the color of a series, the legend color automatically changes to match it. Also notice that when you point to a particular bar, a ScreenTip displays showing the value of that particular bar.

You can also use the Chart menu option to change different parts of the chart. In addition, you can use a number of buttons on the toolbars to change elements in a chart. You can select Chart, Chart Options from the menu to select the chart element that you want to modify.

Summary

In this project, you learned how to create a chart to display numerical data. The process included inserting a new chart slide, activating the Microsoft Graph program, and replacing sample data. You learned to select a chart type, switch columns and rows, and modify various parts of the chart.

You can expand your learning by exploring one of the other options for adding a chart to a presentation. You can use the Chart button on the toolbar to add a chart to a blank slide. You can also try using a layout design that includes a chart on one half of the slide and a bulleted list in the other half of the slide.

Checking Concepts and Terms

True/False

For each of the following, check *T* or *F* to indicate whether the statement is true or false.

__T __F **1.** The New Slide button is one of three Common Tasks buttons. [L1]

__T __F **2.** You can add or delete rows and columns in a chart datasheet. [L1]

__T __F **3.** If you want to chart a series of numbers in PowerPoint, you would use a subprogram called Microsoft Graph. [L1]

__T __F **4.** To delete a row in a datasheet, put the cursor in any cell of that row and press Del. [L1]

__T __F **5.** You know you are in Microsoft Graph when the Data and Chart options are available in the menu. [L2]

__T __F **6.** The type of chart you choose should be determined by the type of data you are going to display. [L2]

__T __F **7.** You can modify a chart using the tools in the regular PowerPoint program. [L1]

__T __F **8.** The legend in a chart is a key that identifies the color code for each series of data. [L4]

__T __F **9.** The value axis is the horizontal line at the bottom of the chart. [L4]

__T __F **10.** The category axis is the horizontal line at the bottom of the chart. [L3]

Multiple Choice

Circle the letter of the correct answer for each of the following.

1. You can tell that the Microsoft Graph program is active when ______________. [L2]

a. the Chart menu option displays

b. the Data menu option displays

c. chart buttons display

d. all of the above

2. The quickest way to switch the data on the category axis from columns to rows is to ______________. [L3]

a. use the By Column button on the Microsoft Graph toolbar

b. reenter the data in the datasheet

c. in the PowerPoint program, drag the columns to display horizontally instead of vertically

d. none of the above

3. ScreenTips ______________. [L3]

a. identify different parts of the chart

b. display when you rest your mouse pointer on one part of a chart

c. help you select the part of a chart you want to modify

d. all of the above

4. The primary purpose of a chart of numerical data is to ______________. [Intro]

a. show the hierarchical relationship in an organization

b. show change over time, parts of a whole, trends, or comparisons

c. show a flow of ideas

d. add visual interest to a presentation

5. When you first activate the Microsoft Graph program ______________. [L1]

a. a line chart displays

b. a datasheet with sample data displays

c. an empty datasheet displays

d. a pie chart displays

Screen ID

Identify each of the items shown in Figure 3.17.

A. Legend
B. Chart Type toolbar
C. Category axis
D. Value axis
E. Shortcut menu
F. Datasheet
G. Sample data
H. Indicates the Microsoft Graph program is active
I. Column label
J. By Column button

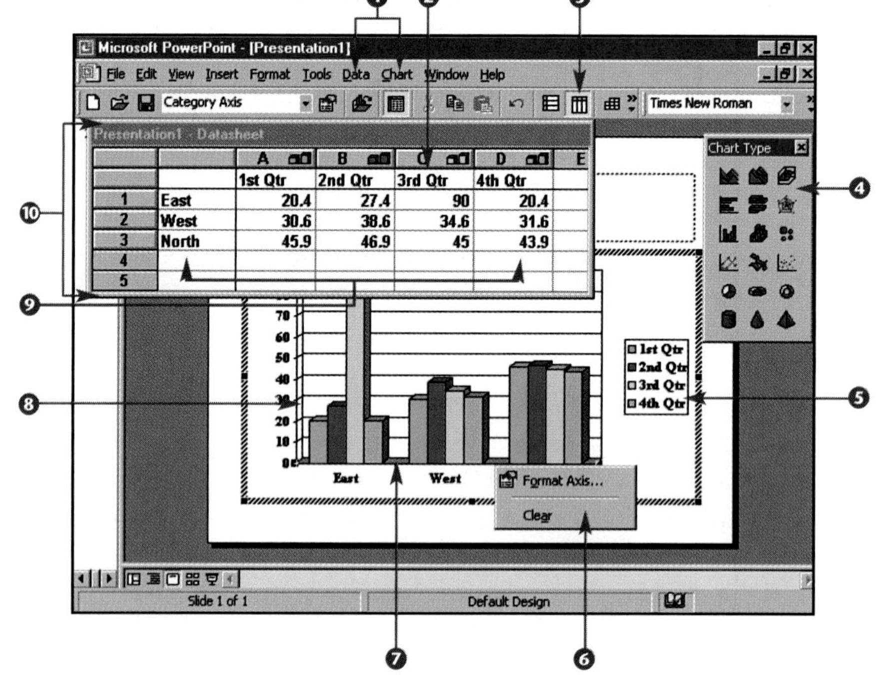

1. ______________ **5.** ______________ **9.** ______________

2. ______________ **6.** ______________ **10.** ______________

3. ______________ **7.** ______________

4. ______________ **8.** ______________

Discussion Questions

1. What kind of data would best be displayed with a pie chart? Would you use a pie chart when your data consists of several columns of numbers? Why or why not?
2. If you wanted to show a trend, what type of chart would you use? What type of charts would be particularly bad for displaying trends?
3. Why is numerical data easier to understand using a chart? Do you think that everyone finds charts easier to understand than tables of numeric data?

Skill Drill

Skill Drill exercises reinforce project skills. Each skill reinforced is the same, or nearly the same, as a skill presented in the project. Detailed instructions are provided in a step-by-step format.

In the following exercises, you open an existing file that is related to the Armstrong Pool, Spa, and Sauna Company. You create a chart that shows the results of the year's activity by product for the Taylor store. Then you make some modifications to the chart. Finally, you print the chart as a slide. Leave the file open from one Skill Drill to the next until you have completed all the exercises.

This set of Skill Drill exercises uses file PO-0302.

1. Adding a New Chart Slide

The first step in the process of creating a new chart is to launch PowerPoint and add a new slide by choosing the Chart slide layout. [L1-2]

1. Launch PowerPoint. Open `PO-0302` from your CD and save it on your floppy disk with the name `Final Year End Report`.
2. Move to Slide 2.
3. Click Common Tasks and click the New Slide button.
4. Select the Chart slide type and click OK.

2. Adding Data to the Chart Datasheet

To create a chart, you have to replace the sample data with your own data. Follow the steps below to replace the sample data. [L1]

1. Double-click to open the Microsoft Graph program to activate it.
2. Enter the text and numbers in the datasheet as shown:

Pools	3	34	47	5
Spas	56	52	44	61
Saunas	23	12	8	24

3. Close the datasheet, but leave the Microsoft Graph program open.
4. Save your changes.

3. Modifying the Chart

After the data is entered, you might want to modify the chart. Follow these steps to modify and print the chart. [L4]

1. Change the chart type to Column Chart.
2. Change the chart to display the data by product rather than by quarter.
3. Change the colors of the bars in the chart to colors of your choice.
4. Right-click the category axis and select Format Axis. Click the Font tab and change the font to Arial.
5. Select the value axis and change the Font to Arial.
6. Select the legend and change the font to Arial.
7. Click the title on the slide and add the title `Taylor Store - Units Sold`.
8. Print a grayscale copy of the Column Chart slide.
9. Save your work and close the file.

Challenge

Challenge exercises expand on or are somewhat related to skills presented in the lessons. Each exercise provides a brief narrative introduction followed by instructions, in a numbered step or bulleted list format, that are not as detailed as those in the Skill Drill section.

In these Challenge exercises, you use the Chart menu option to change chart types, so you can see the additional chart styles that are available. Then you create and modify a line chart and create and modify the pie chart. Challenges 1 and 2 should be done in order and together. Challenges 3 and 4 should also be done in order and together. All files should be saved on your disk and closed at the end of the exercise.

1. Changing Chart Types Using the Menu Options

In this project, you learned how to change chart types by using the Chart Type button. Many more options are available to you when you use the Chart menu option. In this exercise, you change the chart type option by using the Chart menu. [L2]

To change a chart to a line chart by using the Chart menu option, follow these steps:

1. Locate and open the **PO-0303** file found on the CD that came with your book. Save the file on your floppy disk with the name **Line Chart**.
2. Activate the chart and choose Chart, Chart Type. Click the various Chart type options to see the choices that are available. On the Standard Types tab, select the default line chart (the first one in the second row) for this chart.
3. Click the Press and Hold to View Sample button. A sample of the chart displays. The way it currently displays is confusing. Click OK to select the line chart type. You change the line chart in the next Challenge exercise.
4. Save your changes. Leave the file open for use in the next Challenge exercise.

2. Modifying a Line Chart

Just as you learned to modify a column chart, you can also modify a line chart. In this exercise, you modify the line chart you created in the previous exercise. [L3-4]

When you have completed this exercise, you will have a chart that looks similar to the one in Figure 3.18. To modify a line chart, follow these steps:

Figure 3.18

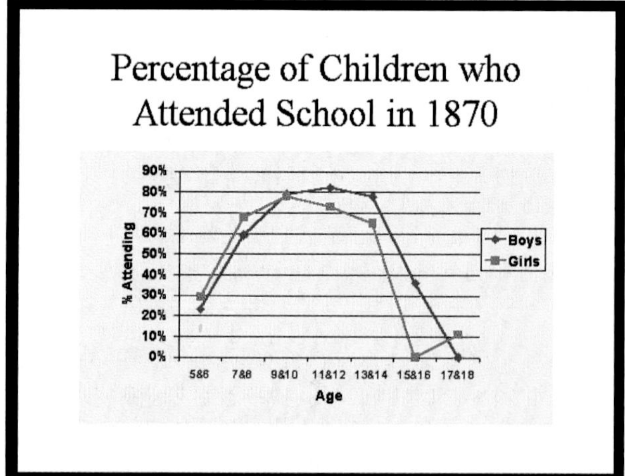

1. If necessary, open the Line Chart file created in Challenge 1.
2. Change the chart to display the data By Column.
3. Select Chart, Chart Options from the menu, and add **Age** as the label for the category axis and **% Attending** as the label for the value axis. Click OK to accept your changes and close the Chart Options dialog box.

4. Select the line for the boys and open the Format Data Series dialog box. Change the line color for boys to blue and select the largest Weight option available for the line. Change the Foreground and Background for the bullet object to blue, and increase the Size to 10 points.
5. Select the line for the girls and make the same changes you did for the other line, but use the bright pink as the color choice.
6. Select the category axis, and change the font to Arial and the font size to 14 (not bold).
7. Change the font on each of the following to Arial:

   Category axis title, value axis title, value axis, and legend.
8. Right-click an open area on the chart, and open the Format Chart Area dialog box. Select the Patterns tab and choose a pale, contrasting color for the background of the chart.
9. Save your changes and print the slide. Close the file.

3. Creating a Pie Chart

A pie chart is very useful for showing parts of a whole. It gives the viewer a perspective on how much each part is contributing. In this Challenge exercise, you create a pie chart that shows the total number of casualties (injuries and deaths) caused by tornadoes in the state of Michigan for the past four decades.

To create a pie chart that shows tornado casualties in Michigan, follow these steps: [L2-3]

1. Open a blank presentation and choose the Chart layout option. Add `Michigan Tornado Casualties by Decade` as the title, as shown in Figure 3.19.

Figure 3.19

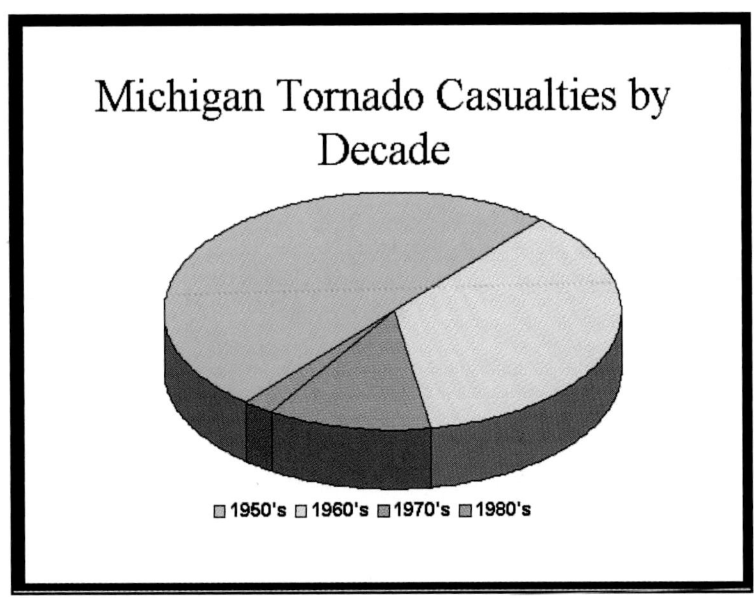

2. Activate the chart, and enter the following data:

   `1950s 1,695`

   `1960s 1,236`

   `1970s 384`

   `1980s 79`
3. Delete the columns that are not used on the datasheet. Delete the titles in the first row. They are not used in this chart. Close the datasheet.
4. Change the chart to display the data By Column.
5. Change the Chart Type to the 3D Pie Chart. Notice the very clear pattern that emerges as you look at this chart.
6. Save the slide on your floppy disk with the name `Tornadoes`. Leave the file open to use in the next Challenge exercise.

4. Modifying a Pie Chart

In this exercise, you make several modifications to the Tornado pie chart that you created in the previous exercise. When you have completed this exercise, you will have a chart that looks similar to the one in Figure 3.19. [L4]

To modify the Tornado pie chart, follow these steps:

1. If necessary, open the Tornadoes file you created in the previous exercise.
2. Click the Plot area, the square around the pie, and drag one of the handles in the corner of the Plot area placeholder to expand the size of the Plot area.
3. Select the legend, and open the Format Legend dialog box. Change the placement to the bottom of the chart. Change the font to Arial. Change the border (found under the Patterns tab) to None.
4. On the green segment of the pie, click once, and click a second time to select the segment. (This is not the same as a double-click.)
5. Right-click the selected segment and choose Format Data Point. In the Format Data Point dialog box, change the color to a color of your choice.
6. Repeat steps 4 and 5 for the other three segments of the pie, selecting new colors for each segment.
7. Use Help to figure out how to change the 3D settings. Set the Elevation at 30 degrees. Rotate the chart to 220 degrees. Click OK to accept your changes.
8. Use the sizing handles in the corner of the placeholder to increase the size of the chart.
9. Open the Format Plot Area dialog box, and select None for the border options.
10. View your slide in the Slide Show view. Save the file and print the slide.
11. Close the file. Exit PowerPoint unless you are going to proceed to the Discovery Zone exercises.

Discovery Zone

Discovery Zone exercises require advanced knowledge of topics presented in *Essentials* lessons, application of skills from multiple lessons, or self-directed learning of new skills.

These exercises are independent of each other and can be completed in any order. They help you learn how to create a table, which is another data presentation tool, and how to import a chart from Excel. In each exercise, you create a separate file that you can close at the end of the exercise.

1. Creating a Table

Another PowerPoint tool you can use to display data is the table. This feature works like tables that you create in Word. Like the Microsoft Graph program, you use a special table editor that enables you to work with the table you create. Open Help and from the Microsoft PowerPoint Help option type `how do I create a table`. Select Create a table and read this introductory information. If necessary, print the topic to use as a reference; then choose Create a simple table and use the instructions provided to create a 3 by 8 table in a new blank presentation. Enter the following data using Tab to move across the table from one cell to the next.

Ages	Boys	Girls
5&6	23%	29%
7&8	59%	58%
9&10	79%	78%
11&12	82%	73%
13&14	78%	65%
15&16	36%	0%
17&18	0%	11%

Increase the font size and add emphasis as appropriate. Click the Table button on the Tables and Borders toolbar and click Select Table; choose Table, Borders and Fill, and eliminate the gridlines. (*Hint*: Click each line in the diagram area to turn it off and on.) Title the slide **`Percentage of`**

Children who Attended School in 1870. Add a design template of your choice. Save the table as Attended School. Print a copy of the slide and close the file. Your slide should look similar to the one shown in Figure 3.20.

Figure 3.20

Percentage of Children who Attended School in 1870

Ages	Boys	Girls
5 & 6	23%	29%
7 & 8	59%	58%
9 & 10	79%	78%
11 & 12	82%	73%
13 & 14	78%	65%
15 & 16	36%	0%
17 & 18	0%	11%

2. Inserting a Microsoft Excel Chart as an Object

Sometimes it is preferable to insert a chart that has been previously created in another program, such as Microsoft Excel. One advantage of this approach is that the data does not have to be reentered, thereby reducing the risk of error. A second advantage is that the chart can be linked to the original file so that any changes to the data in the source file are also reflected in the chart object in the PowerPoint presentation.

Before you proceed with this exercise, copy the Excel file entitled 1999 Sales from the CD to your floppy disk. This file should be located in the folder for this section of the book. This file contains the chart that you insert in a PowerPoint presentation.

Activate Help and from the Microsoft PowerPoint Help option, type inserting an Excel chart. Click Insert a Microsoft Excel chart in a presentation, and read the instructions. If necessary, print the topic for reference.

Start a new presentation with the Title Only slide and follow the instructions given in Help to insert the chart. Use the Create from file option on the Insert Object dialog box, and use the Browse button to locate the 1999 Sales file that you copied to your floppy disk. Select the Link check box on the Insert Object dialog box to make sure the chart links to the data source file. Adjust the size of the chart to fill the maximum space without overlapping the title area of the slide. Title the slide Real Estate Brokers.

Double-click the chart that you inserted. This launches Excel, which enables you to make changes to the data. The same charting tools that are used in PowerPoint are used in Excel. Click the 1999 Sales tab at the bottom of the screen. (Maximize your screen if you do not see the tabs at the bottom.) Double-click the cell for the 2nd Qtr for the South (cell C5), and change the data from 42.1 to 82.1. Press ←Enter and notice the change in the totals. Click the Chart1 tab at the bottom of the screen to see the changes in the Excel chart. Use the taskbar to go back to PowerPoint. The chart no longer displays. You have to update the link to display the change. Right-click on the small gray box and choose Update link to see the chart. Save the file as 1999 Sales Chart. Close and reopen the PowerPoint file. Choose Yes to update the link. Print the slide and close both files.

3. Using Paste Special to Copy an Excel Worksheet to PowerPoint

Activate Help and look for information on linked and embedded objects. Several options are available to you for sharing information between applications. Read the content on the options for sharing information. Specifically, review the topic Create a linked or embedded object from information in an existing file.

If you completed Discovery Exercise 2, you can use the same file you created for that exercise; otherwise, open a new PowerPoint presentation. Choose the Title Only slide layout for a new slide. Title the slide **1999 Sales ($million)**. Launch Excel and open the file 1999 Sales. If necessary, select the 1999 Sales tab at the bottom of the worksheet. Click and drag across the data in cells A3 through F8 to select it. Choose Edit, Copy. Use the taskbar to return to PowerPoint. Click the open area on the slide and choose Edit, Paste Special. In the Paste Special dialog box, select the Paste option, if necessary, and select Microsoft Excel Worksheet Object in the As box. This action inserts the selected area as an object in the presentation. Click OK.

Expand the chart to fill the available space. With this type of Paste Special option, when you double-click the inserted object it launches a small spreadsheet that you can use to edit the data. Any changes made to the data using this method will *not* be reflected in the original source file. Save the file as **1999 Sales Chart**. Print a copy of the slide; close the file and exit PowerPoint.

Project 4

Adding Animations for the Slide Show

Objectives

In this project, you learn how to

- **Use the Slide Sorter View to Change Sequence**
- **Animate the Transition from One Slide to the Next**
- **Animate Text**
- **Dim Previously Displayed Text**

Key terms introduced in this project include

- animate
- animation features
- Custom Animations
- dim
- transition

Why Would I Do This?

After you create a presentation, you should review it using the Slide Show view to see whether you can make it better. You may want to rearrange the slides so that they are presented in a different order. When photographers rearrange a set of traditional 35mm slides, they place them side-by-side on a piece of glass that has a light behind it. This method enables them to see all the slides at the same time and make judgments about how they look as a group or how the sequence flows from one slide to another. PowerPoint uses the same type of layout in the Slide Sorter view to let you make similar decisions about a set of slides.

Another aspect of your slide show that you can control is the ***transition*** between slides—the way the entire slide moves onto your screen. For example, each slide can appear to fly in from any direction, dissolve from one slide to the next, or change from the center of the slide out to the edge.

You might also want to animate your slide presentation to give it greater visual appeal and to provide you with more control over the pace of the presentation. When you ***animate*** a slide, you set the way each bulleted point, graphic, or chart element appears on the screen. You can also specify a length of time for the point to remain on the screen before the next animation occurs. PowerPoint includes a variety of animation features that you can apply to individual slides, as well as to an entire slide show. ***Animation features*** are controls for the direction, speed, and sound used when a new object or line of text appears on a slide. Bulleted points can come onto the screen from the top, sides, or bottom of the screen. They can move onto the screen at a fast, medium, or slow speed. One popular animation feature is to dim the current bulleted point when a new bulleted point appears on the screen. When you ***dim*** a bulleted point, you change it to a color with less contrast, so it appears to fade into the background and is less dominant on the screen. This helps the audience focus on the next point in your presentation, which is in a brighter color.

In this project, you rearrange some slides using the Slide Sorter view, add transitions between slides, add animation to text, and dim bullet points.

Visual Summary

When you are done, you will have animated a bulleted list, so that the points appear one at a time and the previous points are shown in a new color. Your slide will look like Figure 4.1.

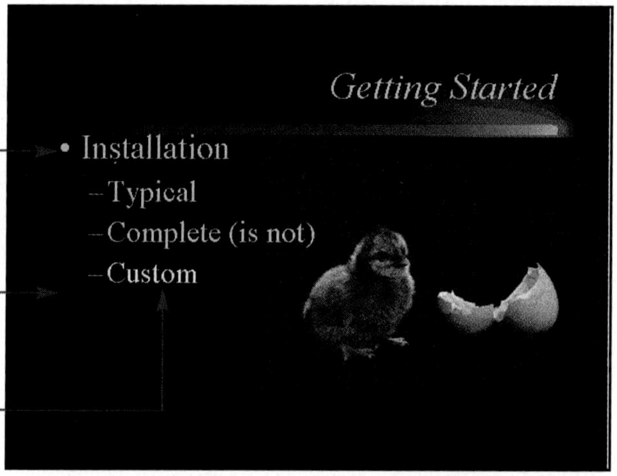

Figure 4.1
Animations add visual appeal to the Slide Show.

Animations are used to display text one line at a time

Listed items change color as a new point is introduced

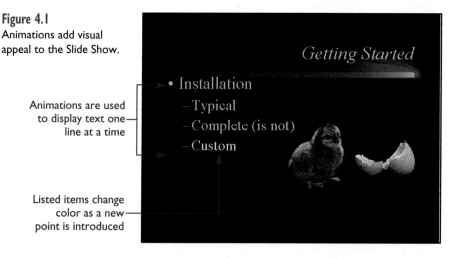

Lesson 1: Using the Slide Sorter View to Change Sequence

Most slide shows benefit from review and revision. The Slide Sorter view enables you to see several slides at one time, so you can examine the sequence of the slides and see how they look next to each other. Slide Sorter view is also the best place to rearrange the order of the slides.

In this lesson, you use the Slide Sorter view to change the order of the slides in a presentation.

To Use the Slide Sorter View to Change Sequence

1. **Launch PowerPoint. Locate and open `PO-0401` from your student disk. Save the file on your floppy disk as `Install Office`.**

2. **Click the Slide Sorter View button.**
   The slides display side-by-side (see Figure 4.2). Use the scrollbar to view Slides 7–11.

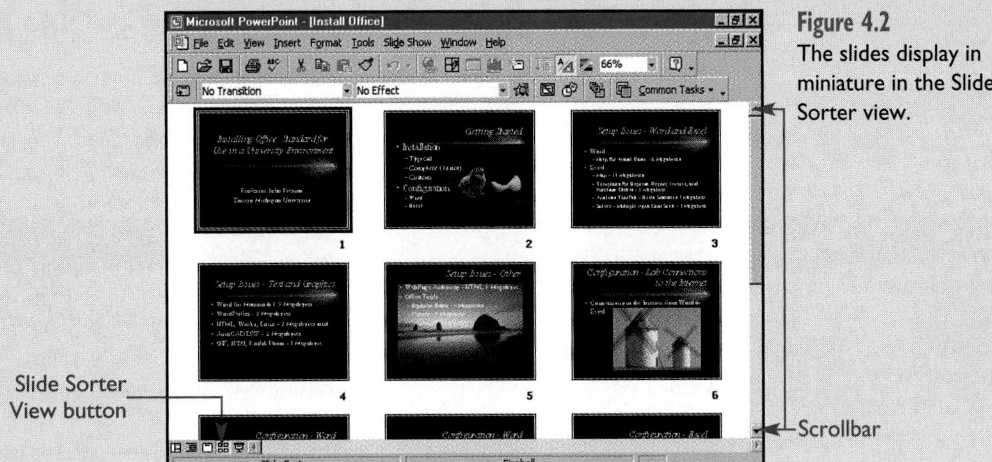

Figure 4.2
The slides display in miniature in the Slide Sorter view.

3. **Click the list arrow on the right side of the Zoom box and click 33%.**
   All the slides in this presentation display on one screen, but they are difficult to read.

4. **Click the Show Formatting button on the Standard toolbar to turn off the details of the slide's formatting.**
   The slide's title is still displayed, but in a larger font (see Figure 4.3). Upon examination of the sequence, you decide that the sixth slide, which deals with Internet connections, should be moved to the second-to-last position.

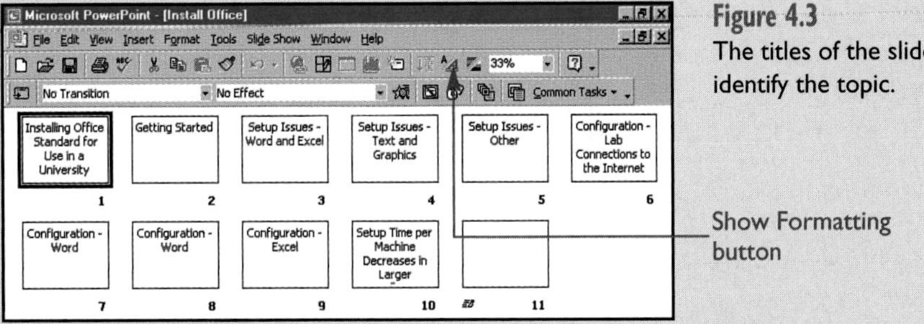

Figure 4.3
The titles of the slide identify the topic.

5. **Click and drag the slide to a position between Slides 9 and 10. Release the mouse button when a vertical line displays between these two slides.**
   The Internet slide is now Slide 9, and all the affected slides are renumbered (see Figure 4.4).

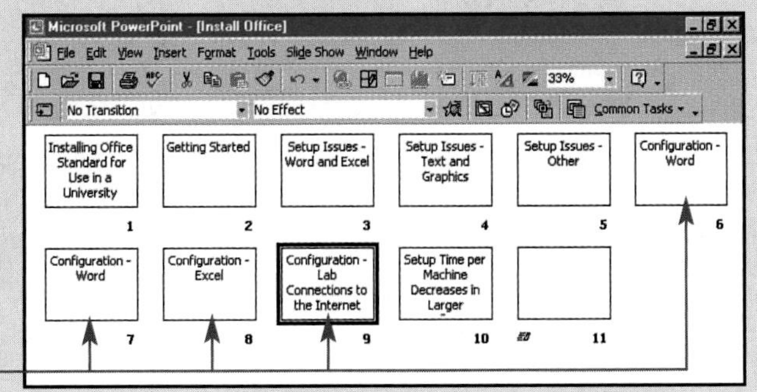

Figure 4.4
The Internet slide is now slide number 9.

continues ▶

To Use the Slide Sorter View to Change Sequence (continued)

6 **Click Save to save your changes**
Leave the file open for use in the next lesson.

Lesson 2: Animating the Transition from One Slide to the Next

When you run the Slide Show, it presents the slides one after the other when you click the mouse button or press Spacebar. The slides simply appear on the screen in their entirety. You can control the way a slide comes into view by animating this transition between slides.

In this lesson, you set the transitions from one slide to the next.

To Animate Transitions

1 **In the Slide Sorter view, choose Edit, Select All from the menu.**
All the slides are selected.

2 **Click the drop-down arrow on the right side of the Slide Transition Effects box to reveal a list of transition options.**
The transition option you select from the list is applied to the selected slides.

3 **Select Box Out.**
This transition opens the slide from the center outward in a boxed shape. A small icon appears beneath each slide to indicate that a transition has been applied (see Figure 4.5).

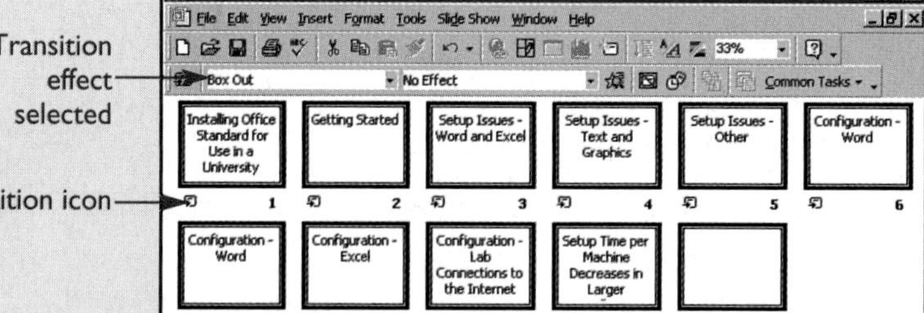

Figure 4.5
The transition icon displays beneath each slide.

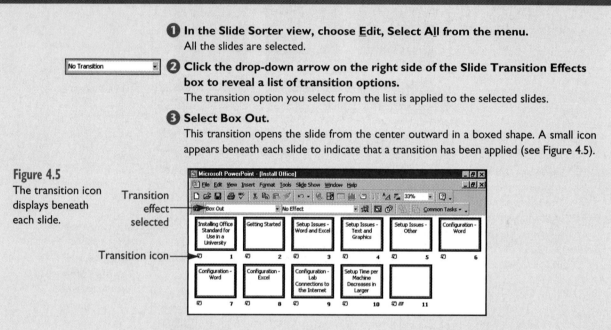

4 **Click the Show Formatting button to show the slide details again.**

5 **Click the list arrow on the right side of the Zoom box. Click 66%.**
The slides enlarge (see Figure 4.6).

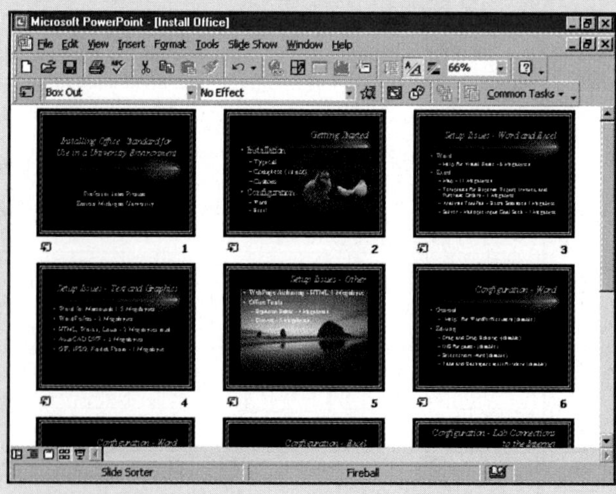

Figure 4.6
The slides show the details and enlarge to demonstrate the transition effect.

6 If necessary, scroll to display the first slide. Click in a white space between the slides to deselect the slides, and click the first slide to select it.
The dark border around the slide indicates that it is selected.

7 Click the Slide Transition icon below Slide 1.
The Box Out transition is demonstrated on Slide 1. This gives you the opportunity to review the transition style that you selected.

8 With Slide 1 selected, click the Slide Show button to start the slide show. Click the mouse button to advance from one slide to the next to observe the Box Out transition.
Stop at Slide 9 entitled `Configuration – Lab Connections to the Internet` (see Figure 4.7).

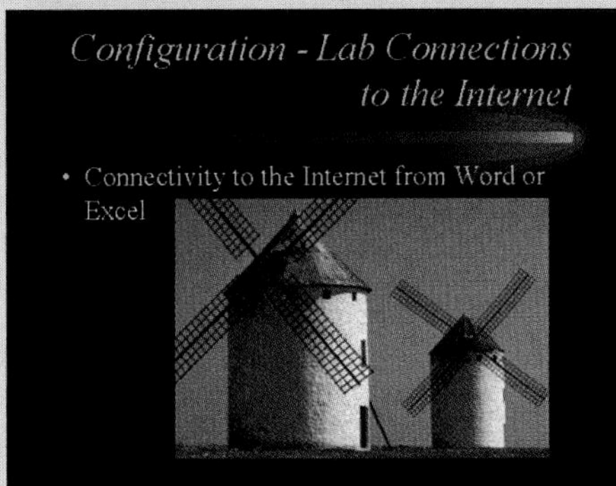

Figure 4.7
A Box Out transition is used between the slides.

9 Right-click to reveal the shortcut menu. Click End Show to return to Slide Sorter view.
You can use the shortcut menu to end a slide show or you can press Esc.

10 Click the Save button to save your work.
Leave the file open for use in the next lesson.

Setting Slide Transition Styles
Slide transitions can be different for each slide. You can select the Random option, which varies the transition randomly, or you can individually select a slide and set the transition. The transition names convey some idea of what the transition looks like. Often a direction is used to indicate whether the transition moves down the slide, from top to bottom, or across the slide from left to right. To try different transition, simply select a slide and select a transition style. If you don't like the results, try another one.

Lesson 3: Animating Text

Just as you selected an animation style for the transitions between your slides, you can also control the manner in which text displays on the slide. For example, people read text from left to right, so you might want to reveal the text from left to right. It is also desirable to display your bulleted points one at a time to prevent your audience from reading ahead.

In this lesson, you animate the appearance of the text. You also learn how to remove the transition effect from individual slides.

To Animate Text

1 Select Edit, Select All from the menu.
A dark border displays around each slide.

continues ▶

To Animate Text (continued)

No Effect

2. **Click the list arrow on the right side of the Preset Animation box, and scroll to the bottom of the list of options.**
3. **Select Wipe Right.**
   This effect reveals the text from left to right during a slide show. Look at Figure 4.8 and observe the text animation icon below each slide, with the exception of Slide 8.

Figure 4.8
Preset animation icons display below the slides.

No Animation icon here

Animation style selected

Preset animation icon

4. **Click in an open space to deselect all the slides and click Slide 1. Click the Slide Show button to start the slide show. Click the mouse repeatedly to observe the text transition.**
   Notice that the text transition is probably not necessary on the title slide.
5. **Right-click, and click End Show to return to the Slide Sorter view.**
6. **Click Slide 1 to select it. Click the list arrow on the right side of the Preset Animation box and scroll to the top of the list.**
7. **Select No Effect.**
   Figure 4.9 shows that the text animation icon is removed from Slide 1.

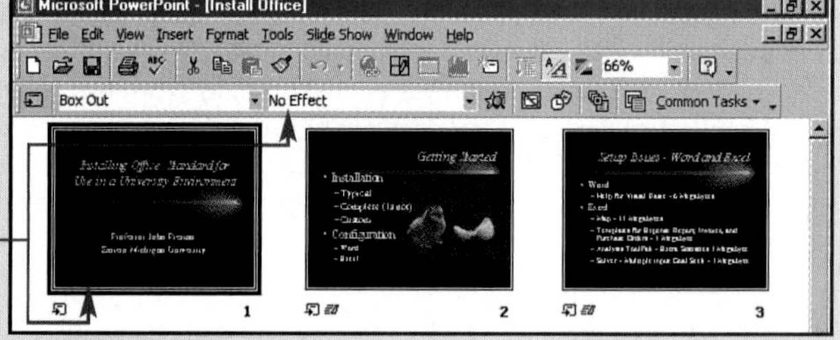

Figure 4.9
The animation can be added or removed from slides one at time.

Animation effect removed from Slide 1

Leave the file open for use in the next lesson.

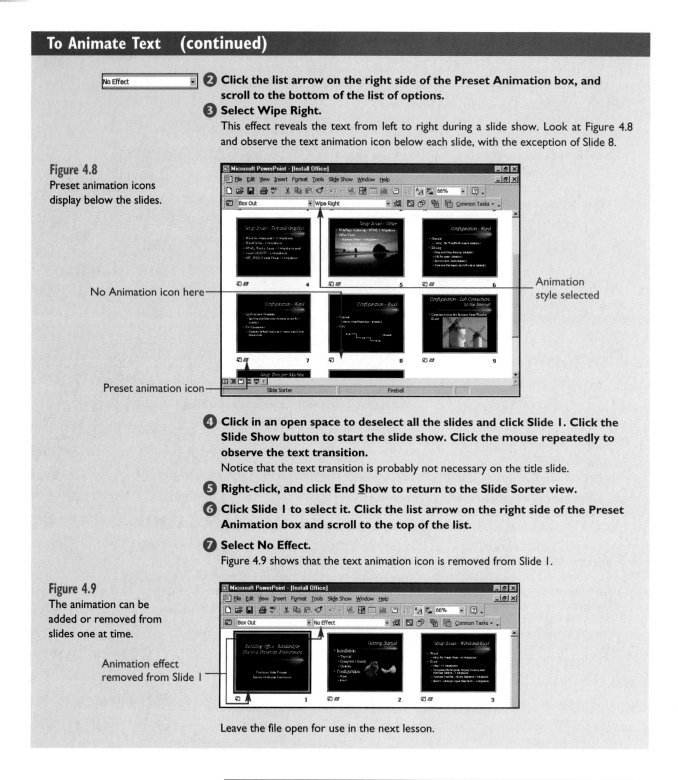

Where's the Animation Icon?

Slide 8 does not show the animation icon because the original file contains a custom animation for no effect for this slide. The Select All option does not override custom animations. When a slide has a custom animation, the Preset Animation box is blank. If you click Slide 8, you see that the Preset Animation box is blank.

Using Animation Effects

As with the transition effects, a wide variety of animation effects can be used. Again the name of the effect gives you some idea of how the effect displays the text and the direction in which it moves. For example, with a fly effect the entire bulleted point moves quickly onto the screen as a group; with the crawl effect the words move onto the screen very slowly. When animating text, it is best to stick with one or two styles for the entire presentation. Otherwise, you run the risk that your audience will watch the animations and miss the point of your presentation.

Lesson 4: Dimming Previously Displayed Text

You can emphasize the text you are currently talking about by dimming the bulleted points you already discussed. This helps the audience keep track of where you are in your presentation, and makes sure they focus on the current point. You might also want to reveal the subpoints of a section one at a time. You can individually control the timing of items that appear on your slide using the Custom Animation feature. The ***Custom Animation*** feature enables you to control a slide by assigning a particular animation technique to each element on the slide.

In this lesson, you use the Custom Animation feature to dim previous points and to reveal subpoints one at a time.

To Dim Previously Displayed Points

1. **Click Slide 2 to select it, and then click the Slide View button.**
2. **Point at the text and right-click.**
   The text area is selected and a shortcut menu opens.
3. **Click Custom Animation.**
   The Custom Animation dialog box displays. Make sure the Effects tab is selected, as shown in Figure 4.10.

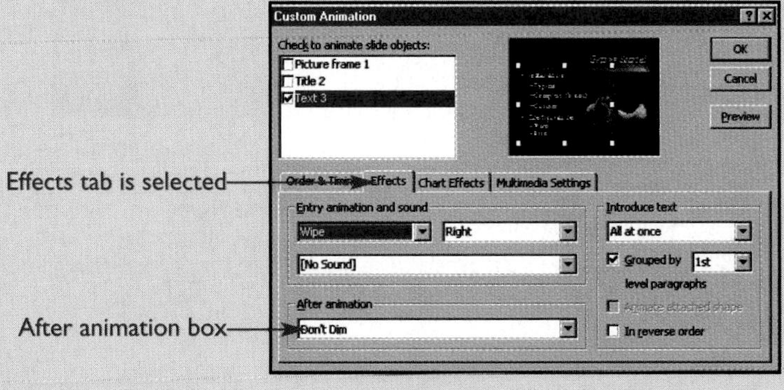

Figure 4.10
Use the Custom Animation dialog box to control individual elements in a slide show.

4. **Click the list arrow on the right side of the After animation box.**
   Several options display.
5. **Select the fifth color box from the left to select a darker color than the yellow that is used for the text.**
6. **Click the list arrow on the right side of the Grouped by level paragraphs box and select 2nd from the list.**
   This type of animation lists the second level subpoints of the bulleted text one at a time. Compare your selections to Figure 4.11.

continues ►

To Dim Previously Displayed Points (continued)

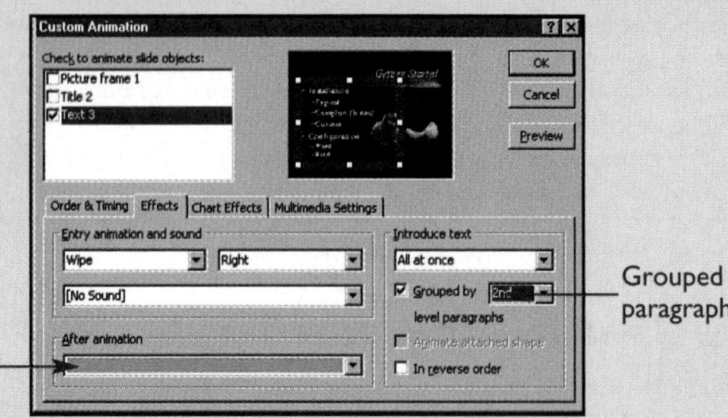

Figure 4.11
Use the Custom Animation dialog box to set how your text is introduced.

❼ **Click OK to return to Slide view.**

❽ **Click the Slide Show button. Click repeatedly to reveal each bulleted point and its subpoints individually.**
Notice that each point changes color after the next point is presented (see Figure 4.12).

Figure 4.12
Color changes after the next point is selected.

❾ **Right-click to display the shortcut menu and click End Show.**
The slide displays in Slide view.

❿ **Click the Save button to save your changes. Close the file and exit PowerPoint.**

Summary

In this project, you learned how to rearrange slides using the Slide Sorter view. You then added a box out transition to the slides and a wipe right animation for the bulleted points in the slide. Finally, you learned how to add one type of custom animation by dimming previously displayed bulleted points.

You can expand your learning by trying some other transition and preset animation effects. Try using different transition and animation effects for different slides to see how it affects a slide show. Use Help and explore the topic **`About animating text and objects`** to get an overview of different capabilities of the PowerPoint program.

Checking Concepts and Terms

True/False

For each of the following, check *T* or *F* to indicate whether the statement is true or false.

__T__F **1.** You can change the sequence of slides by clicking and dragging a slide to a new position in Slide Show view. [L1]

__T__F **2.** In Slide Sorter view, you turn off the details of a slide and just show the slide's title by clicking the Show Formatting button. [L1]

__T__F **3.** The Slide Transition Effects box displays how each line of bulleted text will be revealed. [L2]

__T__F **4.** If you are in Slide Sorter view and want to see how a particular slide transition looks, you can click the small icon below the slide to preview the transition. (Show Formatting must be turned on.) [L2]

__T__F **5.** The After animation option dims the previous slide during a slide show. [L3]

__T__F **6.** Animation can be applied to each bulleted point, graphic, or chart in a presentation. [L3]

__T__F **7.** Animation features include the direction, speed, and even the sound that is used when something new appears on a slide. [Intro]

__T__F **8.** Bulleted points can come onto the screen from the top or bottom of the screen but not from the side. [L3]

__T__F **9.** When you dim a bulleted point, you change it to a different color so that it is less dominant on the screen. [L4]

__T__F **10.** Transitions between slides have to be the same for the entire presentation. [L2]

Multiple Choice

Circle the letter of the correct answer for each of the following.

1. A transition is best described as ____________. [Intro]

a. the way a bullet point appears on the screen

b. the way a slide appears on the screen

c. the change from one bullet point to the next

d. none of the above

2. If you set a custom animation for a slide, the preset animation box __________ for that slide. [L3]

a. displays the words custom animation

b. displays the words no effect

c. is blank

d. displays the name of the effect you have added

3. Text animation effects control how bulleted points appear in a presentation by specifying __________. [L3]

a. direction

b. speed

c. sound used

d. all of the above

4. In the Slide Sorter view, the Show Formatting button is used to __________. [L1]

a. turn the details of the slide on or off

b. show the animation effects

c. show the transition effects

d. identify the font styles, size, and emphasis for each bulleted point

5. The Slide Sorter view is used to __________. [L1]

a. rearrange the order of slides

b. add transition effects to slides

c. add preset animations to slides

d. perform all of the above tasks

Screen ID

Identify each of the items shown in Figure 4.13.

Figure 4.13

A. Show Formatting button
B. Slide Show button
C. Slide Sorter View button
D. No animation is set for this slide
E. Slide View button
F. Slide Transition icon
G. Preset Animation icon
H. Slide Transition Effects box
I. Zoom box
J. Preset Animation box

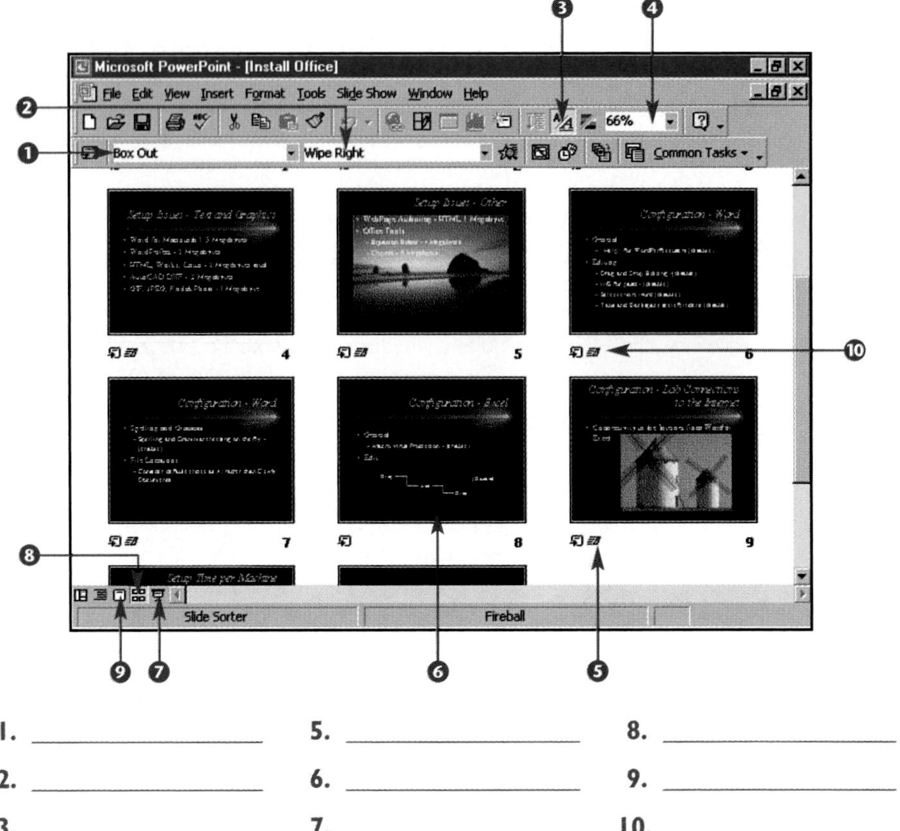

1. ____________
2. ____________
3. ____________
4. ____________
5. ____________
6. ____________
7. ____________
8. ____________
9. ____________
10. ____________

Discussion Questions

1. In the process of creating a presentation, when would it be best to add transitions and animation effects?
2. Describe a presentation that you have seen that did not use animation effects. Would the presentation have been improved if it had been animated? Why?
3. You have seen just a small part of what can be done with animations. What additional kinds of animations would you like to learn about?

Skill Drill

Skill Drill exercises reinforce project skills. Each skill reinforced is the same, or nearly the same, as a skill presented in the project. Detailed instructions are provided in a step-by-step format.

These exercises all use the same presentation. Leave the presentation open at the end of each exercise for use in the next. Launch PowerPoint. Open the file `PO-0402` and save it on your disk as `Nucleus in the News`. (This is a presentation created by the author to help people understand current events that are related to nuclear physics.)

1. Rearranging a Slide Show Using the Slide Sorter

It is easier to work with the slides as a group using the Slide Sorter view. In this exercise, you turn off the formatting, so it is easier to see the slides you want to move and then you rearrange some of the slides. To rearrange the slides follow these steps: [L1]

1. Click the Slide Sorter button.
2. Change the Zoom to 33%.
3. Click the Show Formatting button to turn off the details and display only the slide titles.
4. Slides 21, 22, and 23 deal with the Radon issue. Move these three slides to the end of the presentation. The last three titles should be `Radioactive Isotopes Turn Into Stable Isotopes`, `Radon`, and `Radon`.
5. Choose File, Print from the menu.
6. Choose Slides, and type **22-27**.
7. Select Handouts in the Print what box, and select 6 in the Slides per page box.
8. Select Pure black & white, and Frame slides. Click OK to print. Leave the file open.

2. Applying a Slide Transition to All the Slides

In this exercise, you apply a transition to the slides. To add a transition effect to the slides follow these steps: [L1–2]

1. Click the Show Formatting button to display the details of the slides, and change the Zoom back to 66%.
2. Choose Edit, Select All from the menu.
3. Click the list arrow on the right side of the Slide Transition Effects box and select Cover Right.
4. Click the small transition icon below one of the slides to preview the transition.
5. Choose File, Print from the menu.
6. Choose Current slide. (It doesn't matter which slide you print.) Select Slides in the Print what box. Select Pure black & white. Click OK to print the slide.
7. Below the printed slide, write a description of what the Cover Right transition looks like. Draw an arrow to indicate the direction of motion.

3. Animating Text Transitions

In this exercise, you add a preset animation effect to the slides and then view the results of the change. To add a preset animation, follow these steps: [L2]

1. If necessary, click the Slide Sorter button to show the slides.
2. Choose Edit, Select all from the menu.
3. Click the list arrow on the right side of the Preset Animation box.
4. Select Dissolve from the list.
5. Click between the slides to deselect them.
6. Click Slide 4 to select it.
7. Click the Slide Show button to start the slide show.
8. Click the mouse button repeatedly to display each line of text using the Dissolve transition.
9. Press Esc to end the slide show. Click Slide 4 to select it again.
10. Choose File, Print from the menu.
11. Choose Current slide. Select Slides in the Print what box. Select Pure black & white. Click OK to print.
12. Below the printed slide, write a description of what the Dissolve transition looks like.

4. Dimming Previous Points

To help your audience focus on the current point in the presentation, it is helpful to dim points that you already covered. To dim previously displayed points, follow these steps: [L4]

1. Click the Slide View button to display Slide 4 in Slide view.
2. Right-click the text portion of the slide and choose Custom Animation from the shortcut menu. Click the Effects tab if necessary.
3. Click the list arrow on the right side of the After animation box.
4. Select a gray color.
5. Click OK.
6. Click the Slide Show button to display this slide. Click the mouse button repeatedly to see how the previous points are dimmed. Press Esc to return to Slide view.
7. Save your changes and close the file. Leave PowerPoint running if you are proceeding to the Challenge exercises.

Challenge

Challenge exercises expand on or are somewhat related to skills presented in the lessons. Each exercise provides a brief narrative introduction followed by instructions, in a numbered step or bulleted list format, that are not as detailed as those in the Skill Drill section.

In these exercises, you use the Random transition effect, which uses a variety of transitions between slides. You then learn how to add animations to other objects in a presentation, such as text boxes and connectors, charts, and WordArt objects. Three different files are used for the four exercises. Each file should be opened from the disk that came with your book and then saved under the suggested filename on your student floppy disk.

1. Using Random Transitions

In this project, you learned to apply the same transition to all the slides in a presentation. In this exercise, you select the Random Transition, which varies the transition automatically between slides, creating more visual interest. Then you describe one of the transitions in the slide show that you particularly liked. [L2]

To apply the Random Transition to slides in a presentation, follow these steps:

1. Locate and open the `PO-0403` file. Save the file with the name `Office Demo`.
2. Add your name to the first slide after the words `Presented by`.
3. Change to Slide Sorter view and select all the slides. Change the transition to the Random Transition option, which is located at the bottom of the list of transitions.
4. Start with Slide 1 and view the slide show to see the various transitions that are used by the Random Transition option. Choose one of the transitions you liked and write a sentence that describes the transition. What would you name the transition?
5. Save your changes and close the presentation.

2. Animating Drawing Objects

In this project, you learned how to animate bulleted points. You can also animate drawing objects. If drawing objects are used to show a connection or a sequence, it is useful to animate them to demonstrate their relationship. This enables you to show the flow of ideas from one to the next by displaying each part of a diagram one piece at a time. For this exercise, you use a slide that was part of the Installing Office file you worked on during the project. You set the sequence of text and object animation using the Custom Animation options. [L3]

To animate text boxes and connectors on a slide, follow these steps:

1. Locate and open file `PO-0404`. Save the file on your floppy disk with the name `Object Animations`.
2. Make sure the first slide displays and select the text portion of the slide. Right-click to open the shortcut menu.
3. Click Custom Animation to open the Custom Animation dialog box. Click the Order & Timing tab to select it.
4. Click the check box next to Text 3 in Check to animate slide objects list. Text box 3 is added to the Animation order box at the bottom of the dialog box. The selected object is outlined in the Preview window.
5. Click the check box next to Elbow connector 6. It is added to the Animation order box.
6. Animate the rest of the objects in the following order:

   Text 4

   Elbow connector 7

   Text 5

   Text 8
7. Click the Effects tab and click Text 3.
8. Hold down Shift and click Elbow connector 7. This selects the first five objects in the drawing.
9. In the Entry animation and sound area, click the list arrow on the right side of the box on the left. Scroll down and select Wipe.
10. In the same area, click the list arrow on the box on the right and select Right.
11. Click the Preview button to see a demonstration of how the animations will work.
12. Click OK to finish the custom animation and return to Slide view.
13. Save your changes; leave the file open for use in the next exercise.

3. Animating a Chart

Another type of object in a presentation that you might want to animate is a chart. To animate a chart, you use the Custom Animation feature. Charts are used to communicate the relationship between numbers. If the relationship is based on a time sequence, you may want to animate the parts of your chart to emphasize this sequence. [L3]

To animate the individual parts of a chart, follow these steps:

1. Open the Object Animations file used in the previous Challenge exercise, if necessary. If you did not complete Challenge 2, locate and open file **PO-0404** and save it on your disk as **Object Animations**.
2. Move to Slide 2 and right-click the chart.
3. Click Custom Animation and select the Chart Effects tab, if it is not already selected.
4. Click the list arrow on the right side of the Introduce chart elements box and select by Element in Series.
5. Click the Animate grid and legend box so that those elements are also animated.
6. Click OK to return to Slide view.
7. Click the Slide Show button and click the mouse button several times to see how the individual elements of the chart display one at a time.
8. Close the Slide Show; save your changes and close the file.

4. Removing Background Graphics and Animating a WordArt Slide

You use WordArt to create special effects that can be on a slide by itself or part of another slide. Because you want the visual appeal of the WordArt to standout, it is useful to remove any background design graphics so that they don't compete with the WordArt. Then you can apply a custom animation that takes advantage of the WordArt shape. [L2–3]

To remove background graphics from a WordArt slide and apply custom animations suited to the shape of the graphics, follow these steps:

1. Locate and open the **PO-0405** file. Save the file with the name **WordArt Animation**.
2. Change to the Slide Sorter view, if necessary, and select all the slides. Click Format, Background and check the Omit background graphics from master box in the dialog box, and then apply it to the slides.
3. Use the Custom Animation dialog box to apply a different animation to each slide. Choose something that takes advantage of the shape of the WordArt. Options you might consider include Spiral, Swivel, and Zoom.
4. Using the Slide Transition dialog box, change the speed of the transition for each slide.
5. View the results in the slide show.
6. Save your changes; close the file, and exit PowerPoint unless you are going to move to the Discovery Zone exercises.

Discovery Zone

Discovery Zone exercises require advanced knowledge of topics presented in *Essentials* lessons, application of skills from multiple lessons, or self-directed learning of new skills.

These Discovery Zone exercises are independent of each other and can be completed in any order. They help you learn other techniques for changing and animating a slide show. You learn how to change the order of animated objects using the move arrows in the Custom Animation dialog box. In the second exercise, you learn how to change the order of topics in an outline. In the third exercise, you set a presentation to run continuously. In the last exercise, you add sound effects to some animations. In each exercise, you create a separate file that you can close at the end of the exercise.

1. Changing the Order of Animated Objects

If you have a slide that is mostly objects, it is important that the objects appear in the order in which you will be discussing them. This may not match the order in which they were created, or the random number that was applied to each object. You can use the move arrows in the Custom Animation dialog box to change the order of animated objects.

Locate and open the **PO-0406** file found on the disk that came with your book. Save the file with the name **Access Intro**. Each object on this slide has been animated, but the order needs to be corrected. Use the move arrows to the right of the Animation order box in the Custom Animation dialog box to correct the order of the objects. The objects should appear in the following order:

1. `Text 1`
2. `Text 2`
3. `Straight Connector 11`
4. `Text 3`
5. `Shape 7`
6. `Elbow Connector 8`
7. `Text 4`
8. `Shape 9`
9. `Elbow Connector 10`
10. `Text 5`
11. `Text 6`
12. `Oval 12`
13. `Text 13`
14. `Line 14`

Print the slide and number each object on the slide to indicate the order that it appears in the presentation. Save your changes. Close the presentation.

2. Changing the Order of Topics in an Outline

In this project, you learned how to change the order of slides using the drag-and-drop method in the Slide Sorter view. Sometimes you need to change the order of topics within a slide. You can use the drag-and-drop technique to move topics within a slide, but it requires a little more finesse. Generally, it is easier to use the Outline toolbar to move topics.

Locate and open **PO-0407**. Save the file on your disk with the name **Office Demo2**. Add your name to the first slide after the words **Presented by**. Open Help and type **rearrange topics**. Select Change the order of paragraphs in an outline and read the resulting Help screen. Change to the Outline view and open the Outlining toolbar. On Slide 3, select the second topic and make it the first topic. You can drag the selected text to the new location or use the move up arrow on the Outline toolbar. On Slide 4, select the first topic, including any subpoints, and use the down arrow to move it down to the second topic. Make sure the entire topic moves. On Slide 5, move the first topic to the third position. Save your changes and print Slides 3 through 5. Close the file.

3. Setting a Presentation to Run Continuously

One of the features of PowerPoint you can use is to have a slide show run continuously. Using this technique, you can create a slide show to highlight the features and benefits of your product and have it play continuously at a trade show or convention booth. This gives potential customers something to look at when they stop by your booth. It can be created to run with or without assistance.

To learn more about a self-running presentation, open Help and type **self-running presentations**. Select the appropriate topic to read, and print it. Locate and open **PO-0407**, located on the CD that came with this book. Save the file on your disk with the name **Office Demo2**. If necessary, add **your name** to the first slide after the words **Presented by**. Follow the procedure described in Help to set this presentation to run automatically. Choose either the manual or rehearsal option to set the timing for each slide. Be sure to set the timing in seconds, not minutes. The timing applies to each item on the slide. View the slide show to see how the automatic timing works. Make any adjustments necessary. Save your changes and close the file.

4. Adding Animation Sounds

PowerPoint has several animation sounds that you can add to a presentation for special effects. It is advisable to limit the use of these animation sounds, so they do not detract from your message. An animated sound in the beginning or end of a presentation can add some humor and grab the audience's attention.

Locate and open **PO-0408**. Save the file on your disk with the name **Access Intro2**. Using the Animation Effects button on the toolbar, or the Slide Show, Custom Animation menu, add sound animation to at least two text boxes and three lines. If necessary, use Help for instructions on how to add sounds. Preview the changes using the Slide Show view and make any adjustments that are necessary. Save your changes, and close the file. Exit PowerPoint.

Part V Access

Access

1 Creating a Database

2 Entering and Editing Data

3 Querying Your Database

4 Creating and Using Forms

5 Creating and Printing Reports

6 Interacting and Connecting

7 Customizing Fields and Tables

8 Making Data Entry Easier and More Accurate

Working with Databases

Microsoft Access is a database program that enables you to store, retrieve, analyze, and print information. Companies use databases for many purposes: to manage customer files, to track orders and inventories, and for marketing purposes. An individual might set up a database to track household expenses or manage a list of family, friends, and business addresses. Teachers often set up a database to track student grades and other class information. A database enables you to access and manage thousands, even millions, of pieces of data in an organized, efficient, and accurate manner.

Tables are the foundation of the database because they store the data in the database. Each table stores a set of related data. Tables are made up of records that are all the related information about one person, event, or transaction. Records display in rows. Each category of information in a record is known as a field. Fields display in columns, and the field name appears in the database table as a column heading.

Tables can also be connected to each other, enabling you to use fields from more than one table in a report. Linking tables is a feature of a relational database.

When you first open an Access database, the database window displays. The various database objects, such as tables, forms, and reports, display as buttons down the left side of the window. You can choose to create or open tables from this window. You can also choose to change the design of existing tables.

The look of the Access window changes, depending on what you are doing with the program. You might recognize many parts of the Access screen as familiar parts of every Windows program—elements such as the Minimize, Maximize/Restore, and Close buttons, as well as the scrollbars.

Project 1

Creating a Database

Objectives

In this project, you learn how to

- ➤ **Create a New Database**
- ➤ **Create a New Table**
- ➤ **Save a Table Design and Create a Primary Key**
- ➤ **Add Fields**
- ➤ **Edit Fields**
- ➤ **Change Views and Move Fields**
- ➤ **Delete Fields**

Key terms introduced in this project include

- data type
- database
- Datasheet view
- Design view
- field
- field selector
- index
- Object Linking and Embedding (OLE)
- primary key
- properties
- read-only
- record
- relationship
- table

Why Would I Do This?

With Access, you can set up databases to perform a wide variety of tasks. For example, you might want a database (similar to the one you create in this project) to keep track of staff training for your company. You can set up various databases to store different sets of related information, and you can create as many databases as you need.

Think of the database as the shell that holds together all of the related objects. The fundamental type of object in an Access database is a table. You use ***tables*** to store data and organize the information into a usable structure. You can also create other objects, such as queries, forms, and reports. You learn about these other database objects later in this book.

In this project, you learn how to create a database and table from scratch. You also learn how to edit the structure of the table. When you finish this project, you will have created a database table structure like the one in Figure 1.1

Visual Summary

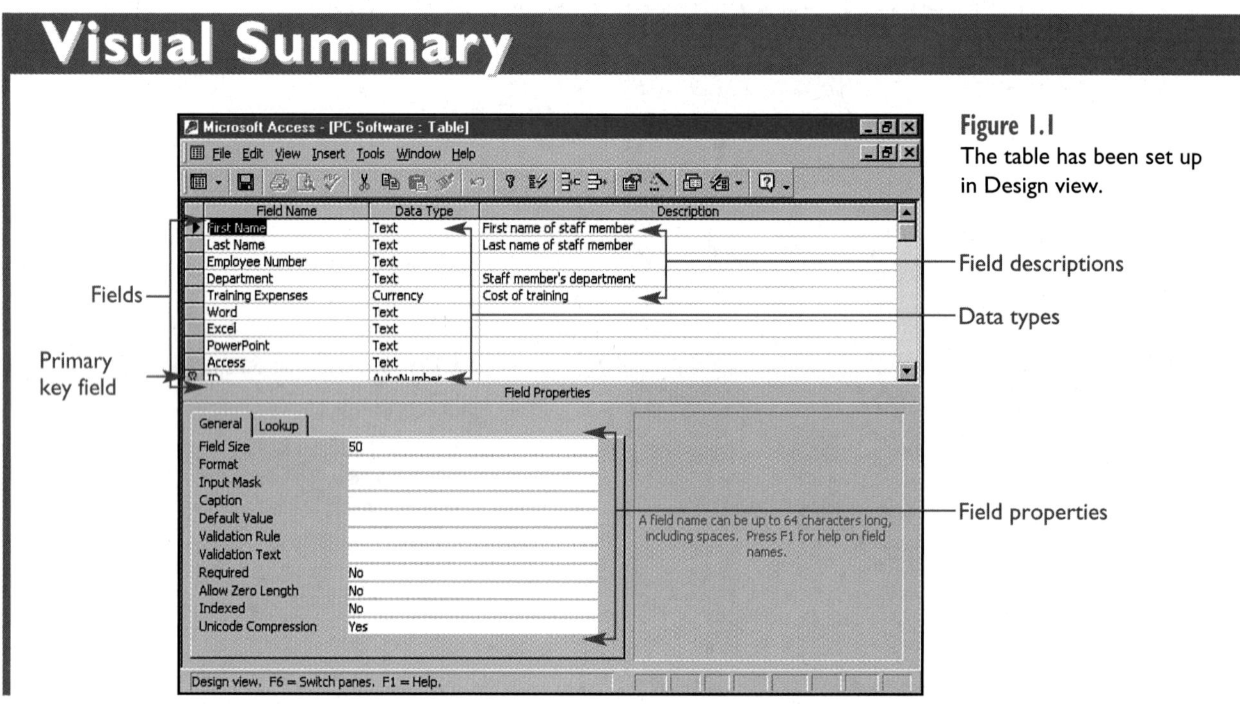

Figure 1.1
The table has been set up in Design view.

Lesson 1: Creating a New Database

Remember that the table is the object in which you actually store and define the structure for your data, and the database is the shell that houses all the related tables and other objects.

Creating a New Database from a Blank Database

In this exercise, you create a new database to keep track of the personal computer software training received by your staff. You start with a blank database and create the shell that will eventually contain your tables, queries, forms, and reports.

To Create a New Database

1. **Click the Start button on the taskbar; move the pointer to the Programs option, and select Microsoft Access to launch Access.**
   When you start Access, a Microsoft Access dialog box appears.
2. **Click the Blank Access database option and click OK.**
   Access displays the File New Database dialog box and suggests a default name (such as db1 or db2) for the new database; however, you can assign a more descriptive name here, and you can also tell Access where you want to store the database.
3. **In the File name text box, type `Training`.**
   This is the name you want to use for the new database. After you name the database the first time, you won't have to name it again. As you add or edit records, Access updates the database automatically. As you add new objects such as tables, forms, or reports, however, you have to save each of them. When you add a table, for example, you have to save it. Access then updates the database to incorporate this new database object.
4. **Click the arrow next to the Save in box and select your drive or folder.**
   Access suggests a default drive and folder for saving the new database. Select drive A unless otherwise instructed (see Figure 1.2). Make sure you have a disk in drive A.

Figure 1.2 You use the File New Database dialog box to assign a name to your database.

continues ▶

To Create a New Database (continued)

5 Click the Create button.

Access opens the database window (see Figure 1.3). Notice that there are no tables shown because you have not created any database objects (tables, queries, and so on). Three methods for creating a new table are displayed.

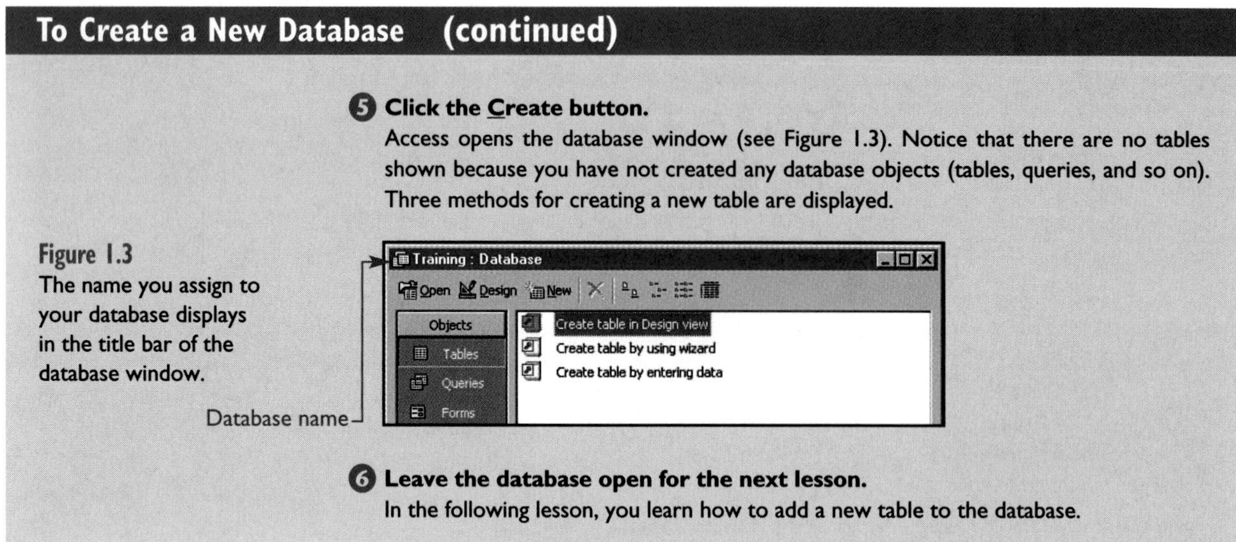

Figure 1.3
The name you assign to your database displays in the title bar of the database window.

6 Leave the database open for the next lesson.

In the following lesson, you learn how to add a new table to the database.

Alternative Ways to Perform the Same Function
Access usually gives you more than one way to perform each function. For example, to create a new database, you can press Ctrl+N, select New from the File menu, or click the New button on the toolbar.

Lesson 2: Creating a New Table

After you create your database, you can add tables to store your information. A database is built on one or more tables, each of which holds a distinct set of information. Several small tables, each containing data about a specific topic, are preferable to a large table containing a lot of duplicate information. The table defines the structure of the data—what pieces of data you enter and in what order. You should spend some time planning the structure of your database. How many fields do you need? What are their data types? Who will be using the database and how will they be using the information? If necessary, you can add fields later if you need them, but it is very important to map out the fundamental structure of the table before you get started.

Building a database without a plan is like building a house without a blueprint. The more work you invest in the initial design, the less time you spend in patchwork repairs later. Design your table structures first, so that you can immediately put the database to work with confidence.

When you create a new table, you can add any fields you want. Remember that the table consists of ***records*** (one set of information—such as the name, address, and phone number for one person) and fields. ***Fields*** are the individual pieces of information that together make up a record; for example, an address is a field. To add a field, you type a field name and then select a ***data type***, which defines the kind of information you can enter into that field. Table 1.1 describes the various data types you can use. You can also type a description for the field and set field ***properties***, which are the characteristics of a screen element.

Table 1.1 Data Types and What They Mean

Data Type	Explanation
Text	The default data type. You can enter up to 255 numbers or letters.
Memo	This type of field is useful when you want to include sentences or paragraphs in the field—for example, a long product description. This type of field can hold 64,000 characters.
Number	You can enter only numbers.
Date/Time	You can enter only dates or times.
Currency	You can enter numbers. Access formats the entry as currency. If you type 12.5, for example, Access displays it as $12.50.
AutoNumber	Access enters a value that is incremented automatically with each new record added to a table.
Yes/No	A Yes/No field type limits your data to one of two conditions. You can enter only Yes or No, True or False, or On or Off. For example, you may have a Sent Christmas Card field in your address database that would work best as a Yes/No field.
OLE Object	You can insert ***Object Linking and Embedding (OLE)*** objects, which are objects such as pictures or charts created in another application package.
Hyperlink	A field that enables you to enter active Web addresses.
Lookup Wizard	A field that looks up data from another source.

In this lesson, you create a table containing fields for first names, last names, and department names.

To Create a New Table

1. **In the Tables window in the Training database window, click the New button.**
   Access displays the New Table dialog box (see Figure 1.4). You can choose between two views of a blank database, or you can launch one of three wizards to create a new table. The wizards walk you through the process of setting up a table, bringing in a table from another source, or linking the database to another data source without actually moving the information into the database.

   You could also create a new table by double-clicking the Create a new table in Design view option.

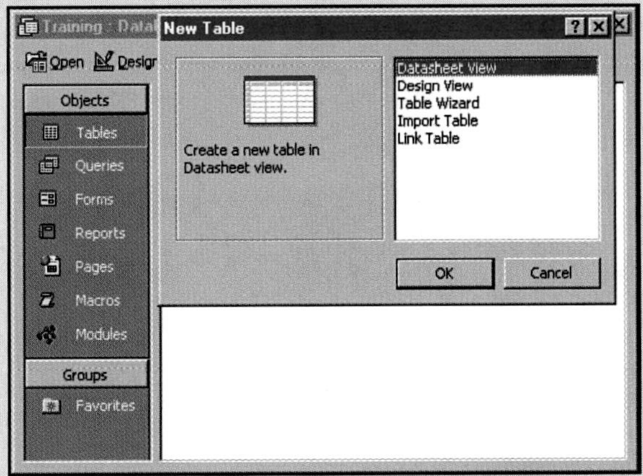

Figure 1.4
The New Table dialog box offers five choices for creating a table.

continues ▶

To Create a New Table (continued)

2 Select Design View and click OK.

You see the table in ***Design view*** with the default name of Table1 (see Figure 1.5). The new table contains no fields. To add fields to the table, you must enter the field names, data types, and descriptions (if desired). The blinking insertion point displays in the first row of the Field Name column. Here you type the first field name.

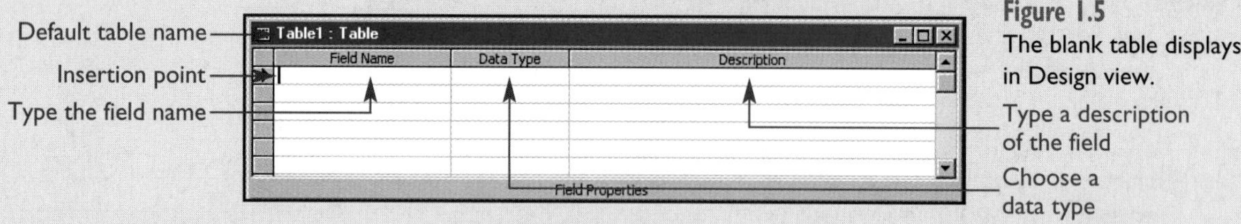

Figure 1.5
The blank table displays in Design view.

3 Type `First Name` and press Enter.

Access enters the field name for the first field. In the lower half of the window, Access displays the field properties that you can set (see Figure 1.6). Access moves the insertion point to the Data Type column, so that you can choose the type of data you want the field to contain. The most common data type is Text, which is the default. You can click the down arrow (which displays when you move to the Data Type column) to display a drop-down list of data types. For First Name, leave the data type as the default, which is Text.

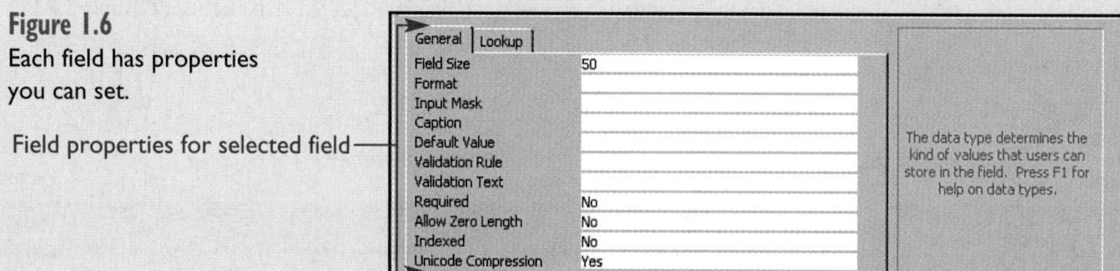

Figure 1.6
Each field has properties you can set.

4 Press Enter.

Access accepts the Text data type, and the insertion point moves to the Description column.

5 Type `First name of staff member` and press Enter.

Access enters the field description and moves the insertion point to the next row (see Figure 1.7). The description column comes in handy when you are in ***Datasheet view*** and enter a value in the First Name field. The field description displays in the status bar. You are now ready to enter the next field name.

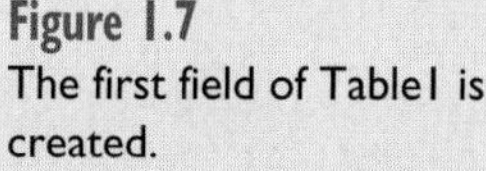

Figure 1.7
The first field of Table1 is created.

6. **Type `Last Name` and press Enter twice.**
Access enters the name for the field, accepts the default, Text, as the data type, and moves the insertion point to the Description column.

7. **Type `Last name of staff member` and press Enter.**
As before, Access enters the field description for this second field and moves the insertion point to the next row, so that you can add another field. Adding a field description is optional. If you do include a description, however, it displays in the status bar whenever you are in Datasheet view or Form view and place the insertion point in that field. The information in the status bar provides the user with a more complete description of the purpose of the field.

8. **Type `Department` and press Enter twice.**
Again, this step enters the field name, accepts Text as the data type, and moves the insertion point to the Description column. You can also type the field name and press ↓ to accept the Text data type and skip the description.

9. **Type `Staff member's department` and press Enter.**
This is the description for the third field of your table (see Figure 1.8). By adding these fields to the database table, you have taken the first steps toward creating a database to track staff training. Keep this table and the Training database open. You learn how to save the table in the next lesson.

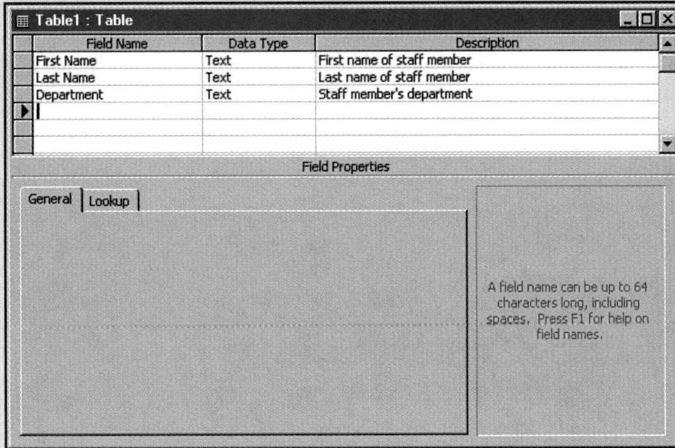

Figure 1.8
The Design view of a database table contains three fields.

Determing Which Fields to Use

When you design a table, you need to decide which fields to include. To determine this, you consider what kinds of information should be included in a printed report or what information you want to see if you looked at a single record on the screen. Consider how you may want to sort or filter the records. For example, if you want to print a list of employee names that is sorted by employee seniority, you need to have a field that indicates the hire date.

An Access database consists of parts that interact with each other, and it is hard to design one part until you know what the other parts can do. You will have a much better idea of what fields to include in a table after you learn how to create queries, forms, and reports in later projects.

Field Name Restrictions

You can create a field name using up to 64 characters. Try to use names that are short but meaningful. You can use any combination of letters, numbers, spaces, and characters, with a few exceptions: periods (.), exclamation points (!), single quotation marks ('), and brackets ([ ]) cannot appear anywhere in the name. Spaces are allowed, but not as the first character of the field name.

You can also use Tab in place of Enter when adding fields, choosing field types, and entering descriptions in the table Design view.

Lesson 3: Saving a Table Design and Creating a Primary Key

The first time you save the table's design, you are prompted to assign a name. After you save and name the table the first time, it takes only a moment to save changes whenever necessary. If you make changes to the design, such as adding new fields, you must save the changes to the design.

In addition to saving new tables, you should assign or create a ***primary key*** field for each table in your database. Each record's primary key field contains a value that uniquely identifies it; no two records can have the same value in their primary key field. Examples of good primary key fields are things like Social Security Numbers, student ID numbers, or automobile part numbers. You can use this feature to your advantage when you need to establish a ***relationship*** between one table and another. A relationship connects a field in one table to a field in a second table. Relationships enable you to draw information from more than one table at a time for forms or reports.

Assigning a primary key also ensures that you won't enter the same information for the primary key field more than once in a table (because it won't accept a duplicate entry). Because Access automatically builds an ***index*** for primary keys, it can easily search for information and sort tables based on the primary key field. An index is a location guide built by Access for all primary key fields that helps speed up searching and sorting for that field. Indexes can also be created for other fields, as long as they are not OLE or Memo fields.

If you have a unique field, such as an ID number, in your table, you can use that as the primary key field. Otherwise, you can have Access create a simple AutoNumber field.

In this lesson, you have Access create an AutoNumber field to use as the primary key field because you cannot ensure that fields such as First Name, Last Name, and Department contain unique information.

To Save a Table Design and Create a Primary Key

1 In the Training database, with Table1 open, click the Save button on the toolbar.

You could also open the File menu and choose the Save command. You see the Save As dialog box, which prompts you to type a name for the table (see Figure 1.9). As you can see, the default name that Access provides doesn't tell you much, so you want to provide a more descriptive name.

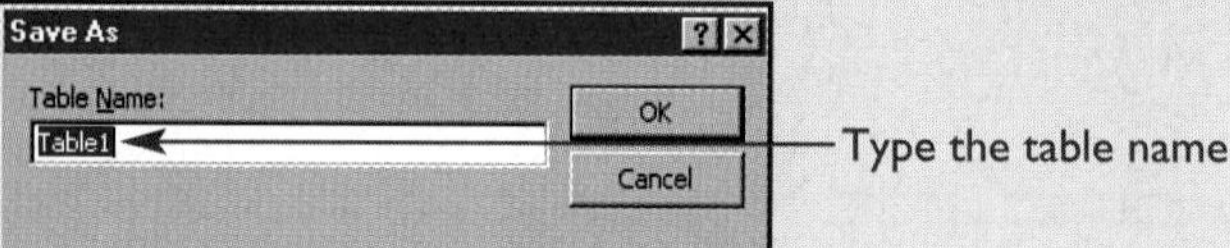

Figure 1.9
You must give the table a name the first time you save it.

2 Type `PC Software` and click OK.

This is the name you want to assign to the table for this example. The next time you see the list of tables in the database window, this name displays. The size of a table name isn't limited to eight characters. You can use up to 64 characters, including spaces.

Access displays a reminder that no primary key has been defined (see Figure 1.10). You are not required to use a primary key, but it is a good idea to include one. An easy way to create a primary key field is to have Access create an AutoNumber field that automatically assigns a different number to each record in your table.

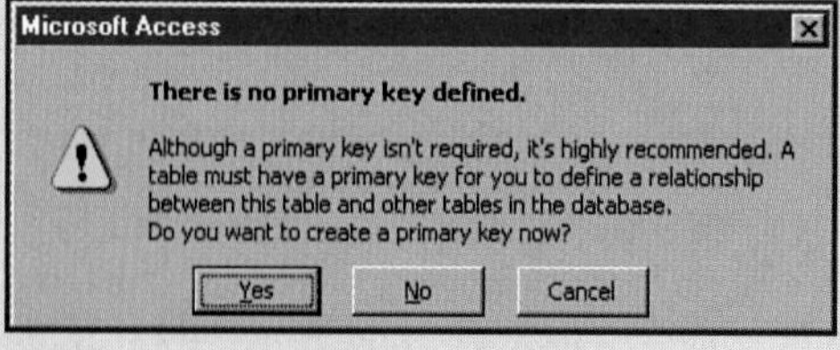

Figure 1.10
A dialog box warns you that you haven't defined a primary key field.

If you have the Office Assistant turned on, your dialog box looks different from the one shown. You can turn the Office Assistant off by choosing Help, Hide the Office Assistant from the menu.

3 Click the Yes button.
Access saves the table and adds an AutoNumber field named ID with an AutoNumber data type. This field is now the primary key field. Access automatically places sequential numbers in this field as you add new records. Your table Design view should look like the one shown in Figure 1.11. Notice the key symbol in the ***field selector*** for the ID field. The key indicates that the ID field is the primary key field for this table.

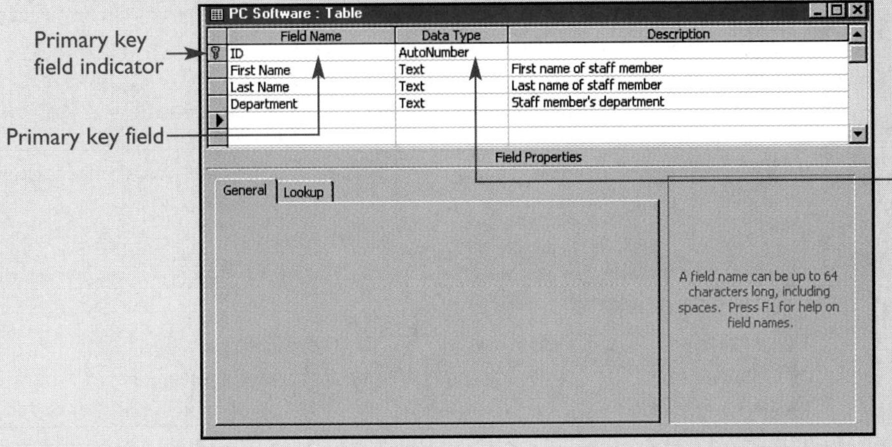

Figure 1.11
The key symbol indicates the field designated as the primary key.

4 Click the Close Window button.
Keep the Training database open. In the next lesson, you learn how to add new fields to the table.

Changing the Primary Key Field
To make another field in the database the primary key, click the field selector for the field you want, and click the Primary Key button on the toolbar. You can also open the Edit menu and choose the Primary Key command. The primary key field is indicated by the key symbol in the field selector.

To save a table quickly, press Ctrl+S.

Lesson 4: Adding Fields

What happens if you decide you want to track more information than you included in your original PC Software table? You can add new fields to store this additional data. Keep in mind, however, that if you have already added records to the table, any new fields in those existing records are empty until you type information into them. Other database objects, such as queries, forms, or reports, that are based on the table do not automatically update to include the new fields. Because you have not yet created any other database objects that use this table, now is a good time to make changes.

In this lesson, you add seven new fields to your PC Software table—one for training expense, one for employee number, one for employee's supervisor, and one each for four of the Microsoft Office software applications.

To Add Fields to a Table

1 Select the PC Software table and click the Design button. Position the insertion point in the next blank row of the PC Software table.
This is the row in which you want to enter the first new field name. The field selector arrow displays next to this row (see Figure 1.12).

continues ▶

To Add Fields to a Table (continued)

Figure 1.12
The field selector arrow indicates the current row.

Field selector arrow

Insertion point

Current row

❷ **Click the Maximize button to maximize the Design view window. Type `Cost` and press Enter twice.**
Access enters the name of the field, accepts Text as the data type (you change it later), and moves to the Description column.

❸ **Type `Cost of training` and press Enter.**
This is the description for the new field. When you press Enter, Access moves the insertion point to the next row.

❹ **Type `Employee Number` and press Enter three times.**
By pressing Enter three times you enter a name for this field, accept Text as the data type, and skip the Description column. Again, the insertion point is in position to add a new field to the table.

❺ **Type `Supervisor` and press Enter three times.**
Once again, you added another new field to the table, accepting Text as the data type, skipping the description, and moving to the next row.

❻ **Type `Word` and press Enter three times. Use the same procedure to enter fields for `Excel`, `PowerPoint`, and `Access`.**
You added seven additional fields to the table. Your table should look similar to the one in Figure 1.13, although you might have to scroll up or down to see all the fields.

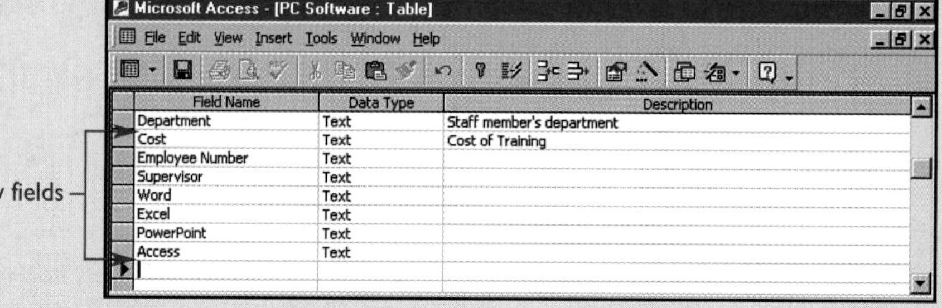

Figure 1.13
You added seven new fields to the PC Software table.

❼ **Click the Save button to save your work, and leave both the PC Software table and the Training database open.**
In the next lesson, you learn another way to alter the structure of your PC Software table.

Lesson 5: Editing Fields

As you create your database, you might want to modify the structure. For example, you might want to change field names, choose a different data type, or edit (or add) a description. You make these changes in Design view.

Changing the field type might have an effect on the data in your table. For example, if you type text into a field and change that field to a Yes/No field, you might encounter problems. Access prompts you to let you know when changes in the field type are made and when they might result in a loss of data. Be sure that you want to make the change before you confirm it.

In this lesson, you edit the name of a field, add a description, and change a field type.

To Edit Fields

❶ **In the Design view of the PC Software table, position the pointer on the fifth field name, `Cost`, and double-click.**
This action selects the word you want to change (see Figure 1.14). You might have to scroll up to get to this field.

Microsoft Access - [PC Software : Table]

Selected field name

Field Name	Data Type	Description
Department	Text	Staff member's department
Cost	Text	Cost of Training
Employee Number	Text	
Supervisor	Text	
Word	Text	
Excel	Text	
PowerPoint	Text	
Access	Text	

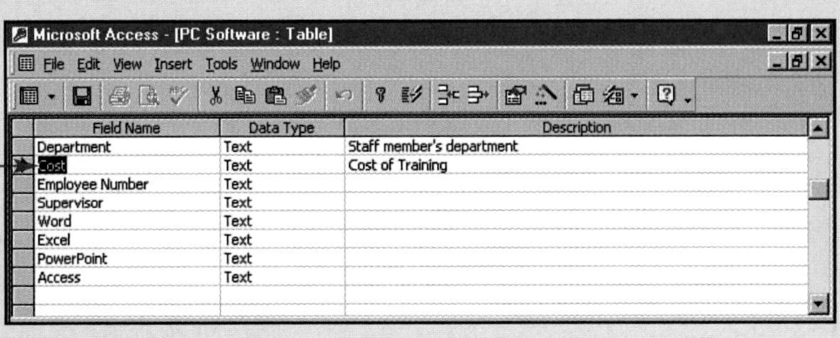

Figure 1.14
To change a field name, you first select it.

❷ **Type `Training Expense`.**
The new text replaces the highlighted text.

❸ **Click the Description column for the Supervisor field.**
After moving the insertion point to this field, you can add a description.

❹ **Type `Reporting Supervisor`.**
The description that you enter provides information about what is stored in this field.

❺ **Click the Data Type column for the Training Expense field.**
Notice that a list arrow displays, which indicates that a list of data type options is available.

❻ **Click the list arrow.**
A list of choices displays (see Figure 1.15).

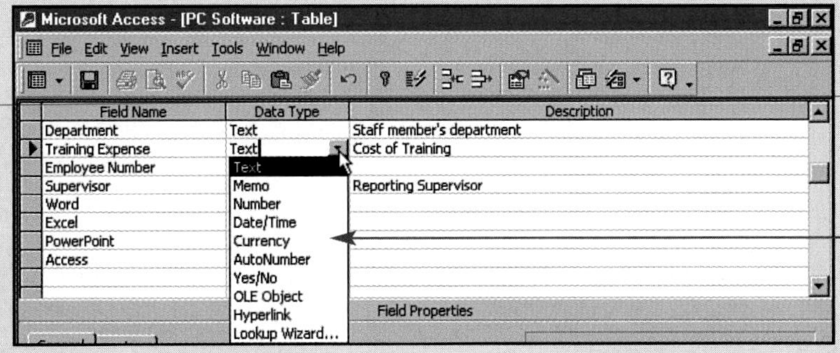

Figure 1.15
When you click the list arrow in the Data Type column, a list of data types displays.

❼ **From the list, click `Currency`.**
You changed the data type to a type that is more appropriate for the information in this field. All data in the field now displays with a dollar sign, commas (if needed), and two decimal places.

❽ **Click the Save button on the toolbar to save your work.**
Leave both the PC Software table and the Training database open. In the next lesson, you learn how to move fields from one location in the table to another.

A Shortcut for Entering the Data Type

If you know the name of the data type you want to enter in the Data Type column, you don't have to use the mouse to open the drop-down list. Instead, if the Data Type column is highlighted, you can type the first letter of the data type you want. Access fills in the rest of the characters for you. When you type the letter "c," for example, Access fills in Currency.

The Consequences of Changing a Field Name
Changing the field name or description does not have any effect on the data you already entered in the table. Changing the field name might have an unintended effect, however. If any forms, queries, or reports refer to the field name, you might have to manually change the references to reflect the new name. Otherwise, these database objects no longer work as they did before.

Lesson 6: Changing Views and Moving Fields

In addition to changing the name and data type of a field, you can change the order in which the fields display in your database. When you enter records, you might want the fields in a different order. In the PC Software table, for example, you might find it easier to enter the employee's number immediately after you enter the employee's name. You may also want to move the ID (counter) field to the end because you never have to enter anything in this field.

In this lesson, you first look at the table in Datasheet view—the view you use to enter records. You then change to Design view to rearrange the fields.

To Change Views and Move Fields

1. **Click the View button on the toolbar to change from Design view to Datasheet view.**
   If you have not saved your changes to the table, Access prompts you to save them. Notice that the View button looks different in Datasheet view than it did in Design view. The icon on the View button indicates the view that displays when you click it.

If the Table Design toolbar is not showing, choose View, Toolbars, Table Design from the menu.

Your view of the database changes to Datasheet view (see Figure 1.16). Datasheet view is the view you use to enter, sort, and edit the records in the database.

The datasheet you see is blank, except for the field names because you haven't added any records yet. You learn how to work with records in Access Project 2, "Entering and Editing Data." In Datasheet view, you cannot make any changes to the structure of the table, although you can change column widths.

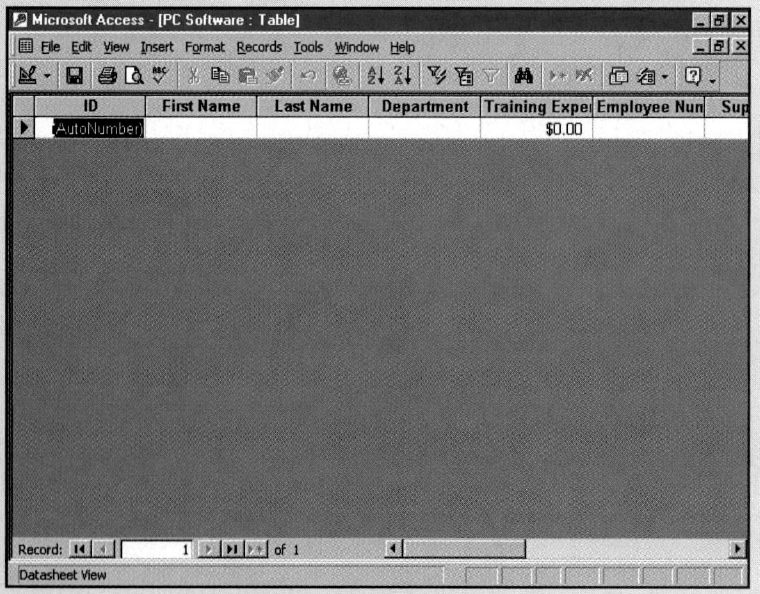

Figure 1.16
The PC Software table displays in Datasheet view.

2 Click the View button on the toolbar.
You return to Design view, so that you can make changes.

3 Click the field selector for the Employee Number field.
This step selects the field you want to move. Notice that the entire row is highlighted (see Figure 1.17). You move this field, so that it immediately follows the Last Name field.

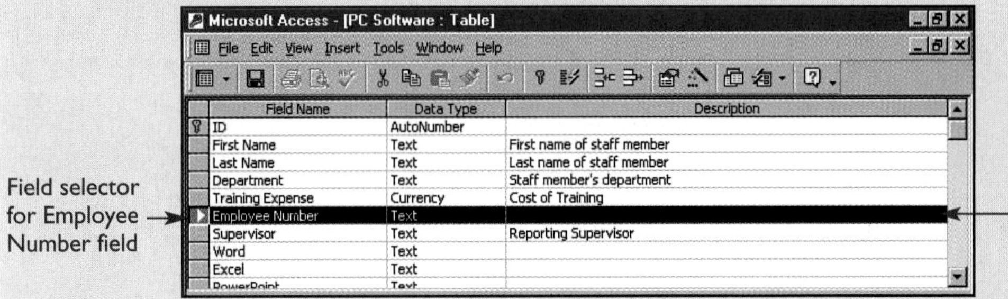

Figure 1.17
Click the field selector to select the row you want to move.

4 Click the field selector again. Hold the mouse button down while you drag the row to its new position under Last Name. Release the mouse button.
As you drag, a small gray box displays under the mouse pointer, along with a horizontal line showing where the row will be placed. When you release the mouse button, Access places the row in its new spot (see Figure 1.18).

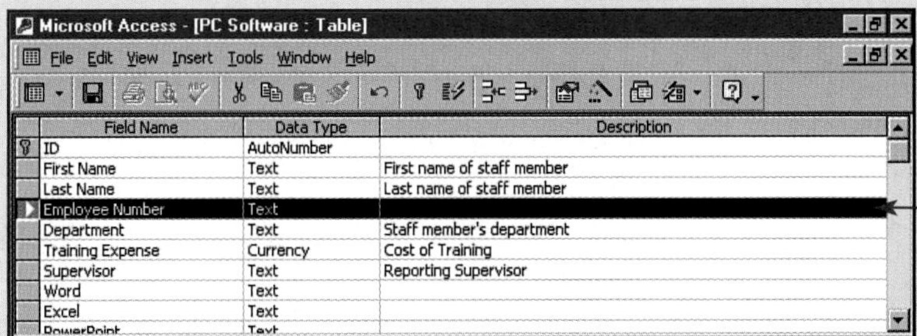

Figure 1.18
The Employee Number field appears in its new location.

If the field that you move displays in the wrong place after you drag and drop it, don't worry. Just move the field again.

If you see a double-headed arrow as you try to position the mouse, the mouse pointer isn't in the correct spot. If the double-headed arrow displays, Access thinks that you want to resize the row height or the Design View window.

If, when you drag, you accidentally resize rather than move your row, click the Undo button (or open the Edit menu and choose the Undo command). The Undo command reverses your most recent action, such as moving a row. Only the most recent change can be undone.

If your window is too small to see all the rows, maximize the window by clicking the Maximize button in the upper-right corner of the table window.

5 Select the ID row and drag it down to the first empty row of the table.
The ID or AutoNumber field moves to the last position in the table. Next, try undoing the move.

With the number of fields in this table, you might not be able to see the ID field and the first empty row at the same time. If you try to drag the ID field down, the screen scrolls quickly when you reach the bottom of the field area. To overcome this problem, drag the field down near the bottom and drop it there. Scroll down so that you can see both the field and the first blank row, and then move the field the rest of the way.

continues ▶

To Change Views and Move Fields (continued)

6 Click the Undo button.
With Access, you can undo some of the changes you make to the database. In this example, however, you decide that you really do want the ID field at the end of the table.

7 Select the ID row again and drag it back to the end of the table.
The ID field moves back to the end of the table.

8 Click the Save button to save your work. Keep both the Training database and the PC Software table open in Design view.
In the next lesson, you learn how to delete fields from your table structure.

Lesson 7: Deleting Fields

Another significant change that you can make to the structure of your PC Software table is to remove fields you no longer need. Suppose that you decide you don't really need a field for the supervisor. Instead of having it take up space in the table design, you can delete the field.

Keep in mind that deleting a field from your table also deletes all the data in that field. Because this might not be what you intend to do, Access displays a warning that asks you to confirm the change. Read the warning carefully, and be sure that you want to delete all the data before you delete the field. If you have already created other database objects, such as forms or reports that use this field, you have to revise them individually.

To Delete a Field

1 In the PC Software table of the Training database, click the field selector for the Supervisor field.
The entire Supervisor row is highlighted, showing that the Supervisor field is selected. This is the field you want to delete.

2 Click the Delete Rows button to delete the row from your table.
Access removes the field from the table and deletes any data in that field (see Figure 1.19). If you had entered any data into this field in the Datasheet view, Access warns you that the data will be lost.

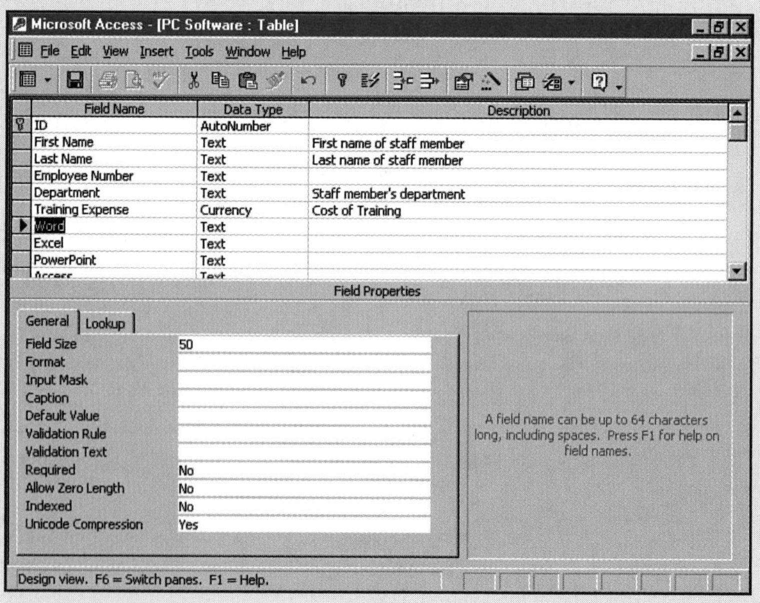

Figure 1.19
The Supervisor field has been deleted.

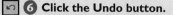

3 Click the Save button to save your changes.

4 Close the PC Software table by clicking the Close button in the upper-right corner of the table window.

5 Close the Training database by clicking the Close Window button in the upper-right corner of the database window.

If you are finished with your session at the computer, click the Close button in the upper-right corner of the Access window. Otherwise, continue with the Checking Concepts and Terms section.

Summary

In this project, you were introduced to some of the steps required to create a new database. You created your first database, table, and primary key field. You saved the new table and went back into Design view to modify the structure of the table, by adding, editing, moving, and deleting fields.

To expand your knowledge of the table creation process, use the Office Assistant to get more information about the different data types and in what situations each might be used. There is a link to a summary of field data types near the bottom of the Help window. Click this link (it will be in blue) and look at the expanded data type definitions. Click the double arrow to get more information about defining the Number data type.

Checking Concepts and Terms

True/False

For each of the following, check *T* or *F* to indicate whether the statement is true or false.

__T__F **1.** In Design view you can move a field by grabbing the field selector and dragging the field up or down the field list. [L6]

__T__F **2.** You can include only eight characters in a table name. [L2]

__T__F **3.** The most common data type is Text, the default. [L2]

__T__F **4.** You must have a primary key field. [L3]

__T__F **5.** You can enter only numbers in a Number field. [L2]

__T__F **6.** After you save your table structure, you cannot edit or change it. [L4]

__T__F **7.** A Yes/No field type limits your data to one of two conditions. [L2]

__T__F **8.** When planning a database, you should gather information from the people who will use the database to make sure you understand their needs. [L2]

__T__F **9.** It is best to build one large database with everything in one table. [L2]

__T__F **10.** If you add a new field to a database that already has data in other fields, the new field is empty until you enter the information. [L4]

Multiple Choice

Circle the letter of the correct answer for each of the following.

1. How do you select a row in the table Design view? [L6]

a. Drag across the entire row.

b. Click the field selector next to the row.

c. Click the Select Row button on the toolbar.

d. Press Ctrl+R.

2. If you let the program create a primary key for you, what field name does it use? [L3]

a. Counter

b. ID

c. MDB

d. Primary

3. In Design view, how can you tell that a field is the primary key? [L3]
   a. The status bar displays text when you have the field selected.
   b. There is no way to tell in Design view.
   c. The field name is underlined.
   d. The key symbol appears on the Field Selector button.
4. Why is the Description entry in table Design view handy? [L2]
   a. It appears in the status bar when you enter data in the field in Datasheet view.
   b. It appears as a pop-up label when you place the mouse pointer on the field in Datasheet view.
   c. Access uses it to automatically test the data you enter into the field.
   d. It serves no real purpose at all.
5. A table consists of ______________. [Intro]
   a. rows called records and columns called fields
   b. free-form information about each database item
   c. rows called fields and columns called records
   d. queries, reports, forms, and other database objects

Screen ID

Refer to Figure 1.20 and identify the numbered parts of the screen. Write the letter of the correct label in the space next to the number.

Figure 1.20

- **A.** Primary key symbol
- **B.** Primary key field
- **C.** Primary key button
- **D.** Properties area
- **E.** View button
- **F.** Field selector indicator
- **G.** Save button
- **H.** Delete field button
- **I.** Undo button
- **J.** Database name

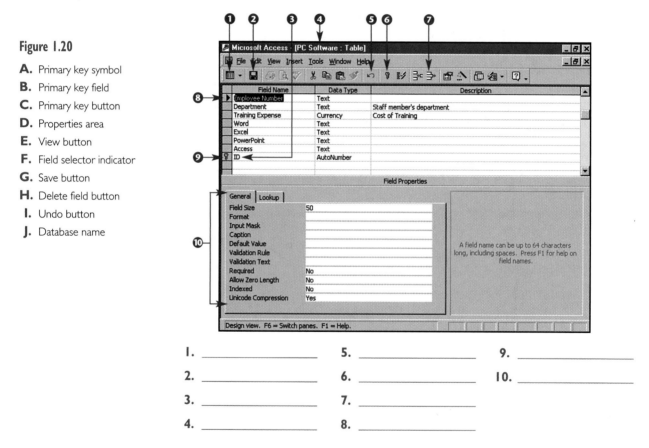

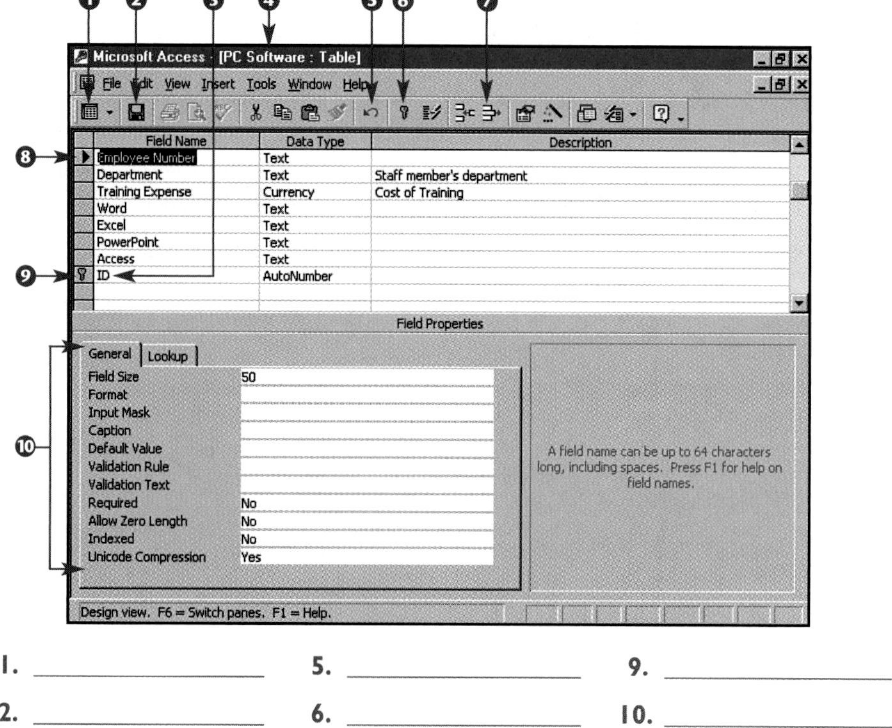

1. ______________
2. ______________
3. ______________
4. ______________
5. ______________
6. ______________
7. ______________
8. ______________
9. ______________
10. ______________

Discussion Questions

1. Access is a powerful database that can be used in the most complex business applications. It can also be used for personal information. If you were to create a database to keep track of your personal information, what tables would it contain?
2. If you wanted to create a table of people to send birthday cards to, what fields would you need to include? Could you get all the information into one table, or should you split it up into two tables?
3. Assume you have been hired to set up a database for a small used bookstore. This bookstore prides itself on giving its customers great information. With each book that they sell, they also hand the customer a printout giving the following information: author, name of the book, year of publication, number of pages, publisher, illustrator, author's nationality, and author's date of birth and death. How many tables would you set up for this database? Which fields would go in which table?

4. In the used bookstore database you set up in question 3, what would be a good primary key field for each table?
5. In this project, you created a table that had the first name and last name in separate fields. What might be the advantage of separating the first and last names? Why wouldn't it be just as good to have a single field for "Jane Smith?" How about "Smith, Jane?" Should you also create a separate field for the middle name? It might help to think about how you would use the names if you were putting together an address list for a club or other organization.

Skill Drill

Skill Drill exercises reinforce project skills. Each skill reinforced is the same, or nearly the same, as a skill presented in the project. Each exercise includes a brief narrative introduction, followed by detailed instructions in a step-by-step format.

1. Keeping Track of Your Books

You are an avid reader and have been collecting books for years. You've also borrowed books from the library over the years, and sometimes you can't remember whether you own the book or not. To make matters worse, you read a lot of mysteries and sometimes pick up a book and can't remember whether you've read it. You decide it is time to create a database to keep track of your collection. [L1]

To create a book collection database, complete the following steps:

1. Launch Access, and select the Blank Database option.
2. Type **Book Collection** in the File name text box.
3. Use the Save in box to select the drive and/or folder you want to save your database in.
4. Click the Create button.

2. Creating a Table to Store Book Information

Now that you have created an empty database, it is time to decide what fields you want to include. Give this a little thought. [L2, 4]

To create the Book Collection Database, complete the following steps:

1. Click the New button to create a new table.
2. Select Design view.
3. Type **Author Last Name** in the Field Name column.
4. Accept Text as the Data Type.
5. Type **Last name of the author** in the Description column.
6. Add the following fields. Make them all Text fields, and add a short description in the Description column.

   Author First Name
   Book
   Year Published
   Type of Book
   Publisher
   Pages

3. Saving the Table Design and Adding a Primary Key Field

Now that you have put this much work into your new database, it is probably a good time to save what you've done. You could press the Save button, but you can click the View button and get the same results. [L3]

To save your table design and add a primary key field, follow these steps:

1. Click the View button on the toolbar.
2. Click Yes to save your changes.
3. Name the table **Books**.
4. Click Yes to have Access insert a primary key field.
5. Maximize the table window. If necessary, scroll to the right to see your fields.
6. Click the View button to return to the Design view.

4. Adding and Deleting Fields

After some thought, you decide that you would like to make some changes to your database. You find that you are spending far more time typing than you'd like, and the name of the publisher is the culprit. You can't imagine a need for this field in the future, so you decide to eliminate it. You also realize that you should have included a field for whether or not you have read the book. [L4, 7]

To add and delete fields in your book table, follow these steps:

1. Place the insertion point in the first empty row in the list of fields.
2. Type **Read?** in the Field Name column.
3. Accept Text as the Data Type.
4. Type **Enter Y or N only!** in the Description column.
5. Click the field selector in the Publisher field.
6. Click the Delete Rows button to remove the field.
7. Click the Save button to save your changes to the structure of the table.

5. Editing the Data Type of Fields

Two of the fields, Pages and Year Published, are always going to be numbers. You decide that it would be a good idea to change the data type. [L5]

To change the data types of fields, complete the following steps:

1. Click the Data Type column of the Year Published field.
2. Click the list arrow to display the drop-down menu.
3. Select Number from the list.
4. Highlight the data type in the Data Type column of the Pages field.
5. Type the letter **n** to change the data type to Number.
6. Click the Save button to save your changes to the structure of the table.

6. Moving a Field

After some more thought, you decide that you'd like the Pages field to follow the Book field. [L6]

To move a field, complete the following steps:

1. Click the field selector of the Pages field.
2. Click the field selector of the Pages field again, and drag the field up between the Book field and the Year Published field.
3. Click the View button to change to Datasheet view.
4. Click Yes to save your changes.
5. Check the order of the fields in Datasheet view to make sure the Pages field is in the right place.
6. Close the database, and close Access unless you are going to continue with the Challenge section.

Challenge

Challenge exercises expand on or are somewhat related to skills presented in the lessons. Each exercise provides a brief narrative introduction followed by instructions, in a numbered step or bulleted list format, that are not as detailed as those in the Skill Drill section.

You will use the CD database AO-0101 in the following exercises. (*Note*: You cannot make any changes to the databases on your CD-ROM. On the CD-ROM, the database is Read Only, which means that the file can be opened but not changed.)

1. Adding a Table to an Existing Database by Entering Data

You have decided to expand an Alaska database by adding tables that record other information about the Alaskan environment. The first table you want to add is about the wildlife you have seen in your travels. [L2]

To add a table by entering data, complete the following steps:

1. Copy **AO-0101** from your CD-ROM to drive A (or other location). Right-click the filename; deselect Read-Only, and select the Archive check box. Right-click the file; select Rename from the shortcut menu and rename it **Alaska Environment**.
2. Open the Alaska Environment database and double-click Create table by entering data.

3. Enter **Black Bear**, **Garbage Dump**, **Seward**, **1995** in the first four fields.
4. Click the View button and name the table **Wildlife I Have Seen**. Do not add a primary key field.
5. In Design view, name the four fields **Animal**, **Surroundings**, **Location**, and **Year**.
6. Close the table and save your changes.

2. Adding a Table to an Existing Database Using a Wizard

Now that you have added a wildlife table, you decide you ought to have a table for plants you have seen. You know the common names, but decide you ought to leave a place for the scientific names when you get around to looking them up. [L2]

To add a table using a wizard, complete the following steps:

1. In the database window, double-click Create table by using wizard.
2. Choose the Personal category and select Plants from the Sample Tables options.
3. For fields, choose **CommonName**, **Genus**, **Species**, **LightPreference**, **TempPreference**, **Photograph**, and **Notes**.
4. Name your table **Plants I Have Seen**. Have the program set a primary key.
5. Do not relate this table to any other table.
6. Choose to enter information directly into the table.
7. Enter **Dandelion** as the Common Name and type **Seen all over the place** for the Notes field. Leave all the other fields blank.
8. Close the table.

3. Adding a Primary Key Field to an Existing Table

Two of your three tables now have primary key fields, and you decide that maybe the third one should, too. [L3]

To add a primary key field to an existing table, complete the following steps:

1. Select the Wildlife I Have Seen table and open it in Design view.
2. Add a new field called **ID**. Add it at the end of the document and move it to the top of the field list.
3. Make the data type of the new field AutoNumber.
4. Click the Primary Key button.
5. Close the table and save your changes.

4. Deleting More than One Field at a Time

Looking at your Plants I Have Seen table, you realize that you are just doing this for fun, and the odds of you ever looking up the genus and species are very small. Therefore, you decide you want to remove these fields from your table. [L7]

To delete more than one field at a time, complete the following steps:

1. Select the Plants I Have Seen table and open it in Design view.
2. Click the field selector for the Genus field and hold the mouse button down.
3. Drag down and select the Species field as well.
4. Press Del.
5. Close the table and save your changes.

5. Adding Check Boxes to a Table

You just saw a friend's database that has really neat check boxes for Yes/No fields and decide you'd like to add one to one of your tables. The obvious choice would be a check box in the Geography table for places you have visited. [L4]

To add check boxes to a table, complete the following steps:

1. Open the Geography table in Design view.
2. Add a new field called `Visited`.
3. Select Yes/No as the data type.
4. Click the View button and save your changes.
5. Scroll to the right edge of the table.
6. Click the check boxes for the first two records.
7. Close the table.

6. Adding a Hyperlink Field

One of the data type options is called Hyperlink. You are not sure exactly what this is or how it can be used in an Access database.

To explore the use of Hyperlink fields, complete the following steps:

1. Use the Office Assistant to figure out exactly what a Hyperlink field is and how it works. If you are still unsure, go online and check the Microsoft Web site.
2. Open the Geography table.
3. Go out onto the Web and find a site about one of the cities listed in the table.
4. Add a new Hyperlink field called `Local Information`.
5. Enter the URL that you found on the Web for an Alaskan city.
6. Scroll to the right edge of the table.
7. Test the URL.
8. Close the table.

Discovery Zone

Discovery Zone exercises help you gain advanced knowledge of project topics and/or application of skills. These exercises focus on enhancing your problem-solving skills.

1. Creating a Lookup Wizard Field

The Lookup Wizard data type is unlike any of the other data types. It enables you to choose information from a drop-down list.

Goal: Create a Lookup Wizard field that categorizes the animals listed in the Wildlife I Have Seen table.

Use the program's Help features and online Help to figure out how to use a Lookup Wizard field. You can use this type of field in two different ways—you choose which one you want to use. You should create at least three categories for the wildlife types. One of your categories might be Birds.

2. Creating a Primary Key Field Using More than One Field

Sometimes you want to use information in your database for your primary key field, but no one field is unique. Access offers you a way to use more than one field in combination as a primary key.

Goal: Create a primary key using two fields.

Use the Geography table and create a primary key field out of the Latitude and Longitude fields. (Two places might have the same latitude or the same longitude, but no two places have both the same latitude and longitude. If they do, the entries should be combined.)

Hint: You need to remove the existing primary key field before you can proceed.

Project 2

Entering and Editing Data

Objectives

In this project, you learn how to

- **Add Records**
- **Move Among Records**
- **Edit Records**
- **Insert and Delete Records**
- **Adjust Column Widths and Hide Columns**
- **Find Records**
- **Sort Records**

Key terms introduced in this project include

- current record indicator
- pencil icon
- record selector

Why Would I Do This?

After you create a database and table, you want to be able to put them to work. For your database to be useful, you must enter data into the table (or tables). You can use the Training database you created in Access Project 1, "Creating a Database," to keep track of training that your staff receives by entering information about the employees and the training they received into the PC Software table. As you learned in Project 1, the set of information you enter for each row in a table is called a record.

One reason databases are so useful is that you can work with and modify the records after you enter them. With a paper filing system, you have to cross out, erase, or redo a record when the information changes. With database software, however, you can easily change a record in the table to correct a mistake or to update the information. You can delete records you no longer need, search for a particular record, and sort the records—all quickly and with little effort on your part.

In this project, you learn how to add records to your table, move around in the records within the table, and edit and delete records. You also learn how to search for a particular record and sort your records according to a system that you determine. When you finish this project, you will have created a database like the one in Figure 2.1.

Visual Summary

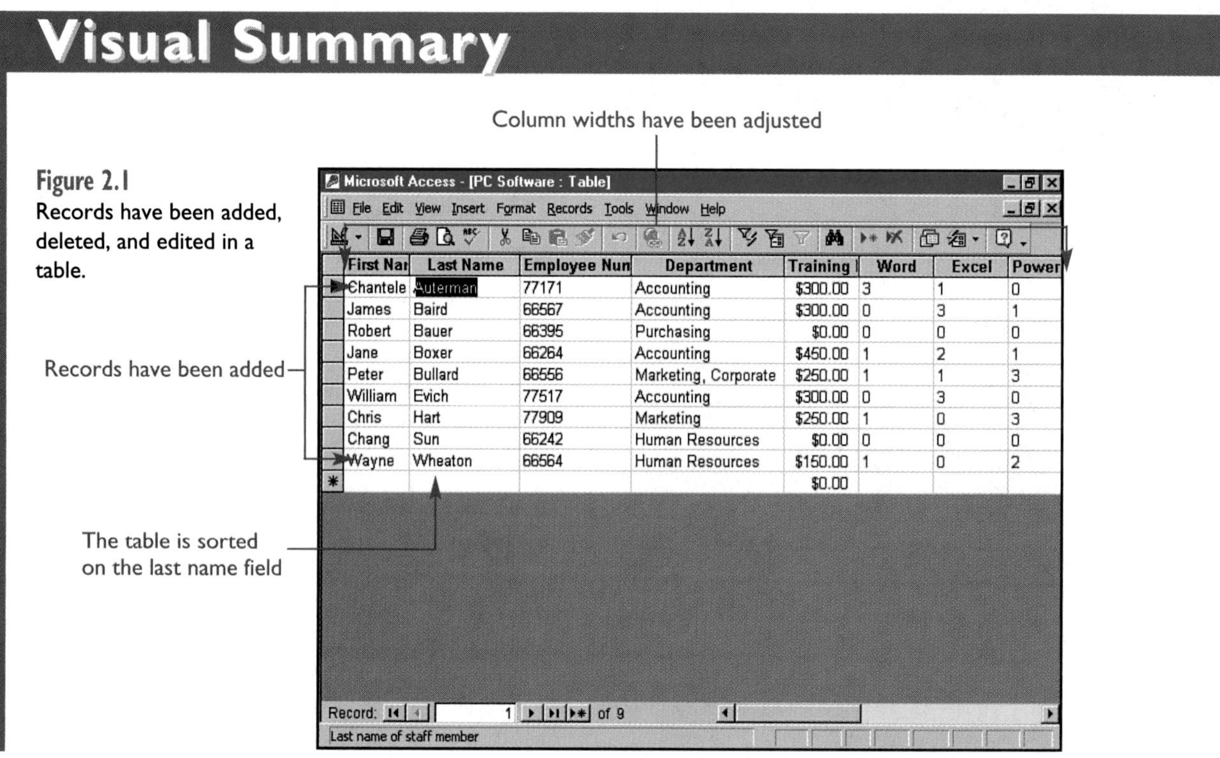

Column widths have been adjusted
Records have been added
The table is sorted on the last name field
Microsoft Access - [PC Software : Table]
File Edit View Insert Format Records Tools Window Help
First Nai | Last Name | Employee Num | Department | Training | Word | Excel | Power
Chantele | Auterman | 77171 | Accounting | $300.00 | 3 | 1 | 0
James | Baird | 66567 | Accounting | $300.00 | 0 | 3 | 1
Robert | Bauer | 66395 | Purchasing | $0.00 | 0 | 0 | 0
Jane | Boxer | 66264 | Accounting | $450.00 | 1 | 2 | 1
Peter | Bullard | 66556 | Marketing, Corporate | $250.00 | 1 | 1 | 3
William | Evich | 77517 | Accounting | $300.00 | 0 | 3 | 0
Chris | Hart | 77909 | Marketing | $250.00 | 1 | 0 | 3
Chang | Sun | 66242 | Human Resources | $0.00 | 0 | 0 | 0
Wayne | Wheaton | 66564 | Human Resources | $150.00 | 1 | 0 | 2
$0.00
Record: 1 of 9
Last name of staff member

Figure 2.1
Records have been added, deleted, and edited in a table.

Lesson 1: Adding Records

As you recall from Project 1, you worked in Design view when you set up your table structure. In Design view, you can make changes to the fields in the table, such as change a field name, add a field, change the data type, and so on. When you want to work with the data in the table, you switch to Datasheet view. In this view, you can add records or edit them.

In this lesson, you open a database, Employee Training, which is a corrected version of the database and PC Software table from Project 1. You switch to Datasheet view and add records to the database.

To Add Records

1. **Launch Access. Click OK to open an existing file.**
   Make sure you have a disk in drive A.

2. **Find the `AO-0201` file on your CD-ROM; right-click it, and copy it to the floppy drive. Move to drive A; remove the Read Only status; rename the file `Employee Training`, and open the new database.**
   The database should open to the Tables object button, and a PC Software table should be listed.

If you are using a drive other than drive A, you must substitute the correct drive letter where drive A is referenced. To remove a file's read-only status, right-click the filename; deselect Read-Only, and select the Archive check box.

3. **Select the PC Software table in Datasheet view and click the Open button.**
   In this project, you use the Training database you created in Project 1. (Employee Training is a completed version of your work from Project 1.) The PC Software table should be displayed onscreen in Datasheet view. Each of the field names appears along the top of the window. At this point, the table consists of only one row, and it is blank. The insertion point is in the first field, and you see a small black arrow next to the first field. This arrow indicates the current record (see Figure 2.2).

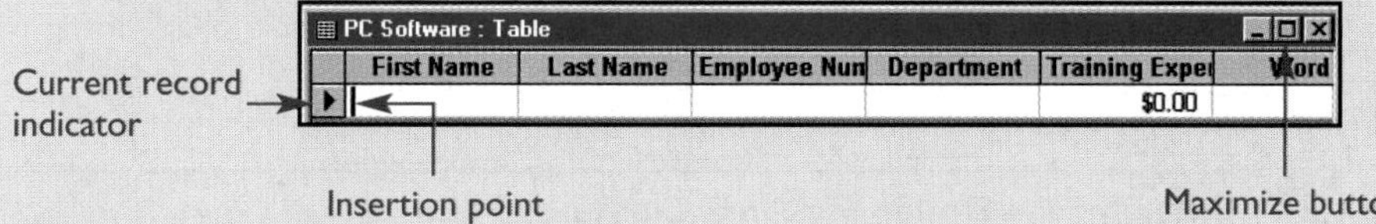

Figure 2.2
A blank database table displays in Datasheet view.

4. **Maximize the Table window. Type `Chantele` in the First Name field and press ↵Enter.**
   As you type, Access displays a pencil icon in the ***record selector,*** which is the gray area to the left of the record. You can also use Tab in place of ↵Enter when you add data to the table.

5. **Type `Auterman` and press ↵Enter.**
   The staff member's name is entered, and the insertion point moves to the Employee Number field.

6. **Type `77171` and press ↵Enter.**
   The employee number is entered, and the insertion point moves to the Department field.

7. **Type `Accounting` and press ↵Enter.**
   The department is entered, and the insertion point moves to the Training Expense field.

8. **Type `300.00` and press ↵Enter.**
   The expense for training this employee is entered, and the insertion point moves to the four fields for specific software training. Notice that Access formats the entry as Currency because in Project 1 you set the data type to Currency after you created this field.

9. **Type `3` and press ↵Enter; type `1` and press ↵Enter; type `0` and press ↵Enter; and finally type `1` and press ↵Enter.**
   The levels of completed classes are recorded in the four application fields. When you press ↵Enter the last time, Access moves to the counter field, which has a value that was automatically entered when you started entering data in the first field.

10. **Press ↵Enter.**
    Access saves the record and moves to the next row so that you can add another record (see Figure 2.3). Whenever you move the insertion point off the record you are editing, Access immediately saves the record or any changes you made to the record.

continues ▶

To Add Records (continued)

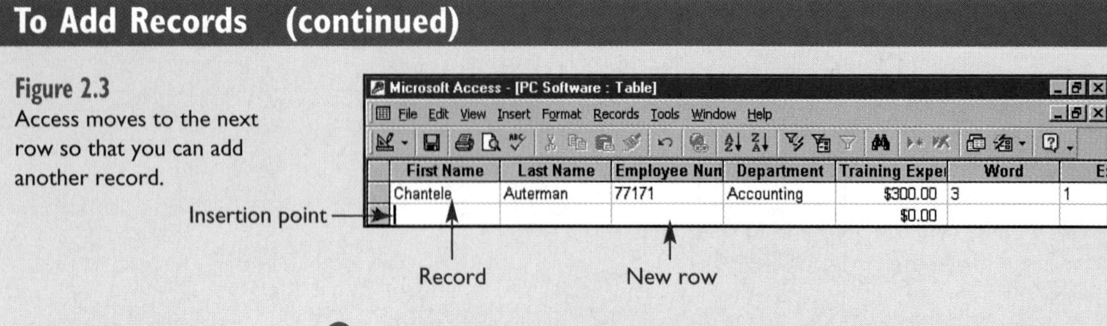

Figure 2.3
Access moves to the next row so that you can add another record.

⑪ **Use the following list of data to add more records to the database table. (Because of the number of fields in each record, the items are separated by commas. Do not type the commas.)**

```
Chang,Sun,66242,Human Resources,0,0,0,0,0
Jane,Boxer,66264,Purchasing,450,1,2,1,3
Robert,Bauer,66395,Purchasing,0,0,0,0,0
Peter,Bullard,66556,Marketing,250,1,1,3,0
James,Baird,66567,Accounting,300,0,3,1,1
Wayne,Wheaton,66564,Human Resources,150,1,0,2,0
Chris,Hart,77909,Marketing,250,1,0,3,1
```

Access adds these records to the database table. You don't have to worry about saving the records because Access does that each time you press Enter and move to the next row to add a new record.

Keep the Employee Training database and the PC Software table open. In the next lesson, you learn how to move among the records in your table.

Entering the Dollar Sign in a Currency Field

You do not need to enter the dollar sign ($) into a currency field. Access adds it automatically. Adding the dollar sign does not hurt anything, but if you learn to leave it off, it saves you time if you have to enter large amounts of data. Also, if a dollar amount is a whole number, the program adds the .00 automatically, even if you don't type it.

Lesson 2: Moving Among Records

Earlier, you noticed that Access displays an arrow next to the current row. When you want to do something with a record, such as edit a field to change or update its information, you first must move to the row containing the record that you want to change. You can tell what row you have moved to because a black triangular arrow, called the ***current record indicator***, displays in the record selector box to the left of the current row.

Access gives you several ways to move among the records. If you can see the record you want on the screen, you can simply click it to select it. If you have numerous records in your table, however, you may have to scroll through the records until you can get to the one you want.

To move to a particular record, you can use the vertical scroll bar, the navigation buttons at the bottom of the window, or the arrow keys on the keyboard. Table 2.1 explains how these navigation buttons and keys work.

Table 2.1 Moving Among Records with the Navigation Buttons and Keys

To Move To	Buttons	Keyboard
First record in table	⏮	Ctrl + Home
Previous record in table	◀	↑
Next record in table	▶	↓
Last record in table	▶|	Ctrl + End
New record at end of table	▶*	Ctrl + +

In this lesson, you move among the records in your table by using each of these navigational methods.

To Move Among Friends

1. **With the PC Software table of the Employee Training database open, move the pointer to the record selector at the left of the `Wayne Wheaton` record and click.**
   The record is selected.

2. **Press Ctrl+Home. Access moves you to the first record in the database table. Notice the current record indicator arrow to the left of the active record (see Figure 2.4).**

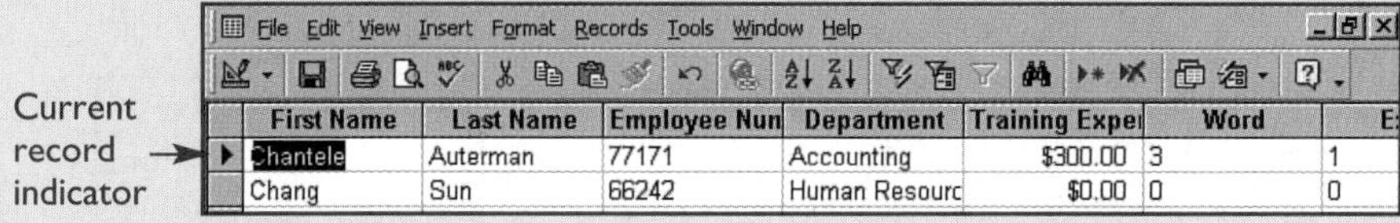

Figure 2.4
Pressing the Control and Home keys moves you to the first record.

3. **Press ↓.**
   Access moves to the next record in the table.

4. **Click the Last Record button.**
   Access moves to the last record in the table.

5. **Click the Previous Record button.**
   Access moves to the previous record in the table.

6. **Click the First Record button.**
   Access moves to the first record in the table.

7. **Click the New Record button.**
   The pointer moves to the next empty record.

Now that you know how to move among the records in your table, the next lesson shows you how to make changes to the records. Keep the Employee Training database and the PC Software table open as you continue with Lesson 3.

Lesson 3: Editing Records

As you work with the data in the database table, you find that you need to make changes from time to time. In your PC Software table, for example, you might want to correct a typing mistake or change other information. You can update or correct any of the records in your table while you are in Datasheet view.

The first step in making any change is to move to the record that you want to change. Next, you have to move to the field that you want to edit. To move among fields using the mouse, click the field to which you want to move. When you click, Access places the insertion point in the field and does not select the entire field.

You can also use the keys listed in Table 2.2 to move among fields. When you use these keys, Access moves to the specified field and selects all the text in that field.

Table 2.2 Moving Among Fields with the Keyboard

To Move To	Press
Next field	Tab or →
Previous field	Shift+Tab or ←
First field in record	Home
Last field in record	End

After you are in a field, you can add to the current entry, edit the current entry, or delete the current entry. Try moving among the fields and making changes now.

To Edit Records

1 With the PC Software table of the Employee Training database open, click after the word `Marketing` in the Department column of the record for Peter Bullard.

The insertion point appears where you are going to add new text in the field.

2 Type a comma (,). Press Spacebar and type `Corporate`.

As you start typing, notice that Access displays a ***pencil icon*** in the record selector next to the record. This icon reminds you that you are editing the record and that the change has not yet been saved (see Figure 2.5).

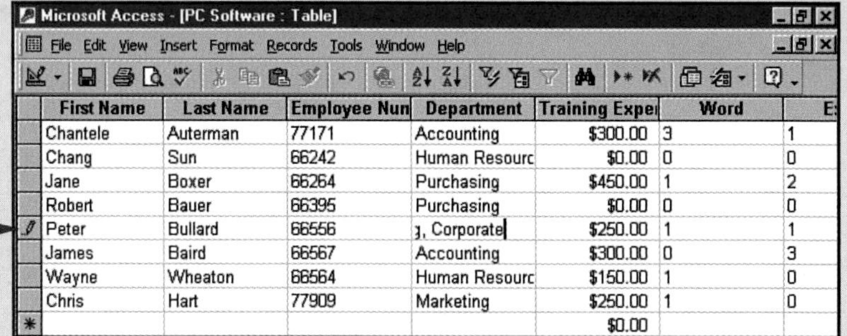

Figure 2.5
The pencil icon indicates that that the field you are editing has not been saved.

3 Press ↑ twice.

This moves you to the Department field in the record for Jane Boxer. When you move to another record, Access automatically updates the record you changed.

The text in that field is selected, as shown in Figure 2.6. Anything you type replaces the selected text.

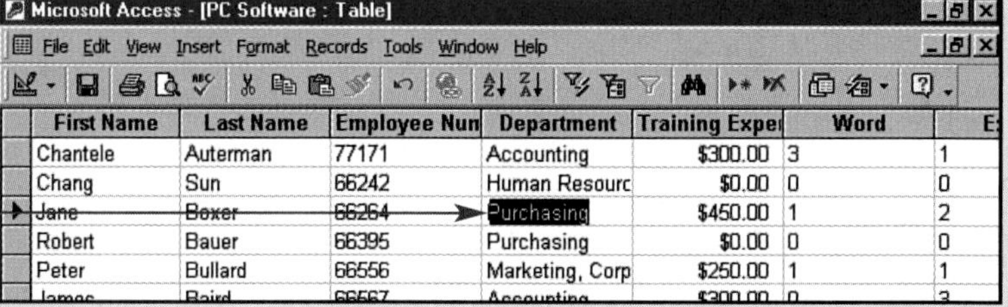

Figure 2.6
Typing replaces the selected text.

4 Type `Accounting`.

The record is updated for this employee, who has been transferred to a new department.

5 Press ↓.

Access updates the record you edited and moves to the next record.

Keep the Employee Training database and the PC Software table open. In Lesson 4, you learn how to insert new records and delete records you no longer need.

If you click a field in the table and enter the editing mode, the Ctrl+Home and Ctrl+End commands only move to the beginning and end of the current field. These commands move to the beginning and end of the table if you select a field or record.

If you make a change by mistake, you can undo it by immediately clicking the Undo button, or by opening the Edit menu and choosing the Undo command. If you are editing a field and decide you don't want the changes, press Esc and Access ignores your changes.

Saving Data Changes
When you move the insertion point off the record you are editing, Access saves the change to that record immediately. You can also save the change you make by pressing Shift+Enter while still on the record you are editing. To save a record using the menu, choose the Records, Save Record command.

Lesson 4: Inserting and Deleting Records

When you first create your database table, you can't always predict exactly what information you want to include in it. As you use your database, you will probably want to insert new records or delete outdated records.

With Access, you don't have to add all your records at one time. You can add a new record to the end of the table at any time. If you want to enter several records containing similar data, you can enter the data for one record, copy that record, paste the new record into your table, and then edit the data in the new record.

You can delete a record by removing the row from the database table. In this lesson, you insert new records and delete a record you no longer need.

To Insert and Delete Records

1. **With the PC Software table of the Employee Training database open, click the First Name field of the row marked by an asterisk.**
The insertion point is placed in the First Name field of the empty record where the new record will be added. The current record indicator arrow replaces the asterisk and a new empty record is added (see Figure 2.7).

Microsoft Access - [PC Software : Table]

File Edit View Insert Format Records Tools Window Help

First Name	Last Name	Employee Nun	Department	Training Expe	Word	E:
Chantolo	Auterman	77171	Accounting	$300.00	3	1
Chang	Sun	66242	Human Resourc	$0.00	0	0
Jane	Boxer	66264	Accounting	$450.00	1	2
Robert	Bauer	66395	Purchasing	$0.00	0	0
Peter	Bullard	66556	Marketing, Corp	$250.00	1	1
James	Baird	66567	Accounting	$300.00	0	3
Wayne	Wheaton	66564	Human Resourc	$150.00	1	0
Chris	Hart	77909	Marketing	$250.00	1	0
				$0.00		

Current record indicator

Figure 2.7
Access inserts new records at the bottom of the table.

2. **Type the following data for your new record. Press Enter after each entry. After the last entry, press Enter twice.**

```
William, Evich, 77517, Accounting, 300, 0, 3, 0, 2
```

Access adds the new employee record to the end of your table. You can also copy a record and add the copy, so that you have two versions of the same record. You might want to do this if you have two or more similar records. This might be appropriate for an inventory database of computer hardware. To practice this skill, you can copy the record you just added.

3. **To copy the new record, click the record selector to select the entire row.**
Access highlights the entire row.

4. **Click the Copy button.**
Onscreen, you won't notice anything different after you copy the record. Access places a copy of the selected record onto the Clipboard, which is a temporary storage location for whatever you have copied or cut from your document. Next, you paste the copy of the record into your table.

continues ▶

To Insert and Delete Records (continued)

5. **Click the record selector to highlight the empty record at the end of the table and click the Paste button.**
   Access adds, or appends, the record to the end of the table. Now that you have the basic data in place, you can make any changes necessary for this record. Rather than edit this duplicate record just now, you use it to practice deleting a record.

6. **Click the record selector next to the new record you inserted.**
   The record you pasted is selected. You can also select the record by opening the Edit menu and choosing Select Record when the insertion point is anywhere in the record.

7. **Click the Delete Record button.**
   Access wants to be sure that you intend to delete the record, so you are prompted to confirm the deletion (see Figure 2.8). You cannot undo record deletions, so be absolutely sure that you want to delete a record before you confirm the deletion.

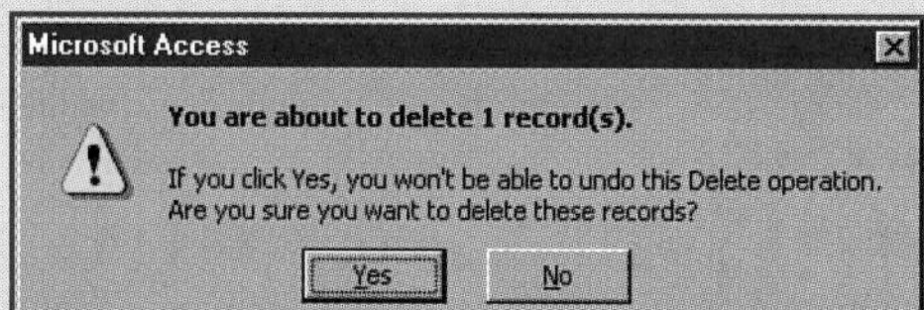
Microsoft Access
You are about to delete 1 record(s).
If you click Yes, you won't be able to undo this Delete operation.
Are you sure you want to delete these records?
Yes
No

Figure 2.8
Access prompts you to confirm the deletion.

8. **Click the Yes button.**
   Access deletes the record and saves the changes to the database table.

Keep the PC Software table open. In Lesson 5, you learn how to change the width of the columns in your table and how to hide and unhide columns.

Copying Entries from One Field to Another
In addition to copying entire records, you can also copy an entry from one field to another. If you want to enter another record for someone from the Marketing Department, for example, you can copy `Marketing` from the Department field and paste it in the new record.

To copy an entry, move to the appropriate field and select the text you want to copy by dragging across it. Click the Copy button. Move to the location where you want to place the copied text, and click the Paste button. Access pastes the selected text.

You can also use shortcut keys: Ctrl+C for Copy and Ctrl+V for Paste.

To delete a record, you can select the record and press Del, or place the insertion point anywhere in the record, and choose Delete Record from the Edit menu.

To add a new record, you can click the New Record button on the toolbar.

Lesson 5: Adjusting Column Widths and Hiding Columns

By default, Access displays all the columns in your table with the same width. You can change the column width, making some columns wider, so that you can see the entire entry and making other columns narrower so that they don't take up as much space. The easiest way to adjust the column width is to use the mouse, but you can also adjust it using Format, Column Width from the menu.

In addition to changing the column width, you can also hide columns that you don't want to display, such as the AutoNumber field, which is never used for data entry. Adjusting the column width does not change the field size. You learn how to change the field size in Access Project 4, "Creating and Using Forms."

To Adjust Column Widths and Hide Columns

1 With the PC Software table of the Employee Training database open, place the mouse pointer on the line between the First Name and Last Name field selectors.

The mouse pointer changes to a thick vertical bar with arrows on either side (see Figure 2.9). This pointer indicates that you can now move the column borders.

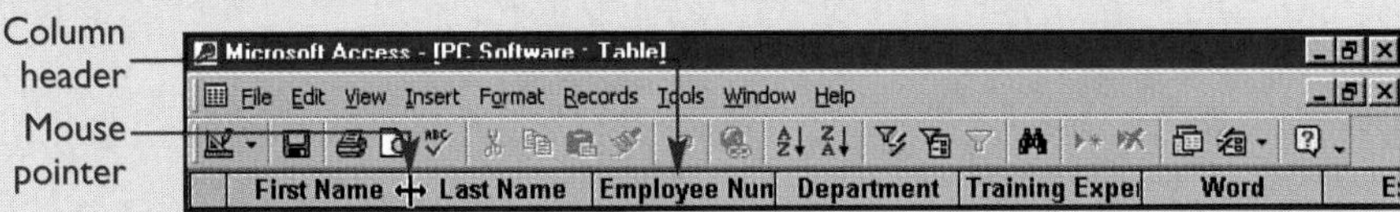

Figure 2.9
The appearance of the mouse pointer changes when you are preparing to resize a column.

2 Press and hold the mouse button, and drag to the left until you think the column is narrow enough, and you can still see all the entries in the column. Release the mouse button.

The new width is set. As you drag to the left, you make the column narrower. Notice that you can see the border of the column move as you drag. Don't worry if you cover part of the field name.

If you don't see the thick bar with the arrows, you don't have the pointer in the correct spot. Be sure that you are within the gray area of the field selectors and that your pointer is sitting directly on the border separating the two columns.

3 Move the pointer to the border between the Department and Training Expense columns, and double-click.

Double-clicking is a shortcut method that automatically adjusts the column to fit the longest entry currently displayed onscreen in that column. This often creates a problem when you use long field names, because double-clicking widens the column to show the whole field name if it is the longest entry in the column.

4 Drag across the field selectors for the Training Expense, Word, Excel, PowerPoint, Access, and ID fields. Use the horizontal scrollbar to view the selected columns.

When you drag across the headings, you select all six columns (see Figure 2.10). You can then adjust the width of the six columns at one time.

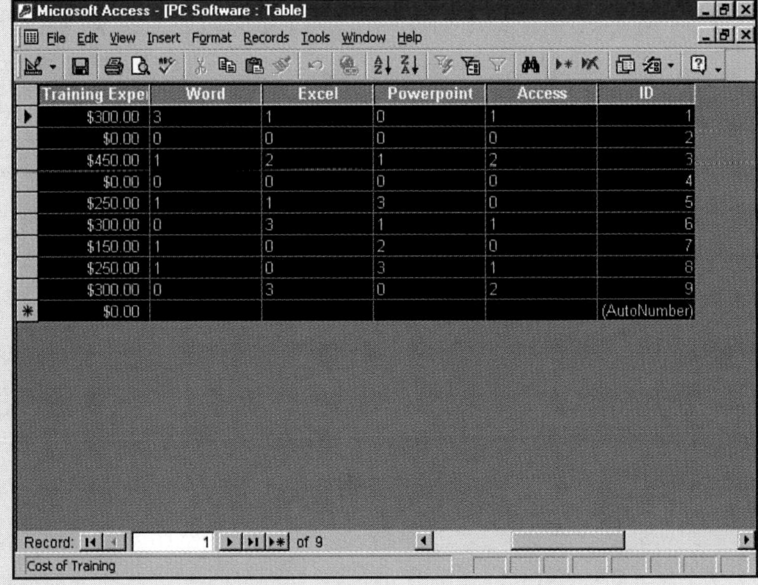

Microsoft Access - [PC Software : Table]

Training Expe	Word	Excel	Powerpoint	Access	ID
$300.00	3	1	0	1	1
$0.00	0	0	0	0	2
$450.00	1	2	1	2	3
$0.00	0	0	0	0	4
$250.00	1	1	3	0	5
$300.00	0	3	1	1	6
$150.00	1	0	2	0	7
$250.00	1	0	3	1	8
$300.00	0	3	0	2	9
$0.00					(AutoNumber)

Record: 1 of 9
Cost of Training

Figure 2.10
You can select several columns and resize them together.

continues ▶

To Adjust Column Widths and Hide Columns (continued)

5. **Drag the border on the right of the Training Expense column, so that it is just big enough to hold the longest entry.**
   Notice that dragging one of the borders resizes all six columns.
6. **Click anywhere in the table to deselect the columns.**
7. **Scroll to the left and click the field selector of the Employee Number field.**
   Now that you have selected this column, you can practice hiding it.
8. **Open the Format menu and choose the Hide Columns command.**
   Access hides the selected column.
9. **Open the Format menu and choose the Unhide Columns command to unhide the column.**
   Access displays the Unhide Columns dialog box (see Figure 2.11). If the column has a check mark next to its name, the column is displayed. If there is no check mark, the column is hidden.

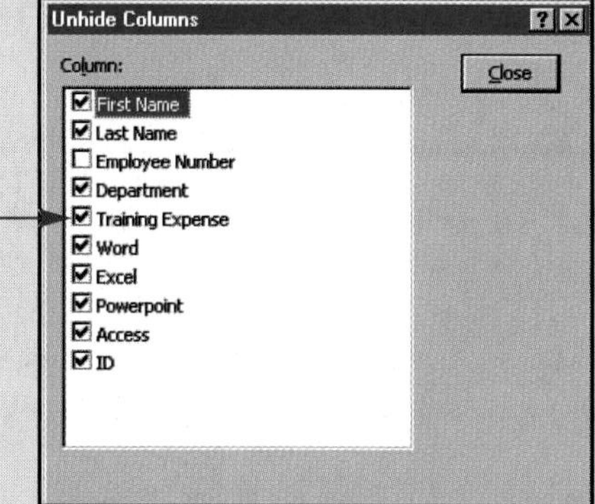

Figure 2.11
Use the Unhide Columns dialog box to unhide a column.

A check mark indicates that the column is displayed

10. **Click the Employee Number check box, and click the Close button.**
    Access closes the Unhide Columns dialog box. The Employee Number column reappears on the screen.

    Save your work and keep the PC Software table open. In Lesson 6, you search for specific records in your database.

Adjusting Column Widths and Hiding Columns
You can also use the menus to adjust the column width. Move the insertion point to the column you want to adjust. Open the Format menu and choose the Column Width command. Type the width of the column in points, and click the OK button.

You can also hide multiple columns by selecting them and selecting the Hide Columns command from the Format menu. In addition, you can use the Unhide Columns dialog box to hide columns. In the list displayed in the dialog box, click the check box next to a column to deselect it. This hides the column.

Lesson 6: Finding Records

In a table with many records and fields, it might be time-consuming to scroll through the records and fields to find a specific record. Instead, you can search for a specific field entry to find and move quickly to a record.

For example, if you want to find the Wayne Wheaton record, you can search for Wheaton. It is always faster to select the field you want to use for your search and search only that field, but you can also search for text in any field in the table. In this lesson, you find a record; first you search a single field, and then you search all fields.

To Find a Record

1 With the PC Software table of the Employee Training database open, click the Last Name field.

It doesn't matter which row you click. Clicking anywhere in the field tells Access that you want to search for a particular record using the Last Name field only. The field with the insertion point is searched by default.

2 Click the Find button.

Access displays the Find and Replace dialog box (see Figure 2.12). Here you tell Access what you want to find and where you want to look.

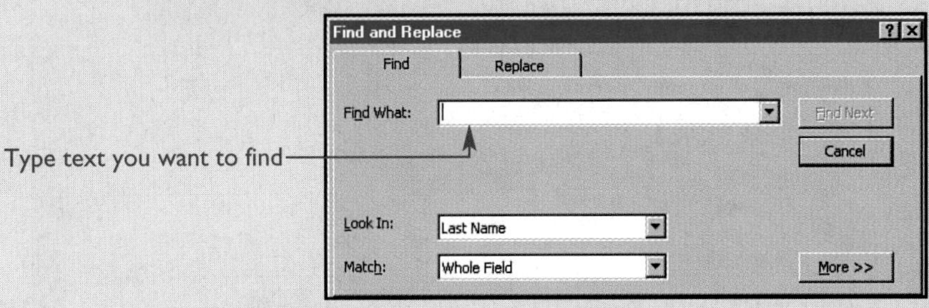

Figure 2.12
You use the Find and Replace dialog box to prepare for your search.

3 Type `Wheaton` and click the Find Next button.

Access moves to the first match, and the dialog box remains open. You can continue to search by clicking the Find Next button until you find the record you want.

If you can't see the match because the dialog box is in the way, move the dialog box by dragging its title bar.

4 Drag across the text in the Find What text box to select it, then type `Resources`.

This is the next entry you want to find.

5 Click the arrow in the Look In box and select PC Software : Table.

Instead of restricting the search to the current field, you are telling Access to look in all fields.

6 Click the arrow in the Match box and select Any Part of Field.

The text you want to find (`Resources`) won't be the entire entry; it is only part of the field. For this reason, you have to tell Access to match any part of the field. Figure 2.13 shows the options you requested for this search.

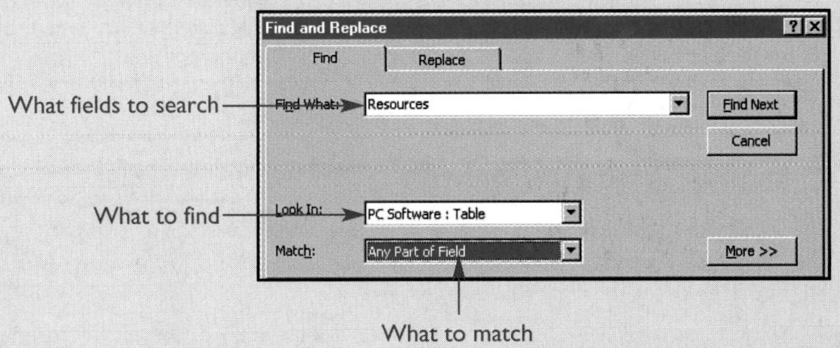

Figure 2.13
You can change your search options in the Find and Replace dialog box.

7 Click the Find Next button.

Access moves to the first occurrence and highlights `Resources` in the Department field in the record for Wayne Wheaton (see Figure 2.14). The program starts searching from the selected record.

continues ▶

To Find a Record (continued)

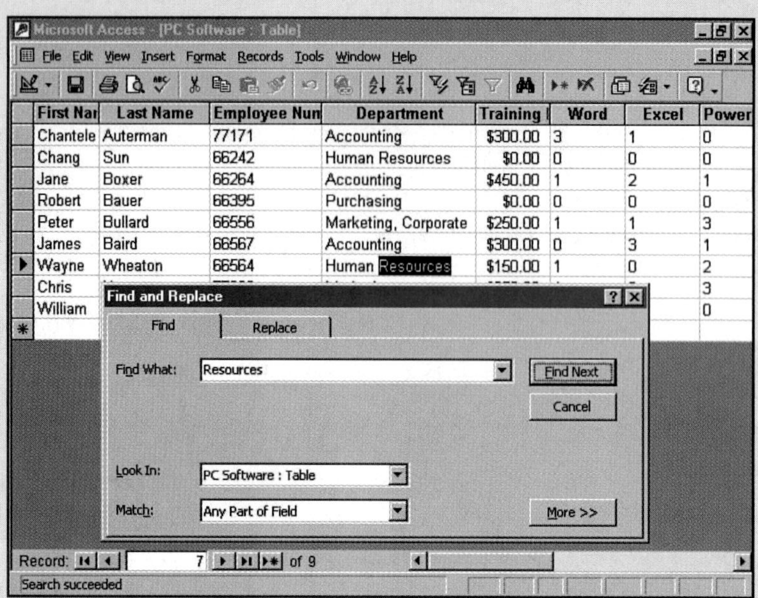

Figure 2.14
The Find feature can find information in any part of a field.

8. **Click the Find Next button.**
   Access moves to the next occurrence and highlights `Resources` in the Department field in the record for Chang Sun.
9. **Click the Cancel button.**
   The Find and Replace dialog box closes. The last record found remains selected.

   Save your work and keep the PC Software table open. In Lesson 7, you learn how to sort the records in your table.

The Way Access Searches for Data

If you see a message telling you that Access has reached the end of the records and asking whether you want to start searching from the beginning, click the Yes button. By default, Access searches from the current record down through the database. The record you want may be located before the current one.

If you see another message telling you that Access reached the end of the records, Access did not find a match. Try the search again. Be sure that you typed the entry correctly. You may need to change one or more of the options.

Lesson 7: Sorting Records

Access displays the records in your table in an order determined by the primary key. You learned how to create a primary key in Project 1. If your table has no primary key, Access displays the records in the order in which they were entered.

If you use a primary key, Access sorts the entries alphabetically or numerically based on the entries in that field. (If a counter field is your primary key, your records display in the order in which they were entered.) Fortunately, however, you aren't restricted to displaying your data only in the order determined by your primary key. With Access, you can sort the display by using any of the fields in the database table. You can also sort the display by multiple, adjacent fields.

In this lesson, you first sort your data on the Last Name field. Then you use the toolbar to sort by the Employee Number field.

To Sort Records

1 With the PC Software table of the Employee Training database open, click the Last Name field.
Clicking in this field tells Access that you want to base your sort on the Last Name field.

2 Click the Sort Ascending button.
Access sorts the records in ascending alphabetical order (a to z) based on the entries in the Last Name field (see Figure 2.15).

Microsoft Access - [PC Software : Table]

File Edit View Insert Format Records Tools Window Help

First Nar	Last Name	Employee Nun	Department	Training	Word	Excel	Power
Chantele	Auterman	77171	Accounting	$300.00	3	1	0
James	Baird	66567	Accounting	$300.00	0	3	1
Robert	Bauer	66395	Purchasing	$0.00	0	0	0
Jane	Boxer	66264	Accounting	$450.00	1	2	1
Peter	Bullard	66556	Marketing, Corporate	$250.00	1	1	3
William	Evich	77517	Accounting	$300.00	0	3	0
Chris	Hart	77909	Marketing	$250.00	1	0	3
Chang	Sun	66242	Human Resources	$0.00	0	0	0
Wayne	Wheaton	66564	Human Resources	$150.00	1	0	2
				$0.00			

Sort Ascending button

Sort Descending button

Sorted field

Figure 2.15
Access displays the results of an ascending sort based on the Last Name field.

3 Click the Employee Number field.
Clicking this field tells Access that you now want to base your sort on the Employee Number field.

4 Click the Sort Ascending button on the toolbar.
Access sorts the table by using the entries in the Employee Number field. Keep in mind that the sort order displayed onscreen does not affect the order in which the records are actually stored.

5 Close the PC Software table.
A dialog box asks whether you want to save your changes, which in this case, were the changes to the sort order.

6 Click the Yes button.
If you have completed your session on the computer, exit Access and Windows before turning off the computer. Otherwise, continue with the Checking Concepts and Terms section.

Using the Menu to Sort Records

You can also use the Records, Sort command from the menu and select the Sort Ascending or Sort Descending option. As with the buttons, you must first have the insertion point in the field you want to sort.

Sorting Records Using Multiple Fields

To sort by multiple, adjacent fields (for example, last name and then first name) select the field name for the first sort, hold down Shift and select the second field to sort. (The second field must be adjacent and to the right of the first field.) You can also click the first field selector and drag to the right to select the second field. Click the Sort Ascending or Sort Descending button to perform the sort.

When you have completed a sort, if you want to return records to their original order, choose Records from the menu and click Remove Filter/Sort.

If the fields you want to sort are not in the proper order (for example, your database Employee Training displays the first name field followed by the last name field), you can move the fields in Design view prior to the sort. By moving the field so that the last name column appears first in your table, with the first name field as the next field immediately to the right, you can then sort the table by last name, and then by first name. You can also move a field by selecting the field, clicking the field name, and dragging the field to the desired location.

Summary

In this project, you worked with records in a table. You added, edited, inserted, and deleted records, and learned how to move around quickly in a table. You used two of the more important features of a database to find and sort records. You also adjusted the widths of the columns to make the table more readable and learned to hide columns without deleting the field.

You can extend your knowledge of tables by asking the Office Assistant how to design a table. Several topics are available about table design, and some of the basic design concepts are discussed in the topics on creating a table.

Checking Concepts and Terms

True/False

For each of the following, check *T* or *F* to indicate whether the statement is true or false.

__T__F **1.** You can edit records in Design view. [L1]

__T__F **2.** When the pencil icon appears in the record selector, it reminds you that the record is being edited and the change has not been saved. [L3]

__T__F **3.** When you change the column width, you also change the field size. [L5]

__T__F **4.** When you add a new record, it is added to the end of a table. [L1]

__T__F **5.** You can undo record deletions. [L4]

__T__F **6.** The only way to delete a record is to use the Delete Record button. [L4]

__T__F **7.** You can hide a column, so that it does not appear on the screen. [L5]

__T__F **8.** When using the Find and Replace dialog box, the default choice is to search in the field where the insertion point is located. [L6]

__T__F **9.** You can hide only one column at a time. [L5]

__T__F **10.** Multiple sorts can be created by choosing non-adjacent fields. [L7]

Multiple Choice

Circle the letter of the correct answer for each of the following.

1. Which of the following is not a way to adjust the column width? [L5]

a. Double-click the column border.

b. Drag the column border.

c. Open the View menu and choose the Column Size command.

d. Open the Format menu and choose the Column Width command.

2. Access automatically saves the data you enter to disk when you do which of the following? [L3]

a. Press Shift + Enter.

b. Leave the field in which you entered the data.

c. Choose Save Record from the Record menu.

d. all of the above

3. To hide a column, you should do which of the following? [L5]

a. Select the column and press Del+H.

b. Select the column and double-click the right column separator on the border.

c. Place the insertion point in the column and select Hide Columns from the Format menu.

d. Place the insertion point in the column and select AutoHide from the Format menu.

4. Access identifies the record you are editing by which of the following? [L3]

a. the arrow on the record selector

b. the asterisk on the record selector

c. the key symbol on the record selector

d. the pencil icon on the record selector

5. What does the New Record button look like? [L2]

a. an arrow pointing to an asterisk

b. a folder with an arrow on it

c. a folder with a star on it

d. an arrow pointing to a line

Screen ID

Refer to Figure 2.16 and identify the numbered parts of the screen. Write the letter of the correct label in the space next to the number.

Figure 2.16

A. First Record button
B. Paste button
C. Next Record button
D. Sort Ascending button
E. Pencil icon
F. New Record button
G. Sort Descending button
H. Previous Record button
I. Empty Record icon
J. Last Record button

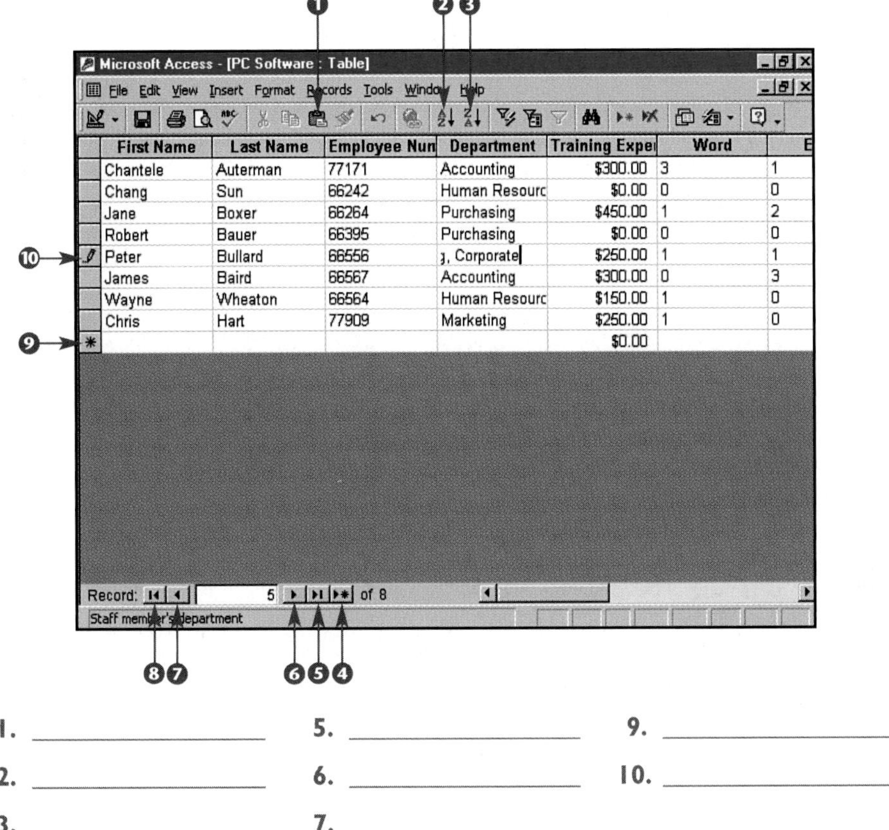

1. ______
2. ______
3. ______
4. ______
5. ______
6. ______
7. ______
8. ______
9. ______
10. ______

Discussion Questions

1. Access does not enable you to insert records into the middle of a table—just at the end. Does the order in which you enter records really matter? If so, why? If not, why not?
2. Assume for a moment that you are designing a database table for automobile parts for use in a store. This table can be used by both the sales personnel at the counter and by the customers at a self-help computer. The table contains the make of the car, part name, description, number sold year-to-date, quantity in stock, retail price, sale price, and cost. Which, if any, of the fields would you hide? Why?
3. Forms are also used to enter data. With forms, you can lay out the fields so that many fields are on the screen at a time, but for only one record at a time. When would you want to use a form rather than a table? When would a table be preferable?
4. In this project, you learned about several different methods of moving around in a table. When might it be preferable to use buttons? Keyboard shortcuts? The mouse?
5. Sorting records is done often in a database. Sorting by last name and first name is an example of sorting on more than one field at a time. Can you think of any other instances when you might need to sort on two fields at once? Would there ever be a reason to sort on three fields?

Skill Drill

Skill Drill exercises reinforce project skills. Each skill reinforced is the same, or nearly the same, as a skill presented in the project. Each exercise includes a brief narrative introduction, followed by detailed instructions in a step-by-step format.

You are working for a company that does research for other companies. Your current project is to conduct a survey for a cable TV company to find out how subscribers feel about five of the channels offered in their basic cable package. You are just starting out and testing your survey with a small number of families. You have set up a preliminary survey and are recording the results in an Access database.

1. Adding Records

You have decided you need ten families for your trial run, so you need to add two more families to your survey. [L1]

To add records, complete the following steps:

1. Find the `AO-0202` database file on your CD-ROM; copy it to drive A; remove the read-only status, and name it `Television Survey`. Open the database and open the Questionnaire table.
2. Click the View button to switch to Design view and read the Description column to see what each of the categories means. Click the View button again to return to Datasheet view.
3. In Datasheet view, click the New Record button. Use either the one on the toolbar or the one included with the navigation buttons
4. Enter the following information into the Questionnaire table. (*Note*: You can enter check boxes by clicking them with the mouse or by pressing Spacebar.)
5. Close the table but leave the database open.

Adults	Children	Use	Hours	#1	#2	#3	Doing	Comments
4	0	N	8	DISCOVERY	CNN	SCIFI	Great	More nature shows
1	2	Y		DISNEY	SCIFI		Good	More cartoons!!!

2. Editing Records

While looking over the paper survey forms you have received, you find that you made a couple of mistakes entering the data. [L3]

To edit records, complete the following steps:

1. Open the Questionnaire table in the Television Survey database. Make sure you are in Datasheet view.
2. Move down to the 8th field (the one that has only CNN in the favorite channel fields).
3. Highlight CNN and type `TNT`.
4. Move to the Improve field and type `No opinion`.
5. Leave the table open for the next exercise.

3. Inserting and Deleting Records

After discussing your sample data with representatives from the cable company, you find that they feel that every household must have at least one of the five channels being tested in their list of favorites. This means that you have one record that needs to be deleted, and you need to find another one to take its place. [L4]

To insert and delete records in a table, complete the following steps:

1. Click the record selector next to the record with no favorite channels listed. This should be the fourth record.
2. Press Del to remove the record.
3. Click the New Record button.
4. Add the following information:

Adults	Children	Use	Hours	#1	#2	#3	Doing	Comments
2	2	Y	2	TNT	CNN	DISCOVERY	Good	Would like more news & nature shows

4. Adjusting Column Widths and Hiding Columns

You would like to be able to see more of your survey information on the screen at one time. The best way to do that is to reduce the width of several columns, and to hide the ID column. [L5]

To adjust column widths and hide columns, complete the following steps:

1. Click the field selector of the ID field and drag until you select the ID, Adults, Children, Use, and Hours fields.
2. Grab the column separator between any two of the fields, and reduce the column width to the smallest size needed to show all the data. You cut off part of the field names.
3. Place the insertion point in the ID field.
4. Choose Format, Hide Columns from the menu.
5. Leave the table open for the next exercise.

5. Finding a Record

Although this is a small sample, you want to be prepared to find data when the full survey is completed. [L6]

To find records in a table, complete the following steps:

1. Place the insertion point in the Improve field of the ninth record (the Disney Channel record you entered in the first exercise).
2. Type **Nature** in the Find What box. Click the Find button on the toolbar.
3. Select Any Part of Field from the Match drop-down menu.
4. Click the Find Next button. If the first instance is hidden, move the Find and Replace dialog box out of the way. Notice that the first record found is the last record in the table.
5. Click the Find Next button again. A second match is found.
6. Click the Find Next button. When no more matches are found, click OK and close the Find and Replace dialog box.
7. Leave the table open for the next exercise.

6. Sorting and Printing Records

Your client wants to see the sample survey data in two different orders. [L7]

To sort and print records in a table, complete the following steps:

1. Place the insertion point in the Children field and click the Sort Descending button.
2. Select File, Page Setup, and move to the Page tab.
3. Select Landscape orientation and click OK.
4. Click the Print button to print the table.
5. Click the Use field, and click the Sort Ascending button. You could print this table, although it is not necessary to do so at this time.
6. Close the table and save your changes. Close the database and close Access unless you plan to complete the Challenge section now.

Challenge

Challenge exercises expand on or are somewhat related to skills presented in the lessons. Each exercise provides a brief narrative introduction followed by instructions, in a numbered step or bulleted list format, that are not as detailed as those in the Skill Drill section.

The table you use in the Challenge section is a list of your CDs in a database called CD Collection. This table has fields for the artist, title, year, label, serial number, and category.

1. Freezing Columns

You have to use the horizontal scrollbar to scroll back and forth to look at all the fields for a record. When you scroll to the right, the name of the artist disappears from view. You would like to keep the name of the artist and title on the screen at all times. [L5]

To freeze columns, complete the following steps:

1. Copy the `AO-0203` database file to drive A; remove the read-only status, and rename it `CD Collection`.
2. Open the database, and open the CD Collection table in Datasheet view.
3. Select both the Artist/Group and the CD Title fields.
4. Choose Format, Freeze Columns from the menu.
5. Scroll to the right to make sure the first two columns don't move off the screen.
6. Close the table and save your changes.

2. Finding and Replacing Data

When you show a friend a printout of your CD collection, she points out that you misspelled the name of classical composer Gustav Holst, which you spelled "Holzt." You can scan the entire 371 records and try to make sure you find all the misspelled words, or you can use the Find and Replace feature to do the hard work for you. You decide to try the latter option. [L6]

To find and replace data, complete the following steps:

1. Open the CD Collection table in Datasheet view.
2. Highlight the CD Title column.
3. Choose Edit, Replace from the menu.
4. Type **`Holzt`** in the Find What text box and **`Holst`** in the Replace With text box. Make sure that you match any part of the field and look in only the CD Title field.
5. Click Find Next to find the first instance of the misspelled word. Replace it with the correct spelling. You cannot undo this action.
6. Click Replace All to find the rest of the misspelled words.
7. Close the table and save your changes, if necessary.

3. Copying and Pasting Records

At times, you might have a CD to enter into the table that is very similar to another one you have already entered. Try copying and pasting a record to save work. [L4]

To copy and paste records, complete the following steps:

1. Open the CD Collection table in Datasheet view. Use the Find button to find the CD Title called "Too Long in Exile" by Van Morrison. (*Hint*: you can type the first word or two in the Find What box.)
2. Click the record selector to select the whole record.
3. Use the Copy button to copy the record.
4. Click the New Record button and click the record selector to select the whole record.
5. Click the Paste button to paste the whole record you copied.
6. Change the Title field to **`Days Like This`**. Change the Year field to **`1995`**. Change the Serial number field to **`31452 7307 2`**.
7. Close the table.

4. Removing Sorts

You just noticed that there is a command to remove a sort, and you wonder how it works. Does it remove only the previous sort? Does it go back to the original order even after two sorts? Does it work after you have saved your changes and left the table? Look at the first three records so you can remember which records came first. [L7]

To remove a sort, complete the following steps:

1. Open the CD Collection table in Datasheet view. Place the insertion point anywhere in the Artist/Group column and sort in ascending order.
2. Now sort on the Label field in descending order.
3. Choose Records, Remove Filter/Sort from the menu. Notice that the records are back in their original order.
4. Sort by Artist/Group, and close the table and save your changes.
5. Open the CD Collection table again; notice that the sort on Artist/Group is still in effect.
6. Choose Records, Remove Filter/Sort from the menu. Did the records go back to their original order?
7. Close the table and save your changes.

5. Changing Column Widths Using the Menu

The column widths are not quite right in the CD Collection table. Try the menu option to change the column widths. [L5]

To change column widths using the menu, complete the following steps:

1. Open the CD Collection table in Datasheet view. Select the Year column.
2. Choose Format, Column Width from the menu.
3. Click the Best Fit button to narrow the column.
4. Select the Serial number field; choose Format, Column Width from the menu.
5. Select the Standard Width check box and click OK.
6. Select the Artist/Group field and choose Format, Column Width from the menu. Notice that the column width is shown as `22.5`. Change the number to **`30`** and click OK.
7. Use the Help option from your computer or online to find out exactly what the numbers in the Column Width box are. Could they be points? Eighths of inches? Some other measurement?
8. Use what you found out from Help to make the CD Title column exactly 3" wide.
9. Close the table and save your changes.

6. Formatting Text in a Table

You have seen text formatting on text in word-processing programs and spreadsheets, and you wonder whether the same thing can be done with text in Access. [L3]

To format text in a table, complete the following steps:

1. Open the CD Collection table in Datasheet view.
2.  Use the Access Help or online Help to find out how to turn on the Formatting toolbar in the Datasheet view.
3. Change the background color to a pale blue (or other light background color of your choice).
4. Change the text to a very dark blue (or other dark font color of your choice).
5. Highlight any CD Title and click the Italic button. What happened?
6. Close the table and save your changes.

Discovery Zone

Discovery Zone exercises help you gain advanced knowledge of project topics and/or application of skills. These exercises focus on enhancing your problem-solving skills.

1. Sending a Database to the Desktop as a Shortcut

You buy CDs all the time, and you find that you are opening this database several times a week. It would be a good idea to place an icon representing the database right on your desktop. That way, you can boot your computer and double-click the CD Collection icon to move directly to the database, saving several steps!

Goal: Create, test, and delete a desktop shortcut to a specific database.

Create a desktop shortcut for your CD Collection database; test it, and delete it from your desktop.

Hint: You can do this in two ways: one within Access and one using Windows. Try to figure out both of them.

2. Using Access Tools

Access has all sorts of tools available to help you enter data quickly and proof information when you are finished. The most commonly used tool is the Spelling checker, which can be very important to people who are weak in this area. A second, lesser-known tool can be of at least as much help. This is the AutoCorrect feature.

Goal: Use the Spelling checker to check spelling and add words to the dictionary. Use the AutoCorrect tool to simplify the entry of long text entries.

Spelling checker goals:

- Find two ways to activate the Spelling checker.
- Check the spelling of several words in the CD Title column.
- Add one of the words to your dictionary.

AutoCorrect tool goals:

- Have the program automatically capitalize the first letter of a sentence.
- Turn on the feature that changes the second letter of two capital letters to lower case, and make an exception for CD.
- Create a shortcut that enables you to type `ASMF` and have it replace those letters with `Academy of St. Martins on the Field (Sir Neville Marriner)`.
- Test the three features you just worked with.

Also, look at some of the other tools available for use with your table.

3. Analyzing Your Table

When you look at your fields in the CD Collection table, you notice that the names of the artists are repeated frequently. Knowing that this probably isn't good database design, you'd like to have the table analyzed. You've heard that Access has a procedure to analyze tables.

Goal: Discover how to have Access analyze your table, and run the analysis option.

Use Help to find out where the Table Analysis tool is located. Run the analyzer to see whether the program feels your table should be split into two tables. If Access suggests splitting the table, read why, but do not actually go through with it.

Project 3

Querying Your Database

Objectives

In this project, you learn how to

- ➤ **Create a New Query**
- ➤ **Choose Fields for a Query**
- ➤ **Save the Query**
- ➤ **Edit the Query**
- ➤ **Change the Field Order and Sort the Query**
- ➤ **Match Criteria**
- ➤ **Save the Query with a New Name and Open Multiple Queries**

Key terms introduced in this project include

- column selector
- criteria
- design grid
- dynaset
- query
- Select Query

Why Would I Do This?

The primary reason you spend time entering all your data into a database is so that you can easily find and work with the information. In an address book database, for example, you might want to display all your contacts in Indiana. To do so, you would create a ***query***. A query asks a question of the database, such as, "Which records have IN as the state?" and then pulls those records from the database into a subset of records. The subset is called a ***dynaset***. You can then work with (or print) only those records selected by your query.

You can also create queries that display all the records but show only selected fields. For example, you can display only the Last Name and Employee Number fields in the Employee Training database. You can create a query that searches for values in one field, such as the Indiana example, but displays only selected fields in the result. You can also create more complex queries. For example, you can query your Employee Training database to display all staff members who received training in either Microsoft Excel or PowerPoint. You create queries and save them, so that you can use them over and over.

In this project, you create, save, edit, and use a query like the one in Figure 3.1.

Visual Summary

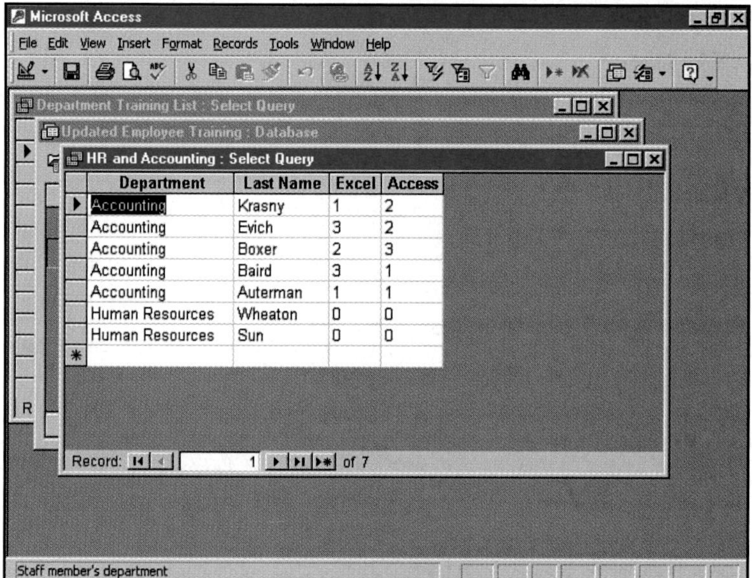

Figure 3.1
Queries enable you to select the information you need from a table or tables.

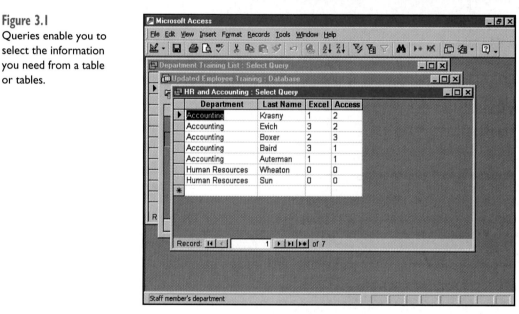

Lesson 1: Creating a New Query

A table is the most basic type of object you can include in a database, but as mentioned in Access Project 1, "Creating a Database," several other types of objects exist. A query is one of the other database objects, and you can have many queries based on a single table.

You might remember that when you open the database, you see the Database window that lists the tables contained in the database and also displays object buttons for queries, forms, reports, and so on. If you want to add a query to the table, you can start from the Database window.

In this lesson, you work with the data in the PC Software table of your Employee Training database. The PC Software table on disk that you copy and use in this project includes the records you entered in Access Project 2, "Entering and Editing Data," as well as some additional records. The headings in the revised table have been modified slightly to adjust the size of each column, allowing more information to appear on the screen. To start the procedure you create a query, and then you add the table (or tables) with which you want to work.

To Create a New Query

1. **Launch Access. Click OK to open an existing file.**
   Make sure you have a disk in drive A.

2. **Find the `AO-0301` file on your CD-ROM; right-click it, and copy it to the floppy drive. Move to drive A; remove the Read Only status; rename the file `Updated Employee Training`, and open the new database.**
   The database should open to the Tables object button, and a PC Software table should be listed.

3. **Click the Queries object button.**
   The Queries list displays no queries because you haven't created and saved any queries yet (see Figure 3.2).

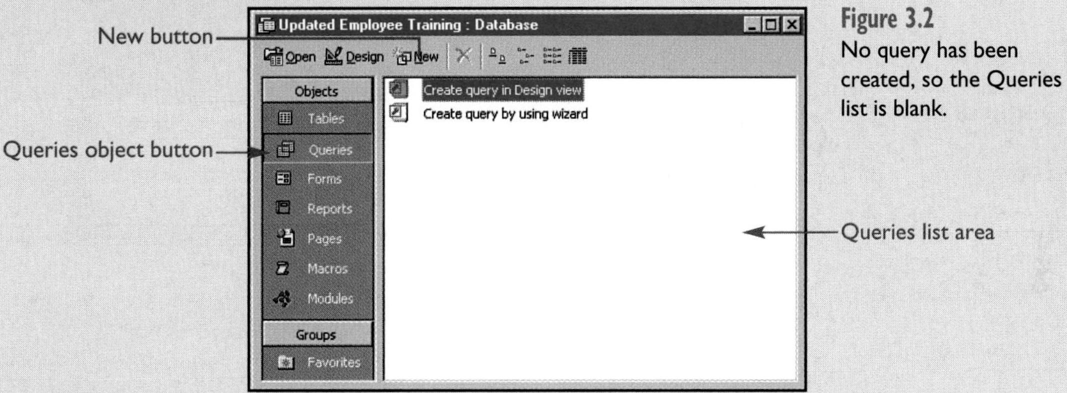

Figure 3.2
No query has been created, so the Queries list is blank.

4. **Click the New button.**
   The New Query dialog box opens (see Figure 3.3). You can use one of the query wizards to create a query. This method works best for specific kinds of queries, such as finding duplicate records. You could use the Simple Query Wizard to complete this lesson, but the more general Design View method gives you a better feel for how a query works.

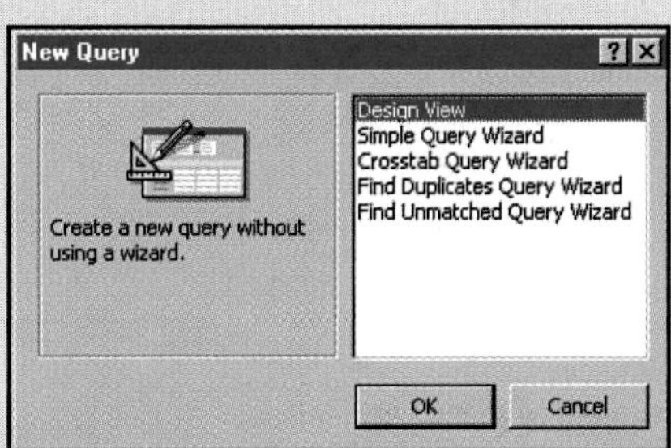

Figure 3.3
Choose the method you want to use to create a new query.

5. **Click Design View and click OK.**
   The Show Table dialog box displays (see Figure 3.4). Here you select the table(s) you want to use in your query. For complex queries, you can pull information from more than one table.

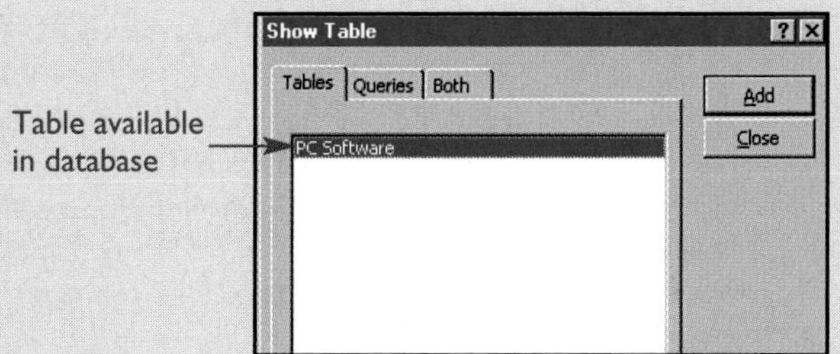

Figure 3.4
Select the table you want to use from the Show Table dialog box.

continues ▶

To Create a New Query (continued)

6 The PC Software table is already selected, so click the Add button.
This step selects the table you want to use. The Show Table dialog box remains open, so that you can add other tables if necessary.

7 Click the Close button in the Show Table dialog box.
Access closes the Show Table dialog box and displays the Select Query window (see Figure 3.5). Leave the Select Query window open and continue with Lesson 2.

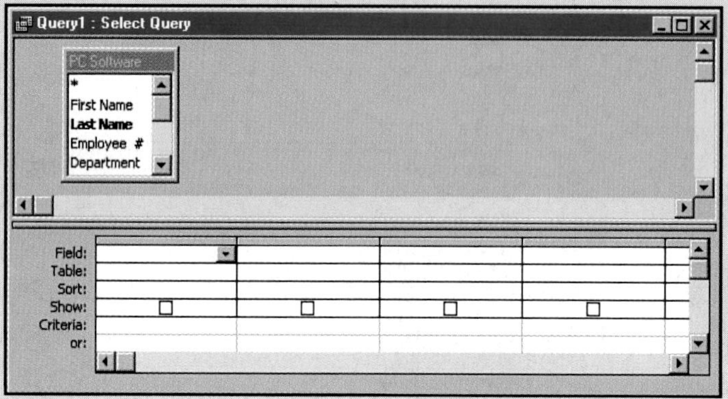

Figure 3.5
Use the Select Query window to create a new query.

Lesson 2: Choosing Fields for a Query

After you open a new query and select a table, you see a window divided into two parts. The top half of the Select Query window displays a scroll box containing a list of the fields from the table you selected. Notice that the primary key field appears in bold type. (In this version of the database, the Last Name field is designated as the primary key.) You can use this Field list to choose the fields you want to include in your query.

In the lower half of the Select Query window, you see the ***design grid*** with rows for Field, Table, Sort, Show, Criteria, and Or. All the columns are blank. You use the design grid to control which fields you include in your query. The simplest type of query, and the one you will probably use most often, is the ***Select Query***, which displays data that meet conditions that you set.

You add the fields you want to include in the query to the Field row in the design grid. You can include as many fields as you want in the query, but you must include at least one field.

In this lesson, you create a query that contains only the Last Name and Department from your PC Software table. This list might be handy if you need to know who has received training in each department. You can use one of several methods to add fields to your query.

To Choose Fields for a Query

1 In the Field list in the top half of the Select Query window, click the Last Name field.
The Select Query window should still be open from the preceding lesson. This step selects the field you want to add to the design grid.

2 Drag the selected field from the field list to the first column in the Field row of the design grid.
As you drag, a little field box displays. When you release the mouse button, Access displays the field name in the Field row, and the table name in the Table row (see Figure 3.6). The Show row in this column displays a check mark in the check box, indicating that this field will display in the query. (You may want to use a field to set a condition or to sort on, but not display its contents. In that case, you click the Show check box to deselect it.)

To Choose Fields for a Query

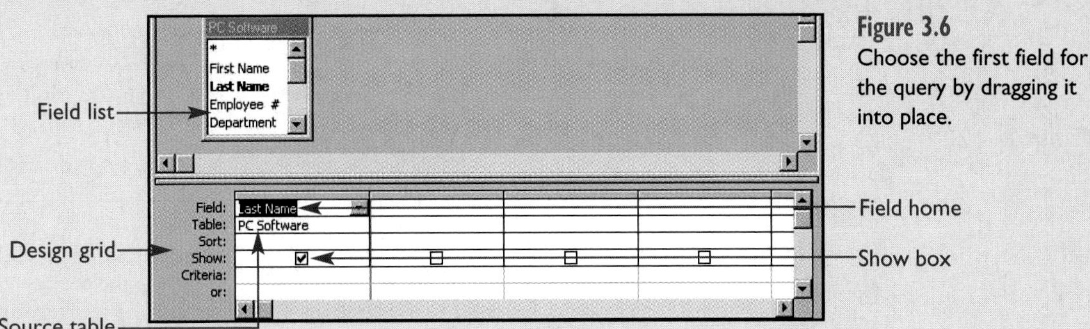

Figure 3.6
Choose the first field for the query by dragging it into place.

3. **Click in the second column of the Field row in the design grid.**
   A list arrow displays; clicking this arrow activates a drop-down list of available fields.

4. **Click the list arrow.**
   Access displays the drop-down list of fields (see Figure 3.7). The top entry in this menu is the table name, displayed with an asterisk. If you select the table name, all the fields display when the query runs.

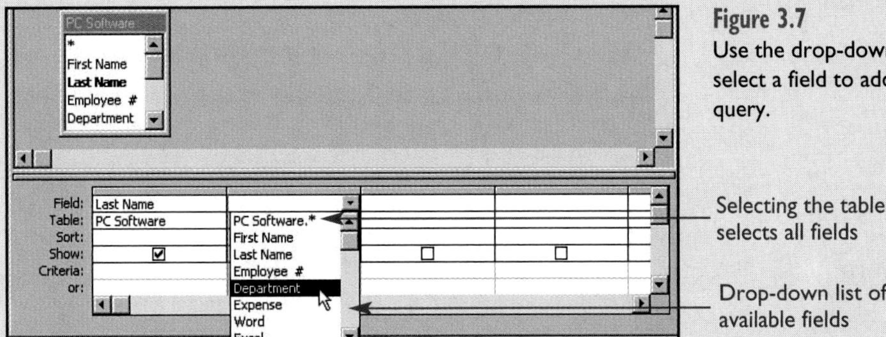

Figure 3.7
Use the drop-down list to select a field to add to the query.

5. **Click `Department` in the list.**
   The Department field is added to the query. This action has the same result as dragging the field from the field list.

6. **Click the View button on the toolbar.**
   The records display in Datasheet view and use the fields you selected in the query (see Figure 3.8). Notice that the title bar displays Select Query to remind you that you are viewing a dynaset, not the actual table. The difference between a table and a dynaset is that the table consists of all the records with all the fields; the dynaset consists of a subset of the records.

Query1 : Select Query

Last Name	Department
Auterman	Accounting
Baird	Accounting
Bauer	Purchasing
Baylis	Branch 3
Boxer	Accounting
Bullard	Marketing,Corporate
Dobbs	Payroll
Evich	Accounting
Hart	Marketing
Hill	Branch 2
Krasny	Accounting
Lord	Payoll
Nolan	Branch 1

Record: 1 of 21

Figure 3.8
In Datasheet view, you can see that the query now includes two fields.

continues ▶

To Choose Fields for a Query (continued)

7 Click the View button on the toolbar.
The View button now has a different look. You return to Design view for the query. Keep the Select Query window open in Design view. You learn how to name and save the query in the next lesson.

Alternative Query Procedures
If you would rather use the menus, you can open the View menu and select the Datasheet View or the Design View command, instead of clicking the toolbar View buttons. You can also add fields to the query by double-clicking the field name or by typing the field name in the Field row of the design grid.

Using Query Shortcuts
You can select several fields and add them all at one time from the field list. If the fields are listed next to each other, click the first field in the field list; hold down Shift, and click the last field in the field list. Access selects the first and last fields, and all fields in between. You can also select fields that aren't listed next to each other. Click the first field you want to select. Hold down Ctrl and click the next field you want to select. Continue pressing Ctrl while you click each subsequent field. After you select all the fields you want, drag them to the design grid, and place them in the first empty space in the Field row. This adds all the selected fields to the query.

When you switch from Design view to Datasheet view, you run your query. Instead of switching views, you can open the Query menu and select the Run command or click the Run button on the toolbar.

Lesson 3: Saving the Query

As with any object you add to a database, you must save and name the object if you want to keep it. When you save a query, you save the structure of the query, not the dynaset. The dynaset is the result of running the query, which can be different each time it runs because it is based on the data in your table. If the records in the table change, the resulting dynaset reflects those changes.

The first time you save a query, Access prompts you to give it a name. After that, you can save changes to the query without retyping the name. You can open the File menu and choose the Save command, or you can click the Save button on the toolbar. You can also close the Select Query window, at which point the program asks whether you want to save the query.

In this lesson, you save the query and name it.

To Save the Query

1 The Select Query window, based on the PC Software table, should still be open from the preceding lesson. Click the Save button on the toolbar.
The Save As dialog box displays with the name Query1 (see Figure 3.9). Access suggests Query1 as a default name, but as you can see, it isn't a very descriptive name.

Figure 3.9
Replace the default name with a more descriptive name for the query.

2 Type `Department Training List`.
Access assigns this name to the query. You can type up to 64 characters, including numbers, letters, spaces, and special characters.

If Access does not accept your query name, it means that you have used one of the forbidden characters—a period (.), an exclamation point (!), an accent (‘), or square bracket ([ ]). Also, you cannot include leading spaces in the query name.

3. **Click the OK button.**
   Access saves the query and the database. The name of the query displays in the title bar of the Select Query window and also in the Queries list in the Database window.

4. **Click the Close Window button in the upper-right corner of the Select Query window.**
   Access closes the Select Query window. The Department Training List query displays in the Database window (see Figure 3.10).

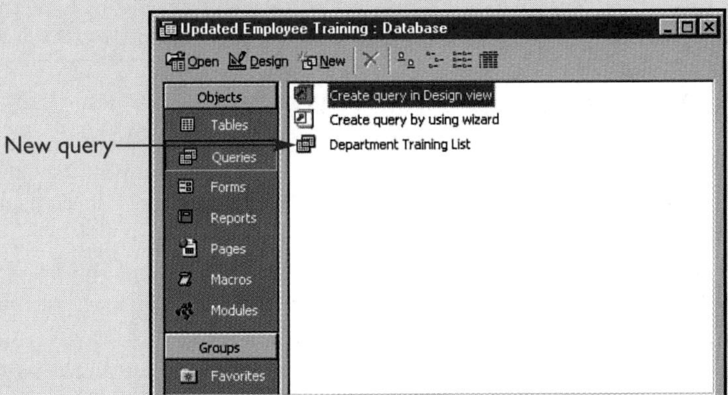

Figure 3.10
The new query displays in the database window.

5. **Select Department Training List and click the Open button.**
   This reopens the query. The query displays in Datasheet view, instead of Design view. Keep the Department Training List query open for the next lesson.

Renaming a Query
If you don’t like the name you used—for example, suppose that you accepted the default Query1 name—you can change the name. To do this, move to the Database window; right-click the object you want to rename, and select Rename from the shortcut menu.

Saving a Query
You don’t have to save the query if you’re sure you won’t use it again. Just close the Select Query window without saving. When Access prompts you to save, click the No button.

If you decide to save the query, you can do so by choosing File, Save from the menu or by pressing Ctrl+S.

Lesson 4: Editing the Query

Creating a query takes some practice and a little trial and error. You choose some fields, view the query, make some changes, view the query again, and so on, until you get the results you want.

You can edit the query to add or delete fields. In this project, you add three fields and delete a field.

To Edit the Query

1. **With the Department Training List Select Query window displayed, click the View button on the toolbar.**
   When you opened the query in the preceding lesson, it displayed in Datasheet view. To make changes, you first have to change to Design view. Now you should see the Select Query window with the field list box at the top and the design grid at the bottom.

continues ▶

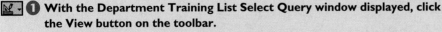

To Edit the Query (continued)

2 Click the Excel field in the field list. (You might have to scroll down to find it.) Drag the Excel field to the third column of the design grid.
Access adds this field to the design grid.

3 Click the PP field in the Field list, and drag this field to the third column of the design grid (the same column that currently contains the Excel field).
Access adds the PP field as the third column and moves the Excel field over one column to the right. You now have four fields in the query.

If the PP field appears in the wrong location, drag across the PP name in the column where it appears, and press Del. Repeat step 3. If you want to fill an empty column, click the Field row of the empty column; click the drop-down arrow, and select the appropriate field for that column from the drop-down field list.

4 Double-click Access in the Field list.
Access is added in the next empty field. You now have five fields in the query. In your window, you may not be able to see part, or even any, of the fifth column, depending on the size and settings of your computer monitor. Use the horizontal scrollbar to view the field you just added, if necessary.

5 In the design grid, click the column selector over the PP column.
When you are in the ***column selector*** (the thin gray bar above the field names), you see a black down arrow for the mouse pointer. Clicking the column selector selects the entire column (see Figure 3.11). After you select a column, you can move it or delete it. Try deleting this column.

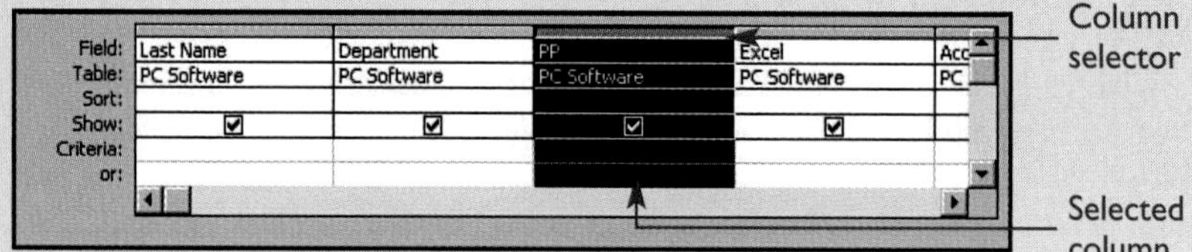

Figure 3.11
You can select a column by clicking the column selector.

6 Press Del.
You can also open the Edit menu and choose the Delete command. Access removes the field from the design grid.

7 Click the Save button on the toolbar.
Access saves the query with the changes you made. Keep the Department Training List query open in Design view. In the next lesson, you rearrange the order of the columns in your query.

Using Undo with Column Deletions
You cannot use the Undo command to undo the deletion of a column. If you delete a column by mistake, simply add it again by dragging the name from the field list, double-clicking the field name in the field list, or using the drop-down list in the design grid.

Lesson 5: Changing the Field Order and Sorting the Query

The way your query results are arranged depends on two factors. First, the order in which you add fields to the Field row in the design grid determines the order in which the fields display. If you don't like the order, you can rearrange the fields into a different order. Second, the primary key determines the default order in which the records display. You can change the query's sort order by using the Sort row in the design grid.

To Change the Field Order and Sort the Query

1 In the Department Training List query in Design view, click the column selector above the Department field.
The entire column is selected. After you select a column, you can move it or delete it.

2 Place the pointer on the column selector and drag Department until it is the first column in the design grid.
A dotted box displays as part of the pointer to signify that you are dragging the column (see Figure 3.12). A dark vertical line also displays to indicate the insertion point for the selected column. When you release the mouse button, Access rearranges the columns in the new order.

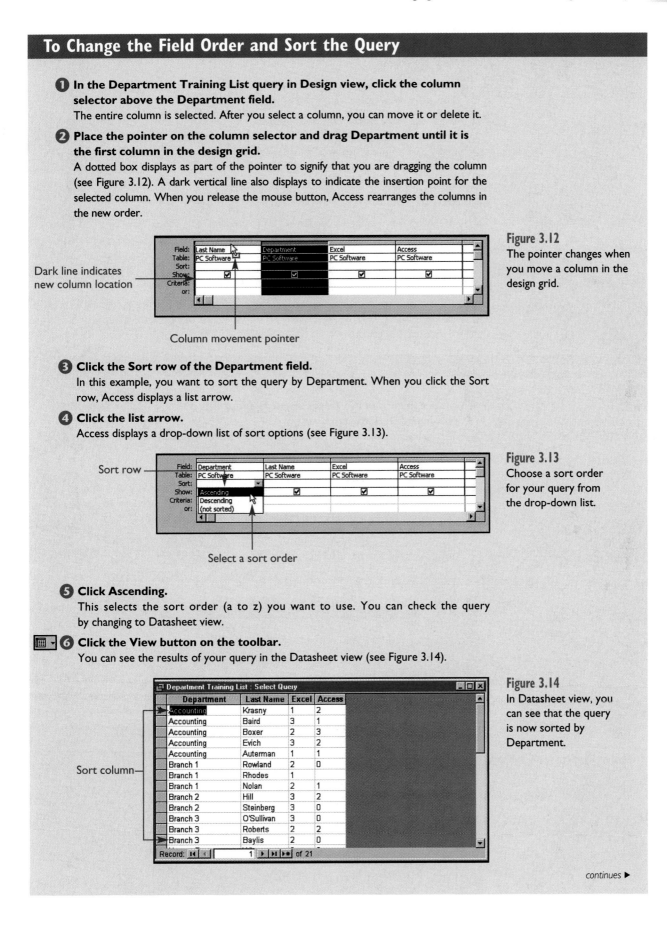

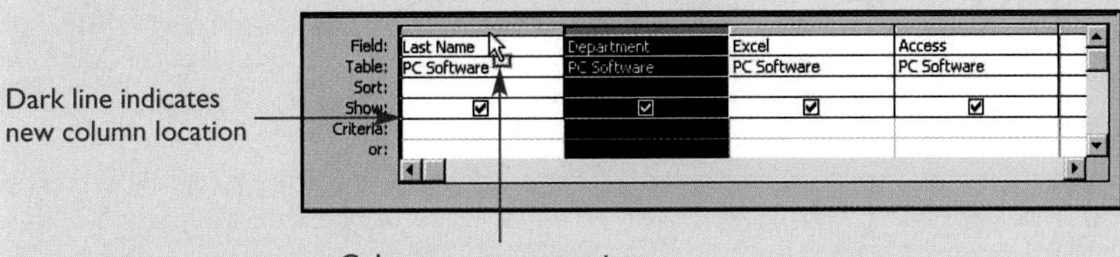

Figure 3.12
The pointer changes when you move a column in the design grid.

3 Click the Sort row of the Department field.
In this example, you want to sort the query by Department. When you click the Sort row, Access displays a list arrow.

4 Click the list arrow.
Access displays a drop-down list of sort options (see Figure 3.13).

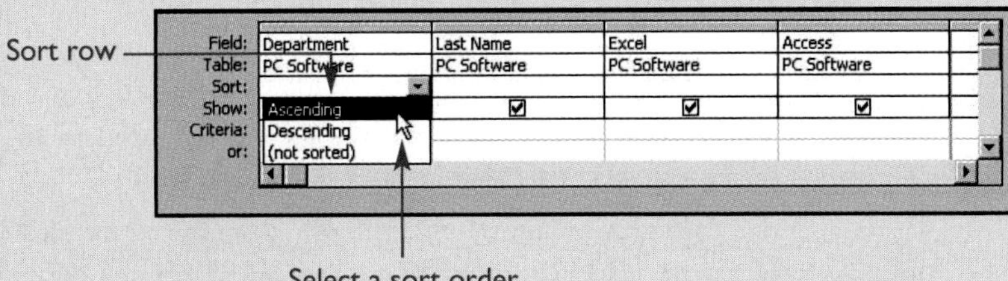

Figure 3.13
Choose a sort order for your query from the drop-down list.

5 Click Ascending.
This selects the sort order (a to z) you want to use. You can check the query by changing to Datasheet view.

6 Click the View button on the toolbar.
You can see the results of your query in the Datasheet view (see Figure 3.14).

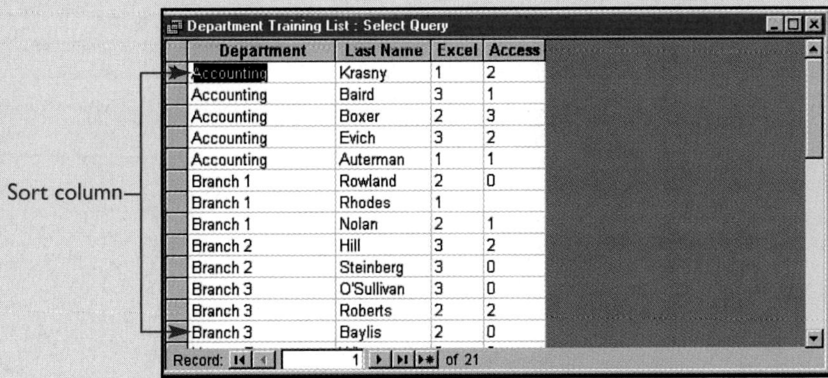

Department	Last Name	Excel	Access
Accounting	Krasny	1	2
Accounting	Baird	3	1
Accounting	Boxer	2	3
Accounting	Evich	3	2
Accounting	Auterman	1	1
Branch 1	Rowland	2	0
Branch 1	Rhodes	1	
Branch 1	Nolan	2	1
Branch 2	Hill	3	2
Branch 2	Steinberg	3	0
Branch 3	O'Sullivan	3	0
Branch 3	Roberts	2	2
Branch 3	Baylis	2	0

Figure 3.14
In Datasheet view, you can see that the query is now sorted by Department.

continues ▶

To Change the Field Order and Sort the Query (continued)

7. **Click the View button on the toolbar again.**
   The query once again displays in Design view.

8. **Click the Save button on the toolbar.**
   This saves the changes you made to the query. Keep the Department Training List query open in Design view as you continue with the next lesson.

Lesson 6: Matching Criteria

So far, the query you have created displays all the records contained in the Updated Employee Training database, but it shows only the fields you selected. You can also use a query to display only certain records—records that match certain ***criteria***. Criteria are a set of conditions that limit the records included in a query. A single condition is called a criterion.

You can match a criterion, such as the last names of staff members who have received training in Excel, or you can match multiple criteria, such as staff members in the Marketing or Human Resources departments who have received training in Access or Excel. In this lesson, you practice using the various types of criteria.

To Match Criteria

1. **In Design view of the Department Training List query, click the Criteria row in the Department column.**
   The insertion point moves to this location of the design grid. Here you can type the value that you want to match.

2. **Type `Human Resources`, and press Enter.**
   Access automatically adds quotation marks around the criterion that you entered (see Figure 3.15). However, in some cases, such as when you enter values that contain any punctuation marks, you must type the quotation marks.

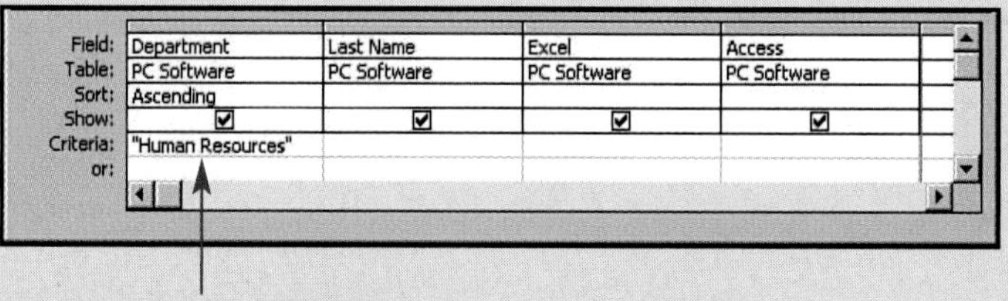

Figure 3.15
Enter the criterion you want to match.

3. **Click the View button.**
   You see the results of the query. Notice that the dynaset includes only the staff members in the Human Resources Department (see Figure 3.16).

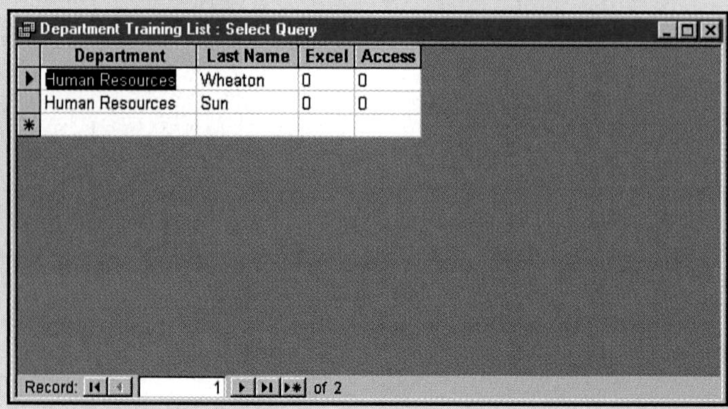

Figure 3.16
The query now lists all the people in Human Resources who are listed in the PC Software table.

4. **Click the View button again.**
This returns you to the design grid, so you can make a change to the query.

5. **Move to the Or row immediately below the Criteria row where you previously typed Human Resources. Click the Or row.**

> **X** If the Criteria row is not large enough to display more than one line of criteria, the list may automatically scroll down, and some of the criteria may disappear from view. Click the Maximize button before proceeding, if necessary.

If you want to match more than one condition, use this row to specify the second value. For this example, you might want to specify staff members in Human Resources or Accounting who have received training.

6. **Type `Accounting` and press Enter.**
When the entry you want to match is one word and contains no punctuation, as in this example, you don't have to type quotation marks. Access adds them automatically.

7. **Click the View button.**
You see the results of the query. Notice that the dynaset now includes trained staff members from Human Resources and Accounting (see Figure 3.17). Keep the Department Training List query open. In the next lesson, you save the query with a new name.

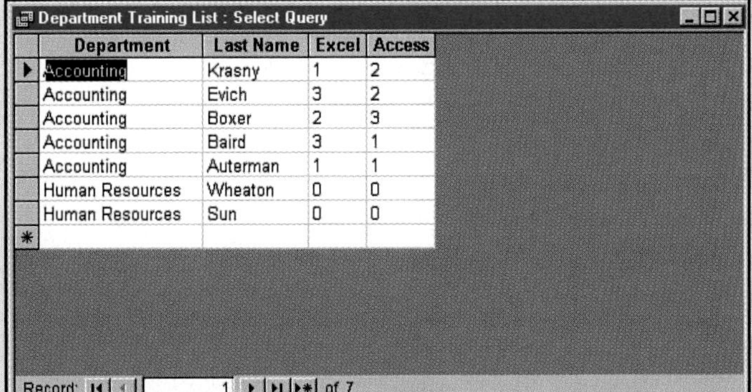
Department Training List : Select Query

Department	Last Name	Excel	Access
Accounting	Krasny	1	2
Accounting	Evich	3	2
Accounting	Boxer	2	3
Accounting	Baird	3	1
Accounting	Auterman	1	1
Human Resources	Wheaton	0	0
Human Resources	Sun	0	0

Record: 1 of 7

Figure 3.17
The query now lists all the people in Human Resources and Accounting.

> **X** If you see a blank dynaset when you switch to Datasheet view, it means that Access found no matching records. Be sure that you typed the value you are trying to match exactly as you entered it in the database table. For example, you can't type "Humans Resources" to match "Human Resources". Check your typing and try again.
>
> If Access displays a syntax error message when you enter text into the Criteria rows to make a match, it means that you did not type the entry in the correct format. Remember that if the text entry contains punctuation, you must supply quotation marks.

Using Other Query Types and Criteria

Access has many types of queries you can use. You can, for example, match a range of values, as you would if you asked Access to display all staff members who received training in Excel at a level 2 or above. You can also create other types of queries, such as a query to display all duplicate records in a table.

You can use other types of criteria besides a direct match. You can use comparisons such as <, which means less than, or >, which means greater than. If you use < to make a comparison in a text field, it uses alphabetical order. For example, if your criterion is **<**Jones, you would get all the names that come before Jones in the alphabet. Similarly, if you use **<**1/1/95 in a date field, you would get all the dates before January 1, 1995. For more examples of different criteria, use the Access Help index to look up Criteria and explore some of the different categories.

Lesson 7: Saving the Query with a New Name and Opening Multiple Queries

In some cases, you might modify a query and want to keep both versions of the query—the original and the modified query—for future use. In this lesson, you learn how to save a query with a new name.

You can also open a query from the Database window, and you can have more than one Select Query window open at a time. This lesson explains how to open multiple queries.

To Save the Query with a New Name and Open Multiple Queries

1. **In the Department Training List query, open the File menu option, and choose the Save As command.**
   The Save As dialog box displays, with the current name listed in the New Name text box (see Figure 3.18).

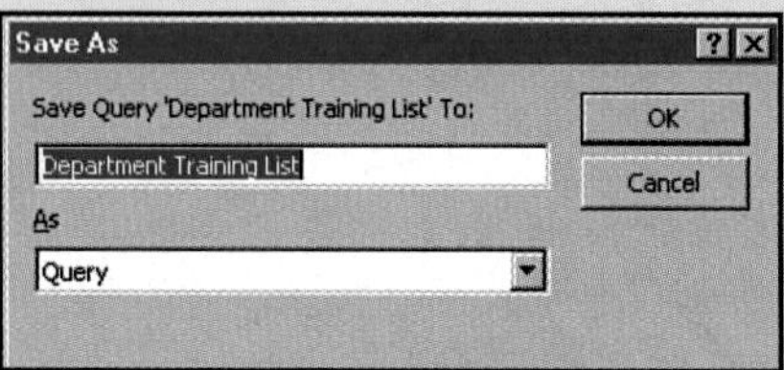

Figure 3.18
The Save As dialog box displays the current query name as the default new name.

2. **Type `HR and Accounting`.**
   This is the name you want to use for the new query.

3. **Click the OK button.**
   Access saves the query with the new name, and the new name displays in the title bar. The original query remains unchanged in the database.

4. **Click the Close Window button in the Select Query window.**
   This returns you to the Database window. The Queries object button should be selected, and you should see the two queries displayed in the Queries list (see Figure 3.19).

Figure 3.19
More than one query displays for the Updated Employee Training database.

5. **Select the Department Training List query and click the Open button.**
   The Department Training List query opens. Notice that the query displays all departments, not just the ones for Human Resources and Accounting because you did not save the criteria.

6. **Click the Database Window button on the toolbar.**

7. **Select and open the HR and Accounting query.**
   Your modified query opens. Now both queries and the Database window are open onscreen.

8 Open the Window menu and choose Cascade.

This step arranges the windows so that you can see which windows are currently open (see Figure 3.20). You can work on more than one query at a time by moving among windows.

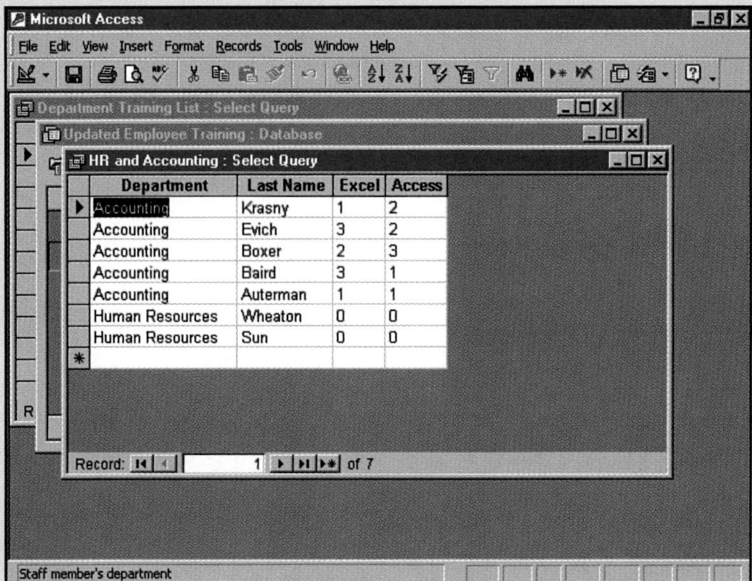

Figure 3.20
The open windows cascade on top of each other with the title bars displayed.

9 Close both query windows and the database.

If you have completed your session on the computer, exit Access. Otherwise, continue with the Checking Concepts and Terms section.

Using Shortcuts to Copy and Open a Query

You can also make a copy of a query in the Database window by selecting the query, clicking the Copy button, and clicking the Paste button. A Paste As dialog box opens so you can give the query copy a new name.

After a query has been saved, you can open it in Design view instead of in Datasheet view. To open a query in Design view, click the query to select it, and click the Design button.

Summary

This project focused on extracting a subset of information from a table. You learned how to create a query in Design view, select the appropriate fields, and save your query. You changed the fields and structure of the query and had the query display only records that met conditions that you set. Finally, you duplicated a query and saved it with a different name.

You can expand your understanding of the use of queries by looking at the Help available in the Office Assistant on some of the features that make queries more powerful. For example, you can type "How do I enter criteria" in the Office Assistant, look through the various Help topics, and find examples of criteria expressions. These examples give you a better idea of the many criteria features available in an Access query.

Checking Concepts and Terms

True/False

For each of the following, check *T* or *F* to indicate whether the statement is true or false.

__T __F **1.** You must include at least one field in a query. [L2]

__T __F **2.** You define the conditions of a query in the design grid. [L6]

__T __F **3.** The data for a dynaset is stored on disk separately from its source table. [L3]

__T __F **4.** You cannot include spaces or punctuation in a query name. [L3]

__T __F **5.** If you see a blank dynaset when you run a query, Access found no matching records. [L6]

__T __F **6.** The first time you save a query, the Save As dialog box appears. [L3]

__T __F **7.** You must include all fields in a query, even though you might not want to display them. [L2]

__T __F **8.** If you accidentally delete a field from the query, you can click the Undo button to restore the field. [L4]

__T __F **9.** A query can use only one table. [L1]

__T __F **10.** As you drag a field name from the Field list to the query, the mouse pointer changes to an arrow with a little box attached. [L5]

Multiple Choice

Circle the letter of the correct answer for each of the following.

1. Which of the following can you do to add a field to the query? [L2]

a. Double-click the field name in the Field list.

b. Use the drop-down list in the Field row of the design grid.

c. Drag the field name from the Field list to the design grid.

d. all of the above

2. How should you enter criteria for text fields if the criterion contains punctuation? [L6]

a. in all uppercase

b. in all lowercase

c. in bold

d. within quotation marks

3. In what order are fields included in a query? [L5]

a. the order in which you add them

b. the order in which they appear in the table

c. alphabetical order

d. numerical order

4. How do you change the order of the fields in a query? [L5]

a. Select one field; select a second field while pressing Ctrl, and choose Swap from the Edit menu.

b. Select the field's column selector and drag it to the new location.

c. Drag the field from the field list to the new location. The other references in the query are automatically deleted.

d. You can't change the order of the fields. They must appear in the same order as they do in the Field list.

5. Which of the following is not a way of creating another query? [L7]

a. altering the current query and saving it with a new name

b. selecting New in the Query window and building a query from scratch

c. selecting Duplicate from the Edit menu and saving the duplicate query with a new name

d. copying and pasting the query in the Database window and renaming the copy with a new name

Screen ID

Refer to Figure 3.21 and identify the numbered parts of the screen. Write the letter of the correct label in the space next to the number.

Figure 3.21

A. Field list
B. View button
C. Show check box
D. Sort order
E. Run button
F. Criterion
G. Source table of field
H. Field name
I. Column sector
J. Design grid

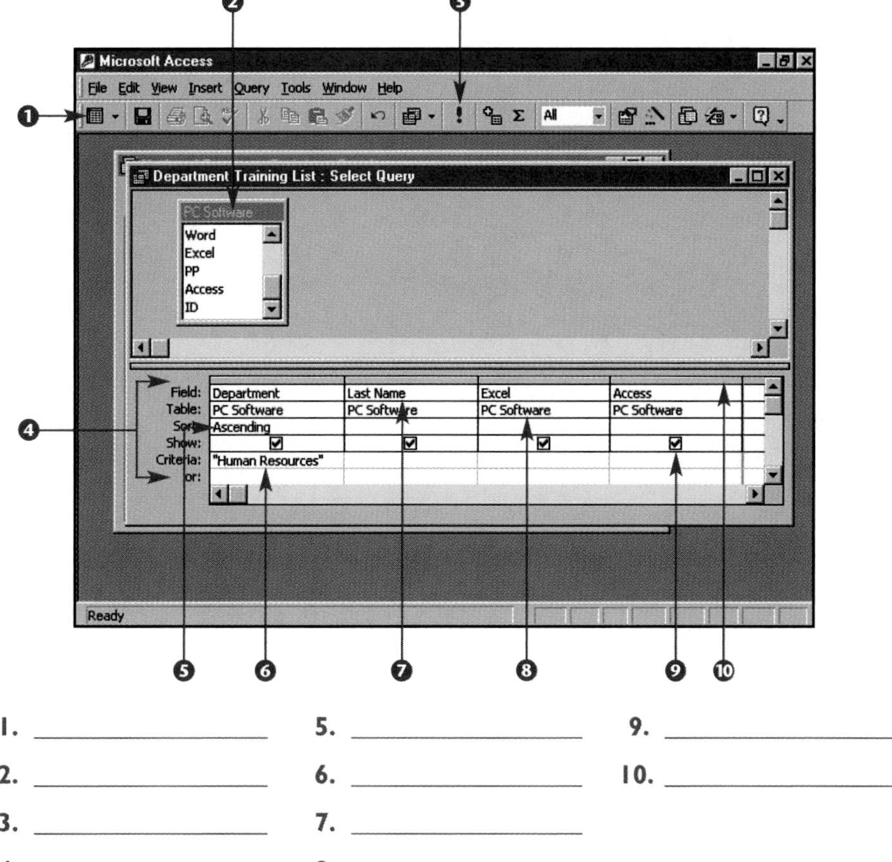

1. ____________ 5. ____________ 9. ____________
2. ____________ 6. ____________ 10. ____________
3. ____________ 7. ____________
4. ____________ 8. ____________

Discussion Questions

1. You have created a home inventory using the following fields: room, category (for example, furniture, appliances, clothes), description, year purchased, serial number, and cost. What fields might you use queries on?
2. In the home inventory example in question 1, assume that some of your possessions are fairly valuable, and you want to submit a list of them to your insurance company. Which field would you set a criterion for, and which fields would you include in the query?
3. You have developed the table for the automobile parts store, containing fields for the make of the car, part name, description, number sold year-to-date, quantity in stock, retail price, sale price, and cost. You now want to create a query or queries that you can use repeatedly. What queries would you create, and what fields would each contain?
4. In the automobile parts store exercise in the previous question, can you think of a query that might include a field that you don't show in the dynaset (in other words, turn off the Show check box)?
5. You can sort data in either a table or a query, using different procedures. Which sort procedure is easier if you are sorting on a single field? Which sort procedure is easier if you want to sort on multiple, nonadjacent fields?

Skill Drill

Skill Drill exercises reinforce project skills. Each skill reinforced is the same, or nearly the same, as a skill presented in the project. Each exercise includes a brief narrative introduction, followed by detailed instructions in a step-by-step format.

You created a database and table to store the information on your vast collection of history books. The collection is divided into four categories: United States, Ancient, World, and England & Empire with fields for Author, Title, Year (either written or published), Pages, and Category. You would like to be able to sort your query, and also print the information by category.

1. Creating a Simple Query

You would like to create a query from which you can build other queries. First, you need to create a basic query. [L1]

To create a simple query, complete the following steps:

1. Find the **AO-0302** database file on your CD-ROM; copy it to drive A; remove the Read-Only status, and name it **History Books**. Select and Open the History Books table and look at the fields. Click the Close Window button to close the table.
2. Click the Queries object button, and click New to create a new query.
3. Choose Design View, and click Add to add the History Books table. Close the Show Table dialog box.
4. Double-click the Author field to add it to the design grid.
5. Drag the Title field to the design grid as the second field.
6. Add the Year and Category fields to the design grid, but do not add the Pages field.
7. Click the View button to see the results of your query.
8. Save the query as **All History Books**. Close the query.

2. Editing Your Query

In your All History Books query, you have decided that you would really like to see the number of pages in the books, but don't care to see the year of publication. [L4]

To add a field and hide a field in a query:

1. Select the All History Books table and click the Design button.
2. Click the Pages field in the Field box and drag it on top of the Year field. The Pages field should be between the Title field and the Year field.
3. Click the View button to view the results. Click the View button again to return to Design view.
4. Click the Show button for the Year field to hide the field in this query.
5. Click the View button to see the results of your change.
6. Save your changes and close the query.

3. Changing the Field Order in a Query

You have decided that you really should display the Year field, but you want to change the order of the fields. [L5]

To change the field order, complete the following steps:

1. Select the All History Books table and click the Design button. Notice that the Year field disappears from the query because it was not shown or used for anything (sorting or criteria).
2. Double-click the Year field to add it to the end of the fields in the design grid.
3. Click the Year column selector. Let go of the mouse button; then click the column selector again and drag the field to the right of the Title field.
4. Use the same procedure to move the Category field to the first field position. The order of fields should now be: Category, Author, Title, Year, Pages.
5. Click the View button to view the new query layout. Save your changes and close the query.

4. Sorting the Query and Saving It with a New Name

You want to look at your history books in a couple of different orders. The query design grid makes it easy to do this. [L5]

To sort the query and save it with a new name, complete the following steps:

1. Select the All History Books table and click the Design button.
2. Click the Sort row for the Pages field in the design grid.
3. Click the list arrow in the Pages Sort row, and select Descending to look at your largest books first.
4. Click the View button to see a list of your books from largest to smallest.
5. Click the View button to return to Design view.
6. Click the list arrow in the Pages field to turn off the sorting on this field.
7. Click the list arrow on the Title field Sort row, and select Ascending order.
8. Click the View button to see a list of your books in alphabetical order by title.
9. Choose File, Save As from the menu. Save the query as **Sorted by Title**. Close the query.

5. Matching a Single Criterion

You have divided your history books into four categories, and you frequently want to look at the books by category. It would be good to have a query for each one. [L6]

To match a single criterion, complete the following steps:

1. Select the All History Books table and click the Design button.
2. Type **Ancient** in the Criteria row of the Category field.
3. Choose File, Save As from the menu. Save the query as **Ancient History Books**.
4. Delete Ancient from the Criteria row, and type **United States** in its place. Choose File, Save As from the menu. Save the query as **United States History Books**.
5. Delete United States from the Criteria row and type **World** in its place. Choose File, Save As from the menu. Save the query as **World History Books**.
6. Delete **World** from the Criteria row, and type **England & Empire** in its place. Choose File, Save As from the menu. Save the query as **England & British Empire History Books**.
7. Close the query. Highlight each of the four new queries and open them to make sure you typed the criteria information correctly. If one of the queries does not work, select it and go to Design view to edit the criterion.

6. Matching More than One Criterion

You decide that you'd like to quickly see if you have any U.S. history book published in 1977. [L6]

To match more than one criterion, complete the following steps:

1. Select the All History Books table and click the Design button.
2. Type **United States** in the Criteria row of the Category field.
3. Type **1977** in the Criteria row of the Year field.
4. Click the Run button to run the query.
5. Close the query, but don't save your changes. Close the database unless you are planning to move on to the Challenge section.

Challenge

Challenge exercises expand on or are somewhat related to skills presented in the lessons. Each exercise provides a brief narrative introduction followed by instructions, in a numbered step or bulleted list format, that are not as detailed as those in the Skill Drill section.

The database you use for the Challenge section is the same database of history books you used in the Skill Drill section.

1. Creating a Query Using a Wizard

You have decided to try some of the more advanced query features on your history books database, but just to be safe, you decide to create a second database with the same data. The first feature you want to try out is the Simple Query Wizard. Make sure you read each wizard screen and read the directions. [L1]

To add a query using a wizard, complete the following steps:

1. Copy the **AO-0302** database file to drive A; remove the Read-Only status, and rename it **History Books 2**.
2. Select Simple Query Wizard from the New Query dialog box.
3. Select all the fields for this query. Display all the fields in the query.
4. Call your query **History Book Collection** and close it.

2. Sorting on Multiple Fields

It would be very convenient to use a query to sort the data in the table on more than one field. In this case, you want to first sort by category, and then sort alphabetically by title within each category. [L5]

To sort on multiple fields, complete the following steps:

1. Open the History Book Collection query in Design view.
2. Move the Category field to the first field in the design grid.

3. Move the Title field to the right of the Category field.
4. Select both the Category and the Title field at the same time.
5. Sort in ascending order.
6. Save the query as `Sorted by Category and Title`. Close the query.

3. Limiting Records by Looking for a Part of a Text Field

For years, you have made a special collection of books on Michigan history. You have given them special titles—all the titles begin with "Michigan:" followed by the title of the book or pamphlet. All these special titles are saved in the United States category. You would like to create a query to separate the titles in your Michigan history collection from the rest of the United States history books. [L6]

To limit records based on a part of a text field, complete the following steps:

1. Open the History Book Collection query in Design view.
2. Go to Help, either on your computer or online, and find instructions on entering text criteria in a query.
3. In the Criteria row of the Title field, type the expression used to find all titles that begin with "Michigan:".
4. Run the query to make sure only the books beginning with "Michigan:" are included. (*Hint*: There should be 184 records in this query.)
5. Save the query as `Michigan History Books`. Close the query.

4. Limiting Records by Setting Limits to Numeric Fields

In the previous Challenge, you limited the records by setting a criterion that included only part of the Title field. It would also be nice to be able to set beginning and ending limits to a numeric field, such as the Year field in the current database. [L6]

To limit records by setting limits to a numeric field, complete the following steps:

1. Open the History Book Collection query in Design view.
2. Go to Help, either on your computer or online, and find instructions on entering number criteria in a query.
3. In the Criteria row of the Year field, type the expression used to find all titles that were published between World War I and World War II.

   Note: World War I ended in 1918, and World War II began for the U.S. in 1941. Your query should include books published between 1919 and 1940. Both 1919 and 1940 should be included.
4. Sort on the Year field in ascending order.
5. Run the query to make sure only the books from 1919 to 1940 are included. (*Hint*: There should be a total of 59 books when you successfully set up the query.)
6. Save the query as `Books Published between the Wars`. Close the query.

5. Including or Excluding Records by Searching for Words Anywhere in a Text Field

In an earlier Challenge, you found all the titles beginning with "Michigan:". You might also want to find words or phrases anywhere in a field or be able to exclude all records with a certain word in the title. In this case, you look for the word "revolution" anywhere in the title. [L6]

To include or exclude records by searching for words anywhere in a text field, complete the following steps:

1. Open the History Book Collection query in Design view.
2. Go to Help, either on your computer or online, and find instructions on entering text criteria in a query.
3. In the Criteria row of the title field, type the expression that locates records that have the word "revolution" in them.

4. Run the query to make sure all the books include the word "revolution." (*Hint*: There should be a total of 17 books when you successfully set up the query.)
5. Go back to your help source and figure out how to exclude those 17 records that have the word "revolution" in them. Type the expression to remove those 17 records from your list of books. You should have 1136 records that don't include that word.
6. Change the Criteria row in the Title field back to include only those books with "revolution" in the title.
7. Save the query as **`Books about Revolution`**. Close the query and the database unless you are going to proceed to the Discovery Zone exercises.

Discovery Zone

Discovery Zone exercises help you gain advanced knowledge of project topics and/or application of skills. These exercises focus on enhancing your problem-solving skills.

1. Creating a Crosstab Query

Crosstab queries are powerful tools for summarizing data from large databases. They summarize the relationship between two (or more) fields. For example, if you sent out a survey with ten questions, you would enter each person's responses in a single record. If you got 1,000 responses, you would have 1,000 records, each with a numeric response (for example, a 1 to 5 rating scale) to the ten questions. Counting the number of times each response was given for each question would take a long time. A Crosstab query can give you a table of responses in seconds.

Goal: Create a Crosstab query that counts the books published each year by category of book; sort the Crosstab in descending order.

Use the **`AO-0302`** file to create a new database called **`History Books 3`** on your disk. Use Help from your computer or online to understand how Crosstab queries work and how to build them. Save the query as **`Category by Year Crosstab`**.

Hint 1: Use the Year field down the left side of the crosstab table, and use the Category field as column headers. If you do it the other way, it is extremely difficult to read.

Hint 2: Have the program Count the instances, not add them up!

Hint 3: You do not perform the sort until after you build and run the Crosstab query.

2. Using Queries to Delete Records from Tables

You can use queries for more than creating dynasets of tables. You can also use them to directly affect the information in tables. For example, you can use them to append records to existing tables, update the information in tables, and even delete records in tables. Perform such actions with care! Any time you are going to use one of these special query types, always back up your database first, in case you change more than you anticipated.

Goal: Use a query to delete records from a table.

Use the History Books 3 database you used in the first Discovery Zone exercise. (If you did not do the first exercise, copy **`AO-0302`** and create a new database on your disk.) Create and run a Delete Query that removes all titles beginning with "Michigan:" from the History Books table. Do not save the query.

Hint 1: Look for the Query Type button on the Design view toolbar.

Hint 2: Use what you learned in the Challenge section to identify those records that begin with "Michigan:".

Hint 3: Run the query from the Design view window.

Hint 4: You'll know you're on the right track when you run the query and the program warns you that you are about to delete 184 rows and won't be able to get them back.

Project 4

Creating and Using Forms

Objectives

In this project, you learn how to

- **Create an AutoForm**
- **Enter and Edit Data Using a Form**
- **Save, Close, and Open a Form**
- **Create a New Form from Scratch**
- **Add Fields to Forms**
- **Move and Resize Fields in Forms**
- **Add a Form Header and Label**

Key terms introduced in this project include

- AutoForm
- control
- field label
- field text box
- form
- form footer
- form header
- label
- selection handles
- tab order

Why Would I Do This?

When you enter records in a table, all records are diplayed, each in a row. If the table has many fields, you might not be able to see all the fields on the screen, and you might find it difficult to locate the record you want with all the records displayed. You use a ***form*** to display one record at a time, and you can place the fields anywhere on the screen. Even if a record has many fields, you might be able to see them all on one screen. You can move the fields around and add text to the form so that it resembles paper forms that are already in use. It is much easier for people to transfer data from paper forms to a form on the screen that looks the same.

Using a form offers the following advantages:

- You can select the fields you want to include in the form, and you can arrange them in the order you want.
- You can choose to display only one record at a time, which makes it easier to concentrate on that record.
- You can make the form visually appealing.

Access provides an ***AutoForm*** that you can create quickly without a great deal of work. The AutoForm is a wizard that sets up an input screen that includes all the fields in the table. If this form isn't what you need, you can also create a form from scratch. In this project, you use both methods to create forms. When you have completed this project, you will have created a form like the one in Figure 4.1.

Visual Summary

Figure 4.1
Access enables you to quickly create forms for data entry.

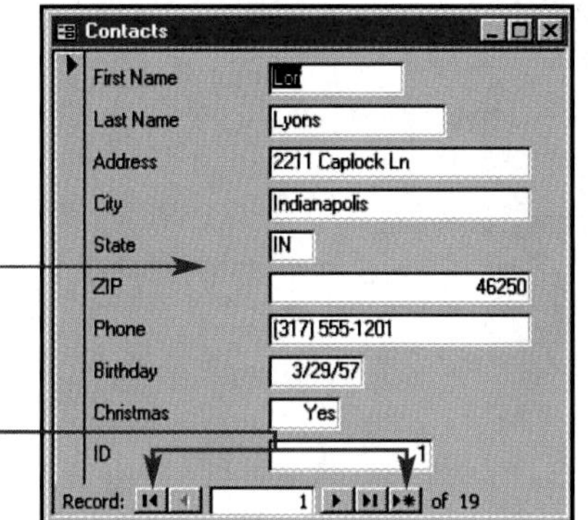

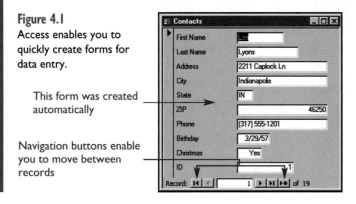

Lesson 1: Creating an AutoForm

If you want a simple form that lists each field in a single column and displays one record at a time, you can use one of the Access form wizards to create an AutoForm. The form wizards look at the structure of your database table and create a form automatically. You simply choose the commands to start the wizards.

To Create an AutoForm

1. **Launch Access. Click OK to Open an existing file.**
   Make sure you have a disk in drive A.
2. **Find the `AO-0401` file on your CD-ROM, right-click it, and copy it to the floppy drive. Move to drive A; remove the Read-Only status, rename the file `New Address List`, and open the new database.**
   The Database window displays, showing the Contacts table.
3. **Click the Forms object button.**
   No forms are listed because you haven't created and saved any (see Figure 4.2).

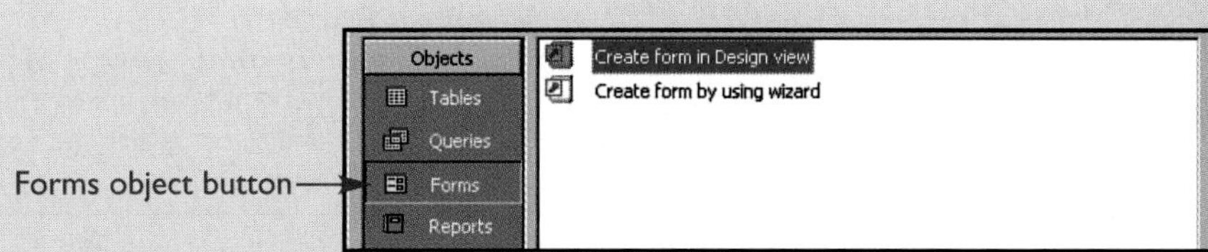

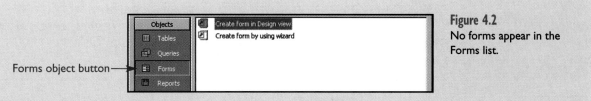

Figure 4.2
No forms appear in the Forms list.

4 Click the New button.
The New Form dialog box displays. First, you have to select a table to use with the form. Next you must decide whether you want to use one of the form wizards or start with a blank form.

5 Click the down arrow in the Choose the table or query where the object's data comes from drop-down list box.
You see a list of the tables and queries available in the database (see Figure 4.3). You can base a form on either a query or a table. You must select the Contacts table, even though it is the only table or query available.

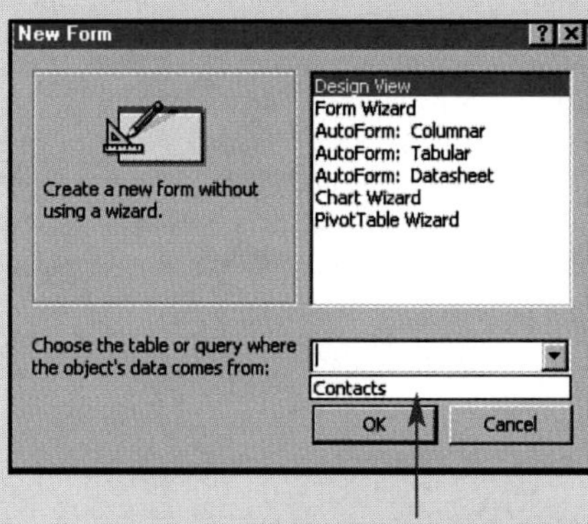

Figure 4.3
From the drop-down list, choose the table or query on which you want to base the form.

6 Click Contacts.
This step selects the table you want to use.

7 Click the AutoForm: Columnar option; then click OK.
The Form Wizard creates the form; this step may take several seconds. The status bar displays the progress so that you can see that Access is working. After building the AutoForm, Access displays the table's first record. Notice that the fields display in a column in the form. Your screen might not have the same background settings. The navigation buttons display at the bottom of the form to enable you to move through the records (see Figure 4.4). Keep this form onscreen as you continue to the next lesson, where you learn more about the navigation buttons.

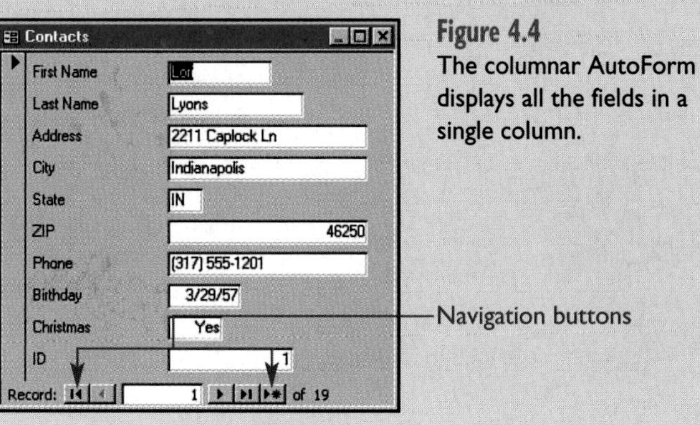

Figure 4.4
The columnar AutoForm displays all the fields in a single column.

Using the New Object Button to Create a Form
You can also create a new form by clicking the drop-down arrow to the right of the New Object button on the toolbar in the Database window. When you are in the table Datasheet view, you can click the New Object list button and select either the Form button or the AutoForm button to create a new form.

Lesson 2: Entering and Editing Data Using a Form

Forms often make it easier to enter and edit data. Before you save the form, you might want to enter some data to be sure that you like the structure of the form. If you don't like the way the form is set up, you can change it or create a new one, as you learn to do later in this project.

You can use the same tools to enter, find, sort, and display records in a form that you use in a table. In this lesson, you add and edit a record using a form.

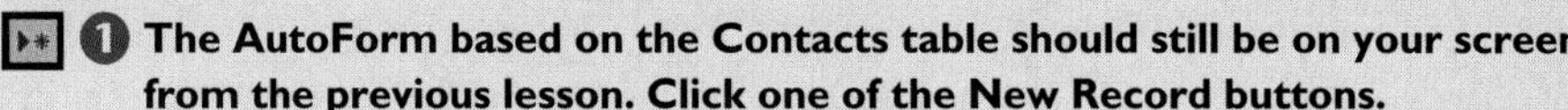

To Enter and Edit Data Using a Form

1 The AutoForm based on the Contacts table should still be on your screen from the previous lesson. Click one of the New Record buttons.
New Record buttons appear on the toolbar and with the navigation buttons on the bottom of the Form window. This step adds a new record, and a blank form displays (see Figure 4.5). The insertion point appears in the first field of the form.

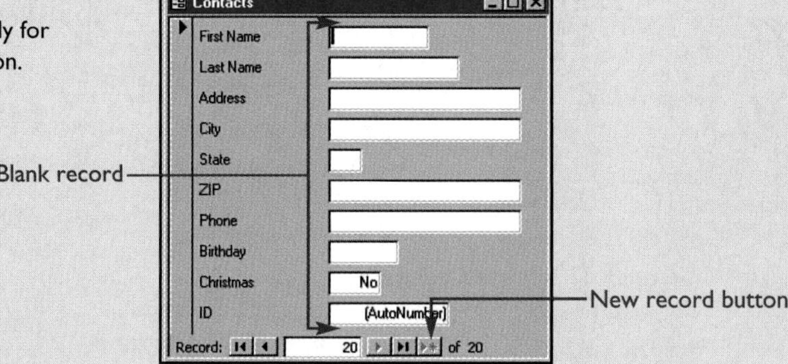

Figure 4.5
The new form is ready for you to add information.

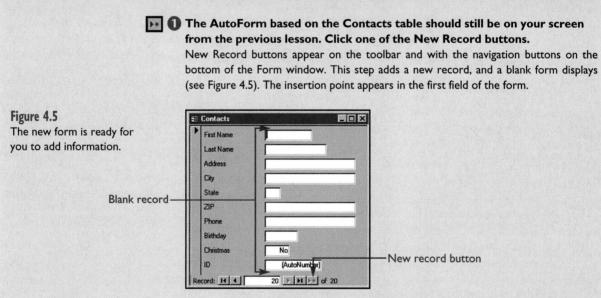

2 Type the following data; press Tab after each entry to move to the next field:

```
Janet
Eisenhut
455 Sheridan
Indianapolis
IN
46204
317 555 6588
3/29/60
Yes
```

Notice that when you type the phone number, Access automatically provides parentheses around the area code, moves you over so that you can type the exchange, and provides a hyphen after the exchange.

You might have to scroll down to see all the fields in the form. When you reach the last field—the ID field—you do not have to enter a value because it is a counter field. Also, remember that when you move to another record, Access automatically saves the record you entered. Keep in mind that the record is saved in the underlying Contacts table. You don't have to worry about updating the table separately.

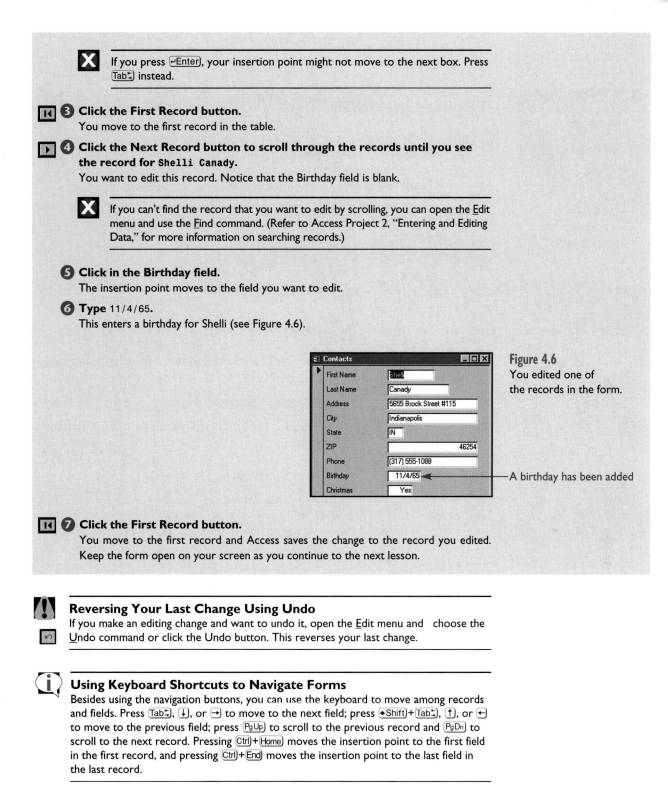

If you press ↵Enter, your insertion point might not move to the next box. Press Tab instead.

3. **Click the First Record button.**
   You move to the first record in the table.

4. **Click the Next Record button to scroll through the records until you see the record for `Shelli Canady`.**
   You want to edit this record. Notice that the Birthday field is blank.

If you can't find the record that you want to edit by scrolling, you can open the Edit menu and use the Find command. (Refer to Access Project 2, "Entering and Editing Data," for more information on searching records.)

5. **Click in the Birthday field.**
   The insertion point moves to the field you want to edit.

6. **Type** `11/4/65`**.**
   This enters a birthday for Shelli (see Figure 4.6).

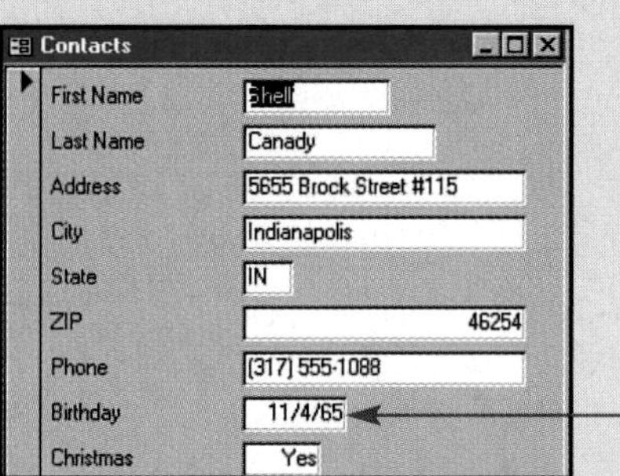

Figure 4.6
You edited one of the records in the form.

7. **Click the First Record button.**
   You move to the first record and Access saves the change to the record you edited. Keep the form open on your screen as you continue to the next lesson.

Reversing Your Last Change Using Undo
If you make an editing change and want to undo it, open the Edit menu and choose the Undo command or click the Undo button. This reverses your last change.

Using Keyboard Shortcuts to Navigate Forms
Besides using the navigation buttons, you can use the keyboard to move among records and fields. Press Tab, ↓, or → to move to the next field; press ⇧Shift+Tab, ↑, or ← to move to the previous field; press PgUp to scroll to the previous record and PgDn to scroll to the next record. Pressing Ctrl+Home moves the insertion point to the first field in the first record, and pressing Ctrl+End moves the insertion point to the last field in the last record.

Lesson 3: Saving, Closing, and Opening a Form

If you use the form and like its organization, you can save the form so that you can use it again later. If you try to close the form without saving it, Access reminds you to save. You don't have to save the form; you should save it only if you intend to use it again. If you accidentally close the form without saving it, you can simply recreate it. (Follow the steps in Lesson 1 of this project.)

As with the other objects you create, you are prompted to type a name the first time you save the form. You can type up to 64 characters, including spaces. In this lesson, you save, close, and open a form.

To Save, Close, and Open a Form

1 The AutoForm that uses the Contacts table should still be open on your screen. Click the Save button.
The Save As dialog box displays (see Figure 4.7). The default name, Contacts, is the name of the table on which the form is based.

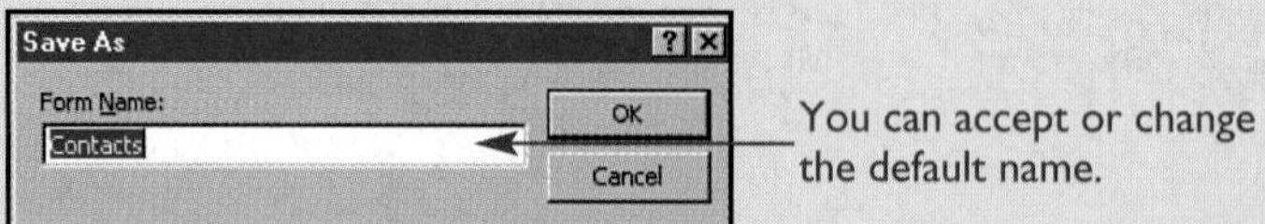

Figure 4.7
Give the form a name before you save it.

2 Type `Contacts AutoForm` and click OK.
Access saves the form.

3 Click the Close button in the upper-right corner of the Form window to close the form.
The Form window closes, and you see the Database window again. Notice that your new form is included in the Forms list (see Figure 4.8).

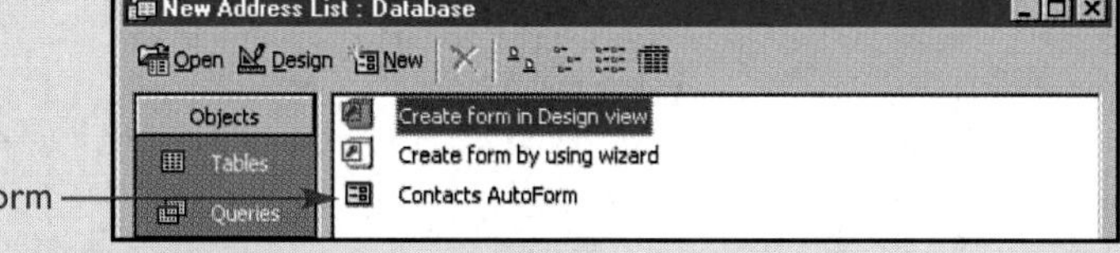

Figure 4.8
The name of your form appears in the Forms list.

4 Double-click Contacts AutoForm to open it.
Access displays the first record in the table on which the form is based. You can add, modify, or delete records. As you move from field to field, Access automatically saves any changes you make.

5 Click the Close button to close the Contacts Autoform.
Access closes the form. Keep the New Address List database open, and continue to the next lesson.

Alternative Ways to Save a Form
You can choose File, Save from the menu or press Ctrl+S to save the form instead of using the Save button.

Lesson 4: Creating a New Form from Scratch

Sometimes the form wizards do not create the form you need. When that happens, you can start from a blank form and create exactly the form you want. The form can include any text, fields, and other ***controls*** you want to incorporate. Controls are any objects selected from the Toolbox, such as text boxes, check boxes, or option buttons.

A form consists of many different elements. Each part of the form is called a section. The main, or Detail, section is the area in which records display. You can also add ***form headers*** (top of form) or ***form footers*** (bottom of form). Anything you include in these sections displays onscreen in Form view when you use the form. You can also add page headers and page footers, which are not visible onscreen in Form view, but appear if you print the form.

The rest of this project covers some of the common features you can use when you create a form from scratch. Keep in mind, however, that Access offers many form features, such as drop-down lists, groups of option buttons, graphic objects, and much more.

In this lesson, you create a new, blank form.

To Create a New Form from Scratch

1. **In the New Address List database window, click the Forms object button (if necessary), and click the New button.**
   The New Form dialog box displays. Before you choose whether you want to use a form wizard or start with a blank form, you should select the table you want to use for the form.

2. **Click the down arrow in the Choose the table or query where the object's data comes from drop-down list and select the Contacts table.**

3. **Select the Design View option from the top of the list, and click OK.**
   The form displays in Design view. To work on a blank form, it is useful to have the rulers turned on and the Field list and Toolbox open. Whether they display on your screen depends on whether the last person to use this view turned them on or off. Examine your screen and compare it to Figure 4.9. Perform the following steps as needed.

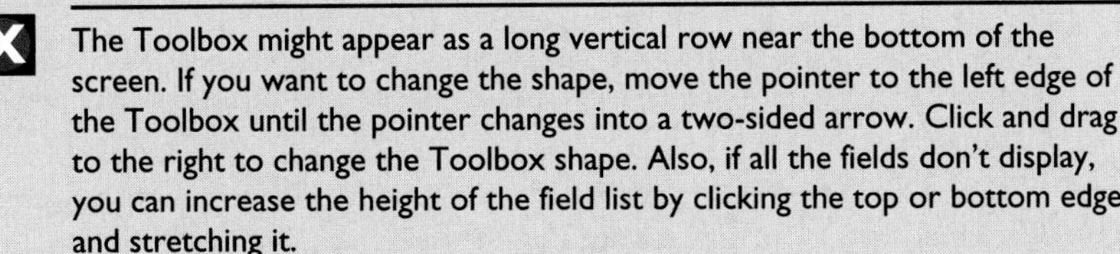

The Toolbox might appear as a long vertical row near the bottom of the screen. If you want to change the shape, move the pointer to the left edge of the Toolbox until the pointer changes into a two-sided arrow. Click and drag to the right to change the Toolbox shape. Also, if all the fields don't display, you can increase the height of the field list by clicking the top or bottom edge and stretching it.

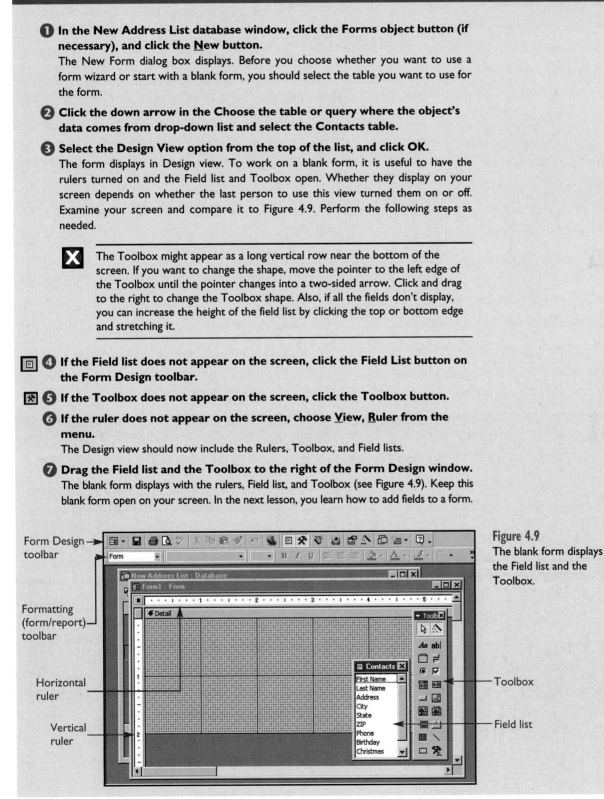

4. **If the Field list does not appear on the screen, click the Field List button on the Form Design toolbar.**

5. **If the Toolbox does not appear on the screen, click the Toolbox button.**

6. **If the ruler does not appear on the screen, choose View, Ruler from the menu.**
   The Design view should now include the Rulers, Toolbox, and Field lists.

7. **Drag the Field list and the Toolbox to the right of the Form Design window.**
   The blank form displays with the rulers, Field list, and Toolbox (see Figure 4.9). Keep this blank form open on your screen. In the next lesson, you learn how to add fields to a form.

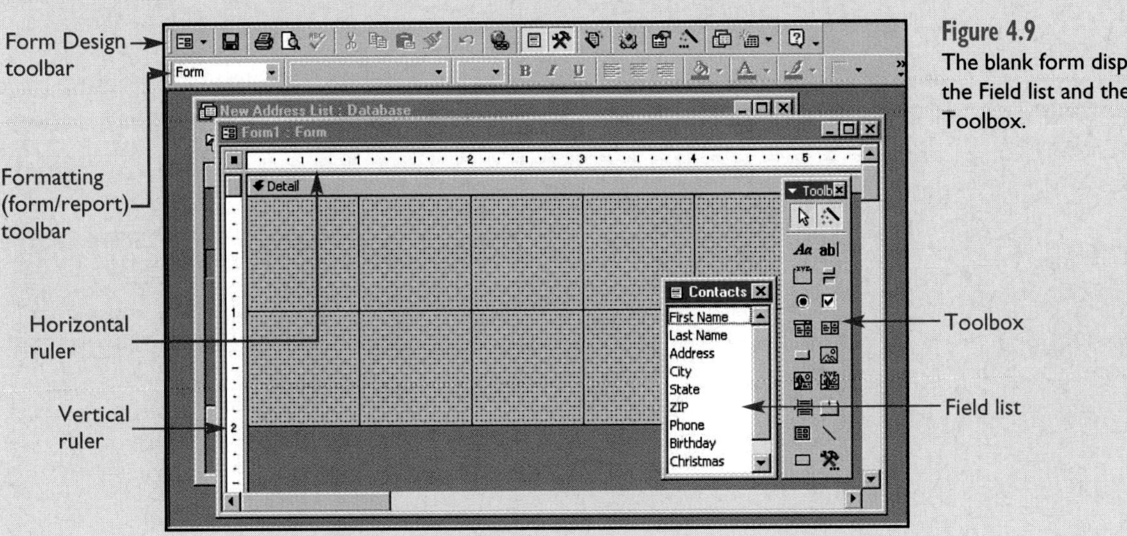

Figure 4.9
The blank form displays the Field list and the Toolbox.

Understanding Controls
Some controls are bound to the fields in the table. If you create a text box for a field and enter data in the field in the form, for example, Access updates the field in the table. Other controls are not tied to the table but, instead, are saved with the form. For example, you may want to add a descriptive title to the form. This type of text is called a ***label*** and is not bound to the table.

Lesson 5: Adding Fields to Forms

You decide it would be a good idea to send birthday greetings to your customers to help maintain good relations. You added a Birthday field to your Contacts table, but your table is not convenient for the purpose of sending birthday greetings. To make sure that birthday greetings are sent to your customers, you want to create a simple form that lists just the person's name and his or her birthday. This form should include three fields: Last Name, First Name, and Birthday, and a label in the form's header.

When you want to set up or change the structure of a form, you must use Design view. Access includes the following items to help you design the form:

- Toolbar—Use the toolbar to access some form design commands. You can click the Save button to save the form, the View button to view the form, and so on. If you place the pointer on a button, the button name appears directly under the button.
- Toolbox—Use the Toolbox to add items, such as labels or images, to the form. As with the toolbar, you can place the mouse pointer over a Toolbox button to see its name. The Toolbox might not display when you create a new form. If it does not, click the Toolbox button to display it.
- Field list—Use the Field list to add fields to the form. The Field list might not display when you create a new form. If it does not, click the Field List button on the toolbar.
- Rulers—Use the rulers to help position controls on the form.

In this lesson, you use the Field list to add fields to the form. The new, blank form you are creating for the Contacts table should still be on your screen from the preceding lesson.

To Add Fields to Forms

1. **Click and drag the First Name field from the Field list to the Detail area of the form.**
   As you drag, your pointer becomes a small, boxed field name. You can use this to help place the field onscreen. The ***field text box***, which holds a place for the contents of the field you selected, appears where you release the box attached to your pointer.
2. **Release the mouse button, and drop the field at approximately the 1-inch mark on the horizontal ruler, and down about 1/4" from the top of the Detail area.**
   This places the field text box and ***field label***, which is the field name, on the form (see Figure 4.10). The field label will be placed to the left of the field text box so you need to leave space for it.

If you see only one field text box when you drag the field from the Field list, you might have placed the field too far to the left (beyond the 1-inch horizontal mark, for example), or the field text box and field label might be on top of one another. You have to move or resize the field so that you can see both the field label and the field text box.

You can delete the field and start again if you run into problems. To delete a field, click it to select it, and press Del. This removes the field from the form, but it doesn't delete the field or its contents from the table.

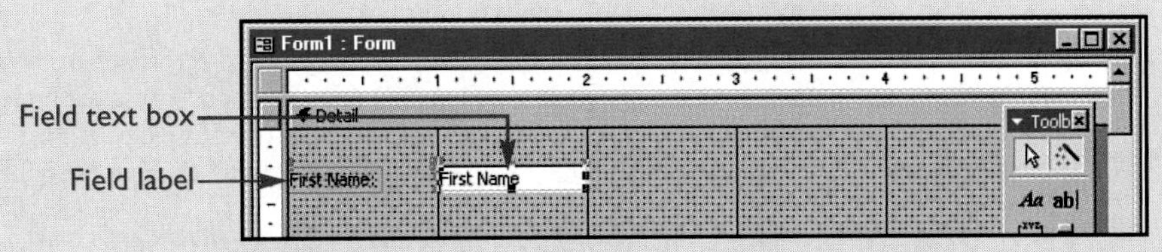

Figure 4.10
You add a field to the form by dragging it from the Field list.

3 Drag the Last Name field to the form; place this field below the First Name field, at the same horizontal location (the 1-inch mark) and about 1/4" below the First Name field.
This step adds a second field to the form. As you drag and drop the field, try to align the field with the field above it. Make sure that you leave enough room between the two fields; don't drop the fields on top of one another.

4 Drag the Birthday field to the form. Place this field below the Last Name field (also at the 1-inch horizontal mark).
Your form now includes three fields (see Figure 4.11). You can save and name the form, so that these changes won't be lost.

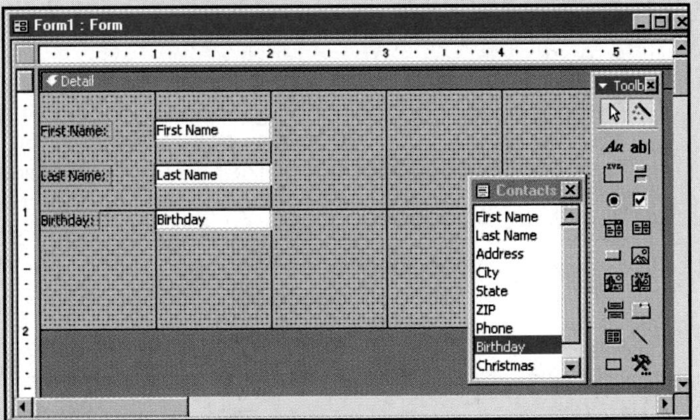

Figure 4.11
The new form contains three fields.

5 Click the Save button.
The Save As dialog box displays.

6 Type `Birthdays` and click OK.
Access saves the form and returns you to Design view. You can continue building the form, or you can display the form.

7 Click the View button on the toolbar.
The form displays as it will appear when you use it (see Figure 4.12). You can see whether you need to make any adjustments, such as adding a label or resizing the fields. Keep the Birthdays form open and continue with the next lesson.

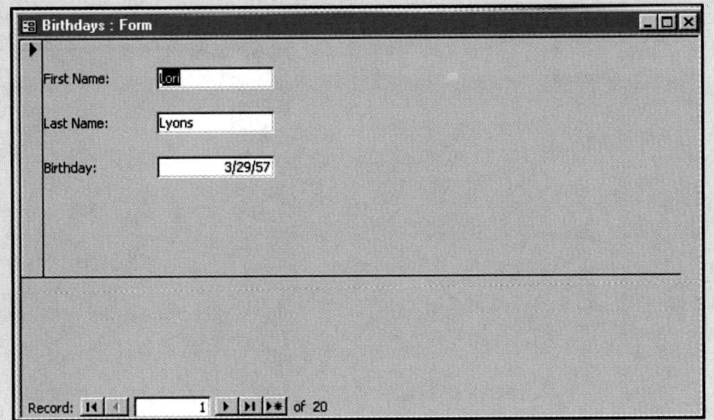

Figure 4.12
Your new form displays in Form view.

Creating and Editing Forms
In addition to creating a blank form, you can use the Form Wizard to create other types of forms, such as columnar, tabular, charts, and pivot tables.To modify an existing form, click the name of the form in the Database window, and click the Design button. Alternatively, you can open the form and change to Design view by clicking the View button.

Lesson 6: Moving and Resizing Fields in Forms

When you create your form, you might find that it is difficult to get the fields in the right place the first time. That's OK; you can move or resize the fields after you add them to the form. You can drag and place them visually, using the ruler as a guide. Or you can have Access align the fields with an underlying grid—making them an equal distance apart.

In this lesson, you move the Birthday field up next to the First Name field.

To Move and Resize Fields in Forms

1. **In the Birthdays form, click the View button.**
To make changes to the form design, you must return to Design view.

2. **If the Birthday field is not selected, click the Birthday field text box.**
Selection handles appear around the borders (see Figure 4.13). Selection handles are small squares that appear at the corners and on the sides of control boxes. You use handles to change the size of the control box. Notice that both the field label and the field text box are selected because these two items are attached. However, handles appear around only the object you clicked. The other one (in this case the field label) has one large handle in the upper-left corner. Most of the time you want to keep the field label and the field text box together.

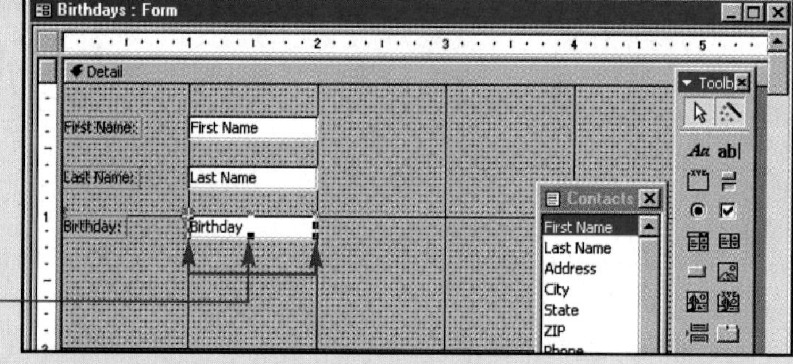

Figure 4.13
You must click a field to select it before you can move it.

3. **Place the mouse pointer on one of the borders, but not on one of the handles.**
When the pointer is in the correct spot, it should resemble a small hand (see Figure 4.14). If you see arrows rather than the hand, the pointer isn't in the correct spot. Move it around until you see the hand.

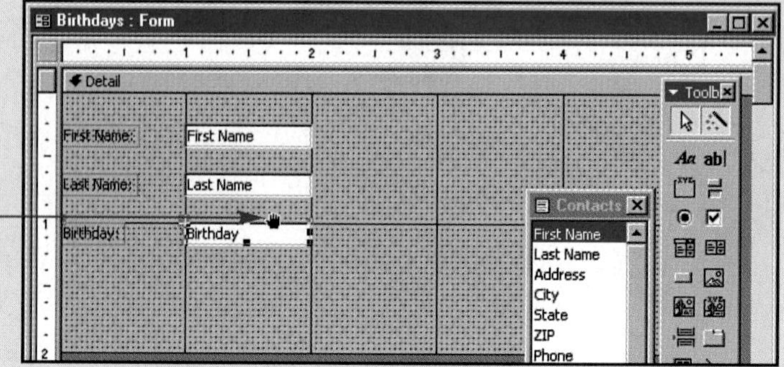

Figure 4.14
To move the field, the pointer must look like a hand.

4. **Drag the Birthday field up next to the First Name field and place it so that the left edge of the Birthday field label is at approximately the 2 1/2-inch mark on the horizontal ruler.**
Notice that as you drag, you see the outline of the field label and the field text box. When you release the mouse button, Access moves the field next to the First Name field. (You might need to drag the field list box out of the way so that you can see where you are positioning the Birthday field.)

5. **Move the pointer to the right side of the Birthday field and place it on the center handle. The pointer turns into a two-headed arrow (see Figure 4.15).**
The Birthday field is longer than necessary, so you are going to change the size to approximately 1/2" wide.

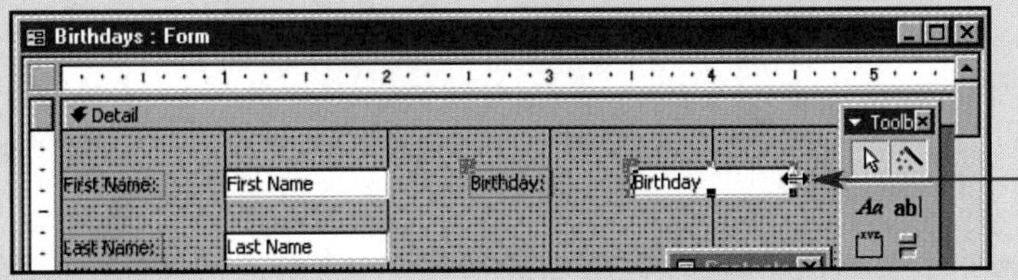

Figure 4.15
Use the selection handles to resize a field.

6. **Make the field smaller by dragging the right side of the field text box to the left. Stop at the 4" mark on the horizontal ruler, so that the field is about 1/2" wide.**
The Birthday field is now about the right size to contain a date.

If you find that the field text box is not large enough to display the data completely, you can return to form Design view and increase the size of the field text box.

7. **Click the View button to return to Form view to make sure the date fits in the new field text box.**

8. **Click the Save button.**
Access saves the form and your changes. Keep the Birthdays form open. In the next lesson, you add a form header to the form.

If you see arrows in the form when you begin to drag, you are resizing the field. If you resize by accident, click the Undo button to undo the change.

When you want to move a field, be sure to place the pointer on the edge of the field and wait until it changes to a hand; don't place the pointer on one of the selection handles.

Moving the Field Label Box Separately from the Field Text Box

If you want to move the field label box separately from the field text box, point to the large handle in the upper-left corner of the field label box. When the pointer turns into a pointing finger, you can click and drag the field label box to a new location. You can move the field text box independently of the field label box by using the same technique. Point to the large handle in the upper-left corner of the field text box until the pointer turns into a pointing finger. Click and drag the field text box to the desired location.

Changing the Tab Order

When you enter data into a form, the insertion point jumps from one box to the next each time you press Tab. The order in which the insertion point moves is called the ***tab order***. When you move fields around on a form, you might need to change the tab order. In Design view, select View, Tab Order from the menu and a list of fields displays. Click once on the field that you want to move to select it; click and drag the field to the desired position on the list. You can also click the Auto Order button, which often (but not always) sets the tab order the way you want it.

Lesson 7: Adding a Form Header and Label

The final step for this form is to add a form header at the top of the form and a label showing the name of the form. Form headers appear at the top of every form. Form footers are similar to form headers, but they appear at the bottom of every form.

In this lesson, you first add a new section to the form, the Form Header section, and then you add a label to the form. In addition to adding the label, you can change the font and font size of the text so that the label stands out.

To Add a Form Header and Label

1. **Click the View button to return to Design view of the Birthdays form.**

2. **Choose View, Form Header/Footer from the menu.**
Access adds two sections to the form: a form header and a form footer (see Figure 4.16). You want to include the form label in the header, but the section is too small. Therefore, you need to adjust the size of the section.

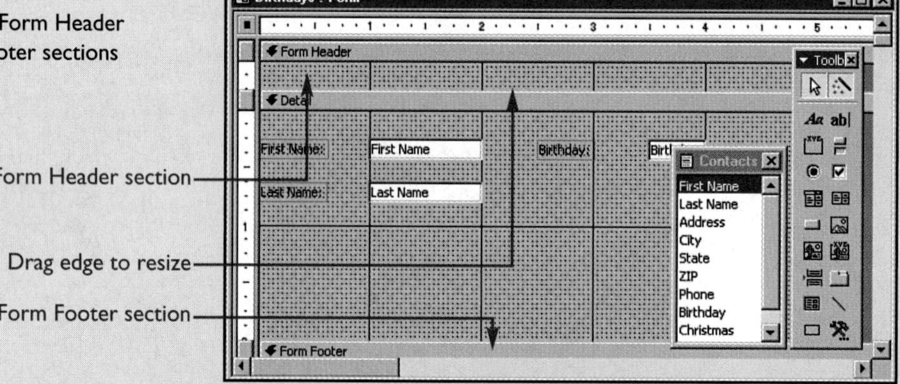

Figure 4.16
You can add Form Header and Form Footer sections to the form.

3. **Place the mouse pointer on the bottom edge of the Form Header section (the top edge of the Detail area).**
The pointer should change to display a thick horizontal bar with a two-headed arrow crossbar (see Figure 4.17). This pointer shape indicates that you are about to resize this section.

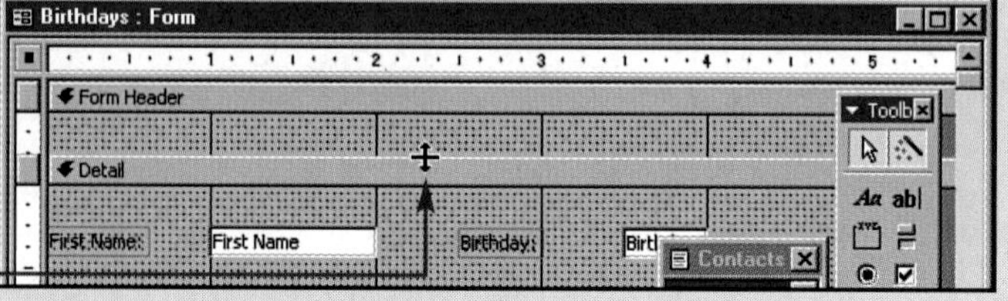

Figure 4.17
The two-headed arrow pointer indicates that you are about to resize the Form Header area.

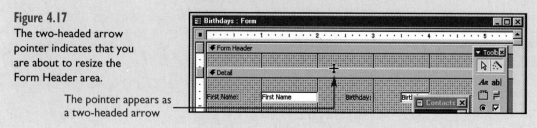

4. **Drag down until the form header is about an inch tall.**
You can use the rulers along the left edge of the form Design view to gauge the size of the section. Don't worry if the size isn't exact. Now that the header is a little bigger, you can add a label to the form.

5. **Click the Label button in the Toolbox.**
Remember that you can place your pointer on a button to see its name.

6. **Position the crosshairs of the pointer near the upper-left corner of the Form Header section. Drag to the right and down to draw a box. Make the box approximately 2 inches wide and 1/2 inch tall.**
The pointer should appear as a small crosshair with an A underneath it while you are positioning it (see Figure 4.18). When you release the mouse button, you see a label text box with the insertion point inside.

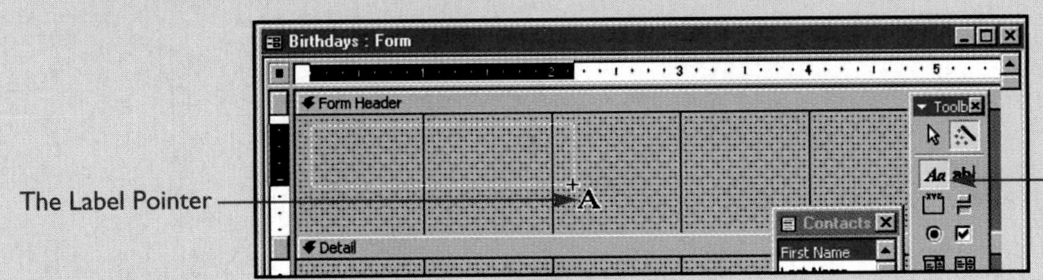

Figure 4.18
Use the Label pointer to place and size the label text box.

If you make the label text box too small, you can always resize it. Click the label text box to select it; place the pointer on one of the selection handles and drag to resize.

7. **Type `Birthdays!`. Click outside the label text box to exit the text-editing mode.**
This is the text you want to include as the label. As you can see, the text is fairly small, but you can change it.

8. **Click inside the label text box to select it.**
Notice that the Formatting toolbar displays the font and font size in the Font and Font Size drop-down lists. You can use these lists to change the font and the font size (see Figure 4.19).

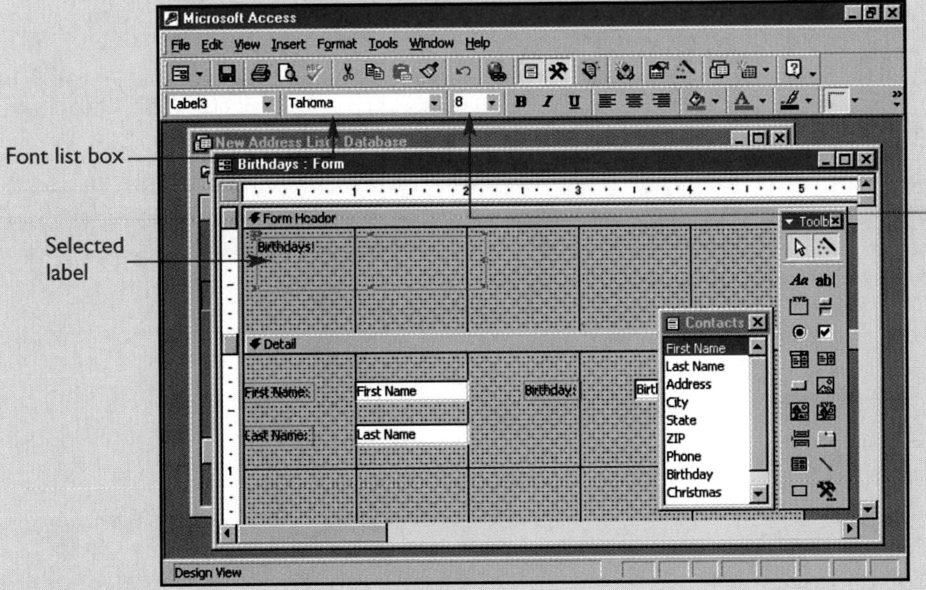

Figure 4.19
You can change the font type and font size of a label using the Formatting toolbar.

continues ▶

To Add a Form Header and Label (continued)

9. **Click the down arrow next to the Font Size box. Select 24.**
This changes the font in the label text box to 24-point type. You don't have to change the actual font, but you can make the text bold.

10. **Click the Bold button on the toolbar.**
Access makes the text bold.

11. **Click the Save button on the toolbar.**
Access saves the form with the changes you made.

12. **Click the View button on the toolbar.**
You switch to Form view, so that you can see the form you created (see Figure 4.20).

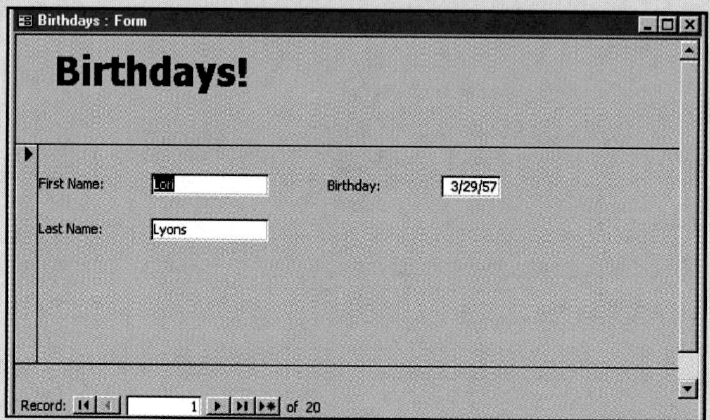

Figure 4.20
The Form view shows the results of your design changes.

13. **Close the Birthdays form, and then close the New Address List database.**
If you have completed your session on the computer, exit Access. Otherwise, continue with the Checking Concepts and Terms section.

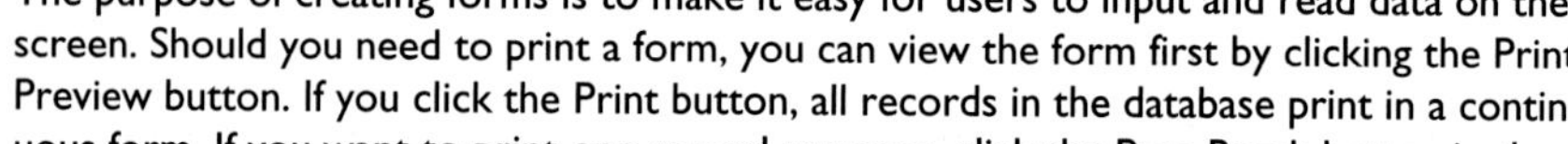

Printing a Form

The purpose of creating forms is to make it easy for users to input and read data on the screen. Should you need to print a form, you can view the form first by clicking the Print Preview button. If you click the Print button, all records in the database print in a continuous form. If you want to print one record per page, click the Page Break button in the Toolbox and drag the small Page Break symbol onto the form.

If you want to print a selected record, move to that record and select File, Print from the menu. Choose the Selected Record(s) radio button in the Print dialog box. Choosing this option prints the current record.

Summary

This project focused on the use of the various form features built into Access. You learned how to create an AutoForm from a table and how to create a new form in Design view. You entered and edited information in a form and modified the form structure by adding fields, moving and resizing fields, and adding form headers and labels.

To enhance your ability to create effective forms, look for help on adding page headers and footers. Pay particular attention to the procedure for adding current information, such as the date, time, or page numbers to headers and footers.

Checking Concepts and Terms

True/False

For each of the following, check *T* or *F* to indicate whether the statement is true or false.

__T __F **1.** AutoForm creates a form using all the fields in your table. [L1]

__T __F **2.** When you use a form to enter data, that data is saved in the form. You also have to update the table. [L2]

__T __F **3.** You must save a form if you want to use it again. [L3]

__T __F **4.** You can have only one section in a form. [L4]

__T __F **5.** To delete a field from a form in form Design view, click the field once to select it, and press Del. [L5]

__T __F **6.** By pressing Ctrl+Alt in Form view, you can use the mouse to make changes to the form without switching to Design view. [L5]

__T __F **7.** If you accidentally close a form without saving it, you can simply click the Undo button to restore the form. [L3]

__T __F **8.** In the Toolbox of Form Design view, the Label button has both an uppercase and a lowercase A on it. [L7]

__T __F **9.** When a field text box is selected, its associated label is also selected. [L6]

__T __F **10.** After you generate a form, you cannot change it. You must generate a new form in Design view. [L6]

Multiple Choice

Circle the letter of the correct answer for each of the following.

1. Which type of section includes the record information? [L4]

a. Detail

b. Page Header

c. Page Footer

d. Form Header

2. What should the pointer look like to move a field? [L6]

a. a hand

b. a white cross

c. a two-headed arrow

d. a crosshair

3. To save data to the table after you have entered several records using a form, you must do which of the following? [L2]

a. Choose Save from the File menu.

b. Choose Update from the File menu.

c. Click the Save button on the toolbar.

d. none of the above (because data is saved automatically).

4. Which of the following is a fast way to create a form based on the current table? [L1]

a. Use the QuickForm.

b. Use an AutoForm.

c. Open a blank form and drag the fields onto it from the Field List window.

d. Click NewForm in the Toolbox.

5. How can you add the Toolbox to the Design View window if the Toolbox is not already present? [L4]

a. Select Open Toolbox from the Tools menu.

b. Choose Insert Toolbox from the menu.

c. Click the Toolbox button on the Form Design toolbar.

d. Press ↵Enter.

Screen ID

Label each element of the Access screen shown in Figure 4.21.

Figure 4.21

A. Label pointer
B. Toolbox
C. Field text box
D. Label button
E. Toolbox button
F. Font button
G. Field list button
H. Field label
I. Font size button
J. Field list

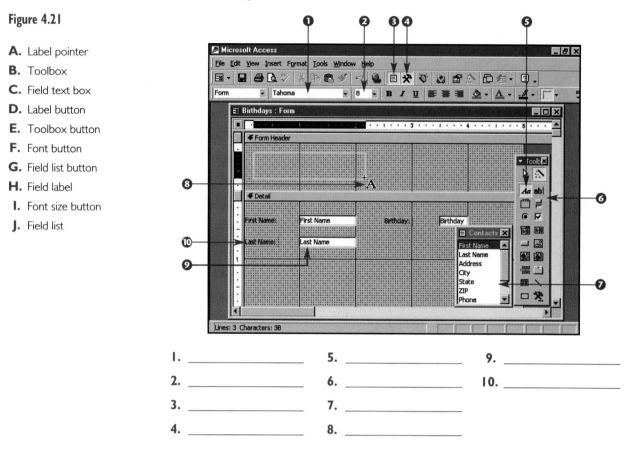

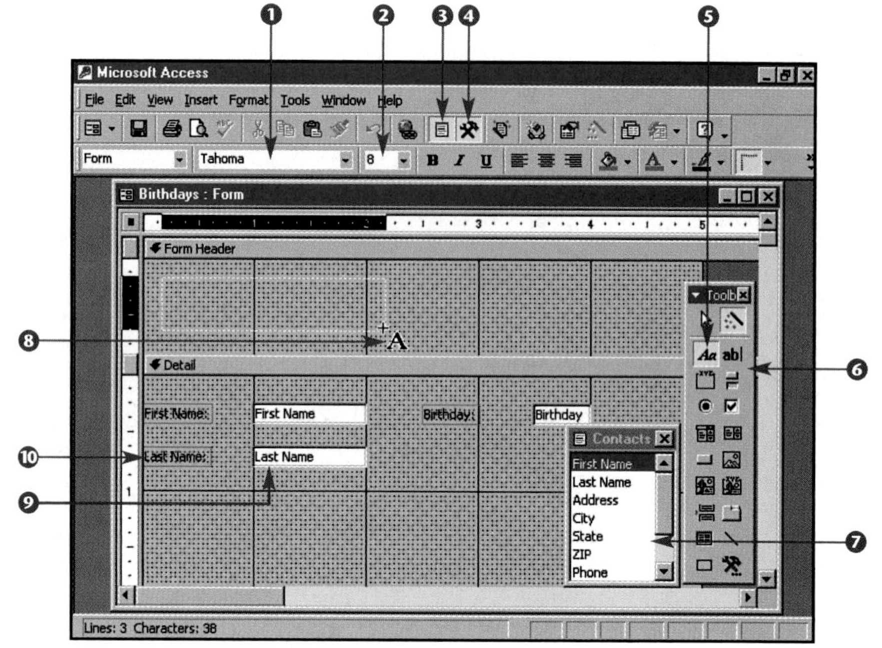

1. ________________
2. ________________
3. ________________
4. ________________
5. ________________
6. ________________
7. ________________
8. ________________
9. ________________
10. ________________

Discussion Questions

1. In Access Project 3, "Querying Your Database," you answered a question about when you might use forms and when you might want to enter data directly into the table. Now that you have some experience with forms, has your opinion changed? Do you think you will use forms or tables (or some combination) for data entry into tables you anticipate using in the future?
2. If you have a table with a few fields (fewer than 10), what would be the advantage of using one of the form wizards to create a columnar or tabular form? Would there be any advantage to creating the form in Design view?
3. The tabular form looks a lot like the table Datasheet view. Can you think of any reason why you would want to create this type of form instead of simply entering the text into the table?
4. You can add form headers and footers and page headers and footers. When would you use page headers and footers? When would you use form headers and footers?
5. In what type of situations would you print information in the Form view? Can you think of any place you might have received a Form view printout from a database?

Skill Drill

Skill Drill exercises reinforce project skills. Each skill reinforced is the same, or nearly the same, as a skill presented in the project. Each exercise includes a brief narrative introduction, followed by detailed instructions in a step-by-step format.

The database you use for these exercises contains two tables: one with information about short story books, and the other with information about the authors of these books.

1. Creating an AutoForm

Entering the data into the Book information table is not easy because the fields scroll off the field to the right. It would be a good idea to create a form to make data entry easier. You decide to use the AutoForm feature to create the new form. [L1]

To create an AutoForm, complete the following steps:

1. Find the `AO-0402` database file on your CD-ROM; copy it to drive A; remove the Read-Only status, and name it **`Short Story Books`**. Select and open the Book information table, and look at the fields. Click the Close Window button to close the table.
2. Click the Forms object button and click New to create a new form.
3. Select the Book information table from the Choose the table or query where the object's data comes from drop-down list.
4. Select the AutoForm: Columnar wizard and click OK.
5. Close the form and save it as **`Book information data input`**.

2. Adding Data to the Form

You just found a short story book at the local used bookstore and can't wait to try out that new form you just created. [L2]

To add data to the form, complete the following steps:

1. Select the Book information data input form, and click the Open button.
2. Click the New Record button on the toolbar.
3. Press ↵Enter to skip the BookID field, which is entered automatically.
4. Enter **`Rinehart, Mary Roberts`** in the Author field.
5. Enter **`Affinities and Other Stories`** in the Title field.
6. Enter **`1920`** for the Year field, **`282`** for the Page field, and **`Review of Reviews`** for the Publisher field.
7. Close the form.

3. Editing Data in the Form

When looking more carefully at the book you entered, you find that the publisher that you listed was a reprint house, and that the original publisher was George H. Doran. You also found out that the date of publication for *Auld Licht Idylls*, by J. M. Barrie (also the author of the children's classic *Peter Pan*) was 1888. You need to go into your form and change this information. [L2]

To edit data in the form, complete the following steps:

1. Select the Book information data input form and click the Open button.
2. Place the insertion point in the Title field and click the Find button.
3. Type **`Affinities`** in the Find What text box; select Start of Field from the Match box.
4. Click Find Next. Move the Find and Replace dialog box, if necessary, and change Review of Reviews to **`George H. Doran`** in the Publisher field.
5. Place the insertion point in the Title field and type **`Auld`** in the Find What box.
6. Click Find Next. Type **`1888`** in the Year field.
7. Close the Find and Replace dialog box, and close the Book information form.

4. Creating a New Form in Design View

Now that you've created a form for the Book information table, you decide that you also want one for the Author information table. [L4]

To create a new form in Design view, complete the following steps:

1. Click the Forms object button, and click New to create a new form.
2. Select the Author information table from the Choose the table or query where the object's data comes from drop-down list.
3. Select Design View and click OK.
4. Maximize the Form window. Click the Toolbox and Field List buttons, if necessary. Select View, Ruler to turn the rulers on, if necessary.

5. Drag the Author field onto the form about 1/4" down and 3/4" to the right of the left edge.
6. Drag the DOB field to the 3" mark and line it up to the right of the Author field.
7. Place the Birth City, State, and Birth Country fields under the Author field, about 1/4" apart. Use the hand pointer to adjust the field locations, if necessary.
8. Click the View button to see your form.
9. Save the form as **`Author information data input`**, and close it.

5. Moving and Resizing Fields

You decide that you don't like the look of the form. You'd like the last three fields to line up across the screen. [L6]

To move and resize fields, complete the following steps:

1. Open the Author information data input form in Design view.
2. Grab the State field and move it just to the right of the Birth City field.
3. Grab the Birth Country field and move it to the right of the State field. Don't worry if the field overlaps the edge of the work area—the work area automatically widens.
4. Click the View button to see your form.

6. Deleting Field Labels and Adding a Label

Your form still does not look right. It would look much better without the field names and with a single label describing all three fields. [L7]

To delete field labels and add a label, complete the following steps:

1. Click the View button to return to Design view.
2. Click the Birth city field label. Handles should appear around the label on the left, but not the field text box (which should have one large handle in the upper-left corner).
3. Press Del to remove the Birth city label.
4. Select and delete the field labels for the State and Birth Country fields.
5. Select all three fields in the second row and move them down about 1/2" and over to the left edge of the form. (*Note*: Click the Birth city field; hold down ⇧Shift, and click the State and Birth Country fields.)
6. Click the Label button, and click and drag the crosshair pointer to place a label text box above the three fields you just moved.
7. Type **`Place of Birth:`** in the label text box.
8. Click outside the label text box; click the label text box again to select it. Click the Bold button. Resize the text box as necessary. Your Design window should look like Figure 4.22.
9. Click the View button, and click the Next Record button a few times to see how your form works. The fourth and fifth records should contain data in all five fields.
10. Save your changes and close the form.

Figure 4.22

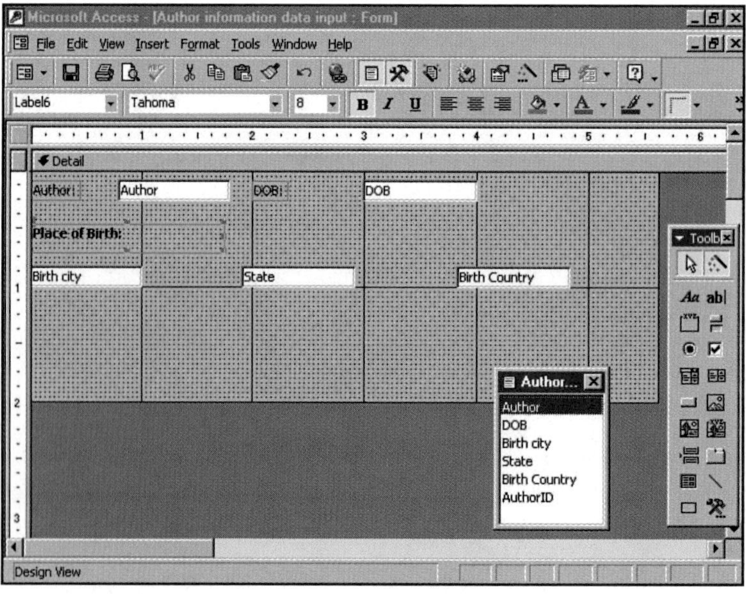

Challenge exercises expand on or are somewhat related to skills presented in the lessons. Each exercise provides a brief narrative introduction followed by instructions, in a numbered step or bulleted list format, that are not as detailed as those in the Skill Drill section.

The database you use for the Challenge section is the same database of short story books and authors you used in the Skill Drill exercises. The Book information data input form has been modified. Before you start the Challenge exercises, spend a little time looking at the form in Form view, and then look at it in Design view. Notice how it has been laid out and how some of the field labels have been deleted and replaced by other labels.

1. Adding the Date and Time to the Form Header

You have decided to make your Book information data input form more user-friendly. Because you expect to frequently print out single forms, you'd also like to make the forms more informative. The first thing you want to do is add the current date to the form header. [L2]

To add the date and time to a form header, complete the following steps:

1. Copy the `AO-0403` database file to drive A; remove the Read-Only status, and rename it `Revised Short Story Books`.
2. Open the database, and open the Book information data input form in Form view. Maximize the Form window and examine the form layout.
3. Move to Design view and examine the layout of the form.
4. Use the Insert menu to place the date (in the 12/31/99 format) and the time (in the 11:59 PM format) in the form.
5. Click the View button. If the date and time are not in the upper-left corner of the form header, return to Design view, and move them to that location.
6. Save your changes, and close the form.

2. Adding a Page Number to a Page Footer

You have added the date and time to the form header, now you want to keep track of the page numbers. [L5]

To add the page number to a page footer, complete the following steps:

1. Open the Book information data input form in Design view. Maximize the Form window.
2. Scroll down, if necessary, until you can see the Form Footer area.
3. Use the Insert menu to place the page number (in the Page N of M format).
4. Place the page number at the bottom of the page and center align it.
5. Notice that the program added Page Header and Page Footer sections, and the page number is in the Page Footer section.
6. Click the View button to look at the page number. Notice that the page number does not appear. Use the Help menu to find out why it does not show up here, and what possible use this feature might be.
7. Save your changes and close the form.

3. Adding an Image to a Page Header

You have added the date and time to the form header and the page number to the page footer. Now you want to improve the appearance of your form. The first thing you want to do is to add a small graphic image to the form header. [L7]

To add an image to a page header, complete the following steps:

1. Open the Book information data input form in Design view. Maximize the Form window.
2. Use the Help menu or online Help to figure out how to add the Books image file (Books.wmf) included on the CD-ROM to your form.
3. Turn on the ruler, if necessary, and use it to help you resize the image to about 1/2" high.

4. Move the image to the upper-right side of the form header.
5. Click the View button to see how the image looks on the form.
6. Save your changes, and close the form.

4. Customizing the Look of the Form

You have added an image to the form, now you would like to make some changes to the overall form design. You decide to try to change the background color of the Detail area and give the field labels and field text boxes a special effect. [L5]

To customize the look of a form, complete the following steps:

1. Open the Book information data input form in Design view. Maximize the Form window.
2. Find the Fill/Back Color button, and change the background color to a pale blue.
3. Select all the field labels and field text boxes. (*Hint*: You can move the pointer to the vertical ruler near the top of the Detail area. It changes to a right arrow. Click and drag down to below the last row of fields and release the mouse button. All the field labels and field text boxes are selected.)
4. Use the right mouse button on any one of the selected field labels or field text boxes. Find the option that enables you to customize these boxes and select Sunken.
5. Click the View button to see how your changes look on the form. Your form should look like Figure 4.23.

Figure 4.23

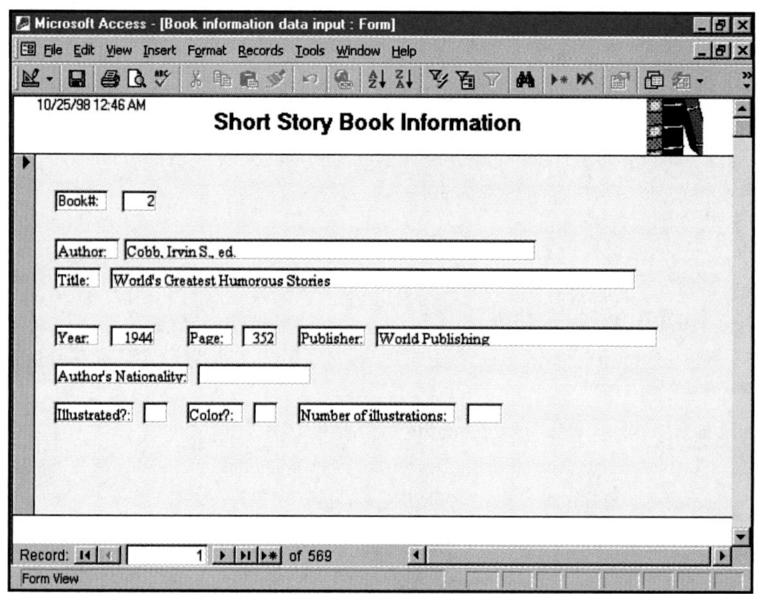

6. Save your changes and close the form.

5. Inserting a Page Break and Printing a Form

You have created your form, and now you want to make it more readable. You also want to make some copies. You decide to add page breaks for clarity, and then print the result. [L3]

To insert a page break and print a form, complete the following steps:

1. Open the Book information data input form in Design view. Maximize the Form window.
2. Find and click the Page Break button in the Toolbox.
3. Move the new pointer, and click about 1/4" under the last row of fields.
4. Click the View button to move to Form view.
5. Choose File, Print from the menu.
6. Make sure that the correct printer is selected and the printer is turned on.
7. Choose the Selected Record(s) option to print only the current record, and click OK.
8. Save your changes and close the form.

6. Copying a Form and Basing It on a Query

Your collection includes books by a number of different publishers, but you specialize in the books published by Scribner's. You would like to create a query that would show only the Scribner's books and use the new query as the source for a copy of the form on which you have been working. [L1]

To copy a form and base it on a query, complete the following steps:

1. Create a query in Design view. Add all the fields from the Book information table. Use `Scribner's` as the criteria in the Publisher field; sort on Author and Title. Save the query as `Scribner's Books`.
2. Find and click the Page Break button in the Toolbox, and enter a page break at the bottom of the form.
3. Move to the Form window. Use Access Help to find out how to make a copy of the Book information data input form and paste it as `Scribner's information`.
4. Switch to the Scribner's information Design view. Use Access Help to find out how to view the Properties box for the entire form. (*Hint*: If you want to use the shortcut menu, the ruler must be turned on. If you want to use the menus, the whole form must be selected.)
5. Change the Record Source from the Book information table to the Scribner's Books query.
6. Switch to the Form view and scroll through a few records to make sure the only books shown are those published by Scribner's.
7. Save your changes and close the form.

Discovery Zone

Discovery Zone exercises help you gain advanced knowledge of project topics and/or application of skills. These exercises focus on enhancing your problem-solving skills.

1. Adding a Drop-Down List to a Field in a Form

In many cases, fields in tables have a limited number of possible entries. Examples of these would be fields that ask for the name of a state or a department in a company. Access has a feature that enables you to create a drop-down menu, so that you can choose from a list of choices. These drop-down menus are called combo boxes.

Goal: Create a combo box in the Publisher field that enables you to select from a list of the most common publishers.

Use the `AO-0404` file to create a new database called `Short Story Books with a Combo Box` on your disk. Use Help from your computer or online to understand how combo boxes are set up. Go to the Book information table Design view and change the Publisher field text box to a combo box. Include the following publishers in the list:

```
Century
Colliers
Dodd, Mead
Grosset & Dunlap
Harpers
Scribner's
```

Hint 1: A shortcut menu option helps you determine which type of field text box to use.

Hint 2: Use the Properties box for the Publisher field text box to determine where the information for the combo box comes from. You can create a table to use as the source, or you can type the value list in another box in the Properties box.

Hint 3: A Value List is usually best when there are only a few items, while a table is best for a larger number of items.

Your combo box should look like Figure 4.24.

Figure 4.24

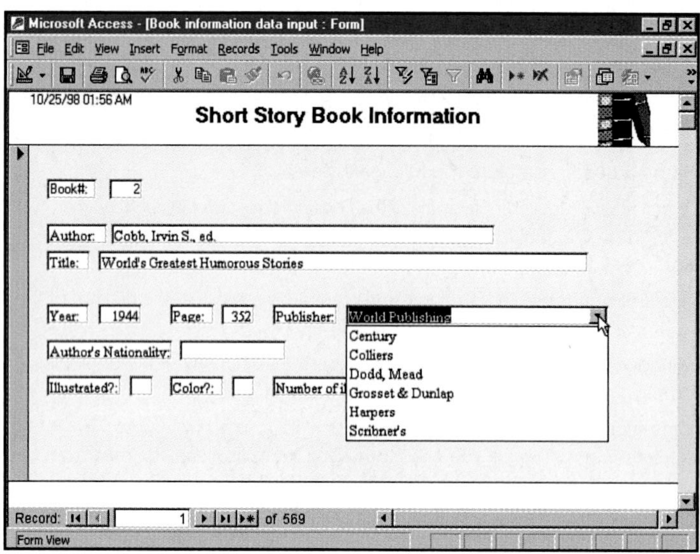

2. Using Multiple Pages with Tabs on a Form

When a table has a large number of fields or can be easily divided into more than one category, Access includes a feature that enables you to divide a form into pages. These pages have tabs at the top, and all you have to do to move between pages is to click a tab.

Goal: Create two tabbed pages on a form based on a table showing the number of cars and trucks by location in the United States.

Use the `AO-0405` file to create a new database called `US Motor Vehicle Statistics`. Use Help from your computer or online to understand how Tab Control works. Create the new form in Design view and save it as `US Cars and Trucks`. Your form should have the following:

- Two pages, with the tabs labeled `Cars` and `Trucks`.
- The Location, Privately Owned Cars, and Publicly Owned Cars fields on the Cars tab.
- The Location, Privately Owned Trucks, and Publicly Owned Trucks fields on the Trucks tab.
- Identical field labels for both occurrences of the Location field. (*Hint*: You need to change the field name on one of them.)

Hint 1: This is much easier than it sounds! Look in the Toolbox to get started.

Hint 2: Most of your time will be spent resizing the field labels and the field text boxes and lining them up.

Your tabbed form should look like Figure 4.25.

Figure 4.25

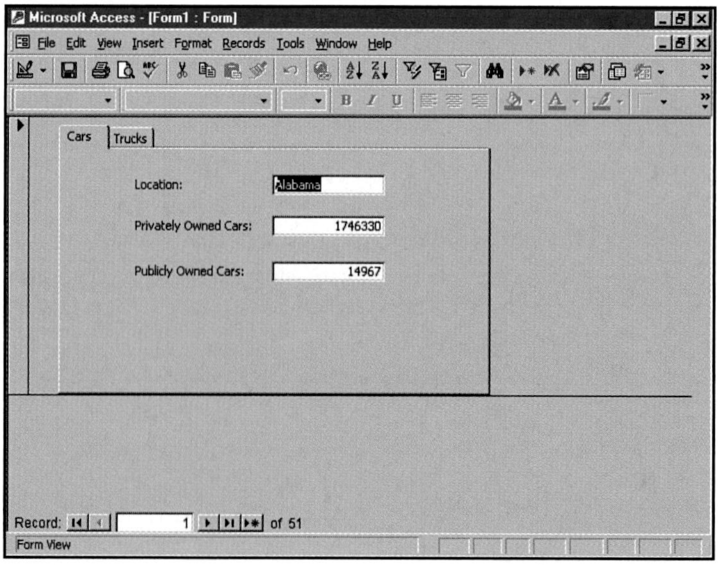

Project 5

Creating and Printing Reports

Objectives

In this project, you learn how to

- **Print the Table Data**
- **Create a Report Using the Report Wizards**
- **Print and Rename a Report**
- **Modify a Report Design**
- **Save the Report with a New Name**
- **Add Labels to Reports**

Key terms introduced in this project include

- AutoReport
- expression
- landscape orientation
- portrait orientation
- report
- section

Why Would I Do This?

You can display the information in your database several ways. You can print a form or print copies of tables or queries. These printouts are limited in format and flexibility. To produce flexible printouts from tables or queries, you need to learn how to use ***reports***. Reports are database objects designed to print and/or summarize selected fields. They are divided into ***sections*** that can contain controls, labels, formulas, and even images. In this project, you learn the fundamental tasks involved in creating, modifying, saving, and printing a simple report.

Before you create a report, think about why you need the printed data. Do you want to check the entries to make sure they are correct? Do you need an address list or phone list? Do you need to pass the information along to someone else? If so, what information does that person need and in what order? If you spend a few moments determining the purpose of the report, you can design a report that truly meets your needs.

Access provides many tools for creating a report; you can create an ***AutoReport***, use the report wizards to create other common report types (single-column report, mailing labels, and so on), or create a blank report that you add information to later. You can also change the layout of an existing report design and add report labels to help make the report more self-explanatory. This project shows you how to use the report tools included with Access. When you have finished this project, you will have created a report like the one in Figure 5.1.

Visual Summary

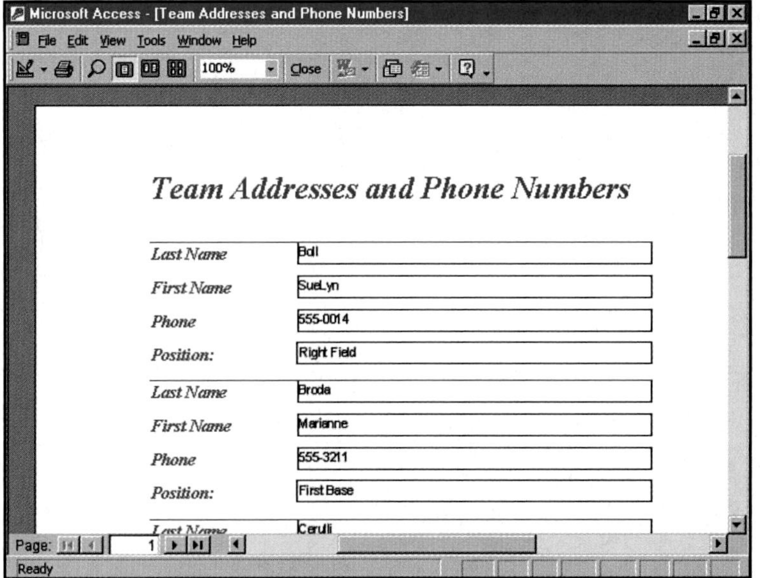

Figure 5.1
You can create reports easily using report wizards.

Lesson 1: Printing the Table Data

If all you need is a printout of the entire table or query, it is faster to print the table without using a report. For example, you might want to print the data in a table so that you can check the accuracy of the records. In this case, you don't have to create a report.

To Print the Table Data

1. **Launch Access. Click OK to open an existing file.**
   Make sure you have a disk in drive A.
2. **Find the AO-0501 file on your CD-ROM; right-click it, and copy it to the floppy drive. Move to drive A; remove the read-only status; rename the file `Softball Team`, and open the new database.**

The Softball Team database includes a table of team members and a table of game information. After you open the Softball Team database, you should see the two tables displayed in the Tables list. In this project, you work with the Team table.

3. **Select the Team table and click the Open button. Maximize the Table window.**
The table opens in Datasheet view. You might want to scroll through the table to see how it is set up. The table includes fields for the first and last name of each player, along with his or her position, phone number, address, and dues. You can print this information; but before you print, preview the printout, so that you have some idea of what the printed list will look like.

4. **Click the Print Preview button.**
A preview of the printed list displays (see Figure 5.2). The structure of the printout is fairly simple; each record displays as a row in a grid. The navigation button that enables you to scroll to the next page is active, which indicates that the printout will be more than one page. This means that all the table columns don't fit on one page width when the report prints.

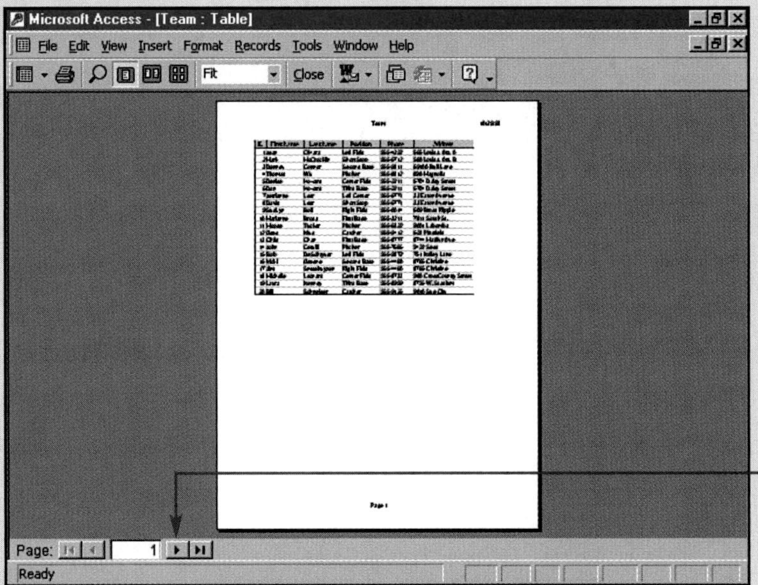

Figure 5.2
You can preview the table before you print it.

5. **Click the Next Page button, which is the same as the Next Record button in a form or table.**
The second page of the printout, which shows the remaining column, displays. This is a problem with printing all the fields in the table. If the table is too wide by just a few columns, you can still get a usable printout by changing the orientation of the page so that Access prints across the long edge of the page, rather than down the page. Using ***landscape orientation***, you can fit more columns across the page.

6. **Choose File, Page Setup from the menu.**
The Page Setup dialog box lists options for setting margins and page layouts.

7. **Make sure the margins are all 1", and click the Page tab to display the page orientation (see Figure 5.3).**

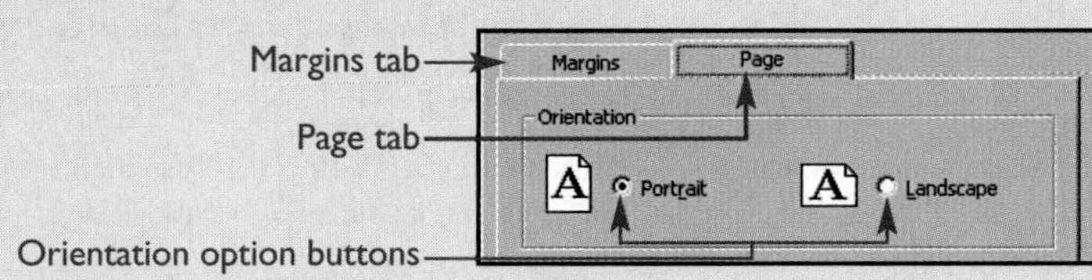

Figure 5.3
Use the Page Setup dialog box to change the page orientation.

continues ▶

To Print the Table Data (continued)

8. **In the Orientation area, click the Landscape option button, and click OK.**
The orientation of the page changes to landscape, which is the horizontal orientation of a page. The standard vertical orientation of a page is called ***portrait orientation***. Now when you print the report, all the columns fit on a single page.

9. **Click OK. From the File menu, choose Print.**
The Print dialog box displays (see Figure 5.4). Here you can control which pages and how many copies print, and select other options. The default settings work fine for this one-page printout.

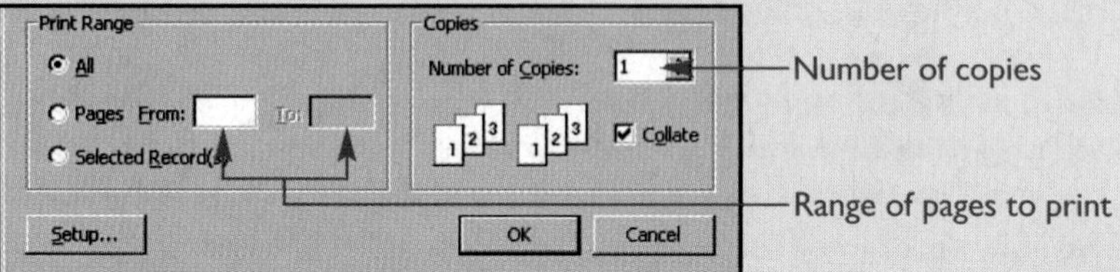

Figure 5.4
Use the Print dialog box to choose the pages and the number of copies you want to print.

10. **Click OK.**
The table data prints. If you don't have access to a printer, click Cancel.

11. **Click the Close Window button.**
The Preview window and the table close. Leave the Softball Team database open for the next lesson.

Other Ways to Print a Table
You don't have to preview the printout, but previewing is a good idea. You can print directly from Datasheet view. Simply click the Print button on the toolbar or open the File menu, and choose the Print command. Access prints the table. The keyboard shortcut for the Print command is Ctrl+P.

Making the Data Fit on a Page
If the data doesn't quite fit on the page, you can do one of several things to make it fit. You can reduce the width of the columns. If this cuts off some of the data, you can reduce the font size using Format, Font from the menu.

Lesson 2: Creating a Report Using the Report Wizards

Simple table printouts are limited in what they can do. Access provides several reporting options to make it easy to create more sophisticated reports. Using the New Report feature, you can create the reports described in Table 5.1.

Table 5.1—Common Report Creation Options

New Report Option	Description
Design View	Opens a Design window where you can add fields or text. This option does not use a wizard.
Report Wizard	Guides you through the process of creating a report. A report wizard has several options for layout and grouping of data.
AutoReport: Columnar	Places all the fields in a table in a single-column report.
AutoReport: Tabular	Places all the fields of the table in a row-and-column format similar to the layout of a datasheet.

New Report Option	Description
Chart Wizard	Guides you through the process of selecting fields that you want to summarize in a graphical form. The Chart Wizard enables you to choose from several chart types, such as pie, line, and bar.
Label Wizard	Enables you to set up and print mailing labels in more than 100 different label styles.

A report wizard leads you step by step through the process of creating a report, asking you which fields to include in the report, which sort order to use, what title to print, and so on. After you make your selections, the wizard creates the report.

In this lesson, you create a columnar report for your Team table in the Softball Team database. This report works well as an address list.

To Create a Report Using the Report Wizards

1 Click the Reports object button.
No reports are listed because you haven't created any yet (see Figure 5.5).

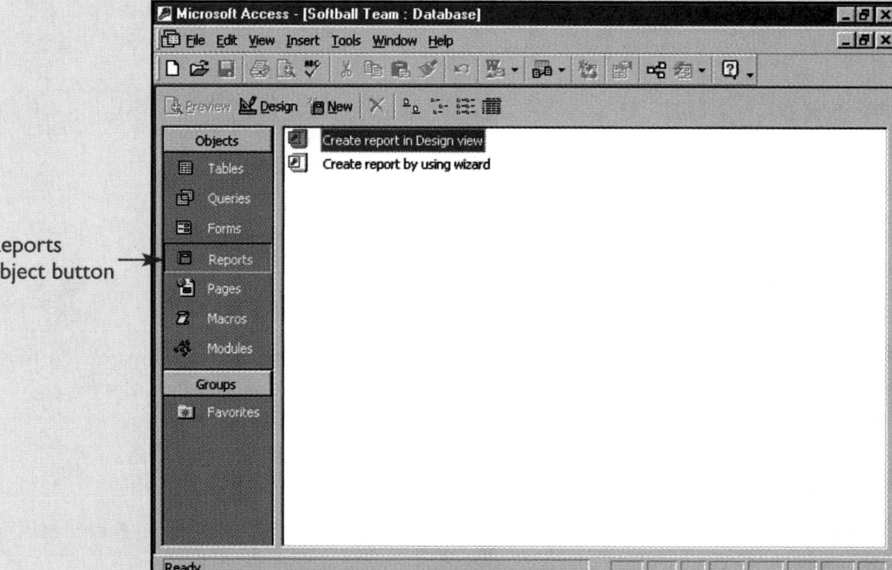

Figure 5.5
No reports are listed in the Reports Object window.

2 Click the New button.
The New Report dialog box displays (see Figure 5.6). You need to select the method of creating the report and the table or query on which you want to base the report. You used the same procedure to create a form.

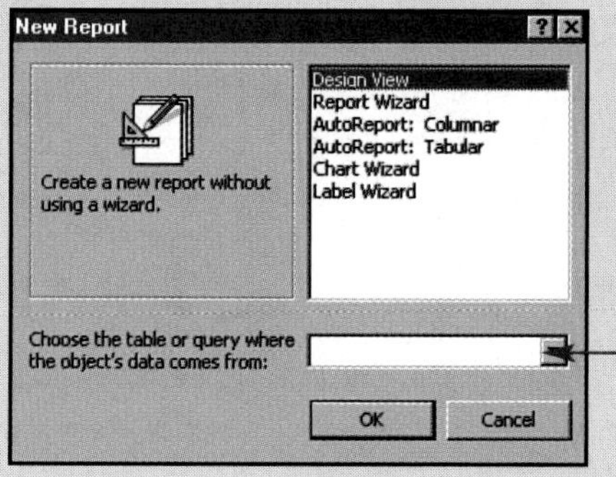

Figure 5.6
You choose the method you want to use to create a new report and the table or query on which to base the report.

continues ▶

To Create a Report Using the Report Wizards (continued)

3 Select Report Wizard and choose the Team table as a source. Click OK.

The first Report Wizard dialog box displays.

4 In the Available Fields list, click the First Name field, and click the Add button.

The wizard removes the field from the Available Fields list and places the field in the Selected Fields list (see Figure 5.7). The fields appear in the report in the order you select them. The First Name field, for example, will be the first field listed in the current report.

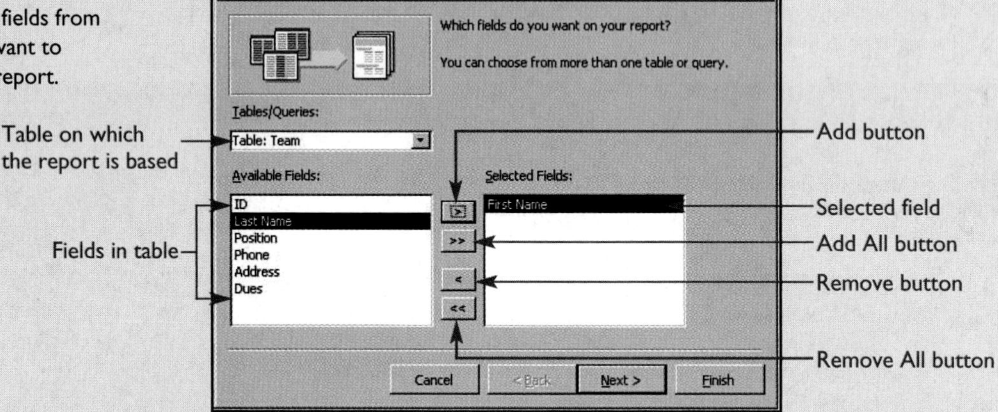

Figure 5.7
Choose which fields from the table you want to include in the report.

5 Highlight and add the Last Name, Address, and Phone fields to the Selected Fields list.

Your report now includes four fields. These are all the fields you want to include.

6 Click the Next button.

The second Report Wizard dialog box displays. You use this step to group similar records together, such as grouping the team by position played. However, in this example, we have not included any fields that need to be listed together as a group.

7 Click Next button again.

The third Report Wizard dialog box enables you to sort the data on one or more fields.

8 Click the down arrow next to the first sort selection text box to reveal the available fields. Select Last Name as the field to sort. Click Next.

The fourth Report Wizard dialog box enables you to select the layout, orientation, and fit (see Figure 5.8).

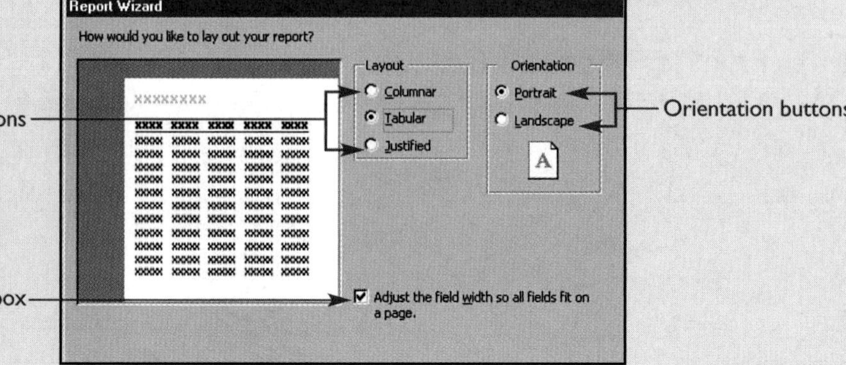

Figure 5.8
Select the layout and orientation options.

9 **Select a Columnar layout, Portrait orientation, and fit the report to one page. Click the Next button.**
The fifth Report Wizard displays. In this dialog box, you select a report style.

10 **Select the Corporate option and click the Next button.**
The final Report Wizard dialog box displays. In this screen, you enter the title for the report. By default, the wizard uses the table name and prints the title on the first page.

If you make a mistake or change your mind about an option anywhere in the wizard, you can back up by clicking the Back button in the Wizard dialog box.

11 **Type `Team Addresses and Phone Numbers`, and click the Finish button.**
A preview of the report displays (see Figure 5.9). You can print, zoom, and save the report, as you learn in the next lesson. Notice that the default label at the top of the report is also the name of the table from which the report was taken. Keep the report open for the next lesson, where you print and rename a report.

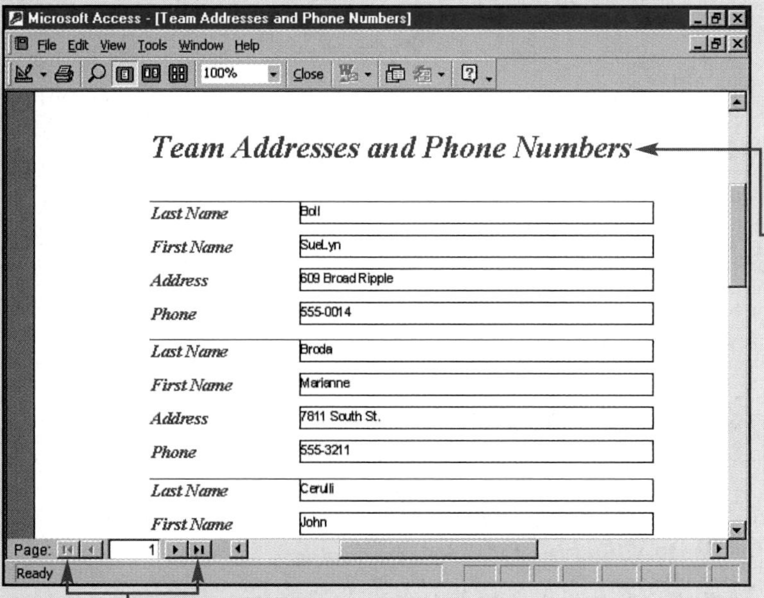

Figure 5.9
You can review the columnar report onscreen.

Creating an Auto Report
In Access Project 4, "Creating and Using Forms," you used the Form Wizard to quickly create an AutoForm. You can also create an AutoReport using the report wizards. An AutoReport includes all the fields from the table in the report. The report is in either a one-column or tabular format with as many records on the page as possible. The report also includes a header with the table name and current date, and a footer with the page number. To create this type of report, choose AutoReport from the list of new objects displayed in the New Objects list box.

Lesson 3: Printing and Renaming a Report

The next step is to print your report. However, before you print, it's always a good idea to preview the report. In the Print Preview mode, you can use the navigation buttons to check for unexpected additional pages, and check the font, the font size, and the actual data in the report. If you click the Zoom button on the toolbar, you can view the entire report to determine, generally, how the printed report will look on the page. If you do not like the way the report is set up, you can make changes before you print it. This strategy can save you time and paper.

You can also rename a report in the Database window to ensure that it's not confused with other database objects with the same name.

To Print and Rename a Report

1 With the Preview window still active, click the pointer anywhere in the report.
Access displays a full-page view of the report so that you can see the entire page (see Figure 5.10).

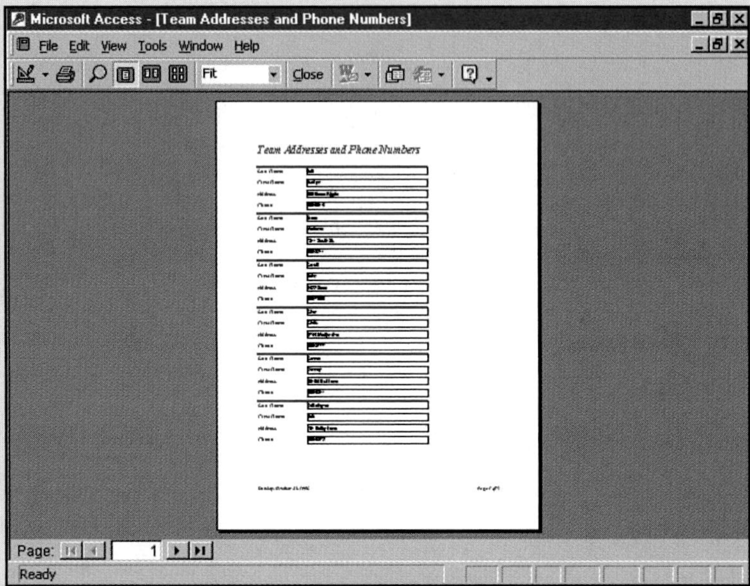

Figure 5.10
You can use the full-page view to preview the report.

2 Click the report again.
Access zooms in so that you can read the text of the report. It centers on the spot you clicked, so you might need to use the scrollbars to get back to the section you want to see. Now you are ready to print.

3 Click the Print button on the toolbar.
The report prints. If you do not have access to a printer, skip this step.

This report is three pages long. If you are restricted to printing one page, select File, Print from the menu; choose to print from pages 1 to 1 in the Print Range section.

Close **4 Click the Close button on the toolbar to close the Preview window.**
The program returns to the report Design view.

5 Click the Close Window button to close the report.
The new report displays in the Database window under the Reports tab. You decide that the name you gave the report could be improved.

6 Right-click the Team Addresses and Phone Numbers report, and select Rename from the shortcut menu.
The name changes to edit mode so that you can change it.

7 Type the name `Team Roster`.

8 Press ↵Enter or click outside the Name box to save the change.
The report name is now Team Roster. Keep the database open for the next lesson, where you modify a report design.

Lesson 4: Modifying a Report Design

After you create a report, you might decide you want to modify it. The finished report might not be exactly what you intended. Rather than start over with a wizard or a blank form, you can modify the report design so that the report includes the information you want.

When you look through the report Design view, you notice some unusual-looking things in the Page Footer. These are ***expressions***, which are predefined formulas that perform calculations, display built-in functions, or set limits.

Suppose that you need a phone list in addition to the team roster. You can modify the Roster report to create this new report. Start by deleting the Address field, which you don't need in your phone list. Add the Position field so you have a list that includes the name, phone number, and position played for each member of the team.

To Modify a Report Design

1 Select the Team Roster report, and open it in Design view.

The report displays in Design view (see Figure 5.11). This view is similar to the Design view you used when you created a form. The same tools are available onscreen. You can use the ruler to place items on the report, the Toolbox to add controls, and the Field list to add fields.

If your rulers are not turned on, choose View, Ruler from the menu. You can also turn on the Toolbox and the Field list using the appropriate buttons, as you did when you worked with forms in Project 4.

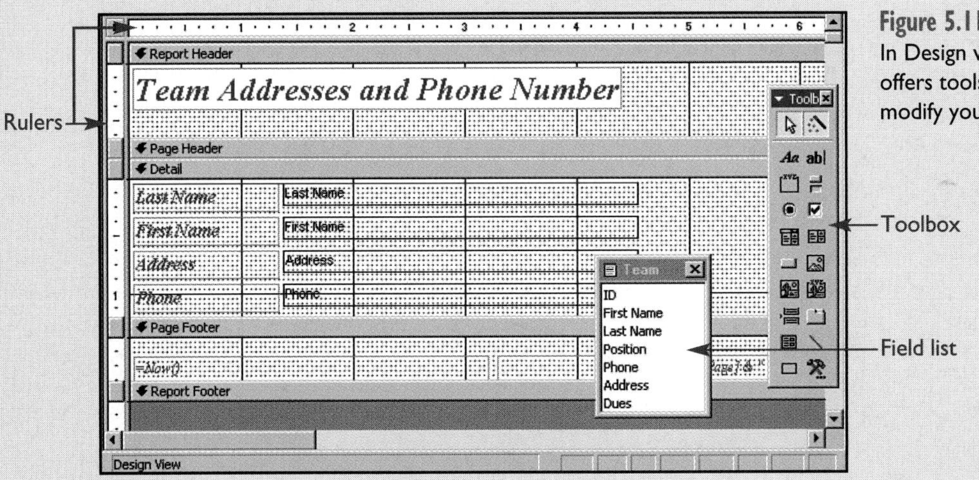

Figure 5.11
In Design view, Access offers tools to help you modify your report.

2 Click the scroll arrows to scroll through the report to see how it is structured.

Notice that the report includes a page footer with the date and page number. The expression =NOW() inserts the current date (see Figure 5.12). An expression is similar to a function in spreadsheet software. Access provides many expressions that you can include in your report.

continues ▶

To Modify a Report Design (continued)

The expression, `="Page" & [Page] & "Of" & [Pages]`, on the right side of the page footer prints the current page and the total number of pages. Remember that you placed this expression in the form in Access Project 4.

The Detail section includes four fields: Last Name, First Name, Address, and Phone.

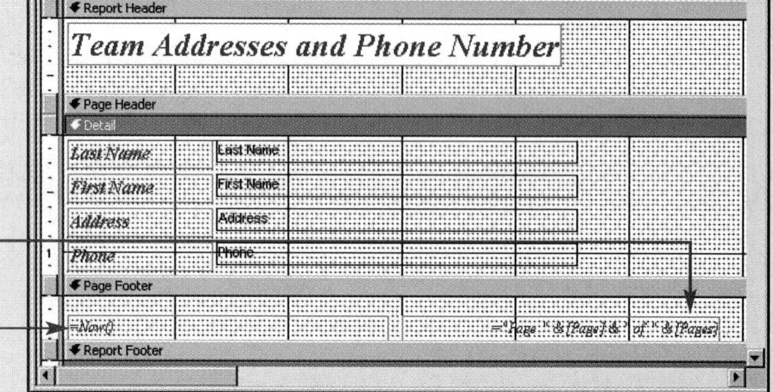

Figure 5.12 Expressions add calculations or functions to a report.

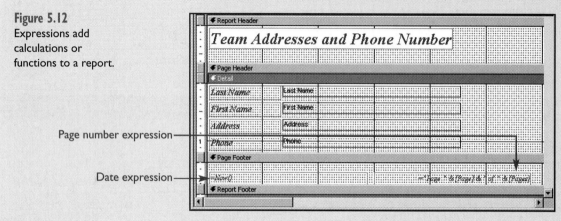

3 Maximize the window, and click the Address field text box.
The field label is on the left, and the field text box is on the right. If you click the Address field text box, handles appear at the sides and corners of the field text box and in the upper-left corner of the field label box.

4 Press Del.
Access removes the field and its label from the report. Now you have a gap between two of the fields. To fix this gap, you can move the Phone field up.

5 Click the Phone field to select it.
Position the pointer on the field, so that it turns into an open hand.

6 Drag the Phone field directly under the First Name field.
The Phone field moves up closer to First Name. Now you add the Position field to the report.

7 In the field list box, click the Position field and drag it directly below the Phone field text in the Detail section of the report and release the mouse.
The pointer turns into a small field box when you drag the field onto the report. As soon as you release the mouse, the field text box is positioned under the Phone text box and the field label for the new field is added to the left of the field (see Figure 5.13). Next you need to format the new field to match the ones on the report.

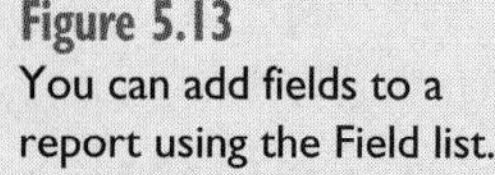

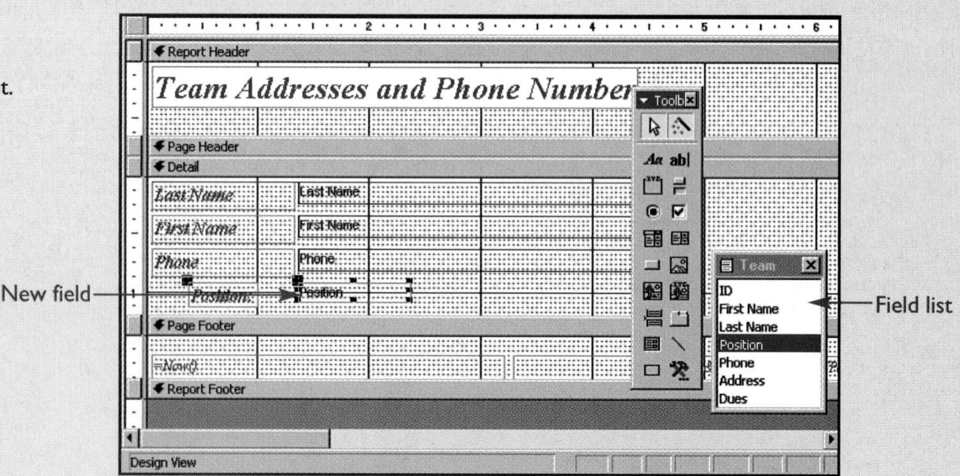

Figure 5.13 You can add fields to a report using the Field list.

8. **Point to the Phone field text box above the new Position text box. Hold down Shift, and click. The Phone and Position boxes should both be selected.**
9. **Choose Format, Size, To Widest to match the length of the two boxes.**
10. **Choose Format, Size, To Tallest to match the height of the two boxes.**
11. **Choose Format, Align, Left to match the alignment of the two boxes.**
12. **Click in an unused space in the Detail area to deselect the boxes.**
13. **Select the field label box for Position. Grab the center handle on the left edge of the field label box and drag to the left until it is lined up with the left edge of the Phone field label box.**
14. **Click the Print Preview button on the toolbar.**
    The new field should now match the other boxes in size and alignment. However, the other field text boxes have a border. Next you add the border to the Position text box.
15. **Click the Close button to return to Design view, and click the Position field text box to select it.**
16. **Click the down arrow to the right of the Line/Border Width button (see Figure 5.14).**

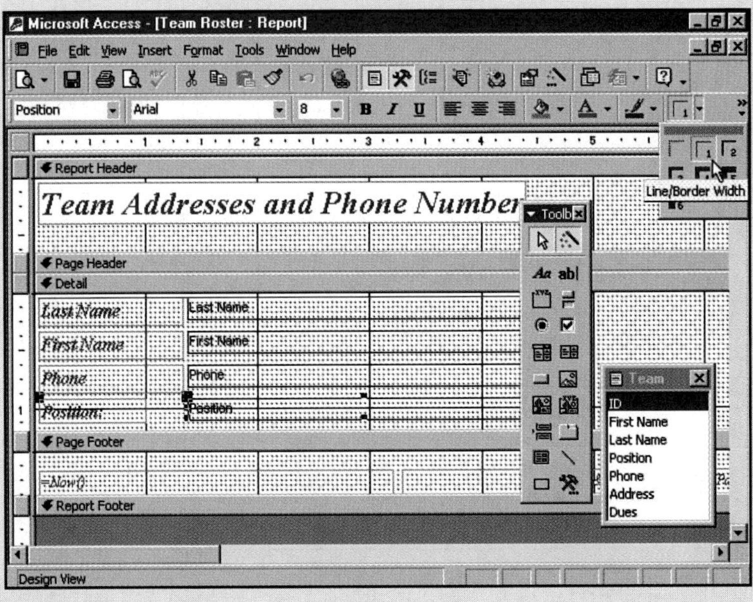

Figure 5.14
Use the Line/Border Width button to add a border or to change the color of a border of a selected control.

17. **Select border option 1. Keep this report open for the next lesson.**
    You might want to use the Print Preview option to make sure the Position field now has a border that matches the other fields.

Modifying Reports Created by Wizards

The report wizards provide you with all the necessary elements of a report and enable you to place these elements in their proper locations. The wizards save you time, but seldom provide finished reports. You almost always need to modify field lengths, add or format labels, modify the spacing between fields, and change locations of some of the elements. If you are asked to create a report using a wizard, make sure you use the Print Preview feature to scan through the data and look for fields that might have been cut off and need to be modified.

Lesson 5: Saving the Report with a New Name

As you modify a report, you might decide that you want to keep the original report as well as your modified version. If this is the case, you can save the modified report with a new name. Doing so enables you to use both reports.

In addition to saving the report with a new name, you should change the report header to reflect the purpose of the new report.

To Save the Report with a New Name

1. **With the Roster report still onscreen, choose File, Save As from the menu.**
   The Save As dialog box displays with the original name listed (see Figure 5.15).

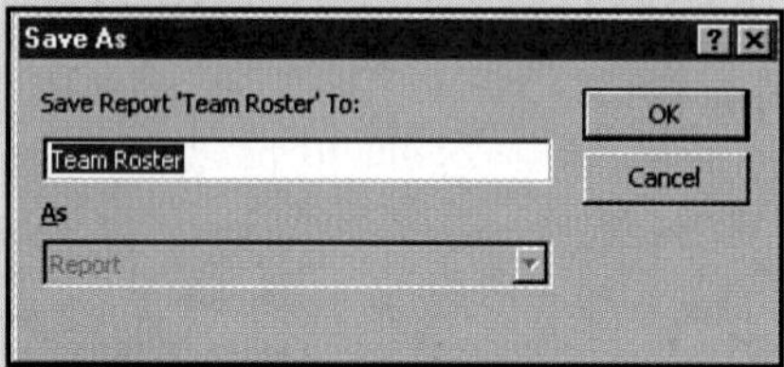

Figure 5.15
When you choose Save As, Access displays the original name in the New Name box.

2. **Type `Phone List` and click OK.**
   The report is saved with a new name.
3. **Click the label box in the Report Header section.**
   Here you want to replace the existing text with a more descriptive title.
4. **Drag across the existing text to select it; type `Phone List`.**
   The new text replaces the selected text.

5. **Click the Save button.**
   This step saves your changes to the Phone List report by writing over the report with that name. Keep the Phone List report open and continue to the next lesson, where you learn to add labels to a report.

Creating a Duplicate Report
You can also create a duplicate report from the Database window. With the Reports tab selected, right-click the report name, and select Copy from the shortcut menu. Right-click again in an open area of the window, and select Paste from the shortcut menu. Give the duplicate report a new name when prompted.

Lesson 6: Adding Labels to Reports

When you create a report using a wizard, the labels tend to be short and nondescriptive. After you modify the report, as you did in Lesson 4, you often find that additional labels are necessary to explain exactly what is on the report. Access gives you an easy way to add labels to either the report header or the page header. Labels you add to the report header show up on the first page of the report; labels you add to the Page Header area appear at the top of every page.

In this lesson, you add the team name to the Page Header area.

To Add Labels

1. **With the Phone List report open in Design view, grab the line between the Page Header and the Detail section and drag down to make the Page Header area about 1/2" high.**
   You use this space to place the new text label.

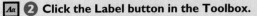

2 Click the Label button in the Toolbox.

When you move the pointer over an open area of the Design window, the pointer turns into a large A with a crosshair attached.

3 Click in the Page Header section and drag down and to the right until you have a text box about 2" wide and 1/4" high.

You can enter text in this label box (see Figure 5.16).

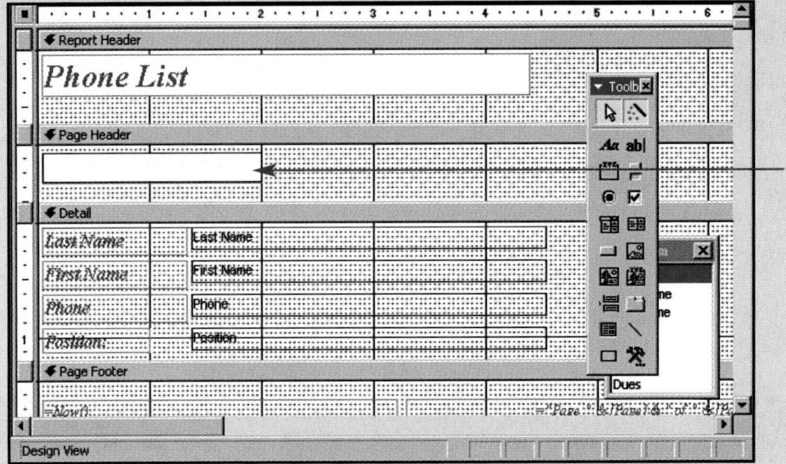

Figure 5.16 The Label button in the Toolbox enables you to add new labels.

4 Type `The Oakville Tigers` in the label box.

If the text is too long for the box you created, you can select the box and resize it to fit.

5 Click in an open area of the Page Header section.

This action turns off the text-editing mode.

6 Click the Print Preview button.

The original title and the new title you just added display at the top of the report (see Figure 5.17). You can advance to the second page to view the report heading and the page header.

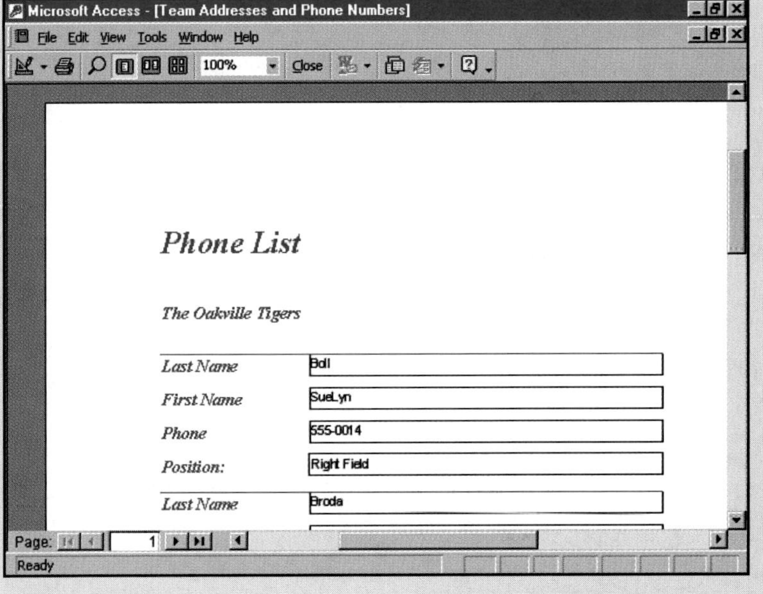

Figure 5.17 The new label appears at the top of every page of the report.

continues ▶

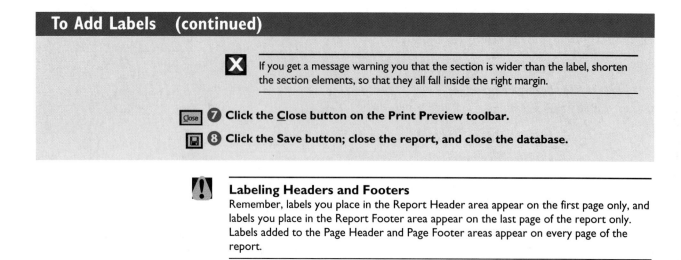

To Add Labels (continued)

If you get a message warning you that the section is wider than the label, shorten the section elements, so that they all fall inside the right margin.

7. **Click the Close button on the Print Preview toolbar.**

8. **Click the Save button; close the report, and close the database.**

Labeling Headers and Footers
Remember, labels you place in the Report Header area appear on the first page only, and labels you place in the Report Footer area appear on the last page of the report only. Labels added to the Page Header and Page Footer areas appear on every page of the report.

If you have completed your session on the computer, exit Access and Windows before you turn off the computer. Otherwise, continue with the Checking Concepts and Terms section of this project.

Summary

The main output component of Access is the report. Although you can print a table, as you did in this project, reports are designed to be printed for presentation to others. In this project, you created a report using the Report Wizard. You printed the report and renamed it. You then learned some of the techniques that you can use to modify a report, such as how to add and resize fields. After modifying a report you saved it with a new name using the Save As command. Finally, you used the Label tool to add a label to the report.

Access includes several different report styles and options that you can use, as you saw when you used the wizard. To expand your knowledge, create a report, and explore the different options that display in the wizard to see the alternatives. Use Help, and read the topic, `Reports: What they are and how they work`. Also review the topic, `Print a report`. Continue with the exercises at the end of this project to practice creating reports.

Checking Concepts and Terms

True/False

For each of the following, check *T* or *F* to indicate whether the statement is true or false.

__T __F **1.** To print table data, you have to use a Report Wizard. You can't print directly from the table. [L1]

__T __F **2.** You can modify the report layout in Print Preview mode. [L4]

__T __F **3.** To rename a report in the Database window, click the report name and type the new name. [L3]

__T __F **4.** You cannot add new fields to an existing report. [L4]

__T __F **5.** To add a label to a report, you use the Label tool in the Toolbox. [L6]

__T __F **6.** When you drag a field name into a report, the mouse pointer turns into a small field box. [L4]

__T __F **7.** To save a report with a new name, select Save As from the File menu. [L5]

__T __F **8.** If you delete a field text box, its label box is also deleted. [L4]

__T __F **9.** The expression [#Pages] in the footer inserts page numbers in the Page X of Y format in your report. [L4]

__T __F **10.** If the data in a report is too wide to fit in Portrait orientation, it may fit in Landscape orientation. [L3]

Multiple Choice

Circle the letter of the correct answer for each of the following.

1. Which of the following choices is not one of the selections when you select New from the Reports window? [L2]

a. Report Wizard

b. Double-column

c. AutoReport: Tabular

d. AutoReport: Columnar

2. To change the orientation of the report, which command do you use under the File menu? [L1]

a. Print Setup

b. Print Orientation

c. Page Setup

d. Printer Setup

3. How do you delete a control from a report? [L4]

a. Click it and press Del.

b. Drag it off the report.

c. Double-click it and press Del.

d. Press Backspace.

4. To make a group of text boxes the same dimension from top to bottom, select Format, Size, and ______________. [L4]

a. Tallest

b. Highest

c. Height, Tallest

d. Largest

5. An AutoReport includes which of the following? [L2]

a. All nonautomatic fields in the table or query

b. All fields in the database

c. The fields you designate in the third dialog box

d. All fields in the source table or query

Screen ID

Label each element of the Access screen shown in Figure 5.18.

Figure 5.18

A. Expression

B. Label button

C. Field label

D. Ruler

E. Field list

F. Print preview button

G. Field list button

H. Toolbox button

I. Field text box

J. Label

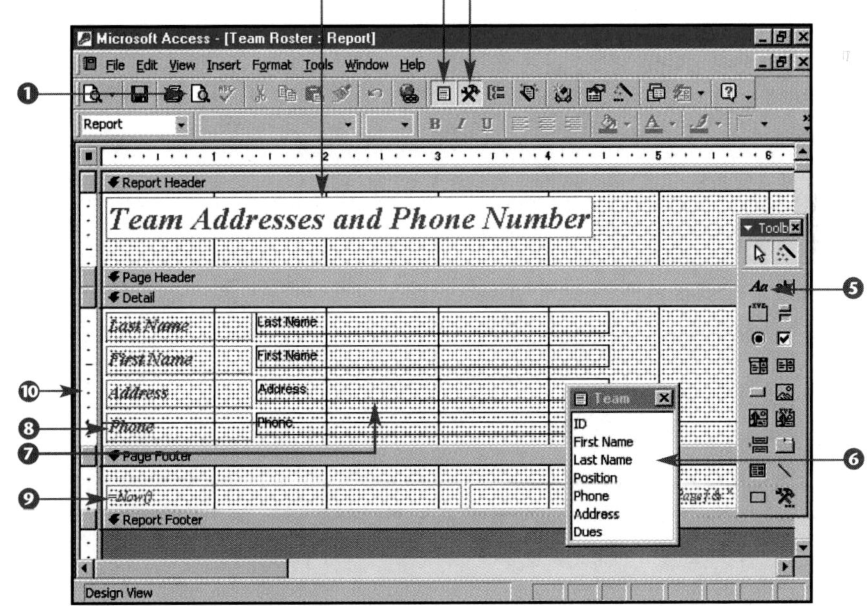

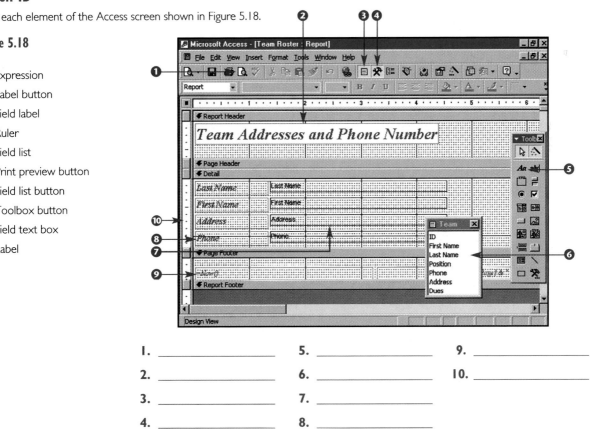

1. ______________ **5.** ______________ **9.** ______________

2. ______________ **6.** ______________ **10.** ______________

3. ______________ **7.** ______________

4. ______________ **8.** ______________

Discussion Questions

1. Why do companies produce reports? What are some of the goals or purposes of reports that are created from databases?
2. In databases that you use, what are the reports that are produced? How are they organized? How are they sorted?
3. What formatting has been applied to reports you use that make them easier to read and understand? What techniques have you seen in Access reports that are comparable to the formatting in the reports you use?
4. If you were to redesign a report that you currently receive, how would you organize the information? Think about bank statements, utility bills, and other bills that you might receive. These statements are reports to customers.
5. Look for an example of a report that you think is well done and share it with class members; point out what makes this report easy to understand.

Skill Drill

Skill Drill exercises reinforce project skills. Each skill reinforced is the same, or nearly the same, as a skill presented in the project. Each exercise includes a brief narrative introduction, followed by detailed instructions in a step-by-step format.

The database you use for these exercises contains tornado data for the state of Arizona. These records cover a 45-year time span and include all the confirmed sightings during that period. The records are an abbreviated form of records produced by the National Oceanic and Atmospheric Administration (NOAA). The fields included in this sample table include the year, date, time of day, number of people killed, number of people injured, a damage scale, the county, and the F-scale (a measure of tornado intensity). Many of the fields are blank because there were no casualties or damage, or because the F-scale was not recorded.

1. Printing Data from a Table

You want a quick printout of the tornadoes in Arizona over the past 45 years. The layout is not important, and because there are not a lot of fields, you decide to print the information directly from the table. [L1]

To print data from a table, complete the following steps:

1. Find the AO-0502 database file on your CD-ROM; copy it to drive A. Remove the read-only status, and name it **Arizona Tornadoes**. Select and open the Arizona Tornadoes table and examine the fields. Notice that the records display in chronological order.
2. Click the Print Preview button to make sure the fields fit across the page in the portrait orientation.
3. Click the View button to return to Datasheet view.
4. Select File, Print from the menu.
5. Print only the second page.
6. Close the table.

2. Creating a Report Using the Report Wizard

Printing directly from the table enabled you to quickly scan the data, but it did not give you any real control over the final product. You decide to use the Report Wizard to build a more useful, attractive report. [L2]

To create a report using the Report Wizard, complete the following steps:

1. Click the Reports object button.
2. Click the New button.
3. Select the Arizona Tornadoes table and choose the Report Wizard.
4. Select all the fields.
5. Group on the County field.
6. Sort on the Year field first and then on the Date field.
7. Choose the Block layout.
8. Select the Soft Gray style.
9. Edit the report title to read **Arizona Tornadoes**.
10. Maximize the Print Preview window and scroll down to look at your new report. Leave the report open for the next exercise.

3. Printing a Report

Reports are created with one thing in mind—publishing, to either paper or the Web. You decide you would like to see how your report looks on paper. [L3]

To print a report, complete the following steps:

1. Click the Preview window to see the whole page. You want to set it up with a wider left margin so that it can be put in a binder.
2. Select File, Page Setup from the menu.
3. Change the Left margin to 1.25" and the Right margin to 0.75".
4. Select File, Print from the menu.
5. Print only page 1.

4. Modifying a Report

The report you created using the wizard looks pretty good, but the title is not terribly descriptive. You decide to add the period of time covered by the report. [L4–5]

To modify a report label, complete the following steps:

1. Click the View button to move to the report Design view.
2. In the report header, click the title to select it.
3. Grab the center handle on the right edge of the title and drag it to the 6" mark. (If your rulers are not turned on, choose View, Ruler from the menu.)
4. Modify the title so it reads **Arizona Tornadoes, 1951-1995**.
5. Click the View button to see your changes.
6. Save your changes and close the report.

5. Changing Character Formatting in a Report

The report is looking better and better, but a few more changes would make it really easy to read. First, the text in the Detail area is a little small, and second, the names of the counties could be emphasized a little more. [L4]

To change character formatting in a report, complete the following steps:

1. Open the Arizona Tornadoes table in Design view.
2. Move the pointer to the ruler to the left of the Detail area until it changes to an arrow pointing right.
3. Click to select all the fields.
4. Click the Font Size button and change the font size from 11 points to 12 points.
5. Click in an open area to deselect the fields, and click the County field to select it.
6. Click the Bold and Italic buttons to add character formatting to the county names.
7. Click the View button to see the changes to your report. Leave the report open for the next exercise.

6. Adding a Label to a Report

One last thing is needed to finish the report—a subtitle to show where the information came from. It is always good form to give your sources, even when the sources are public domain. [L5]

To add a label to a report, complete the following steps:

1. Click the View button to return to Design view.
2. Click the Label button and draw a label box about 1/4" high and 3" wide just below the title in the report header.
3. Type **National Oceanic and Atmospheric Administration (NOAA)** in the text box. Notice what happens when you get to the end of the text box.
4. Click in an open area to deselect the label, and then click the label box to select it again.
5. Click the Italic button.
6. Click the Font/Fore Color button, and select white to change the color of the font to match the title.
7. Click the View button to see the results of your changes. Your report should look like Figure 5.19.
8. Choose File, Print from the menu and print page 1.
9. Save your changes and close the report.

Figure 5.19

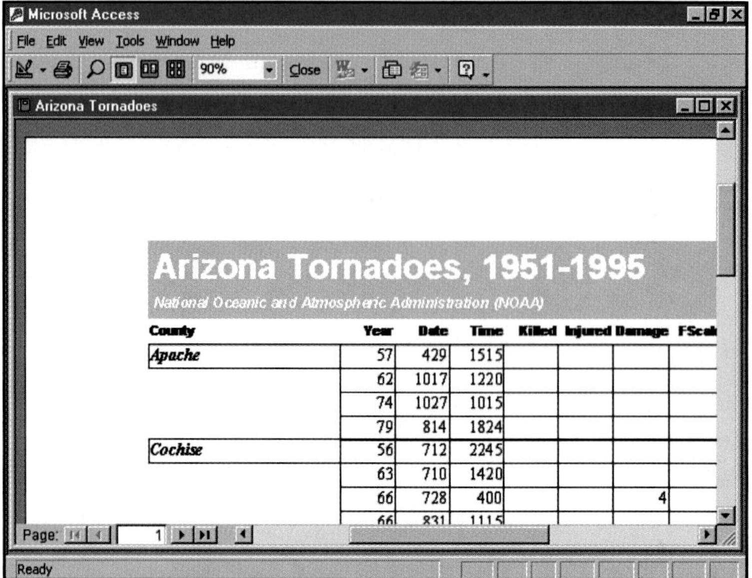

Challenge

Challenge exercises expand on or are somewhat related to skills presented in the lessons. Each exercise provides a brief narrative introduction followed by instructions, in a numbered step or bulleted list format, that are not as detailed as those in the Skill Drill section.

The database you use for the Challenge section is the same one you used in the Skill Drill section, including the changes you made.

1. Creating a Report Using the AutoReport: Columnar Option

Access has several other ways to create reports that you have not yet tried. You decide to try a couple of them just to see what they look like. The first one you try is the AutoReport: Columnar option. [L2, 5]

To create a report using the AutoReport: Columnar option, complete the following steps:

1. Copy the **`AO-0503`** database file to drive A; remove the read-only status, and rename it **`Arizona Tornadoes 2`**.
2. Switch to the Reports window and create a new report.
3. Create an AutoReport: Columnar report based on the Arizona Tornadoes table.
4. Scroll down and look at the layout of the report. Move to Design view, and examine the structure of the report.
5. Print the first page of the report. Save the report as **`Column Report`** and close it.

2. Creating a Report Using the AutoReport: Tabular Option

You've tried the AutoReport: Columnar option and can't figure out how you'd ever use it. Maybe the AutoReport: Tabular option would produce better results. [L2, 5]

To create a report using the AutoReport: Tabular option, complete the following steps:

1. Create a new report.
2. Create an AutoReport: Tabular report based on the Arizona Tornadoes table.
3. Scroll down and look at the layout of the report. Move to Design view, and examine the structure of the report. Which of the two AutoReports do you think would be the most useful the majority of the time?
4. Print the first page of the report. Save the report as **`Tabular Report`** and close it.

3. Summarizing Data in a Report

As you create reports in the future, you will often want to summarize the data grouped on a field. Access enables you to print all the data along with summaries, or just the summaries themselves. In this exercise, you create a report that summarizes tornado data by county. [L2]

To summarize data in a report, complete the following steps:

1. Create a new report based on the Arizona Tornadoes table using the Report Wizard.
2. Select all the fields and group by county. Don't sort the records, but click the Summary Options button on the Sorting dialog box.
3. In the Summary Options dialog box, choose to Sum the Killed and Injured fields, and Avg (average) the Damage and FScale fields.
4. In the same dialog box, choose to display the Summary Only.
5. Use the Outline 2 layout and the Portrait orientation. Select the Bold style.
6. Name the new report **`County Summaries`**. Notice that some of the categories are empty and some are shown with seven decimal places. A part of the second page is shown in Figure 5.20.

Figure 5.20

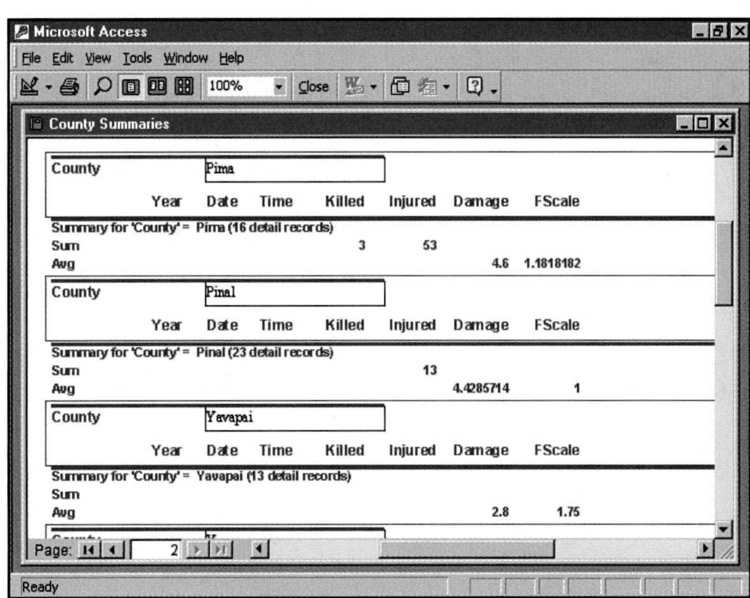

7. Leave the report open for the next exercise.

4. Formatting the Numbers on Reports

The number of decimal places in the Damage and FScale fields are inconsistent. You would like to fix them so that both fields display the results to one decimal place. [L4–5]

To format the numbers in a report, complete the following steps:

1. In Design view, select both the Damage and the FScale summary fields in the County Footer area.
2. Click the Properties button.
3. Use the Help menu to figure out how to set the numbers to a fixed format, and the decimal places to 1.
4. Click the View button to make sure you set both formatting options.
5. Print the first page of the report. Save your changes and close the report.

5. Changing the Report Sort Order

You like the Arizona Tornadoes report in general, but you wonder what the results would be if you deleted some data and shifted some of the information around. [L2]

To change the report sort order, complete the following steps:

1. Open the Arizona Tornadoes report in Design view.
2. Find the Sorting and Grouping button.
3. Use the Help options available to you to help you delete the Year and Date fields from the sorting area. Add the FScale field and sort in descending order.
4. Look at a preview of your report.
5. Print the first page of the report. Save your changes and close the report.

6. Draw Lines in a Report

Looking at the report entitled Tabular Report that you created earlier in this Challenge section, you decide that you would like to try adding a line under the title. [L2]

To draw lines in a report, complete the following steps:

1. Open the Tabular Report in Design view.
2. Find the Line button and draw a straight line under the title in the report header.
3. If the line is not solid, use the available Help to figure out how to change the line to a solid line. (*Hint*: The line style is a property of the line.)
4. Change the line color to red.
5. View your changes. Save the report and close it.

Discovery Zone

Discovery Zone exercises help you gain advanced knowledge of project topics and/or application of skills. These exercises focus on enhancing your problem-solving skills.

1. Changing the Grouping of Report Data and Keeping the Groups Together

When you finally get your report finished, you might decide that you want to change its focus. You might also consider copying and pasting the report to save you the work of creating another one. You can then use the new copy to display the data in a different manner. For example, in the Arizona Tornadoes report, you grouped the data on the County field and sorted on the Year and Date fields. Suppose you also wanted to be able to examine the data by year, and you wanted to make sure the tornadoes of one year did not overlap from one page to the next.

Goal: Change the grouping field in an existing report and have the report keep the data from the grouped field together (on the same page) in the report.

Use the AO-0504 file to create a new database called `Arizona Tornadoes by Year` on your disk. Use Help from your computer or online to understand how to change the grouped field and how to keep the data together for each of the grouped items. You modify the Arizona Tornadoes report. To modify this report you should:

- Change the grouping to the Year field, rather than the County field.
- Change the sort field to the Date field only.
- Change the character formatting to bold for the Year field and remove the bold formatting from the County field.
- Swap the locations of the County field and the Year field.
- Have the county name show in every record, but have the year display only when it changes. (That is, each year should be displayed only once.)

Hint 1: A button on the Report Design toolbar can lead you to a way to make several of the changes.

Hint 2: You can eliminate duplicate years in the Properties box.

Your grouped report should look like Figure 5.21.

Figure 5.21

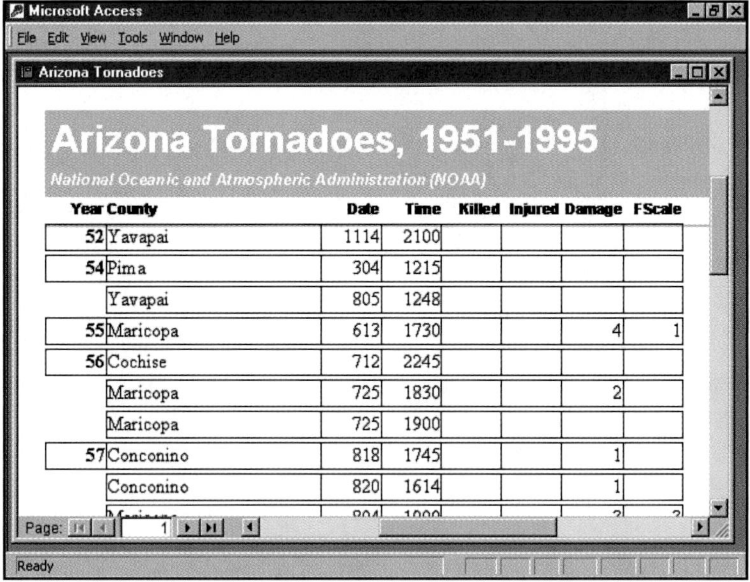

2. Creating Mailing Labels Using the Label Wizard

If you are creating a database for a business, a church, or an organization, you might often use your reports to create mailing labels. Mailing labels are usually printed on special sheets that contain ready-to-use labels in various sizes. The Avery company specializes in making labels that fit every need, from folder labels to nametags. Each of the different types of label has its own "Avery number." When you set up your mailing label, you need to know which Avery label you are using. The wizard asks for the Avery number and automatically sets up the page for you.

Goal: Create a report using the Label Wizard that generates mailing labels from a table of addresses.

Use the `AO-0505` file to create a new database called `Address Labels` on your disk. Read through the Access Help on mailing labels to understand how the wizard works. Also, carefully read the Help provided on each of the wizard screens. Use the following guidelines:

- The report should use Avery #5160 labels.
- The font should be normal (no special character formatting), 10 point.
- The first row should contain the First Name and Last Name fields with a space between them.
- The second row of the labels should contain the Address field.
- The third row of the labels should contain the City field, followed by a comma and a space, and then the State field, a space, and finally the ZIP field.
- Name your report `Contact Mailing Labels`.

Preview the page and print the labels.

Your report should look like Figure 5.22.

Figure 5.22

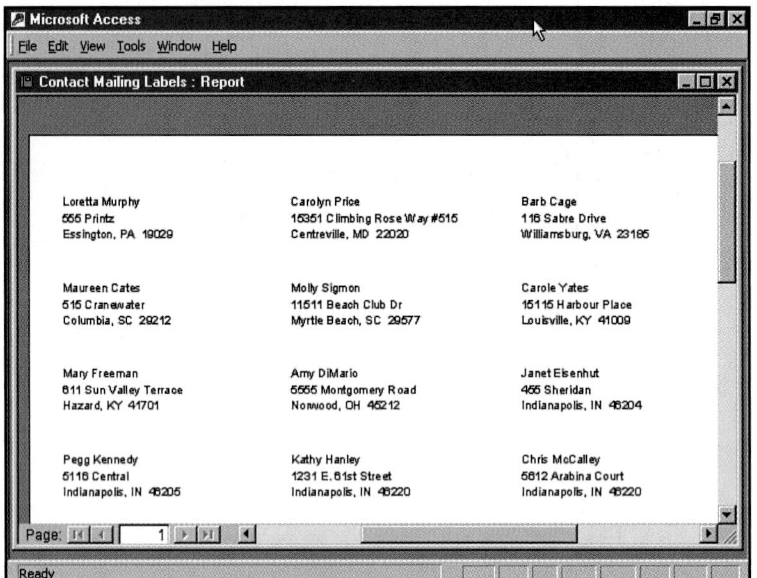
Microsoft Access
File Edit View Tools Window Help
Contact Mailing Labels : Report
Loretta Murphy
555 Printz
Essington, PA 19029
Carolyn Price
15351 Climbing Rose Way #515
Centreville, MD 22020
Barb Cage
116 Sabre Drive
Williamsburg, VA 23185
Maureen Cates
515 Cranewater
Columbia, SC 29212
Molly Sigmon
11511 Beach Club Dr
Myrtle Beach, SC 29577
Carole Yates
15115 Harbour Place
Louisville, KY 41009
Mary Freeman
811 Sun Valley Terrace
Hazard, KY 41701
Amy DiMario
5555 Montgomery Road
Norwood, OH 45212
Janet Eisenhut
455 Sheridan
Indianapolis, IN 46204
Pegg Kennedy
5116 Central
Indianapolis, IN 46205
Kathy Hanley
1231 E. 61st Street
Indianapolis, IN 46220
Chris McCalley
5812 Arabina Court
Indianapolis, IN 46220
Page: 1
Ready

Project 6

Interacting and Connecting

Objectives

In this project, you learn how to

- **Convert a Database from a Previous Version of Access**
- **Link an Access Table to a Form Letter in Word**
- **Merge an Access Table with a Form Letter**
- **Import a Table from Excel**
- **Save a Form as a Data Access Page**
- **Use a Browser to Interact with the Database**

Key terms introduced in this project include

- delimiter
- mail merge

Why Would I Do This?

As you have seen, the data in a database may come from another source—another database, a spreadsheet, or even the Internet. The files you interact with might be on your computer or on a computer anywhere in the world. The tornado information that you used in an earlier project, for example, was obtained over the Internet from the U.S. Storm Data Center. You can also use the power of Access in combination with Microsoft Word to produce form letters so that you can send data to people individually.

The reports, queries, and forms you create might need to be seen by others. Access is capable of placing information on the World Wide Web so that it can be accessed from anywhere in the world.

Visual Summary

When you have completed this lesson, you will have created a document that merges data from a table of addresses, imported a table of data from a non-Access source, and set up the database for use on the Internet. The merged document, the imported table, and a form as a Web page look like Figures 6.1, 6.2, and 6.3.

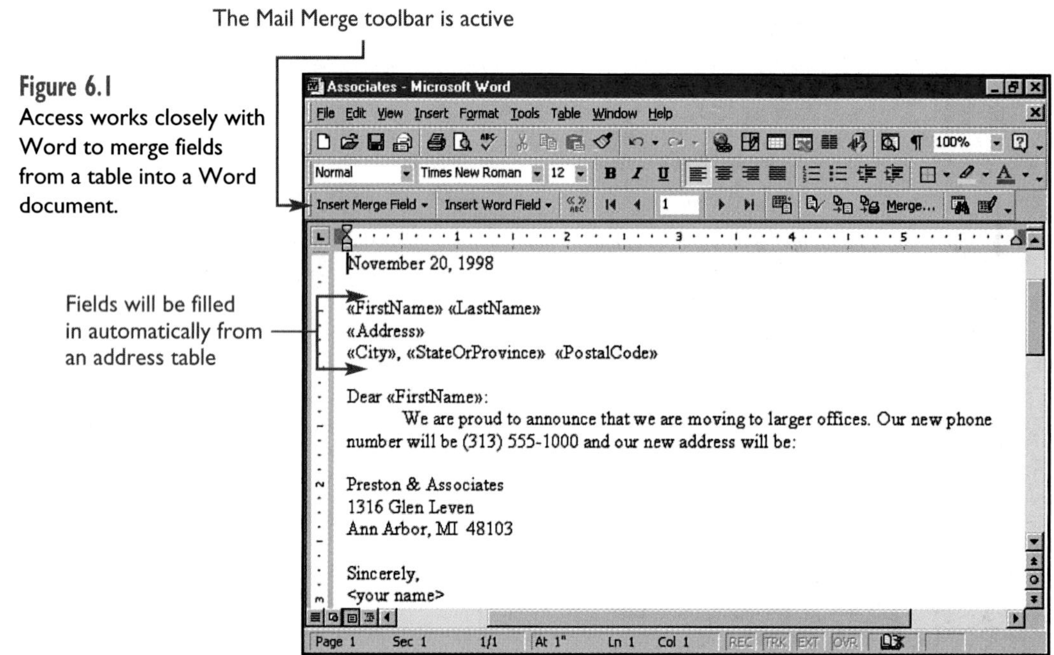

The Mail Merge toolbar is active
Fields will be filled in automatically from an address table
Associates - Microsoft Word
Insert Merge Field
Insert Word Field
Merge...
November 20, 1998
«FirstName» «LastName»
«Address»
«City», «StateOrProvince» «PostalCode»
Dear «FirstName»:
We are proud to announce that we are moving to larger offices. Our new phone number will be (313) 555-1000 and our new address will be:
Preston & Associates
1316 Glen Leven
Ann Arbor, MI 48103
Sincerely,
<your name>

Figure 6.1
Access works closely with Word to merge fields from a table into a Word document.

Excel column headings become Access field names

A primary key field has been added

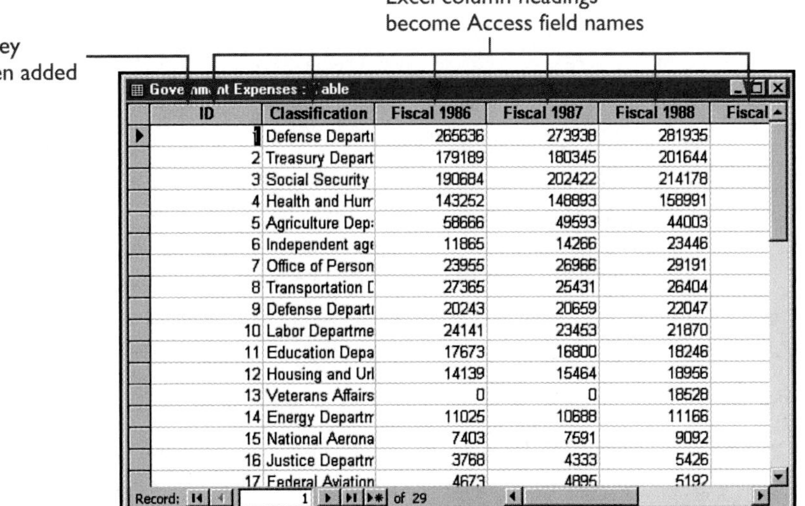

Government Expenses : Table

ID	Classification	Fiscal 1986	Fiscal 1987	Fiscal 1988	Fiscal
1	Defense Departı	265636	273938	281935	
2	Treasury Depart	179189	180345	201644	
3	Social Security	190684	202422	214178	
4	Health and Hurr	143252	148893	158991	
5	Agriculture Dep:	58666	49593	44003	
6	Independent agı	11865	14266	23446	
7	Office of Person	23955	26966	29191	
8	Transportation [	27365	25431	26404	
9	Defense Departı	20243	20659	22047	
10	Labor Departme	24141	23453	21870	
11	Education Depa	17673	16800	18246	
12	Housing and Url	14139	15464	18956	
13	Veterans Affairs	0	0	18528	
14	Energy Departrr	11025	10688	11166	
15	National Aerona	7403	7591	9092	
16	Justice Departrr	3768	4333	5426	
17	Federal Aviation	4673	4895	5192	

Record: 1 of 29

Figure 6.2 Information has been imported from an Excel worksheet.

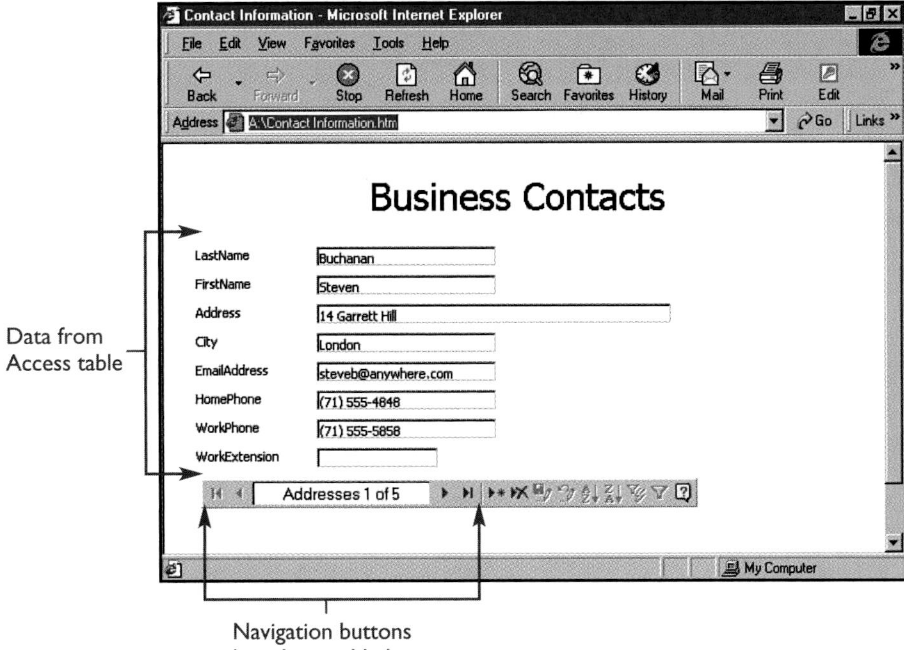

Data from Access table

Navigation buttons have been added

Figure 6.3 Access data can be displayed on the Web.

Lesson 1: Converting a Database from a Previous Version of Access

Access has changed its basic file structure to conform to an international standard that supports several languages. Access converts databases stored in previous versions of Access to the new version. Older versions of Access cannot read this data structure, and no program provided at this time can convert entire Access 2000 databases into older versions of Access, although Access can covert all but the new features from Access 2000 to Access 97. Access does not have a Save As option like the other Office products.

In this lesson, you convert a database from the Access 97 format.

To Convert a Database from a Previous Version of Access

1 Launch Access. Click OK to open an existing file.
Make sure you have a disk in drive A.

2 Find and select the `AO-0601` file on your CD-ROM. Click Open.
The Convert/Open Database dialog box displays (see Figure 6.4).

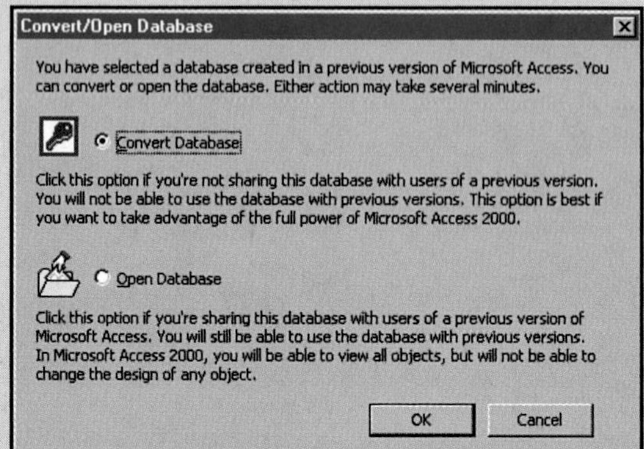

Figure 6.4 The Convert/Open Database dialog box enables you to convert databases created in older versions of Access.

3 Select the Convert Database option, and click OK.
The Convert Database Into window displays.

4 Choose 3 1/2 Floppy (A:) in the Save in box. Change the name to `Associates` in the File name box.
The dialog box should look like Figure 6.5.

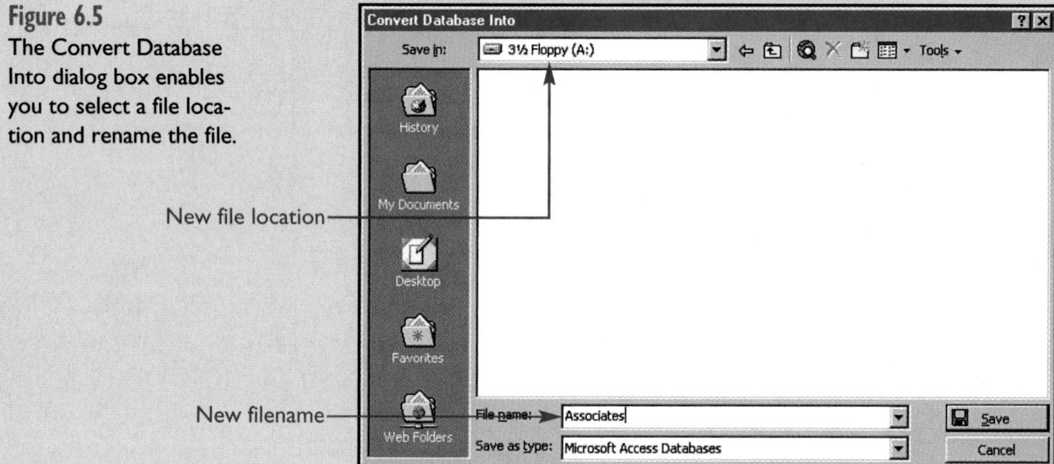

Figure 6.5 The Convert Database Into dialog box enables you to select a file location and rename the file.

5 Click Save.
The file is converted and placed on your disk. The process may take a while, depending on the speed of your computer. When it is done, the file opens automatically.

6 Leave the Associates database open for use in the next task.

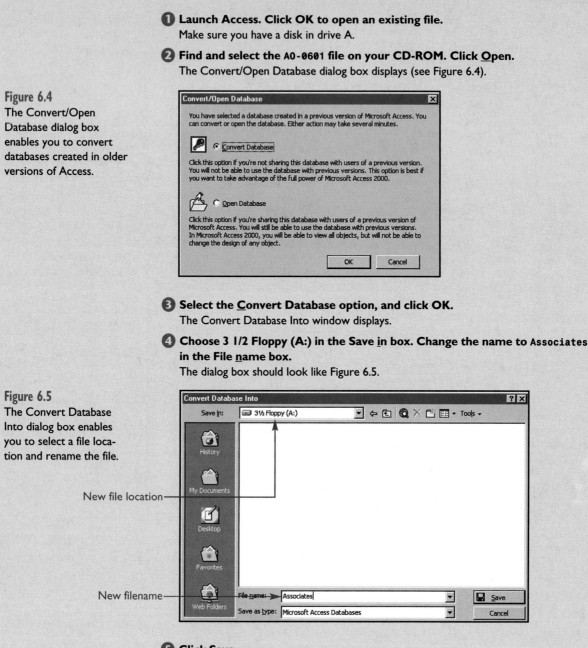

Sharing an Older Database

The Convert/Open Database window also enables you to use the database without updating it to Access 2000. This is particularly important if you are sharing the database with someone who is still using an older version of the program. The limitation is that you cannot change the design of any of the objects in the database. If you need to make structural changes, they must be made by the person using the older version.

Lesson 2: Linking an Access Table to a Form Letter in Word

You can merge databases that contain names and addresses with Microsoft Word documents to create a series of documents where each document contains data that is unique to that individual. This feature is known as ***mail merge***. We have all received mail that has a label attached with our names and addresses on it, and most of us have received letters that have our names, birthdays, addresses, or phone numbers embedded in the text. An organization can communicate with its members in a similar manner. Such mailings are not limited to the postal service—you can also create mailings that use fax or email.

In this lesson, you create a letter to notify your business associates that you are moving and will have a new address and phone number.

To Link an Access Table to a Form Letter in Word

1. **If it is not already highlighted, select the Addresses table. Click the list arrow to the right of the Office Links button on the Standard toolbar.**
   A list of links to other Microsoft Office programs displays.

2. **Click Merge It with MS Word.**
   The Microsoft Word Mail Merge Wizard dialog box displays (see Figure 6.6).

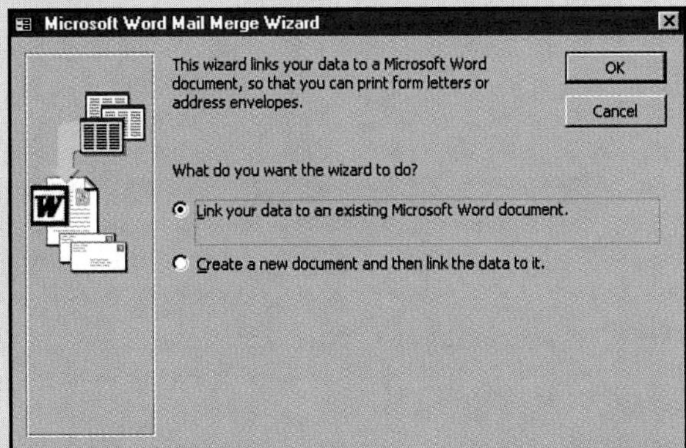

Figure 6.6
The Microsoft Word Mail Merge Wizard dialog box enables you to link to an existing document or to create a new one.

3. **Click the Create a new document and link the data to it button. Click OK.**
   Microsoft Word launches, and a new document opens. Notice that the Mail Merge toolbar displays (see Figure 6.7).

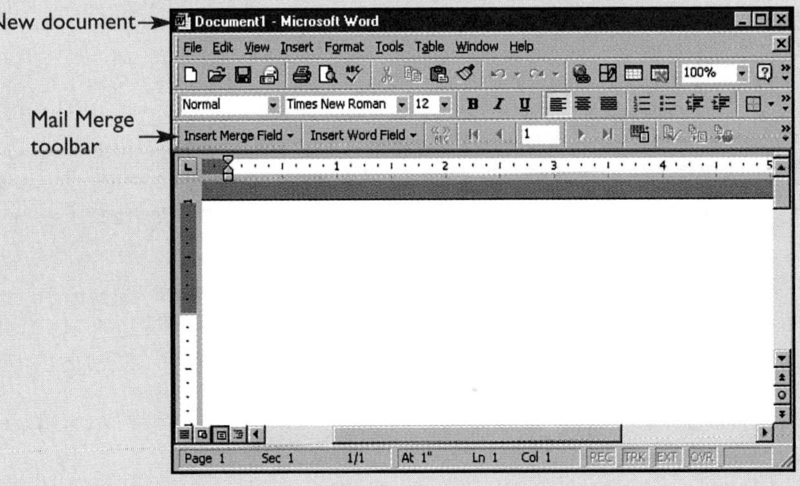

Figure 6.7
A new Microsoft Word document opens with the Mail Merge toolbar displayed.

continues ▶

To Link an Access Table to a Form Letter in Word (continued)

The Mail Merge toolbar should open. It might be above or below the Formatting or Standard toolbar. If it does not open, you can open it by choosing View, Toolbars from the menu and clicking Mail Merge to open the toolbar.

4. **Maximize the Word window, change the Zoom to 100%, and set the Font Size to 12.**

5. **Type today's date in the first line and press ↵Enter twice.**
   Notice that when you begin typing the date, Word automatically suggests the month and the date. You can press ↵Enter to accept the month, and press Spacebar. Press ↵Enter again when today's date appears. Word completes the date for you. Press ↵Enter twice more to move the insertion point down two lines.

6. **Click the Insert Merge Field button on the Mail Merge toolbar.**
   A list of fields from the Addresses table in the Associates database displays.

7. **Click FirstName.**
   The name of the field is placed in the document.

8. **Press Spacebar to enter a blank space after the first name. Click the Insert Merge Field button again and click LastName.**

9. **Press ↵Enter to move to the next line of the address. Refer to Figure 6.8 to create the rest of the document.**
   Type your name in the last line rather than <your name>.

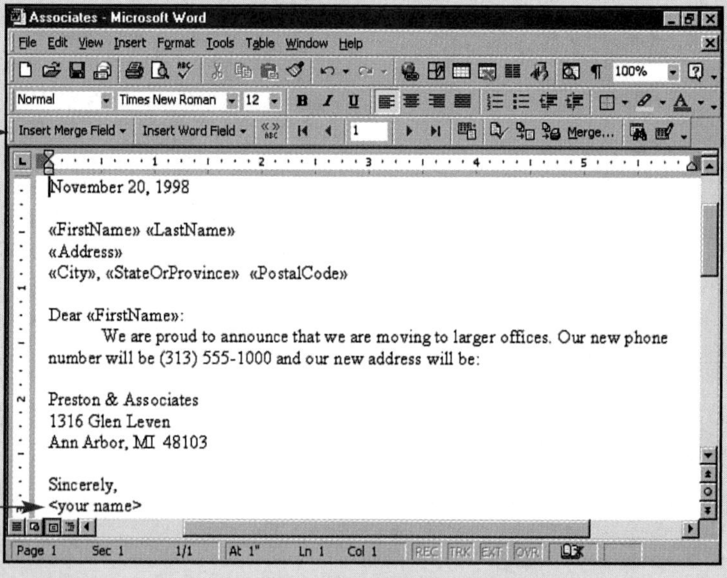

Figure 6.8
The Word document has been set up to use the Mail Merge feature.

Insert Merge Field button

Type your name here

November 20, 1998

«FirstName» «LastName»
«Address»
«City», «StateOrProvince» «PostalCode»

Dear «FirstName»:
We are proud to announce that we are moving to larger offices. Our new phone number will be (313) 555-1000 and our new address will be:

Preston & Associates
1316 Glen Leven
Ann Arbor, MI 48103

Sincerely,
<your name>

The font size on your letter might revert to 10 point or whatever default font is set for your computer. If this happens, don't worry about it. The goal of this lesson is to show you how to merge a database file with a Word document, and the formatting of the letter is not critical to this purpose.

10. **Click the Save button. The Save As window opens.**

11. **Type `Associates` in the File name box, and use the Save in box to select the folder that you are using for your files.**

12. **Click Save.**
    The document is saved as Associates for later use. Leave the document and the database open for use in the next lesson.

Office File Extensions
Microsoft Word documents are automatically saved with a file extension of .doc and Access databases are saved with an .mdb extension. You can use the same name for the Word document and the Access database because they have different extensions, even though the extensions might not appear on your screen.

Lesson 3: Merging an Access Table with a Form Letter

After you link the database field names to a Word document, you can create a series of documents with each one containing the data from a record in the database table. This process creates a file of the merged, personalized letters. You also learn how to print a few of the letters to ensure that they do not contain errors before you send the rest of them to the printer.

In this task, you merge the database file into the letter and print two of the documents.

To Merge an Access Table with a Form Letter

1. **Click the View Merged Data button.**
   The data from the first record in the Addresses table is inserted into the document (see Figure 6.9).

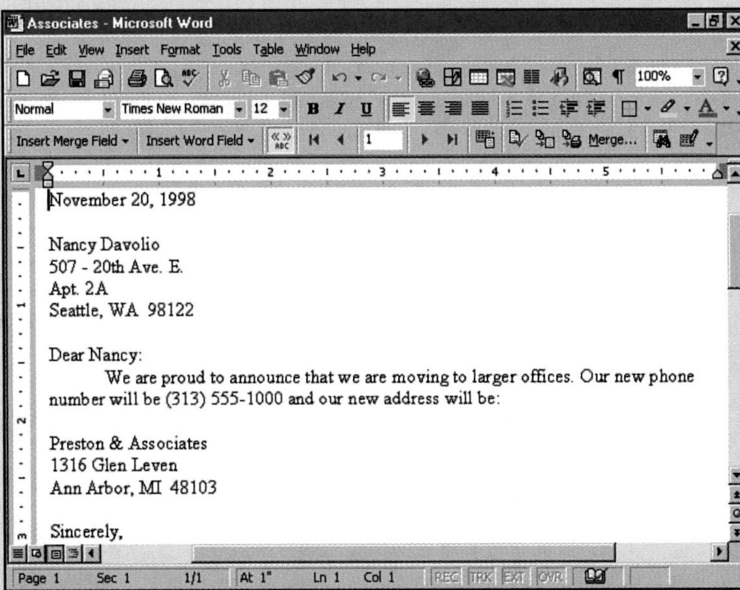
Associates - Microsoft Word
File Edit View Insert Format Tools Table Window Help
Normal
Times New Roman
12
100%
Insert Merge Field
Insert Word Field
Merge...
November 20, 1998
Nancy Davolio
507 - 20th Ave. E.
Apt. 2A
Seattle, WA 98122
Dear Nancy:
We are proud to announce that we are moving to larger offices. Our new phone number will be (313) 555-1000 and our new address will be:
Preston & Associates
1316 Glen Leven
Ann Arbor, MI 48103
Sincerely,
Page 1 Sec 1 1/1 At 1" Ln 1 Col 1 REC TRK EXT OVR

Figure 6.9
The Word document displays the data from the first record in the table.

2. **Click the Next Record button.**
   The data from the second record displays. Notice that the address of the first person takes two lines, while the second person's address takes only one line. Word adjusts for multiple line addresses and for empty fields.

3. **Click the Start Mail Merge button.**
   The Merge dialog box displays.

4. **Click the list arrow next to the Merge to box.**
   Notice that you can send this letter electronically by email or fax as well as by traditional postal service (see Figure 6.10).

continues ▶

To Merge an Access Table with a Form Letter (continued)

Figure 6.10
You can send the mail merge document by fax or to email addresses.

Optional document destinations

5 **Click Printer. Click the From box in the Records to be merged section and type `1`. Type `2` in the To box.**

6 **Click the Merge button to print the letters to the first two people in the Addresses table.**
The Print dialog box displays.

7 **Click OK.**
The first two letters print.

8 **Close the Associates Word document.**
Save any changes when prompted. Close Microsoft Word. Leave the Associates database open for use in the next task.

Lesson 4: Importing a Table from Excel

Excel has some database management features, such as the capability to sort and filter data. Therefore, many people use Excel as a crude database management program. At times, you might need to import data that is stored in an Excel worksheet and use it with an Access database.

In this task, you import an Excel worksheet that contains budget information for the U.S. government into the Associates database that is open from the previous task. The Associates database is being used for convenience—the information you import in the next task is not related to the address table in the database.

To Import a Table from Excel

1 **Launch Excel, and open `AO-0602` from the CD. Scroll down the rows and examine the data.**
Notice that each row is a record of a type of government expense. The column headings will become field names (see Figure 6.11).

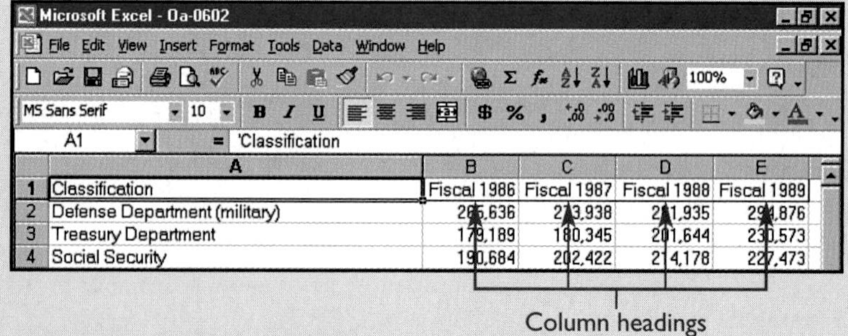

Figure 6.11
The Excel column headings will become Access field names.

2 **Close the file and close Excel.**
Switch to Access and the Associates database.

3 **Choose File, Get External Data, Import.**
The Import dialog box displays.

❹ **Click the list arrow next to the Files of type box and select Microsoft Excel. Locate and select the `AO-0602` Excel file on the CD.**

Your Import dialog box should look like Figure 6.12.

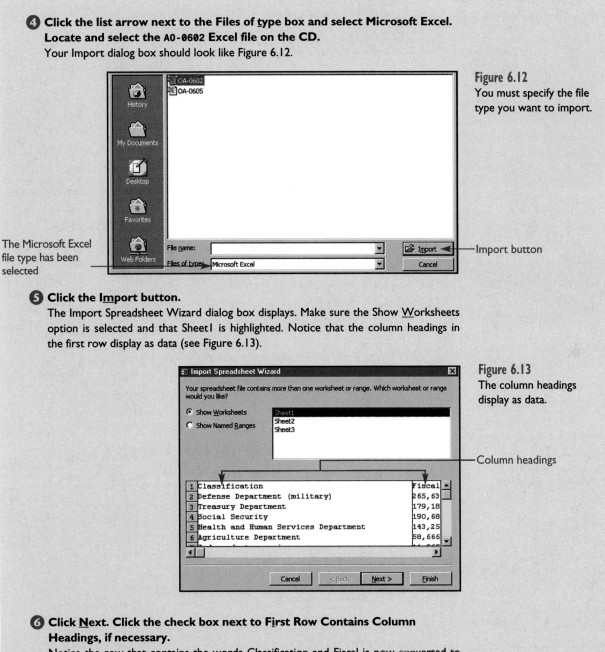

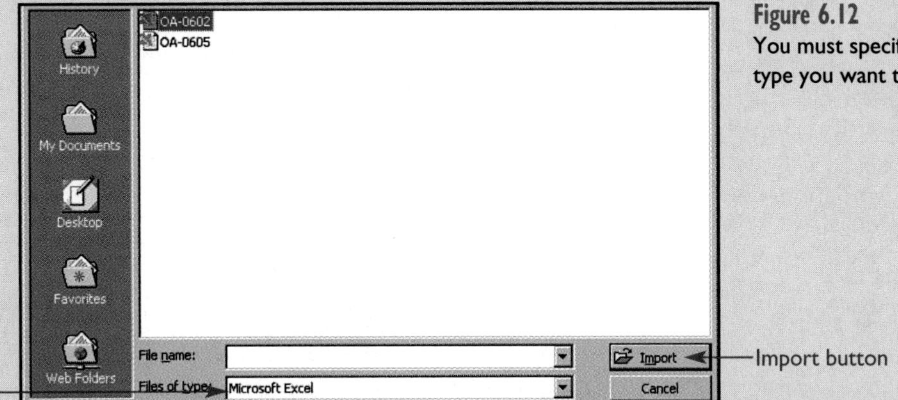

Figure 6.12
You must specify the file type you want to import.

❺ **Click the Import button.**

The Import Spreadsheet Wizard dialog box displays. Make sure the Show Worksheets option is selected and that Sheet1 is highlighted. Notice that the column headings in the first row display as data (see Figure 6.13).

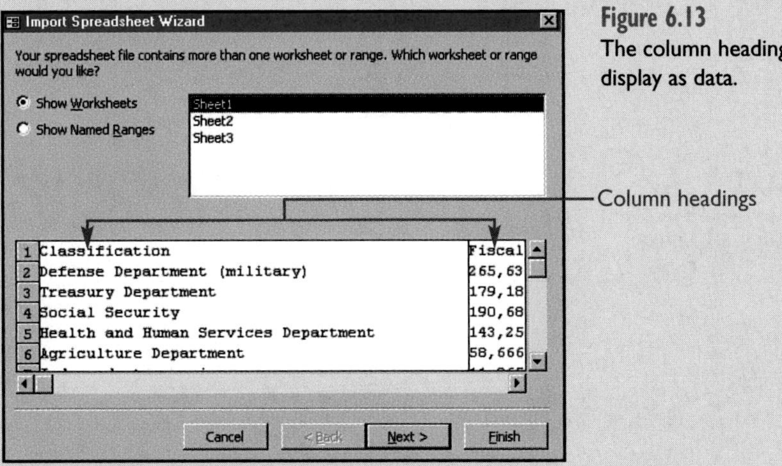

Figure 6.13
The column headings display as data.

❻ **Click Next. Click the check box next to First Row Contains Column Headings, if necessary.**

Notice the row that contains the words Classification and Fiscal is now converted to headers. These words will appear as field names in the database table (see Figure 6.14).

continues ▶

To Import a Table from Excel (continued)

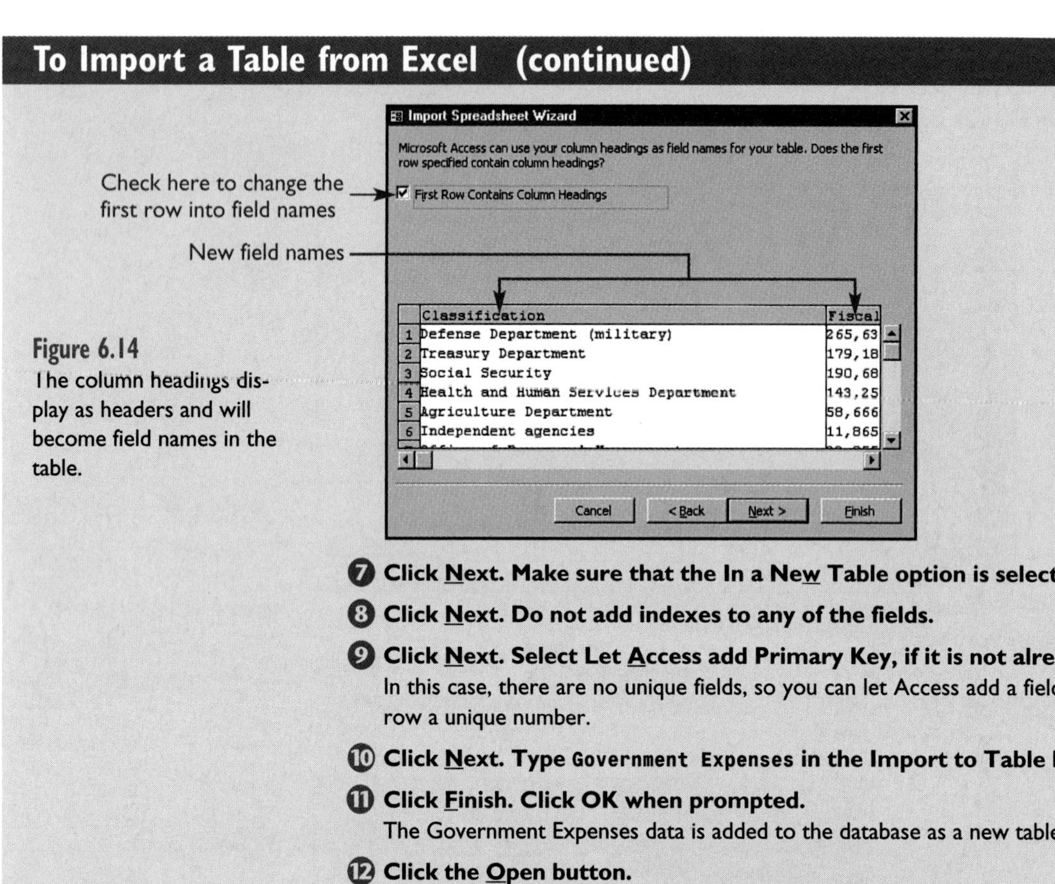

Figure 6.14
The column headings display as headers and will become field names in the table.

❼ **Click Next. Make sure that the In a New Table option is selected.**

❽ **Click Next. Do not add indexes to any of the fields.**

❾ **Click Next. Select Let Access add Primary Key, if it is not already selected.**
In this case, there are no unique fields, so you can let Access add a field that gives each row a unique number.

❿ **Click Next. Type `Government Expenses` in the Import to Table box.**

⓫ **Click Finish. Click OK when prompted.**
The Government Expenses data is added to the database as a new table.

⓬ **Click the Open button.**
The Government Expenses table displays (see Figure 6.15).

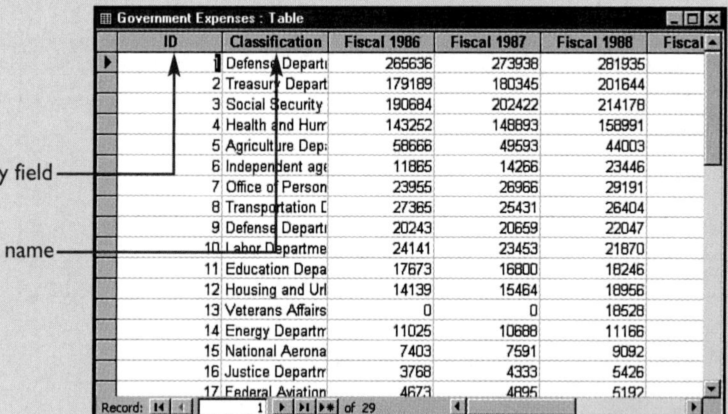

ID	Classification	Fiscal 1986	Fiscal 1987	Fiscal 1988	Fiscal
1	Defense Departi	265636	273938	281935	
2	Treasury Depart	179189	180345	201644	
3	Social Security	190684	202422	214178	
4	Health and Hum	143252	148893	158991	
5	Agriculture Dep	58666	49593	44003	
6	Independent age	11865	14266	23446	
7	Office of Person	23955	26966	29191	
8	Transportation D	27365	25431	26404	
9	Defense Departi	20243	20659	22047	
10	Labor Departme	24141	23453	21870	
11	Education Depa	17673	16800	18246	
12	Housing and Url	14139	15464	18956	
13	Veterans Affairs	0	0	18528	
14	Energy Departm	11025	10688	11166	
15	National Aerona	7403	7591	9092	
16	Justice Departm	3768	4333	5426	
17	Federal Aviation	4673	4895	5192	

Figure 6.15
The Excel worksheet has become an Access table.

⓭ **Click the Close Window button.**
This table is now available for use. Leave the Associates database open for the next lesson.

Setting Up the Excel Worksheet
A worksheet must be set up like a database table if you are going to import it successfully. Check to make sure that the Excel data is arranged in rows and columns, where each column is a field type and each row is a record. If necessary, copy the data to a new worksheet. Remove blank rows or rows that contain decorative characters such as long rows of dashes set up to look like a line.

Lesson 5: Saving a Form as a Data Access Page

Access 2000 is capable of saving forms as interactive Web pages that can be viewed with an Internet browser that supports XML features. You can place a database on a Web server and interact with it using a Web page.

In this lesson, you create a Web page that would allow your sales people to look up contact information.

To Save a Form as a Data Access Page

1. **Click the Pages object button and click New.**
   The New Data Access Page window displays.

2. **Select Page Wizard; choose the Addresses table as the data source, and click OK.**
   The first page of the Page Wizard displays.

3. **Use the Add button to select the following fields: FirstName, LastName, Address, City, EmailAddress, HomePhone, WorkPhone, WorkExtension, and FaxNumber.**
   Your dialog box should look like Figure 6.16.

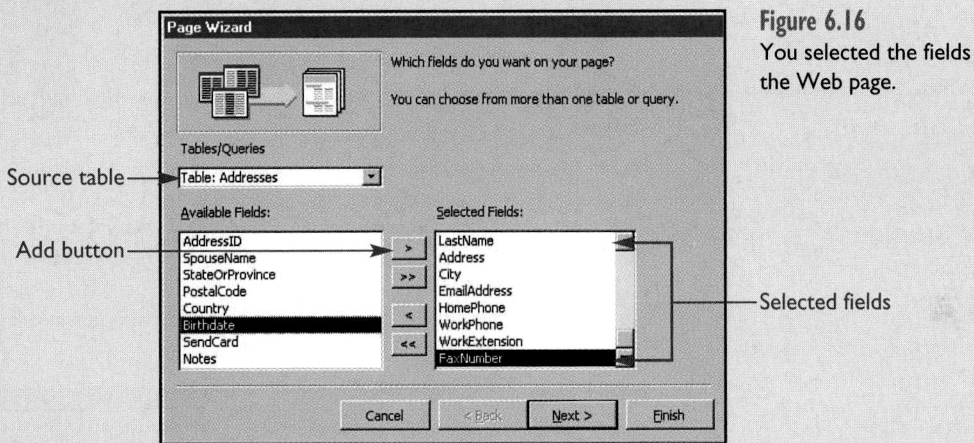

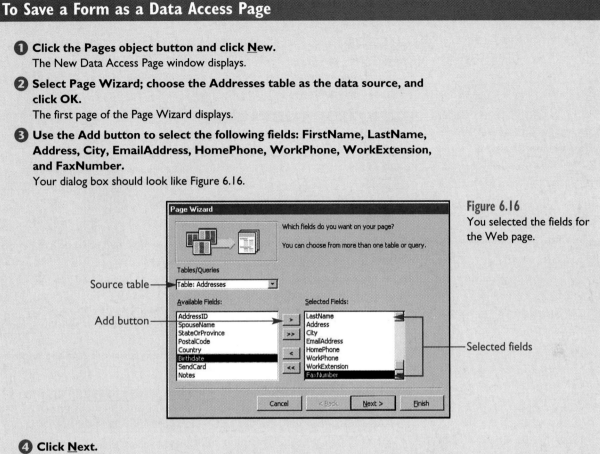

Figure 6.16
You selected the fields for the Web page.

4. **Click Next.**
   The second Page Wizard dialog box displays. Do not use the grouping option at this time.

5. **Click Next.**
   The third Page Wizard dialog box displays (see Figure 6.17).

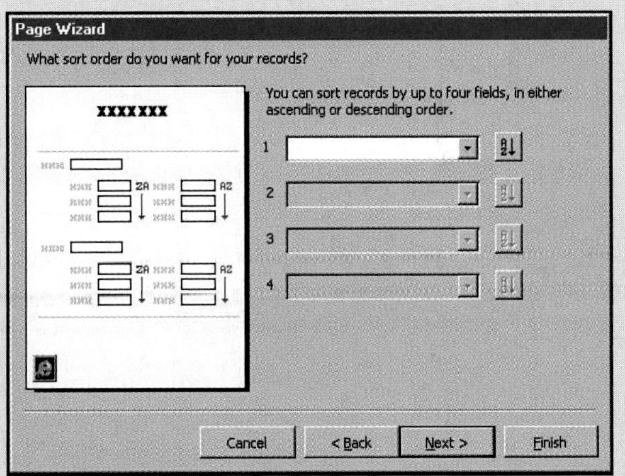

Figure 6.17
The third Page Wizard dialog box enables you to sort the records.

6. **Click the list arrow next to the first sorting box and select LastName. Click Next.**
   The fourth Page Wizard dialog box displays, asking you to name the page.

7. **Name the page `Contact Information` and click Finish.**
   The wizard creates the Contact Information data access page, which opens in Design view.

continues ▶

To Save a Form as a Data Access Page (continued)

8 Click in the Click here and type title text area at the top of the window and type `Business Contacts`.

You may have to move toolbars to get to the text box. A placeholder for introductory text appears just above the Data area (see Figure 6.18).

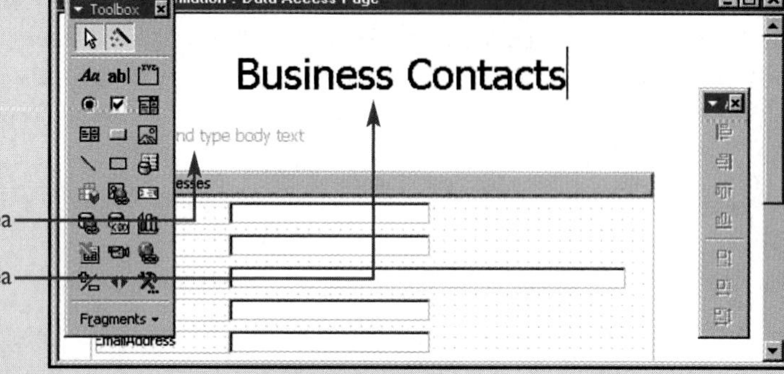

Figure 6.18
The Design view of the Page window enables you to add titles and supplementary text to the page.

9 Click the View button to switch to Page view. Maximize the window.

The title displays at the top of the page, and the first record shows. A set of navigation buttons displays below the data (see Figure 6.19). The page is also saved separately with an .htm extension in the same location as your database. In this case, the filename is Contact Information.htm.

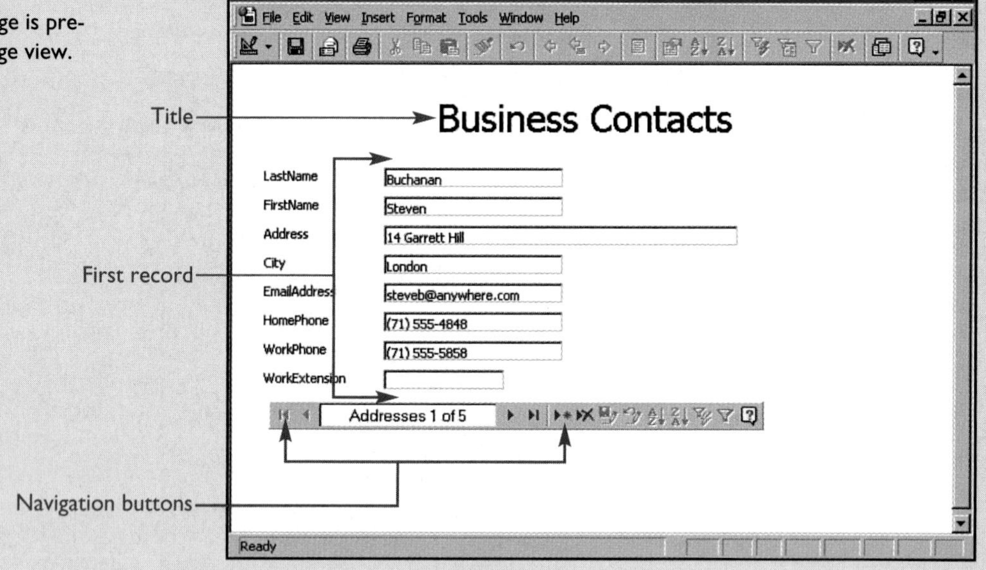

Figure 6.19
The Web page is previewed in Page view.

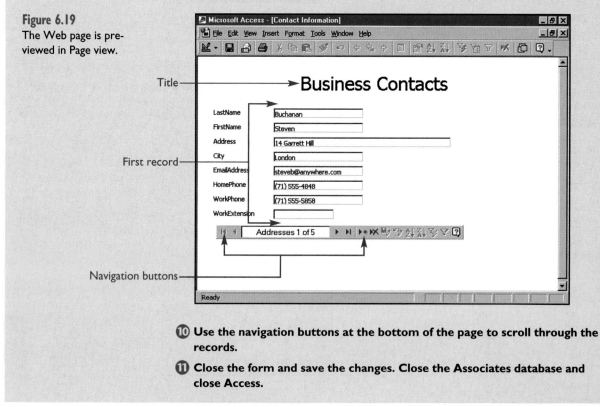

10 Use the navigation buttons at the bottom of the page to scroll through the records.

11 Close the form and save the changes. Close the Associates database and close Access.

Lesson 6: Using a Browser to Interact with the Database

If the database table and a related interactive Web page are placed on a Web server (or in a shared folder on a local area network), others can use the database with a Web browser. When you interact with the table on the Web, you can browse through the data. You can also sort and filter the data using any field, and you can even change the data.

In this task, you use Internet Explorer to interact with the database on your disk as though it was placed on a Web server.

To Use a Browser to Interact with the Database

1. **Launch Internet Explorer.**
   You must have Internet Explorer 5.0 or greater to run the Web page you created in Lesson 5.
2. **Type the disk location and name of your Web page in the Address box (for example, `a:\Contact Information.htm`). Press Enter.**
   The browser displays the page and a toolbar (see Figure 6.20).

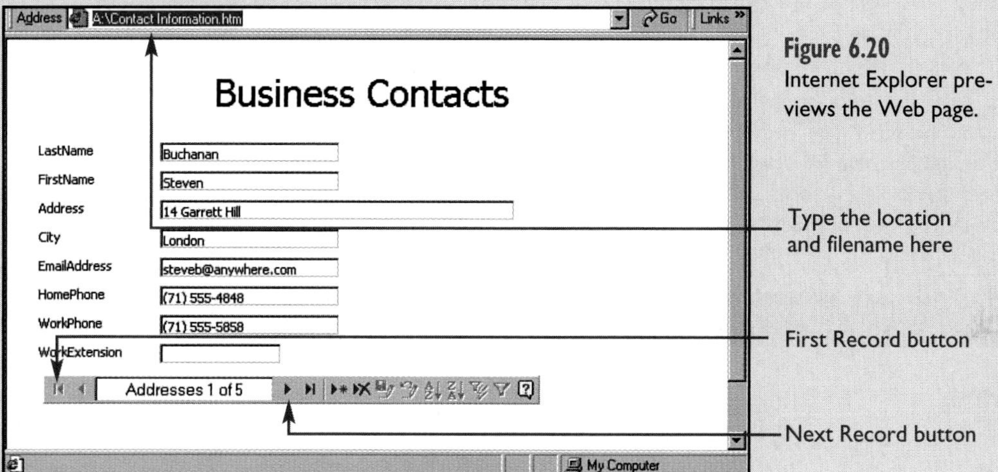

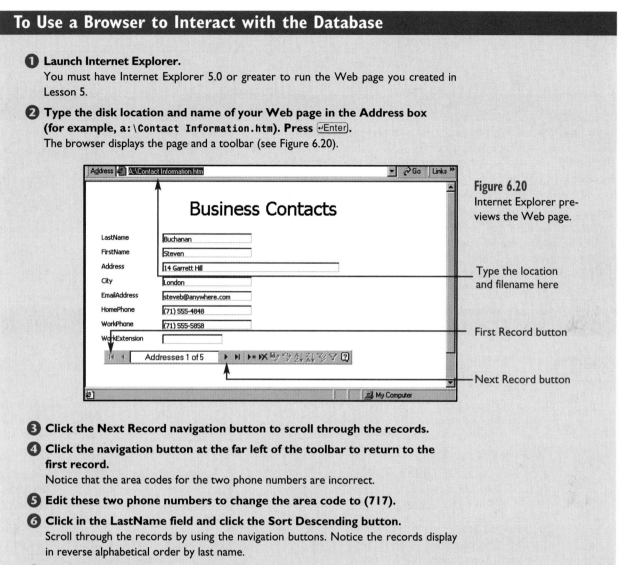

Figure 6.20
Internet Explorer previews the Web page.

3. **Click the Next Record navigation button to scroll through the records.**
4. **Click the navigation button at the far left of the toolbar to return to the first record.**
   Notice that the area codes for the two phone numbers are incorrect.
5. **Edit these two phone numbers to change the area code to (717).**
6. **Click in the LastName field and click the Sort Descending button.**
   Scroll through the records by using the navigation buttons. Notice the records display in reverse alphabetical order by last name.
7. **Close the browser.**
   The Access program did not run during this task.
8. **Launch Access and open the Associates database.**
9. **Open the Addresses table and scroll to the right until you can see both telephone numbers.**
   Both area codes that you changed on the Web page are changed in the database table (see Figure 6.21).

Postal Code	Country	Email Address	Home Phone	Work Phone	W
98122-	USA	nancyd@anywh	(504) 555-9857	(504) 555-9922	
98401-	USA	andrewf@anywh	(504) 555-9482	(504) 555-9933	
98033-	USA	janetl@anywher	(504) 555-3412	(504) 555-9944	
98052-	USA		(504) 555-8122	(504) 555-9955	
SW1 8JR	UK	steveb@anywhe	(717) 555-4848	(717) 555-5858	
*					

The area codes have been changed

Figure 6.21
The area codes that you changed on the Web page are also changed in the table.

10. **Close the table and close the database.**
    If you have completed your session on the computer, exit Access and Windows before you turn off the computer. Otherwise, continue with the "Checking Concepts and Terms" section of this project.

Typing an Address in Internet Explorer
As you are typing the address in Internet Explorer, it might determine that you are typing a drive name and offer you a drop-down menu. For example, after you type `A:\` (if your page was saved on drive A), a drop-down menu displays, showing all the files available on that drive.

Summary

In this project, you were introduced to some of the tools and techniques that enable you to work with information from other sources and to publish Access files for use as Web pages. Specifically, you learned to convert an existing Access database to the current version, Access 2000. You also imported data from an Excel worksheet into Access. Finally, you created a data access page and viewed it using a Web browser.

To learn more about the capability of Access to import data from other sources, go to Help and look at the topic `Data sources Microsoft Access can import or link`. Also examine the topic `Data access pages: What are they and how do they work`. Reading these topics can expand your knowledge about design considerations when you want to make your database accessible using a Web browser.

Checking Concepts and Terms

True/False

For each of the following, check *T* or *F* to indicate whether the statement is true or false.

__T __F **1.** To merge an Access database with a Word document, you must first create the document and then open the database and merge it with the document. [L3]

__T __F **2.** One reason to view your merged document before printing is to ensure that the document looks the way you intended. [L3]

__T __F **3.** When you print a merged Word/Access document, you must print all the records, rather than just a few records. [L3]

__T __F **4.** The Merge function in Access adjusts for multiple address lines and empty fields when it prints a merged document. [L3]

__T __F **5.** Excel files cannot be imported into an Access database. [L4]

__T __F **6.** When importing a worksheet file into Access, it is important to set up the first row of the worksheet as field names, and each subsequent row as a record. [L4]

__T __F **7.** If you want to use an Access 2000 database on a computer that has Access 97, you can use the Save As option on the File menu. [L1]

__T __F **8.** Saving a form as a Web page produces a file that can be viewed by an Internet browser such as Internet Explorer 5.0. [L5]

__T __F **9.** It is possible to change the data in the database by using a browser and a Web page. [L6]

__T __F **10.** You can sort the data on a Web page in ascending or descending order. [L6]

Multiple Choice

Circle the letter of the correct answer for each of the following.

1. With a database created using an older version of Access, you can _______________. [L1]

a. enter data with Access 2000 but not change any objects

b. convert it to Access 2000

c. share the database with people using different versions of Access

d. all of the above

2. To set up a Microsoft Word mail merge document while you are using Access, _______________. [L2]

a. click the Mail Merge button in the toolbar

b. select the appropriate table; click the OfficeLinks button, and choose Merge It with MS Word

c. select the appropriate table; open MS Word, and choose Link to Access from the Tools menu

d. open the appropriate table; click the OfficeLinks button, and choose Merge It with MS Word

3. You can send a mail merge document using _______________. [L3]

a. a fax machine

b. a printer

c. email

d. all of the above

4. When you create a Web page using the Page Wizard, the Web page is saved _______________. [L5]

a. as a separate file only

b. both in the database and as a separate file

c. only in the database

d. on a file server only

5. When you open an Access table on the Web, you can _______________. [L6]

a. edit the data

b. sort the records using any field

c. filter the data

d. all of the above

Screen ID

Label each element of the Access screen shown in Figures 6.22 and 6.23.

Figure 6.22

A. Merged database field

B. Returns to first record on Web page

C. Sort Descending button

D. Displays next record on Web page

E. Places an Access field in a Word document

F. Start mail merge button

G. Displays next merged record

H. Location of Web page on your disk

I. View Merged Data button

J. Web form title

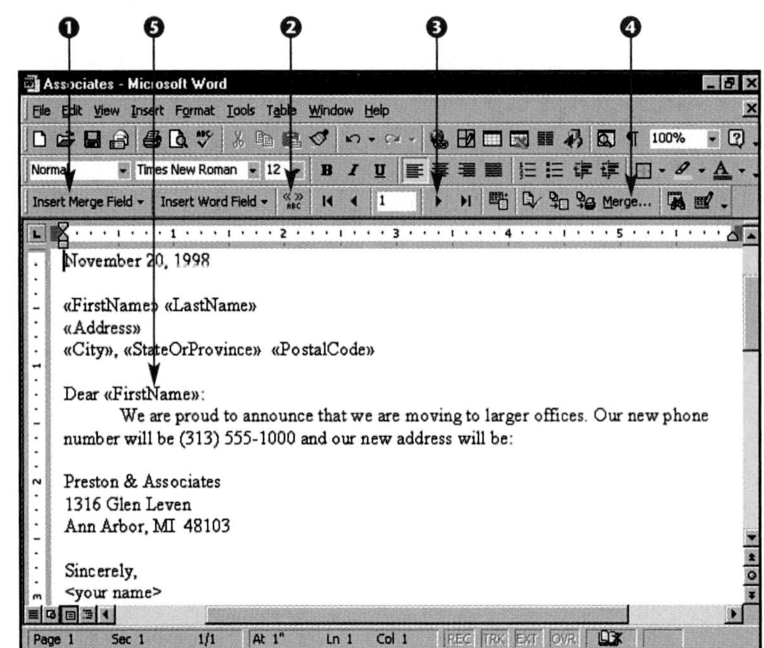

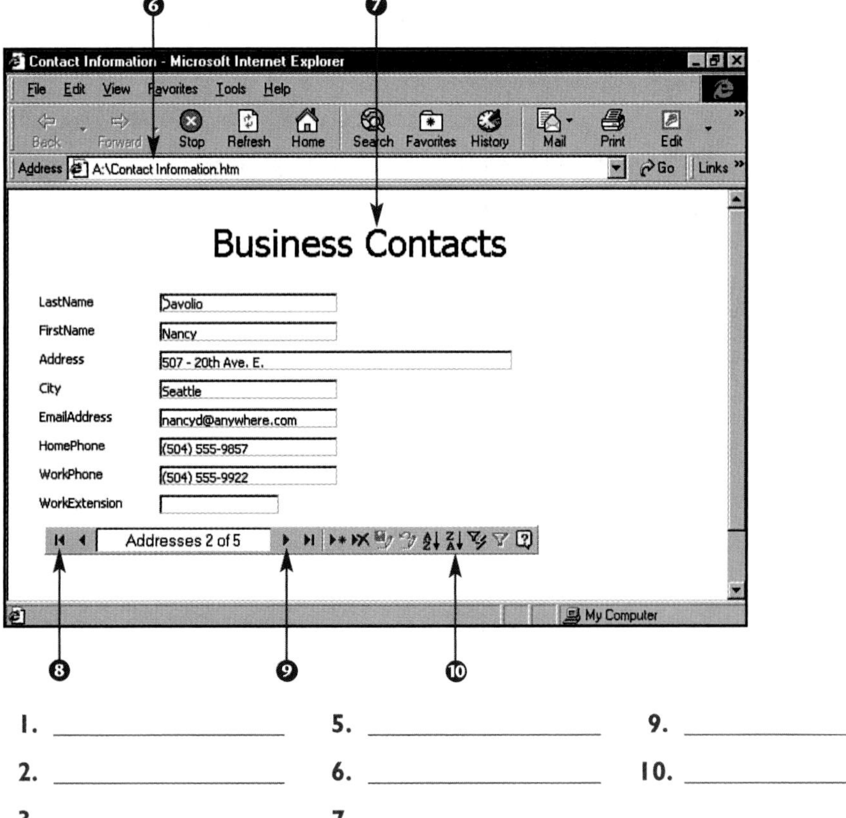

1. ________________
2. ________________
3. ________________
4. ________________
5. ________________
6. ________________
7. ________________
8. ________________
9. ________________
10. ________________

Discussion Questions

1. What methods have been commonly used in the past for sharing files and information between co-workers? What was done before people used personal computers? What was done before people used networks and the Internet?
2. How has the communication technology used today impacted businesses? How does it affect the way we work? How does it affect the chance for success of a business?
3. Of the various communications technologies used today, which do you think has had the greatest impact? Why?
4. For databases that you commonly use, how would the capability to share the data with co-workers affect your work? What are some of the issues involved in sharing databases?
5. What are some possible problems with allowing people to change data on a Web page?

Skill Drill

Skill Drill exercises reinforce project skills. Each skill reinforced is the same, or nearly the same, as a skill presented in the project. Each exercise includes a brief narrative introduction, followed by detailed instructions in a step-by-step format.

1. Opening a Database Created in an Older Version of Access

To practice converting databases from older versions of Access, convert this database of Michigan Tornadoes and give it a new name. [L1]

To open a database created in an older version of Access, complete the following steps:

1. Launch Access.
2. Find and select the file `AO-0603` on your CD-ROM.
3. Click the Open button.
4. Give the file a new filename of `Michigan Tornadoes`.
5. Choose to save the file to drive A.
6. Open the Michigan Tornadoes—Last Decade table to make sure the file translated properly.
7. Close the table and close the database.

2. Creating a Memo Using Mail Merge

Your company is going to have a summer picnic. You have already invited all your employees, but you decide it would also be a nice gesture to invite your business contacts. You use a new version of the Associates database you worked with throughout this project to create a quick memo to send to the people in the Addresses table. [L2]

To create a memo using mail merge, complete the following steps:

1. Find the `AO-0604` database file on your CD-ROM; copy it to drive A; remove the read-only status, and name it `Associates2`. Open the database and select the Addresses table.
2. Edit the Addresses table, and enter `a guest` in the empty spouse field.
3. Click the OfficeLinks button, and select Merge It with MS Word. Create a new document in Word and click Open.
4. Create a mail merge memo announcing a company picnic. Invite each person by name, and invite their spouse by name. Use Figure 6.24 as a guide.
5. Type your name at the bottom of each letter where it says <your name>.
6. Save the document as `Picnic Invitation`. Leave it open for the next exercise.

Figure 6.24

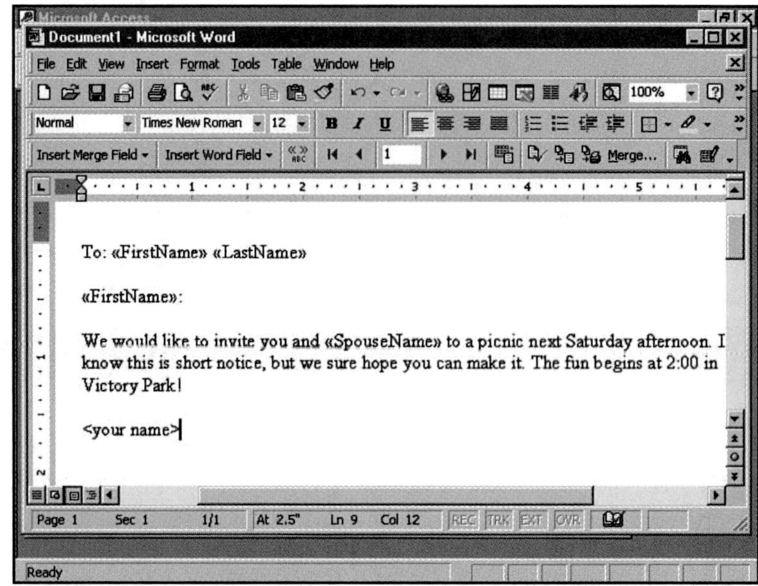

3. Merging and Printing a Mail Merge Document

Now that you have created the mail merge document to invite your contacts to the company picnic, make sure it works properly before you print the memos. [L3]

To merge and print a mail merge document, complete the following steps:

1. Click the View Merged Data button to test your mail merge document.
2. Scroll through the records to make sure the record you edited flows smoothly.
3. Click the Print button, and print the first and last pages. To do this in one step, type **1,5** in the Pages box.
4. Close the Picnic Invitation document, but leave the Associates2 database open.

4. Importing a Table from Excel

Your company's sales are based on population growth, so you would like to have some population forecasts available to make long-range sales projections. One of the marketing people has put the information into an Excel worksheet. You want to move it into your Associates database. [L4]

To import a table from Excel, complete the following steps:

1. Choose File, Get External Data, and Import from the menu.
2. Specify Microsoft Excel in the Files of type box.
3. Find the **AO-0605** Excel file and Import the first sheet.
4. Specify that the first row contains column headings.
5. Check the Choose my own primary key button, and select the Year column as the primary key.
6. Name the table **Population Projection**.
7. Open the table and review it to make sure it translated properly.
8. Print the table and close it.
9. Leave the database open for use in the next exercise.

5. Creating a Data Page for Use on the Web

You want to put the government budget information on a Web page. The first step is to create the data page and decide what information you want to include. [L5]

To create a data page for use on the Web, complete the following steps:

1. Click the Pages object button and click New.
2. Select Page Wizard and choose the Government Expenses table.
3. Select the Classification, Fiscal 1987, Fiscal 1988, and Fiscal 1989 fields. You do not use the ID and Fiscal 1986 fields.
4. Sort by Classification.
5. Call the data page **Government Budget**.
6. Add a title called **U.S. Government Budget**.
7. Save your changes and close the Data Access Page Design window; close the Associates2 database.

6. Opening a Data Page Using a Web Browser

Now that you have created a data access page, you need to open it using an Internet browser to make sure it is working properly. [L6]

To open a data page using a Web browser, complete the following steps:

1. Open the Windows Explorer (or My Computer) and find the Government Expenses data access page.
2. Double-click the Government Expenses file to open it.
3. Use the navigation buttons to scroll through the records. What could you do to improve the quality of this page?
4. Close Internet Explorer.

Challenge

Challenge exercises expand on or are somewhat related to skills presented in the lessons. Each exercise provides a brief narrative introduction followed by instructions, in a numbered step or bulleted list format, that are not as detailed as those in the Skill Drill section.

1. Opening and Adding Data to an Older Version of Access

You and your sister have been collecting CDs for years and putting them into a single database. She has a computer that uses Access 97; you upgraded to Access 2000. You still want to keep up the combined database, so you have to open the old version without converting it. You would also like to add another field to help keep track of who owns which CD. [L1]

To open and add data to an older version of Access, complete the following steps:

1. Copy the **AO-0606** file to drive A, remove Read -Only status, and change the name to **CD Collection**.
2. Open the CD Collection database. Choose the Open Database option, not the Convert Database option.
3. Open the CD Collection table, and add the following record:

   Rollins, Sonny
   Saxophone Colossus
   1956
   Prestige
   OJCCD-291-2
   Jazz/Big Band
4. Go to the table Design view and scroll to the first empty field.
5. Add a field called **Whose?** and make it a text field.
6. Switch back to Datasheet view. Is the new field displayed? Why?
7. Close the table and close the CD Collection database.

2. Importing a Table from an Old dBASE III Plus Database

A common database for personal computers in the 1980s was dBASE III. Many database records from that period are still stored in that format, as are many data sources on the Web. In this exercise, you import data from a 1987 database that shows statistics about retail establishments and their employees in Michigan by postal code. (Sales and Payroll figures are in 1000s.) [L4]

To import a table from an old dBASE III Plus database, complete the following steps:

1. Create a new database and call it **Michigan Retail Statistics**.
2. Choose File, Get External Data, and Import from the menu.
3. Specify that you are looking for dBASE III file types and select the file, **AO-0607.dbf**.
4. Close the Import dialog box. Rename the new table **Retail Statistics**. If you do not remember how to do this, use Help.
5. Open the Retail Statistics table. Click the record selector to the left of the first record. Press and hold Shift while you click the record selector for the tenth record (zip code is 48009) to select the first ten records.
6. Choose File, Print, Selected Records(s), and print the first ten records.
7. Close the table and leave the database open for use in the next exercise.

3. Importing a Text File

Data is frequently found in text files where the fields are separated by tabs, commas, spaces, or some other character. These data separators are known as ***delimiters***. If fields are separated by tabs, for example, the file is referred to as tab-delimited. Access can import such files using the Import Wizard.

To import a text file, complete the following steps:

1. Find the `AO-0608.txt` file on your student disk. Open it in Microsoft Word to find out what kind of delimiter is used. Close the file.
2. Create a new database and call it `Hardware Supplies`.
3. Check the available Microsoft Help to figure out how to import a text file into a table. Let Access add a primary key field.
4. Name the new table `Plumbing`. Print the table.
5. Close the table and the database.

4. Creating a Data Access Page Based on a Query

You can base a data access page on a query as well as a table. This gives you the ability to use query features, such as criteria, to restrict the information you place on the Web. In the following three challenges, you use the CD collection information that you worked with in the first exercise in the Challenge section.

To create a data access page based on a query, complete the following steps:

1. Copy the `AO-0609` database onto drive A; remove the read-only status, and rename it `New CD Collection`.
2. Create a new query based on the CD Collection table. Include all the fields. Call the query `The Last 10 Years`.
3. Set the criteria so that the query shows only CDs from after 1988.
4. Create a new data access page based on The Last 10 Years query. Do not group or sort.
5. Add a title that reads `CDs Since 1988`.
6. Close the database, and preview your Web page on your browser.

5. Editing an Existing Data Access Page

You might look at your new Web page and decide that you should make some changes. You can always go back to Access and edit your work.

To edit an existing data access page, complete the following steps:

1. Open the New CD Collection database and click the Pages object button, if necessary.
2. Select the New CD Collection page and open it in Design view.
3. Add `From the Collection of <your name>` as body text (type your name for <your name>).
4.  Use the available Help to figure out how to add a clip art image to the page. Find an appropriate image and resize it to about 1" high. Place it to the right of the title.
5. Save your changes and close the document.
6. Go to Windows Explorer or My Computer and look at the file you just saved. There should be a new folder that contains a copy of the image you placed in the page. This folder needs to be kept with the page file.
7. Leave the page open in the browser for the next exercise.

6. Sorting and Filtering Information on a Data Page

When you open a data access page on the Web, Access gives you some control over the data. You can sort on any field, and you can filter the data by category.

To sort and filter information on a data page, complete the following steps:

1. With the New CD Collection open in the browser, click in the Artist/Group field.
2. Sort by Artist/Group in ascending order.
3. Scroll to the first record listed as Classical; click in the Classical field.
4. Click the Filter by Selection button. You should have 132 classical CDs listed in the navigation bar. Scroll through a few records to make sure that the filter worked.
5. Click the Remove Filter button to turn off the filter. All 373 records should be listed in the navigation bar.
6. Close your browser.

Discovery Zone

Discovery Zone exercises help you gain advanced knowledge of project topics and/or application of skills. These exercises focus on enhancing your problem-solving skills.

1. Copying Part of a Table to a Word Document

A convenient way to transfer data from a database table to a document is a simple copy and paste. Try this procedure with the data from the Addresses table in the Associates database that you worked with earlier in this project.

Goal: Copy columns of data from an Access table to a table in Word.

- Create a simple Microsoft Word document (not linked) that refers to the list of associates.
- Open the **AO-0604** database as Associates3 on drive A. Move the Home Phone and Work Phone fields to the right of the Last Name field.
- Select and copy the First Name, Last Name, Home Phone, and Work Phone fields; switch to Word and paste.
- Use the Table, AutoFormat feature to adjust the size and spacing of the table. Choose a format that you like.
- Print the document and save it as **Associates3**.
- Close the report and leave the database open for use in the next exercise.

2. Updating a Table by Pasting Cells from a Worksheet

You might want to send a table of data to someone who does not have the Access program but who does have Excel.

Goal: Export a table to Excel; make changes to it in Excel. Paste the new cells back into the Access table.

- Make a copy of the Addresses table (right-click it and use the shortcut menus). Name the copy **Address Updates.**
- Export the table to Excel. Name it **Address Updates**.
- Add comments to the Notes field in the Excel sheet.
- Copy the updated cells in the Excel sheet. (Do not include the heading.)
- Open the Addresses table; click the Notes column selector, and paste.
- Close the database and Excel.

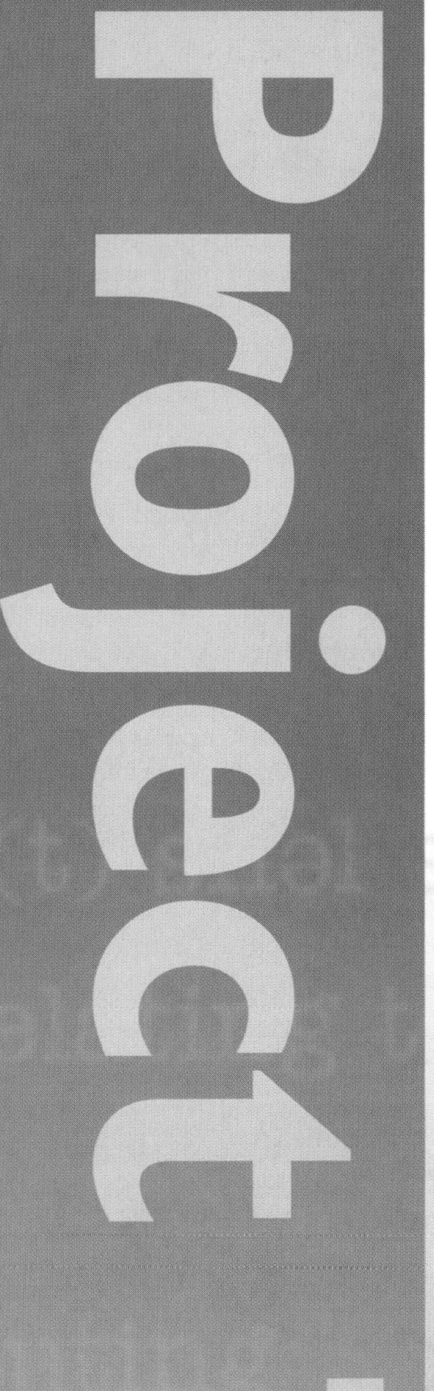

Project 7

Customizing Fields and Tables

Objectives

In this project, you learn how to

- **Modify a Table Design**
- **Enter a Default Value**
- **Change a Field Type and Select a Format**
- **Change a Field Size**
- **Work with More Than One Table**
- **Create Table Relationships**
- **Create a Multiple Table Query**

Key terms introduced in this project include

- enforce referential integrity
- Input masks
- join
- one-to-many

Why Would I Do This?

Access provides many features to help you customize your database table. You can select the field size, enter a default value, or select how data in that field is displayed.

When you first create a database, you may not be sure which of these options you want to use. After you have entered several records, however, you may find that you need to make changes, and you can make them by modifying the table design. You can add fields to the table or delete fields. You can also change the field properties, which are the defining attributes of a field, of the table entries. In this project, you learn how to modify a table design and change some of the field properties.

Another way you can customize tables is by connecting two or more tables together. Access is a relational database, which means that data is stored separately in tables and then connected or related by common fields in each table. Connecting tables enables you to set up a sophisticated database system and makes managing the information easier.

The connection between the two tables is called a relationship. The most common type of relationship is called a ***one-to-many***. If two tables have a one-to-many relationship, it means that each record in the first table can be related to more than one record in the second table. Records in both tables must share a field that can be used to relate them. Other types of relationships are possible. For instance, in a one-to-one relationship one record from a table is related to one record in another table through a common field.

The advantage of using two tables can be demonstrated by a database designed for a small company. The company sells supplies to 20 different retail outlets. Each month, the company sends several orders to each outlet. The company wants to record the mailing address of each of the outlets and information about each order. If a single table is used with all the fields in it, the company will have to enter all of the address information of the outlet every time an order is sent. If the database is designed with two tables, the mailing address information can be entered once for each outlet in one table, and the specific order information can be entered in a second table.

This project examines some of the relational features of a database.

Visual Summary

When you have completed this project, you will have created a query that looks like Figure 7.1:

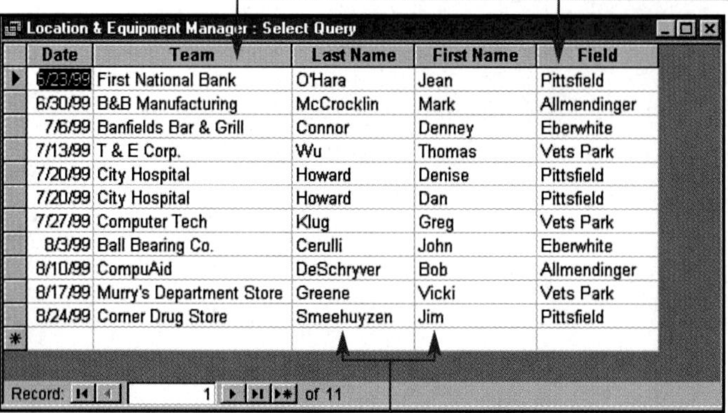

Date	Team	Last Name	First Name	Field
6/23/99	First National Bank	O'Hara	Jean	Pittsfield
6/30/99	B&B Manufacturing	McCrocklin	Mark	Allmendinger
7/6/99	Banfields Bar & Grill	Connor	Denney	Eberwhite
7/13/99	T & E Corp.	Wu	Thomas	Vets Park
7/20/99	City Hospital	Howard	Denise	Pittsfield
7/20/99	City Hospital	Howard	Dan	Pittsfield
7/27/99	Computer Tech	Klug	Greg	Vets Park
8/3/99	Ball Bearing Co.	Cerulli	John	Eberwhite
8/10/99	CompuAid	DeSchryver	Bob	Allmendinger
8/17/99	Murry's Department Store	Greene	Vicki	Vets Park
8/24/99	Corner Drug Store	Smeehuyzen	Jim	Pittsfield

Figure 7.1
The query consists of fields from two tables.

Lesson 1: Modifying a Table Design

It is a good idea to spend some time planning your database structure—thinking about which fields to include and in which order. If you had only one chance to get the database table right, however, you probably would get frustrated quickly, because it is difficult to anticipate all of the features that need to be included in a table.

Fortunately, Access lets you make changes to a table design even after you have created the table. Consequently, you can add fields, delete fields, or modify field properties as the need arises.

If the field already contains data and you make a change to the field, the data will be affected. Sometimes the change doesn't cause any problems. For example, if you have already entered numbers in a field and then decide you want to format them as currency, you won't lose any data.

However, if you enter a note in a field and then change that field type to a Yes/No field, you will lose most of the data in the field when Access reformats it to the new type. Just be sure that you understand the changes you are making and that you realize how they will affect your data. Back up your database before you change data types.

You begin this lesson by modifying the Team table of the Softball database by adding a few new fields.

To Modify a Table Design

1. **Launch Access. Click OK to open an existing file.**
   Make sure you have a disk in drive A:.

2. **Find the AC1-0701 file on your CD-ROM, right-click on it, and send it to the floppy drive. Move to drive A:, remove the read-only status, rename the file `Softball2`, and open the new database.**
   The Softball Team database includes a table of team members and a table of game information. After you open the Softball database, you should see the two tables displayed in the Tables list. In this lesson, you work with the Team table.

3. **Click the Team table, and then click the Design button. Maximize the Design window.**
   The Team table opens in Design view so that you can make changes (see Figure 7.2). When you first created the table, you didn't include the city, state, or ZIP code for the players, because most of them live in the same city; you didn't think you needed to track this information.

   After using the database for some time, however, you have decided that you want to include the city, state, and ZIP Code in the table so that you can have complete addresses for mailings. Now you want to add these three fields to the table, and you want to place them after the address field.

continues ▶

To Modify a Table Design (continued)

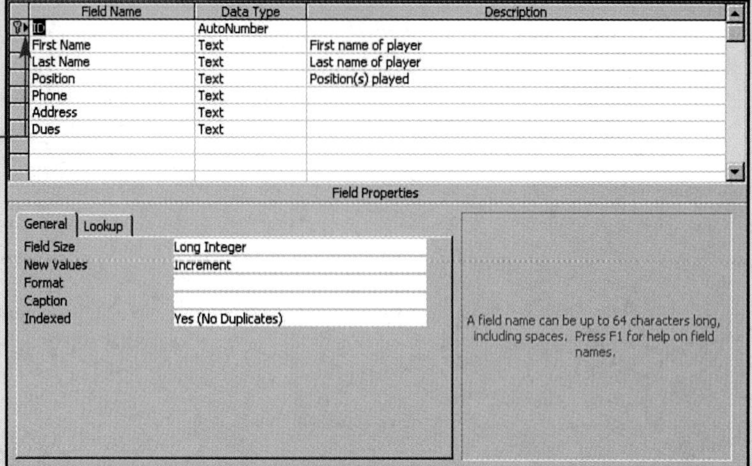

Figure 7.2
Open the table in Design view so that you can modify its design.

4. **Click the row selector next to the Dues field and click the Insert Rows button three times.**
   Access inserts three rows in which you can enter the City, State, and ZIP Code fields. You can also insert a row by selecting the Insert menu and choosing the Rows command.

5. **Click in the first empty Field Name column box, and type `City`. Press Tab three times.**
   This enters the field name, accepts Text as the field type, skips the Description column, and moves you to the next row.

6. **Repeat this step to enter the State and ZIP Code fields.**
   When you have finished, you will have inserted three new fields (see Figure 7.3).

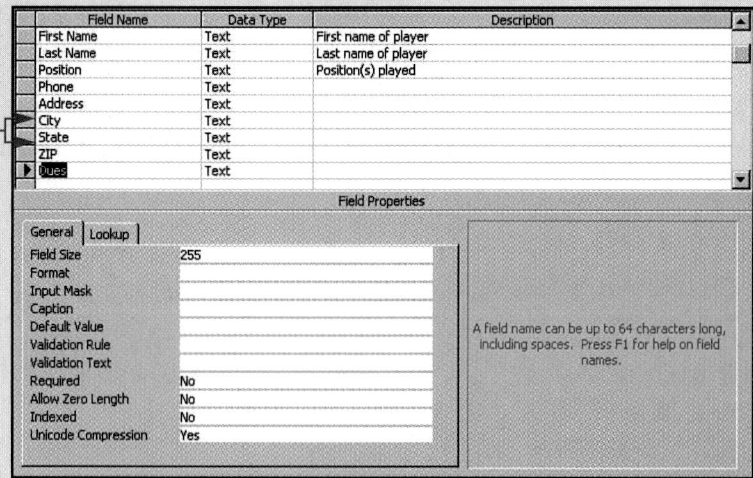

Figure 7.3
You can add new fields to a table by inserting new rows.

7. **Click the Save button on the toolbar, and close the table. Leave the Softball2 database open.**
   The Team table is saved with the modifications you have made.

8 Click the Games table to select it; then click Design.

Notice that the table has a counter field that is used as the Primary key. Because the team never plays more than one game on any given day, the Date field can serve as the Primary key field.

9 Click the row selector for the Date field, and then click the Primary Key button on the toolbar.

The Primary key icon is now displayed on the row selector button next to the Date field.

10 Click the row selector button for the ID field and press the Delete Rows button on the toolbar.

A warning message will appear that tells you all data in this field will be deleted permanently (see Figure 7.4).

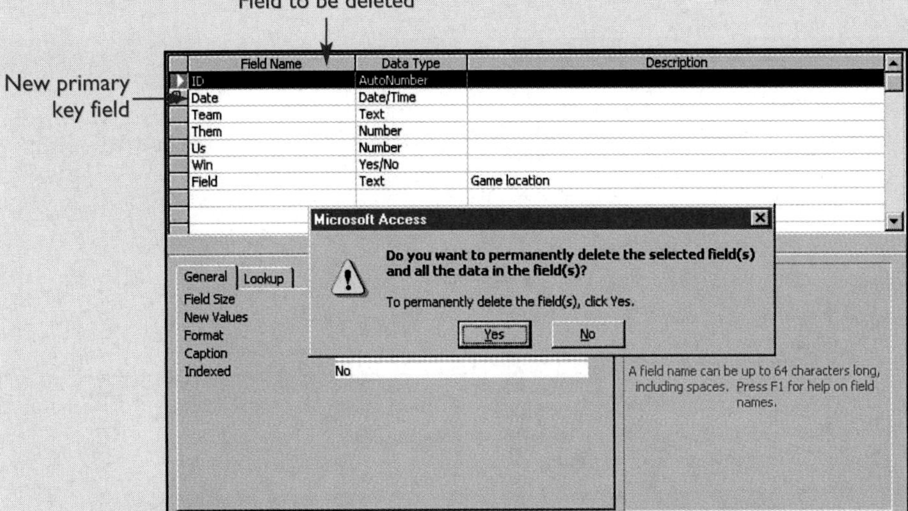

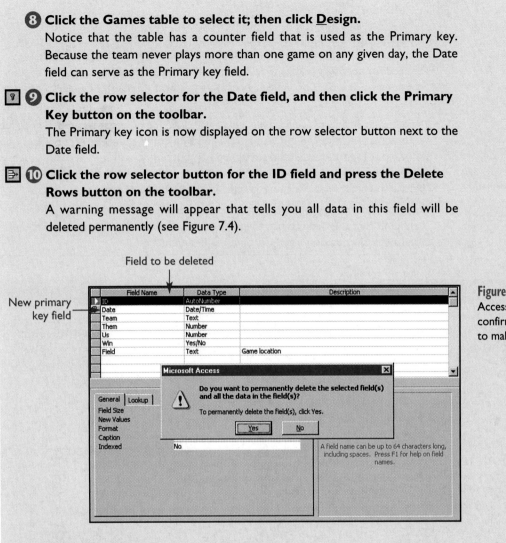

Figure 7.4
Access asks you to confirm that you want to make the deletion.

11 Click Yes to confirm the deletion of the fields. Close the table and save your changes.

Keep the database open for use in the next lesson, where you learn to enter a default value.

Lesson 2: Entering a Default Value

At times, you may want a particular value to appear in a specific field for most of the records in your table. In the three new fields you entered in the preceding lesson, for example, you want to use the same city, state, and ZIP Code for nearly all the records. You can type the entry over and over again for each record, or you can enter a default value.

When you enter a default value, Access automatically uses that field entry for all new records. (All records you entered previously, however, are not affected.) If you are entering a record with a different value, simply type over the default value.

Creating Small Database Fields

One of the rules of database design is to create the smallest usable fields. In this table, the Address field contains the street number and the street name. This practice reduces the number of fields in the table but it also reduces your options for sorting the data. For example, if you wanted to sort the addresses by street name, it would be difficult because the street number comes first in the field.

Another illustration would be to use a single field for a person's name. If you entered names with the last name followed by a comma and the first name (**Preston, John**), they would sort properly, but you would have trouble when you wanted to print mailing labels, because the last name would always be listed before the first name. Once again, two fields are best.

In general, do not group two types of data into the same field unless you are confident that the need to use them separately is unlikely to occur. It is difficult to change this decision once the data has been entered.

To Enter a Default Value

1 Select the Team table and click Design. Click in the record selector next to the City field.

This step selects the field you want to modify. When a field is selected, you see the appropriate field properties for that field type in the lower half of the window. The available properties vary, depending on the data type. In this area, you can enter a default value (see Figure 7.5).

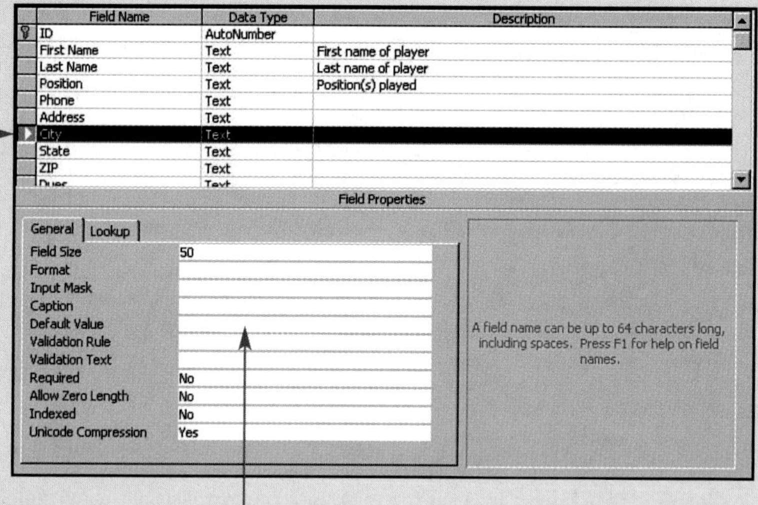

Figure 7.5
You can enter default values in the property boxes in the Field Properties area.

2 Click the Default Value property box in the Field Properties area. Type `Ann Arbor` and press Enter.

Notice that Access has placed quotation marks around the default value. They are automatically added to all text entries.

All records you add to the table from here on will default to Ann Arbor in the City field. Typing in the city name will overwrite this field.

In some cases, you must surround the default value with quotation marks, or Access may display an error message if the entry is mistaken for a command. For example, when you type only `IN` as the default value for the state field, Access thinks you are creating an expression (formula) rather than entering a default value for Indiana. Quotation marks indicate to Access that this is not an expression.

If you see a syntax error message, it means that you forgot to type the quotation marks around the default value in the table design. Click the OK button, and then edit the entry in Design view to include the quotation marks.

3. **Click in the row selector next to the State field.**
   This selects the next field you want to modify.

4. **Click the Default Value property box for this field, and type `MI`.**
   Here is where you enter the value you want to use for all new records.

5. **Click the row selector next to the ZIP Code field.**
   This selects the ZIP Code field and displays its properties.

6. **Click the Default Value property box for this field and type `48103`.**

7. **Click the Save button.**
   This saves the changes you have made to the table design. Now try adding a new record.

8. **Click the View button on the toolbar. Then click the New Record button.**
   This switches you to Datasheet view and moves the insertion point to a new row so that you can enter a new record.

9. **Press Tab to skip the Counter field; then type the following entries, pressing Tab after each one.**

```
Steve
Rasche
First Base
555-8177
8409 Evanston
```

   Notice that when you get to the City, State, and ZIP Code fields, the values have already been entered (see Figure 7.6).

continues ▶

To Enter a Default Value (continued)

Last Name	Position	Phone	Address	City	State
Wu	Pitcher	555-8812	890 Magnolia		
Howard	Center Field	555-2211	6704 Daisy Street		
Howard	Third Base	555-2211	6704 Daisy Street		
Lear	Left Center	555-6771	33 Eaton Avenue		
Lear	Short Stop	555-6771	33 Eaton Avenue		
Boll	Right Field	555-0014	609 Broad Ripple		
Broda	First Base	555-3211	7811 South St.		
Tucker	Pitcher	555-6322	9001 Labomba		
Klug	Catcher	555-5412	623 Pittsfield		
Chan	First Base	555-8777	8744 Marilyn Ave		
Cerulli	Pitcher	555-7666	5422 Seed		
DeSchryver	Left Field	555-9872	751 Kelley Lane		
Greene	Second Base	555-4460	8766 Christine		
Smeehuyzen	Right Field	555-4460	8766 Christine		
Leonard	Center Field	555-8733	98A CrossCountry Street		
Kenney	Third Base	555-8999	8756 W. Stadium		
Schneider	Catcher	555-9126	9010 Sue City		
Rasche	First Base	555-8177	8409 Evanston	Ann Arbor	MI
				Ann Arbor	MI

Record: 21 of 21

City, State, and ZIP are entered automatically

Figure 7.6
Your default values are entered automatically.

10 Press Tab three times to move past the three fields that have default values and type 50 in the Dues field. Press Tab to move back to the first field.

This record is saved when you press Tab to move to the next record. Keep the Team table open, and continue with the next lesson.

Lesson 3: Changing a Field Type and Selecting a Format

In addition to adding fields to the table, you can also modify existing fields. Suppose that when you first added fields to your table, you were unfamiliar with the other data types, so you used Text as the data type for all your fields. A Text field type is the most common type and works well in many cases.

Now you have a better understanding of the various field types, and you want to change a particular field type so that it more accurately reflects the format of the data being entered. In this case, you can modify the table design and change the field type.

In this lesson, you change the Dues field to a Number data type and then select a format to display the number as currency. The format controls how the data in that field is displayed and what kind of data can be entered.

To Change a Field Type and Select a Format

1 With the Team table still open, click the View button to return to Design view.

Remember that you can't make changes to the structure of the table in Datasheet view; you must switch to Design view.

2 Click in the Data Type column of the Dues field.
This is the field you want to change. You see a down arrow, and the field properties for this field are listed in the lower half of the window. This field currently has a Text field type, but you have entered numbers in this field. You can change it to a Number field.

3 Click the down arrow.
A drop-down list appears, showing the available data types (see Figure 7.7).

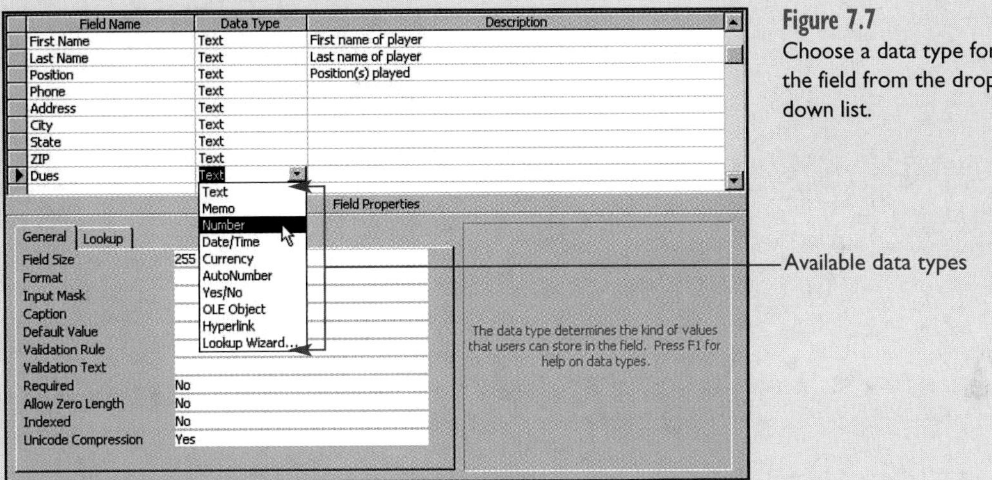

Figure 7.7
Choose a data type for the field from the drop-down list.

4 Click Number in the list.
This selects Number as the data type. You could have selected Currency; however, this method will show you several other options for formatting numbers as well as currency.

5 Click the Format property box in the Field Properties area.
A down arrow is displayed in the text box.

6 Click the down arrow.
A drop-down list appears showing the available display formats (see Figure 7.8). The listed formats vary depending on the data type of the selected field.

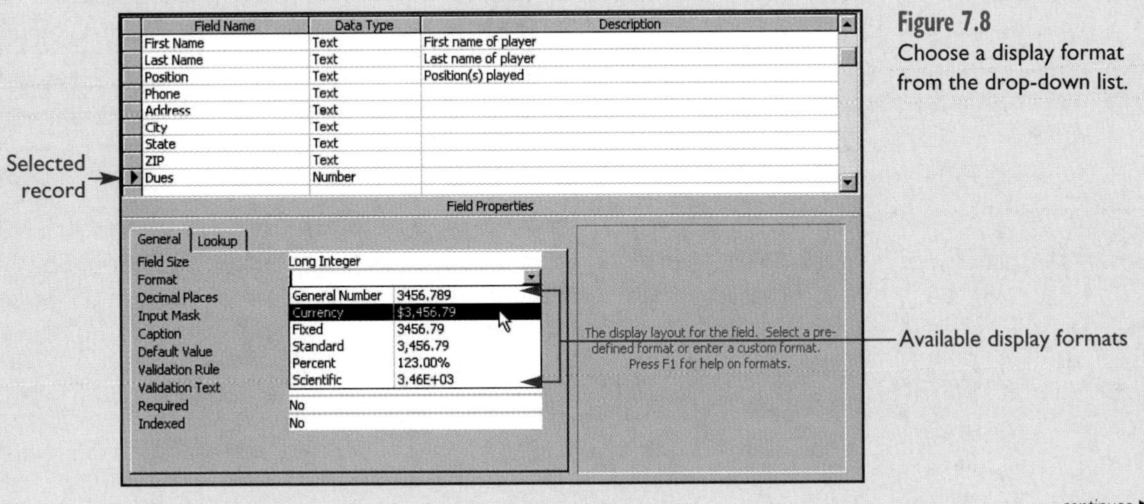

Figure 7.8
Choose a display format from the drop-down list.

continues ▶

To Change a Field Type and Select a Format (continued)

7. **Click Currency in the list.**
   This selects Currency as the display format for the selected field.

8. **Click the Save button on the toolbar.**
   This saves the changes you have made to the table design. To take a look at how these changes affected your table, switch to Datasheet view.

9. **Click the View button on the toolbar.**
   Scroll to the Dues column and notice how the data is now formatted (see Figure 7.9). Keep the Team table open, and continue to the next lesson, where you learn how to change a field size.

Figure 7.9
The Dues column is now displayed using the Currency display format.

Address	City	State	ZIP	Dues
565 Louisa, Apt. A				$50.00
560 Louisa, Apt. B				$50.00
6910A Bull Lane				$50.00
890 Magnolia				$50.00
6704 Daisy Street				$50.00
6704 Daisy Street				$50.00
33 Eaton Avenue				$50.00
33 Eaton Avenue				$50.00
609 Broad Ripple				$50.00
7811 South St.				$50.00
9001 Labomba				$50.00
623 Pittsfield				$50.00
8744 Marilyn Ave				$50.00
5422 Seed				$50.00
751 Kelley Lane				$50.00
8766 Christine				$50.00
8766 Christine				$50.00
98A CrossCountry Street				$50.00
8756 W. Stadium				$50.00

Record: 1 of 21

Field with Currency display format

Setting Decimal Places and Currency Signs
The Field Properties area is also the place to choose the number of decimal points to use for a number field. The default is Auto, which works well if you are using currency with two decimal places. If you wanted a field displaying dollar signs and commas every third number, but with no cents, you would use the drop-down menu in the Decimal Places box and choose `0`.

Lesson 4: Changing a Field Size

Another property of your table that you may want to change is the field size. When a field is added to a form or report, the size of the field's text box is determined by the field size. Setting field sizes in the table for fields such as State will reduce the modifications you will have to make to forms and reports later.

Be careful that you do not choose a field size that is too small; doing so limits what you can enter in that field. In the State field, for example, you want to type the two-letter state abbreviation. You can change the field size and then add a description to the field so that anyone who uses this table is aware of this restriction.

To Change a Field Size

1 With the Team table still open on your screen, click the View button.
This switches to Design view, which is where you have to be to change the table.

2 Click the Description column for the State field.
This is the field you want to change. The field properties for this field are listed in the lower half of the window.

3 Type `Enter two-letter abbreviation.`
This description will appear in the Status bar in Datasheet view when the insertion point is in the State field.

4 Click the Field Size property box in the Field Properties area.
The default for text fields is 50, which will be too long for many fields.

5 Delete 50, and type 2.
The new field size is large enough for a two-letter abbreviation for the state (see Figure 7.10).

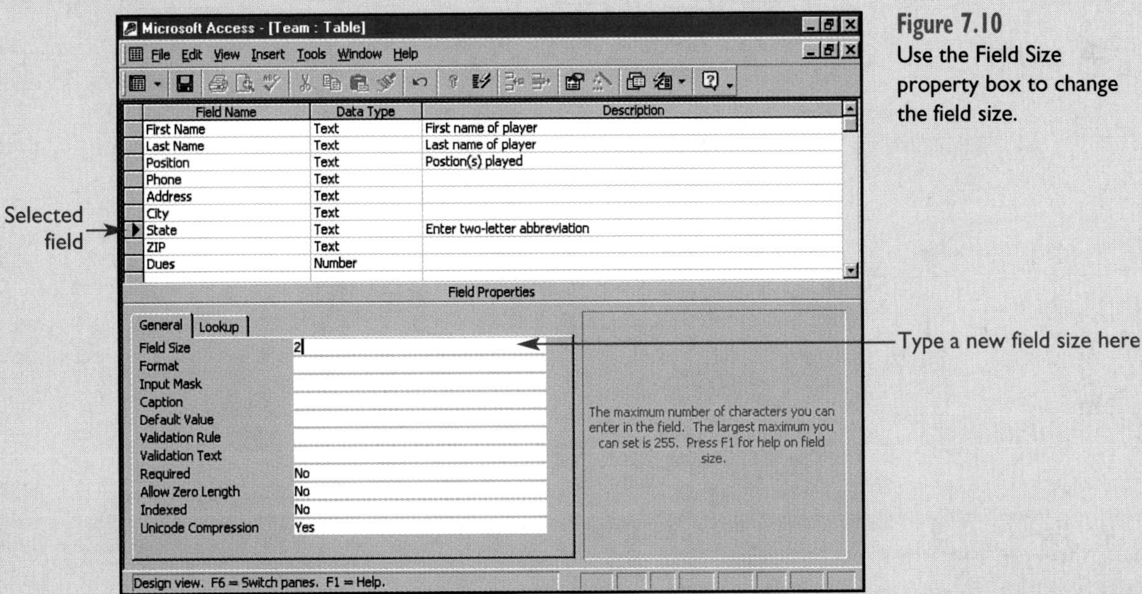

Figure 7.10
Use the Field Size property box to change the field size.

6 Click the Save button.
Access prompts you to let you know that you may lose some data by reducing the field size (see Figure 7.11). In this case, none of the entries is longer than two characters, so it is safe to proceed.

Figure 7.11
The program warns you that reducing the field size could result in loss of data.

continues ▶

To Change a Field Size (continued)

7 Click Yes to confirm the change in field size.
Now when you enter a state in the table, you will be able to type only two characters. Keep the Team table open, and continue with the next lesson, where you work with more than one table.

Effect of Column Width on Field Size
Remember that changing the column width in Datasheet view has no effect on the field size. To change the field size, you must change the field property.

Lesson 5: Working with More Than One Table

Rather than lumping all the information you want to maintain in your Access database into one large table that may be difficult to manage, you can keep your data in more than one table. You can create separate tables and connect them by setting relationships.

In order to relate tables, the tables must share at least one common field. The data type for the common field must be the same for both tables. You cannot, for example, relate a Text field to a Date/Time field. Once the relationship is established, you can take advantage of it by creating queries that use data from several tables at the same time.

In the rest of this project, you first add a common field you can use to relate two tables; then you enter the data, set the relationships, and use the two tables to create a query.

For this lesson, you want to relate the Games table to the Team table to see who is responsible for the equipment at each game. So that one person doesn't have to be responsible for the equipment all season, the job is rotated to a new player for each game. Start by adding a new field called Equipment Date. This field shows the date on which a specific player acts as equipment manager. This date field will then be related to the date field in the Games table.

To Work with More Than One Table

1 With the Team table still open on your screen, click in the row selector next to the Dues field. Click the Insert Rows button.
Access inserts a new row in which you can enter the new field information.

2 Click in the Field Name column, and type `Equipment Date`. Press Tab.
The field name is entered, and Access moves you to the Data Type column.

3 Click the down arrow.
A drop-down list appears, showing the available data types.

4 Click Date/Time in the list.
This selects a Date data type for the Equipment Date field (see Figure 7.12).

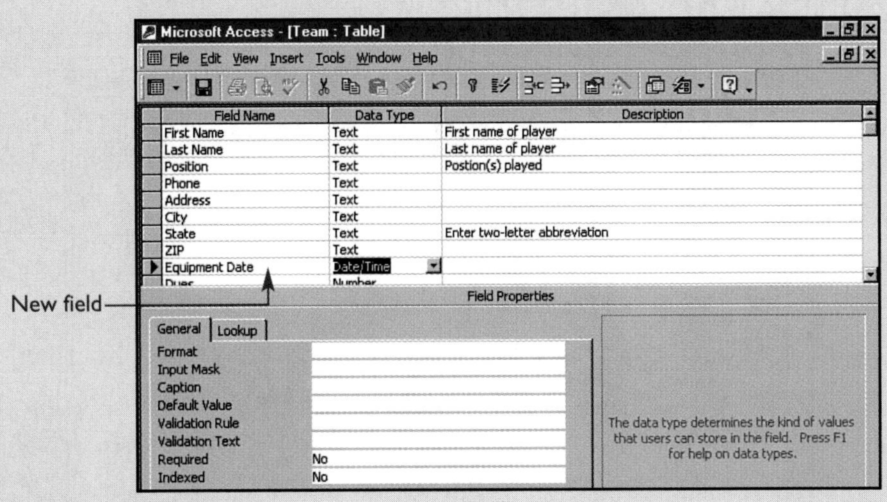

Figure 7.12
A field has been added that will be used to relate the tables.

5 Click the Save button.

This saves the changes you have made to the table design. Next, you need to enter values in the field you just added.

6 Click the View button.

Access displays the table in Datasheet view so that you can enter values into the new field.

There is a problem with entering the Equipment Dates. The new field is several columns away from the column with the players' names.

7 Point to the field selector for the first column. Click and drag across the first three columns (ID, First Name, and Last Name) to select them.

8 Select Format, Freeze Columns from the menu.

This will keep these columns on the screen while you scroll through the other columns.

9 Click anywhere in the table to deselect the columns, and scroll the table columns until you can see the name columns and the Equipment Date column at the same time (see Figure 7.13).

continues ▶

To Work with More Than One Table (continued)

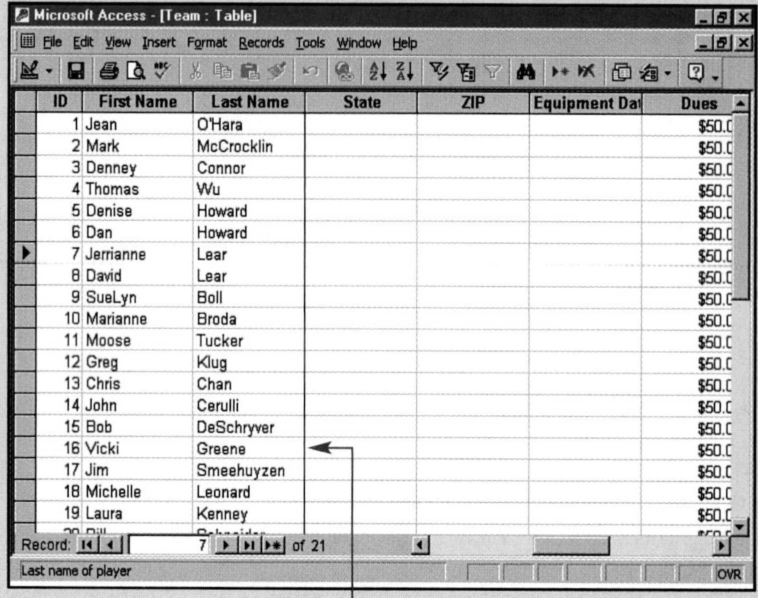

Figure 7.13
The names and equipment date fields are onscreen at the same time to simplify the addition of the dates.

Heavier line indicates that columns are frozen

10 Enter the following dates for the appropriate team players.

Player	Equipment Date
O'Hara	6/23/99
McCrocklin	6/30/99
Connor	7/6/99
Wu	7/13/99
Howard, (Denise)	7/20/99
Howard, (Dan)	7/20/99
Klug	7/27/99
Cerulli	8/3/99
DeSchryver	8/10/99
Greene	8/17/99
Smeehuyzen	8/24/99

These dates match the dates in the Date field of the Games table. Notice that Dan and Denise Howard are sharing the responsibility on July 20, because they ride to the game together (see Figure 7.14). Access saves your entries automatically as you type an entry and move to the next row.

ID	First Name	Last Name	State	ZIP	Equipment Dat	Dues
1	Jean	O'Hara			6/23/99	$50.0
2	Mark	McCrocklin			6/30/99	$50.0
3	Denney	Connor			7/6/99	$50.0
4	Thomas	Wu			7/13/99	$50.0
5	Denise	Howard			7/20/99	$50.0
6	Dan	Howard			7/20/99	$50.0
7	Jerrianne	Lear				$50.0
8	David	Lear				$50.0
9	SueLyn	Boll				$50.0
10	Marianne	Broda				$50.0
11	Moose	Tucker				$50.0
12	Greg	Klug			7/27/99	$50.0
13	Chris	Chan				$50.0
14	John	Cerulli			8/3/99	$50.0
15	Bob	DeSchryver			8/10/99	$50.0
16	Vicki	Greene			8/17/99	$50.0
17	Jim	Smeehuyzen			8/24/99	$50.0
18	Michelle	Leonard				$50.0
19	Laura	Kenney				$50.0

Record: 17 of 21

Figure 7.14
The equipment dates have been added to the table.

11 Close the table by clicking the Close button in the upper-right corner of the table window (not the Access window).
Confirm that you want to save your changes to the layout. This preserves the Freeze Columns feature.

The table closes and the database window is displayed. From this window, you can set the relationship between the tables, which you do in the next lesson.

Relating a Number Field to a Counter Field
There is a possibility that the two fields that are used to relate the tables may be different. When the primary key in one table is a counter field and it is used as one of the related fields, it must be related to a number field stored as a long integer in the other table. Counter fields are actually stored as long integers, so this exception still conforms to the "same data type" rule, but it isn't obvious.

Creating Common Fields Among Tables
Setting up common fields among tables that you want to relate is an idea you should consider when you are creating a new database. You can always edit the table to include a linking field, if necessary, and you can use an existing field if it is an appropriate data type.

Lesson 6: Creating Table Relationships

When you want to relate two tables, you choose a field in each table that contains the same values. For example, in the Team table, you now have a list of game dates in the Equipment Date field. These are the same dates contained in the Date field of the Games table.

Often the fields have the same name, but that isn't a requirement for establishing a relationship between the two. The fields must, however, be the same data type.

You can create various types of relationships. In this lesson, you create a one-to-many relationship between the dates in the Games table to the dates in the Team table.

A one-to-many relationship requires that the field in the table on the "one" side of the relationship does not contain any duplicate values. The Date field that is used as the primary key for the Games table has this property. The field that will be on the "many" side of the relationship may use the same date more than once. In this example, Dan and Denise Howard are both assigned to take care of the equipment on the same game date.

To Create Table Relationships

1 Click the Relationships button on the Database toolbar.
You can also select the Tools menu and choose the Relationships command. The Show Table dialog box is displayed (see Figure 7.15). The first step in the process is to choose the tables you want to relate.

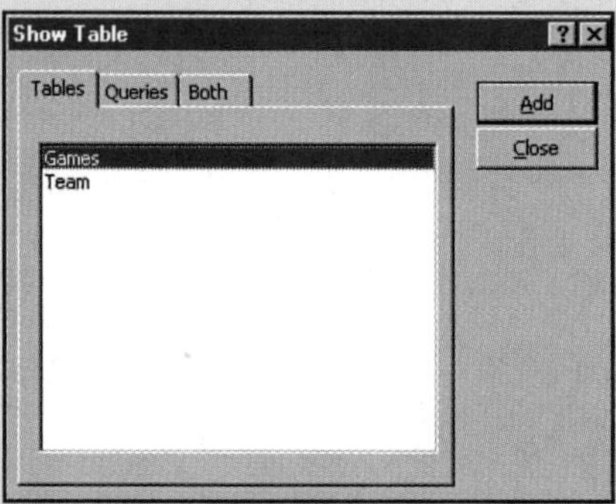

Figure 7.15
In the Show Table dialog box, you choose the tables you want to relate.

In some cases, such as after you have deleted relationships, the Show Table dialog box will not be displayed when you click the Relationships button. If this happens, click the Show Table button in the Relationship toolbar.

2 Click the Games table, and then click the Add button.
Access adds the table to the Relationships window; the dialog box remains open.

3 Click Team, and then click the Add button.
Access adds the Team table to the Relationships window. (The Team table will probably be hidden behind the Show Table dialog box.)

4 Click the Close button in the Show Table dialog box.
This closes the dialog box and displays both tables listed in the Relationships window.

5 Place the pointer on the bottom border of the Team field list and drag down until all the fields are visible (see Figure 7.16). Do the same thing to the Games field list.
The primary key fields of each table are displayed in boldface type.

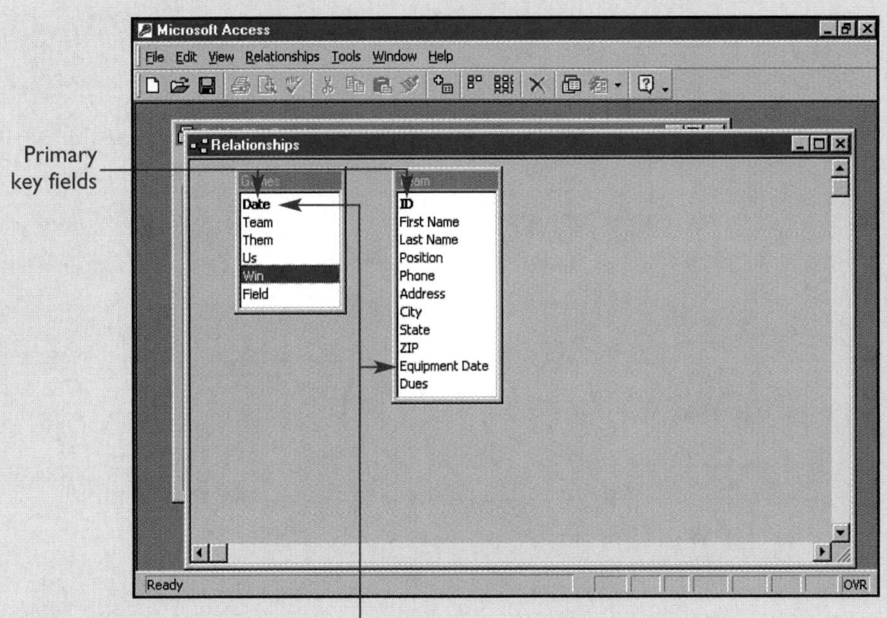

Figure 7.16
The Relationships window may be used to establish links between similar fields in two or more tables.

6 Click the Date field in the Games table and drag it to the Equipment Date field in the Team table.
When you release the mouse button, the Relationships dialog box is displayed (see Figure 7.17). In this dialog box, you can confirm that the relationship is correct. You can also set other options, such as the type of relationship you want. For this lesson, the default settings are acceptable.

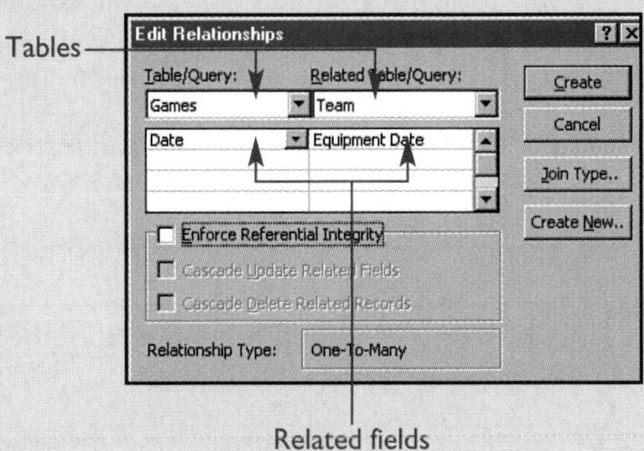

Figure 7.17
Use the Relationships dialog box to confirm whether you have selected the correct fields for the relationship.

Referential Integrity
When you create a one-to-many relationship, you can elect to ***enforce referential integrity***. This is used to ensure that each record in the related table is connected to a record in the primary table. This helps prevent orphan records. It also prevents you from adding records that are not connected to an existing record in the primary table.

7 Click the Create button.
Access creates the relationship. A line connects the two fields (see Figure 7.18).

continues ▶

To Create Table Relationships (continued)

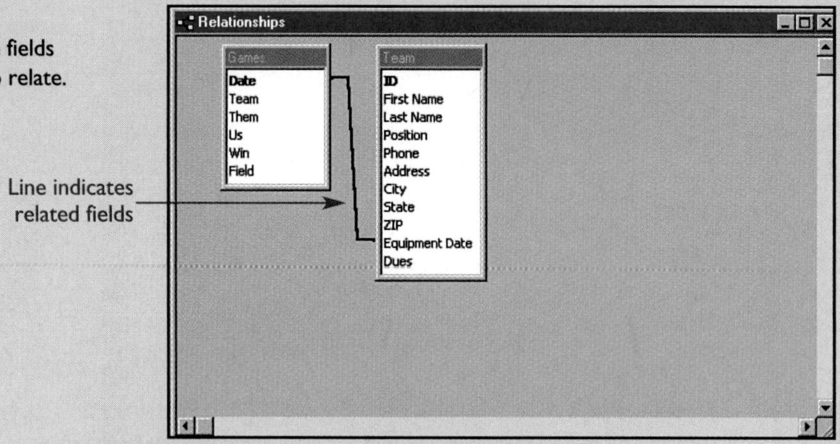

Figure 7.18
A line connects the fields you have chosen to relate.

Line indicates related fields

Relationships

Games	Team
Date	ID
Team	First Name
Them	Last Name
Us	Position
Win	Phone
Field	Address
	City
	State
	ZIP
	Equipment Date
	Dues

8 **Click the Save button on the toolbar.**
This saves the relationship you just created; the Relationships window remains open.

9 **Close the Relationships window.**
You return to the database window. Keep the Softball2 database open as you continue to the next lesson, where you create a multiple-table query.

Deleting or Changing a Relationship
To delete a relationship, click the line connecting the two tables and press Del. Access prompts you to confirm the deletion. Click the OK button. Once the relationship has been deleted, the relationship can be re-created by dragging the field name from one table onto the field name in the second table.

If you want to change the relationship options, right-click on the line, then choose Edit Relationship from the shortcut menu. This option is also available in the Relationships menu choice.

Changing the Field Size of a Joined Field
You cannot change the field size of a field that is part of a relationship. If you want to change the field size of a field in a relationship, you need to remove the relationship first.

Lesson 7: Creating a Multiple-Table Query

After you have established a relationship between tables, you can create forms and queries using data from both tables. When you have defined a relationship, Access automatically knows how to relate the data in the two tables and creates a ***join***.

When you create a query that involves two or more tables, Access gives you a choice of three types of joins. The most commonly used join includes only those records with matching values in the common field in both tables. For example, your Games table includes the dates for all the Softball matches. Access uses these dates to create the join and pulls only the records with matching date entries from the Equipment Date field of the Team table. The other two types of joins include all the records from one table and just the matching records from the other table.

In this lesson, you create a query that lists three fields from the Games table: Date, Team, and Field; and one field, Equipment Manager, from the Team table.

To Create a Multiple-Table Query

1. **Click the Queries object button in the Softball2 database window, and click the New button.**
   The New Query dialog box is displayed, showing the different query design options.

2. **Select Design View and click OK.**
   The Show Table dialog box is displayed with the Query window in the background.

3. **Click the Games table, and then click the Add button.**
   This adds the Games table to the query window.

4. **Click the Team tables, and then click the Add button.**
   This adds the Team table to the query window.

5. **Click the Close button.**
   Notice that the relationship between the two tables is displayed. Also displayed are field lists for each table; you will need to scroll the list of Team fields to see the related field (see Figure 7.19).

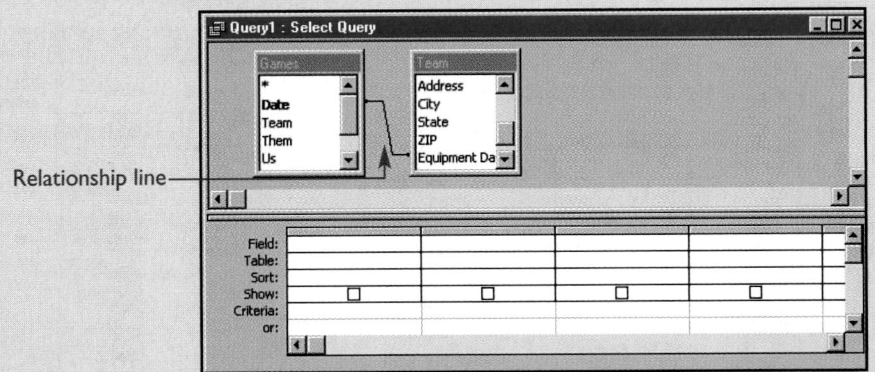

Figure 7.19
Related tables are displayed in the Design window.

6. **From the Games field list, drag the Date field to the first column in the design grid. Then drag the Team field from the Games field list to the second column.**
   The Date and Team fields are added to the query.

7. **Drag the Last Name field from the Team field list to the third column in the design grid.**
   The Last Name field is added to the query.

8. **Drag the First Name field from the Team field list to the fourth column in the design grid.**
   The First Name field is added to the query.

continues ▶

To Create a Multiple-Table Query (continued)

9 Drag Field from the Games field list to the fifth column of the design grid.

You may have to scroll down the field list and scroll to the right to find the fifth column. You now have added all the fields you want to include in the query (see Figure 7.20). Check the results of the query.

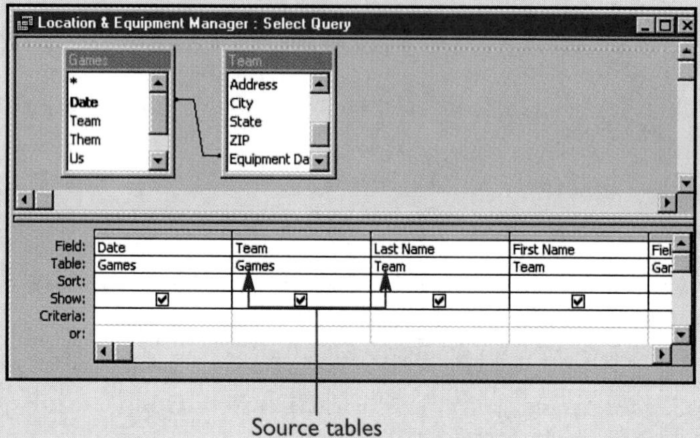

Figure 7.20
Five fields have been added to the query from two tables.

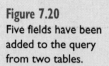

10 Click the View button on the toolbar.

The results of your query are displayed (see Figure 7.21). The query lists the game date, team played, equipment manager's last and first name, and playing field location. You can save this query.

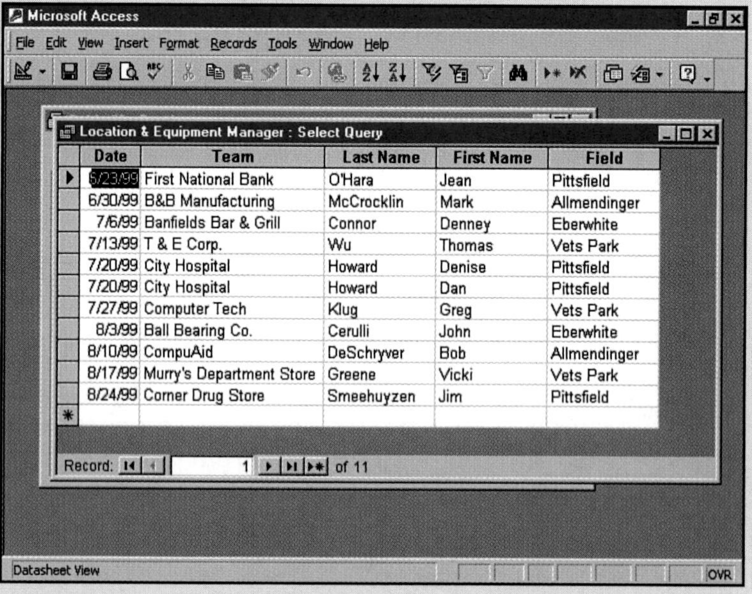

Date	Team	Last Name	First Name	Field
6/23/99	First National Bank	O'Hara	Jean	Pittsfield
6/30/99	B&B Manufacturing	McCrocklin	Mark	Allmendinger
7/6/99	Banfields Bar & Grill	Connor	Denney	Eberwhite
7/13/99	T & E Corp.	Wu	Thomas	Vets Park
7/20/99	City Hospital	Howard	Denise	Pittsfield
7/20/99	City Hospital	Howard	Dan	Pittsfield
7/27/99	Computer Tech	Klug	Greg	Vets Park
8/3/99	Ball Bearing Co.	Cerulli	John	Eberwhite
8/10/99	CompuAid	DeSchryver	Bob	Allmendinger
8/17/99	Murry's Department Store	Greene	Vicki	Vets Park
8/24/99	Corner Drug Store	Smeehuyzen	Jim	Pittsfield

Figure 7.21
Here is your completed multiple-table query.

11 Click the Save button.

The Save As dialog box is displayed.

12 Type `Location & Equipment Manager` and click the OK button.

This step saves the query with the name Location & Equipment Manager.

⓭ **Close the query so that you are back in the Softball2 database window; then close the database.**

If you have completed your session on the computer, exit Access. Otherwise, continue with the "Checking Concepts and Terms" section in this project.

Removing Joins Between Tables in a Query

You can also remove the joins between tables in a query. To do this, click on the line that joins the field lists. The line becomes much thicker, indicating that the relationship has been selected. Press Del. The line (and the relationship) is removed. This does not affect any relationships between the tables other than in this one query.

Summary

You can use the field properties in a table to help control the data that is entered. In this project, you learned how to modify a table by changing the field size, type, and format. You also learned how to work with more than one table by creating a relationship between tables and by using more than one table in a query.

To expand your knowledge, examine some of the other property options in the table design view. Notice how the properties that are available depend on the data type of the field that is selected. Use Help to look for information on table field properties. Use the Field Properties Reference page, select a property that is of interest to you, and read how it works. Some of the properties are set in the table; others are set in a form or report.

Checking Concepts and Terms

True/False

For each of the following, check *T* or *F* to indicate whether the statement is true or false.

__T __F **1.** To relate two fields, they must be the same data type. [L5]

__T __F **2.** The properties for a field are always the same, no matter what the data type. [L2]

__T __F **3.** You can change the field size by adjusting the column width in Datasheet view. [L4]

__T __F **4.** To create a relationship between two tables, the two tables must have at least two pairs of similar fields. [L6]

__T __F **5.** To create a relationship, the matching fields must have the same name. [L6]

__T __F **6.** You can't make changes to the structure of a table in Datasheet view. [L3]

__T __F **7.** Using the Format, Freeze Columns menu selection, you can freeze columns onscreen so that they will always be visible. [L5]

__T __F **8.** Click the Show Table button if you open the Relationships dialog box and the Show Table dialog box is not displayed. [L6]

__T __F **9.** If you change the data type for a field that already contains data, you always lose the data you have already input. [L1]

__T __F **10.** When you enter a default value in a field for a table that already contains data, Access inserts the default value in all the existing records. [L2]

Multiple Choice

Circle the letter of the correct answer for each of the following questions.

1. Which button do you use to insert a new field into a table in Design view? [L1]
   a. Insert Rows
   b. Insert Fields
   c. New Record
   d. Field Design

2. What is the default field size for text fields? [L4]
   a. 100
   b. 50
   c. 20
   d. 25

3. How are related tables displayed in the relationship or query window? [L6]
   a. Related fields are in boldface.
   b. Related fields are underlined.
   c. Related fields are connected by a line.
   d. Related fields are aligned next to each other.

4. When you define a default value for a field, how or when is that value used? [L2]
   a. for all existing records
   b. only for new records
   c. only for records that contain a blank field
   d. only when you select a special command

5. In which view can you modify the structure of a table? [L3]
   a. any view
   b. Datasheet view
   c. Design view
   d. Query view

6. Which of the following is the most commonly used relationship? [L6]
   a. one-to-one
   b. one-to-many
   c. many-to-one
   d. many-to-many

7. Why must you be careful about how you designate the information you use as default values? [L2]
   a. You can't use default values.
   b. The information must be used for every new record that follows.
   c. Even though you designate the information, you must Paste it each time you are in that field.
   d. Some words are reserved for Access commands and must be enclosed by quotation marks.

8. After you have defined a field in a table, which of the following can you change? [Intro]
   a. the size
   b. the data type
   c. the default value
   d. all of the above

9. Where are default values entered? [L2]
   a. in the dialog box that appears when you select the Properties button on the toolbar
   b. in the Default Value box in the Field Properties area of the table Design view window
   c. in the Default Value box next to the Data Type box in the field definition area of the Table Design view window
   d. in the dialog box that appears when you select Default Values from the Edit menu

10. The currency data type: [L3]
    a. must always use two decimal places
    b. is the default data type for numbers
    c. displays a dollar sign and commas when necessary
    d. is a property of a text field

Screen ID

Label each element of the Access screen shown in Figure 7.22 and Figure 7.23.

Figure 7.22

A. Insert Rows button

B. Delete Rows button

C. Field selector indicator

D. Primary key indicator

E. View button

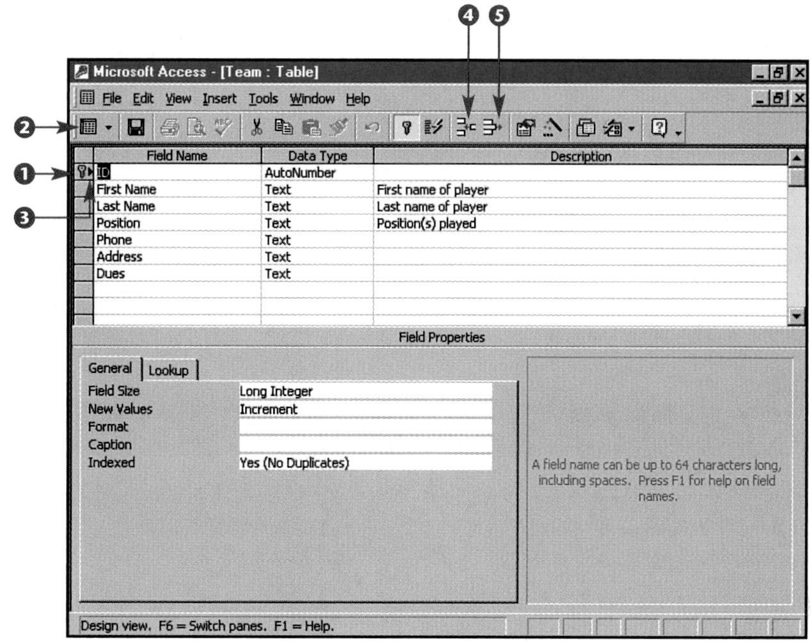

Figure 7.23

F. Source tables

G. Relationship line

H. Primary key field

I. Show Table button

J. Table name

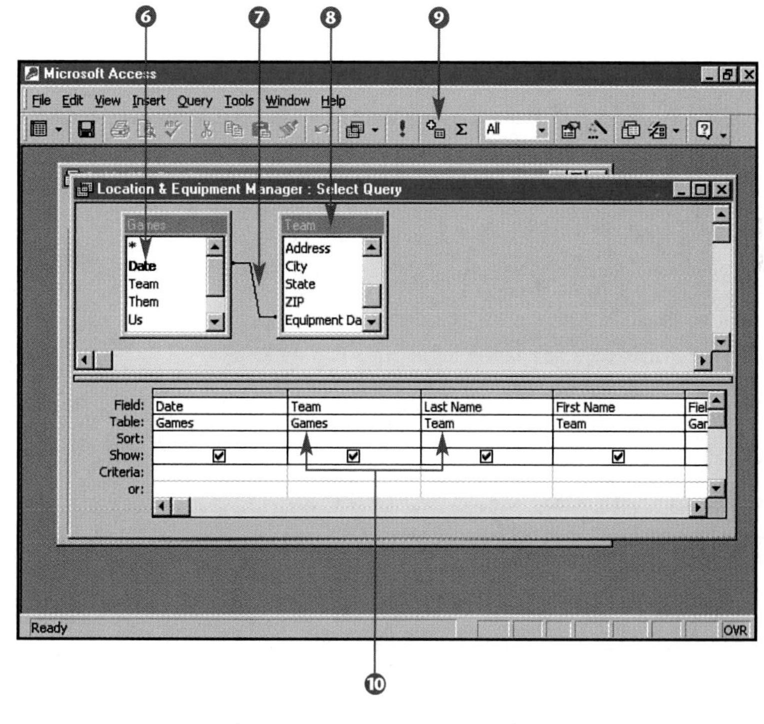

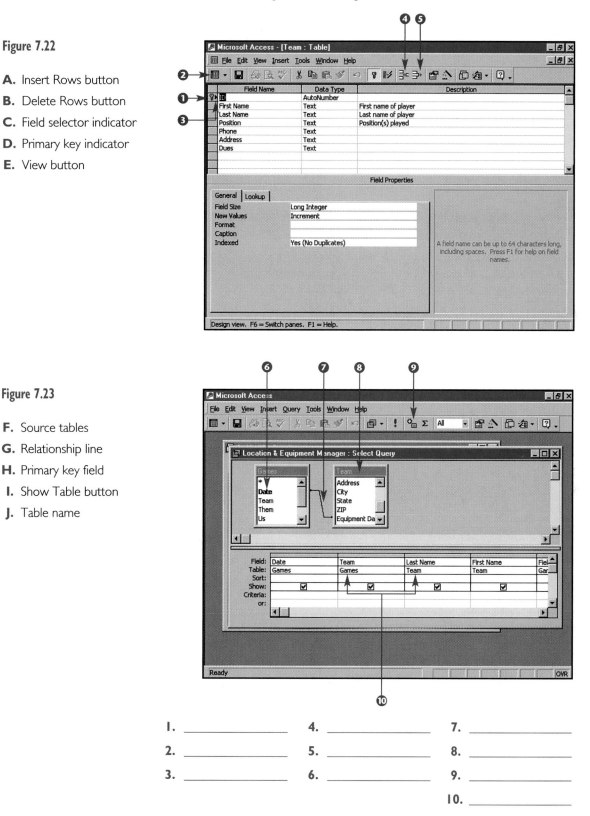

1. ____________ **4.** ____________ **7.** ____________

2. ____________ **5.** ____________ **8.** ____________

3. ____________ **6.** ____________ **9.** ____________

10. ____________

Discussion Questions

1. In the databases with which you are familiar, how is data integrity maintained? What steps and procedures are used?
2. In the databases with which you are familiar, are there controls that restrict the type of data that can be entered in each field? How does this help to ensure that good data is entered? What are some of these controls?
3. When would it make sense to use a default value for a field? When would you not use a default for a field?
4. If you were a sales representative for a company and you had an assigned list of customers you were responsible for, what kind of information would you want to maintain about your customers?
5. In the above example, how might the company use a relational database to keep track of their sales force and their customers? How would these two sets of records be related?

Skill Drill

Skill Drill exercises reinforce project skills. Each skill reinforced is the same, or nearly the same, as a skill presented in the project. Each exercise includes a brief narrative introduction, followed by detailed instructions in a step-by-step format.

The database you will use in the Skill Drill exercises contains a short table of suppliers for a small swimming pool, spa, and sauna company. It also contains a table containing a list of swimming pool parts.

1. Adding a Field to a Table

For billing purposes, you find that you need the tax number of your suppliers. There is no field for a tax number, so you will need to create one. It will need to go between the Phone field and the Billing field.

To add a field to a table, complete the following steps:

1. Find the AC1-0702 database file on your CD-ROM, send it to drive A:, remove the read-only status, and name it **`Pool Store`**. Select the Parts Suppliers table and click the Design button.
2. Click anywhere in the Billing field and click the Insert Rows button to insert a row between the Phone field and the Billing field.
3. Add a new field called **`Tax Number`**.
4. Accept Text as the Data Type.
5. Close the table and save your changes.

2. Adding a Default Value

There is a field in the Parts Supplier table that contains billing data. The various suppliers give you 30, 45, or 60 days to pay for your orders. Most of the suppliers use 30 Day billing, so to save time, you decide it would be a good idea to add a default value to the field.

To add a default value, complete the following steps:

1. Select the Parts Supplier table and click the Design button.
2. Click anywhere in the Billing field.
3. Click in the Default Value box in the Field Properties area.
4. Enter **`30 Day`** for the Billing default value.
5. Close the table and save your changes.

3. Changing the Field Type

Because both the Price and Sale Price fields are dollar amounts, you would like to add dollar signs and decimal places to the fields. The easiest way to do this is to change the field types.

To change the field type, complete the following steps:

1. Select the Pool Parts Inventory table and click the Design button.
2. Move to the Data Type column of the Price field.
3. Click the drop-down arrow and select Currency from the drop-down list.
4. Move to the Data Type column of the Sale Price field.
5. Click the drop-down arrow and select Currency from the drop-down list.
6. Click the View button to switch to Datasheet view. Save your changes when prompted. Look at the two fields you just changed.
7. Close the table.

4. Changing the Field Size

All of the fields in the Parts Supplier table are text fields, and most of them are too large.

To change the field size, complete the following steps:

1. Select the Parts Suppliers table and click the Design button.
2. Click anywhere in the Contact field.
3. Delete the Field Size in the Field Properties area and type **30** to change the field size to 30 characters.
4. Repeat the above procedure to change the field size of the City field to **20** characters.
5. Change the Phone, ZIP, and Billing fields to **10** characters and the State field to **2** characters.
6. Close the table and save your changes.

5. Creating Table Relationships

You want to eventually be able to create a query that shows the contact person for each of the pool parts. The first step in this process is to create a relationship between the tables. The only fields that contain the same information are the Name field in the Parts Supplier table and the Distributor field in the Pool Parts Inventory field.

To create table relationships, complete the following steps:

1. From the Database window, click the Relationships button. If the Show Table dialog box is not displayed, click the Show Table button.
2. Select the Parts Suppliers table and click the Add button.
3. Select the Pool Parts Inventory table and click the Add button.
4. Click the Close button to close the Show Table dialog box.
5. Click the Name field in the Parts Suppliers field list and drag it on top of the Distributor field in the Pool Parts Inventory field list.
6. Click the Create button to create the relationship.
7. Close the Relationships window and save your changes.

6. Creating a Multiple-Table Query

You want to be able to print out a list of pool parts along with the names and telephone numbers of the contact person at the company that sells the parts. To do this, you need to create a query that is based on both tables in the Pool Store database.

To create a multiple-table query, complete the following steps:

1. Click the Queries object button, then click the Design button.
2. Select the Parts Suppliers table in the Show Table dialog box, and click the Add button.
3. Select the Pool Parts Inventory table and click the Add button.
4. Click the Close button to close the Show Table dialog box.
5. Click the Contact field from the Parts Suppliers field list, and drag it into the first empty field of the query design table.
6. Click and drag the Phone field from the Parts Suppliers field list into the next empty field.
7. Click and drag the Part Name field from the Pool Parts Inventory field list into the next empty field.
8. Click and drag the Description field from the Pool Parts Inventory field list into the next empty field.
9. Click the View button to see the results of your query in Datasheet view.
10. Close the query, and save it as `Contacts and Parts`.

Challenge

Challenge exercises expand on or are somewhat related to skills presented in the lessons. Each exercise provides a brief narrative introduction followed by instructions in a numbered step or bulleted list format that are not as detailed as those in the Skill Drill section.

You will be using two databases for the Challenge exercises. The first is a modified version of the one you used in the Skill Drill exercises. The two tables could benefit from a few modifications, such as lists and drop-down boxes for fields with common entries. They could also use an input format for telephone number entry.

The second database contains some information you are becoming familiar with—tornado data. You will use this database to link three tables together. You will also create both a report and a form that draw information from more than one table.

1. Formatting Fields Using Input Masks

Input masks are special formatting features that make data entry easier. For example, when typing in a phone number, it helps to have the various parts set up in a (999)000-0000 format. Other types of data that can benefit from input masks are Social Security numbers, 9-digit ZIP Codes, dates, and time. In the Parts Suppliers table, the phone number has been entered as a long string of numbers. You will add an input mask to the Phone field.

To format a field using an input mask, complete the following steps:

1. Copy the AC1-0703 database file to drive A:, remove the read-only status, and rename it `Pool Store2`.
2. Open the Pool Store2 database and open the Parts Suppliers table in Design view.
3. Select the Phone field, and click in the Input Mask box of the Field Properties area.
4. Click the Build button (the one with three dots) on the right edge of the Input Mask box.

You may get a message that Access can't start this wizard. This feature is not installed as part of the standard installation. You will be asked if you want to install it now. Check with your instructor for directions if you are in a computer lab. If you are using your own machine, insert the CD-ROM that came with your software and choose Yes.

5. Select the Phone Number input mask from the Input Mask Wizard dialog box.
6. Accept the defaults in the other wizard dialog boxes.
7. Switch to Datasheet view to look at the results of your new input mask.
8. Close the table.

2. Creating a List Box

When there are only a few choices that can be made in a field, you can place a list on the screen from which the user can choose. This is called a list box. List boxes have the advantage of making sure that data that is entered is entered consistently and with no typographical errors. Nothing can be entered into the field except those items shown in the list box. List boxes can also be added to forms.

To create a list box, complete the following steps:

1. Open the Parts Suppliers table in Design view.
2. Click anywhere in the Billing field, and click the Lookup tab in the Field Properties area.
3. Use the Display Control drop-down arrow to select List Box.
4. Select Value List from the Row Source Type drop-down menu.
5. In the Row Source box, type `"30 Day";"45 Day";"60 Day"` exactly as shown. The quotation marks identify each item in the list, and the semicolons separate the list items.
6. Switch to Datasheet view to observe the results of your changes.
7. Close the table.

3. Creating a Drop-Down (Combo) Box

A second useful list type is called a combo box. This creates a list arrow and a drop-down list of choices for a field. The advantages of combo boxes are that they take up no more room than a standard field text box, and you can type in an item that is not included on the list. Combo boxes can also be added to forms.

To create a combo box, complete the following steps:

1. Open the Pool Parts Inventory table in Design view.
2. Select the Distributor field, and click the Lookup tab in the Field Properties area.
3. Change the Display Control to Combo Box.
4. Change the Row Source to the Parts Suppliers table.
5. Switch to Datasheet view, and click in the Distributor field in the empty record at the end of the table.
6. Click the drop-down arrow to see your combo box.
7. Close the table; then close the Pool Store2 database.

4. Linking Three Tables Together

It is possible to link more than two tables at a time. The database you will be working with in the next three exercises contains three tables—one with county names, one with state names, and one with tornado data and codes for the county and state names. The last two exercises involve creating queries and reports using all three tables. The first thing you must do is to create a relationship between the three tables.

To link three tables together, complete the following steps:

1. Copy the AC1-0704 database file to drive A:, remove the read-only status, and rename it `Five Year Tornado Data`.
2. Open the Relationships window; then show the list of tables.
3. Add all three tables to the Relationships window.
4. Increase the size of the 5 Year US Tornado field list so that you can see all of the fields.
5. Move the field lists around in the Relationships window so that the 5 Year US Tornado field list is in the middle.
6. Create a relationship between the CountyID field in the 5 Year US Tornado table and the CountyID field in the County Names table.
7. Create a relationship between the StateID field in the 5 Year US Tornado table and the State field in the County Names table.
8. Close the Relationships window, and save your changes.

5. Creating a Query Using Fields from Three Tables

Now that you have created a relationship between the three tables, you can create a query that eliminates the code numbers for the counties and states and replaces them with the actual county and state names. This will make the data easier to read and understand.

To create a query using fields from multiple tables, complete the following steps:

1. Use the available help features to create a query containing fields from all three tables in the database. Use the Simple Query Wizard.
2. Include all of the fields from the 5 Year US Tornadoes table except the StateID, CountyID, and County fields.
3. Include the State Name field from the State Names table.
4. Include the County Name field from the County Names table.
5. Save the query using the default name.
6. Move the State Name field so that it is displayed in the first column, and display the County Name field in the second column.
7. Sort on four fields in the following order: State Name, County Name, Year, and Date. Preview your query.
8. Close the query, and save your changes.

6. Creating a Report Using Fields from Multiple Tables

A report can be produced in two ways. You can base it directly on the tables that contain the data, or you can base it on a query, where the work of selecting the tables, fields, criteria, and sort order has already been done.

To create a report using fields from multiple tables, complete the following steps:

1. Use the available help features to create a report based on the 5 Year US Tornadoes query. Use the Report Wizard.
2. Accept all of the defaults.
3. Fix any labels or data that are cut off.
4. Put your name in the center of the page footer, then print page 70 of the report.
5. Close the report. Close the database and exit Access unless you are going to try the Discovery Zone exercises.

Discovery Zone

Discovery Zone exercises help you gain advanced knowledge of project topics and application of skills. These exercises focus on enhancing your problem-solving skills. Numbered steps are not provided, but you are given hints, reminders, screen shots, and references to help you reach your goal for each exercise.

1. Creating Your Own Input Mask

Access has pre-set input masks for phone numbers, Social Security numbers, 9-digit ZIP Codes, and several other common data structures. You may have a data structure that is common in your business. Perhaps you would like to create an input mask for that data. You added a Tax Number field to the Parts Suppliers table in the Pool Store database earlier in this project. This field could use an input mask to aid in data entry, because all tax numbers have the same structure.

Goal: Create a new input mask and add it to the list of input masks available in Access.

Use the AC1-0705 file to create a new database called `Pool Store3` on your disk. Use any available help from your computer or online to understand how to add an input mask to the Tax Number field. There should be a dash after the second character in the tax number and a dash before the last character. For example, the tax number for the Compaq Spa and Pool should read `2A-436234-C`. Your input mask should:

- Require the entry of the two letters as letters.
- Require the entry of the all seven numbers as numbers (0 through 9).
- Automatically change any letters entered into the input mask to uppercase.
- Insert a dash after the second character and before the last character.
- Use the underscore character as a placeholder for blanks while data is being entered.
- Store the dashes along with the letters and numbers.
- Show the Compaq Spa and Pool tax number (2A-436234-C) as the sample number in the Input Mask wizard.
- Save the new input mask so that you can use it in future databases.

Hint #1: You can make the input mask work by typing it into the Input Mask box in the Field Properties area of the Tax Number field, but in order to do the last two steps, you will need to use the Tax Number Build button.

Hint #2: You do not want to replace an existing input mask. When you are creating the input mask, no input mask should be displayed.

Enter a new record with the following data (these are in the order of the fields in your Parts Suppliers table): `Twinhead Chemicals`, `William McMahon`, `4722 Edison Lane`, `Port Huron`, `MI`, `48060`, `(810) 986-0000`, `1B-7536222-Z`, `30 Day`. When you enter the tax number, enter lowercase letters to see if the program automatically changes them to uppercase.

2. Creating Validation Rules and Validation Error Messages

All of your suppliers come from Michigan or northern Ohio, which means that all of the ZIP Codes you enter will begin with the number 4. You are also using just the five-digit ZIP Code rather than the nine-digit ZIP Code. To help avoid typographical errors in the future, you would like to have the program automatically detect when an incorrect ZIP Code is added, and include a message on the screen to help the user.

Goal: Create a validation rule for a ZIP Code field and add an error message to be displayed when an incorrect number is entered.

Use the Pool Store3 file that you created in the first exercise of the Discovery section. If you did not do the first exercise, use the Proj0705 file to create a new database called `Pool Store3` on your disk. Read through the Access help on validation rules and validation text to understand how validation works. Use the following guidelines:

- The validation rule should restrict entry to five-digit numbers beginning with the number 4.
- The error message that appears when an incorrect entry is made should say `The ZIP code must be a 5-digit number beginning with the number 4`.

  Hint #1: The ZIP field is a text field, but that does not matter in this case. The procedure would be the same for a text field containing numbers or a numeric field.

  Hint #2: You will need to build an expression for the validation rule so that you test the entry to make sure it is between two numbers.

Add a new record, and try to type in a number that does not meet your conditions to make sure your validation rule and validation text work the way you want.

Project 8

Making Data Entry Easier and More Accurate

Objectives

In this project, you learn how to

- **Create Consistent Data Formats**
- **Create Conditional Formats for Positive, Negative, and Null Values**
- **Change the Data Input Structure Using Input Masks**
- **Restrict Entries to Those That Meet Validation Criteria**
- **Require Entry of Necessary Information**
- **Prevent Duplicate Entries Using Indexed Fields**
- **Create a Lookup Column to Allow Selection from a List**

Key terms introduced in this project include

- Expression Builder
- format
- Indexed field
- Input mask
- null value
- placeholder
- primary key field
- validation rule
- validation text

Why Would I Do This?

It is important that your data is stored in a consistent format. If some phone numbers are entered as (XXX) XXX-XXXX and some as 1-XXX-XXX-XXXX, it may be difficult to sort or extract the data. If one person designs and enters all the data, you may be able to get consistent input, but if that person is on vacation or out due to illness, your database could be filled with useless data by someone unfamiliar with your methods.

You may want your database to call attention to negative numbers or to suppress zeros in empty numeric fields. You learn how to use conditional formats to accomplish these goals.

To save time, you can create a list of possible entries. This allows you to choose an entry from a list rather than enter it from the keyboard.

It is also important to guard against common errors. You can check an entry against a set of rules to see if the entry is within allowable limits or matches a list of possible values. You may want to require that all records contain certain fields and to guard against duplicate entries.

In this project, you learn how to control the ***format*** of your data, check entries against a set of rules, and prevent duplicate entries. The database that you are modifying is designed to track the training employees have received on computer software packages.

Visual Summary

When you have completed this project, you will have created a document that looks like this:

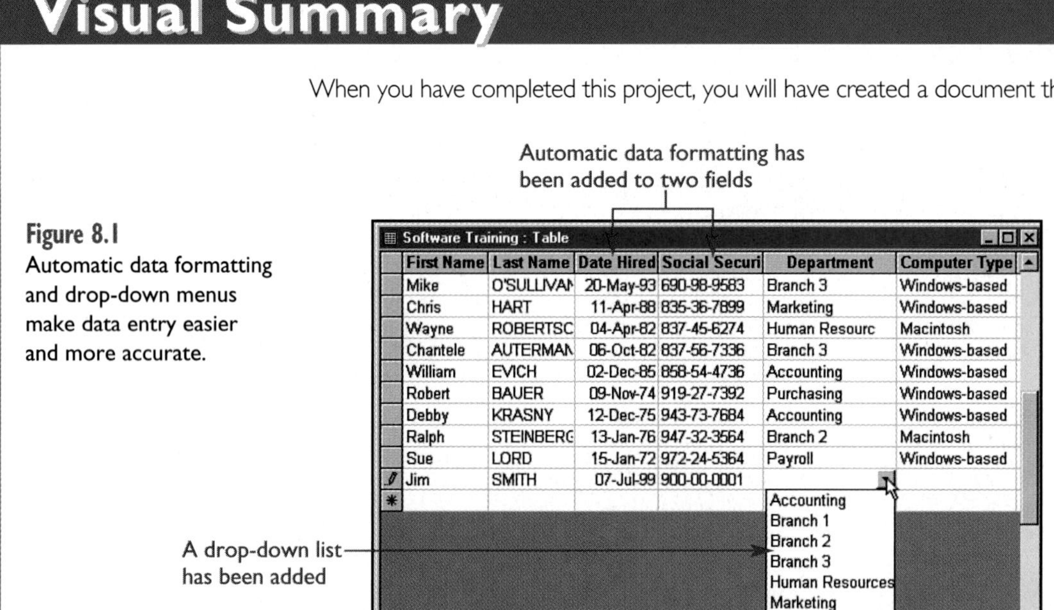

Figure 8.1
Automatic data formatting and drop-down menus make data entry easier and more accurate.

Lesson 1: Creating Consistent Data Formats

On many occasions you will want your data to be displayed in a specific format. For example, you might want to have text displayed in uppercase letters, or you might want dates to appear in a consistent format. Some of these formats can be activated by using a drop-down menu, whereas others require that you enter a symbol in a special format box.

In the following procedure, you learn how to change the appearance of two of the fields in the Software Training table. You change the format of the Last Name field to display all the names in uppercase letters, and modify the date format in the Date Hired field.

To Use a Display Format to Control the Appearance of the Data

1. **Launch Access. Click OK to open an existing file.**
The Open dialog box is displayed. Make sure you have a disk in drive A.

2. **Use the Look in box to locate the AC2-0101 file on your CD-ROM, right-click on it, and use the Send To option to send it to the floppy drive. Move to drive A, right-click on the filename, and select Properties from the shortcut menu. Select Archive and deselect Read-only from the Attributes section. Click OK to close the Properties dialog box.**

3. **Right-click on the filename, and select Properties from the shortcut menu. Select the Rename option, and then rename the file** `PC Training`**. Click OK, and then open the database.**
The database window should now be open to the Tables area (see Figure 8.2).

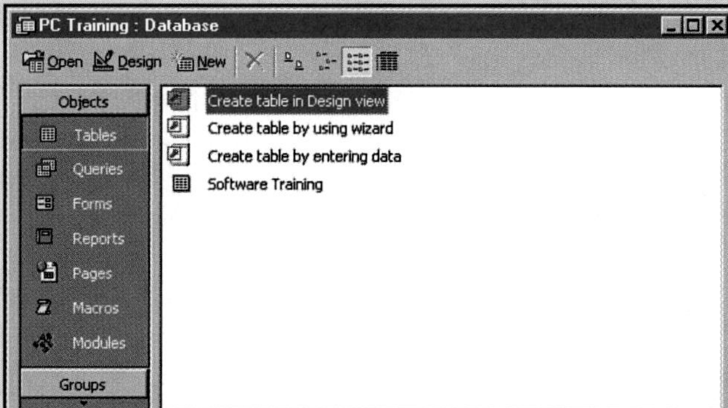

Figure 8.2
The database window displays the Tables area of the PC Training database.

> The file may appear as AC2-0101.mdb. This depends on whether the file extensions have been turned on in Windows. When renaming the file, make sure you add the .mdb extension if your original file shows it. Do not add it if the original file does not show it.

4. **Click the Tables object button, if necessary. Select the Software Training table, and then click the Open button to view the data.**
Notice that the data contained in the Last Name field is a mix of uppercase and lowercase letters, and the Date Hired field is displayed in the mm/dd/yy format.

5. **Click the View button on the toolbar to switch to Design view.**
The Table Design view is displayed (see Figure 8.3).

continues ▶

To Use a Display Format to Control the Appearance of the Data (continued)

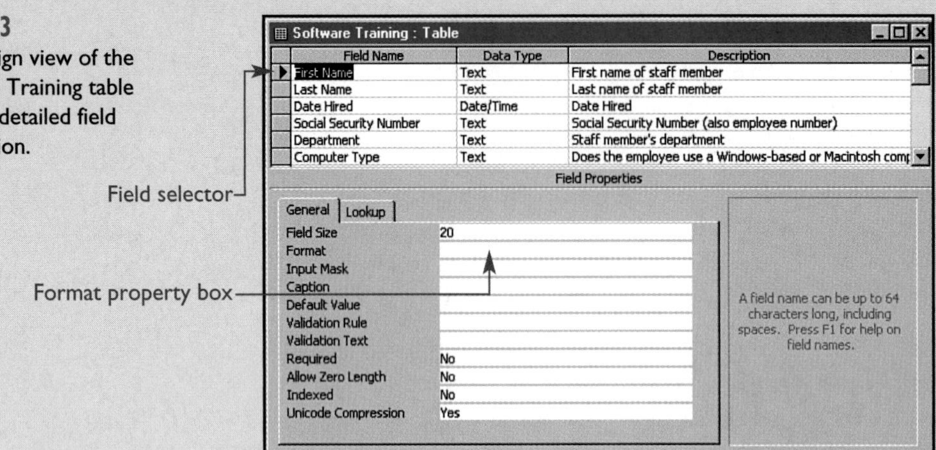

Figure 8.3
The Design view of the Software Training table includes detailed field information.

6 Click anywhere in the Last Name field to select it.
The Field Properties section in the bottom half of the window changes to display the properties of the Last Name field.

7 Click in the Format property box in the Field Properties section.

8 Type the greater than symbol (>) as the Format property.
The greater than symbol tells the program to display all text in the field as uppercase. The less than symbol (<) displays all the text in a field as lowercase. When no entry is made in the Format property box, text is displayed as entered.

9 Click the View button on the toolbar to switch to Datasheet view.
Whenever you make changes in field structures, the program asks if you want to save your changes. Click Yes whenever this message is displayed. Notice that all the last names in the Last Name field are now displayed in capital letters.

10 Click the View button to return to Design view, and then click anywhere in the Date Hired field.

11 Select the Format property box, and then click the drop-down arrow.
The date Format drop-down list is displayed (see Figure 8.4). Notice that a format can be selected for dates and times, or the General Date can be used to display both date and time.

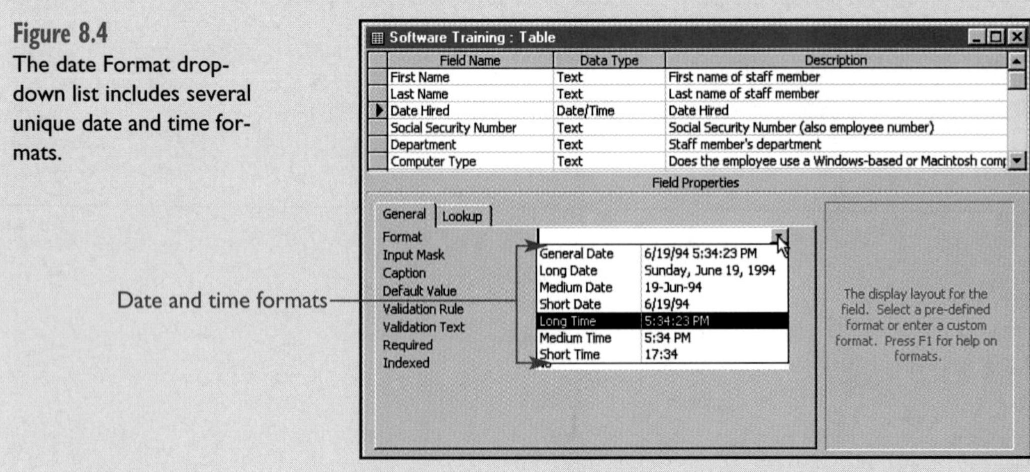

Figure 8.4
The date Format drop-down list includes several unique date and time formats.

⑫ **Select the Medium Date format.**
Each format refers to the relative length of the date entries as they appear in the database.

 ⑬ **Click the View button to return to Datasheet view.**
Once again, you have changed the structure of the table, so you will need to save your changes. The Date Hired field is now displayed in the dd-mmm-yy format (see Figure 8.5).

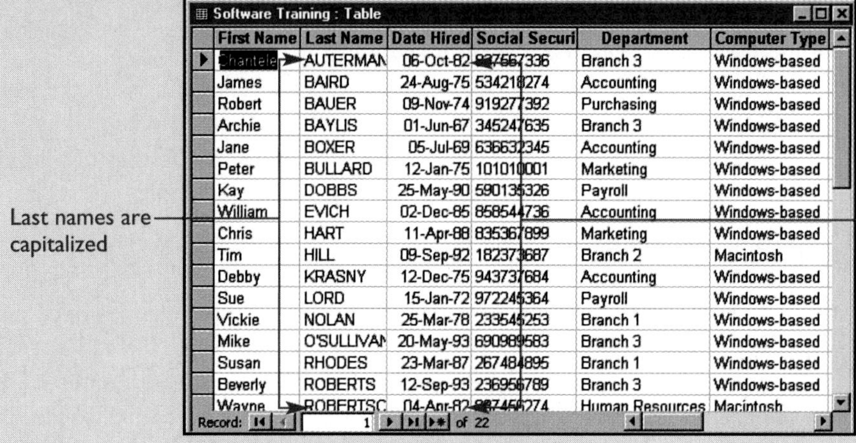

First Name	Last Name	Date Hired	Social Securi	Department	Computer Type
Chantele	AUTERMAN	06-Oct-82	[illegible]7567336	Branch 3	Windows-based
James	BAIRD	24-Aug-75	534218274	Accounting	Windows-based
Robert	BAUER	09-Nov-74	919277392	Purchasing	Windows-based
Archie	BAYLIS	01-Jun-67	345247635	Branch 3	Windows-based
Jane	BOXER	05-Jul-69	636632345	Accounting	Windows-based
Peter	BULLARD	12-Jan-75	101010001	Marketing	Windows-based
Kay	DOBBS	25-May-90	590135326	Payroll	Windows-based
William	EVICH	02-Dec-85	858544736	Accounting	Windows-based
Chris	HART	11-Apr-88	835367899	Marketing	Windows-based
Tim	HILL	09-Sep-92	182373687	Branch 2	Macintosh
Debby	KRASNY	12-Dec-75	943737684	Accounting	Windows-based
Sue	LORD	15-Jan-72	972245364	Payroll	Windows-based
Vickie	NOLAN	25-Mar-78	233545253	Branch 1	Windows-based
Mike	O'SULLIVAN	20-May-93	690989583	Branch 3	Windows-based
Susan	RHODES	23-Mar-87	267484895	Branch 1	Windows-based
Beverly	ROBERTS	12-Sep-93	236956789	Branch 3	Windows-based
Wayne	ROBERTSC	04-Apr-82	[illegible]7456274	Human Resources	Macintosh

Figure 8.5
The Software Training table shows the changes in format.

Date format has been changed

Keep the database open for the next lesson.

How Formatted Data Is Saved
The Format property does not change the contents of the table, just how the data is presented. For example, the last names are still saved on your disk as you originally typed them.

Getting Help on Formatting Fields
Many more options are available for formatting fields. You can click in any of the Field Properties boxes, and then press F1 to get help on options for every data type.

Lesson 2: Creating Conditional Formats for Positive, Negative, and Null Values

More complex procedures are available to format fields than those shown in Lesson 1. These require a succession of components containing instructions separated by semicolons. Each component represents a specific data format for a certain condition.

Conditional formats are particularly useful for dates and numbers. For example, you could set up a conditional format to display positive numbers with black text, negative numbers in red, and zeros or blanks when no data is entered in the field (a ***null value***). In this lesson, you set up the expense field to leave cells blank when you choose not to enter a number.

To Create a Conditional Format

1 In the PC Training database, click the View button on the toolbar to switch to Design view of the Software Training table.

2 Scroll down the list of field names, and then click anywhere in the Expense field to select it.

The Expense field is already formatted as Currency. Unfortunately, this displays fields with no entries as $0.00.

3 Click in the Format box in the Field Properties area.

4 Select the Currency format and delete it.

When formatting numeric fields (such as Number and Currency), the various components are separated by semicolons (;). The first component is always the format of a positive number, whereas the second is the format of a negative number. The third component tells the program how to display null values.

5 Enter the following in the Format property box, exactly as shown:

`$#,##0.00;$#,##0.00[Red];#`

The first component tells the program to display a dollar sign followed by the number for a positive number. The pound signs (#) to the right of the dollar sign tell the program to place a number there if one has been entered. If the number is less than a thousand, a zero will not be forced into that location, and the comma will be dropped. If a number under $1 is entered, a zero is displayed in the first position to the left of the decimal.

Sometimes you want to force a leading zero to identify decimal numbers that may be less than one. There is less possibility of overlooking the decimal point or confusing it with a period if it follows a zero (0.25) than if it does not (.25).

The second component uses the same format but displays negative numbers in red. This is indicated by typing the word `Red` surrounded by square brackets (not parentheses). The third component contains a pound sign (#), which tells the program to leave the field blank if no number is typed in.

The properties area should look like Figure 8.6.

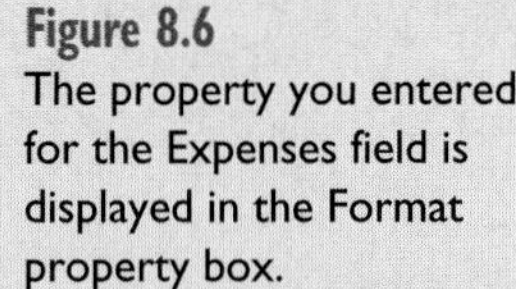

Figure 8.6
The property you entered for the Expenses field is displayed in the Format property box.

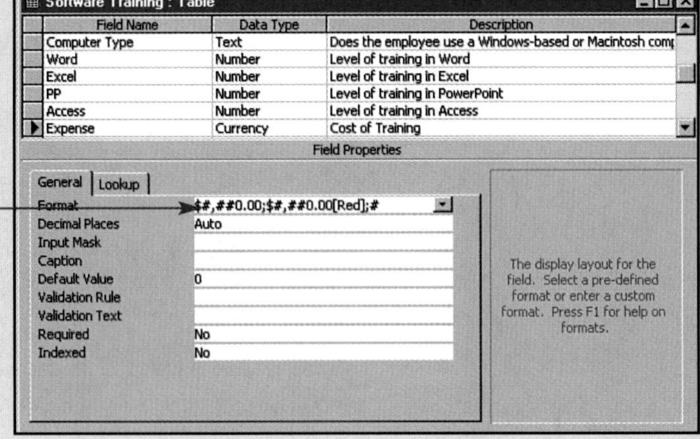

6 Click the View button on the toolbar to switch to Datasheet view.
Click Yes when prompted to save your changes to the table.

7 Scroll to the right and notice that the records that had no entries for the Expense field now display a blank instead of $0 (see Figure 8.7).
Keep the database open for the next lesson.

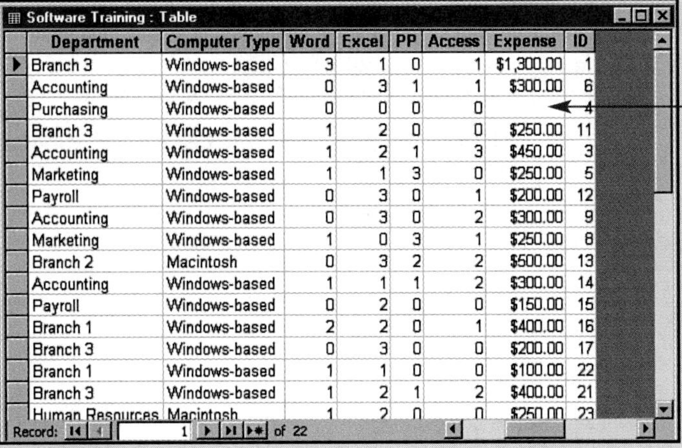

Software Training : Table

Department	Computer Type	Word	Excel	PP	Access	Expense	ID
Branch 3	Windows-based	3	1	0	1	$1,300.00	1
Accounting	Windows-based	0	3	1	1	$300.00	6
Purchasing	Windows-based	0	0	0	0		4
Branch 3	Windows-based	1	2	0	0	$250.00	11
Accounting	Windows-based	1	2	1	3	$450.00	3
Marketing	Windows-based	1	1	3	0	$250.00	5
Payroll	Windows-based	0	3	0	1	$200.00	12
Accounting	Windows-based	0	3	0	2	$300.00	9
Marketing	Windows-based	1	0	3	1	$250.00	8
Branch 2	Macintosh	0	3	2	2	$500.00	13
Accounting	Windows-based	1	1	1	2	$300.00	14
Payroll	Windows-based	0	2	0	0	$150.00	15
Branch 1	Windows-based	2	2	0	1	$400.00	16
Branch 3	Windows-based	0	3	0	0	$200.00	17
Branch 1	Windows-based	1	1	0	0	$100.00	22
Branch 3	Windows-based	1	2	1	2	$400.00	21
Human Resources	Macintosh	1	2	0	0	$250.00	23

Record: 1 of 22

Figure 8.7
The Software Training table shows a blank rather than a zero.

Getting Help with Conditional Formats
The first few times that you use conditional formats, you will probably need to use help. The quickest way to get the right kind of help is to go to Design view, select the field you want to format, place the insertion point in the Format properties box, and press F1. This will take you directly to format help.

Lesson 3: Changing the Data Input Structure Using Input Masks

Input masks are data formats that make data entry more meaningful. They can be used to make certain types of data, such as telephone numbers and Social Security numbers, easy to enter. Input masks can be entered in the Input Mask properties box. They can also be added using the Input Mask Wizard.

In this lesson, you add an input mask to the Social Security Number field to divide the number into the familiar XXX-XX-XXXX format. Input masks can also control the format of the data as it is stored in the table.

To Create an Input Mask

1 In the PC Training database, click the View button on the toolbar to switch to Design view of the Software Training table.

continues ▶

To Create an Input Mask (continued)

2 Click anywhere in the Social Security Number field to select it.

The Social Security numbers in this database have been entered as text. Because all Social Security numbers contain three blocks of numbers of 3, 2, and 4 digits, it would make data entry easier if the field was also set up in this format.

3 Click the Input Mask box in the Field Properties area.

A Build button (the one with three dots) is displayed on the right-hand side of the Input Mask box (see Figure 8.8).

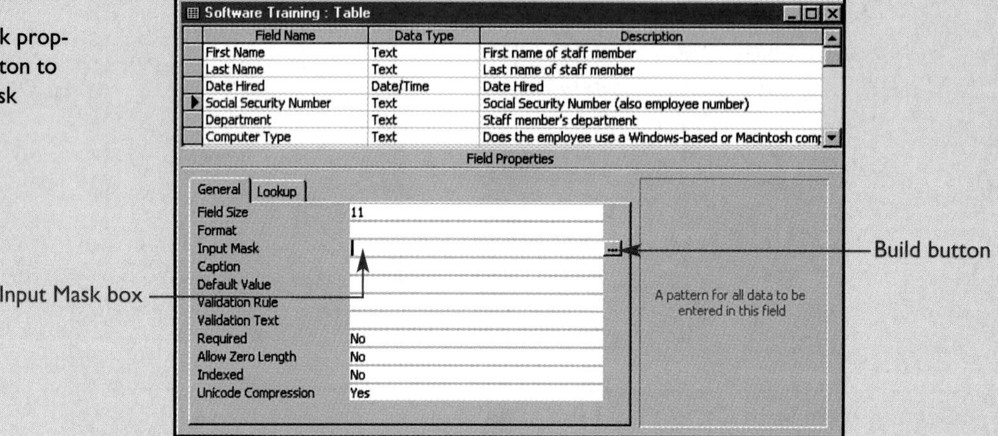

Figure 8.8
Use the Input Mask property box Build button to start the Input Mask Wizard.

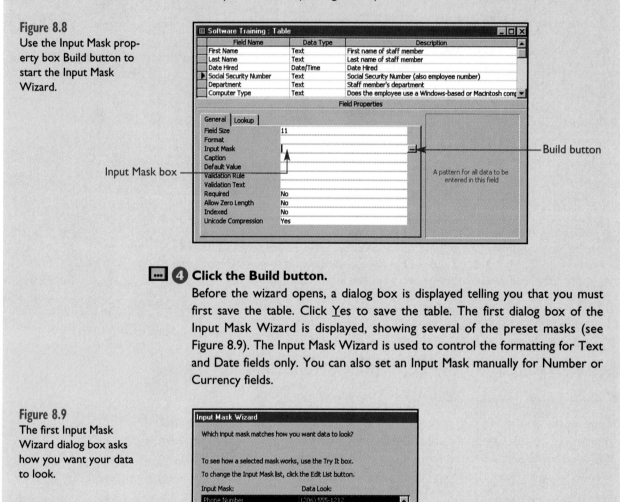

4 Click the Build button.

Before the wizard opens, a dialog box is displayed telling you that you must first save the table. Click Yes to save the table. The first dialog box of the Input Mask Wizard is displayed, showing several of the preset masks (see Figure 8.9). The Input Mask Wizard is used to control the formatting for Text and Date fields only. You can also set an Input Mask manually for Number or Currency fields.

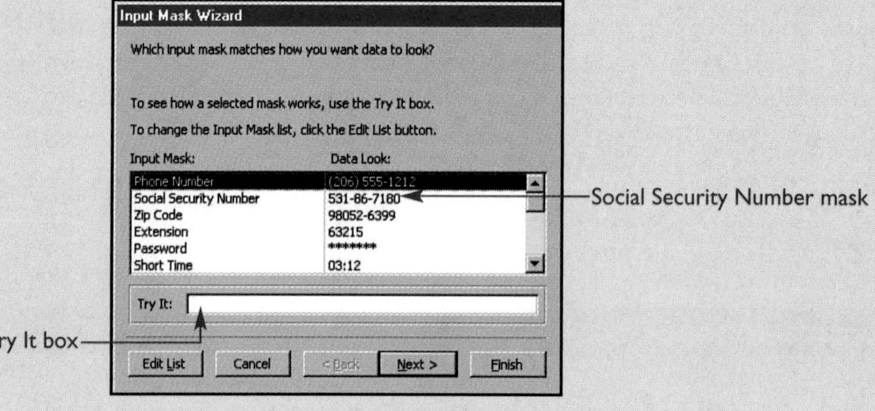

Figure 8.9
The first Input Mask Wizard dialog box asks how you want your data to look.

You might get a message that Microsoft Access cannot start this wizard. This means that the Input Mask Wizard has not been installed on your machine. If this is the case, click Yes to install it. A dialog box will ask for the first Microsoft Office installation CD. Place the CD in your CD drive and click OK. Select Add or Remove Features from the installation window. Expand the Microsoft Access for Windows button and click the drop-down arrow for Typical Wizards. Choose whether you want to run the wizard from the hard disk or the CD, and whether you want to install just the feature you need (in this case the Input Mask Wizard) or all the typical wizards. Click Update Now to complete the installation.

It is not absolutely necessary to use the Input Mask Wizard. If you know the expression you want to use, you can type it directly into the Input Mask property box. Look at the examples of the input masks in the following section and enter the expression directly into the Input Mask property box.

5. **Select the Social Security Number option, and then click in the Try It area to see the format that appears in the field.**

6. **Click the Next button.**
The second Input Mask Wizard dialog box is displayed (see Figure 8.10). The basic format is shown, and you are asked if you are satisfied with the format and the ***placeholders*** used to reserve spaces for the data. In this example, you accept the default settings.

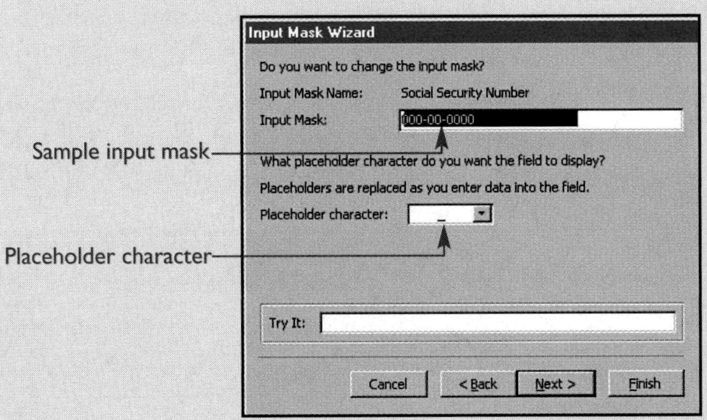

Figure 8.10
The second Input Mask Wizard dialog box enables you to modify the selected input mask.

7. **Click the Next button.**
The third Input Mask Wizard dialog box is displayed (see Figure 8.11). This dialog box asks whether the program should save the characters, in this case dashes, used to separate the three parts of the Social Security number. The dashes will be displayed in forms and reports that use this field but will not be part of the actual data stored in each field. If you export the data to another program, the dashes will not be there. The default choice is not to save the extra characters.

continues ▶

To Create an Input Mask (continued)

Figure 8.11
The third Input Mask Wizard dialog box asks you how you want to store the data.

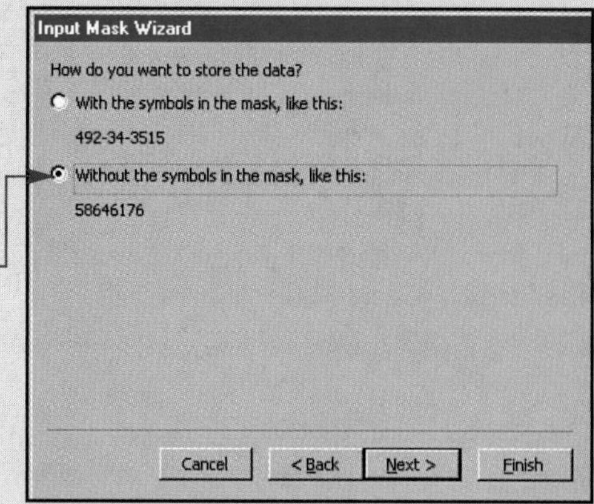

Save without the symbols option

8 **Click the Next button to accept the default.**
The fourth Input Mask Wizard dialog box is displayed. This dialog box tells you that you have completed the Wizard.

9 **Click the Finish button to complete the Input Mask Wizard.**
The Input Mask property box contains the following:

```
000-00-0000;;_
```

The Input Mask contains three components that are separated by semicolons. The first component shows the input format. The next component has nothing in it, which indicates that there is no special format for an empty field. The third component has an underscore to indicate that the placeholder for the field is an underscore.

10 **Click the View button on the toolbar to switch to Datasheet view.**
Click Yes when prompted to save your changes to the table. Notice that the Social Security numbers are now in the familiar format (see Figure 8.12).

Figure 8.12
An Input Mask for the Social Security Number field has been added.

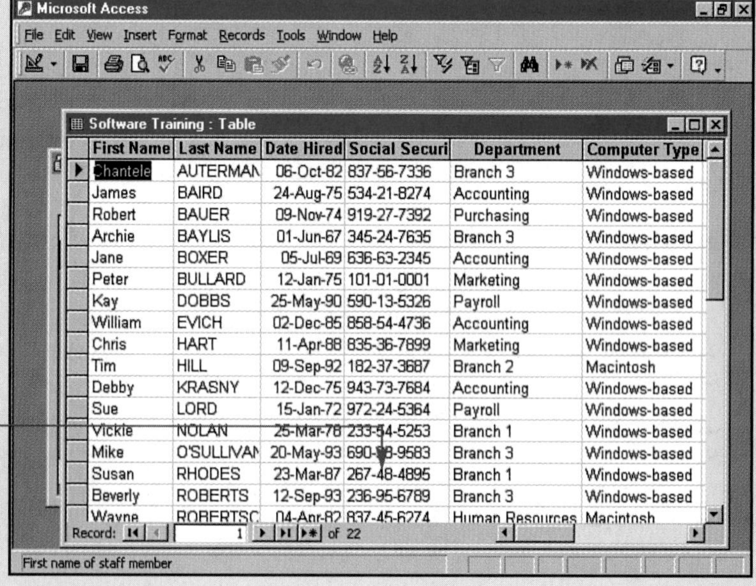

Microsoft Access
File Edit View Insert Format Records Tools Window Help
Software Training : Table
First Name | Last Name | Date Hired | Social Securi | Department | Computer Type
Chantele | AUTERMAN | 06-Oct-82 | 837-56-7336 | Branch 3 | Windows-based
James | BAIRD | 24-Aug-75 | 534-21-8274 | Accounting | Windows-based
Robert | BAUER | 09-Nov-74 | 919-27-7392 | Purchasing | Windows-based
Archie | BAYLIS | 01-Jun-67 | 345-24-7635 | Branch 3 | Windows-based
Jane | BOXER | 05-Jul-69 | 636-63-2345 | Accounting | Windows-based
Peter | BULLARD | 12-Jan-75 | 101-01-0001 | Marketing | Windows-based
Kay | DOBBS | 25-May-90 | 590-13-5326 | Payroll | Windows-based
William | EVICH | 02-Dec-85 | 858-54-4736 | Accounting | Windows-based
Chris | HART | 11-Apr-88 | 835-36-7899 | Marketing | Windows-based
Tim | HILL | 09-Sep-92 | 182-37-3687 | Branch 2 | Macintosh
Debby | KRASNY | 12-Dec-75 | 943-73-7684 | Accounting | Windows-based
Sue | LORD | 15-Jan-72 | 972-24-5364 | Payroll | Windows-based
Vickie | NOLAN | 25-Mar-78 | 233-54-5253 | Branch 1 | Windows-based
Mike | O'SULLIVAN | 20-May-93 | 690-98-9583 | Branch 3 | Windows-based
Susan | RHODES | 23-Mar-87 | 267-48-4895 | Branch 1 | Windows-based
Beverly | ROBERTS | 12-Sep-93 | 236-95-6789 | Branch 3 | Windows-based
Wayne | ROBERTSC | 04-Apr-82 | 837-45-6274 | Human Resources | Macintosh
Record: 1 of 22
First name of staff member

Social Security Number with input mask

 **11 Click on the New Record button and add another record to see how the data is entered into the field. Use your own name and make up the rest of the information.**

Do not use a Social Security number that is a duplicate of a number in the table. You learn how to automatically guard against this type of error in Lesson 6, "Preventing Duplicate Entries Using Indexed Fields."

Keep the database open for the next lesson.

Input Mask Limitations

Adding an Input Mask puts certain limitations on data entry. If you have placeholders for nine characters, you need to enter all nine. If you enter eight or fewer characters, you get an error message, and you are not able to move out of the field until you correct the problem. If you do not have all the characters to enter, don't put any of them in, but press Esc to leave the field blank for now.

Lesson 4: Restricting Entries to Those That Meet Validation Criteria

The data entered in some fields in a database needs to be restricted in some way. For example, a field set up for coded data might only use 0s and 1s, whereas a text field might be used to enter only two possible values. Several fields in the PC Training table fit this category. The Computer Type field has only two possible answers: Windows-based or Macintosh. The four software fields, Word, Excel, PP, and Access, use only four numbers (0, 1, 2, and 3).

Access gives you the option of restricting the information that will be accepted into a field. This is done by constructing a ***validation rule***, which is an expression that the program compares entered data against to see if it is acceptable. If the data is not acceptable, ***validation text*** can be displayed to explain the reason the data is not acceptable.

Validation rules are used for two purposes: to make sure the user does not enter incorrect data, and to help avoid typographical errors. In this lesson you use the ***Expression Builder*** to build a validation rule for the four software fields. You also create validation text to be used as an error message for incorrect data entry.

To Create Validation Rules and Validation Text Using the Expression Builder

1 In the PC Training database, click the View button on the toolbar to switch to Design view of the Software Training table.

2 Click anywhere in the Word field to select it, and then click the Validation Rule box in the Field Properties area.

You may have to scroll down to see the Word field. Notice that a Build button (containing three dots) is displayed to the right of the Validation Rule property box.

continues ▶

To Create Validation Rules and Validation Text Using the Expression Builder (continued)

3 Click the Build button on the right side of the Validation Rule box.
The Expression Builder dialog box is displayed (see Figure 8.13). You now build a Function, which is the default.

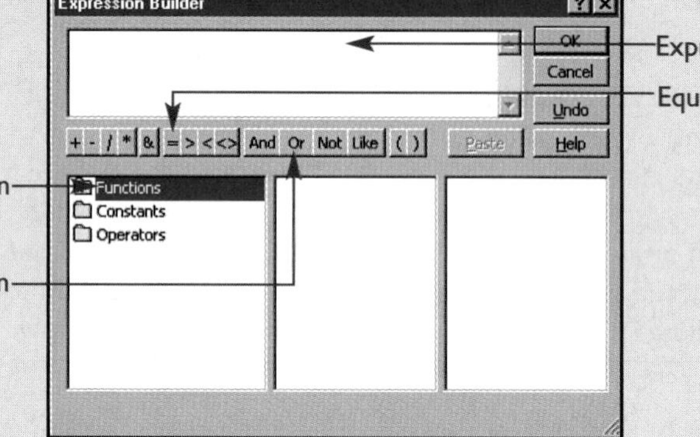

Figure 8.13
Use the Expression Builder dialog box to build a function in a Validation Rule.

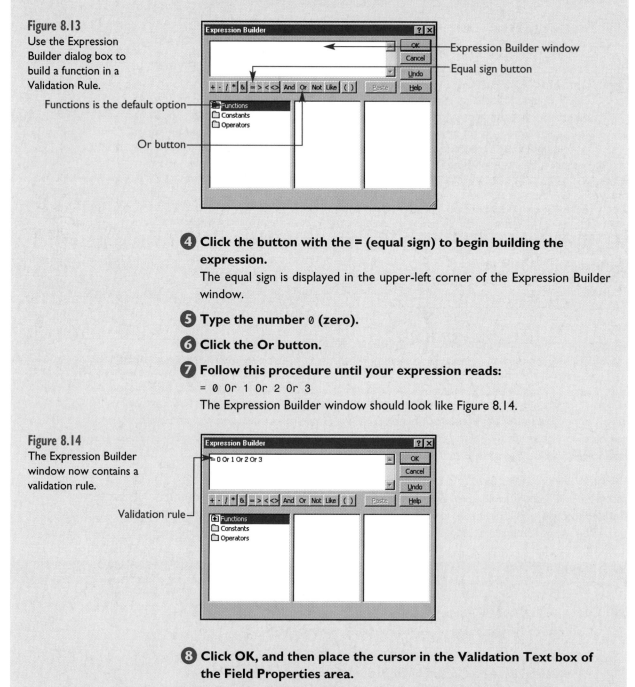

4 Click the button with the = (equal sign) to begin building the expression.
The equal sign is displayed in the upper-left corner of the Expression Builder window.

5 Type the number `0` (zero).

6 Click the Or button.

7 Follow this procedure until your expression reads:
`= 0 Or 1 Or 2 Or 3`
The Expression Builder window should look like Figure 8.14.

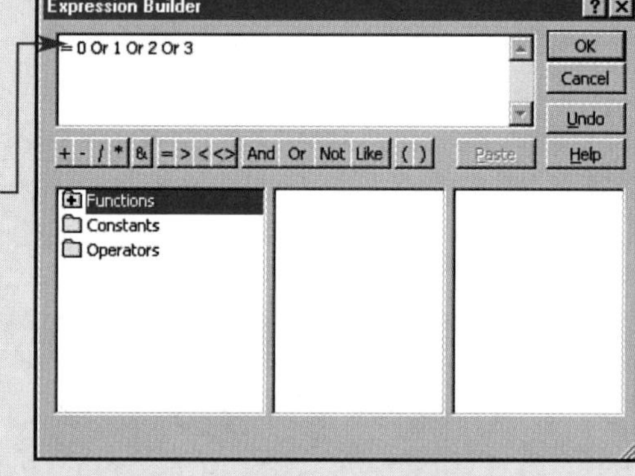

Figure 8.14
The Expression Builder window now contains a validation rule.

8 Click OK, and then place the cursor in the Validation Text box of the Field Properties area.

9 Type the following in the Validation Text property box: `That is not a valid option. Please enter the number 0, 1, 2, or 3.`
You should now have entries in both the Validation Rule box and the Validation Text box (see Figure 8.15).

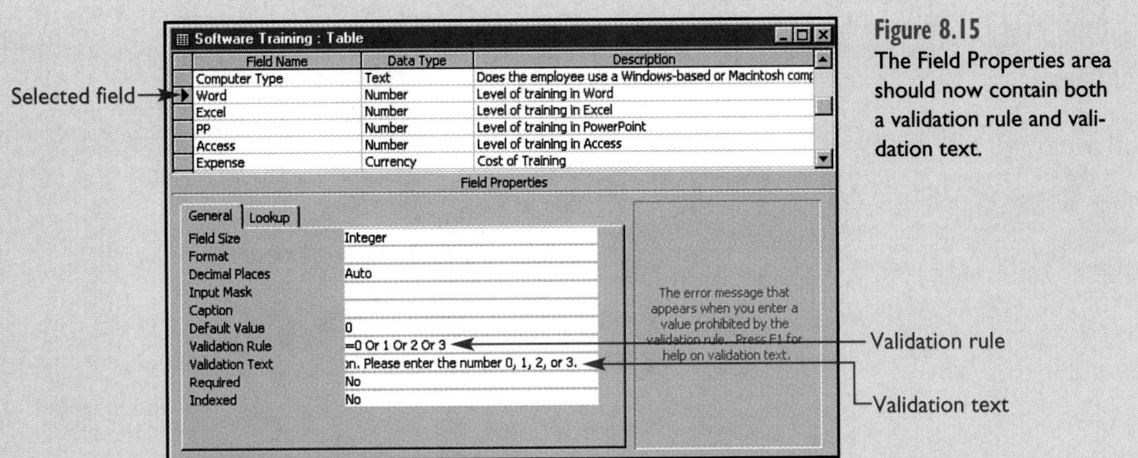

Figure 8.15
The Field Properties area should now contain both a validation rule and validation text.

⑩ **Repeat steps 2 through 9 for the other three software fields (Excel, PP, and Access).**
To save time and effort, you can use the Copy and Paste commands with Field Properties. Highlight the Validation Rule text in the Word property box and click the Copy button. Then select the Excel field, click the Validation Rule property box, and click the Paste button. Do this to the other two fields (PP and Access), and then go back and repeat the procedure with the Validation Text property boxes.

⑪ **Click the View button on the toolbar to switch to Datasheet view.**
Click Yes when prompted to save your changes to the table.

As usual, when you change the structure of the table, you will be prompted to save your changes. This time, however, an additional dialog box is displayed (see Figure 8.16). This dialog box warns you that `Data integrity rules have been changed; existing data may not be valid for the new rules`. Whenever a validation rule is added or modified, this warning is displayed. It is important that you are familiar with the content of your data so you can assess whether, in fact, the data in the table violates the new rule that has just been added. In this case, the data will cause no problem.

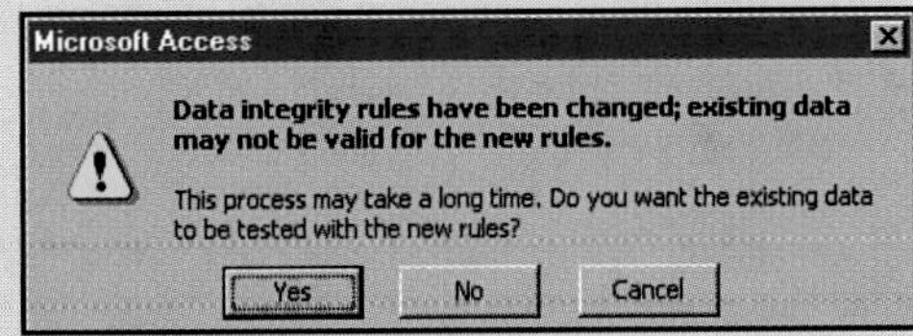

Figure 8.16
The Data Integrity warning dialog box notifies you that data integrity rules have been changed.

⑫ **Click Yes. The program tests your fields to find any conflicting data.**
If data integrity is violated, you receive an additional warning box telling you that data has been detected that violates the rules, but the program does not specifically identify the data. You then need to create a query to search for the data that was outside of the rules and change that data, if appropriate.

⑬ **Attempt to enter the number 5 in one of the software fields and press Enter to move to the next field.**
Notice how the message you typed in the Validation Text property box is displayed in the error message window (see Figure 8.17).

continues ▶

To Create Validation Rules and Validation Text Using the Expression Builder (continued)

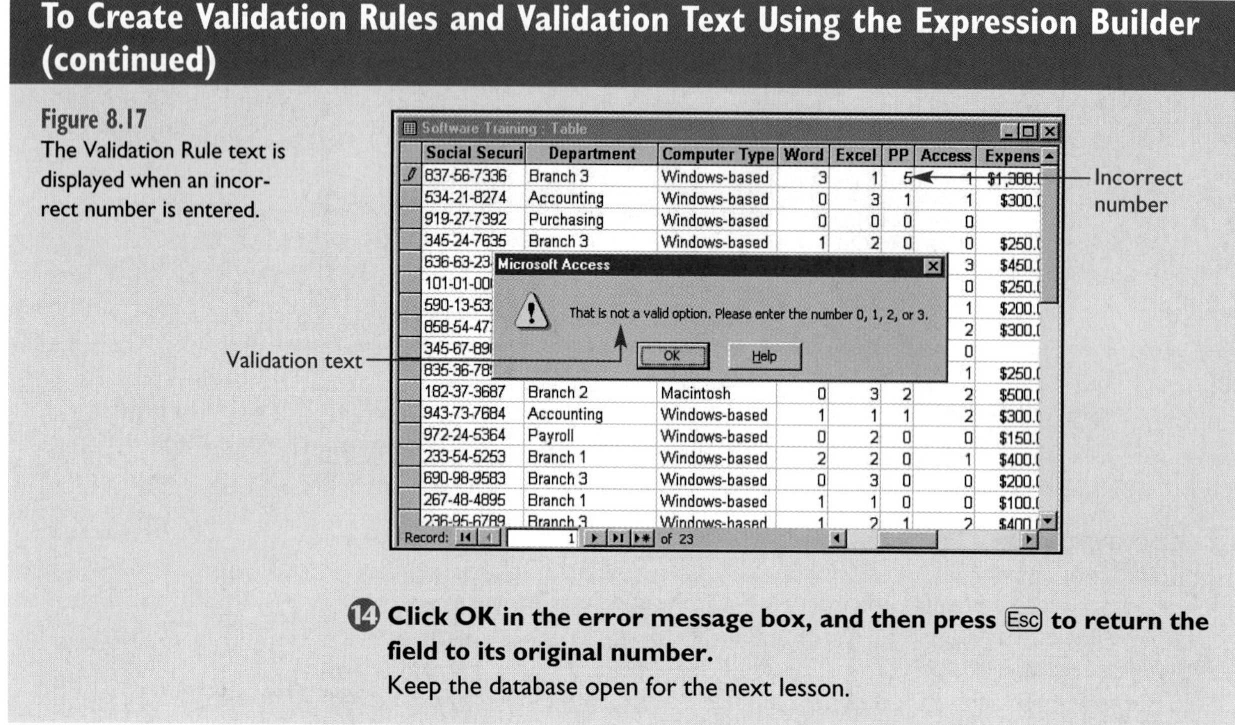

Figure 8.17
The Validation Rule text is displayed when an incorrect number is entered.

⓮ **Click OK in the error message box, and then press Esc to return the field to its original number.**
Keep the database open for the next lesson.

Testing Structural Changes on a Backup File
It is a good idea to test your changes on a backup file before you make major changes to your table structure. If you change the structure of a table on the only file you have and choose yes when it checks for data integrity, it is always possible that some data could be lost. By testing the structure change on a backup file, you can thoroughly test the change without having to worry that you are going to incorrectly change the "real" data.

Lesson 5: Requiring Entry of Necessary Information

At times you will want to force the user to fill in a field. Access enables you to require a data entry in a field. Required responses can be added to all field types except the AutoNumber fields, which are used when sequential numbering is required.

In this lesson, you require that data be entered into the Last Name field.

To Require Entry of Necessary Information

❶ **In the PC Training database, click the View button on the toolbar to switch to Design view, and then click the Last Name field to select it.**
You may have to scroll up to find the Last Name field.

❷ **Click the Required box in the Field Properties area.**

❸ **Click the drop-down arrow to reveal the choices.**
The screen should look like Figure 8.18.

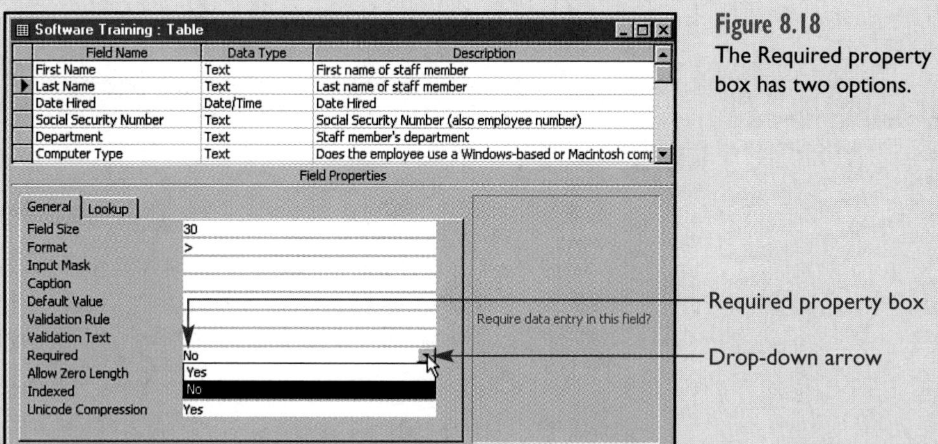

Figure 8.18
The Required property box has two options.

4 Select Yes to make an entry into this field required.

5 Click the View button on the toolbar to switch to Datasheet view.
Click Yes when prompted to save your changes to the table. You are warned about data integrity rule changes as you were when you changed the Validation Rule in Lesson 4, "Restricting Entries to Those That Meet Validation Criteria." Click Yes to move to the datasheet.

> If you entered any records without a last name, you will see another warning box that states `Existing data violates the new setting for the 'Required' property for the field 'Last Name'.` Choose Yes to continue testing with the new setting.

6 Scroll down to the bottom of the table and enter a new record, but leave the Last Name field blank.
The program enables you to continue entering data to the end of the record; however, when you press ↵Enter after the last field, another dialog box is displayed (see Figure 8.19), warning you that the Last Name field cannot contain a Null value.

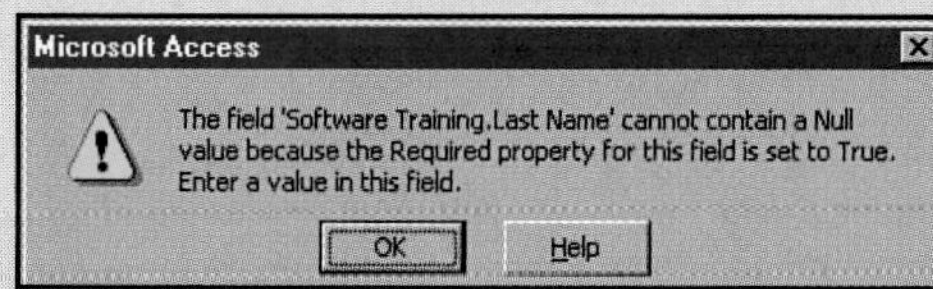

Figure 8.19
The Null value warning dialog box is displayed if you try to skip the Last Name field.

7 Click OK in the warning box.

8 Press Esc to back out of the entry.
Keep the database open for the next lesson.

Lesson 6: Preventing Duplicate Entries Using Indexed Fields

In Access it is possible to build an index for a field. This acts like an index in a book; it speeds up searching and sorting for that field. Indexes can be created for all but Memo, Hyperlink, and OLE fields. ***Indexed fields*** can also be set up to prevent duplicate entries in a field. If a field has been designated as the ***primary key field***, it is automatically indexed, with no duplicate entries allowed. Other fields can also be indexed and set to disallow duplicate entries.

In this lesson, you index the Social Security Number field and prevent duplicate entries, because all Social Security numbers should be unique.

To Prevent Duplicate Entries Using Indexed Fields

1 In the PC Training database, click the View button on the toolbar to switch views to Design view of the Software Training table.

2 Click anywhere in the Social Security Number field to select it, and then click the Indexed property box.

A drop-down arrow is displayed at the right side of the property box.

3 Click the drop-down arrow and select Yes (No Duplicates) from the drop-down list.

The Social Security Number properties area should look like Figure 8.20.

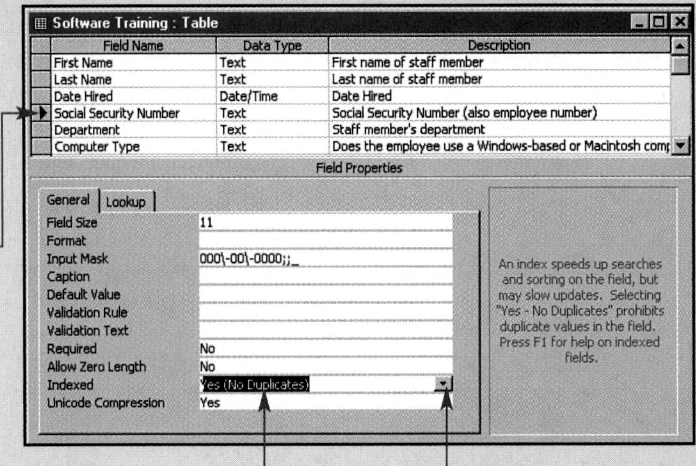

Figure 8.20
The Social Security Number Field Properties area now shows "Yes (No Duplicates)" in the Indexed property box.

4 Click the View button on the toolbar to switch to Datasheet view.

Click Yes when prompted to save your changes to the table.

5 Scroll down to the bottom of the table.

6 Add a new record, but this time enter a Social Security number from a previous record.

When you try to complete the record, an error message is displayed (see Figure 8.21). Notice that the error message tells you that you have entered a duplicate value in an index, primary key, or relationship, but does not tell you in which field the error occurred. This can be a big problem in a database with many indexed fields.

Checking For the Primary Key or Indexed Fields

If you get an error message and can't remember which field is the primary key, switch to Design view and look for the key icon to the left of the list of fields. You can also check to see which fields are indexed by selecting each field and checking the Indexed box in the Field Properties area.

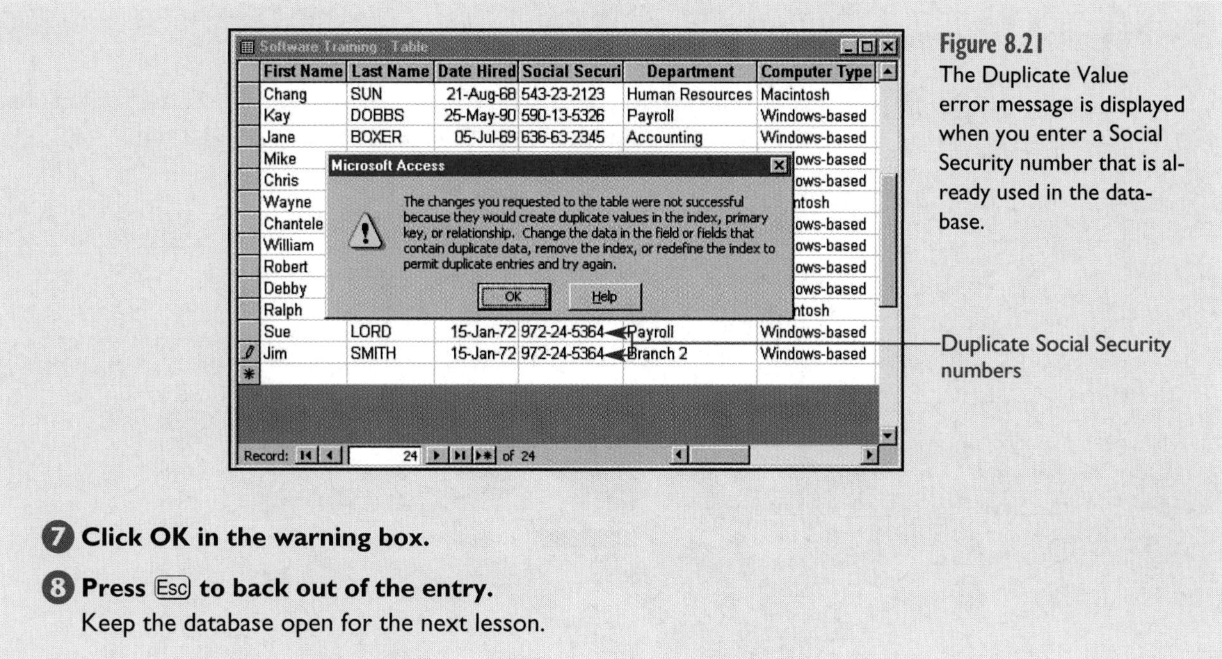

Figure 8.21
The Duplicate Value error message is displayed when you enter a Social Security number that is already used in the database.

7 Click OK in the warning box.

8 Press Esc to back out of the entry.
Keep the database open for the next lesson.

Searching For Duplicate Entries
One way to search for a duplicate entry is to use the Find button on the toolbar. Enter the number or word that caused a problem and search for each occurrence of it. Because the error message does not identify which field contains the duplicate entry, you may need to look at the design of the table to determine which fields are indexed or which field is the primary key. Search for duplicate values in these fields.

Lesson 7: Creating a Lookup Column to Allow Selection from a List

There are times when you will have a field that has several common entries. This is particularly true of fields designed for such things as city or state names, job titles, and military ranks.

Access contains a Lookup Wizard in the Data Type column in the Table Design view. This wizard enables you to either enter the common items or have the program make up a list from a field in another table. Having pre-typed choices available makes data entry far easier, and also prevents the user from making typographical errors. When entering data, if the value you need is not on the list, you can type it in the field.

In this lesson, you add a Lookup list for the Department field. The Lookup Wizard walks you through the steps of creating the data list, and you end up with a drop-down list containing all the department names in the database.

To Create a Lookup Column Using the Lookup Wizard

1 In the PC Training database, click the View button on the toolbar to switch views to Design view of the Software Training table.

2 Click on the Data Type box of the Department field.

A drop-down arrow is displayed on the right side of the box.

3 Click the arrow in the Department Data Type box.

A drop-down menu is displayed (see Figure 8.22). The various data types are shown in this box. At the bottom of the box is the Lookup Wizard choice.

Figure 8.22
The Lookup Wizard option is displayed at the bottom of the drop-down list.

Drop-down arrow

Lookup Wizard option

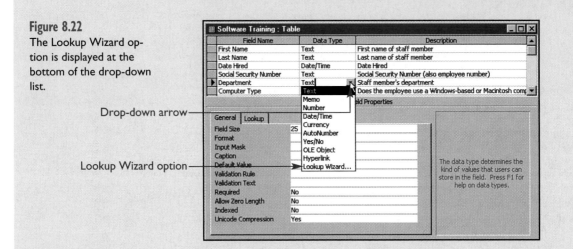

4 Select Lookup Wizard from the drop-down list.

The first Lookup Wizard dialog box is displayed (see Figure 8.23).

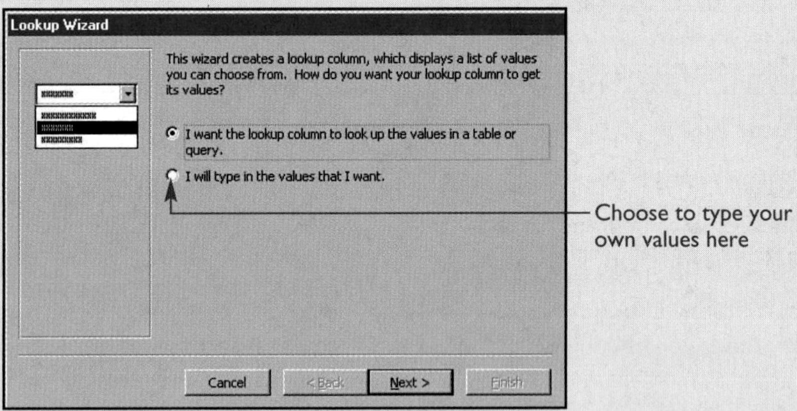

Figure 8.23
The first Lookup Wizard dialog box asks how you want your lookup column to get its values.

5 Choose the second option to type the values you want, and then click Next.

The second Lookup Wizard dialog box is displayed.

6 Accept the default number of columns, and then type the departments listed below in the box labeled Col1:

Do not press ↵Enter after each entry. This takes you to the next dialog box. Use ↓ or Tab to move down. If you accidentally move to the next dialog box before you finish entering the department names, click Back to return to the data entry area.

```
Accounting
Branch 1
Branch 2
Branch 3
Human Resources
Marketing
Payroll
```

As you enter the seven department names (see Figure 8.24), the first one may scroll off the screen. If you need to move up to edit an entry that has scrolled off the screen, use ↑.

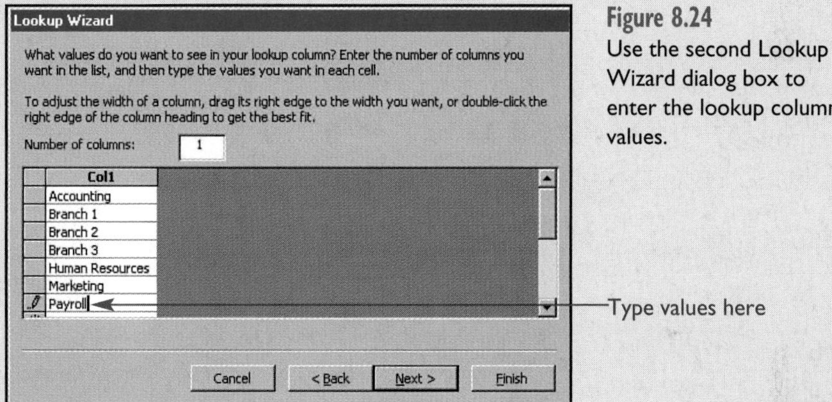

Figure 8.24
Use the second Lookup Wizard dialog box to enter the lookup column values.

7 Click Next to move to the third Lookup Wizard dialog box.

This dialog box asks what you want to name your lookup column (see Figure 8.25).

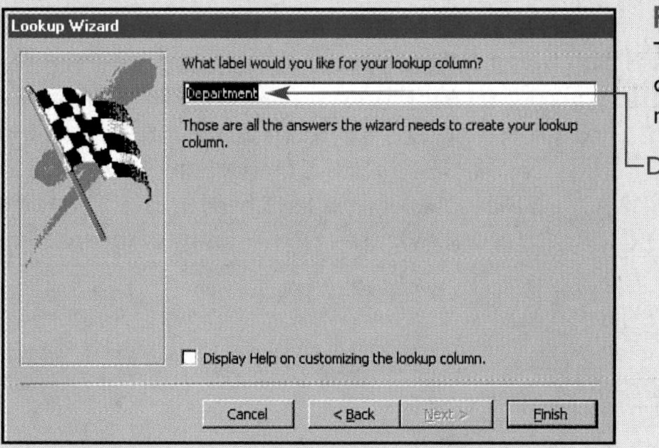

Figure 8.25
The final Lookup Wizard dialog box enables you to name the lookup column.

continues ▶

To Create a Lookup Column Using the Lookup Wizard (continued)

8. **Accept the default, Department, as the lookup column name, and then click Finish.**

9. **Click the View button on the toolbar to switch to Datasheet view.** Click Yes when prompted to save your changes to the table.

10. **Scroll down to the bottom of the table and enter a new record.** When you get to the Department field, notice that a drop-down arrow is displayed.

11. **Click the arrow to display the drop-down box you just created, and then select one of the departments.** You have now created a timesaving feature for your table (see Figure 8.26).

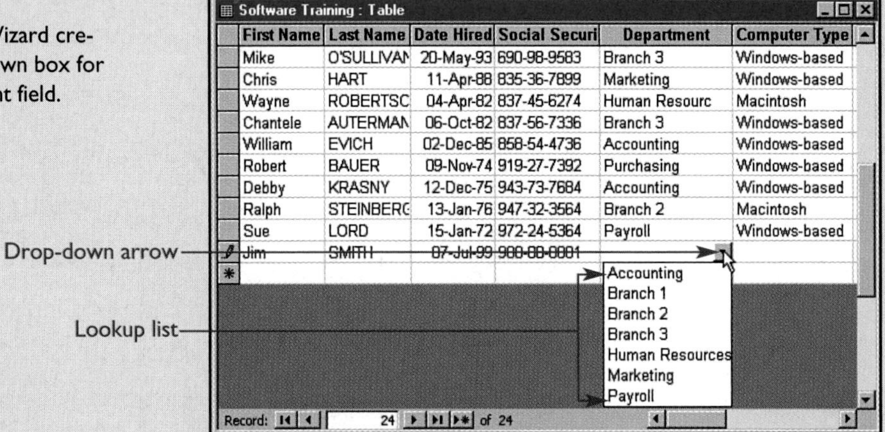

Figure 8.26
The Lookup Wizard created a drop-down box for the Department field.

12. **Press Esc to back out of the entry. Close your table and Exit Access.** If you have completed your session on the computer, select Shut Down from the Start menu. Otherwise, continue with the exercises for this project.

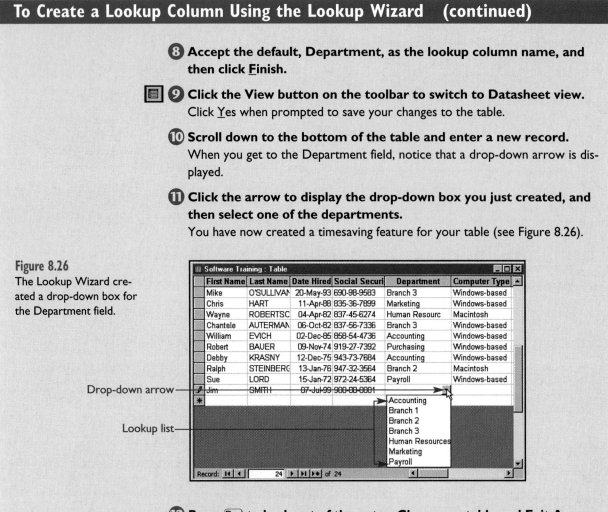

Effects of Format Changes in a Table
The changes made to the text and number formatting in table design carry over to new forms and reports that are based on this table. Some of the changes, such as required fields, validation rules, and default values, also show up in existing forms. It is always best to have the table structure complete before creating other objects to ensure that all the formatting characteristics flow from the table to the objects based on that table. If you make changes to the table structure after other objects have been created, you can add those same formatting characteristics directly to the design of the form, reports, or queries.

Features That Improve Data Accuracy
All the topics in this project were performed and tested in the table view. By changing the text and number formatting in table design, the formatting carries over to new forms and reports. All the following features help improve accuracy in forms, tables, and reports:

- **Consistent data formats**
- **Conditional formats**
- **Input masks**
- **Validation criteria**
- **Required fields**
- **Prevention of duplication**

Summary

In this project, you were introduced to some of the techniques used to refine and control data entry. You learned how to make field entries appear as all upper- or lowercase letters, and how to make data look different depending on data characteristics. You also set up input masks to assist with entry of consistently formatted data. You learned how to set conditions for accepting data entry, how to require the entry of data in a field, and how to avoid duplicate entries by indexing a field. Finally, you created a lookup list to make data entry quicker and more accurate.

You can learn more about taking control of data entry in Access by looking a little more closely at some of the other options available in input masks, conditional and data formatting, and validation criteria in Microsoft Help. The best way to do this is to go to the help index and explore the topic you are interested in. Create a new database and try out these features.

Checking Concepts and Terms

True/False

For each of the following statements, check *T* or *F* to indicate whether the statement is true or false.

__T __F **1.** When you change the display format of a field in an existing table, the data already stored on your disk is changed also. [L1]

__T __F **2.** If you want to show negative numbers in red text, you would create a conditional format. [L2]

__T __F **3.** You must use the Input Mask Wizard to enter an input mask. [L3]

__T __F **4.** Text you enter into the Validation Text property box will appear in an error message dialog box if the Validation Rule is violated. [L4]

__T __F **5.** Data entry can be required in every type of field except AutoNumber. [L5]

__T __F **6.** If you want a text field displayed in all capitals, enter the > (greater than) symbol in the format properties box for that field. [L1]

__T __F **7.** When you add an input mask to a field after data has been entered, it does not change the way the existing data is displayed; you must re-enter the data to have the new format take effect. [L3]

__T __F **8.** If the Input Mask Wizard does not work when you click the Build button, it means that it has not yet been installed on your hard drive. [L3]

__T __F **9.** When indexing a field, the Yes (No duplicates) option can only be used for the primary key field. [L6]

__T __F **10.** A null value is the same as a zero. [L2]

Multiple Choice

Circle the letter of the correct answer for each of the following questions.

1. In a conditional format, components are separated by ______________. [L2]

a. commas

b. semicolons

c. colons

d. quotation marks

2. The Input Mask Wizard creates formats for ______________. [L3]

a. all types of fields

b. all types of fields except OLE

c. text fields only

d. text and date fields only

3. A program that helps the user create formulas for Validation Rules is called a(n)______________. [L4]

a. Expression Builder

b. Validation Text

c. Rule Wizard

d. Restriction Builder

4. If you enter duplicate information in a field where duplicates are not allowed, how do you back out of that entry? [L6]

a. Press Del.

b. You can't delete the record.

c. Press Esc.

d. Press ↵Enter and go on.

5. One way to speed up searching and sorting on a field is to ______________. [L6]

a. prevent duplicate entries in the field

b. make it a required field

c. index it

d. make the data format consistent

6. Validation Text is used to______________. [L4]

a. explain to the person entering data the reason why the data entered is not acceptable

b. verify that only valid data is entered

c. validate text fields only

d. intimidate the user for making a mistake

7. Formats for the Date/Time data type can be set for ______________. [L1]

a. dates

b. times

c. date and time

d. all the above

8. Which of the following best describes a null value? [L2]

a. zero in a number field

b. spaces in a text field

c. $0 in a currency field

d. no entry at all

9. A required property can be set for every type of field except ______________. [L5]

a. Memo

b. OLE

c. AutoNumber

d. Yes/No

10. A lookup list would be most useful for a field that contained ______________. [L7]

a. Social Security numbers

b. department names

c. last names

d. account numbers

Screen ID

Label each element of the Access screens shown in Figure 8.27 and Figure 8.28.

Figure 8.27

A. Build button

B. Allows more than one condition

C. Special format for negative number

D. Begins an expression

E. Conditional format

F. Duplicate entries can be eliminated here

G. Selected field

H. Dialog box text

I. Data must meet this condition

J. Validation condition being built

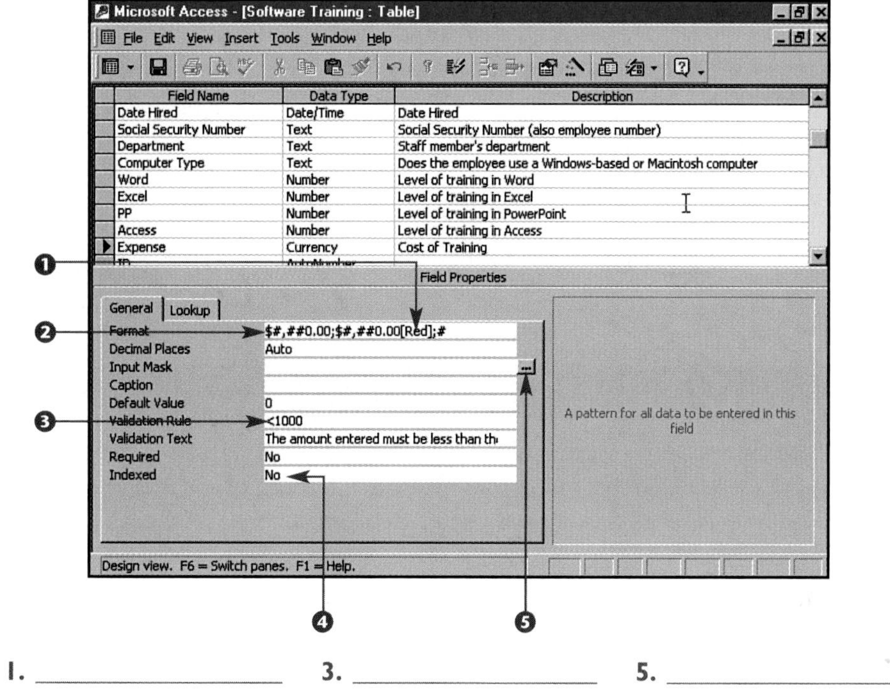

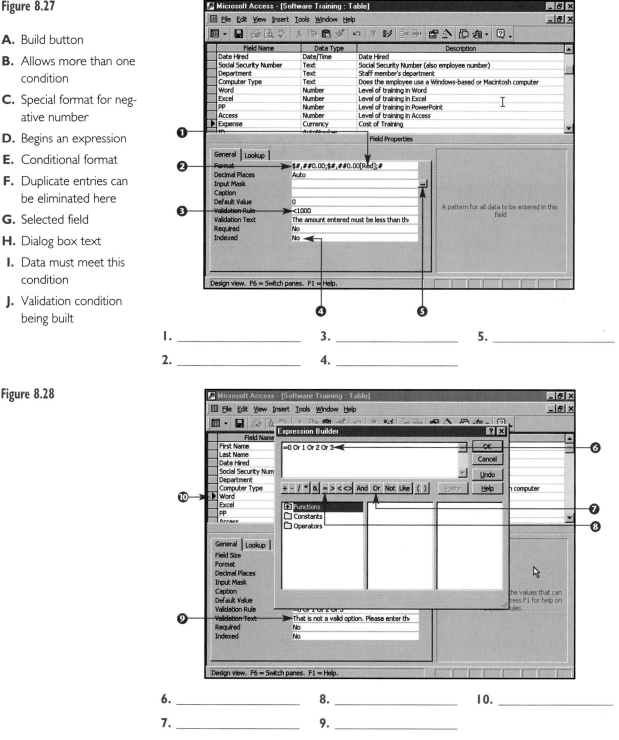

1. ____________ **3.** ____________ **5.** ____________

2. ____________ **4.** ____________

Figure 8.28

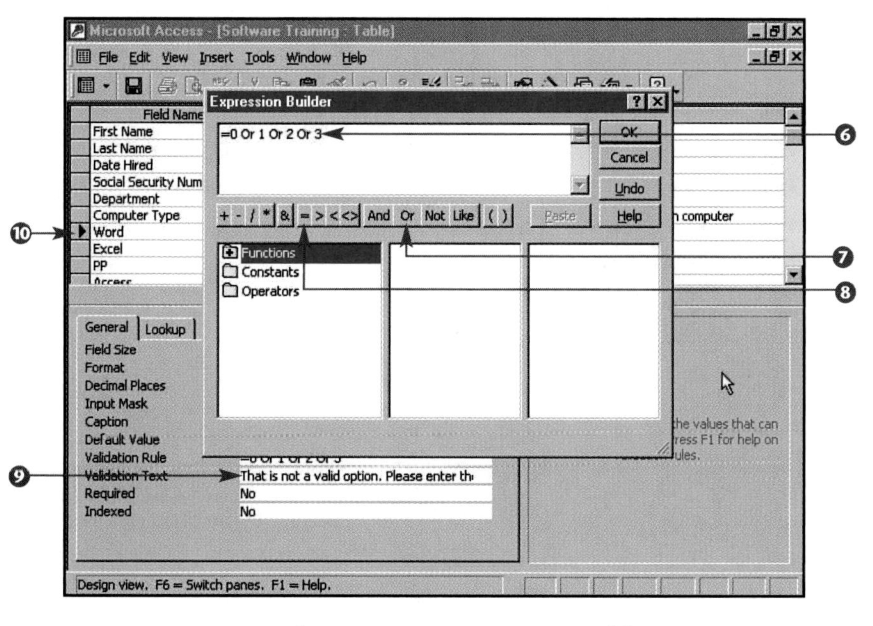

6. ____________ **8.** ____________ **10.** ____________

7. ____________ **9.** ____________

Discussion Questions

1. You learned how to use display formats and input masks in this project. In what situations would you use an input mask rather than a display format, and vice versa? When might you want to use both in the same field?
2. In the Software Training table of the PC Training database you worked with in this project, you used a conditional format on the Expense field. Are there any other fields that could use a conditional format?
3. If you wanted to index on the Last Name field, what would you have to do differently from what you did with the index you used in the Social Security Number field? Why?
4. In the Software Training table, which fields should be required? What problems could arise from making too many of the fields required fields?
5. Which other field(s) should use lookup columns? Would lookup columns be helpful for the Word, Excel, PP, and Access fields? Why or why not?

Skill Drill

Skill Drill exercises reinforce project skills. Each skill reinforced is the same, or nearly the same, as a skill presented in the project. Each exercise includes a brief narrative introduction, followed by detailed instructions in a step-by-step format.

The database you will use in the Skill Drill exercises contains information about a company's computers. It consists of two tables—one with information about the characteristics of the computers and one with information about the vendors who sold you the computers.

1. Creating a Consistent Data Format

The first thing you want to do is set the computer processor type to all capital letters.

To change the format of text in a field, complete the following steps:

1. Find the AC2-0102 file on your CD-ROM, right-click on it, and send it to the floppy drive. Move to drive A, remove the read-only status, and rename the file `Computer Inventory`.
2. Open the Computer Inventory database, and then open the PC Hardware table in Design view.
3. Place the insertion point anywhere in the Processor field.
4. Click in the Format box in the Field Properties area.
5. Type a greater than (>) symbol.
6. Click the View button to move to Datasheet view. Save your changes when prompted.
7. Widen the Processor column so that you can read the data.
8. Close the table. Because you changed the structure of the table (column width), you will be prompted to save your changes.

2. Adding an Input Mask to a Text Field

The Phone Number field in the Vendors table has a text data type. You will want to add an input mask to this field. This will prompt the user to enter an area code for the number.

To add an input mask for a telephone number, complete the following steps:

1. With the Computer Inventory database open, select the Vendors table.
2. Open the Vendors table in Design view.
3. Click anywhere in the Phone Number field.
4. Click in the Input Mask box in the Field Properties area.
5. Click the Build button to start the Input Mask Wizard.
6. Select the Phone Number option and click Next.
7. Accept the default input mask, placeholder, and method of saving, and click Next when necessary.
8. Click Finish to complete the input mask.
9. Click the View button to switch to Datasheet view. Save your changes.
10. Make sure your phone numbers are in the proper format, and then close the table.

3. Adding Validation Rules

All your computers have RAM of one of six sizes—4, 8, 16, 32, 64, or 128 MB. You think it is highly likely that any new machines you add in the near future will fit into one of these categories. Therefore, you want to restrict the data input to one of these numbers. (Note: You can edit or remove validation rules at any time.)

To add validation rules to the RAM field, complete the following steps:

1. With the Computer Inventory database open, select the PC Hardware table.
2. Open the PC Hardware table in Design view.
3. Click anywhere in the RAM field.
4. Click in the Validation Rule box in the Field Properties area.
5. Click the Build button to open the Expression Builder.
6. Click the equal button, or type the = symbol in the Expression Builder work area.
7. Type **4**, and then click the Or button.
8. Repeat this procedure to enter **8**, **16**, **32**, **64**, and **128**. When you are finished, click OK.
9. Click the View button to switch to Datasheet view. Save your changes when prompted, and have the program check for data integrity errors.
10. Add a new field and try to enter a number other than one of those you typed into the Expression Builder. Click OK to acknowledge the error.
11. Back out of the new field and record by pressing Esc twice.

4. Preventing Duplicate Entries Using the Index Property

Many of the entries in the Inventory Code Number field are similar. To make sure the user doesn't type the code number from another computer, you will want to index on the field and prevent duplicates from being entered. (Note: If you were sure that no numbers would ever be duplicated in this field, you could make it a primary key field, which would automatically prevent duplicate entries.)

To prevent duplicate entries using the Index property, complete the following steps:

1. With the Computer Inventory database open, select the PC Hardware table, if necessary.
2. Open the PC Hardware table in Design view.
3. Click anywhere in the Inventory Code Number field.
4. Click in the Indexed box in the Field Properties area.
5. Click the drop-down arrow and select Yes (No Duplicates).
6. Click the View button to switch to Datasheet view, and save your changes when prompted.
7. Enter a new record and enter **B324231** in the Inventory Control Code field. When you press ↵Enter after the last field, notice that the error message does not tell you which field contains the error.
8. Click OK, and then back out of the new record by pressing Esc.

5. Adding a Lookup Column

One of the fields in the PC Hardware table is the name of the vendor that sold you the computers. You have deals with three vendors—Acme Computer, General Comp, and Wilson Electric. Because all your computers will come from one of these three companies, you can add a drop-down list to the field by using the Lookup Wizard.

To add a lookup column to a field, complete the following steps:

1. With the Computer Inventory database open, select the PC Hardware table, if necessary.
2. Open the PC Hardware table in Design view.
3. Click in the Data Type column of the Vendor field.
4. Click the drop-down arrow in the Data Type box and select Lookup Wizard from the data type menu.
5. Choose to type the values yourself.

6. Accept the default of one column, and then type `Acme Computer`, `General Comp`, and `Wilson Electric` and click Next. Use Tab or ↓ to move from one field to the next. If you accidentally press Enter, click the Back button in the dialog box.
7. Accept Vendor as the name of the label.
8. Click the View button to switch to Datasheet view. Save your changes when prompted.
9. Move to the Vendor field and click anywhere in the column. Click the down arrow to see if your lookup column is working.

6. Requiring a Field Entry

Computers are first sent through your company's Receiving department, which places an Inventory Code Number on each computer. Once this is done, the item is placed in the database. An entry into the Inventory Code Number field is required, so you need to make sure that a number is entered for every record.

To require the entry of an inventory code, complete the following steps:

1. With the Computer Inventory database open, select the PC Hardware table, if necessary.
2. Open the PC Hardware table in Design view.
3. Click anywhere in the Inventory Code Number field.
4. Click in the Required box in the Field Properties area.
5. Click the drop-down arrow and select Yes.
6. Click the View button to switch to Datasheet view, save your changes when prompted, and let the program check for data integrity problems.
7. Enter a new record and skip the entry for the Inventory Code Number field. Read the error message you receive, and then click OK.
8. Back out of the new field by pressing Esc.
9. Close the table, and then close the database.

Challenge

These exercises expand on or are somewhat related to skills practiced in the project. Each exercise provides a brief narrative introduction followed by instructions in a numbered step format that are not as detailed as those in the Skill Drill section.

The database you will be using for the Challenge section is for a small online chess club that started out as a chess-by-mail club. Yearly dues help pay for space on a file server where games can be played and saved. Like most clubs, some members have paid in advance, and some are behind in their dues. The database currently contains only one table—a membership list that you are responsible for. You decide that if you must take care of the list, you will set it up the way you want it!

1. Placing Default Text in Empty Fields Using Custom Formats

You have two address fields for each of the members. Some of the members don't have second address lines, and you'd like to place the word 'None' in the field if it is left empty.

To place default text in empty fields using a custom format, complete the following steps:

1. Copy the file AC2-0103 from your CD-ROM, place it on your floppy drive, and rename it `Chess Club`. Change it to an Archive file, and deselect the Read-only attribute.
2. Open the database and the Membership Information table. Notice that two of the records have no entry in the Address2 field.
3. Switch to Design view, select the Address2 field, and click in the Format properties box.

4. Type `@;"None"` in the Format properties box.
5. Press F1 to find out what each of the two sections of the custom format do.
6. Switch to Datasheet view and look at the Address2 fields that were formerly blank to make sure your custom format is working.

2. Creating a Two-Column Lookup Column

You want to save the State field in the standard two-character format, but you sometimes have trouble remembering what code is used for what state. You decide to add a lookup column that contains both the two-character state code and the full state name. Right now, you have members from Colorado, Georgia, Indiana, and Michigan. You are also pretty sure a person from Missouri will be joining soon.

To create a two-column lookup column, complete the following steps:

1. Select the Design view of the Member Information table and select the State field.
2. Change the Data Type to Lookup Wizard.
3. Indicate that you want to type the values, but change the number of columns to **2**.
4. Enter the following information in the columns:

Col1	Col2
CO	Colorado
GA	Georgia
IN	Indiana
MI	Michigan
MO	Missouri

5. Double-click on the line between the Col1 and Col2 column headings to reduce the width of the Col1 column.
6. Continue through the rest of the wizard. Choose to store the value from Col1 in your table and accept the default name.
7. Switch to Datasheet view and add another member. The membership information should read: `9998765`, `Ms.`, `Hawken`, `Charity`, `S.`, `1885 Burtchville Rd.`, [leave Address2 blank], `Jeddo`, `MO`, `63460`, `(573) 555-1234`, `25`, `9/9/99`, `47`. Use the lookup column for the State field. Notice that the two-character code and the state name both appear, but only the code is entered into the table.

3. Using Validation Rules to Set a Minimum Value for a Field

By club rules, the minimum membership age is 18 years. You want to make sure that you don't accidentally type an incorrect age, so you want to create a validation rule to have the program tell you if you type a number less than 18.

To set a minimum value for a field, complete the following steps:

1. With the Chess Club database open, open the Member Information table in Design view.
2. Use the available help to make sure that the number entered is 18 or greater. There are two ways to do this—either way will do.
3. Type `The age must be at least 18` as validation text.

4. Switch to Datasheet view and change the age in the first record (Mr. Jones) from 24 to **15**. Try changing it to **17** (this is the critical one in determining whether your validation rule is correct).
5. Change the age back to **24**.

4. Using Conditional Formats to Emphasize Negative Numbers

You want to display the negative numbers in the Dues field in red. In Lesson 2, "Creating Conditional Formats for Positive, Negative, and Null Values," you set up a conditional format that included red for negative numbers, but there were no negative numbers in the field. In the Dues field, use the available help to figure out how to display the negative numbers in red and with no decimal places. Also, have the negative numbers surrounded by parentheses.

5. Indexing Multiple Fields

You can create indexes for more than one field in a table. You can also create an index that is based on multiple fields. Because you are anticipating a lot more members in the future, you want to create an index on the Last Name and First Name fields so that the program will sort on these fields faster.

To index on more than one field at a time, complete the following steps:

1. With the Chess Club database open, open the Member Information table in Design view.
2. Click the Indexes button on the toolbar. The Indexes dialog box shows two current indexes.
3. Type **Name** in the first available Index Name box.
4. Select the Last Name field from the drop-down list in the Field Name column.
5. Move down one row and select the First Name field from the drop-down list in the Field Name column. Leave the Index Name box blank in this row.
6. Switch to Datasheet view. The multiple-field index will make little difference with only a few fields, but will be very important when you work with tables with many records.

Discovery Zone

Discovery Zone exercises help you gain advanced knowledge of project topics and application of skills. These exercises focus on enhancing your problem-solving skills. Numbered steps are not provided, but you are given hints, reminders, screen shots, or references to help you reach your goal for each exercise.

The database you will be using in this Discovery Zone is a slightly modified version of the Chess Club database you used in the Challenge section.

1. Creating Your Own Input Mask

The Member ID# is set up with the last two digits of the year the member joined followed by a randomly generated five-digit number. You would like to create an input mask that would separate the first two digits from the last five digits with a dash.

Copy the file AC2-0104 from your CD-ROM, place it on your floppy drive, and rename it `Chess Club 2`. Change it to an Archive file and deselect the Read-only attribute.

Goal: Create a custom input mask that results in a Member ID # with the following format: `ID 92-23434` (this is the Member ID # for the first record in the table). The input mask should

- Start each Member ID # with the following characters: `ID`.
- Use a dash to separate the first two digits (the year) from the last five digits.
- Make all seven digits required entries.
- Use the underscore as a placeholder.
- Not store the literal characters (for example, the dash) in the table.

Hint #1: All the information you need is in the Input Mask help section.

Hint #2: You will need three sections for this input mask.

2. Creating Your Own Custom Date Format

Date fields give you great flexibility in customizing formats. You want to show as much information as possible for the Date Joined field in your Member Information table.

Goal: Create a custom display format that results in the Date Joined field with the following format: `Monday, January 9, 1995` (this is the Date Joined for the first record in the table). This format will be displayed even though you only type in `1/9/95`. The format should

- Include commas after the weekday and the date, as shown above.
- Display just the number of digits needed for the date (January 9 should not read January 09).
- Display the full year.
- Include a single space after each of the commas.

Hint #1: The table of custom formats in the Format Property-Date/Time Data Type help will give you all the necessary information to create this date format.

Hint #2: It may not seem logical, but the same symbol is used for two of the four parts of this input mask.

Part VI Actrix

ACTRIX

1 Drawing Skill Opportunities

Project 1

Drawing Skill Opportunities

Objectives

In this project, you learn how to

- **Draw Circles in a Rectangle**
- **Draw a Simple Circuit**
- **Draw Triangles**
- **Draw Pipes**
- **Draw a Parallel Circuit**
- **Use the Explode Command**
- **Draw a Circle Inside a Circle**
- **Draw a Parabola**
- **Draw a Schematic Symbol**
- **Select Colors**
- **Draw a Right Triangle**

Lesson I: Drawing Circles in a Rectangle

This Drawing Skill Opportunity provides step-by-step instructions for creating a drawing of a circle placed inside of a rectangle.

Drawing a rectangle

1. **Select the Basic Drawing Template on the General Tab of the New Drawing Dialog box.**
2. **With your left mouse button, click on the Rectangle shape.**
3. **Holding the button down, drag the rectangle into the drawing editor**
4. **To resize the rectangle, click on it with the left mouse button, select one of the corners and stretch to the desired size.**
5. **At this stage, you will have created a complete rectangle on the draw screen.**

Inserting a circle into the retangle

1. **Using the mouse, single click on the circle, and holding down on the left mouse button, drag the circle into the drawing of the rectangle.**
2. **At this point, you should have a rectangle on your screen with a circle inside of it.**

   If you recall, the problem that confronted us in the Introduction to Problem Solving concerned the number of circles that could be placed inside of a certain rectangle. Using the drawing software, it is possible to get an approximation to this answer. We can now move the circle that we just created and begin inserting others.

Moving the circle

1. **To move the circle, click on it with the left mouse button, hold the button down, and move the circle to the new location.**

Lesson 2: Drawing a Simple Circuit

In this Drawing Skill Opportunity, we will learn how to draw the simple circuit that was the focus of Thought Project 1. We will begin with the battery and move clockwise around the circuit.

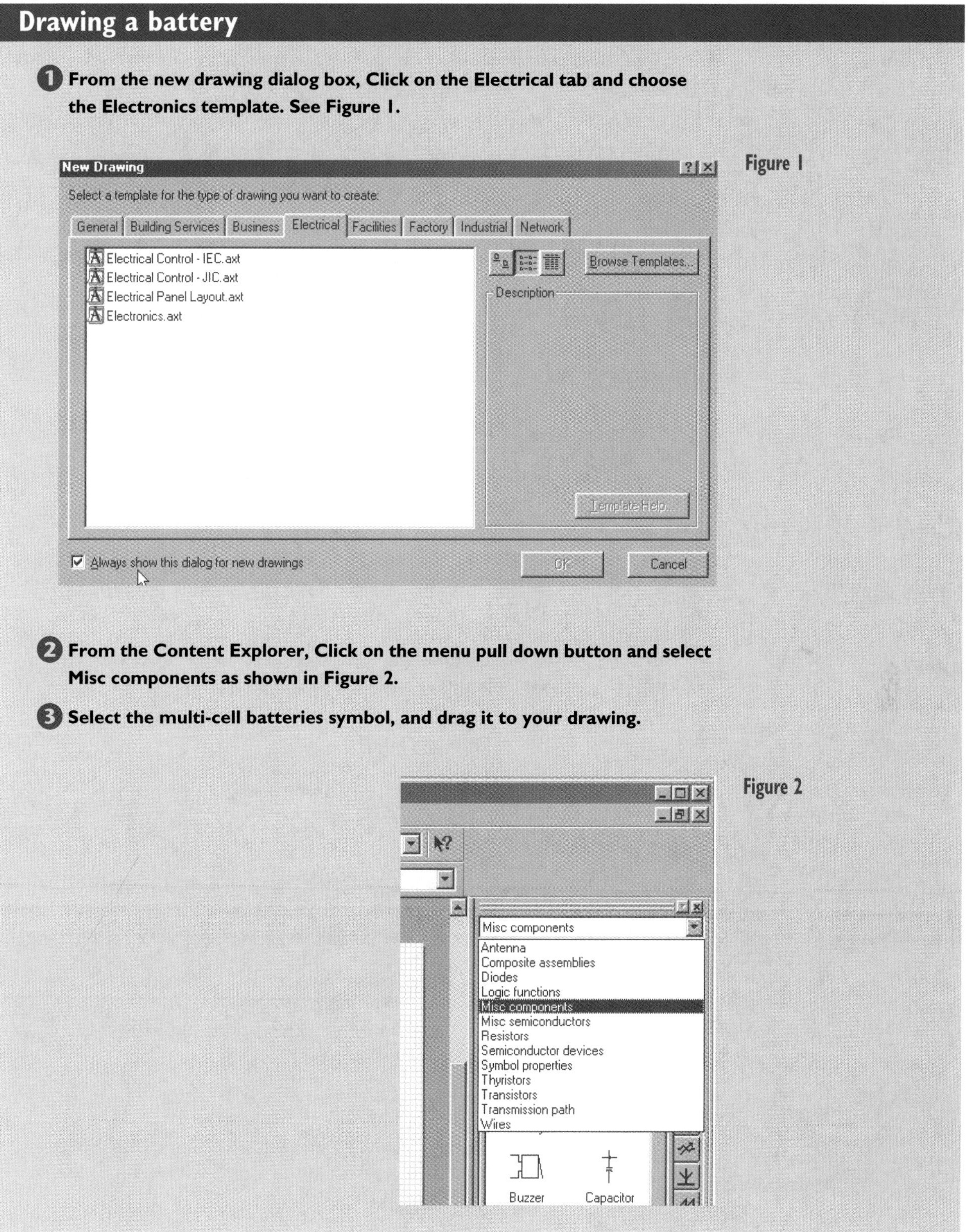

Drawing a battery

1. **From the new drawing dialog box, Click on the Electrical tab and choose the Electronics template. See Figure 1.**

Figure 1

2. **From the Content Explorer, Click on the menu pull down button and select Misc components as shown in Figure 2.**
3. **Select the multi-cell batteries symbol, and drag it to your drawing.**

Figure 2

Adding the resistor

1 From the Content Explorer, Click on the menu pull down button and select Resistors. See Figure 3.

2 Select the Series Resistor and drag it to your drawing. Next the Resistor will need to be rotated, select the resistor and right click to bring up the properties dialog box. Select rotate on this menu. See Figure 4. Rotate the resistor to the vertical position shown in Figure 5.

3 To draw the connection lines use the Connector Tool located on the main menu.

Figure 3

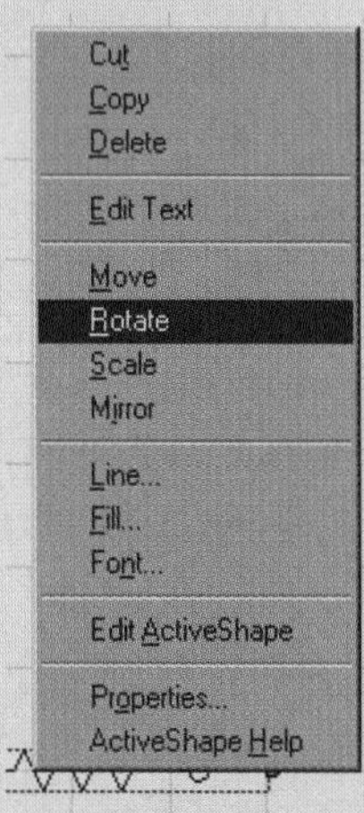

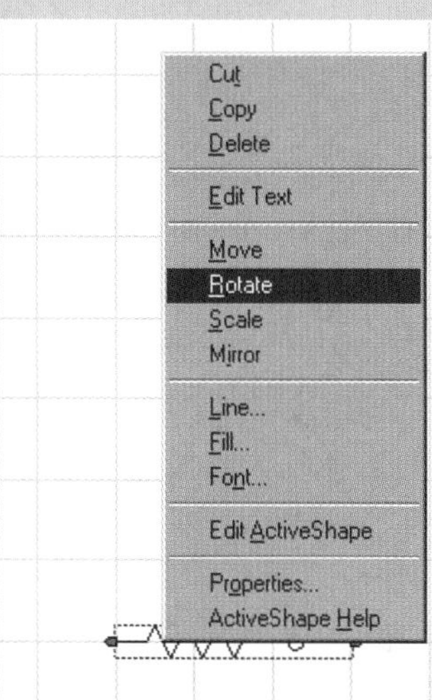

Figure 4

Select the Connection Tool, select the end of the resistor, and then select the end of the battery. A line will be formed between each of the components. Use the same procedure to complete the schematic drawing shown in Figure 5.

Figure 5

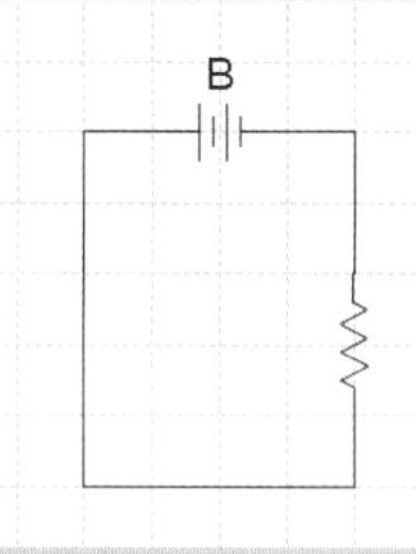

Lesson 3: Drawing Triangles

Although there are many different angles from which to view the exterior of a pyramid, we will examine the front face in this Drawing Skill Opportunity. Although it may appear complex, drawing this view of a pyramid is nothing more than an exercise in drawing triangles.

Drawing an equilateral triangle

1. **In the New Drawing Dialog box, Select the General Tab and the Basic Drawing Template.**
2. **Select the Triangle from the Content Explorer and drop into the drawing.**
3. **To change the size, select the triangle, select the green corner and stretch to the new size.**

Lesson 4: Drawing Pipes

There are many methods for drawing pipes of varying widths, lengths, etc. The following sequence of commands is one of a number of sequences that will generate pipe drawings.

Drawing a pipe

1. **Select the Plumbing and Piping—Small Layout template from the Building Services Tab of the New Drawing Dialog.**
2. **Drag and Drop the Horizontal Pipe symbol into the drawing. Continue adding symbols to complete the drawing shown in Figure 1.**

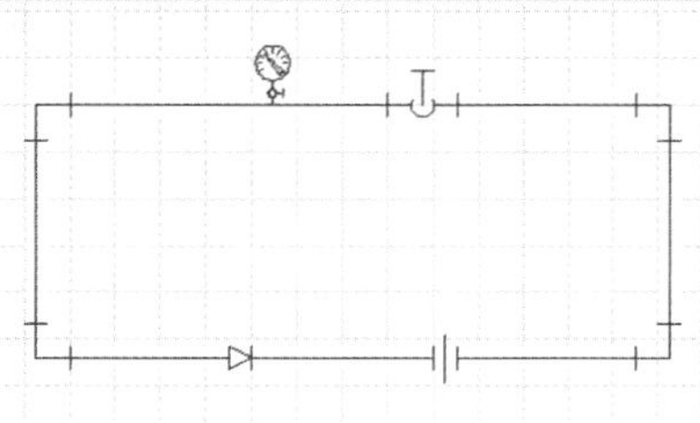

Figure 1

Drawing Skill 5: Drawing a Parallel Circuit

Our goal in this Drawing Skill Opportunity associated with Thought Project 14 is to use the drawing software to draw a circuit with three parallel resistors. This problem is an extension of the drawing we created in Drawing Skill Opportunity 2. This time, we will add two more resistors to our previous drawing. As a reminder, let's again look at the sequence of commands that we used to generate the battery drawing:

Drawing the battery

1. **From the new drawing dialog box, click on the Electrical tab and choose the Electronics template.**
2. **From the Content Explorer, click on the menu pull down button and select Misc components**
3. **Select the multi-cell batteries symbol, and drag it to your drawing and rotate it 90°.**

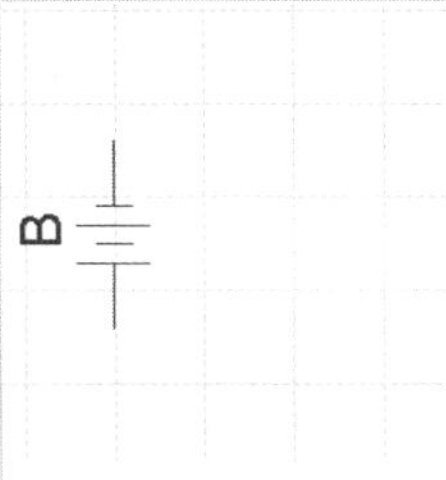

Adding the Resistor

1. **From the Content Explorer, click on the menu pull down button and select resistors.**
2. **Draw, drop, and rotate 3 resistors as shown below.**

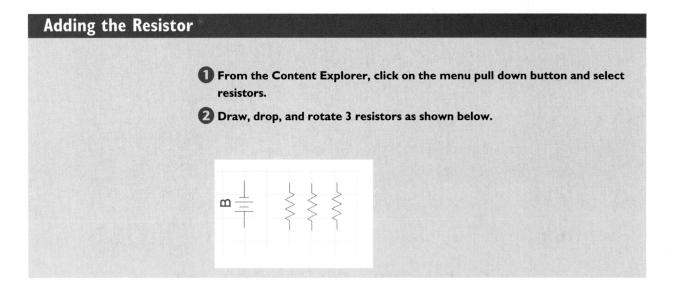

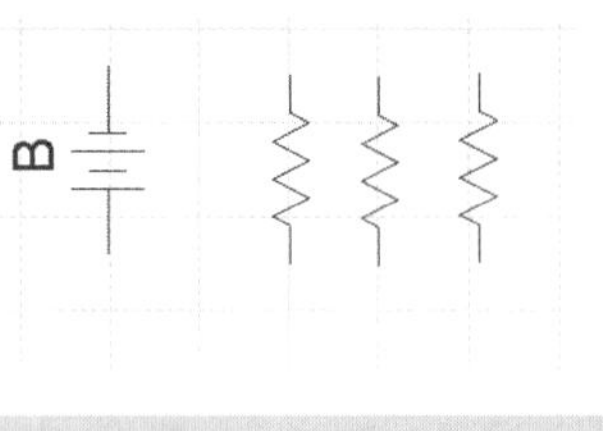

Drawing the wires that connect the battery and the resistors

Select the Connection Tool, select the end of the resistor, and then select the end of the battery. A line will be formed between each of the components. Use the same procedure to complete the schematic drawing shown in below.

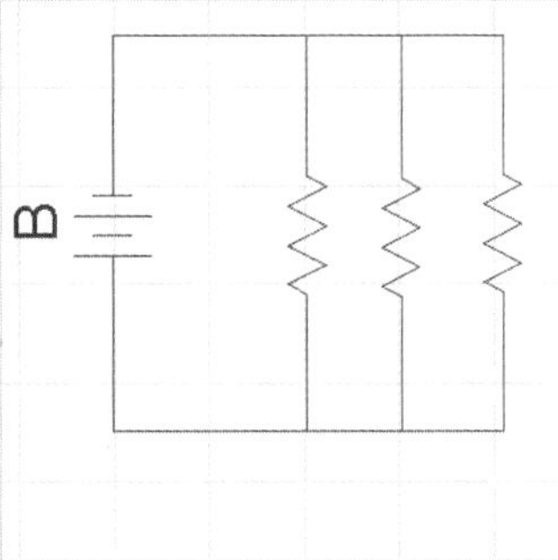

To add the connection points

Use the circle icon to place a circle at each intersection and right click to bring up the menu. See Figure 1.

Select Fill and set fill color to black. See Figure 2.

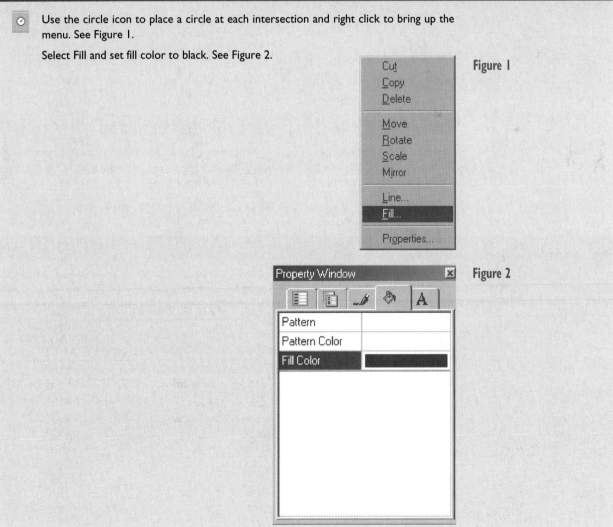

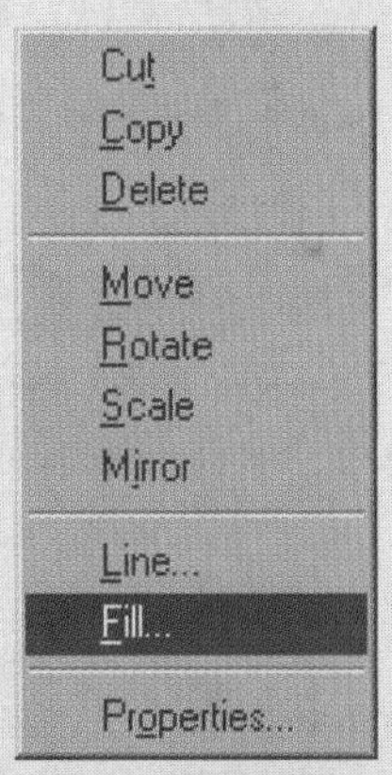

Figure 1

Figure 2

To add the connection points (continued)

Your completed circuit should look like Figure 3.

Figure 3

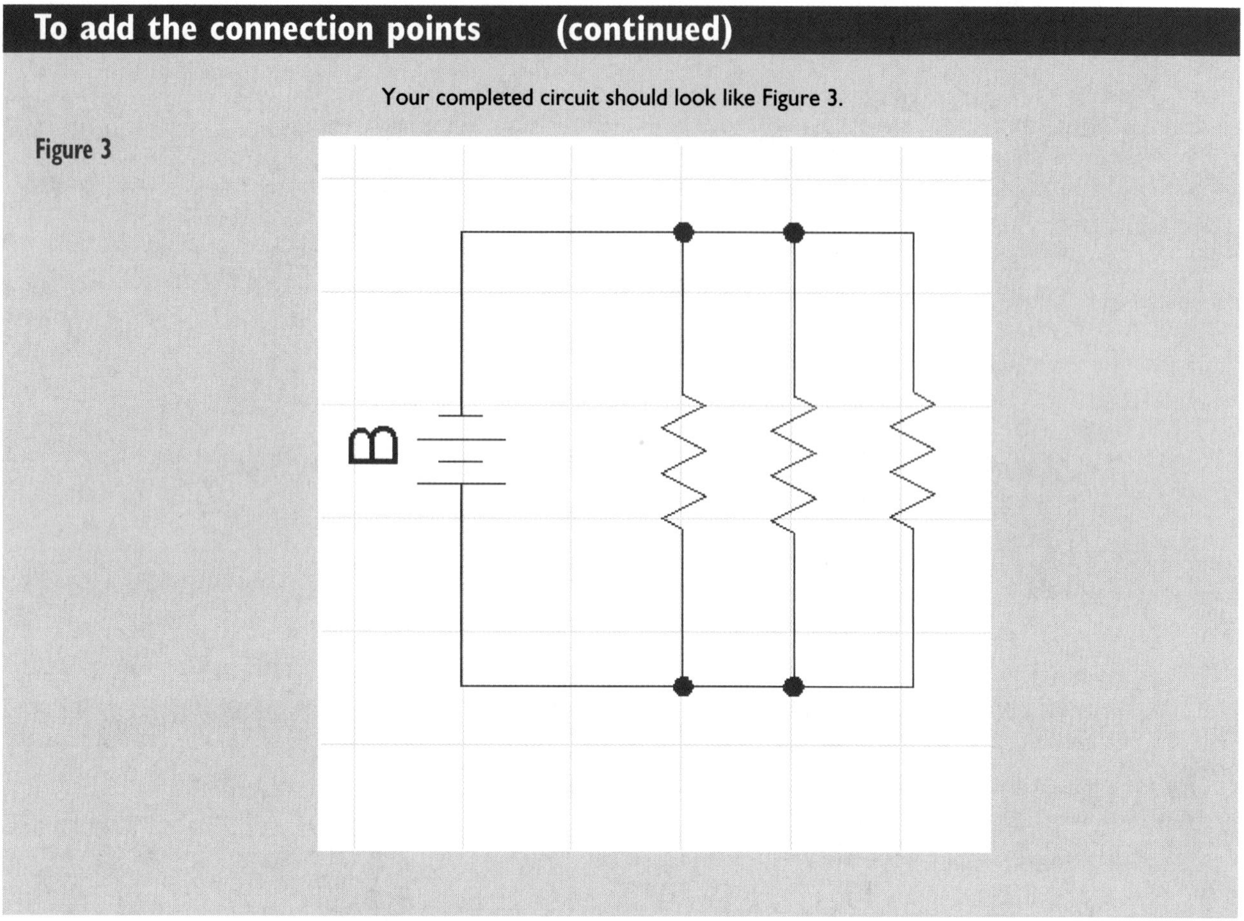

Drawing Skill 6: Using the Explode Command

Our goal in this Drawing Skill Opportunity is to acquire an introductory understanding of the Explode command. To understand the uses of this command, we must begin by opening our drawing from Drawing Skill 5.

Employing the Explode command

1. **Open the Parallel Circuit from Drawing Skill 5.**
2. **Click on the battery and select Modify and Explode from the pull down menu. See Figure 1.**

   By executing this command, you have now broken the battery into its different parts.
3. **Select the "B" by the battery and press the delete key on the keyboard.**

   Your schematic should now look like Figure 2.

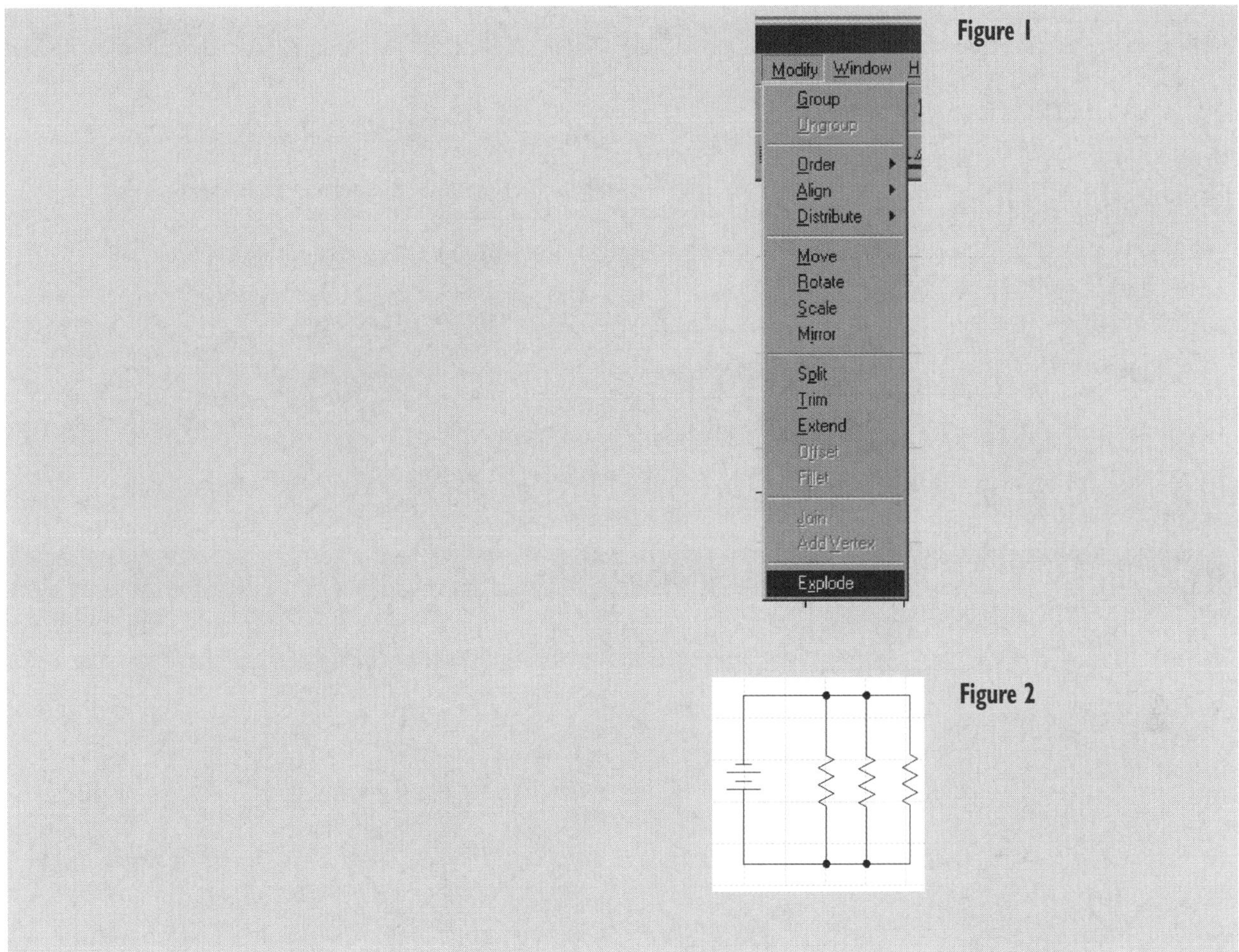

Figure 1

Figure 2

Drawing Skill 7: Drawing a Circle Inside a Circle

In this Drawing Skill Opportunity, we will use our drawing software to create a portion of the Power Wheel that was discussed in Thought Project 19. Recall that the Power Wheel contained both lettering and equations. Because this is intended to be only an introduction to the software package, we will not take on the more difficult tasks of inserting the equations or text that surrounds the outer portion of the wheel. These are advanced concepts that will be covered in later coursework at ITT Technical Institute. Instead, we will focus on inscribing circles.

We will accomplish this task thorough a three stage process. First, we will execute the commands necessary to generate the three circles. Second, we will insert the radial lines of the wheel. Lastly, we will insert the four letters P, I, V, and R into their respective locations.

Creating the three circles

1. **Select the Basic Drawing Template in the Create New Drawing dialog box.**
2. **Select the circle shape, drag it to you drawing and position it so that it is located approximately in the center of your screen.**
3. **Stretch the circle so that it has a radius of approximately 3/4 of an inch.**

   We must now create the next largest circle. Our goal is to make this new circle have the same center as our first one.

4. **Select the circle shape again and drag it to the center of the first circle. Notice that one circle "blocks out" the circle below it. Right click and set the fill for both circles to none.**
5. **Both circles should now appear on your screen.**
6. **Finally add the third circle.**

Drawing the radial lines

7. **Draw a vertical and horizontal line trough the axis of the circle. See Figure 1.**

Figure 1

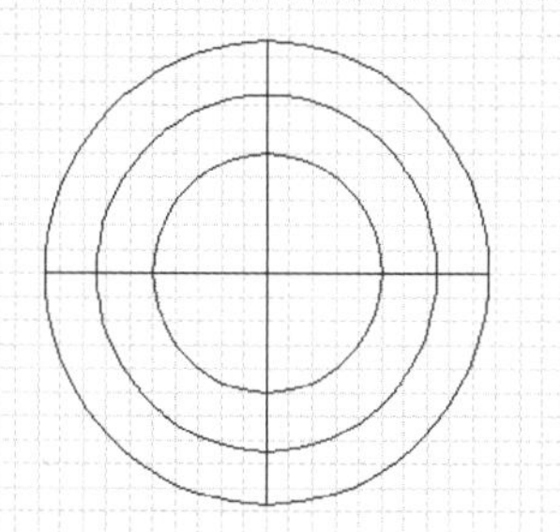

Inserting the letters P, I, V, and R

8. **Select the text and font size appropriate to your circle size and add the letters P, I, V, and R. Use the cursor to position your letters. See Figure 2.**

Figure 2

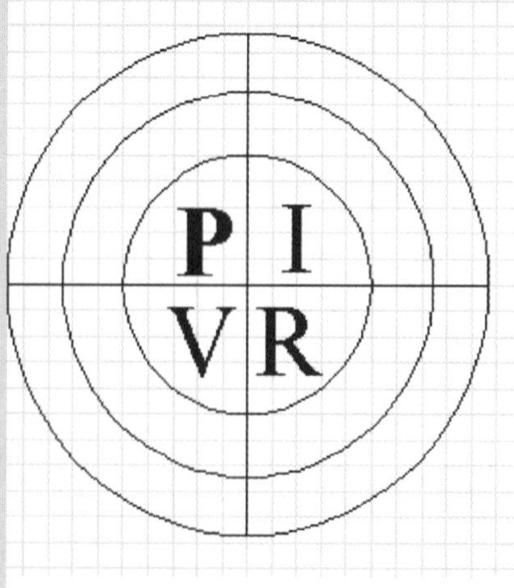

Drawing Skill 8: Drawing a Parabola

Now that we've completed Thought Project 23 and 24 on Projectile Motion, let's use the drawing software to draw the trajectory of one of our projectiles. Namely, let's learn how to draw a parabola. This exercise will use the Spline command.

Creating a parabola

1. **Select the Basic Drawing Template from the Create New Drawing dialog box.**
2. **Select the Spline Icon.**
3. **Begin by selecting grid points; try to make the curve as smooth as possible.**
4. **After the parabola is complete, convert it to an active shape by clicking on the Tools pull down menu and selecting Make ActiveShape. Select OK. You can now change the size and position of the parabola.**

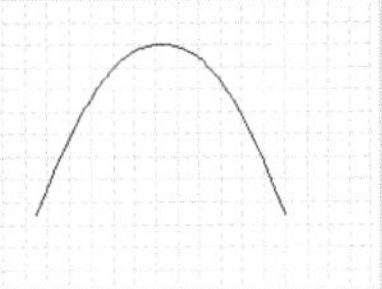

Drawing Skill 9: Drawing a Schematic Symbol

We have been adding resistors and batteries to our schematic, it is now time to look at a new component: the capacitor. If you return to Thought Project 26, you will see the symbol for a capacitor.

Adding the capacitor symbol

1. **Select the electronics template from the Create New Drawing dialog box.**
2. **From the Content Explorer, click on the menu pull down button and select Misc components.**
3. **Notice that we only have one capacitor, called *capacitor shunt;* this symbol will need some editing.**
4. **Drag the capacitor shunt into you drawing.**
5. **Right click on the symbol and select edit ActiveShape. Remove the "C" as well as the intersection and connection point.**
6. **Finally rotate the capacitor 90°. See Figure 1.**

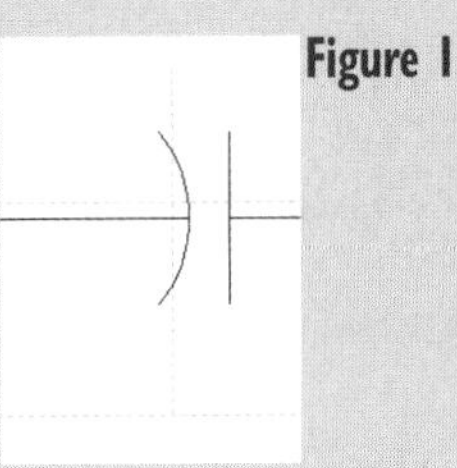

Figure 1

Drawing Skill 10: Selecting Colors

As with most software programs, colors can be easily added and changed in our drawings. In this Drawing Skill Opportunity, we will learn the commands that control the colors and thickness of objects in our drawings.

Figure 1

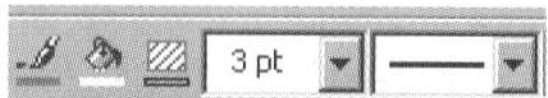

1. Figure 1 shows the toolbar items that control the color and thickness of objects in the Actrix software.
2. To draw a red line with a thickness of 3 pt, change the toolbar to the settings shown in Figure 1.
3. Draw several lines and circles of different colors and thickness as shown in Figure 2.

Figure 2

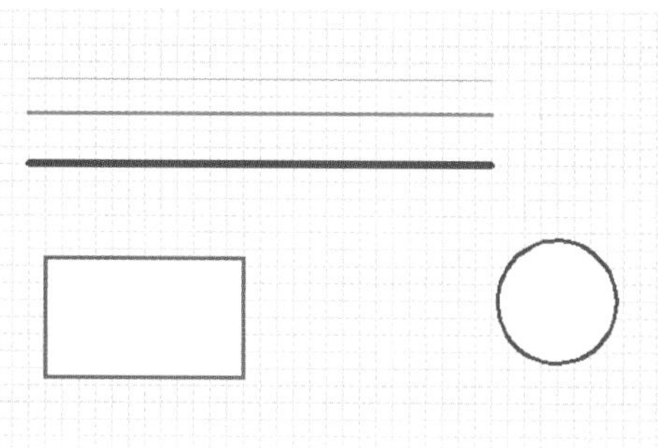

Additional opportunity:

If class time permits, return now to a Drawing Skill Opportunity of your choosing and rework it varying the colors of the shapes and lines that your drew.

Drawing Skill 11: Drawing a Right Triangle

The subject of Thought Project 35 provides a perfect setting to illustrate another useful property of the drawing software. In this Drawing Skill Opportunity, we will use the software to calculate the hypotenuse of a right triangle. By executing the appropriate commands, we may avoid the calculations associated with the Pythagorean Theorem.

This exercise has two components. First, we will draw the two legs of the right triangle. After they are created, we will find the length of the hypotenuse to complete the triangle.

Drawing the legs of the triangle

1. **Open the Basic Drawing Template from the Create New Drawing Dialog Box.**
2. **Select the Line icon from the toolbar.**
3. **Pick a point on the lower, left portion of the draw screen.**
4. **Count over 5 squares on the grid and select the point.**

   (Side note: These steps may be somewhat familiar. If you recall from the Thought Projects on graphing, you always used a horizontal and a vertical axis. By selecting the point 5 units over and moving 0 units in the Y direction, you instructed the computer to make the line representing the bottom leg of the right triangle to achieve a length of 5 units out the x-axis, and 0 units up the y-axis.)
5. **Now, to create the vertical leg of the triangle, again access the Line command.**
6. **Pick the point on the end of the horizontal line.**
7. **Count up 12 squares and pick the point.**

   At this point, you should have the two legs of your right triangle on the screen.

Creating the hypotenuse of the triangle

8. **Connect the end point of the vertical line to the end point of the horizontal line.**
9. **Count the number of squares that the angled line passes through. You should get 13. See Figure 1.**

   Let's now use the Pythagorean Theorem to verify that the software is correct:

$$a^2 + b^2 = c^2$$

$$5^2 + 12^2 = c^2$$

$$25 + 144 = c^2$$

$$169 = c^2$$

$$\sqrt{169} = c$$

It works!

Creating the hypotenuse of the triangle (continued)

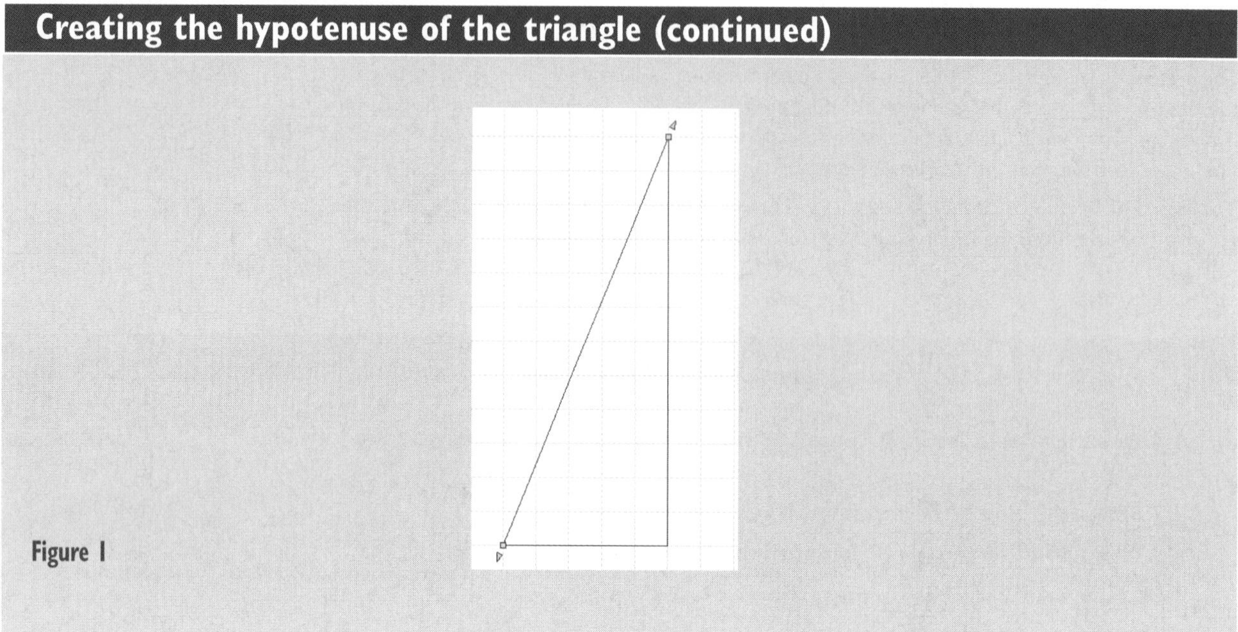

Figure 1

Part VII Instant AutoCAD Essentials for AutoCAD 2000

AutoCAD

1 The Big Picture: Ready . . .

2 Always Be Prepared: . . . Set . . .

3 Every Journey Begins with a Single Line: . . . Go!

4 Alterations Done Here: Modifying

5 WYSIWYG (What You See is What You Get): Viewing

Introduction

AutoCAD is a very complex and powerful software program, and it takes many years to become expert in it. Happily, the business of learning does not have to be a grave and studious one and you don't have to be an expert to make great strides in improving your work quality and productivity. It is just as instructive to learn the program with simple exercises, lighter language, and friendly graphics. In fact, for some it may be more instructive to learn a complex topic in this nonthreatening way.

Now, we're sure you can understand that a book this size will only touch on the basics of AutoCAD study—the very beginning of your CAD learning. Some topics, those you need to perform basic operations within AutoCAD, are explained more fully while others leave you to do extensive exploration on your own. We hope that this will be the start of a journey that will never end. In fact, we hope that this book will lead you directly to more specialty areas in AutoCAD.

The layout of the book is explained fully in Chapter 1, but it is essential to emphasize the various components that comprise a chapter. The first section in each chapter lists key ideas that will be covered in the chapter. Throughout the chapter you may see a variety of things: stylized print lifting an idea from the pages for emphasis, tip boxes that stress a certain fact about the program, command sequences in a very simple print that present the user's desired input in bold letters, and hands-on exercises to reinforce a new idea. As well, at the end of each chapter you will find a short-answer test, a series of questions requiring longer answers, and a number of assignments. Remember that the more you put into it in effort, study, and exercise completion, the more you'll take away from it in learning. It's up to you.

We have no doubt that if you enjoy anything in the field of graphics drawing and design, you will love the versatility that comes with a tool such as AutoCAD.

Take Note

It would seem you would be correct in assuming that it would be impossible to even introduce a complex subject such as AutoCAD in a mere 200 pages. "How do we do it?" you are most likely asking yourself. Well, we'll share our secret at this early stage of the game. The CD that accompanies this text makes ALL the difference.

The CD provides you with myriad images for samples, symbols, and exercises. In fact, there are over 700 files in all.

The CD gives you visual help to bridge a gap in understanding: It provides the details you may need when creating complex drawings; it offers hands-on reinforcement for your newly mastered skills. So, how do we present so much information in 200 pages?—we don't! By using the accompanying CD in concert with the text, you get the benefit of so much more.

Chapter 1

The Big Picture: Ready . . .

Key topics

- Screen Layout
- Selecting Objects
- Viewing Basics
- Clean Your Room—File Management

Welcome!

If you're like most of us, you are living in a fast-paced world. With this in mind, we want to teach you to use AutoCAD in the fastest and most effective way possible. We've stripped down all the bells and whistles of learning AutoCAD into a concise, condensed, and practical approach we call Instant AutoCAD. We want you to start using AutoCAD right away, so that your confidence grows as quickly as your knowledge does.

AutoCAD can be a daunting program with its many advanced features and capabilities. But, since you'll be introduced to commands as you need them, you'll be amazed at how fast you'll be using AutoCAD to create drawings and designs. Once you've mastered the basics, you'll be more apt to tackle all those advanced features that make AutoCAD such a powerful design tool.

Let's start by moving around in the AutoCAD drawing environment and reviewing basic concepts in the areas of creating objects, selecting and modifying objects, and viewing commands. Let's go!

"...you will be amazed at how fast you will be using AutoCAD..."

A Brief Tour

Our goal is to provide you with background knowledge of AutoCAD's commands as well as to teach you the practical applications of its features. Each command or procedure introduced to you is followed, in most cases, by hands-on practical application. Although this hands-on approach is essential for physical learners, the concrete tasks make the experience beneficial for relational and mental learners as well.

The hands-on sections are easily identified by the **hands-on** heading. Any time you see the **hand**, you'll know it's time to practice using AutoCAD.

You will also notice **icons** in the left margin. These icons represent AutoCAD commands that are picked from menus and help you identify the actual commands in the program.

The **lightbulb/idea** symbol, attached to tip boxes throughout the text, provides tips on items that help you avoid beginner pitfalls.

Your **CD-ROM** includes numerous drawings, symbols, and template files to make learning easier and faster. Be sure to copy these files into the ICAD folder (subdirectory) on your computer.

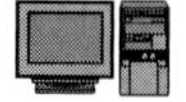

The end of each chapter provides you with **questions** and **assignments** to reinforce what you've learned.

Hands-On: Starting AutoCAD

1. **Start AutoCAD by**

   a. **locating the AutoCAD 2000 shortcut icon and double-clicking on it**

   or

   b. **picking the Windows ® Start button, entering into the Programs sub-menu, finding the AutoCAD 2000 menu, and picking the AutoCAD 2000 menu item**

   After a few moments the AutoCAD logo will appear. It will quickly disappear and be replaced with the AutoCAD drawing editor.

2. **A Startup dialog box may appear in the center of the screen. (See Figure 1.1). (However, if the small box in the lower-left corner of the dialog box**

has been unchecked, this dialog box is skipped and a blank drawing screen appears.) The Startup dialog box is used to assist you in starting a drawing. (We'll talk more about this later.) For now, pick on the Start from Scratch button and OK it. This will give you a blank drawing file from which to start. Now you are able to roam freely around the AutoCAD screen.

❸ Get to know the layout of the AutoCAD drawing editor screen. Look at your screen and the following text, but do not exit AutoCAD.

Screen Layout

The words across the top of the screen are the items in the pull-down menu bar; below it are the standard toolbar and any docked toolbars. As you can see from Figure 1.2, docked toolbars can run along the sides of the screen as well. The floating command window and status bar run along the bottom of the screen. The dominant portion in the center of the screen, referred to as the graphics area, displays the geometry, the moving crosshair cursor, and floating toolbars. Now compare Figure 1.2 and your screen, matching up the various areas. (Your screen may not appear exactly as

Figure 1.1
The Startup dialog box

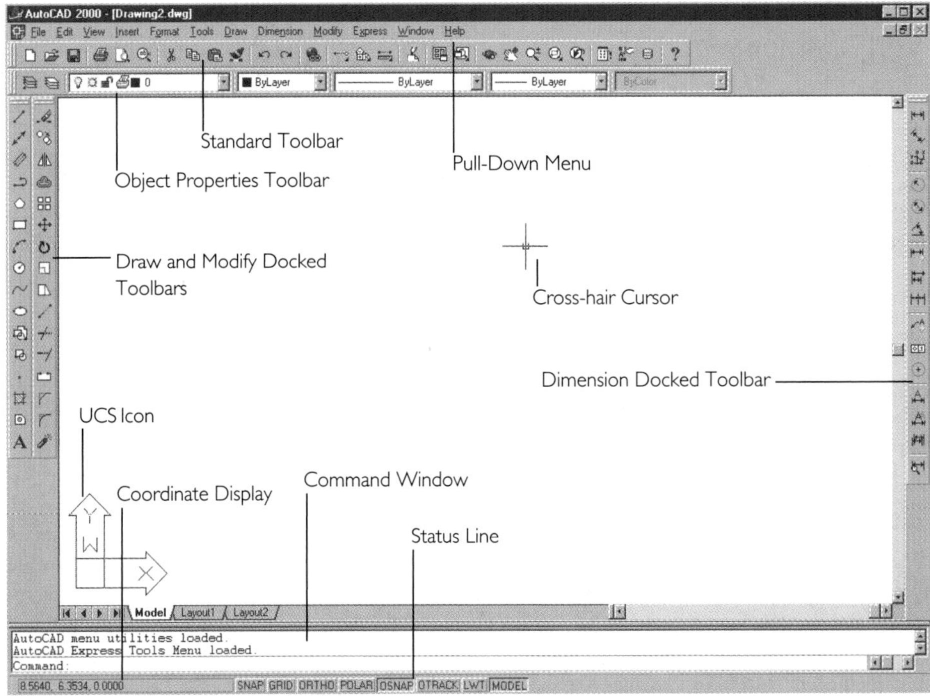

Figure 1.2
The AutoCAD drawing editor screen

Figure 1.2, but that's OK.) Although the words may be new to you, as you get familiar with all the parts of the screen, it won't sound nearly as confusing!

Using the Mouse

Although your household cat may be fascinated by a mouse's movement, this isn't the kind of mouse you'll need to trap. This mouse controls the movement of the cursor to access commands, select objects, or enter coordinates. This is what the mouse buttons do:

Left button The left mouse button is used to pick commands, locations on the screen, or objects. To *pick* an item, the cursor is placed over the item and the left button is pressed once.

Right button Pressing the right mouse button displays a Context menu. This menu changes depending on where the cursor is located and what command is currently active. You should practice with this menu because it may present command options that you might not know are available.

Double-click If you move the cursor over a file name when opening files and double-click with the left mouse button, that file will open.

Cursor menu If you hold down the Shift key and press the right mouse button, an Object Snap menu will appear on the screen. This menu is used to snap onto objects (explained later).

Get to know this mouse — it's your new best friend!

Pull-Down Menu Bar

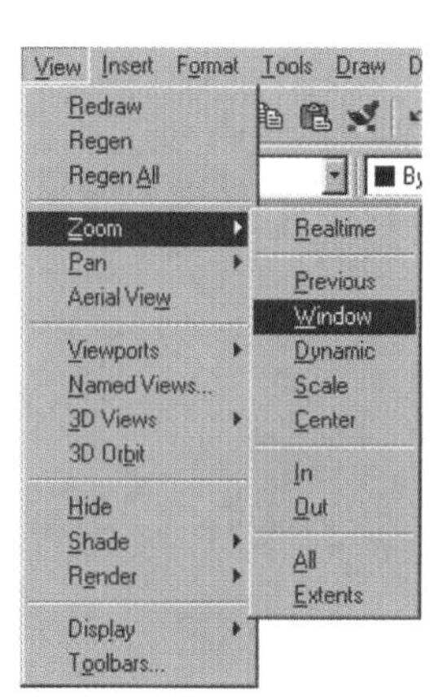

The pull-down menu bar contains most of the commands that control drawing in AutoCAD. By picking on a menu heading, a list of menu items is *pulled down* onto the screen; move your cursor along the list to pick the desired command. Some of the menu items have a ▶ symbol to the right of the item. This signifies that another "cascading menu" is attached, giving you more related options to this item. A checkmark next to an item signifies it is active, and if an item is grey, it means it is not selectable at the current time.

Docked Toolbars and Floating Toolbars

A *toolbar* is a set of related icons that pictorially describe a command, making them more of an international language. They are linked to form a bar, which may run horizontally, vertically, or in the form of a rectangle. They can be resized by picking on their edges, and reshaped by moving the cursor. The toolbar may *float* about the screen or become *docked* along the top, bottom, right, or left side of the graphics area. To move a toolbar, pick on its edge and drag it to wherever you want it to go. Toolbars are displayed by using the Toolbars dialog box shown in Figure 1.3. The View/Toolbars pull-down menu item (refer to Figure 1.2) is used to display this dialog box. The Draw and Modify toolbars are normally docked along the left side of the screen but can be moved if desired.

By picking on the associated icon tool, that particular command is activated. Tools with a small black triangle have *flyouts* that contain more commands. If you hold down on the pick button, a flyout menu bar is displayed. By dragging your cursor along the bar you can select from these additional commands.

If you pause the movement of the cursor on a tool, a *tooltip* will appear and display a word describing the tool and a line of text on the status line at the bottom of the screen. Tooltips can be turned on or off by checking the appropriate box in the Toolbars dialog box.

Floating Command Window

The floating command window, normally located at the bottom of the graphics screen, contains the command line. This line lets you know when a command can be entered and what type of command option can be entered, as well as providing feedback after a command is entered. Pay constant attention to what is displayed here. When the command line states "Command:" it's ready to receive a command from a menu or keyboard entry.

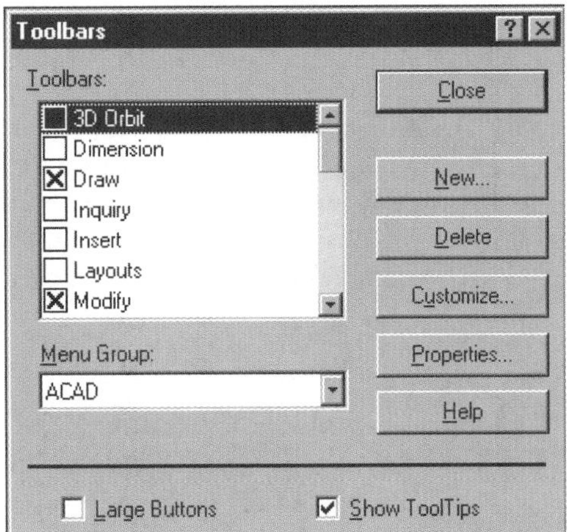

Figure 1.3
The Toolbars dialog box

Tip: Toolbars?... oh, toolbars?...
Toolbars can be hidden underneath each other. If you try to display a toolbar and it doesn't show up, it's probably just hidden underneath another. Keep dragging the top toolbar out of the way until you reveal the one you want.

Status Bar and Coordinate Display

The status bar gives you the current status of various options, such as the current coordinate location, grid and snap modes, and others. The coordinate display shows the X, Y, and Z axes coordinate location (Cartesian coordinate system). As you move the cursor the coordinates will change to reflect the cursor location. The status bar also gives further information on toolbar commands when you highlight a tool icon. Like the command line, it's always useful to keep an eye on the status bar.

Some other items that will appear on the screen include the graphics cursor, which moves about on the screen in response to the pointing device (mouse); the cursor menu, which can appear at the cursor location on the graphics screen; and the UCS icon, which can appear at the lower left of the screen to give the orientation of the X and Y axes. Figure 1.4 shows the Cartesian coordinate systems and the UCS icon. Of course, you're going to make all sorts of other fabulous things appear on your screen, but that's discussed in lessons to come!

Tip: Canceling a Command
To cancel a command, use the Esc (Escape) key. You'll know a command is fully canceled when there are no options next to the Command: prompt.

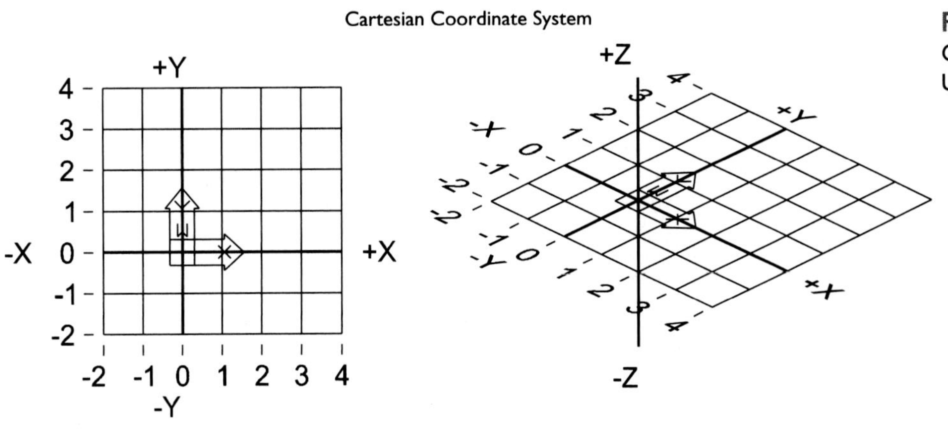

Figure 1.4
Coordinate system and UCS icon

Hands-On: Moving About the Screen

1 The AutoCAD drawing editor should be on your screen with the Startup dialog box closed. You are going to practice moving around the screen and accessing commands, but before you start drawing you will first need to turn on blips. Blips are markers that tell you where you have picked on the screen. Proceed with the following:

Command: **BLIPMODE**

ON/OFF **<OFF>: ON**

2 Look at the coordinate display at the lower left of the screen. If the numbers displayed are grey, they have been turned off. To turn them on or off, press F6, the Ctrl D key combination, or double-click inside the coordinate box. Make sure they are turned on (black).

Move your cursor around the graphics area and look at the coordinate display as you do so. The X and Y axes coordinates should change as you move the cursor. They show you where you are in the drawing. The X axis is represented by the first number and runs horizontally across the screen. The Y axis is the second number and is vertical, running up and down the screen. At the start of a new drawing the 0,0 (0X,0Y) location is in the lower left of the graphics screen.

3 Type the word SNAP on the command line and enter 1 for the value as in the following:

Command: **SNAP**

Snap spacing or ON/OFF/Aspect/Rotate/Style <0.500>: **1**

4 SNAP controls the intervals or increments the cursor moves. Move the cursor down into the status line area and over the word SNAP. If the word is grey it means SNAP is off. Make sure it's on by double-clicking on the word until it is black. Practice double-clicking to turn it on and off.

Now move the cursor around the screen again. Notice how it jumps. Look at the coordinate display. The X and Y numbers move in 1 unit increments. This gives you more accuracy in moving the cursor and picking points. You can set this to any value to ensure specific coordinate locations.

Leave SNAP on for now.

Remember, ● to be grey is to be inaccessible; ● to be black is to be accessible.

Pull-Down Menu

5 Move your cursor up to the pull-down menu area and pick on the word Draw. The Draw menu will pull down onto the screen.

Move the cursor down the menu and pause on the word Circle. A cascading menu should appear to the right showing the various commands to draw a circle.

Move your cursor onto the Center Diameter item and pause. Look at the status line. It explains what the command is for.

Pick on the Center Radius command. The command line now shows that the Circle command is active and should look similar to the following:

```
Command: _circle Specify center point for circle or [3P/2P/Ttr
    (tan tan radius)]:
```

The command (Circle) is shown, followed by options (3P/2P/TTR/<Center point>).

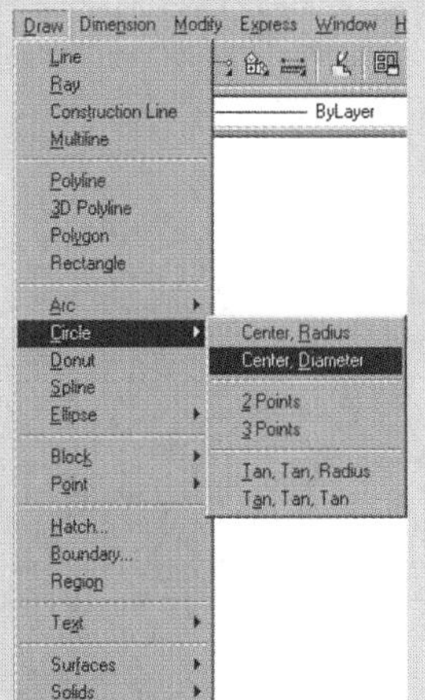

Sometimes you will see a value inside the brackets <>. This is what is referred to as the default value. Sometimes it will be the last value that you entered. If you want to keep the default value, just press the Enter button. You can enter the X,Y location either from the keyboard or you can pick the location using the cursor.

Move your cursor to the middle of the screen and pick a point using the left mouse button.

The command line now gives you further information:

Specify radius of circle or [Diameter}

The command is now asking you to specify the radius. This can be done by picking on the screen or entering a numeric value. Note the word Diameter in brackets. If instead you wanted to enter the diameter you would enter D (the capitalized letter of Diameter) and you would be prompted to enter the diameter.

Drag the cursor and watch the circle change size. Refer to Figure 1.5 and pick the location that matches the circle in the figure. You don't have to be exact at this stage.

6. **Note the small crosses at the center of the circle and at the edge of the circle where you picked the radius. These are the blips we mentioned earlier. To clear the screen of blips, enter R (for Redraw) on the command line. They should disappear, leaving only the circle.**

Icon Tools

7. **The default setup of AutoCAD has two toolbars at the left of the screen. Of these two, the leftmost is the Draw toolbar and the other is the Modify toolbar. If they are not visible, use the View/Toolbars pull-down menu item to display the dialog box. Check the Draw and Modify boxes to display those toolbars.**

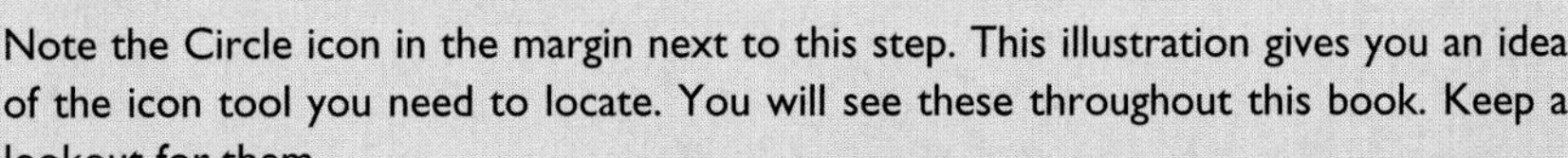

Note the Circle icon in the margin next to this step. This illustration gives you an idea of the icon tool you need to locate. You will see these throughout this book. Keep a lookout for them.

Move your cursor onto the Draw toolbar and place it on the Circle tool. If you rest the cursor for a moment on a tool, a tooltip appears labeling the tool. Also, look at the status line. As with the pull-down menu, a further description of the command appears there.

Pick on the Circle tool and draw a second circle on the screen as shown in Figure 1.6.

Command Line

8. **Press the Esc key several times to make sure that there are no commands active and observe the command line. It should read:**

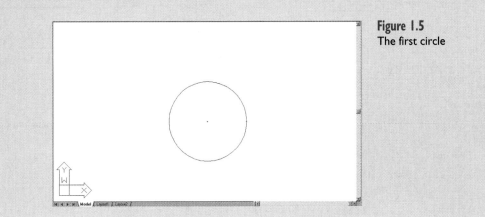

Figure 1.5
The first circle

Hands-On: Moving About the Screen (continued)

Command:

Now type the word CIRCLE (in all upper- or lowercase letters) on the command line as shown in the following and press Enter:

Command: **CIRCLE**

The CIRCLE command is activated. Draw a third circle as shown in Figure 1.7. Almost every command has a command line equivalent. Some people who are proficient with the keyboard prefer this method of entering commands.

9. **With a blank command line, enter only the letter C, as in the following:**

Command: C

This method of using the command line is called an alias because it is a short form of the command term. There are aliases for many of the AutoCAD commands. You don't have to feel that you're being sneaky when you use this kind of alias!

Using the circle alias, draw a fourth circle as shown in Figure 1.8.

Figure 1.6
Drawing the second circle

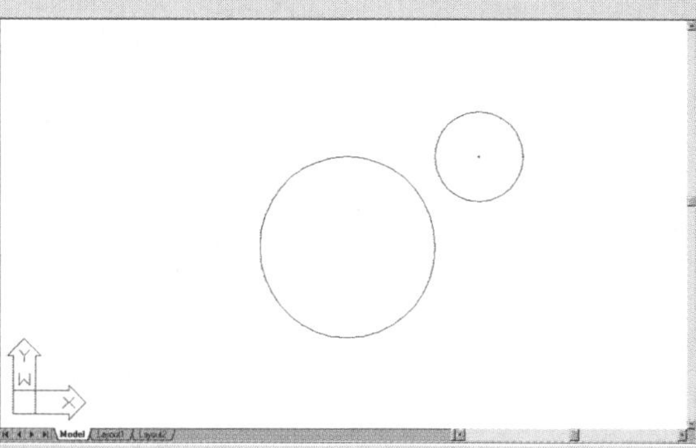

Figure 1.7
Drawing the third circle

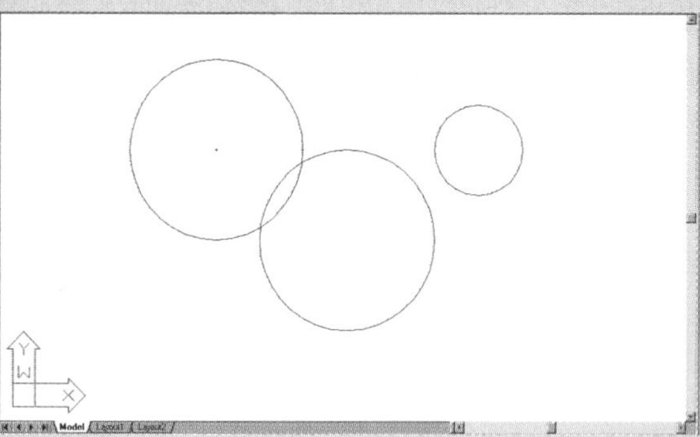

Figure 1.8
Drawing the fourth circle

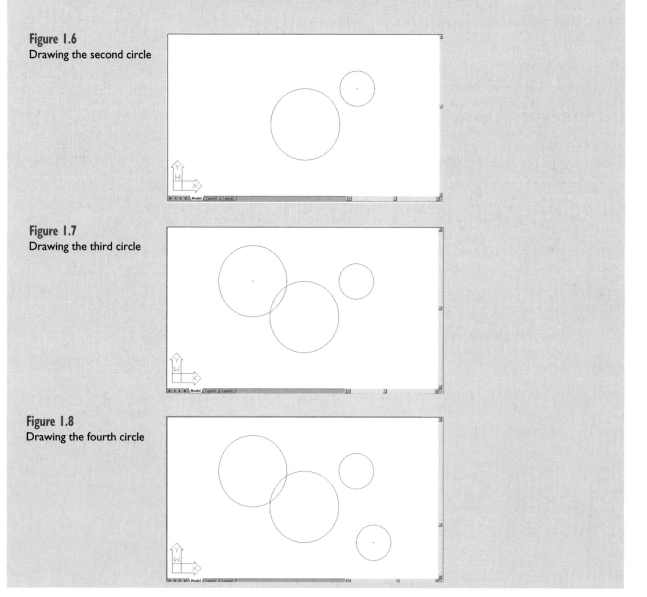

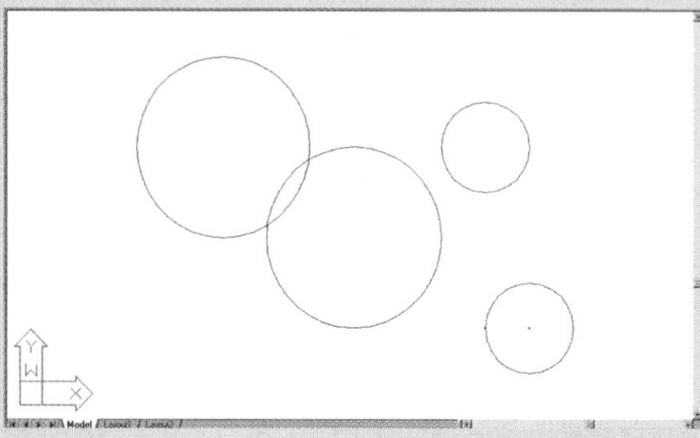

As you can see, whether you are using a pull-down menu, an icon tool, or the command line, the behavior of the command is the same. The method you choose to select a command is up to you.

The command line method will be shown in most cases because it best illustrates the various options. But you can use the pull-down menu or icon tools — whatever suits you best.

...whether you are using a pull-down menu, an icon tool, or the command line, the behavior of the command is the same.

Don't worry about saving this drawing yet, just keep it on the screen for now. However, if for some reason you have to exit out of the program, you'll need to redraw the four circles on the screen when you come back, before continuing on.

Tip: Changing the size of the pickbox
You can change the size of the pickbox by entering, strangely enough, PICKBOX on the command line. You enter the size of the box in pixels. Commonly, a size of 3 to 5 is used. But you can set it to any size at any time for your own strange purposes.

Selecting Objects

The most common objects, particularly to a beginning student of AutoCAD, are lines, circles, text, and dimensions. These will be discussed here. More advanced objects, such as blocks, xrefs, and polylines, will be discussed near the end of the section, once you feel comfortable with the basics. You may not believe us yet, but you will use these basic and advanced objects with ease and in an amazing variety of combinations to create your final designs.

Often in the design process, you will need to select an object for modification, manipulation, or information extraction, that is, you may need to change it in some way, move it around, or find out something about it. The group of objects selected, even including a single object, is called a *selection set*. When a command is used that requires a selection set, you will be prompted as follows:

Select objects:

The program is asking you to pick the objects you want to make changes to. You can select objects in a variety of ways, but the most common is to move the cursor, which appears as a small *pickbox*, over the object and pick it. When an object is selected, it will be highlighted so that it stands out from nonselected objects (see Figure 1.9).

Once you have selected (highlighted) all the objects you want, press Enter to complete the selection process.

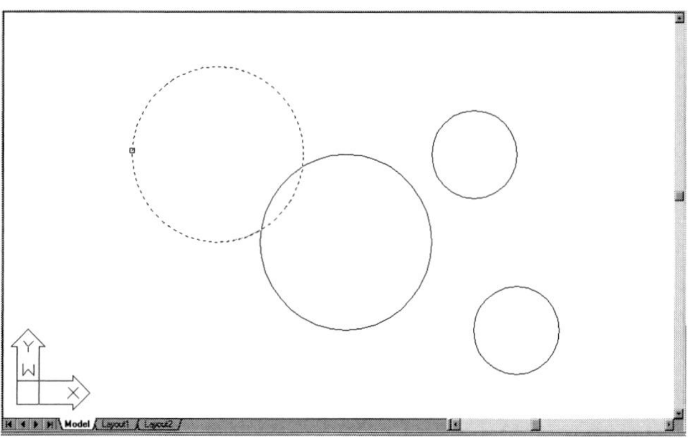

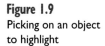

Figure 1.9
Picking on an object to highlight

Selection Options

There are various options that can make selection easier; two of these are window and crossing. When you're asked to select an object, if you pick in open space (no object), and drag the cursor, a rectangular window will form. To set the size of the window, pick the opposite corner of the window. If you drag the cursor toward the right, it will display a solid outlined window. If you drag the cursor toward the left, it will display a dash outlined window.

With the solid window (referred to as *window*), only objects completely within the window are picked. With the dashed window (referred to as *crossing*), objects crossed by the window, as well as those inside, are picked. Figure 1.10 shows both window and crossing.

More options that can be accessed by entering a letter or group of letters are available. You will want to review these, once you're comfortable with using window and crossing. However, if you'd like to see a list of the options when selecting objects, enter a ? at the Select Objects prompt. It returns an error message, but is followed by a list of the possible options, as shown below:

Select objects: **?**

Invalid Selection

Expects a point or

Window/Last/Crossing/BOX/All/Fence
Wpolygon/Cpolygon/Group/Add/Remove/Multiple/Previous /Undo/AUto/SIngle

Select objects:

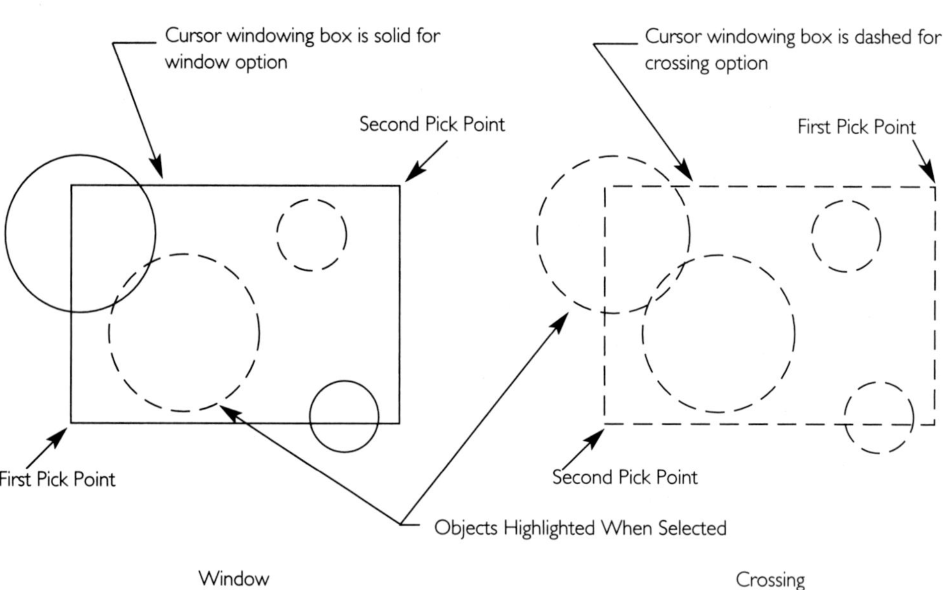

Figure 1.10
Window and crossing selection of objects

Hands-On: Selecting and Modifying Objects

1. **The AutoCAD drawing editor should be visible and the four circles you created earlier should be on the screen. If they aren't, create four circles to match Figure 1.8 and then proceed.**

2. **Move your cursor into the pull-down menu and pick on the Modify heading. From the presented list of MODIFY commands, pick the ERASE command. The small pickbox should replace the cursor.**

   Move the cursor over one of the circles. It must be over part of the arc that describes the circle to select it. Use the pick button on the mouse to select the circle. The display should have many dashed lines to show it has been selected. Press Enter to complete the selection. The circle should disappear.

3. **Now you are going to erase the rest of the circles using the Window Selection options. Remember you need to make the window completely surround the object, starting in the lower left and going to the upper right. Proceed with the following, noting that the bold text is what you type in or pick:**

Command:	**ERASE**
Select objects:	**Pick in the lower-left corner, outside the circles to be erased.**

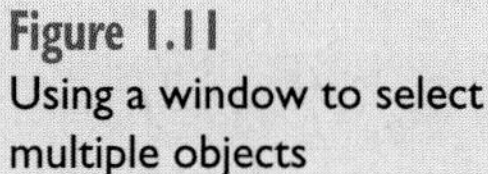

Figure 1.11
Using a window to select multiple objects

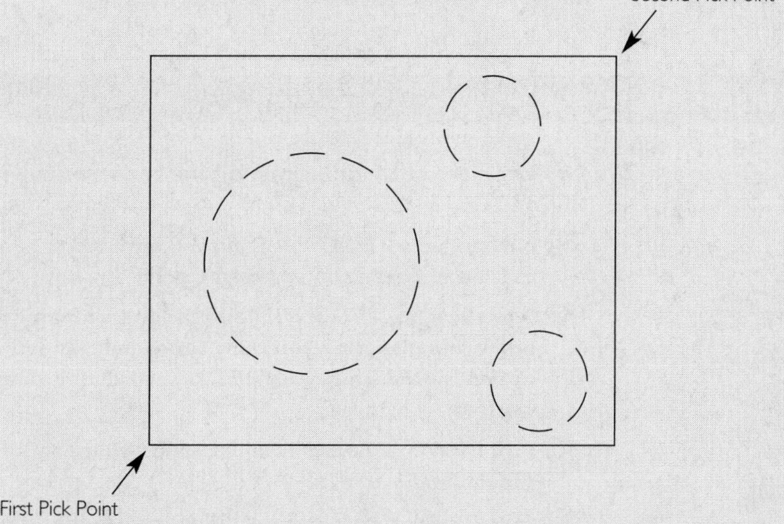

Other corner:	**Drag the cursor to the upper right, totally enclosing the circles as shown in Figure 1.11. When the window totally encloses the circles, pick the point to complete the box.**
Select objects:	**Press Enter to complete the selection.**

As you can see, the Window option makes it easier and faster to select many objects at one time.

4. **Now you are going to try something that makes learning AutoCAD even easier. If you make a mistake, fear not. You can easily undo commands or operations. To bring back the circles you erased, simply enter a U on the command line. Each time it is entered a command sequence is reversed. You may have to enter the U several times to bring all the circles back. Try it! Now doesn't that make your AutoCAD life less worrisome?**

View Manipulation

To create any drawing, you must be able to move around the drawing and view it with different amounts of detail. Several commands allow this type of display movement, including REDRAW and ZOOM. Both of these commands can be found under the View pull-down menu.

The REDRAW Command

You will use the REDRAW command often to refresh what is currently viewed on the screen. When the screen gets cluttered with blips (temporary location markers) or previously erased objects, the REDRAW command lets you see what remains. (This would be a very handy tool for everyday life — when your life gets cluttered with blips, just press R!) This is a perfect example of the Redraw alias, R. If you enter R on the command line, the REDRAW command is implemented.

The ZOOM Command

The ZOOM command is used to magnify the viewing of an area or to reduce an area to let you see the big picture.

To magnify a portion of a drawing, pick the View/Zoom/Window pull-down menu item and then, using the cursor, place a window around the portion you want to modify.

To see all the objects that are currently shown in the drawing, pick the View/Zoom/Extents pull-down menu item. This command sizes the viewing area to the extent of the objects. The display of the objects will expand or reduce until all the objects can be seen.

Hands-On: Changing the View

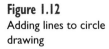

1. **Using the circle drawing you have been working on, draw some other lines and circles on the screen as shown in Figure 1.12.**
2. **Now use the REDRAW (R alias) command to refresh the screen. Any blips that were visible should now be gone.**
3. **Pick the View/Zoom/Window pull-down menu item and make a small window around an area you want to magnify, as shown in Figure 1.13. This option is used when you need to get a closer view of objects you want to work on.**
4. **Pick the View/ Zoom/Extents pull-down menu item and all your objects should fill the screen.**
5. **Experiment with drawing objects, redrawing, zooming in with window, and zooming out with extents, until you are comfortable with them. You will be using them often as you become more proficient.**

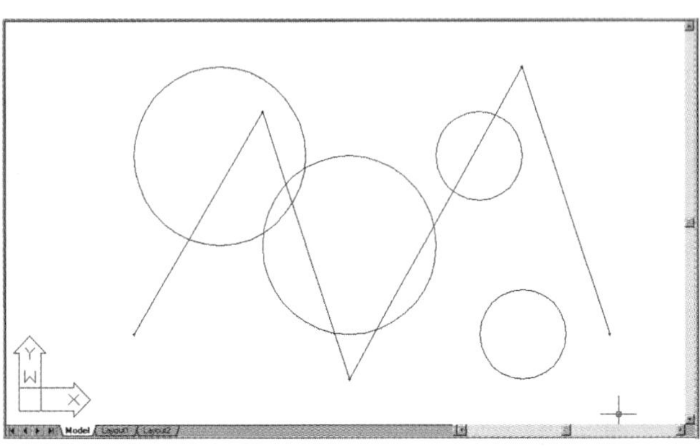

Figure 1.12
Adding lines to circle drawing

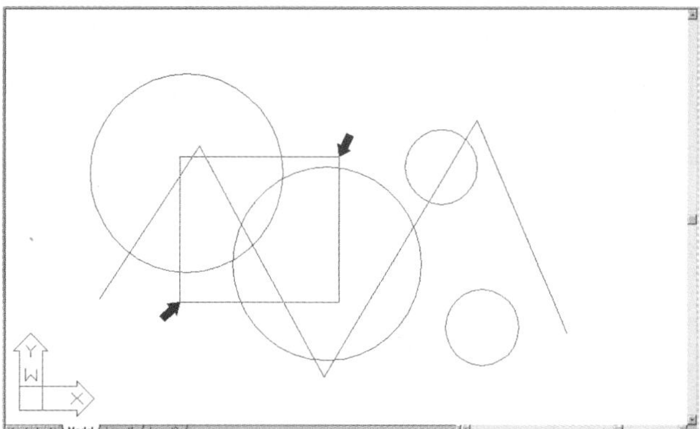

Figure 1.13
Using the Window option of the ZOOM command

File Management

You have now reached a point where you may be wondering how to save or recall a drawing.

Once you are in the drawing editor, you can retrieve previous drawings by *opening* them to allow manipulation.

When it is time to store the drawing, you can *save* it either by the name under which it was created, or under a new name, which allows you to retain the original. The following sections explain commands to do just that.

The NEW Command

Under normal conditions (is there any such thing? Well, other conditions are explained later), when you enter the AutoCAD drawing editor, you begin with a new, unnamed drawing. This new drawing matches the default settings in either English or metric units as set by Start from Scratch.

When you want to start a new drawing while another drawing is on the screen, you enter the NEW command, which is found in the File pull-down menu. If you have not saved the first drawing, you will be prompted with a dialog box similar to Figure 1.14. Once you have responded, or if you have previously saved the current drawing, you will be prompted with the Create New Drawing dialog box similar to Figure 1.15.

If you pick the Start from Scratch button, you will begin a new blank drawing, which is assigned the default name of Drawing.

The Use a Template button starts a new drawing with previously established settings stored in a template file. You will be using a series of template files that comes with this book, which will assist in and speed up your learning.

The Use a Wizard button leads you through the common procedures needed to set up a drawing. Chapter 2 will explain the simple set of steps to actually start a drawing. Following the simple set of steps will help you understand the choices you're making.

Tip: Dialog Boxes Playing Hide-and-Seek?
Note that file dialog boxes will appear only if the FILEDIA variable is set to 1. Sometimes this can inadvertently become set to 0. Enter FILEDIA on the command line and enter 1. If other dialog boxes do not appear, make sure the CMDDIA variable is also set to 1.

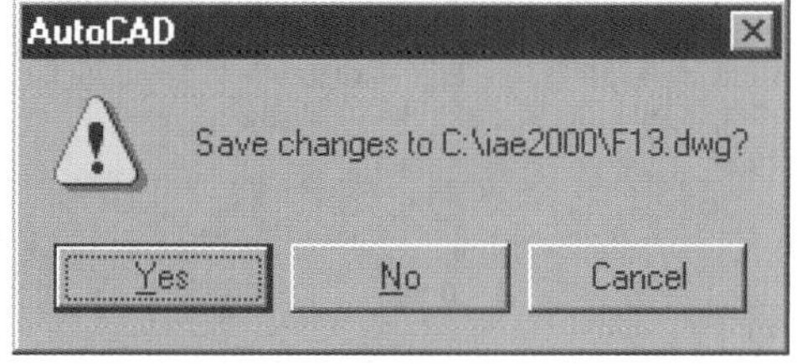

Figure 1.14
Drawing Modification dialog box

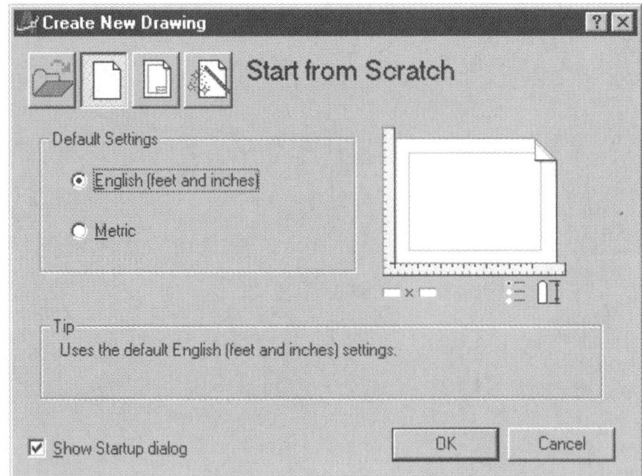

Figure 1.15
Create New Drawing dialog box

The Open Command

The OPEN command is used to recall existing drawings into the editor. Like the NEW command, if you have not saved the current drawing you'll be asked whether or not you would like to. You will then be presented with the Select File dialog box similar to Figure 1.16.

The following is a brief explanation of the different areas of the Select File dialog box:

Look in: Sets the subdirectory where you will find your files. Below this is a list of subdirectories and files contained in the *Look in:* subdirectory.

File name: You can enter the name of the file you want to open in this box. When you pick a name from the list above, it will appear in this box.

Files of type: This area sets the file extension type. Drawings have the extension .DWG, templates are .DWT, and drawing exchange files are .DXF. To simplify things at this point, just keep in mind the drawing file extension .DWG, as in PLAN.DWG.

Preview If you highlight a drawing file name that was created using Release 13 or above, you'll see a small picture of the drawing in the preview box to help you identify it.

Locate This button will search for a drawing of the name you entered in the File Name box. If you're in the root directory of the disk, the Locate feature will search the drive until it locates the file. If you're in a subdirectory, the Locate feature will only search the directories contained in the subdirectory. So don't panic if your file isn't found on the first try.

Find File... This button is used to perform a more extensive search, as well as to allow you to visually browse the files.

Open Once you have found the drawing you want, pick the Open button.

Partial Open This button allows you to load parts of a drawing instead of the complete drawing.

The SAVE, QSAVE, SAVEAS Commands

When you want to retain the drawing you're working on, you must save it. There are several ways to do this.

If you pick the SAVE command from a menu, the QSAVE (quick save) command is executed. If you have already named your file, it will be saved to the location where it was first loaded. If you haven't named the drawing, you'll be presented with the Save Drawing As dialog box, so that you can name the drawing and indicate where it is to be saved, as shown in Figure 1.17.

Save frequently... Save often... and, most importantly, remember to save frequently and often.

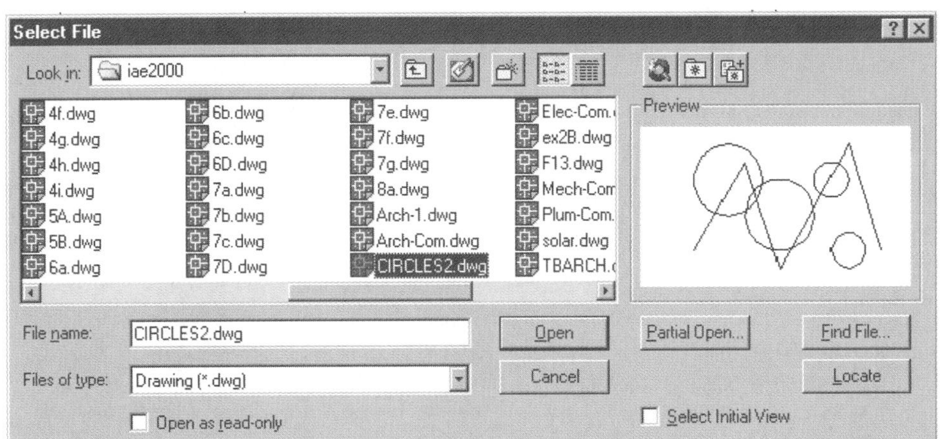

Figure 1.16
Select File dialog box to open a drawing

If you pick the SAVEAS command, you can change the name of the file and its location before saving it. This is useful if you want to retain the original drawing and save the changes to a new drawing file. The Save as type box allows you to set the type of format in which the drawing will be saved. Normally you would want it set to AutoCAD 2000 Drawing, but you have other choices, such as previous versions of AutoCAD, AutoCAD LT, and a Template File. Refer to Figure 1.17, which shows the Save Drawing As dialog box.

Remember to save your drawing often, so that no information is lost. For added safety, when you are finished with the current drawing, save it in two locations—for example, the hard disk, micro disk, or network drive, if available.

Tip: Saving a Drawing to A: Drive

If you want to save your drawing to a removable disk, such as A: drive, you should type the SAVE command on the command line. This lets you save the drawing without logging onto the location or changing the name of the current drawing.

If you use the menu Save As, it logs onto the location you set. If the location is a removable disk drive, the operation of AutoCAD slows down to the speed of the removable disk drive.

The EXIT or QUIT Commands

Either the EXIT or QUIT command leaves the drawing editor and closes AutoCAD. If you have not saved the current drawing, you will be prompted to do so before AutoCAD is closed.

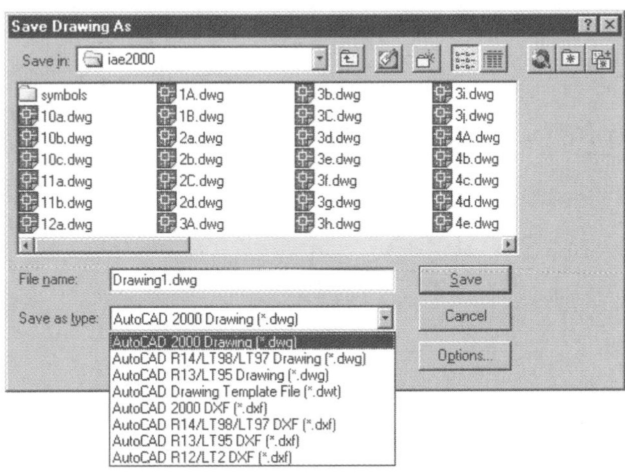

Figure 1.17
Save Drawing As dialog box

Hands-On: Saving and Opening a Drawing

1. **If the Circle drawing is still on the screen, move to Step 2. If it is not, draw some geometry on the screen. It doesn't matter what, as long as you can recognize it when you open the drawing again.**

Saving

2. **Go to the File pull-down menu and pick the Save As item. You'll be presented with the dialog box shown in Figure 1.18. Using the Save in: box, find the subdirectory where you are supposed to save your drawings. If this is your own computer, look for the IAE2000 subdirectory created for this book. If you are a student, your instructor may have told you where to save your files. Set that directory as the Save in: directory.**
3. **In the File name: box, enter C1D1, which stands for Chapter 1, Drawing 1, for the drawing name. Pick the Save button to save your drawing.**

New

4. **Select the NEW command. If the Start Up dialog box appears, pick the Start from Scratch button and OK it.**

Open

5. **Select the OPEN command and the Select File dialog box appears. As with the Save Drawing As dialog box, the Look in: box needs to show the directory where you saved your drawing. Usually it will highlight the location of the last save. It should show IAE2000 (or your directory). If it does not, use the Look in: box to find it. See Figure 1.19.**

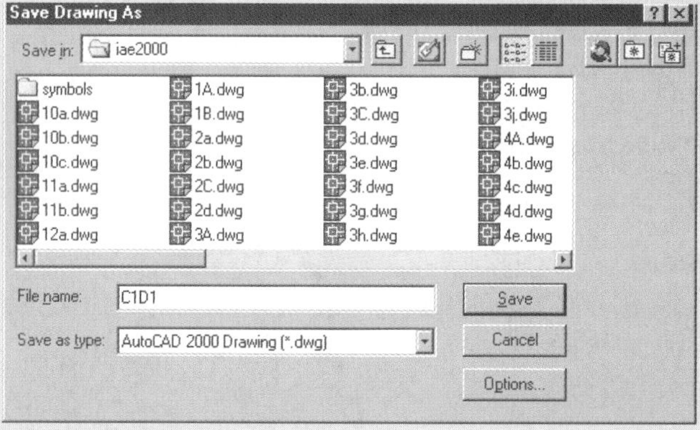

Figure 1.18
Using Save Drawing As dialog box to save C1D1 drawing

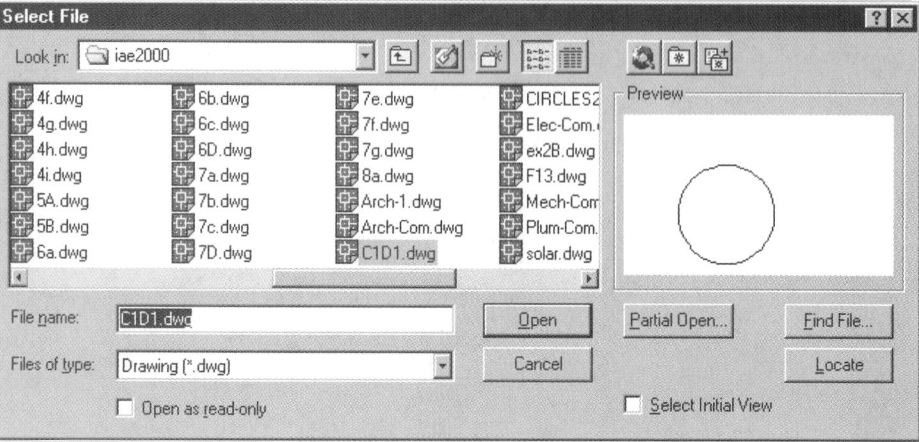

Figure 1.19
Using the Select File dialog box to open the C1D1 drawing

Once you have found the directory, the name of your file should appear in the list. Look for it, and pick on it once to highlight it. A picture of it should appear in the preview. If you double-click on it, it will load automatically without picking the Open button. Open your C1D1 drawing.

Saving and opening drawings are as easy as that. You didn't even need to use the NEW command — it just gave you a blank screen before you opened your drawing for the practice.

Template Files

Throughout your work you are going to use a form of template files to do most of your practical work. *Template files* are drawing files that already contain settings and geometry for you to work with. Although some files appear blank, they actually have numerous settings already established for you. You are going to test start a new drawing with a template drawing.

❻ **Select the NEW command. From the Start Up dialog box, pick the Use a Template File button. Beside the button a list of template files will appear. You need to find the IAE2000 subdirectory where this book's template files are located.**

With the Use a Template File button pushed in, pick on the Browser button. You will be presented with a Select a template file dialog box similar to Figure 1.20.

❼ **Using the Look in: box, find the IAE2000 subdirectory. Once you have done that, the dialog box should look similar to Figure 1.21. Pick on the C1T1 template file and open it. A new drawing is created called Drawing that matches what is contained in template file C1T1. This screen should also look similar to Fig 1.21.**

When you use a template file, you should immediately use the SAVEAS command to change the name of the drawing from Drawing to your file name. Do this now, and save the drawing as C1D2. Once you have saved the drawing, open it again, just for practice.

Remember that drawings have the file extension .DWG, and templates have the extension .DWT.

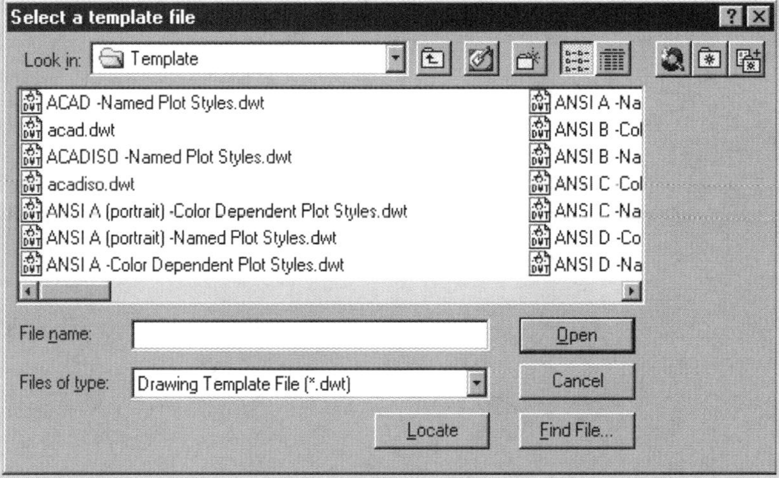

Figure 1.20
Select a template file dialog box

Hands-On: Saving and Opening a Drawing (continued)

Figure 1.21

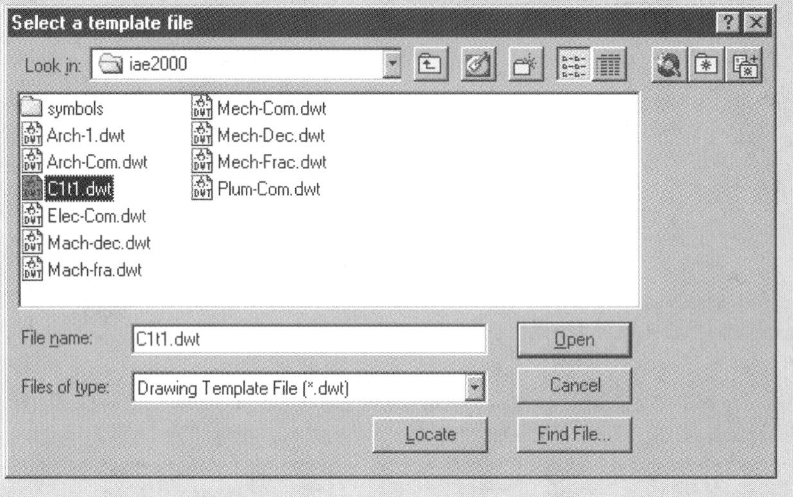

In a Nutshell

You have now gone over the initial groundwork for creating drawings. You should be comfortable moving around the menus and screen, and be able to save and open your own drawings. You may want to practice with the commands that you have learned in this chapter. The easiest way to do this is to repeat the Hands-On sections and to add to them. Once you are ready, move on to Chapter 2.

Testing... testing... 1, 2, 3

At the end of each chapter you'll find a short-answer test with the above title. It could have items that are true or false, multiple choice, fill in the blank, or matching. It may even require you to write a list. In this section, there is often a question called Remember. This is a review test question that is drawn from material in the previous chapter, just to keep you on your toes.

Fill in the blank.

Write the word(s) in the blank that most appropriately completes the following sentences.

1. The __________ command starts a drawing from scratch whereas the __________ command recalls a drawing previously drawn and saved.
2. C is the __________ for circle.
3. The __________ command lets you change the name of a file and save it.

True or False

Indicate whether the following statements are true or false by circling T or F.

1. Template files may appear blank but they can have many settings already established. T or F
2. Comprising a little over one-third of the space, the command line is the dominant part of the display screen. T or F
3. It is possible to alter the size of the pickbox. T or F

Matching

Match the item in column A with the one it belongs with in column B.

Column A	Column B
___1. Press right mouse button	a. picks commands
___2. Shift key + right mouse button	b. opens Draw pull-down menu
___3. Left mouse button	c. <enters>
___4. Double-click left mouse button	d. activates object SNAP menu
	e. opens files

Multiple Choice

Choose the best answer to complete each of the following statements.

1. A set of related pictures describing a command and linked together in a line is
   a. the Command line.
   b. a pull-down menu.
   c. a toolbar.
   d. a cursor menu.
   e. none of the above

2. A small black triangle on a tool indicates that it has
   a. additional commands associated with it.
   b. a flyout.
   c. a buried menu bar.
   d. all of the above

3. When a toolbar gets lost under another toolbar you can
   a. yell toolbar, oh toolbar!
   b. drag the imposing one out of the way.
   c. send out a toolbar search party.
   d. quit and go to lunch.
   e. all of the above

What?

At the end of each chapter, following the Testing, testing section, you'll find a What? exercise. These are longer answer questions that may require anything from a few words to a few sentences or paragraphs. Remember to organize your thoughts well. And remember, we may spring a "Remember" question on you in this section as well!

1. What different methods are there to access a command?

   ____

2. List the four main parts of the drawing screen and explain the importance of each.
   1. ____
   2. ____
   3. ____
   4. ____

3. What is the difference between window and crossing when used to select a group of objects?

   ____

   ____

4. Explain the axes of the Cartesian coordinate system.

____

____

5. Why would you want to type the SAVE command on the command line instead of picking from a menu?

____

____

6. What two functions does the right mouse button serve?

 1. ____
 2. ____

7. Explain the function of the REDRAW command.

____

____

8. Explain the Zoom options window and extents.

____

____

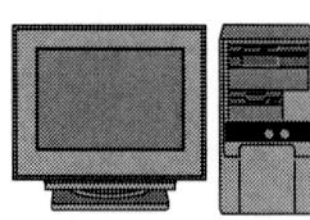

Let's Get Busy!

Finally, at the end of every chapter, you'll find a few assignments to extend your learning. The Let's Get Busy section focuses on your cumulative knowledge, so, for instance, the Chapter 4 section will require you to do everything you've learned up to and including that chapter.

1. Draw a line on the screen and move it about on the screen using the MOVE command. Make a list of all the paths you can follow to arrive at the MOVE command.

2. Study the objects in Figure 1.22. Reproduce the drawing to the best of your ability and save it as STUFF. Now erase one of the objects and move another to a different location of your choice. Save the second drawing as STUFF2.

3. Study the objects in Figure 1.23. Reproduce the drawing to the best of your ability and save it as STUFF3. Now use the Window option of the ERASE command to erase only the circles. Now use the Crossing option of the ERASE command to erase the vertical lines. (*Hint:* Draw the crossing box through the tops of the lines.)

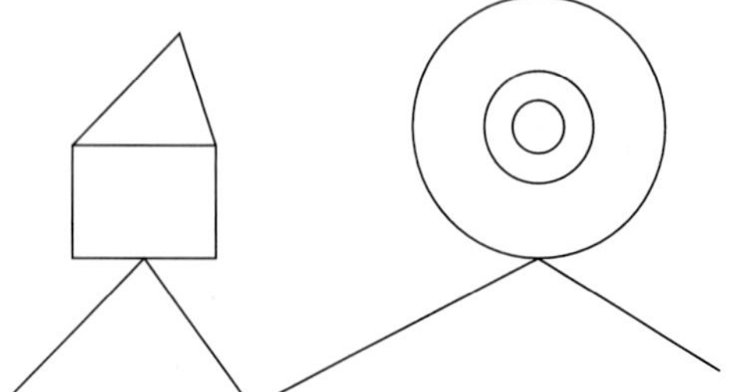

Figure 1.22
Assignment 2 STUFF2

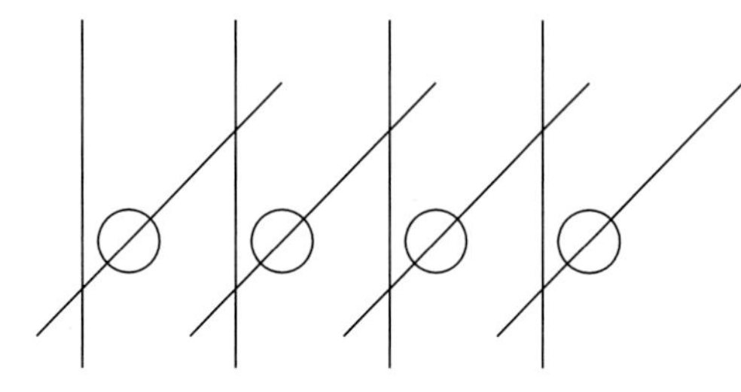

Figure 1.23
Assignment 3 STUFF3

Chapter 2

Always Be Prepared: . . . Set . . .

Key topics

- Units
- Layers
- Limits
- Templates
- Drawing Aids

Where to Begin?

In no time at all, you'll be using AutoCAD to develop and draw your own ideas and fantastic creations. But to get there, you need firm footing. This footing is the initial preparation of a drawing and the various settings that make your drawing experience a lot easier and a lot faster. Remember the Boy Scout motto: Always be prepared. It has never been more important than it is now. Once you understand the settings and creation aids laid out in this chapter, you will be well prepared to start any drawing. (Don't worry if you weren't a Boy Scout—we have every confidence you can still learn the principle.)

Preparing the Drawing File

Every new drawing needs a new bunch of settings to organize it and prepare it for the type of drawing you want to create. The typical initial settings involve units, layers and linetypes, and limits. Most of these can be stored in a template file. The Format pull-down menu will give you access to most of the settings that you will need when starting a drawing. The Wizard from the Startup dialog box goes through some of the settings to begin a drawing. After you have become familiar with the various settings, you may decide to use the Wizard to get some of the settings out of the way during start up. Read on for a description of these settings.

Units

AutoCAD has a simple way of dealing with distance. It has only one type of distance measurement, the *unit*. This measurement, however, gives you a great deal of freedom because, in a drawing, a unit may represent any value you desire: 1 micron (one millionth of a meter), 1 inch, or 1 parsec (the distance light travels in one year). Also, you aren't restricted by the size of paper you have; your 8 1/2" × 11" sheet can contain a city block or even an entire galaxy.

AutoCAD ... has one type of distance measurement ... the unit

---

To make things even easier, AutoCAD has several preset unit formats. A *unit format* is the way AutoCAD displays values on the screen, and the way it expects you to enter values. (However, it is possible to enter values in different formats depending on the current format.) The following chart shows the unit formats available in AutoCAD.

Format	Example of Display	Method of Input
Scientific	2.75E+01	2.75E+01
Decimal	27.50	27.50
Engineering	2'-3.5"	2'3.5"
Architectural	2'-3 1/2"	2'3-1/2"
Fractional	27 1/2"	27-1/2"

Note how the method of input is different from the display for some of the formats, especially those with fractions—during input, you need a hyphen to separate integers and fractions.

You can also choose the way you want to display angle values. The following chart shows the angle formats available in AutoCAD.

System of Angle Measure	Example of Display
Decimal Degrees	45.00
Degrees/Minutes/Seconds	45d0'0"
Grads	50.00g
Radians	0.7854r
Surveyor's Units	N45d0'0"E

By default, angles are measured positively in a counterclockwise direction from 0 as shown in Figure 2.1.

Units and angles are set using the Drawing Units dialog box (see Figure 2.2). Note the precision settings for units and angles. This controls the number of decimal places or fraction denominators

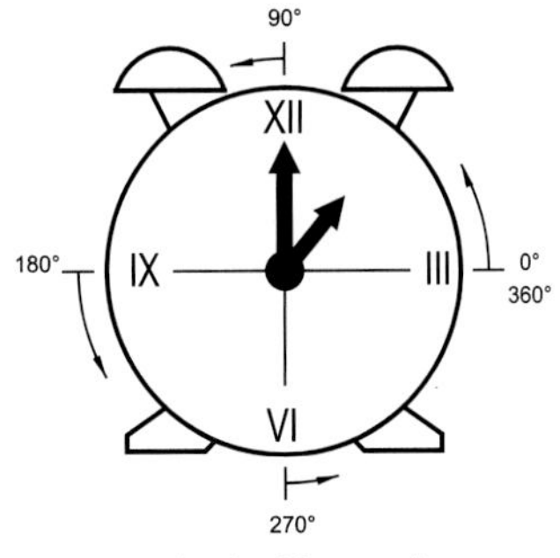

Figure 2.1
Angular measurement direction

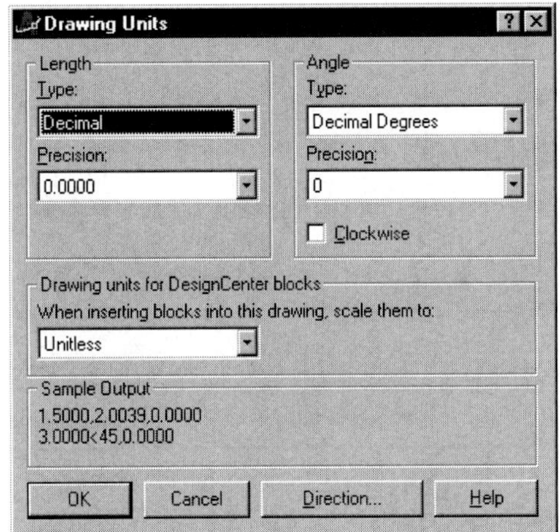

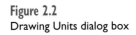

Figure 2.2
Drawing Units dialog box

used in a drawing. For the beginner (that's probably you) it's usually best to set the units to 3 decimal places (or 1/16) and the angular precision to 2 decimal places.

You can find Units in the Format pull-down menu or you can type UNITS on the command line.

For the beginner, it's usually best to set the units to 3 decimal places (or 1/16) and the angular precision to 2 decimal places.

Layers

Think of layers as a series of transparent sheets glued together like a pad. Remember the transparent overlays in encyclopedias, showing all of the body's interconnected systems—circulatory, respiratory, digestive, and the rest? In AutoCAD each layer/sheet has a unique name that establishes its purpose, and you can control the display of any layer less clumsily than you can with a pad of vellum. By displaying your layer choice combinations, you form the desired drawing like the one in Figure 2.3.

When adding any object to your drawing, it's placed on a layer of your choice. For instance, a mechanical drawing may have individual layers for object lines, hidden lines, dimensions, and so on, whereas an architectural drawing may have layers divided for walls, doors, windows, and the rest.

You can create as many layers as you want but you should name them in a logical fashion so that both you and others will easily recognize their functions. Layer 1, 2, 3, and so on may be a wonderful no-brainer when you initially assign a name, but it won't be nearly as pleasing when you're trying to recall what you placed on Layers 1, 2, and 3 a month after naming them.

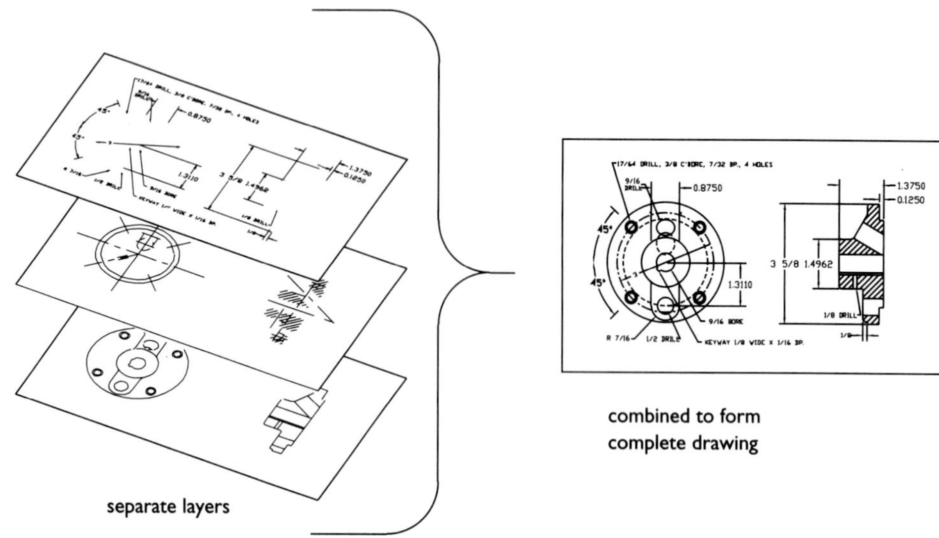

Figure 2.3
Using different layers to create a complete drawing

Linetypes

Each object you draw uses a linetype which controls the appearance of the object, as shown in Figure 2.4. You assign a linetype to an object before you draw it. The easiest way to assign linetypes is to assign them to a layer; then, when you draw on a layer, the object will use that layer's linetype.

Linetype and color are usually assigned to drawing layers.

There is also a scale that you assign to linetypes which controls the size of dashes. The global value that controls all the objects in a drawing is called LTSCALE (see Figure 2.5). Changing this value changes the linetype scale of all the objects in the drawing; this is the easiest and most common way to set the linetype scale. You can also set the linetype scale of individual objects, but this should be reserved for special circumstances. A value too small or too large for the global LTSCALE can result in a line that looks continuous (refer to Figure 2.5). The value of the LTSCALE is usually based on the size of the objects you're drawing; that is, small objects use a small LTSCALE, while large objects use a large value.

You can also set the color for each layer. Then, when you look at your combined drawing, you can immediately tell which objects come from which layer.

Figure 2.4
Some available linetypes

CONTINUOUS

HIDDEN

CENTER

PHANTOM

Figure 2.5
The same line with different LTSCALE values

LTSCALE = 0.01

LTSCALE = 0.5

LTSCALE = 1

LTSCALE = 2

LTSCALE = 45

Layers are created with the Layer Properties Manager dialog box shown in Figure 2.6. This is accessed from the Format pull-down menu or the Layer tool. To draw on a layer, you make it Current. There are several ways to do this (what else is new!). The easiest way is to use the Layer Control tool shown in Figure 2.7. Simply pick on the name of the layer on which you want to draw. (You'll get more on Layer options when we arrive at Chapter 4.)

There are two methods for controlling the thickness of lines. You can control the thickness by the color of the object when plotted or you can assign a lineweight property. Refer to Figure 2.6 and the lineweight column. Normally it is set to default, which means that you use the color to control the thickness. If you pick in the Lineweight column next to a layer, you will get a Lineweight dialog box similar to Figure 2.8a. You can select the thickness from the list. Refer to Figure 2.8b showing a drawing illustrating different line thicknesses and linetypes.

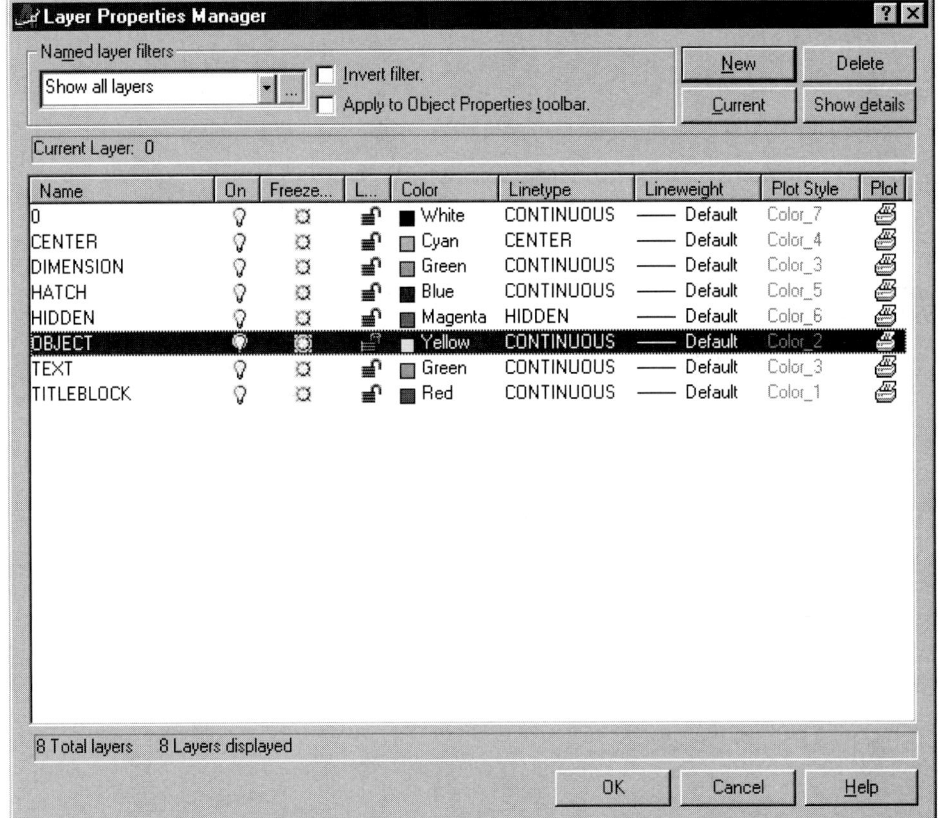

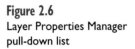

Figure 2.6
Layer Properties Manager pull-down list

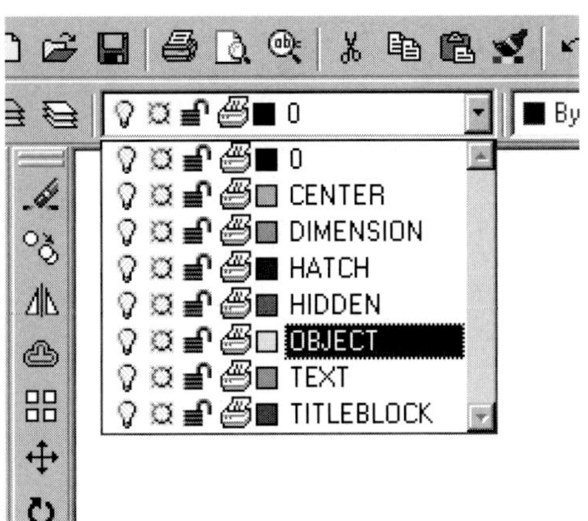

Figure 2.7
Layer control

Figure 2.8
(a) Lineweight dialog box and (b) drawing showing linetypes and line thicknesses

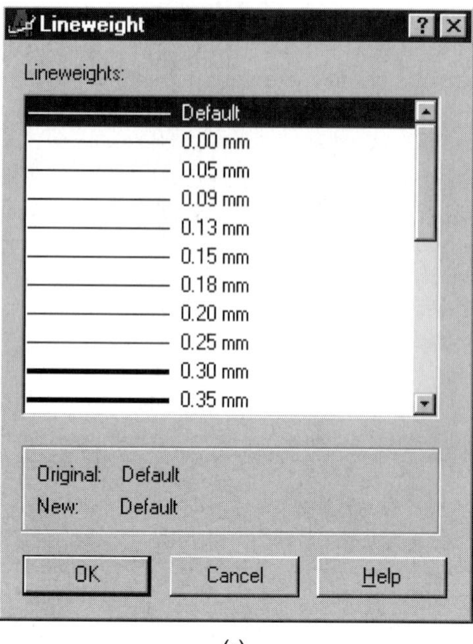

(a)

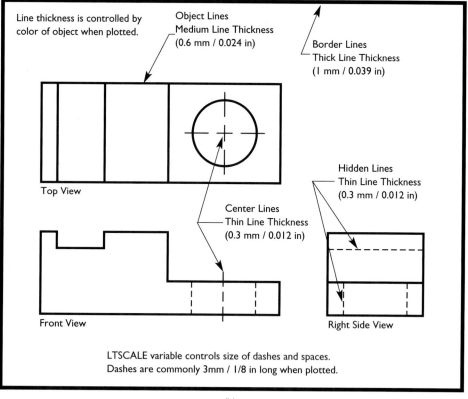

Line thickness is controlled by color of object when plotted.

Object Lines
Medium Line Thickness
(0.6 mm / 0.024 in)

Border Lines
Thick Line Thickness
(1 mm / 0.039 in)

Top View

Hidden Lines
Thin Line Thickness
(0.3 mm / 0.012 in)

Center Lines
Thin Line Thickness
(0.3 mm / 0.012 in)

Front View

Right Side View

LTSCALE variable controls size of dashes and spaces.
Dashes are commonly 3mm / 1/8 in long when plotted.

(b)

Limits

The idea of limits is usually hard for the beginner to grasp; but, never fear, it is actually quite straightforward. When you're drawing on a physical piece of paper, you can see how much area you have to work with and you can clearly understand that an object occupies, perhaps, one-half of that space. However, when working on an electronic screen, because you can zoom in and out, the object occupies a constantly differing proportion of screen space.

To help with this, AutoCAD allows you set a working limit that defines the area where you are working. By setting a lower-left and upper-right corner, you decide the size of your work area. In this way you can correlate how big or small objects are based on the limits. It should be noted that you can change your limits at any time. Once you're familiar with electronic drawing, you may find you stop using limits altogether.

Templates

As mentioned before, templates are drawing files that contain pre-established settings such as layers and linetypes. Whenever you start a new drawing, to save time use a template file. However, since limits change for practically every drawing, they are not usually set in a template. Once you load the template file, you'll then need to set the limits.

For your convenience, units and layers have been pre-established for this book in the form of template files.

Tip: To What Size Should LTSCALE Be Set?
An easy guideline to follow is to initially set the LTSCALE to what you think your plot scale is going to be. For instance, if you were going to plot your drawing out on paper at a scale of 1:1, initially set the LTSCALE to 1. Then you can adjust it up or down in small increments of say 0.25. In you were going to plot your drawing at 1:48, then initially set the LTSCALE to 48 and adjust it up or down in increments of 5.

Hands-On: Starting from Nothing and Then Some

This exercise will show you how to set up a drawing manually, and then show you how to use the Instant AutoCAD Hands-On Exercises Loader to automatically load your exercises.

Starting a New Drawing from Scratch

New

1. **Start a new drawing from scratch by typing NEW on the command line, selecting New from the File pull-down menu, or picking the New tool shown in the margin to the left of this step. When the Startup dialog box appears, make sure the Start from Scratch button is depressed and the units are set to English. Then pick OK. The graphic portion of the screen will go blank. This starts a new, blank drawing.**

Units

2. **Open the Drawing Units dialog box shown in Figure 2.9 either by typing UNITS on the command line or by selecting Units from the Format pull-down menu.**
3. **Experiment by selecting different units and identifying them by the coordinate readout displayed in the lower-left of the screen. The readout changes to reflect the unit format.**
4. **Now set the units to Fractional. This establishes that you will be working with fractional units.**

Hands-On: Starting from Nothing and Then Some (continued)

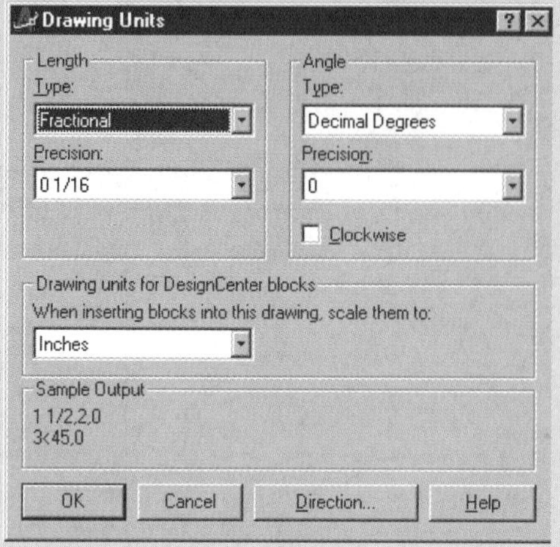

Figure 2.9
Drawing Units dialog box

Layer

5 Open the Layer dialog box by typing LAYER on the command line, by selecting Layer from the Format pull-down menu, or by picking the Layers tool shown in the margin to the left of this step. When the dialog box appears, make sure that the Details portion is displayed, as shown in Figure 2.10. If it isn't, pick on the Details button.

Create the layer Object using the New button, as shown in Figure 2.10. Give it the color cyan; create a layer called Hidden and give it the color blue.

To set the linetype to Hidden, you must load it first. Pick in the Linetype column aligned with the Hidden layer. You will be presented with the Select Linetype dialog box. Pick Load from this dialog box. A list of possible linetypes will appear. Scroll down until you see Hidden. Highlight it and then pick OK. You will return to the

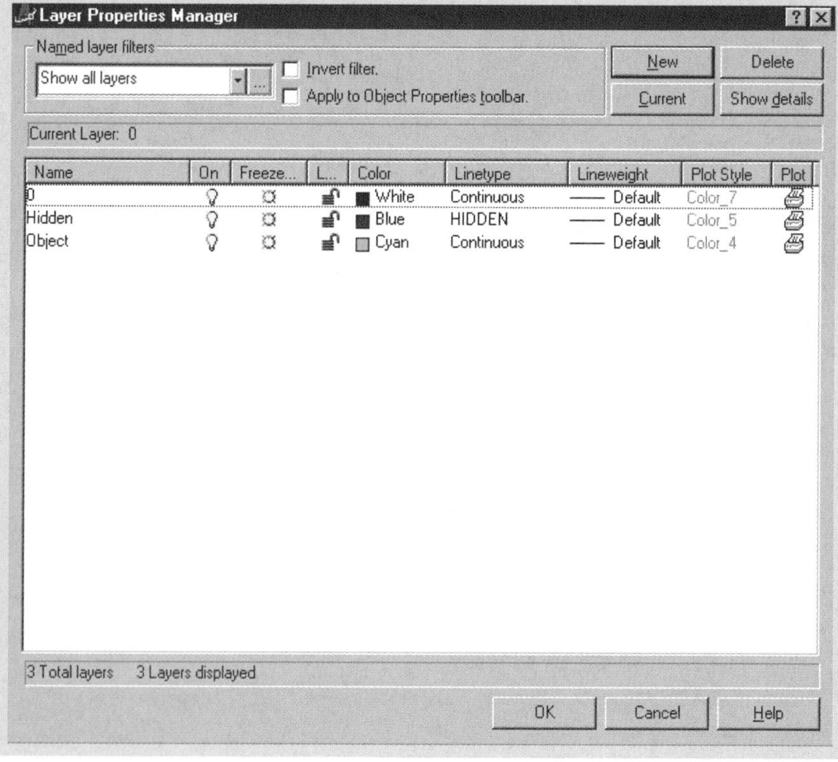

Figure 2.10
Layer Properties Manager dialog box with layers created

Select Linetype dialog box. The linetype hidden is now available. Highlight it and pick OK to return to the Layer Properties Manager. You can see that it has now been added to the layer properties for the Hidden layer.

You have now created two layers upon which to draw—just like that! Before you close the dialog box, look at the upper-right corner. There is a button that reads either Show details or Hide details. This button is used to give you a list of information about the highlighted layer. Experiment with showing details and hiding details for the two layers you just created.

Close the dialog box by picking OK.

Limits

6. **Set the limits to 0,0 for the lower-left corner and 10-1/4, 7-1/4 for the upper-right corner. Type LIMITS on the command line.**
7. **Using the Layer Control pop-up list, pick on the layer name Object to make it current. Using the LINE command, draw the continuous (solid) lines shown in Figure 2.11.**
8. **Using the Layer Control pop-up list, pick on the layer name Hidden to make it current. Draw the hidden lines shown in Figure 2.11. Note how the lines take on the color and linetype of the current layer.**
9. **Save your drawing as EX2.**

Using Hands-On Exercise Loader

You are now going to learn how to use the Instant AutoCAD Hands-On Exercise Loader. [If, for some reason, you cannot access the exercises with the loader, all is not lost. Simply open the desired drawing (for instance 2A.DWG for the lab in Chapter 2) in the IAE2000 subdirectory.]

Note: The Instant AutoCAD Hands-On Exercise Loader will not work if you have multiple drawings open at the same time. If you try to run the exercise loader and you get an error, close all your drawings and start a single drawing from scratch. Once this is done, use the Instant AutoCAD tool to load the exercise.

1. **Pick the Instant AutoCAD tool, shown in the margin on the left. A dialog box similar to Figure 2.12 will appear.**
2. **Pick on the Chapter pop-up list and highlight Two (for Chapter 2) from the list. The Exercise list on the right should now be showing 2A. If it is not, pick on the list then pick on 2A. A picture of the exercise will appear at the top of the dialog box and a description of the exercise will appear at the bottom.**
3. **Pick on the Start Exercise button. You will be notified that the file is read-only. This is to protect the original file from being accidentally modified. Answer Yes to open the file as read-only. Exercise 2A will then appear. See how easy it is?**

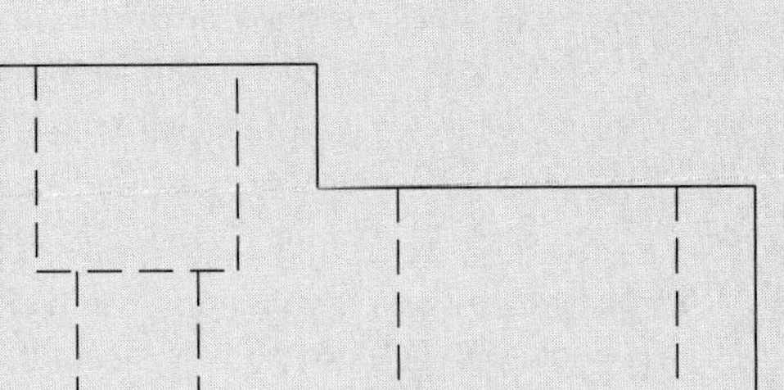

Figure 2.11
Practice geometry using two layers

Hands-On: Starting from Nothing and Then Some (continued)

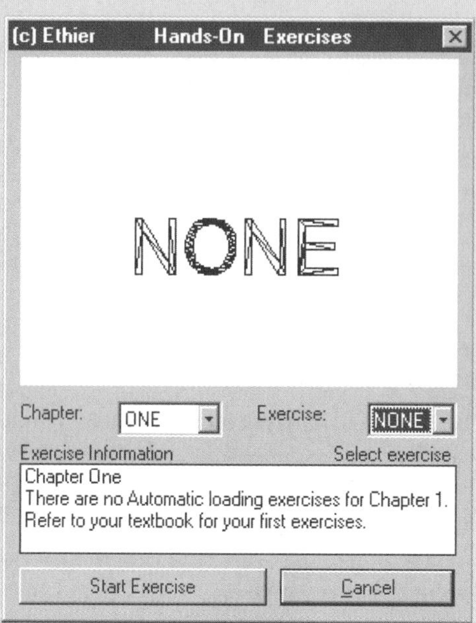

Figure 2.12
Hands-On Exercises dialog box

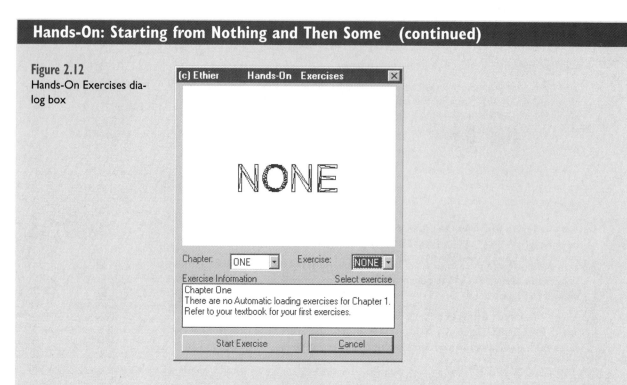

❹ **Observe the geometry in the top box labeled A. Using the Layer Control tool and the LINE command, draw the same geometry shown in the box labeled B.**

❺ **Once you have drawn the geometry, try freezing (invisible) and thawing (visible) the two layers using the Layer dialog box. Note how the icons of the sun (thaw) and snowflake (freeze) change, depending on the state of the layer. Experiment using the Layer Control tool to perform the same task.**

Throughout this section you will be asked to load and work on exercises in this manner. In this way you can see on the screen what you are being asked to do.

Using a Template File

To save time when setting up a drawing, use a template file that has pre-established settings. You can create your own just by setting up a drawing and then saving it as a template file. We've created a number of templates for your use, but the world won't always be this nice—sometime soon you'll have to make your own. The following is the procedure to use an already created template file.

❶ **Select the NEW command and pick the Use a Template file. Beside the button, a list of template files will appear. You need to find the IAE2000 subdirectory where this book's template files are located. (*Note:* If the Startup dialog box does not appear, cancel the command by using the Esc key and open the Options dialog box by typing OPTIONS on the command line. Pick on the Systems tab and locate the Show Startup Dialog box under General Options. Make sure the box is checked. Pick the Apply button if it is black and pick OK to exit. Try the NEW command again.)**

With the Use a Template file button pushed in, pick on the Browse button as shown in Figure 2.13. You will be presented with a Select template file dialog box similar to Figure 2.14.

❷ **Using the Look in: box, find the IAE2000 subdirectory. Once you have done that, the dialog box should look similar to Figure 2.14. Pick on the ARCH-1 template file and click Open. A new drawing is created called Drawing that matches what is contained in the ARCH-1 template.**

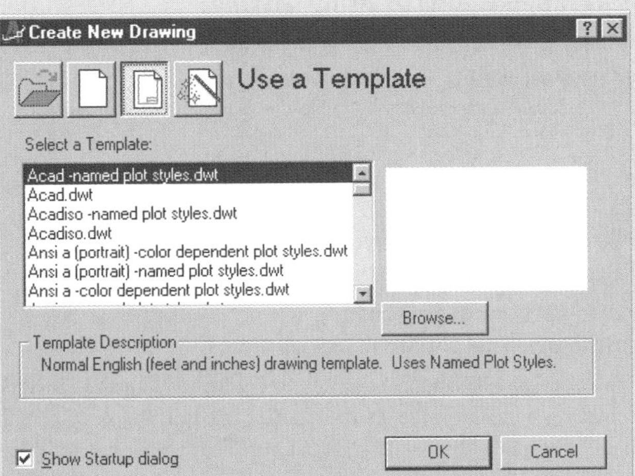

Figure 2.13
Create New Drawing dialog box

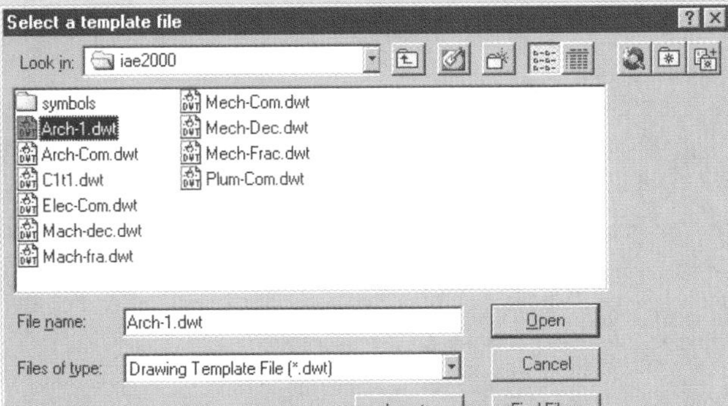

Figure 2.14
Setting the Select template subdirectory to ICAD

3. **Using the Layer Control tool, observe the numerous layers that have already been created for you.**

Using Hands-On Exercises to Load Template Files

To save even more time for learning, Hands-On template files have been created to make starting new drawings even faster.

1. **Pick the Instant AutoCAD tool and the Hands-On dialog box will appear.**

2. **Pick on the Chapter pop-up list and highlight Templates from the list. The Exercise list is on the right and should now be showing ARCH-1. Pick on the list and review it. It contains a variety of templates pre-established for you. You can use them any time you want to start a new drawing with your layers already set. Pick on ARCH-1. A description of the template will appear at the bottom of the dialog box.**
3. **Pick on the Start Exercise button, answer yes to Open as read-only, and the template will appear. You won't see any objects but, have a little confidence in us, layers have been created. You should immediately save the drawing using Save As and give it the name of your new drawing (in this case: PRAC2A). There you have it—Instant Templates!**
4. **Using the Layer Control tool, observe that the architectural layers have been created for you. This allows you to start drawing immediately. Try drawing on the different layers to see the effect of color and linetype.**

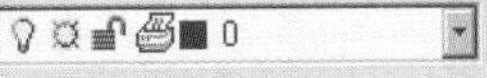

Drawing Aids and Drafting Settings

Before you get into the thick of drawing, you'll be happy to know that there are special drawing aids and drafting settings that make drawing tasks much easier. Refer to Figure 2.15a. The Drafting Settings dialog box is accessed from the Tools pull-down menu. From this dialog box, you can control snap, grid, polar tracking, and object snap.

The Snap options control the movement of the cursor in incremental values. Normally you set the X and Y spacing to the same values. As a beginner, it is best not to change the snap angle from 0 or the X and Y base from 0.

The Grid options display a grid of dots on the screen to give you a visual spacial reference. If the X and Y values are set to 0, the grid spacing will match that of the snap spacing. If the spacing is too close together, the dots won't display.

The Polar Tracking options are used to control the angular movement. Refer to Figure 2.15b, which shows the buttons on the status line. You can turn the snap, grid, and polar tracking on or off using these buttons. If you right-click on the buttons, you can get access to the dialog box.

Notice the ORTHO button. When this is on (pressed in), the movement is limited to moving along the X or Y axis. This is useful for drawing or moving straight along only one axis.

The five drawing aids that you should concern yourself with now are: Snap, Grid, Ortho, Blips, and Object Snaps. Blips are temporary markers that appear in the drawing area when you select objects or locations. You turn their application on or off by typing BLIPMODE on the command line.

Object Snap

Object snap is probably one of the most important drawing aids ever. Its purpose is to locate coordinates on existing objects automatically. Any time you want to locate a point at the end of a line, center of a circle, or intersection of two objects, you make use of object snap. This makes it a precision tool for even the most imprecise user. See Figure 2.16 for a graphic description of the various types of object snaps. Do you see that there is a type of snap for almost every possibility? Let's review a typical application that involves snapping to the end of a line in order to draw another line (see Figure 2.17). Proceed with the following:

Command: LINE

From point: ENDP You can enter the object snap short form or use other methods to access it (explained later). A small box called the *aperture* will appear. This is used to

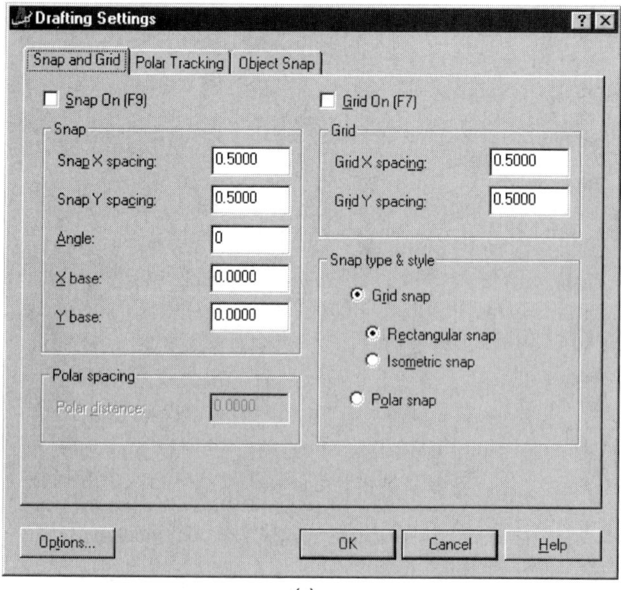

(a)

SNAP GRID ORTHO POLAR OSNAP OTRACK LWT MODEL

(b)

Figure 2.15
(a) Drafting Settings and (b) status line dialog box

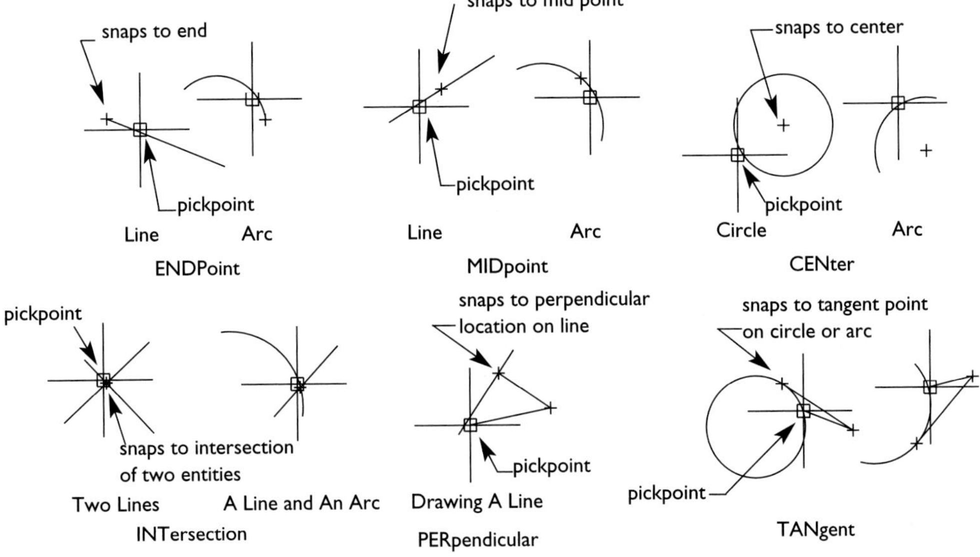

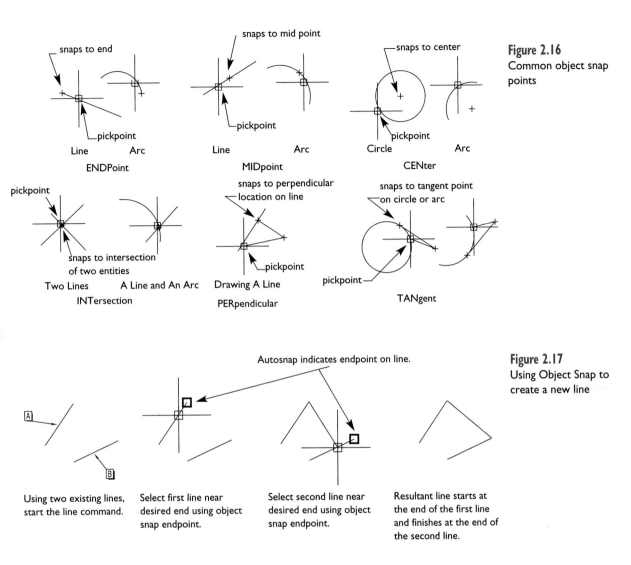

Figure 2.16 Common object snap points

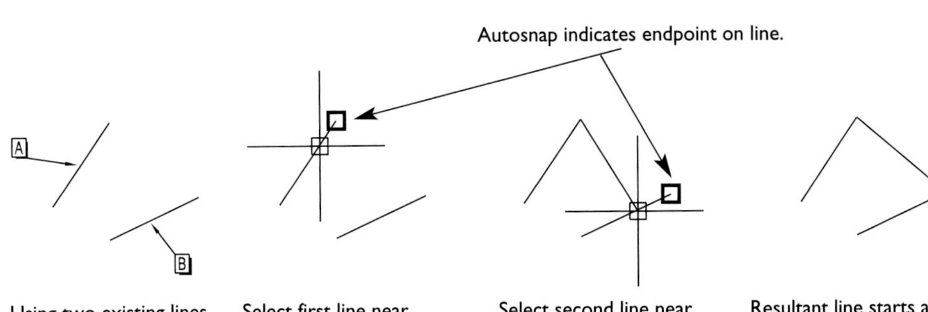

Figure 2.17 Using Object Snap to create a new line

identify the snap location. As you move near the snap location, an identifying symbol may appear, such as □ for endpoint. The symbol for each is shown in Figure 2.18.

Pick near the end of the line you want to snap to. The cursor automatically snaps to the end of the line.

Methods of Accessing Object Snap

There are many methods to access object snaps. The one you choose depends on both your preference and its application. Whenever you are prompted to locate a point on an existing object, you can access an object snap with any of the following methods:

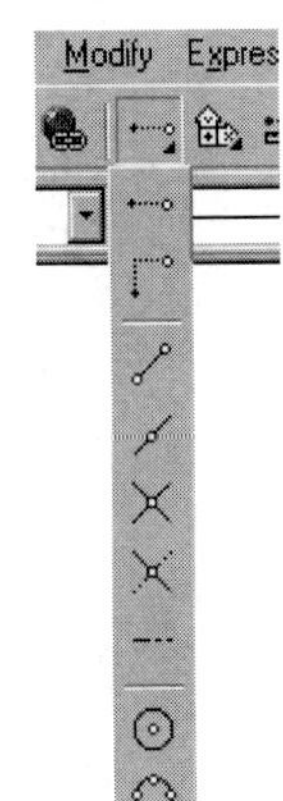

Command Line Type the Object Snap option in full or abbreviated form (e.g., CEN for center).

Standard Toolbar Refer to the Toolbar flyout in the margin on the next page. Near the center of the toolbar is a flyout that contains all the various object snaps. To use, pick and hold on the first tool. When the flyout appears, drag the cursor until you are on top of the desired object snap and release the pick button.

Cursor Menu When using a mouse, hold down the keyboard Shift key and press the right mouse button, then release both. A menu will appear listing the various object snaps. Simply pick from the list.

Running Object Snaps These are special object snap settings that remain on. (Refer to Figure 2.18 for the dialog box showing the four most common snaps turned on.) The dialog box can be accessed by right-clicking on the OSNAP button on the status line. Running snaps can be useful but care must be taken when trying to perform some windowing operations because they can get in the way. To avoid windowing problems when running snaps are in operation, pick in open areas that have no objects that might be inadvertently snapped to. You can turn the running object snaps on or off by picking the OSNAP button on the status line.

Tip: How Do I Identify the Object Snap I'm Using?
When using object snaps, it is always useful to have AutoSnap turned on. AutoSnap displays a unique object snap symbol at the various locations on the object, such as a box for endpoint or a triangle for midpoint. If the AutoSnap symbol does not appear when you are object snapping, open the dialog box using the OSNAP command. Pick on the AutoSnap tab and check the displayed settings. All should be turned on.

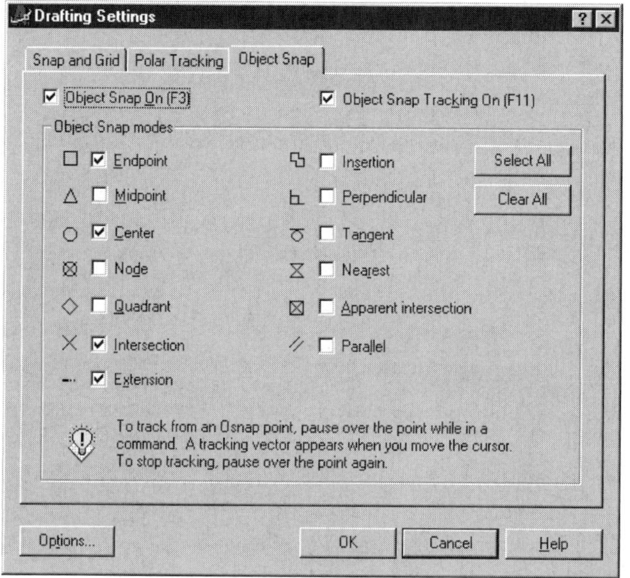

Figure 2.18
Drafting Settings dialog box

Hands-On: Using Drawing Aids

The following Hands-On exercises deal with the use of drawing aids and object snaps. Practice them several times until you are comfortable with each operation.

Drawing Aids

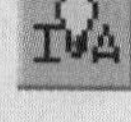

❶ Pick on the Instant AutoCAD icon and start Exercise 2B. It should look like Figure 2.19. Save it as EX2B.

❷ Try drawing the figure shown in Box A in the empty Box B. Do this first without any drawing aids. Draw only the first few lines. Not very easy, is it? Erase the lines you drew.

❸ Type SNAP on the command line and enter 0.25 for the snap. This forces the cursor to move in 0.25 unit jumps.

SNAP GRID ORTHO PO

❹ The three drawing aid boxes, SNAP, GRID, and ORTHO, at the bottom of the screen, should be turned on (pushed in). To turn them on or off, pick on

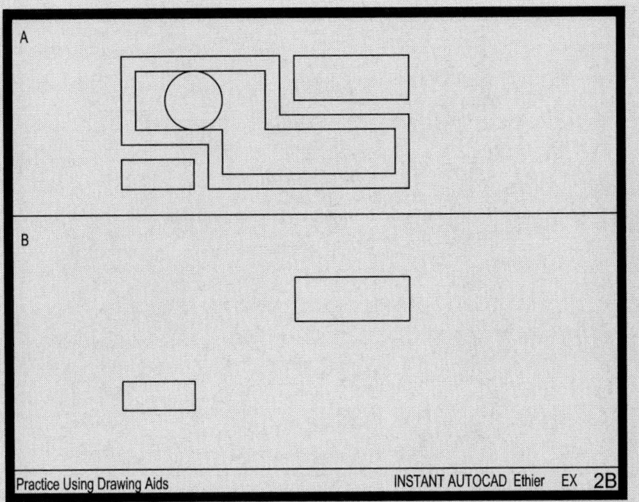

Figure 2.19
Using drawing aids (2B)

the buttons. SNAP controls the movement of the cursor. GRID displays guide dots across the screen. ORTHO forces the cursor to move along the X and Y axes.

5. **Now draw the geometry with the help of drawing aids. A lot easier, wouldn't you say? Using increment snap and grid can be very helpful when initially laying out geometry. Once the initial lines are drawn, you can make use of object snaps.**
6. **Save your drawing as EX2B.**

Object Snaps

Now you are going to practice using various object snaps with existing objects to show you how snaps can increase precision and speed when drawing.

1. **Pick on the Instant AutoCAD tool and start Exercise 2C. It should look like Figure 2.20. Save it as EX2C.**

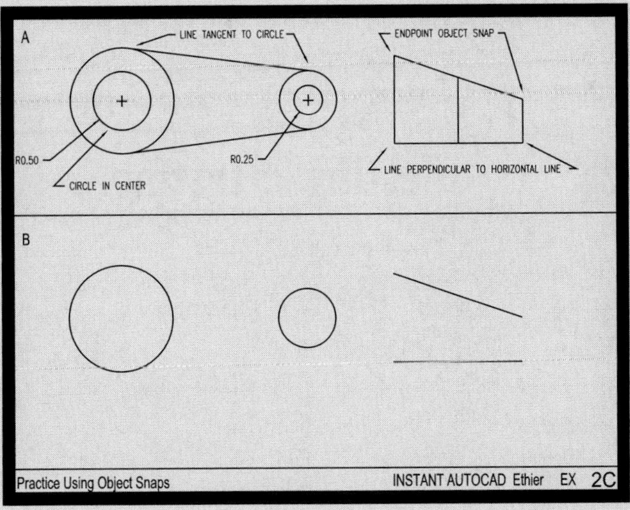

Figure 2.20
Using object snaps (2C)

Figure 2.21
Using object snaps (2D)

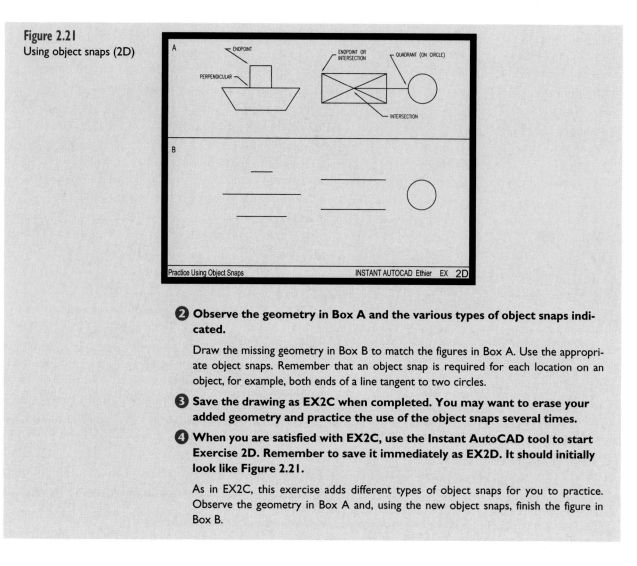

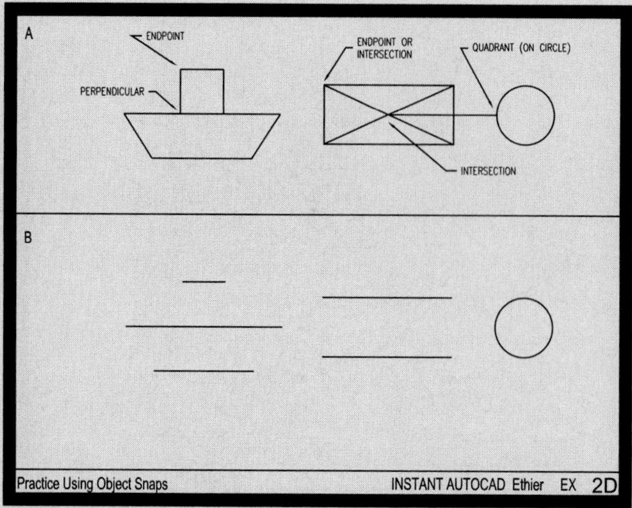

2 Observe the geometry in Box A and the various types of object snaps indicated.

Draw the missing geometry in Box B to match the figures in Box A. Use the appropriate object snaps. Remember that an object snap is required for each location on an object, for example, both ends of a line tangent to two circles.

3 Save the drawing as EX2C when completed. You may want to erase your added geometry and practice the use of the object snaps several times.

4 When you are satisfied with EX2C, use the Instant AutoCAD tool to start Exercise 2D. Remember to save it immediately as EX2D. It should initially look like Figure 2.21.

As in EX2C, this exercise adds different types of object snaps for you to practice. Observe the geometry in Box A and, using the new object snaps, finish the figure in Box B.

In a Nutshell

Chapter 1 put us in the *ready* position and you've now moved to the *set* position. *Go* is just over the horizon where, in Chapter 3, you will learn how to enter drawing data, how to create new entities, and how to manipulate them. But, before we do that, let's review some of the new skills you just learned.

Testing... testing... 1, 2, 3

Matching

Match the unit format with its method of display.

Format	Display
____1. Engineering	a. 1'-2.25"
____2. Scientific	b. 14.25
____3. Decimal	c. 1.425E+01
____4. Architectural	d. 14 1/4"
____5. Fractional	e. 19-2 1/4"

Fill in the blank.

1. During input, a(n) __________ must separate integers and fractions.
2. Type __________ on the command line to activate units.
3. The LTSCALE controls __________.
4. Using a(n) __________ makes it easier to start a drawing quickly.
5. __________ is the most important drawing aid.

Multiple Choice

Choose the best answer to complete each of the following statements:

1. To snap to the end of a line to draw another line you would use:
   a. Snapend.
   b. Endp.
   c. Snapline.
   d. Endline.
   e. none of the above
2. You can access Snap from
   a. the command line.
   b. the isometric snap/grid.
   c. the left mouse button.
   d. all of the above
   e. none of the above
3. On each drawing layer you can store different
   a. limits.
   b. limits and colors.
   c. limits, colors, and linetypes.
   d. limits and linetypes.
   e. linetypes and colors.
4. A displayed cross marker at each picked location is called:
   a. a crosshair.
   b. a cursor.
   c. a blip.
   d. a snap.
   e. an aperture.
5. *Remember:* The size of the pickbox is expressed in
   a. units.
   b. millimeters.
   c. fractions of an inch.
   d. pixels.
   e. any of the above

(A *Remember* question can come from any of the material in the previous chapter.)

What?

1. What are the advantages of using template files?

____

____

2. Explain the purpose of LTSCALE.

____

____

3. How do you name drawing layers and why do you name them this way?

____

____

4. What is the purpose of establishing drawing limits?

____

____

5. List the five drawing aids that are of concern to the current material.
   1. _______________
   2. _______________
   3. _______________
   4. _______________
   5. _______________
6. Explain three ways to access Object Snap.
   1. _______________
   2. _______________
   3. _______________
7. How can you tell which object snap you have activated?

____

____

Let's Get Busy!

1a. First, draw the following exercise without using any drawing aids. Then, turn on Ortho, Snap, Grid, and Object Snaps. Now draw the same exercise. Record your time. What is the increase in speed when you have drawing aids available? Express this as a percentage of the total time.

b. Draw four circles like the ones you see in Figure 2.22, which are 5 units in diameter. Next, draw the interior lines, the exterior lines, and, finally, the lines tangent to the corners.

2. First, redraw Figure 2.23 using nothing but relative coordinates. Next, use Grid and Snap. Last, use only Object Snaps. Which methods did you use? Which method took the least time?

3. Decide which drawing aids are most useful for drawing the simple geometry in Figure 2.24.

Figure 2.22
Practicing drawing aids

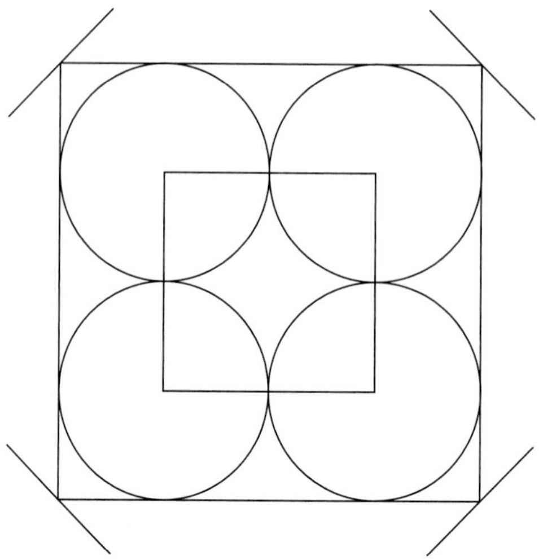

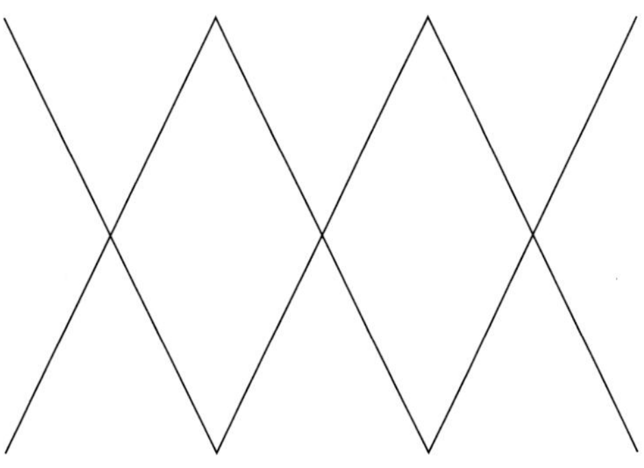

Figure 2.23
What is the best method?

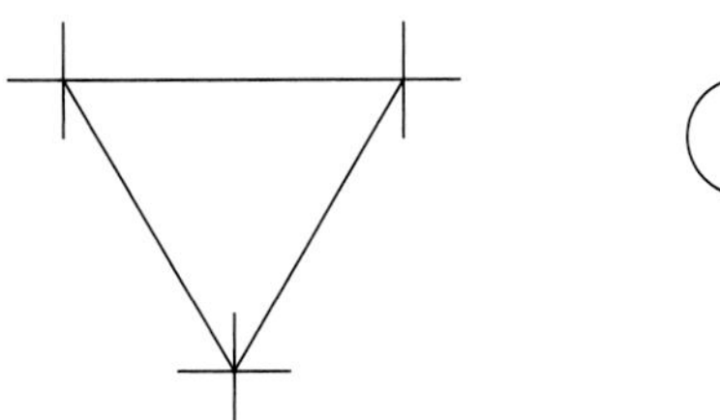

Figure 2.24
Choosing the drawing aids

Chapter 3

Every Journey Begins with a Single Line: . . . *Go!*

Key topics

- Coordinate Input
- Object Properties
- Basic Objects
- Making New from Old

Where Are You?

The key to drawing is knowing where the objects you draw must be located. The first line has to have a starting point. (Before computerized drafting, this point was known as the point of terror.) You need to know where the line begins, how far it's going, and in what direction. All of this is based on the Cartesian coordinate system.

Creation in two dimensions makes use of the Cartesian coordinate system. Figure 3.1 shows the X and Y coordinate grid. The 0,0 location is called the *UCS* (User Coordinate System) origin. Objects may be placed along either the positive or negative axis. To place an object, you can choose from the five methods of coordinate input: absolute, relative, polar, cylindrical, and spherical. Cylindrical and spherical methods deal solely with three-dimensional applications. We won't get to that in this particular journey; however, we need to learn a lot about the other three.

There are five methods of coordinate entry.
We are interested, at this stage, in three:
absolute, relative, and polar.

Coordinate Input

Absolute Coordinate Entry

Absolute coordinates are based on the UCS origin 0,0. You identify a point on an object by its X and Y distances from the origin point. Think of it this way, if you placed a salt shaker on a checkered tablecloth and identified this as the starting point for all objects, to locate a point on the cloth, you would travel in the specified directions, always starting from the salt shaker. The following input demonstrates drawing two lines using absolute coordinates (see Figure 3.2):

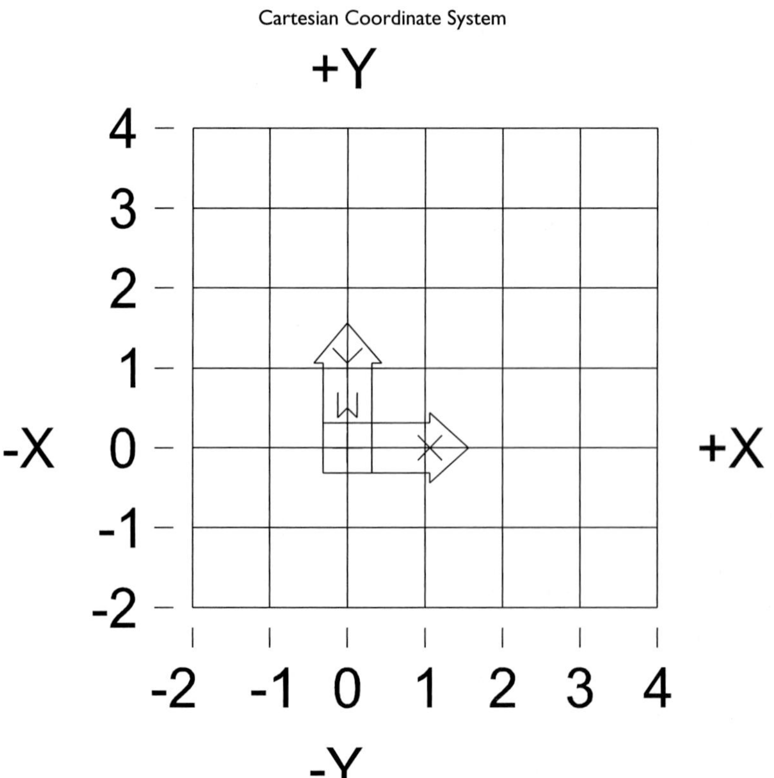

Figure 3.1
The Cartesian grid showing the X and Y axes and the UCS origin point.

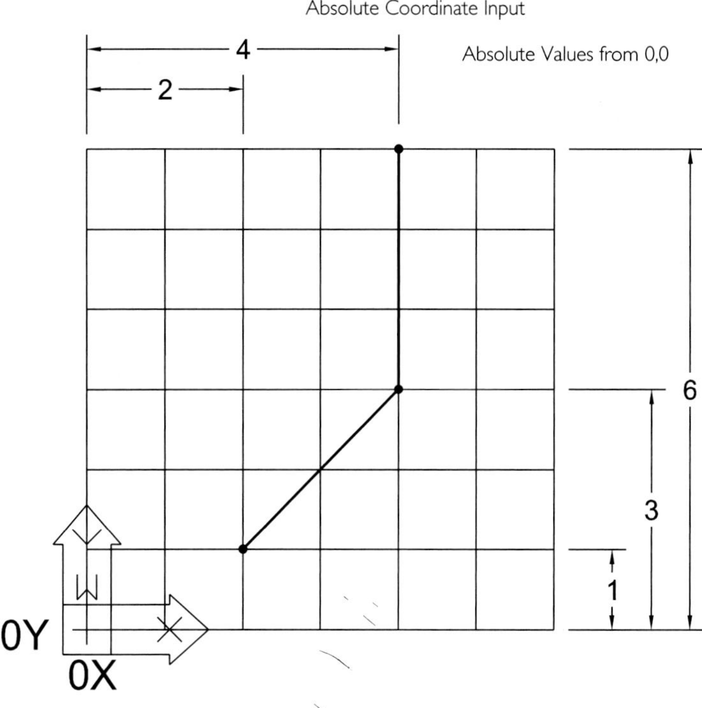

Figure 3.2
Drawing a line using absolute coordinates

Command: **LINE**

From point: **2,1** (The 2 means 2 units along the positive X axis, and the 1 means 1 unit along the positive Y. Both are measured from the 0,0 origin.)

To point: **4,3** (The 4 is 4 units along the positive X axis from the origin point, and the 3 is 3 units along the positive Y.)

To point: **4,6** (The 4 is 4 units along the positive X axis from the origin point, and the 6 is 6 units along the positive Y. Since the 4 in the X direction matches the 4 from the previous entry, the line will run straight along the Y axis. It has no movement along the X axis.)

Entering numbers, either positive or negative, specify absolute locations on the X, Y grid.

Relative Coordinate Entry

Relative coordinates are based on the "last point," that is, the last set of coordinates entered. In this way you can specify a series of locations using relative values all based on the previous point entered. Getting back to our tablecloth, each time you move, you carry the salt shaker with you. Then, when you move again, you measure the distance from the last salt shaker location. Refer to Figure 3.3 and to the following example:

Command: **LINE**

From point: **1,2** (In this case, you start a series of relative coordinates with an absolute coordinate. Later you'll learn other ways to begin a line.)

To point: **@4,2** (The @ sign tells AutoCAD that you are using relative coordinates. The 4 represents 4 units in the positive X direction from the "last point," which happens to be the endpoint snapped to in the last entry. The 2 represents 2 units in the positive Y direction from the "last point" entered.)

To point: **@0,–3** (Again, notice the @ sign. The 0 means that the line will not travel at all along the X axis. The negative 3 means that the line will travel downward (negative Y axis) from the "last point" from the previous entry. This creates a line pointing vertically downwards.)

Entering numbers, either positive or negative, after the @ sign specify relative distances from the "last point" entered.

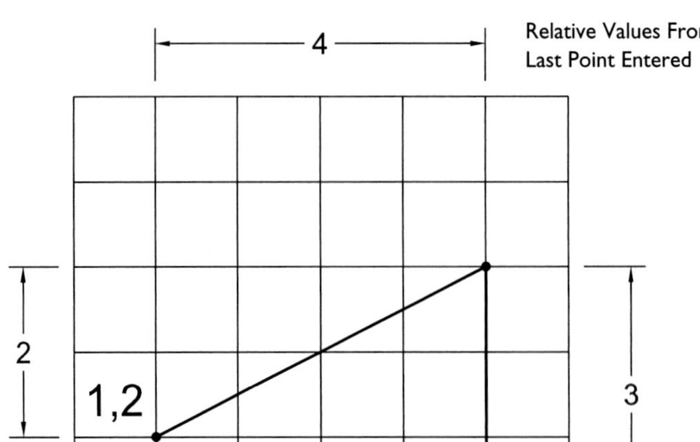

Figure 3.3
Drawing a line using relative coordinates

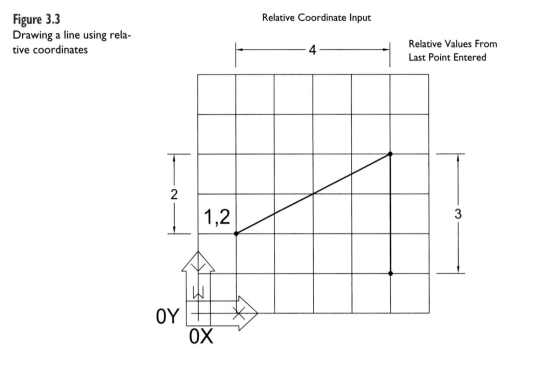

Polar Coordinate Entry

Polar coordinates function like relative coordinates, except that you enter a vector distance and an angle from the "last point." (In this case, bringing up the salt shaker will just confuse the issue.) Refer to Figure 3.4 and to the following example:

Command: **LINE**

From point: **2,1**	(Starting at an absolute coordinate once more.)
To point: **@3<45**	(Again the @ sign signifies relative coordinates, a distance of 3 units from the "last point." However, the 45 represents the 45 degree angle along which the line will travel the 3 units. You must include the < sign to separate the distance from the angle.)
To point: **@2<90**	(Now, the distance is 2 units and the direction is 90 degrees. This means the line will travel 2 units upward from the "last point.")

Entering distance and angle numbers, either positive or negative, after the @ sign specifies polar distance from the "last point" entered.

Tip: A Quick Way to Draw Lines
Here is a neat way to draw lines very quickly. Start the LINE command and indicate the first point of the line as usual. When prompted to specify the next point, move the cursor in the direction you want the line drawn but don't pick a point, just enter the distance for the length of the line. The line will be drawn the specified distance in the direction indicated by the cursor. With the Ortho option turned on, it makes drawing horizontal or vertical lines a snap!

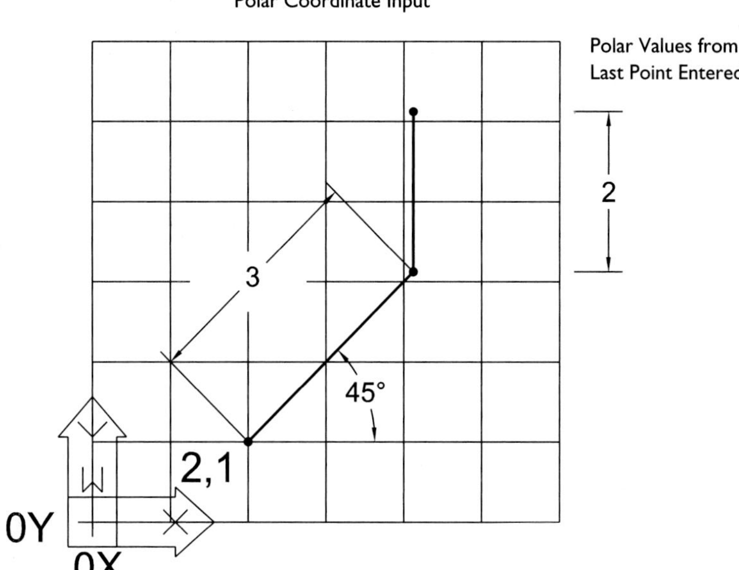

Figure 3.4
Drawing a line using polar coordinates

Object Properties

All objects have properties attached to them that control location, size, and display. Let's talk about some of the typical ones.

Color

Color is used to help distinguish the various objects and to establish line thickness when printing your drawing onto paper. Normally an object's color matches its layer color (BYLAYER). But you can override this and display an object in a different color from its layer. This is used for special circumstances.

Layer

Every object is drawn on a layer to efficiently organize the drawing. You do not normally draw on layer 0; it is reserved for special applications (explained later).

Linetype

Linetype is similar to color in that it normally matches the layer (BYLAYER). However, like color, you can override the setting and create an object whose linetype doesn't match its layer linetype.

Linetype Scale

The appearance of a linetype is controlled by its linetype scale. Normally you would use the global LTSCALE value to control appearance of all the linetypes. However, when you want to "fine-tune" an individual line, you can use the object's individual linetype scale property, which acts as a multiplication factor. Since a value of 1 is 1 times the global LTSCALE, a value of 0.5 is 0.5 times the global LTSCALE. Normally, one keeps the individual object's linetype scale value at 1.

Every object has a series of properties like color, layer, linetype, and linetype scale.

Tip: Controlling Linetype and Color
For most applications, the linetype and color settings should be set to BYLAYER. This means that they will match the current layer settings. If you draw an object, and the linetype or color don't match the layer on which you're drawing, the offending property has been set to a specific option and not to BYLAYER. You should change the setting and modify the object so that it too is set to BYLAYER. To make changes to linetype or color, you can use the Property toolbar at the top of the screen or type LINETYPE and COLOR on the command line and set them to BYLAYER.

Modifying an Object's Properties

Commonly, you set an object's properties, such as layer, and then you draw the object. However, there may be times when you forget to set the properties or you want to change an object's properties mid-drawing. This can be done with the Object Properties dialog box, shown in Figure 3.5. To use this dialog box either select the Modify/Properties pull-down menu or pick the Properties tool. When the Properties dialog box is visible, select any object to highlight it. To undo the selection, press the Esc key several times.

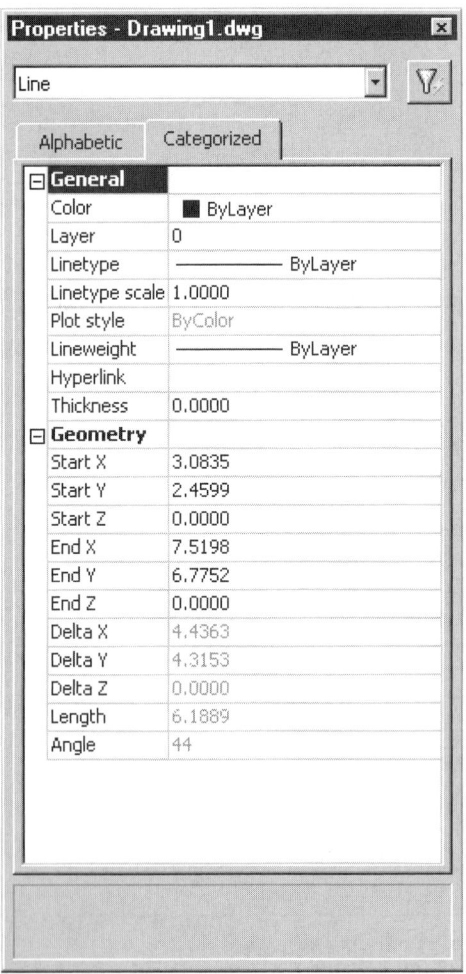

Figure 3.5
Properties dialog box showing Line Properties

Figure 3.6
Properties dialog box with three selected objects

Hands-On: Moving in a Coordinated Fashion

Get ready. You're going to practice creating some geometry using absolute, relative, and polar coordinates.

Absolute Coordinates EX3A

1. **Open the Hands-On Exercises dialog box and start Exercise 3A from Chapter 3.**

The screen is divided into four separate boxes. At the top of each box is a figure drawn in red; the absolute coordinates are blue and the actual points are green. These are all placed on special locked layers so that you can't accidentally erase them. A layer called Working has been created for your exercise.

2. **Save the drawing as EX3A in your subdirectory.**
3. **Note the UCS icon with a cross in the middle. When the cross is visible, the icon is showing you where the origin 0,0 is located. That is your reference point for all the absolute coordinate values.**
4. **A red cross is located in each box. These are your starting points. Using these starting points, draw the identical figure below the sample one in a clockwise direction. It is important to follow the points successively along the line since that is the pattern you wish to draw. Entering them in a random order will result in a very different line.**

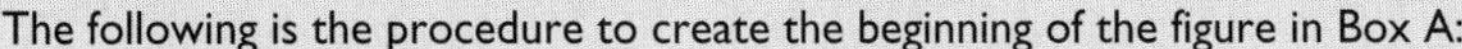

The following is the procedure to create the beginning of the figure in Box A:

Command: **LINE**
From point: **1,4**
To point: **1,5**
To point: **2,5**
To point: (Now you follow the rest and press Enter when you are finished.)

5. **Do the same with Boxes B and C. Remember that the crosshair indicates the starting coordinates. Note the extra challenge in B—can you do it? It involves starting the CIRCLE command, locating the center, and then using the radius indicated.**
6. **Note that Box D is blank. Create your own enclosed figure. The lowest and the highest points must be 6,0 and 9,1.5, respectively. See what you can come up with by just using absolute coordinates.**
7. **Save your drawing as EX3A in your subdirectory.**

Relative Coordinates EX3B

Now that we're well practiced with absolute coordinates, let's do similar exercises with relative coordinates and polar coordinates. Then, you'll be ready to make some educated judgements.

1. **Open the Hands-On Exercises dialog box and start Exercise 3B from Chapter 3.**
2. **Save the drawing as EX3B in your subdirectory.**
3. **Starting in Box A, draw the figure using relative coordinates. (*Note:* The start point is given in absolute coordinates.) Begin like this:**

Command: **LINE**
From point: **5,16**
To point: **@0,5** (That's 0 units in the X direction and 5 units in the Y.)

Hands-On: Moving in a Coordinated Fashion (continued)

To point: **@2,0**	(Now you're going 2 units in X and 0 units in the Y.)
To point: **@0,–3**	(A minus sign means the line travels in a negative direction.)
To point:	(You finish the rest and press Enter at the end.)

4 Create the figures in Boxes B and C. Note in Box C that you are moving along both X and Y axes.

5 In Box D, create a figure using relative coordinates. It must start at absolute 24,1 and go through absolute 40,12.

6 Save your drawing as EX3B in your subdirectory.

Polar Coordinates EX3C

Now, let's do some work with polar coordinates. Because there are angles involved, these can be a little trickier but, since you're becoming a better problem solver already, we have every confidence that you'll be equal to the challenge.

1 Open the Hands-On Exercises dialog box and start Exercise 3C from Chapter 3 and immediately save it as EX3C in your subdirectory.

2 Starting in Box A, draw the figure using polar coordinates. (*Note*: The starting point is given in absolute coordinates.) The following is how to start:

Command: **LINE**
From point: **14,16**

To point: **–90**	(A minus distance of 9 units and an angle of 0 degrees.)
To point: **@490**	(A distance of 4 units and an angle of 90 degrees.)
To point:	(You finish the rest and press Enter to end.)

3 Create the figures in Boxes B and C. What does the figure in Box C remind you of? Hmmm? You'll notice that Mickey is a little rough around the edges. When we explore arcs and you can apply what you've learned, he'll feel better and he'll be a more well-rounded character.

4 In Box D, try creating a star shape using polar coordinates. It must fit within the absolutes 24,1 and 40,12.

5 Save your drawing as EX3C.

Basic Objects

Points

A point, formally called a node point, is a small, simple entity like a dot. It is handy mainly because Object Snap can snap immediately to a point using node object snap. Locate a point by simply entering its coordinate location. The dialog box in Figure 3.7 shows how to set PDMODE and PDSIZE variables, which control the appearance of the points. Type DDPTYPE to access the dialog box.

Lines

Lines are very popular objects in drawings, and they are easy to use as well. You probably have a very good idea of how the command works from your practice with various coordinate systems, but let's review.

Command: **LINE**

From point:	(Move the cursor until the tracking display reads the correct coordinates or enter the coordinates.)
To point:	(Move the cursor to the correct coordinates or enter absolute, relative, or polar coordinates.)

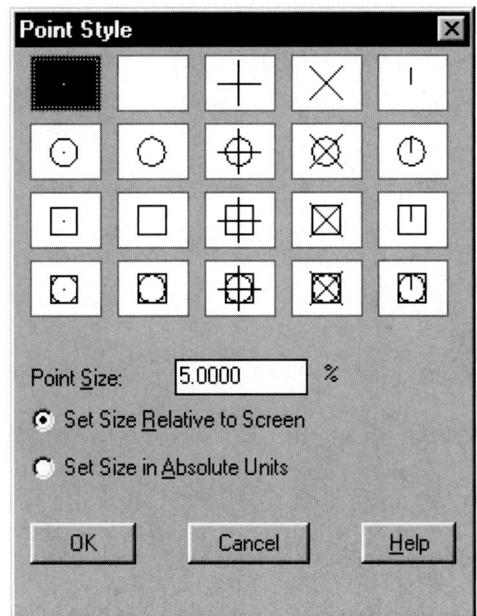

Figure 3.7
Point Style dialog box

To point:	(Do this repeatedly until the desired shape appears.)
To point:	(Press Enter to exit from the LINE command.)

When prompted for the From point, you can snap to the last created line or arc by answering the request with a return or a space. In the case of a line, the line will simply continue in the same direction. However, with an arc, the line will run tangentially from the arc. This wonderful time saver is called line continuation. (See Figure 3.8.)

This is not, however, the only special feature of the line command. The Close option automatically closes a polygon as long as the shape has been drawn in the same LINE command. This makes certain that you have a closed figure even if your coordinates are slightly off. As well, a built-in line undo allows you to undo the LINE command a step at a time until you reach the command itself. (There is even a SKETCH command that allows you to draw as if you are holding a pencil, but that is for another time and place.)

Circles

There are no less than five ways to generate a circle in AutoCAD, and you have to be comfortable with all of them in order to choose the right one for the application. Let's review the methods now.

The center/radius method is more common than the center/diameter method, which involves specifying coordinates for the center and a distance for the radius either by entering a value or by picking a point. (See Figure 3.9.)

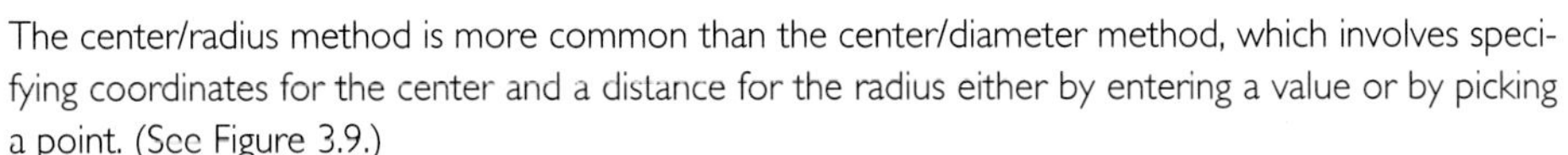

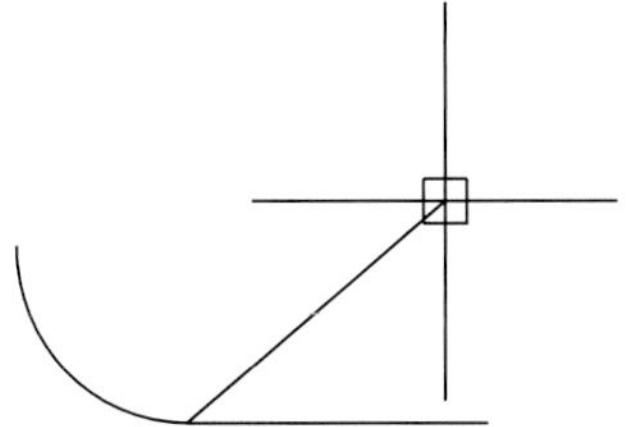

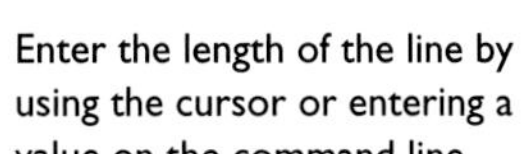

Draw an arc

Start the line command and use the continue option—a rubber band connects the cursor to the end of the arc

Enter the length of the line by using the cursor or entering a value on the command line

Figure 3.8
Line continuation feature

Figure 3.9
Circles created by center and radius and TTR (Tangent, Tangent Radius)

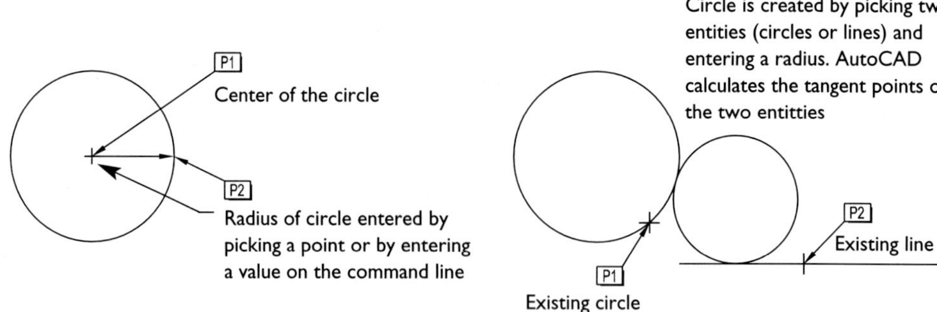
P1
Center of the circle
P2
Radius of circle entered by picking a point or by entering a value on the command line
Circle is created by picking two entities (circles or lines) and entering a radius. AutoCAD calculates the tangent points on the two entitties
P2
Existing line
P1
Existing circle

Command: **CIRCLE**	
Specify center point for circle or [3P/2P/Ttr (tan tan radius)]:	**Enter absolute coordinates of the center, such as 5,5**
Specify radius of circle or [Diameter]:	**Enter a value for the radius, such as 3**

Use the center/diameter method when you wish to include the diameter in the formula.

Command: **CIRCLE**	
Specify center point for circle or [3P/2P/Ttr (tan tan radius)]:	**Enter absolute coordinates of the center, such as 5,5**
Specify radius of circle or [Diameter]:	**D** (for diameter)
Specify diameter of circle:	**6** (Enter the desired diameter.)

The next two methods are similar to each other and very different from the first two methods.

In the 3-point method, the three points that you specify all become points on the circumference of your circle.

Command: **CIRCLE**	
Specify center point for circle or [3P/2P/Ttr (tan tan radius)]:	**3P**
Specify first point on circle:	**Enter desired coordinates**
Specify second point on circle:	**Enter desired coordinates**
Specify third point on circle <last given value>:	**Enter desired coordinates**

The 2-point method is almost the same except that you type 2P instead and you only specify 2 points.

The last circle creation method, the tangent, tangent radius method, requests two objects to which the circle will be tangent and a value for the circle's radius. (See Figure 3.9.)

Command: **CIRCLE**	
Specify center point for circle or 3P/2P/TTR (tan tan radius)]:	**TTR**
Specify point onobject for first tangent of circle:	**Pick a line or circle**
Specify point on object for second tangent of circle:	**Pick another line or circle**
Specify radius of circle <last given value>::	**Enter the desired value**

Arcs

There are many methods you can use to generate an arc, eleven in fact, but the most common is the 3-point method, which uses a start, second, and third point to define an arc. Experiment with the options your instructor emphasizes. The fact is it's usually easier to make an arc by trimming a circle—then you don't have to remember which method you're using and which direction you're going. See Figure 3.10 for the start, center, and end method.

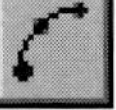

Command: **ARC**

Specify start point of arc or [Center]:

Tip: Drawing to Scale

When drawing with traditional manual methods, you choose the scale. A small mechanical part may be at a scale of 1 = 1 (full size), whereas a residential home may be at a scale of 1/4″=1′-0″ (1:48).

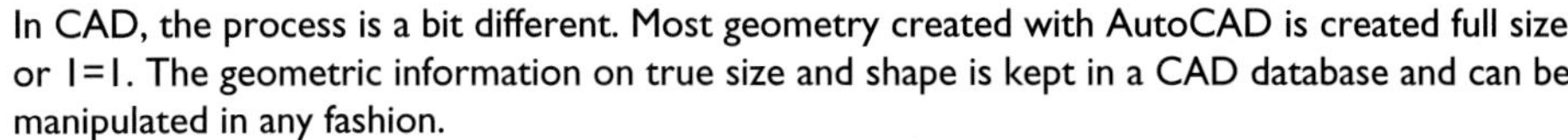

In CAD, the process is a bit different. Most geometry created with AutoCAD is created full size, or 1=1. The geometric information on true size and shape is kept in a CAD database and can be manipulated in any fashion.

When you want to draw a line that represents a wall 40 feet long, you enter its length as 40′. Entering all the geometry at full size gives the geometry total interchangeability.

The only time the size of objects is critical is when you are about to enter text, dimensioning, or hatching. The physical size of those objects controls their readability, so it makes no difference that comparably the text may be as tall as your front door. For now, draw everything full size.

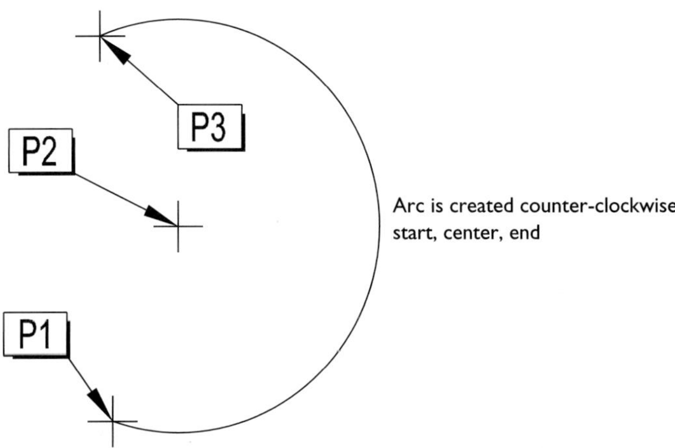

Figure 3.10
Arc creation takes place in a counter-clock wise direction.

Hands-On: Drawing Circles and Arcs

You've had quite a bit of practice drawing lines; now, it's time to practice the creation of circles and arcs.

Circles EX3D

To draw a circle by indicating its center, radius, and diameter is quite straightforward so this exercise will concentrate on the 2P, 3P, and TTR method.

1. **Open the Hands-On Exercises dialog box and, start Exercise 3D from Chapter 3, and save the drawing as EX3D in your subdirectory.**

2. **Review the slot shown at the left in Box A. It was formed by using two circles, object snapped onto the ends of the two lines, using the 2P method. The circles were then trimmed. This will demonstrate how easy it is to draw circles and trim them to create the desired arcs.**
3. **Complete the slot at the left in Box B. The following is the procedure to trim the circles after you have drawn them.**

Command:	**TRIM**
Current Settings: Projection=UCS Edge=Extend	
Select cutting edges...	
Selected objects:	**Pick the two vertical lines to be used as cutting edges and press Enter.**
Select object to trim or [Project/Edge/Undo]:	**Pick the inner parts of the circles to trim away and press Enter.**

(More on trimming is explained in Chapter 4.)

4. **Complete the other two figures using the 3P and TTR methods. Remember to use object snaps to identify pick points for 3P; just pick the circles for the TTR method.**
5. **Save your drawing as EX3D.**

Arcs EX3E

You'll probably find that it's easier to draw circles and trim them than to draw arcs. However, this lab will give you some practice in creating arcs, just in case.

1. **Open the Hands-On Exercises dialog box and start Exercise 3E from Chapter 3, and save the drawing as EX3E in your subdirectory.**

2. **The first figure in Box A uses the default method of creating arcs, that is, the 3-point method. Using the ARC command, complete the figure in Box B. Remember to use object snaps for the start and endpoints.**
3. **The middle figure in Box A uses the center, start, end method, which is useful for creating door swings. Create the matching figure in Box B. Again, use object snaps.**
4. **The right figure in Box A uses one of the less used methods— start, end, angle—in order to demonstrate one of the many possibilities. Complete the figure in Box B (with the aid of object snaps).**
5. **Save your drawing as EX3E.**

Once you can draw points, lines, circles, and arcs,
there is practically nothing you can't draw!

Tip: Getting Information
There are several commands that access information about your drawing. Three useful ones are: LIST, DIST, and AREA. LIST lists properties, such as size and location, about objects you select. DIST retrieves distance and angular information between two points you pick, whereas AREA displays area and perimeter information about objects or selected points.

New from Old

Copy

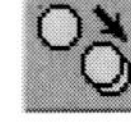

The COPY command acts just like the MOVE command except that when the copy moves to its new location it leaves the original object in its place. You can even make multiple copies with just an extra flick of the wrist, as long as that wrist flick depresses the M key at the right moment as shown in Figure 3.11.

Command:	**COPY**
Select objects:	**Pick objects to copy and press enter.**
Specify base point or displacement, or [Multiple]:	**Pick start point**

(If you respond with M, you can make a copy every time you pick a second point.)

Specify second point of displacement or <use first point as displacement>:	**Pick destination point**

(Press Enter to exit the command.)

Offset

OFFSET copies objects parallel to existing ones at a given distance or point. This is really handy for laying out center-to-center distances like those used when drawing buildings. (See Figure 3.12.)

Command: **OFFSET**

Specify offset distance or [Through] <last given value>:	**Enter a value to set the distance between an object and its offset copy** (Picking Through prompts you to choose a point through which you want the copy to pass.)

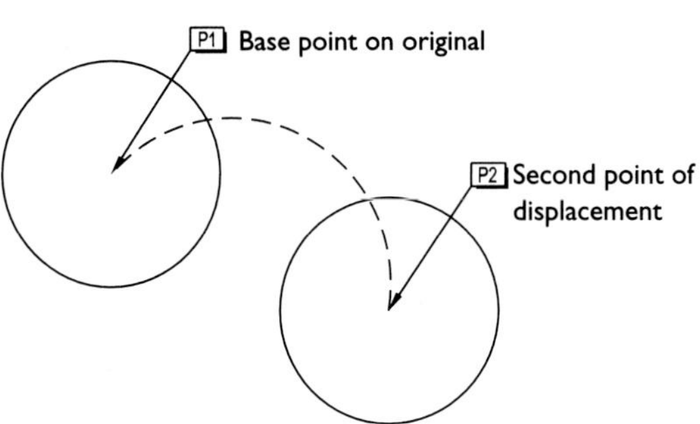

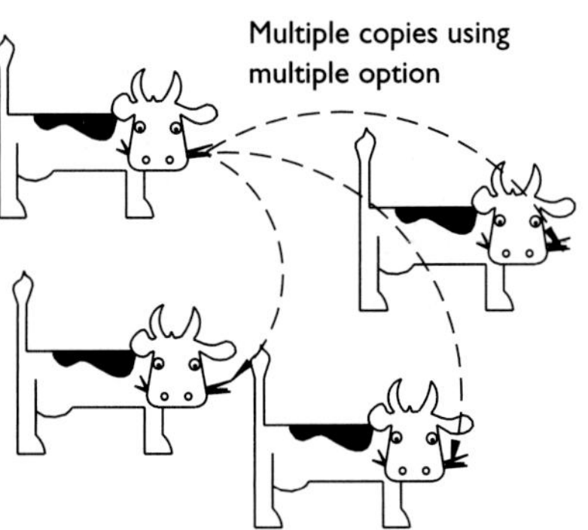

Figure 3.11
Creating single and multiple copies

Figure 3.12
Creating parallel copies at a distance

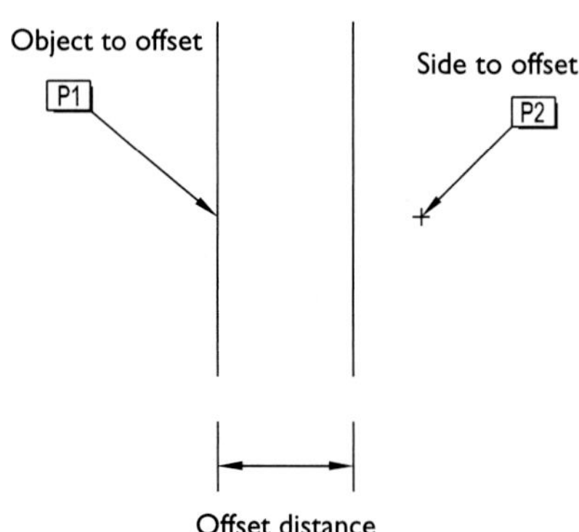

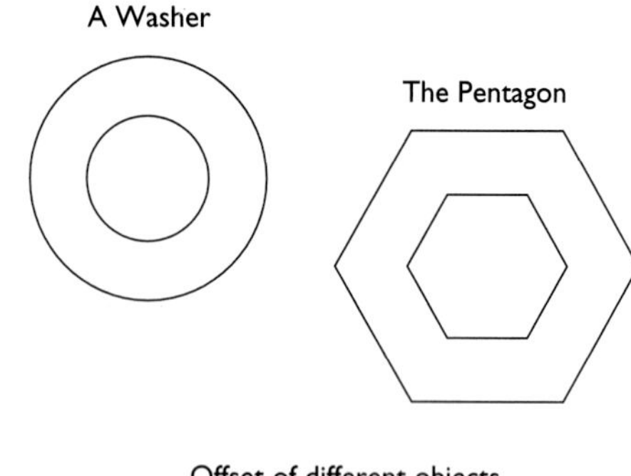

Select object to offset or <exit>::	**Pick a line, circle, or so on**
Specify point on side to offset:	**Pick the side where you want the copy to appear**
Select object to offset or <exit>:	**You can continue to pick objects to offset or press Enter to exit**

Mirror

The MIRROR command will produce a mirrored image on the other side of a mirror line that you specify, or it will mirror a copy while erasing the original, performing a flip-flop of an image. Aside from its obvious usefulness in manufacturing Rorschach tests, this has a number of important drawing uses. (See Figure 3.13.)

Command:	**MIRROR**
Select objects:	**Pick objects to mirror and press Enter**
Specify first point of mirror line:	**Pick the start point of the mirror line**
Specify second point of mirror line:	**Pick the end point of the mirror line**
Delete source objects? [Yes/No] <N>:	**(N performs mirror, Y performs flip-flop)**

Array

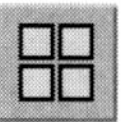

The ARRAY command is a special kind of COPY command that organizes multiple copies in a specified pattern—either rectangular or circular (polar). (See Figures 3.14 and 3.15.) This is great for any repetitive item or symbol that requires an ordered pattern, like the windows of a high rise or the keys on a piano.

Figure 3.13
Creating mirror image copies

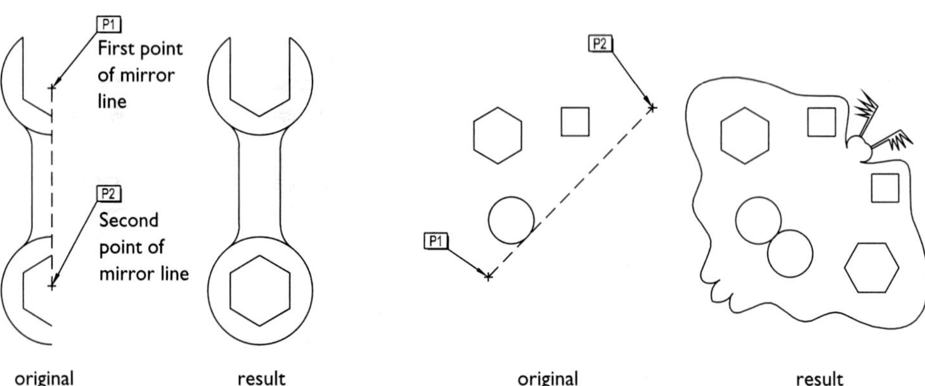

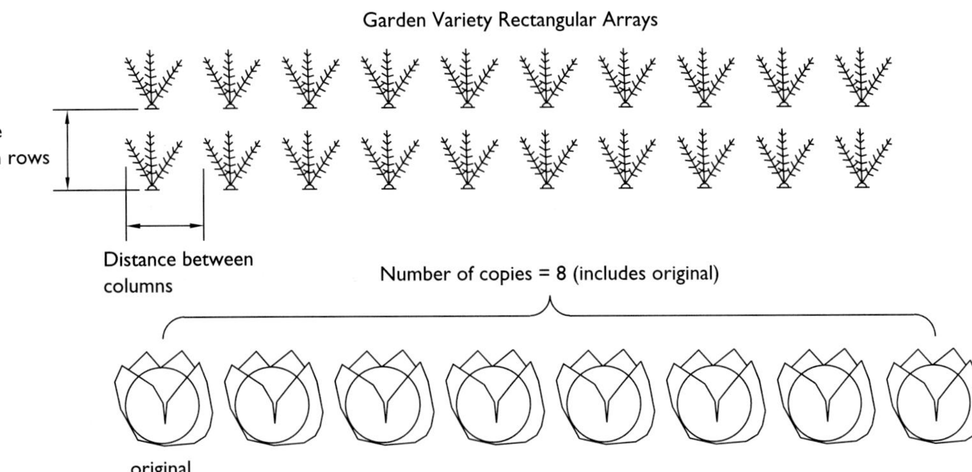

Figure 3.14
Creating a series of copies with rectangular array

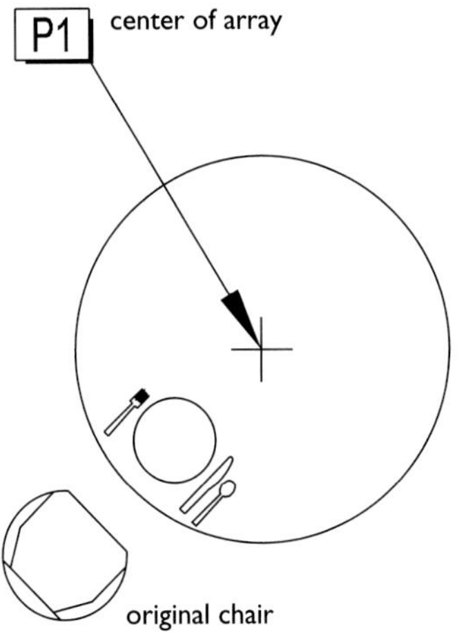

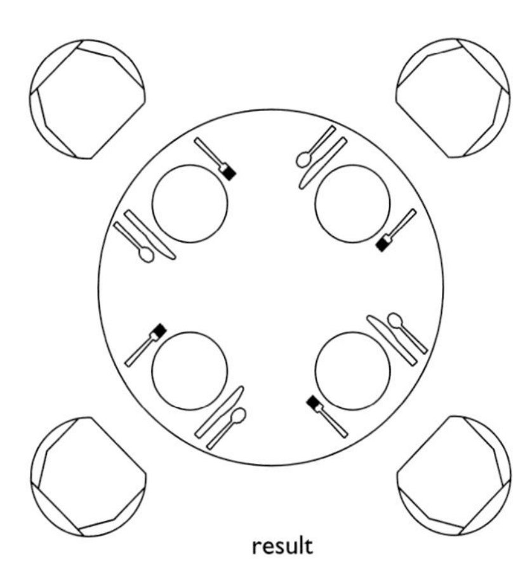

Polar Array

Figure 3.15
Creating a series of copies with polar array

Rectangular

Command:	**ARRAY**
Select objects:	**Pick objects to copy**
Enter the type of array [Rectangular/Polar] <R>:	**R**
Enter the number of rows (- - -) <1>:	**Enter desired number of horizontal rows**
Enter the number of columns (|||) <1>:	**Enter desired number of vertical columns**
Enter the distance between rows or specify unit cell (- - -):	**Enter the Y axis distance spacing**
Specify the distance between columns (|||):	**Enter the X axis distance spacing**

(Positive distance will follow positively along the axis and negative distances will do the reverse.)

Polar

Command:	**ARRAY**
Select objects:	**Pick objects to copy**
Enter the type of array [Rectangular/Polar] <R>:	**P**
Specify center point of array:	**Pick a point**
Enter the number of items in the array:	**Enter the total number of copies you wish, including the original**
Specify the angle to fill (+=ccw, –2=cw) <360>:	**Enter the angle to be filled by copies (360 is the whole circle, 90 is one-quarter of the circle, and so on) and the direction you want them to travel (+ is counterclockwise and –2 is clockwise).**
Rotate arrayed objects? [Yes/No] <Y>:	**Enter yes for copies to be rotated or no to keep their orientation.**

Fillet

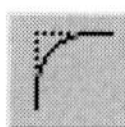

The FILLET command allows you to connect two lines, circles, arcs, or polylines with an arc, using a radius you specify, and resulting in a rounded corner. As well, a fillet with a 0 radius will connect two selected objects with a 90-degree angle. (See Figure 3.16.) Filleting is an extremely useful drawing tool and it's another tool that people, particularly parents of children just learning to walk, wish they could apply to the real world.

Command:	**FILLET**
Current settings: Mode = TRIM, Radius = 0.5000	
Select first object or [Polyline/Radius/Trim]:	**R**
Specify fillet radius <0.5000>:	**Enter value for the radius**
Command:	**FILLET**
Current settings: Mode = TRIM, Radius = 3.0000	
Select first object or [Polyline/Radius/Trim]:	**Pick the first object**
Select second object:	**Pick the second object**

Chamfer

CHAMFER is a lot like FILLET except that, instead of using an arc, it uses a sloped line. (See Figure 3.17.) Your job is to specify a distance along each line and an angle. The options are:

Angle: You provide a length and an angle
Trim: You choose to keep or discard excess lines

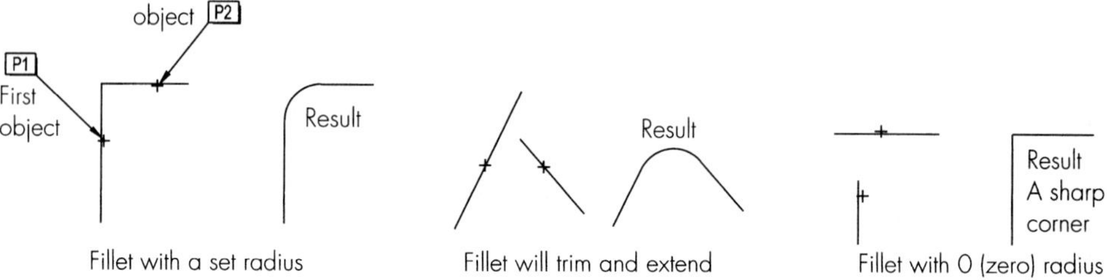

Figure 3.16
Rounding sharp corners

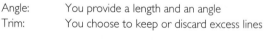

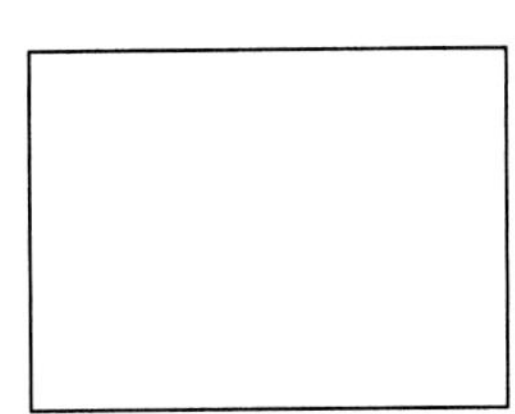

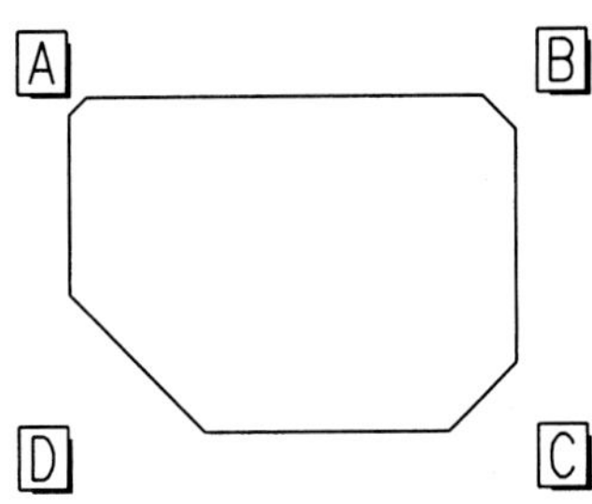

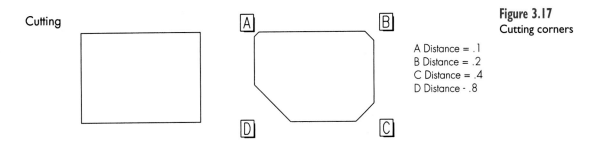

Figure 3.17
Cutting corners

Method: You wish to choose a distance method over an angle method chamfer
Polyline: You can chamfer the entire polyline based on distances entered previously

Command:	**CHAMFER**
(TRIM mode) Current chamfer Dist1 = 0.5000, Dist2 = 0.5000	
Select first line or [Polyline/Distance/Angle/Trim/Method]:	**D**
Specify first chamfer distance <0.5000>:	**Enter distance along the first line**
Specify second chamfer distance <1.0000>:	**Enter distance along the second line**
Command:	**CHAMFER**
(TRIM mode) Current chamfer Dist1 = 1.0000, Dist2 = 2.0000	
Select first line or [Polyline/Distance/Angle/Trim/Method]:	**Pick the first line**
Select second line:	**Pick the second line**

Hands-On: Creating New Objects from Existing Ones

These exercises will offer experience in using the various commands that make use of existing objects to create new ones, such as COPY and OFFSET.

Copy EX3F

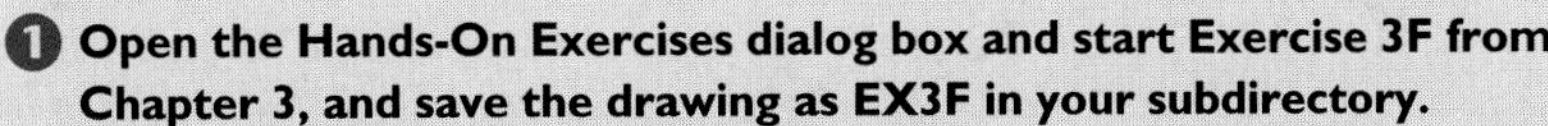

1. **Open the Hands-On Exercises dialog box and start Exercise 3F from Chapter 3, and save the drawing as EX3F in your subdirectory.**

2. **Use the COPY command to copy the hole and center lines to the new location. Use the following procedure:**

Command:	**COPY**
Select objects:	**Pick the circle and center lines.**
Specify base point or displacement, or [Multiple]:	**CENTER** (Identify the center of the circle using center object snap.)
Specify second point of displacement or <use first point as displacement>: **@1-1/4,0**	(Use relative coordinates to place the copy at an exact location.)

3. **Use the Multiple option of the COPY command to copy the single tree into a group of three trees.**
4. **Save your drawing as EX3F.**

Hands-On: Creating New Objects from Existing Ones (continued)

Offset EX3G

1. **Open the Hands-On Exercises dialog box, start Exercise 3G from Chapter 3, and save the drawing as EX3G in your subdirectory.**
2. **To create the office, use the OFFSET command, first to create the outside walls, and then to create the inside walls. Use the TRIM command to cut the doorway.**
3. **To create the miniature racetrack, use the OFFSET command. The outside of the track is a closed polyline. When you pick it, the whole outside of the track will be copied.**
4. **Save your drawing as EX3G.**

Mirror EX3H

1. **Open the Hands-On Exercises dialog box, start Exercise 3H from Chapter 3, and save the drawing as EX3H in your subdirectory.**

2. **To create the right-hand glove, use the MIRROR command. (To make it simpler for you, the green line represents the mirror line.) Snap to each end to define the mirror.**
3. **To change the swing of the door from right to left, use the MIRROR command again, only this time answer Yes to delete original. In this way, the mirror copy replaces the original.**
4. **To create the other half of the angle bracket, use the two corners of the bracket. Can you see that the mirror line can be at any angle?**
5. **Save your drawing as EX3H.**

Array EX3I

1. **Open the Hands-On Exercises dialog box and start Exercise 3I from Chapter 3, and save the drawing as EX3I in your subdirectory.**

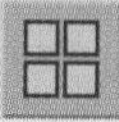

2. **Use the Rectangular option of the ARRAY command to create the series of desks and chairs. When asked to select objects, pick both the desk and the chair. In this way you can array both at the same time.**
3. **Use the Polar option of the ARRAY command to create the rest of the bolt holes around the circular flange. Don't forget to include the center line in the array.**
4. **Save your drawing as EX3I.**

Fillet and Chamfer EX3J

1. **Open the Hands-On Exercises dialog box and start Exercise 3J from Chapter 3, and save the drawing as EX3J in your subdirectory.**

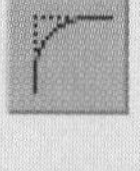

2. **The first figure requires the use of the FILLET command. Note the two different radii.**
3. **The second figure uses a 0 (zero) radius with the FILLET command. This allows you to create sharp corners efficiently by extending or/and trimming.**

4. **The third figure requires the use of the CHAMFER command. There are two different chamfers.**
5. **Save your drawing as EX3J.**

In a Nutshell

Now, with a few basic objects under our belts, we can begin to draw in fine style. Chapter 4, moving right along, teaches you to be a master manipulator of the objects you create. You'll be spinning and stretching with the best pizza makers! On with the fun.

Testing... testing... 1, 2, 3

Matching

Match the following coordinates with their system name.

___1. 2.3, 1.7 to -8.0<50	a. absolute coordinates
___2. 6.6, 1.4 to @ 4.1, 2.2	b. relative coordinates
___3. 3,4 to 11,9	c. polar coordinates
___4. 1,1 to @ 0,5	
___5. 0,0 to 0,5	
___6. 0,0 to @ 3.1<90	

True or False

Indicate whether the numbered statements are true or false by choosing T or F:

1. Drawing in two and three dimensions involves the absolute, relative, and polar Cartesian coordinate system. T or F
2. You don't normally draw on layer 1. T or F
3. Pick the Properties tool to change an object's properties mid-drawing. T or F
4. The Close option of the ARC command will close any arc into a semicircle. T or F
5. The COPY command acts exactly like the MOVE command. T or F

Fill in the blank.

1. The point entity is formally called the __________.
2. There are __________ methods for creating a circle including __________ and __________.
3. Every object is drawn on a(n) __________ to facilitate better organization.
4. *Remember:* The AutoCAD program allows you to establish __________ to define the area in which you're working.
5. To copy an object several times in random locations use the __________ command, but when you want the objects copied in a round pattern use the __________ command.

What?

1. Explain the procedure for moving from point A at 0,0 to point B at 0,4 to point C at 8,8 using relative coordinates. Record what the command sequence would read.

   ____

   ____

2. Do the same as above using polar coordinates.

   ____

   ____

3. What are the five methods for generating a circle? Give a full explanation of two of them.

   1. ____
   2. ____
   3. ____
   4. ____
   5. ____

4. Under what circumstances does the Line Continuation option work?

5. Explain the use of the MIRROR command and its options.

6. Compare and contrast the FILLET and CHAMFER commands.

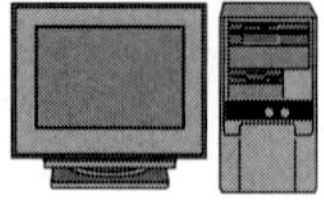

Let's Get Busy!

1. Draw the geometry in Figure 3.18 using circles, lines, and arcs with the help of various object snaps. Save assignment as C3A1.
2. Draw the L bracket shown in Figure 3.19. Remember to use the proper layers for object, hidden, and center lines. Don't dimension it. Use the MECH-1 Hands-On template file. Save assignment as C3A2.
3. Draw the window illustrated in Figure 3.20. Remember to set the units to architectural and the limits larger than the overall size of the window. Use the ARCH-1 Hands-On template file. Save assignment as C3A3.

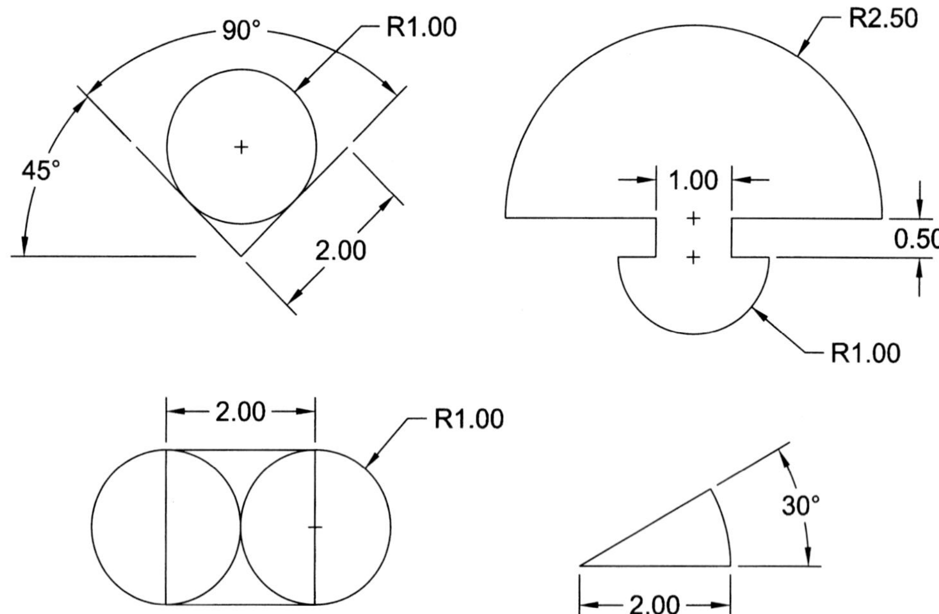

Figure 3.18
Lines, circles, and arcs

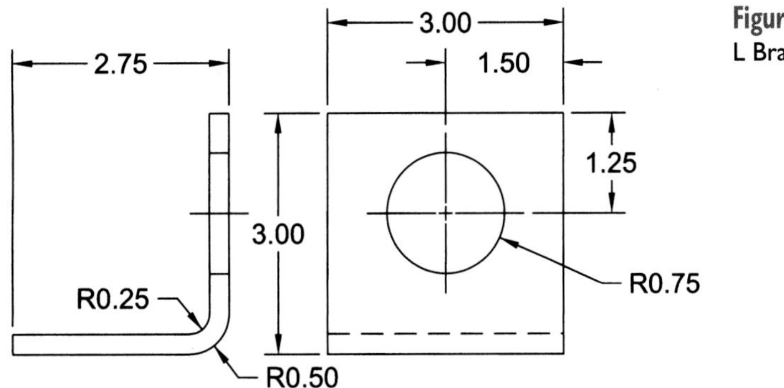

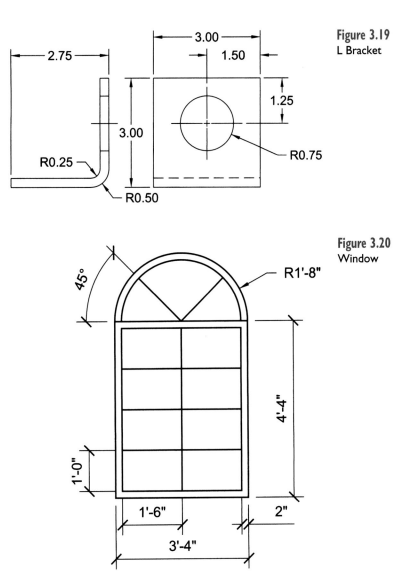

Figure 3.19
L Bracket

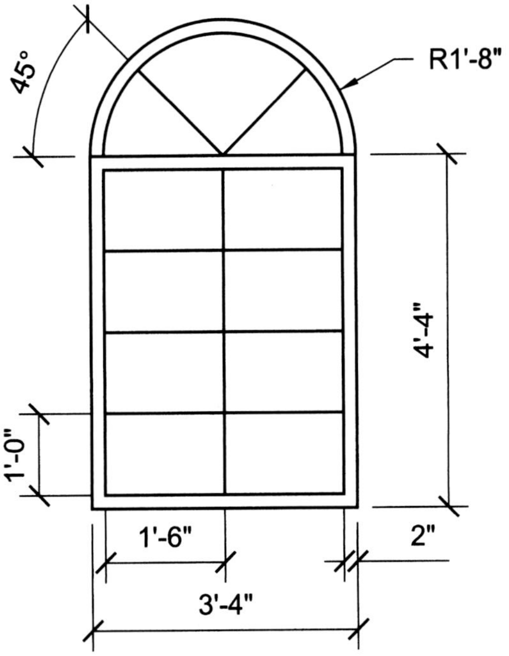

Figure 3.20
Window

Chapter 4

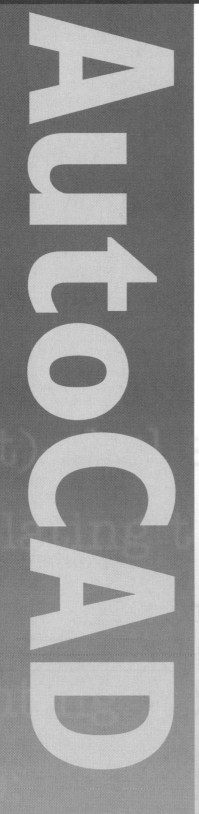

Alterations Done Here: Modifying

Key topics

- Trim, Extnd, Break
- Move, Rotate
- Scale, Stretch, Lengthen
- Grips

Selecting Objects

Remember so very long ago in Chapter 1 we talked about selecting individual and group objects? Because you may need to alter objects or move them around, some commands require you to choose a selection set—a single object or a group of objects that you want the command to affect. You can pull those objects into the group by picking on them with the pick-box, by windowing around them, or by using other methods. (See Figure 4.1.) Once you have them in your grasp, there are many things you can do with them as the following chapter demonstrates.

TRIM, EXTEND, and BREAK

In Chapter 3, you had a little experience with the FILLET command. Well, TRIM, EXTEND, and BREAK work in a similar manner. In fact, if you use the FILLET command with a 0 radius, the command will perform both trim and extend to form sharp corners.

TRIM

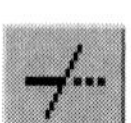

When you want to get rid of unwanted bits of objects on the screen, particularly if those bits are intersecting other objects, you use the TRIM command. Identifying the cutting edge, the first stage of the command, tells the program where to cut the offending pieces; identifying the objects that you wish trimmed, the second stage, trims those objects that intersect with the cutting edge. Just think of your bangs as the offending hairs and your eyebrows as the cutting edge. Every hair is cut off at that point. (See Figure 4.2.)

Command:	**TRIM**
Current settings: Projection=UCS Edge=Extend	
Select cutting edges ...	
Select objects:	**Pick one or more cutting edges**
n found	
Select objects:	**Press Enter to proceed to trimming**
Select object to trim or [Project/Edge/Undo]:	**Pick 1 + objects to trim**
Select object to trim or [Project/Edge/Undo]:	**Press Enter to exit command**

The projmode allows edge trimming in 3D, while the edgemode makes allowance for objects that don't intersect the cutting edge.

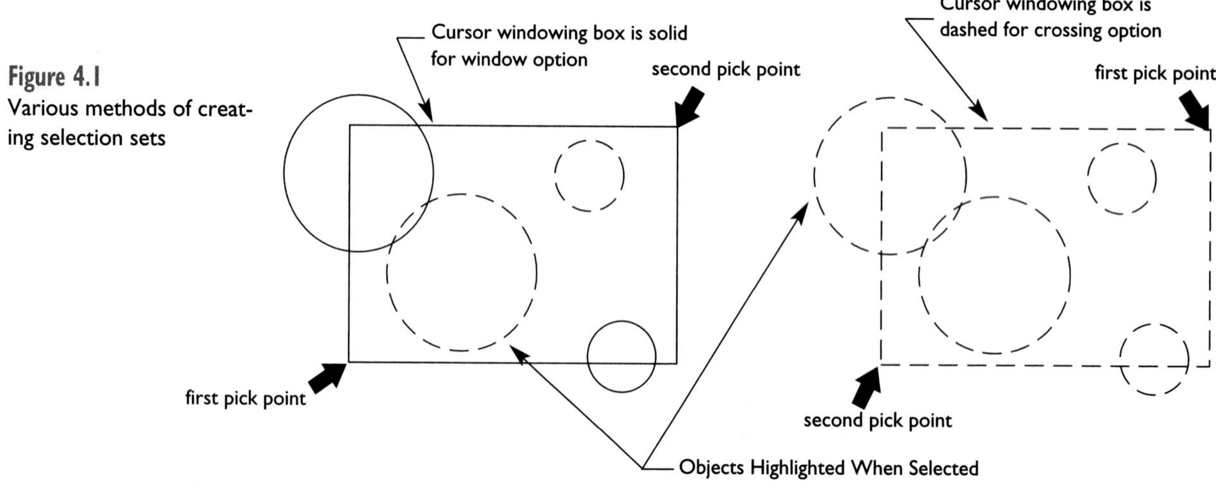

Figure 4.1
Various methods of creating selection sets

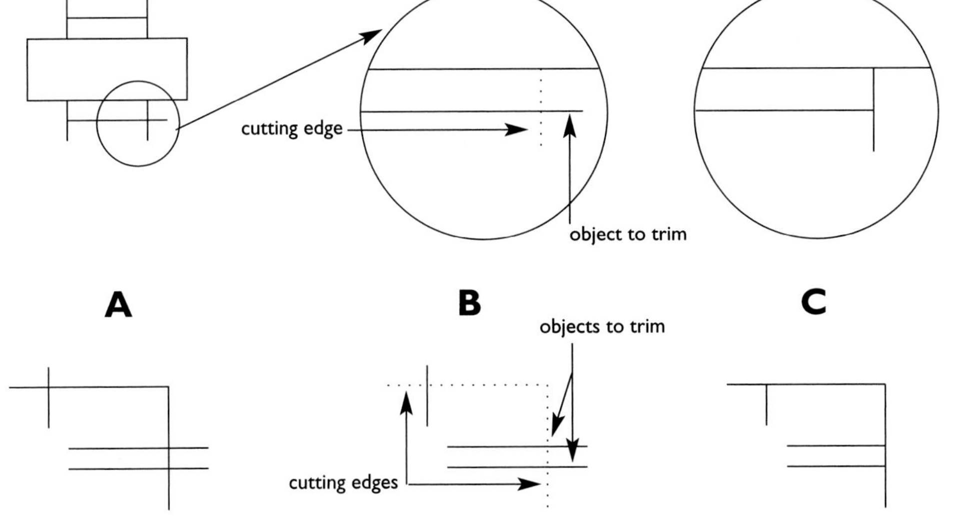

Figure 4.2
Trimming

EXTEND

The EXTEND command, you guessed it, extends objects until they intersect with others. This two-stage command begins with identifying the boundary to which the objects will extend and then, naturally, with picking the objects you want to extend. (See Figure 4.3)

Command:	**EXTEND**
Current settings: Projection=UCS Edge=Extend	
Select boundary edges ...	
Select objects:	**Pick one or more objects for the boundary**
n found	
Select objects:	**Press Enter to proceed to extend**
Select object to extend or [Project/Edge/Undo]:	**Pick 1+ objects to extend**
Select object to extend or [Project/Edge/Undo]:	**Press Enter to exit command**

Remember, FILLET with a 0 radius works better for certain trims and certain extends.

BREAK

Finally, the BREAK command breaks away pieces of an object or breaks the object into two pieces. (See Figure 4.4.)

Command:	**BREAK**
Select object:	**Pick an object** (This will be the first break point unless you use the First option and choose another.)
Specify second break point or [First point]:	**Pick the location of the second break point**

If you enter **F** rather the second break point, you will be asked to pick the first break point location again. This is used when the break point overlaps another object. In that case, you would select the break object where it doesn't overlap and then use the First option to identify the intersecting break point.

Figure 4.3
Extending

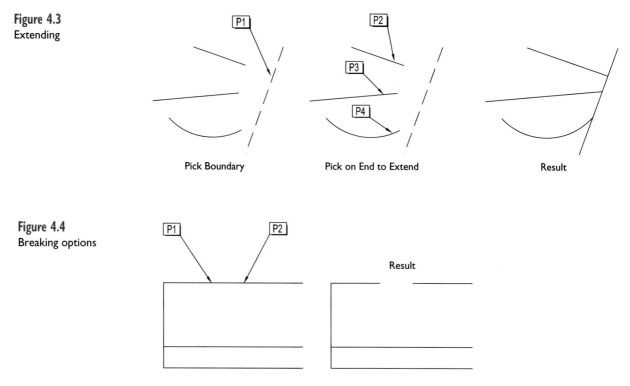

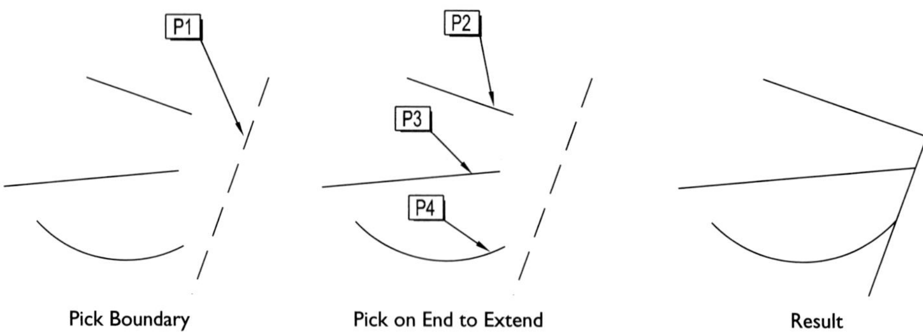

Figure 4.4
Breaking options

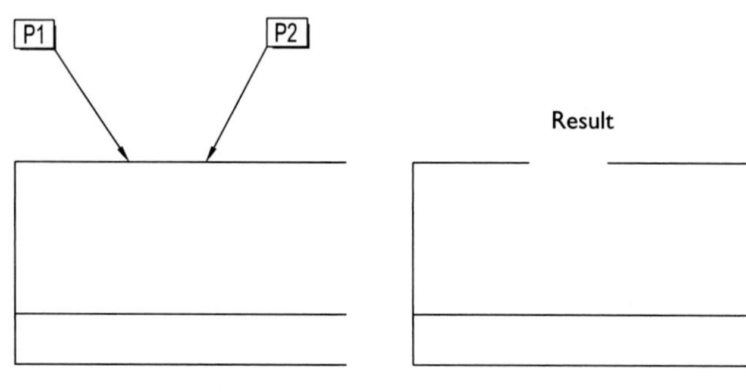

If you enter an **@** rather than the second break point, the object will be broken in half at the first break point.

Let's take a look at some BREAK options:

Option	**Result**
1 Point	Use the @ option—breaks an object at the select object pick point.
1 Point Select	Use the First and @ options—selects an object and breaks it at the defined point.
2 Points	Use select object point as the first pick point—breaks and removes a portion of the object between the two picked points.
2 Points Select	Use the First option—defines the two break points and removes the broken object.

Hands-On: Using TRIM, EXTEND, and BREAK

These exercises will offer experience in using similar modify commands to cut away and add to existing objects.

TRIM EX4A

1 Open the Hands-On Exercises dialog box, start Exercise 4A from Chapter 4, and save the drawing as EX4A in your subdirectory.

2 The first two figures in Box A show two circles bisected by two lines. Using the TRIM command, the circles were used as the cutting edges. With the first circle, the inner lines were trimmed; with the second circle the outer lines were trimmed. It's your turn to do the same in Box B. The following is the way to do it:

Command:	**TRIM**
Current settings: Projection=UCS Edge=Extend	
Select cutting edges ...	
Select objects:	**Pick the circle and then press Enter to move on**
Select object to trim or [Project/Edge/Undo]:	**Pick the part of the line to trim away.**
Select object to trim or [Project/Edge/Undo]:	**Press enter when you are finished.**

3. **The center figure shows crossing lines. All the lines were used as cutting edges and the unwanted portions were trimmed away. Try doing this within Box B.**
4. **The far-right figure shows how you can use text as a cutting edge and how the unwanted lines crossing through the text are trimmed away. Do the same in Box B.**
5. **Save your drawing as EX4A.**

EXTEND EX4B

1. **Open the Hands-On Exercises dialog box, start Exercise 4B from Chapter 4, and save the drawing as EX4B in your subdirectory.**
2. **The first figure in Box A shows how many lines can be extended to one boundary line. Do the same in Box B using the following procedure:**

Command:	**EXTEND**
Current settings: Projection=UCS Edge=None	
Select boundary edges ...	
Select objects:	**Pick horizontal line as the boundary to extend to and press Enter to continue on**
Select object to extend or [Project/Edge/Undo]:	**E** (Enter E for edge option)
Enter an implied edge extension mode [Extend/No extend] <No extend>:	**Extend**
Select object to extend or [Project/Edge/Undo]:	**Pick on the lines near the end to extend and press Enter to exit**

3. **The second figure demonstrates how an arc can be extended, and the third figure shows how even a dimension line can be extended. For the third figure use the vertical line on the box as the boundary and then pick the dimension line to extend. Proceed to extend the various geometry in Box B.**
4. **Save your drawing as EX4B.**

BREAK EX4C

1. **Open the Hands-On Exercises dialog box, start Exercise 4C from Chapter 4, and save the drawing as EX4C in your subdirectory.**
2. **The first figure in Box A shows a circle with a piece broken out. Try doing this in Box B using the BREAK command. Just pick the two points on the circle, in a counterclockwise direction.**

Hands-On: Using TRIM, EXTEND, and BREAK (continued)

3. **The second figure demonstrates breaking a line at a point and then erasing one-half of the broken line. To do this follow this procedure:**

Command:	**BREAK**
Select object:	**Pick on the line anywhere to identify the line**
Specify second break point or [First point]:	**F** (Use the F option to identify where the break point should occur.)
Specify first break point:	**Pick the location of break point**
Specify second break point: @	(Entering the @ sign tells AutCAD to break the Object "at" the first point.)
Command: **ERASE**	(Use the ERASE command to get rid of one-half of the line.)

4. **Try the same thing with the last figure. Only this time, instead of erasing half of the line, change its properties so that it is on the Hidden layer.**
5. **Save your drawing as EX4C.**

MOVE and ROTATE

Without the capability of moving objects around in a drawing, the whole process would be much like it was before AutoCAD revolutionized the drawing world. In the past, when you started to draw, you had to make certain that you were starting to draw in exactly the right place. Revisions were costly, messy, and time consuming. Not so anymore; stand back and just watch us move.

MOVE

In the case of the MOVE command, you can take one or more objects and move them from a start point to a destination point. AutoCAD calls these points the base point and the second point of displacement, respectively. If you don't enter any response for the second point, the program uses your first point as a relative movement distance. (See Figure 4.5.)

Command:	**MOVE**
Select objects:	**Pick objects to move and press Enter**
Specify base point or displacement:	**Pick the start point**
Specify second point of displacement or <use first point as displacement>:	**Pick the destination point**

It's that simple to change the entire layout of your drawing.

Figure 4.5
Using the MOVE command

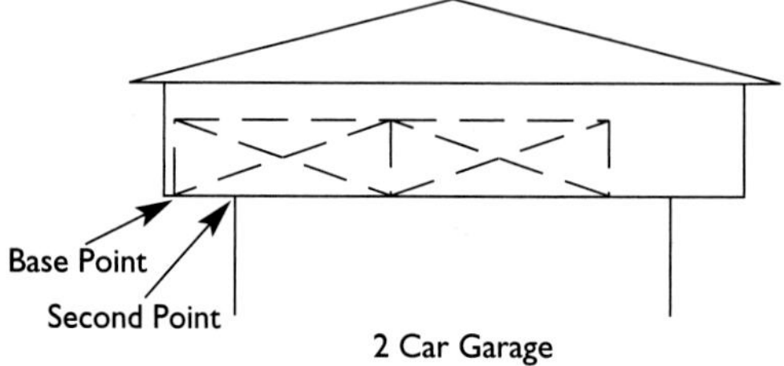

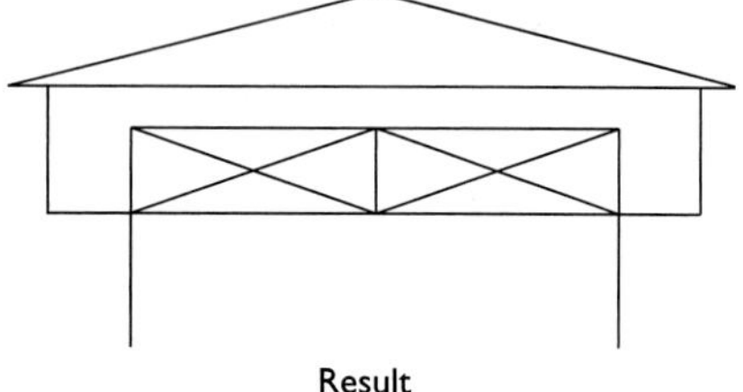

ROTATE

The ROTATE command is just another way to move an object. However, rather than moving an object in a straight line, you pivot it around a rotation point, which AutoCAD calls the base point. (If you are sitting in a comfortable, modern computer chair, you're probably quite familiar with rotation.) All you do is provide a rotation angle, positive or negative. If you want to, you can provide a reference angle whereby you identify the current angle and then the new rotation angle. (See Figure 4.6.)

Command:	**ROTATE**
Current positive angle in UCS: ANGDIR=counterclockwise ANGBASE=0	
Select objects:	**Pick objects to rotate and press Enter**
Specify base point:	**Pick the pivot point**
Specify rotation angle or [Reference]:	**Enter a relative angle or R for reference**

Hands-On: Using MOVE and ROTATE

In these exercises you will practice moving and rotating objects.

MOVE EX4D

1. **Open the Hands-On Exercises dialog box, start Exercise 4D from Chapter 4, and save the drawing as EX4D in your subdirectory.**
2. **In the first figure a circle was moved onto the center of a second circle using MOVE and object snaps. Try this by using the following procedure:**

Command:	**MOVE**
Select objects:	**Pick the circle to move and press Enter to continue**
Specify base point or displacement:	**center** (Use the Center object snap.)
	Pick the edge of circle to move
Specify second point of displacement or <use first point as displacement>:	**center** (Again, use the Center object snap.)
	Pick the edge of the circle that you are moving to

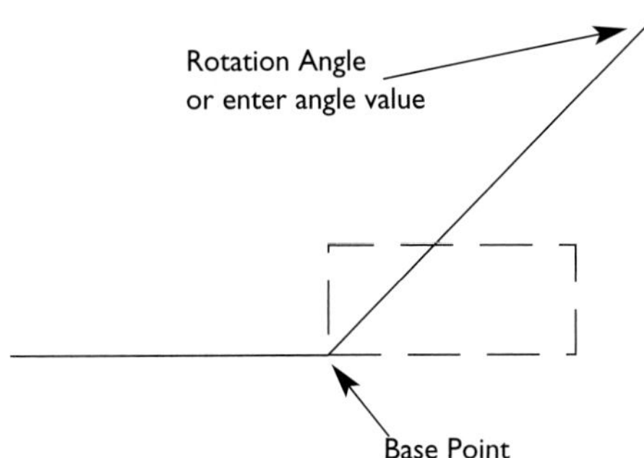

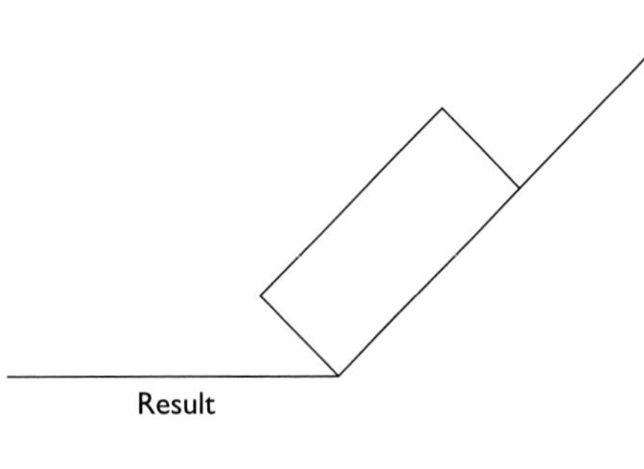

Figure 4.6
Rotating an object

Hands-On: Using MOVE and ROTATE (continued)

3 The figure in the middle requires the same kind of move using endpoints as the object snaps.

4 The moving truck in the right figure requires the use of a relative coordinate entry to facilitate the move. For the base point, pick the corner of the truck using object snaps; for the second point, enter in the distance using relative coordinates @3,0.

5 Once you have made all the right moves, save your drawing as EX4D.

ROTATE EX4E

1 Open the Hands-On Exercises dialog box, start Exercise 4E from Chapter 4, and save the drawing as EX4E in your subdirectory.

2 In the first figure, a line that was at 0 degrees was rotated to 45 degrees. The following is the procedure for you to try:

Command:	**ROTATE**
Current positive angle in UCS: ANGDIR=counterclockwise ANGBASE=0	
Select objects:	**Pick the horizontal line and press Enter to continue**
Specify base point:	**endpoint** (Use endpoint object snap.)
	Pick the end of the line to use as the pivot base point
Specify rotation angle or [Reference]:	**45** (Enter the rotation angle.)

3 Try to close the door in the second figure using a negative rotation angle of –90 degrees.

4 In the far-right figure, use object snaps to identify the base point and the rotation angle to rotate the skateboard onto the slope.

5 Save your drawing as EX4E.

SCALE, LENGTHEN, and STRETCH

Have you every eaten a holiday dinner, pushed away from the table, and wished you could enlarge your clothes to accommodate the extra turkey; or have you taken a cotton shirt out of the dryer and longed for the ability to stretch the arms to their former dimensions? These next commands take one or more objects and manipulate their dimensions, again making revision easier. Although these commands could certainly make everyday life much easier, they are still available only in the CAD program.

SCALE

The SCALE command changes an object's dimensions by an equal factor. A scale of 3 would triple the size of the current object, while a scale of .25 would make the object one-fourth its former size. (See Figure 4.7.)

Command:	**SCALE**
Select objects:	**Pick objects to scale**
Specify base point:	**Pick the fixed point from which the scaling will occur**
Specify scale factor or [Reference]:	**Enter a value or R** (allows you to enter a reference length, then a new length.)

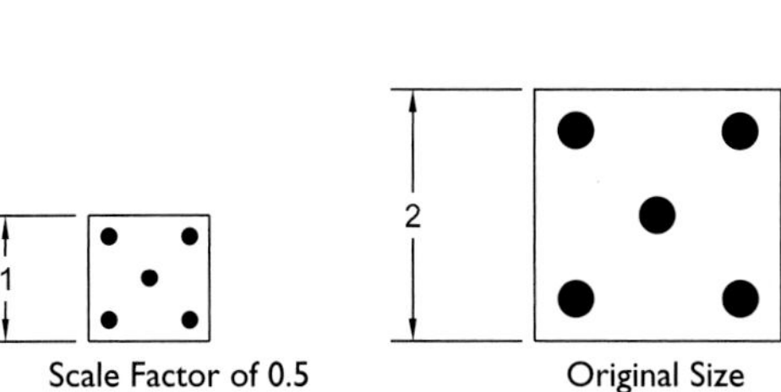

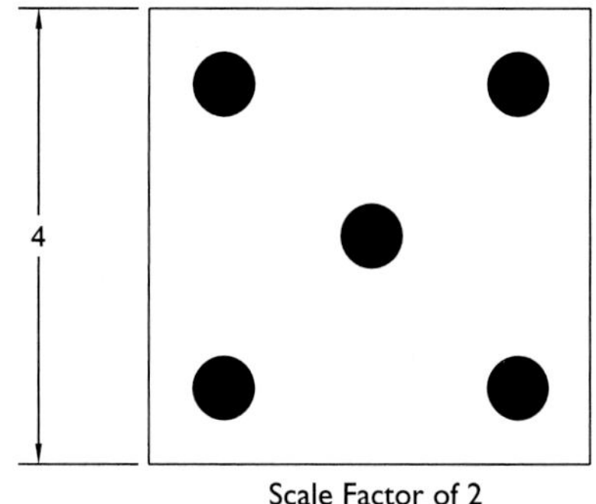

Figure 4.7
Changing the size of an object with the SCALE command

LENGTHEN

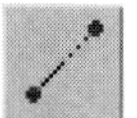

The LENGTHEN command lets you change the lengths of lines and arcs. A look at some of the options will give you a good idea of how the command can work. However, you can also pick and drag dynamically to get the results you want. (See Figure 4.8.)

Command:	**LENGTHEN**
Select an object or [Delta/Percent/Total/DYnamic]:	

To change length you:

Option	**Result**
Delta	Specify a value >1 or < 1 for lines, or an angle for arcs
Percent	Specify a percentage >100 to increase or <100 to decrease
Total	Enter the desired length
DYnamic	Drag the object to the desired size

STRETCH

Finally, the STRETCH command is a complex command that's simple to use. When you use this command, you can move some objects to a new location while stretching or shrinking others that are connected to the objects moved. Just think how useful that could be in the real world—no more flood pants or altering hem lines! When you window around a group of objects using the Window Crossing option, those that are completely surrounded by your window will be moved based on the movement from the base point to the second point of displacement. Those objects that appear in your window but also continue out of it will be stretched or shrunk to meet those objects that you moved. (See Figure 4.9.)

Command:	**STRETCH**
Select objects to stretch by crossing-window or crossing-polygon...	
Select objects:	**Use Crossing option to window around the area to be stretched (P1,P2)**
Specify base point or displacement:	**Pick a location from which to stretch objects or enter a distance to be moved (P3)**

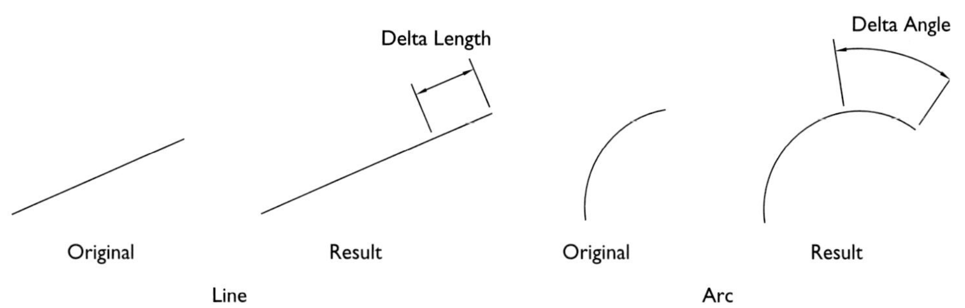

Figure 4.8
Lengthening a line and arc

Figure 4.9
Enlarging a room with the STRETCH command

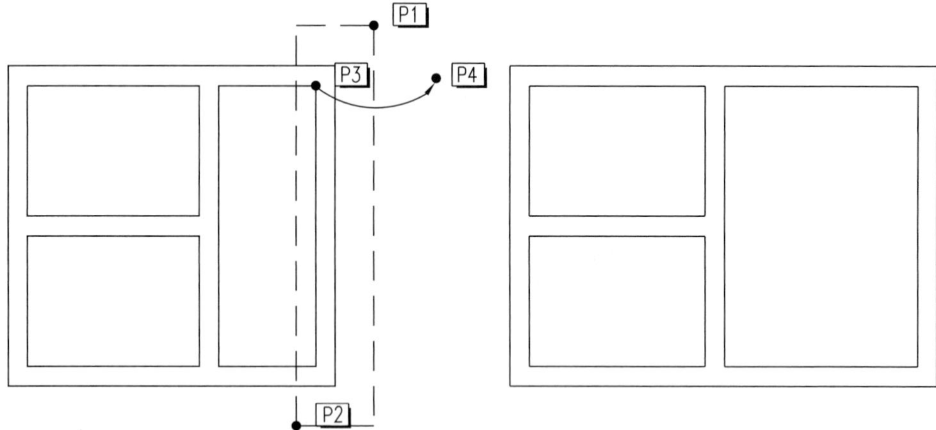

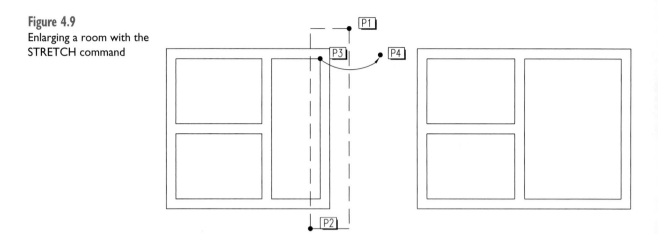

Specify second point of displacement: **Pick a location to which to stretch, or press Enter to use the distance set in the previous line (P4)** (Note the rubberband mode allowing you to get a look at your choice before you commit.)

The STRETCH command works even better with dimensions. However, when stretching objects that have already been dimensioned, make sure you include the start point for the extension line within the window and leave the other extension line at the original location. Then you'll get a correct update on the new dimensions. (See Figure 4.10.)

Figure 4.10
Using STRETCH with dimensions

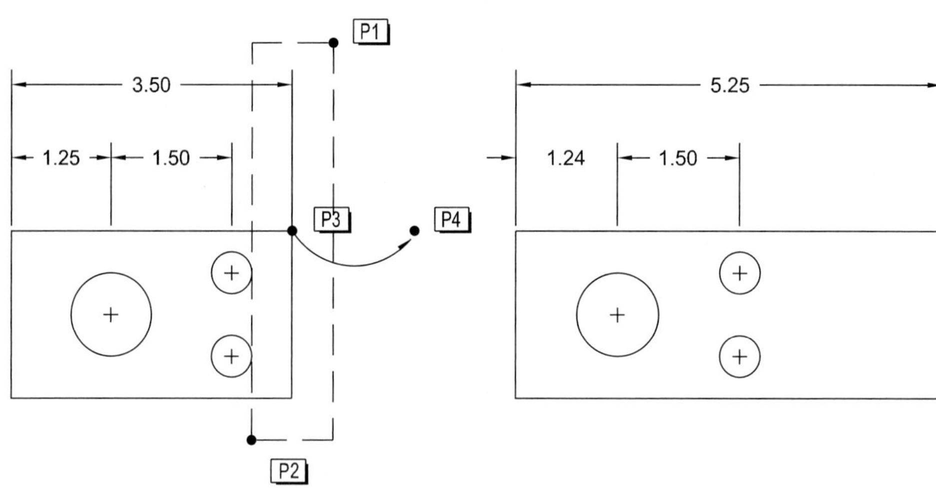

Hands-On: Using SCALE, LENGTHEN, and STRETCH

These exercises will offer experience in altering the size of objects using three different methods.

SCALE EX4F

❶ **Open the Hands-On Exercises dialog box, start Exercise 4F from Chapter 4, and save the drawing as EX4F in your subdirectory.**

❷ **To scale the tree, simply identify its center as the base point and slowly drag the cursor back and forth until you get the size you want.**

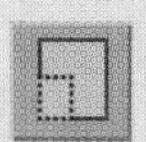

❸ **To scale the circle, the centerlines, and the radial dimension, select them all, identify the center of the circle as the base point, and enter 1.5 as the scale factor.**

❹ **To scale the door to its new size is a little tricky but you can learn to do it by doing the following:**

Command:	**SCALE**
Select objects:	**Pick the door** (it's all one object) **and press Enter**
Specify base point:	**endpoint** (Use Endpoint object snap.)
	Pick the hinge point of the door
Specify scale factor or [Reference]:	**R** (Enter the R option to specify a reference length.)
Specify reference length <1>:	**endpoint** (Use Endpoint object snap.)
	Pick the hinge point again for the start of the reference length.
Specify second point:	**endpoint** (Use Endpoint object snap.)
	Pick the end of the arc to establish the current length of the door
Specify new length:	**endpoint** (Use endpoint object snap.)
	Pick the end of the door opening that you want to scale to

LENGTHEN EX4G

❶ **Open the Hands-On Exercises dialog box, start Exercise 4G from Chapter 4, and save the drawing as EX4G in your subdirectory.**

❷ **In this exercise you are going to lengthen the bars in the bar graph. Lengthen the first bar using the Delta option with a value of 1. Lengthen the second bar using the Percent option and a value of 200%. Lengthen the third bar by using the Total option and value of 2. (*Hint:* Set the delta, percent, or total before selecting an object by picking its edge.)**

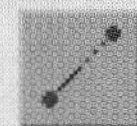

❸ **Save your drawing as EX4G.**

STRETCH EX4H

❶ **Open the Hands-On Exercises dialog box, start Exercise 4H from Chapter 4, and save the drawing as EX4H in your subdirectory.**

❷ **The first figure shows a hole in a part and the corresponding dimensions. Using the STRETCH command, increase the distance as shown in Box A. The following is the procedure:**

Hands-On: Using SCALE, LENGTHEN, and STRETCH (continued)

Command:	**STRETCH**
Select objects to stretch by crossing-window or crossing-polygon...	
Select objects:	**C** (Enter C to enforce the crossing-window mode.)
Specify first corner:	**Pick the lower-left corner** (Refer to the green dashed box.)
Specify opposite corner:	**Pick the upper-right corner to create a box enclosing the hole and hole location dimension** (Refer to the green dashed box.)
Select objects:	**Press Enter**
Specify base point or displacement:	**Object snap on the corner to stretch**
Specify second point of displacement:	**@1′,0**

3. **The second figure shows a door in a wall. Using the STRETCH command, move the door along the wall a relative distance of 4′,0.**
4. **Save your drawing as EX4H.**

Grips

We'll avoid the temptation of telling you to get a grip, and move right on to the important stuff—Grips. These terrific and adaptable tools will increase your modification speed and provide the creative part of the process with more positive reinforcement. Using Grips, you can stretch, rotate, copy, scale, and mirror without going through the standard commands. Figure 4.11 illustrates various objects and their grip points.

Turn Grips on by using the DDGRIPS command and making certain the Enable grips boxed is selected under Grips. (See Figure 4.12.) Note that you can change grip color, but they are normally blue (cold) when unselected and red (hot) when active. As well, you can change the size of the grip box if you desire. Now, to use grips, pick on an object and its grips will be highlighted.

Take a look at the following section. It will explain a variety of grip manipulations that will help you to manipulate objects as the need arises (see Figure 4.13).

Option	**Result**
To move option	Highlight grips, pick a central grip box—like the middle of a line or the center of a circle—and drag the object to a new location. (You will notice that the grip you picked, now called the base grip, will fill with color.)
To copy	While moving, press the Shift key when you reach the new location—this activates Multiple Copy.
To place copies at a fixed distance	Hold the Shift key down during the move and the copies will be placed equadistantly a distance set by the first copy.
To stretch	Pick a grip on the end of a line and stretch to the new location. (For other objects, see Stretch mode.)
To scale	Pick an object's outer grip and drag to a new location.

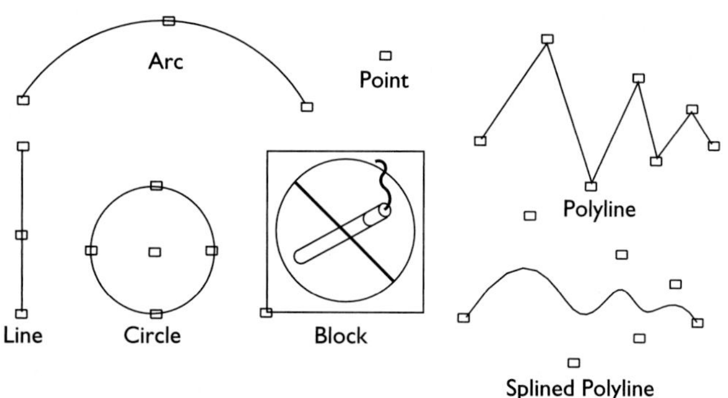

Figure 4.11
Grip locations on selected objects

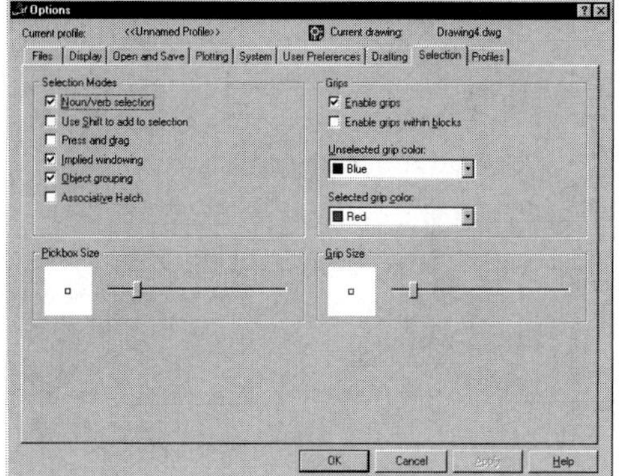

Figure 4.12
Options dialog box showing Selection tab for grips

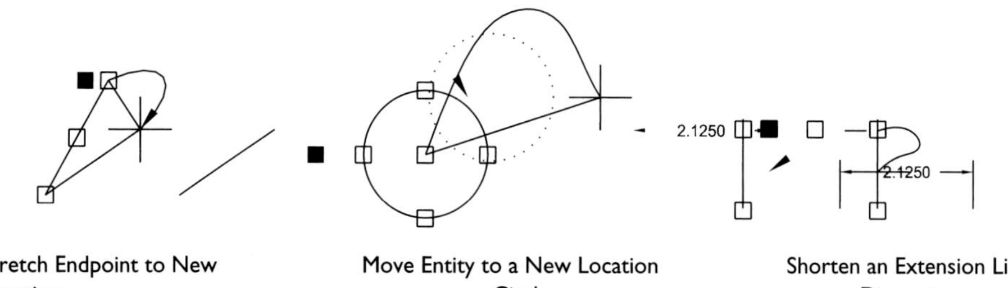

Figure 4.13
Grip manipulations

Option	**Result**
To select multiple objects	Hold down the Shift key when picking grip boxes and then release the Shift key to select the base grip.
To select Grip modes	Right-click when hot grip is active.
To change dimensions	Pick on a dimension and alter any element including text, extension lines, and dimension lines.

Hands-On: Starting Using Grips

In this exercise you will get some practice moving objects by their grip points.

Grips EX4I

1. **Open the Hands-On Exercises dialog box, start Exercise 4I from Chapter 4, and save the drawing as EX4I in your subdirectory.**
2. **Check to make sure grips are active by entering DDGRIPS on the command line. The Enable Grips box should be checked.**
3. **The first figure shows a dimension moved to a new location. Pick on the dimension with no command active. Blue boxes should appear identifying the blue grips on the dimension. Pick on the grip beside the arrowhead, turning it red, and drag the dimension to the new location. Press the Esc key twice to cancel the grips.**
4. **In the second figure a line was rotated and lengthened with the use of a grip. Pick on the line to highlight the blue grips. Pick on the grip at the end of the line, turning it red, and drag the end of the line to the new location. Press the Esc key twice to cancel the grips.**
5. **In the third figure a circle was scaled to touch a corner. Pick on the circle to turn on the blue grips. Pick on the grip on the outer edge of the circle, turning it red, and drag the edge to the corner. It will scale to the new size. Press the Esc key twice to cancel the grips.**
6. **Save your drawing as EX4I.**

In a Nutshell

Well, you've completed all the basic moves—and you didn't think you'd get here! Now it's time to take a look at what you've worked so hard to create. Once you master Chapter 5 on viewing, you'll never get lost again.

Testing... testing... 1, 2, 3

Multiple Choice

Choose the best answer to complete each of the following statements:

1. You can choose a selection set by
   a. typing <ss> on the command line.
   b. windowing around the objects.
   c. picking each with the pickbox.
   d. a and b
   e. b and c

2. AutoCAD calls the beginning and endpoints of the MOVE command the
   a. base point and second point.
   b. base point and the second point of displacement.
   c. base point of displacement and the second point of displacement.
   d. start point and the second point.
   e. base point and the destination point.

3. The LENGTHEN command includes the options:
   a. Percent, Total, DYspeptic.
   b. DExter, Total, DYnamic.
   c. DElta, Percent, DYspeptic.
   d. DElta, Percent, Total.
   e. DExter, Percent, DYspeptic.
4. The BREAK command option that breaks and removes a portion of an object is the
   a. one-point option.
   b. two-point option.
   c. breakpoint option.
   d. removal option.
   e. none of the above

Fill in the blanks.

1. Selected grips are usually colored __________ while unselected grips are usually colored __________.
2. In the STRETCH command the __________ mode allows you to see your choice before fully committing.
3. The __________ command with a(n) __________ allows you to both extend and trim to form a 90 degree corner.
4. To move an object by pivoting it around a fixed center involves the __________ command.
5. The __________ command changes an object's __________ by an equal factor.

True or False

Indicate whether the numbered statements are true or false by choosing T or F.

1. The LENGTHEN command is effective only on lines and circles. T or F
2. TRIM is very effective at eliminating intersecting entities. T or F
3. BREAK removes pieces of objects or breaks objects into many pieces. T or F
4. (*Remember*) The ARRAY command has two options: rectangular and circular. T or F
5. Turn on Grips using the ENABGRIPS command. T or F

What?

1. Explain the difference between the SCALE and the LENGTHEN commands.

   ____

   ____

2. What are the advantages of enabling Grips?

   ____

   ____

3. Explain how to put a group of objects into a selection set.

   ____

   ____

4. Describe the command sequence for the BREAK command. List and explain each of the options.

   ____

   ____

5. What happens when you use the STRETCH command?

____

____

6. Pick four of the grip manipulations, name them, and explain how each one works.

   1. ______________________________
   2. ______________________________
   3. ______________________________
   4. ______________________________

Let's Get Busy!

1. Draw the geometry shown in Figure 4.14 using various modifying commands such as TRIM, BREAK, and FILLET. Do not dimension. Save assignment as C4A1.
2. Draw the support plate shown in Figure 4.15. Note that it's symmetrical. Draw one-half and use MIRROR to create the other half. Don't dimension! Save assignment as C4A2.
3. Draw the bedroom shown in Figure 4.16. (Using the OFFSET command will make the job a lot easier.) Add more furniture to the room. Save assignment as C4A3.

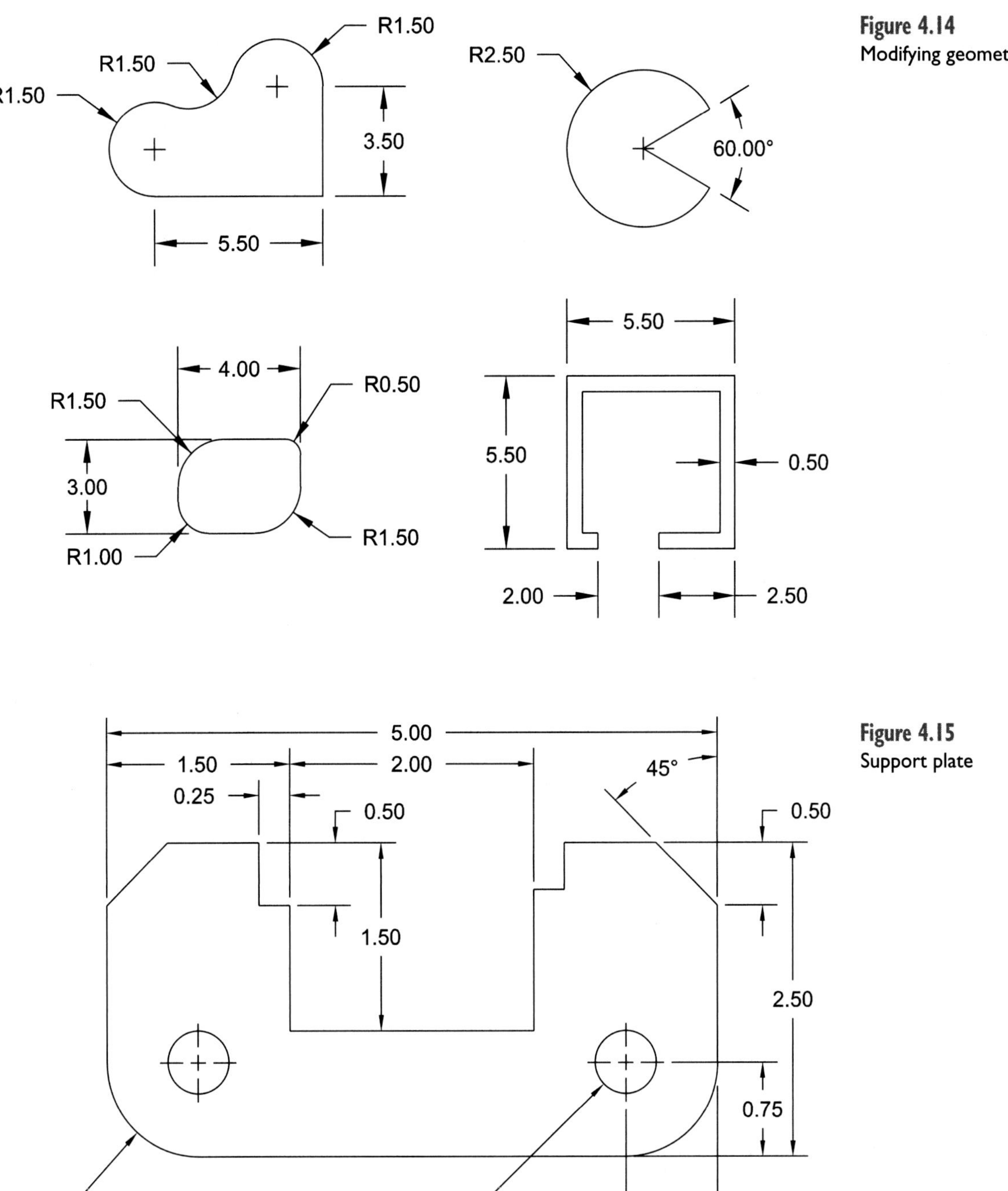

Figure 4.14
Modifying geometry

Figure 4.15
Support plate

Figure 4.16
Bedroom

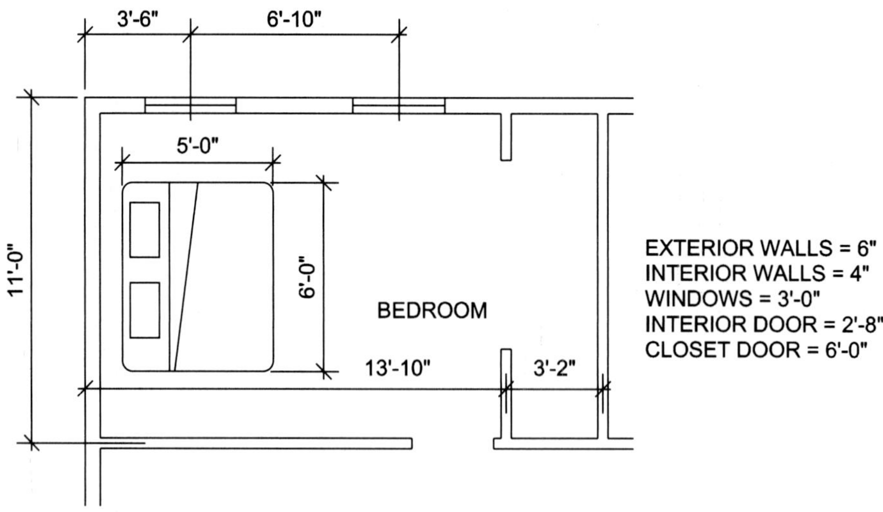

Chapter 5

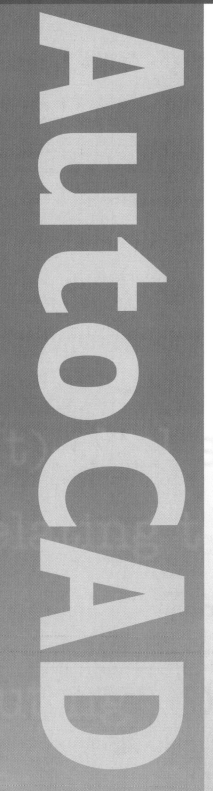

WYSIWYG (What You See Is What You Get): Viewing

Key topics

- Viewing
- Pan
- Redraw versus Regen
- Layer Options

Before We Get Started

It's important, before we start to view our drawings in a variety of ways, that you understand something about the two working environments in AutoCAD—model space and paper space. Get ready for a little bit of theory with little or no sugar coating. Model space is used to create the objects to form the contents of your drawing. Paper space activities include arranging drawing views and plotting those views together as one drawing.

Figure 5.1 shows a partial view of a drawing, with the Model tab active. Check the tab line at the bottom of the graphics screen for the word Model. Also, look at the status line at the right of the figure. The word MODEL appears, signifying that you are working in model space. This is the way you have been drawing so far.

Figure 5.2 shows the paper space environment. You can see two separate views and the "set-square" paper space icon. Observe the tab line in this figure. Note that one of the Layout tabs has been activated. The layouts are used to work in paper space. Look at the status line in the figure. The word Model has been replaced with the word Paper, signifying that you are working in paper space.

Figure 5.3 shows an active model space inside the paper space environment. Note the paper space "set-square" is gone but there are now two UCS icons in the *viewports*. Observe the status line. The word PAPER has been replaced with MODEL, while the Layout tab is still active.

Use the tabs Layout and Model to switch from your paper space layout to model space. Use the Model/Paper button if you want to work within a Model Space viewport with the Paper Space layout tab still active.

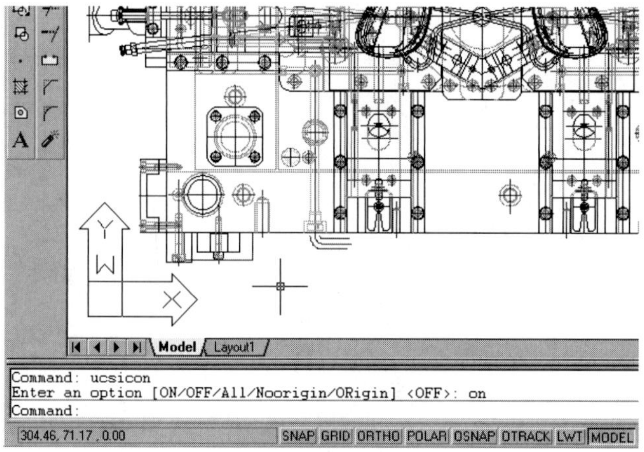

Figure 5.1
Partial view of drawing in model space with TILEMODE 1

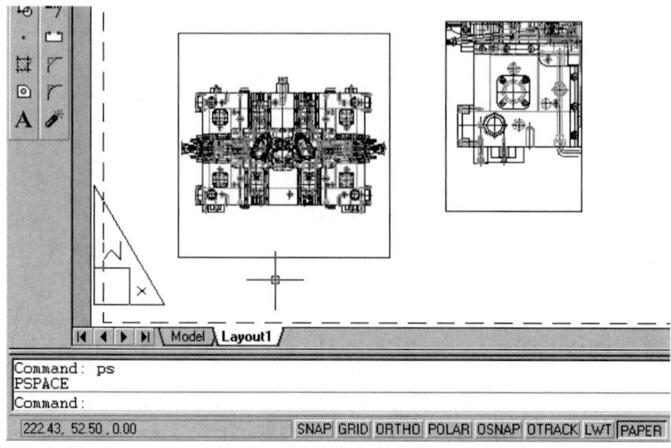

Figure 5.2
Partial view of drawing in paper space with TILEMODE 0

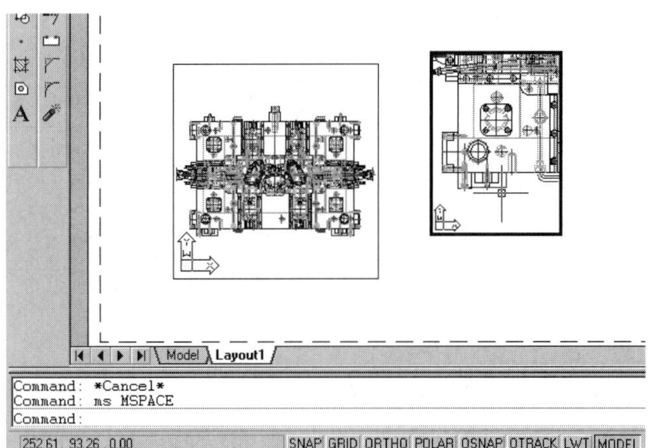

Figure 5.3
Partial view of drawing in model space with TILEMODE 0

A word of warning: When you first switch from model space to paper space, the screen will go blank. Don't worry, your drawing hasn't been lost. It's just that the viewports haven't been created. For now, it's easier to remain with the Model tab active. Study Figures 5.1, 5.2, and 5.3 to familiarize yourself with the look of model space and paper space environments.

For now, it's easier to remain with the Model tab active.

Viewing

There are lots of ways to change the display of your drawing to showcase it in its best light. The following takes a look at all the basic facilities.

ZOOM Realtime and PAN Realtime

AutoCAD has a wonderful new zooming feature called Realtime Zooming. With ZOOM Realtime you can zoom in and out simply by moving the cursor vertically up and down. Take a look at Figure 5.4.

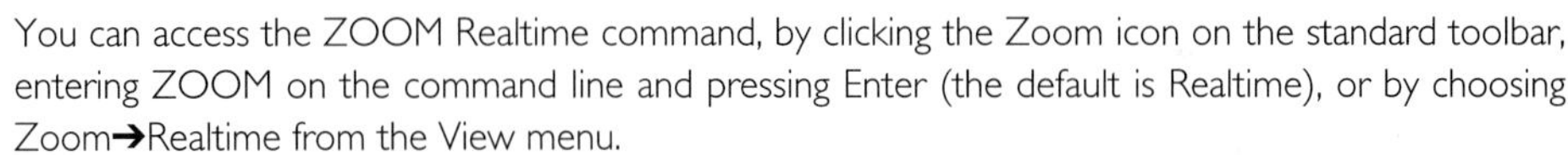

You can access the ZOOM Realtime command, by clicking the Zoom icon on the standard toolbar, entering ZOOM on the command line and pressing Enter (the default is Realtime), or by choosing Zoom→Realtime from the View menu.

If you hold down the pick button at the midpoint of your drawing and then move the cursor up to the top, you will zoom in by 100%(2×). If you do the reverse, you will zoom out by 100%(.5×). The program will cease to display the plus (+) sign when you have enlarged the view to its capacity, and it will no longer display the minus (-) sign when you have shrunk the view to its capacity. Remember, however, that what is being changed isn't the true size of the drawing, just the portion that you get to see on the graphics screen.

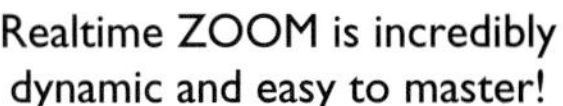

Realtime ZOOM is incredibly dynamic and easy to master!

Other Realtime ZOOM options are available by right-clicking to the cursor menu and choosing the command, while Realtime ZOOM is active.

ZOOM Previous

You can step back up to ten views by restoring the previous view in AutoCAD. Just choose Zoom→Previous from the View menu. You can even step back to the last ZOOM Realtime by using the right-click cursor menu and choosing ZOOM Previous.

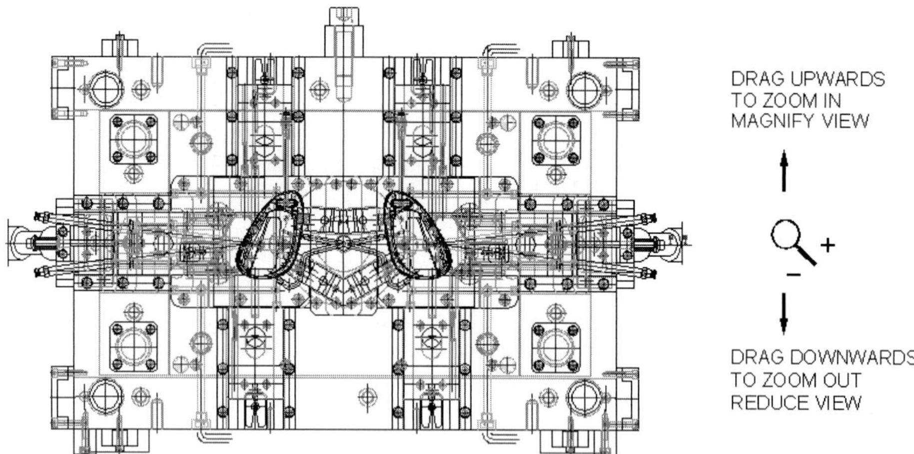

Figure 5.4
Realtime ZOOM In and Out

ZOOM DYNAMIC

The ZOOM DYNAMIC command option creates a separate viewing window where you can change the magnification and location of your view all at one time. You look at the entire drawing and then magically hop to an entirely different place and view by choosing a new viewing window.

The program uses a colorful way to help you make sense of the new viewing window. The extents of the drawing are shown within a solid white or black box. The view that was displayed before you entered ZOOM Dynamic is encased in either green or magenta, and the newly generated zooming area has four red corners. Figure 5.5 shows ZOOM Dynamic.

Tip: Fast Zoom Mode

It is important to understand that some facilities, particularly Realtime ZOOM and PAN and Aerial View Realtime ZOOM and PAN, will not operate unless Fast Zoom mode is on, which it is by default.

To turn Fast Zoom on and off:

1. Type **viewres** at the Command: prompt.
2. Enter y to turn on Fast Zoom and **n** to turn it off.
3. Press Enter.

To use the option, pick the ZOOM Dynamic tool or enter ZOOM, then D, on the command line. The screen will change to display your entire drawing, with a green box showing the area you were currently looking at. A floating window is attached to the cursor. To pan to a different area, move the box over the area to view and press Enter. If you want to change the size of the window, pick on the screen while the window is floating, move the cursor to change the size, and pick again.

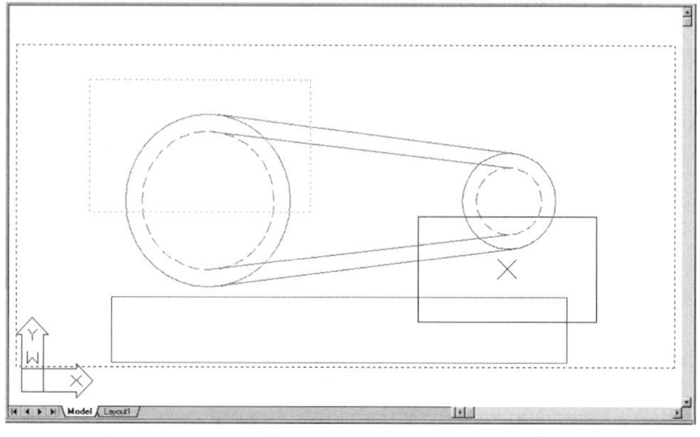

Figure 5.5
ZOOM Dynamic

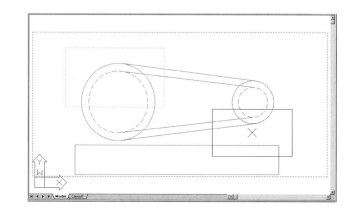

Aerial View

With Fast Zoom mode on, Aerial View displays a view of the drawing in a separate window while working in model space. This view, which you can leave open while you work, allows you to realtime zoom or pan within the drawing without entering a command. The view changes when AutoCAD regenerates a drawing, but zooming or panning within the window doesn't cause a regeneration.

To open Aerial View, choose Aerial View from the View menu. To close, click the upper-right corner of the created window. It's as simple as that.

It's just as easy to zoom in Aerial View. In the aerial view window, choose Zoom from the Mode menu. Then, pick and drag to create a new window. Panning in Aerial View works much the same way. However, when you pick Pan from the Mode menu, the cross-hairs turn into a broken line box that is the same size as the current viewing box. You then drag the box to a new location, or pick and drag for realtime panning. Look at Figure 5.6.

Some of the options in the Aerial View include:

Option	Result
Global	Displays the entire drawing
Zoom In or Out	Increases or decreases the size of the image
Dynamic Update	Turns dynamic updating on or off
Auto Viewport	Turns viewport updating on or off

Saving and Recalling

After doing so much work to arrange the view you want—panning to just the right angle and zooming to the perfect size—you need to be able to save your creation for posterity. You can save paper space views if you are in paper space; you can save single viewports; and you can save the current viewport if you are working in multiple viewports.

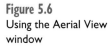

To name and save a view:

1. Choose Named Views from the View menu, type VIEW on the command line, or use the Name Views tool.
2. Choose New in the View dialog box.
3. Enter your name in the New View dialog box. The name can have up to 255 characters including letters, numbers, and three special signs: $, -, and _.
4. You can leave the Current display button checked to save the current view by name. You can also check the Define window button, pick the Define View window, and window in on an area to store as a view.

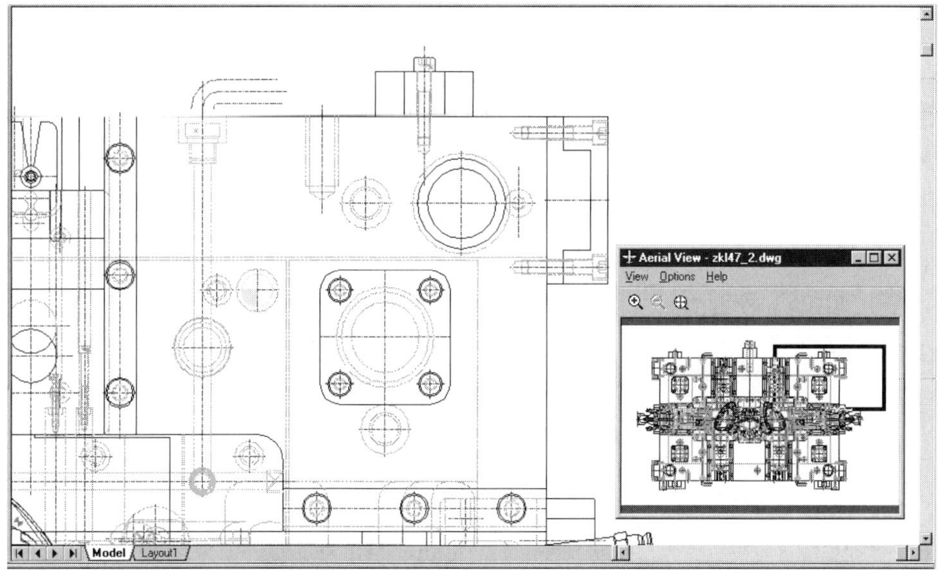

Figure 5.6
Using the Aerial View window

5. Pick the OK button to save the named view.
6. Choose OK in the View Control dialog box.

To make a named view current:

1. Click into the viewport whose view you want to replace.
2. Choose Named Views from the View menu.
3. In the View dialog box, choose the view you want to make current.
4. Select Make Current. Choose OK.

Refer to Figure 5.7 for the View Control dialog box.

Tip: Renaming Views

Objects in your drawing such as views and layers can be renamed. The command RENAME will display a dialog box from which you can select the category of named objects such as View. From the presented items list, you can highlight the item whose name you want to change. The old name will appear in a box below the list. Below the old name, you type in the new name and then press the Rename To: button.

PAN

With PAN Realtime, just a click on the image and a movement of the cursor allows you to pan around the object.

To PAN Realtime, click Pan on the Standard toolbar, enter PAN on the command line, or choose Pan→Realtime from the View menu. When you hold down the pick device on the object around which you want to pan, the panning hand will appear. When you reach the drawing edge, the cursor will display an angle.

REDRAW versus REGEN

The REDRAW command refreshes the current display screen. The REGEN command regenerates the virtual screen buffer from the entire CAD database. If the latter one sounds more complex, you're right, and complexity takes more time. (It's like doing the entire shower and shave rather than just running a comb through your hair and some toothpaste over your teeth.) Sometimes the image is regenerated automatically, but some commands need to be followed by a REGEN command. (We'll tell you about those as we come to them.) If you want to perform the operations on all the viewports and not just the current one, you have to use REDRAWALL or REGENALL.

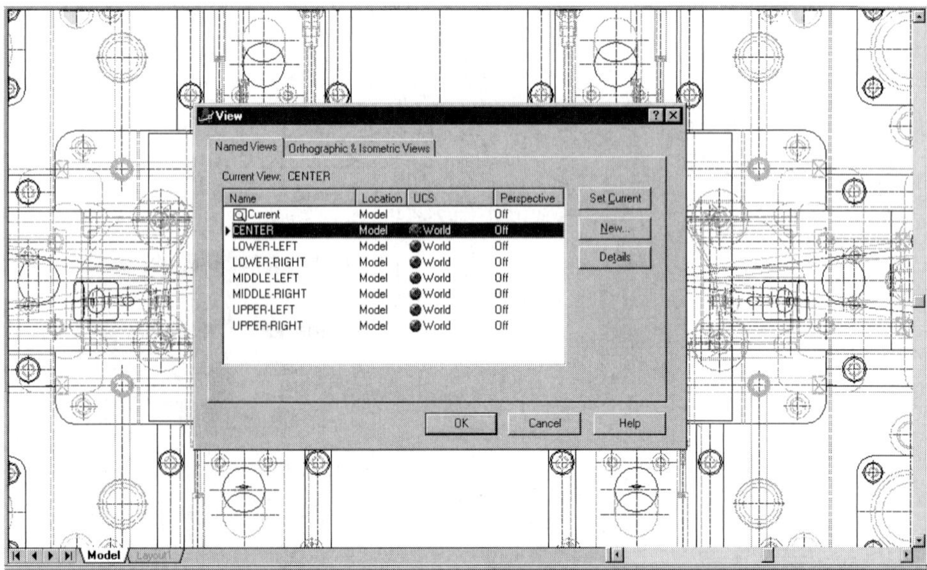

Figure 5.7
View dialog box

If REDRAW is a quick comb of the hair, REGEN is the entire shower!

Hands-On: Using Various Viewing Commands EX5A

1. **Open the Hands-On Exercises dialog box, start Exercise 5A from Chapter 5, and save the drawing as EX5A in your subdirectory. A floor plan should be displayed on your screen.**

ZOOM PREVIOUS

2. **Using the ZOOM WINDOW command, window in on the kitchen area. Zoom closer to the sink area. You can zoom in as close as you like.**
3. **Now use the ZOOM PREVIOUS to reverse your zooming steps. Anytime you've zoomed several times successively, you can use ZOOM PREVIOUS to reverse the process one zoom at a time.**

ZOOM Realtime and PAN Realtime

4. **Using the ZOOM WINDOW command, zoom back in on the kitchen area.**

5. **Select the ZOOM REALTIME command and notice how the cursor changes to a magnifying glass. Pick on the screen and drag upward to increase magnification and downward to decrease magnification. When you release the cursor, the zooming stops. To start zooming again, pick and drag. To stop zooming, press the Esc key.**

6. **Select the PAN REALTIME command. This time the cursor changes to a hand. Pick on the screen and drag the hand. The screen will slide (pan) in the direction you drag. The Esc key exits the command.**

ZOOM DYNAMIC

7. **Zoom in on Bedroom 3.**

8. **Select the ZOOM DYNAMIC command. The screen will change to display a full view of your drawing. There will be a dashed green box showing the area on which you had zoomed in, and a floating window attached to the cursor.**

   Move the window/cursor until it encloses Bedroom 2 and then press Enter. The screen now shows the view of Bedroom 2. In this way, you can pan to any area of your drawing.

9. **Enter the ZOOM DYNAMIC command again. This time move the window/cursor over the kitchen area but *don't* press Enter. Pick on the screen and drag your cursor slowly back and forth (right and left). The window/cursor changes size allowing you to change the magnification. Pick on the screen again to lock the size. Move the window/cursor to a new location and press Enter to display the view. Using these options you can pan and zoom at the same time.**

Aerial View

10. **Select Aerial View from the View pull-down menu. A small window will appear on your screen showing the total view of your drawing.**

Hands-On: Using Various Viewing Commands EX5A (continued)

The aerial view is similar to the ZOOM DYNAMIC command except the total view of your drawings stays on the screen all the time. This is useful if your screen is large enough to display both your drawing and the aerial view. If you have a smaller screen, you may opt to use the ZOOM DYNAMIC command.

⑪ **When the aerial view is displayed, you can window in on an area inside the aerial view and the corresponding view will appear on the screen. Experiment with this process. Try using the other tools in the Aerial View window and see what happens.**

Close the Aerial View window when you have finished experimenting.

Named Views

⑫ **You can save and restore any view (magnification and location) you display on the screen. Select the Named Views tool and a dialog box will appear. In this exercise various views have already been created.**

At any time you can turn the Current view into a Named view just by picking the New button. Try this now and name the view MYVIEW.

When you return to the View Control dialog box, highlight the view Garage, pick the Set Current button, and then pick the OK button. The view of the garage will be displayed.

Now do the same but this time restore MYVIEW. See how easy it is?

Experiment by displaying different views around the house.

Layers

Many things have multiple layers—an onion, people's personalities, that really good salsa dip some people make for parties; layers add a depth and complexity that couldn't have existed otherwise. The same can be said of an AutoCAD drawing. We put things on different layers in drawings because it is the nature of drawing and design that the pictorial display is a very busy area with many intersecting lines that are difficult to follow. When this drawing is placed on a variety of layers, it is easy to isolate one particular aspect in order to edit it, or simply to view it.

For instance, it is very difficult to edit a drawing's geometry when all the hatch lines are visible. If you place the hatch lines on a different layer in a mechanical drawing, you can turn that layer off while you edit the drawing. Or, in an architectural drawing, you can isolate plumbing, heating, and electrical systems.

Tip : Multiple Layers
You can also add multiple layers by entering a new name in the list of layers and then following the name with a comma. Every time you enter a comma, the new name is added to the layer list.

Layer Options and Their Icons

There are quite a few Layer options used to manipulate your drawing. Some of these are hidden from view when the Layer Properties Manager dialog box is displayed. You can get access to all the options by using the Show Details button. Some items may be greyed out because you cannot use them until certain conditions are met. The following is a description of the most common Layer options:

On/Off If you turn off a layer, it is not displayed or plotted; however, it is still regenerated as part of the drawing. The advantage is that if you are moving quickly between visible and invisible layers you don't have to regenerate the drawing as you do every time you thaw a layer.

To turn a layer on or off:

1. Format menu➔Layer (choose Layer from the Format menu).
2. Layer Properties Manager dialog box➔layers upon which you want to act (select the layers you want to influence from the Layer Properties Manager dialog box). Use Select All on the cursor context menu if you want to select all of the layers. (See Figure 5.8.)
3. Click the On/Off icon.
4. OK (choose OK).

Thaw/Freeze If you freeze a layer, it does not display, plot, or regenerate the layer until it has been thawed. So, don't freeze and thaw layers frequently, the way you can turn them on and off. The major advantage of freezing a layer is that it speeds up the operation of such things as zoom and pan.

Tip: Manipulating Layers

You can also turn layers on and off, freeze and thaw layers, and lock and unlock layers from the Object Properties toolbar using the Layer Control list. Just click on the appropriate icon for each layer. (See Figure 5.9.)

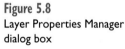

To freeze or thaw a layer:

1. Format Menu➔Layer (choose Layer from the Format menu).
2. Layer Properties Manager dialog box➔layers upon which you want to act.
3. Click Freeze/Thaw icon.
4. OK (choose OK).

Figure 5.8
Layer Properties Manager dialog box

Lock/Unlock The objects on a locked layer are still visible; however, they cannot be edited. This is useful when you want to edit objects on other layers while continuing to see the other objects.

To lock or unlock a layer:

1. Format menu➔Layer (choose Layer from the Format menu).
2. Layer Properties Manager dialog box➔layers upon which you want to act.
3. Click Lock/Unlock icon.
4. OK (choose OK).

Plot/Do Not Plot You can cause objects on individual layers not to plot. This can be useful when you have objects used to lay out the drawing but do not want to have them plotted out on paper.

Layer Control List Use the Layer Properties Manager dialog box when you want to create layers, but use the Layer Control list when you want to switch between layers. To use the Layer Control list, pick on the list and a list of layers is pulled down onto the screen (see Figure 5.9). If you pick on one of the names, it will become the current layer on which to draw. To change the state of a layer, pick on the appropriate tool beside the layer. For instance, if the layer named *Wall* was frozen, pick on the snowflake symbol and it will change to a sun, thawing the layer. Then, when you exit the list, the change will occur.

Tip: Changing an Object's Layer to Match Another Object

To make your job of making corrections easier, there is a command that will take a source object and change any other object's properties to match the source. This can be very useful when you create something on the wrong layer and want to switch it to the correct layer. The process is as follows:

Command: **MATCHPROP**
Select Source Object: **Pick object to use as the source for the properties**
Current active settings = color layer ltype ltscale thickness text dim hatch
Settings/<Select Destination Object(s)>: **Pick on the objects you want to change and press Enter, or you can enter S to adjust the properties to change**

Figure 5.9
Layer Control list

Hands-On: Layer Options EX5B

1. **Open the Hands-On Exercises dialog box, start Exercise 5B from Chapter 5, and save the drawing as EX5B in your subdirectory. A floor plan should be displayed on your screen.**

Layer Freeze and Thaw

2. **Open the Layers Properties Manager dialog box and make sure that the Instant-AutoCAD layer is current.**
3. **Right-click over the list of layer names and a small Context menu will appear. Pick on the Select All item. This will highlight all the layers in the list.**

   Pick on any of the sun icons. A message will appear stating you cannot freeze the current layer. OK this box and you will notice that all the suns have been replaced with snowflakes, freezing all the layers except the Instant-AutoCAD layer that was current.

   Click OK to exit this dialog box and the display will be empty except for the Instant-AutoCAD border and text.
4. **Using the Layer Control list, thaw the Wall layer by picking on the corresponding snowflake, turning it into a sun. Pick on the screen to exit from the list and the walls should appear.**
5. **Repeat for the other layers.**

Layer Lock and Unlock

6. **You may have noticed that all the layers have been locked. Using the ERASE command, try to erase anything from a locked layer. You will find that you cannot even select an object on a locked layer. This protects objects from being changed accidentally.**
7. **Unlock the Fixture layer using the Layer Control list. Pick in the Lock icon to display it in an unlocked position.**
8. **Now try to erase one of the water closets (toilets) from one of the bathrooms. It should work this time.**
9. **Make sure you undo any erasures you may have performed.**

In a Nutshell

Well, now that you know how to look at things in the world of AutoCAD, let us see how your knowledge of AutoCAD has grown.

Testing... testing... 1, 2, 3

Matching

Match the colors to the appropriate sections of the ZOOM Dynamic viewing window.

ZOOM Dynamic Views	Colors
___1. Newly generated viewing area	a. black or white
___2. Extents of the drawing	b. four red corners
___3. View previous to ZOOM Dynamic	c. green or magenta

Fill in the blanks.

1. Name the following options of the Aerial View option.
   a. __________ displays the entire drawing.
   b. __________ turns dynamic updating on or off.
   c. __________ turns viewport updating on or off.
   d. __________ increases or decreases the size of the image.
2. In Tilemode __________ you can only work within __________ space.
3. In the PAN command, the crosshair cursor is replaced with a(n) __________.
4. The __________ command refreshes the graphics screen whereas the __________ command recreates the drawing from the AutoCAD database.

Multiple Choice

Choose the best answer to complete each of the following statements:

1. A layer that is frozen is still
   a. visible.
   b. able to be edited.
   c. able to be plotted.
   d. all of the above
   e. none of the above
2. A layer that is locked is still
   a. visible.
   b. able to be edited.
   c. frozen.
   d. all of the above
   e. none of the above
3. When you wish to switch between layers use
   a. the Layers Properties Manager dialog box.
   b. the Layer Control list.
   c. the Layer Control dialog box.
   d. none of the above
   e. a and c

What?

1. Explain the difference between turning off a layer, locking a layer, and freezing a layer. Name a circumstance under which you would use each to your benefit.

   ____
   ____
   ____
   ____
   ____
   ____

2. Why would you use REGEN rather than REDRAW?

   ____
   ____

3. Explain the procedure for returning to model space.

   ____
   ____

4. List the procedure for accessing Realtime ZOOM. What happens?

____

____

5. What is the advantage of having Aerial View turned on?

____

____

6. What is the purpose of Fast Zoom?

____

____

Let's Get Busy!

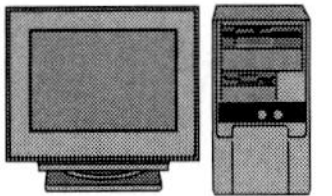

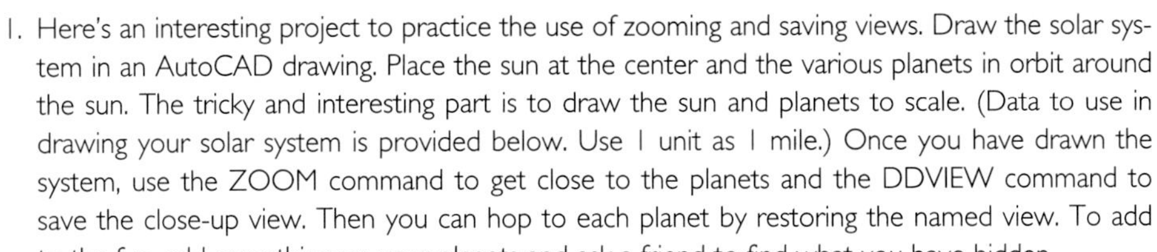

1. Here's an interesting project to practice the use of zooming and saving views. Draw the solar system in an AutoCAD drawing. Place the sun at the center and the various planets in orbit around the sun. The tricky and interesting part is to draw the sun and planets to scale. (Data to use in drawing your solar system is provided below. Use 1 unit as 1 mile.) Once you have drawn the system, use the ZOOM command to get close to the planets and the DDVIEW command to save the close-up view. Then you can hop to each planet by restoring the named view. To add to the fun, add something on your planets and ask a friend to find what you have hidden.

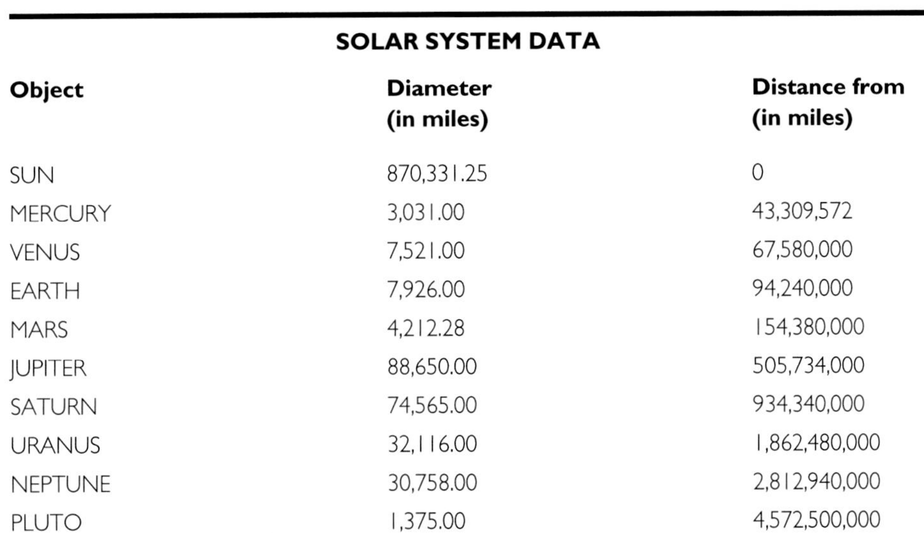

SOLAR SYSTEM DATA

Object	**Diameter (in miles)**	**Distance from (in miles)**
SUN	870,331.25	0
MERCURY	3,031.00	43,309,572
VENUS	7,521.00	67,580,000
EARTH	7,926.00	94,240,000
MARS	4,212.28	154,380,000
JUPITER	88,650.00	505,734,000
SATURN	74,565.00	934,340,000
URANUS	32,116.00	1,862,480,000
NEPTUNE	30,758.00	2,812,940,000
PLUTO	1,375.00	4,572,500,000

If you have trouble, find the file called SOLAR.DWG located on the CD-ROM. It has the solar system drawn for you with pre-named views.

Part VIII Electronics Workbench/MultiSIM

MultiSIM

1 Introduction to MultiSIM

2 Power Supply Circuits

3 The Transistor Amplifier

4 Operational Amplifiers

5 Digital Logic Circuitry

Lab 1

Introduction to MultiSIM

MultiSIM

Performance Objectives

Upon completion of this exercise, you will be able to

1. Discuss the advantages of electronic simulation.
2. Explain how a circuit can be setup and simulated with Electronics Workbench (multiSIM).

Background Information

The purpose of this exercise is to examine the features of an electronic circuit simulation application called Electronics Workbench (or simply multiSIM). With this application, you can setup a virtual electronic circuit, complete with a power source, resistors, capacitors, switches, indicator lights, or even transistors and integrated circuits. After completing the schematic of the circuit, you can also connect different virtual instruments as well, such as voltmeters, ammeters, or even an oscilloscope for viewing waveforms. Then, with the click of a button, actually simulate the electronic circuit, in real time. The results of the simulation are very accurate, practically eliminating the need to setup a real circuit in a laboratory, or wire it up on a circuit board. Plus, the entire circuit can be saved as a file and loaded and worked with again at later time. It is not so easy to leave a circuit unattended on a laboratory workbench. Furthermore, the price of a single copy of Electronics Workbench is much less than the cost of the instruments and supplies required for an actual laboratory workbench, and the virtual instruments will not go out of calibration like their real-world counterparts.

Part I: Getting Started

Figure I.1 shows a screen shot of the multiSIM simulation window. A simple series circuit is being simulated. The ammeter indicates 5.000 mA of current is flowing.

The title bar of the window contains the name of the circuit file being simulated (Circuit1). The rocker switch near the upper right corner of the circuit window is used to start and stop the simulation. While the simulation is running, the simulation time is displayed in the status area at the bottom of the simulation window.

Down the left side of the simulation window are 14 buttons that provide access to the built-in parts bins containing all of the components that can be used to construct a circuit. Holding the mouse pointer still over a button will cause a small pop-up window to appear showing the name of the parts bin (such as Sources, Diodes, or Indicators).

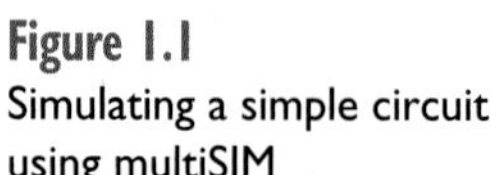

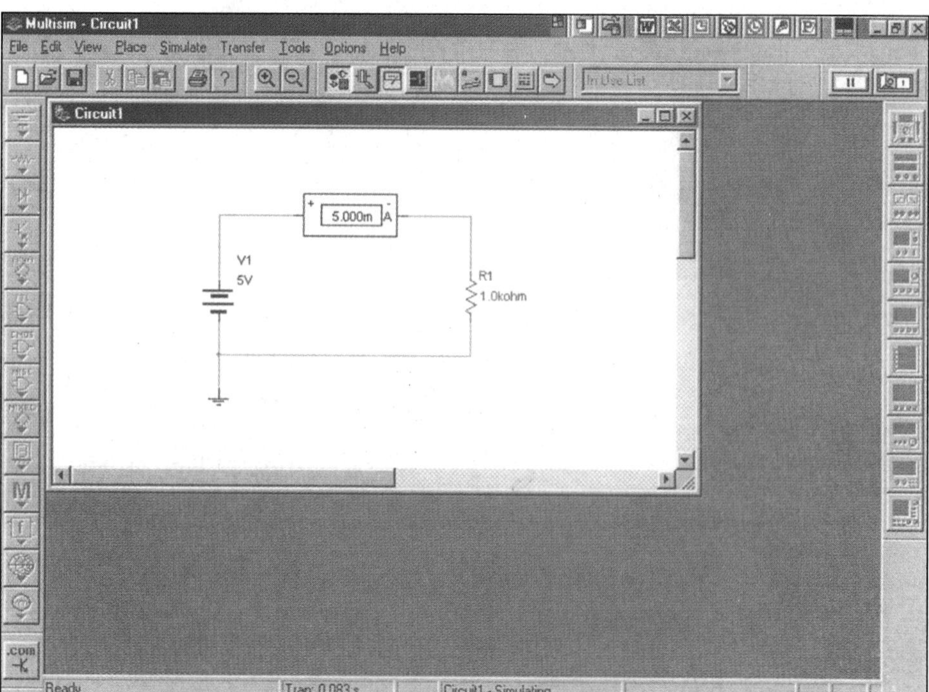

Figure I.1
Simulating a simple circuit using multiSIM

Normally, multiSIM colors components of a circuit based on their properties. For example, active components such as transistors are colored green, whereas passive components (resistors, capacitors) are colored blue. Wires are usually colored black. You can change the assigned colors, or select a different color scheme for the background (black on white, white on black, etc.). This is accomplished by left-clicking Edit and then User Preferences to get to the color selection window. For the purposes of discussion in this exercise, all components are colored black.

Placing Components

Components are placed in the circuit window by selecting them from the desired parts pin and then left-clicking on the desired screen position. When the mouse pointer moves over a parts bin button, the parts bin will automatically pop up and allow you to choose a component. For example, to select and place a DC voltage source, do the following:

1. Move the mouse pointer over the Source button (the top button on the left side of the simulation window).
2. After the parts bin pops up, move the mouse pointer over the icon for the DC voltage source (the second icon in the first column) and left-click once.
3. The mouse pointer will change to indicate you are in the middle of a placement operation. Move the mouse pointer to the location where you would like the DC source and left-click again to place the source on the screen.

Figure 1.2 shows the DC source after it has been placed. Note that its voltage is automatically set to 12 V. It is often necessary to change the voltage value of the source. To do this, left double-click on the DC source. The Battery properties window will open up, as shown in Figure 1.3. Enter '5' in the Voltage box and click OK.

Adding a Resistor

Choose a resistor from the Basic parts bin (the second button down on the left side of the simulation window). The resistor icon is the first icon in the first column.

The properties window for the resistor opens up automatically when the resistor is selected. This window is shown in Figure 1.4. It is necessary to change the value of the resistor before it is placed. This is done by selecting the desired ohm amount in the Component List. Set the resistor value to 1.0 K ohms and then place it in the circuit window. To change the value of a resistor after it has been placed, left double-click on it to bring up the properties window and then choose Replace.

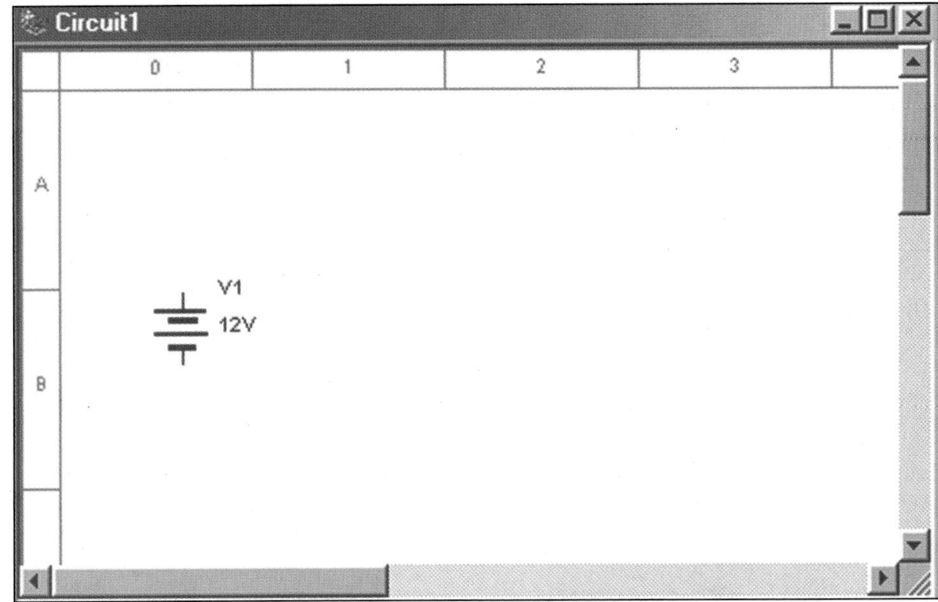

Figure 1.2
Placing a DC voltage source

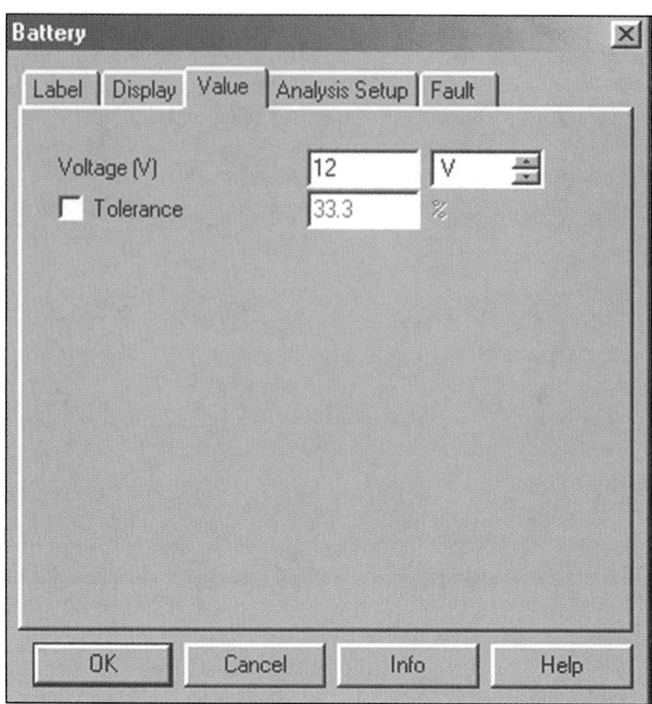

Figure 1.3
Battery properties

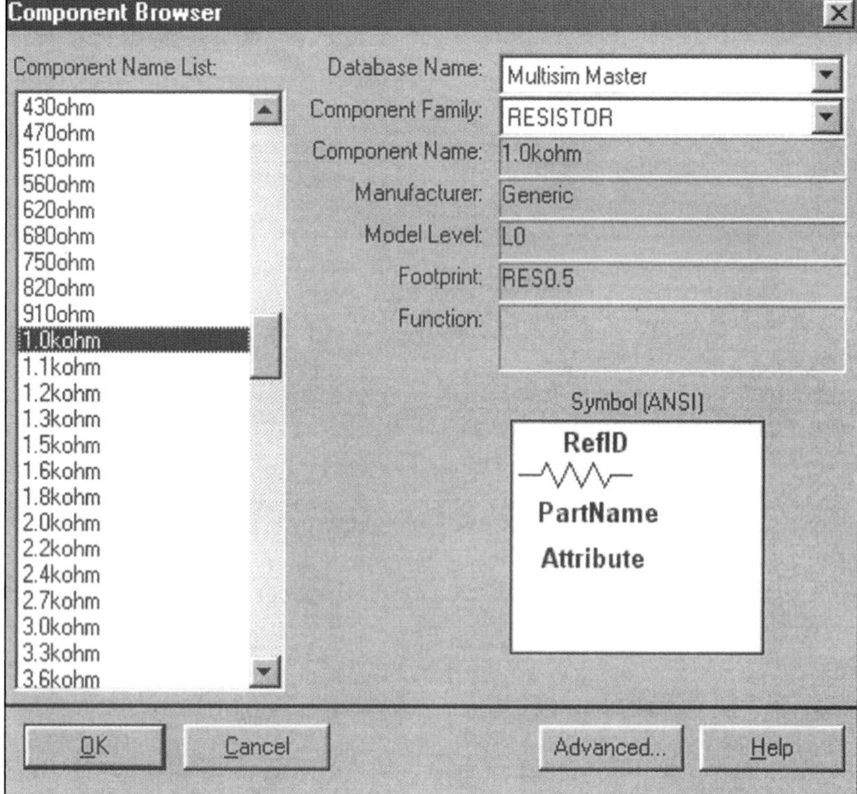

Figure 1.4
Setting the resistor properties

The resistor is oriented horizontally after placement, as indicated in Figure 1.5. To change its orientation to vertical, select the resistor with a single mouse click and then press Control-R on the keyboard to rotate it. Note that the component identifier (R1) and its value (1.0kohm) will also move around when the resistor is rotated. If necessary, grab the identifier or value (left click and hold) and drag it to the desired location and release the left mouse button.

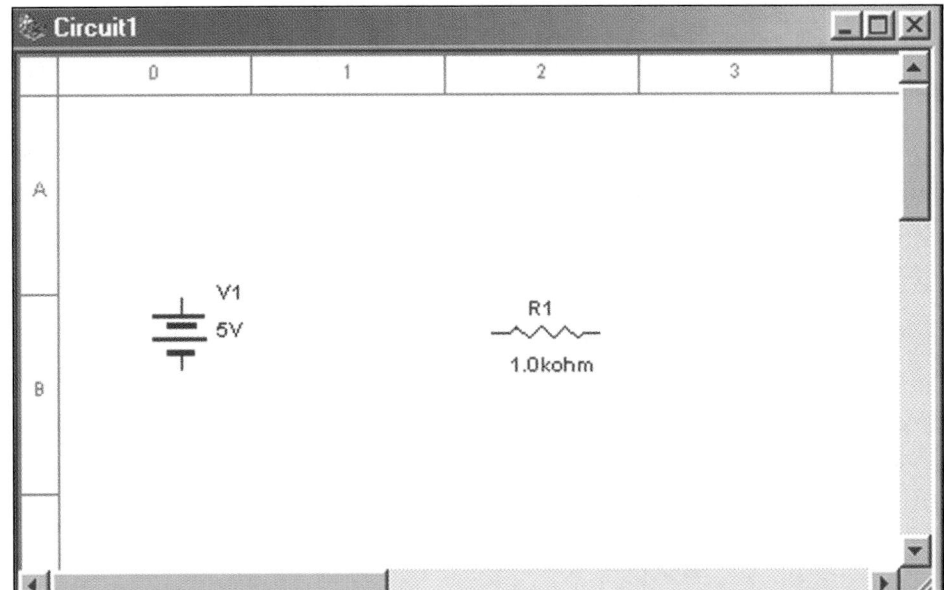

Figure 1.5
Placing a resistor

Adding a Voltmeter

Voltmeters are used to measure voltage. They must be connected in parallel to work properly. The voltmeter is found in the Indicators parts bin (the button with the red figure 8 on it, the fifth button from the bottom). It is the first icon in the first column (it has a V in it). When the voltmeter is selected, it properties window will automatically open up. Choose the VOLTMETER_V setting to orient the voltmeter vertically. Figure 1.6 shows the resulting circuit window after the voltmeter is placed.

Note that a component may not be in the exact position where you want it after placing it. To move the component, grab it and drag it to the new location.

Adding an Ammeter

Ammeters are used to measure current and must be connected in series. Select an ammeter from the Indicators parts bin (it has an A in it) and place it on the screen as indicated in Figure 1.7.

Now that we have placed all the components for our circuit we must connect them with wires.

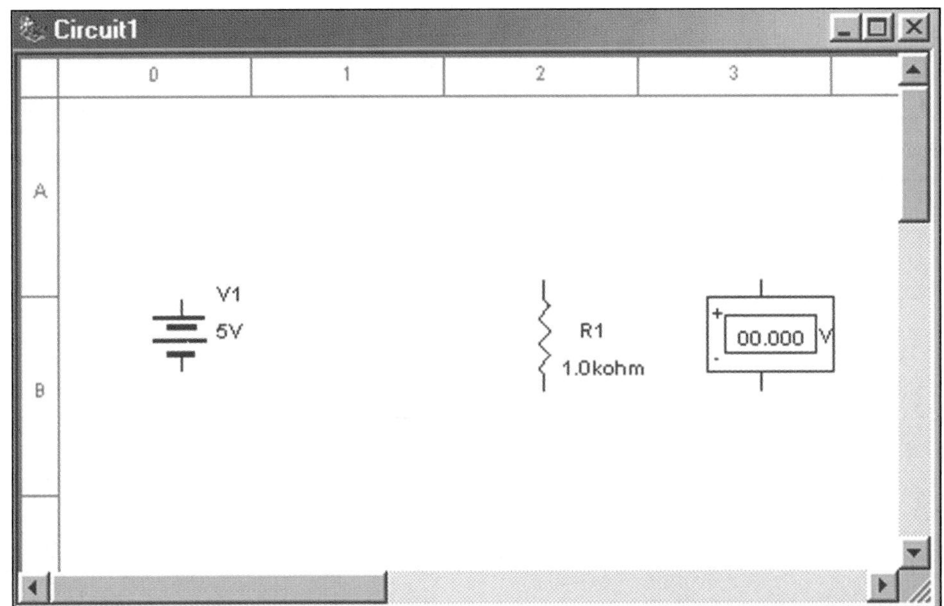

Figure 1.6
Adding a voltmeter

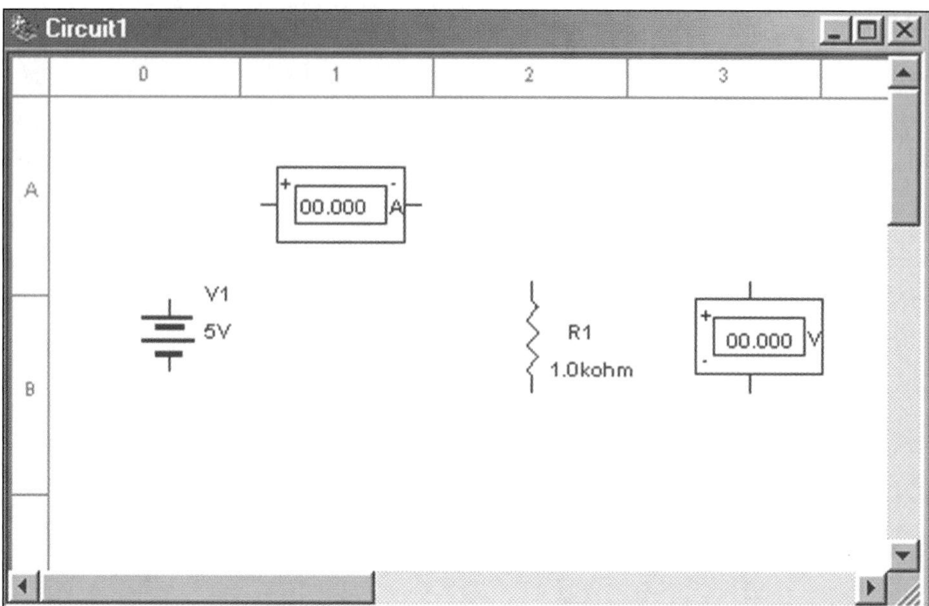

Figure 1.7
Adding an ammeter

Adding Wires

To add a wire to the circuit, move the mouse pointer over the component terminal and left click once. This sets the starting point of the wire. Then move the mouse pointer to the location for the ending point of the wire. As you do this, a dashed line representing the wire will appear and follow the mouse pointer around. Left click again to make the second wire connection. This process is illustrated in Figure 1.8.

If you make a mistake adding a wire, or simply want to delete a wire that has already been added, move the mouse pointer over the wire, right click on it and choose Delete from the pop-up menu. If you are in the middle of adding a wire, right clicking will erase it. Also, there will be times when it is difficult to connect a wire to a component that already has a wire connected to it. In this case, drag the connected wire to make it longer to give more room for an additional connection. Left click once on the wire to select it, then drag portions of the wire to adjust it.

Add the remaining wires to the circuit so that it looks like Figure 1.9.

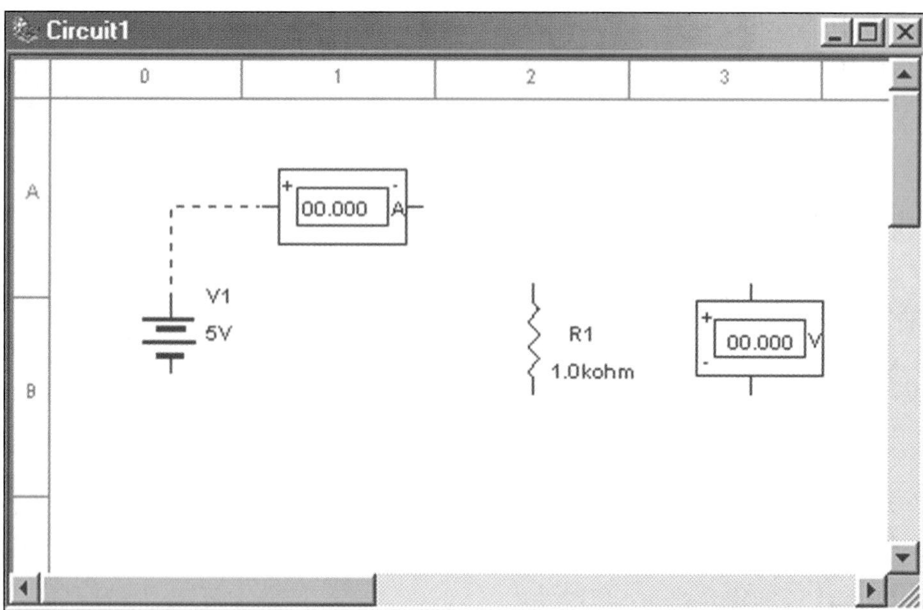

Figure 1.8
Adding a wire

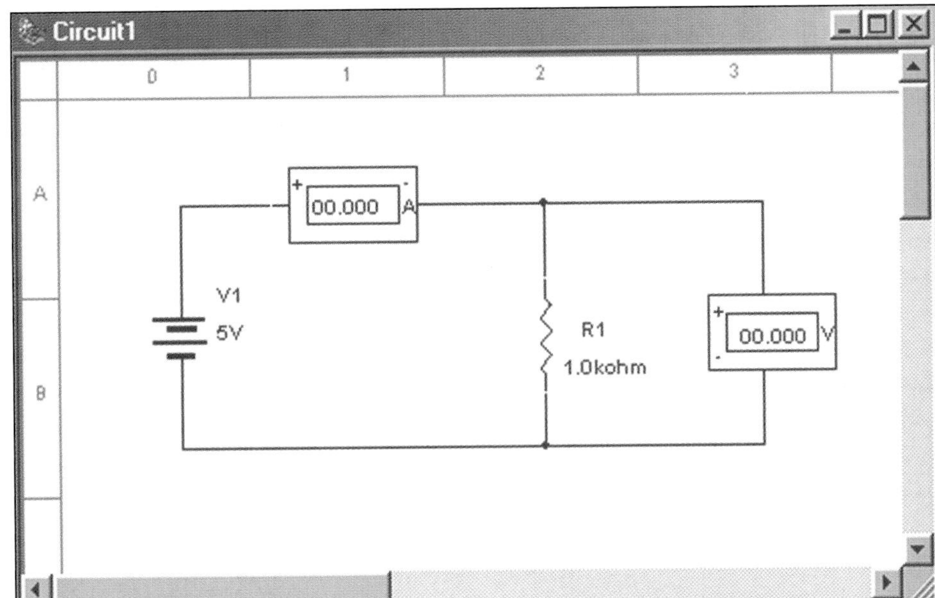

Figure 1.9
All wires have been added to the circuit

Adding a Ground Terminal

Most circuits require a *ground* connection to properly simulate. The ground symbol is found in the Sources parts bin (the first icon in the first column) and is usually connected to the negative side of the voltage source. Figure 1.10 shows the final circuit with the ground terminal included.

Simulating the Circuit

The circuit can be simulated by left clicking the power switch. The results are indicated by the numbers displayed in the voltmeter and ammeter, as indicated in Figure 1.11. The circuit can be saved by choosing Save from the File menu, or by clicking on the icon of a floppy disk near the upper left corner of the simulation window. In a similar fashion, you can also load a circuit that has been previously saved.

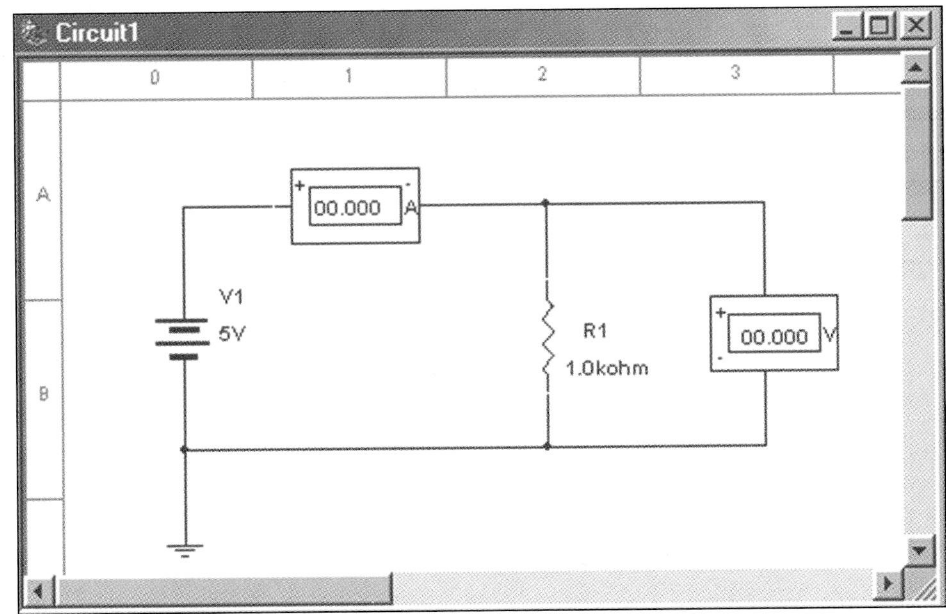

Figure 1.10
Adding the ground terminal

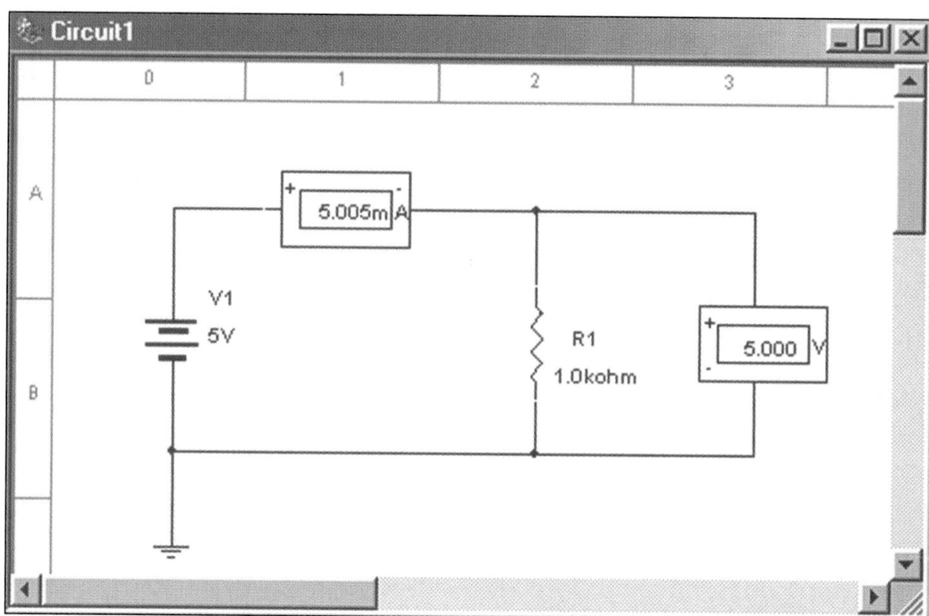

Figure I.11
The results of the simulation

The Two-Resistor Series Circuit

Figure I.12 shows a two-resistor series circuit. You will setup and simulate this circuit, as well as the remaining ones in this exercise, when you perform the Familiarization Activity.

One characteristic of a series circuit is that the voltages measured across each resistor add up to the supply voltage. The voltmeter values in Figure I.12 (4.002 V and 5.998 V) indicate that this is true. Another characteristic of a series circuit is that each resistor has the same current flowing through it (there is only one current in a series circuit). If you multiply the circuit current (2.004 mA, which equals 0.002004 A) by the individual resistor values (2.0 K ohms and 3.0 K ohms, or 2000 ohms and 3000 ohms) you will get the indicated voltage values.

The Two-Resistor Parallel Circuit

The same two resistors from the series circuit in Figure I.12 can be connected differently to form a two-resistor parallel circuit. This type of circuit is shown in Figure I.13.

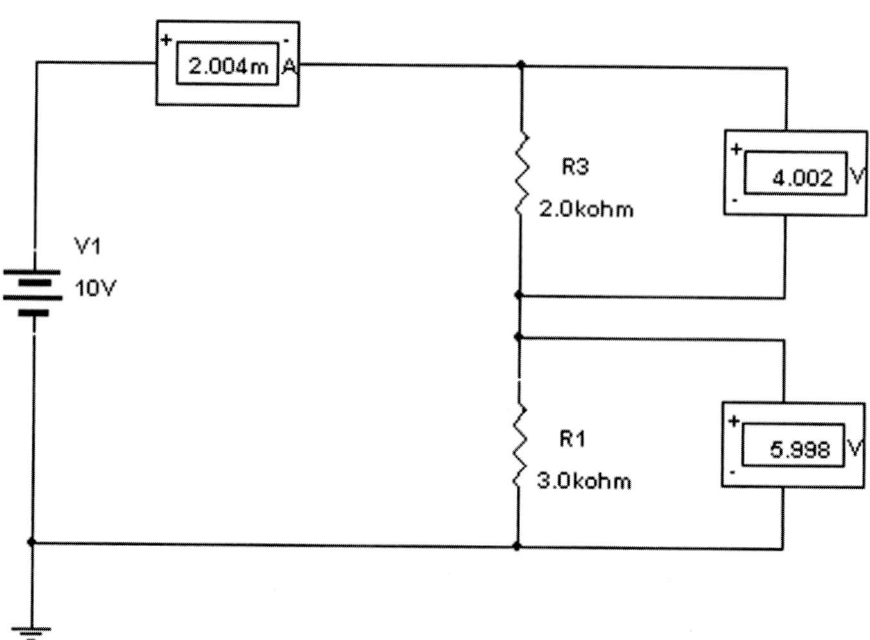

Figure I.12
Two-resistor series circuit

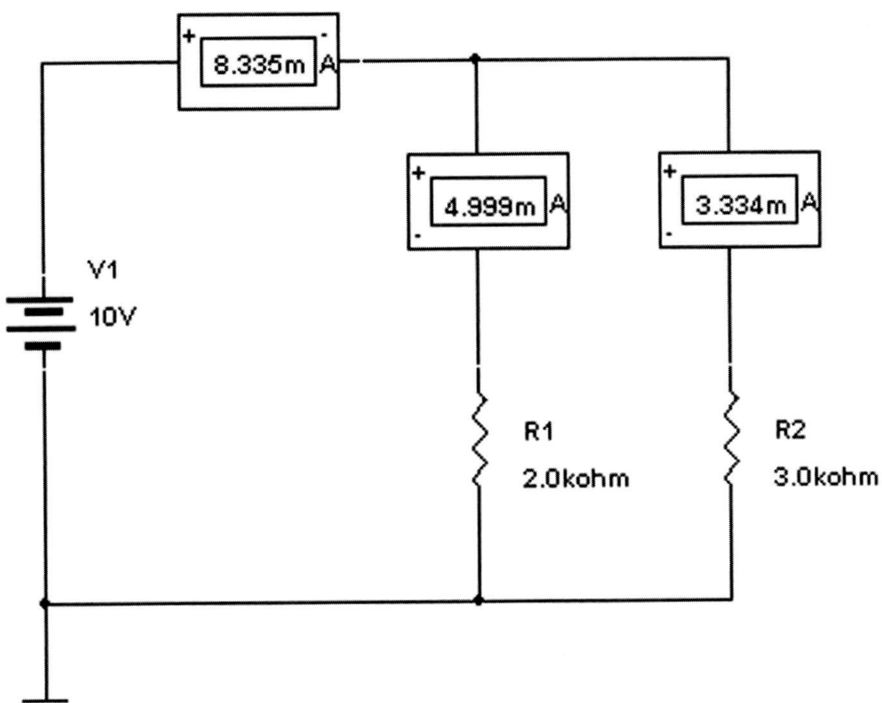

Figure 1.13
Two-resistor parallel circuit

Note that three ammeters are used to measure the circuit currents, and that each ammeter has a different current measurement displayed. Furthermore, the sums of the currents through R1 and R2 add up to the current in the ammeter at the top of the circuit. This is an important characteristic of parallel circuits. The sum of the individual resistor currents (also called *branch* currents) add up to the current supplied by the voltage source.

Another characteristic of a parallel circuit is that there is only one voltage present (10 V in this case). If you divide 10 V by the value of R1 (2000 ohms), you get 0.005 A (5 mA). Note that the ammeter for R1's branch measures 4.999 mA. Check the current in R2 using this same method. You should get 3.333 mA.

Part II: Adding a New Twist: Time

The DC voltage source, together with a resistive circuit, produces a steady current that does not change. There are, however, other electrical and electronic components that have characteristics that produce a time varying change in voltage or current. One of these components is the capacitor.

The Capacitor

The capacitor is essentially used to store electrical energy. When a capacitor is connected in series with a resistor and a DC voltage source, as indicated in Figure 1.14, the capacitor 'charges' from 0 V to the DC supply voltage (10 V in this case) over a certain period of time. This time is based on the time constant of the R-C circuit. The time constant equals the product of R and C. For the circuit in Figure 1.14, the time constant is 4.7 K ohms times 5.1 micro-Farads, or just under 24 milli-seconds (0.024 seconds). The capacitor will become fully charged after five time constants, which equals 120 milli-seconds. Because the capacitor voltage is constantly changing (causing a change in current as well), it is not appropriate to measure the capacitor voltage with a voltmeter. Instead, an instrument called an oscilloscope is used.

The Oscilloscope

The oscilloscope is an instrument that is used to display a voltage waveform. Refer back to Figure 1.1. There is a group of nine large buttons across the top of the simulation window. Left clicking on the third button from the left opens up the Instruments window shown in Figure 1.15. Any technician would be jealous of the instruments provided by multiSIM, since many of them are typically

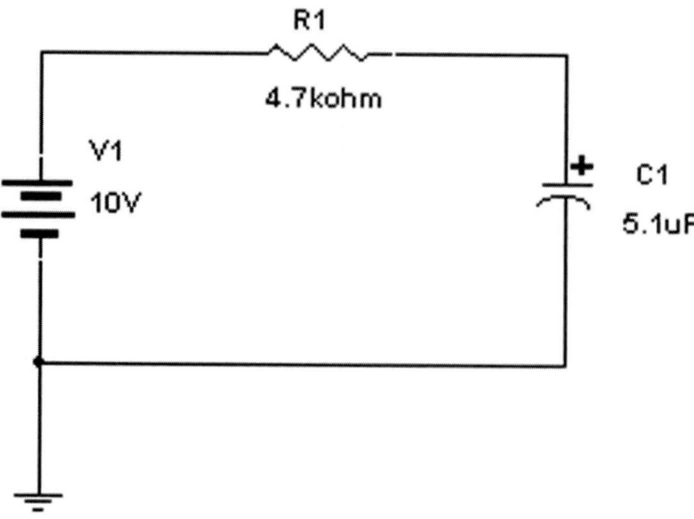

Figure 1.14
Resistor-capacitor charging circuit

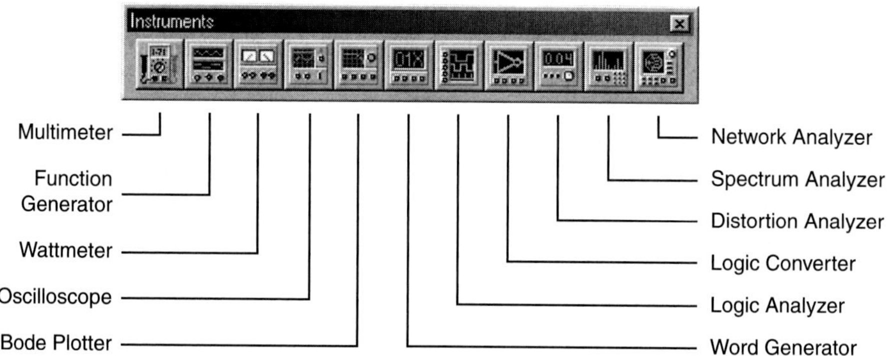

Figure 1.15
Instruments available in multiSIM

very expensive.

The oscilloscope is very useful for displaying time-varying waveforms. The oscilloscope provided by multiSIM has two channels, each capable of displaying its own waveform. Figure 1.16 shows how the oscilloscope is connected to the R-C circuit. Notice that the DC voltage source has been replaced by an AC square wave source set to 10 V and a frequency of 5 Hz. This means that the source will output 10 V for 100 milli-seconds, and 0 V for 100 milli-seconds. This will allow the capacitor to charge for 100 milli-seconds and discharge for 100 milli-seconds, over and over again. This effect will be captured with the oscilloscope.

To view the oscilloscope controls, left double-click the oscilloscope and it will open up into the instrument panel shown in Figure 1.17. The Timebase Scale (currently 10 ms/Div) controls how much time passes between horizontal divisions on the display screen. The Channel A and Channel B Scale values (both set to 5 V/Div) control the vertical size of the waveform as it is displayed.

Simulate the circuit for a few seconds and watch what happens on the oscilloscope display. Then stop the display and use the horizontal scroll bar in the oscilloscope display window to view the waveform over time. Figure 1.18 shows a sample display. Experiment with the vertical settings (V/Div and Y position) to get the desired display.

Capacitive Reactance

When an AC signal is applied to a capacitor, it exhibits opposition to current similar to resistance, but the amount of opposition depends on the frequency of the AC signal. This opposition is called capacitive reactance. To determine the reactance of a capacitor, divide the voltage across the capacitor by the current through it. Figure 1.19 shows a 1 micro-Farad capacitor being operated at 5000 Hz. Dividing the capacitor voltage (0.225 V) by the circuit current (7.071 mA) gives 31.8 ohms of capacitive reactance. Note that the voltmeter and ammeter must be changed to read AC values. This is accomplished by left double-clicking on the meter, and then choosing the AC mode from the Value tab.

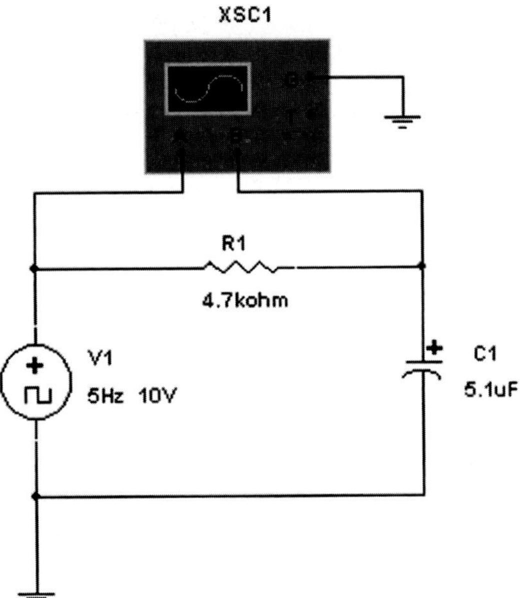

Figure I.16
Using the oscilloscope

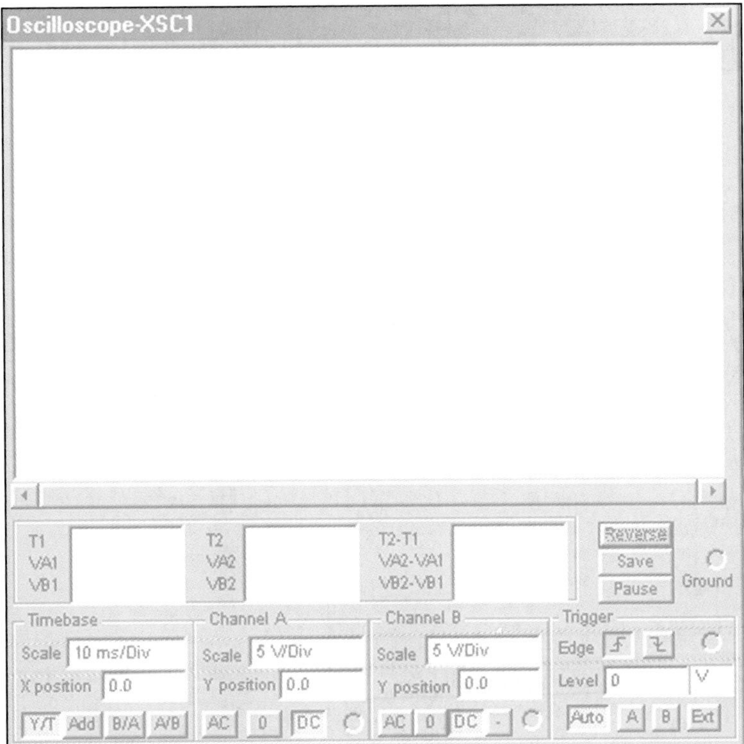

Figure I.17
The oscilloscope controls

Part III: Special Components

In this last part we examine the operation of four additional components. Three of these components are called semiconductors, due to the special way they must be operated. These are the diode, transistor, and light emitting diode. Before looking at these components, let us take a look at one more AC component, the transformer.

The Transformer

The transformer is an AC device that relies on magnetic fields to couple a signal from the input side (the primary) to the output side (the secondary). The number of turns of wire in the primary and

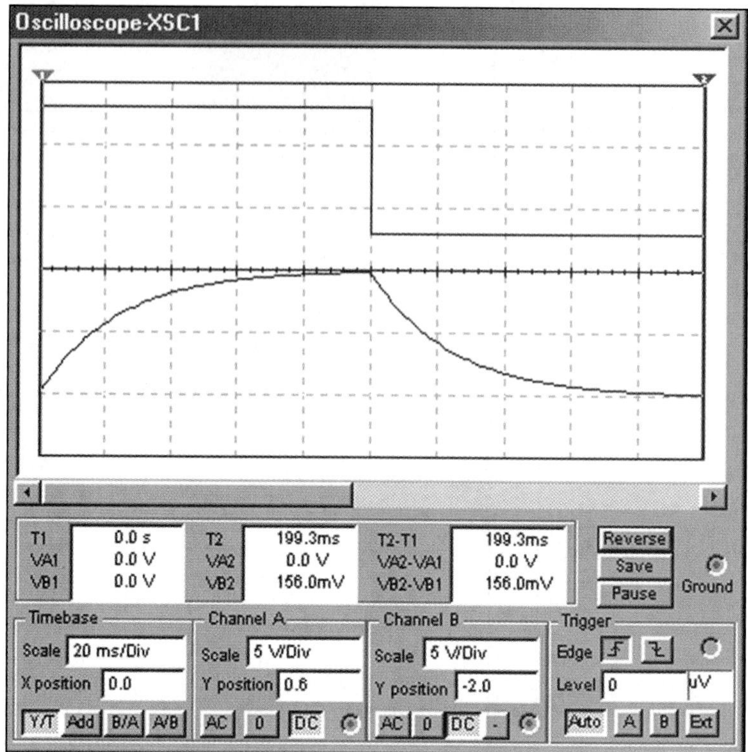

Figure 1.18
R-C charge/discharge waveforms

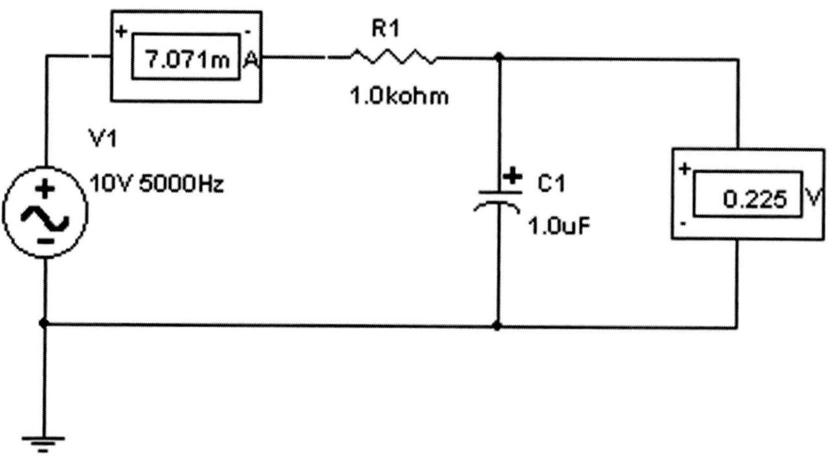

Figure 1.19
R-C circuit with AC voltage source

secondary determine if the output voltage is higher (a step-up transformer) or lower (a step-down transformer) than the input voltage.

Figure 1.20 shows a simple step-down transformer circuit. The input voltage of 10 V (7.07 VAC) is stepped down to 0.616 VAC. The number of turns in the primary of the transformer is 141. The secondary contains 1622 turns (this information is available in the transformer menu that pops up when a transformer is selected). Dividing 1622 by 141 gives 11.5. Thus, the *turns ratio* of the transformer is 11.5 to 1. So, dividing the input voltage of 7.07 VAC by 11.5 gives 0.615 VAC, practically the same result found during simulation.

Transformers are used in power supplies to help convert the high voltage 120 VAC from the wall outlet to a lower AC voltage that can be rectified (by a diode) and regulated.

The Diode

The diode is the most basic type of semiconductor, containing a single P-N junction. An important property of the diode is that it only allows current to pass through it in one direction. This happens

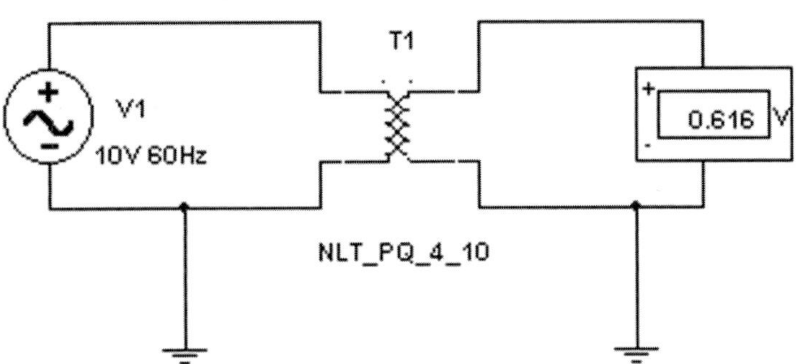

Figure I.20
Step-down transformer

when the diode is *forward biased*. This means that the anode of the diode is more positive than the cathode. Figure I.21 shows two diode circuits. In Figure I.21(a) the diode is forward biased and is conducting current. The anode (the triangular part) is 0.7 V more positive than the cathode.

In Figure I.21(b) the diode is *reversed biased*. Notice that no current is flowing now (the 1.77 micro-ampere reading is considered to be zero current) and that the resistor voltage is practically zero (10 nano-volts). This property of the diode makes it useful in circuits called rectifiers, where an AC voltage is converted into a pulsating DC voltage through the action of a diode.

The Transistor

The transistor is essentially a current amplifier. A small amount of input current is able to control a large amount of output current. The simple transistor biasing circuit shown in Figure I.22 indicates that an input current of 89 micro-amperes produces an output current of 4.489 mA. This is a current gain of 50.4. An individual transistor may have a current gain anywhere from 20 to 300.

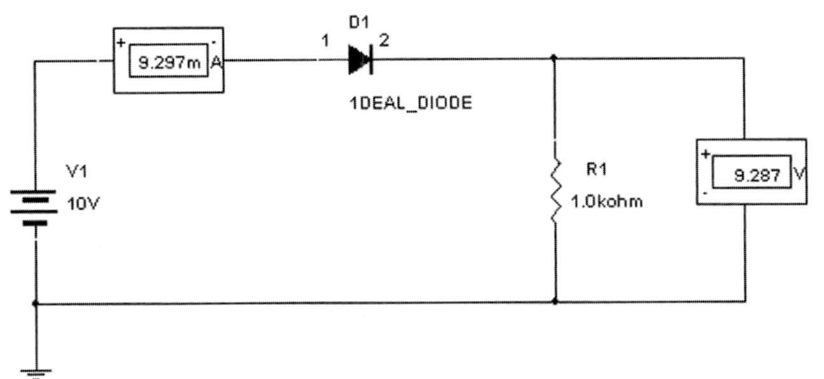

Figure I.21(a)
Forward-biased diode

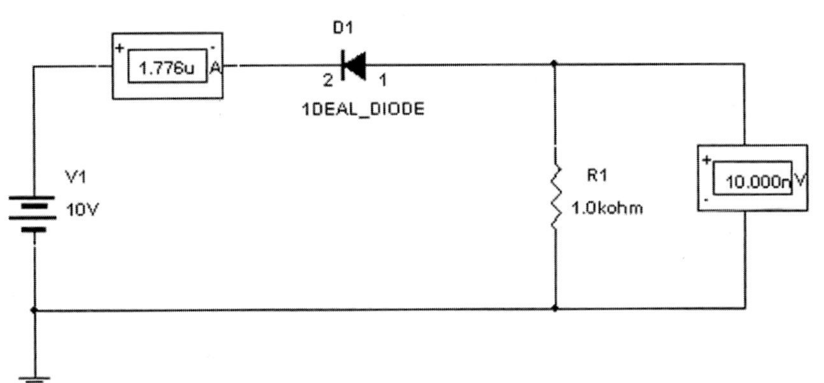

FIGURE I.21(b)
Reverse-biased diode

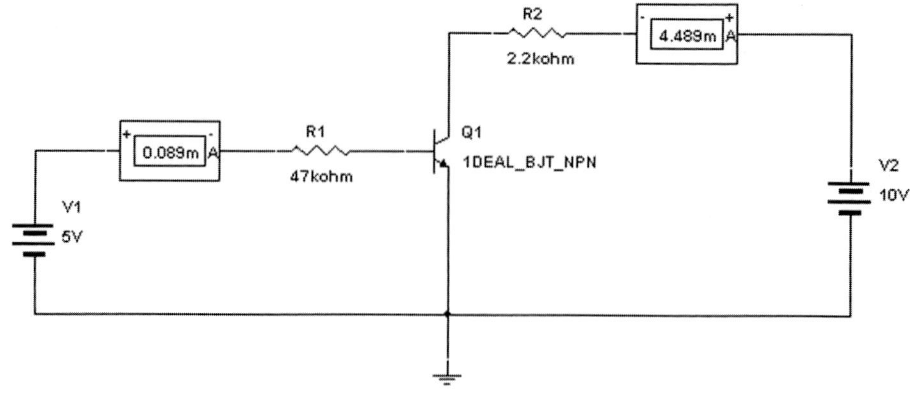

Figure I.22
Transistor biasing circuit

The Light-Emitting Diode

The light emitting diode (LED) is a special diode that gives off light when it is turned on. Figure I.23 shows a simple LED circuit. During simulation, the two arrows coming out of the LED glow if the LED is on. LEDs are used in all sorts of electronic equipment, from toys to alphanumeric displays.

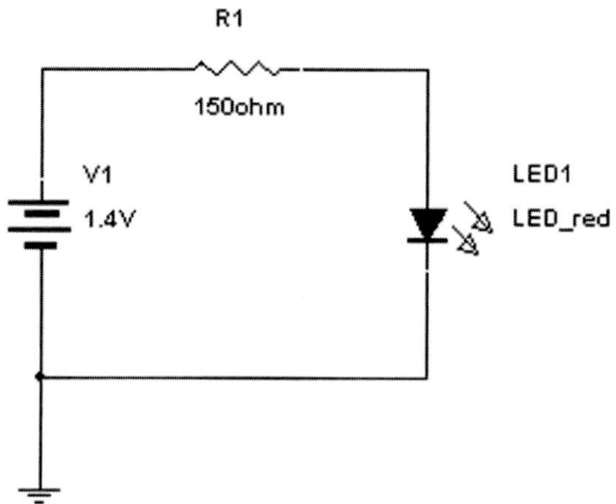

Figure I.23
Light emitting diode circuit

Research Questions / Activities

1. Search the web for other electronic simulation applications.
2. What disadvantages are there to electronic simulation?

Review Quiz

1. Discuss the advantages of electronic simulation.
2. Explain how a circuit can be setup and simulated with Electronics Workbook (multiSIM).

Lab 2

Multisim

Power Supply Circuits

Introduction

Power supplies are the most important component of an electronic system. Without a source of stable DC voltage, many electronic circuits will function poorly or not at all. In this laboratory, we examine several ways to convert the 120 Vac, 60 Hz sinusoidal voltage from a wall outlet into a stable, low DC voltage.

Performance Objectives

Upon completion of this exercise, you will be able to:

1. Describe the three basic rectifier circuits.
2. Explain how a zener diode helps maintain a constant power supply voltage.

Background information

A DC power supply creates its DC output voltage by rectifying the 60 Hz AC power line voltage. One or more diodes are used to rectify AC into pulsating DC, which is then smoothed out with the aid of a filter capacitor. A step-down transformer converts the high-voltage 120 Vac power line voltage into a lower amplitude AC voltage (12 Vac for example with a 10:1 transformer), which is then rectified and smoothed out.

Procedure

1. Start multiSIM.
2. Setup the half-wave rectifier circuit shown in Figure 2.1
3. The peak voltage at the anode of the diode is 16.97 volts, one tenth of the primary voltage on the 10:1 transformer. Subtracting 0.7 volts for the diode drop gives a peak voltage of 16.27 volts across the load resistor. The equation to predict the average DC output voltage of the half-wave rectifier is:

$Vdc = 0.318 \cdot Vpo$

where Vpo is the peak output voltage. Thus, the predicted output voltage is 0.318 times 16.27 volts, or 5.17 volts. Note from Figure 2.1 that the actual voltage is very close to the predicted value. How does the output voltage of your simulation compare?

4. Add a 100 uF capacitor in parallel with the load resistor. What is the new DC output voltage?
5. Remove the capacitor, add a second diode, and rewire the circuit to make the full-wave center-tap rectifier shown in Figure 2.2

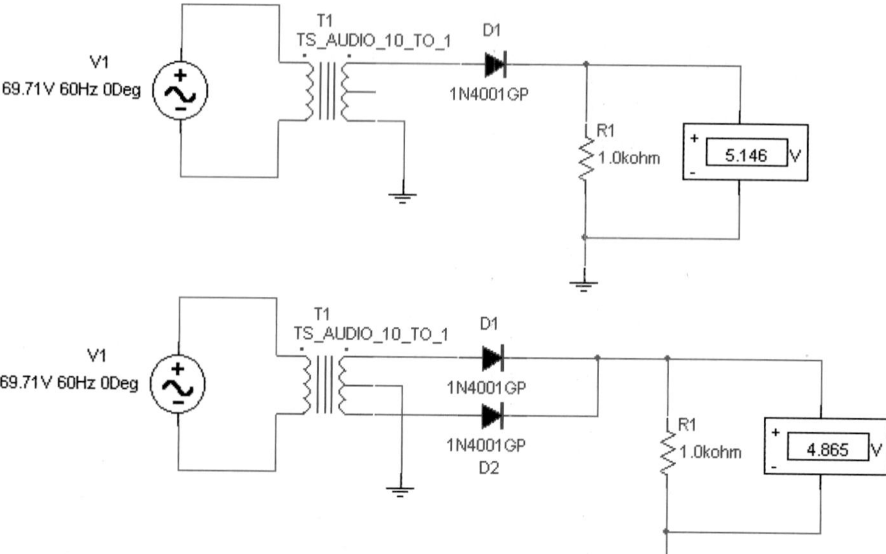

Figure 2.1
Half-wave rectifier

Figure 2.2
Full-wave center-tapped rectifier

6. The output voltage of the full-wave center-tapped rectifier is found by this equation:

$$Vdc=0.636 \cdot Vpo$$

The peak voltage at the anode of each diode is 8.5 volts (due to the center tap on the secondary of the transformer). Taking away 0.7 volts for the diode drop gives a peak output voltage of 7.8 volts. Thus, the DC output voltage is predicted to be 5 volts. This compares well with the value indicated on the meter in Figure 2.2. How does the actual value in your simulation compare?

7. Connect the 100 uF capacitor again and re-measure the output voltage.
8. Disconnect the capacitor, add two more diodes, and setup the full-wave bridge rectifier circuit illustrated in Figure 2.3.
9. The peak voltage output voltage of the bridge rectifier is 16.97 volts minus 1.4 volts (for two diode drops), or 15.57 volts. This gives an average DC output voltage of 9.9 volts. The actual voltage indicated in Figure 2.3 is very close. How does your simulation compare?
10. Setup the zener-based voltage regulator shown in Figure 2.4.
11. The zener diode will maintain a constant voltage when reverse biased, so the voltage across the 2.2 K ohm load resistor will also be constant, since it is 'in parallel' with the zener. The diode D1 is used to cancel the 0.7 V base-emitter drop of the transistor. The 1N4732 has a zener voltage of 4.7 volts, which is the voltage that will appear across the load resistor, even if the resistor value changes. Change the load resistor to 1.5 K ohms and 4.7 K ohms. What is the load voltage in each case? Has it changed?
12. Add the necessary components to make the op-amp controlled adjustable voltage regulator shown in Figure 2.5.
13. The ratio of R2 and R3 determine the output voltage according to the following formula:

$$Vdc=Vz \cdot \left(1+\frac{R2}{R3}\right)$$

Vz for the 1N4732 is 4.7 volts, which gives a DC output voltage prediction of 6.7 volts. Compare this with the actual reading shown in Figure 2.5 and with your own simulation.

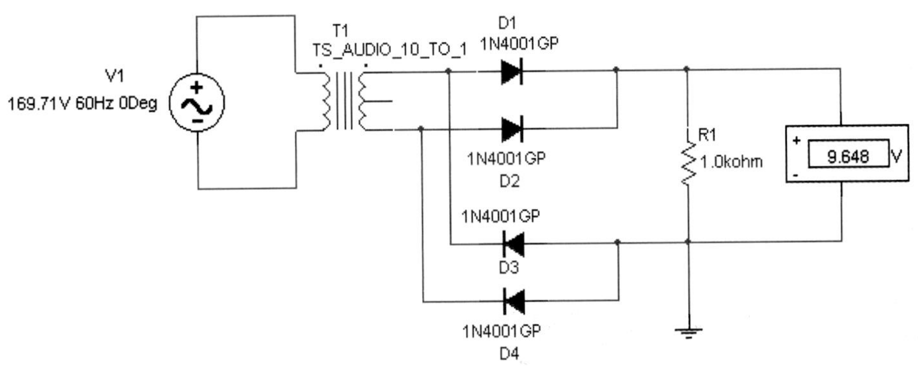

Figure 2.3
Full-wave bridge rectifier

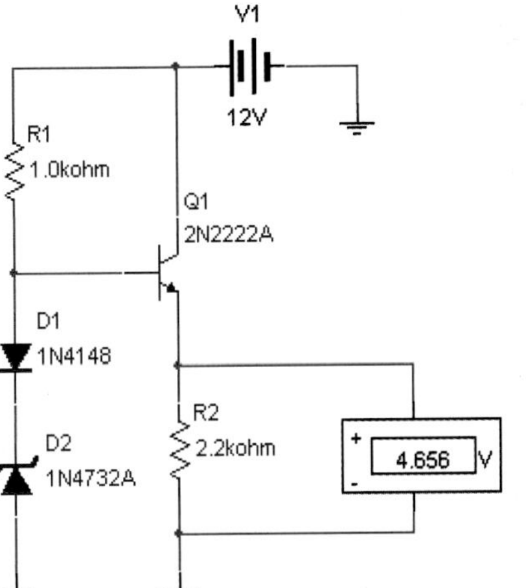

Figure 2.4
Zener-based fixed DC voltage regulator

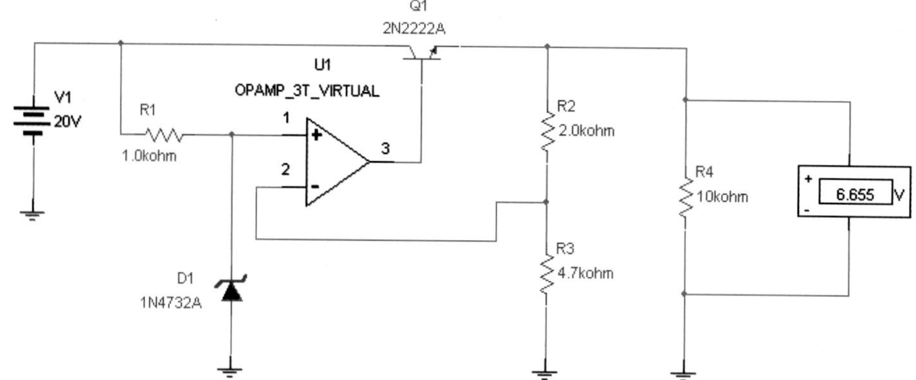

Figure 2.5
Regulated DC power supply with adjustable output voltage.

14. Change R2 to 1.5 K ohms and 4.7 K ohms. What is the output voltage in each case?
15. Change R3 to 2.0 K ohms and 10 K ohms. What is the output voltage in each case?
16. Exit multiSIM.

Research Questions / Activities

1. What is a switching power supply? Where are they used?
2. Name one source of DC voltage that does not contain a rectifier.

Review Quiz

Under the supervision of your instructor,

1. Describe the three basic rectifier circuits.
2. Explain how a zener diode helps maintain a constant power supply voltage.

Lab 3

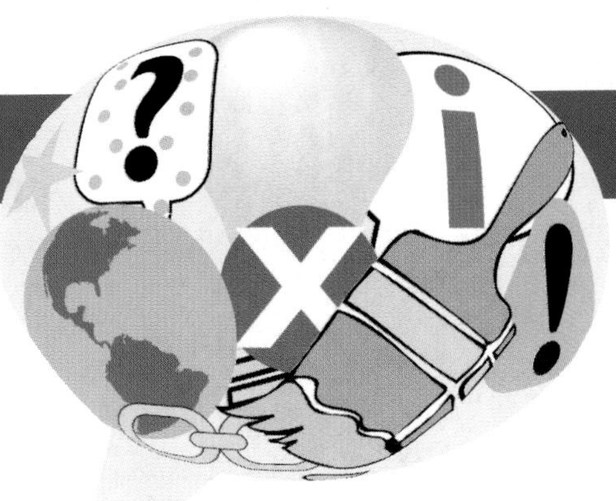

Multisim

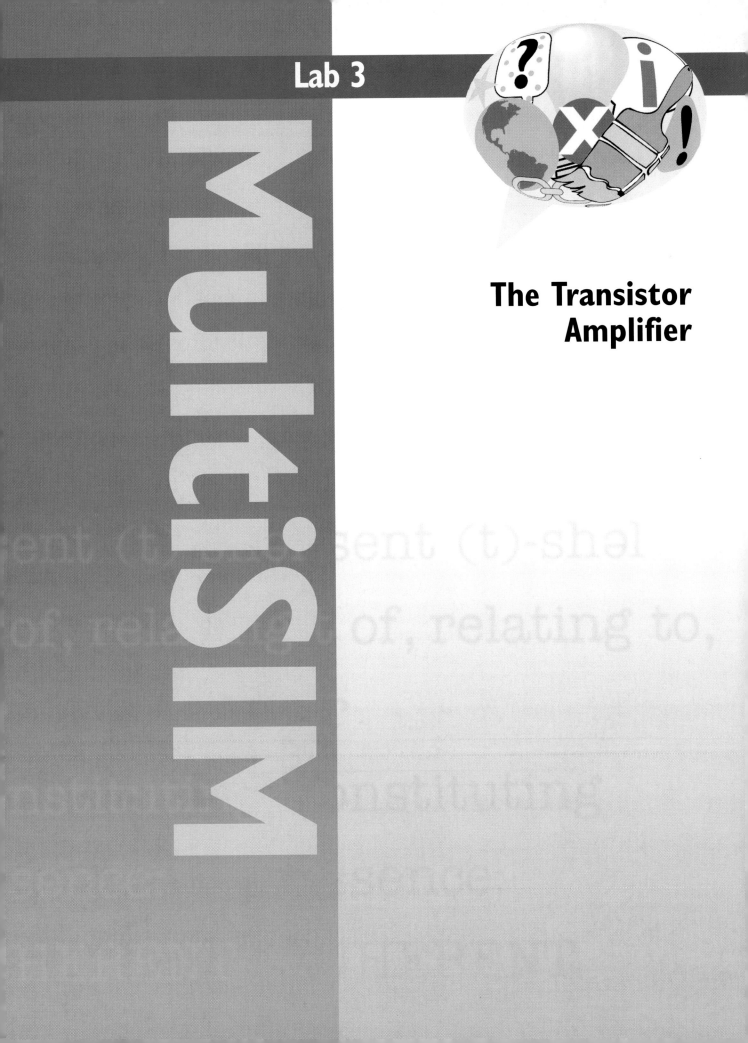

The Transistor Amplifier

Introduction

The Bipolar Junction Transistor (BJT) is a current-controlled, 3-terminal semiconductor that can be used in high-speed analog or digital circuits. The transistor operates reliably as an analog amplifier or a digital switch, and can be manufactured so small that millions of them can fit on the silicon ship that resides inside an integrated circuit. In this exercise, we will see how a specific type of transistor, the NPN transistor, behaves as an amplifier.

Performance Objectives

Upon completion of this exercise, you will be able to:

1. Calculate the gain of the common emitter amplifier (loaded and unloaded).
2. Explain how a transistor is used as a switch.

Background Information

There are two types of BJTs: NPN and PNP. An NPN transistor has two N-type semiconductors and one P-type semiconductor. The collector and emitter leads of the NPN transistor are the N-type semiconductors, and the base is the P-type. A small base current controls a larger collector current, as follows:

$$Ic = B \cdot Ib$$

where B stands for Beta, the transistors forward current gain. The base-emitter junction (a PN junction) must be forward biased with 0.7 volts for the transistor to operate.

Procedure

1. Start multiSIM.
2. Enter the BJT common-emitter amplifier circuit shown in Figure 3.1.
3. The voltage gain of the common-emitter amplifier is a function of the transistor's Beta (or Hfe), the collector resistor (R3), and the internal transistor resistance Hie. To predict the voltage gain, use the following equation:

$$Av = -\frac{Hfe \cdot R3}{Hie}$$

The minus sign on the equation indicates that the common-emitter amplifier is an inverting amplifier, with its output 180 degrees out-of-phase with its input signal. Hie depends on the q-point emitter

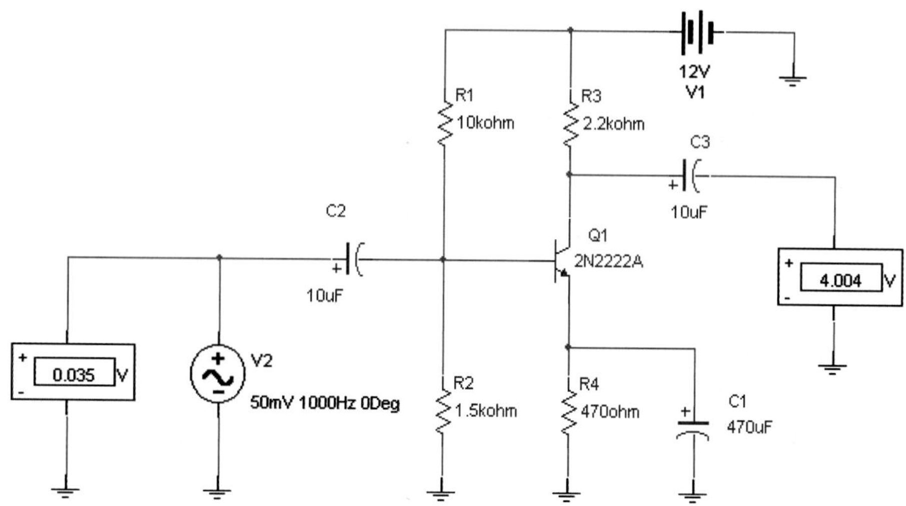

Figure 3.1
BJT common-emitter amplifier configuration

current Ieq. A voltage divider made up of R1 and R2 sets the base voltage of the transistor, which in turn sets the voltage across the emitter resistor (R4).

$$Hie = \frac{26mV \cdot (1 + Hfe)}{Ieq} \qquad Ieq = \frac{VI \cdot \frac{R2}{R1 + R2} - 0.7}{R4}$$

Using Hfe = 220, the equations give the following results: Ieq = 1.84 mA, Hie = 3123 ohms, and Av = -155. Compare this with the actual gain found by dividing the output and input voltages shown in Figure 3.1. The actual voltage gain is -114, 36% lower than the predicted value. Compare these results with those of your own simulation.

4. Use the Oscilloscope tool to view the input and output waveforms. They should look similar to those shown in Figure 3.2.
5. Add a 1.5 K ohm load resistor to the output of the common-emitter amplifier. Determine the new voltage gain via measurement and calculation. Is the gain lower with the load resistor connected?
6. Compare the actual loaded gain with the gain predicted by the following equation:

$$Av = -\frac{Hfe \cdot \left(\frac{R3 \cdot Rload}{R3 + Rload}\right)}{Hie}$$

7. Disconnect the load resistor and change the frequency of the input signal to 10 Hz. Determine the new voltage gain via measurement and calculation.
8. The BJT is used as a switch (on / off states only, no amplification) by saturating the transistor when it is turned on. This is accomplished easily by using a small base resistor to make the base current large enough to saturate the transistor (reach the maximum collector current possible in the circuit). The BJT is slammed on when a positive voltage is applied to the base resistor, and shut off when the voltage drops to zero.

Setup the two-transistor switching circuit shown in Figure 3.3.

9. What happens when you toggle the SPDT switch? Can you determine which transistor is on when the switch is up and which one is on when the switch is down?
10. Exit multiSIM.

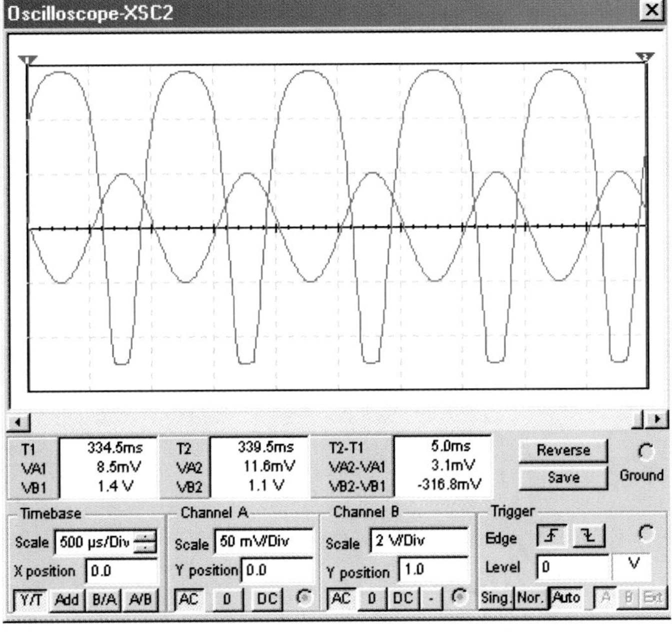

Figure 3.2
Input (smaller waveform on Channel A) and output (larger waveform on Channel B) for the BJT common-emitter amplifier

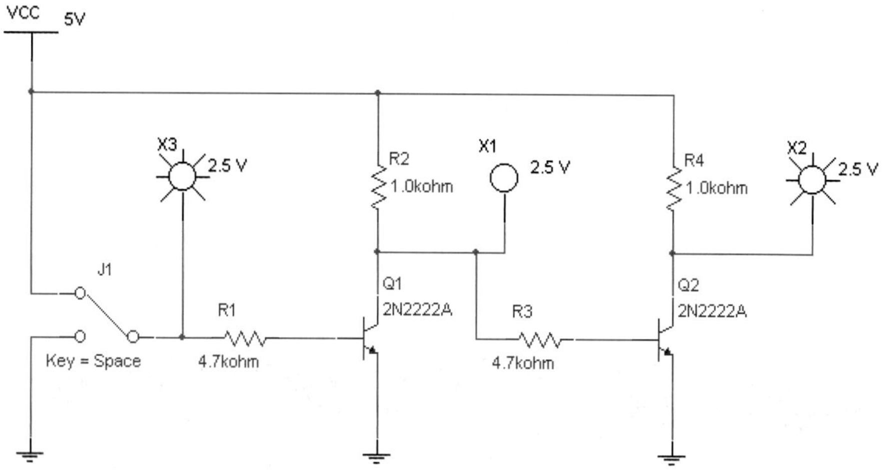

Figure 3.3 Two-stage cascaded transistor inverters

Research Questions / Activities

1. What is different about PNP transistors?
2. How does a JFET differ from the BJT?

Review Quiz

Under the supervision of your instructor,

1. Calculate the gain of the common emitter amplifier (loaded and unloaded).
2. Explain how a transistor is used as a switch.

Lab 4

MultiSIM

Operational Amplifiers

Introduction

Operational amplifiers (op-amps for short) are amazing devices that have a wide range of applications in electronic circuits. In this laboratory we will examine several basic op-amp configurations.

Performance Objectives

Upon completion of this exercise, you will be able to:

1. Name the four standard op-amp configurations.
2. Calculate the gain and output voltage for an op-amp circuit.

Background Information

An operational amplifier contains a very high open-loop voltage gain (100,000 or more), a very high input resistance (10 M ohms or higher), and a low output resistance (50 ohms). In short, the op-amp comes close to an ideal amplifier. By adding feedback, the op-amp can be used as an amplifier (negative feedback), or as an oscillator (positive feedback). When used as an amplifier, it is possible to calculate the exact voltage gain of the op-amp circuit. Compare this feature with the gain of the common-emitter amplifier, which depends on a number of factors and is not as accurate.

Procedure

1. Start multiSIM.
2. Enter the inverting amplifier circuit shown in Figure 4.1.
3. The voltage gain of the inverting amplifier is found as follows:

$$Av = -\frac{R2}{R1} = -\frac{4.7K}{1.0K} = -4.7$$

Note from Figure 4.1 that Vin = 2 volts and Vout = -9.4 volts. Dividing Vout by Vin gives a gain of -4.7, which matches the gain predicted by the equation. Does the gain in your circuit match the predicted gain of -4.7?

4. Change R1 to 2.2 K ohms. Calculate the new gain and compare against measured values.
5. Re-arrange the components to form the non-inverting amplifier shown in Figure 4.2.
6. The gain of the non-inverting amplifier is found as follows:

$$Av = 1 + \frac{R2}{R1}$$

Determine the expected gain and verify that the circuit in Figure 4.2, as well as your own simulation, has the same gain.

7. A nice feature of the op-amp is that its output voltage does not change when a *reasonable* load resistance is attached. Recall from Laboratory 3 that this is not the case for the common-emitter

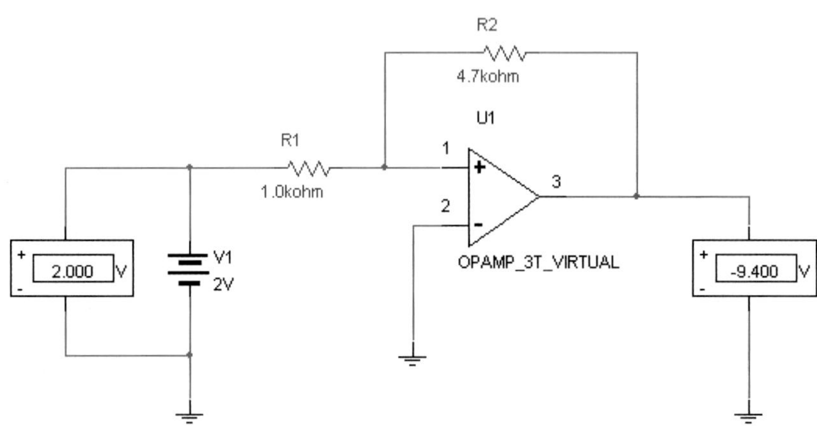

Figure 4.1
Inverting amplifier configuration

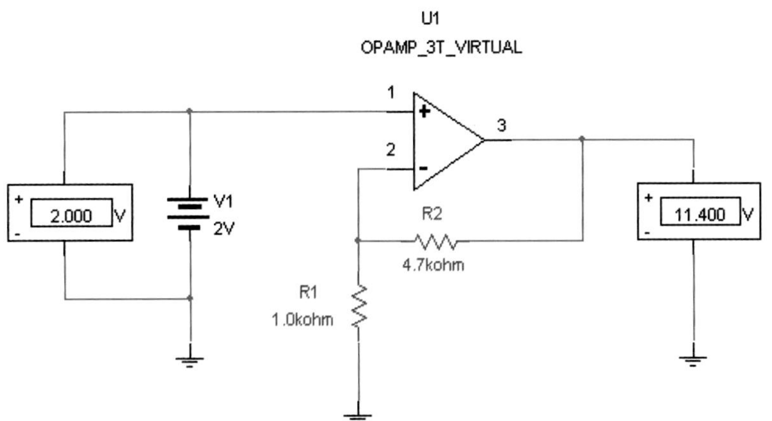

Figure 4.2
Non-inverting amplifier configuration

amplifier, whose gain drops when a load is connected. A reasonable load resistance is one that does not draw a significant amount of output current from the op-amp. For example, a 10 K ohm load resistor only draws 1 mA when the output voltage is 10 volts. This seems reasonable. Connect a 10 K ohm load resistor to the output. Does the gain change?

8. Rewire the circuit to make the mixer amplifier shown in Figure 4.3.
9. The output voltage of the mixer is found by this equation:

$$Vout = -R3\left(\frac{V1}{R1} + \frac{V2}{R2}\right)$$

Verify that the output voltage is correct in Figure 4.3 (and in your own simulation).

10. Add a fourth resistor and rewire the circuit to create the difference amplifier illustrated in Figure 4.4.

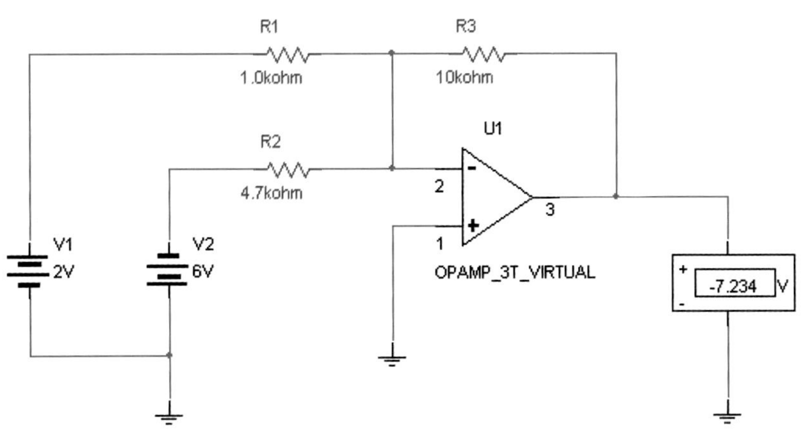

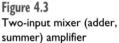

Figure 4.3
Two-input mixer (adder, summer) amplifier

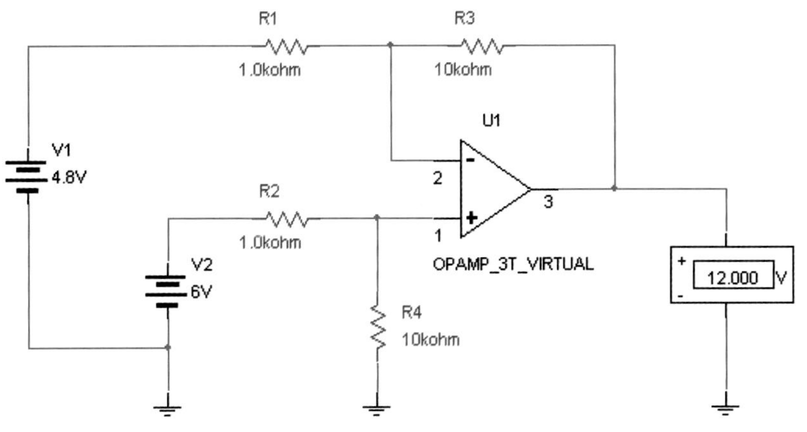

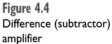

Figure 4.4
Difference (subtractor) amplifier

11. The output voltage of the difference amplifier is found as follows:

$$Vout = \frac{R4}{R2}(V2 - V1)$$

This equation is only valid if R1 = R2 and R3 = R4. Verify that the output voltage is correct in Figure 4.4 (and in your own simulation).

12. Exit multiSIM.

Research Questions / Activities

1. Search the Internet for additional types of op-amp circuitry.
2. What does the term 'operational' refer to in the operational amplifier? *Hint:* Find out about analog computers.

Review Quiz

Under the supervision of your instructor,

1. Name the four standard op-amp configurations.
2. Calculate the gain and output voltage for an op-amp circuit.

Lab 5

MultiSIM

Digital Logic Circuitry

Introduction

Digital logic circuitry is found in personal computers, FAX machines, vending machines, telephones, radio and television receivers, and countless other devices. In this laboratory we examine several practical digital logic circuits.

Performance Objectives

Upon completion of this exercise, you will be able to:

1. List several types of logic gates and functions.
2. Explain how 0s and 1s may be input to a digital circuit in multiSIM.

Background Information

There are several basic types of logic gates: The inverter (or NOT function), the AND gate, and the OR gate. Combinations of these basic gates lead to other logic functions, such as NAND (not AND), NOR (not OR), and XOR (exclusive OR). Each gate uses one or more binary inputs (0 or 1) to generate a logical binary output. Table 5.1 is a truth table that shows the output of each type of logic function.

Table 5.1
Truth table showing the basic logic functions

Input A	Input B	NOT A	A AND B	A OR B	A NAND B	A NOR B	A XOR B
0	0	1	0	0	1	1	0
0	1	1	0	1	1	0	1
1	0	0	0	1	1	0	1
1	1	0	1	1	0	0	0

The basic logic functions are the building blocks of more complex digital circuits, even powerful microprocessors.

Procedure

1. Start multiSIM.
2. Enter the basic logic gates circuit shown in Figure 5.1
3. Use the A and B keys to change the switch positions from their up (logic 1) position to down (logic 0) and apply all four input combinations of A and B to the circuit. Note the state of the output for each input combination. Do the outputs match their associated truth table entry?
4. Connect four NAND gates as shown in Figure 5.2 Add SPDT switches and a logic indicator as in Figure 5.1.
5. Apply all input combinations and determine which single 2-input logic gate can be used to replace all four NAND gates.

Figure 5.1
Basic logic functions

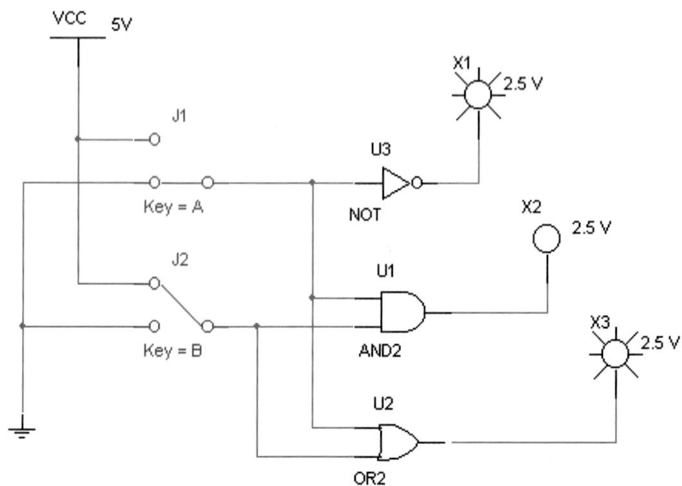

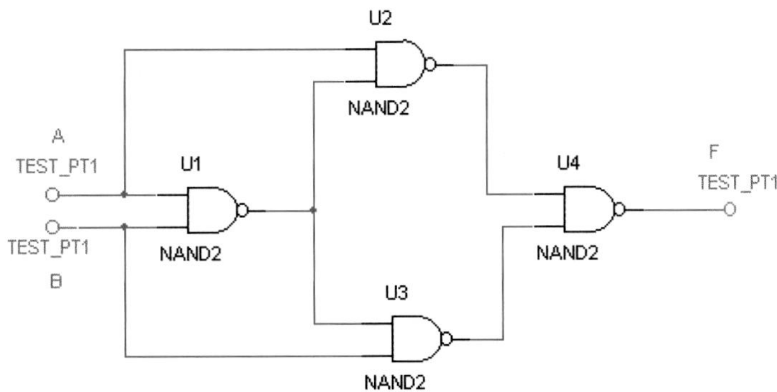

Figure 5.2
NAND gate circuit for investigation

6. Enter the 3-bit counting circuit shown in Figure 5.3.
7. Does the circuit count from 0 (000) to 7 (111) or from 7 to 0?
8. Enter the 4-bit counting circuit shown in Figure 5.4.
9. What is the counting sequence for the circuit?
10. Exit multiSIM.

Research Questions / Activities

1. What is DeMorgan's Theorem?
2. When was the first integrated circuit invented?

Review Quiz

Under the supervision of your instructor,

1. List several types of logic gates and functions.
2. Explain how 0s and 1s may be input to a digital circuit in multiSIM.

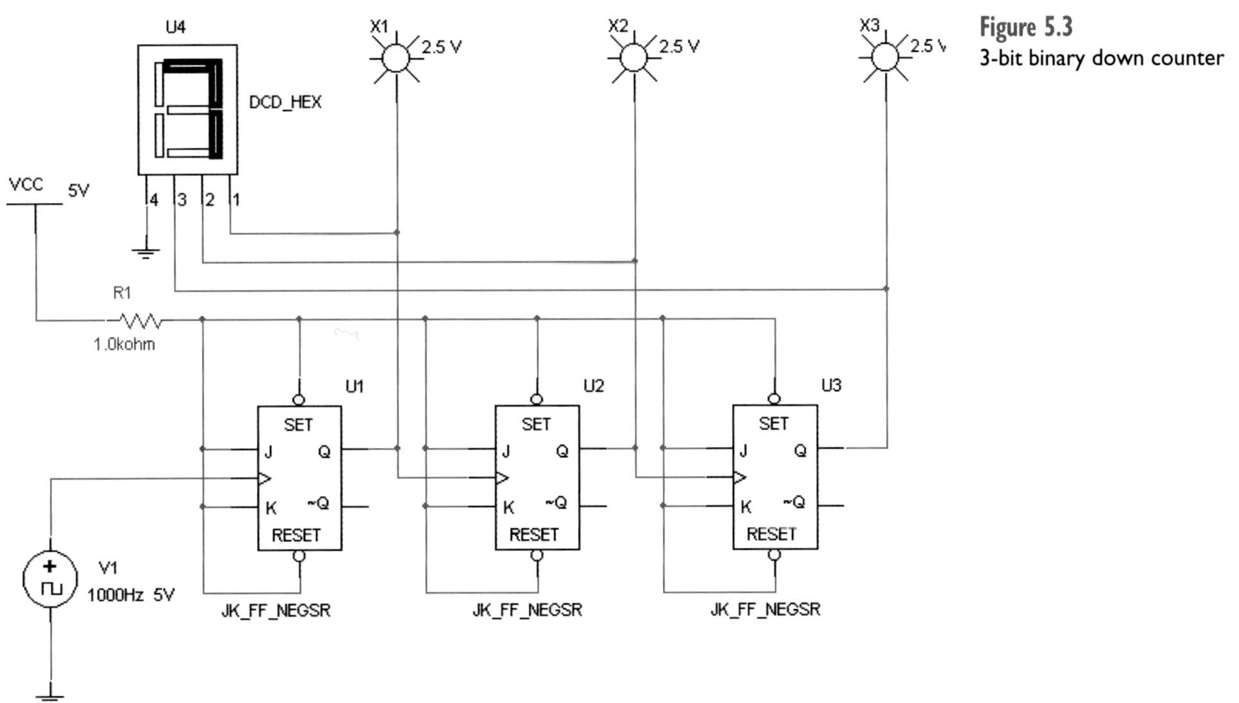

Figure 5.3
3-bit binary down counter

Figure 5.4
4-bit decimal counter with 7-segment decoder/display

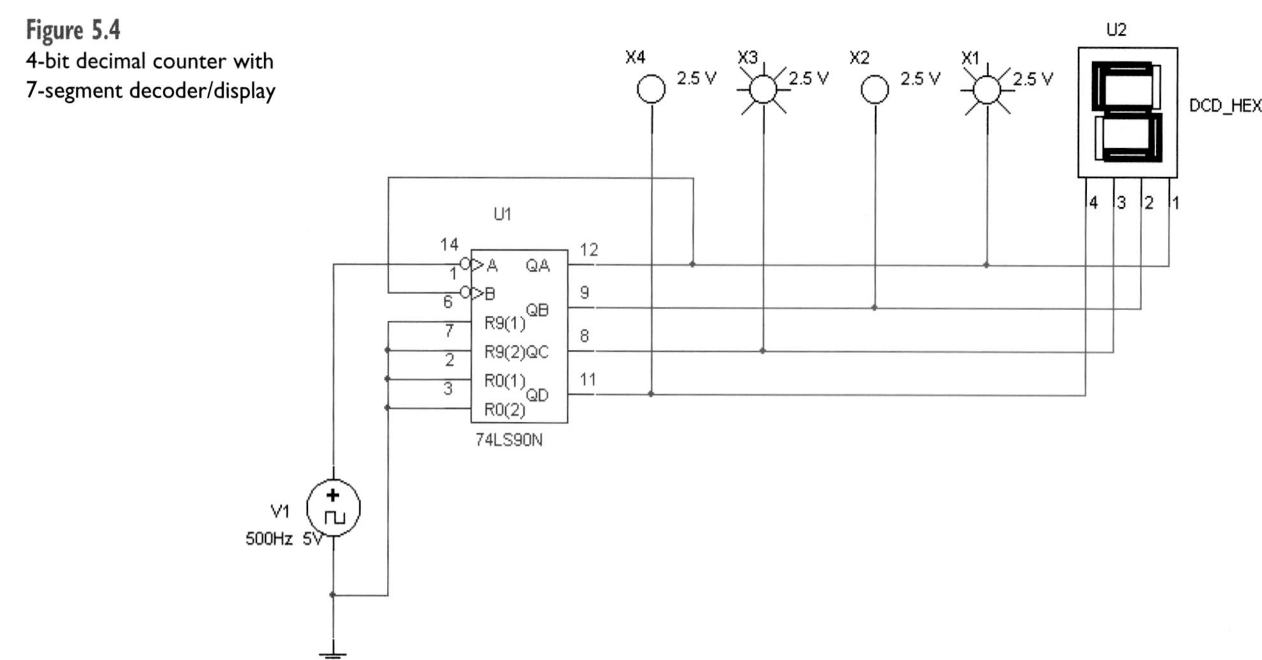

Appendices

A Basics

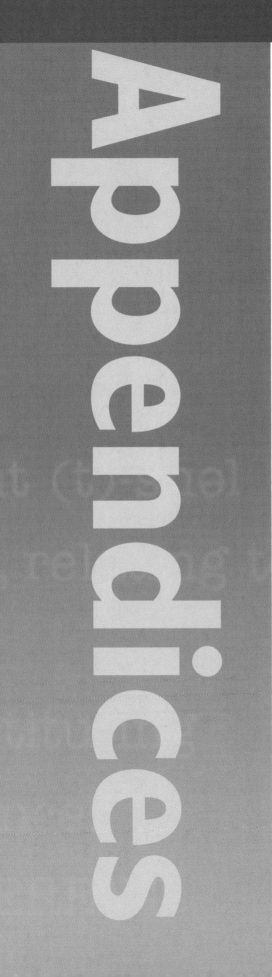

B Microcomputer Hardware

C MathPro

D Task Guide

E Glossary

Appendix A Basics

Basics

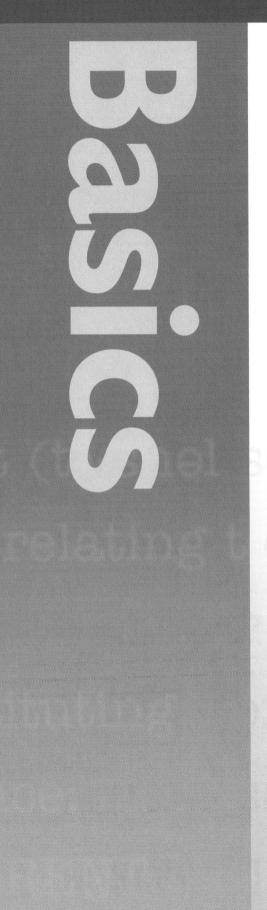

1 Working with Windows

2 Windows Disk and File Management

3 Working with Office 2000

Working with Windows and Office

This book is not about Windows; entire books about each of the Windows versions exist. However ,you must have a basic understanding of Windows to use Microsoft Office 2000 effectively. Microsoft Windows is a computer operating system that is required if you want to run Microsoft Office 2000. It works behind the scenes, doing the housekeeping and enabling you to do such things as save your work and print a document while you use an Office application.

Microsoft Office 2000 works with four different versions of Windows: Windows 95, Windows 98, Windows 2000, and Windows NT. The version of Windows you use does not make a difference in the way any of your Office 2000 programs work. The version does, however, influence the look of your screen. For example, the Help topics are rearranged, as is the Help window layout. Also, some of the Windows utilities are made to look more like Web pages in the newer versions.

The first project in this section provides you with a basic introduction to Microsoft Windows. It covers such topics as using the mouse, taskbar, and Start button, as well as resizing, moving, maximizing, and minimizing windows. It also introduces you to Windows Help. The second project deals with managing your files and disk drives. The third project in this section is a basic introduction to Microsoft Office 2000.

Project 1

Working with Windows

Objectives

In this project, you learn how to

- **Start Windows and Use the Mouse**
- **Use the Start Button**
- **Resize and Move a Window**
- **Scroll a Window**
- **Maximize, Restore, Minimize, and Close a Window**
- **Use the Taskbar to Work in Multiple Windows**
- **Use the Windows Help System**
- **Shut Down Your Computer**

Key terms in this project include

- desktop
- dialog box
- graphic user interface (GUI)
- horizontal scrollbar
- icon
- maximize
- menu bar
- minimize
- mouse pointer
- My Computer
- restore
- scroll box
- shortcut menu
- Start button
- status bar
- submenu
- taskbar
- title bar
- toolbar
- vertical scrollbar
- window
- Windows Explorer

Why Would I Do This?

To use Microsoft Office 2000 effectively, you need to have a basic familiarity with the Microsoft Windows operating system. You need to know how to work with the Start button and taskbar, and how to open, close, move, and resize windows. You also need to know how to use both the left and right buttons on your mouse.

If you are familiar with Microsoft Windows and feel comfortable using the mouse, move to the Checking Concepts and Terms section at the end of the project. If you can answer the questions, you might want to move to the next project.

In this project, you learn how to use the mouse. You also learn how to use the Start button and the taskbar, and how to manipulate windows. You learn how to use some of the help features available in Windows. Finally, you learn how to shut down your computer.

Lesson 1: Starting Windows and Using the Mouse

In most cases, starting Windows is an automatic procedure. You turn on the machine and Windows (whichever version you are using) eventually appears. The mouse and keyboard are two of the common input devices you use to interact with Windows.

Your screen might look different from the Windows screens displayed throughout this project because your computer has different software installed and different shortcuts on the desktop.

To Start Windows and Use the Mouse

1. **Turn on your computer.**

After showing several screens of text and the Windows opening screen, the Windows desktop displays. The look of the screen varies depending on which version of Windows you are using. A window might be open on your screen if the window was left open by the last person to use the computer (see Figure 1.1).

If you are using a computer in a lab or on a network, a box, called a dialog box, may appear asking for a user name and password. In many cases, you can press Esc or click the Cancel button, which bypasses the security. If this doesn't work, ask your instructor or network administrator how to proceed.

Using the Mouse Buttons

Unless expressly stated otherwise, "click" means to press and release the left mouse button; "right-click" refers to pressing and releasing the right mouse button.

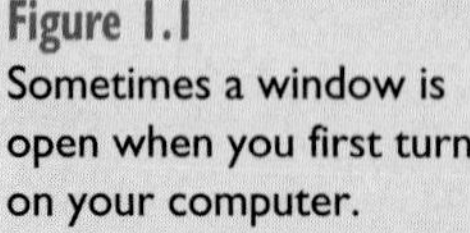

Figure 1.1
Sometimes a window is open when you first turn on your computer.

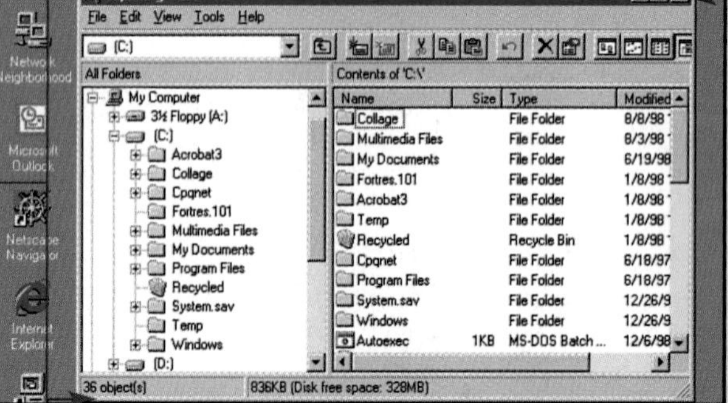

2 If a window is open, click the Close button (the button with the X on it) in the upper-right corner of the window.

The window closes, and the Windows ***desktop*** displays (see Figure 1.2). The desktop consists of shortcut ***icons*** (small graphic symbols that represent programs) that run programs, the ***taskbar*** at the bottom of the screen, and the ***Start button*** on the left edge of the taskbar. Shortcut icons also appear on the right side of the taskbar. Finally, somewhere on the desktop, you see an arrow. This is the ***mouse pointer***, often just called the pointer, which you use to select or activate things on the screen.

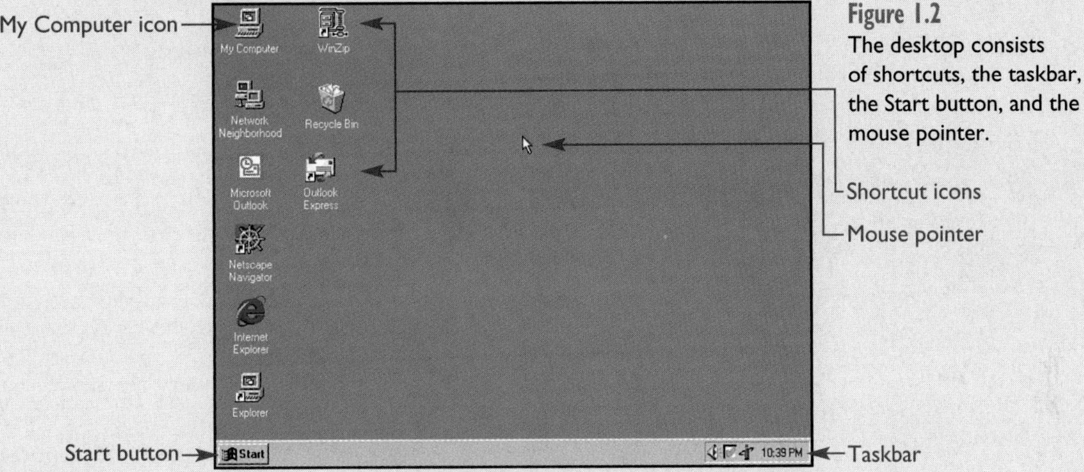

Figure 1.2
The desktop consists of shortcuts, the taskbar, the Start button, and the mouse pointer.

The taskbar might not appear at the bottom of the desktop. If you cannot see the taskbar, it may be hidden. To see it, move the mouse pointer to the bottom of the screen; the taskbar should pop up.

The taskbar also might not appear at the location shown in the figure. Someone might have moved it to the top or one of the sides of the desktop.

3 Move the mouse pointer until it points to the center of the My Computer icon on the desktop.

My Computer is one of two ways to get at the programs and documents stored on your computer. The My Computer icon looks like a miniature computer. The name of this icon might have been changed. If more than one icon looks like a miniature computer, ask your instructor which one is My Computer.

4 Click once on the My Computer icon.

The icon turns dark, indicating that it has been selected.

5 Click twice on the My Computer icon.

The My Computer ***window*** displays (see Figure 1.3). A window is a box that displays information or a program. A window consists of a ***title bar*** containing the window name, a ***menu bar***, and usually one or more ***toolbars***. A ***status bar*** at the bottom of the window gives additional information.

X

The My Computer window can be customized in many ways. Your window might look like a Web page, it might display smaller buttons, or it might even consist of a list of folders and filenames. You can change the look of the window by using the View menu option. You learn more about using menus in Project 3.

continues ▶

To Start Windows and Use the Mouse (continued)

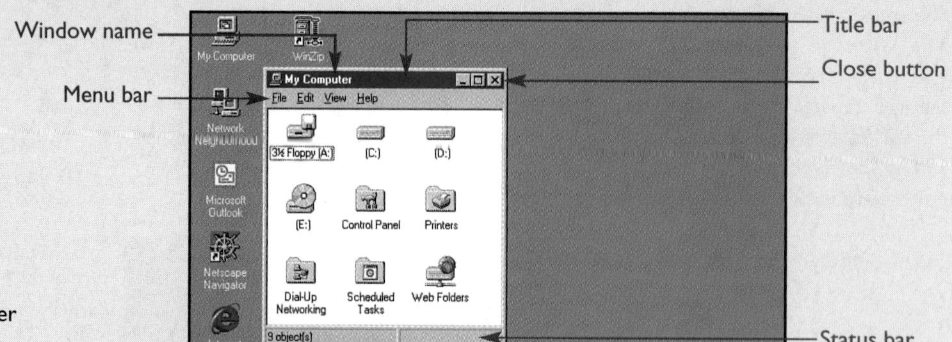

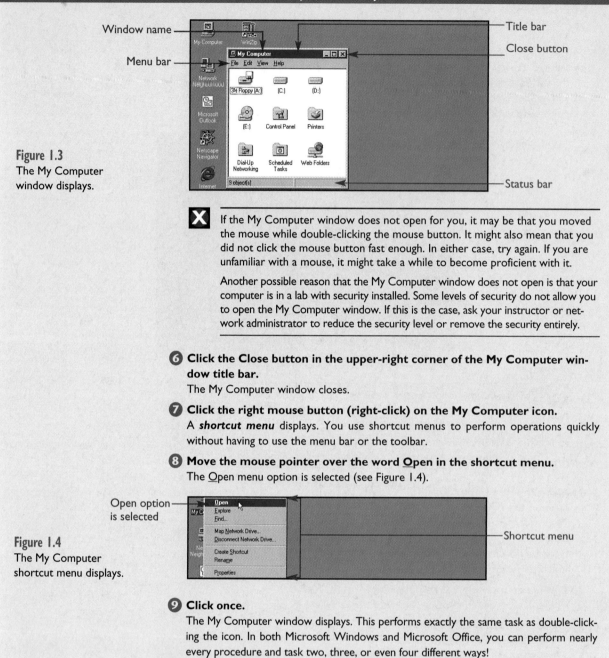

Figure 1.3
The My Computer window displays.

> If the My Computer window does not open for you, it may be that you moved the mouse while double-clicking the mouse button. It might also mean that you did not click the mouse button fast enough. In either case, try again. If you are unfamiliar with a mouse, it might take a while to become proficient with it.
>
> Another possible reason that the My Computer window does not open is that your computer is in a lab with security installed. Some levels of security do not allow you to open the My Computer window. If this is the case, ask your instructor or network administrator to reduce the security level or remove the security entirely.

6. **Click the Close button in the upper-right corner of the My Computer window title bar.**
   The My Computer window closes.
7. **Click the right mouse button (right-click) on the My Computer icon.**
   A ***shortcut menu*** displays. You use shortcut menus to perform operations quickly without having to use the menu bar or the toolbar.
8. **Move the mouse pointer over the word Open in the shortcut menu.**
   The Open menu option is selected (see Figure 1.4).

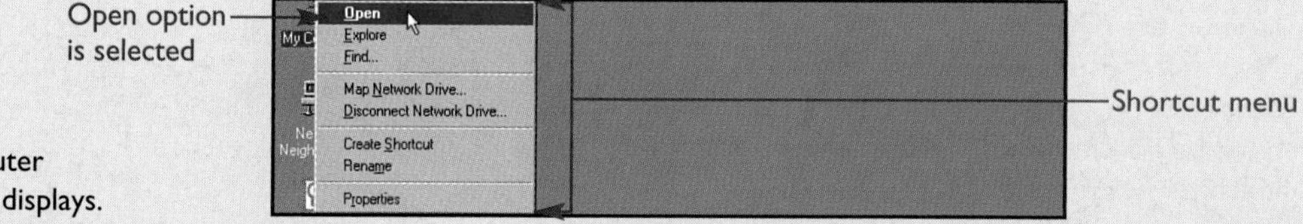

Figure 1.4
The My Computer shortcut menu displays.

9. **Click once.**
   The My Computer window displays. This performs exactly the same task as double-clicking the icon. In both Microsoft Windows and Microsoft Office, you can perform nearly every procedure and task two, three, or even four different ways!
10. **Click the Close button in the My Computer window title bar.**
    The window closes. Leave your computer on for the next lesson.

Understanding Windows, Windows, and Dialog Boxes

It is important to understand the distinction between Windows, windows, and dialog boxes. Windows (with a capital W) is the operating system you are using. It might be Windows NT, Windows 95, Windows 98, or Windows 2000. These operating systems are all similar and use what is known as a ***graphic user interface (GUI)***. The graphic user interface lets you see your document formatting as it looks when you print the document. It also uses small graphic objects (icons) to represent commands or files.

A window, on the other hand, is a box on the screen that contains some sort of program, whereas a dialog box gives you a message or asks for a decision.

Using Shortcut Menus

The shortcut menu you activated by right-clicking the mouse works on nearly all objects in Windows and in Microsoft Office applications. Before you go to the toolbar or menu to do something to an object on the screen, try right-clicking it first. Shortcut menus are great timesavers.

Lesson 2: Using the Start Button

The Start button is a very important part of the Windows desktop. You can use it to launch programs, set up your printer, get help, and shut down your computer.

In this lesson, you use the Start button to open a built-in application that acts as an online calculator.

To Use the Start Button

1 Move the pointer to the Start button and click it once.

The Start menu displays (see Figure 1.5). Notice that some of the options have arrows on the right. These arrows indicate that there is a ***submenu*** containing programs or folders that contain more options. A submenu is a second-level menu activated by selecting a menu item.

The items at the top of the Start menu are different from those on your screen. The user can customize the shortcuts to programs at the top of the Start menu. After the Start menu displays, you can let go of the mouse button.

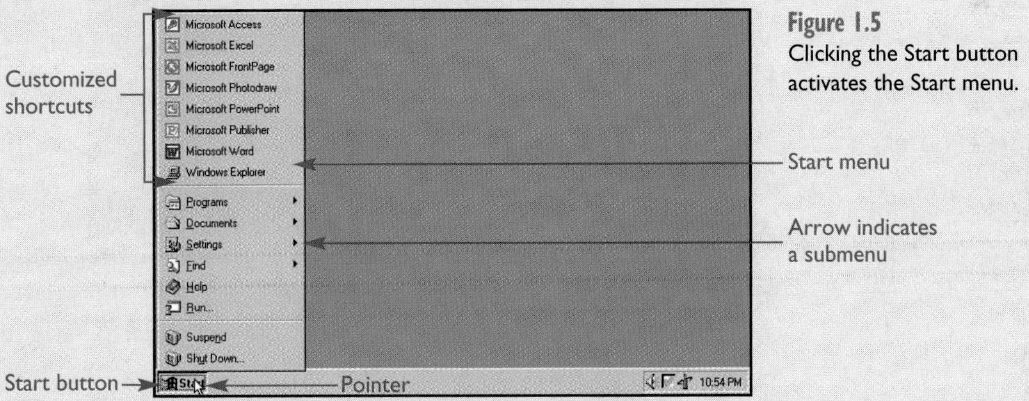

Figure 1.5
Clicking the Start button activates the Start menu.

2 Move the pointer to the Programs menu option, but do not click the mouse button.

The Programs menu displays (see Figure 1.6). Your program menu might look somewhat different because your computer has different programs installed. The folders at the top contain programs, more folders, or both.

continues ▶

To Use the Start Button (continued)

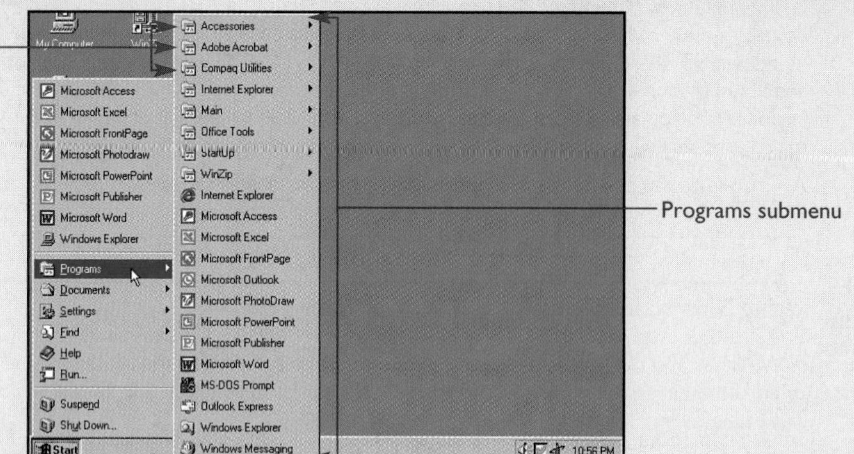

Figure 1.6
The Programs menu option contains a submenu with more options.

❸ **Move the pointer over and up to the Accessories menu option, but do not click the mouse button.**
The Accessories submenu displays.

If the Accessories option is not visible, move the pointer to the top of the menu and hold it above the up arrow. The menu should scroll up to the top.

❹ **Move the pointer into the Accessories submenu and move down to the Calculator option.**
The Calculator option is highlighted (see Figure 1.7).

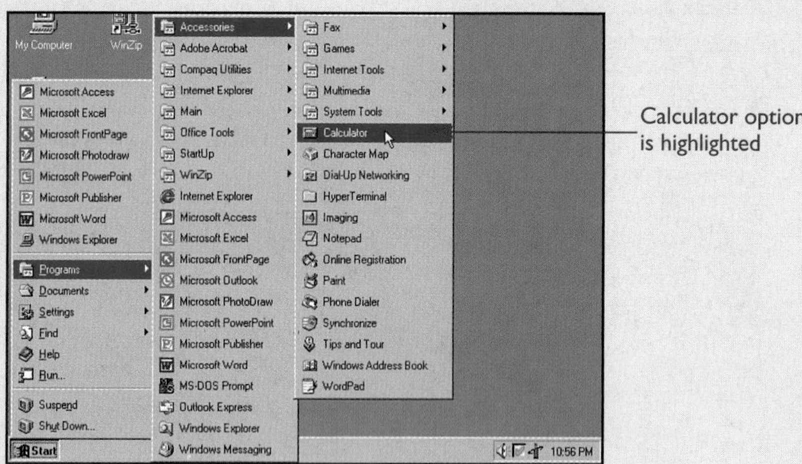

Figure 1.7
The Calculator program is ready to be opened.

❺ **Click the Calculator option.**
The Calculator window displays (see Figure 1.8). Try using the Calculator.

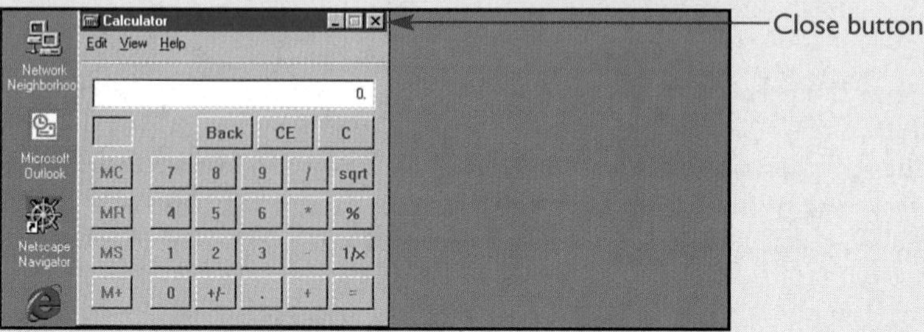

Figure 1.8
The Calculator window displays.

❻ **Click the Close button to close the Calculator.**
Leave the computer on for the next lesson.

Using More Than One Program at a Time
You can use the Accessories programs from the Start menu while you are using one of the Office programs. For example, you might want to make a quick calculation while you are typing a document into Microsoft Word. You can go to the Start button and open the Calculator (as you did previously), make the calculation, and then place the answer in your Word document without ever closing Word!

Lesson 3: Resizing and Moving a Window

In Lesson 2, you opened the Calculator window using the Start button. You can also use the Start button to get to the ***Windows Explorer***. The Windows Explorer is another way to access programs and documents, as well as copy, move, delete, and rename files.

In this lesson, you open, resize, and move the Windows Explorer. You use the Windows Explorer in the next three lessons.

To Resize and Move a Window

1. **Move the pointer to the Start button and click once.**
   The Start menu displays.

2. **Move the pointer up to the Programs menu option.**
   The Programs submenu displays. Near the end of the menu you see Windows Explorer (see Figure 1.9). Your Programs submenu might look different from the one shown in the figure, but the Windows Explorer option should display.

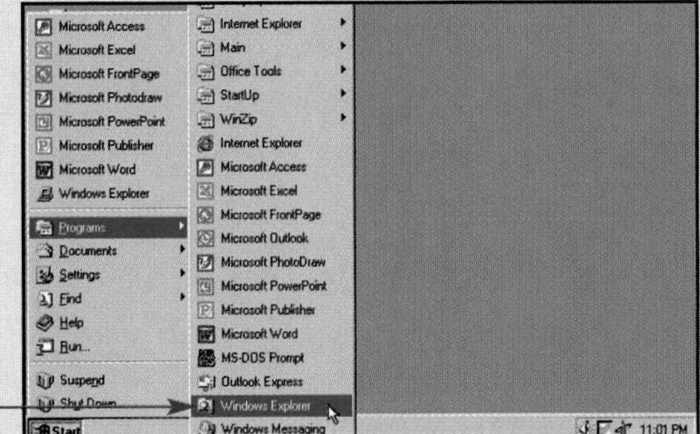

Windows Explorer option

Figure 1.9
The Windows Explorer is a menu choice in the Programs submenu.

3. **Move the pointer to the Windows Explorer option and click.**
   You might have to scroll down to find the Windows Explorer option if you are using Windows 98. The Windows Explorer window displays. It consists of a title bar, a menu bar, a toolbar, a list of drives and folders, and a list of the contents of the default disk drive (see Figure 1.10).

Your screen might look considerably different from the one shown in the figure. The size and shape might be different; the general look and feel might be different, and you might not see the toolbar. Take the following steps to get your screen to look something like the one in the figure:

- If the Windows Explorer takes up the entire screen, click the middle button in the set of three buttons in the upper-right corner of the screen. You learn more about these buttons in Lesson 5.
- If the toolbar does not display, choose View, Toolbar from the menu. To use the menu, click the command you want with the left mouse button (in this case View) and release the mouse button. Move the pointer down the list of choices in the drop-down menu. When the option you want is highlighted (in this case Toolbar), click it.
- If icons appear instead of folders and files in the right side of the window, choose View, Details from the menu.
- If you see other differences, don't worry about them.

continues ▶

To Resize and Move a Window (continued)

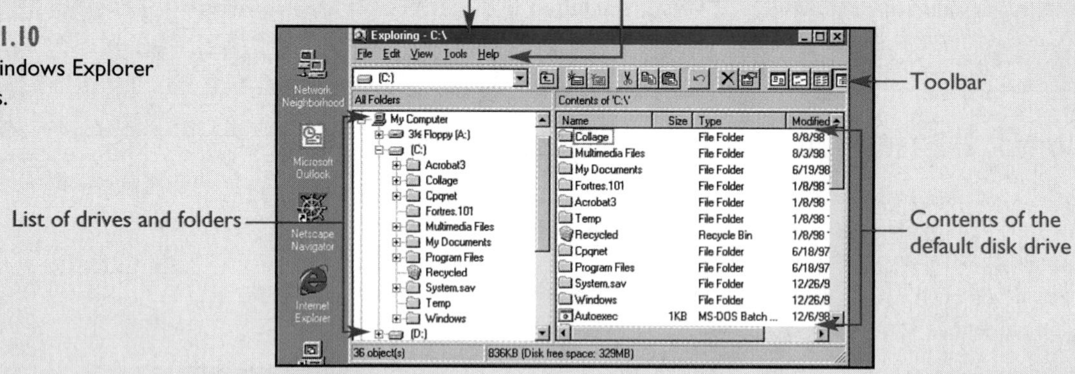

Figure 1.10
The Windows Explorer displays.

4. **Move the pointer to the edge of the lower-right corner of the Windows Explorer window.**
   The pointer changes to a diagonal two-headed arrow.

5. **Click and hold down the left mouse button; drag up and to the left.**
   When you release the left mouse button, the Windows Explorer window will be resized to the dimensions of the thick gray outline (see Figure 1.11). Resize your window to approximately the same size as the one in the figure.

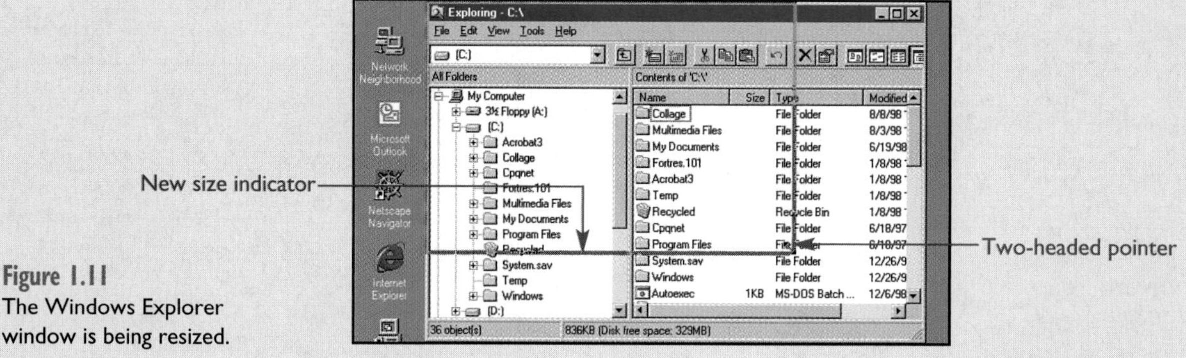

Figure 1.11
The Windows Explorer window is being resized.

6. **Release the left mouse button.**
   The Windows Explorer window is resized.

7. **Move the pointer to the Windows Explorer title bar. Click and drag down and to the right.**
   When you release the left mouse button, the Windows Explorer window will be moved to the location indicated by the thick rectangle (see Figure 1.12).

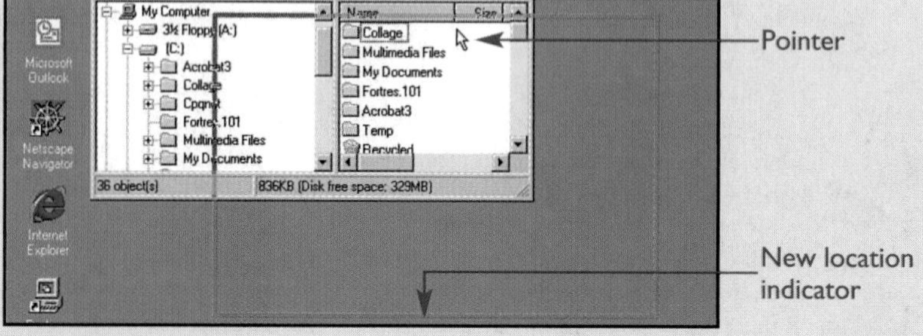

Figure 1.12
The Windows Explorer window is being moved.

8. **Release the left mouse button.**
   The Windows Explorer window is moved. Leave the Windows Explorer window open for the next lesson.

Making the Windows Explorer Look Like a Web Page
You might want the Windows Explorer to look like a Web page, although the figures in this lesson are not set up that way. If you want to see what the Windows Explorer looks like in a Web page format (or want to turn that feature off), choose View, as Web Page from the menu. This does not work if you are using Windows 95 or Windows NT version 4.

Lesson 4: Scrolling a Window

In many cases, your computer cannot display all the information contained in a window, whether that window contains a word-processing document, a Web page, or the Windows Explorer. Scrollbars are included if the information in a window stretches beyond the right or bottom edges of the window. The ***horizontal scrollbar*** enables you to move left and right to view information too wide for the screen. The ***vertical scrollbar*** enables you to view information too long for the screen.

In this lesson, you use the scrollbars in the Windows Explorer window to look at information that won't fit on the screen.

To Scroll a Window

1. **With the Windows Explorer window open, click and hold down the left mouse button on the down arrow at the bottom of the vertical scrollbar in the middle of the window.**
   The items at the bottom of the window scroll up so that you can see the folders and files that were not visible before (see Figure 1.13). The Windows Explorer window consists of two windows, both of which can have vertical and horizontal scrollbars.

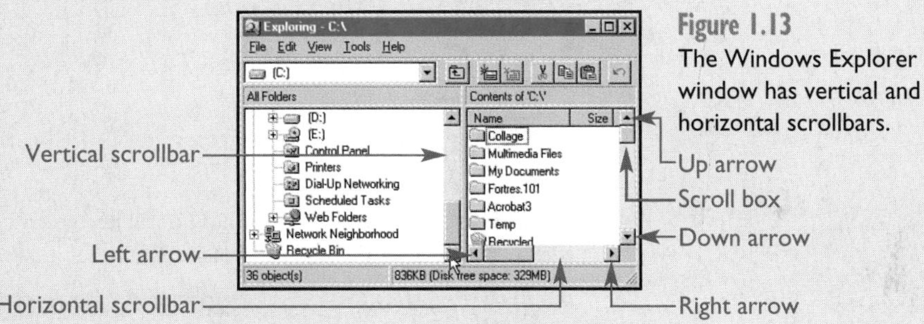

Figure 1.13
The Windows Explorer window has vertical and horizontal scrollbars.

2. **Click and hold down the left mouse button on the up arrow on the same scrollbar.**
   You move up in the list until the first item (the Desktop) displays.
3. **Click and hold down the right arrow in the horizontal scrollbar at the bottom right-hand corner of the window.**
   The window scrolls to display the information on the right.
4. **Click and hold down the left arrow in the same horizontal scrollbar.**
   The window scrolls back to the left edge of the information.
5. **In the vertical scrollbar on the right side of the window, click the scroll box with the left mouse button and drag down.**
   The ***scroll box*** enables you to move quickly up or down a window (see Figure 1.14). The relative location of the scroll box also indicates your relative location in the window. The vertical scrollbar also contains a scroll box in the middle of the window. Leave the Windows Explorer open for the next lesson.

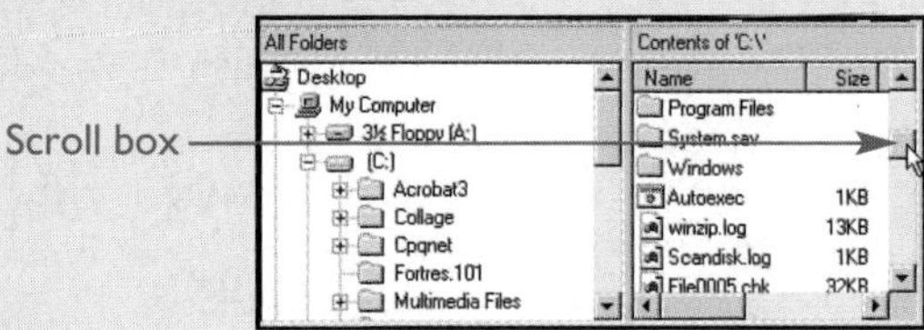

Figure 1.14
Use the scroll box to move quickly on a scrollbar.

Moving a Screen at a Time
You can move up or down a screen at a time by clicking in the gray area above or below the scroll box.

Lesson 5: Maximizing, Restoring, Minimizing, and Closing a Window

In Lesson 4, you resized the Windows Explorer window. You can also ***maximize*** the window, which enables the window to take up the whole screen, and ***restore*** the window, which takes it back to the size it was before being maximized. You can also ***minimize*** a window, removing it entirely from the screen and storing it in the taskbar until it is needed again.

In this lesson, you maximize, restore, minimize, and finally close the Windows Explorer window.

To Maximize, Restore, Minimize, and Close a Window

1. **Place the pointer on the Maximize button in the upper-right corner of the Windows Explorer window.**
   The Maximize button is the middle button in the group of three (see Figure 1.15).

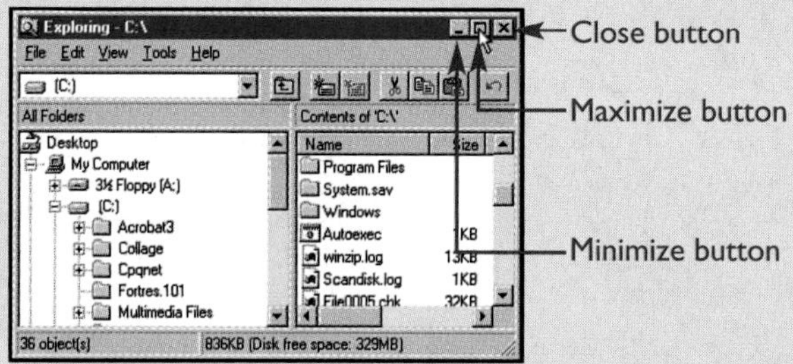

Figure 1.15
The Maximize button makes the window take up the entire screen.

2. **Click the Maximize button.**
   The Windows Explorer window now occupies the entire screen. The Maximize button is now the Restore button, and has a different look (see Figure 1.16).

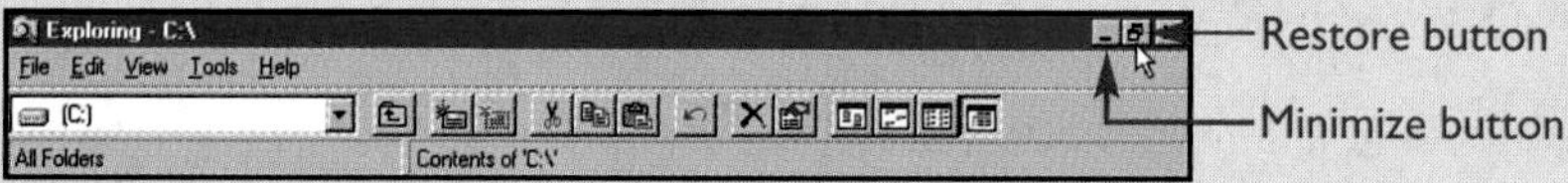

Figure 1.16
The Maximize button changes to a Restore button.

3. **Click the Restore button.**
   The window returns to the size it was before you clicked the Maximize button.
4. **Click the Minimize button.**
   The Windows Explorer window is still open, but is stored on the taskbar at the bottom of the screen (see Figure 1.17). The window has not been closed, just temporarily hidden.

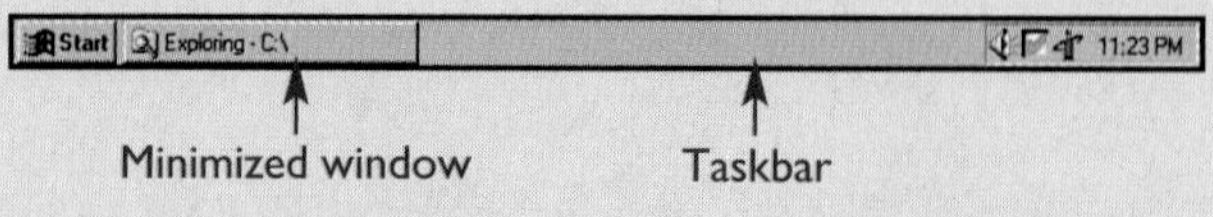

Start | Exploring - C:\ | 11:23 PM

Minimized window Taskbar

Figure 1.17
The Minimize button places the window in the taskbar, but does not close the window.

5. **Click the Exploring icon in the taskbar.**
   The window reappears in the same location it was in when you clicked the Minimize button.
6. **Click the Close button in the upper-right corner of the Windows Explorer window.**
   The Windows Explorer window closes.

Differences Between Dialog Boxes and Windows
Dialog boxes and windows serve two different purposes. Dialog boxes ask you for some type of decision: Do you want to accept changes? What size should something be? Or, how do you want this item formatted? These responses always deal with a single item or task. A window, on the other hand, contains information that can be used over and over again: a document, a list of available programs, the Calculator. Because windows can be used multiple times, they all have Minimize buttons so they can be stored on the taskbar but not closed. Dialog boxes do not have Minimize buttons because they focus on a particular task.

Lesson 6: Using the Taskbar to Work in Multiple Windows

One of the really nice features of the Windows operating system is that it enables you to have more than one window open at a time. This is particularly important when using Microsoft Office, because you can have more than one application open at a time and easily move information between applications.

In this lesson, you open two of the Office applications and quickly move from one to the other.

To Use the Taskbar to Work in Multiple Windows

1. **Click the Start button and move the pointer to the Programs menu choice.**
   The Programs submenu displays.

2. **Move the pointer to Microsoft Word and click.**
   Microsoft Word opens. A Microsoft Word button is also located on the taskbar (see Figure 1.18). The Word window might or might not be maximized. If it is not, click the Maximize button.

Microsoft Word button

Figure 1.18
A Microsoft Word button displays on the taskbar.

The way you open the Microsoft Office applications depends on how your computer is set up. You might have a shortcut so that you can start the programs from the top of the Start menu. You might also have shortcuts on the desktop. If there is a shortcut for Microsoft Word on the desktop, you can double-click it instead of using the Start menu. You might also have a toolbar at the top of your screen with icons that open Office applications.

3. **Click the Start button; go to the Programs option, and select Microsoft Excel.**
   Microsoft Excel opens. You now have buttons for both Word and Excel in the taskbar (see Figure 1.19). The Excel window might or might not be maximized. If it is not, click the Maximize button.

   The buttons on the taskbar display from left to right in the order you opened the programs.

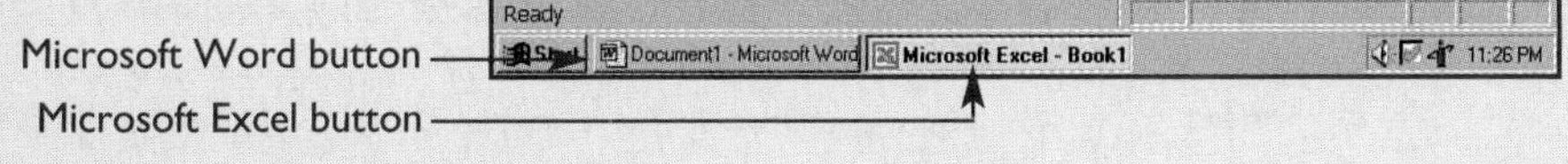

Figure 1.19
Buttons display on the taskbar for both open programs.

4. **Click the Microsoft Word button.**
   You are immediately taken to the Microsoft Word window. The program was hidden, not closed, so you didn't have to reopen it.

5. **Click the Microsoft Excel button.**
   The Excel window displays. You can have more than two programs open at the same time.

continues ▶

To Use the Taskbar to Work in Multiple Windows (continued)

6 Click the Close button to close Excel.

Make sure you click the Close button on the right side of the title bar that says Microsoft Excel and not the Close Window button on the workbook (the lower X button).

The Microsoft Word window displays again.

7 Click the Close button to close Word.

You know that no more programs are open because the taskbar is empty.

Lesson 7: Using the Windows Help System

Windows enables you to perform many different tasks. If you want to do something in Windows but don't know how, Windows has a Help feature that can guide you. Three separate help functions are included in the Windows Help file. The first is a Contents section that reads like a book. The second is an Index of key terms that might help you find a topic if you know the proper terminology. The third is a Find (Search) feature that enables you to look for individual words in the help text. This is particularly important if you don't know the correct words and phrases to use with the Index feature.

In this lesson, you look up a topic in the Contents section, and then move to the Index section to look for help on a specific topic.

To Use the Windows Help Screen

1 Click the Start button and select the Help option. Click the Contents tab, if necessary.

The Help Topics dialog box has three tabs (see Figure 1.20): Contents, Index, and Find (called Search in the newer versions of Windows). The Contents dialog box contains help in a book-like format.

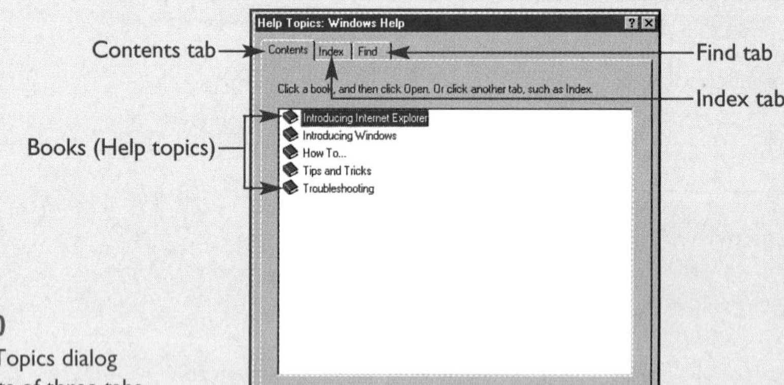

Figure 1.20
The Help Topics dialog box consists of three tabs.

2 Double-click the `Introducing Windows` book if you are using Windows 95; single-click if you are using a newer version.

The Introducing Windows book opens to display chapters that are also in the form of books.

The look of the Help Topics window varies depending on which version of Windows you are using. For example, the Contents tab contains five books in Windows 95 and ten books plus an introduction in Windows 98. The way these books are activated is also different. In Windows 95, you need to double-click the book or select the book and click the Open button. If you are using Windows 98, you simply need to single-click the book. This demonstrates the movement of the Windows operating system toward a Web look.

3 Open any one of the books until you see a chapter displayed.
The chapter consists of a page with a question mark (see Figure 1.21). The chapters are different for different versions of Windows.

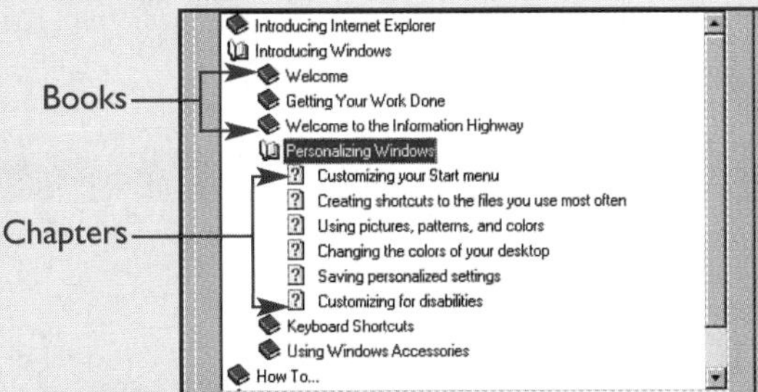

Figure 1.21
Each Help book consists of books or chapters on the topic.

4 Open a chapter and move through the help for the topic you have chosen. When you are through, click the Close button to close the Help Topics window.

5 Click the Start button; select the Help option, and click the Index tab, if necessary.
The Help Topics dialog box displays (see Figure 1.22). The Index tab enables you to type the word or phrase that you are looking for help on. Related topics display in the bottom part of the window. The Index tab limits you to searches for predetermined words and phrases.

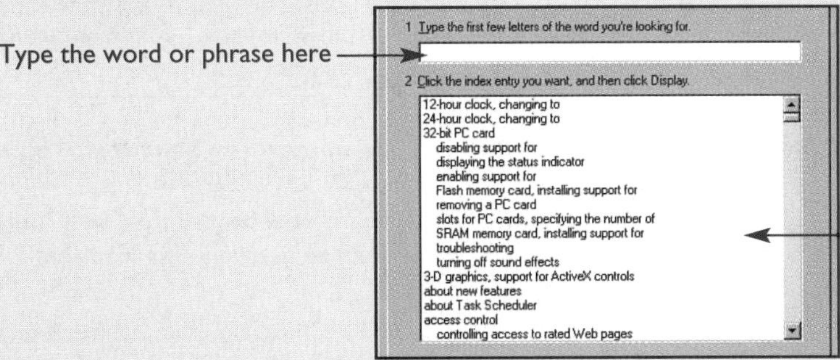

Figure 1.22
The Help Index tab enables you to type a word or phrase to find help.

Once again the look of the dialog box depends on the version of Windows you are using. The Help Topics dialog box Index tab displayed in the figure is from Windows 95.

6 Type `Start` in the text box at the top of the dialog box.
Related topics display in the drop-down list box below.

7 Double-click `customizing` from the Start menu topic.
Go through the instructions about adding a program to the Start menu. When you are through, close the Help dialog box.

As with the Contents tab, the look of the Index tab differs depending on your Windows version. The exact wording differs also, but you should be able to determine which option to use.

8 When you are through, click the Close button to close the Help dialog box.

Using the Find/Search Tab
The third (Find/Search) tab in the Windows Help dialog box enables you to look through the Help text for individual words. This is particularly useful when you don't know the proper terminology for what you want to do.

Lesson 8: Shutting Down Your Computer

It is important that you close your computer properly. To do this, you need to use the Shut Down option from the Start menu. The Shut Down option gives the computer a chance to close many of the programs that are active in the background—programs that you probably don't even know are running. Simply turning off the computer can cause problems.

In this lesson, you shut down your computer using the proper procedure.

To Shut Down Your Computer

1. **Click the Start button.**
   The Start menu displays.

2. **Select Shut Down from the Start menu.**
   The Shut Down Windows dialog box displays (see Figure 1.23).

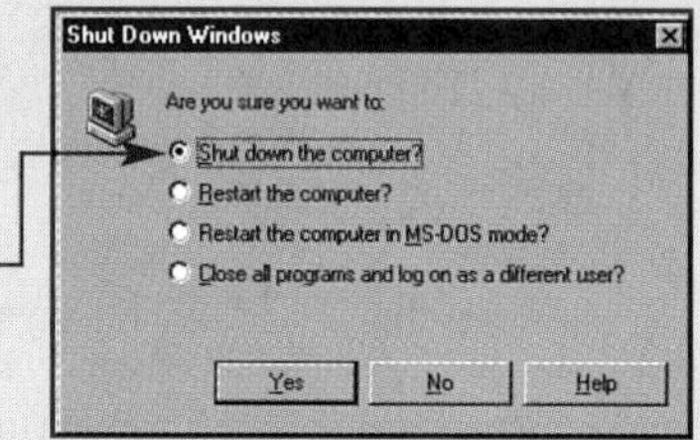

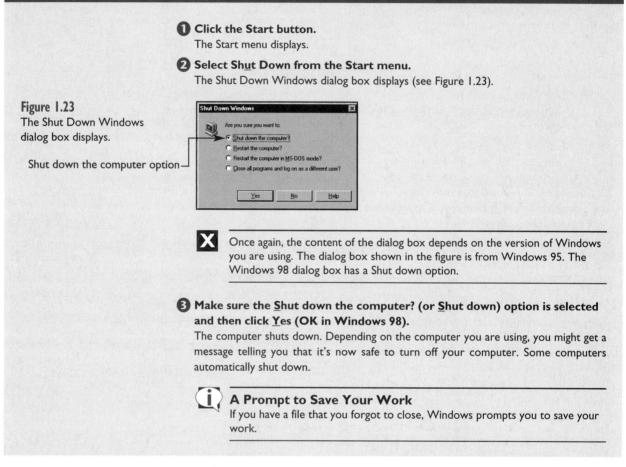

Figure 1.23
The Shut Down Windows dialog box displays.

Shut down the computer option

Once again, the content of the dialog box depends on the version of Windows you are using. The dialog box shown in the figure is from Windows 95. The Windows 98 dialog box has a Shut down option.

3. **Make sure the Shut down the computer? (or Shut down) option is selected and then click Yes (OK in Windows 98).**
   The computer shuts down. Depending on the computer you are using, you might get a message telling you that it's now safe to turn off your computer. Some computers automatically shut down.

A Prompt to Save Your Work
If you have a file that you forgot to close, Windows prompts you to save your work.

Summary

The project began with an introduction to Windows. The first project in this section provided you with a basic introduction to Microsoft Windows. You learned how to use the mouse, taskbar, and Start button; and to resize, move, maximize, and minimize windows. You also were introduced to Windows Help.

Checking Concepts and Terms

True/False

For each of the following, check *T* or *F* to indicate whether the statement is true or false.

__T__F 1. The mouse pointer, which is shaped like a hand with a pointed finger, is used to select or activate objects on the screen. [L1]

__T__F 2. To select the My Computer icon on the desktop, click it once with the left mouse button. [L1]

__T__F 3. The Start button can be used to launch programs, set up printers, get help, and shut down your computer. [L2]

__T__F 4. When you move the pointer to the lower-right corner of a window to change the size of the window, the pointer changes to a four-way arrow. [L3]

__T__F 5. To move a window on the desktop, click and hold down the mouse in the status bar and drag to the new location. [L3]

__T__F 6. The vertical scrollbar enables you to view information too wide to fit in a window. [L4]

__T__F 7. Minimizing a window hides the window but leaves it open and available on the taskbar. [L5]

__T__F 8. If you are using one Office program and want to use another program, you need to close the first program before you open the new one. [L6]

__T__F 9. The Contents tab in the Help window can be used like a book. [L7]

__T__F 10. It is very important to shut the computer down using the Shut Down option from the Start menu. [L8]

Multiple Choice

Circle the letter of the correct answer for each of the following questions.

1. If the taskbar is not displayed on the screen, you can ______________. [L1]
   a. choose View, Taskbar from the menu
   b. move the pointer to the bottom of the screen
   c. click the Taskbar button
   d. turn off your computer, and then turn it on again

2. If you double-click the My Computer icon and it does not open, it could be that ______________. [L1]
   a. you didn't click fast enough
   b. you moved the mouse while you were clicking
   c. a security program won't allow you to use My Computer
   d. all of the above

3. An arrow to the right of a menu option in the Start menu means ______________. [L2]
   a. if you select that option, you see a submenu of programs and/or files
   b. you right-click the mouse to activate that command
   c. you must double-click to activate that command
   d. that menu option is currently unavailable

4. In a scrollbar, the following enables you to see information that is not currently on the screen: ______________. [L4]
   a. up and down arrows
   b. left and right arrows
   c. scroll box
   d. all of the above

5. If you don't know the correct terminology to find help on a topic, the best place to look would be ______________. [L7]
   a. the Contents tab of the Help menu
   b. the Index tab of the Help menu
   c. the Find (or Search) tab of the Help menu
   d. the Book tab of the Help menu

Screen ID

Label each element of the Windows screen shown in Figure 1.24.

Figure 1.24

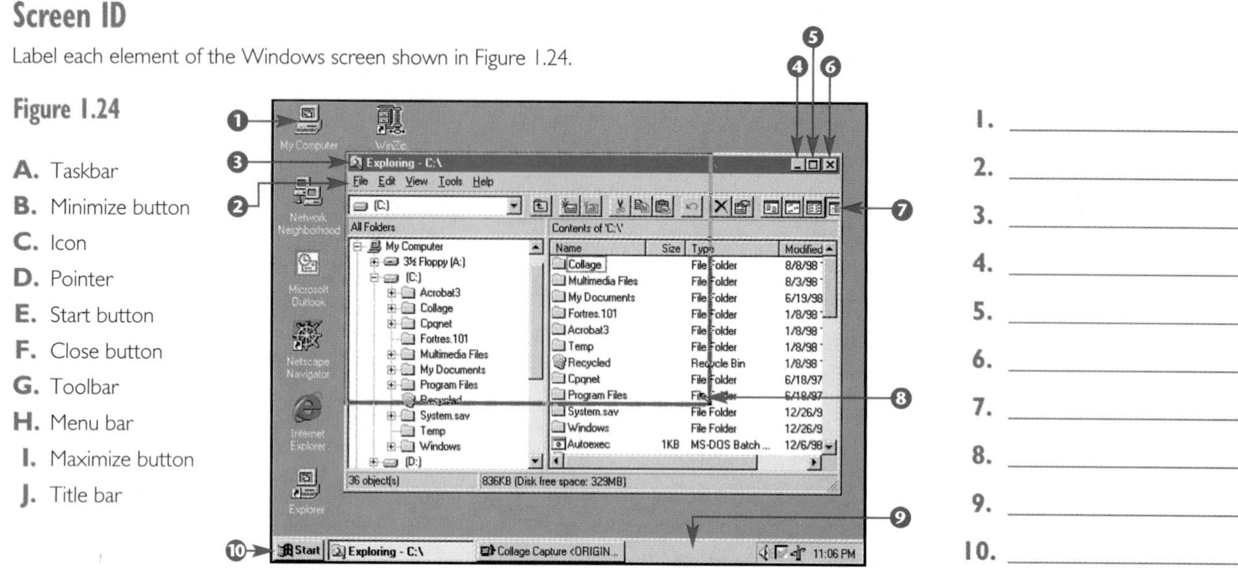

A. Taskbar
B. Minimize button
C. Icon
D. Pointer
E. Start button
F. Close button
G. Toolbar
H. Menu bar
I. Maximize button
J. Title bar

1. ______
2. ______
3. ______
4. ______
5. ______
6. ______
7. ______
8. ______
9. ______
10. ______

Skill Drill

Skill Drill exercises reinforce project skills. Each skill reinforced is the same, or nearly the same, as a skill presented in the project. Each exercise includes a brief narrative introduction, followed by detailed instructions in a step-by-step format.

1. Starting WordPad by Using the Start Menu

In Lesson 2, you used the Start menu to open the Calculator. The Accessories menu contains other programs, including two easy-to-use word processors with limited options. When you just need to type a quick note, NotePad or WordPad works well. [L2]

1. Click the Start button on the taskbar.
2. Select the Programs option.
3. Choose Accessories from the submenu.
4. Select and click WordPad (or NotePad) from the Accessories submenu.
5. Look around in the program; when you are through, click the Close button.

2. Changing the View in the My Computer Window

The My Computer window usually opens with large icons displayed. If someone has changed the view, however, it may open showing small icons or lists of disk drives and folders. You can easily change the look of the My Computer window. [L5]

1. Double-click the My Computer icon.
2. Choose View, Details from the menu. If your computer already shows details, choose View, List.
3. Click the lower-right corner of the My Computer window and resize the window so that you can see all the information.
4. Click the Maximize button to increase the size of the window to take up the whole screen.
5. Click the Minimize button to hide the My Computer window but leave the window available in the taskbar.
6. Click the My Computer button in the taskbar, and then click the Close button to close the window.

3. Using Help to Find Information About Setting Up Printers

In Lesson 7, you used two of the three tabs in the Help window. The third is the Find (or Search) tab, which enables you to type a word and find all the topics related to that word in the Help file. [L7]

1. Click the Start button on the taskbar.
2. Select the Help option.
3. Click the Find (Search) tab.
4. Type `print` in the text box provided. If nothing appears in the drop-down list box below, press Enter.
5. Scroll down until you find a topic about setting up your printer, and then click to select it.
6. Click the Display button and read the instructions.
7. When you are through, click the Close button.
8. If you are through using the computer, click the Start button and select Shut Down. Follow your shutdown procedure to turn off your computer.

Project 2

Windows Disk and File Management

Objectives

In this project, you learn how to

- ➤ **Format a Disk**
- ➤ **Create a Folder**
- ➤ **Copy a File**
- ➤ **Rename a File or Folder**
- ➤ **Move a File**
- ➤ **Delete a File or Folder**
- ➤ **Copy a Floppy Disk**

Key terms introduced in this project include

- destination disk
- file extension
- folder
- format
- source disk
- subfolder

Why Would I Do This?

If you are going to use computers on a regular basis, you need to know how to use disks and files effectively. If you are using a floppy disk to store your files for this book, it is especially important that you know how to copy, move, rename, and even delete files. If you are using unformatted or old disks, you also need to know how to set them up to receive data.

In this project, you format a floppy disk and then create two folders. You copy files from your CD-ROM onto this floppy disk, and then you rename, move, and delete files and folders. You also learn how to create ***folders***, which store data files, programs, and folders inside of folders, called ***subfolders***. Folders enable you to organize the information on storage devices, including hard drives, Zip drives, network drives, and 3 1/2" disks. You need two floppy disks to complete this project.

Lesson 1: Formatting a Disk

When you purchase a floppy disk, it is likely to be formatted for use on a Windows-based machine. At times, however, you need to ***format*** a disk yourself. Formatting a disk sets it up to receive data. It also identifies and automatically isolates any bad spots on the surface of the disk and sets up an area for a disk directory. Formatting erases any information that might be on the disk. If you have any previously used disks lying around that don't contain important data, it is probably a good idea to reformat them before you use them.

In this lesson, you format a floppy disk.

To Format a Disk

1 Place a floppy disk in drive A.

Drive A is the floppy drive on your computer. It doesn't matter if the disk you use is brand new or not.

2 Click the Start button, move to the Programs option, and select Windows Explorer.

The Windows Explorer opens. It may or may not be maximized. For the purposes of this lesson, it does not matter. Your Windows Explorer window should look similar to Figure 2.1, although the names in the All Folders column (on the left) should be different. Also, the contents of your disk should be different from the contents in the Contents of A:\ column (on the right). The files and folders contained on drive A are the ones you add to the disk by the end of Lesson 3.

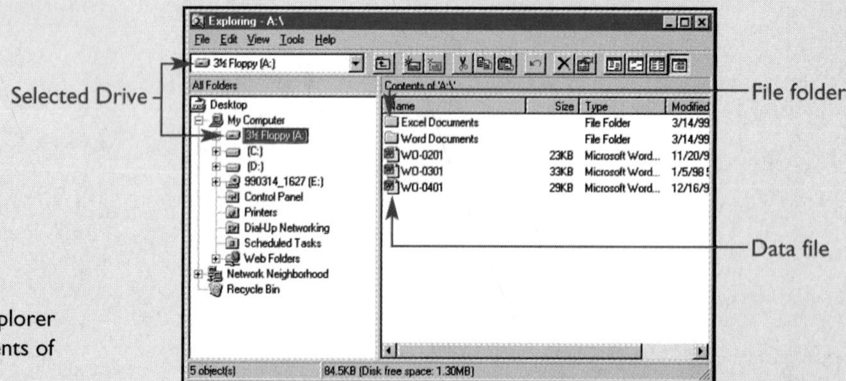

Figure 2.1
The Windows Explorer displays the contents of drive A.

Your Windows Explorer screen might have a different look from the one in Figure 2.1. The version of Windows that you use makes a difference in the look and feel of the window. (This figure displays a Windows 95 screen.) Also, the files and folders in the Contents area might be displayed as large icons, or as text with a different level of detail.

3 If you can't see the icon that says 3 1/2 Floppy (A:), use the up arrow on the scrollbar to move to the top of the list of folders.
The drive A icon should be visible in the All Folders area of the Windows Explorer window. In this example, no files or folders are in the drive A Contents area.

4 Right-click the floppy disk icon or name.
A shortcut menu displays (see Figure 2.2). One of the options is Format. The options available in the shortcut menu vary depending on which version of Windows you are using and what other programs you have installed on your computer.

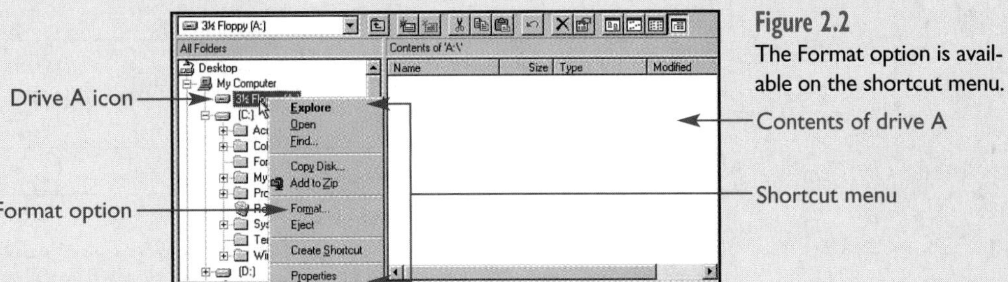

Figure 2.2
The Format option is available on the shortcut menu.

5 Click the Format option.
The Format dialog box displays and makes several options available to you (see Figure 2.3). You can do a Quick (erase) format, which erases the existing files on a previously formatted disk. You can also Copy system files only to a previously formatted disk, so that the disk can be used to boot your computer. By far the most common format used is the default, Full format.

The Capacity of the disk is detected automatically. If you are formatting a very old disk, the capacity might be 720 Kb instead of 1.44 Mb.

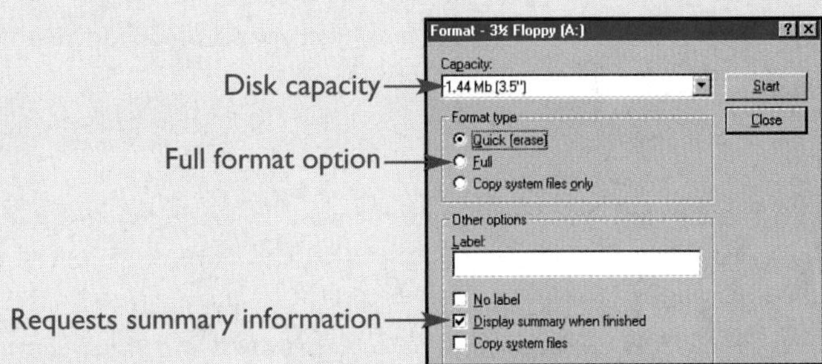

Figure 2.3
The Format dialog box gives you several formatting options.

6 Select the Full format option and the Display summary when finished option, if necessary, and then click Start.
Windows begins to format the disk. A bar at the bottom of the Format window shows you the progress of the format, which takes a couple of minutes. When it is through, a Format Results dialog box displays (see Figure 2.4).

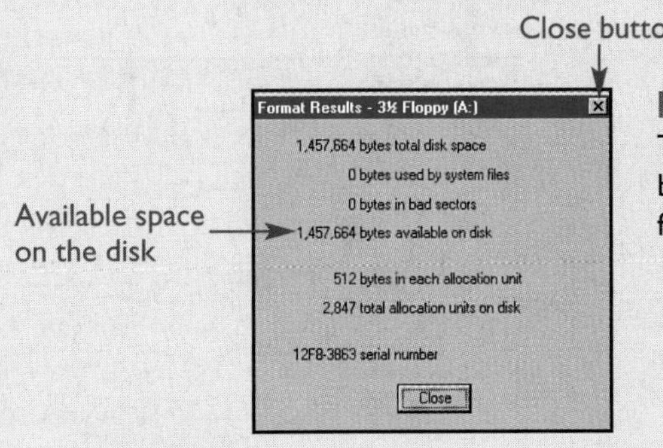

Figure 2.4
The Format Results dialog box displays when the formatting is complete.

continues ▶

To Format a Disk (continued)

7. **Click the Close button in the Format Results dialog box.**
The dialog box has two Close buttons: a big one at the bottom, and the standard X button in the upper-right corner. Both do the same thing. The program returns to the Format dialog box.

8. **Click either Close button in the Format dialog box.**
You now have a clean disk ready to use.

Trying to Open an Unformatted Disk
If you try to open a disk that the computer cannot read, Windows automatically asks if you want to format the disk.

Reformatting a Macintosh Disk
If you are ever in need of a disk and don't have any Windows disks around, you can format a Macintosh disk. The formatting removes all the data on the disk and sets it up to be readable by a Windows computer.

Lesson 2: Creating a Folder

You use folders to organize files or other folders (called subfolders). As you use the computer more and more, you build up a collection of files that you want to save. If you put all the files in one place, finding the right one might be difficult. Folders enable you to store your important files by type or by subject and make handling your files more manageable. In most cases, you use folders on hard drives or other drives with large capacities. You can, however, create folders on floppy disks. The procedure is the same no matter where you want to create them.

In this lesson, you create two folders on the floppy disk you formatted in Lesson 1.

To Create a Folder

1. **With the Windows Explorer window open, click the icon for drive A.**
You may have to scroll up to find the drive A icon. The Contents area is empty because you just formatted the disk.

2. **Move the pointer to the Contents area and right-click.**
A shortcut menu displays. The contents of the shortcut menu depend on the version of Windows that you are using.

3. **Move the pointer to the New option.**
A submenu displays, showing the things that you can create from this shortcut menu (see Figure 2.5). The top of the submenu gives you the option of creating a new folder or shortcut; the lower part of the submenu reflects the programs that you have installed on your computer.

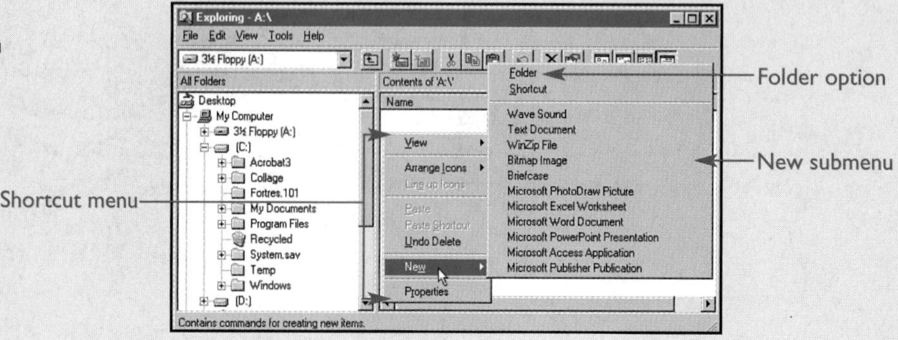

Figure 2.5
The New submenu displays.

4 Select the Folder option by clicking it.
A new folder is created. The folder name is in edit mode, which enables you to change it.

5 Type `Word Documents` over the default `New Folder` name and press Enter.
The folder now has a meaningful name (see Figure 2.6).

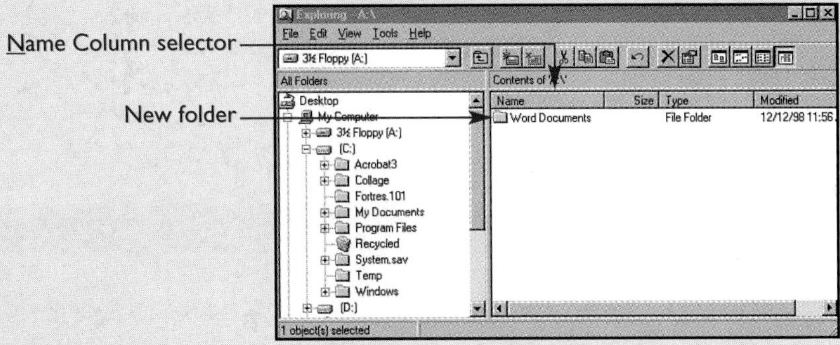

Figure 2.6
The new folder is renamed.

If you accidentally press Enter before you have a chance to name the folder, you can rename it. Click the folder once to select it, and choose File, Rename from the Windows Explorer menu. Type a new name.

6 Choose File, New from the Windows Explorer menu.
The same submenu you used in the shortcut menu displays.

7 Select Folder from the submenu. Name the new folder `Excel Documents` and press Enter.
You now have two folders and no files on your disk.

8 Click the Name column selector in the Contents area of the Windows Explorer window.
The folders are sorted in alphabetical order (see Figure 2.7). If you click the Name column selector again, it will sort the folders in descending (z-to-a) order.

Leave the Windows Explorer window open for the next lesson.

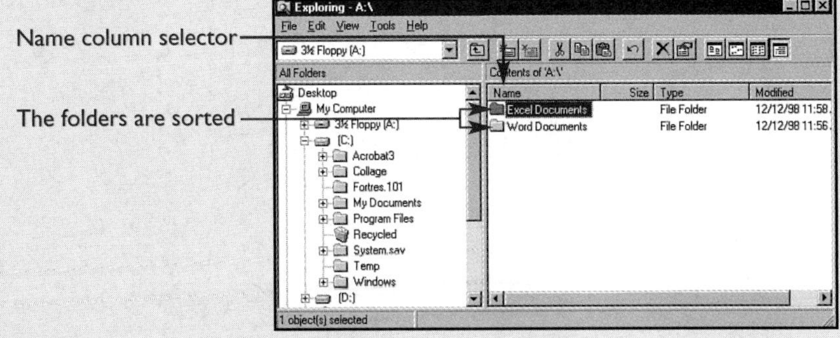

Figure 2.7
The folders are sorted alphabetically.

Sorting Columns in the Contents Area

You can click any of the column selectors in the Contents area to sort the files and folders. Clicking the Size column selector once, for example, sorts the files by size, smallest to largest. Clicking it again sorts the files from largest to smallest. Because folders have no size, they are either all shown first or all shown last. You can use the same procedure to sort by date modified or by file type.

Lesson 3: Copying a File

You will often need to copy files from one location to another. As you work on your computer, you need to make backup copies of important files. You can do this by copying a file from a hard disk to a floppy disk, a network drive, a Zip disk, or even a recordable CD. Throughout the remainder of this section, you frequently need to copy files from your student CD-ROM to a floppy drive (or other drive, depending on your situation).

When you copy a file directly to a floppy disk, the My Documents folder, the desktop, or a Zip disk, you can use the Send To option from a shortcut menu. If you are copying to a hard drive, or to a folder on any drive, you need to select and copy the file, and then move to the desired location and paste it.

In this lesson, you copy a file from your student CD-ROM to the floppy disk you formatted in Lesson 1.

To Copy a File

1. **Scroll down the All Folders column (on the left side of the Windows Explorer window) and select the CD-ROM drive where you have placed your student disc.**
   The Windows Explorer displays the folders and files that are on that CD (see Figure 2.8). You can also select the CD-ROM from the list of folders in the All Folders section of the Windows Explorer window. The drive letter of your CD-ROM might be different from the one shown.

The name of your CD-ROM is different from the one shown, which is an early version of the disc that came with your book. You might also have a slightly different list of files and folders. These factors do not affect the following lesson.

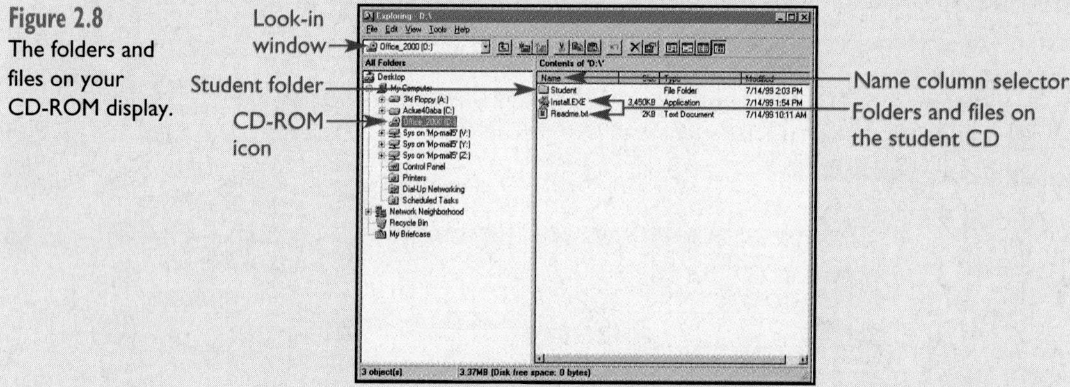

Figure 2.8 The folders and files on your CD-ROM display.

2. **Double-click the Student folder.**
   A list of files used in this book displays (see Figure 2.9).

Figure 2.9 The files used in this book display.

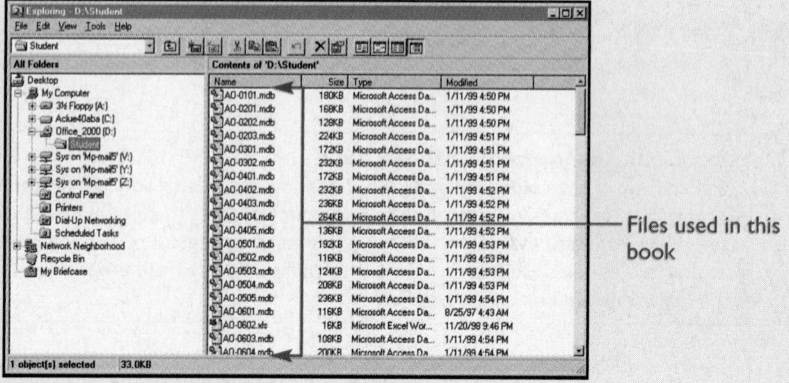

3 Scroll downward to locate the `WO-0201` file. Right-click the file.
A shortcut menu displays.

You may not see a file called WO-0201. Instead, there may be a file called WO-0201.doc. The three letters following the filename are called a ***file extension***, and nearly all files have these extensions. If you want to turn them off, choose View, Options from the menu, and then click the View tab. Click the Hide MS-DOS file extensions for file types that are registered check box.

Files created by Microsoft Office programs have a standard set of extensions. For example, Microsoft Word documents end in .doc; PowerPoint presentations end with .ppt, and so on. This book assumes that the file extensions are turned off.

4 Select Send To from the shortcut menu.
A submenu displays showing the locations to which you can send the file (see Figure 2.10). You want to send this file to your floppy drive.

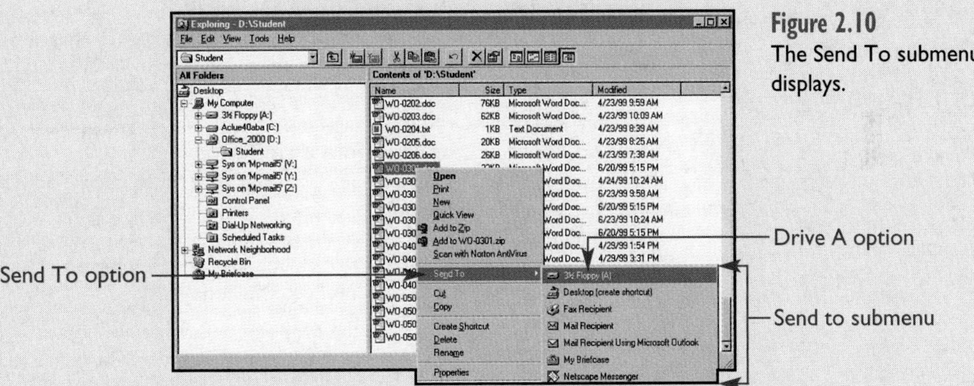

Figure 2.10
The Send To submenu displays.

If you are using disk space on a hard drive or network drive to store your files, you need to use a different procedure. There are several methods you can use, but the easiest is to select the file, use the Edit, Copy command from the menu (or click the Copy button), go to the destination drive and folder, and use the Edit, Paste command from the menu (or click the Paste button).

5 Select and click the 3 1/2 Floppy (A) option.
The file is copied to your floppy drive. Repeat the procedure to copy two more files.

6 Right-click the `WO-0301` file; choose Send To from the shortcut menu, and select and click the 3 1/2 Floppy (A) option.
The WO-0301 file is copied to your floppy disk.

7 Right-click the `WO-0401` file; choose Send To from the shortcut menu, and select and click the 3 1/2 Floppy (A) option.
The WO-0401 file is copied to your floppy disk.

8 Click the icon for drive A in the All Folders section of the Windows Explorer.
Notice that your files are now on the floppy disk (see Figure 2.11). They also remain on the CD-ROM. Copying does not remove the original files from their original location, no matter where you are copying from and to. Leave your Windows Explorer open to drive A for the next lesson.

continues ▶

To Copy a File (continued)

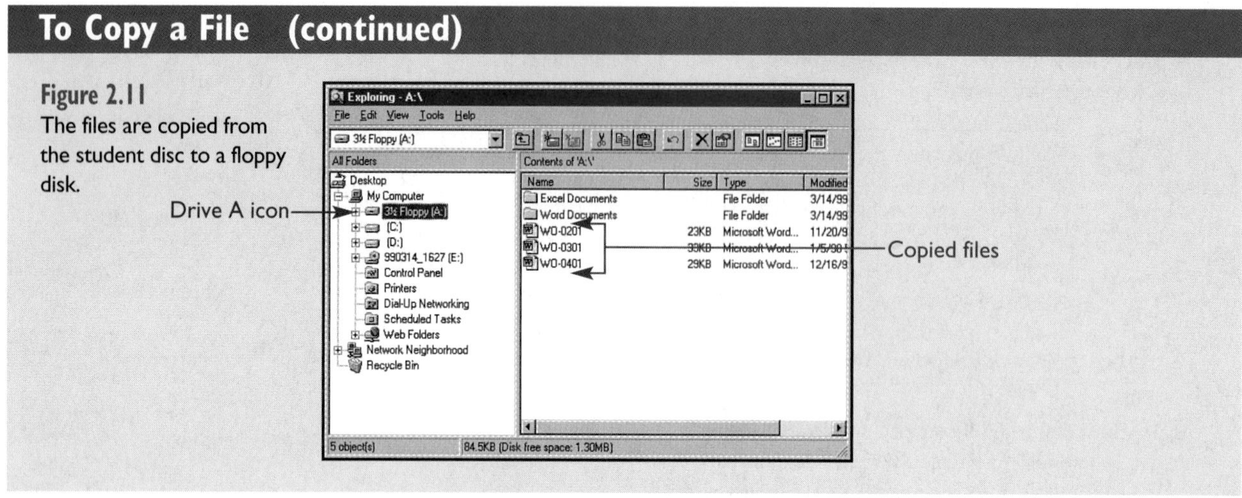

Figure 2.11
The files are copied from the student disc to a floppy disk.

Dragging Files from Your CD to Drive A

You can also copy files from the CD-ROM to the floppy disk by dragging the file from the CD-ROM and dropping it on the icon for drive A or whatever drive and folder you are using.

Copying More Than One File at a Time

You might need to copy several files from one disk to another. You can copy them one at a time, as you did in this lesson, or you can copy multiple files. If the files are all next to each other, you can click the first one, press and hold down Shift, and then click the last file. The first and last file and all the files in between are selected. You can then right-click any of the selected files and send them to the floppy disk.

If the files are not together, click the first one; press and hold down Ctrl, and click each of the files you want to copy. You can then right-click any of the selected files and send them to the floppy disk.

Lesson 4: Renaming a File or Folder

In Lesson 3, you copied a file from one location to another. You can copy files to make backups. You can also copy files that you want to change. In such a case, you want to rename the file after you copy it.

In this lesson, you rename a file you copied to your floppy drive in Lesson 3. You also rename a folder.

To Rename a File or Folder

1. **With the Windows Explorer window open, click the drive A icon, if necessary.**
   The files and folders on your floppy drive are listed on the right side of the Windows Explorer window.

2. **Right-click the `WO-0201` file.**
   The file is selected and a shortcut menu displays (see Figure 2.12).

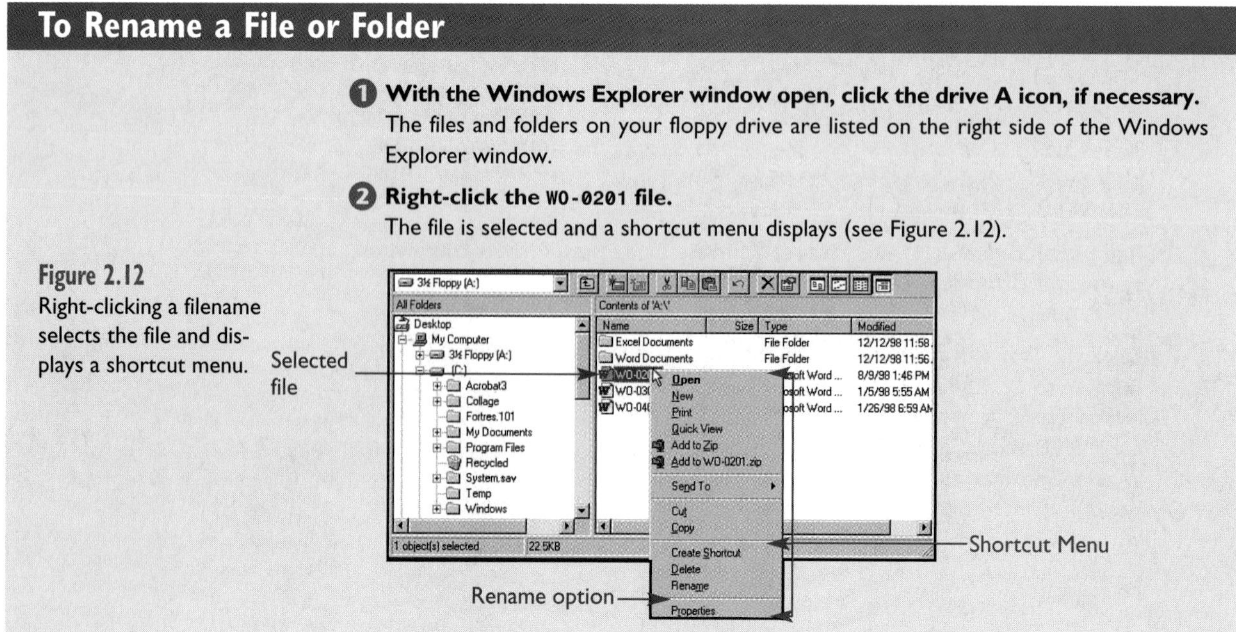

Figure 2.12
Right-clicking a filename selects the file and displays a shortcut menu.

3 Select Rena_m_e from the shortcut menu.
The shortcut menu disappears and the filename is in edit mode.

4 Type `Sample Word Document` over the existing name and press ↵Enter.
The first letter you type removes the entire original name. You might be asked to confirm that you want to rename a Read Only file because the source of the file is a Read Only CD. Click Yes to complete the name change.

If you have file extensions turned on, you get an error message telling you that if you change a filename extension, the file may become unusable. If you get this message, click the No button, and then add .doc to the filename you typed.

If your filename is longer than the Name column in the Contents area of the Windows Explorer window, the right side of the filename appears to be cut off. Don't worry, it's still there. If you want to see the whole filename, click the line to the right of the Name column selector and drag to the right. You can resize any of the columns in the Contents area.

5 Click the Excel Documents folder.
The folder is selected.

6 Choose File, Rena_m_e from the menu.
The folder name is now in the edit mode.

7 Click to the left of the word `Documents` in the folder name and drag to the right until you have selected the whole word.

8 Type `Spreadsheets` over the word `Documents`, and press ↵Enter.
If you accidentally select the space before the word `Documents`, you have to put a space back in. The name of the folder changes to `Excel Spreadsheets` (see Figure 2.13). It doesn't matter which of the two methods for renaming files and folders you use; use whichever is most comfortable for you. Leave the folder selected for the next lesson.

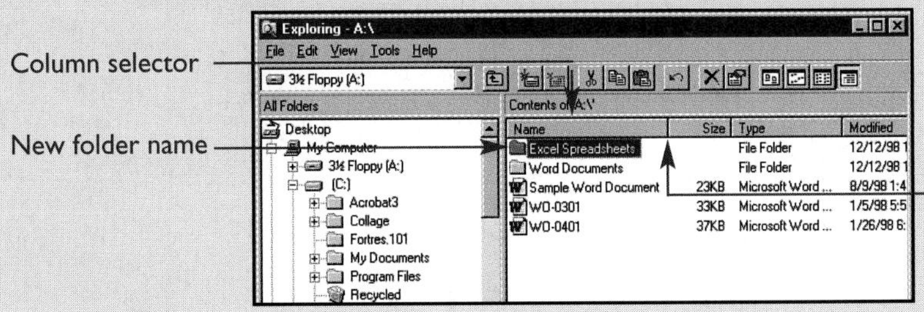

Figure 2.13
The folder name is changed.

Filename Restrictions
Several restrictions for naming files or folders exist. A filename can contain up to 255 characters, including spaces, although the filename cannot begin with a space. It also cannot contain the following characters: \ / : * ? " < > |.

Another Way to Rename a File or Folder
A third way to rename a file or folder is to click the filename or folder name, wait a second, and then click it again and type in a new name. However, if you click too quickly, you open the file or folder.

Lesson 5: Moving a File

You have copied three files to your floppy disk. They are all Microsoft Word documents that should be in the Word Documents folder. You can move files, or even folders, from one folder to another, or up or down one folder level on the same disk drive.

In this lesson, you move the three documents into the Word Documents folder.

To Move a File

1 **With the Windows Explorer still active, click the drive A icon.**
The files and folders on your floppy drive are listed on the right side of the Windows Explorer window.

2 **Click the Sample Word Document file and drag it over the top of the Word Documents folder in the All Folders column.**
The Word Documents folder is selected, and the Word icon appears over the folder (see Figure 2.14).

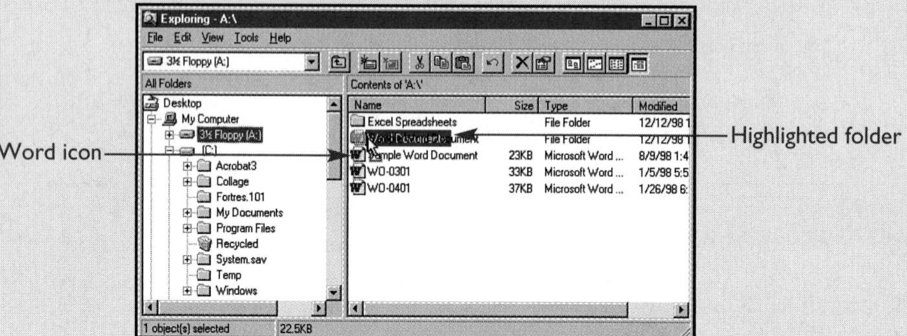

Figure 2.14
Dragging the file over a folder highlights the folder.

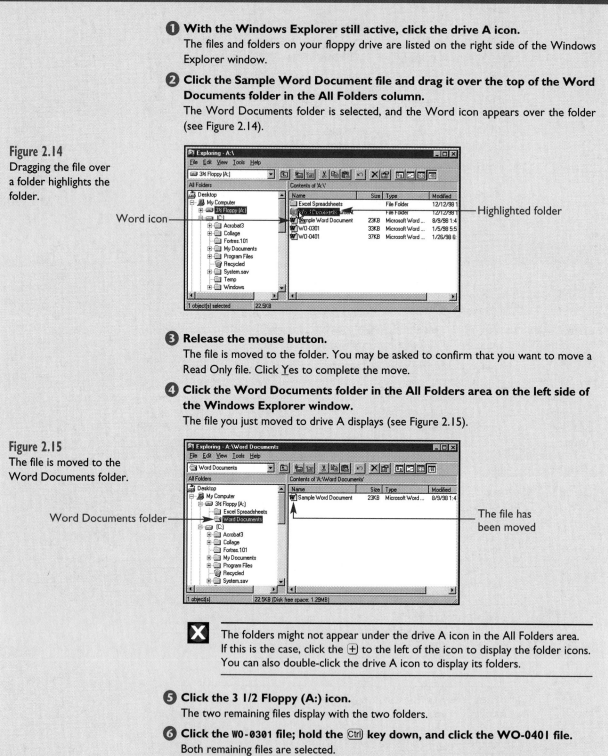

3 **Release the mouse button.**
The file is moved to the folder. You may be asked to confirm that you want to move a Read Only file. Click Yes to complete the move.

4 **Click the Word Documents folder in the All Folders area on the left side of the Windows Explorer window.**
The file you just moved to drive A displays (see Figure 2.15).

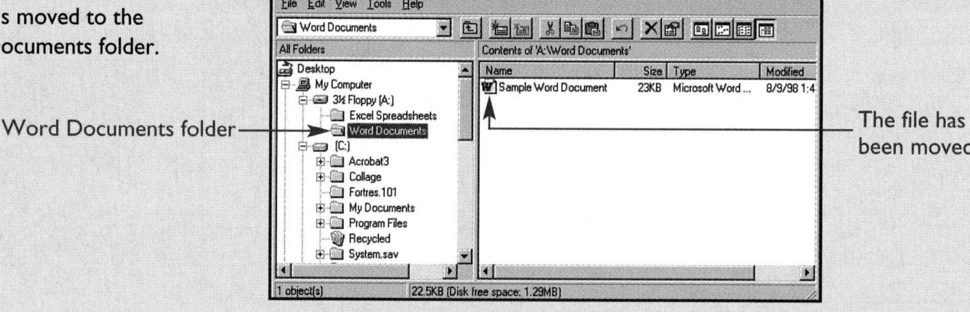

Figure 2.15
The file is moved to the Word Documents folder.

The folders might not appear under the drive A icon in the All Folders area. If this is the case, click the + to the left of the icon to display the folder icons. You can also double-click the drive A icon to display its folders.

5 **Click the 3 1/2 Floppy (A:) icon.**
The two remaining files display with the two folders.

6 **Click the `WO-0301` file; hold the Ctrl key down, and click the WO-0401 file.**
Both remaining files are selected.

7 **Click and hold down the left mouse button on one of the two files; drag them up to the Word Documents folder until it is selected, and release the mouse button.**
Both files move to the Word Documents folder. Once again, you may be asked to confirm the move of each file.

Using Cut-and-Paste to Move a File
You can also move a file using the cut-and-paste method. To do this, select the file, and choose Edit, Cut from the menu (or click the Cut button on the Windows Explorer toolbar). Move to the new drive or folder, and then choose Edit, Paste from the menu (or click the Paste button on the toolbar).

8. **Click the Word Documents folder in the All Folders area on the left side of the Windows Explorer window.**
All three files are now in the Word Documents folder (see Figure 2.16). Leave the Windows Explorer open for the next lesson.

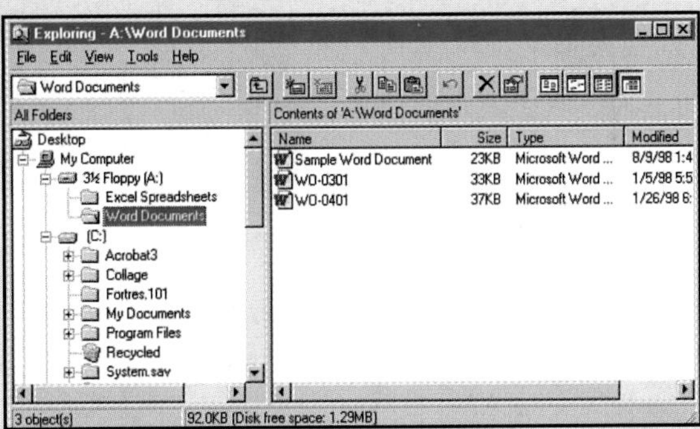

Figure 2.16
All three files now appear in the Word Documents folder.

Lesson 6: Deleting a File or Folder

When you are certain you no longer need a file, it is a good idea to remove it from the disk, whether it is a floppy disk or a hard drive. If you leave it on a disk too long, you tend to forget what was in the file and it just sits there taking up space. If you don't remove files, your disks can fill up. You can delete files in several ways.

In this lesson, you delete a file and a folder from your floppy disk.

To Delete a File or Folder

1. **Right-click the Sample Word Document file.**
A shortcut menu displays (see Figure 2.17).

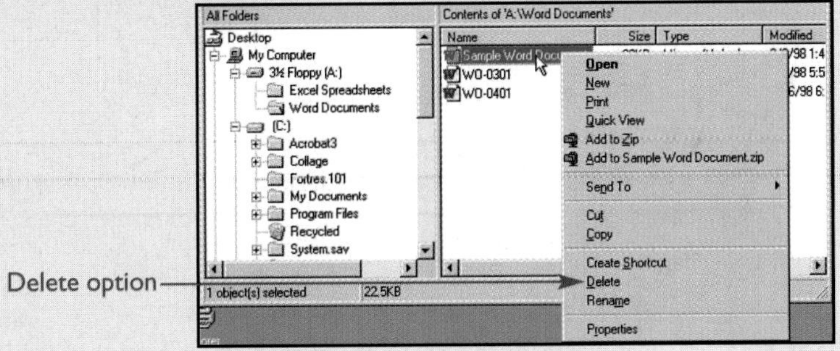

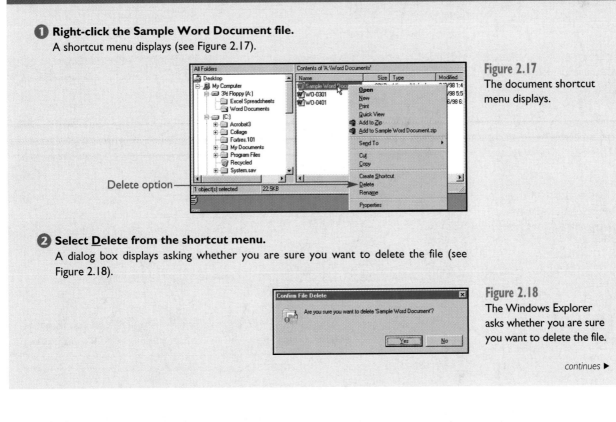

Figure 2.17
The document shortcut menu displays.

2. **Select Delete from the shortcut menu.**
A dialog box displays asking whether you are sure you want to delete the file (see Figure 2.18).

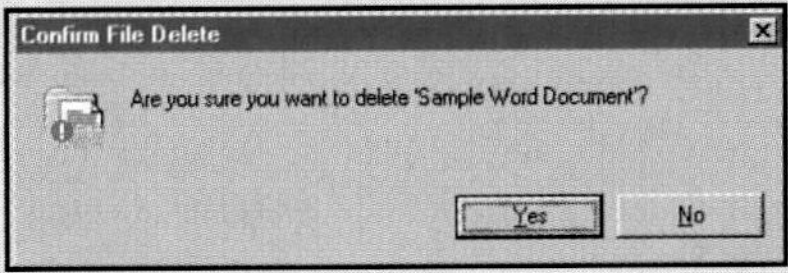

Figure 2.18
The Windows Explorer asks whether you are sure you want to delete the file.

continues ▶

To Delete a File or Folder (continued)

3 Click the Yes button.
The file is deleted from the disk.

4 Click the 3 1/2 Floppy (A:) icon.
The two file folders display.

5 Click the Excel Spreadsheets folder.
The folder is selected.

6 Press Del.
A dialog box asks whether you are sure you want to delete the folder and all its contents (see Figure 2.19). When you delete a folder, you also delete any files in that folder.

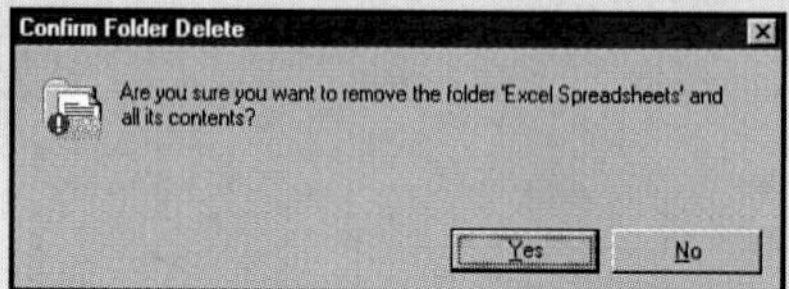

Figure 2.19
A dialog box asks whether you want to remove the folder and all its contents.

7 Click the Yes button to confirm the deletion.
The folder is deleted from the disk. Leave the Windows Explorer open for the next lesson.

Trying to Delete an Open File
Sometimes when you try to delete a file, Windows Explorer displays a dialog box that says the file cannot be deleted. This usually means that the file is open. You must close an open document before you can delete it.

Lesson 7: Copying a Floppy Disk

If you are saving your files on a floppy disk, you should make backup copies of your files. If you have access to a hard drive, you can copy files from a floppy disk to a temporary location on the hard drive and then put a new floppy disk in the drive and copy the files from the hard drive to the new disk. An easier way to duplicate an entire floppy disk is to use the Copy Disk option from a shortcut menu.

In this lesson, you make a copy of an entire floppy disk.

To Copy a Floppy Disk

1 Right-click the 3 1/2 Floppy (A:) icon.
A shortcut menu displays.

2 Select Copy Disk from the shortcut menu.
A dialog box asks what you want to copy from and to (see Figure 2.20). If your system has a Zip drive, it also displays here.

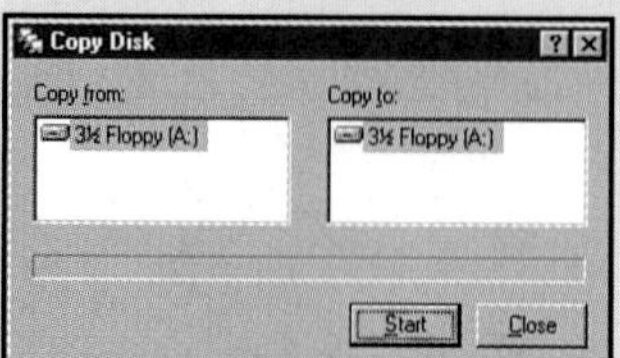

Figure 2.20
A dialog box asks where you want to copy from and to.

3 Click the Start button.
The program reads the disk you want to copy, known as the ***source disk***, into memory, and then asks you to insert the disk you want to copy to, which is called the ***destination disk*** (see Figure 2.21).

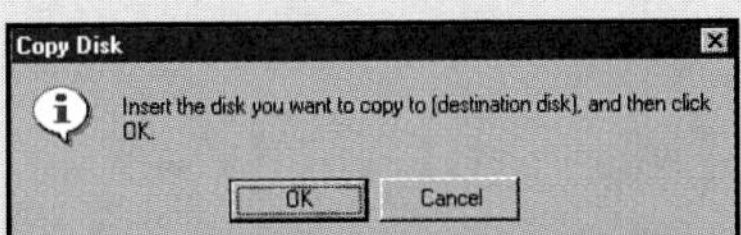

Figure 2.21
The Copy Disk dialog box prompts you to insert the destination disk.

4 **Remove the source disk and insert the destination disk, and then click OK.**
The contents of the source disk are copied to the destination disk. When the Copy Disk procedure finishes, the Copy Disk dialog box displays a message that the copy was successful (see Figure 2.22).

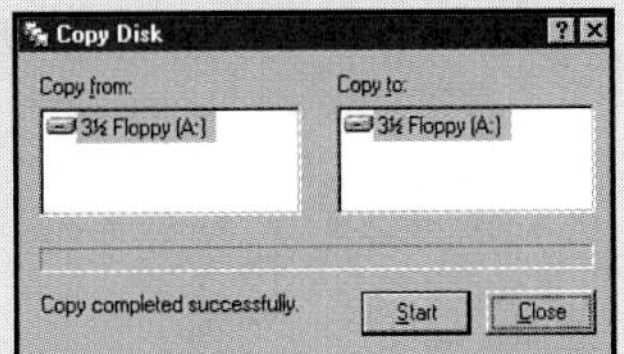

Figure 2.22
A dialog box tells you the copy was successful.

5 **Click the Close button to close the Copy Disk dialog box.**
You now have an identical copy of your original disk.

6 **Click the Close button to close the Windows Explorer. If you are through using the computer, click the Start button and select Shut Down.**

Copying a Disk Copies Everything
The Copy Disk procedure does not simply copy the files from the source disk and write them to the destination disk. It actually makes a duplicate of the source disk, which means that it deletes any files that are on the destination disk!

Summary

In this project, you worked with Windows disk and file management. You formatted a disk to prepare it to receive data. You used the Windows Explorer to create folders to hold files, then copied, moved, renamed, and deleted files and folders. Finally, you made an exact copy of a floppy disk.

You might want to expand your file management skills by using Windows Help to find out how to use the My Computer feature to work with files and folders.

Checking Concepts and Terms 

True/False

For each of the following, check *T* or *F* to indicate whether the statement is true or false.

__T __F **1.** Formatting a disk sets it up to receive data. [L1]

__T __F **2.** You cannot format a Macintosh disk for use in a Windows computer. [L1]

__T __F **3.** You can create folders on hard disks but not on floppy disks. [L2]

__T __F **4.** To sort the file and folder names in alphabetical order, you can click the column selector of the Name column in the Windows Explorer Content area. [L2]

__T __F **5.** A quick way to copy a file from a hard disk or CD-ROM to a floppy disk is to right-click the filename and select Send To from the shortcut menu. [L3]

__T __F **6.** A file extension consists of three characters at the end of a filename that identify the size of the file. [L3]

__T __F **7.** You can rename a file, but not a folder. [L4]

__T __F **8.** You can use the cut-and-paste method to move a file from one folder to another. [L5]

__T __F **9.** One way to remove a file from a disk is to select it and press Del. [L6]

__T __F **10.** Copying a floppy disk is a good way to back up your work. [L8]

Multiple Choice

Circle the letter of the correct answer for each of the following questions.

1. If you put an unreadable disk in the floppy drive, ______________. [L1]

a. you are immediately asked whether you want to format it

b. it is automatically formatted

c. you cannot use it

d. you are asked whether you want to format it the first time you try to select it

2. To rename a file or folder, you can ______________. [L4]

a. right-click the filename and select Rename from the shortcut menu

b. click the filename or folder name, wait a second, and click it again

c. choose File, Rename from the menu

d. all of the above

3. When naming a file or folder, you can use ___________. [L4]

a. numbers

b. more than 255 characters

c. a space as the first character

d. a question mark (?) or asterisk (*)

4. To move a file from one folder to another, you can ______________. [L5]

a. use the shortcut menu and select the Move option

b. click the Move button on the toolbar

c. drag the file and drop it on the new folder icon

d. all of the above

5. When you use the Copy Disk procedure, ______________. [L7]

a. you can copy the contents of a floppy disk, a CD-ROM, or a hard disk

b. all the data on the source disk is deleted and replaced by the data on the destination disk

c. all the data on the destination disk is deleted and replaced by the data on the source disk

d. the destination disk is automatically reformatted

Screen ID

Label each element of the Windows screen shown in Figure 2.23.

Figure 2.23

A. Place to look for disk location

B. Prepares a disk to receive data

C. Column selector

D. Makes a duplicate of the original disk

E. Floppy disk

F. Removes a file or folder from the disk

G. Quick way to copy a file to a floppy disk

H. Shortcut menu

I. Displays folders and files in the selected disk or folder

J. Enables you to change the name of a file or folder

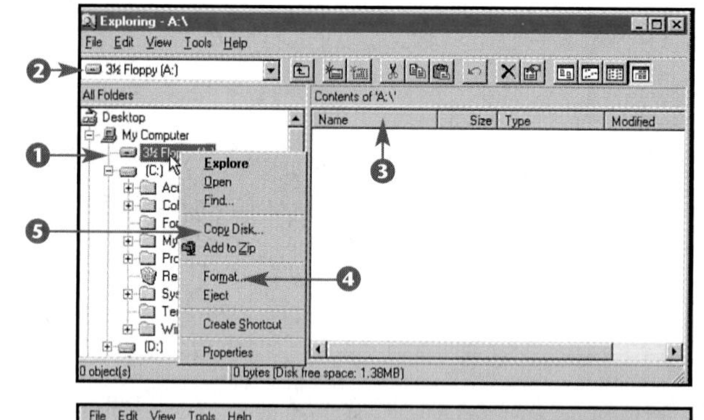

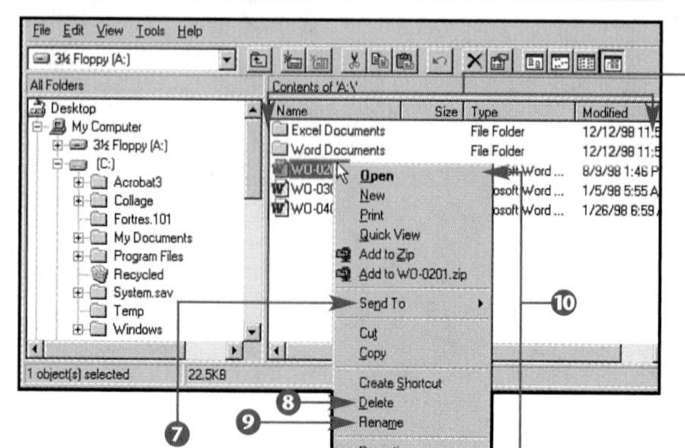

1. ______________

2. ______________

3. ______________

4. ______________

5. ______________

6. ______________

7. ______________

8. ______________

9. ______________

10. ______________

Skill Drill exercises reinforce project skills. Each skill reinforced is the same, or nearly the same, as a skill presented in the project. Each exercise includes a brief narrative introduction, followed by detailed instructions in a step-by-step format.

The following exercises should be done in order. It does not matter which disk you use.

1. Using the Quick Format Option

In Lesson 1, you did a full format on a disk. You can also do a quick format, which gets rid of all the files on your disk, but doesn't do the magnetic setup necessary for a full format. The quick format is much faster than the full format. [L1]

To do a quick format on a disk, complete the following steps:

1. Place one of the floppy disks you used in this project into the disk drive.
2. Click the Start button; choose the Programs option, and open the Windows Explorer, if necessary.
3. Right-click the 3 1/2 Floppy (A:) icon in the All Folders area of the Windows Explorer.
4. Select Format from the shortcut menu.
5. Choose Quick (erase) from the Format type area of the Format dialog box.
6. Click the Start button.
7. Close the Format Results dialog box and the Format dialog box when the format is complete.

2. Copying and Renaming Files to a Floppy Disk

You copied Word files to your floppy disk in Lesson 3 and renamed them in Lesson 4. In this exercise, you practice moving and renaming files. [L3–4]

To copy and rename files, complete the following steps:

1. With the Windows Explorer active, find and select the CD-ROM that came with this book.
2. Open the Student folder and find the Excel sample files. Right-click `EO-0301`.
3. Select the Send To option and choose the 3 1/2 Floppy (A) option.
4. Use the same procedure to copy `EO-0401` to the floppy disk.
5. Find the PowerPoint sample files and send `PO-0301` and `PO-0401` to the floppy disk.
6. Click the icon for drive A.
7. Right-click the `EO-0301` file and choose Rename from the shortcut menu. Rename the file `Excel Sample File 1`.
8. Use the same procedure to rename `EO-0401` `Excel Sample File 2`.
9. Rename `PO-0301` `PowerPoint Sample File 1` and `PO-0401` `PowerPoint Sample File 2`.

3. Backing Up a Disk

The Copy Disk procedure is very important, particularly if you are using floppy disks for data storage. This exercise gives you one more chance to practice backing up your disk. If you do not have access to space on a hard drive or network drive, this is the only way you can back up your work. [L7]

To back up your disk, complete the following steps:

1. Place your disk in the floppy drive and click it once to make sure it is the one you want to copy.
2. Right-click the 3 1/2 Floppy (A:) icon and select Copy Disk from the shortcut menu.
3. Make sure the Copy Disk dialog box shows your floppy disk drive in the Copy from and Copy to areas.
4. Click the Start button. Place a new disk in drive A when prompted.
5. Click the drive A icon to make sure the entire disk copied correctly.
6. When you finish, click the Start button and choose Shut Down from the Start menu. Don't forget to remove your floppy disk from drive A.

Project 3

Working with Office 2000

Objectives

In this project, you learn how to

- **Launch and Exit an Office Application**
- **Open, Edit, and Save an Existing Document**
- **Use Menus and Toolbars**
- **Save a Document with a New Name**
- **Print a Document Using the Toolbar Button and the Menu**
- **Get Help Using the Office Assistant**
- **Get Help Online**

Key terms introduced in this project include

- application
- database
- desktop publisher
- Formatting toolbar
- graphics software
- HTML
- information manager
- insertion point
- launching
- Office Assistant
- presentation manager
- program
- spreadsheet
- Standard toolbar
- Web creation and management
- word processor

Why Would I Do This?

Many of the techniques and procedures you use in one Office 2000 application work in most or all of the other applications. (*Note*: the term ***application*** refers to one of the parts of the Office suite, such as Word or Excel. In this book, it is used synonymously with the word ***program.***) For example, you use the same procedures to activate a menu in Word as you do in Excel and PowerPoint. You use the toolbars in the same way, and some of the more common buttons (Print, Copy, Paste, and several others) that you learn about in the following projects are exactly the same in every application.

However, differences do exist among the applications. No two have exactly the same menu options, although all have many similarities. Some buttons are common to many of the programs, but are missing from one or two others. For example, PowerPoint does not use the Print Preview feature, which is used in many other applications.

One of the main strengths of using the Microsoft Office 2000 suite is consistency of the programs and the way they work together. You can create a chart in Excel and easily insert it into a Word document or a PowerPoint presentation. You can use an outline in Word as the backbone of a PowerPoint presentation. You can send a table of data in Access to Excel for numerical anaylsis.

Another strength of the Office suite is that you can save the products of the applications in a format that can be read on the World Wide Web. You can create a Web page using Word, Publisher, or Front Page. You can create a Web slideshow using PowerPoint, and you can publish Access data files that can be read, searched, and sorted by people all over the world.

In this project, you look at some of the features common to all (or nearly all) of the Microsoft Office 2000 applications.

The Office Suite of Applications

Several versions of Microsoft Office 2000 are available: the Small Business edition, the Standard edition, the Professional edition, and the Premium edition. These come with a variety of programs, although all versions include Word and Excel. The version that is installed on your computer determines which of the following Office components you have access to (see Table 3.1).

Table 3.1 Office 2000 Components

Program	What the Program Does
Word	Word is a program known as a ***word processor***. Word processors are the most commonly used productivity programs. You use them to create documents that are mainly text-based, although you can add graphics to documents. Use word processors to create letters, memos, research papers, simple newsletters, and even Web pages.
Excel	Excel is a ***spreadsheet*** program, which is a program usually used to process, analyze, and chart numbers, although it can be used to sort through lists of data. Using spreadsheets, you can track sales, create financial models, or create a home or business budget.
PowerPoint	PowerPoint is a ***presentation manager***. Presentation managers enable you to create professional-quality computer slide presentations, overhead transparencies, and even Web slide shows.
Access	Access is a ***database*** program. Databases store and present large amounts of information. This information can be sorted, searched, and categorized. You could use a database for such things as inventories, address lists, and research data.
Outlook	Outlook is an ***information manager***—a program that can take charge of your day-to-day scheduling. You can use is to track business contacts, supervise your email, keep track of appointments, and store task lists. Outlook helps busy people organize their activities.

Program	What the Program Does
Publisher	Publisher is a ***desktop publisher***, which is a program that organizes and presents different kinds of information. Desktop publishing programs combine text and graphics to create such things as newsletters, posters, greeting cards, and even Web pages.
Front Page	Front Page is a sophisticated, powerful ***Web creation and management*** tool. It gives you maximum flexibility in the design and layout of Web pages and provides the oversight tools to manage the site once it goes online.
PhotoDraw	PhotoDraw is a ***graphics software*** package. With it, you can create original drawings and enhance and modify images from a scanner, a digital camera, or even downloaded (copyright-free) images.

The version of Office that you have installed determines the combination of programs. One of the great strengths of Office 2000 is the interchangeability of information among the various programs. For example, you might create a document using Word and then place a logo that you created in PhotoDraw at the top of the first page. You can also insert a small data set created in Access, and a table or chart created in Excel. Finally, you might put the new document on the Web as a Web page.

With Office 2000, you can save your documents in an ***HTML*** (Hypertext Markup Language) file format, which is the format of the Web. Anyone with a Web browser can view your documents. You can also edit the documents as necessary because of the ability to "round trip" the documents to the Web and then back into the original Office program without losing any of the functionality of the Office file formats.

This book covers Word, Excel, PowerPoint, and Access in detail. Each section contains a longer introduction to the program. Lesson 3 of this Basics section also contains basic assumptions about the setup of each of the programs.

Lesson 1: Launching and Exiting an Office Application

Starting up a Microsoft Office 2000 program is referred to as ***launching*** the program. Usually, you launch a program using the Start button on the taskbar. All Office applications can be launched in exactly the same way. The exit procedure is also consistent for all Office applications.

In this lesson, you launch Microsoft Word and exit it.

To Launch and Exit an Office Application

1. **Click the Start button and move to the Programs option.**
   A submenu displays. It doesn't matter whether the Windows Explorer or any program is open. You can launch any Office application with one or more programs open. The look of the program list differs, depending on which version of Windows you are using.

2. **Select Microsoft Word from the Programs submenu.**
   The Microsoft Word window opens to a new document. The document has a default name, such as Document1 or Document2 (see Figure 3.1). This name displays in the title bar and the taskbar.

   You might have two toolbars displayed on two different rows, instead of the one that is shown in the figure. This issue is addressed in Lesson 3. Your work area might also look different and have a ruler down the left side of the screen. Several different views are available for you to choose from when you work in Word, and the one that displays is the last one that was used on that machine. This is addressed in the Word section of this book. Finally, you might have a paper clip icon somewhere on your screen. This is the Office Assistant; ignore it for now.

   In some of the applications, such as Access and PowerPoint, you have to answer questions before you get to the window in which you enter information. In Word and Excel, however, a blank document (or worksheet) displays as soon as the program launches.

continues ▶

To Launch and Exit an Office Application (continued)

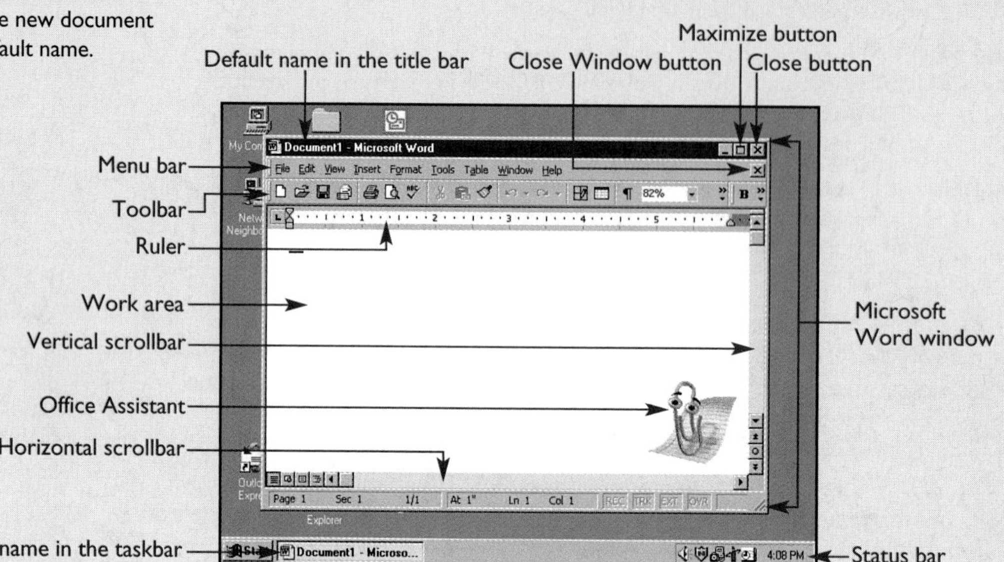

Figure 3.1
The Microsoft Word window opens, and the new document receives a default name.

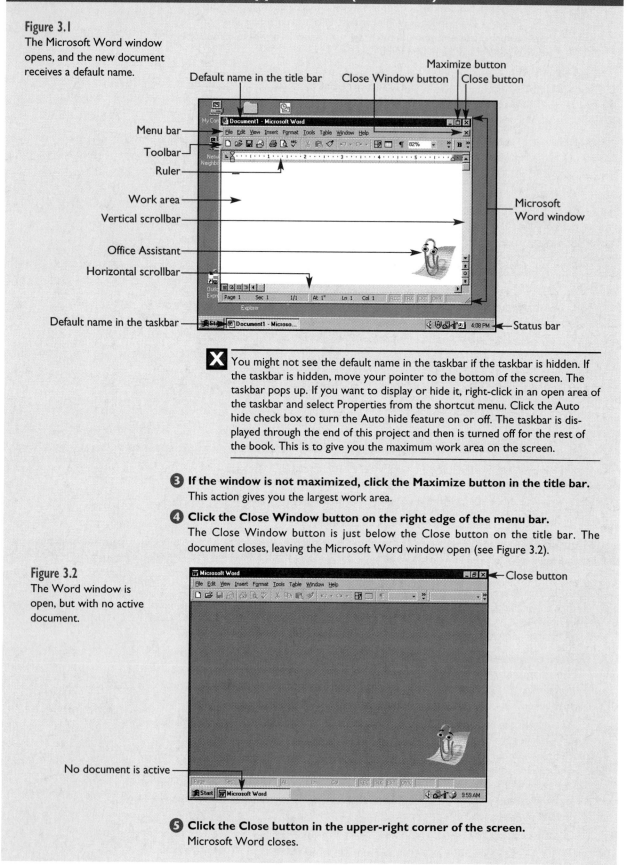

You might not see the default name in the taskbar if the taskbar is hidden. If the taskbar is hidden, move your pointer to the bottom of the screen. The taskbar pops up. If you want to display or hide it, right-click in an open area of the taskbar and select Properties from the shortcut menu. Click the Auto hide check box to turn the Auto hide feature on or off. The taskbar is displayed through the end of this project and then is turned off for the rest of the book. This is to give you the maximum work area on the screen.

3. **If the window is not maximized, click the Maximize button in the title bar.**
   This action gives you the largest work area.

4. **Click the Close Window button on the right edge of the menu bar.**
   The Close Window button is just below the Close button on the title bar. The document closes, leaving the Microsoft Word window open (see Figure 3.2).

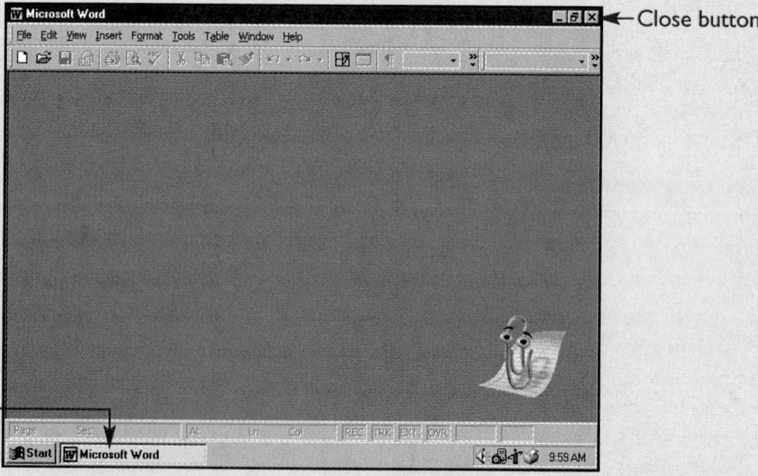

Figure 3.2
The Word window is open, but with no active document.

5. **Click the Close button in the upper-right corner of the screen.**
   Microsoft Word closes.

Different Ways to Launch Office Applications
You can launch an Office application several ways. The most common way is to use the Start menu, where you can get to the program using the Programs option. You can also add Office application shortcuts to the top of the Start menu or to the desktop. Use Windows Help if you want to use one of these shortcut methods. In this book, you are instructed to launch the application. It is up to you to decide which method you use.

Lesson 2: Opening, Editing, and Saving an Existing Document

In Lesson 1, you launched Microsoft Word and in the process created a blank document. When you have created a document and want to edit it, you can use the same procedure but add one more step. When you make a change to an existing document, you can save the change with the click of a button.

In this lesson, you copy a file from the CD-ROM to your floppy disk. You then open the document, make a change, and save the change. You use the document for the rest of this project.

To Open and Save an Existing Document

1. **Click the Start button; choose the Programs option, and select Windows Explorer.**
The Windows Explorer window displays.

2. **Find the drive containing your CD-ROM; then locate and right-click the `IO-0301` file.**
A shortcut menu displays. Make sure you have a floppy disk in the floppy disk drive.

3. **Select the Send To option from the shortcut menu and select 3 1/2 Floppy (A).**
The file is copied to your floppy disk.

4. **Click the Start button; move to the Programs option, and select Microsoft Word.**
Microsoft Word opens and displays a blank document with a default name, such as Document1 or Document2.

5. **Click the Open button on the toolbar.**
The Open dialog box displays (see Figure 3.3).

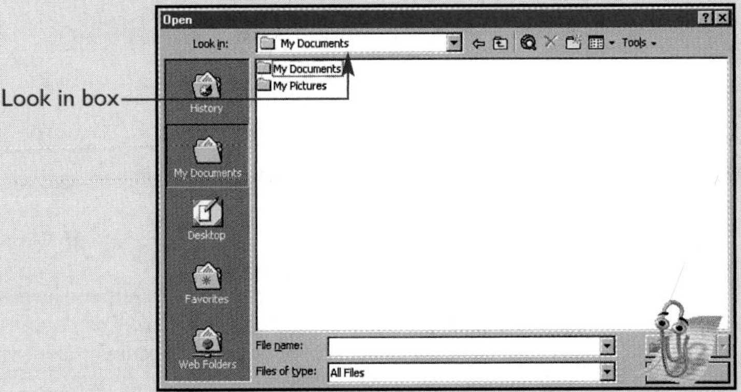

Figure 3.3
The Open dialog box enables you to open an existing document.

6. **Click the arrow on the right side of the Look in box; find and select drive A in the drop-down list, and then double-click the `IO-0301` file.**
The existing document opens. The filename appears in the title bar and the taskbar (see Figure 3.4).

continues ▶

To Open and Save an Existing Document (continued)

Figure 3.4
An existing document has been opened.

Document name

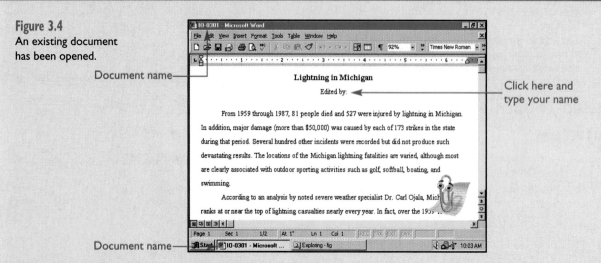

Click here and type your name

Document name

⑦ **Click the pointer to the right of `Edited by:` and type your name.**
The pointer is now in the form of an I-bar. When you position the I-bar pointer and click, a flashing vertical line, called the ***insertion point,*** appears (see Figure 3.5). When you start typing, the text appears at the insertion point, not at the pointer location. This is true in all Office programs.

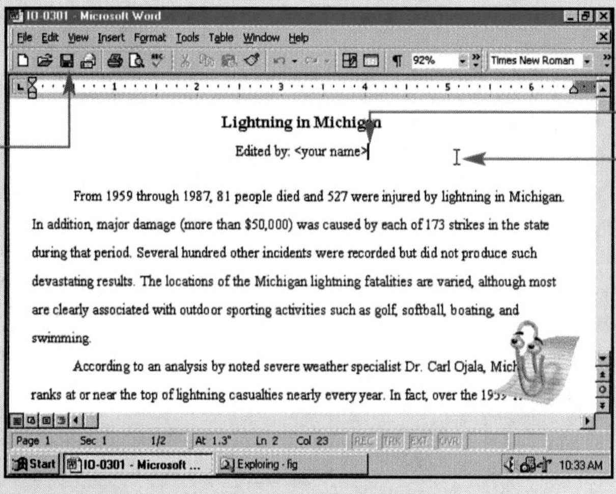

Figure 3.5
The insertion point appears in the document.

Save button

Insertion point

Pointer

 ⑧ **Click the Save button on the toolbar.**
The changes that you made to the document are saved. Leave the document open for the next lesson.

An Easier Method for Opening a File
After you save the document on your floppy disk, you can use an easier method to open it in the future. Open the Windows Explorer, find the file, and double-click it. The application that created the file (in this case Word) opens automatically, along with the document.

Lesson 3: Using Menus and Toolbars

You already used menus and toolbars in the introductory projects of this section. In Basics Project 2, "Windows Disk and File Management," for example, you used the File menu option to create a new folder. Earlier in this project you clicked buttons on a toolbar. The toolbars and menu bar have features that you need to know to help you understand the way Office 2000 works.

In this lesson, you learn how to use the menu and how to use and modify a toolbar.

To Use Menus and Toolbars

1 With the IO-0301 document open, click the Tools option in the menu bar.

A fairly short drop-down menu displays (see Figure 3.6). The options shown are the most commonly used Tools options and the ones most recently used on your computer. Other Tools options are not visible yet. Two toolbars are active in most office applications. The ***Standard toolbar*** is usually on top (or on the left if you are using a single toolbar). It includes such things as the Save, Print, Copy, Paste, and Help buttons. The ***Formatting toolbar*** includes such things as the Bold, Italic, Align Left, Font, and Font Size buttons.

The underline under a letter in the menu bar refers to a keyboard shortcut for that menu option. An alternative way to activate the menu is to press Alt and press the underlined letter, which activates the drop-down menu. You can then use the up and down arrows to move to menu choices and press ↵Enter to select a command. Some people prefer this method because they don't have to take their hands off the keyboard.

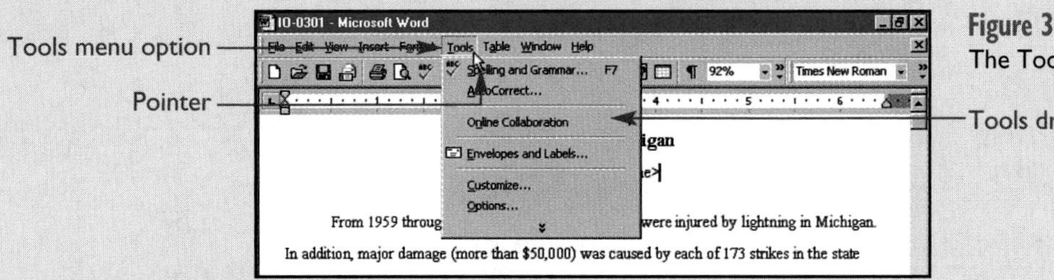

Figure 3.6
The Tools menu displays.

2 Leave the pointer on the Tools menu option for a couple of seconds.

The Tools drop-down menu expands (see Figure 3.7). The options with the dark gray background are the options that were visible in the unexpanded drop-down menu. Those with a light gray background are less commonly used options. This feature enables you to choose the most commonly used commands from a short menu, but offers other options if you need them; if you use one of the other options on a regular basis, it shows up in the short menu.

Notice that some of the options in the Tools menu have arrows on the right side. This means that there is a submenu for that option.

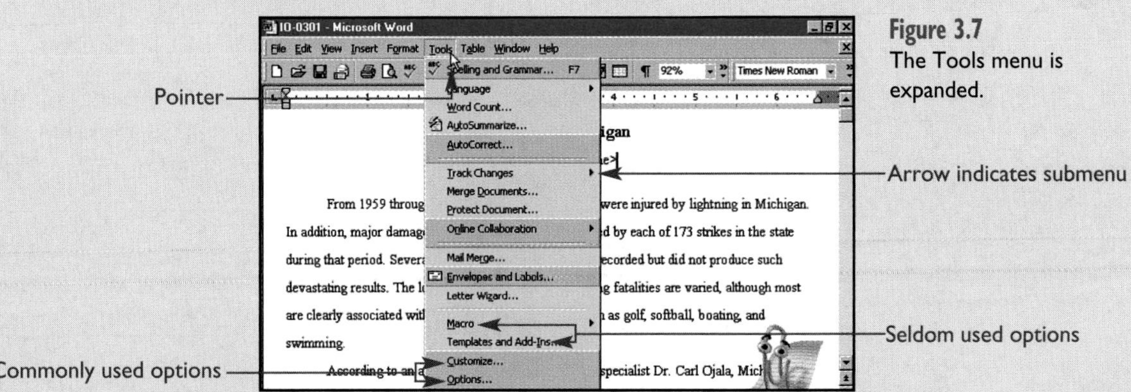

Figure 3.7
The Tools menu is expanded.

3 Move the pointer anywhere in the document and click.

When you have a menu open and want to close it, clicking outside the menu turns it off. You can also press Esc to turn off a menu.

4 Click View and move the pointer down to the Toolbars option.

A submenu displays showing the toolbars that are available. The ones that are open have check marks to the left. A Customize option is available at the bottom of the submenu (see Figure 3.8).

continues ▶

To Use Menus and Toolbars (continued)

Both the Standard and Formatting toolbars are on the same line in this figure. This is the default toolbar setting for several Office programs, including Word, Excel, and PowerPoint. You can stretch or shrink toolbars by grabbing the vertical bars at the left ends of the toolbars and dragging to the left or right. The problem with using a single row for the two most commonly used toolbars is that you probably don't recognize each of the buttons or remember where they are located. It is much easier to use these two toolbars on separate rows.

Figure 3.8
The View, Toolbars submenu displays.

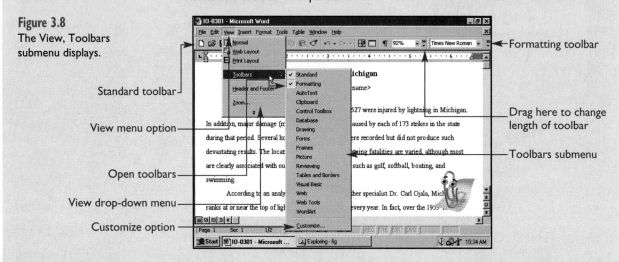

Standard toolbar
View menu option
Open toolbars
View drop-down menu
Customize option
Formatting toolbar
Drag here to change length of toolbar
Toolbars submenu

5 Move the pointer to the Toolbars submenu and select Customize.
The Customize dialog box displays. This dialog box consists of three tabs: Toolbars, Commands, and Options (see Figure 3.9).

Figure 3.9
The Customize dialog box consists of three tabs.

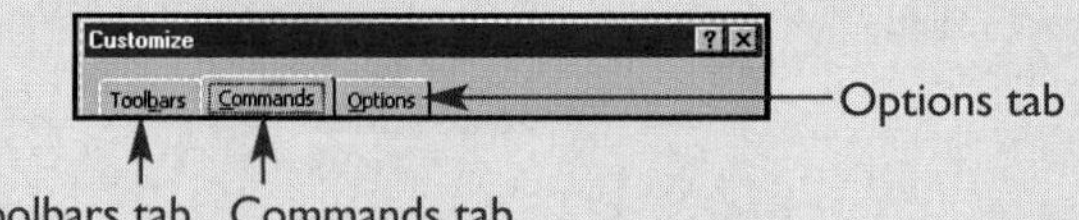

Options tab
Toolbars tab
Commands tab

If you move the pointer outside of the menu and submenu, they disappear. Make sure you keep the pointer inside the menus, particularly as you move from the View drop-down menu to the Toolbars submenu. If you are not used to using a mouse, it might take some time before you are comfortable with this procedure. If you accidentally turn the menu off, simply reselect View, Toolbars, Customize.

6 Click the Options tab, if necessary.
The various toolbar options display.

7 Click the check box to turn off the Standard and Formatting toolbars share one row option, if necessary (see Figure 3.10).
The Standard and Formatting toolbars display on separate rows. The second toolbar decreases your work area slightly, but the convenience of seeing all the buttons more than makes up for that. You should use this procedure to separate the main toolbars when you start the Excel and PowerPoint sections of this book. All the figures from this point on show the double toolbars when appropriate.

Figure 3.10
The row-sharing option is turned off.

Row-sharing option

Some computer labs are set up with a security system that prevents you from changing the program defaults. If you are working in a lab, check with the lab manager before you try to customize program settings.

8. **Click the Close button in the dialog box to turn it off.**
   Notice that you now have two rows of toolbars. Also notice that some buttons on the toolbar have down arrows on the right side.

9. **Click the down arrow on the Font button on the Formatting toolbar and release the mouse button.**
   A drop-down menu displays, showing some of the available fonts (see Figure 3.11). A vertical scrollbar is at the right of the drop-down menu. Try scrolling up and down to see the different fonts you can use. The most recently used fonts appear at the top of the list.

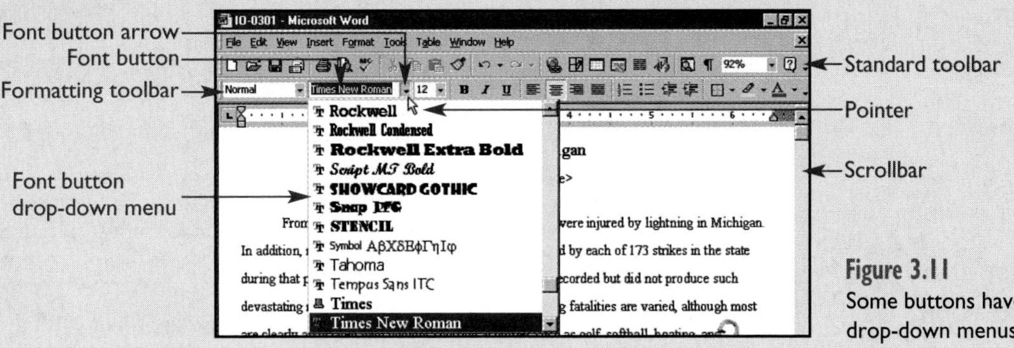

Figure 3.11
Some buttons have drop-down menus.

10. **Click anywhere in the document to close the Font menu.**
   Leave the document open for the next lesson.

Adding and Removing Toolbars
You can add or remove toolbars by right-clicking any toolbar. This activates a shortcut menu that displays all the available toolbars and the Customize option. Scroll down and select the toolbar you want to turn on or off and click it once.

Lesson 4: Saving a Document with a New Name

In Lesson 2, you copied the IO-0301 file from your CD-ROM to a floppy disk. You use the copy procedure often in this book. Because these filenames are not very descriptive, you can change the names of the files. The filename restrictions you learned about in Project 2 are also in effect in the Office applications. A filename can contain up to 255 characters, including spaces, although the filename cannot begin with a space. It also cannot contain the following characters: \ / : * ? " < > |.

In this lesson, you save a copy of your document with a new name.

To Save a Document with a New Name

1. **With the IO-0301 document still open, choose the File option from the menu. Make sure you have a disk in drive A.**
   The File drop-down menu displays.

2. **Select Save As from the File menu.**
   The Save As dialog box displays.

3. **Change the location in the Save in drop-down list box to 3 1/2 Floppy (A:), if necessary.**

continues ▶

To Save a Document with a New Name (continued)

4 Replace `IO-0301` with `Lightning Data` in the File name text box.

Your Save As dialog box should look like Figure 3.12. If you are using a disk that you used in Project 2, the files and folders from that project also display.

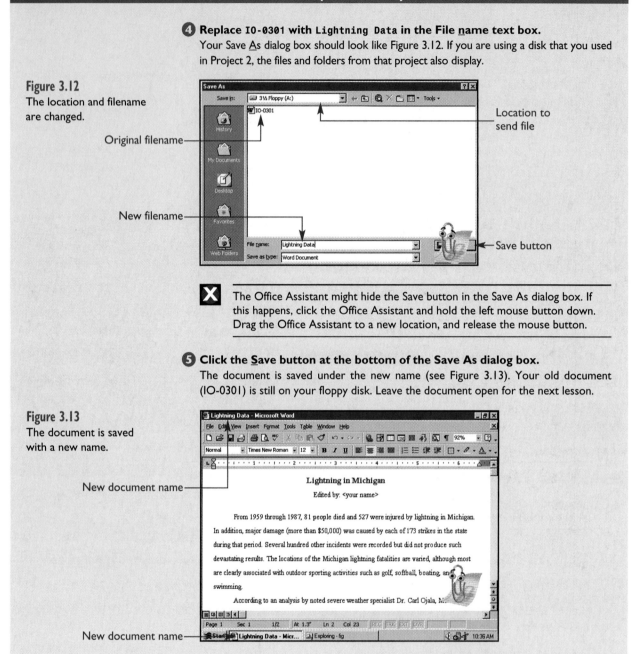

Figure 3.12
The location and filename are changed.

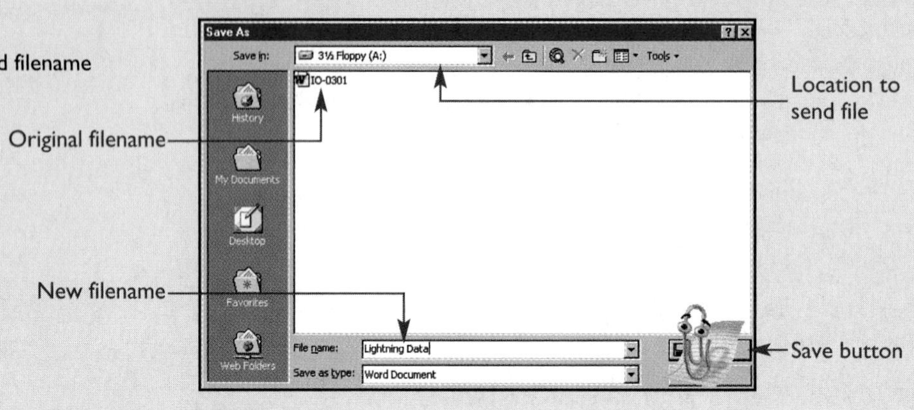

The Office Assistant might hide the Save button in the Save As dialog box. If this happens, click the Office Assistant and hold the left mouse button down. Drag the Office Assistant to a new location, and release the mouse button.

5 Click the Save button at the bottom of the Save As dialog box.

The document is saved under the new name (see Figure 3.13). Your old document (IO-0301) is still on your floppy disk. Leave the document open for the next lesson.

Figure 3.13
The document is saved with a new name.

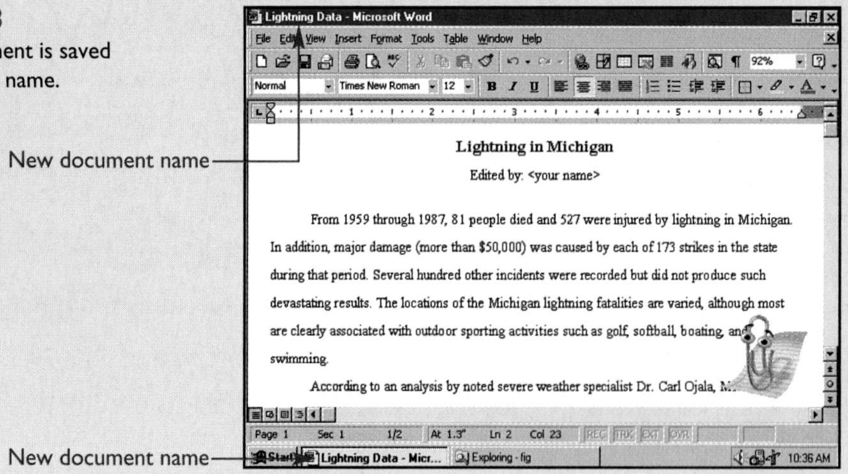

Lesson 5: Printing a Document Using the Toolbar Button and the Menu

You print documents for many different reasons—as draft copies for proofing, or as final documents, handouts, or overhead transparencies. Most Office applications have two different printing levels. The easiest way to print is to simply click the Print button. This sends a complete document to the printer. The problem with using the Print button is that it gives you little control over the process. You can also print using the Print command from the File menu. This gives you much more control and enables you to print specific pages or ranges of information. It also enables you to specify a printer and set the page layout.

In this lesson, you print the document you've been working on in this project using both the Print button and the menu command.

To Print a Document by Using the Toolbar Button and the Menu

 **1 With the Lightning Data document still active, make sure your printer is turned on, and then click the Print button on the Standard toolbar.**

The entire document goes to the printer.

> If the document does not print, it could mean that your printer is not turned on or is not connected properly. Check your connections and try again. If this does not work, you need to make sure the correct printer is chosen in the Print dialog box, which you open in Step 2. If several printers are available, ask your instructor or lab administrator which printer you should use.

2 Choose File, Print from the menu.

The Print dialog box displays (see Figure 3.14). This dialog box enables you to choose a printer, specify the number of copies to be printed, select specific pages to print, and select several other important options.

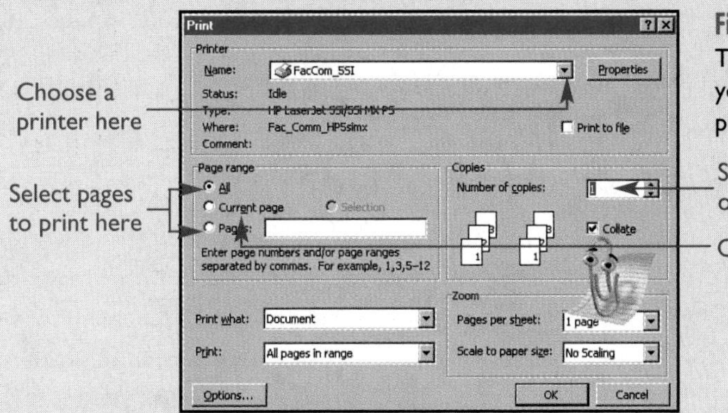

Figure 3.14
The Print dialog box gives you control over the print process.

3 Click the Current page option in the Page range section.

The page you print might not be the page showing on the screen. The program prints whichever page the insertion point is currently in.

4 Click OK to print the current page.

The page containing the insertion point prints. Leave the document open for the next lesson.

Variations in the Print Dialog Box

The Print dialog box contains different elements in different Office applications. For example, the PowerPoint Print dialog box has special sections for printing slides and audience handouts, putting frames around slides, and printing a color image in grayscale; whereas Word enables you to collate your copies and print multiple pages per sheet.

Lesson 6: Getting Help Using the Office Assistant

In Project 1, "Working with Windows," you learned how to use Microsoft Help for Windows. You can get help with your questions several ways in any of the Office programs, including some of the procedures you used with Windows Help. The two major help sources are the Office Assistant and online resources. The ***Office Assistant*** is a program that enables you to ask questions by typing in sentences or phrases. When you ask a question of the Office Assistant, a series of possible related topics displays. You pick one of the topics and expand on it.

In this lesson, you use the Office Assistant to get help on centering text.

To Get Help Using the Office Assistant

1 If the Office Assistant is not displayed on your screen, select Help, Show the Office Assistant from the menu.
The Office Assistant displays on the screen, usually in the lower-right corner (see Figure 3.15). You can move it by clicking and dragging it to a new location.

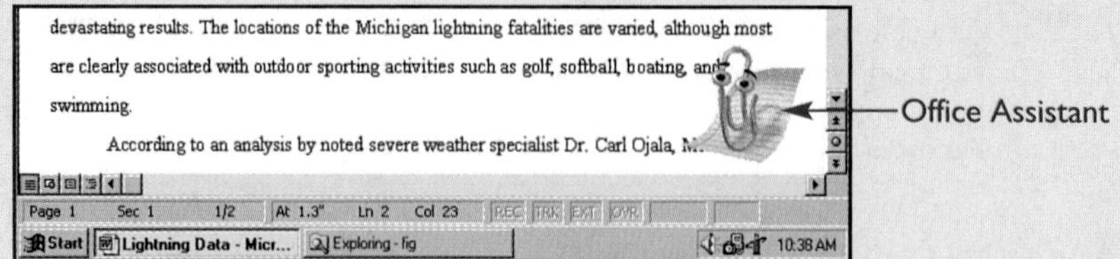

Figure 3.15
The Office Assistant displays on the Word screen.

2 To get help on a topic, click the Office Assistant.
A small search dialog box displays, asking you what you would like to do.

3 Type `How do I center text` in the question box.
The Office Assistant looks for key words in your question and tries to come up with answers. Notice that you do not have to add a question mark to your question (see Figure 3.16).

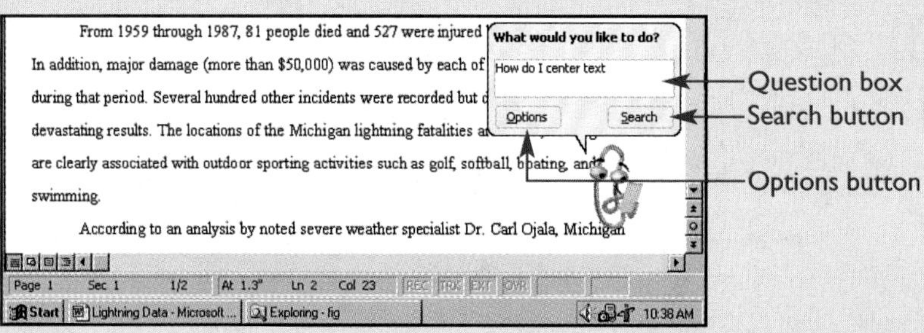

Figure 3.16
The Office Assistant has been asked a question.

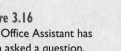

If you start to use the Office Assistant and change your mind, you can remove the search dialog box from the screen by clicking anywhere outside of the search dialog box.

4 Click the Search button.
The Office Assistant looks at your question and anticipates possible answers. The most likely answers display on the screen (see Figure 3.17). If the topic you are searching for does not appear in this list, click the See more button. The most likely answer to your question appears at the top of the list. Notice that by the end of the list, the topics are not as closely related to the topic you entered as those at the top of the list.

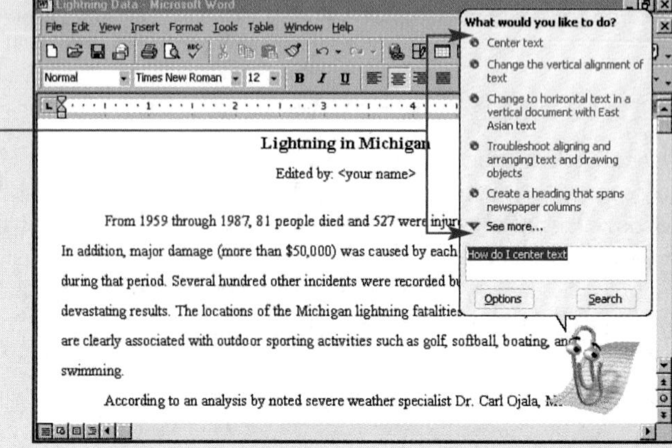

Figure 3.17
A list of possible answers displays.

5 Click the button for the `Center text` topic.

Two things happen: The document you are working on decreases in size and a Help window displays on the right side of the screen (see Figure 3.18). Notice that some of the text is in blue, meaning that the text is a hyperlink and more help is available if you click the word or phrase. You can use the vertical scrollbar to move down the Help window. A Show button provides access to the Index and Contents tabs.

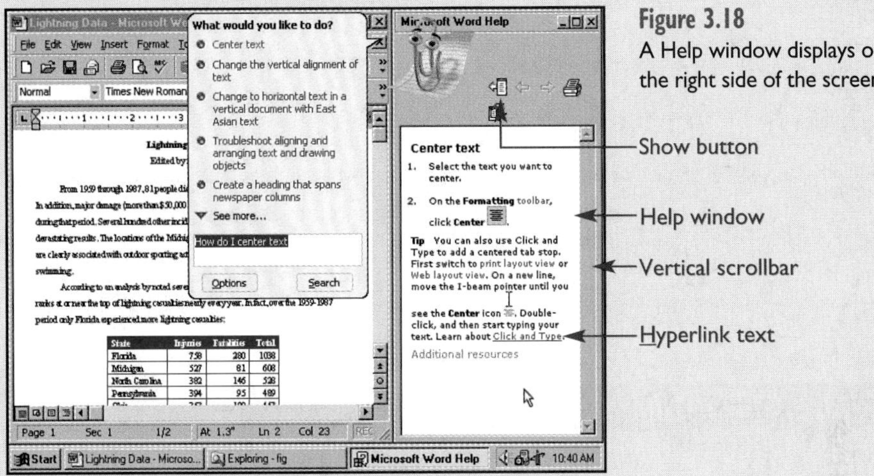

Figure 3.18
A Help window displays on the right side of the screen.

6 Click the Show button.

The Help window expands to include different types of Help (see Figure 3.19). This Help is similar to the Windows Help you used in Project 1. On the Index tab, you can type a word and see whether it matches a predefined topic; the Contents tab reads like a book with chapters and topics. The Answer Wizard tab works like the Office Assistant; you type a question and the wizard displays a list of related topics. To move between these features, simply click the tabs at the top of the window. The Show button changes to the Hide button. If you click the Hide button, the additional Help screen is removed from the screen.

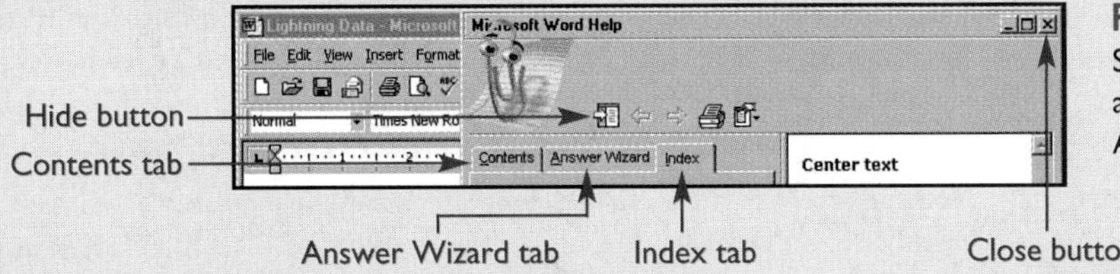

Figure 3.19
Several types of help are available in the Office Assistant Help window.

7 Click the Close button to close the Office Assistant Help window.

The document again appears full-size, and the Office Assistant remains at the bottom of the screen.

Changing the Office Assistant

If you don't like the look of the Office Assistant, you can change it. Click the Office Assistant Options button and click the Gallery tab. Click the Next and Back buttons to view your options, and click OK when you find one you like. The Office CD might need to be in the CD-ROM drive in order to have access to the different Assistants.

Some people do not like to have the Office Assistant on the screen at all. You can hide the Office Assistant by choosing Help, Hide the Office Assistant. To turn it off completely, click the Office Assistant and click the Options button. Click the check box for the Use the Office Assistant option at the top of the dialog box.

Help Tips Might Appear Automatically

Occasionally, when you are typing a document or trying to perform a procedure, the Office Assistant appears, even though you haven't called for it. Don't worry; the Office Assistant is just trying to be helpful. Read through the comment, and if it looks like it might be helpful, follow the onscreen instructions. If you do not want this help, you can simply close the Help window. If you do not like these hints appearing on your screen, click the Office Assistant and click the Options button and turn off the check boxes for the Show tips features.

Lesson 7: Getting Help Online

At times you can't find an answer using the Office Assistant or other Office Help. Microsoft has set up an online Help service that enables you to search through a larger help resource. It also enables you to look at a particular topic and see what kinds of problems and questions other people have been experiencing.

The Microsoft online Help has been evolving for years, and every few months the structure and layout change. Chances are excellent that the screens you see won't match the ones shown in the figures in this lesson. The procedures for obtaining help might even be different. Use this lesson as a guideline for how online Help works, and then follow the onscreen instructions when you go online.

In this lesson, you try out the Microsoft Office online Help feature.

To Use Office Online Help

1. **Select Help, Office on the Web from the menu.**

   You are taken to a Web page that asks you to register for support.

For Office online Help to work, you need to have a connection to the Internet and a browser, such as Netscape Navigator or the Internet Explorer, set up on your computer. Also, the exact steps you need to follow to get help vary depending on which browser you are using.

2. **Fill in the registration information. After you have registered, you can enter the Support Online area.**

   You only need to register one time. After that, you can type your email address and password and get in immediately. This screen enables you to search through many different types of Help (see Figure 3.20). You can look at frequently asked questions, view popular topics, or select a program and do a search just like you did with the Office Assistant. (***Note:*** You need to scroll down the screen to view all the options.)

   You can also join a newsgroup, where other people interested in the same topic get together and exchange ideas and problem solutions. This is a great idea if you have to learn one of the Office applications very well.

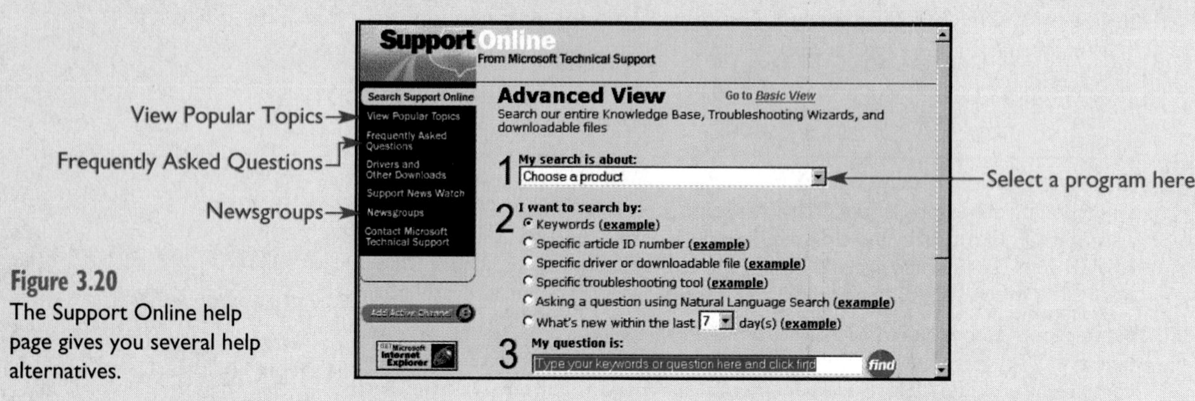

Figure 3.20
The Support Online help page gives you several help alternatives.

3 Click `Frequently Asked Questions`. Select `Access` from the product list.
You are now ready to look at the frequently asked questions about Microsoft Access (see Figure 3.21).

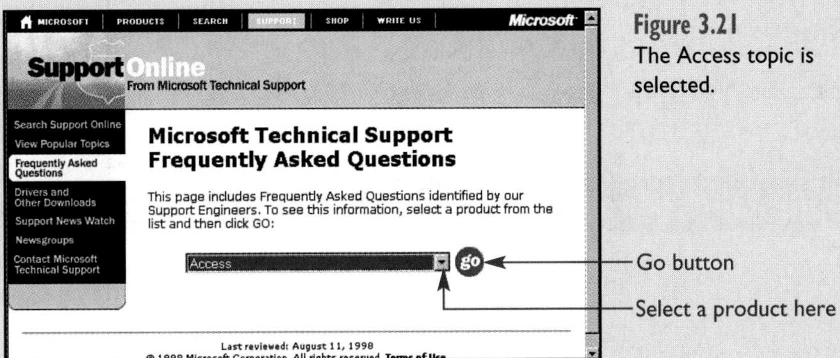

Figure 3.21 The Access topic is selected.

4 Click the Go button.
Several topic areas display. You might have to scroll down the screen to see them all.

5 Select one of the topic areas.
Another list of general topics displays.

6 Select one of the general topics.
A list of specific topics displays (see Figure 3.22).

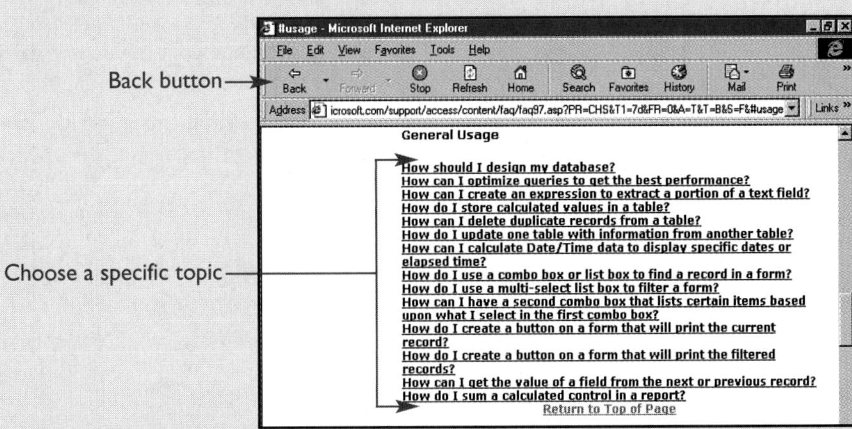

Figure 3.22 Specific Access topics display.

7 Click the Back button three times to return to the Support Online home page.

8 Click the Newsgroups option and follow the screen instructions to enter a newsgroup of your choice.
You can participate in this group, search for answers, respond to questions, or ask your own questions. Explore the other online Help features in the same manner.

9 When you are through with online Help, click the Close button to close your browser. Click the Close button to close Microsoft Word.
Leave your computer on for the exercises.

Getting a Working Knowledge of Online Help

Because of the constant changes in the Online Support pages, you have to explore this topic on your own. Try each of the major categories so you know what features are available and how to use them. A working knowledge of online Help can be a great benefit to you, both in completing the exercises in the rest of this book and in your personal and business applications.

Summary

In this project, you worked with one of the Microsoft Office applications—Word 2000. You launched and exited an application, and opened and closed an existing document. You used menus and toolbars that are similar in all Office applications. You saved a document with a new name, and you printed a document using two different procedures. Finally, you used the Help built in to the program, and looked at the Help you can get online.

You might want to expand your Office skills by using the Office Assistant to explore topics of interest to you.

Checking Concepts and Terms

True/False

For each of the following, check *T* or *F* to indicate whether the statement is true or false.

__T __F **1.** One of the strengths of Office 2000 programs is that they interact easily with the Web. [Intro]

__T __F **2.** To launch an Office program you need to close any other Office program that is running at the time. [L1]

__T __F **3.** When you start typing in a document, the text appears at the pointer location. [L2]

__T __F **4.** You can activate the menu bar by pressing Alt. [L3]

__T __F **5.** To expand a menu, double-click the menu choice in the menu bar. [L3]

__T __F **6.** One way to turn toolbars on or off is to right-click anywhere in the toolbar area and click one of the toolbar choices. [L3]

__T __F **7.** When you use the Save As option, you can change the program name, which deletes the old version. [L4]

__T __F **8.** Using File, Print from the menu gives you more control over printing than using the Print button. [L5]

__T __F **9.** You can type questions in sentence form when you use the Office Assistant. [L6]

__T __F **10.** When you see blue text in a Help window, it means that more help is available by clicking the text. [L6]

Multiple Choice

Circle the letter of the correct answer for each of the following questions.

1. Which of the following is a good reason to use the Microsoft Office suite of programs? [Intro]

a. The various programs share many of the same menu items.

b. The various programs share many of the same buttons.

c. Items developed in one program can be inserted into another program.

d. all of the above

2. After a document has been saved on a floppy disk, you can move to the Windows Explorer and open it by ____________. [L2]

a. single-clicking it with the left mouse button

b. single-clicking it with the right mouse button

c. double-clicking it with the left mouse button

d. double-clicking it with the right mouse button

3. If a document doesn't print when you click the Print button, it could be that ____________. [L5]

a. your printer is not turned on

b. the printer is not connected to your computer

c. the correct printer has not been chosen in the Print dialog box

d. all of the above

4. If the Office Assistant is not displayed on your screen, you can ____________. [L6]

a. click the Office Assistant button

b. press Esc

c. select Help, Show the Office Assistant from the menu

d. select View, Office Assistant from the menu

5. To expand the Office Assistant Help window so you can use the Contents and Index tabs, ____________. [L6]

a. click the Show button in the Microsoft Word Help dialog box

b. double-click the Office Assistant icon

c. select Show from the Help menu

d. select Index from the View menu

Screen ID

Label each element of the Microsoft Word screens shown in Figure 3.23 and Figure 3.24.

Figure 3.23

A. Filename
B. Menu
C. Toolbar
D. Insertion Point
E. Pointer
F. Office Assistant
G. Hide button
H. Save button
I. Open button
J. Print button

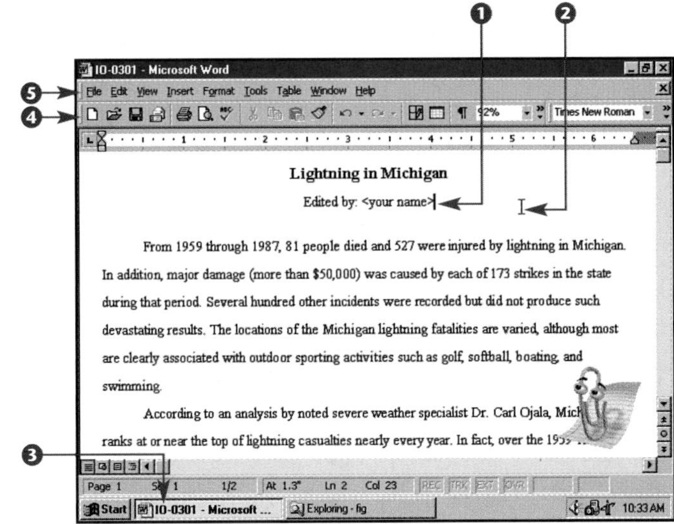

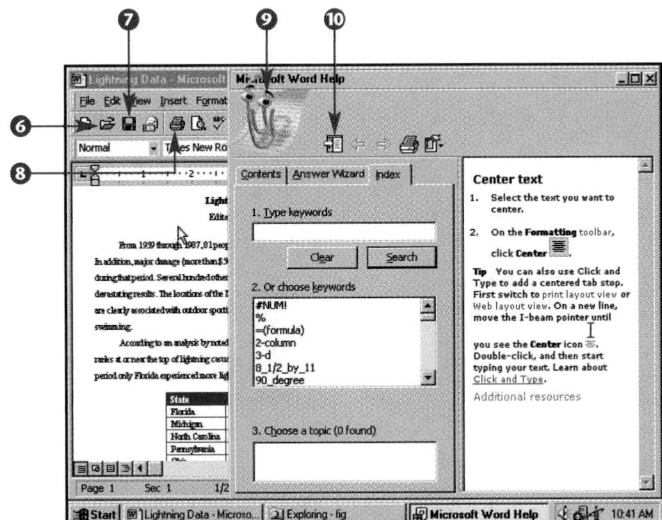

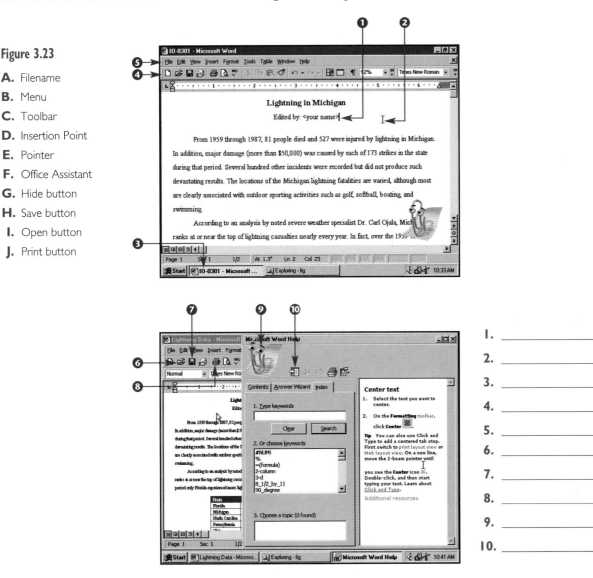

1. ______________________
2. ______________________
3. ______________________
4. ______________________
5. ______________________
6. ______________________
7. ______________________
8. ______________________
9. ______________________
10. ______________________

Skill Drill

Skill Drill exercises reinforce project skills. Each skill reinforced is the same, or nearly the same, as a skill presented in the project. Each exercise includes a brief narrative introduction, followed by detailed instructions in a step-by-step format.

1. Launching Microsoft Excel and Saving a File

In the first two lessons of this project, you launched Microsoft Word. You also made changes to a Word file and saved the changes. In this exercise, you do the same things, but with a different Office application. [L1–2]

1. Click the Start button and move to the Programs option.
2. Select Microsoft Excel from the Programs submenu. The Microsoft Excel window opens to a new document. Excel is a spreadsheet and is commonly used for analyzing numerical data.
3. Type your name. It appears just under the toolbars and in the upper-left corner of the work area (in a box called a cell). Press ↵Enter.
4. Click the Save button on the toolbar. Because the document has not been saved before, the Save As dialog box displays.

5. Type **`My First Excel File`** in the File name text box.
6. Locate drive A (or wherever you want to save your document) in the Save in drop-down list box.
7. Click the Save button at the bottom of the dialog box. Notice that the name of the document appears in the Excel title bar. Leave the document open for the next exercise.

2. Using Menus and Adding a Toolbar

All the Microsoft Office applications have a similar-looking menu. In fact, most have several of the same options; so learning one application means that you have a head start on learning all the others. Most applications also have several toolbars available at any one time, although many of them are hidden because they are not used often and would just take up space on the screen if displayed. [L3]

1. Click the Format menu option. Notice that the first option, Cells, is followed by three dots. This means that clicking the option opens a dialog box.
2. Click Cells in the Format menu to open the Format Cells dialog box. This dialog box has several tabs, each with a different purpose.
3. Click the Patterns tab in the Format Cells dialog box. A cell-shading palette displays.
4. Click the bright red button. The color displays in the Sample preview box.
5. Click the down arrow in the Pattern button. Choose one of the dot patterns and click it. Click OK to see how your changes look. Notice that the only cell that is affected is the one that is selected.
6. Click the View menu option, and then select Toolbars. Select Drawing from the submenu. The Drawing toolbar displays at the bottom of the screen.
7. Right-click anywhere on the Drawing toolbar, and then move up and click Drawing again. The toolbar is turned off. (*Note:* You could have right-clicked any toolbar to turn off any other toolbar.)

3. Using the Office Assistant and the Index

In Lesson 6, you clicked the Show button in the Office Assistant. This doubled the size of the Help window and gave you the option of clicking one of three tabs to get help in different ways. Probably the most commonly used tab is the Index tab. [L6]

1. Click the Microsoft Excel Help button to open the Office Assistant.
2. If you have turned off the Office Assistant in the Options dialog box, click the Show button so you can see the Index tab.

   If the Office Assistant appears, click the Options button. Click the Use the Office Assistant check box to turn it off. Click the Help button again and click the Show button, if necessary, so you can see the Index tab.
3. Click the Index tab, if necessary. (*Note*: The characteristics of the Help window depend on previous use. The Index tab might already be active.)
4. Type **`color`** into the Type keywords text box.
5. Click the Search button. A list of topics displays in the bottom box.
6. Click the Shade cells with solid colors topic. The box on the right of the screen displays help on filling a cell with color. Notice that this method uses a button to do what you did in the second exercise using the menu.
7. Click the Close button to close the Help window, and then click the Close button in the title bar to close Excel. Save your changes when prompted.

Appendix B Microcomputer Hardware

1 Microcomputer Hardware

This appendix provides an overview of microcomputer hardware devices.

Background Information

One of the most common ways of getting information into a computer is through a keyboard. A computer keyboard consists of separate keys that, when tapped, send specific codes to the computer. Essentially, such a code tells the computer that a key is depressed, what key is being depressed, and when the key is no longer depressed.

Another device used for getting information into a computer is a computer **mouse.** A mouse is simply a device that moves a cursor to any desired area of the screen. The computer always knows at what position on the screen the cursor is located. On the mouse itself, there are buttons (usually three). When a button is depressed, this—along with the position of the cursor on the screen—gives the computer specific information. Usually the screen contains information as to what that particular area of the screen means to the mouse user. For instance, it could mean to begin or terminate a process. Figure 1 shows actions of a keyboard and a mouse.

As you can see from Figure 1, both these devices are input devices. The major disadvantages of the keyboard are the typing skill required to use it and the need to know specific key sequences to initiate computer actions (such as DIR in order to get the directory listing of a disk).

The disadvantages of the keyboard are overcome through the use of a mouse. Using the mouse does not require any typing skills or knowledge of special key sequences (such as the DOS commands). Windows essentially requires only the use of the mouse for system interaction. Windows allows you to execute multiple programs simultaneously, and quickly change from one application to another, with a single mouse click.

The Keyboard

A new keyboard, used with most PCs, contains 101 keys. The function keys are located horizontally along the top of the keyboard, where there are now 12 of them. The ESC key is at the upper left. The keyboard contains duplicate cursor-movement and other similar keys. This is sometimes referred to as the **enhanced keyboard** (Figure 2).

Identifying Keys

There are four ways of identifying a key on an IBM keyboard: by the **character** on the cap of the key, by the **character code** associated with each key-cap character, by the scan code of the key, and by the decimal key–location number. These are illustrated in Figure 3.

During the power-on self-test, the first part of the keyboard scan code is displayed if there is a problem with that particular key. Figure 4 shows the scan codes for the IBM 101-key keyboard, and

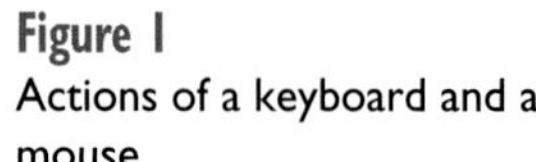

Figure 1
Actions of a keyboard and a mouse

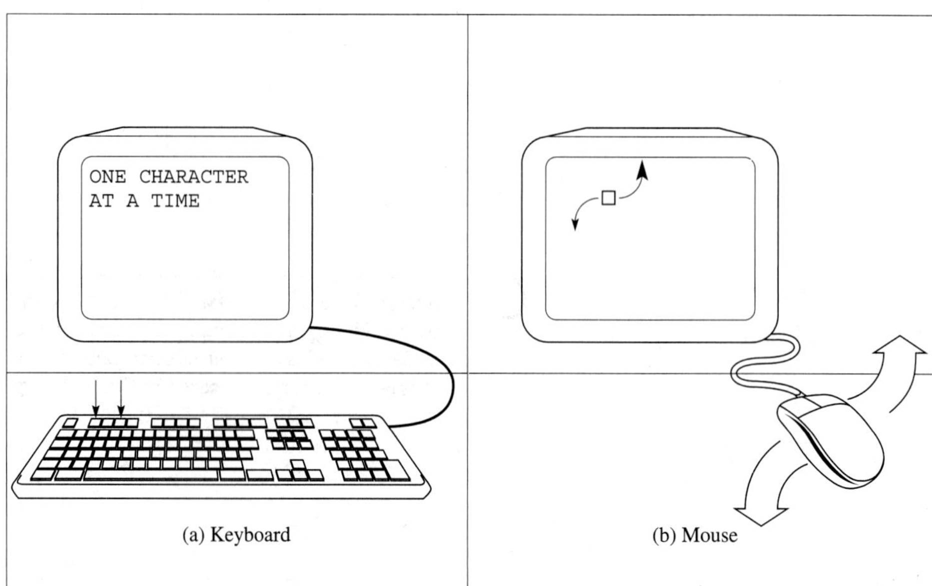

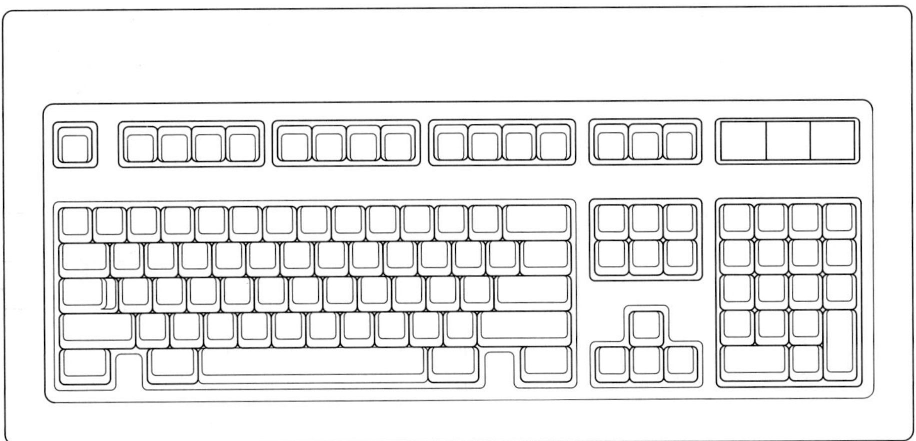

Figure 2
The 101-key enhanced keyboard

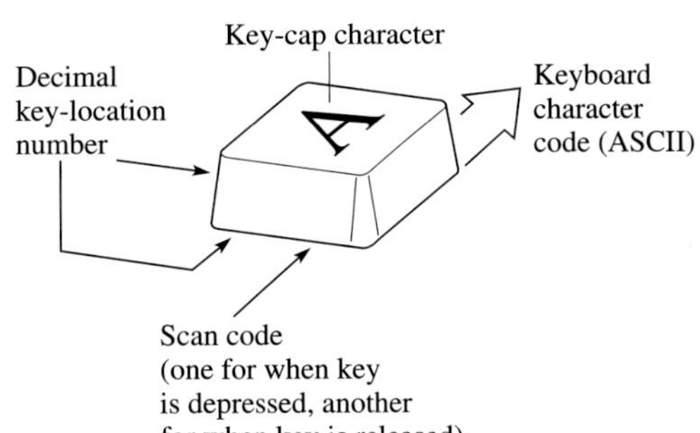

Figure 3
Four ways of identifying a key on an IBM keyboard

Figure 4
Scan codes for 101-key keyboard

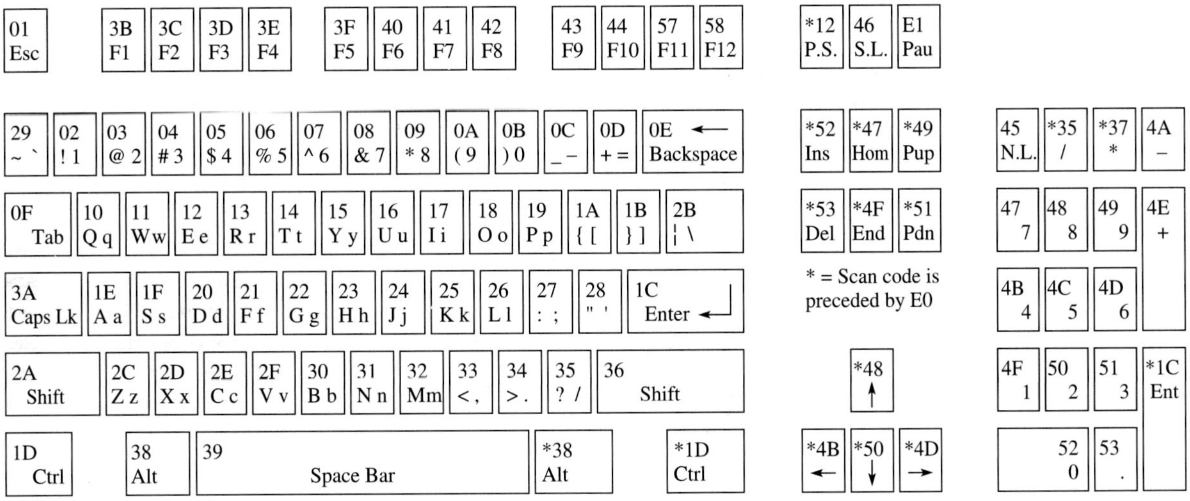

01 Esc | 3B F1 | 3C F2 | 3D F3 | 3E F4 | 3F F5 | 40 F6 | 41 F7 | 42 F8 | 43 F9 | 44 F10 | 57 F11 | 58 F12 | *12 P.S. | 46 S.L. | E1 Pau

29 ~ ` | 02 ! 1 | 03 @ 2 | 04 # 3 | 05 $ 4 | 06 % 5 | 07 ^ 6 | 08 & 7 | 09 * 8 | 0A (9 | 0B) 0 | 0C _ – | 0D + = | 0E ← Backspace | *52 Ins | *47 Hom | *49 Pup | 45 N.L. | *35 / | *37 * | 4A –

0F Tab | 10 Q q | 11 W w | 12 E e | 13 R r | 14 T t | 15 Y y | 16 U u | 17 I i | 18 O o | 19 P p | 1A { [| 1B }] | 2B ¦ \ | *53 Del | *4F End | *51 Pdn | 47 7 | 48 8 | 49 9 | 4E +

3A Caps Lk | 1E A a | 1F S s | 20 D d | 21 F f | 22 G g | 23 H h | 24 J j | 25 K k | 26 L l | 27 : ; | 28 " ' | 1C Enter ↵ | 4B 4 | 4C 5 | 4D 6

* = Scan code is preceded by E0

2A Shift | 2C Z z | 2D X x | 2E C c | 2F V v | 30 B b | 31 N n | 32 M m | 33 < , | 34 > . | 35 ? / | 36 Shift | *48 ↑ | 4F 1 | 50 2 | 51 3 | *1C Ent

1D Ctrl | 38 Alt | 39 Space Bar | *38 Alt | *1D Ctrl | *4B ← | *50 ↓ | *4D → | 52 0 | 53 .

Enhanced Keyboard Scan Codes

Figure 5 shows the key-location numbers for the same keyboard.

As shown in Figure 5, each key is assigned a decimal number that is used as a key-location reference on most IBM drawings. These numbers are used only as convenient guides for the physical location of the various keys and bear no relationship to the actual characters generated by the corresponding keys.

Keyboard Servicing

Outside of routine cleaning of the keyboard, there is little you can do to service it. In many cases, the keyboard assembly is a sealed unit. The major hazards to a keyboard are spilled liquids. Periodically you can use a chip puller to pull the keytops off the keyboard. (Be sure to have a similar keyboard to use as a reference when replacing these key caps.) Then hold the keyboard upside down and blow it out with compressed air.

The keyboard is connected to the computer through a cable to the **keyboard interface connector.** This connector is shown in Figure 6.

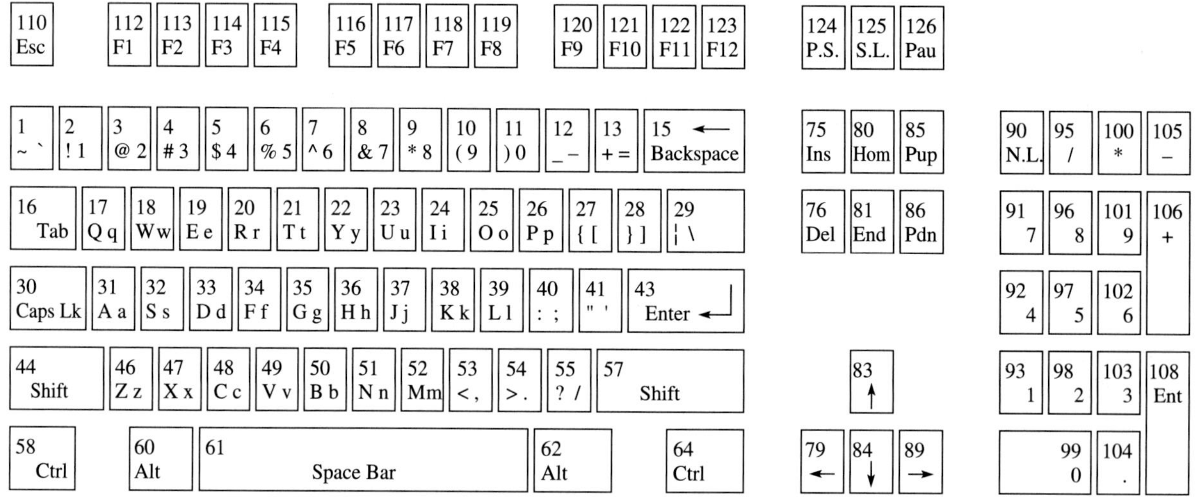

Enhanced Keyboard Location Numbers

Figure 5
Key-location numbers for IBM 101-key keyboard

Figure 6
Keyboard interface connector (socket)

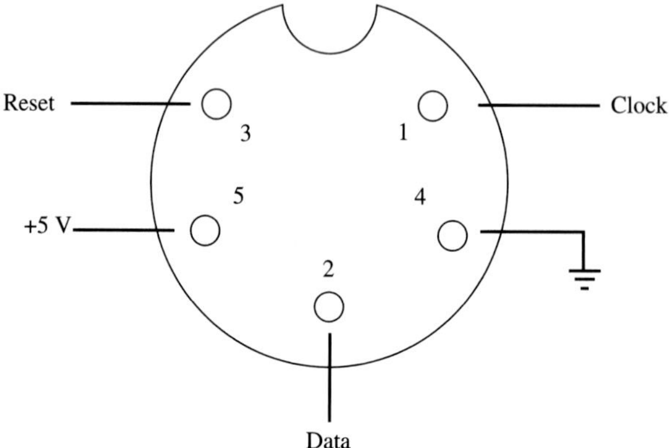

You can use a voltmeter to test the operation of the keyboard interface connector. Voltages between all pins and pin 4 of the connector should be in the range of 2 to 5.5 V DC. If any of these voltages are wrong, the problem is usually in the computer's system board. If these voltages are correct, the problem may be in the keyboard or its connector cable. Some keyboards have one or more switches (on the bottom side) to make them compatible with the computer to which they are connected. Check these switch settings as well as the documentation that comes with the keyboard.

If you find that only one key is malfunctioning, you can check the small spring on the key. Simply remove the key cap, under which you will see a small spring. Try pulling the spring slightly and then replace the key cap. You can check the cable continuity by carefully removing the bottom plate of the keyboard and observing how the cable interfaces with the computer.

Because new keyboards are so inexpensive, it is usually cheaper to replace a bad keyboard.

Today, you can purchase custom keyboards that have themes (a *Star Trek* keyboard), keyboards with infrared transmitters and no cables, or a keyboard with the keys arranged into two groups, one for each hand. You can even buy a keyboard with a built in scanner.

The Mouse

There are basically two types of mouse drivers used with PCs: one is a **serial mouse** and the other is a **parallel mouse.** The serial mouse interfaces with the computer through the serial port; the parallel mouse interfaces through a parallel port. In the PC, the mouse is typically connected to the 9-pin male plug on the COM1 serial port. A 9- to 25-pin adapter is available if the serial port has a 25-pin connector.

Figure 7 shows a typical computer mouse.

Trackballs

A trackball is similar to a mouse except the device does not move. Instead, the user pushes a round trackball around inside its case, allowing the same movement as a mouse but not requiring a mousepad or large surface for movement. Many laptop and notebook computers have trackball mouse devices built in.

Video Monitors and Video Adapters

The computer display system used by your computer consists of two separate but essential parts: the monitor and the video adapter card as shown in Figure 8. Note from the figure that the monitor does not get its power from the computer; it has a separate power cord and its own internal power supply.

The video adapter card [Figure 8(b)] interfaces between the motherboard and the monitor. This card processes and converts data from the computer and allows you to see all the things you are used to seeing displayed on the screen.

It is very important to realize that there are many different types of monitors and that each type of monitor essentially requires its own special video adapter card, as shown in Figure 9. Connecting a monitor to an adapter card not made for it can severely damage the monitor or adapter card, or both.

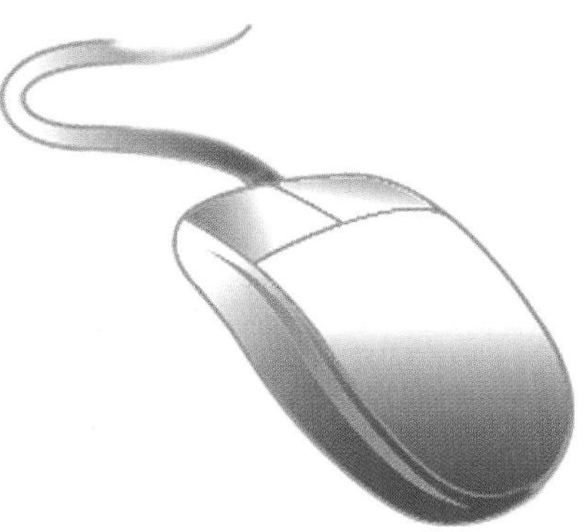

Figure 7
Typical computer mouse

Figure 8
The two essential parts of a computer display system

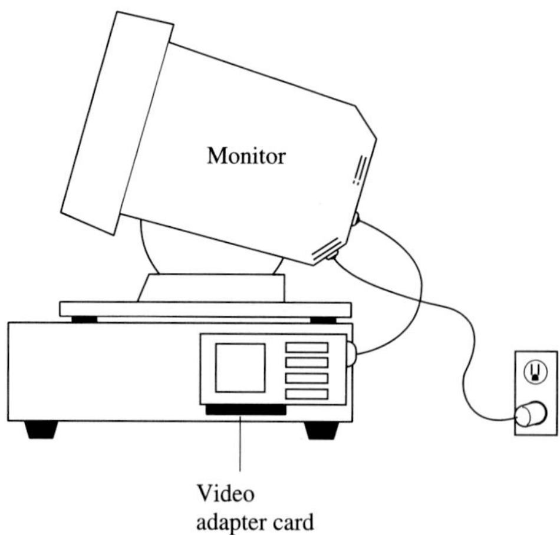

(a) Video adapter card with companion monitor

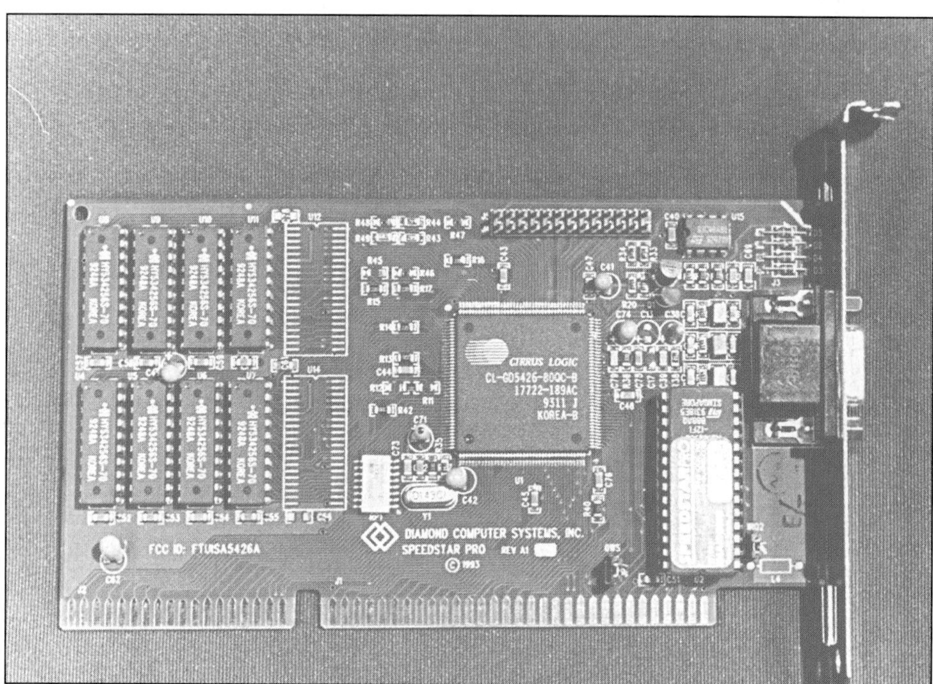

(b) SVGA graphics accelerator card (*photograph by John T. Butchko*)

Figure 9
Necessity of each computer monitor having its own matching adapter

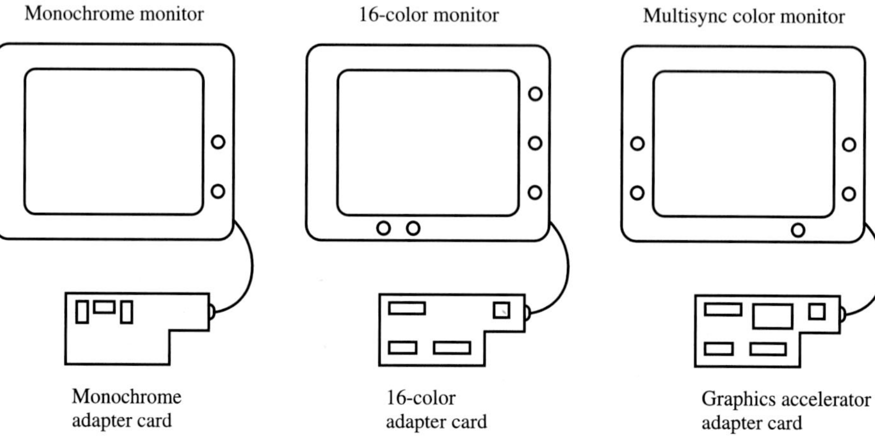

Monitor Servicing

Very seldom is the computer user expected to repair a computer monitor. Computer monitors are very complex devices that require specialized training to repair. These instruments contain very high and dangerous voltages that are present even when no power is being applied. The servicing of the monitor itself is, therefore, better left to those who are trained in this specialty.

What you need to know is what kinds of monitors are available, their differences, and how they interface with the computer. Then you need to know enough about hardware and software in order to tell if a problem that appears on the monitor is in the monitor itself, its adapter card, the computer, or the monitor cabling—or is simply a lack of understanding about how to operate the computer.

Monitor Fundamentals

All monitors have the basic sections shown in Figure 10. Table 1 lists the purpose of each of the major sections of a computer monitor.

Monochrome and Color Monitors

One of the differences between a monochrome (single-color) monitor and a color monitor is in the construction of the CRT. The differences are illustrated in Figure 11.

As shown in the figure, the color CRT contains a triad of color phosphor dots. Even though this consists of only three color phosphors, all the colors you see on a color monitor are produced by means of these three colors (including white, which is produced by controlling the intensity of the three colors: red is 30%, green is 59%, and blue is 11%). This process, called **additive color mixing,** is illustrated in Figure 12.

The other differences between monochrome and color monitors are the circuits inside these systems as well as their adapter cards. Some of these differences are the high voltages in a color monitor that are several times higher than those found in a monochrome monitor. Usually, these voltages are on the order of 30,000 V or more. You should note that this high voltage can be stored by the color CRT and still be present even when the set is unplugged from the AC outlet. A special probe is used to discharge the CRT.

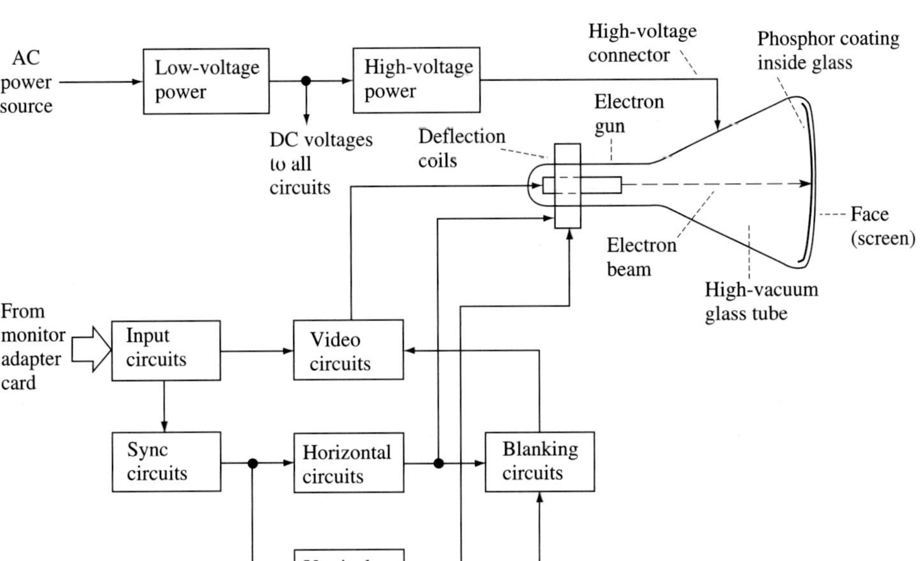

Figure 10
Major sections of a computer monitor

Table 1
Major sections of a computer monitor

Section	Purpose
Glass CRT	The cathode-ray tube (CRT) creates the image on the screen. It is so named because the source of electrons is called the cathode and the resulting stream of electrons is called its rays (cathode rays).
Electron gun	Generates a fine stream of electrons that are attracted toward the glass face of the CRT (the screen) by the large positive voltage applied there.
Phosphor coating	A special kind of material that emits light when struck by an electron beam.
High-voltage power source	Supplies the large positive voltage required by the CRT to attract the electrons from the electron gun.
Deflection coils	Generate strong magnetic fields that move the electron beam across the face of the CRT.
Horizontal circuits	Generate waveforms applied to the deflection coils, causing the electron beam to sweep horizontally across the face of the CRT from left to right.
Vertical circuits	Generate waveforms applied to the deflection coils, causing the horizontal sweep of the electron beam to move vertically across the face of the CRT from top to bottom and creating a series of horizontal lines.
Blanking circuits	Cause the electron beam to be cut off from going to the face of the CRT so that it isn't seen when the electron beam is retracing from right to left or from bottom to top. (This is similar to what you do when writing. You lift your pen from the surface of the paper after you finish a line and return to the left side of the paper to begin a new line just below it.)
Video circuits	Control the intensity of the electron beam that results in the development of images on the screen.
Sync circuits	Electrical circuits that help synchronize the movement of the electron beam across the screen.
Low-voltage power supply	Supplies the operating voltages required by the various circuits inside the monitor.

Energy Efficiency

Energy-efficient PCs are designed with energy efficiency in mind. The system BIOS, monitor video card, and other hardware must support either the Advanced Power Management (APM) or VESA BIOS extensions for power management (VBE/PM) standards. Some computers may support limited power management or energy saving features.

It is estimated by the U.S. Environmental Protection Agency (EPA) that the average office desktop computer or workstation uses around $105 of electrical power annually. When all desktops are considered, the total consumption adds up to around 5 percent of all electrical energy consumed in the United States. The EPA estimates that by using energy-efficient equipment, as much as $90 a year per computer can be saved.

The EPA has proposed a set of guidelines for energy-efficient use of computers, workstations, monitors, and printers. The EPA *Energy Star* program requires the computer and monitor to use less than 30 watts each when they are not being used (for a total of 60 watts including both the system unit and the monitor). Personal computers adhering to the Energy Star recommendations are also called *green* PCs.

Each computer can be set up to automatically reduce energy usage using the standby and sleep modes. The standby mode is activated after a user-specified period of inactivity. The sleep mode is

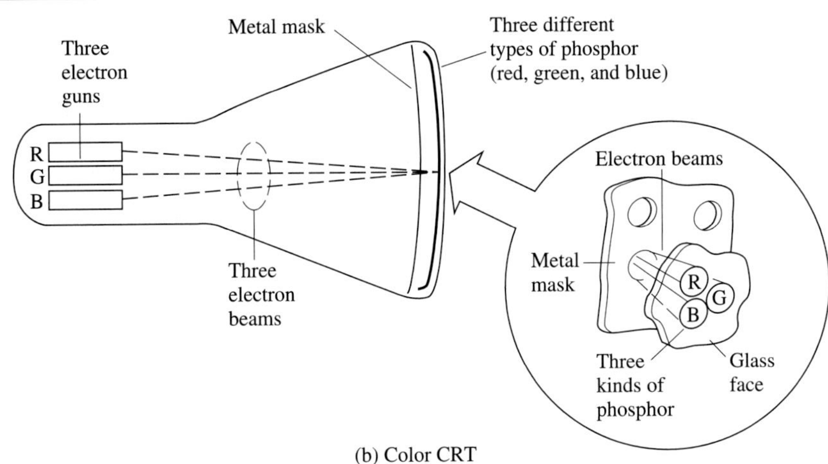

Figure 11
Monochrome and color CRTs

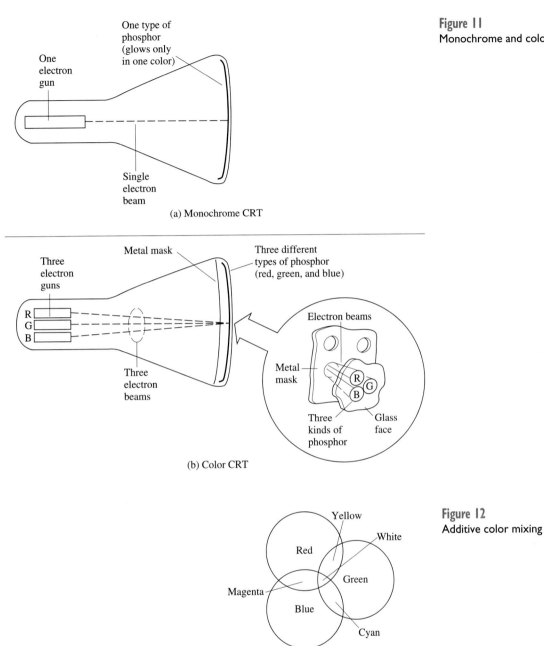

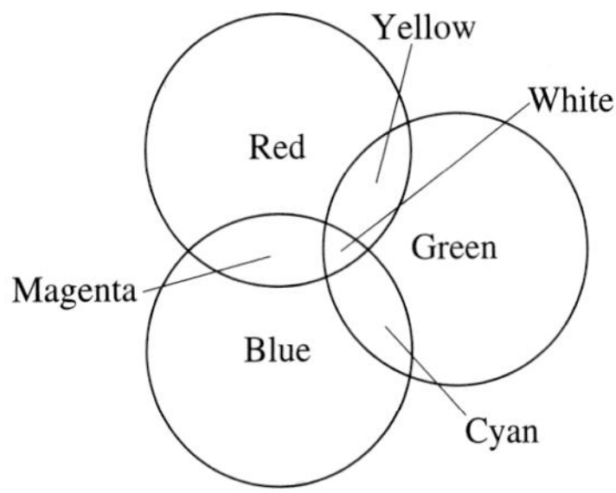

Figure 12
Additive color mixing

automatically activated after the standby time has expired. If the computer is used during standby energy saving mode, it takes just a short period of time before the monitor is usable. Sleep mode is similar to a power-down of the monitor and requires some additional time before the monitor is usable.

The EPA Web site located at http://www.epa.gov/energy_star maintains a list of all energy-efficient computer products. Look for the Energy Star trademark on product packaging and the marketing materials supplied by most manufacturers.

Video Controls

Table 2 lists some of the major video controls and their purposes.

Pixels and Aspect Ratio

Figure 13 illustrates two important characteristics of computer monitors. As shown in the figure, a pixel (or pel) is the smallest area on the screen whose intensity can be controlled. The more pixels

Table 2
Major video controls

Control	Purpose
Contrast	A gain control for the circuits that determine the strength of the signal used to place images on the screen. It affects the amount of difference between light and dark.
Brightness	Controls the amount of high voltage applied to the CRT, which controls the strength of the beam. The higher the voltage, the stronger the beam and the brighter the picture.
Vertical size	Controls the output of the vertical circuit, changing the amount of the vertical sweep of the CRT and thus changing the vertical size of the displayed image.
Horizontal size	Controls the output of the horizontal circuit, changing the amount of horizontal sweep of the CRT and thus changing the horizontal size of the displayed image.
Vertical hold	Helps adjust the synchronous circuits so the image is stable in the vertical direction.
Horizontal hold	Helps adjust the synchronous circuits so the image is stable in the horizontal direction.

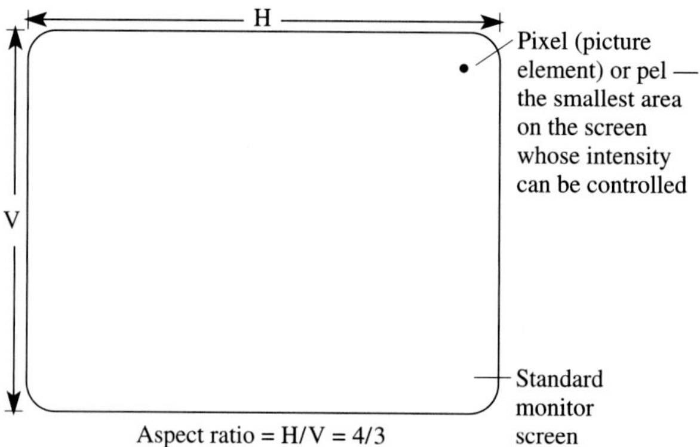

Figure 13
Pixels and aspect ratio

available on the screen, the greater the detail that can be displayed. The number of pixels varies among different types of monitors; the more pixels, the more expensive the monitor. The aspect ratio indicates that the face of the CRT is not a perfect square. It is, instead, a rectangle. This is important to remember, especially if you are developing software for drawing squares and circles; you may wind up with rectangles and ellipses. The size of a pixel is referred to as its *dot pitch* and is a function of the number of pixels on a scan line and the distance across the display screen.

Monitor Modes

There are two fundamental modes in which the monitor operates: the **text mode** and the **graphics mode.** Figure 14 illustrates the difference.

In the text mode, the CRT display gets its information from a built-in ROM chip referred to as the **character ROM.** This may not be a separate ROM chip but part of another, larger one. This ROM contains all the characters on your keyboard, plus many more. This group of characters is known as the **extended character set** and may, among other things, be used in combination to form squares, boxes, and other shapes while your computer is still in the text mode. To get any of these extended characters on the screen (or to get *any* character on the screen), simply hold down the SHIFT and ALT keys at the same time and then type in the character number. For example, to get the character ö, hold down the SHIFT and ALT keys and type in 148 on the keypad; when you lift up on the SHIFT and ALT keys, the character appears (and can also appear on the printer, depending on the type of printer).

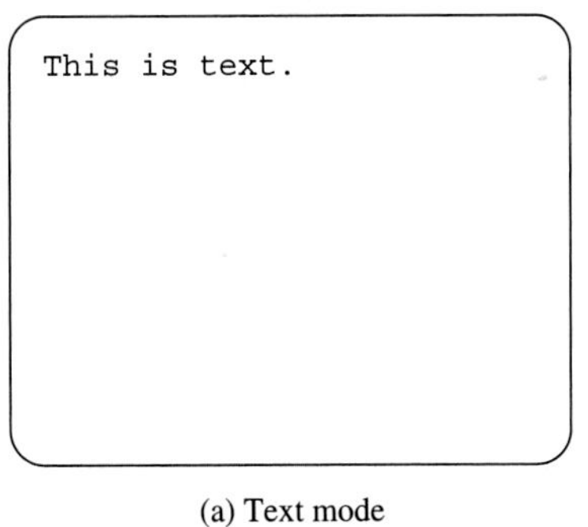

(a) Text mode

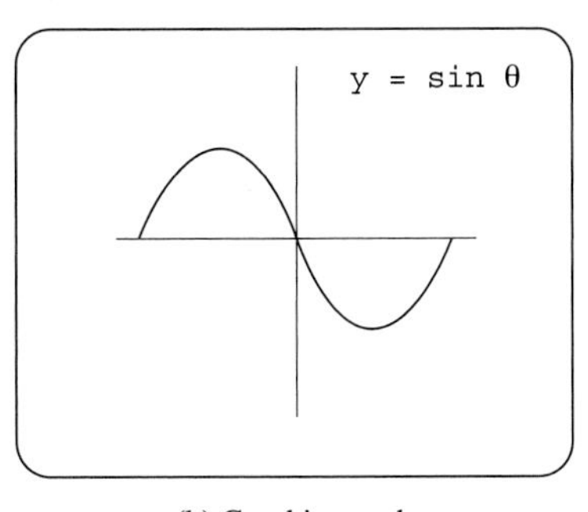

(b) Graphics mode

Figure 14
Text and graphics modes

The advantage of the text mode is that it doesn't take much memory and the visual results are predictable and easy to achieve (you need only to press a key on the keyboard). The size of the text screen is 80 × 25 or 40 × 25. The text screen is sometimes referred to as the **alphanumeric mode.**

When the monitor and its circuits are in the graphics mode, an entirely different use of memory is required. RAM is used because a program has complete control over the intensity and (in the case of color) the color of each pixel. The more pixels available on the monitor, the more memory required; the more memory required, the longer it takes to display a complete picture on the face of the CRT, which in turn means that your whole computer must be able to operate at a very high speed. In order to display detailed graphics, you must have a big and powerful machine, which means a more expensive system as well as a more expensive monitor.

Just to give you an idea of the memory requirements for graphics, if your monitor has 640 horizontal pixels and 480 vertical pixels, the total number of pixels that must be addressed by RAM is 640 × 480 = 307,200, which is more than a third of a megabyte for just one screen. If color is not used in the graphics mode, less memory is required (because the computer needs to store less information about each pixel).

Types of Monitors

In order to understand the differences among the most common types of computer monitors, you must first understand the definitions of the terms used to describe them. Table 3 lists the major terms used to distinguish one monitor from another.

Now that you know the definitions of some of the major terms used to distinguish one monitor from another, you can be introduced to the most common types of monitors in use today. Table 4 lists the various types of monitors and their distinguishing characteristics.

VGA Monitor The **video graphics array (VGA) monitor** is one of the most popular color monitors; it provides high color resolution at a reasonable price. More and more software with graphics is making use of this type of monitor. The associated cards have a high scanning rate, resulting in less eye fatigue both in text and in graphics modes.

SVGA Monitor Higher screen resolution and new graphics modes make the **Super VGA (SVGA) monitor** even more popular than the VGA monitor.

Multiscan Monitor The **multiscan monitor** was one of the first monitors that could be used with a wide variety of monitor adapter cards. Since this type of monitor can accommodate a variety of adapter cards, it is sometimes referred to as the *multidisplay* or *multisync* monitor.

Display Adapters

As previously stated, a computer monitor must be compatible with its adapter card. If it is not, damage to the monitor or adapter card, or both, could result.

VGA Adapter The **VGA (video graphics array card)** was the fastest-growing graphics card in terms of popularity until the SVGA card became available. The VGA adapter card uses a 15-pin high-density pin-out, as shown in Figure 15. The VGA 15-pin adapter can be wired to fit the standard 9-pin graphics adapter, as shown in Figure 16.

Table 3
Computer monitor terminology

Term	Definition
Resolution	The number of pixels available on the monitor. A resolution of 640 × 480 means that there are 640 pixels horizontally and 480 pixels vertically.
Colors	The number of different colors that may be displayed at one time in the graphics mode. For some color monitors, more colors can be displayed in the text mode than in the graphics mode. This is possible because of the reduced memory requirements of the text mode.
Palette	A measure of the full number of colors available on the monitor. However, not all the available palette colors can be displayed at the same time (again, because of memory requirements). You can usually get a large number of colors with low resolution (fewer pixels) or a smaller number of colors (sometimes only one) with much higher resolution—again, because of memory limitations.
Display (digital or analog)	There are basically two different types of monitor displays, **digital** and **analog.** Some of the first computer monitors used poor-quality analog monitors. Then digital monitors, with their better overall display quality, became more popular. Now, however, the trend is back to analog monitors because of the increasing demand for high-quality graphics, where colors and shades can be varied continuously to give a more realistic appearance.

Table 4
Common types of computer monitors

Type	Resolution*	Colors	Palette	Display
Monochrome composite	640 × 200	1	1	Analog
Color composite	640 × 200	4	4	Analog
Monochrome display	720 × 350	1	1	Digital
RGB (CGA)	640 × 200	4	16	Digital
EGA	640 × 350	16	64	Digital
PGA	640 × 480	Unlimited	Unlimited	Analog
VGA	640 × 480	256	262,144	Analog
SVGA	1280 × 1024	Varies	Varies	Digital/ analog
Multiscan	Varies	Unlimited	Unlimited	Digital/ analog

*In general, the higher the resolution, the higher the scan frequency. For example, the typical scan frequencies of EGA and VGA monitors are 21.5 KHz and 31.5 KHz, respectively.

SVGA Adapter The Super VGA graphics interface uses the same connector that VGA monitors use. However, more display modes are possible with SVGA than with VGA.

VESA The **VESA** (Video Electronics Standards Association) specification has been developed to guide the operation of new video cards and displays beyond VGA. New BIOS software that supports the VESA conventions is contained in an EPROM mounted on the display card. The software also supports the defined VESA video modes. Some of these new modes are 1024 × 768, 1280 × 1024, and 1600 × 1200, with up to 16 million possible colors.

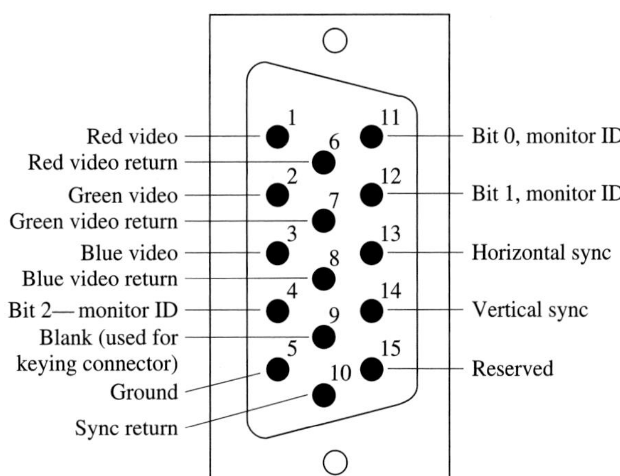

Figure 15
Pin diagram for VGA adapter

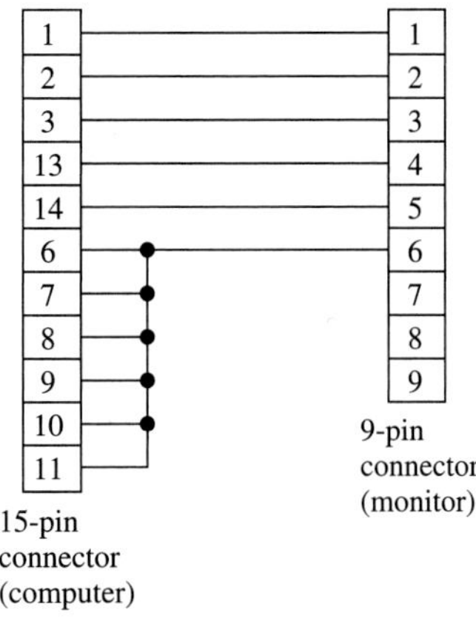

Figure 16
Nine-pin adapter cable for VGA

Graphics Accelerator Adapters

A graphics accelerator is a video adapter containing a microprocessor designed specifically to handle the graphics processing workload. This eliminates the need for the system processor to handle the graphics information, allowing it to process other instructions (nongraphics related) instead.

Aside from the graphics processor, there are other features offered by graphics accelerators. These features include additional video memory, which is reserved for storing graphical representations, and a wide bus capable of moving 64 or 128 bits of data at a time. Video memory is also called VRAM and can be accessed much faster than conventional memory.

Many new multimedia applications require a *graphics accelerator* to provide the necessary graphics throughput in order to gain realism in multimedia applications. Table 5 illustrates the settings available for supporting many different monitor types and refresh rates.

Most graphics accelerators are compatible with the new standards such as Microsoft DirectX, which provides an application programming interface, or API, to the graphics subsystem. Usually, the graphics accelerators are also compatible with OpenGL for the Windows NT environment.

AGP Adapter

The **Accelerated Graphics Port (AGP)** is a new interface specification developed by Intel. The AGP adapter is based on the PCI design but uses a special point-to-point channel so that the graphics controller can directly access the main system memory. The AGP channel is 32 bits wide and runs at 66 MHz. This provides a bandwidth of 266 MBps as opposed to the PCI bandwidth of 133 MBps.

AGP optionally supports two faster modes, with throughput of 533MB and 1.07GB. Sending either one (AGP 1X), two (AGP 2X), or four (AGP 4X) data transfers per clock cycle accomplishes these data rates. Table 6 shows the different AGP modes. Other optional features include AGP texturing, sideband addressing, and pipelining. Each of these options provides additional performance enhancements.

Table 5
Common monitor support

Resolution	Colors	Memory	Refresh Rates
640 x 480	256 65K 16M	2MB 2MB 2MB	60, 72, 75, 85
800 x 600	256 65K 16M	2MB 2MB 2MB	56, 60, 72, 75, 85
1024 x 768	256 65K 16M	2MB 2MB 4MB	43 (interlaced), 60, 72, 75, 85
1280 x 1024	256 65K 16M	2MB 4MB 4MB	43 (interlaced), 60, 75, 85

Table 6
AGP graphics mode

Mode	Throughput (MB/s)	Data Transfers per Cycle
1x	266	1
2x	533	2
4x	1066	4

AGP graphics support is provided by the new NLX motherboards, which also support the Pentium II microprocessor (and above). It allows for the graphic subsystem to work much closer with the processor than previously available by providing new paths for data to flow between the processor, memory, and video memory. Figure 17 shows this relationship.

AGP offers many advantages over traditional video adapters. You are encouraged to become familiar with the details of the AGP adapter.

The Computer Printer

Two fundamental types of printers are used with personal computers: the **impact printer** and the **nonimpact printer.** The impact printer uses some kind of mechanical device to impart an impression to the paper through an inked ribbon. The nonimpact printer uses heat, a jet of ink, electrostatic discharge, or laser light. Nonimpact printers form printed images without making physical contact with the paper. These two types of printers are illustrated in Figure 18.

Impact Printers

The most common type of impact printer is the **dot-matrix printer.** The dot-matrix printer makes up its characters by means of a series of tiny mechanical pins that move in and out to form the various characters printed on the paper.

The Dot-Matrix Printer The dot-matrix printer, one of the most popular types of printers, uses a mechanical printing head that physically moves across the paper to be printed. This mechanical head consists of tiny movable wires that strike an inked ribbon to form characters on the paper. There are two popular kinds of dot-matrix print heads: one consists of 9 pins (the movable wires) and the other consists of 24 pins. A 9-pin print head is shown in Figure 19.

The 24-pin dot-matrix printer is more expensive than the 9-pin model. However, because both types have modes of operation that allow for an *overstrike* of the image (with the head moving slightly and the image being struck again), the 9-pin model can produce close to what is known as letter-quality printing. The 24-pin model can produce an even sharper character when operated in

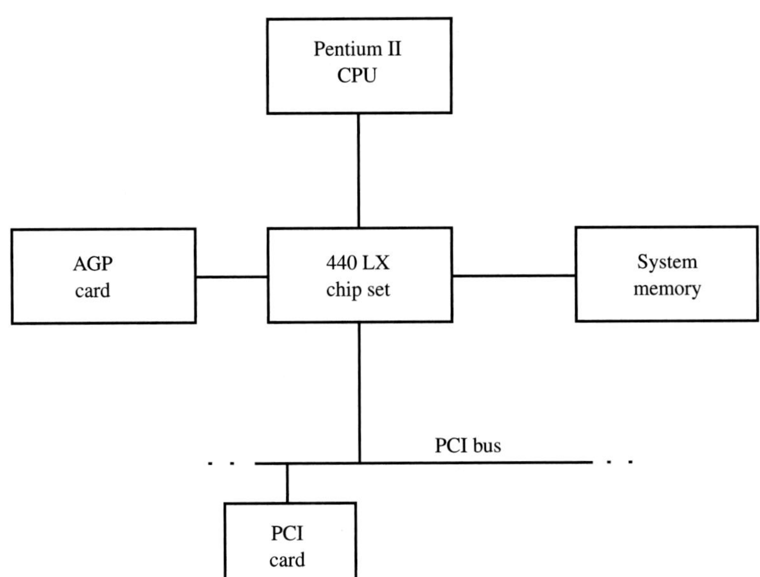

Figure 17
AGP configuration

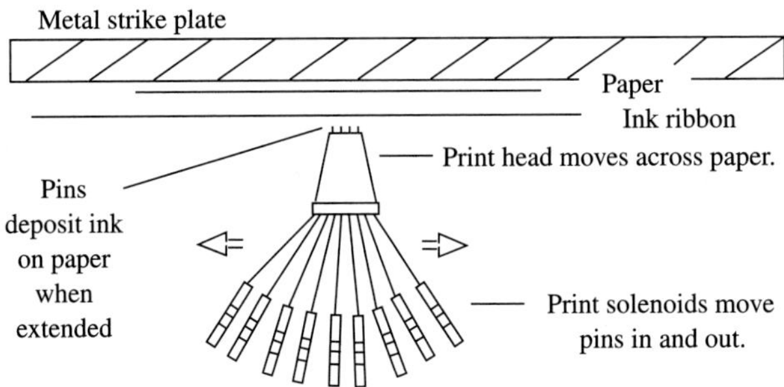

(a) Impact (Dot-matrix Illustration)

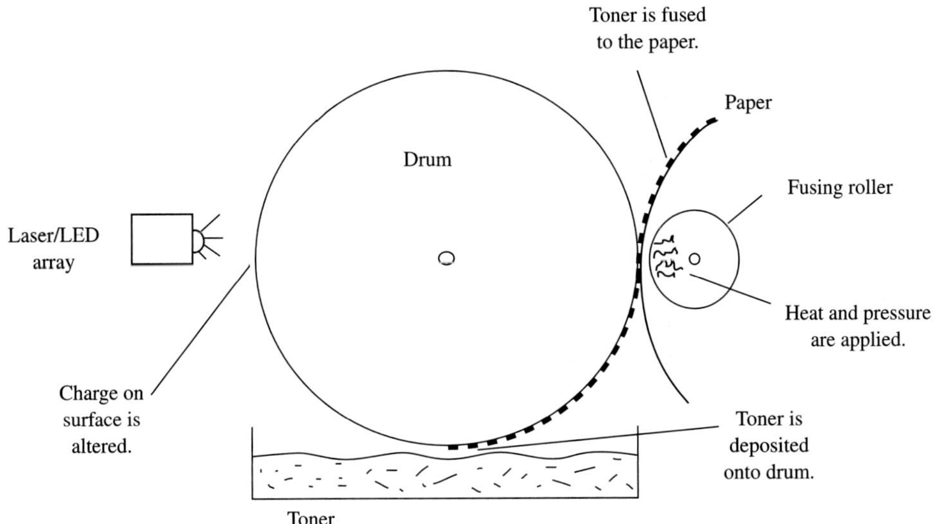

(b) Nonimpact (Laser Illustration)

Figure 18
Two fundamental types of printers

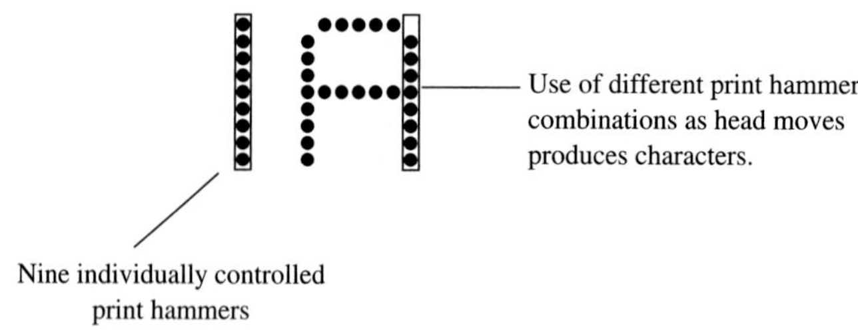
Use of different print hammer combinations as head moves produces characters.
Nine individually controlled print hammers

Figure 19
Nine-pin dot-matrix print head

the same overstrike mode. Because of the manner in which characters are formed in this type of printer, the printing of graphic images is possible.

Nonimpact Printers

The most popular nonimpact printers are the *ink-jet printer, bubble-jet printer,* and the *laser printer.* The ink-jet printer uses tiny jets of ink that are electrically controlled. The laser printer uses a laser to form characters. The laser printer resembles an office photocopying machine.

Ink-Jet and Bubble-Jet Printers An **ink-jet printer** uses electrostatically charged plates to direct jets of ink onto paper. The ink is under pressure and is formed by a mechanical nozzle into tiny droplets that can be deflected to make up the required images on the paper. A **bubble-jet printer** uses heat to form bubbles of ink. As the bubbles cool, they form the droplets applied to the paper. Ink-jet and bubble-jet printers cost more than impact printers but are quieter and can produce high-quality graphic images.

Laser Printers Through the operation of a laser and mirror (controlled by software), an electrical image is impressed on a photoreceptor drum. This drum picks up powdered toner, which is then transferred to paper by electrostatic discharge. A second drum uses high temperature to bond this image to the paper. Table 7 shows the six step process which is used by laser printers. The result is a high-quality image capable of excellent characters and graphics.

Because of their high-quality output, laser printers find wide application in desktop publishing, computer-aided design, and other image-intensive computer applications. Laser printers are usually at the high end of the price range for computer printers.

Technical Considerations

Most printer problems are caused by software. What this means is that the software does not match the hardware of the printer. This is especially true when the printing of graphics is involved. Software troubleshooting for printers is presented last in this section. When there is a hardware problem with printers, it is usually the interface cable that goes from the printer adapter card to the printer itself. This is illustrated in Figure 20.

Table 7
Laser printer six step electrophotographic process

Step	Purpose
1. Charging	The photoreceptor drum is charged with static electricity.
2. Exposure	The print image is exposed onto the drum using a laser.
3. Developing	Toner is applied to the exposed parts of the drum.
4. Transfer	Toner is transferred from the drum to the paper.
5. Fusing	The toner is heated and bonded to the paper.
6. Cleaning	The photoreceptor drum is cleaned in preparation for the next image.

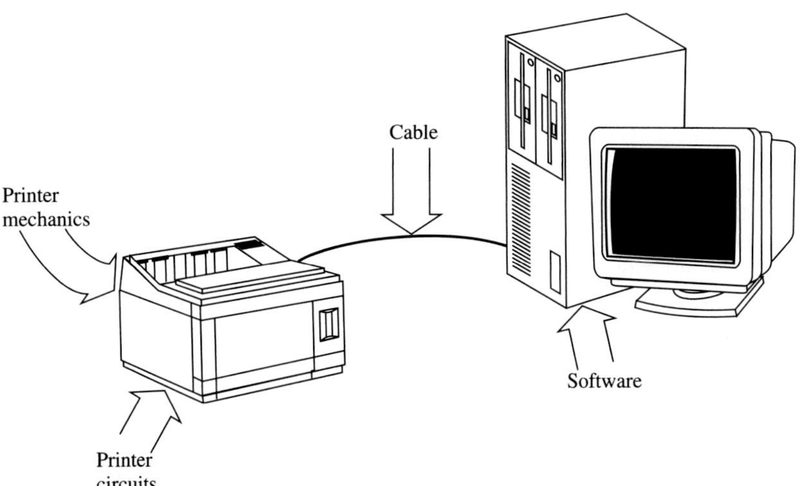

Figure 20
Problem areas in computer printers

Printer Cables The interface cable is used to connect the printer to the computer. Previously, there was limited communication between the printer and computer. The computer received a few signals from the printer such as the online or offline indicator, the out-of-paper sensor, and the print buffer status. As long as the printer was sending the correct signals to the computer, the computer would continue to send data.

Advances in printer technology now require a two-way communication between the computer and printer. As a result of these changes, a new bidirectional printer cable is required to connect most new printers to the computer. The bidirectional cables may or may not adhere to the new IEEE standard for Bidirectional Parallel Peripheral Interface. The IEEE 1284 Bitronic printer cable standard requires 28 AWG construction, a Hi-flex jacket, and dual shields for low EMI emissions. The conductors are twisted into pairs to reduce possible cross talk.

Check the requirements for each printer to determine the proper cable type. Figure 21 shows two popular parallel printer cable styles. Many different lengths of printer cables are available. It is usually best to use the shortest cable possible in order to reduce the possibility of communication errors.

Types of Printer Connections and Configurations

A printer directly connected to the computer is called a *local* printer. A printer accessed over the network is a *network* printer. A printer must be shared to make it a network printer. Table 8 shows several types of common printer connection types.

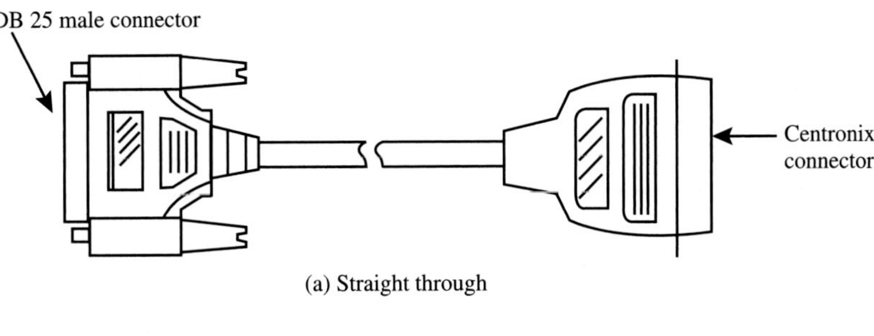

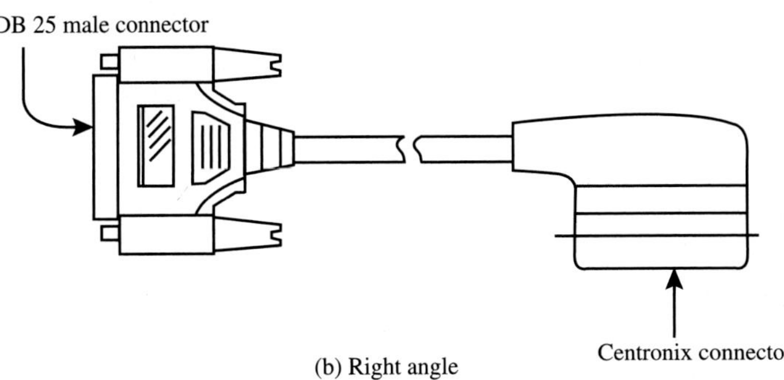

Figure 21
Typical printer cables

Table 8
Printer connection types

Connection	Explanation/Details
Parallel	A cable containing a male DB25 connector on one end and a 36-pin male Centronix connector on the other is required. The DB25 connector plugs into the printer/parallel port. Most printers use the parallel connection due to its high speed.
Network	A network printer is a printer that is shared by the computer it is connected to. Stand-alone print servers are also used to provide network printer capability. Users must establish a connection to the network printer before using it. Note that network printing is slower than parallel printing, since it is serial by nature and must compete with other network traffic.
Infrared	A laptop (or desktop) computer may use its Infrared port to print to an IrDA compatible printer. The IrDA drivers must be installed on the laptop before installing the printer drivers. Although the infrared serial connection is slower than parallel, it is point-to-point and thus does not compete with other network traffic.
USB	A USB cable is required.
Serial	A serial cable containing a 9-pin connector on each end is required. The serial cable plugs into a free COM port. This is the slowest printer connection and rarely used.

Printer Hardware A printer requires periodic maintenance. This includes vacuuming out the paper chaff left inside the printer. A soft dry cloth should be used to keep the paper and ribbon paths clean. It is a good idea to use plastic gloves when cleaning a printer, because the ink or toner is usually difficult to remove from the skin. With dot-matrix printers, be careful of the print heads. These heads can get quite hot after extended use. Make sure you do not turn the print platen rollers when the power is on because a stepper motor is engaged when power is applied. This little motor is trying to hold the print platen roller in place. If you force it to move, you could damage the stepper motor.

Laser Hardware Essentially, laser printers require very little maintenance. If you follow the instructions that come with the printer, the process of changing the cartridge (after about 3500 copies) also performs the required periodic maintenance on the printer.

When using a laser printer, remember that such a machine uses a large amount of electrical energy and thus produces heat. So make sure that the printer has adequate ventilation and a good source of reliable electrical power. This means that you should not use an electrical expansion plug from your wall outlet to run your computer, monitor, and laser printer. Doing so may overload your power outlet.

When shipping a laser printer, be sure to remove the toner cartridge. If you don't remove it, it could open up and spill toner (a black powder) over the inside of the printer, causing a mess that is difficult to clean up.

Testing Printers

When faced with a printer problem, first determine if the printer ever worked at all or if this is a new installation that never worked. If it is a new installation and has never worked, a careful reading of the manual that comes with the printer is usually required to make sure that the device is compatible with the printer adapter card. Table 9 lists some of the most direct methods for troubleshooting a computer printer.

System Software

Many types of commands are sent to the printer while it is printing. Some of these commands tell the printer what character to print; others tell the printer what to do, such as performing a carriage

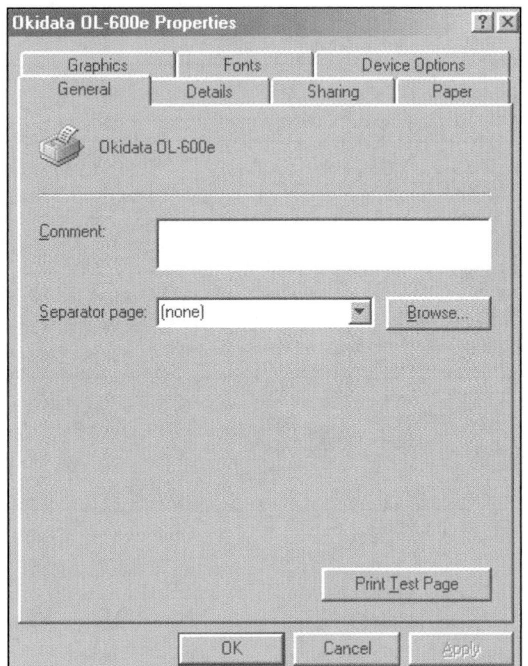

Figure 22
Print Test Page option

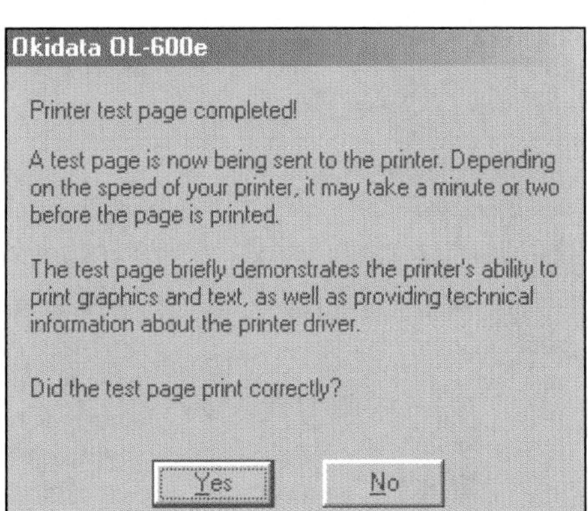

Figure 23
Printer test page confirmation

Windows 98
Printer Test Page

Congratulations!

If you can read this information, you have correctly installed your Okidata OL-600e.

The information below describes your printer driver and port settings.

```
Printer name:   Okidata OL-600e
Printer model:  Okidata OL-600e
Driver name:    HPPCLB.DRV
Driver version: 4.00
Color support:  No
Port name:      LPT1:
Data format:    EMF

Files used by this driver:
 C:\WINDOWS\SYSTEM\msprint2.cat
 C:\WINDOWS\SYSTEM\HPPCLB.DRV    (4.10.1998, GPC 3.04)
 C:\WINDOWS\SYSTEM\FINSTALL.DLL  (4.0.2.01)
 C:\WINDOWS\SYSTEM\FINSTALL.HLP
 C:\WINDOWS\SYSTEM\UNIDRV.DLL    (4.10.1998)
 C:\WINDOWS\SYSTEM\UNIDRV.HLP
 C:\WINDOWS\SYSTEM\ICONLIB.DLL   (4.10.1998)
```

This is the end of the printer test page.

Figure 24
Printer test page output

Table 9
Printer troubleshooting methods

Checks	Comments
Check if printer is plugged in and turned on.	The printer must have external AC power to operate.
Check if printer is online and has paper.	Printers must be *online,* meaning that their control switches have been set so that they will print (check the instruction manual). Some printers will not operate if they do not have paper inserted.
Print a test page.	Select the Print Test Page option as shown in Figure 22. Confirm that the page printed properly, see Figure 23. Figure 24 shows the printer test page output.
Do a printer self-test.	Most printers have a self-test mode. In this mode, the printer will repeat its character set over and over again. You must refer to the documentation that comes with the printer to see how this is done.
Do a Print Screen.	If the printer self-test works, then with some characters on the computer monitor, hold down the SHIFT key and press the PRINTSCRN key at the same time. What is on the monitor should now be printed. Do not use a program (such as a word-processing program) because the software in the program may not be compatible with the printer.
Exchange printer cable.	If none of the above tests work, the problem may be in the printer cable. At this point, you should swap the cable with a known good one.
Replace the printer adapter card.	Try replacing the printer adapter card with a known good one. Be sure to refer to the printer manual to make sure you are using the correct adapter card.
Check parameters for a serial interface.	If you are using a serial interface printer from a serial port, make sure you have the transmission rate set correctly, along with the parity, number of data bits, and number of stop bits. Refer to the instruction manual that comes with the printer and use the correct form of the DOS MODE command.
Check the configuration settings.	Check all the configuration settings available on the printer.
Check the software installation.	When software is installed (such as word-processing and spreadsheet programs), the user may have had the wrong printer driver installed (the software that actually operates the printer from the program).

return, making a new line, or doing a form feed. This is all accomplished by groups of 1s and 0s formed into a standard code that represents all of the printable characters and the other commands that tell the printer what to print and how to print it.

The ASCII Code Table 10 lists all the printable characters for a standard printer. The code used to transmit this information is called the ASCII code. ASCII stands for American Standard Code for Information Interchange.

As you can see in Table 10, each keyboard character is given a unique number value. For example, a space is number 32 (which is actually represented by the binary value 0010 0000 when transmitted from the computer to the printer). The number values that are less than 32 are used for controlling the operations of the printer. These are called **printer-control codes,** or simply **control codes.** These codes are shown in Table 11.

The definitions of the control code abbreviations are as follows:

ACK	Acknowledge	GS	Group separator
BEL	Bell	HT	Horizontal tab
BS	Backspace	LF	Line feed
CAN	Cancel	NAK	Negative acknowledge
CR	Carriage return	NUL	Null
DC_1–DC_4	Device control	RS	Record separator
DEL	Delete	SI	Shift in
DLE	Data link escape	SO	Shift out
EM	End of medium	SOH	Start of heading
ENQ	Enquiry	SP	Space
EOT	End of transmission	STX	Start text
ESC	Escape	SUB	Substitute
ETB	End of transmission block	SYN	Synchronous idle
ETX	End text	US	Unit separator
FF	Form feed	VT	Vertical tab
FS	Form separator		

The way you can enter an ASCII control code is by holding down the ALT key and the SHIFT key at the same time and using the numeric keypad to enter the ASCII control code. You will see the corresponding character on the screen when you release the ALT and SHIFT keys. (The top row of numbers on your keyboard will not work—only the ones on the numeric keypad portion of the keyboard.)

Table 10
Standard printable ASCII codes

Dec	Hex	Char	Dec	Hex	Char	Dec	Hex	Char
32	20		64	40	@	96	60	'
33	21	!	65	41	A	97	61	a
34	22	"	66	42	B	98	62	b
35	23	#	67	43	C	99	63	c
36	24	$	68	44	D	100	64	d
37	25	%	69	45	E	101	65	e
38	26	&	70	46	F	102	66	f
39	27	'	71	47	G	103	67	g
40	28	(	72	48	H	104	68	h
41	29	)	73	49	I	105	69	i
42	2A	*	74	4A	J	106	6A	j
43	2B	+	75	4B	K	107	6B	k
44	2C	,	76	4C	L	108	6C	l
45	2D	–	77	4D	M	109	6D	m
46	2E	.	78	4E	N	110	6E	n
47	2F	/	79	4F	O	111	6F	o
48	30	0	80	50	P	112	70	p
49	31	1	81	51	Q	113	71	q
50	32	2	82	52	R	114	72	r
51	33	3	83	53	S	115	73	s
52	34	4	84	54	T	116	74	t
53	35	5	85	55	U	117	75	u
54	36	6	86	56	V	118	76	v
55	37	7	87	57	W	119	77	w
56	38	8	88	58	X	120	78	x
57	39	9	89	59	Y	121	79	y
58	3A	:	90	5A	Z	122	7A	z
59	3B	;	91	5B	[	123	7B	{
60	3C	<	92	5C	\	124	7C	|
61	3D	=	93	5D	]	125	7D	}
62	3E	>	94	5E	^	126	7E	~
63	3F	?	95	5F	–			

Table 11
ASCII control codes

Dec	Hex	Char	
0	0	^@	NUL
1	1		SOH
2	2	☺	STX
3	3	♥	ETX
4	4	♦	EOT
5	5	♣	ENQ
6	6	♠	ACK
7	7	•	BEL
8	8	◘	BS
9	9	○	HT
10	A	█	LF
11	B	♂	VT
12	C	♀	FF
13	D	♪	CR
14	E	♫	SO
15	F	☼	SI
16	10	►	DLE
17	11	◄	DC_1
18	12	↕	DC_2
19	13	‼	DC_3
20	14	¶	DC_4
21	15	§	NAK
22	16	■	SYN
23	17	↨	ETB
24	18	↑	CAN
25	19	↓	EM
26	1A	→	SUB
27	1B	←	ESC
28	1C	∟	FS
29	1D	↔	GS
30	1E	▲	RS
31	1F	▼	US
32	20		SP

For example, to create a text file that will cause the printer to eject a sheet of paper (a form feed), using an editor, you would press

```
ALT-SHIFT-12
```

What will appear on the screen when you release the ALT-SHIFT keys is

```
^L
```

This may not be exactly what you expected, but it is your monitor's way of interpreting what you have just entered. If you put this into a text file (say it is called FORMFED.TXT), then when it is sent to the printer, it will be interpreted as a form feed, and the printer will feed a new sheet of paper. You can then make a batch file that prints this form-feed text file (called FORMFED.BAT) as follows:

```
PRINT FORMFED.TXT
```

To test the printer's form feed, you would simply enter

```
A> FORMFED
```

and the printer (if on and ready) should then feed a sheet of paper through. You could also make up your own custom batch files to perform other types of printer tests or put your name in them (so the name appears printed on the sheet).

Extended ASCII Codes

If you set up your printer to act as a graphics printer (by setting the appropriate configuration; refer to the user manual that comes with the printer), you can extend the character set to include many other forms of printable characters. These characters are shown in Table 12.

Table 12
Extended ASCII character set

Dec	Hex	Char	Dec	Hex	Char	Dec	Hex	Char	Dec	Hex	Char
128	80	Ç	160	A0	á	192	C0	└	224	E0	åα
129	81	ü	161	A1	í	193	C1	┴	225	E1	åβ
130	82	é	162	A2	ó	194	C2	┬	226	E2	
131	83	â	163	A3	ú	195	C3	├	227	E3	°Γ
132	84	ä	164	A4	ń	196	C4	─	228	E4	Σ
133	85	à	165	A5	Ń	197	C5	┼	229	E5	åσ
134	86	ȧ	166	A6	ª	198	C6	╞	230	E6	åµ
135	87	ç	167	A7	º	199	C7	╟	231	E7	åτ
136	88	ê	168	A8	¿	200	C8	╚	232	E8	åf
137	89	ë	169	A9	⌐	201	C9	╔	233	E9	åu
138	8A	è	170	AA	¬	202	CA	╩	234	EA	Ω
139	8B	ï	171	AB	½	203	CB	╦	235	EB	åδ
140	8C	î	172	AC	¼	204	CC	╠	236	EC	∞
141	8D	ì	173	AD	¡	205	CD	═	237	ED	Ø
142	8E	Ä	174	AE	"	206	CE	╬	238	EE	–
143	8F	Ȧ	175	AF	"	207	CF	╧	239	EF	∩
144	90	É	176	B0	░	208	D0	╨	240	F0	≡
145	91	æ	177	B1	▒	209	D1	╤	241	F1	±
146	92	Æ	178	B2	▓	210	D2		242	F2	≥
147	93	ô	179	B3	│	211	D3	╥	243	F3	≤
148	94	ö	180	B4	┤	212	D4	╘	244	F4	⌠
149	95	ò	181	B5	╡	213	D5		245	F5	⌡
150	96	û	182	B6	╢	214	D6	╒	246	F6	+
151	97	ù	183	B7	╖	215	D7	╓	247	F7	=
152	98	ÿ	184	B8	╕	216	D8	╪	248	F8	°
153	99	Ö	185	B9	╣	217	D9	┘	249	F9	•
154	9A	Ü	186	BA	║	218	DA	┌	250	FA	.
155	9B	¢	187	BB	╗	219	DB	█	251	FB	√
156	9C	£	188	BC	╝	220	DC	▄	252	FC	η
157	9D	¥	189	BD	╜	221	DD	▌	253	FD	2
158	9E	₧	190	BE	╛	222	DE	▐	254	FE	■
159	9F	ƒ	191	BF	┐	223	DF	▀	255	FF	

You can write these extended character codes to your printer by creating text files. To do this, again hold down the ALT and SHIFT keys and type the number code into the numeric keypad on your keyboard. For example, to get the Greek letter $\sum$, simply press ALT-SHIFT-228; when you lift up on the ALT-SHIFT keys, a $\sum$ will appear on the monitor. If you include this in a text file (or do a Print Screen), you can transfer it to the printer. The extended characters 176 through 223 are used for creating boxes, rectangles, and other shapes on the monitor or printer while it is still in the text mode. If you can't get these extended characters on the printer, it is either because you haven't set the printer to the graphics mode or your printer simply can't perform the functions required by this mode.

Other Printer Features

Recall that most printers allow you to get different kinds of text (such as 80 or 132 characters of text across the page) or change the page orientation from portrait to landscape. You can also create batch files to test the capabilities of the printer to print the following:

- Bold text
- Underscores
- Overscores
- Superscripts
- Subscripts
- Compressed or expanded text
- Italics

For example, suppose a new printer does not do bold text. You could move the printer to a different computer to see if the problem is in the printer, or you could have a batch file you created that will quickly test if the printer really is capable of producing bold text. If the printer can do it, the problem is probably in the software, because a new printer driver needs to be installed (which comes from the software vendor). To do this, you need to understand what printer manufacturers do in order to get their printers to create features such as **bold text,** subscripts, and superscripts.

Printer Escape Codes

The ESC (escape) character is used by printer manufacturers as a preface. It is an easy way for them to get a whole new set of printer commands. The character ESC generally doesn't do anything by itself; what it does is to tell the printer that the character or set of characters that follows is to be treated in a special way. As an example, an <ESC>E means to begin bold text and <ESC>F means to end the bold text. The exact escape sequence is different for different printer manufacturers, and you need to find the sequence for your printer in the user's manual.

You could have a batch file calling a text file that tests for bold printing, such as

> Mickey Brown's Printer test:
> This is normal text.
> <ESC>E
> This is now bold text.
> <ESC>F
> This is back to normal text.

The problem in creating this kind of text file is to actually enter the ESC key into it (just pressing the ESC key doesn't do it). The secret to doing this is to enter a CTRL-V (hold down the CTRL key while pressing the V key) and then follow it with the [(left bracket). So when you see the text

```
<ESC>E
```

it really means CTRL-V[E, which will start boldface printing. Remember, for the printer you are using, the escape code may be different. All you need to do is to use the operator's manual that comes with the printer to determine the proper escape code for each printer's unique features.

Multifunction Print Devices

It is becoming more and more common to see printers bundled with other common products, like a fax machine. For example, a fax machine usually prints any faxes received. With some modifications, it can print data received from a computer. These types of printers generally use either ink-jet or bubble-jet printer technology.

Similarly, when sending a fax, the image or text that is sent must be scanned. Again, by making some additional modifications, the scanner can provide the scanned data to a computer instead of a fax. These three features—printing, faxing, and scanning—are available on most multifunction printers. Other features such as an answering machine may also be included. Multifunction devices can save a lot of money while offering the convenience of many products in one package.

Energy Efficiency

Like computers and monitors, printers can waste a tremendous amount of energy. This is because printers are usually left on 24 hours a day but are active only a small portion of the time. The EPA Energy Star program recommends that a printer automatically enter a sleep mode when not in use. In sleep mode, a printer may consume between 15 and 45 watts of power. This feature may cut a printer's electricity use by more than 65 percent.

Other efficiency options recommended by the EPA include printer sharing, duplex printing, and advanced power management features. Printer sharing reduces the need for an additional printer. Power management features can reduce the amount of heat produced by a printer, contributing to a more comfortable workspace and reduced air-conditioning costs. Consider turning off a printer at night, on weekends, or during extended periods of inactivity.

Definition of the Motherboard

The main system board of the computer is commonly referred to as the **motherboard.** A typical motherboard is shown in Figure 25. Sometimes the motherboard is referred to as the **system board,** or the **planar.**

Table 13 shows the common motherboard form factors names and their dimensions.

Contents Of The Motherboard

The motherboard holds and electrically interconnects all the major components of a PC. The motherboard contains the following:

- The microprocessor
- The math coprocessor (only on older 386 motherboards)
- BIOS ROM
- RAM (Dynamic RAM, or DRAM, as well as level-2 cache)
- The expansion slots
- Connectors for IDE drives, floppies, and COM ports

Table 14 lists these major parts and gives a brief overview of the purpose of each part.

Figure 26 shows a typical motherboard layout and the locations of the major motherboard parts.

In this section, you will have the opportunity to learn more details about the microprocessor and the coprocessor. You will also learn about the other areas of the motherboard.

Table 13
Motherboard Form Factors

Form Factor	Size
Baby AT	8 1/2" X 11"
ATX	8 1/2" X 11"
LPX	9" X 10.6"
NLX	Generic Riser Card

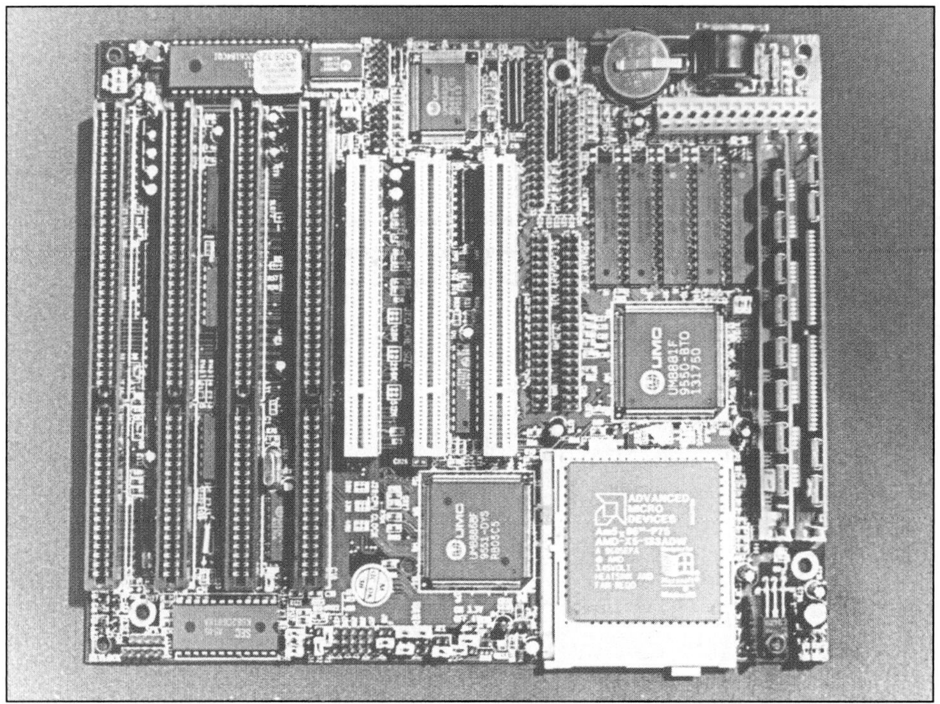

Figure 25
Typical PC motherboard (photo by John T. Butchko)

Table 14
Purposes of major motherboard parts

Part	Purpose
Microprocessor	Interprets the instructions for the computer and performs the required process for each of these instructions.
Math coprocessor	Used to take over arithmetic functions from the microprocessor.
BIOS ROM	Read-only memory. Memory programmed at the factory that cannot be changed or altered by the user.
RAM	Read/write memory. Memory used to store computer programs and interact with them.
Expansion slots	Connectors used for the purpose of interconnecting adapter cards to the motherboard.
Connectors	Integrated controller on motherboard provides signals for IDE and floppy drives, the printer, and the COM ports.

Figure 26
Motherboard layout

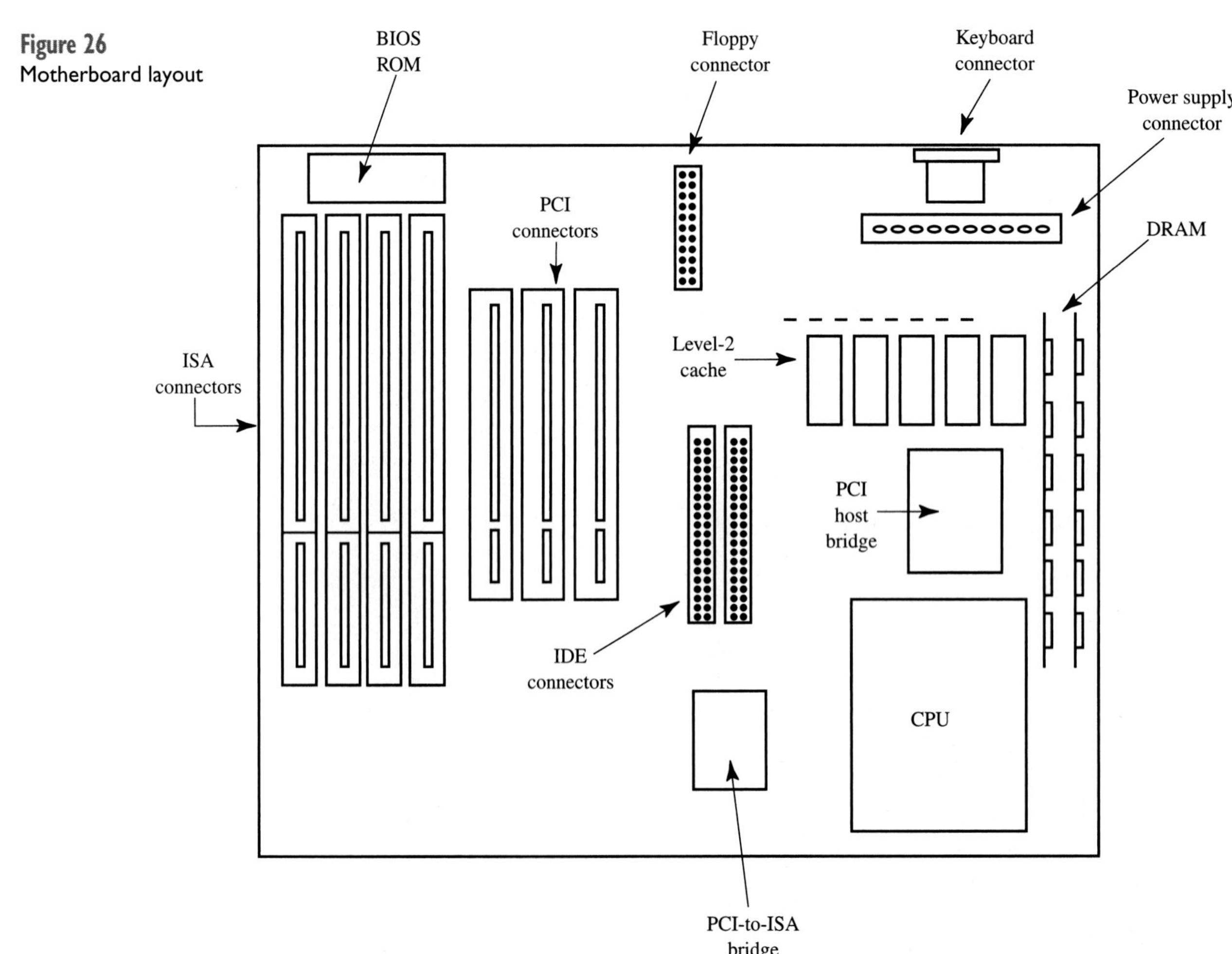

Motherboard Resources

Peripherals request and use system resources. A resource is an IRQ line, I/O port, DMA channel, or block of memory, not to mention every other hardware device in the system. Each device uses a different set of resources. Only under special circumstances (PCI adapters) may resources be shared by two or more devices. Table 15 shows the motherboard devices and the IRQ and I/O port settings.

Standard IRQ settings

Each peripheral must be assigned a unique IRQ or conflicts will occur that will prevent one or more devices from operating correctly. Note that Network adapters typically use IRQ 10. SCSI adapters may use IRQ 11 or 12.

Modems

The modem may use IRQ 4, and I/O ports 3E8 through 3EF. Since the modem is a serial device, it will take over the resources of COM1 or COM2.

Floppy drive controllers

The floppy controller uses IRQ 6, DMA channel 2, and I/O ports 3F2 through 3F5. Windows installs a standard floppy controller driver when the operating system is installed.

Hard drive controllers

There are two hard drive controllers: Primary and Secondary.

- Primary controller: IRQ 14, and I/O ports 1F0 through 1F7.
- Secondary: IRQ 15, and I/O ports 170 through 177.

Table 15
Motherboard IRQ and I/O Port Resources

Device	IRQ	I/O Ports
System timer	0	40-5F
Keyboard	1	60-6F
Cascade to IRQs 8-15	2	A0-AF
COM2, COM4	3	2F8-2FF, 2E8-2EF
COM1, COM3	4	3F8-3FF, 3E8-3EF
LPT2 or Sound card	5	278-27F
Floppy controller	6	3F2-3F5
LPT1	7	378-37F
Real-time clock	8	70-7F
Free	9	
Free	10	
Free	11	
PS/2 Mouse	12	238-23F
Math coprocessor	13	F8-FF
Primary hard disk controller	14	1F0-1F7
Secondary hard disk controller	15	170-177

Both controllers are typically part of a single integrated controller. The integrated controller may interface the IDE drives to the PCI bus. The resources used by the integrated controller are those used by the Primary and Secondary controllers.

USB ports

The USB host controller may use IRQ 11, and I/O ports 1860 through 187F.

Infrared ports

The infrared port may use IRQ 3, I/O ports 2F8, and DMA channel 3. The infrared port must be enabled in the BIOS setup program.

The Microprocessor

You can think of the **microprocessor** in a computer as the central processing unit (CPU), or the "brain," so to speak, of the computer. The microprocessor sets the stage for everything else in the computer system. Several major features distinguish one microprocessor from another. These features are listed in Table 16.

You can think of a **bus** as nothing more than a group of wires all dedicated to a specific task. For example, all microprocessors have the following buses:

Data bus	Group of wires for handling data. This determines the data path size.
Address bus	Group of wires for getting and placing data in different locations. This helps determine the maximum memory that can be used by the microprocessor.
Control bus	Group of wires for exercising different controls over the microprocessor.
Power bus	Group of wires for supplying electrical power to the microprocessor.

Figure 27 shows the bus structure of a typical microprocessor.

Since all the data that goes in and out of a microprocessor is in the form of 1s and 0s, the more wires used in the data bus, the more information the microprocessor can handle at one time. For example, some microprocessors have eight lines (wires or pins) in their data buses, others have 16, and some have 32 or 64.

The number of lines used for the address bus determines how many different places the microprocessor can use for getting and placing data. The *places* that the microprocessor uses for getting and placing data are referred to as **memory locations.** The relationship between the data and the address is shown in Figure 28.

The greater the number of lines used in the address bus of a microprocessor, the greater the number of memory locations the microprocessor can use. Table 17 lists the common microprocessors used in the PC. All of these microprocessors are manufactured by Intel Inc.

Table 16
Microprocessor features

Feature	Description
Bus structure	The number of connectors used for specific tasks.
Word size	The largest number that can be used by the microprocessor in one operation.
Data path size	The largest number that can be copied to or from the microprocessor in one operation.
Maximum memory	The largest amount of memory that can be used by the microprocessor.
Speed	The number of operations that can be performed per unit time.
Code efficiency	The number of steps required for the microprocessor to perform its processes.

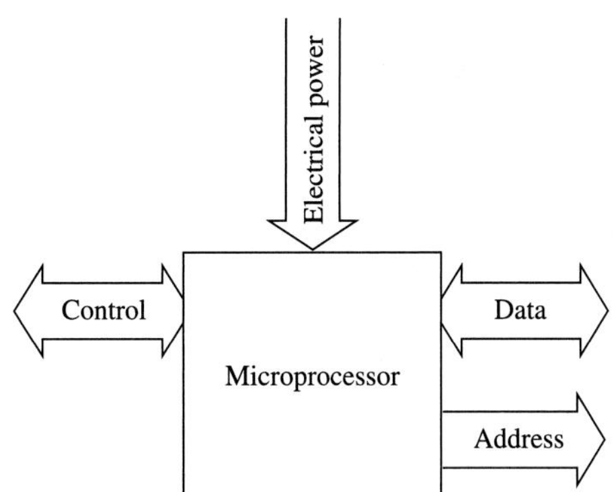

Figure 27
Typical microprocessor bus structure

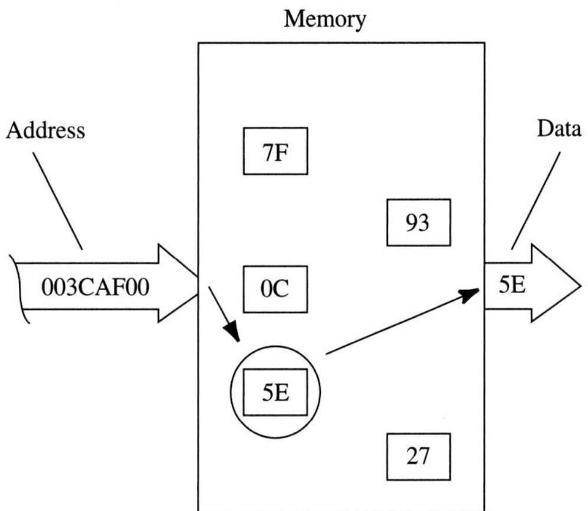

Figure 28
Relationship between data and address

Table 17
Types of microprocessors used in the PC

Microprocessor	Lines		Maximum Clock Speed	Addressable Memory
	Data	Address		
8088	8	20	8 MHz	1MB
8086	16	20	8 MHz	1MB
80286	16	24	20 MHz	16MB
80386SX	16	24	20 MHz	16MB
80386	32	32	31 MHz	4GB
80486	32	32	66 MHz	4GB
Pentium	64	32	233+ MHz	4GB
Pentium Pro	64	36	200+ MHz	64GB
Pentium II/III/IV	64	36	400+ MHz	64GB

Note from Table 17 that the greater the number of address lines, the more memory the microprocessor is capable of addressing. In the table, 1MB = 1,048,576 memory locations, and 4GB = 4,294,967,296 memory locations.

PC Bus Architectures

ISA Bus The ISA (industry standard architecture) is the first bus used in the PC and is still supported today. Recall that a bus is nothing more than a group of conductors treated as a unit; as a data bus, it is a group of conductors used to carry data. In terms of an expansion slot, a bus can be thought of as a group of connectors that is connected to the bus on the motherboard.

AT (16-Bit ISA) Bus This bus is designed to accommodate the older 8-bit ISA expansion cards as well as the newer AT expansion cards. The reason for the two different types of slots is to accommodate the PC expansion card containing the skirt, which comes down to the board level. The 16-bit ISA expansion slots are divided into two sections. The first section has the 62 pins that are electrically identical to the 62 pins of the 8-bit ISA expansion slots. The second section contains an additional 36 pins. This gives a total of 98 electrical connections. The additional 36 pins are used to handle the additional requirements of the 80286 microprocessor used by the AT systems.

PCI Bus PCI stands for Peripheral Component Interconnect, and it is Intel's offering in the world of standardized buses. The PCI bus uses a bridge IC to control data transfers between the processor and the system bus. In essence, the PCI bus is not strictly a local bus, since connections to the PCI bus are not connections to the processor, but rather a special PCI-to-host controller chip. Other chips, such as PCI-to-ISA bridges, interface the older ISA bus with the PCI bus, allowing both types of buses on one motherboard, with a single chip controlling them all. The PCI bus is designed to be processor independent, plug-and-play compatible, and capable of 64-bit transfers at 33 MHz and above. PCI connectors are physically different from all other connectors.

Table 18 shows a summary of the common buses found in the PC and portable computers.

Compatible CPUs

A number of companies manufacture processors that compete with Intel for use in PC motherboards and other applications. Two of these companies are AMD and Cyrix. Table 19 shows recent sets of compatible CPUs.

Having more than one processor to choose from allows you to examine pricing, chip features, and other factors of importance when making a decision.

Table 18
Common PC bus characteristics

Expansion Bus	Data Width	Speed	Addressing	Features
ISA	8	4.77 MHz	1MB	Original PC bus
AT	16	8MHz	16MB	Wider data path, higher speed, larger address space
MCA	32	10MHz	16MB	Proprietary (obsolete)
EISA 32	8	MHz	4 GB	Larger address space
VESA Local	32/64	33/50 MHz	4GB	Local, high speed bus
PCI	32/64	33 MHz	4GB	Bus Mastering
PCMCIA	16	8MHz	64MB	Hot swapping
AGP	32	528MB/s	16–32MB	Video bus only
USB	1	12 Mbps*	127 devices	Serial bus
FireWire	1	400 Mbps	63 devices	Serial bus

*USB version 2.0 operates at 480 Mbps.

Table 19
Comparing CPUs

Intel	AMD	Cyrix
Pentium	K5	5x86*
Pentium II	K6	6x86MX

*Pentium performance, pin compatible with the 80486.

About the 80x86 Architecture

The advanced nature of the Pentium microprocessor requires us to think differently about the nature of computing. The Pentium architecture contains exotic techniques such as branch prediction, pipelining, and superscalar processing to pave the way for improved performance. Let us take a quick look at some other improvements from Intel:

- Intel has added MMX technology to its line of Pentium processors (Pentium, Pentium Pro, and Pentium II/III/IV). A total of 57 new instructions enhance the processors' ability to manipulate audio, graphic, and video data. Intel accomplished this major architectural addition by *reusing* the 80-bit floating-point registers in the FPU. Using a method called **SIMD** (single instruction multiple data), one MMX instruction is capable of operating on 64 bits of data stored in an FPU register.
- The Pentium Pro processor (and also the Pentium II/III) uses a technique called *speculative execution*. In this technique, multiple instructions are fetched and executed, possibly out of order, in order to keep the pipeline busy. The results of each instruction are speculative until the processor determines that they are needed (based on the result of branch instructions and other program variables). Overall, a high level of parallelism is maintained.
- First used in the Pentium Pro, a bus technology called Dual Independent Bus architecture uses two data buses to transfer data between the processor and main memory (including the level-2 cache). One bus is for main memory, the second is for the level-2 cache. The buses may be used independently or in parallel, significantly improving the bus performance over that of a single-bus machine.
- The five-stage Pentium pipeline was redesigned for the Pentium Pro into a *superpipelined* 14-stage pipeline. By adding more stages, less logic can be used in each stage, which allows the pipeline to be clocked at a higher speed. Although there are drawbacks to superpipelining, such as bigger branch penalties during an incorrect prediction, its benefits are well worth the price.

Spend some time on the Web reading material about these changes, and others. It will be time well invested.

CPU chips produced by different hardware manufacturers come in many different shapes, sizes, speeds, and voltages. As a computer technician you should be aware of the similarities as well as the differences between them. Using this knowledge, a technician can identify a processor in a computer system to determine an upgrade path or simply choose a processor for a new computer system.

Characteristics

The characteristics of microprocessors are broken down into the following categories: form factor (size), chip speed, bus speed, cache memory availability and cache memory size as shown in Table 20.

Sockets

The socket a CPU chip plugs in to determines what processor a motherboard can support. There currently exists many different motherboard sockets such a Socket 4, Socket 5, Socket 7, Super Socket 7, Socket A, and Socket 370. The various socket details are shown in Table 21.

The Coprocessor

Each Intel microprocessor released before the 80486 has a companion to help it do arithmetic calculations. This companion is called a **coprocessor.** For most software, the coprocessor is optional. However, some programs (such as CAD, computer-aided design, programs) have so many math calculations to perform that they need the assistance of the math coprocessor; the main microprocessor simply cannot keep up with the math demand.

These **math chips,** as they are sometimes called, are capable of performing mathematical calculations 10 to 100 times faster than their companion microprocessors and with a higher degree of accuracy. This doesn't mean that if your system is without a coprocessor it can't do math; it simply means that your microprocessor will be handling all the math along with everything else, such as displaying graphics and reading the keyboard.

Table 22 lists the math coprocessors that go with various microprocessors. Note that the 80486 and higher processors have built-in coprocessors.

For a math coprocessor chip to be used by software, the software must be specifically designed to look for the chip and use it if it is there. Some spreadsheet programs look for the presence of this

Intel CPUs

Processor	Max Clock	Bus	Volts	Connector	Cache (Speed)	Size	Max Temp	Power	Transistors	Multimedia Support
Mobile Celeron	933	100	1.7	BGA/PGA	L2: 128kB (Full) L1: 32kB	0.18μ	100°C	<3W	28 million	SSE
Celeron	1200	100	1.475	Socket 370 (FC-PGA)	L1: 32kB L2: 256kB (Full)	0.13μ	69°C	30W	28 million	SSE
Pentium III-M	1200	133	1.4	μFCPGA / μFCBGA	L1: 32kB L2: 512kB (Full)	0.13μ	100°C	10-22W	44 million	SSE
Pentium III	1266	133	1.45	FC-PGA2	L1: 32kB L2: 512kB (Full)	0.13μ	69°C	31W	44 million	SSE2
Pentium III Xeon	1000	133	2.8/5/12	Slot 2	L1: 32kB L2: 256kB (Full)	0.18μ	55°C	33-35W	28 million	SSE
Pentium 4	2000	400	1.75	Socket478	L1: 8kB Data + 12kB ETC L2: 256kB (Full)	0.18μ	76°C	75W	42 million	SSE2
Xeon	2000	400	1.7	Socket-603	L1: 8kB Data + 12kB ETC L2: 256kB (Full)	0.18μ	78°C	78W		SSE2

AMD CPUs

Processor	Max Clock	Bus	Volts	Connector	Cache (Speed)	Size	Max Temp	Power	Transistors	Multimedia Support
K6-2	550	100	2.2/3.3	Super 7	L1: 64kB *(L2: 1024kB) (Bus)*	0.25μ	70°C	15-25W	9.3 million	3DNow!
Mobile Duron	950	200	1.2-1.45	Socket A	L1: 128kB L2: 64 kB (Full)	0.18μ	95°C	2-24W	25 million	3DNow ! Pro
Duron	1200	200	1.75	Socket A	L1: 128kB L2: 64 kB (Full)	0.18μ	90°C		25.2 million	3DNow!+ SSE
Athlon	1400	266	1.75	Socket A	L1: 128kB L2: 256 kB (Full)	0.18μ	95°C	65-72W	37 million	3DNow!+
Athlon 4	1200	200	1.2-1.35	Socket A	L1: 128kB L2: 256 kB (Full)	0.18μ	95°C	2-25W	37.5 million	3DNow! Pro
Athlon MP	1533	266	1.75	Socket A	L1: 128kB L2: 256 kB (Full)	0.18μ	95°C	66W	37.5 million	3DNow! Pro
Athlon XP	1600	266	1.75	Socket A	L1: 128kB L2: 256 kB (Full)	0.18μ	90°C	68W	37.5 million	3DNow! Pro

VIA (Cyrix) CPUs

Processor	Max Clock	Bus	Volts	Connector	Cache (Speed)	Size	Max Temp	Power	Transistors	Multimedia Support
Cyrix III	700	133	1.9	Socket 370	L1: 128kB	0.18μ	70°C	17W	11.2 million	3DNow!
C3E	733	133	1.5	Socket 370	L1: 128kB L2: 64kB	0.15μ			15 million	3DNow!
C3	866	133	1.5	Socket 370	L1: 128kB L2: 64kB	0.13μ		7-12W	15 million	3DNow!

Table 20
Popular CPU characteristics

Table 21
CPU socket specifications

Sockets	Pin Holes	Range of Bus Speeds	Processors
486 Socket 486 bus	 168 pin LIF	20MHz 33MHz	486
Socket 1 486 bus	169 pin LIF 169 pin ZIF	16MHz 33MHz	486
Socket 2 486 bus	238 pin LIF 238 pin ZIF	25MHz 50MHz	486
Socket 3 486 bus	237 pin LIF 237 pin ZIF	25MHz 50MHz	486
Socket 4 P5 bus	273 pin LIF 273 pin ZIF	60MHz 66MHz	Pentium
Socket 5 P54C bus	296 pin LIF 296 pin ZIF 320 pin LIF 320 pin ZIF	50MHz 66MHz	Pentium K5 K6
Socket 6 486 bus	235 pin ZIF	25MHz 40MHz	486
Socket 7 P54C bus P55C bus	296 pin LIF 321 pin ZIF	40MHz 124MHz	Pentium K6-2 K6-III
Socket 8 P6 bus	387 pin LIF 387 pin ZIF	60MHz 75MHz	Pentium Pro Pentium II
Slot 1 P6 bus	242 pin SECC 242 pin SECC2 242 pin SEPP	60MHz 133MHz	Celeron Pentium II Pentium III
Slot 2 P6 bus	330 pin SECC	100MHz 133MHz	Pentium II Xeon Pentium III Xeon
Socket 370 P6 bus	370 pin ZIF	66MHz 133MHz	Celeron
Slot A EV6 bus	242 pin SECC	100MHz (x2) 133MHz (x2)	Athlon
Socket A EV6 bus	462 pin ZIF	100MHz (x2) 133MHz (x2)	Athlon Duron
Socket 423 P6.8 bus	423 pin ZIF	100MHz (x4)	Pentium 4
Socket 478 P6.8 bus	478 pin ZIF	100MHz (x4) 133MHz (x4)	Celeron Pentium 4

chip and use the microprocessor for math if the coprocessor is not present. If the coprocessor is present, the software uses it instead. Some programs, such as word-processing programs, have no use for the math functions of the coprocessor and do not use the coprocessor at all. Therefore, the fact that a system has a coprocessor doesn't necessarily mean that the coprocessor will improve the overall system performance. Improvement will take place only if the software is specifically designed to use the coprocessor and there are many complex math functions involved in the program.

BIOS ROM

Beginning with the AT model computer, the old way of configuring the system with motherboard-mounted DIP switches was eliminated in favor of a CMOS RAM that stored system parameters.

Table 22
Matching math coprocessors

Microprocessor	Math Coprocessor
8086	8087
8088	8087
80286	80287
80386	80387
80386SX	80387SX
80486DX	Built-in coprocessor enabled
80486SX	Coprocessor disabled
Pentium, Pentium Pro, and Pentium II/III	Built-in coprocessor enabled always

There were simply too many options to be set with switches. The CMOS RAM stores 64 bytes of data and uses a battery backup circuit so that it retains its information when the computer is turned off. During the boot sequence, the CMOS RAM is read by the BIOS software to establish the required hardware configuration for the computer system. The BIOS setup program allows you to modify the CMOS RAM and thereby reconfigure your system.

CMOS (complementary metal oxide semiconductor) is a special logic family that operates at low power. Thus, is it not difficult to preserve the CMOS RAM data, even if the PC is turned off, through the use of a battery backup circuit. If the operation of the computer system becomes erratic, or the CMOS parameters do not survive a cold-boot, this may be an indication that the CMOS battery is failing and should be replaced. The same battery powers the real-time clock that retains the time and date when the computer is off.

The BIOS setup program contains many menu options, each designed to control a different aspect of the hardware and software installed on the system. To enter the BIOS setup program you must reboot the computer and press a certain key or combination of keys. The keys are different for each BIOS manufacturer. Three of the most popular BIOS manufacturer's are Award, AMI (American Megatrends), and Phoenix.

The program stored in the BIOS ROM is referred to as firmware. The firmware is an integral part of the system, since it both begins the boot sequence, and also contains the low-level hardware drivers used to access the system board peripherals.

The role of BIOS in the boot sequence begins as soon as power is turned on. The POST code checks and initializes hardware, reporting any errors encountered, and possibly halting the system. When the specialized BIOS programs of the installed peripherals complete, memory is tested. This is where BIOS will identify the amount of RAM available. Next, Plug-and-Play BIOS code initializes any Plug-and-Play devices (as well as detecting new ones). BIOS then searches for a boot drive in the order specified in its internal settings (such as C, then CD-ROM, then A), and loads and executes the boot sector of the selected drive. If the boot sector is infected with a boot sector virus, the system is already compromised, and the spread of infection is likely.

New BIOS programs, called "Plug-and-Play" BIOS, work together with add-on peripherals (sound cards, modems, etc.) to automatically recognize new hardware when it is added to the machine. The user does not have to fool around with DIP switch settings or tiny option jumpers. Windows 95/98 contains built-in support for Plug-and-Play BIOS, and does a nice job of detecting and configuring new plug-and-play hardware. The BIOS setup program allows you to change the Plug-and-Play settings (IRQs, DMAs, etc). Plug-and-Play BIOS allows PCI-based adapter cards to share an IRQ (called IRQ steering). If the wrong IRQ is shared, problems may occur with non-PCI devices. Figure 29 shows a flowchart of the operation of the BIOS program.

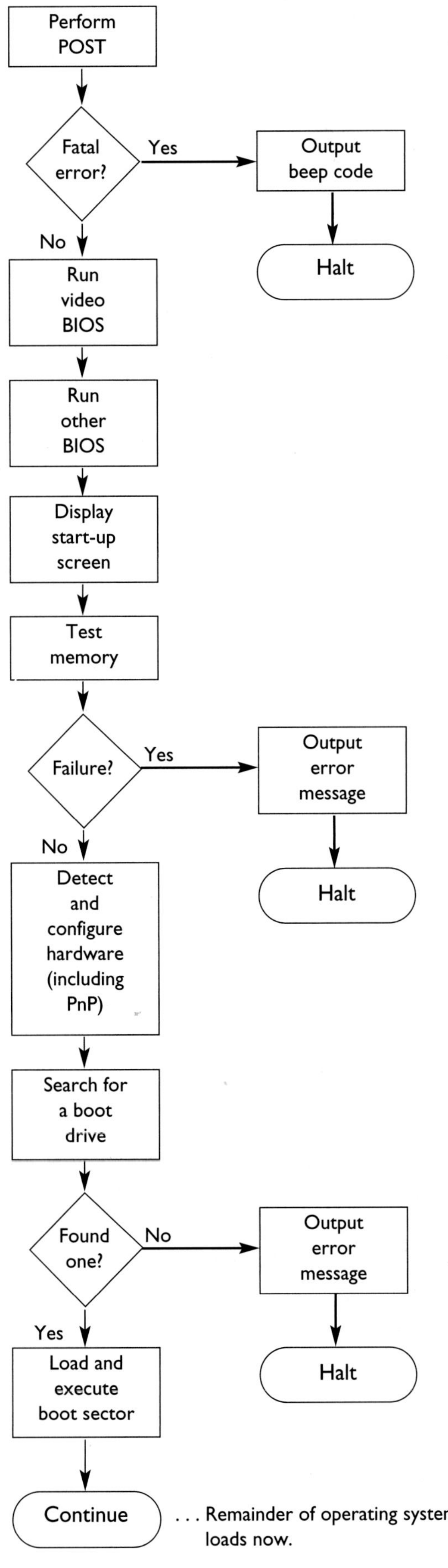

Figure 29
Flowchart of BIOS Operation

Computer Memory

Computer memory consists of any device capable of copying a pattern of 1s and 0s that represent some meaningful information to the computer. Computer memory can be contained in *hardware,* such as in chips, or in **magneticware,** such as floppy and hard disks (or other magnetic material such as magnetic tape). Computer memory is not limited to just these two major areas. For example, a laser disk uses light to read large amounts of information into the computer; this too is a form of computer memory. For the purpose of discussion here, computer memory will be divided into two major areas: hardware memory and magneticware memory.

The hardware memory of a computer is referred to as **primary storage.** The magneticware of a computer is referred to as **secondary storage,** or **mass storage.** Here are some facts about each.

Primary Storage

- Immediately accessible to the computer.
- Any part of the memory may be immediately accessed.
- Short-term storage.
- Limited capacity.

Secondary Storage

- Holds very large amounts of information.
- Not immediately accessible.
- May be sequentially accessed.
- To be used, must be transferred to primary storage.
- Long-term storage.

In this section, you will see how primary and secondary computer memories are used (see Figure 30) and how they can work with each other to produce an almost unlimited amount of computer memory. First, let us learn about primary storage.

PRIMARY STORAGE—RAM AND ROM

There are two basic kinds of primary storage: one kind that the computer can quickly store information in and retrieve information from and another kind that the computer can only receive information from. Figure 31 shows the two basic kinds of primary storage memory.

The kind of memory that the computer can get information (read) from but cannot store information (write) to is called **read-only memory** (ROM). The advantage of having ROM is that it can contain programs that the computer needs when it is first turned on; these programs (called the **Basic Input/Output System,** or BIOS) are needed by the computer so it knows what to do each time it turns on (such as reading the disk and starting the booting process). Obviously, these programs should not be able to be changed by the computer user, because doing so could jeopardize the operation of the system. Therefore, ROM consists of chips that are programmed at the fac-

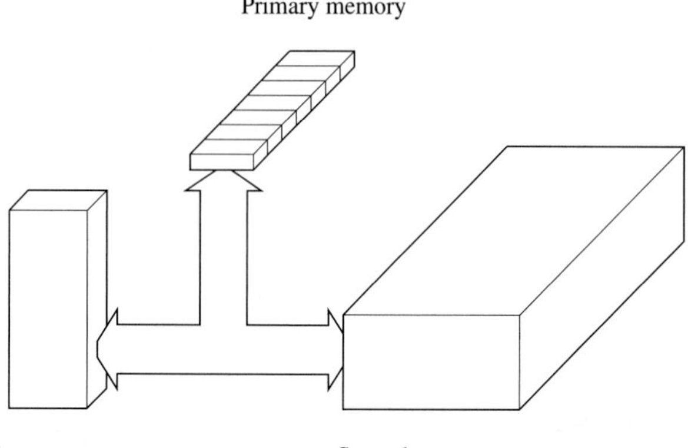

Figure 30
Two major areas of computer memory

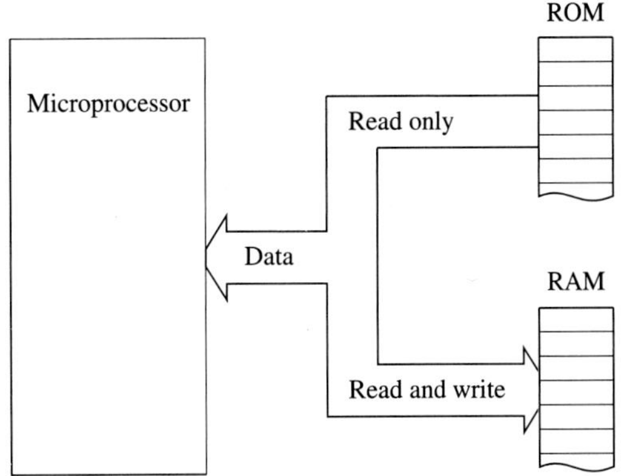

Figure 31
Two basic kinds of primary storage memory

tory. The programs in these chips are permanent and stay that way even when the computer is turned off; they are there when the computer is turned on again.

The kind of memory that the computer can write to as well as read from is called **read/write memory.** The acronym for read/write memory is RWM, which is hard to say. Because of this, read/write memory is called RAM, which stands for **random access memory.** Both ROM and read/write memory are randomly accessible, meaning that the computer can get information from any location without first going through other memory locations. However, read/write memory is traditionally referred to as RAM.

Unlike ROM, RAM loses anything that is stored in it when the power is turned off. Because the information in RAM is not permanent, it is referred to as **volatile memory.** Figure 32 shows this difference.

The system ROM chip for the PC contains two main programs, the **Power-On Self-Test** (POST) and the **Basic Input/Output System** (BIOS). The programs in the ROM chip set the personality of the computer. As a matter of fact, how compatible a computer is can be determined primarily by the programs in these ROM chips. The ROM chips have changed over time as systems have been improved and upgraded. There have been, for example, more than 20 changes in the ROM BIOS programs by IBM for its different PCs.

You may need to update your old BIOS to use new hardware in your system (large IDE hard drives, for example). To upgrade your BIOS ROM, you may (1) replace the ROM with a new one or (2) run a special upgrade program (typically available for download off the Web) that makes changes to a *flash EPROM*, an EPROM that can be electrically reprogrammed.

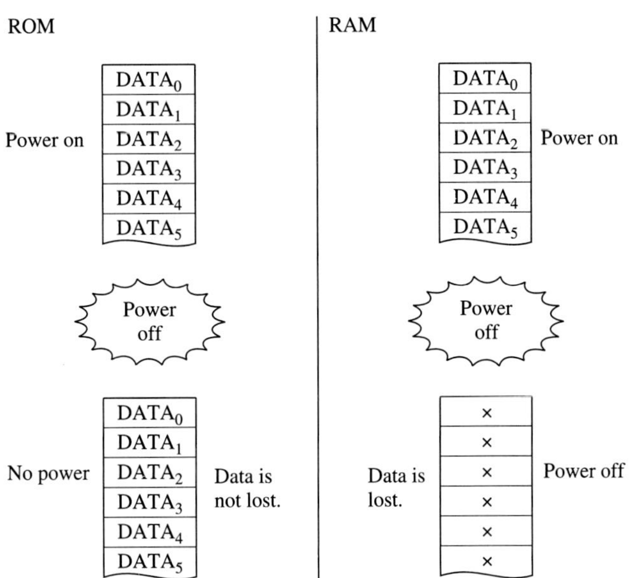

Figure 32
ROM and RAM

BITS, BYTES, AND WORDS

Recall that a bit is a single binary digit. It has only two possible conditions: ON and OFF. Everything in your computer is stored and computed with ONs and OFFs. The bits inside your computer are arranged in such a way as to work in units. The most basic unit, or group, of bits is called a **byte.** A byte consists of 8 bits. Mathematically, 8 bits have 256 unique ON and OFF combinations. You can figure this out with your pocket calculator—just calculate 2^8, which is 2 multiplied by itself eight times. A **word** is 16 bits, or 2 bytes. When 4 bytes are taken together, such as in 32-bit microprocessors, they are called a **double word.** These different arrangements are shown in Figure 33.

In PCs a method called **parity checking** is used to help detect errors. There are times when, in the process of working with computer bits, a bit within a byte may accidentally change from ON to OFF or from OFF to ON. To check for such an error, parity checking uses an extra bit called the **parity bit.** IBM and most compatibles use what is called **even parity** to check their bits. Even parity means that there will always be an even number of ONs for each byte, including the parity bit. Even parity checking is illustrated in Figure 34.

SIMM

The **Single-In-Line Memory Module,** or SIMM, is another way of physically organizing memory. It is a small "boardlet" with several memory chips soldered to it. This boardlet is inserted into a system slot. Figure 35 shows a SIMM.

Figure 33
Arrangement of computer data

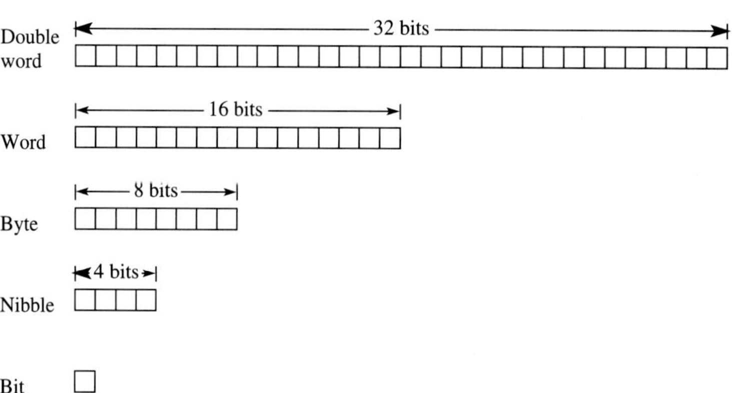

Figure 34
Even parity checking

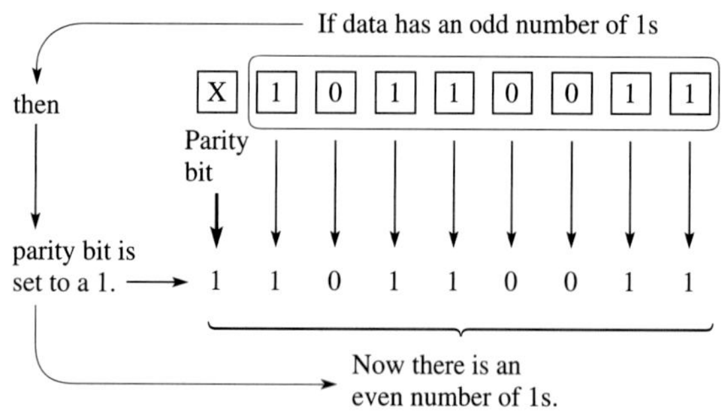

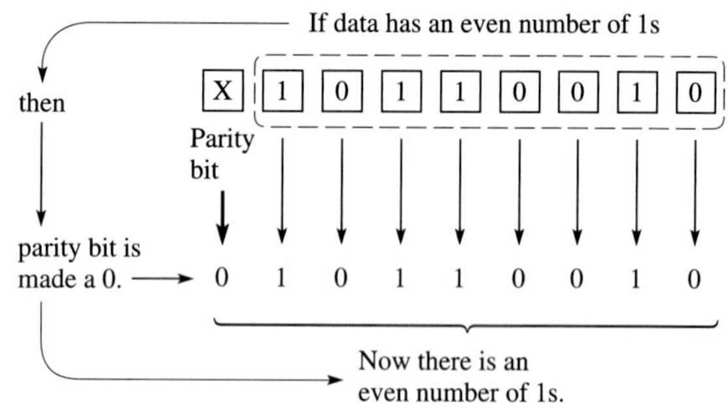

Figure 35
Single-In-Line Memory Module (SIMM)

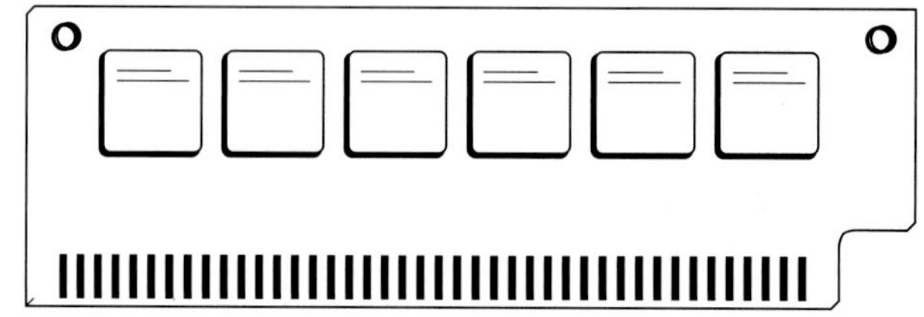

SIMMs came about in an attempt to solve two problems. The first problem was "chip creep." Chip creep occurs when a chip works its way out of a socket as a result of thermal expansion and contraction. The old solution to this problem—soldering memory chips into the board—wasn't a good solution, because it made them harder to replace. So the SIMM was created. The only problem with the SIMM is that if only 1 bit in any of its chips goes bad, the whole SIMM must be replaced. This is more expensive than replacing only one chip. SIMMs come in 256KB, 1MB, 4MB, and 16MB sizes. A similar type of memory module, called a SIPP, contains metal pins that allow the SIPP to be soldered directly onto the motherboard.

Regarding parity bits in a SIMM, a 32-bit SIMM is nonparity, and a 36-pin SIMM stores one parity bit for each byte of data. Pentium processors incorporate parity in their address and data buses.

DIMM

The Dual In-Line Memory Module (DIMM) was created to fill the need of Pentium-class processors containing 64-bit data buses. A DIMM is like having two SIMMs side by side, and come in 168-pin packages (more than twice that of a 72-pin SIMM). Ordinarily, SIMMs must be added in pairs on a Pentium motherboard to get the 64-bit bus width required by the Pentium.

SDRAM

Synchronous DRAM (SDRAM) is very fast (up to 100-MHz operation) and is designed to synchronize with the system clock to provide high-speed data transfers.

EDO DRAM

Extended Data Out DRAM (EDO DRAM) is used with bus speeds at or below 66 MHz and is capable of starting a new access while the previous one is being completed. This ties in nicely with the bus architecture of the Pentium, which is capable of back-to-back pipelined bus cycles. Burst EDO (BEDO RAM) contains pipelining hardware to support pipelined burst transfers.

VRAM

Video RAM (VRAM) is a special *dual-ported* RAM that allows two accesses at the same time. In a display adapter, the video electronics needs access to the VRAM (to display the Windows desktop, for example) and so does the processor (to open a new window on the desktop). This type of memory is typically local to the display adapter card.

Level-2 Cache

Cache is a special high-speed memory capable of providing data within one clock cycle and is typically ten times faster than regular DRAM. Although the processor itself contains a small amount of internal cache (8KB for instructions and 8KB for data in the original Pentium), you can add additional level-2 cache on the motherboard, between the CPU and main memory, as indicated in Figure 36. Level-2 cache adds 64KB to 2MB of external cache to complement the small internal cache of the processor. The basic operation of the cache is to speed up the average access time by storing copies of frequently accessed data.

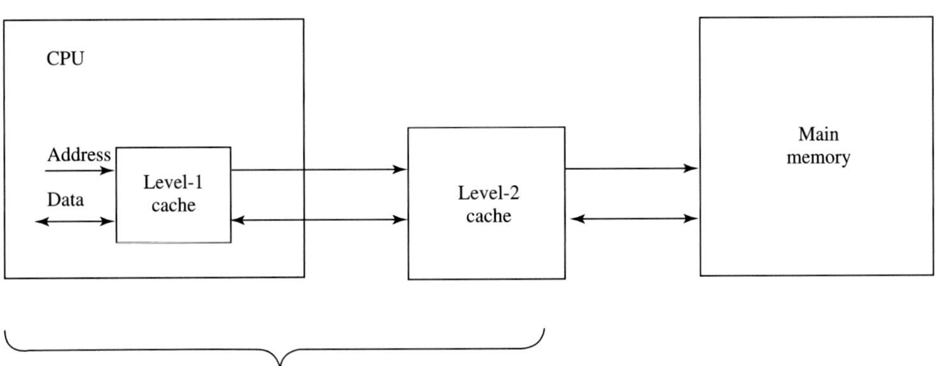

Figure 36 Using cache in a memory system

Chip Speed

When replacing a bad memory module, you must pay attention to the *speed* requirements of that module. If you do not, the replacement will not work. You can use memory chips that have a higher speed or the same speed as the replacement, but not a lower speed. The faster the memory, the more it costs. Adding faster memory to your system may not improve overall performance at all because the speed of your computer is determined by the system clock, among other things.

Memory chip speed is measured in **nanoseconds.** A nanosecond is 0.000000001 second. To check the speed rating of a RAM chip, look at the coding on the top of the chip. Typical DRAM speeds are 60 ns and 70 ns.

How Memory Is Organized

It is important that you have an understanding of the organization of memory in the computer. The 8088 and 8086 microprocessors are able to address up to 1MB of memory. Since some of the first PCs used the 8088 and 8086 microprocessors, when the 80286, 80386, 80486, and Pentium microprocessors were introduced, they were made **downward compatible** with their predecessors. This meant that software that worked on an older PC would still work on the newer systems.

In order to keep downward compatibility, the newer microprocessors (80286, 80386, 80486, and Pentium) come with two modes of operation (there is one other mode that will be presented later). One mode is called the **real mode,** in which the microprocessors behave like their earlier models (and are limited to 1MB of addressable memory). The other mode, called the **protected mode,** allows the microprocessors to use the newer power designed into them (such as addressing up to 16MB for the 80286 and 4GB for the 80386, 80486, and Pentium).

All PCs and compatibles have what is called a **base memory,** which is the 1MB of memory that is addressable by the 8088, 8086, and newer microprocessors running in real mode. A common way of viewing the organization of memory is through the use of a **memory map.** A memory map is simply a way of graphically showing what is located at different addresses in memory. Figure 37 shows the memory map of the PC in real mode.

As you can see from the memory map, several areas of memory are designated for particular functions; not all the 1MB of memory is available for your programs. As a matter of fact, only 640KB can be used by DOS-operated systems. Table 23 lists the definitions of the various memory sections.

The memory above the conventional 640KB of memory is referred to as **upper memory.**

How Memory Is Used

There are three ways memory can be allocated: as **conventional memory, extended memory,** or **expanded memory.** Figure 38 shows the relationships among the three types of memories.

Table 24 explains the uses of the three different memory allocation methods. It is important to note that DOS and systems that use DOS are limited to 1MB of addressable space. The reason for this is

Figure 37
Memory map of PC in real mode

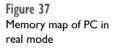

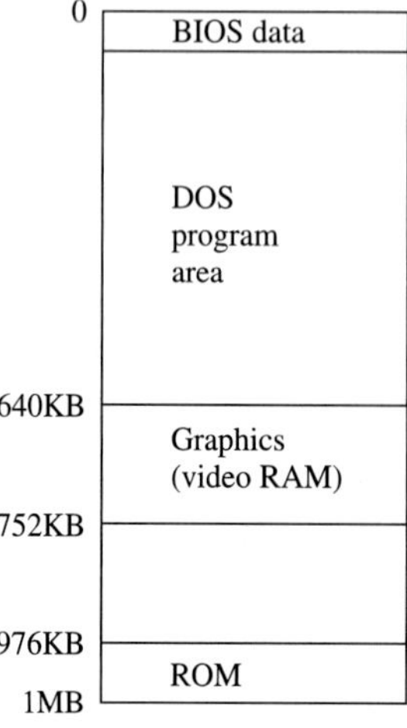

Table 23
Purpose of allocated memory

Assignment	Definition
Base memory	This refers to the amount of memory actually installed in the conventional memory area.
Conventional or user memory	This is the 640KB of memory that is usable by DOS-based programs.
Video or graphics memory	This area of memory (128KB) is reserved for storing text and graphics material for display on the monitor.
Motherboard ROM	This is space reserved for the use of the ROM chips on the motherboard.

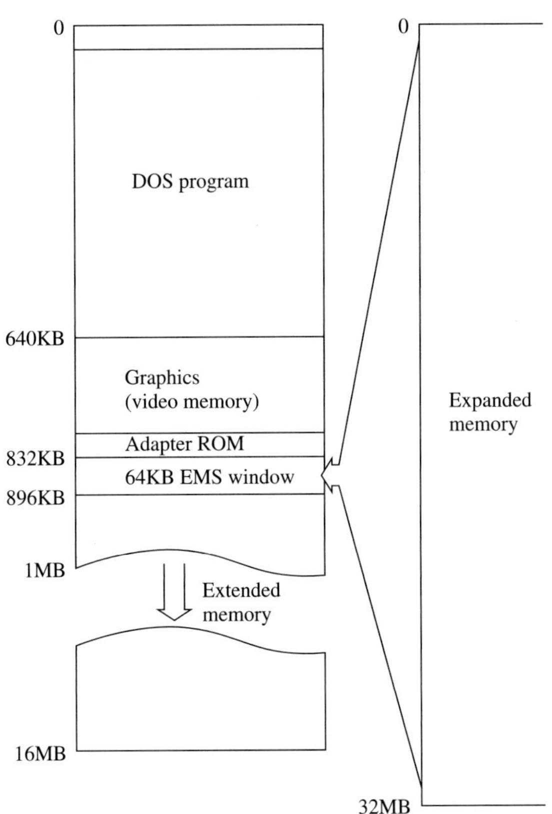

Figure 38
Relationships among conventional, extended, and expanded memory

that DOS is made for microprocessors running in the real mode. This memory limit exists because computer and program designers thought that 1MB of memory would be all that anyone would ever need on a PC for years to come. Since 340KB of the 1MB of addressable DOS memory is reserved by the system, DOS really has only 640KB left for user programs. Thus, DOS is said to have a 640KB limit. However, as you will see, there are ways of allowing DOS to store data in an addressable memory location that is beyond this DOS limit.

Virtual Memory

Another method of extending memory is through the use of **virtual memory.** Virtual memory is memory that is not made up of real, physical memory chips. Virtual memory is memory made up of mass storage devices such as disks. In the use of virtual memory, the computer senses when its usable real memory is used up, stores what it deems necessary onto a disk (usually the hard disk), and then uses what it needs of the freed-up real memory. If it again needs the data it stored on the disk, it simply frees up some more real memory (by placing its contents on the disk) and then reads what it needs from the disk back into the freed-up memory. The concept of virtual memory is illustrated in Figure 39. Windows uses demand-paging virtual memory to manage memory, a technique supported by features of protected mode.

Table 24
Memory allocation methods

Memory Type	Comments
Conventional	1. Memory between 0KB and 1MB, with 640KB usable and 384KB reserved. 2. Completely usable by DOS-based systems. 3. Uses real mode of 8086, 8088, 80286, 80386, 80486, and Pentium.
Extended	1. Uses protected mode of 80286 (up to 16MB), 80386, 80486, and Pentium (up to 4GB). 2. Cannot be used by DOS-based systems (which are limited to 1MB of memory). 3. Can all be accessed by the IBM OS/2 operating system. 4. Can be used by a virtual disk in DOS systems. 5. Is the type of memory to use with the 80386, 80486, and Pentium microprocessors.
Expanded	1. Uses "bank-switching" techniques. 2. Requires special hardware and software. 3. Is not a continuous memory but consists of chunks of memory that can be switched in and out of conventional memory. 4. Sometimes referred to as EMS (expanded memory specification) memory.

Figure 39
Virtual memory

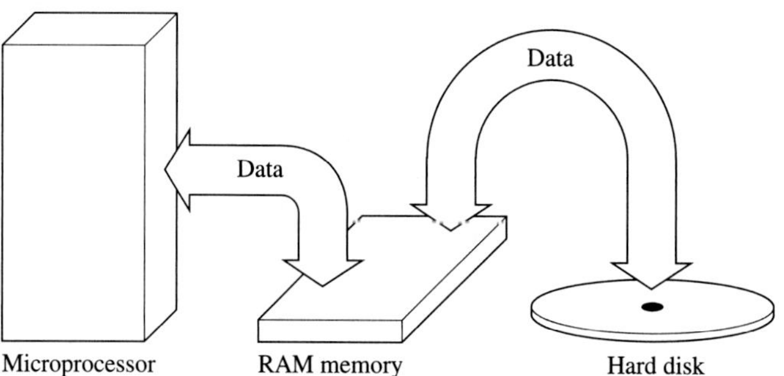

Memory Usage in Windows

It is not difficult to determine why an operating system performs better if it has 32MB of RAM available, rather than only 8MB. With 32MB of RAM, the operating system will be able to support more simultaneous processes without having to use the hard drive for virtual memory backup. Additional memory will also be available for the graphical user interface (multiple overlapped windows open at the same time).

It is no secret that the Windows 3.x architecture did not use memory efficiently, typically requiring at least 8MB or 16MB to get a reasonable amount of performance on a 386 or 486 CPU. Windows 95/98 also performs much better when given a large amount of RAM to work with. A minimum of 16MB or 32MB is recommended.

What does Windows 95/98 use memory for? Conventional memory, the first 640KB of RAM, still plays an important role supporting real-mode device drivers and DOS applications. For instance, if you want DOSKEY installed as part of your DOS environment under Windows 95, place its command line in AUTOEXEC.BAT as you normally would.

Upper memory, the next 360KB of the first 1MB of RAM, can be used to place DOS and other memory-resident applications above the 640KB limit, freeing more RAM for DOS applications.

Extended memory, everything above the first 1MB of RAM (4096MB total), is where Windows 95/98 runs most applications, using an addressing scheme called *flat addressing*. The flat addressing model uses 32-bit addresses to access any location in physical memory, without the need to worry about the segmented memory scheme normally used.

Windows 95/98 provides the Resource Meter (in the System Tools folder under Accessories) to monitor system resources. As indicated in Figure 40, the amount of resources available is shown graphically. The display is updated as resources are used and freed up.

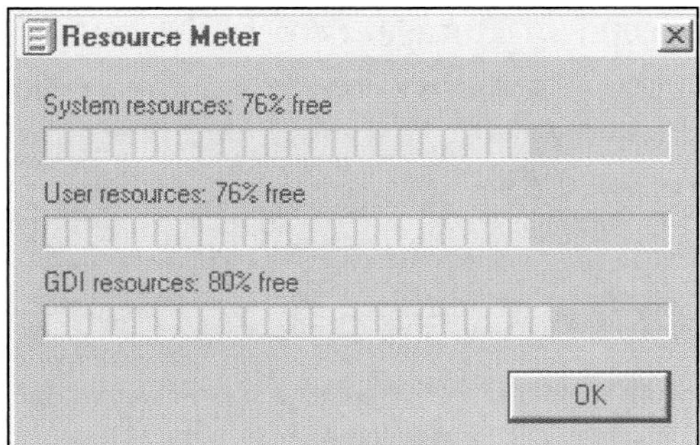

Figure 40
Resource Meter display

Another useful tool is the System Monitor in Windows 95/98 and the Performance Monitor in Windows NT (shown in Figure 41), which display a running tally of resource usage over a period of time. The display format is selectable (bar, line, or numeric charts), as are the colors and type of information displayed.

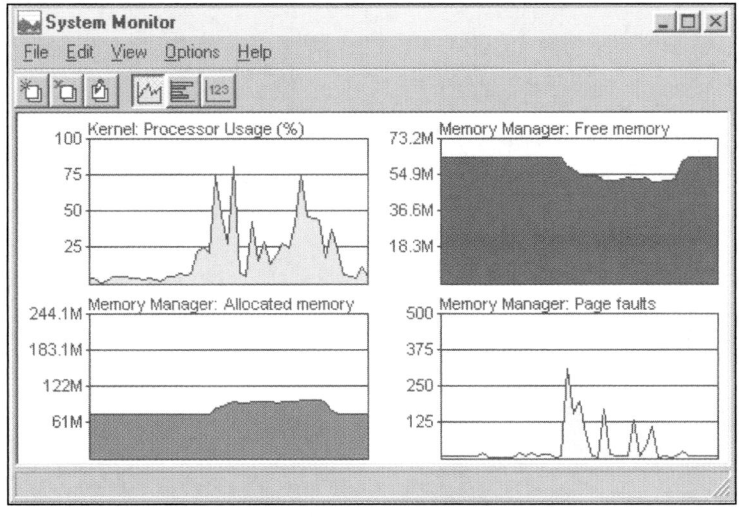

(a)

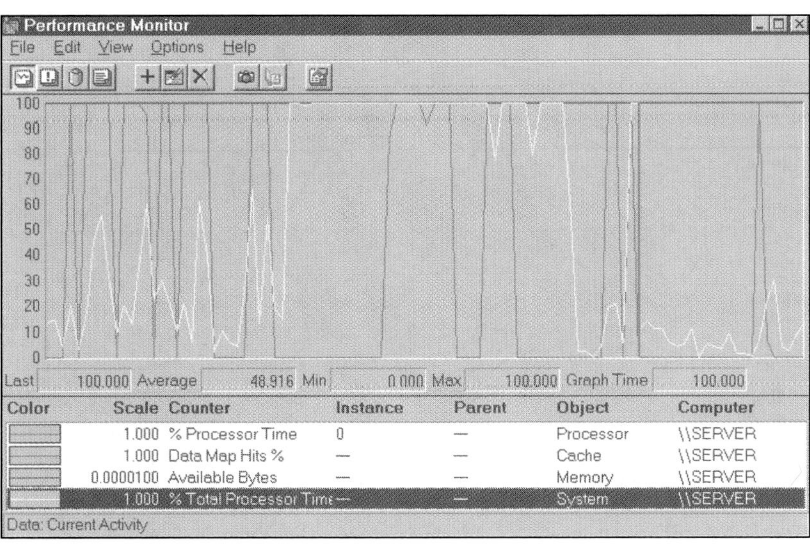

(b)

Figure 41
(a) Windows 95/98 System Monitor display, and (b) Windows NT Performance Monitor display

Secondary Storage, Part I: The Floppy Disk Drive

A floppy disk drive is a device that enables a computer to read and write information on a floppy disk.

Floppy disk drives (FDDs) are located at the front panel of the computer. The most common is the 3 1/2" drive (the old 5 1/4" drive is almost obsolete). These two disk drives are illustrated in Figure 42.

How A Floppy Disk Drive Works

Figure 43 is a simplified drawing of an FDD with its major components. Table 25 summarizes the purpose of each major component of the FDD.

Operating Sequence

The operating sequence of a typical 3½" drive is as follows. Pushing the floppy disk into the drive causes the disk to be properly seated. The initial start-up for the drive consists of determining where track 0 is located. This is usually accomplished by a mechanical device, which is activated once the drive head is over track 0. When information is read, the stepping motor moves the read/write heads to their proper location. When information is written, the disk's write-protect status is checked and then new information is added to the disk.

Figure 42
Typical floppy disk drives

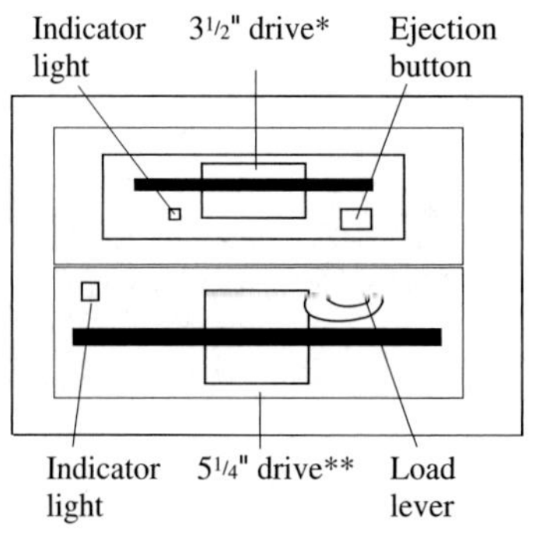

*Most frequently used now.
**Rarely used now.

Figure 43
Major components of a floppy disk drive

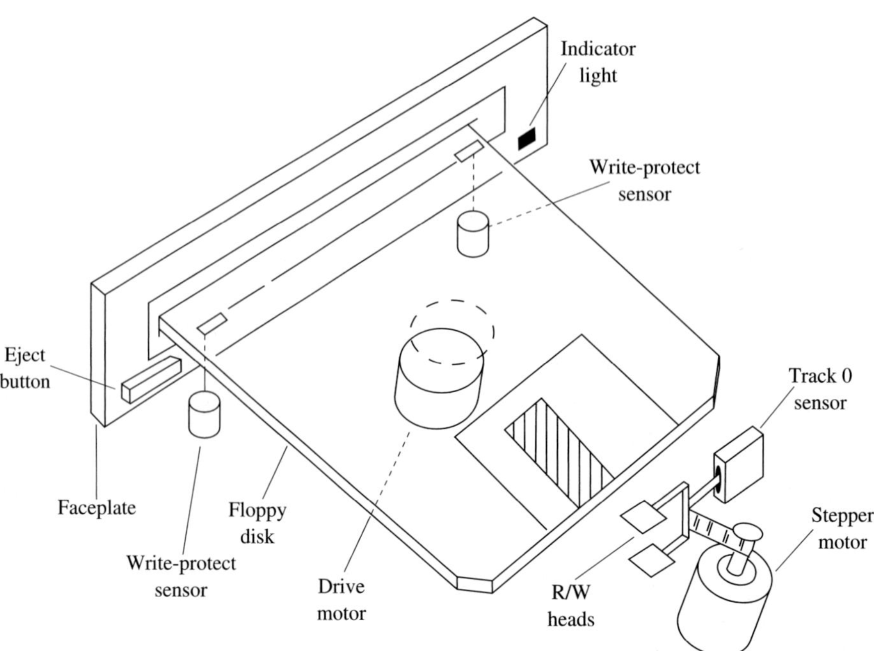

Table 25
Main parts of an FDD

Part	Purpose
Eject button	Used to eject a disk from the drive.
Write-protect sensor	Checks the condition of the floppy disk's write-protect system.
Read/write heads	Read and write information magnetically on the floppy disk. The heads move together, each working from its own side of the disk.
Track 0 sensor	Indicates when the read/write head is over track 0 of the floppy disk.
Drive motor	Spins the floppy disk inside the FDD.
Stepper motor	Moves the read/write head to different positions on the floppy disk.
Indicator light	Indicates if the disk drive is active.

Disk Drive Support System

For proper operation, each part of the FDD support system must function properly.

1. *OS.* The operating system must be compatible with the media on the floppy disks.
2. *Floppy disk.* The disk itself must contain accurately recorded information in the proper format.
3. *Disk drive controller.* The drive controller conditions the signals between the motherboard and the FDD. Originally, a controller card that plugged into the motherboard was used to control the floppy drive. Most motherboards now have the floppy controllers built in.
4. *Disk drive electronic assembly.* This assembly consists of circuit boards that control the logical operations of the FDD. They act as an electrical interface between the disk drive controller and the electromechanical parts of the FDD.
5. *Disk drive mechanical assembly.* This assembly ensures proper alignment of the disk and read/write heads for reading and writing information.
6. *System power supply.* The power supply provides electrical power for all parts of the FDD, including the motors.
7. *Interconnecting cable.* Ribbon cable is used to transfer signals between the disk drive electrical assembly and the disk drive controller card.
8. *Power cable.* The DC power cable supplies electrical power to all parts of the FDD.

Let us take a closer look at many of these important components.

The OS

The operating system plays an important role in the operation of the floppy drive. Beginning with the system BIOS, all drive parameters must be known by the operating system so that data can be properly exchanged. Windows contains many applications designed specifically for disk drive operations. For example, right-clicking the drive A: icon in the My Computer window produces a Properties window similar to that shown in Figure 44. A pie chart is used to graphically illustrate used/free space on the drive. The volume label can be changed by entering a new one in the text box.

The Floppy Disk

There are several built-in Windows tools available for working with floppy disks. These tools are contained in the Tools submenu, as indicated in Figure 45.

The disk can be scanned for errors (using ScanDisk), backed up, or *defragmented.* A disk that has had many files created and deleted on it eventually becomes fragmented, with the files broken up into groups of sectors and scattered all over the disk (but still logically connected through the use of the FAT). This fragmentation increases the amount of time required to read or write entire files to the disk. By defragmenting the disk, all the files are reorganized, stored in consecutive groups of sectors at the beginning of the storage space on the disk.

A fourth tool is included that allows you to *compress* the data on your floppy, increasing the amount of free space available. The Compression submenu shown in Figure 46 indicates what will be gained by compressing the current disk.

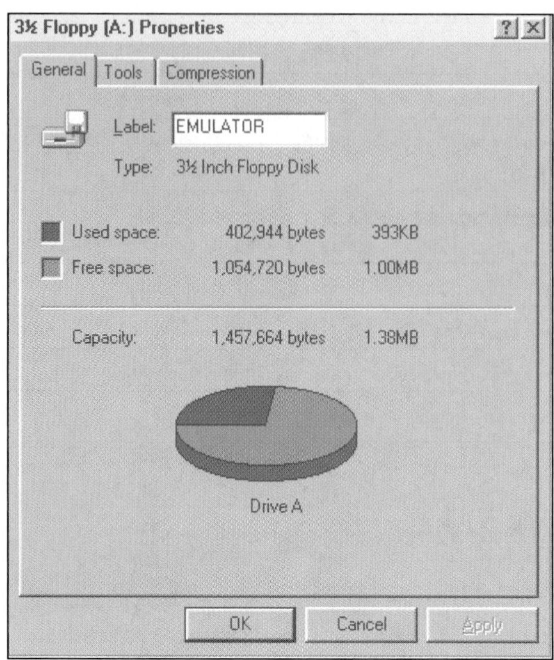

Figure 44
Drive A: Properties window

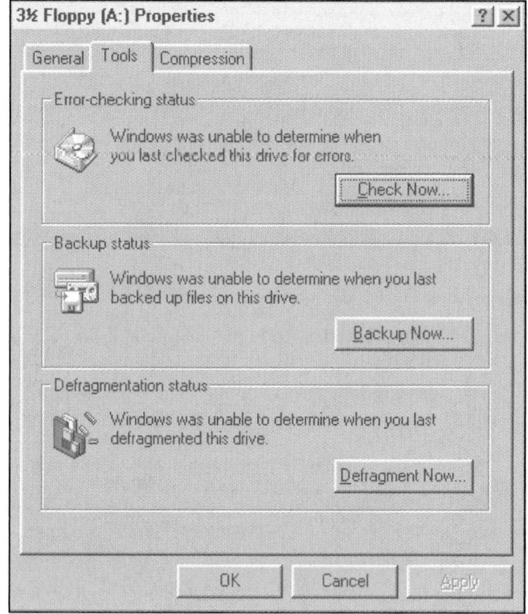

Figure 45
Floppy disk tools

The Disk Drive Controller

The disk drive controller used to be an individual chip on a controller card. Now, the controller is just one part of a multifunction peripheral IC designed to operate the floppyand hard drives, the printer, and the serial ports. As always, I/O ports and interrupts are used to control the floppy disk drive. The settings used by Windows 95/98 can be examined/changed by using the Device Manager submenu of System Properties. The settings used by Windows NT can be examined from the Windows NT Diagnostics menu. Figure 47 shows the hardware configuration of a typical A: drive. These settings can be changed if necessary.

The Drive Cable

A 34-conductor ribbon cable is used to connect one or two disk drives to the controller. A twist in the cable between the two drive connectors reverses the signals on pins 9 through 16 at each connector. This twist differentiates the two drive connectors, forcing them to be used specifically for drive A: or drive B:. Figure 48 shows the cable details.

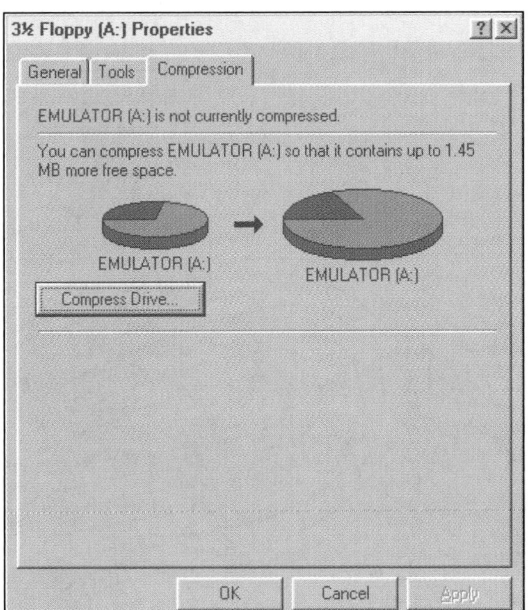

Figure 46
Compression submenu

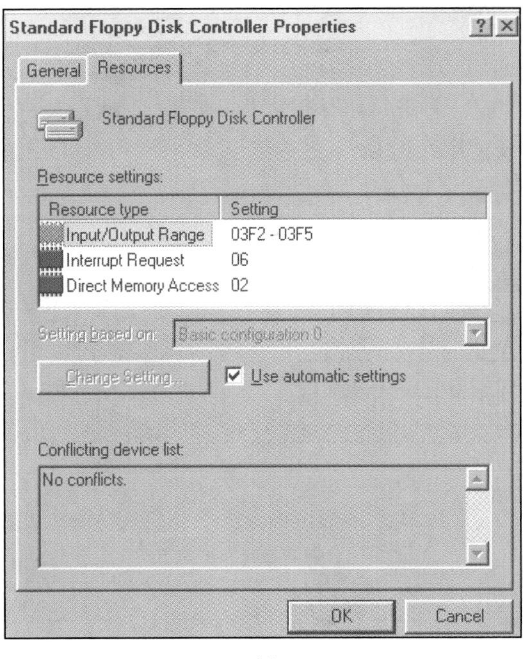

(a)

Figure 47
(a) Hardware settings for floppy drive, and
(b) Windows NT Floppy Properties

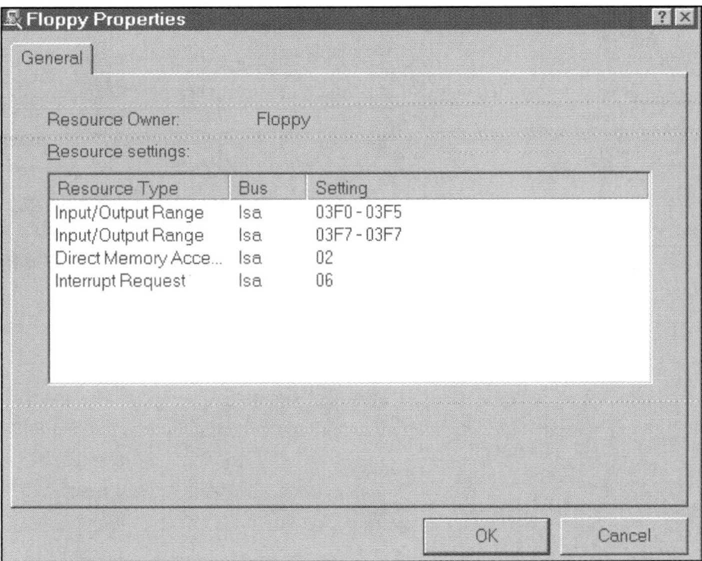

(b)

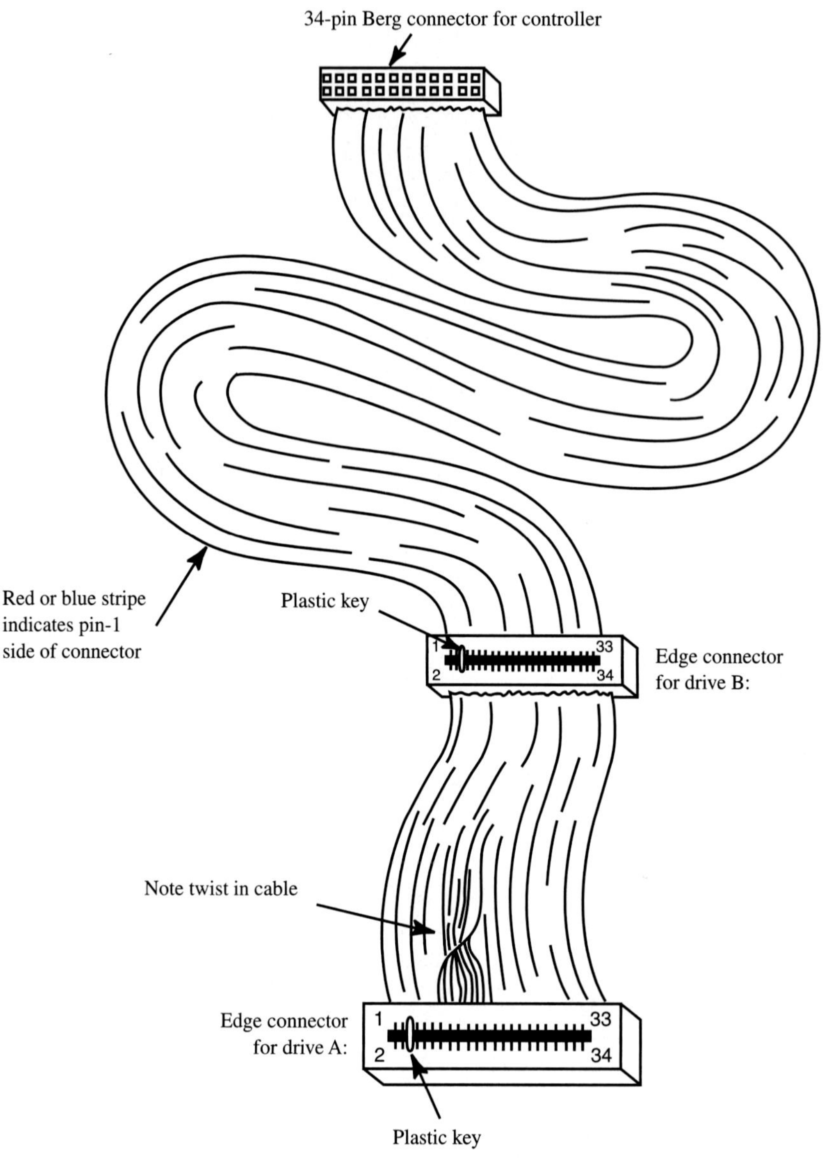

Figure 48
Floppy drive cable

The meanings of the signals on the drive cable are shown in Table 26. Note that the signals affected by the twist in the cable are the select and enable signals for each drive.

The Power Cable

Like any other peripheral, the disk drive needs power to operate the drive and stepper motors, the read/write amplifiers and logic, and the other drive electronics. Figure 49 shows the pinout of the standard power connector used on the floppy drive. The connector is keyed so that it only plugs in one way.

Zip Drives

A device similar to the floppy drive is the Zip drive, manufactured by Iomega. Zip drives connect to the printer port, have removable 100MB cartridges, and boast a data transfer rate of 60MB/minute (using an SCSI connection). The 100MB disks spin at 2941 RPM, have an average access time of 29 milliseconds, and are relatively inexpensive. Newer 250MB cartridges are also available.

The software driver for the Zip drive uses the signal assignments shown in Figure 50 to control the Zip drive through the printer port. Using the printer port to control the Zip drive allows you to easily exchange data between two computers.

Table 26
Floppy drive cable signals

Conductor (Pin)	Signal
1–33 odd	Ground
2	Unused
4	Unused
6	Unused
8	Index
10	Motor Enable A
12	Drive Select B
14	Drive Select A
16	Motor Enable B
18	Stepper Motor Direction
20	Step Pulse
22	Write Data
24	Write Enable
26	Track 0
28	Write Protect
30	Read Data
32	Select Head 1
34	Ground

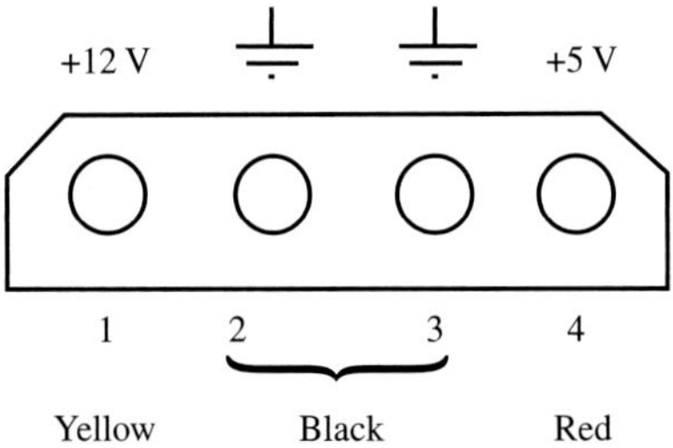

Figure 49
Floppy drive power connector

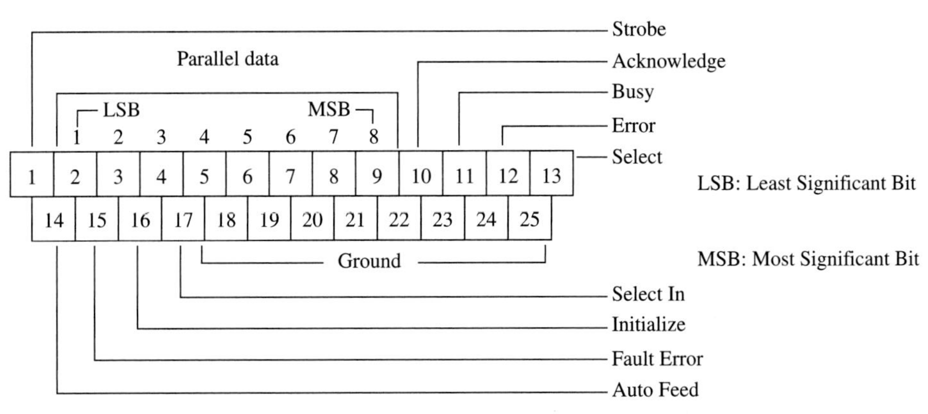

Figure 50
Zip drive parallel interface

Jaz Drives

Similar to the Zip drive, the Jaz drive uses a 1GB removable cartridge that spins at 5400 RPM, has an average seek time around 10 milliseconds, and has a sustained data transfer rate of more than 6MB/second. A Jaz drive operates similarly to a hard drive, except the drive media is removable.

The 120MB SuperDisk

The SuperDisk is a new type of floppy drive with a 120MB capacity. SuperDisk drives can read/write both 120MB SuperDisk floppies and 1.44/2.88 MB 3½" disks.

Working with Floppies

A few tips to keep in mind when working with floppy drives:

- Sometimes disks that are formatted on one system cannot be read by another. This may be due to differences in the read/write head alignments between both drives.
- If a floppy gives unexpected read errors, try ejecting the floppy and reinserting it.
- Run ScanDisk or some other suitable disk tool (such as Norton Utilities) to check a troublesome floppy.
- Always beware of disks given to you by someone else. Before you begin using them, scan them for viruses. This is especially important in an educational setting, where students and instructors often exchange disks as a normal part of class or lab.

Secondary Storage, Part 2: The Hard Drive

The construction of a hard disk system is much different from that of a floppy disk system. With the floppy disk system, data is stored on each side of the disk, but in a hard disk system, there is usually more than one disk, or **platter.** Figure 51 shows the structure of a two-platter hard disk system, in which there are four sides for storing data.

As you can see from Figure 51, the four sides are labeled 0 through 3. Figure 52 shows how a floppy disk organizes its data in single concentric tracks, as compared with a hard disk system, which organizes its data in a combination of tracks called **cylinders.**

Partitions

A hard disk can be formatted so that it acts as two or more independent systems. As an example, it is possible for a hard disk to operate under two entirely different operating systems, such as Windows and UNIX. Doing this is called **partitioning** the disk, as shown in Figure 53. This is sometimes necessary when a computer is part of a collection of computers connected together over a network.

In the early versions of DOS, no disk partition could be larger than 32MB, and no one operating system could access more than one partition. This means that no matter how much data the hard disk could hold, early versions could make use of only 32MB of the disk surface. DOS 4.0 broke the 32MB limitation on hard disks.

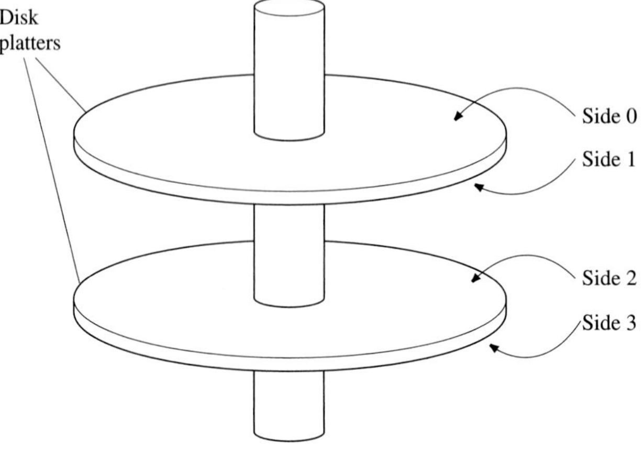

Figure 51
Typical hard disk structure

Track 0

Track N
where N = number of tracks − 1

(a) Floppy disk

Cylinder 0
Side 0, track 0
Side 1, track 0
Side 2, track 0
Side 3, track 0

Cylinder N
Side 0, track N
Side 1, track N
Side 2, track N
Side 3, track N

(b) Hard disk system

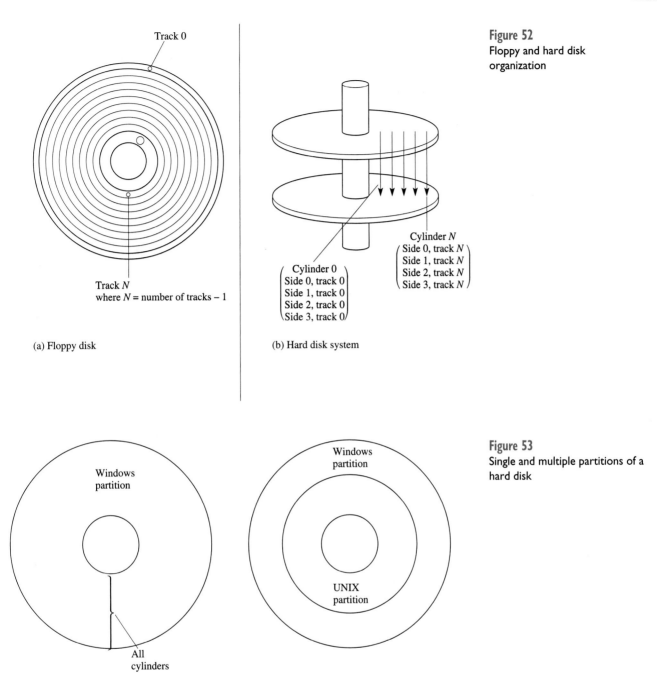

Figure 52
Floppy and hard disk organization

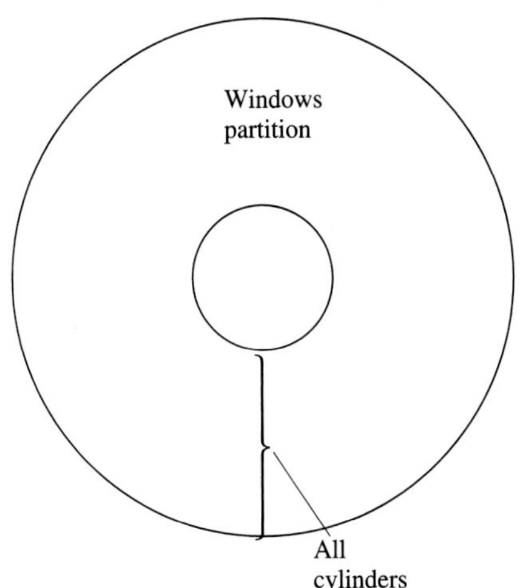

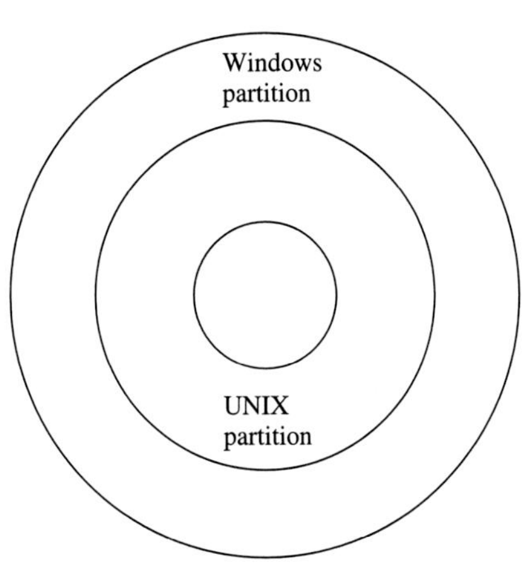

Figure 53
Single and multiple partitions of a hard disk

When a disk is partitioned, its **primary partition** (the one from which it boots) is called the C: drive, and the remaining partitions are referred to as D, E, F, and so on.

Every disk may be partitioned differently, but there are a few rules that must be followed. For example, Windows 95 Version A can recognize disks as large as 2.1GB. Windows 95 Version B and above can address disks as large as 4TB (terabytes). The operating system determines the maximum size that can be handled. Updates to an operating system add capabilities for new technology.

The FDISK tool supplied by DOS and Windows is used to create partitions on the hard disk. Figure 54 shows the Windows 98 FDISK menu. It looks very similar to the old DOS FDISK program. FDISK is used to create, modify, or delete partitions on a hard drive. Extreme caution must be observed when working with the FDISK program.

There are also many specialty programs designed to make the disk partitioning process easier and more flexible than the FDISK program. For example, PartitionMagic by PowerQuest allows for a hard drive to be partitioned dynamically, saving time and disk space. Figure 55 shows the PartitionMagic main window. Information about the default drive is displayed automatically, showing

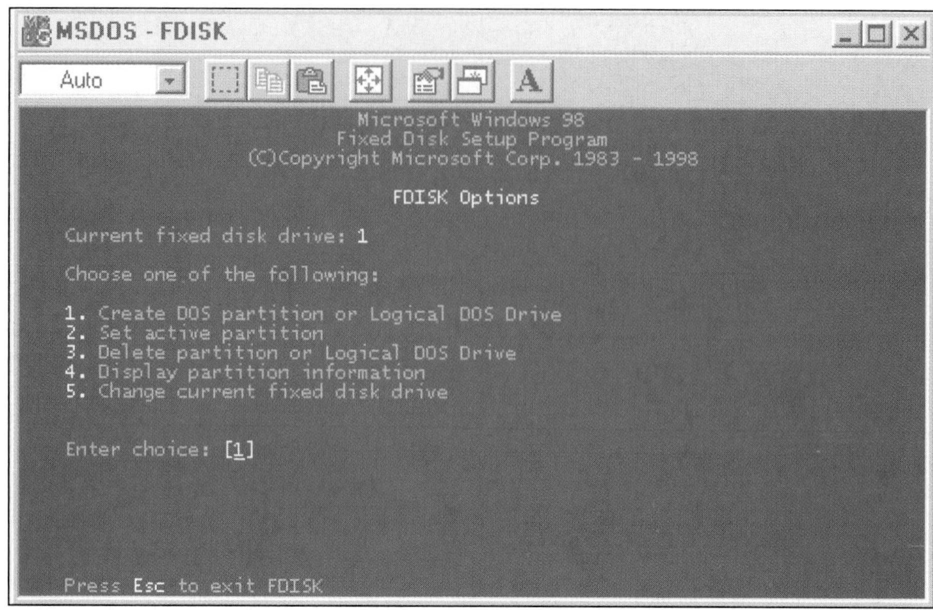

Figure 54
Windows 98 FDISK utility

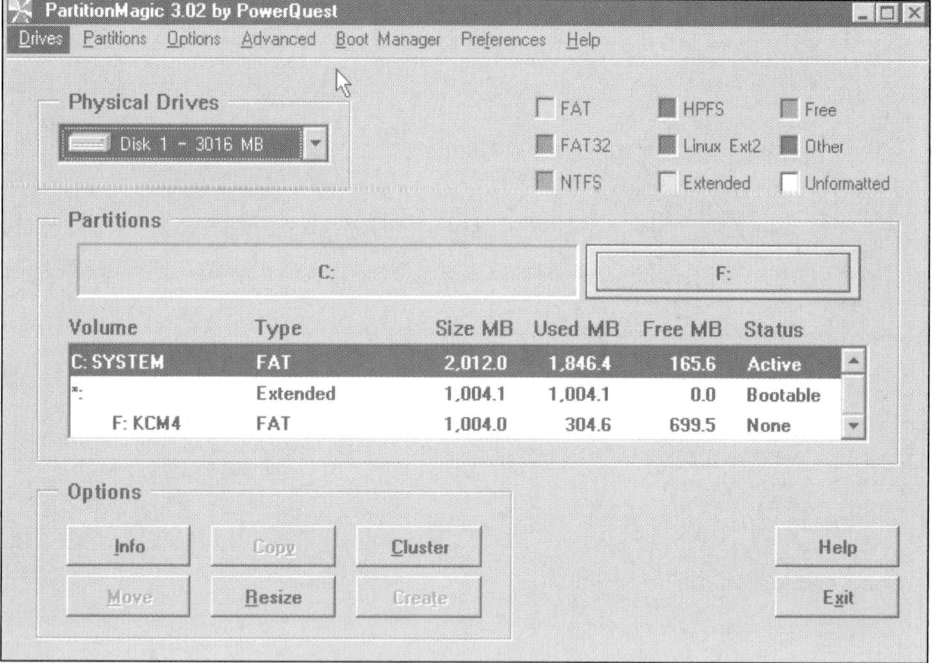

Figure 55
PartitionMagic main window

the size of each partition and associated disk format. By selecting the Info Options button, the Partition Information window is displayed showing the default disk usage statistics, as shown in Figure 56.

The Cluster Waste tab shows the current amount of disk space that is wasted. This waste is attributed to the smallest amount of disk space that can be allocated by the operating system. For example, if we want to store one character in a file, it will be stored in a 32K chunk of space on a computer with 32K clusters (shown in Figure 57). The cluster size is determined by the type of file structure used on the disk, such as FAT16 or FAT32, which will be discussed shortly.

PartitionMagic can also display information about the physical layout of a partition, as shown in Figure 58. The first, last, and total physical sectors are displayed along with the corresponding cylinder and head information. The disk physical geometry is also indicated on the Partition tab.

Details about the FAT are available on the FAT Info tab shown in Figure 59. This window contains

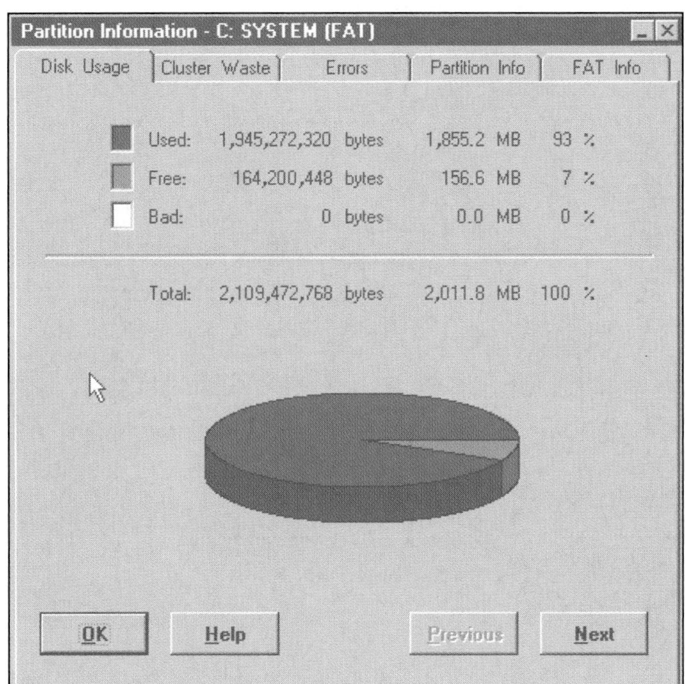

Figure 56
Disk Usage Partition Information

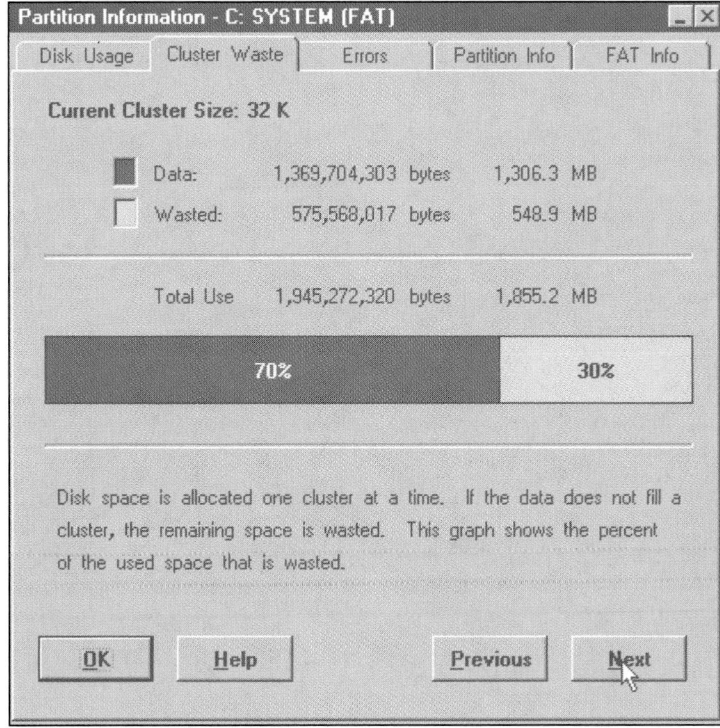

Figure 57
Cluster Waste Partition Information

the details of the FAT structure, such as the number of FATs, root directory capacity, First FAT sector, First Data sector, and other interesting information.

PartitionMagic can also change partition information dynamically, such as changing the cluster size. Figure 60 shows the common cluster sizes and associated wasted space. In this case, since the disk is close to capacity, PartitionMagic cannot recommend any type of changes; otherwise, the user may select a new cluster size and change the partition size. If it is necessary to change disk partition size frequently, it may be a good idea to invest in a software package.

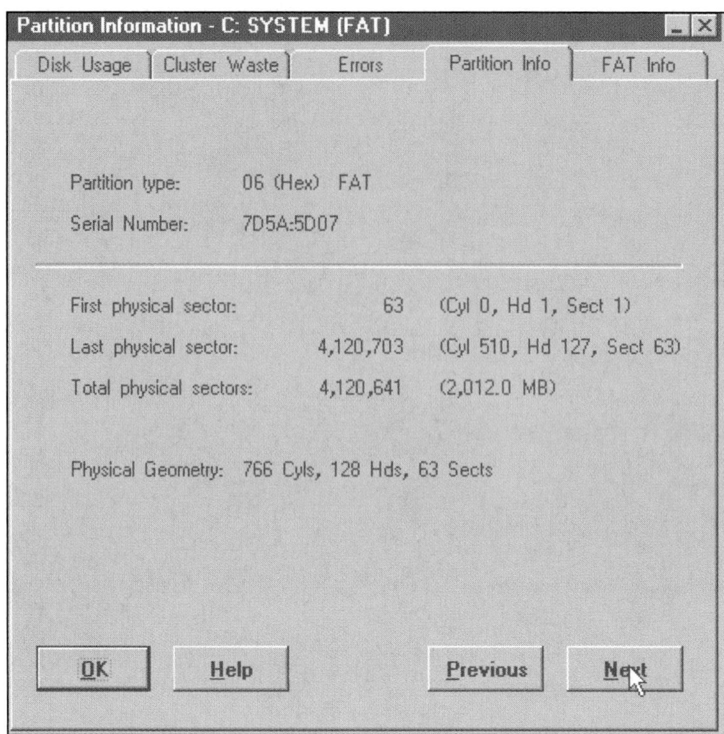

Figure 58
Physical Partition Information

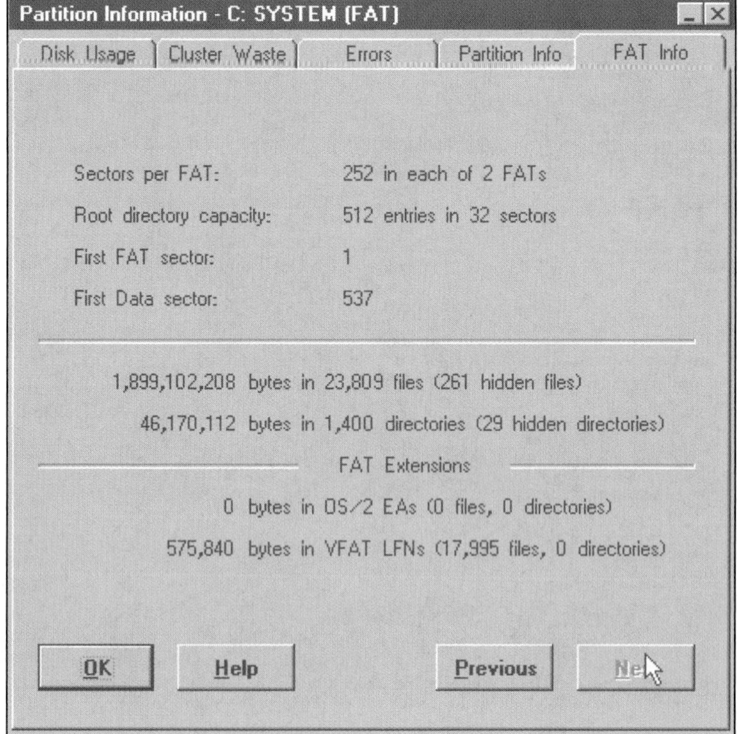

Figure 59
FAT Info tab

Windows NT Disk Administrator

Windows NT provides a different method to deal with the chore of managing disks and disk partitions. The Disk Administrator utility, located in the Windows NT Administrative Tools (Common) menu, offers many advantages over running the traditional FDISK program in a DOS window. Figure 61 shows a graphical display of the physical partitions on a computer system. Notice how Disk 0 contains an NTFS partition at the beginning of the disk labeled "C:" and an unknown partition at the

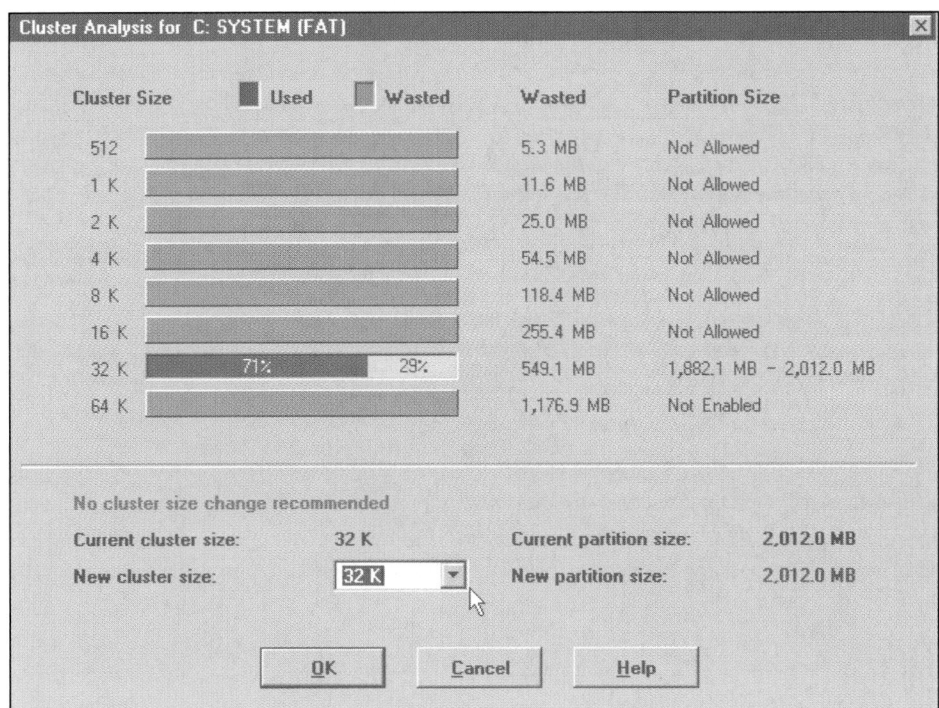

Figure 60
Cluster Analysis window

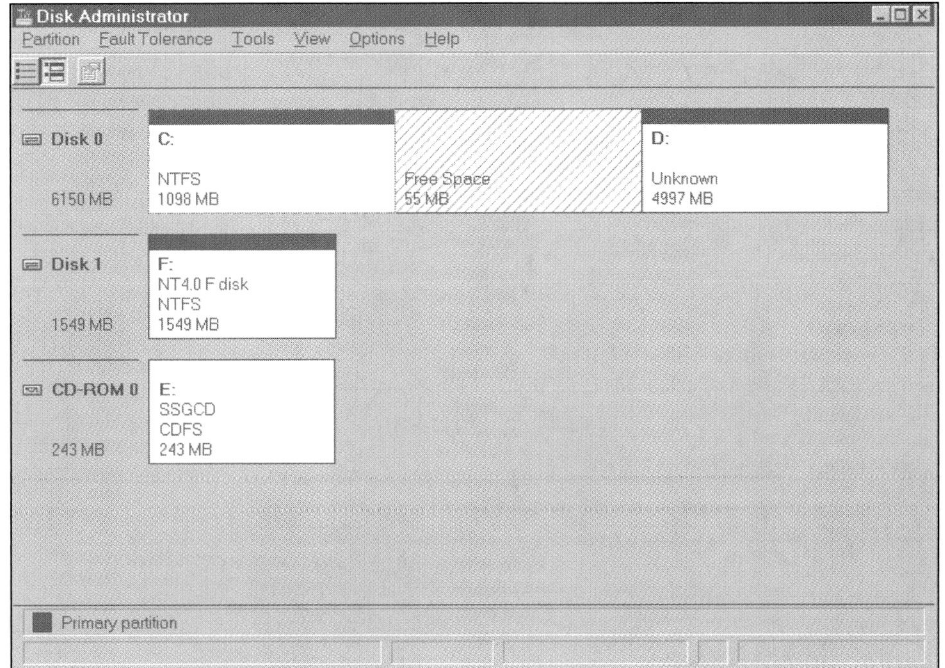

Figure 61
Windows NT Disk Administrator window

end of Disk 0 labeled "D:" with 55MB of free space remaining. Also note from the figure that Disk 1 contains an NTFS partition and a label of "F:" with no free space and the CD-ROM 0 reports information about the CD currently in the drive. On this computer, the D: disk is actually the Windows 98 operating system, but because the format is FAT32, Windows NT cannot read it. Likewise, Windows 98 cannot see the NTFS partitions.

You are encouraged to explore the capabilities of the Disk Administrator utility.

LBA

Logical block addressing (LBA), is a method to access IDE (Integrated Drive Electronics) hard disk drives. Using LBA, disks larger than 504MB (1024 cylinders) can be partitioned using FDISK or PartitionMagic. Actually, LBA has been around for quite some time now, and has been incorporated into system BIOS on most PCs. Before this, BIOS limitations prevented FDISK from using the entire drive and it was necessary to use custom software, called a Dynamic Drive Overlay. The last option was to simply stay under the limit.

LBA may be implemented in four ways. For example:

1. ROM BIOS support for INT 13h.
2. Hard disk controller support for INT 13h.
3. Use only 1024 cylinders per partition.
4. Real-mode device driver support for geometry translation.

Windows 95 and Windows 98 support the first three methods directly. The last method requires a special version of the Dynamic Drive Overlay software.

IDE disks using the ATA interface also use BIOS INT 13h services. The disk drive identifies itself to the system BIOS specifying the number of cylinders, heads, and sectors per track. The number of bytes in each sector is always 512.

FAT32

As hard drives grew in storage capacity, they quickly reached the maximum size supported by DOS and Windows (initially only 32MB, then 504MB, then 2.1GB). This limitation was based on the number of bits used to store a cluster number. The original FAT12 used a 12-bit FAT entry. FAT16 added four more bits, allowing for up to 65,536 clusters. With each cluster representing 16 sectors on the disk, and each sector storing 512 bytes, a cluster would contain 8KB. The total disk space available with 65,536 clusters of 8KB is 512MB, a small hard drive by today's standards.

One way to support larger partitions is to increase the size of a cluster. Storing 32KB in a cluster allows a 2048MB (2.048GB) hard drive, but also increases the amount of wasted space on the hard drive when files smaller than 32KB are stored. For example, a file of only 100 bytes is still allocated 32KB of disk space when it is created because that is the smallest allocation unit (one cluster). You would agree that most of the cluster is wasted space. Some disk compression utilities reclaim this wasted file space for use by other files. In general, however, large cluster sizes are not the solution to the limitation of the FAT16 file system.

FAT32 uses 32-bit FAT entries, allowing 2200GB hard drives without having to result to using large cluster sizes. In fact, FAT32 typically uses 4KB clusters, which helps keep the size of the FAT small and lowers the amount of wasted space. FAT32 is only used by Windows 95 Version B (OEM Service Pack 2) and Windows 98. Several utilities, such as PartitionMagic, are able to convert a FAT16 disk into a FAT32 disk. Windows NT has its own incompatible file system called NTFS.

NTFS

The **NT file system,** or NTFS, is used on Windows NT computers. Using NTFS, it is possible to protect individual items on a disk and therefore prevent them from being examined or copied. This is a feature commonly found on multiuser computers such as Windows NT.

Hard Drive Interfaces

Many companies manufacture hard drives for personal computers. Even though each company may design and build its hard drives differently, the interface connectors on each drive must conform to one of the accepted standards for hard drive interfaces. These interface standards are illustrated in Figure 62.

The first popular hard drive interface scheme was invented by Shugart Technologies. Called **ST506,** it requires two cables (control and data) between the controller card and the hard drive. This is shown in Figure 62(a). Serial data passes back and forth between the controller and hard drive over the data cable. A second hard drive is allowed; the second drive shares the control cable with the

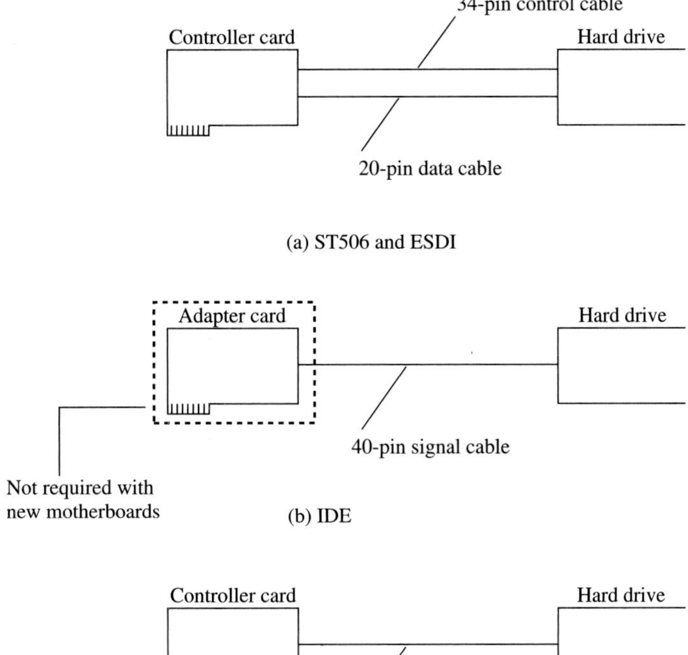

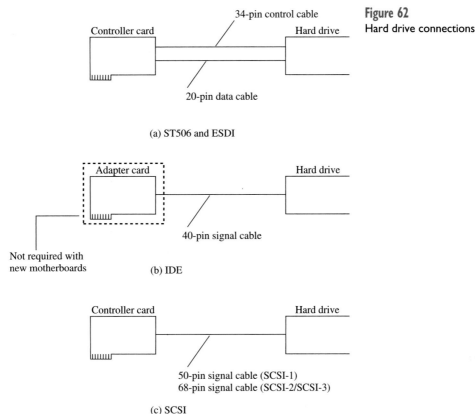

Figure 62
Hard drive connections

first drive, but has its own data cable. Jumpers must be set on each drive for proper operation, and the last drive needs to contain termination resistors.

An improvement on the ST506 standard was developed by Maxtor, another hard drive manufacturer. Called **ESDI** (Enhanced Small Device Interface), this interface uses the same two cables as the ST506, but allows data to be exchanged between the controller and hard drive at a faster rate. Although similar in operation to ST506, ESDI is not electrically compatible with it. Thus, ST506 hard drives require ST506 controllers, and ESDI hard drives require ESDI controllers.

The **IDE** (Integrated Drive Electronics) interface, shown in Figure 62(b), has virtually replaced the older ST506 standard. A single cable is used to exchange parallel data between the adapter card and the hard drive. A second hard drive uses the same cable as the first, with a single jumper on each drive indicating if it is the primary drive. A significant difference in the IDE standard is that the controller electronics are located *on the hard drive itself.* In a two-drive system, the primary drive controls itself and the other hard drive as well. The adapter card plugged into the motherboard merely connects the hard drive to the system buses, using parallel data transfers. This allows typical data transfers with an IDE hard drive of up to 8MB per second.

New motherboards have built-in **EIDE** (enhanced IDE) controllers, which provide signals for four EIDE connectors. This eliminates the need for an adapter card. One pair of connectors are the *primary* connectors, the other pair are the *secondary* connectors. Each pair can support two IDE hard drives (CD-ROM and tape backup drives as well) in a master/slave configuration. Figure 63 shows the pin and signal assignments for the EIDE interface, and a typical IDE hard drive.

The earlier IDE interface lacked the upper eight data lines D_8 through D_{15}. The IDE specification also limited hard drive capacity to just 504MB. The EIDE specification increases drive capacity to more than 8GB, expands the maximum number of drives from two to four, and increases the data transfer rate to over 16MB/second.

IDE/EIDE devices consist of hard drives, CD-ROM drives, and tape drives. Installation procedures include mounting the device into the computer chassis, connecting power and signal cables, and installing the associated software drivers. When mounting an IDE hard drive or CD-ROM, be sure to use screws of the proper length. Using a screw that is too long may damage the internal circuitry of the drive. When inserting the 40-pin IDE connector, look for the colored stripe on the cable to locate pin-1. The connector may also be keyed so that it can only be inserted one way.

Right-clicking on My Computer and then choosing Properties allows you to check the system properties. In Device Manager, double-click on the Hard disk controller entry and then the primary IDE controller entry. You should get a settings window similar to that shown in Figure 64. In Windows NT, this information is available in the Windows NT Diagnostics window.

Figure 63
(a) Primary EIDE connector pin/signal assignments, and (b) typical IDE hard drive (photograph by John T. Butchko)

Signal	Pin	Pin	Signal
$\overline{\text{RESET}}$	1	2	GND
D_7	3	4	D_8
D_6	5	6	D_9
D_5	7	8	D_{10}
D_4	9	10	D_{11}
D_3	11	12	D_{12}
D_2	13	14	D_{13}
D_1	15	16	D_{14}
D_0	17	18	D_{15}
Ground	19	20	Key (missing pin)
DRQ3	21	22	GND
$\overline{\text{IOW}}$	23	24	GND
$\overline{\text{IOR}}$	25	26	GND
IOCHRDY	27	28	ALE
DACK3	29	30	GND
IRQ14*	31	32	IO16
A_1	33	34	GND
A0	35	36	A_2
CS0	37	38	CS1
SLV/ACT	39	40	GND

* IRQ15 for the secondary IDE connector

(a)

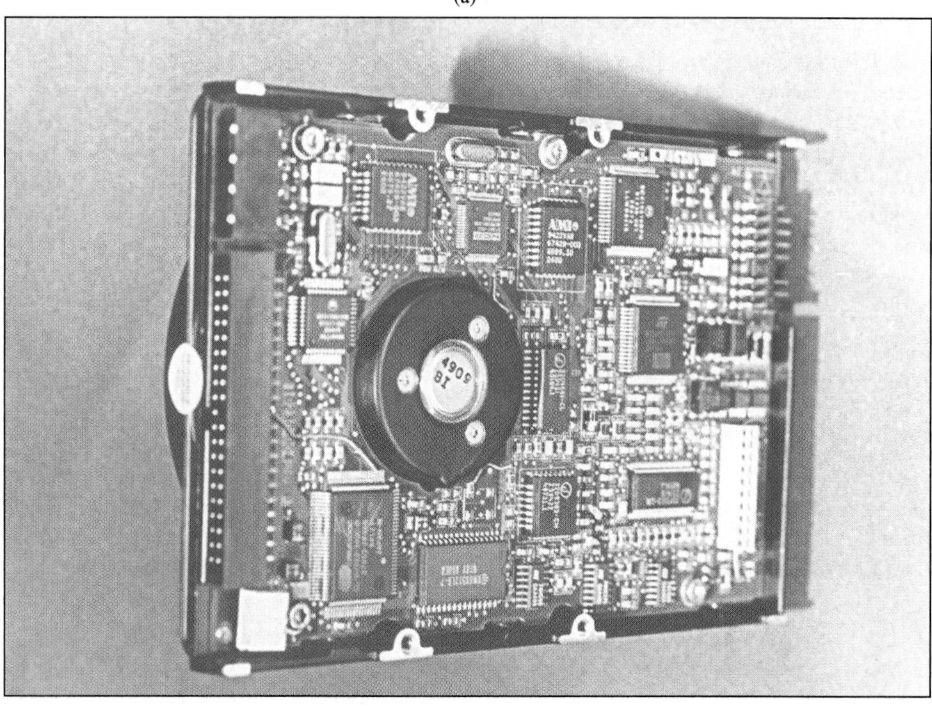

(b)

As indicated in Figure 64, the primary IDE controller uses interrupt 14. A handful of I/O ports are required as well, to issue commands and read data from the controller.

The **SCSI** (Small Computer System Interface) standard, shown in Figure 62(c), offers more expansion capability than any of the three previously mentioned standards. Like the IDE standard, the SCSI standard uses a single cable to control the hard drive. But where all three previous standards allowed at most two hard drives, the SCSI standard allows up to *seven* devices to be daisy-chained on the single 50-pin cable. Each device can be a hard drive, if necessary. This difference is important to computer users who have large storage requirements and might require **gigabytes** (1GB = 1024MB) of hard drive capacity. SCSI is used to connect a wide variety of devices together on a shared bus. For example, several disk drives, a tape drive, and a scanner can be connected to one SCSI bus. Each device on the bus and the controller card itself requires an address and the end of the SCSI cable, or the last device on the bus, must be terminated. Figure 65 shows a daisy chain of SCSI devices. The last device contains a terminator.

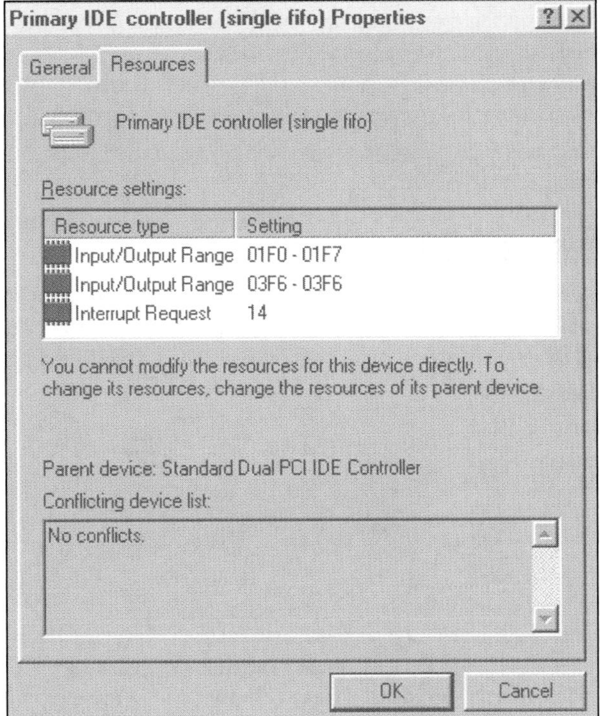

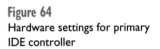

Figure 64
Hardware settings for primary IDE controller

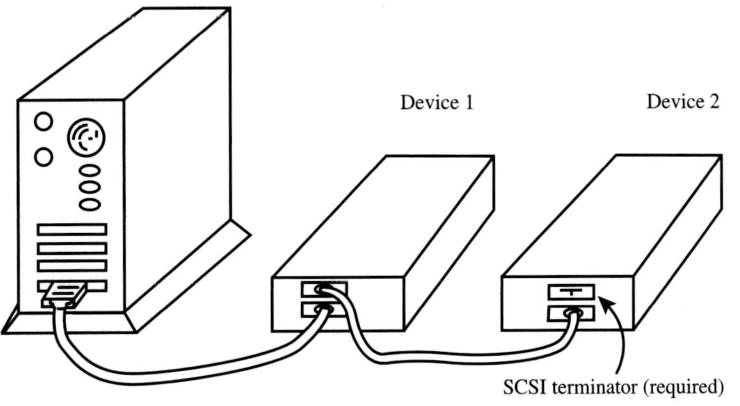

Figure 65
A daisy chain of SCSI devices

There are several different types of SCSI buses, each allowing for a specific cable type, transfer rate, bus width, and so on. Table 27 shows the different SCSI standards.

SCSI buses also have specific length requirements falling into two categories: single-ended and differential. A single-ended SCSI bus is cheap and fast over short distances. Differential SCSI can be used over longer distances. Table 28 shows the SCSI bus length requirements.

There are also different types of connectors used to connect SCSI devices together. Check the individual requirements for each SCSI device to determine the appropriate type. Note that SCSI devices are generally more expensive than non-SCSI devices, but they provide for combinations of devices not possible with standard PC technology.

Table 29 shows the capabilities of all the various SCSI buses. Note the maximum speed, bus width, and the maximum number of devices that are supported.

Jumper block settings (binary equivalents)

When configuring a SCSI device to the proper address setting, a jumper block is provided to allow the device address to be set. It is necessary for the system administrator to put jumpers in place to represent the proper address. This representation is coded using the binary number system. Table 30 lists decimal to binary equivalent values. A jumper must be installed on the pins to set the device address. SCSI-1 buses contain up to 8 devices (including the controller) and SCSI-2/SCSI-3 buses may contain up to 16 devices (also including the controller).

On some SCSI devices, a thumb wheel may be used to set the SCSI device address to the proper decimal value. Both of these methods are equivalent.

DATA STORAGE

Although there are differences between IDE hard drives and SCSI hard drives (and all the other types), there is also something in common: each hard drive uses the flux changes of a magnetic field to store information on the hard drive platter surface. A number of different techniques are used to read and write 0s and 1s using flux transitions. Some of the more common techniques are listed in Table 31.

Table 27
SCSI bus standards

Standard	Bus Width	Max Transfer Rate (Mbps)	Cable Type
SCSI-1	8	4	Not specified
SCSI-2	8 16	5 10	A B
SCSI-3	16 32	10 20	P P, Q

Table 28
SCSI bus lengths

Bus Type	Single-Ended	Differential
SCSI-1	6 meters	25 meters
SCSI-2	6 meters	25 meters
SCSI-3	3 meters	25 meters

SCSI Term	Bus Speed, MBytes/Sec. Max.	Bus Width, bits	Max. Bus Lengths, Meters (1)			Max. Device Support
			Single-ended	LVD	HVD	
SCSI-1	5	8	6	12	25	8
Fast SCSI	10	8	3	12	25	8
Fast Wide SCSI	20	16	3	12	25	16
Ultra SCSI	20	8	1.5	12	25	8
Ultra SCSI	20	8	3	-	-	4
Wide Ultra SCSI	40	16	-	12	25	16
Wide Ultra SCSI	40	16	1.5	-	-	8
Wide Ultra SCSI	40	16	3	-	-	4
Ultra2 SCSI	40	8	-	12	25	8
Wide Ultra2 SCSI	80	16	-	12	25	16
Ultra3 SCSI or Ultra160 SCSI	160	16	-	12	-	16
Ultra320 SCSI	320	16	-	12	-	16

Table 29
SCSI (Wide, Fast, Ultra, LVD (Low Voltage Differential)) characteristics

Decimal Address Value	SCSI-1	SCSI-2 and SCSI 3
0	000	0000
1	001	0001
2	010	0010
3	011	0011
4	100	0100
5	101	0101
6	110	0110
7	111	0111
8	n/a	1000
9	n/a	1001
10	n/a	1010
11	n/a	1011
12	n/a	1100
13	n/a	1101
14	n/a	1110
15	n/a	1111

Table 30
SCSI address values

Table 31
Data recording techniques

Technique	Meaning/Operation
MFM	Modified Frequency Modulation. Magnetic flux transitions are used to store 0s and 1s.
RLL	Run Length Limited. Special flux patterns are used to store *groups* of 0s and 1s.
Advanced RLL	Advanced Run Length Limited. Permits data to be recorded at higher density than RLL.

DISK CACHING

Because of mechanical limitations (rotational speed of the platters; movement and settling time of the read/write head), the rate at which data can be exchanged with the hard drive is limited. It is possible to increase the data transfer rate significantly through a technique called **caching.** A hardware cache is a special high-speed memory whose access time is much shorter than that of ordinary system RAM. A software cache is a program that manages a portion of system RAM, making it operate as a hardware cache. A computer system might use one or both of these types of caches, or none at all.

The main idea behind the use of a cache is to increase the *average* rate at which data is transferred. Let us see how this is done. First, we begin with an empty cache. Now, suppose that a request to the hard drive controller requires 26 sectors to be read. The controller positions the read/write head and waits for the platters to rotate into the correct positions. As the information from each sector is read from the platter surface, a copy is written into the cache. This entire process may take a few *milliseconds* to complete, depending on the drive's mechanical properties. If a future request requires information from the same 26 sectors, the controller reads the copy from the cache instead of waiting for the platter and read/write head to position themselves. This means that data is accessed at the faster rate of the cache (whose access time might be as short as 10 *ns*). This is called a cache *hit.* If the requested data is not in the cache (a *miss*), it is read from the platter surface and copied into the cache as it is outputted, to avoid a miss in the future. The cache uses an algorithm to help maintain a high hit ratio.

The same method is used for writing. Data intended for the hard drive is written into the cache very quickly (8MB/second), and then from the cache to the platter surface at a slower rate (2.5MB/second) under the guidance of the controller.

Many hard drives now come with 256KB of onboard hardware cache. In addition, a program called SMARTDRV can be used to manage system RAM as a cache for the hard drive. To use SMARTDRV, a line such as

```
C:\DOS\SMARTDRV.EXE 2048
```

must be added to your AUTOEXEC.BAT file. This command instructs SMARTDRV to use 2MB of expanded or extended memory as a cache. Small programs that are run frequently (DOS utilities stored on the hard drive) load and execute much more quickly with the help of SMARTDRV.

DISK STRUCTURE

The information presented here applies equally well to floppy disks as to hard disks. Figure 66 shows how a disk is divided into **sectors.** From the figure, you can see that a sector is a specified pie-slice area on the disk.

Disk sectors and tracks are not physically on the disk, just as data is not physically on the disk. They are simply magnetic patterns placed on the disk by electrical impulses. The number of tracks available on the disk varies. For example, a standard 3½-in. floppy disk has 80 tracks, whereas a hard disk may contain 650. The number of sectors a disk has also varies. This is illustrated in Table 32.

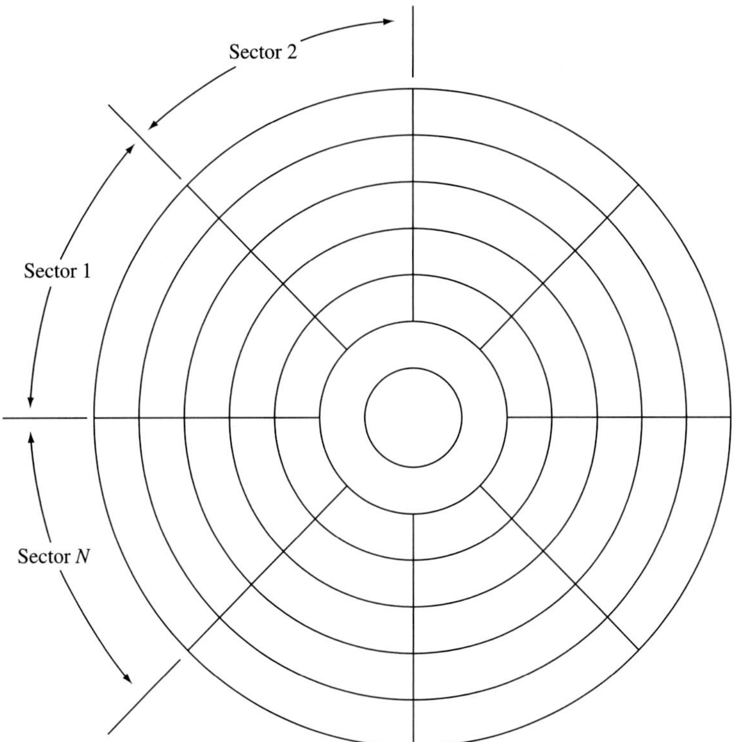

Figure 66
Disk sectors

Table 32
Floppy disk configurations

Disk Size	Disk Type	Tracks/Side	Total Sectors*
5.25	Single-sided—8 sectors per track	40	320
5.25	Single-sided—9 sectors per track	40	360
5.25	Double-sided—8 sectors per track	40	640
3.5	Double-sided—9 sectors per track	40	720
3.5	Quad-density—9 sectors per track	80	1440
5.25	Quad-density—15 sectors per track	80	2400

*Common sector sizes for disks are 128, 256, 512, and 1024 bytes.

DISK STORAGE CAPACITY

You can calculate the storage capacity of a disk as follows:

$$\text{DSC} = \text{sides} \times \text{tracks} \times \text{sectors} \times \text{size}$$

where

DSC = disk storage capacity
sides = number of disk sides used
tracks = number of disk tracks per side
sectors = number of disk sectors per track
size = size of each sector in bytes (usually 512)

As an example, consider a double-sided, double-density (nine-sector-per-track) disk. From Table 32, you can see that such a disk has 40 tracks per side and nine sectors per track, where each sector stores 512 bytes. Thus, for this type of disk, the total disk storage capacity is

$$\text{DSC} = 2 \times 40 \times 9 \times 512 = 368{,}640 \text{ bytes (or 360KB)}$$

Recall that each disk contains a boot sector. This boot sector is contained in sector 1, side 0, track 0, as illustrated in Figure 67. Table 33 lists the information contained in a boot sector.

Following the boot sector, there is a file allocation table (FAT). This table is used by DOS to record the number of disk sectors on the disk that can be used for storage as well as bad sectors that must not be used for storage. Several sectors are reserved for the FAT. All hard disks come from the factory with a certain number of bad sectors. During final product testing, these bad sectors are usually found and are usually then labeled on the hard drive unit itself.

In order to ensure reliability, each disk contains a duplicate copy of the FAT. This means that if one copy of the FAT goes bad, the backup copy is available for use.

DISK FRAGMENTATION

Disk fragmentation is the result of one or more disk files being contained in scattered sectors around the disk, as shown in Figure 68. Observe that the read/write heads may take more than one revolution of the disk to read all the file information scattered across the various sectors as a result of disk fragmentation.

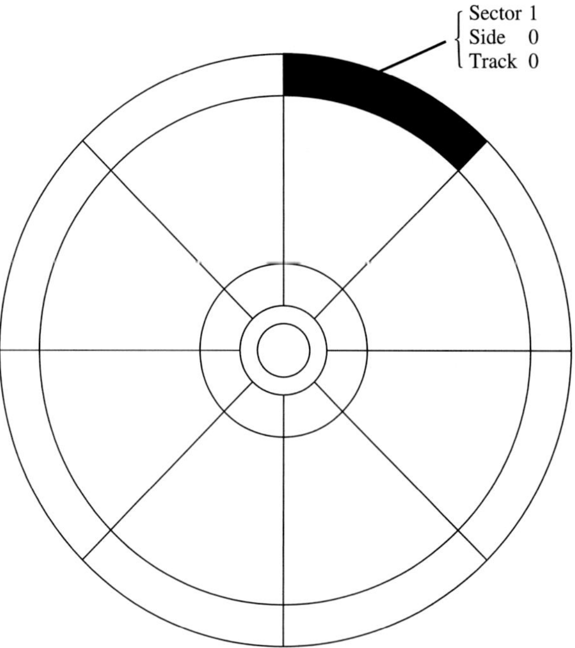

Figure 67
Location of the boot sector

Table 33
Information in a boot sector

Information	Size
• Microprocessor jump instruction • Manufacturer's name (IBM or Microsoft) and version number • Number of bytes per disk sector • Number of sectors per cluster • Number of reserved sectors • Number of maximum root directory entries • Total number of sectors • Description of the disk media • Number of sectors per track • Number of disk heads • Number of hidden sectors • The BOOTSTRAP program	512 bytes

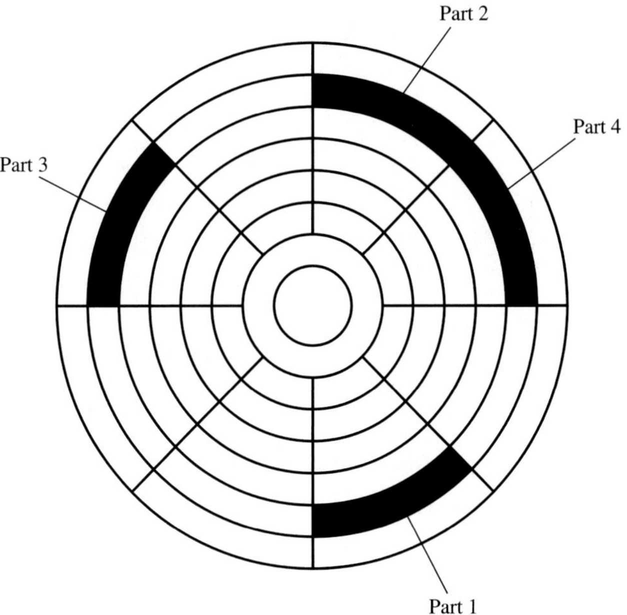

Figure 68
Disk fragmentation

Next, consider the file data distributed in contiguous sectors around the disk, as shown in Figure 69. The way the data is distributed here, it is conceivable that it could all be read in one revolution of the disk. The difference between fragmented data and contiguous data is that it takes longer to read fragmented data.

You must keep in mind that disk drives are slow when compared with the rest of the computer system. If information is fragmented over the hard disk, it takes longer to read the disk and significantly slows the entire computer system (because it takes longer to read and write the information). Disk fragmentation occurs when files are repeatedly added and deleted on a disk. Once disk fragmentation occurs (especially on the hard drive), your system will begin to run more slowly when it interacts with the hard drive. To eliminate this, you must use a hard disk utility program to defragment the disk. It is important now to realize that you must do this periodically in order to maximize system performance.

The defragmentation process can be automated in Windows 95/98 using the system agent. During periods of inactivity, the system agent will periodically run the disk utility tools, keeping the disk in reasonably good condition. The defragmentation process can also be run on demand by selecting Disk Defragmenter from the System Tools submenu (located under Accessories on the Start menu). Figure 70 shows the initial defrag screen presented by Windows.

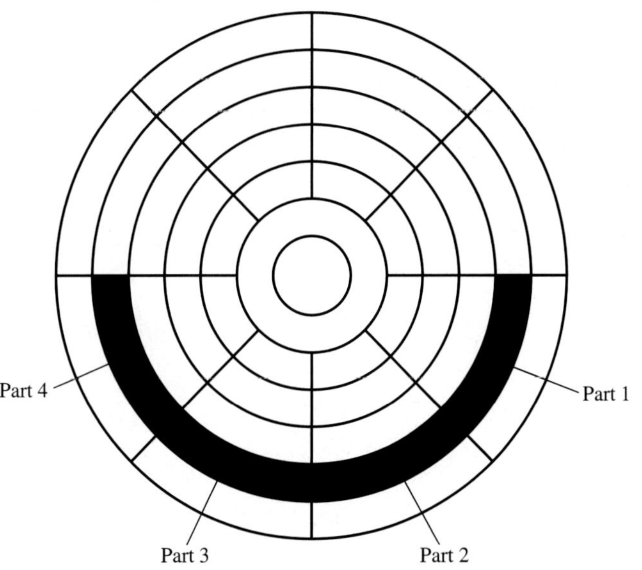

Figure 69
Contiguous file data on the same disk track

Figure 70
Selecting a disk to defragment

From this menu, it is very easy to start the defragmentation process, select another drive, check or modify the advanced parameters, or exit. Figure 71 shows the Disk Defragmenter Settings window.

Figure 72 shows the brief status of the defragmentation process. By clicking the Show Details button, we can also view the details of the defragmentation process as shown in Figure 73. Notice how each of the disk clusters is presented on the screen. It is interesting to watch the defragmentation process. Depending on the amount of fragmentation, the process may last just a few minutes or as long as a few hours. Select Legend to view the legend shown in Figure 74 to help you identify the different types of disk clusters. As you can see, there are many different possible states for a disk cluster.

FILE ALLOCATION

Every time DOS has to get space on the disk for a file, it looks at the FAT for unused disk **clusters.** A cluster is a set of contiguous disk sectors. DOS will always try to minimize disk fragmentation, if possible. Every file written to the disk has a directory entry that is a 32-byte record, which contains the following information:

- Name of file
- File extension
- Attribute byte
- File time
- File date

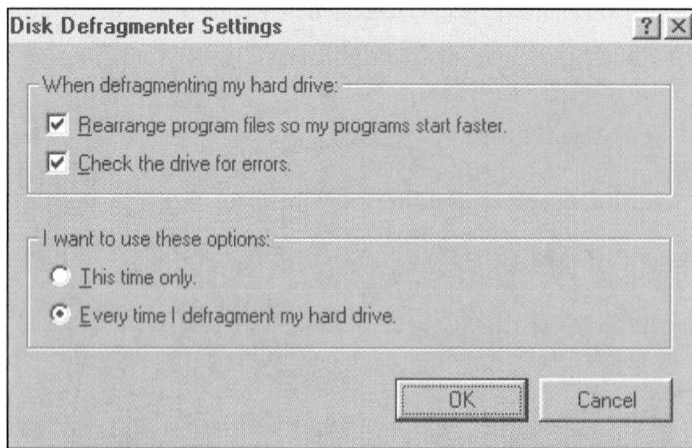

Figure 71
Disk Defragmenter Settings window

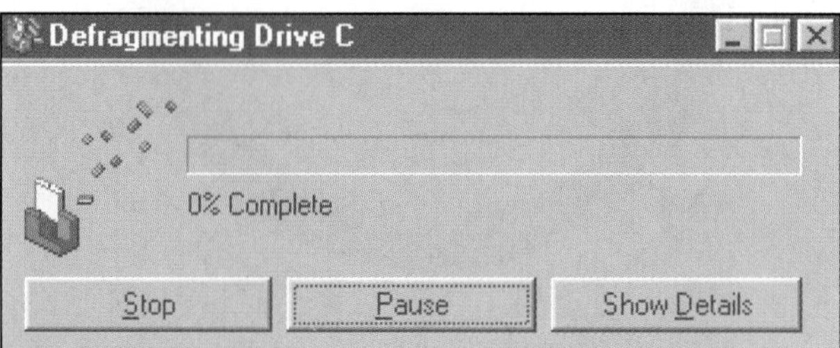

Figure 72
Defragmentation status window

- Number of the starting cluster
- Size of the file

DOS allocates disk space for directory entries in a special directory area that follows the FAT. This means that a disk can hold only a certain number of files, depending on the size and density of the disk. To DOS, a subdirectory is treated simply as a standard DOS file. This means that DOS stores subdirectory information in the same manner as it stores file information. Because of this, the number of subdirectories is also limited by the amount of free file space on the disk.

SECONDARY STORAGE, PART 3: THE CD-ROM DRIVE

A CD-ROM stores binary information in the form of microscopic *pits* on the disk surface. The pits are so small that a CD-ROM typically stores more than 650MB of data. This is equivalent to more than 430 1.44MB floppies. A laser beam is shined on the disk surface and either reflects (no pit) or does not reflect (pit), as you can see in Figure 75.

These two light states (reflection and no reflection) are easily translated into a binary 0 and a binary 1. Since the pits are mechanically pressed into a hard surface and only touched by light, they do not wear out or change as a result of being accessed.

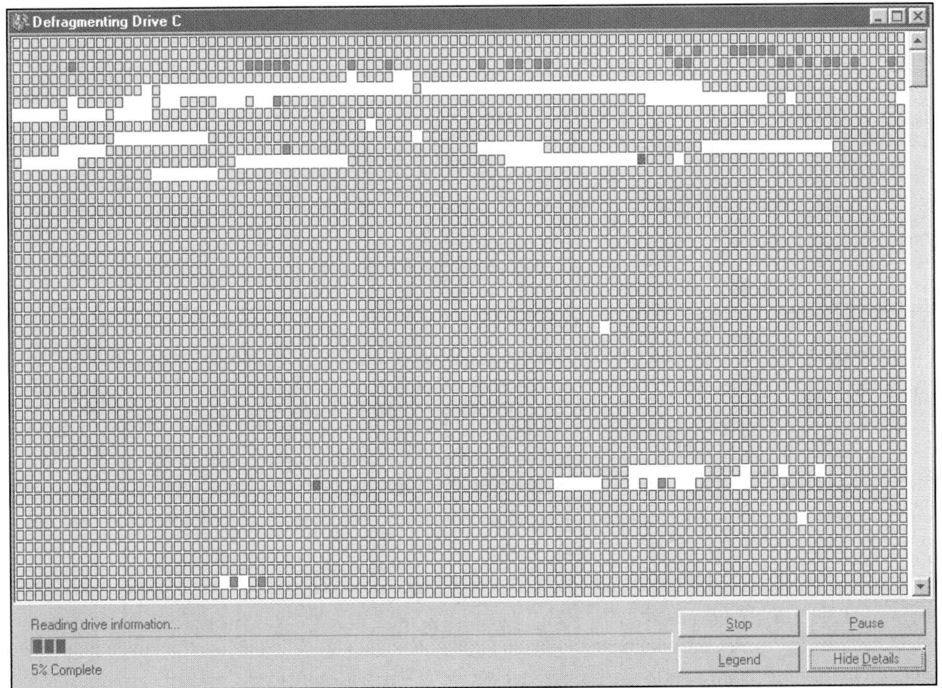

Figure 73
Details of the defragmentation process

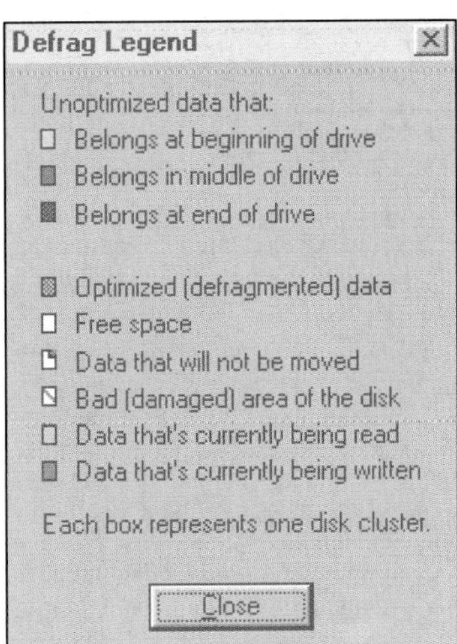

Figure 74
Defragmentation details legend

Figure 75
Reading data from a CD

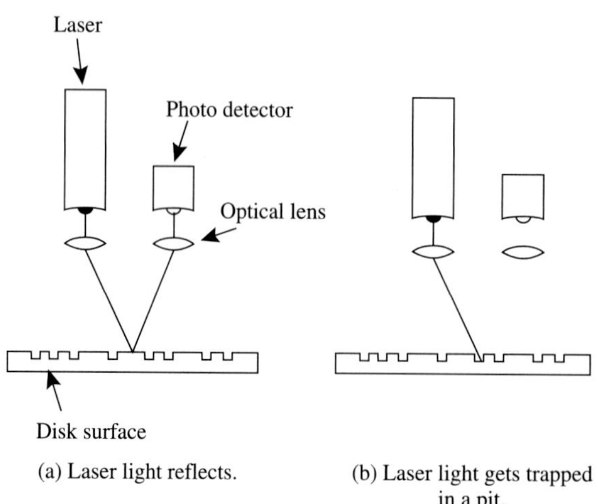

(a) Laser light reflects.

(b) Laser light gets trapped in a pit.

Physical Layout of a Compact Disk

Figure 76 shows the dimensions and structure of a compact disk. The pits previously described are put into the reflective aluminum layer when the disk is manufactured. Newer recordable CDs use a layer of gold instead of aluminum so that they can be written to using a low-power laser diode.

The High Sierra Format

The High Sierra format specifies the way the CD is logically formatted (tracks, sectors, directory structure, file name conventions). This specification is officially called ISO-9660 (International Standards Organization).

CD-ROM Standards

The evolution of the CD-ROM is documented in several *books*. These are described in Table 34. The red book describes the method used to store digital audio on the CD-ROM. Pulse code modulation (PCM) is used to sample the audio 44,100 times/second with 16-bit sampling.

The green book specifies the CD interactive format typically used by home video games. Text, audio, and video are interleaved on the CD-ROM, and the MPEG-1 (Motion Picture Entertainment Group) video encoding method requires special hardware inside the player to support real-time video. The CD-ROM-XA (extended architecture) format is similar to CD-I.

The orange book provides the details on recordable CD-ROM drives. Gold-based disks are used to enable data to be written to the CD-ROM, up to 650MB. A *multisession* CD-ROM allows you to write to the CD more than once, and requires a multisession CD-ROM drive. Compact disks that only allow one recording session are known as WORM drives, for write once, read mostly.

The yellow book describes the original PC-based CD-ROM format (single spin), which specifies a data transfer rate of 150KB/s. 2x CD-ROMs transfer at 300KB/s. 4x CD-ROMs transfer data at 600KB/s. Currently there are 48x CD-ROM drives on the market, with faster ones coming.

Table 34
CD-ROM standards

Book	Feature
Red	CD-DA. Digital audio. PCM encoding.
Green	CD-I. Interactive (text, sound, and video). ADPCM and MPEG-1 encoding.
Orange	CD-R. Recordable.
Yellow	CD-ROM. Original PC CD-ROM format. 150Kbps transfer rate.

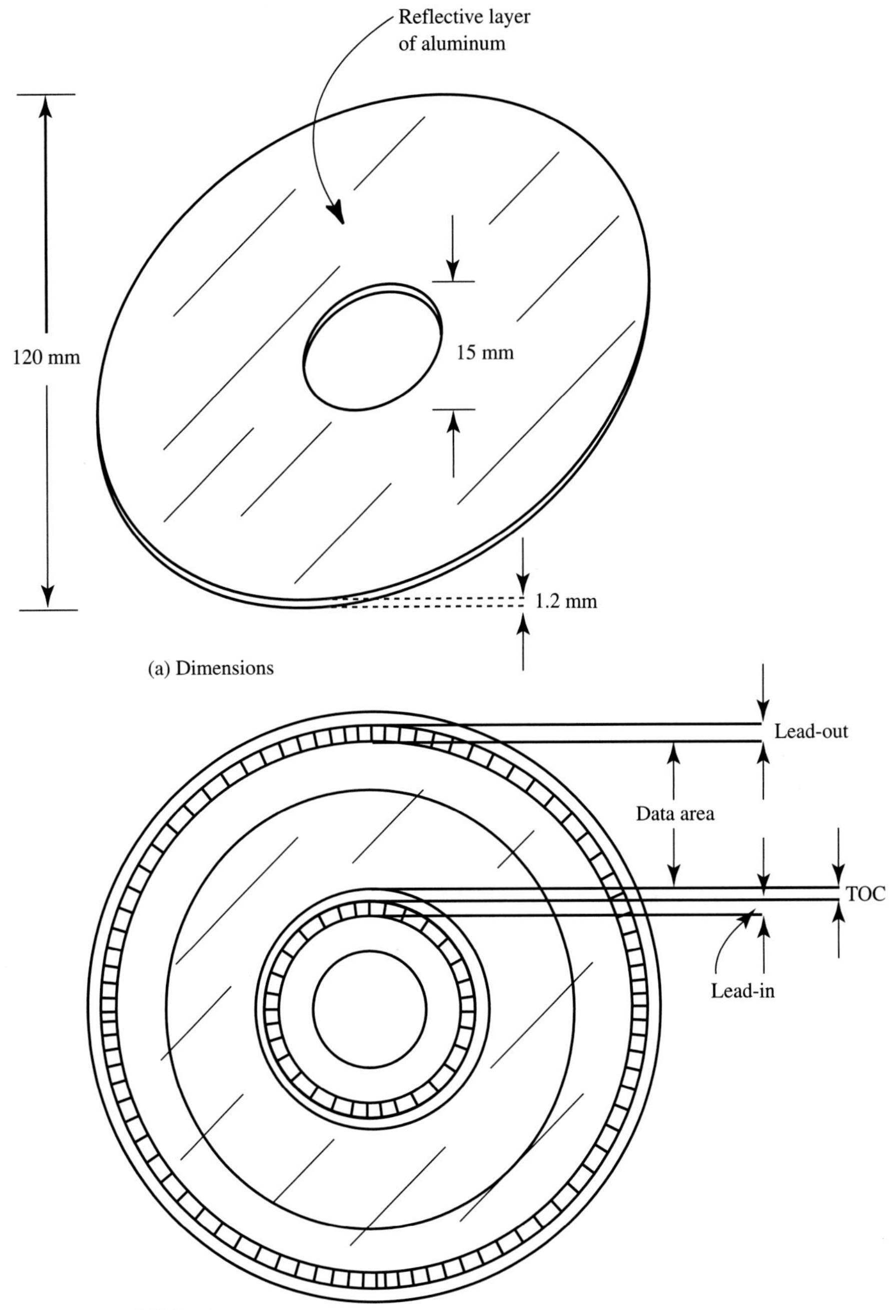

Reflective layer of aluminum
120 mm
15 mm
1.2 mm
(a) Dimensions
Lead-out
Data area
TOC
Lead-in
(b) Structure

Figure 76
Compact disk

Photo CD

Developed by Kodak, the photo CD provides a way to store high-quality photographic images on a CD (using recordable technology) in the CD-I format. Each image is stored in several different resolutions, from 192 × 128 to 3072 × 2048, using 24-bit color. This allows for around 100 images on one photo CD.

ATAPI

ATAPI stands for AT Attachment Packet Interface. ATAPI is an improved version of the IDE hard drive interface, and uses *packets* of data during transfers. The ATAPI specification supports CD-ROM drives, hard drives, tape backup units, and plug-and-play adapters.

I/O, PART I: EXPANSION BUSES

Expansion buses (slots) serve a very important function in personal computers. They allow you to plug in electronic cards to expand and enhance the operation of your computer. The concept of expansion slots is simple; however, in practical terms, there are many things to consider. Figure 77 is a simple illustration of the function of expansion slots.

An expansion slot must be able to communicate with the computer. This communication usually includes access to the microprocessor. In achieving this access, the expansion bus must not interfere with the normal operation of the microprocessor. This means that the expansion bus must have access not only to the address and data lines used by the microprocessor but also to special control signals.

You need to be familiar with the functions of the various types of expansion buses that provide the means to add new features to your computer. Most of these added features, such as extra memory, additional types of monitor displays, extra or different disk drives, telephone communications, and other enhancements, are added in part by cards that fit into expansion slots on the computer (peripheral cards). However, as you will soon see, not all expansion slots are the same. It is important that you know their differences.

MAKEUP OF AN EXPANSION SLOT

Expansion slots have more similarities than differences. Table 35 lists the purposes of the different lines that are connected to the expansion slots. It should be noted that not all expansion slots use every one of these lines. The terminology used in this table does, however, apply to all expansion slots that use any of these lines.

ISA Expansion Slots

Figure 78 shows the ISA (Industry Standard Architecture) expansion slot. True PC compatibles also use the same kind of expansion slot. Pin assignments are shown in Figure 79.

The major features of the ISA expansion slots are listed in Table 36. The features are described in terms of a *bus.* Recall that a bus is nothing more than a group of conductors treated as a unit; as a *data bus,* it is a group of conductors used to carry data. In terms of an expansion slot, a bus can be thought of as a group of connectors that is connected to the bus on the motherboard.

Figure 77
Expansion slots

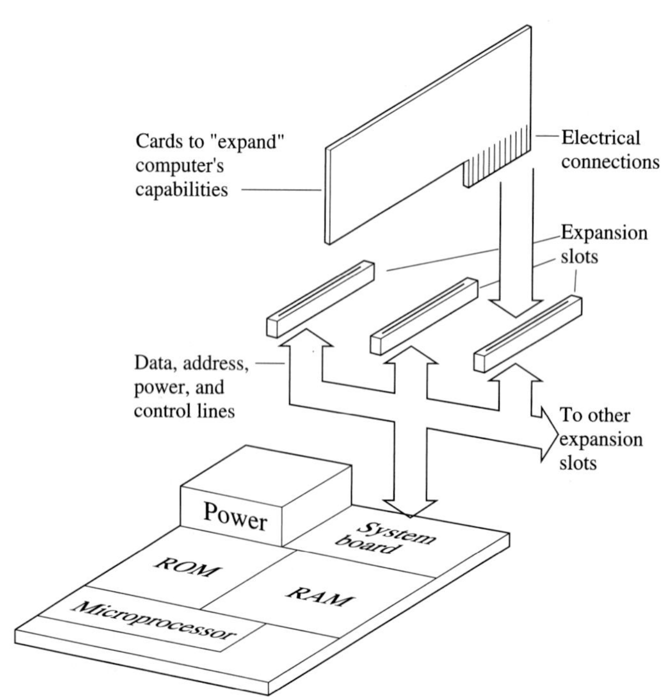

Table 35
Expansion slot terminology

Connections	Purpose
Power lines	Power lines supply the voltages that may be needed by the various expansion cards. The power lines are +5 V DC, –5 V DC, +12 V DC, –12 V DC, and ground.
Data lines	Data lines are used to transfer programming information between the expansion card and the computer. One of the major differences among expansion slots in different computers is the number of data lines available.
Address lines	Address lines are used to select different memory locations. Another major difference among expansion slots is the number of address lines available.
Interrupt request lines	Interrupt request lines are used for hardware signals. These signals come from various devices, including the expansion card itself. Interrupt request signals are used to get the attention of the microprocessor. This is done so that the expansion card can temporarily use the services of the microprocessor.
DMA lines	DMA stands for *direct memory access.* DMA lines are control lines that provide direct access to memory (without having to go through the microprocessor, which tends to slow things down). DMA lines are also used to indicate when memory access is temporarily unavailable because it is being used by some other part of the system. DMA lines are used to indicate that direct memory access is being requested (called a DMA request line) and to acknowledge that request (called a DMA acknowledge).
NMI line	NMI stands for *nonmaskable interrupt.* This line is so called because it cannot be "masked," or switched off, by software. It is primarily used when a parity check error occurs in the system.
Memory-read, memory-write lines	The memory-read and memory-write lines are used to indicate that memory is either being written to or read from.
I/O read, I/O write lines	The I/O read and write lines are used to indicate that an input or output device (such as a disk drive) is to be written to or read from.
Special lines	Another one of the major differences among expansion slots in different types of computers is the number (and the types) of specialized lines used. For example, some of the OS/2 systems offer an *audio channel line* for the purpose of carrying a sound signal.

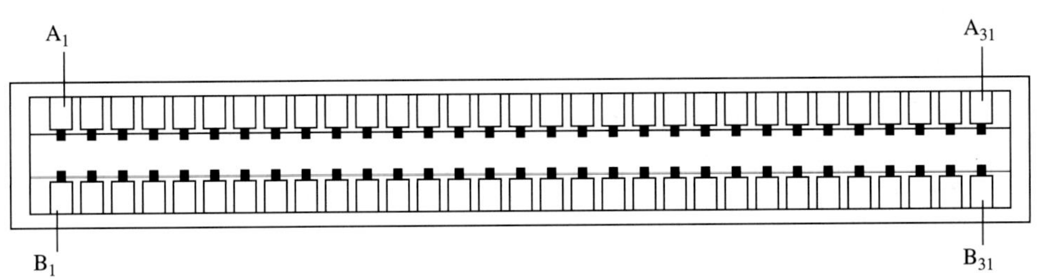

Figure 78
ISA expansion slot and pin numbering

Figure 79
ISA expansion slot pin assignments

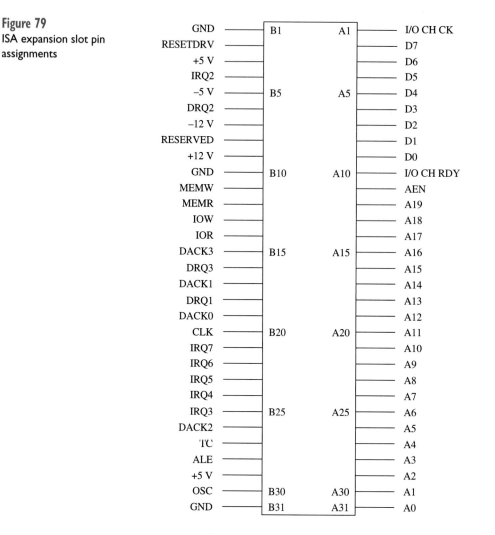

GND	B1	A1	I/O CH CK
RESETDRV			D7
+5 V			D6
IRQ2			D5
–5 V	B5	A5	D4
DRQ2			D3
–12 V			D2
RESERVED			D1
+12 V			D0
GND	B10	A10	I/O CH RDY
MEMW			AEN
MEMR			A19
IOW			A18
IOR			A17
DACK3	B15	A15	A16
DRQ3			A15
DACK1			A14
DRQ1			A13
DACK0			A12
CLK	B20	A20	A11
IRQ7			A10
IRQ6			A9
IRQ5			A8
IRQ4			A7
IRQ3	B25	A25	A6
DACK2			A5
TC			A4
ALE			A3
+5 V			A2
OSC	B30	A30	A1
GND	B31	A31	A0

Table 36
Major features of ISA expansion slots

Type of Bus	Comments
Total pins	62 separate connectors
Data bus	8 data lines
Address bus	20 address lines (1MB addressable memory)

Figure 80 shows the design of an expansion card used in a PC. Note that there are two major types of PC expansion cards: one type goes straight back from the connector and the other has a skirt that dips back down to the board level. This distinction becomes important in the design of expansion slots used in other types of computers to accommodate PC expansion cards.

THE LOCAL BUS

The EISA connector supports 80386, 80486, and Pentium microprocessors by providing a full 32-bit data bus. Three special bus-controlling chips are used to manage data transfers through the EISA connectors. Thus, data that gets transferred between an expansion card and the CPU must go through the bus controller chip set. This effectively reduces the rate at which data can be transferred.

To get around this problem, a new bus architecture was introduced, called the **local bus.** A local bus connector provides the fastest communication possible between a plug-in card and the machine by bypassing the EISA chip set and connecting directly to the CPU. Local bus video cards and hard drive controllers are popular because of their high-speed data transfer capability.

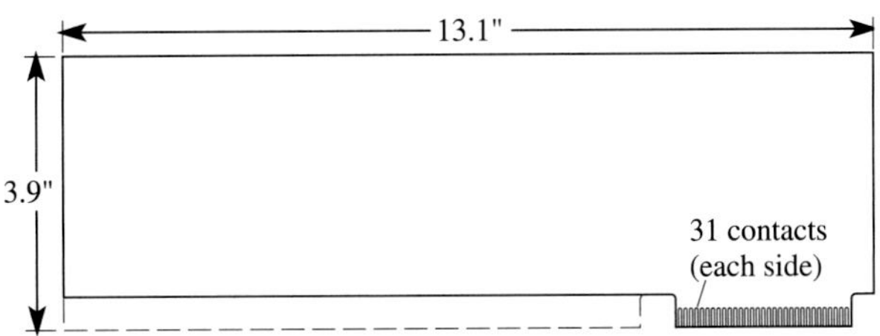

Figure 80
Typical ISA expansion card

One initial attempt to define the new local bus was the VESA local bus. VESA stands for Video Electronics Standards Association, an organization dedicated to improving video display and bus technology. VESA local bus cards typically run at 33-MHz speeds, and were originally designed to interface with 80486 signals. VESA connectors are simply add-ons to existing connectors; no special VESA local bus connector exists.

The PCI Bus

PCI stands for Peripheral Component Interconnect, and it is Intel's offering in the world of standardized buses. The PCI bus uses a *bridge* to control data transfers between the processor and the system bus, as indicated in Figure 81.

In essence, the PCI bus is not strictly a local bus, since connections to the PCI bus are not connections to the processor, but rather a special PCI-to-host controller chip. Other chips, such as PCI-to-ISA bridges, interface the older ISA bus with the PCI bus, allowing both types of buses on one motherboard, with a single chip controlling them all. The PCI bus is designed to be processor independent, plug-and-play compatible, and capable of 64-bit transfers at 33 MHz and above.

PCI connectors are physically different from all other connectors. Refer to Figure 25, which shows four ISA connectors and three PCI connectors. Figure 82 shows the pinout for a 32-bit PCI connector.

THE PCMCIA bus

The PCMCIA (Personal Computer Memory Card International Association) bus, now referred to as *PC card bus,* evolved from the need to expand the memory available on early laptop computers. The standard has since expanded to include almost any kind of peripheral you can imagine, from hard drives, to LAN adapters and modem/fax cards. Figure 83 shows a typical PCMCIA Ethernet card.

The PCMCIA bus supports four styles of cards, as shown in Table 37.

All PCMCIA cards allow *hot swapping,* removing and inserting the card with power on.

A type I connector is shown in Figure 84. The signal assignments are illustrated in Tables 38 and 39. The popularity of laptop and notebook computers suggests the continued use of this bus.

AGP

The Accelerated Graphics Port (AGP) is a new technology that improves multimedia performance on Pentium II/III/IV computers. Figure 85 shows where the AGP technology fits into the other bus hardware.

The heart of the AGP is the 440LX AGPset hardware, a *quad-ported* data switch that controls transfers between the processor, main memory, graphics memory, and the PCI bus. AGP technology uses a connector similar to a PCI connector.

With growing emphasis on multimedia applications, AGP technology sets the stage for improved performance.

USB

The universal serial bus is a new peripheral bus designed to make it easier to connect many different types of devices to the PC. These devices include audio players, joysticks, keyboards, scanners, telephones, data gloves, tape and floppy drives, modems, and printers. Motherboards manufactured

Figure 81
PCI bridge in a Pentium system

Pentium
Data
Address
Level-2 cache
PCI-to-host bridge
DRAM
PCI video adapter card
PCI bus
SCSI controller
Ethernet adapter
PCI-to-ISA bridge
ISA bus
ISA adapter card

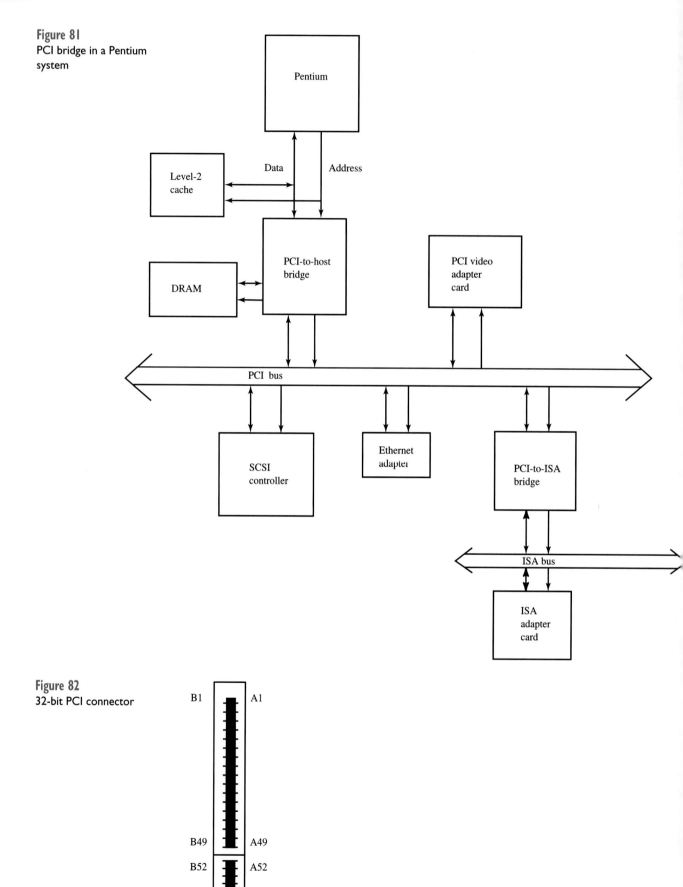

Figure 82
32-bit PCI connector

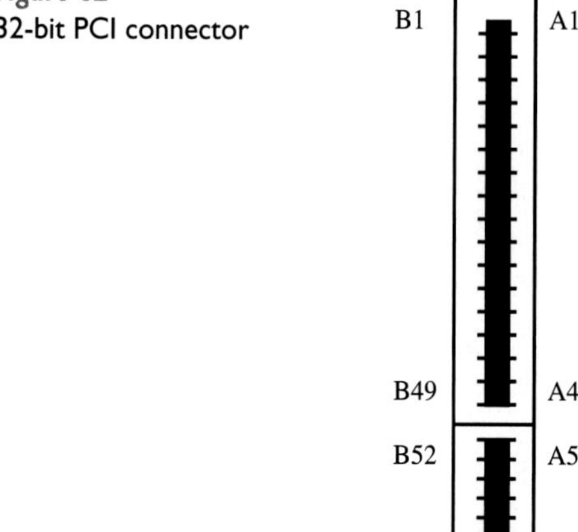

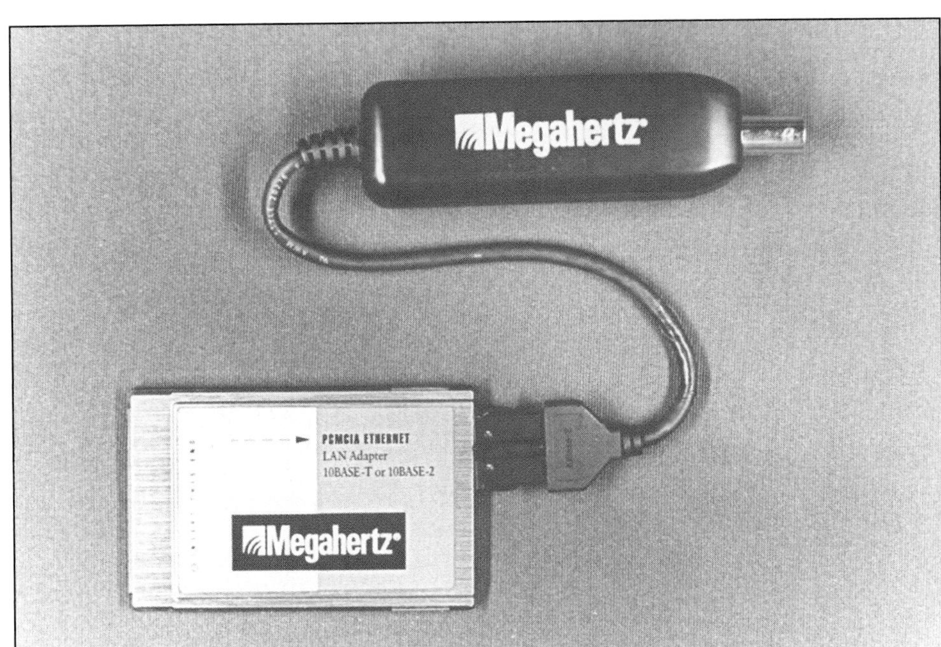

Figure 83
PCMCIA Ethernet card (photograph by John T. Butchko)

Table 37
PCMCIA slot styles

Slot Type	Meaning
I	Original standard. Supports 3.3-mm cards. Memory cards only.
II	Supports 3.3-mm and 5-mm cards.
III	Supports 10.5-mm cards, as well as types I and II.
IV	Greater than 10.5 mm supported.

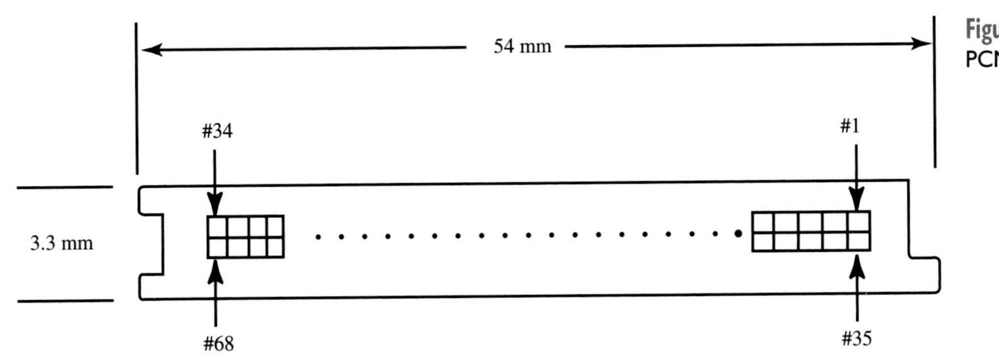

Figure 84
PCMCIA connector

Table 38
PCMCIA pin assignments (available at card insertion)

Pin	Signal	Pin	Signal	Pin	Signal
1	GND	24	A_5	47	A_{18}
2	D_3	25	A_4	48	A_{19}
3	D_4	26	A_3	49	A_{20}
4	D_5	27	A_2	50	A_{21}
5	D_6	28	A_1	51	Vcc
6	D_7	29	A_0	52	Vpp2
7	CE1	30	D_0	53	A_{22}
8	A_{10}	31	D_1	54	A_{23}
9	OE	32	D_2	55	A_{24}
10	A_{11}	33	WP	56	A_{25}
11	A_9	34	GND	57	RFU
12	A_8	35	GND	58	RESET
13	A_{13}	36	CD1	59	WAIT
14	A_{14}	37	D_{11}	60	RFU
15	WE/PGM	38	D_{12}	61	REG
16	RDY/BSY	39	D_{13}	62	BVD2
17	Vcc	40	D_{14}	63	BVD1
18	Vpp1	41	D_{15}	64	D_8
19	A_{16}	42	CE2	65	D_9
20	A_{15}	43	RFSH	66	D_{10}
21	A_{12}	44	RFU	67	CD2
22	A_7	45	RFU	68	GND
23	A_6	46	A_{17}		

Table 39
PCMCIA signal differences

Pin	Memory Card	I/O Card
16	RDY/BSY	IREQ
33	WP	IOIS16
44	RFU	IORD
45	RFU	IOWR
60	RFU	INPACK
62	BVD2	SPKR
63	BVD1	STSCHG

today have USB support built in (as does Windows 98). USB support can be added to older systems through the use of an adapter card. Some of the features of the USB are:

- Serial bus (simple four-wire cable).
- Up to 127 devices may be connected at the same time.
- 12 Mbps data rate (USB version 2.0 operates at 480 Mbps).
- Devices may be attached with power on.
- Plug-and-play compatibility.
- Data is transmitted in packets.
- USB hubs are used to expand connections to the bus.
- PC acts as host, controlling the USB connection.

Using a USB device eliminates the need to go inside the PC (to install an adapter card) or share COM1 or the printer port with another device.

IEEE 1284

The IEEE 1284 standard provides a method for increasing the data transfer speed of the parallel/printer port, while still being backward compatible with older parallel port devices and printers. The 1284 standard defines 5 modes of data transfer.

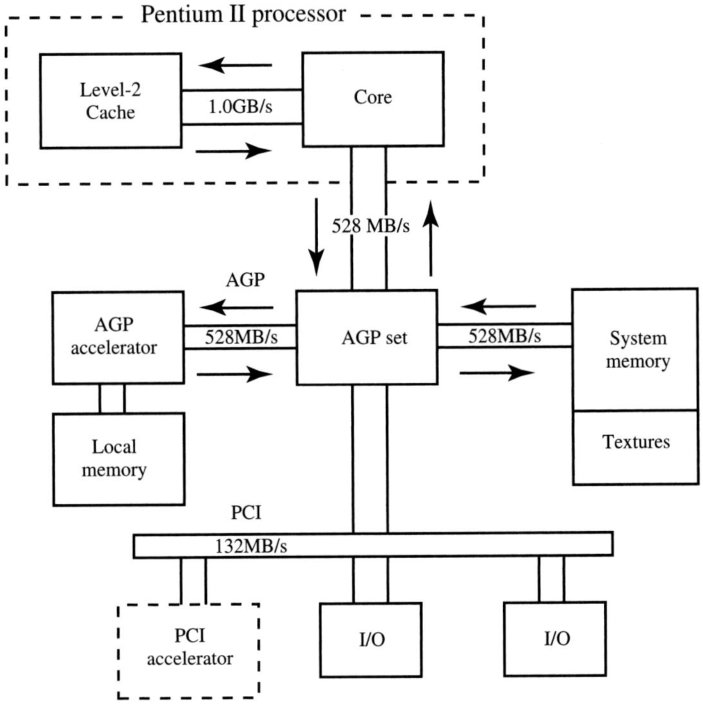

Figure 85
AGP interface

1. Compatibility mode (forward direction only, PC to device). This is also called the standard, or Centronics mode.
2. Nibble mode (reverse direction only, device to PC, 4-bits at a time).
3. Byte mode (reverse direction only, 8-bits at a time).
4. EPP (Enhanced Parallel Port, bidirectional, used for external tape drives, CD-ROMs, etc.).
5. ECP (Extended Capability Port, used on new printers and scanners).

The mode of the parallel/printer port can be changed using the BIOS setup program.

IEEE 1394

Firewire (IEEE-1394) is a very fast external bus standard that supports data transfer rates of up to 400 million bits per second over a distance of 4.5 meters. FireWire is aimed at higher-speed multimedia peripherals such as video and music equipment, and hard disks. Apple, which originally developed the technology, uses the trademarked name FireWire. A single 1394 port can be used to connect up 63 external devices. In addition to its high speed, 1394 also supports delivering data at a guaranteed rate called isochronous data transfer that is used by devices that need to transfer high quantities of data in real-time, such as video devices.

IEEE-1394 is expensive compared to USB although it extremely fast and flexible. Firewire supports both Plug-and-Play and hot plugging, and also provides power to peripheral devices. The standard Firewire cable consists of six wires. Data is sent via two separately-shielded twisted pair transmission lines that are crossed in each cable assembly to create a transmit-receive connection. Two additional wires carry power (8 to 40 v, 1.5 a max.) to remote devices. The standard cable uses 28 AWG signal pairs with 40 twist/meter. The power pair in the standard cable is 22 AWG. Note that the power lines are not used by all FireWire products and this is why FireWire cables come in 4 wire and 6 wire combinations.

I/O, Part 2: The Modem

This section has to do with communications between computers. The user of one computer may interact with another computer—which may be located thousands of miles away—as if it were sitting right in the same room.

In order for computers to communicate in this manner, four items must be available, as shown in Figure 86. There must be some kind of link between the computers. The most convenient link to use is the already-established telephone system lines. Using these lines and a properly equipped computer allows communications between any two computers that have access to a telephone. This becomes a very convenient and inexpensive method of communicating between computers.

There is, however, one problem. Telephone lines were designed for the transmission of the human voice, not for the transmission of digital data. Therefore, in order to make use of these telephone lines for transmitting computer data, the ONs and OFFs of the computer must first be converted to sound, sent over the telephone line, and then reconverted from sound to the ONs and OFFs that the computer understands. This concept is shown in Figure 87.

Modem Definition

The word *modulate* means to change. Thus an electronic circuit that changes digital data into sound data can be called a *modulator.* The word *demodulate* can be thought of as meaning "unchange," or restore to an original condition. Any electronic circuit that converts the sound used to represent the digital signals back to the ONs and OFFs understood by a computer can, therefore, be called a demodulator. Since each computer must be capable of both transmission and reception, each computer must contain an electrical circuit that can modulate as well as demodulate. Such a circuit is commonly called a modulator/ demodulator, or **modem.**

Figure 86
Four items necessary for computer communications

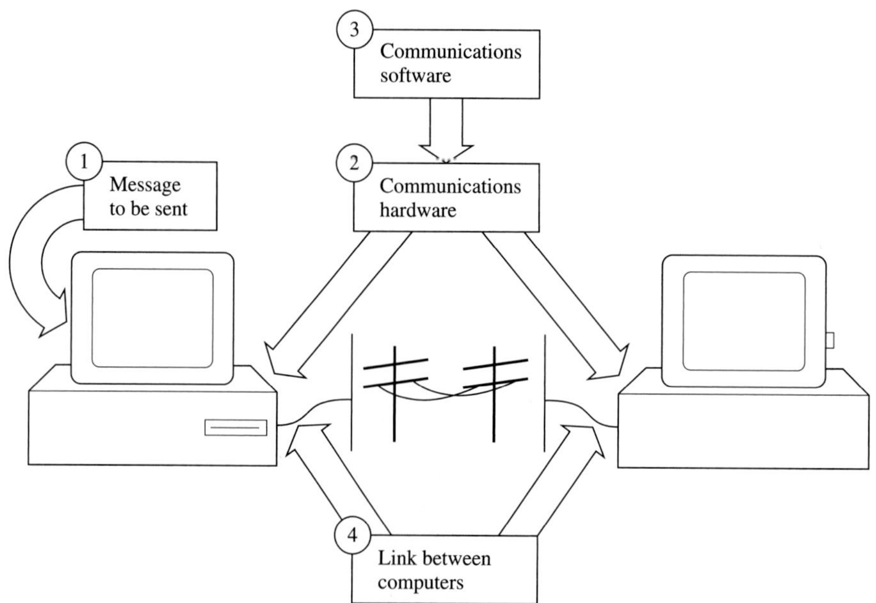

Figure 87
Basic needs for the use of telephone lines in computer communications

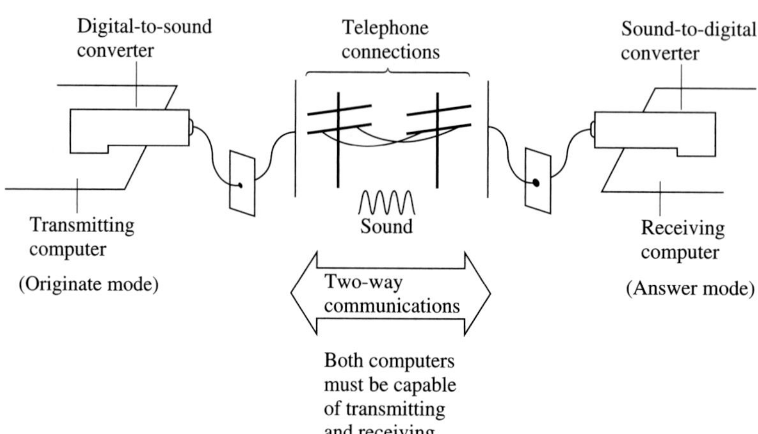

For personal computers, a modem may be an internal or an external device—both perform identical functions.

The RS-232 Standard

The EIA (Electronics Industries Association) has published the EIA *Standard Interface Between Data Terminal Equipment Employing Serial Binary Data Interchange*—specifically, EIA-232-C. This is a standard defining 25 conductors that may be used in interfacing **data terminal equipment** (DTE, such as your computer) and **data communications equipment** (DCE, such as a modem) hardware. The standard specifies the function of each conductor, but it does not state the physical connector that is to be used. This standard exists so that different manufacturers of communications equipment can communicate with each other. In other words, the RS-232 standard is an example of an interface, essentially an agreement among equipment manufacturers on how to allow their equipment to communicate.

The RS-232 standard is designed to allow DTEs to communicate with DCEs. The RS-232 uses a DB-25 connector; the male DB-25 goes on the DTEs and the female goes on the DCEs. The RS-232 standard is shown in Figure 88.

The RS-232 is a digital interface designed to operate at no more than 50 feet with a 20,000-bit/second bit rate. The **baud,** named after J. M. E. Baudot, actually indicates the number of *discrete* signal changes per second. In the transmission of binary values, one such change represents a single bit. What this means is that the popular usage of the term *baud* has become the same as bits per second (bps). Table 40 shows the standard set of baud rates.

Telephone Modem Setup

The most common problem with telephone modems is the correct setting of the software. There are essentially six distinct areas to which you must pay attention when using a telephone modem:

1. Port to be used
2. Baud rate
3. Parity
4. Number of data bits
5. Number of stop bits
6. Local echo ON or OFF

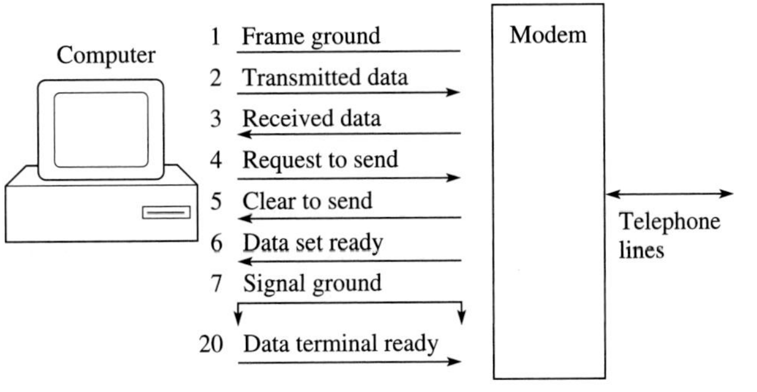

Figure 88
The RS-232 standard

Table 40
Standard baud rates

Low Speed	High Speed
300	
600	
1200	14,400
2400	28,800
4800	33,600
9600	56K

Most telephone modems have a default setting for each of these areas. However, as a user you should understand what each of these areas means. You will have to consult the specific documentation that comes with the modem in order to see how to change any of the above settings. For now it is important that you understand the idea behind each of these areas.

Port to Be Used

The most common ports to be used are COM1 and COM2. Other possible ports are COM3 and COM4. The port you select from the communications software depends on the port to which you have the modem selected. On most communications software, once you set the correct port number, you do not need to set it again.

Baud Rate

Typical values for the baud rate are between 9600 and 56K. Again, these values can be selected from the communications software menu. It is important that both computers be set at the same baud rate.

Parity

Parity is a way of having the data checked. Normally, parity is not used. Depending on your software, there can be up to five options for the parity bit, as follows:

Space: Parity bit is always a 0.
Odd: Parity bit is 0 if there is an odd number of 1s in the transmission and is a 1 if there is an even number of 1s in the transmission.
Even: Parity bit is a 1 if there is an odd number of 1s in the transmission and is a 0 if there is an even number of 1s in the transmission.
Mark: Parity bit is always a 1.
None: No parity bit is transmitted.

Again, what is important is that both the sending and receiving units are set up to agree on the status of the parity bit.

Number of Data Bits

The number of data bits to be used is usually set at 8. There are options that allow the number of data bits to be set at 7. It is important that both computers expect the same number of data bits.

Number of Stop Bits

The number of stop bits used is normally 1. However, depending on the system, the number of stop bits may be 2. Stop bits are used to mark the end of each character transmitted. Both computers must have their communications software set to agree on the number of stop bits used.

Windows Modem Software

Windows has built-in modem software, accessed through the Control Panel. Clicking on the Mouse icon displays the window shown in Figure 89. Notice that Windows indicates the presence of an external Sportster modem. To test the modem, click the Diagnostics tab. Figure 90 shows the Diagnostics window.

Selecting COM2 (the Sportster modem) and then clicking More Info will cause Windows to talk to the modem for a few moments, interrogate it, and then display the results in a new window, shown in Figure 91.

Specific information about the modem port is displayed, along with the responses to several AT commands. The *AT command set* is a standard set of commands that can be sent to the modem to configure, test, and control it. Table 41 lists the typical **Hayes compatible** commands (first used by Hayes in its modem products). An example of an AT command is:

```
ATDT 778 8108
```

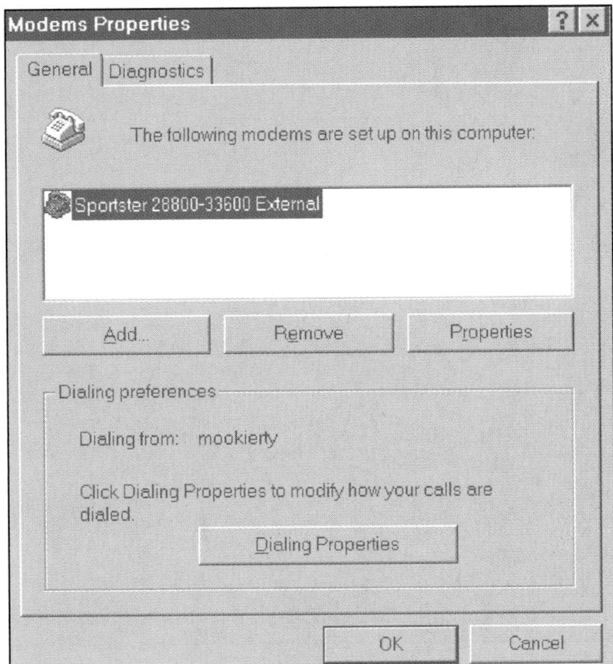

Figure 89
Modems Properties window

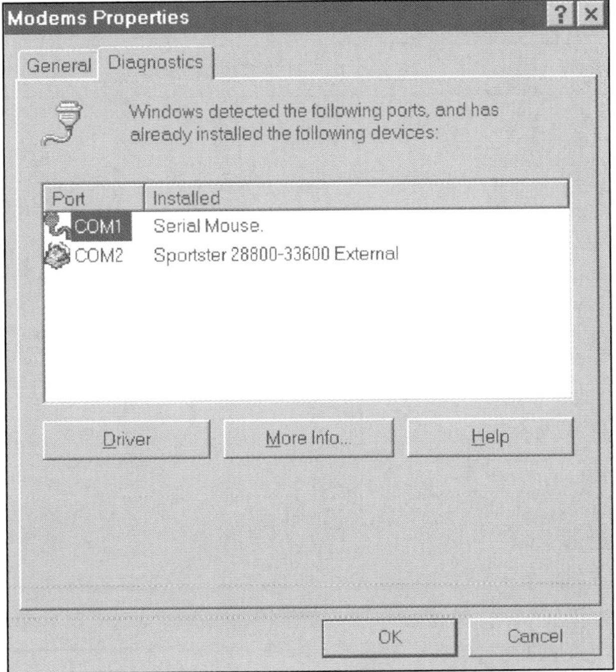

Figure 90
Modems Diagnostics window

which stands for AT (attention) DT (dial using tones). This AT command causes the modem to touch-tone dial the indicated phone number. Many modems require an initial AT command string to be properly initialized. This string is automatically output to the modem when a modem application is executed.

TELEPHONE MODEM TERMINOLOGY

In using technical documentation concerning a telephone modem, you will encounter some specialized terminology. Figure 92 illustrates some of the ideas behind some basic communication methods. As you can see from the figure, **simplex** is a term that refers to a communications channel in which information flows in one direction only. An example of this is a radio or a television station.

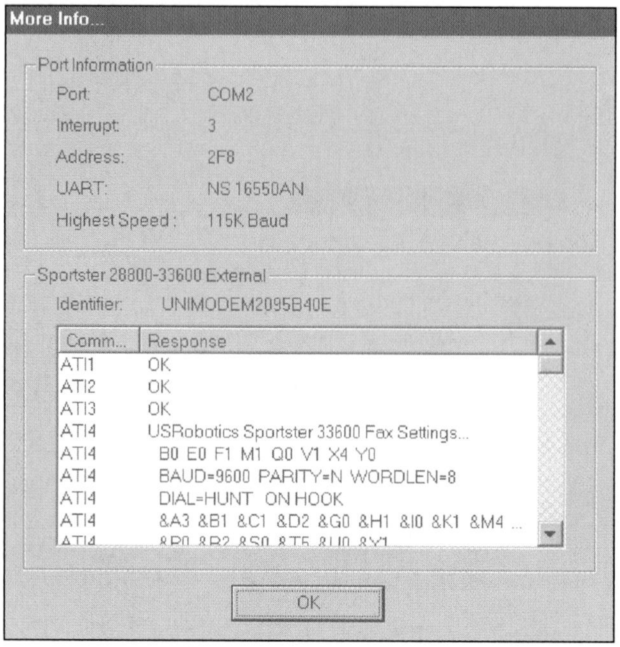

Figure 91
Modem diagnostic information

More Info...

Port Information
Port: COM2
Interrupt: 3
Address: 2F8
UART: NS 16550AN
Highest Speed: 115K Baud

Sportster 28800-33600 External
Identifier: UNIMODEM2095B40E

Comm...	Response
ATI1	OK
ATI2	OK
ATI3	OK
ATI4	USRobotics Sportster 33600 Fax Settings...
ATI4	B0 E0 F1 M1 Q0 V1 X4 Y0
ATI4	BAUD=9600 PARITY=N WORDLEN=8
ATI4	DIAL=HUNT ON HOOK
ATI4	&A3 &B1 &C1 &D2 &G0 &H1 &I0 &K1 &M4 ...

OK

Table 41
Selected AT commands

Command	Function	Command	Function
A/	Repeat last command	Xn	Result code type
A	Answer	Yn	Long space disconnect
Bn	Select CCITT or Bell	Zn	Recall stored profile
Cn	Carrier control option	&Cn	DCD option
D	Dial command	&Dn	DTR option
En	Command echo	&F	Load factory defaults
Fn	Online echo	&Gn	Guard tone option
Hn	Switch hook control	&Jn	Auxiliary relay control
In	Identification/checksum	&M0	Communication mode option
Kn	SRAM buffer control	&Pn	Dial pulse ratio
Ln	Speaker volume control	&Q0	Communication mode option
Mn	Speaker control	&Sn	DSR option
Nn	Connection data rate control	&Tn	Self-test commands
On	Go online	&Vn	View active and stored configuration
P	Select pulse dialing	&Un	Disable Trellis coding
Qn	Result code display control	&Wn	Stored active profile
Sn	Select an S-register	&Yn	Select stored profile on power-on
Sn=x	Write to an S-register	&Zn=x	Store telephone number
Sn?	Read from an S-register	%En	Auto-retrain control
?	Read last accessed S-register	%G0	Rate renegotiation
T	Select DTMF dialing	%Q	Line signal quality
Vn	Result code form	-Cn	Generate data modem calling tone

Duplex

The **duplex** mode refers to two-way communication between two systems. This term is further refined as follows. **Full duplex** describes a communication link that can pass data in two directions at the same time. This mode is analogous to an everyday conversation between two people either face-to-face or over the telephone. The other mode, which is not commonly available with telephone modems, is the **multiplex** mode. Multiplex refers to a communications link in which multiple transmissions are possible.

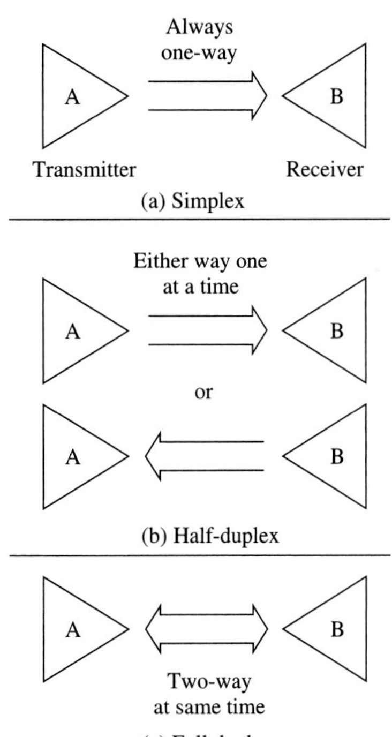

Figure 92
Some basic communication methods

Echo

Terminology used here has to do with how the characters you send to the other terminal are displayed on your monitor screen. The term **echo** refers to the method used to display characters on the monitor screen. First, there is a **local echo.** A local echo means that the sending modem immediately returns or echoes each character back to the screen as it is entered into the keyboard. This mode is required before transmission, so that you can see what instructions you are giving the communications software. Next there is **remote echo.** Remote echo means that during the communications between two computers, the remote computer (the one being transmitted to) sends back the character it is receiving. The character that then appears on your screen is the result of a transmission from the remote unit. This is a method of verifying what you are sending. To use the remote-echo mode, you must be in the full-duplex mode. This idea is illustrated in Figure 93.

Modulation Methods

Many different techniques are used to encode digital data into analog form (for use by the modem). Several of these techniques are:

- AM (amplitude modulation)
- FSK (frequency shift keying)
- Phase modulation
- Group coding

Figure 94 shows how the first three of these techniques encode their digital data.

To get a high data rate (in bits per second) over ordinary telephone lines, group coding techniques are used. In this method, one cycle of the transmitted signal encodes two or more bits of data. For example, using *quadrature modulation,* the binary patterns 00, 01, 10, and 11 encode one of four different phase shifts for the current output signal. Thus, a signal that changes at a rate of 2400 baud actually represents 9600 bps!

Another technique, called *Trellis modulation,* combines two or more other techniques, such as AM and quadrature modulation, to increase the data rate.

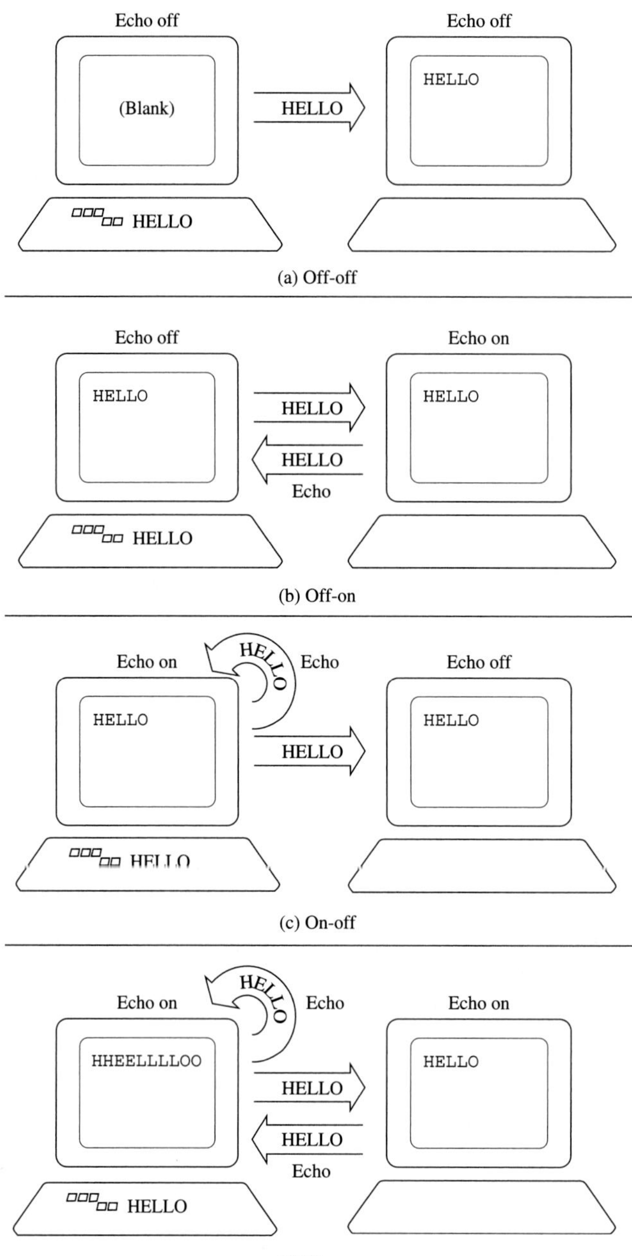

Figure 93
Echo modes

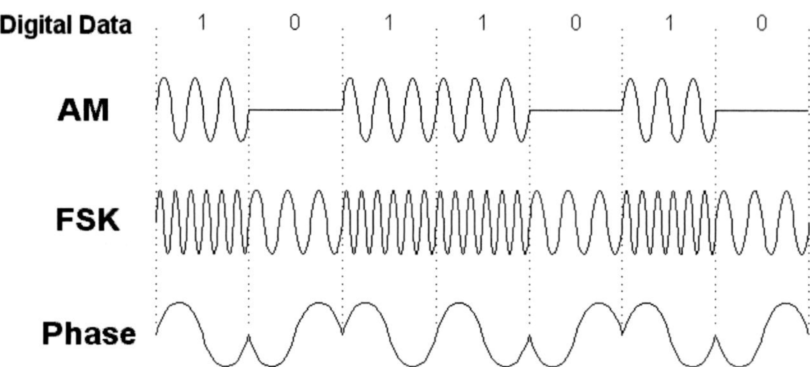

Figure 94
Modulation techniques

MNP Standards

MNP (Microcom Networking Protocol) is a set of protocols used to provide error detection and correction, as well as compression, to the modem data stream. Table 42 lists the MNP classes and their characteristics.

MNP classes 4 and above are used with newer, high-speed modems. When two modems initially connect, they will negotiate the best type of connection possible, based on line properties, and the features and capabilities of each modem. The CCITT standards supported by the modem are also part of the negotiation. Let us look at these standards as well.

CCITT Standards

CCITT (French abbreviation for International Telegraph and Telephone Consultive Committee) standards define the maximum operating speed (as well as other features) available in a modem (which is a function of the modulation techniques used). Table 43 lists the CCITT standards.

Earlier, low-speed standards not shown are the Bell 103 (300 bps using FSK) and Bell 212A (1200 bps using quadrature modulation). V.22 is similar in operation to Bell 212A, and is more widely accepted outside the United States.

The V.90 standard, finalized in early 1998, outlines the details of modem communication at 56K bps, currently the fastest speed available for regular modems. Fax modems have their own set of standards.

Table 42
MNP standards

Class	Feature
1	Asynchronous, half-duplex, byte-oriented
2	Asynchronous, full-duplex, byte-oriented
3	Synchronous, full-duplex, byte-oriented
4	Error correction, packet-oriented
5	Data compression
6	Negotiation
7	Huffman data compression
9	Improved error correction
10	Line monitoring

Note: There is no MNP-8 standard.

Table 43
CCITT standards

Standard	Data Rate (bps)
V.22	1200
V.22 bis	2400
V.32	9600
V.32 bis	14,400
V.32 terbo	19,200
V.34	28,800/33,600
V.90	56K

ISDN Modems

ISDN (Integrated Services Digital Network) is a special connection available from the telephone company that provides 64K bps digital service. An ISDN modem will typically connect to a *basic rate ISDN* (BRI) line, which contains two full-duplex 64Kbps B channels (for voice/data) and a 16Kbps D channel (for control). This allows up to 128Kbps communication. ISDN modems are more expensive than ordinary modems, and require you to have an ISDN line installed before you can use it.

Cable Modems

One of the most inexpensive, high-speed connections available today is the cable modem. A cable modem connects between the television cable supplying your home and a network interface card in your computer. Two unused cable channels are used to provide data rates in the hundreds of thousands of bits per second. For example, downloading a 6MB file over a cable modem takes less than 20 seconds (during several tests of a new cable modem installation). That corresponds to 2,400,000 bps! Of course, the actual data rate available depends on many factors, such as the speed the data is transmitted from the other end and any communication delays. But unlike all other modems, the cable modem has the capability to be staggeringly fast, due to the high bandwidth available on the cable. In addition, a cable modem is typically part of the entire package from the cable company, and is returned when you terminate service. The cost is roughly the same as the cost of basic cable service.

Fax/Data Modems

It is difficult to find a modem manufactured today that does not have fax capabilities built into it. Since fax/data modems are relatively inexpensive, it does not make sense to purchase a separate fax machine (unless it is imperative that you be able to scan a document before transmission). Word-processing programs (such as WordPerfect) now support the use of a fax/data modem, helping to make the personal computer almost an entire office by itself.

Protocols

A **protocol** is a prearranged communication procedure agreed upon by two or more parties. When two modems are communicating over telephone lines (during a file transfer from a computer bulletin board or an America Online session), each modem has to agree on the technique used for transmission and reception of data. Table 44 shows some of the more common protocols. The modem software that is supplied with a new modem usually allows the user to specify a particular protocol.

Computer Networks

A computer network is a collection of computers and devices connected so that they can share information and services. Such networks are called local area networks or LANs (networks in office buildings or on college campuses) and wide area networks or WANs (networks for very large geo-

Table 44
Modem communication protocols

Protocol	Operation
Xmodem	Blocks of 128 bytes are transmitted. A checksum byte is used to validate received data. Bad data is retransmitted.
Xmodem CRC	Xmodem using Cyclic Redundancy Check to detect errors.
Xmodem-1K	Essentially Xmodem CRC with 1024-byte blocks.
Ymodem	Similar to Xmodem-1K. Multiple files may be transferred with one command.
Zmodem	Uses 512-byte blocks and CRC for error detection. Can resume an interrupted transmission from where it left off.
Kermit	Transmits data in packets whose sizes are adjusted to fit the needs of the other machine's protocol.

graphical areas). LANs are connected together using routers, while the computers within a LAN are connected using switches, hubs, or other devices.

Sharing files and printers is a common activity on a LAN. For example, many users in an office may use a single printer that is shared on the network (either by a user on his or her computer, or through a stand-alone print server).

Computers (or other networked devices) communicate with each other using a standard set of protocols (both hardware and software). Hardware protocols handle the job of electronic communication, such as representing 1s and 0s electrically, managing flow control, and error detection. Software protocols are used to perform higher-level communication, such as the correct transfer of an email message from a server to a client.

Each computer or network device has a unique binary address, called a MAC address (for media access control), that is assigned to its network interface. On Windows machines, MAC addresses are called adapter addresses. MAC addresses are 48-bits long. An example MAC address is 00-C0-F0-24-67-E2. Data can not be sent to a destination computer until its MAC address is known. The MAC address is a physical address.

A second address, used for logical addressing, is a device's IP (Internet protocol) address. IP addresses are 32-bits wide and usually represented as four decimal numbers between 0 and 255 separated by periods, as in 192.168.1.105 (also called dotted-decimal notation). IP addresses are used by routers to guide a data packet to the correct destination computer over a WAN.

The WINIPCFG utility (available in Windows 9x) displays a network computer's MAC (adapter) and IP addresses as shown in Figure 95.

The IPCONFIG utility displays similar information in Windows 2000.

```
C:\>ipconfig
Windows IP Configuration
Ethernet adapter Local Area Connection:
        Connection-specific DNS Suffix  . :
        IP Address. . . . . . . . . . . . : 192.168.1.10
        Subnet Mask . . . . . . . . . . . : 255.255.255.0
        Default Gateway . . . . . . . . . : 192.168.1.1
C:\WINDOWS>
```

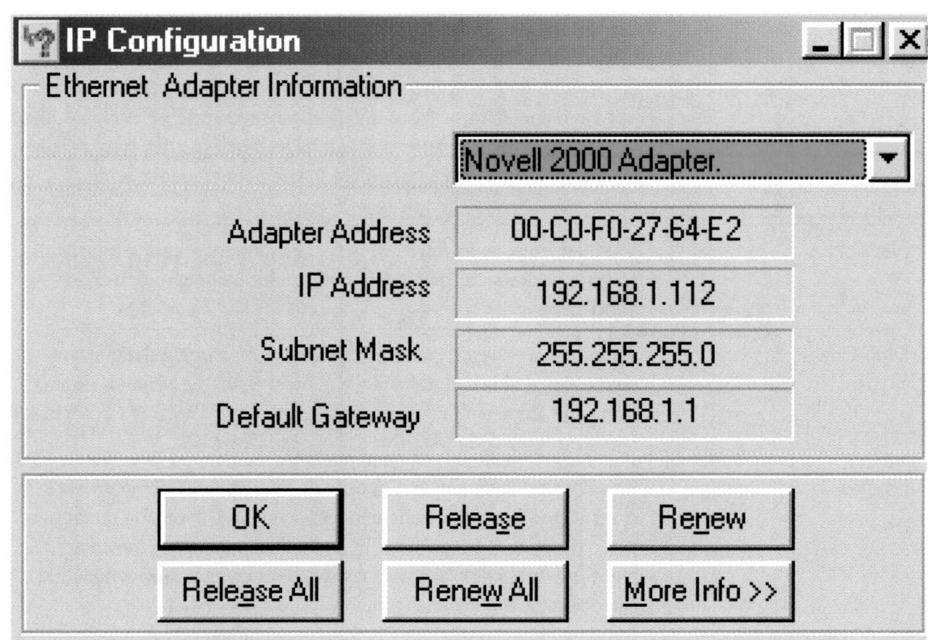

Figure 95
Network information displayed by WINIPCFG

Just throwing 1s and 0s onto a communication link is not enough to establish coherent communication between two nodes in a network. Both nodes must agree in advance on what the format of the information will look like. This format is called a protocol and is firmly defined. The OSI (Open Systems Interconnection) reference model defines seven layers required to establish reliable communication between two nodes, and is one of the accepted standards governing the use of protocols in computer networks. Different protocols are used between layers to handle such things as error recovery and information routing between nodes. Table 45 shows the ISO/OSI protocol stack which defines the responsibilities of each network layer.

Ways to network a PC

A PC may be networked in any of the following ways:

1. Direct connection to one other PC (using parallel, serial, infrared, or even NIC-to-NIC with a crossover UTP cable).
2. To a remote network using a modem.
3. To a LAN using a network adapter.
4. Through the air with a wireless connection (wireless NIC and wireless access point required).

New, home networking products, allow you to network multiple machines over the existing telephone wiring in the home. The network traffic does not interfere with the telephone, which can be used while the network is operating.

Table 45
ISO/OSI Layered Protocol Stack

OSI Model Layer	**Function**
Application	The Application layer (layer 7) is where the actual user program executes and makes use of the lower layers.
Presentation	The Presentation layer (layer 6) deals with matters such as text compression, conversion, and encryption.
Session	The Session layer (layer 5) handles communication between processes running on two different nodes. For example, it allows two mail programs running on different nodes to establish a session to communicate with each other.
Transport	The Transport layer (layer 4) is the first layer that is not concerned with how the data actually gets from node to node. Instead, the Transport layer assumes that the physical data is error-free, and concentrates on providing correct communication between applications from a logical perspective. For example, the Transport layer guarantees that a large block of data transmitted in smaller chunks is reassembled in the proper order when received.
Network	The Network layer (layer 3) is responsible for routing protocol-specific packets to their proper destination using logical IP addressing.
Data-Link	The Data-Link layer (layer 2) takes care of framing data, error detection, and it maintains flow control over the physical connection. The Data-Link layer consists of two sublayers: LLC (Logical Link Control) and MAC (Media Access Control).
Physical	The Physical layer (layer 1) controls how the digital information is transmitted between nodes. In this layer, the encoding technique, the type of connector used, and the data rate, all of which are physical properties, are established. This layer is responsible for transmitting and receiving bits.

Physical Network topographies

Network topography or topology has to do with the way the components of the network are connected. The topology of a computer network is the way the individual computers or devices (called nodes) are connected.

There are four main types of network topologies (illustrated in Figure 96):

1. Mesh, or partially connected, where each node connects to one or more other nodes. A special form of mesh is full mesh (or fully connected), where each node connectes to all other nodes.
2. Star, where groups of nodes are connected to a central hub or switch.
3. Bus, where all nodes share access to the same communication channel.
4. Ring, where all the nodes are connected to form a closed ring, with each node connected to two other nodes (one before and one after).

Hardware protocols

Hardware protocols are used to electrically encode the digital data being carried over the network. There are several different hardware protocols in use, with Ethernet being the most popular and widely used. They are:

1. Ethernet (available in 10-, 100-, 1000-, and 10,000-Mbps speeds).
2. Token Ring (4-Mbps and 16-Mbps).
3. RS-232 (used to encode low-speed serial data).
4. FDDI (fiber distributed data interconnect, a 100Mbps fiber ring technology with a large ring diameter).
5. ATM (asynchronous transfer mode, also called cell relay, uses fixed-size cells of data at speeds of 155 Mbps or 622 Mbps).
6. SONET (synchronous optical network, a fiber ring technology, with speeds from 51 Mbps up to 2.4 Gbps).
7. ISDN (integrated services data network, provides two 64Kbps data channels).
8. ASDL (asymmetrical digital subscriber line, a technology that uses ordinary telephone lines to provide high-speed digital services. It is asymmetric because the upload speed is slower than the download speed, such as 256 Kbps upstream versus 1.5 Mbps downstream).

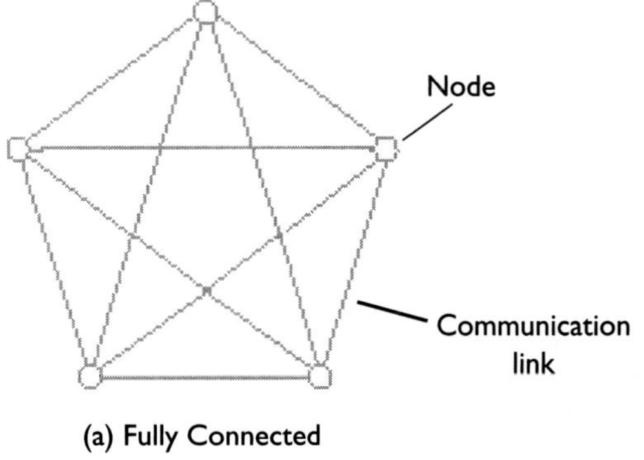

(a) Fully Connected

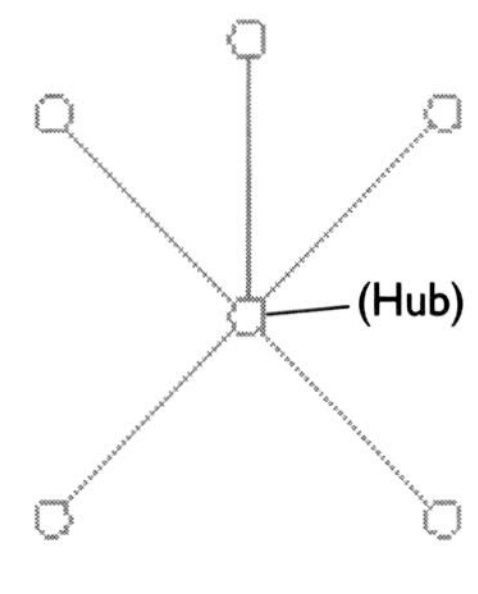

(b) Star

Figure 96
Types of network topologies

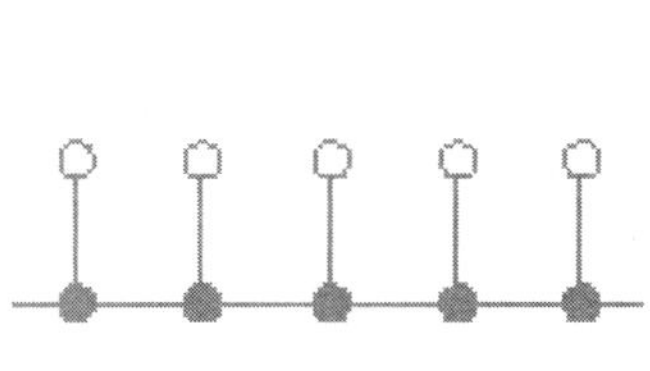
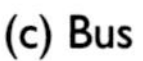

(c) Bus

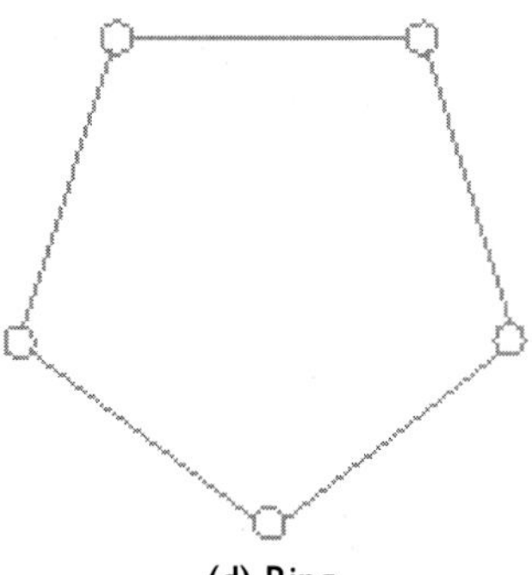

(d) Ring

I/O, Part 3: The Sound Card

Along with CD-ROM drives, sound cards for PCs have also increased in popularity. Currently, 16-bit sound cards are available that provide multiple audio channels and FM-quality sound, and are compatible with the MIDI (Musical Instrument Data Interface) specification.

The basic operation of the sound card is shown in Figure 97. Digital information representing samples of an analog waveform are inputted to a *digital-to-analog* converter, which translates the binary patterns into corresponding analog voltages. These analog voltages are then passed to a *low-pass filter* to smooth out the differences between the individual voltage samples, resulting in a continuous analog waveform. All of the digital/analog signal processing is done in a custom **digital signal processor** chip included on the sound card.

Sound cards also come with a microphone input that allows the user to record any desired audio signal.

MIDI

MIDI stands for Musical Instrument Digital Interface. A MIDI-capable device (electronic keyboard, synthesizer) will use a MIDI-in and MIDI-out serial connection to send messages between a *controller* and a *sequencer.* The PC operates as the sequencer when connected to a MIDI device. MIDI messages specify the type of note to play and how to play it, among other things. Using MIDI, a total of 128 pitched instruments can generate 24 notes in 16 channels. This can be accomplished in a PC sound card by using frequency modulation or *wave table synthesis,* the latter method utilizing prerecorded samples of notes stored in a data table. The output of a note is controlled by several parameters. Figure 98 illustrates the use of attack, delay, and release times to shape the output waveform envelope. Each of the four parameters can be set to a value from 0 to 15.

Figure 97
How binary data is converted into an analog waveform

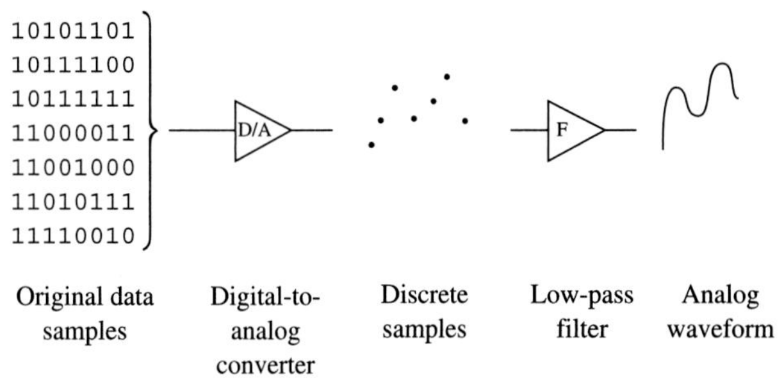

Figure 98
Note envelope

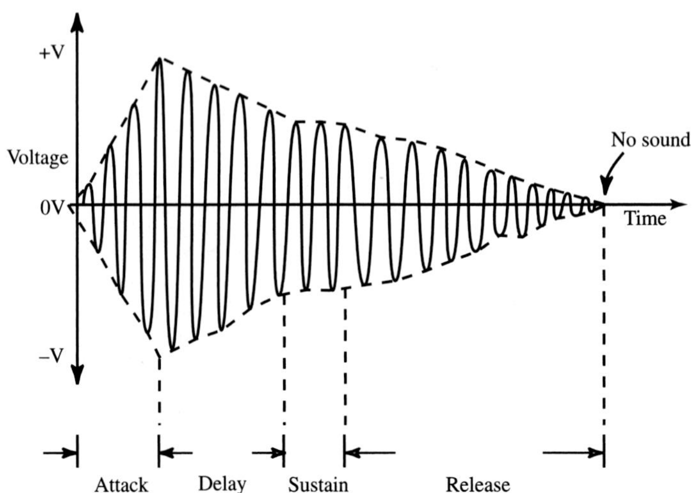

Troubleshooting Techniques

It is a good idea to write down a troubleshooting problem and its eventual solution in a problem/solution journal. Keep track of all the strange things that happen to your computer. Often, a problem comes back again, and you may not remember exactly what you did to fix it. Windows problems are especially notorious in this regard and also difficult to diagnose. Keeping a journal of your repair (and installation) efforts will be rewarding in the long run.

Troubleshooting the Mouse

Usually the biggest problem with a mouse-to-computer connection is improper installation of the mouse software. To correct this problem, read the literature that comes with the mouse. In order for the mouse to interface effectively with the computer, the software that comes with the mouse must be installed in the system as directed by the manufacturer. If you are running DOS, you also want to make sure that the system's CONFIG.SYS and AUTOEXEC.BAT files have been properly set up so that the mouse driver is automatically installed each time the system is booted up. Again, this information is included in the literature that comes with the mouse. The important point here is that you read the literature and follow the directions.

Usually, there is an optional utility program with the software that comes with the mouse that helps you test and adjust the mouse interface (by means of software). These utilities are perhaps one of the best tests of mouse performance.

Windows supplies its own mouse drivers, eliminating the need for any setup in CONFIG.SYS and AUTOEXEC.BAT, and provides a great amount of control over how the mouse appears and operates.

Clicking on the Mouse icon in Control Panel brings up the Mouse Properties window shown in Figure 99. Here you can adjust such important parameters as the double-click speed and left/right-handed operation. Figures 100 and 101 show two additional control windows dealing with the appearance of the mouse pointer. If the mouse is not responding correctly, it may be necessary to change its driver or hardware properties. In Control Panel, double-clicking the System icon and then selecting the Device Manager tab will allow you to double-click Mouse and check the driver information. This information is illustrated in Figure 102. Mouse information is available under the Devices icon in the Windows NT Control Panel. Figure 103 shows the associated Windows NT mouse information.

Troubleshooting the display

Most monitors produced today can be controlled by software. In order to take advantage of this feature, the monitor must be recognized by the operating system. Windows 95/98 will display the

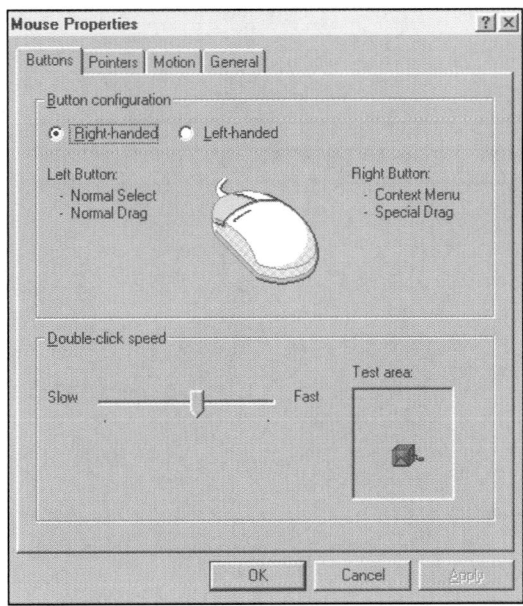

Figure 99
Initial Mouse Properties window

Figure 100
Mouse pointer types

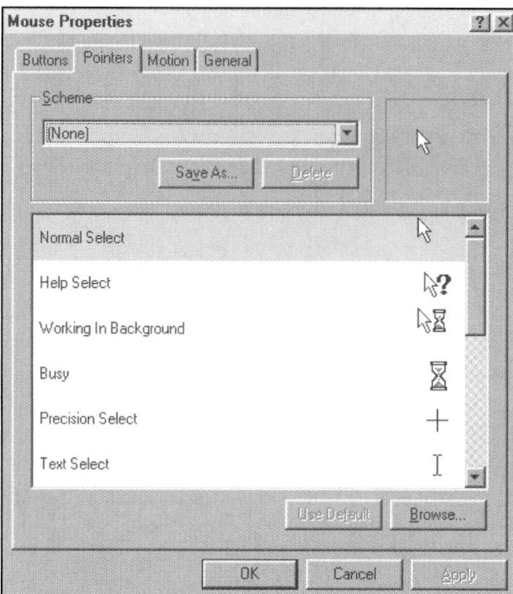

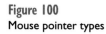

Figure 101
Additional pointer controls

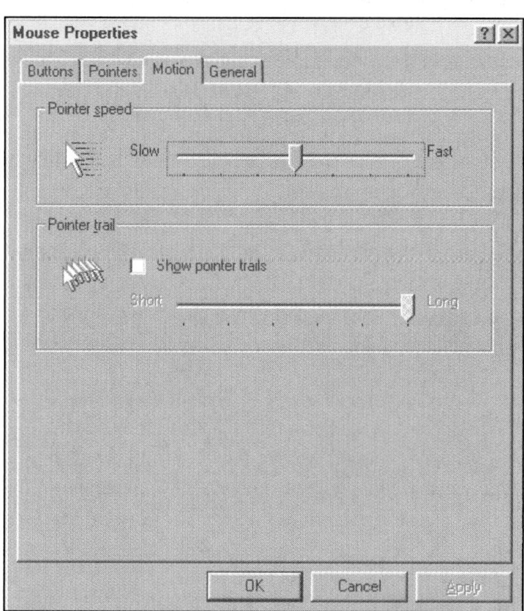

Figure 102
Examining the mouse driver information

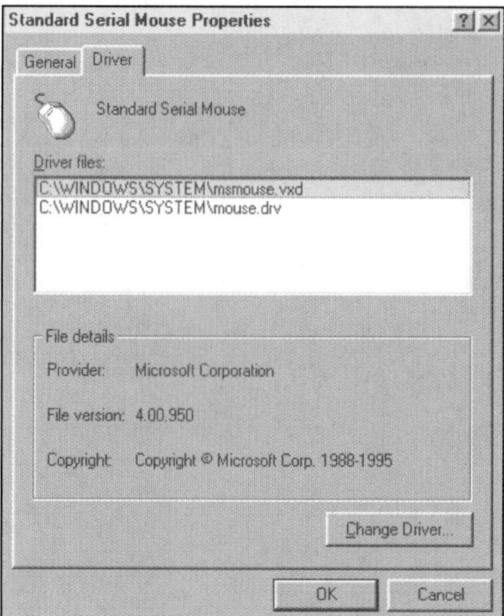

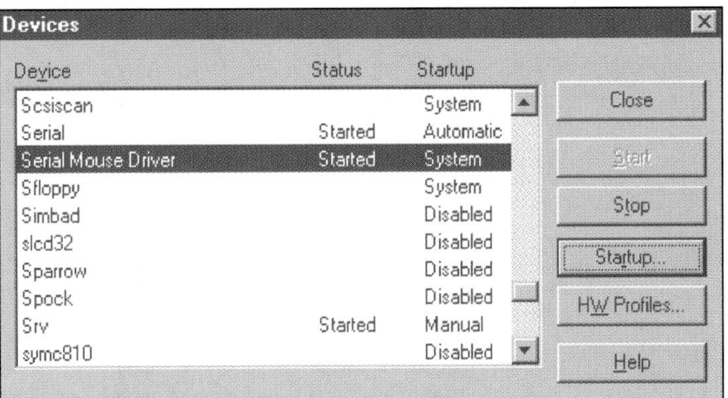

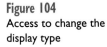

Figure 103
Windows NT Mouse Driver status

monitor's specific information when the Change Display Type button is selected from the Display Properties screen as shown in Figure 104.

The Change Display Type window shows the current settings of the display adapter and the monitor type, as illustrated in Figure 105. Note the additional check box setting used to inform Windows the monitor is Energy Star compliant. If enabled, the monitor may be shut down during a period of inactivity. Be sure to verify the system, video card, and monitor can support Energy Star features before enabling them. Windows NT provides similar screens to accomplish the same tasks.

Troubleshooting the Printer

The most common problems with printers usually involve the quality of the output. Many problems are associated with the supply of ink or toner. Printers also contain many mechanical components that are a common point of failure. In the case of a dot-matrix printer, the ribbon may need to be replaced, the print head may need to be replaced, or the pin feeds may occasionally require some adjustment. For an ink-jet printer, the ink cartridge may become clogged with dried ink and may need to be cleaned to restore the print quality. There is no set schedule for these events to occur.

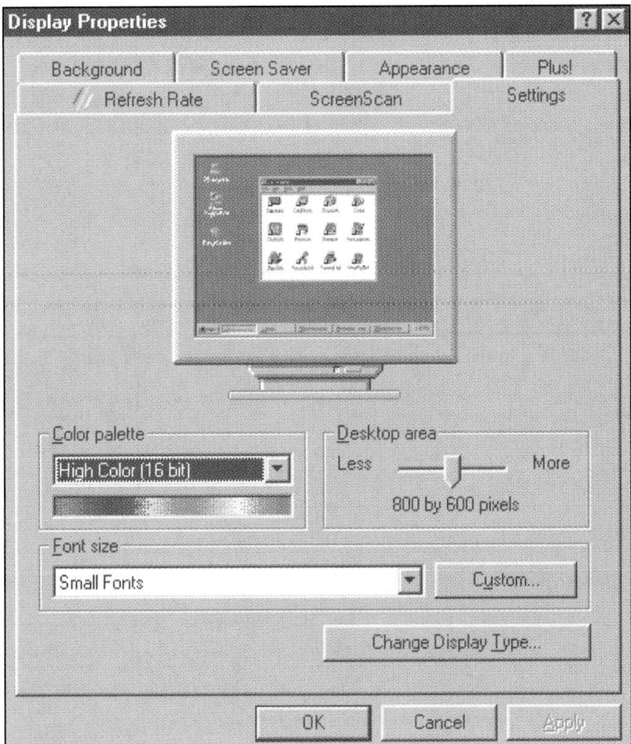

Figure 104
Access to change the display type

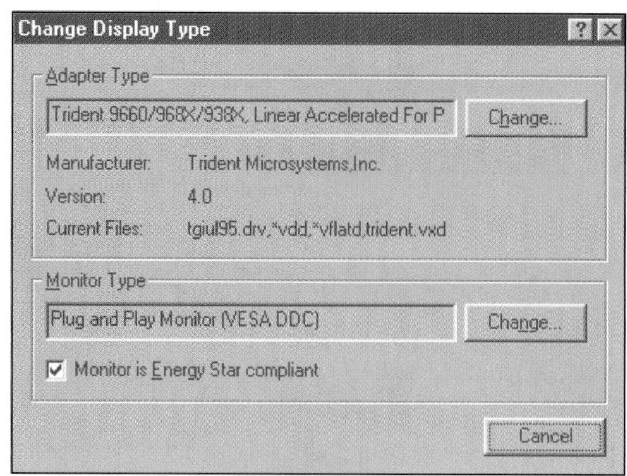

Figure 105
Setting the monitor type

The best course of action is to be prepared for common problems that can be encountered. For example, it is a good idea to keep printer supplies on hand, so when a problem occurs, it can be remedied quickly. Table 46 contains a list of items that should be kept on hand. Remember, many of these items have a certain shelf life. Rotate the stock regularly.

Troubleshooting Memory

One of the simplest ways to determine whether your Windows system has enough RAM to handle its workload is to watch the hard drive light. No or little activity, except when opening or closing an application, is a good sign.

If the hard drive activates sporadically, doing a little work every now and then, the system is borderline. If the activity increases when additional applications are opened, there is a definite lack of RAM.

Frustrated with hard drive activity when only a few applications were open, one user increased the amount of RAM in his system from 32MB to 128MB (taking advantage of a drop in memory prices at that time). Now, even with a taskbar full of applications, the hard drive remains inactive.

Troubleshooting Floppy Drives

Probable causes of what appears to be an FDD failure may be in one of the areas shown in Figure 106. This figure illustrates the relationship of the FDD to the entire computer system. At one end is the software on the disk; at the other extreme is the power cord connection to the electrical outlet. Every part of this system must be functioning properly for the disk drive to do its part. What is important here is to ensure that what appears to be a disk drive problem is not actually a problem caused by one of these other areas.

Troubleshooting Logic

The first step in troubleshooting the disk drive is to classify the problem as occurring in one of the areas shown in Figure 106. Once the area at fault is determined, corrective action may be taken. Figure 107 is a troubleshooting diagram for determining which of these areas may be at fault.

Table 46
Common printer types and supplies

Printer Type	Supplies
Dot matrix	Ribbons, pin-feed paper
Ink jet and bubble jet	Black ink cartridges, color ink cartridges, single-sheet ink-jet paper
Laser	Toner cartridges, single-sheet laser-quality paper
Color laser	Cyan, yellow, magenta, and black toner cartridges, single-sheet color laser-quality paper

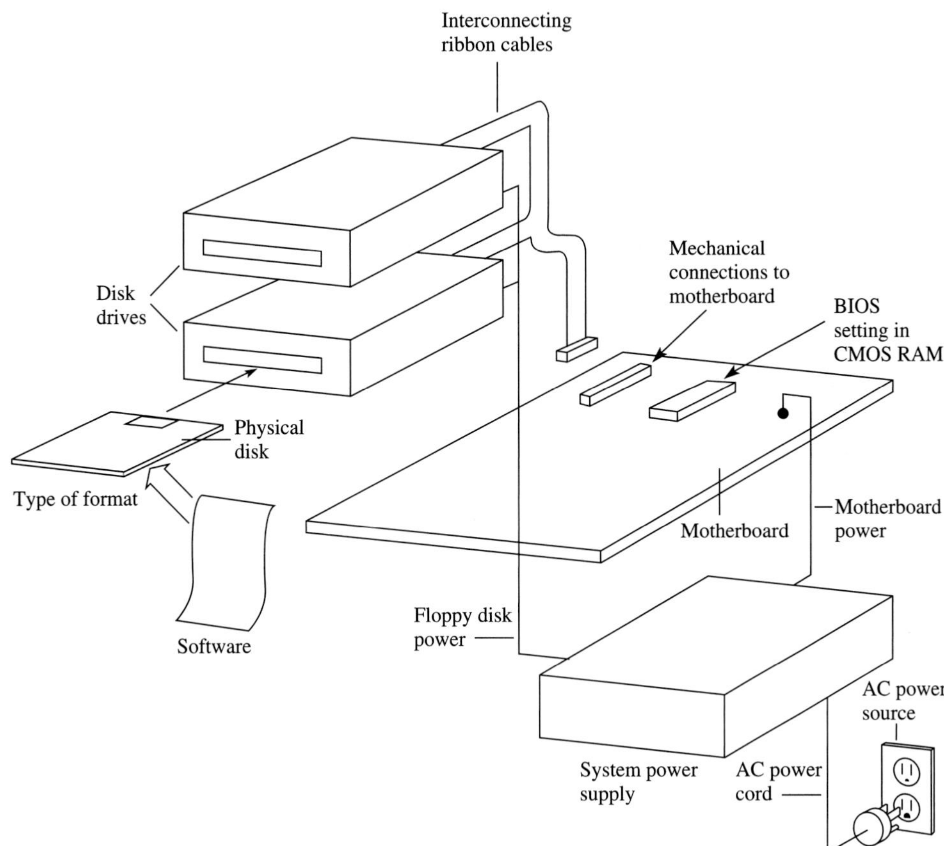

Figure 106
System relationship to floppy disk drive

Troubleshooting Steps

1. *Ask questions.* With all computer servicing, inquire about the history of the system. Was it recently modified? Did anyone attempt to make any changes or repairs? Did the user buy the system used? For example, if the disk drive was recently installed, it may be that certain settings need to be set differently. In this case, you will need to refer to the documentation for the system as well as the newly installed FDD. Asking questions may help you quickly spot the problem, saving you time and money.
2. *Try again.* Sometimes reseating the floppy in the drive fixes any read errors encountered. You could also try using the floppy in a different drive.
3. *Visual inspection.* A good visual inspection may reveal a burned component, an improperly seated cable, a dirty read/write head, or other mechanical evidence of the problem. Remember, a good visual inspection is an important part of any troubleshooting process.
4. *Check BIOS settings.* The system must be aware that a floppy drive exists. This is accomplished by running the BIOS setup program at boot time.
5. *Swap FDD with known good drive.* You need to take some precautions when doing this. It may be that the A: drive has a terminating resistor. You need to refer to documentation for the disk drive in question.
6. *Check drive cable.* In a one-drive system, make sure the connector with the twist is connected to drive A:. In a two-drive system, make sure both connectors are in the correct drives.
7. *Replace drive ribbon cable.* Here, another good visual inspection may be needed. Make sure you refer to the servicing manual to ensure that the cable was correctly installed in the first place. Replacing the cable with a known good one will help determine if the original cable or its connectors are at fault.
8. *Replace drive power cable.* This may be difficult on some systems because the power cable may be permanently attached to the power supply. If this is the case, skip this step and go on to the next one.
9. *Replace system power unit.* Doing this will help eliminate the problem of a power unit supplying the correct voltages when the power demands on it are small, but failing, as a result of the increased

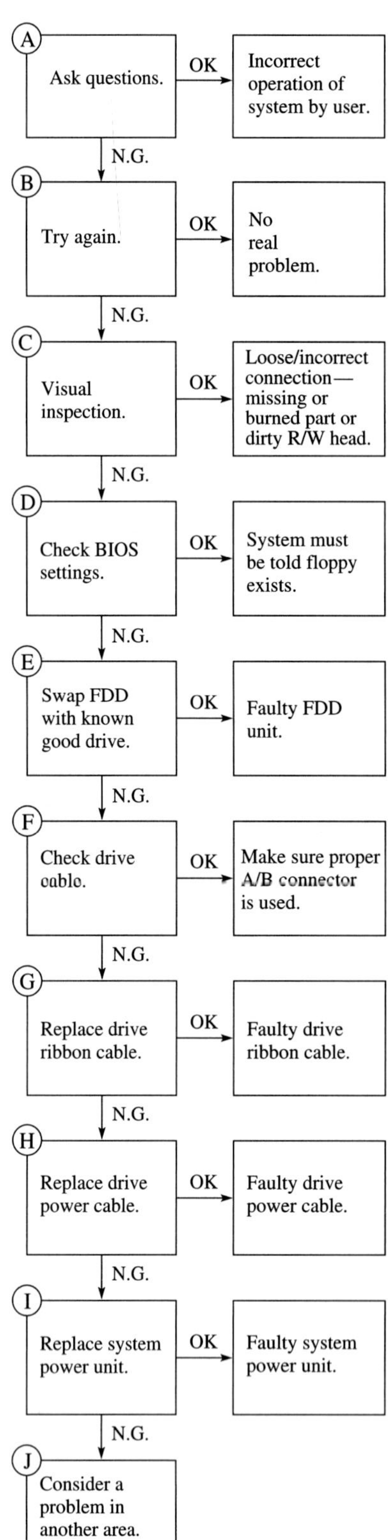

Figure 107
FDD troubleshooting chart

power demand, when a disk drive motor is activated (such as when the FDD is attempting to read a disk). Make a note of the power rating of the power supply; if it is below 100 W, substitute another known good power unit with a higher power rating.

10. *Consider a problem in another area.* If all the preceding steps fail to locate the problem, the problem is in another area of the unit. The most likely area in this case is the motherboard.

Troubleshooting Modems

Table 47 lists some of the most common problems encountered in telephone modems. As you will see, most of the problems are software related.

Other common problems encountered involve very simple hardware considerations. For example, telephone modems usually come with two separate telephone line connectors.

The purpose of the phone input is to connect a telephone, not the output line from the modem, to the telephone wall jack. The phone input is simply a convenience. It allows the telephone to be used without having to disconnect a telephone line from the computer to the wall telephone jack. If you mistakenly connect the line from the wall telephone jack to the phone input, you will be able to dial out from your communications software, but your system will hang up on you. Make sure that the telephone line that goes to the telephone wall jack comes from the *line output* and not the *phone output* jack of your modem.

Another common hardware problem is a problem in your telephone line. This can be quickly checked by simply using your phone to get through to the other party. If you can't do this, then neither can your computer.

A problem that is frequently encountered in an office or school building involves the phone system used within the building. You may have to issue extra commands on your software in order to get your call out of the building. In this case you need to check with your telecommunications manager or the local phone company.

Sometimes your problem is simply a noisy line. This may have to do with your communications provider or it may have to do with how your telephone line is installed. You may have to switch to a long-distance telephone company that can provide service over more reliable communication lines. Or you may have to physically trace where your telephone line goes from the wall telephone jack. If this is an old installation, your telephone line could be running in the wall right next to the AC power lines. If this is the case, you need to reroute the phone line.

Troubleshooting Sound Cards

One of the most common reasons a new CD-ROM drive or sound card does not work has to do with the way its interrupts and/or DMA channels are assigned.

Figure 108 shows the location of the sound card in the hardware list provided by Device Manager. The AWE-32 indicates that the sound card is capable of advanced wave effects using 32 voices.

Figure 109 shows the interrupt and DMA assignments for the sound card. Typically, interrupt 5 is used (some network interface cards also use interrupt 5), as well as DMA channels 1 and 5. If the standard settings do not work, you need to experiment until you find the right combinations.

Table 47
Common telephone modem problems

Symptom	Possible Cause(s)
Can't connect	Usually this means that your baud rates or numbers of data bits are not matched. This is especially true if you see garbage on the screen, especially the { character.
Can't see input	You are typing in information but it doesn't appear on the screen. However, if the person on the other side can see what you are typing, it means that you need to turn your local echo on. In this way, what you type will be echoed back to you, and you will see it on your screen.
Get double characters	Here you are typing information and getting double characters. This means that if you type HELLO, you get HHEELLLLOO; at the same time, what the other computer is getting appears normal. This means that you need to turn your local echo off. In this way, you will not be echoing back the extra character. With some systems *half-duplex* refers to local echo on, whereas *full duplex* refers to local echo off.

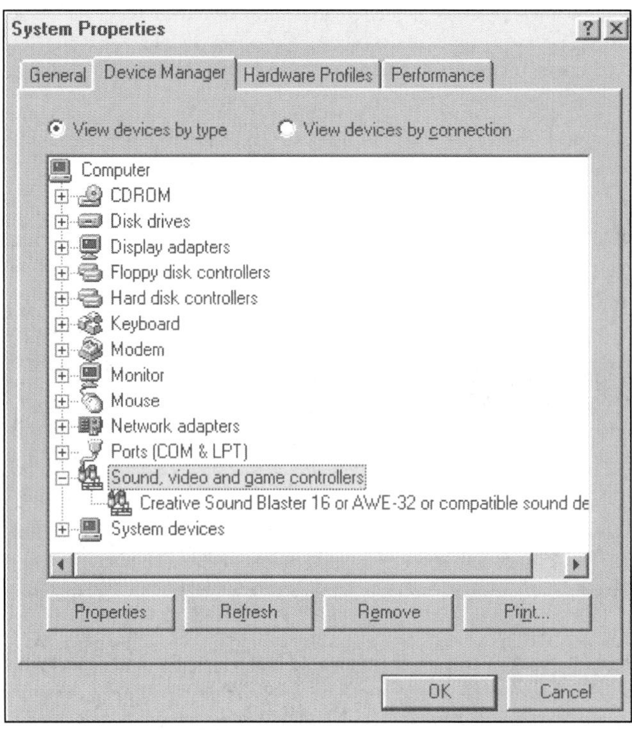

Figure 108
Selecting the sound card

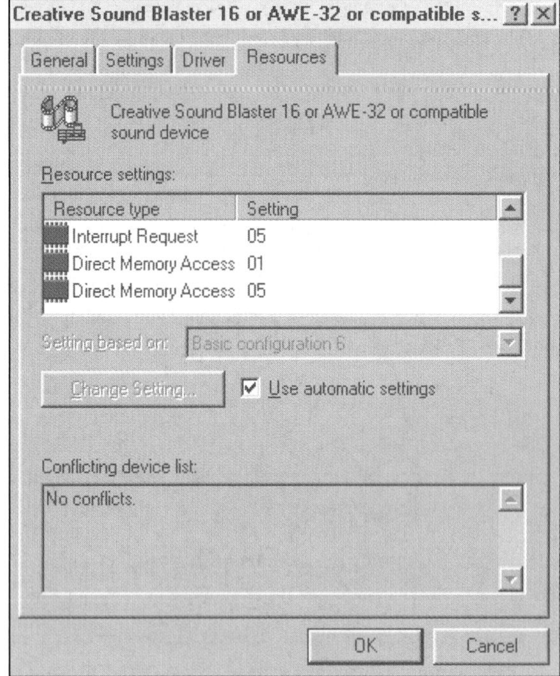

Figure 109
Sound card settings

Troubleshooting CD-ROM Drives

CD-ROM drives are usually reliable and are not prone to actual failure of the device. Usually trouble is more likely to be a matter of configuration or software drivers. A CD-ROM drive that is not recognized by the system indicates a potential problem with cabling, master/slave jumper settings or software drivers. A CD-ROM drive that is not detected at boot time indicate that a BIOS setting may be incorrect or a system resource is in conflict. Check the Device Manager display to determine if a resource issue exists.

If you are trying to use IDE bus mastering drivers, refer to the instructions that came with them and look for a section listing specific models of CD-ROM drives that will not work by themselves on a channel with bus mastering drivers installed. If the drive is listed, then the bus mastering drivers must be removed, or move your CD-ROM to be a slave to a hard disk on one of your channels.

Troubleshooting DVD Drives

Problems with DVD drives are similar to CD-ROMs. Check BIOS settings, cable connections, master/slave jumper settings and software drivers.Check the Device Manager display to determine if a resource issue exists.

Troubleshooting BIOS

Problems with system BIOS typically prevent a computer system from booting. On a system with a static copy of BIOS included on an integrated circuit, it is usually necessary to obtain a new BIOS chip. If the BIOS settings are stored in a flash memory, then it is necessary to update to a newer version of the system BIOS available from the manufacturer website. Perform the BIOS update according the manufacturer instructions and take advantage of an opportunity to save a copy of the currently installed BIOS to disk in case there are problems encountered while updating the BIOS.

Troubleshooting USB Problems

Problems with the USB port prevent USB devices from working properly. It is always a good idea to verify the system resource settings to ensure that the problem is not attributed to a conflict with the IRQ, or I/O addresses. Examine the Device Manager display for the USB device to verify the settings.

Because USB devices are Plug and Play devices, there are no opportunities to configure the devices. Most of the time the problems can be traced to one of the following conditions:

- Malfunctioning or incorrectly configured hardware
- Malfunctioning, incorrectly configured, or missing device driver
- Mismatched cabling
- Out-of-date firmware or basic input/output system (BIOS)
- Improperly configured root hub

Typical Methods to identify and correct USB problems

For a malfunctioning or incorrectly-configured device plugged into a USB port, the computer will stop responding. Often it is necessary to turn off the computer and turn it back on to reset the bus. Unfortunately, it is usually difficult to identify which device is malfunctioning or incorrectly configured. Try to use another computer that is working correctly to see if that computer encounters the same problem.

If the device is plugged into a secondary hub, unplug the device from the hub and then plug the device directly into the root hub. Check the Device Manager to be certain that the root hub is functioning correctly. If the root hub is displayed with an exclamation point in a yellow circle, verify that the BIOS is assigning an interrupt request (IRQ) to the root USB controller. This is required for the device driver to be loaded. The IRQ line is assigned in the computer's BIOS, and usually IRQ 9 is assigned.

Check the Power tab in USB Root Hub properties to verify that the power requirements of the bus are not being exceeded. USB devices can draw a maximum of 500 milliamps for each connection. If a USB device attempts to draw more power the specification recommends that the computer disable that specific port until the computer power is cycled.

For a malfunctioning, incorrectly configured, or missing device driver, the computer may prompt for a device driver, check with the manufacturer of the device to determine if a driver is available.

For a mismatched cabling problem, there are two types of USB cables, high speed and low speed. Low-speed cables differ from high-speed cables in the shielding. If a high-speed device uses a low-speed cable, you can cause signal distortion over longer distances.

Verify the entire USB chain is working correctly to be certain that a device that requires the ability to draw power from the hub is not plugged into the chain on the other side of a non-powered hub. This causes that hub and all of the devices down the chain to be suspended. If the hub is a powered hub, verify that the power supply for that hub is configured properly.

For out-of-date Firmware or BIOS check to make sure the most up-to-date firmware is installed for the system BIOS as well as each individual device. The symptoms of incorrectly configured firmware are duplication of the USB devices. This is a common problem with USB printers and modems.

Troubleshooting NIC Cards

A problem with a NIC card is typically associated with cabling, mismatched system resources, and conflicts. For a new installation, it is not unusual for many different problems to surface. In general, it is a good idea to perform a cold boot to see if the device drivers will load properly. Check the Device Manager to confirm that no conflicts are present and that the system indicates the device is working properly. Many times, it is necessary to reinstall the NIC and associated network protocols.

In a system that suddenly reports problems, check the cabling and try to determine what modifications have been made to the system.

Troubleshooting CMOS

A worn-out battery will cause the CMOS to lose its configuration information. Typically a system will always display the same date and restart the clock at midnight. Make sure to replace the battery with the same type.

Troubleshooting Power Supplies

If power is turned on and nothing happens, the cause may be an incorrectly seated adapter card. It is also possible that the AC power connector is not fully seated in its socket. A bad smell (from an overheated component) is a sign that the power supply must be replaced.

Troubleshooting Post Error Codes

POST errors are reported by BIOS using a series of beeps and/or a numeric code. Look up the POST error code to determine which component is causing the problem. In almost all personal computer POSTs, the numeric error codes can be broken into two major parts: a device number and a two-digit error code. The device number followed by two zeros (such as 100 for the system board) indicates that no errors have been detected. Specific error codes should be referenced using the manuals that come with the computer system. Table 48 lists the major error codes and their causes. The table uses numbers such as 4xx. This means that a 4 represents an error in the monochrome display adapter. The xx represents any value from 00 (meaning no problem) to 99, indicating the specific problem in that part of the computer system. Thus, error codes for the monochrome display adapter are between 400 and 499.

Table 48
POST Error Codes

Error Code	Cause
01x	Undetermined problem
02x	Power supply errors
1xx	System board errors
2xx	RAM memory errors
3xx	Keyboard errors
4xx	Monochrome display adapter errors
4xx	On PS/2 systems, parallel port errors
5xx	Color graphics adapter card errors
6xx	Floppy drive or adapter card errors
7xx	Math coprocessor errors
9xx	Parallel printer adapter errors
10xx	Alternate parallel printer adapter errors
11xx	Asynchronous communications adapter errors
12xx	Alternate asynchronous communications adapter errors
13xx	Game adapter control errors
14xx	Printer errors
15xx	Synchronous data link control: communications adapter errors
16xx	Display emulation errors (specifically 327x, 5520, 525x)
17xx	Fixed disk errors
18xx	I/O expansion unit errors
19xx	3270 PC attachment card errors
20xx	Binary synchronous communications adapter errors
21xx	Alternate binary synchronous communications adapter errors
22xx	Cluster adapter errors
24xx	Enhanced graphics adapter (EGA) errors
29xx	Color or graphics printer errors
30xx	Primary PC network adapter errors
31xx	Secondary PC network adapter errors
33xx	Compact printer errors
36xx	General-purpose interface bus (GPIB) adapter errors
38xx	Data acquisition adapter errors
39xx	Professional graphics controller errors
48xx	Internal modem errors
71xx	Voice communications adapter errors

Error Code	Cause
73xx	3.5-inch external disk drive errors
74xx	On PS/2 systems, display adapter errors
85xx	IBM expanded memory adapter (XMA) errors
86xx	PS/2 systems point device errors
89xx	Music card errors
100xx	PS/2 multiprotocol adapter errors
104xx	PS/2 fixed disk errors
112xx	SCSI adapter errors

Appendix C MathPro

1 MathPro

One of the most useful tools that is included in your first quarter ITT Technical Institute instructional materials is the MathPro software package. This software is an invaluable tool for acquiring the mathematical skills that you will need to succeed in the Problem Solving course. In addition to offering an abundance of problems on which you may practice, MathPro contains short instructional video clips for each topic. These mini-lectures are given by the author of the mathematics portion of your Problem Solving Tools book, K. Elayn Martin-Gay.

Because accessing a particular program on the computer is discussed in your Introduction to Computers course, our focus here is on using the software. Once you have opened the software, click on the chapters button on the toolbar to see the following screen:

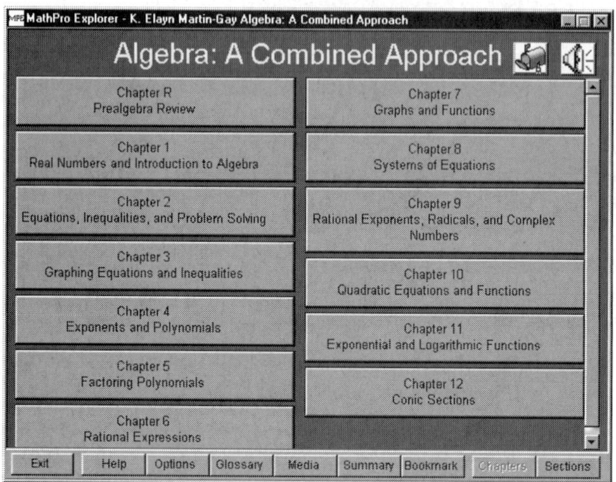

This screen is organized by the chapter titles from Part V of your Tools book. The numbering scheme for the software matches the chapters, subsections, and objectives of your book. If you look at the bottom of the window, you will find a button labeled "media." When you click this button, a listing of the video clips included in the software appears in a smaller window.

With your instructor's guidance this term, you will be directed to view specific video clips that may help you in solving a particular Thought Project.

Another important aspect of the software is the algorithmically generated problem sets that may be worked in a number of different modes. You may choose to view a worked-out example before trying a given problem; or you may receive step-by-step assistance with detailed explanations of the math concept under study. As an example, examine a beginning mathematical concept that will allow you to focus on learning the software itself.

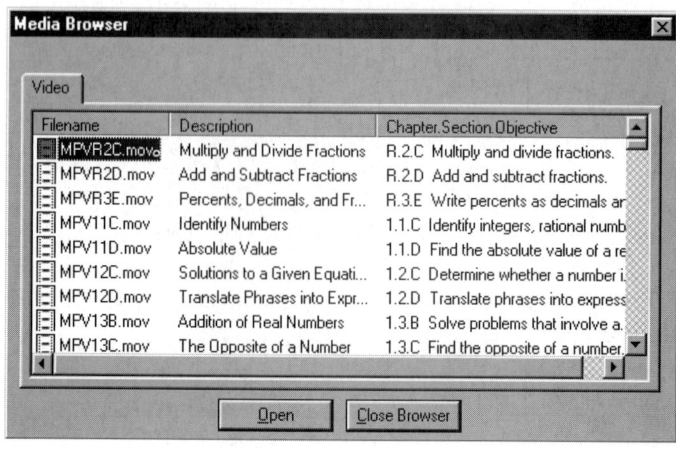

Suppose that while solving a problem, you determine that using mathematics is the best problem solving strategy. However, to use the strategy effectively, you must be comfortable adding, subtracting, multiplying, and dividing signed numbers; recognizing that your skills in this area are rusty, your turn to MathPro. By looking at the introductory MathPro screen, you see that this topic is discussed in Chapter 1. When you click on the Chapter 1 button, the following window appears:

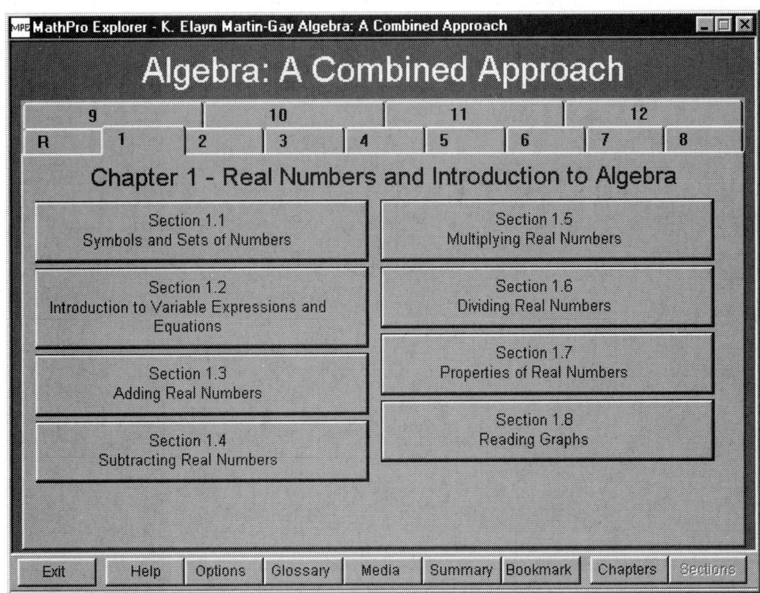

The information on the screen shows that real numbers are covered in several sections, 1.3, 1.4, 1.5, and 1.6. By subdividing the topics, you may focus on learning each new mathematical concept independently. Click on an individual section to study a given subtopic. Notice, that if you click on the media button, the numbering of the video clips corresponds to the chapters and sections from the Tools book.

If you have not already done so, it would be a benefit to become familiar with the MathPro software package. A good place to begin is by watching the Introduction to MathPro video that may be accessed by clicking on the "loud speaker" icon on the chapter menu screen.

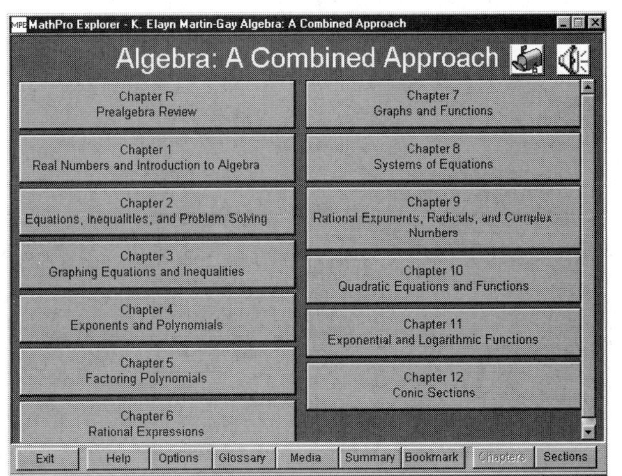

In addition to being a powerful support element for this course, MathPro is a software package that can help you throughout your entire technical career.

Appendix D Task Guide

This book is designed to be kept as a handy reference beside your computer even after you have completed all the projects and exercises. Any time you have difficulty recalling the sequence of steps or a shortcut needed to achieve a result, look up the general category in the alphabetized listing that follows, and quickly home in on your task at hand. For your convenience, some tasks have been duplicated under more than one category.

For the greatest efficiency in using this Task Guide, take a few minutes to familiarize yourself with the order of the applications, the main categories within an application, and keywords before you begin your search. The first three sections—Application and File Management, Customization, and Help—are common to all applications.

To Do This	Use This Command

Tasks Common to All Applications

Application and File Management

To Do This	Use This Command
Exit application	Click the Close button and choose Yes if prompted to save your changes.
Open existing file	Start the application. Click the Open button, locate the file you want, and click Open.
Save file	Click the Save button. Type a name in the File name text box and select the location to save the file in the Save in box. Click Save.
Save file with new name	Choose File, Save As. In the File name text box, type the new name; change the location in the Save in box if necessary. Click Save.
Start an Office application	Click the Start button. Select Programs from the Start menu; find and click the application that you want to launch.

Customization

To Do This	Use This Command
Office Assistant: turn off	Right-click the Office Assistant, and choose Options. Clear the Use the Office Assistant check box, and click OK.
ScreenTips: turn on	Choose Tools, Customize, Options. Check the box or Show ScreenTips on toolbars; click OK.
Toolbars: display or hide	Right-click any visible toolbar; click a toolbar from the list displayed.
Toolbars: separate the Standard and Formatting toolbars	Choose Tools, Customize, Options; uncheck the Standard and Formatting toolbars share one row box.

continues ▶

To Do This	Use This Command
Help	
Access Help	Click the Microsoft Help button or press F1.
Close Help	Click the Close button in the upper-right corner of the Help window.
Expand or contract Help topic	Double-click the book icon.
Find Help topics	Enter a question in the Office Assistant balloon; click Search.
Navigation pane: display or hide	Click the Show button to display; click the Hide button to remove.
Office Assistant: hide or show	Choose Help, Hide the Office Assistant (or Help, Show the Office Assistant).
Office Assistant: how to use	The following procedure can be used for all Microsoft applications. Click the Microsoft Word Help button on the toolbar, or choose Help, Microsoft Word Help from the menu. Type a question, and click Search. If you want to use the Index, click the Show button in the Help window.
Web: Office Help online	Choose Help, Office on the Web. Select an application on which to get help, and choose the type of help for which you are looking. Follow the onscreen instructions.

Basics Task Guide

Basics of Office 2000	
Menu: how to use	Click the menu choice, and click your option from the drop-down menu. If the menu option has an arrow on the right, move the pointer over the option and make a selection from the submenu that displays.
Mouse: how to use	Click the left mouse button once to select an object; double-click to run a program or open a window. Click the right mouse button once on an object to activate the shortcut menu.
Print document using button	Click the Print button. The entire document will print.
Print document using menu	Choose File, Print from the menu. Select the options you want, such as the page numbers and number of copies, and click OK.
Shut down computer	Click the Start button and select Shut Down from the Start menu. Follow the shut-down procedures for your computer.
Start button: how to use	Click the Start button in the taskbar. Release the mouse, and move up to select one of the Start menu options.
Start Windows	Turn on your computer. Press Esc to bypass security or type your user name and password, if necessary. Windows loads automatically.
Files, Folders, and Disks	
Copy file	In Windows Explorer or in the Office application's Open dialog box, right-click the filename and select Copy from the shortcut menu. Select the destination drive and folder, right-click in the Contents area, and select Paste from the shortcut menu.
Copy floppy disk	Place the source disk in the disk drive. In Windows Explorer, right-click the drive A icon and select Copy Disk from the shortcut menu. Follow the instructions in the dialog box.
Create new folder	Select a disk drive in Windows Explorer; right-click the Contents area. Choose New from the shortcut menu and select Folder. Type a new folder name and press ↵Enter.

To Do This	Use This Command
Files, Folders, and Disks	
Delete file or folder	In Windows Explorer, right-click the file or folder and select Delete from the shortcut menu.
Format disk	Put a disk in the floppy drive and open the Windows Explorer. Right-click the drive A icon and select Format from the shortcut menu. Choose from the format options and click Start.
Move file	In Windows Explorer, make sure the destination folder is visible; click the file and drag it to the destination folder.
Rename file or folder	In Windows Explorer, right-click the file or folder and select Rename from the shortcut menu. Type the new name.
Windows	
Close	Click the Close button in the upper-right corner of the window.
Help with Windows	Click the Start button and choose Help. Choose Contents to read the Help menu like a book; choose Index to see Microsoft's preselected categories, and choose Find (or Search) to search on key words.
Maximize and restore	Click the Maximize button to make the window fill the entire screen. Click the Restore button to change back to the previous size.
Minimize	Click the Minimize button. The window is hidden, but is still available on the taskbar.
Move	Point to the window title bar. Click and hold down the left mouse button while dragging the window to a new location.
Multiple windows: working with	Open two or more programs at the same time. Click a button on the taskbar to switch between programs.
Resize	Move the pointer to the lower-right corner of the window until it turns into a two-sided arrow. Click and hold down the mouse button while dragging to resize the window.

Word Task Guide

Application and File Management	
Close document	Click the Close Window button.
Exit Word	Click the Close button.
Open existing document	Click the Open button. Locate the file using the Look in box. Select the file and click Open.
Print document	Make sure the printer is turned on and click the Print button. Or choose File, Print, set the various options, and click OK.
Save document with new name	Choose File, Save As. Choose the location to save the file using the Save in box. Enter a name in the File name box and click Save.
Save new document	Click the Save button. Type a name in the File Name box. Select the location to save the document in the Save in box. Click Save.
Start Word and open new document	Click the Start button; select Programs, Microsoft Word.
Clip Art	
Add clip art	Place your insertion point where you want the clip art to be displayed. Choose Insert, Picture, Clip Art. Select the category and click the image you want. Choose the Insert clip button from the pop-up menu.

continues ▶

To Do This	Use This Command
Clip Art	
Move clip art	Click the clip art image to select it. Move the mouse pointer onto the image and click and drag it to a new location.
Resize clip art	Click the clip art image. Position the mouse pointer over one of the corner sizing handles; click and drag to increase or decrease the size of the image.
Wrap text around clip art	Select the clip art image. Choose Format, Picture. Select the Layout tab. Select the wrapping style you prefer and the alignment option. Click OK.
Display, View, and Movement	
Move insertion point	Scroll to the page you want; position the mouse pointer at the location you want, and click. Use the arrow keys to move up and down one line at a time or one character at a time.
Move up and down a page	Use the vertical scrollbar to move up and down a page by clicking the Next Page or Previous Page arrows, clicking the up or down arrows, or clicking and dragging the scroll box.
Preview document	Click the Print Preview button. Click the document to switch between a full-page view and a close-up view. Click Close.
Preview multiple pages	Click the Print Preview button. Click the Multiple Pages button, and drag the pointer across the page icons to indicate the number of pages you want to view. Click the mouse.
Select Normal view	Click the Normal button on the horizontal scrollbar.
Document	
Footer: create	Choose View, Header and Footer. Click the Switch Between Header and Footer button. Enter the information you want to be displayed in the footer. Use the Header and Footer toolbar buttons to insert date, time, or page numbers. Press Tab to move to the center or right area of the footer. Click OK.
Grammar: correct	Right-click a word or phrase that is underlined with a green, jagged line. Choose the suggested replacement or Ignore from the shortcut menu.
Header or footer: change margin	Choose View, Header and Footer. Click and drag the margin indicator to a new location.
Header or footer: different on first page	Choose File, Page Setup, and click the Layout tab. Click the Different first page check box. Click OK. Move to the first page and create a new header or footer as desired.
Header or footer: format text	Choose View, Header and Footer. Select the text you want to format and use the formatting buttons on the Formatting toolbar.
Header or footer: move tab locations	Choose View, Header and Footer. In either the header or the footer, click and drag the tab indicator to a new location.
Header: create	Choose View, Header and Footer. Type the information you want to be displayed in the header. Press Tab to move to the center or right area of the header. Click OK.
Margins: set	Choose File, Page Setup, and select the Margins tab. Type the margin desired in the boxes for the Top, Bottom, Left, or Right margin. Click OK.
Page breaks: insert	Place the insertion point where you want the new page and press Ctrl+Enter.
Page numbers: insert	Choose Insert, Page Numbers. Select the location where you want the page numbers to display; select the alignment; click OK.
Select the whole document	Press Ctrl and click anywhere in the left margin.

To Do This	Use This Command
Document	
Spelling: correct	Right-click a word that is underlined with a red jagged line. Select the correct word from the shortcut menu, or choose Ignore All, or Add.
Paragraph	
Bulleted list: create	Select the text you want to place in a bulleted list, and click the Bullets button.
Center a line of text	Select the line you want to center, and click the Center button.
Format painter: use	Select the text that displays the format you want to copy. Double-click the Format Painter button. Click and drag across the text you want to format. Select other text to which you want to apply the same formatting. When you are done, click the Format Painter button to turn it off.
Indent: create, hanging	Select the paragraphs that are to be changed. Choose Format, Paragraph. Choose Hanging from the Special drop-down menu. Change the amount in the By box. Click OK.
Indent: first line of a paragraph	Select the paragraph you want to indent; choose Format, Paragraph. Choose First line from the Special drop-down menu. Change the amount of indentation in the By box. Click OK.
Indent: numbered or bulleted list	Select the list and click the Increase Indent button.
Justify a paragraph	Select the paragraph you want to justify, and click the Justify button.
Line spacing: add empty space after paragraphs	Select the paragraphs that are to be changed. Choose Format, Paragraph. Change the spacing in the After box to the setting you want. Click OK.
Line spacing: change	Select the paragraph(s) or text you want to affect; choose Format, Paragraph. Select the spacing preferred from the Line spacing drop-down list.
Numbered list: create	Select the text you want to place in a numbered list, and click the Numbering button.
Numbered or bulleted list: create from scratch	Click the Numbering button or the Bullets button; type the list. Click the same button again to turn off the numbers or bullets.
Select a paragraph	Triple-click anywhere in the paragraph.
Tabs: remove	Click and drag the tab stop indicator down and off of the ruler.
Tabs: set	Select Format, Tabs. Enter the position (in inches) for the first stop in the Tab stop position box. Select the alignment and any leader options. Click Set. Repeat process to set additional tabs. Click OK.
Table	
Add column to table	Place the insertion point in the column where you want to add a new column. Choose Table, Insert, and select the location where you want the column added.
Add row anywhere in table	Place the insertion point in the row where you want to add a new row. Choose Table, Insert, select the location where you want the row added.
Add rows to end of table	Place the insertion point at the end of the last cell and press Tab.
Align text in table	Select the column or row you want to align and click one of the alignment buttons on the toolbar.
AutoFormat: use	Choose Table, Table AutoFormat. Select the format option you prefer, and click OK.
Center table on the page	Choose Table, Select, Table. Click the Center button.

continues ▶

To Do This	Use This Command
Table	
Enter information in a table	Place the insertion point in the first cell in the table and type. Press Tab to move to the next cell and enter the information for the next cell. Continue this process until all information is added.
Insert table	Place the insertion point where you want the table to be inserted. Click the Insert Table button. Move the mouse pointer to indicate the number of rows and columns you want and click the mouse button.
Navigate in table	Press Shift+Tab to move to the previous cell. Use the arrow keys to move up and down the cells.
Select column or row in table	Place your insertion point in the column or row you want to select. Click Table, Select, Column or Table, Select, Row.
Text Characters	
Click and type	Click the Print Layout View button; move the pointer to the location on the page where you want to type, double-click, and type.
Correct errors after insertion point	Position the insertion point; press Del to remove one character at a time to the right of the insertion point.
Correct errors before insertion point	Position the insertion point; press Backspace to remove one character at a time to the left of the insertion point.
Delete a phrase	Click and drag across the text you want to replace to select it, and press Del.
Delete a word	Double-click the word and press Del.
Enter text	Type the text you want, pressing Enter only at the end of a paragraph, or to insert a blank line.
Font: change emphasis	Select the text you want to change; click the Bold, Italic, or Underline button to add that emphasis.
Font: change size	Select the text you want to change; click the down arrow next to the Font Size box, and click the font size you want to use.
Font: change type	Select the text you want to change; click the down arrow next to the Font box, and click the font type you want to use.
Insert text	Place the insertion at the location where you want to insert text and type.
Move text using cut-and-paste	Select the text you want to move; click the Cut button. Move the insertion point to the location where you want to insert the text, and click the Paste button.
Move text using drag-and-drop	Select the text you want to move. Point to the text and click and drag it to the new location. Release the mouse button when the I-beam pointer displays at the location where you want to insert the text.
Redo changes	Click the Redo button to reverse the last undo action. Click the drop-down arrow next to the Redo button, and select the last several actions listed to redo many actions.
Replace text	Click and drag across the text and type the new text.
Replace word	Double-click the word and type the new word.
Select a block of text	Click at the beginning of the block of text, press Shift and click at the end of the block.
Undo changes	Click the Undo button to undo the last change. Click the drop-down arrow next to the Undo button, and select the oldest item you want to undo. All actions up to that point will be undone.

To Do This	Use This Command

Excel Task Guide

Application and File Management

To Do This	Use This Command
Close workbook	Click the Close Window button on the menu bar.
Create new, blank workbook	Choose File, New, or click the New button.
Exit Excel	Click the Close button on the title bar.
Open existing workbook	Start Excel. Click the Open button. Locate the file you want and click Open.
Print worksheet	Click the Print button or choose File, Print from the menu. Change options if necessary in the Print dialog box, and click OK.
Save file with new name	Choose File, Save As. In the File name box, type the new name; change the Save in location box if necessary. Click Save.
Save workbook	Click the Save button. Change the Save in box to the location where you want to save the file. Type a filename in the File name box. Click the Save button.
Start Excel	Click the Start button, Programs, Microsoft Excel.

Cell Contents and Movement

To Do This	Use This Command
Active cell: change	Use the direction arrows on the keypad or click the cell you want.
AutoComplete	Press ↵Enter or an arrow key to accept the entry suggested by Excel; keep typing if the entry suggested by Excel is not correct.
AutoFill: use to create a pattern	Enter a pattern in two consecutive cells (for example, 10, 20, or Week 1, Week 2); select the pattern cells; drag the fill handle in the lower-right corner of the selected cells.
AutoSum	Click the AutoSum button in the toolbar and press ↵Enter to accept the SUM function suggested by Excel or edit the suggested formula.
Copy to adjacent cells	Select the cell(s) you want to copy; click and drag the fill handle to adjacent cells.
Copy to nonadjacent cells	Select the cell(s) you want to copy; click the Copy button. Select the cells to which you want to copy; click the Paste button.
Delete: cell contents only	Select the cell(s) and press Del.
Delete: with options	Select the cell(s); choose Edit, Clear; select among the options.
Edit: entire cell contents	Select the cell and begin typing the new data.
Edit: part of cell contents	Double-click the cell to change to edit mode, press ←Backspace or Del to remove unwanted characters; add others as needed.
Enter text or numbers into cells	Select the cell and type the data. Press ↵Enter to finish the entry.
Fill cells with formulas	Select the cell with the formula you want to replicate; the cell to place the formula in adjacent cells.
Formula: combine operations	Select the cell; type an equal sign, and type the formula. Use parentheses around the operations you want performed first, such as =(A2+B2)/A3.
Formula: create using absolute cell references	Type a dollar sign in front of both the column letter and row number of cell reference you want to be absolute, such as $A$1. Or type the cell reference and press F4.

continues ▶

To Do This	Use This Command
Cell Contents and Movement	
Formula: create using cell references	Type an equal sign, and type the first cell address, math symbol for the operation you want to perform, and type the second cell address. Press ↵Enter.
Formula: create using point and click	Type an equal sign; click the first cell, type the math symbol for the operation you want to perform, and click the second cell. Press ↵Enter.
Function: COUNTIF	Select the cell where you want the count to be displayed. Click the Paste Function button, and choose COUNTIF function from the Statistical category. Select the range to be counted, and enter the criteria in quotation marks. Click OK.
Function: enter by typing	Type an equal sign and the function name, followed by one or more arguments within parentheses. Separate arguments with commas.
Function: paste function	Click the Paste Function button in the toolbar; select a function category, and select a function name within that category, and click OK. Enter the function arguments in the Formula Palette. Click OK when all the arguments are entered.
Function: PMT	Select the cell where you want the payment amount to be displayed. Click the Paste Function button, and choose PMT function from the Financial category. Enter a value or select a cell reference for Rate, Nper, and PV arguments. Click OK.
Labels and numbers	Select the cell; type the desired letters, numbers or other symbols; press ↵Enter or an arrow key.
Merge and center cells	Select the cells you want to merge, and click the Merge and Center button.
Move one cell to the right	Press Tab.
Reference: absolute	Precede the column letter and row number with a dollar sign (for example, $A$4).
Reference: relative	Omit dollar signs in a cell reference (for example, A4).
Select group of contiguous cells	Click the first cell in the group. Hold down the left mouse button and drag to the last cell in the group. Or click the first cell; position the mouse pointer over the last cell; hold down ⇧Shift, and click the last cell in the group.
Select individual cells	Move the mouse pointer to the cell you want to select and click the left mouse button.
Select noncontiguous groups of cells	Click and drag over the first group of cells. Hold down Ctrl and click and drag over the second group of cells.
Sequential text headings: create	Type the first label in a series such as Monday, 1st Quarter, Project 1. Press ↵Enter. Click and drag the fill handle in the lower-right corner of the cell to the connecting cells to complete the sequence.
Series of dates: create	Type the first date in the series and press ↵Enter. Click and drag the fill handle in the lower-right corner of the cell to the connecting cells to complete the series.
Series of numbers: create customized	Enter the numbers necessary to establish a pattern for the series. Select the cells. Click and drag the fill handle in the lower-right corner of the cell to the connecting cells to complete the series.
Chart	
Chart title: change text	Click the title to select it; click and drag the text, and type a new title.
Chart type: change	Right-click an empty area of the chart, and select Chart Type. Select the chart type and subtype you want. Click the Press and Hold to View Sample button to preview the results. Click OK.

To Do This	Use This Command
Chart	
Create chart: from nonadjacent data series	Select the first data range; hold down Ctrl; select the second range of data; continue selecting data series. When all data series are selected, click the Chart Wizard and complete the chart.
Create chart: use Chart Wizard	Select the data range including data labels; click the Chart Wizard button in the toolbar, and complete each of the four Chart Wizard steps (Type, Source Data, Options, and Location). Save as a separate sheet or as part of the worksheet.
Delete chart	Click within a blank area of the chart to select the entire chart, and press Del.
Delete component of a chart	Right-click the specific area of the chart, such as gridlines; select Clear.
Format elements of a chart	Right-click the element you want to format, and select the related format option from the shortcut menu. Use the resulting dialog box to change the font, font size, emphasis, alignment, scale, or other aspect of the selected element.
Position (move) chart	Click any blank area in the chart to select it; move the mouse pointer to the middle of the selected chart until the pointer displays as a four-sided arrow; drag to a new location.
Print: chart only	Select the chart, or click the sheet tab for the chart you want to print. Add a header or footer if desired. Click the Print button or choose File, Print and click the Selected Chart option in the Print what area.
Print: embedded chart and data	Select the range containing the data and associated chart; choose File, Print; click the Selection option in the Print what area.
Resize chart	Click any blank area in the chart to select it; place the mouse pointer on a sizing handle to display a resizing arrow; click and drag to resize.
Columns and Rows	
Column width: change using menu	Click any cell in the column and choose Format, Column; select among Width, AutoFit Selection, and Standard Width.
Column width: change using mouse	Position the mouse pointer on the worksheet frame between the column letter and its adjacent column letter to the right; drag left to narrow; drag right to widen, or double-click to fit the widest entry.
Column/Row: delete	Click the row or column heading to select it, and choose Edit, Delete from the menu.
Column/Row: hide	Select one or more columns; choose Format, Column, Hide; select one or more rows, and choose Format, Row, Hide.
Column/Row: unhide	Select cells to the left and right of a hidden column(s), and choose Format, Column, Unhide; select cells above and below a hidden row(s), and choose Format, Row, Unhide.
Insert new column	Click the column where you want to insert a new column and choose Insert, Columns from the menu.
Insert new row	Click the row where you want to insert a new row, and choose Insert, Rows from the menu.
Row height: change using menu	Click any cell in the row and choose Format, Row; select Height or AutoFit.
Row height: change using mouse	Position the mouse pointer on the worksheet frame between the row number and its adjacent row number below; drag up to reduce height; drag down to increase height, or double-click to fit the tallest entry.

continues ▶

To Do This	Use This Command
Columns and Rows	
Sum a column of numbers	Click the cell where you want the sum to display, and click the AutoSum button; verify that the cells enclosed in the marquee are correct, and press Tab or Enter.
Formatting	
Align text in cell	Select the cell and click the Align Left, Center, or Align Right button.
Bold, italicize, underline	Select part or all of cell contents; click the Bold, Italic, or Underline button on the toolbar.
Borders: add	Select the cells; click the down arrow on the borders button and select the line location you prefer.
Center worksheet on page	Choose File, Page Setup. Click the Margins tab. Click the Horizontally option.
Color: apply to range background	Select the range of cells; click the down arrow to the right of the Fill Color button in the toolbar, and select a color.
Decimal places: change displayed	Select the cells you want to change, and click the Increase Decimal button or Decrease Decimal button to show more and fewer decimal places.
Font emphasis or color: change	Select the cells and click the Bold, Italic, or Underline button. Select the color you prefer from the Font Color drop-down palette.
Font or font size: change	Select the cells you want to change, and select the font typeface from the Font drop-down list; select the size from the Font Size drop-down list.
Footer: add to worksheet	Choose File, Page Setup. Click the Header/Footer tab. Click Custom Footer button, and add the information you want. Click OK.
Format dates	Select the cells you want to format, and choose Format, Cells from the menu. Select Date from the Number page, and select the date format you prefer. Click OK.
Format large numbers	Select the cells you want to format, and click the Comma style button.
Format numbers as currency	Select the cells you want to format, and click the Currency button.
Format text at an angle	Select the cell, and choose Format, Cells. Click the Alignment tab, and click and drag the text orientation indicator to the desired angle.
Gridlines: print on worksheet	Choose File, Page Setup. Click the sheet tab. Click the Gridlines check box.
Header: add to worksheet	Choose File, Page Setup. Click the Header/Footer tab. Click Custom Header button and add the information you want. Click OK.
Number format: change	Select the range of cells; choose Format, Cells; click the Number tab; select a style and set number of decimal places.
Remove formatting	Select the range of cells; choose Edit, Clear, Formats.
Rename worksheet	Double-click the sheet tab, and type the new name. Click anywhere on the worksheet to deselect.
Shading: add	Select the cells; click the down arrow on the Fill button, and choose the fill color you prefer.
Wrap text in cell	Select the cell, and choose Format, Cells. Click the Alignment tab, and click the Wrap Text check box.
Multiple Sheets	
Copy cells between sheets	Select the cells you want to copy, and click the Copy button. Move to the cell in another sheet where you want the first value to be displayed, and click the Paste button.

To Do This	Use This Command
Multiple Sheets	
Hyperlink: insert	Select the cell where you want to add a hyperlink and click the Insert Hyperlink button. Click the File button and locate the file to which you want to link. Click OK twice.
Insert new sheet	Choose Insert, Worksheet.
Label worksheet	Double-click the sheet tab and type a new label. Or right-click a sheet tab; select Rename from the shortcut menu, and type the new name.
Move sheet	Click and drag the sheet tab of the sheet you want to move to a new position in the sheet tab area.
Reference cell in another sheet	Type an equal sign in the cell that will display the results. Click the sheet tab for the sheet you want to use, and click the cell you want to reference. Press ↵Enter or add a mathematical symbol if you are including the cell reference in a formula.
Worksheets: group multiple	To group nonadjacent worksheets, click the worksheet tab of the first worksheet; hold down Ctrl, and click each of the remaining worksheets. To group consecutive worksheets, click the first work-sheet; hold down ⇧Shift, and click the last worksheet.
Worksheets: ungroup	Right-click one of the grouped worksheets, and select Ungroup Sheets.
Printing	
Column to print as label: set	Choose File, Page Setup. Click the sheet tab. Click the Collapse Dialog button for the Columns to repeat at left box. Select the columns you want to repeat on each page. Click the Expand Dialog button, and click OK.
Landscape orientation: set	Choose File, Page Setup. Click the Landscape option and click OK.
Preview printout	Click the Print Preview button.
Range of cells: print	Select the cells you want to print. Choose File, Print, Selection.
Row to print as label: set	Choose File, Page Setup. Click the sheet tab. Click the Collapse Dialog button for the Rows to repeat at top box. Select the rows you want to repeat on each page. Click the Expand Dialog button, and click OK.
View	
Dependent cells: display	Select the cell you want to trace; choose Tools, Auditing, Trace Dependents.
Freeze panes	Click the cell that you want to remain on the screen. Choose Window, Freeze Panes.
Gridlines: display/hide	Choose Tools, Options and select the View tab;check/uncheck Gridlines.
Preview a printout	Click the Print Preview button.
Remove auditing arrows	Choose Tools, Auditing, Remove All Arrows.
Select different sheet	Click the sheet tab at the bottom of the worksheet.
Unfreeze panes	Choose Window, Unfreeze Panes.
View other parts of worksheet	Use the vertical scrollbar to move up and down a worksheet and the horizontal scrollbar to move left to right on a worksheet.
Zoom: change magnification	Click the down arrow on the Zoom button and select the magnification you want to use.
Web Page	
Save Web page as Excel worksheet	Click Export to Excel button. Enter a name and file location, and change the file type to Microsoft Excel Workbook. Click Save.

continues ▶

To Do This	Use This Command
Web Page	
Save worksheet as Web page	Choose File, Save as Web Page. Click the Sheet option and select Add interactivity. Name the file using .htm as the extension and designate the location to save the file. Click Save.
Use Excel Worksheet on the Web	Launch your browser, enter the location and filename of your worksheet in the Address box. Press ↵Enter. Use the tools on the Web toolbar to sort or filter data, total numbers, or perform other operations.

Access Task Guide

To Do This	Use This Command
Application Management	
Convert database	Launch Access. To convert from a previous version, select and open the file. Choose to Convert or Open the database. When prompted, give the database a new name, and specify the location.
Create new database	Launch Access, and click Blank Database; click OK. Type a filename, and select the drive or folder location for the file. Click the Create button.
Form	
AutoForm, create	Click the Forms object button; click the New button; choose a table or a query from which to get the data, and choose an AutoForm style.
Close	Click the Close button.
Create, from scratch	Click the Forms object button; click the New button, and select the table or query you want to use. Choose the Design view option from the list and click OK.
Edit data	Use the navigation buttons to move around the form. Click the field you want to edit and enter new data.
Enter data	Open the form in Form view. Click the New Record button to add a new record.
Field: add	Drag fields from the selected Field list box, and place them on the grid until you have placed all the fields you need. Use the rulers to help align the fields. Save the form with a new name.
Field: move	Work in Design view. Click the field you want to move. When the pointer becomes a hand, you can click and drag the field to a new location.
Field: resize	Click and drag one of the sizing handles of the selected field text box or field label to resize it.
Header and label: add	In Design view, choose View, Form Header/Footer. Adjust the size of the Header area by dragging the edge. Use the Label tool to drag a label box within the header. Type the label text inside the label box. Click elsewhere to deselect the box. Click the box to select it again, and change the font, font size, or other characteristics.
Open	From the Database window, click the Forms object button, and double-click the form you want to open.
Save	Click the Save button. The first time you save a form, type a descriptive name in the Save As dialog box, and click OK.
Integration	
Browse Data Access Page	Open Internet Explorer 5.0 or greater. Type the location of the page in the Address box. Scroll through the records, and make changes as necessary.
Import Excel table	Choose File, Get External Data, Import from the menu. Select Microsoft Excel as the file type and select the file you want. Use the Import Spreadsheet Wizard to refine your table.

To Do This	Use This Command
Integration	
Link table to Word form letter	Select the table; click the Merge It with MS Word from the Office Links button. Click Create a new document. When Word launches, type text and place fields by selecting them from the Insert Merge Field button on the Mail Merge toolbar. Save the Word document.
Merge table with Word form letter	Click the View Merged Data button in the Word Mail Merge toolbar to check for errors. Click the Merge button, and choose a source. Send the document to the printer, email, or fax.
Save form as Data Access Page	Click the Pages object button. Click New and select a table or query. Choose your fields, grouping and sorting options, and page name in the Page Wizard. Make changes in Design view and move to Page view. Your page is saved automatically.
Query	
Create	Open the database and click the Queries object button. Click the New button, Design view, and OK. Select the table(s) you want to use, and click Add. Close the Show Table dialog box.
Criteria, match	Work in Design view. Click in the Criteria row of the field you want to match. Type the criterion you want to match. Add a second criterion by going to the or: row in the design grid. Use quotation marks if punctuation is included in the criteria.
Edit	In query Design view, click and drag fields, or double-click a field to add it to the query. You can insert fields between existing fields in the design grid by clicking and dragging the field. Use the column selector to rearrange columns. You can delete selected columns by opening the Edit menu and selecting Delete.
Field: choose	Click and drag the field from the field list box to the design grid; or, in the design grid, click the drop-down arrow and choose the field you want; or double-click the field in the field list box.
Open, multiple	From the Database window, select and open first one query, then use the Database Window button to select a second query (or more). Open the Window menu, and choose Cascade to view title bars for all queries.
Save	Click the Save button. If it is the first time you have saved the query, the Save As dialog box opens, asking for a query name.
Save, with a new name	Select the query; open the File menu and choose Save As command. Type a new name in the dialog box and click OK.
Sort	In query Design view, click in the Sort row of the design grid of the field to be sorted. Select Ascending or Descending order.
Report	
Create, use Report Wizard	Go to the Reports object tab. Click New, select the wizard you want, and click OK. Select the fields you want included in the report and click the Add button (>). Click Next. The wizard leads you through several more screens. Make your selections; click Next until you reach the final screen; name the report, and click Finish.
Field: add	Work in Design view. In the field box, click and drag the the field you want to add to the desired position. Click the Print Preview button to view the report. Adjust the fields until you are satisfied with the report design.
Label, add to report	Click the Label button in the toolbox. Click and drag where you want to create a label box. Type the text for the new label, and format the text and move it to the desired location.

continues ▶

To Do This	Use This Command
Report	
Modify report design	In report Design view, apply the same techniques used when designing a form. Click and drag the fields you want to move, add, or delete. Use the tools in the toolbox or the Format menu to help align fields, add labels, modify fonts, or change headers and footers.
Print	When you click the Finish button using the wizard, you see a Print Preview of the report. If you are satisfied with the report, click the Print button.
Print table data	In table Datasheet view, click the Print Preview button. Alter the layout by using the Page Setup command in the File menu, if necessary. When the page appears the way you want, open the File menu, and choose Print.
Rename	Select the Reports object button in the Database window. Right-click the report title and choose Rename. The box around the title changes, and you can edit the report title by typing over the existing name.
Save, with a new name	Select the report; open the File menu, and choose the Save As command. Type a new name in the dialog box and click OK.
Table	
Column: adjust width(s)	In table Datasheet view, place the mouse pointer between columns in the field selector area until it changes to a thick vertical bar with arrows on either side. Click and drag the line between the columns to the right or left to adjust the column width. Select several columns at once, and double-click one of the bars between the selected columns for automatic adjustment of all selected columns.
Column: hide or unhide	In table Datasheet view, click the field selector. Open the Format menu, and choose the Hide Columns command. In the Format menu, use Unhide Columns to display the column again.
Column: move (reorder fields)	Select the column, click the field selector, and drag it to its new position.
Create	In the Database window, select the Tables object button. Click the New button; choose Design View, and click OK. Enter the field name; choose the data type, and enter a description for each field.
Field: add	In table Design view, go to the first blank row, and insert the new field name, data type, and description for each field to be added.
Field: delete	In table Design view, use the row selector to select the row you want to delete. Click the Delete Rows button.
Field: edit	In table Design view, go to the field name, data type, or description you want to edit. Select the information you want to change, and type the new information. Use the drop-down box in the Data Type column to change the type of data allowed for that field.
Field: move	In table Design view, use the row selector to select the row you want to move. Click and drag the row to a new location; release the mouse button.
Primary key, create	Use the counter field by clicking Yes when prompted by the save sequence, or use the row selector to select a field and click the Primary Key button.
Print data	In table Datasheet view, click the Print Preview button. Alter the layout by using the Page Setup command in the File menu, if necessary. When the page appears the way you want, open the File menu, and choose Print.

To Do This	Use This Command
Table	
Record: add	In table Datasheet view, type the appropriate information in each field. Move from field to field by pressing Enter or Tab. At the end of the information for one record, press Enter. This moves you to the next row and saves the record you just entered.
Record: delete	In table Datasheet view, click the record selector of the row to be deleted. Click the Delete Record button, and click Yes to confirm.
Record: edit	In table Datasheet view, move to the record and field you want to edit. Click the field, and add, delete, or change the entry as needed. Press Shift+Enter to save your changes.
Record: find	Click the Find button. In the dialog box, type what you want to find. You can search in the current field or all fields. You can also search in Any Part of Field. Click the Find Next button to begin the search.
Record: go to first	Click the First Record button.
Record: go to last	Click the Last Record button.
Record: go to next	Click the Next Record button.
Record: go to previous	Click the Previous Record button.
Record: insert	Click the New Record button.
Records: sort	Click the field you want to sort. Click either the Sort Ascending or Sort Descending button.
Save	Click the Save button. Type a name for the table (on the first save only). Click OK.

PowerPoint Task Guide

To Do This	Use This Command
Animation	
Animate text	In Slide Sorter view, select the slides you want to animate. Click the down arrow next to the Preset Animation box, and select the animation you want.
Dim previously displayed points	In Slide view, select the slide you want to change. Right-click the text and choose Custom Animation. In the Check to animate slide objects area, click the check box for the text you want to dim. In the After animation drop-down list, select a color. Change the Grouped by box to a different paragraph level if you want. Click OK.
Slide transitions: animate	In Slide Sorter view, select Edit, Select All from the menu to add the same transition to all the slides. Click the down arrow on the Slide Transition Effects box, and select a transition style.
Slide transitions: remove	Choose No Transition from the Slide Transitions Effect drop-down list on the Slide Sorter toolbar.
View slide transition	In Slide Sorter view, click the slide transition icon below the slide.
View text animation	In Slide Sorter view, click the animation icon below the slide.
Application and File Management	
Exit PowerPoint	Click the Close button and choose Yes if prompted to save your changes.
Open blank presentation	In the PowerPoint dialog box, choose Blank Presentation and click OK. Select the slide layout you want to use. Click OK.
	If PowerPoint is already open, click the New button. Select the slide layout you want to use. Click OK.

continues ▶

To Do This	Use This Command
Application and File Management	
Open existing presentation	Start PowerPoint. Click Open an existing presentation in the PowerPoint dialog box. Locate the file you want, and click Open.
	When PowerPoint is already open, click the Open button, locate the file you want and click Open.
Print outline	Choose File, Print. In the Print what box, select Outline View. Click OK.
Print slides	Click the Print button.
Save file with new name	Choose File, Save As. In the File name box, type the new name; change location in the Save in box if necessary. Click Save.
Save PowerPoint presentation	Click the Save button. Type a name in the File name text box, and select the location to save the file in the Save in box.
Start PowerPoint	Choose the Start button, Programs, and Microsoft PowerPoint.
Chart Data	
Activate chart	Double-click anywhere in the chart.
Chart: modify	Activate the chart. Right-click on the part of the chart you want to modify. Select the appropriate option from the shortcut menu. Make the changes you desire and click OK.
Chart slide: add	Click Common Tasks, New Slide, and select the Chart option and click OK.
Chart type: change	Activate the chart. Click the More Buttons button, and point to the Chart Type button. Click the style of chart you want to use.
	For greater options, choose, Chart, Chart Type from the menu, and select the chart type and subtype from the dialog box.
Replace sample data	Activate the chart; click in each cell of the datasheet and type the new data. Use Tab to move across the datasheet or the arrow keys to move around on the datasheet.
Switch columns and rows in chart	Activate the chart. Click the By Column button to change to columns. If the data is displayed in columns, click the By Row button to change to rows.
Graphics	
Apply a design	Click Common Tasks, Apply Design Template. Choose the design you want and click Apply.
Clip art: insert	Change to Slide view and select the slide you want to illustrate. Click Insert, Picture, Clip Art. Choose a category; click a clip art image, and choose the Insert clip button from the pop-up menu.
Clip art: move	Click the image and drag it to a new location. Make sure the pointer is not on top of one of the sizing handles.
Clip art: resize	Click the image. Position the pointer on one of the square sizing handles in the corners. Click and drag toward the center of the image to reduce its size, or outward away from the center to increase its size.
Connector line: add	Click the AutoShapes button on the Drawing toolbar and select Connectors. Select the connector style you want. Move the pointer to the desired location on the screen and click and drag from one text box to the next.
Deselect clip art image	Click in another location on the slide.
Picture: insert from file	Choose Insert, Picture, From File.
Text box: add	Click the Text Box button on the Drawing toolbar. Position the pointer on the screen in the desired location; click and drag down and to the right. Type the text you want in the box.

To Do This	Use This Command
Graphics	
Text box: change font	Click the edge of the text box to select it. Use the Font, Font Size, Font Color list boxes to change the font. Use the Bold, Italic, Underline, or Shadow buttons to add emphasis.
Text box: move	Click the edge of the text box and drag it to a new location.
Text box: resize	Click the text box to select it. Position the pointer on one of the sizing handles; click and drag toward the center of the image to reduce the size, or away from the center to increase the size.
WordArt: insert	Choose the slide; click the Insert WordArt button on the Drawing toolbar. Click the option you want, and click OK. Type the text you want in the Edit WordArt dialog box, and click OK.
WordArt: move	Click the image and drag it to a new position. Make sure the pointer is not placed on one of the sizing handles.
WordArt: resize	Click the image to select it. Position the pointer on one of the sizing handles; click and drag toward the center of the image to reduce the size, or away from the center to increase the size.
Navigation	
Delete a slide	Select the slide in Slide Sorter view; press Del.
First slide	Press Ctrl+Home.
Last slide	Press Ctrl+Esc.
Move to a different slide	In the Normal view, click the outline icon for the slide you want to view. In the Slide view click the slide number icon to the left of the slide. Use the vertical scrollbar to move to a specific slide, or use the Next Slide, Previous Slide buttons on the scrollbar to move up or down one slide at a time.
Next slide	Press PgDn or click the Next Slide button.
Previous slide	Press PgUp or click the Previous Slide button.
Specific slide	Drag the scroll box to the corresponding location on the vertical scrollbar.
Presentation Design	
Add a slide	Click the Common Tasks button, New Slide, and select the slide style you want.
Formatting: hide or display	In Slide Sorter view, click the Show Formatting button to turn on or off the formatting and the detailed text.
Number of slides displayed: change	In Slide Sorter view, change the Zoom box to 33 percent or some other option to show more slides on the screen.
Sequence of slides: change	In the Slide Sorter view, click and drag the slide you want to move to the new position in the sequence. When a vertical line displays to show the insertion point, release the mouse.
Slide Layout and Contents	
Demote point to lower level	Select the point in the outline or slide, and press Tab.
Placeholder: change size	Click the placeholder; move the pointer to one of the square sizing handles, click and drag to resize the placeholder.
Placeholder: move on slide	Click the placeholder; position the pointer at the edge of the placeholder and click and drag it to the new position.
Promote point to higher level	Select the point in the outline or slide, and press Shift+Tab.

continues ▶

To Do This	Use This Command
Slide Layout and Contents	
Slide layout: change	Click the Common Tasks and choose Slide Layout. Select the layout you want, and click Apply.
Text: enter in outline	Click the outline pane, and type the text and press Enter to move to the next point.
Text: enter in slide	Click in the placeholder and type the text. Press Tab to move to the next point.
Slide Master	
Bullet color or size: change	Open the Slide Master. Click the level you want to change. Choose Format, Bullets and Numbering. Select one of the bullet options; change the color using the Color drop-down list box, or the size using the Size box. When you have made your selection, click OK.
Bullet type: change	Open the Slide Master. Click the level you want to change. Choose Format, Bullets and Numbering. Select one of the options shown or click the Picture or Character buttons to see more options. When you have selected the bullet you want, click OK.
Font: modify	Open the Slide Master. Click the level you want to change. Use the Font, Font Size, or Font Color list boxes to change the font. Use the emphasis buttons to change the emphasis. The font size should be changed separately for each level. You can select all levels to change the font style.
Footer: add to slide	Open the Slide Master. Choose View, Header and Footer. On the Slide page, choose Update automatically to place the current date on the slide. Type a title or label in the Footer box. Click Don't show on title slide; click Apply to All.
Footer: change font	Open the Slide Master. Click the placeholder you want to change and use the Font, Font Size, or Font Color boxes, or the emphasis buttons to modify the font.
Open the Slide Master	Choose View, Master, Slide Master.
Slide Show	
Advance one slide at a time	Click the left mouse button, Press Enter or PgDn.
Display slide show shortcut menu	Right-click in the slide show.
End slide show	Press Esc or right-click and choose End Show.
Slide show: run continuously	Choose Slide Show, Set Up Show; check Loop continuously until Esc.
View slide show	Move to the first slide and click the Slide Show button. Click the mouse to proceed from one slide to the next.
Speaker Notes and Handouts	
Handouts: print	Choose File, Print. In the Print what box drop-down list, select Handouts. Select the number of Slides per page. Select the Frame slides option and Grayscale if you want; click OK.
Header and footer information: add to handout	Choose View, Master, Handout Master. Select View, Header and Footer from the menu. Choose Update automatically to include the current date. Enter a title or label in the Header box. Add a title or label in the Footer Area. Click Apply to all.
Speaker notes: change font	Choose View, Notes Page; select the notes in the Notes area, and change the font size or style using the Font Size and Font boxes.
Speaker notes: enter	From the Normal or Outline view, expand the Notes pane and type the notes.

To Do This	Use This Command
Speaker Notes and Handouts	
Speaker notes: print	Choose File, Print. Click the Print what drop-down list arrow and choose Notes Pages. Click OK.
Speaker notes: view	Choose View, Notes Page.
View	
Change view	Click the View button next to the horizontal scrollbar for the type of view you want to use.
Datasheet: view or hide	Click the View Datasheet button.
Preview a presentation in black and white	Click the Grayscale Preview button.
Rulers: display	Choose View, Ruler.
Slide master	Choose View, Master, Slide Master.
Slide miniature	Choose View, Slide Miniature.
Slide transitions	Click the Slide Transition icon under the slide (Slide Sorter view).
Speaker notes	Choose View, Notes Page.

Glossary

Many key terms appearing in this book (in bold italic) are listed alphabetically in this Glossary for easy reference.

absolute reference A cell reference in Excel that always refers to a specific cell and does not change when copied or filled into other cells.

active cell The selected cell in Excel; the border of the active cell changes to a darker line.

animate To set the motion for each bullet point, graphic, or chart element appearing on the screen during a PowerPoint presentation. You can also specify a length of time for the point to remain on the screen before the next animation occurs.

animation features Controls for the direction, speed, and sound used when a new object or line of text appears on a PowerPoint slide.

application One of the components of the Microsoft Office 2000 suite, such as Word, Excel, or PhotoDraw. An application is also referred to as a program in this book.

APR Annual Percentage Rate; the method used to calculate most loan interest rates. If the loan payment is made every month, the Excel PMT function needs to use one-twelfth the annual interest rate to calculate the interest cost per month.

arguments The words or values required for a function to perform a calculation.

Arial The default font used in Excel, which is a Microsoft True Type sans serif font.

audience handouts Printouts that display images of PowerPoint slides or an outline. Handouts are useful in a teaching or training environment where specific facts are provided.

AutoContent Wizard A PowerPoint feature that provides step-by-step assistance to help you organize the content of your presentation.

AutoFit A tool in Word's Table menu that changes the width of the columns to best fit the data that has been entered. It is also a check box in the AutoFormat dialog box and is applied by default when an automatic formatting style is applied.

AutoForm A form that is created automatically by Access that includes all the fields in a table.

AutoFormat An option in Word and Excel that enables you to choose from many different table styles, saving you a great deal of time in formatting a table. After you have selected a style, you can make additional formatting changes to suit your needs.

AutoReport A report that is created automatically by Access that includes all the fields of a table in either a one-column or tabular format with as many records on the page as possible.

bar chart A chart type that compares values across categories by using horizontal data bars.

browser A program, such as Netscape Navigator or Microsoft Internet Explorer, that helps you connect to the Internet and view Web pages.

calculations Any mathematical operations involving data in the worksheet cells. The simplest and most commonly used calculation is the sum calculation.

Calendar A part of the Outlook program that records and displays appointments or scheduled events. The default setting displays the current day's appointments and any tasks that have been entered. It can also display scheduled activities for a week, or a month at a time.

category axis The horizontal line on a chart that displays data labels. In Excel, this is also called the X-axis. (see also **X-axis**)

cell Each intersection of an individual row and column in a table or worksheet. The cells can contain text, numbers, or graphics.

cell address The column letter and row number that designates the location of a cell.

centered Alignment of a line of text in the center of the available space. Centering makes titles distinct from other parts of the document and draws the reader's attention.

chart A graphic representation of a series of numbers; sometimes referred to as a graph. A chart or graph helps you see the relationship between numbers.

chart sub-type Variations on the basic chart that you can use to display the data using different emphasis and views of the chart. Each chart type has several chart sub-types.

Chart Wizard A miniprogram that guides you through the steps necessary to create a chart.

clip art A graphic image that you can place in a document to convey an idea.

Clipboard (see **Office Clipboard**)

column chart A chart type that compares values across categories using vertical data columns.

column heading The letter at the top of each column of an Excel worksheet that identifies the column.

column selector In Access, the thin gray line above the field name in the query Design view. When you click the column selector, the whole column is selected.

connector handles Small blue boxes that are used to connect one drawing object to another.

connectors Lines that link drawing objects together. The ends automatically go from a handle on one object to a handle on another.

Contacts The Outlook folder that serves as an address book and information storage area for the people and businesses you want to communicate with. The contacts are automatically alphabetized.

control In Access, any object on a form or report, such as a text box, a label, a line, a check box, or an option button.

copy A command used to duplicate text from one part of a document so that it can be in a second location. This command can be used in all Office applications.

COUNTIF function An Excel function that counts the number of cells within a range that meet the given criteria.

criteria In Access, tests or conditions that limit the records included in a query. A single condition is a called a criterion.

cropping Removing unwanted parts of a graphic image.

current record indicator In Access, an arrow in the record selector that shows which record is currently active.

custom animations Feature that enables you to control a PowerPoint slide by assigning a particular animation technique to each element on the slide.

cut A command to store text (or other objects) temporarily until you designate where in the document to move it using the Paste command. This command can be used in all Office applications.

cut-and-paste A method to move text (or other objects) from one location. You can use the Cut and Paste commands on the menu, or toolbar buttons. This method can be used to move text or objects between Office applications.

data series A group of related data points plotted in a chart.

data type In Access, a definition of the kind of data that can be entered into a field.

database A group of related records.

Database window In Access, a window that displays a list of the table, query, form, report, page, macro, and module objects that comprise a database.

datasheet The part of a PowerPoint chart that contains the data used to build the chart. When you insert a chart into a PowerPoint presentation, the datasheet includes sample row and column data that you change to create the chart.

Datasheet view In Access, the row-and-column view you use when you enter or edit records in a table or a query.

Date Navigator In Outlook Calendar, the section that displays two months at a time in the upper right and includes the current date. It enables you to go to a specific day by clicking the day you want. You can also use the arrows next to the title to change to a different month.

default Common settings used by an application unless they are changed by a specific action. For example, the most common default document margin settings are either an inch for all four sides or an inch at the top and bottom and an inch and a quarter on the left and right.

delimiter A character that separates fields in a text file. Common delimiters are tabs, commas, semicolons, and spaces.

demote To move a bulleted item to a lower level of importance in a PowerPoint outline.

design grid In Access, the area used to define the conditions of a query. You can specify fields, sort order, and criteria to be used to search your database.

design template A background design with preset graphics, fonts, alignments, bullet symbols, and other elements. Using a design template adds a professional appearance to a PowerPoint presentation.

Design view In Access, the view that is used to create or modify an object. In the Design view for a table, you see columns for the field name, data type, and description of each field.

desktop The basic screen from which Windows and programs are run. The desktop consists of program icons, a taskbar, a Start button, and a mouse pointer.

desktop publisher A program that enables you to create sophisticated page layouts for such things as newsletters, cards, posters, and even Web pages. Microsoft Publisher is the Office 2000 desktop publisher.

destination disk The disk to which you want to copy the original (source) disk to in the Copy Disk procedure. All other information on the destination disk is deleted in this procedure.

detail (see **form detail**)

dialog box A box that asks you to make decisions about objects or topics. Dialog boxes do not have Minimize buttons.

dim An animation feature that changes a bulleted point to a color with less contrast, so it appears to fade into the background and is less dominant on the screen. This helps the audience focus on the next point in the presentation, which is in a brighter color.

display settings The default choices that affect such things as how many rows and columns will be shown on the screen.

drag-and-drop A method to move text (or other objects) from one location to another by using the mouse pointer to drag it from the original location and drop it at the desired location on your screen.

dynaset In Access, a subset of records created as a result of a query.

expression A predefined formula that performs calculations, displays built-in functions, or sets limits. You can include expressions in reports and other Access objects, such as macros.

Extensible Markup Language (XML) A Web language that enables a program to attach additional information to data and enables the user to interact with an Excel worksheet or other document using a browser.

field A single category of data or information; the column headings in a database table.

field label In Access, the field name attached to a field text box in a form or report.

field selector The bar at the top of each column in an Access table that contains the field name.

field text box In Access, a placeholder for the contents of a field in the database. Field text boxes show the actual data that has been entered into a table.

file extension The three characters to the right of the period in a filename. Extensions tell the computer what program to use when opening the file. Extensions can be displayed or hidden.

fill A technique that is used to complete a group of adjacent cells with the same values, formulas, or series. Examples of series include dates, numbers, days of the week, and months of the year.

fill handle In Excel, the small black square in the lower-right corner of a selected cell. You can click the fill handle to drag the contents of one cell to other adjacent cells to create a series, such as a series of dates.

folder A directory used to organize files and programs on a computer, represented by icons that look like file folders. Folders are created and named by the user.

font A set of characters of the same typeface style. In Office applications, the Font drop-down list shows the font name in its font style so that you can see what the typeface looks like.

font size The height and width of letters, numbers, and characters. Font size is measured in points; there are 72 points to one inch.

footer The area at the bottom of a document page, slide, or worksheet, that is designed to display information that needs to be shown on every page of a document, with the possible exception of the first page. You can add text to the footer to identify your document, its author, the current version, page numbers, and other relevant information.

Footer Area The placeholder at the bottom of the Notes and Handout masters. These placeholder controls enable you to enter footer text.

form In Access, a type of object you can use to enter, edit, and view records. Think of a form as a fill-in-the-blanks screen.

form detail In Access, the main part of a form, in which the records are displayed.

form footer In Access, an area at the bottom of the form, containing controls such as labels, dates, or page numbers, that appears at the bottom of each form page.

form header In Access, an area at the top of the form, containing controls, such as labels, dates, or graphics, that appears at the top of each form page.

format a disk To set up a floppy disk to receive data. Formatting a disk sets up a special location for a disk directory and marks the disk magnetically, so information can be written and found.

Format Painter A tool that enables you to copy the formatting of one paragraph and paint it onto another paragraph. This tool can help you apply formatting characteristics quickly and easily.

Formatting toolbar A bar of graphical buttons in Office programs that simplify formatting tasks, such as applying Bold, Italic, Align Left, Font, and Font Size, to selected text.

Formula bar The bar near the top of the Excel window that displays the address of the active cell and any data in the cell. Click once on the text in the Formula bar to edit it there.

formula palette The dialog box that guides entry of worksheet functions by displaying and explaining each of its arguments. You enter specifications for arguments in boxes to the right of each argument's name.

frame The container for an object on a Publisher page. All objects, including pictures, clip art, and text, are contained in a frame.

function A predefined Excel formula, such as =SUM(B5:B10), which adds the values in cells B5 through B10.

graphical user interface (GUI) A computer operating system that shows documents as they will look in their final form, and uses icons to represent programs and commands.

graphics software A program that enables you to create drawings, modify clip art images, and work with photographs. Microsoft PhotoDraw is the Office 2000 graphics software.

gridlines Outline of the cells in an Excel worksheet that make it easier to follow rows or columns. The default setting is to omit gridlines when the worksheet is printed.

guides Dotted lines displayed to indicate the boundary and placement of a WordArt object.

Handout Master PowerPoint master that enables you to add header and footer information, such as title, date, time, or presenter's name, on each handout page.

hanging indent Formatting style where the first line of the text is to the left of the rest of the text in the paragraph. For example, it is common for bibliographic references to call for the first line of a bibliographic entry to be a half-inch to the left of the rest of the entry.

header The area at the top of a document page, slide, or worksheet designed to display information that needs to be shown on every page of a document, with the possible exception of the first page. You can add text to the header to identify your document, its author, the current version, page number, and other relevant information.

Header Area Placeholders at the top of the Notes and Handout Master. These placeholder controls enable you to enter header text.

horizontal scrollbar The bar at the bottom of a window that enables you to move left and right to view information too wide for the screen.

HTML Hypertext Markup Language; a computer language used for documents that are put on the Web. You can save Office applications as Web documents, which adds HTML tags for easy translation to a Web site.

hyperlink A connection that enables you to jump from a word or label in one location to a file in another location. When you click a word or label that has been made into a hyperlink, it connects you directly to information in another file.

icon A graphic representation; often a small image on a button that enables you to run a program or program function.

Inbox In Outlook, the folder that displays messages that have been received and is used for sending and receiving email messages.

index A location guide built by Access for all primary key fields that helps speed up searching and sorting for that field. Indexes can also be created for other fields, as long as they are not OLE or Memo fields.

information manager A program that enables you to keep track of contacts, oversee email, and maintain a calendar and task list. Microsoft Outlook is the Office 2000 information manager.

insertion point A flashing vertical line that indicates where text will be entered.

Internet A worldwide communications network of computer connections that enables people to have access to thousands of online resources.

intranet A closed network that uses the same technology as the Internet, but restricts access to authorized users.

justified Alignment where text lines up on both the left and right sides. To accomplish this, the computer adjusts the size of the spaces between the words in each line.

label In Access, text on a form or report that is used to display a description, such as a title or field name. Labels are not bound to the table.

landscape orientation The horizontal orientation of a printed page.

launch To start running an application program, such as Word or Excel.

layout The way the text flows on a page and from one page to the next.

leaders Dots or dashes used to connect two columns of information, such as chapter titles with page numbers in a table of contents.

left-aligned Page alignment where there is a uniform margin between the left edge of the paper and the beginning of each line. Because the words in each line are of different lengths, the right edge of the paragraph is usually uneven.

legend A list that identifies the patterns or colors for each series of data used in a chart.

letter tabs In the Outlook Contacts folder, the alphabet indicators to the right of the window that can be used to scroll directly to the contacts that start with the corresponding letter.

line chart A graph that shows a line running through each data point. A line chart is effective for showing a trend (change over time).

local area network (LAN) A system that uses telephone lines or cables to join two or more personal computers, enabling them to communicate with each other.

logo Special graphic image that companies use on all their correspondence, brochures, and Web pages.

mail merge A word processing feature that enables you to customize documents using information from a database table.

margins The spaces between the main body of text and the edge of the paper. Word enables you to set the left, right, top, and bottom margins independently.

marquee In Excel, a moving dashed line that surrounds the group of cells you want to sum.

masters Pages that display the formatting elements of the active design template. By changing the elements in the master, you have complete control over the way the PowerPoint presentation looks.

mastheads The page headers on a Web page, usually containing the page title, company name, and company motto and/or logo.

maximize To increase the size of a window to fill the screen, using the Maximize button.

menu bar The bar, just under the title bar, that contains command options. These commands are words, not icons.

Microsoft Graph A Microsoft subprogram used to create or edit a PowerPoint chart. When this program is active you can enter the data for your chart in the datasheet.

minimize To remove the window from the screen without closing it, using the Minimize button. Minimized windows can be redisplayed by clicking the appropriate button on the taskbar.

mouse pointer The moving arrow, I-beam, or other shape on the screen that is controlled by movement of the mouse. It is used in combination with the mouse buttons to select or activate objects and programs.

My Computer One of two ways to get at the programs and documents stored on your computer. There is always an icon for My Computer on your desktop, although its name may have been changed.

Name box The box located at the left end of Excel's formula bar, identifying the selected cell, chart item, or drawing object.

navigation bar In Publisher, a frame containing the navigation buttons.

navigation buttons Labeled buttons that enable the user to move easily from page to page in a Web site. Also used in Access to navigate records.

Normal view The most commonly used view in PowerPoint because it is the most flexible. It can be used to enter text in an outline or on a slide, or to add speaker notes.

Notes In Outlook, the folder in which you can jot reminders to yourself, the same as you might use sticky notes.

Notes Master PowerPoint master that enables you to add header and footer information, such as title, date, time, or presenter's name, on each notes page.

Notes Pages view The PowerPoint view where you can see what the notes page will look like when it is printed. The top part of the page displays the slide and the notes show below it.

Notes pane An area in the PowerPoint window that displays any notes that have been added which would be printed in a format known as speaker notes.

object A general term for the components of an Access database, including tables, queries, forms, reports, pages, macros, and modules. The other Office programs also use object as a general term to describe drawing shapes, clip art, or other graphics.

Object Linking and Embedding (OLE) A set of standards that enables you to insert objects, such as pictures or spreadsheets, from one document created with one application into documents created with another application.

Office Assistant A Microsoft Office Help program that enables you to ask questions by typing in sentences or phrases. When you ask a question of the Office Assistant, a series of possible related topics are displayed, from which you can pick one of the topics to expand on it.

Office Clipboard A temporary storage location for text or objects that have been copied or cut. Commonly referred to as just the Clipboard, the Office Clipboard differs from the Windows Clipboard in that it can be used to temporarily store multiple items instead of a single item.

Outline pane The area that displays the outline for your PowerPoint presentation.

Outline view The PowerPoint view used to type in the text of a presentation. Its advantage is that it focuses on the flow of ideas.

Outlook Today A folder that displays a summary of the appointments, tasks, and email listed for the current date shown at the top of the screen.

page break An automatic or artificial break that moves the text following the page break to a new page. This feature enables you to control your document so that lines of text, images, or figures that should be displayed together can be shown on the same page.

paste A command to insert the text (or object) that is stored in the Office Clipboard.

Paste function A button on the Excel Standard toolbar that enables the user to select from a library of preprogrammed calculations.

Payment (PMT) function A formula used to calculate the periodic payment due based on the amount borrowed, interest rate, and number of payments.

pencil icon An icon that looks like a pencil. In Access, it is displayed in the record selector when you are editing a record, and indicates that the current changes have not yet been saved.

picture frame A frame that contains a digitized photograph, clip art image, or drawing.

pie chart A round graph, divided into pie-shaped pieces, or wedges, where each piece displays its size relative to the total. A pie chart shows the contribution of each part to the whole.

placeholder A defined area that has been preformatted by the program to display text using a particular font style, size, and alignment. A placeholder is identified by the dashed outline that changes to diagonal hash marks after you click inside the placeholder.

point A unit of measurement for font height. There are 72 points per inch. The larger the font size, the larger the text looks when you print the document. A 12-point font is standard for most documents and is the default font size that is used in Word 2000.

pointer (see **mouse pointer**)

portrait orientation The vertical orientation of a printed page. This is by far the most common page orientation.

presentation graphics program An application, such as PowerPoint, that provides features and tools for creating a presentation consisting of a collection of slides, overheads, or handouts.

presentation manager A program that enables you to create computer slide presentations, overhead transparencies, and Web slide shows. Microsoft PowerPoint is the Office 2000 presentation manager.

primary key A field in Access that contains a unique value for each record, and is used to identify the record.

Print Preview A screen view that displays the layout of the document the way it will appear when it is printed. This enables you to verify that the text of your document is placed on the pages exactly the way you want.

program One of the components of the Microsoft Office 2000 suite, such as Word, Excel, or PhotoDraw. A program is also referred to as an application in this book.

promote To increase the level of importance of a bullet point to a higher level in a PowerPoint outline.

properties The characteristics of an element in Access. For example, a number has such properties as number of decimal places, format, font size, and others.

query A question posed to the database that determines what information is retrieved. A query can be used to restrict which fields are shown and/or what conditions the displayed data must meet.

Read-Only A database file property that indicates that the file has been opened but cannot be changed. This occurs when you open a database file on a CD-ROM.

record A group of data pertaining to one event, transaction, or person. The categories of information in a record are called fields.

record selector In Access, the gray area to the left of a record. It indicates whether the record is selected or being edited. Clicking it selects the whole record.

relational database A database that has two or more tables that are linked together.

relationship Connection between a field in one table to a field in a second table, enabling you to draw information from more than one table at a time for forms or reports.

relative reference A cell reference that refers to a cell based on its location in relationship to the cell containing a formula. If the formula is moved, the formula refers to a new cell in the same comparative location.

report In Access, a database object designed to print and/or summarize selected fields.

restore To return a window to the size it was before it was maximized.

right-aligned Page alignment where the right margin is straight and the left margin is uneven.

row heading The number to the left of each row in an Excel worksheet that identifies the row.

sans serif Font style without the guiding serif lines. A sans serif font has a clean look and is generally used for headings and other short blocks of text. Arial is a sans serif font

scroll box A small box in a horizontal or vertical scrollbar that indicates the relative location in a window. It can also be dragged to view information off the screen.

scrollbars Navigation tools located on the right side and bottom of the screen that enable you to move a document up and down or side to side on the screen.

section An area of a report, such as the Report header, Page header, Detail, Page footer, and Report footer, that can contain controls, labels, formulas, and images.

select a cell To click a cell to make it the active cell. When it is selected, it is ready to be edited by entering or changing the data in the cell.

select query Lists data that meets conditions set by the user.

selection handles (see **sizing handles**)

serif Font style that refers to the lines at the top and bottom of a letter that helps the reader's eyes move across a line of text. A serif font is typically used for the body of the text. Times New Roman, the default style for Word 2000, is a serif font.

sheet A worksheet in Excel.

shortcut menu A menu activated by placing the pointer over an object and right-clicking.

sizing handles Small square boxes displayed at the corners and along the sides of an object when you click it. When an object is selected, it can be resized, moved, or edited. Sizing handles are used specifically to resize an image or other object. Sometimes they are referred to as selection handles or simply handles.

Slide Master Master that gives you control of all the placeholders on the PowerPoint slides, from the title and bulleted points to the slide background. You can control font, font size, and characteristics of the title and bulleted text on all the slides, change the color of the background, and add graphics that will appear on all but the title slide.

Slide pane The area that displays the layout of the PowerPoint slide.

Slide Show The PowerPoint view that utilizes the full screen and can be used to project the slides for viewing by an audience.

Slide Sorter view The PowerPoint view used to see many slides at one time, to rearrange their order, and to add transitions and animations.

Slide view The PowerPoint view used to view and edit each slide individually. It is the best view for working with graphics.

source disk The original disk that you want to copy in the Copy Disk procedure.

speaker notes Notes used by a speaker during a PowerPoint presentation, helping the speaker ensure that nothing is left out of a presentation. Notes can provide useful reminders about details that need to be mentioned during a presentation and also help a speaker keep on track.

spreadsheet A tabular form divided into vertical columns and horizontal rows. Accountants use spreadsheets to manually keep track of financial data. A spreadsheet program enables you to compute, analyze, and chart numerical data. Spreadsheets can also perform some database functions. Microsoft Excel is the Office 2000 spreadsheet. (see also **worksheet**)

Standard toolbar The main bar of graphical buttons in Office programs that simplifies basic tasks, such as opening, saving, and printing files.

Start button The button on the left side of the taskbar used to launch programs, change system settings, or shut down the computer.

status bar The bar at the bottom of a window that gives additional information about the window.

subfolder A folder that is stored inside another folder; a subdirectory.

submenu A second menu, activated by selecting a menu option.

tab order The order in which the insertion point jumps from field to field on a form in Access.

table One of the objects in an Access database. Tables store data in row-and-column format and are the foundation of the database. A table in Word or Excel also features lists of information set up in a row-and-column format, somewhat like the layout of a spreadsheet.

table frame In Publisher, a frame that holds data in a row-and-column format; similar to an Excel worksheet or an Access table.

Task Pad The section at the lower-right of the Outlook Calendar that shows the tasks that have been entered.

taskbar A bar, usually at the bottom of the screen, that contains the Start button, buttons representing open programs, and other buttons that will activate programs.

Tasks The Outlook folder that serves as a to-do list to help you track assignments. All the tasks display in this window. You can enter new tasks here or use the New Task window if you want to add more details.

text box A drawing object used to add general-purpose free-form text.

text frame Any frame that contains text, including hyperlinks.

Times New Roman A Microsoft True Type serif font, which is the default serif font in Word 2000.

title bar The bar at the top of a window that contains the name of the application and document, along with the Minimize, Maximize/Restore, and Close buttons.

Title Master Master that enables you to control the same elements as the Slide Master, but only on PowerPoint slides that use the title slide layout.

toolbar A bar, usually under the menu bar, that contains command options. These commands are buttons with icons, not words. Toolbars can also display as floating bars on your window.

transition The way the entire PowerPoint slide moves onto your screen. For example, each slide may appear to fly in from any direction, dissolve from one slide to the next, or change from the center of the slide out to the edge.

Uniform Resource Locator (URL) The address of a file on the Internet.

value axis The vertical line on the left side of a chart where values for the chart display. In Excel, this is also known as the Y-axis. (see also **Y-axis**)

vertical scrollbar The bar at the right side of a window that enables you to move up and down to view information too long for the screen.

Web creation and management tool A program that enables you to create and maintain a Web site. Microsoft FrontPage is the Office 2000 Web creation and management tool.

window A box that displays information or a program, such as a letter, a list of programs, or a calculator. Windows usually consist of title bars, toolbars, menu bars, and status bars. A window will always have a Minimize button.

Windows A graphical user interface (GUI) operating system required to run Office 2000. It works in the background while you are using an Office application.

Windows Explorer A window that displays the files and folders on the various drives and computer desktop. You can copy, delete, move, and rename files in the Windows Explorer.

word processor A program that enables you to create documents, such as letters, memos, and research papers. Microsoft Word is the Office 2000 word processor.

word wrap A word-processing function whereby the first word to reach the right margin automatically moves to the next line. You do not press ↵Enter until you get to the end of a paragraph.

WordArt A program within Office applications that creates text as a drawing object, enabling you to add special colors, shadows, and 3D effects. WordArt can be displayed horizontally, vertically, or at angle.

workbook An Excel file that consists of several worksheets.

worksheet A page in an Excel workbook consisting of a set of cells that are identified by row and column headings.

World Wide Web (WWW or Web) A graphical interface that utilizes hyperlinks and makes it much easier to use the Internet.

X-axis The horizontal line at the bottom of a chart that is known as the category axis in an Excel chart.

Y-axis The vertical line at the left edge of the chart. Excel refers to this as the value axis in the chart.

zoom The magnification setting that can be used to increase or decrease the size of the active document. You can use the Zoom control in the Standard toolbar to change the zoom setting for the displayed worksheet.

Index

A

absolute formulas (Excel), filling cells, 256, 257–259, 272
absolute references (Excel), 254
Access
crosstab queries (exercise), 461
columns
freezing (exercise), 439
modifying, 430–432, 438–441
commands
Column Width (Format menu), 430
Delete (Edit menu), 450
Find (Edit menu), 467
Find and Replace, 433
Form Header/Footer (View menu), 474
Get External Data (File menu), 514
Hide Columns (Format menu), 338
Page Setup (File menu), 487
Primary Key (Edit menu), 411
Print (File menu), 488
Remove/Sort (Records menu), 435
Save (File menu), 448
Save As (File menu), 410
Select Record (Edit menu), 430
Sort (Records menu), 435
Toolbars (View menu), 414
Undo (Edit menu), 334, 428, 467
Undo (File menu), 450
data types, 406–407
databases, 402
accessing with browsers, 518–519, 525
adding fields (exercise), 420–421
converting, 509–510
creating, 405–406, 419
creating data pages as Web pages (exercise), 524–526
creating memos with mail merge (exercise), 523
creating shortcuts to desktop (exercise), 441
creating tables (exercise), 419
deleting fields, 416–417, 420
editing data pages (exercise), 526
editing fields, 412–413, 420
fields, 411–412
filtering data pages (exercise), 526–527
importing tables (dBase III Plus Database exercise), 525
importing tables (Excel), 514–516
importing tables (exercise), 524
importing text (exercise), 526
linking tables to form letters (Word), 511–513
merging tables to form letters (Word), 513–514
moving fields, 414–416, 420
naming, 406
opening (exercise), 523–525
printing documents (exercise), 524
saving forms as Web pages, 516–518
saving tables, 410–411, 419
sorting data pages (exercise), 526–527
tables, 406-409
Datasheet view, 408
design grids, 446
Design view, 408
dialog boxes
Convert Database Into, 510
File New Database, 405
Import, 514
Import Spreadsheet Wizard, 515
Merge, 513
New Form, 465
New Query, 445
New Report, 489
New Table, 407
Page Setup, 487
Print, 488
Save As, 410, 448
Show Table, 445
Unhide Columns, 432
dynasets, 447
field labels (exercise), 480
fields
adding hyperlinks (exercise), 422
creating, 408
Lookup Wizard (exercise), 422
Form Design view, 473
Formatting toolbar, 475
forms
adding date/time to headers (exercise), 481
adding drop-down lists (exercise), 483
adding fields, 470–472
adding headers to labels, 474–476
adding images to page headers (exercise), 481
adding page numbers to footers (exercise), 481
AutoForm, 464–466, 479
copying (exercise), 483
creating, 468–470
creating in Design view (exercise), 479
customizing (exercise), 482
editing data, 466–467, 479
entering data, 466–468, 479
headers/footers, 468
inserting page breaks (exercise), 482
moving fields, 472–474, 480
opening, 467–468
printing (exercise), 482
resizing fields, 378-380, 386
tabs (exercise), 484
keyboard shortcuts, 427
labels (exercise), 480
multiple fields (exercise), 421
primary keys
adding (exercise), 421
creating, 410–412, 419–422
queries
creating, 444–445, 458
creating with wizards (exercise), 459
deleting records (exercise), 461
editing, 449–450, 458
matching criteria, 452–453, 459
modifying field order, 450–451, 458
saving, 448–449
saving with new names, 454–455, 458
selecting fields, 446–448
sorting, 450–451, 458
sorting multiple fields (exercise), 459
records
adding, 424–426, 438
copying (exercise), 440
deleting, 429–430, 438
editing, 427–428, 438
excluding/including (exercise), 460
inserting, 429–430, 438
limiting (exercise), 460
navigating, 426–427
pasting (exercise), 440
printing (exercise), 439
replacing data (exercise), 440
searching, 432–434, 439–440
sorting, 434–435, 439
reports
adding labels (exercise), 501
creating, 488–491, 500–501
creating mailing labels (exercise), 505
drawing lines (exercise), 504
formatting (exercise), 503

modifying, 493–495, 501
printing, 492, 501
renaming, 491
saving, 496–498
sorts (exercise), 440
tables
adding check boxes (exercise), 422
analyzing (exercise), 442
copying to Word (exercise), 527
formatting text (exercise), 441
printing, 486–488, 500
updating to Excel (exercise), 527
tools (exercise), 441
views, 414–416
wizards
Form, 465
Page, 517
Report, 488–491
Report (exercise), 500
Simple Query, 445
accessing. *See* opening; starting
Accessories menu, 742
active cells (Excel). *See also* cells
selecting, 189
Actrix, 591–604
colors
selecting, 602
drawing
circle inside a circle, 599–600
circles in a rectangle, 592
parabola, 601
parallel circuit, 596–598
right triangle, 603–604
schematic symbol, 601
simple circuit, 593–594
triangles, 595
explode command, 598–599
adding. *See also* starting
animation sounds (PowerPoint), 400
borders (Excel), 217–219
exercise, 222–223
charts
exercise, 381
PowerPont, 371
colors (Excel), 222–223
connector lines (PowerPoint), 357–359
exercise, 363–365
data labels (Excel), 298
dates (Word), 147
fields (Access), 411–412
exercise, 420–421
forms, 470–472
form headers (Access), 474–476
formulas (Excel), 305–308
hyperlinks (Excel), 308–311
workbooks (exercise), 321
labels (Access), 480
lines (Excel), 217–219
exercise, 222–223
primary keys (Access), 421
records (Access), 424–426
exercise, 438
rows/columns (Word), 171–173
tables (exercise), 180
shading (Excel), 217–219
slides (PowerPoint), 381
spaces after paragraphs (Word), 129–130
speaker notes (PowerPoint), 334–335
exercise, 341
text boxes (PowerPoint), 355–357
colors (exercise), 364–365
exercise, 363
trend lines (Excel), 299
WordArt (PowerPoint), 353–355
exercise, 362–366
aligning. *See also* formatting
cells (Word), 181–182
numbers (Word), 180
text (Excel), 213–215
cells (exercise), 224
text (Word)
paragraphs, 118–120
tables, 175–177
analyzing tables (Access), exercise, 442
animating
charts (PowerPoint), 398–399
drawing objects (PowerPoint), 398
presentations (PowerPoint), 400
text (PowerPoint), 391–393
transitions (PowerPoint), 390–391
exercise, 397
WordArt (PowerPoint), 399
Answer Wizard, 781
applications (Office 2000), 770–771
closing, 772
Help, 779–781
exercise, 786
menus, 774–777
exercise, 786
starting, 771–773
toolbars, 774–777
exercise, 786
Apply Design Template dialog box, PowerPoint, 349
applying
built-in financial formulas (Excel), 261–263
conditional formulas (Excel), 264–266
counting formulas (Excel), 264–266
designs, 362
existing presentations (PowerPoint), 347–349
formulas (Excel), 260–261
exercise, 272–273
random transitions (PowerPoint), 398
transitions (PowerPoint), 397
Arial fonts (Excel), 216. *See also* fonts
artificial page breaks (Word). *See* breaks
As Web Page command (View menu), Office 2000, 745
ascending sorts (Access), 435. *See also* sorting
assigning primary keys (Access), 410
audience handouts (PowerPoint), printing, 359–360
Auditing command (Tools menu), Excel, 252
Auditing tools (Excel), 252
AutoCad, 605–699
basic objects
arcs, 657
circles, 655–656
lines, 654–655
points, 654
commands
new, 619
open, 620
quit (exit), 621
redraw, 618
save (qsave, saveas), 620–621
zoom, 618
coordinate input
absolute coordinate entry, 648–649
polar coordinate entry, 650–651
relative coordinate entry, 649–650
modifying objects
break, 671–672
extend, 671
lengthen, 677
move, 674
rotate, 675
scale, 676–677
stretch, 677–678
trim, 670–671
new from old
array, 660–661
chamfer, 662
copy, 659
fillet, 662
mirror, 660
offset, 659–660
polar, 662
rectangular, 661
object properties
color, 651
layer, 651
linetype, 651
linetype scale, 651
modifying, 652
preparing the drawing file
drawing aids (drafting settings), 638
layers, 629–630
limits, 633
linetypes, 630–632
object snap, 638–640
templates, 633
units, 628–629
selecting objects, 615–617
modifying, 617
screen layout, 609–615
docked toolbar, 610
floating command window, 610–611
floating toolbar, 610
mouse, 610
moving about the screen, 612–615
pull-down menu bar, 610

status bar (coordinate display), 611
viewing objects
aerial view, 691
layers, 694–696
pan realtime, 689, 692
recalling, 691–692
redraw, 692
regen, 692
saving, 691–692
zoom dynamic, 690
zoom previous, 689–690
zoom realtime, 689
AutoFilter (Excel), 313
AutoForm (Access), 464–466
exercise, 479
AutoFormat (Word), 173–174
exercise, 180
AutoReport (Access), 502
AutoShapes (PowerPoint), 358
AutoSum (Excel), 194–195, 259
exercise, 201

B

backgrounds (PowerPoint)
deleting, 399
backing up floppy disks, 764–765. *See also* saving
exercise, 767
backspace keys (Word), deleting, 79
bar charts (Excel). *See also* charts
creating, 282–283
blank databases (Access). *See also* databases
creating new, 405–406
blank presentations (PowerPoint), 326. *See also* presentations
borders (Excel), adding, 217–219
exercise, 222–223
Break command (Insert menu), Word, 150
Break dialog box, Word, 150
breaks (Word), inserting, 150–151
exercise, 163
browsers. See Internet Explorer; Netscape Navigator
built-in financial formulas (Excel), 261–263. *See also* formulas
bulleted lists (Word)
creating, 122–124
exercise, 136
sorting, 139
bullets (PowerPoint)
promoting, 329
Bullets and Numbering command (Format menu)
Word, 123

C

calculating. *See also* summing
cell references (Excel), 249–251
columns of numbers (Excel), 194–195
exercise, 201
loans (Excel), 260–261
exercise, 272–273
statistics (Excel), 274–275
values (Excel), 251–253
exercise, 271
values (Excel), 251. *See also* formulas
wages (Excel), 273
Calculator option, 742
category axis (PowerPoint), 375–376
cells (Excel)
copying, 233–234
data, 190–191
entering (exercise), 202–203
editing, 191–192
formatting, 206–209
modifying (exercise), 321–322
formulas
absolute, 257–259, 272
filling, 253–257
relative, 257–259, 272
modifying, 211–213
protecting (exercise), 226
references, 251–253
creating formulas (exercise), 271
mathematical calculations, 249–251
selecting, 188–190
text, 213–215
aligning (exercise), 224
Word
aligning (exercise), 181–182
merging (exercise), 181
Cells command (Format menu), Excel, 211, 231
center tabs (Word), 137
centering. *See also* formatting
text (Word), 118–120
Chart menu commands (PowerPoint), Chart Type, 375
Chart Type command (Chart menu), PowerPoint, 375
Chart Type dialog box
Excel, 288
PowerPoint, 375
Chart Type toolbar, PowerPoint, 373
Chart Wizard dialog box, Excel, 280
charts
Excel, 282
columns, 295–298
creating, 282–284, 317
documents, 320
editing, 284, 286–290
formulas, 299
line, 279–282, 294–297
PowerPoint, 385
printing, 290–291
types, 288, 295
X-Y, 298
PowerPoint, 368–373
animating, 398–399
flow, 368
formatting, 375–376
line, 382–383
modifying, 376–384
sample data, 370–371
slides, 381
types, 373–374
check boxes (Access), adding (exercise), 422
checking styles (PowerPoint), exercise, 342
Clear All command (Edit menu), Excel, 211
Clear Format command (Edit menu), Excel, 211
Click and Type feature (Word), 81
clicking mouse, 738
clip art. *See also* graphics
PowerPoint
inserting, 350–353, 362, 367
moving, 352–353, 362
resizing, 352–353, 362
watermarks, 475
Word
inserting, 151–152, 162–164
modifying, 153–156
Clip Art command (Insert menu)
PowerPoint, 350
Word, 151
Clipboard
Excel, 234
Word, 102
exercise, 112
closing
applications (Office 2000), 772
documents (Word), 82–83
exercise, 87
Excel, 196–197
exercise, 200
menus, 775
slide shows (PowerPoint), 341
colors
adding, 222–223
text (Excel), 216–217
text boxes (PowerPoint), 364–365
charts (PowerPoint), 379
column charts (Excel). *See also* charts
creating, 282–283
exercise, 294–298
printing, 294
Column Width command (Format menu), Access, 430
columnar options (Access), exercise, 502
columns
Access
documents (Word), 527
freezing, 439
modifying, 430–432, 438–441
Excel
deleting, 193–194
hiding/unhiding, 203
inserting, 193–194, 200–203
modifying, 211–213
summing, 194–195, 201
PowerPoint, 375–376

Word
documents, *166*
tables, *171–173, 180*
text, *111*
combining operations (Excel), 253–257
commands
Chart menu (PowerPoint), Chart Type, 375
Edit menu
Copy, 759
Paste, 759, 763
Edit menu (Access)
Delete, 450
Find, 467
Primary Key, 411
Select Record, 430
Undo, 428, 467
Edit menu (Excel)
Clear All, 211
Clear Formats, 211
Edit menu (PowerPoint)
Select All, 390
File menu
Rename, 757, 761
File menu (Access)
Get External Data, 514
Page Setup, 487
Print, 488
Save, 448
Save As, 410
Undo, 450
File menu (Excel)
Open, 206
Page Setup, 235
Print, 238
Save As, 196, 207
Save as Web Page, 311
File menu (PowerPoint), Print, 337
File menu (Word)
Page Setup, 143
Print, 106, 778
Save As, 94
Format menu (Access)
Column Width, 430
Hide Columns, 432
Format menu (Excel), Cells, 211, 231
Format menu (Word)
Bullets and Numbering, 123
Paragraph, 124
Picture, 155
Tabs, 131
Help menu, Hide the Office Assistant, 781
Help menu (PowerPoint), Microsoft PowerPoint Help, 329
Insert menu (PowerPoint)
Clip Art, 350
Picture, 350
Insert menu (Word)
Break, 150
Clip Art, 151
Page Numbers, 145
Records menu (Access)
Remove/Sort, 435
Sort, 435
Table menu (Word)
Insert Table, 170
Select Column, 175
Table AutoFormat, 173
Table Properties, 177
Tools menu (Excel)
Auditing, 252
Remove all Arrows, 252
Trace Dependents, 252
Tools menu (PowerPoint)
Options, 337
Tools menu (Word), Options, 74
View menu, Toolbars, 775
View menu (Access)
Form Header/Footer, 474
Toolbars, 414
View menu (Excel), Customize, 187
View menu (Office 2000)
as Web Page, 745
Details, 743
Toolbars, 743
View menu (PowerPoint)
Notes Page, 334
View menu (Word)
Header and Footer, 146
Ruler, 131
Toolbars, 103
Window menu (Excel), Unfreeze Panes, 233
conditional formatting (Excel). *See also* formatting
exercise, 226
conditional formulas (Excel), 264–266 *See also* formulas
configuring. *See also* customizing; preferences
margins (Word), 143–144
exercise, 162–165
printers, 752
connector lines (PowerPoint), 357–359
adding (exercise), 363–365
Connectors toolbar, PowerPoint, 358
Contents dialog box, 748
Convert Database Into dialog box, Access, 510
converting
databases (Access), 509–510
text (Word)
table (exercise), 182
Copy command (Edit menu), 759
Copy Disk dialog box, 765
copying
cells (Excel), 233–234
charts (Excel), 385
fields (Access), 414–416
exercise, 420
files, 758–760
exercise, 767
floppy disks, 764–765
exercise, 767
forms (Access), 483
records (Access), 440
tables (Access), 527
text (Word), 110
COUNTIF functions (Excel), 264
calculating wages (exercise), 273
counting formulas (Excel), 264–266. *See also* formulas
criteria (Access), 452–453
matching criteria (exercise), 459
currency. *See* numbers
current record indicators, 426
cursors, 73
Custom Animation dialog box, PowerPoint, 393
Custom Animation feature (PowerPoint), 393–394
exercise, 397
Customize command (View menu), Excel, 187
Customize dialog box, 776
customizing. *See also* configuring; preferences
fill handles (Excel), 246
fill lists (Excel), 245
forms (Access), 482
cutting. *See also* copying; moving; pasting
text (Word), 102–103
exercise, 109

D

data (data entry)
duplicate entries
preventing, 573–575
format
conditional, 563–565
creating consistent, 560–563
input mask, 565
creating, 565–569
lookup column
creating, 575–579
necessary information
requiring entry, 572–573
null value, 563
restricting entries
validation rules, 569, 569–572
Expression Builder, 569–572
validation text, 569
Data Access Pages (Access)
creating, 524–526
editing, 526
filtering, 526–527
forms, 516–518
sorting, 526–527
data labels (Excel), adding (exercise), 298
data series (Excel), 279
data types (Access), 406–407
exercise, 420
databases (Access), 402, 770
browsers, 518–519
accessing (exercise), 525

columns
  freezing (exercise), 439
  modifying (exercise), 438–441
converting, 509–510
creating, 405–406
  exercise, 419
crosstab queries (exercise), 461
data pages
  creating as Web pages (exercise), 524–525
  editing (exercise), 526
  filtering (exercise), 526–527
  sorting (exercise), 526–527
documents (exercise), 524
field labels (exercise), 480
fields
  adding, 411–412, 420–421
  deleting, 416–417, 420
  editing, 412–413, 420
  moving, 414–416, 420
form letters (Word)
  linking tables, 511–513
  merging tables, 513–514
forms
  adding date/time to headers (exercise), 481
  adding drop-down lists (exercise), 483
  adding fields, 470–472
  adding headers to labels, 474–476
  adding images to page headers (exercise), 481
  adding page numbers to footers (exercise), 481
  AutoForm, 464–466, 479
  closing, 467–468
  copying (exercise), 483
  creating, 468–470
  creating in Design view (exercise), 479
  customizing (exercise), 482
  editing data, 466–467, 479
  entering data, 466–467, 479
  headers/footers, 468
  inserting page breaks (exercise), 482
  moving fields, 472–474, 480
  opening, 467–468
  printing (exercise), 482
  resizing fields, 472–474, 480
  saving as Web pages, 516–518
  tabs (exercise), 484
labels, 480
memos (exercise), 523
multiple fields (exercise), 421
naming, 406
opening, 523–525
primary keys
  adding (exercise), 421
  creating, 410–411, 419–422
queries
  creating, 444–445, 458
  creating with wizards (exercise), 459
  deleting records (exercise), 461
  editing, 449–450, 458
  matching criteria, 452–453, 459
  modifying field order, 450–451, 458
  saving, 448–449
  saving with new names, 454–455, 458
  selecting fields, 446–448
  sorting, 450–451, 458
  sorting multiple fields (exercise), 459
records
  adding, 424–426, 438
  copying (exercise), 440
  deleting, 429–430, 438
  editing, 427–428, 438
  excluding/including (exercise), 460
  inserting, 429–430, 438
  limiting (exercise), 460
  navigating, 426–427
  pasting (exercise), 440
  printing (exercise), 439
  replacing data (exercise), 440
  searching, 432–434, 439–440
  sorting, 434–435, 439
reports
  adding labels (exercise), 501
  creating, 488–491, 500–502
  creating mailing labels (exercise), 505
  drawing lines (exercise), 504
  formatting (exercise), 503
  modifying, 493–495, 501
  modifying grouping (exercise), 504–505
  printing, 492, 501
  renaming, 491
  saving, 496–498
shortcuts (exercise), 441
sorts (exercise), 440
tables, 406–409
  adding check boxes (exercise), 422
  analyzing (exercise), 442
  copying to Word (exercise), 527
  creating (exercise), 419
  formatting text (exercise), 441
  printing, 486–488, 500
  saving, 410–411, 419
  updating to Excel (exercise), 527
tables, 525
  Excel, 514–516, 524
text (exercise), 526
tools (exercise), 441
views, 414–416
Datasheet view (Access), 408
datasheets (PowerPoint), 370–371
  exercise, 381
Date and Time dialog box, Word, 147
dates (Excel)
  exercise, 225
  Word, 147
dbase III Plus Database, importing tables to Access (exercise), 525
decimal tabs (Word), exercise, 137
decimals, 210. *See also* numbers
Delete command (Edit menu), Access, 450
deleting
  backgrounds (PowerPoint), 399
  columns/rows (Excel), 193–194
  field labels (Access), 480
  fields (Access), 416–417
    exercise, 420
  files, 763–764
  multiple fields (Access), 421
  records (Access), 429–430
    exercise, 438
  text (Word), 79
    exercise, 87, 109
delimiters (Access), 526
descending sorts (Access), 435. *See also* sorting
design grids (Access), 446
Design view (Access), 408
  creating (exercise), 479
desktop, 739
  Start button, 741–742
destination disks, 764. *See also* disks
Details command (View menu), Office 2000, 743
dialog boxes, 738
  Access
    Convert Database Into, 510
    File New Database, 405
    Find and Replace, 433
    Import, 514
    Import Spreadsheet Wizard, 515
    Merge, 513
    New Form, 465
    New Query, 445
    New Report, 489
    New Table, 407
    Page Setup, 487
    Print, 488
    Save As, 410, 448
    Show Table, 445
    Unhide Columns, 432
  Contents, 748
  Copy Disk, 765
  Excel
    Chart Type, 288
    Chart Wizard, 280
    Format Axis, 286
    Format Cells, 211, 231
    Format Chart Title, 285
    Header, 291
    Insert Hyperlink, 308
    Link to File, 309
    Open, 309
    Page Setup, 235
    Paste Function, 261
    Print, 238
    Save As, 196, 207, 311, 785
  Format, 755
    exercise, 767
  Format Results, 755
  Help, 749
  Help Topics, 748

PowerPoint
- *Apply Design Template, 349*
- *Chart Type, 375*
- *Custom Animation, 393*
- *Edit WordArt Text, 354*
- *Format Axis, 378*
- *Format Data Series, 377*
- *Insert Clip Art, 350*
- *New Slide, 327, 353*
- *Open, 347*
- *Print, 337, 779*
- *Save As, 333*
- *Slide Layout, 331*
- *WordArt Gallery, 353*

Word
- *Break, 150*
- *Date and Time, 147*
- *Format Picture, 155*
- *Insert ClipArt, 152*
- *Insert Table, 170*
- *Mail Merge Wizard, 511*
- *Open, 93, 773*
- *Options, 74*
- *Page Numbers, 145*
- *Page Setup, 143*
- *Paragraph, 120, 125*
- *Print, 106, 779*
- *Save As, 82, 777*
- *Spelling and Grammar, 82*
- *Table AutoFormat, 173*
- *Tabs, 131*

dimming text (PowerPoint), 505–506
- exercise, 509

disks, 754
- copying, 764–765
  - *exercise, 767*
- files, 767
- folders, 756–757
- formatting, 754–756
- Quick Format option (exercise), 767

dividing worksheets (Excel), 303

documents (Word)
- AutoFormat, 173–174
  - *exercise, 180*
- bulleted lists
  - *creating, 122–124, 136*
  - *sorting (exercise), 139*
- charts (Excel), 320
- Click and Type feature, 97
- clip art
  - *inserting, 151–152, 162–164*
  - *modifying, 153–156*
- closing, 82–83
  - *exercise, 87*
- columns of text, 111
- different file formats, 111
- editing (exercise), 87
- entering, 73–76
  - *exercise, 85–86*
- existing
  - *inserting text (exercise), 109*
  - *opening, 93–95, 109*
- fonts, 116–118
  - *modifying (exercise), 136*
- form letters
  - *linking tables (Access), 511–513*
  - *merging tables (Access), 513–514*
- grammar checking, 80–82
  - *exercise, 86*
- headers/footers
  - *adding (exercise), 162–166*
  - *creating, 146–149*
  - *dates, 147*
  - *formatting text, 148*
- Help (exercise), 88
- importing to Access (exercise), 526
- landscape layout (exercise), 89
- Letter Wizard (exercise), 88–89
- line spacing, 120–122
- margins, 143–144
  - *configuring (exercise), 162–165*
- naming, 93–95
  - *exercise, 109*
- navigating, 76–78
- numbered lists (exercise), 137, 139
- opening, 73–76, 773–774
  - *exercise, 85–86*
- outlines (exercise), 343
- page breaks, 150–151
  - *inserting (exercise), 163*
- page numbers, 145
  - *inserting (exercise), 162*
- paragraphs
  - *adding spaces, 129–130*
  - *aligning text, 118–120*
  - *Format Painter, 126–127*
  - *formatting (exercise), 136*
  - *hanging indents, 127–128*
  - *indenting, 124*
- Print Preview, 156–159
  - *exercise, 163*
- printing, 82–83, 778–779
  - *exercise, 87*
- renaming, 777–778
- reports (exercise), 341
- saving, 82–83, 774
  - *exercise, 87–88*
- spell checking, 80–82
  - *exercise, 86*
- subscripts/superscripts (exercise), 138
- tables
  - *adding rows/columns, 173–177, 180*
  - *aligning cells (exercise), 181–182*
  - *aligning numbers (exercise), 180*
  - *aligning text, 175–177*
  - *entering data, 170–171*
  - *formulas (exercise), 182*
  - *inserting, 169–170, 180*
  - *merging cells (exercise), 181*
  - *sorting (exercise), 182*
- tables (Access), 527
- tabs, 130–133
- text
  - *converting to tables (Word), 182*
  - *copying (exercise), 110*
  - *deleting, 79, 87, 109*
  - *drag-and-drop, 104–106, 109*
  - *inserting, 95–96*
  - *moving, 102–103, 109*
  - *pasting (exercise), 110*
  - *printing, 106–107, 111*
  - *replacing (exercise), 109*
  - *selecting, 98–102, 109*
  - *Undo (exercise), 110*
  - *Undo/Redo, 103–104*
- thumbnails (exercise), 112
- title pages (Word), 87
- two columns (exercise), 166
- underlining words (exercise), 137
- worksheets (Excel)
  - *Paste Special (exercise), 319–320*
  - *pasting (exercise), 318*

drag-and-drop (Word), 104–106
- exercise, 109

drawing lines in reports (Access), exercise, 504

drawing objects (PowerPoint), exercise, 398

Drawing toolbar (PowerPoint), exercise, 367

drives, Zip, 764

drop-down lists (Access), adding (exercise), 483

dynasets (Access), 447

E

Edit menu commands
- Copy, 759
- Paste, 759, 763

Edit menu commands (Access)
- Delete, 450
- Find, 467
- Primary Key, 411
- Select Record, 430
- Undo, 428, 467

Edit menu commands (Excel)
- Clear All, 211
- Clear Formats, 211

Edit menu commands (PowerPoint), Select All, 390

Edit WordArt Text dialog box, PowerPoint, 354

editing
- cells (Excel), 191–192
- charts (Excel), 284, 286–290
- Data Access Pages (Access), 526
- documents (Word), 87
- fields (Access), 412–413
  - *exercise, 420*
- forms (Access), 466–467
  - *exercise, 479*

queries (Access), 449–450
exercise, 458
records (Access), 427–428
exercise, 438
text
PowerPoint (exercise), 340
presentations (PowerPoint), 330–332
worksheets (Excel), 200, 223
data
cells (Excel), 190–191
tables (exercise), 420
data
Word, 170–171
Excel, 202–203
forms (Access), 466–467
exercise, 479
formulas (Excel), 251
text
PowerPoint (exercise), 340
presentations (PowerPoint), 328–330
text (Word), 73–76
exercise, 85–86
headers/footers, 146–149, 162–166
EMail, see Outlook Express
dedicated connections, 5
dial-up connections, 5
ethernet, 5
HTTP (Hypertext Transfer Protocol), 27
IMAP (Internet Message Access Protocol), 27
ISP (Internet Service Provider), 5
mail server, 26
modem, 5
POP (Post Office Protocol), 27
server, 5
estimating values (Excel), 299
Excel
absolute references, 254
Auditing tools, 252
borders, 217–219
adding (exercise), 222–223
built-in financial formulas, 261–263
calculating statistics (exercise), 274–275
cell references, 251–253
creating formulas (exercise), 271
mathematical calculations, 249–251
cells, 213–215
aligning text (exercise), 224
copying, 233–234
filling with absolute formulas, 257–259, 272
filling with formulas, 253–257
filling with relative formulas, 257–259, 272
modifying formatting (exercise), 321–322
protecting (exercise), 226
selecting, 206, 209
charts
copying into PowerPoint (exercise), 385
creating, 282–284, 293–294
editing, 284, 286–290
inserting into PowerPoint (exercise), 385
modifying types, 288, 295
pasting into documents (exercise), 320
printing, 290–291, 294
closing, 196–197
exercise, 200
colors (exercise), 222–223
column charts (exercise), 295–298
columns (exercise), 203
combining operations, 253–257
commands
Auditing (Tools menu), 252
Cells (Format menu), 211, 231
Clear All (Edit menu), 211
Clear Formats (Edit menu), 211
Customize (View menu), 187
Open (File menu), 206
Page Setup (File menu), 235
Print (File menu), 238
Remove All Arrows (Tools menu), 252
Save As (File menu), 196, 207
Save as Web Page (File menu), 311
Trace Dependents (Tools menu), 252
Unfreeze Panes (Windows menu), 233
conditional formulas. See *also* formulas,
applying, 264–266
COUNTIF function (exercise), 273
counting formulas, 264–266
data series, 279
dates (exercise), 225
dialog boxes
Chart Wizard, 280
Format Axis, 286
Format Cells, 211, 231
Format Chart Title, 285
Header, 291
Insert Hyperlink, 308
Link to File, 309
Open, 206, 309
Page Setup, 235
Paste Function, 261
Print, 238
Save As, 207, 311, 785
existing worksheets. See *also* worksheets
formatting (exercise), 221–222
files
opening, 206–209
saving, 785
fonts, 216–217
formulas, 260–261
applying (exercise), 272–273
exercise, 274
recalculating, 266–268
trend lines (exercise), 299
frequency distribution (exercise), 275
Goal Seek (exercise), 274
line charts, 279–282
creating (exercise), 294–297
lines, 217–219
adding (exercise), 222–223
numbers
formatting, 210–211
modifying cells/columns, 211–213
series, 229–231
panes, 23, 231
relative references, 254
shading, 217–219
Solver (exercise), 276
starting (exercise), 785
tables, 514–516
exporting to databases (exercise), 524
formatting merge cells (exercise), 223–224
text
creating sequential headings, 228–229
modifying, 216–217
VLOOKUP (exercise), 275
wizards (Chart), 280
word wrapping feature, 215
workbooks
inserting hyperlinks, 308–311, 321
navigating, 186–188
saving, 196–197
saving as Web pages (exercise), 320–321
worksheets
creating (exercise), 199–200
creating charts (exercise), 317
creating lease reports (exercise), 242
creating schedules (exercise), 243–244
creating summary sheets, 304, 316
creating time reports (exercise), 243
customizing fill handles (exercise), 246
customizing fill lists (exercise), 245
deleting columns/rows, 193–194
editing (exercise), 200, 223
editing cells, 191–192
entering data into cells, 190–191, 202–203
header/footer options (exercise), 245
inserting columns/rows, 193–194, 200–203
linking summary sheets, 305–308
moving, 303
Paste Special (exercise), 319–320
pasting into documents (exercise), 318
posting to Web (exercise), 322
previewing printing, 238–239, 246
printing, 196–197, 235–237
projecting population growth (exercise), 224
renaming, 219
saving as Web pages, 311–312
saving summary sheets as Web pages (exercise), 317
selecting cells, 188–190
summing columns, 194–195, 201
XML, 312–314
X-Y charts
adding data labels (exercise), 298
adding trend lines (exercise), 299
y-axis, 286
Y2K
conditional formatting exercise, 226
exercise, 225
zoom, 231–232
executing self-running presentations (PowerPoint), exercise, 400

existing files (Excel), opening, 206
existing documents (Word)
inserting text (exercise), 109
opening, 93–95
exercise, 109
existing presentations (PowerPoint)
designs, 347–349, 362
opening, 347–349, 362
existing worksheets (Excel), exercise, 221–222
exiting. *See* closing
Explorer
disks, 754
files, 743–744
interface, 743
exporting tables (Access), exercise, 527
Extensible Markup Language. *See* XML
extensions, files, 759

F

features
Custom Animation (PowerPoint), 393–394
exercise, 397
fields (Access)
adding, 411–412
exercise, 420–421
creating, 408
deleting, 416–417
exercise, 420
editing, 412–413, 428
exercise, 420
forms
adding, 470–472
moving, 472–474, 480
resizing, 472–474, 480
hyperlinks (exercise), 422
labels (exercise), 480
Lookup wizard (exercise), 422
moving, 414–416
exercise, 420
multiple (exercise), 421
numeric (exercise), 460
primary keys
adding (exercise), 421
creating, 410–411
queries
modifying order, 450–451, 458
selecting, 445–448
text
excluding/including records (exercise), 460
limiting records (exercise), 460
File menu commands, Rename, 757, 761
File menu commands (Access)
Get External Data, 514
Page Setup, 487
Print, 488
Save, 448
Save As, 410
Undo, 450
File menu commands (Excel)
Open, 206
Page Setup, 235
Print, 238
Save As, 196, 207
Save as Web Page, 311
File menu commands (PowerPoint)
Print, 337
File menu commands (Word)
Page Setup, 143
Print, 778
Save As, 94
File New Database dialog box, Access, 405
files, 754
copying, 758–760
exercise, 767
deleting, 763–764
extensions, 759
folders, 756–758
moving, 761–762
renaming, 760–761
exercise, 767
saving (exercise), 767
Windows Explorer, 743–744
files (Excel), exercise, 785
files (Word)
closing (exercise), 87
different formats (exercise), 111
editing (exercise), 87
importing to Access (exercise), 526
navigating, 76–79
opening, 73–76
exercise, 85–86
printing (exercise), 87
saving (exercise), 87–88
text
closing, 82–83
deleting, 79
deleting (exercise), 87
grammar checking, 80–82, 86
printing, 82–83
saving, 82–83
spell checking, 80–82, 86
fill handles (Excel), exercise, 246
fill lists (Excel), exercise, 245
filling cells (Excel)
absolute formulas, 257–259, 272
formulas, 253–257
relative formulas, 257–259, 272
filtering Data Access Pages (Access), exercise, 526–527
financial formulas (Excel), 261–263. *See also* formulas
Find and Replace dialog box, Access, 433
Find command (Edit menu), Access, 467
finding. *See also* searching records
records (Access), 432–434
exercise, 439–440
floppy disks. *See also* disks
copying, 764–765
exercise, 767
files
copying, 767
renaming, 767
folders, 756–757
Quick Format option, 767
exercise, 77
flow charts (PowerPoint), exercise, 368
folders, 754
copying (exercise), 767
creating, 756–757
deleting, 763–764
moving, 761–762
renaming, 760–761
saving (exercise), 767
fonts (Excel), 216–217
fonts (Word), 116–118
exercise, 136
footers (Access), forms, 468
footers (Excel), options, 245
footers (Word)
adding (exercise), 162–166
adding dates, 147
creating, 146–149
text, 148
Form Design view (Access), 473
Form Header/Footer command (View menu), Access, 474
form letters (Word), 511–513
Form Wizard (Access), 465
Format Axis dialog box
Excel, 286
PowerPoint, 378
Format Cells dialog box, Excel, 211, 231
Format Chart Title dialog box, Excel, 285
Format Data Series dialog box, PowerPoint, 377
Format dialog box, 755
exercise, 767
Format menu commands (Access)
Column Width, 430
Hide Columns, 432
Format menu commands (Excel), Cells, 211, 231
Format menu commands (Word)
Bullets and Numbering, 123
Paragraph, 124
Picture, 155
Tabs, 131
Format Painter (PowerPoint), adding (exercise), 365
Format Painter (Word), 126–127
exercise, 136
Format Picture dialog box, Word, 155
Format Results dialog box, 755
formatting
AutoFormat (Word), 173–174
exercise, 180
cells (Excel), 206–209
modifying (exercise), 321–322
charts (PowerPoint), 375–376
columns (Access), 430–432
exercise, 438–439

conditional (Excel), 226
disks, 754–755
Quick Format option, 767
existing worksheets (Excel)
exercise, 221–222
headers/footers (Word), 148
numbers (Excel), 210–211
modifying cells/columns, 211–213
paragraphs (Word)
adding spaces, 129–130
exercise, 136
Format Painter, 126–127, 136
hanging indents, 127–128
tabs, 130–133
reports (Access), 503
tables (Excel), 223–224
text
Access, 441
Word (exercise), 138
text boxes (PowerPoint), 365
Formatting toolbars, 775
Access, 475
forms (Access)
AutoForm, 464–466
exercise, 479
closing, 467–468
copying (exercise), 483
creating, 468–470
customizing (exercise), 482
data
editing, 466–467, 479
entering, 466–467, 479
fields
adding, 470–472
moving, 472–474, 480
resizing, 472–474, 480
footers (exercise), 481
headers, 468
adding date/time (exercise), 481
labels, 474–476
images (exercise), 481
opening, 467–468
page breaks (exercise), 482
printing (exercise), 482
tabs (exercise), 484
formulas (Excel)
applying, 260–261
applying (exercise), 272–273
built-in financial, 261–263
calculating statistics (exercise), 274–275
cell references, 251–253
creating (exercise), 271
cells
absolute, 257–259, 272
filling, 253–257
relative, 257–259, 272
conditional, 264–266
counting, 264–266
entering, 251
exercise, 274
palettes, 262
recalculating, 266–268
summary sheets, 305–308
trend lines (exercise), 299
formulas (Word), exercise, 182
freezing
columns (Access), 439
panes (Excel), 231–233
frequency distribution (Excel), exercise, 275
functions (Excel), 257. See *also* commands; formulas
COUNTIF, 264
calculating wages (exercise), 273
Paste, 261
PMT, 261

G

Get External Data command (File menu), Access, 514
Goal Seek (Excel), exercise, 274
grammar check (Word), 80–82
exercise, 86
graphic user interface. See GUI
graphics (PowerPoint). See *also* clip art
circular WordArt (exercise), 367–368
inserting, 350–353
exercise, 362, 367
moving, 352–353
exercise, 362
resizing, 352–353
exercise, 362
watermarks (exercise), 363
WordArt, 353–355
adding (exercise), 362, 366
moving, 355
graphics (Word), 151–152
inserting (exercise), 162–164
modifying, 153–156
groups, selecting, 206–209
GUI (graphic user interface), 741
guides (PowerPoint), 355
gutter margins (Word). See margins; white space

H

handles (Excel), customizing (exercise), 246
handouts (PowerPoint), printing, 359–360
hanging indents (Word), 124
creating, 127–128
exercise, 136
Header and Footer command (View menu)
Word, 146
Header dialog box, Excel, 291
headers (Access), 474–476
headers (Excel), exercise, 245
headers (Word)
adding (exercise), 162
creating, 146–149
dates, 147
text, 148
headings (Excel), sequential, 228–229
Help, 748–749, 778–781
Answer Wizard, 781
exercise, 786
indexes, 749
Internet, 782–783
outlines (exercise), 342
presentations (PowerPoint), 342
printers, 752
Word (exercise), 88
Help dialog box, 749
Help menu commands
Hide the Office Assistant, 781
Microsoft PowerPoint Help, 329
Help Topics dialog box, 748
Hide Columns command (Format menu), Access, 432
Hide the Office Assistant command (Help menu), 781
hiding
columns (Access), 430–432
exercise, 438–441
columns (Excel), 203
home pages. See Web pages
horizontal scrollbars, 745–746. See *also* scrollbars
HTML (Hypertext Markup Language), 771
hyperlinks (Access), exercise, 422
hyperlinks (Excel)
summary sheets, 305–308
workbooks, 308–311
inserting (exercise), 321
Hypertext Markup Language. See HTML

I

icons, My Computer, 739–740
images. See graphics; pictures
Import dialog box, Access, 514
Import Spreadsheet Wizard dialog box, Access, 515
importing. See *also* moving
tables (dBase III Plus Database), 525
tables (Excel), 514–516
databases (exercise), 524
text (exercise), 526
indenting paragraphs (Word), 124–128
hanging indents (exercise), 136
tabs, 130–133
indexes
exercise, 786
Help, 749
Insert Clip Art dialog box
PowerPoint, 350
Word, 152
Insert Hyperlink dialog box, Excel, 308
Insert menu commands (PowerPoint)
Clip Art, 350

Picture, 350
Insert menu commands (Word)
Break, 150
Clip Art, 151
Page Numbers, 145
Insert Table commands (Table menu), Word, 170
Insert Table dialog box, (Word), 170
inserting. *See also* adding
breaks (exercise), 482
charts (Excel), 385
circular WordArt (PowerPoint), 367–368
clip art (PowerPoint), 350–353
exercise, 362, 367
clip art (Word), 151–152
exercise, 162–164
columns/rows (Excel), 200–203
fields (Access), 411–412
exercise, 420–421
formulas (Excel), 305–308
hyperlinks (Excel), 308–311
workbooks (exercise), 321
page breaks (Word), 150–151
exercise, 163
page numbers (Word), 145
exercise, 162
records (Access), 429–430
exercise, 438
tables (Word), 169–170
exercise, 180
text (Word), 95–96
exercise, 109
insertion points (Word), 73
interface
Excel, 188
PowerPoint, 326–328
Windows Explorer, 743
Internet
data pages (Access)
creating as Web pages (exercise), 524–526
editing (exercise), 526
filtering (exercise), 526–527
sorting (exercise), 526–527
forms (Access), 516–518
Help, 782–783
Web pages (Excel)
saving workbooks as (exercise), 320–321
saving worksheets as, 311–312
viewing worksheets, 312–314
Internet Explorer, 6–9, 311
databases (Access), accessing, 518–519, 525
worksheets (Excel), 312–314

J-K

justifying. *See also* formatting
text (Word), 118–120
justifying. *See also* aligning, 118
keyboard shortcuts. *See also* shortcuts
Access, 427
Excel, 189
My Computer, 740
Word, 78

L

labels (Access)
fields (exercise), 480
forms, 474–476
reports
adding (exercise), 501
mailing (exercise), 505
labels (Excel) (exercise), 298
LAN (local area network), 311
landscape (Word), exercise, 89
launching. *See* opening; starting
layouts (exercise), 89
PowerPoint, 331–332
leaders (Word), 130–133
lease report worksheets (Excel), exercise, 242
left aligned text (Word), 118–120
legends (PowerPoint), 378
Letter Wizard (Word), exercise, 88–89
line charts (Excel). *See also* charts
creating, 279–282
exercise, 294–297
modifying (PowerPoint), 382–383
lines (Excel)
adding, 217–219
exercise, 222–223
trend, 299
lines (PowerPoint), 357–359
adding between objects (exercise), 363–365
line spacing (Word), 120–122
Link to File dialog box, Excel, 309
linking. *See also* hyperlinks
summary sheets (Excel), 305–308
tables (Access), 511–513
workbooks (Excel), 308–311
exercise, 321
lists (Access), exercise, 483
lists (Excel), exercise, 245
lists (Word)
bulleted, 122–124
creating (exercise), 136
sorting (exercise), 139
numbered (exercise), 137–139
loan repayments (Excel), 260–261
applying (exercise), 272–273
local area network. *See* LAN
Lookup Wizard (Access), exercise, 422

M

mail merge (Access)
documents (exercise), 524
form letters (Word), 511–513
memos, 523
Mail Merge Wizard dialog box, Word, 511
mailing labels (exercise), 511
margins (Word). *See also* white space
configuring, 143–144
exercise, 162–165
marquees (Excel), 195
matching criteria (Access), 452–453
queries (exercise), 459
mathematical calculations (Excel)
cell references, 249–251
loan repayments, 244
MathPro, 889–891
maximizing windows, 746, 772
menus
Accessories, 742
bars, 743
closing, 775
exercise, 786
Open, 740
Programs, 741
Start, 741, 752
menus (Word)
documents, 778–779
printing, 106–107
Merge dialog box, Access, 513
merging
cells (Word), 181
databases (Access)
creating memos (exercise), 523
documents (Word), 511–514
tables (Access), 513–514
merging (Excel), 223–224
Microcomputer Hardware, 787–888
AGP (Accelerated Graphics Port), 799–800
ASCII (American Standard Code for Information Interchange), 806–809
coprocessor, 817–821
graphics accelerator adapters, 799
I/O, 856–877
keyboard, 788–791
memory
primary, 822–829
secondary, 822, 830–846
microprocessor, 814–817
motherboard, 811–814
mouse, 791
printers
cables, 803
connections, 803–806
impact printers, 800–802
nonimpact printers, 800, 802
trackballs, 791
troubleshooting, 877–888
video
adapters, 791–792
monitors, 791–799
Microsoft PowerPoint Help command (Help menu), PowerPoint, 329
minimizing windows, 746
mirror margins (Word). *See* margins; white space

modifying
cells (Excel), 211–213
formatting (exercise), 321–322
chart types (Excel), 288
exercise, 295
charts (PowerPoint), 376–379
exercise, 381
formatting, 375–376
clip art (Word), 153–156
columns (Access), 430–432
exercise, 438–439
columns (Excel), 211–213
modifying
documents (Word), 166
field order (Access), 450–451
queries (exercise), 458
files (Windows Explorer), 743–744
fonts (Excel), 216–217
fonts (Word), 116–118
exercise, 136
line charts (PowerPoint), 382–383
line spacing (Word), 120, 122
pie charts (PowerPoint), 383–384
reports (Access), 493–495
exercise, 501
grouping (exercise), 504–505
slide layouts (PowerPoint), 331–332
views (My Computer), 752
views (Access), 414–416
windows, 743–744
zoom (Excel), 231–232
mouse
clicking, 738
pointer, 739
Windows, 738–741
moving. *See also* copying; cutting; pasting; importing
clip art (PowerPoint), 352–353
exercise, 362
clip art (Word), 153–154
fields (Access), 414–416
exercise, 420
forms, 472–474, 480
files, 761–762
text (Word), 102–103
exercise, 109
Windows, 743–744
WordArt (PowerPoint), 355
worksheets (Excel), 303
multiple documents (Word). *See also* documents
exercise, 111
multiple fields (Access). *See also* fields
exercise, 421
multiple queries (Access). *See also* queries
opening, 454–455
multiple windows. *See also* windows
taskbars, 747–748
MultiSim, 701–732
components
ammeter, 707–708
capacitive reactance, 712–713
capacitor, 711
ground terminal, 709
oscilloscope, 711–712
resistor, 705–707
stimulating the circuit, 709–710
time, 711
two-resistor parallel circuit, 710–711
two-resistor series circuit, 710
voltmeter, 707
wires, 708–709
digital logic circuitry, 729–732
operational amplifiers, 725–728
power supply circuits, 717–720
special components
diode, 714–715
transformer, 713–714
transistor, 715–716
transistor amplifier, 721–724
My Computer, 739–740
views, 752

N

naming. *See also* renaming
databases (Access), 406
documents (Word), 93–95
exercise, 105
saving, 777–778
files, 760–761
exercise, 767
queries (Access), 448, 454–455
exercise, 458
worksheets (Excel), 219
navigating
documents (Word), 76–78
interface (PowerPoint), 326–328
multiple windows, 747–748
records (Access), 426–427
Windows, 736, 738–741, 746
workbooks (Excel), 186–188
World Wide Web, 10–14
Netscape Navigator, 311
New Form dialog box, Access, 465
New Query dialog box, Access, 445
New Report dialog box, Access, 489
New Slide dialog box, PowerPoint, 327, 353
New Table dialog box, Access, 407
Normal view (PowerPoint), 328
presentations, 328–330
notes (PowerPoint), speaker, 334–354
adding (exercise), 341
Notes Page command (View menu), PowerPoint, 334
numbered lists (Word), exercise, 137–139
numbers (Excel)
cells
editing, 191–192
entering, 190–191
entering (exercise), 202–203
columns
summing, 194–195
summing (exercise), 197
formatting, 210–211
series, 229–231
numbers (Word)
pages, 145
configuring (exercise), 162
tables (exercise), 180
numeric fields (Access), 460

O

objects (Access)
crosstab queries (exercise), 461
queries
creating, 444–445, 458
creating with wizards (exercise), 459
editing, 449–450, 458
matching criteria, 452–453, 459
modifying field order, 450–451, 458
saving, 448–449
saving with new names, 454–455, 458
selecting fields, 446–448
sorting, 450–451, 458
sorting multiple fields (exercise), 459
objects (PowerPoint)
connector lines, 357–359
adding (exercise), 363, 365
drawing (exercise), 398
text boxes, 355–357
adding (exercise), 363
colors (exercise), 364–365
Office 2000
applications, 770–771
closing, 772
menus, 774–777
starting, 771–773
toolbars, 774–777
commands
As Web Page (View menu), 745
Details (View menu), 743
Toolbars (View menu), 743
menus (exercise), 786
toolbars (exercise), 786
Office Assistant, 771–781. *See also* Help
exercise, 786
online. *See* Internet; Web
Open command (File menu), Excel, 206
Open dialog box
Excel, 206, 309
PowerPoint, 347
Word, 93, 773
Open menu, 740
opening. *See also* starting
documents (Word), 73–76
exercise, 85–86
existing presentations (PowerPoint), 347–349
exercise, 362
forms (Access), 467–468
multiple queries (Access), 454–455

presentations (PowerPoint), 326–328
exercise, 340
previous version databases (Access)
exercise, 523, 525
Windows, 741
WordPad (exercise), 752
worksheets (Excel), 206–209
operating systems. See Windows
operations (Excel), combining, 253–257
options
Calculator, 742
Quick Format (exercise), 767
reports (Access), 488
options (Excel), 245
Options command (Tools menu)
PowerPoint, 337
Word, 74
Options dialog box, Word, 74
orientation slides (PowerPoint), 366
Outline view (PowerPoint), 328
presentations, 330–332
outlines (PowerPoint)
presentations (PowerPoint), 343
printing, 337–338
transitions (exercise), 400
outlines (Word)
importing to PowerPoint (exercise), 342
presentations (PowerPoint), 343
Outlook Express, 21–46
composing, 29–31
configuring, 26–29
deleting, 34–38
inbox, 31
forwarding, 34–38
managing
address book, 38–39
panes, 31–32
reading, 31–33
replying, 34–38
saving, 34–38
sending, 29–31
starting, 23–25

P

page breaks (Word), 150–151
exercise, 163
page numbers (Word), 145
exercise, 162
Page Numbers command (Insert menu), Word, 145
Page Numbers dialog box, Word, 145
Page Setup command (File menu)
Excel, 235
Word, 143
Page Setup commands (File menu), Access, 487
Page Setup dialog box
Access, 487
Excel, 235
Word, 143
Page Wizard (Access), 517
palettes (Excel), 262
panes (Excel), freezing, 231–233
Paragraph command (Format menu), Word, 124
Paragraph dialog box, Word, 120, 125
paragraphs (Word)
Format Painter, 126–127
exercise, 136
formatting (exercise), 136
hanging indents, 127–128
exercise, 136
indenting, 124
spaces, 129–130
tabs, 130–133
text, 118–120
Paste command (Edit menu), 759, 763
Paste function (Excel), 261
Paste Function dialog box, Excel, 261
Paste Special command (Excel)
worksheets (Excel), 319–320
Paste Special command (PowerPoint)
charts (Excel), 385
pasting
charts (Excel), 320
data (Access), 440
text (Word), 109–110
exercise, 110
worksheets (Excel), 318
PhotoDraw, 771
Picture command (Format menu), Word, 155
Picture command (Insert menu)
PowerPoint, 462
Picture toolbar, PowerPoint, 351
pictures. See clip art; graphics
pie charts (Excel), 283–284. *See also* charts
exercise, 293
pie charts (PowerPoint)
creating (exercise), 383
modifying (exercise), 384
placeholders (PowerPoint), 328
PMT function (Excel), 261
pointers, 739
points (Word), 118
population growth (Excel), 244
posting worksheets to the Web (Excel), 322
PowerPoint
animation sounds (exercise), 400
audience handouts, 359–360
AutoShapes, 358
backgrounds (exercise), 399
category axis, 375–376
charts
adding slides (exercise), 381
animating (exercise), 398–399
modifying, 376–381
replacing sample data, 370–371, 381
selecting chart types, 373–374
circular WordArt (exercise), 367–368
clip art
displaying as watermarks (exercise), 363
inserting, 350–353, 362, 367
moving, 352–353, 362
resizing, 352–353, 362
commands
Chart Type (Chart menu), 375
Clip Art (Insert menu), 350
Microsoft PowerPoint Help, 329
Notes Page (View menu), 334
Options (Tools menu), 337
Picture (Insert menu), 350
Print (File menu), 337
Select All (Edit menu), 390
connector lines, 357–359
adding (exercise), 363, 365
Custom Animation feature, 393–394
exercise, 397
dialog boxes
Apply Design Template, 349
Chart Type, 375
Custom Animation, 393
Edit WordArt Text, 354
Format Axis, 378
Format Data Series, 377
Insert Clip Art, 350
New Slide, 327, 353
Open, 347
Print, 337, 779
Save As, 333
Slide Layout, 331
drawing objects (exercise), 398
Drawing toolbar (exercise), 367
Excel charts
copying (exercise), 385
inserting (exercise), 385
existing presentations
applying designs, 347–349, 362
opening, 347–349, 362
flowcharts (exercise), 368
guides, 355
interface, 326–328
legends, 378
line charts (exercise), 382–383
outlines (Word), 342
pie charts
creating (exercise), 383
modifying (exercise), 384
placeholders, 328
presentations
closing slide shows (exercise), 341
creating (exercise), 341–343
creating outlines (exercise), 343
editing text, 330–332
editing text (exercise), 340
entering text, 328–330
entering text (exercise), 340
opening, 326–328, 340
previewing slide shows, 336–337, 341

printing outlines, 337–338
saving, 334–335, 341
random transitions (exercise), 398
self-running presentations (exercise), 400
slides
modifying layouts, 331–332
speaker notes, 334–335
adding (exercise), 341
styles (exercise), 342
tables (exercise), 384
text
animating, 391–393
dimming, 393–394, 397
text boxes, 355–357
adding (exercise), 363
colors (exercise), 364–365
toolbars
Chart Type, 373
Connectors, 358
Picture, 351
transitions
animating, 390–391
animating (exercise), 397
applying (exercise), 397
Slide Sorter view, 388–390, 396–400
transitions in outlines (exercise), 400
value axis, 377
views
Normal, 328
Outline, 328
Slide Show, 328
Slide Sorter, 328
WordArt
adding, 353–355, 362–366
animating (exercise), 399
moving, 355
predefined images. *See* clip art; graphics
presentation managers. *See* PowerPoint; presentations
presentations (PowerPoint)
animation sounds (exercise), 400
audience handouts, 359–360
backgrounds (exercise), 399
charts
adding slides (exercise), 381
animating (exercise), 398–399
modifying, 376–379
modifying formatting, 375–376
replacing sample data, 370–371, 381
selecting chart types, 373–374
circular WordArt (exercise), 367–368
clip art
inserting, 350–353, 362–367
moving, 352–353, 362
resizing, 352–353, 362
connector lines, 357–359
adding (exercise), 363, 365
creating (exercise), 341–343
creating outlines (exercise), 343
drawing objects (exercise), 398
Drawing toolbar (exercise), 367
Excel charts
copying (exercise), 385
inserting (exercise), 385
existing
applying designs, 347–349, 362
opening, 347–349, 362
interface, 326–328
line charts (exercise), 382–383
opening, 326–328
exercise, 340
outlines, 337–338
pie charts
creating (exercise), 383
modifying (exercise), 384
placeholders, 328
random transitions (exercise), 398
saving, 334–335
exercise, 341
self-running (exercise), 400
slide shows
closing (exercise), 341
previewing, 336–337, 341
slides
modifying layouts, 331–332
speaker notes, 334–335
adding (exercise), 341
styles (exercise), 342
tables (exercise), 384
text
animating, 391–393
dimming, 393–397
editing, 330–332, 340
entering, 328–330, 340
text boxes
adding, 355–357, 363
colors (exercise), 364–365
transitions
animating, 390–391, 397
applying (exercise), 397
Slide Sorter view, 388–390, 396–400
views
Normal, 328
Outline, 328
Slide Show, 328
Slide Sorter, 328
WordArt
adding, 353–355, 362, 366
animating (exercise), 399
moving, 355
previewing
slide shows (PowerPoint), 336–337
exercise, 341
worksheets (Excel), 238–239
printing (exercise), 246
previous versions (Access), 509–510
opening (exercise), 523, 525
Print Preview (Word), 156–159
exercise, 163
Primary Key command (Edit menu), Access, 411
primary keys (Access)
adding (exercise), 421
creating, 410–411
exercise, 419, 422
Print command (File menu)
Access, 488
Excel, 238
PowerPoint, 337
Word, 106, 778
Print dialog box
Access, 488
Excel, 238
PowerPoint, 779
Word, 106, 779
Print Layout view (Word) (exercise), 87
Print Preview (Word), 156–159
exercise, 163
printing
audience handouts (PowerPoint), 359–360
charts (Excel), 290–291
databases (Access), 524
documents (Word), 82–83, 778–779
exercise, 87
forms (Access), 482
Help (exercise), 752
outlines (PowerPoint), 337–338
Print Preview (Word), 156–159
exercise, 163
records (Access), 439
reports (Access), 492
exercise, 501
tables (Access), 486–488
exercise, 500
text (Word), 106–107
exercise, 111
thumbnails (Word), 112
worksheets (Excel), 196–197, 235–237
exercise, 245
previewing, 238–239, 246
Programs menu, 741
programs. *See* applications
projecting population growth (Excel), exercise, 244
promoting bullets (PowerPoint), 329
proofreading text (Word), 80–82
exercise, 86
protecting cells (Excel)
exercise, 226

Q

queries (Access)
creating, 444–445
exercise, 458
creating with wizards (exercise), 459
criteria, 452–453
matching (exercise), 459
crosstab (exercise), 461
Data Access Pages (exercise), 526
editing, 449–450
exercise, 458

fields, 450–451
modifying order (exercise), 458
selecting, 446–448
multiple, 454–455
naming, 448
records (exercise), 461
saving, 448–449
saving with new names, 454–455
exercise, 458
sorting, 450–451
exercise, 458
sorting multiple fields (exercise), 459

R

random transitions (PowerPoint), exercise, 398
ranges (Excel), 238–239
exercise, 246
recalculating formulas (Excel), 266–268
recording. *See* entering
records (Access)
adding, 424–426
exercise, 438
copying (exercise), 440
deleting, 429–430
exercise, 438
editing, 427–428
exercise, 438
inserting, 429–430
exercise, 438
navigating, 426–427
numeric fields (exercise), 460
printing (exercise), 439
queries (exercise), 461
searching, 432–434
exercise, 439–440
sorting, 434–435
exercise, 439
sorts (exercise), 440
text fields
excluding/including (exercise), 460
limiting (exercise), 460
Records menu commands (Access)
Remove/Sort, 435
Sort, 435
Redo (Word), 103–104
relationships (Access), 410
relative formulas (Excel), 257–259
filling (exercise), 272
relative references (Excel), 254
Remove All Arrows command (Tools menu), Excel, 252
Remove/Sort command (Records menu), Access, 435
removing. *See* deleting
Rename command (File menu), 757, 761
renaming. *See also* naming
documents (Word), 777–778
files, 760–761
exercise, 767
reports (Access), 491
worksheets (Excel), 219
replacing
data (Access), 440
sample data (PowerPoint), 370–371
exercise, 381
text (Word), 109
Report Wizard (Access), 488–491
exercise, 500
reports (Access)
creating, 488–491
exercise, 500–502
drawing lines (exercise), 504
formatting (exercise), 503
labels (exercise), 501
mailing labels (exercise), 505
modifying, 493–495
exercise, 501
modifying grouping (exercise), 504–505
printing, 492
exercise, 501
renaming, 491
saving, 496–498
sort orders (exercise), 504
reports (Excel), exercise, 242–243
reports (Word), exercise, 341
resizing
clip art (PowerPoint), 352–353
exercise, 362
clip art (Word), 153–154
columns (Access), 430–432
exercise, 438–441
fields (Access), 472–474
forms (exercise), 480
windows, 743–744
WordArt (PowerPoint), 467
restoring windows, 746
results (Excel), linking, 305
revisions
fields (Access), 412–413
exercise, 420
Word, 80–82
exercise, 86
right-aligned text (Word), 118–120
rows (Excel)
deleting, 193–194
inserting, 193–194
exercise, 200–203
rows (PowerPoint), modifying formatting, 375–376
rows (Word), 171–173
adding (exercise), 180
Ruler command (View menu), Word, 131
rulers (Word), 133

S

sample data (PowerPoint), 370–371
replacing (exercise), 381
sans serif (Word), 118. *See also* fonts
sans serif fonts (Excel), 216
Save As command (File menu)
Access, 410
Excel, 196, 207
Word, 94
Save As dialog box
Access, 410, 448
Excel, 196, 207, 311
exercise, 785
PowerPoint, 333
Word, 82, 777
Save as Web Page command (File menu), Excel, 311
Save command (File menu), Access, 448
saving
documents (Word), 82–83, 774
exercise, 87–88
naming, 93–95, 109
renaming, 777–778
files
creating folders, 756–757
exercise, 767
files (Excel)
exercise, 785
forms (Access), 516–518
presentations (PowerPoint), 334–335
exercise, 341
queries (Access), 448–449
new names, 454–455, 458
reports (Access), 496–498
summary sheets (Excel), 317
workbooks (Excel), 196–197
as Web pages (exercise), 320–321
schedules (Excel), exercise, 243–244
scroll boxes, 745
scrollbars, 745–746
scrolling. *See* navigating
searching records (Access), 432–434
exercise, 439–440
security, exercise, 226
Select All command (Edit menu), PowerPoint, 390
Select Column command (Table menu), Word, 175
Select Record command (Edit menu), Access, 430
selecting
cells (Excel), 188–190
groups, 206–209
chart types (PowerPoint), 373–374
fields (Access), 446–448
text (Word), 98–102
exercise, 109
self-running presentations (PowerPoint), exercise, 400
sequential text headings (Excel), creating, 228–229
series (Excel)
data, 279
numbers, 229–231
serif fonts (Word), 118. *See also* fonts
serif fonts (Excel), 216

shading (Excel), adding, 217–219
sheets (Excel)
cells
editing, 191–192
entering data, 190–191, 202–203
selecting, 188–190
columns, 194–195
summing (exercise), 201
moving, 303
printing, 196–197
summary
creating, 304, 316
linking, 305, 308
saving as Web pages (exercise), 317
workbooks
navigating, 186–188
saving, 196–197
shortcut menus (Word)
grammar/spell check, 80–82
exercise, 86
shortcuts. *See also* keyboard shortcuts
Access, 427
Excel, 189
My Computer, 740
Word, 78
Show Table dialog box, Access, 445
Show/Hide button (Standard toolbar), Word, 87
Simple Query Wizard, Access, 445
sizing. *See also* resizing
columns (Access), 430–432
exercise, 438–439
fonts (Excel), 216–217
windows, 743–744
sizing handles (Word), modifying, 153–156
Slide Layout dialog box, PowerPoint, 331
Slide Show (PowerPoint)
random transitions (exercise), 398
self-running presentations (exercise), 400
transitions, 390–391
animating (exercise), 397
applying (exercise), 397
Slide Show view (PowerPoint), 328
transitions, 388–400
Slide view (PowerPoint)
layouts, 331–332
presentations, 330–332
slides (PowerPoint)
animation sounds (exercise), 400
audience handouts, 359–360
backgrounds (exercise), 399
charts
adding (exercise), 381
animating (exercise), 398–399
circular WordArt (exercise), 367–368
clip art
inserting, 350–353, 362–367
moving, 352–353, 362
resizing, 352–353, 362
connector lines, 357–359
adding (exercise), 363, 365
displaying clip art as watermarks (exercise), 363
drawing objects (exercise), 398
layout, 331–332
outlines, 337–338
presentations, 327–328
random transitions (exercise), 398
saving, 334–335
exercise, 341
self-running presentations (exercise), 400
slide shows
closing (exercise), 341
previewing, 336–337, 341
text
animating, 391–393
dimming, 393–394, 397
editing, 330–332, 340
entering, 328–330, 340
text boxes
adding, 355–357, 363
colors (exercise), 364–365
transitions
animating, 390–391, 397
applying (exercise), 397
outlines (exercise), 400
Slide Sorter view, 388–390, 396–400
WordArt
adding, 353–355, 362–366
animating (exercise), 399
moving, 355
Solver (Excel), exercise, 276
Sort command (Records menu), Access, 435
sorting
bulleted lists (Word), 139
Data Access Pages (Access), 526–527
multiple fields (Access), 459
queries (Access), 450–451
exercise, 458
records (Access), 434–435
deleting (exercise), 440
exercise, 439
reports (Access), 504
tables (Word), 182
sounds (PowerPoint), exercise, 400
source disks, 764. *See also* disks
spacing
paragraphs (Word), 119–120
text (Word), 120–122
speaker notes (PowerPoint)
adding, 334–335
exercise, 341
presentations (exercise), 341
spell check (Word), 80–82
exercise, 86
Spelling and Grammar dialog box, Word, 82
spreadsheets. *See* Excel; worksheets
Standard toolbar, Excel, 187
Standard toolbar (Office 2000), 775
Standard toolbar (Word), exercise, 87
Start button, 741–742
Start menu
Start button, 741
WordPad, 752
starting. *See also* opening
applications (Office 2000), 771–773
Excel (exercise), 785
Windows, 738–741
WordPad (exercise), 752
worksheets (Excel), 206–209
statistics (Excel), exercise, 274–275
status bars, 739
styles (PowerPoint), exercise, 342
styles (Word), 173–174
exercise, 180
subfolders, 754
creating, 756–757
submenus, 741
subscripts (Word), exercise, 138
summarizing worksheets (Excel), 303
creating, 304, 316
linking, 305–308
saving as Web pages (exercise), 317
summary sheets (Excel). *See also* worksheets
creating, 136, 304
linking, 305, 308
saving as Web pages (exercise), 317
summing. *See also* calculating
columns (Excel), 194–195
exercise, 201
superscripts (Word), exercise, 138
support. *See* Help, Office Assistant

T

Table AutoFormat command (Table menu), Word, 173
Table AutoFormat dialog box, Word, 173
Table menu commands (Word)
Insert Table, 170
Select Column, 175
Table AutoFormat, 173
Table Properties, 177
Table Properties command (Table menu), Word, 177
tables
default value, 533–536
design
modifying, 531–533
field size
changing, 538–540
field type
changing, 536–538
format
selecting, 536–538
join, 546
multiple tables
creating relationships, 543–546

creating queries, 546–549
working with, 540–543
one-to-many, 530
tables (Access)
analyzing (exercise), 442
check boxes (exercise), 422
creating, 406–409
exercise, 419
crosstab queries (exercise), 461
data (exercise), 420
documents (exercise), 527
fields, 408
form letters (Word)
linking, 511–513
merging, 513–514
printing, 486–488, 500
queries
creating, 444–445, 458
deleting records (exercise), 461
editing, 449–450, 458
matching criteria, 452–453, 459
modifying field order, 450–451, 458
saving, 448–449
saving with new names, 454–455, 458
selecting fields, 446–448
sorting, 450–451, 458
sorting multiple fields (exercise), 459
relationships, 410
saving, 410–411
exercise, 419
text (exercise), 441
wizards (exercise), 421
worksheets (Excel), 527
tables (dbase III Plus Database), 525
tables (Excel)
databases (Access), 514–516
importing (exercise), 524
merge cells (exercise), 223–224
tables (PowerPoint), exercise, 384
tables (Word)
cells
aligning (exercise), 181–182
merging (exercise), 181
data, 170–171
formulas (exercise), 182
inserting, 169–170
exercise, 180
rows/columns, 171–173
adding (exercise), 180
sorting (exercise), 182
text (exercise), 182
tabs (Word), 130–133
exercise, 137
Tabs command (Format menu), Word, 131
Tabs dialog box, Word, 131
tabular options (Access), exercise, 502
taskbars, 739
navigating, 747–748
templates (PowerPoint), 347–349
applying to existing presentations (exercise), 362
text (Access)
records
excluding/including (exercise), 460
limiting fields (exercise), 460
tables (exercise), 441
text (Excel)
cells
aligning, 213–215, 224
editing, 191–192
entering, 190–191, 202–203
cells/columns, 211–213
colors, 216–217
sequential headings, 228–229
text (PowerPoint)
animating, 391–393
dimming, 393–394
exercise, 397
editing, 330–332
exercise, 340
entering, 328–330
exercise, 340
text boxes
adding, 355–357, 363
colors (exercise), 364–365
WordArt, 353–354
exercise, 362, 366
moving, 355
text (Word)
AutoFormat, 173–174
exercise, 180
bulleted lists
creating, 122–124, 136
sorting (exercise), 139
Click and Type, 97
clip art, 154–156
closing, 82–83
columns (exercise), 111
copying (exercise), 110
deleting, 79
exercise, 87, 109
drag-and-drop, 104–106
exercise, 109
entering, 73–76
exercise, 85–86
fonts, 116–118
modifying (exercise), 136
grammar checking, 80–82
exercise, 86
headers/footers, 146–149
entering (exercise), 162–166
importing to Access (exercise), 526
inserting, 95–96
line spacing, 120, 122
moving, 102–103
exercise, 109
naming, 93–95
exercise, 109
numbered lists (exercise), 137–139
paragraphs
adding spaces, 129–130
aligning, 118–120
Format Painter, 126–127, 136
formatting (exercise), 136
hanging indents, 127–128, 136
indenting, 124
tabs, 130–133
pasting (exercise), 110
printing, 82–83, 106–107
exercise, 111
replacing (exercise), 109
saving, 82–83
selecting, 98–102
exercise, 109
spell checking, 80–82
exercise, 86
tables
aligning, 175–177
converting (exercise), 182
Undo (exercise), 110
Undo/Redo, 103–104
thumbnails (Word), exercise, 112
time report worksheets (Excel), exercise, 243
Times New Roman fonts (Excel), 216. *See also* fonts
titles (Excel), 216–217
toolbars, 739
Access, 475
command (View menu), 775
Drawing (exercise), 367
exercise, 786
PowerPoint
Chart Type, 373
Connectors, 358
Picture, 351
toolbars (Excel), 210
toolbars (Office 2000), 774–777
Formatting, 775
Standard, 775
toolbars (Word), 778–779
Toolbars command (View menu)
Access, 414
Office 2000, 743
Word, 103
tools (Access), exercise, 441
Tools menu, 775
Tools menu commands (Excel)
Auditing, 252
Remove All Arrows, 252
Trace Dependents, 252
Tools menu commands (PowerPoint), Options, 337
Tools menu commands (Word), Options, 74
Trace Dependents command (Tools menu), Excel, 252
tracking
lease reports (Excel), 242
schedules (Excel), 243–244

time reports (Excel), 243

transitions (PowerPoint)

animating, 390–391

exercise, 397

applying, 397

outlines (exercise), 400

random (exercise), 398

Slide Sorter view, 388–390

exercise, 396–400

trends (Excel)

exercise, 294–297

formulas (exercise), 299

X-Y charts (exercise), 299

troubleshooting

applications (Help), 779–781, 786

Help, 748–749

printing (exercise), 752

typeface (Excel). ***See also*** **fonts**

modifying, 216–217

typeface (Word), 116–118

types (exercise), 295

U

underlining words (Word), exercise, 137

Undo command (Edit menu), Access, 428, 467

Undo command (Word), 103–104

exercise, 110

Unfreeze Panes command (Windows menu), Excel, 233

Unhide Columns dialog box, Access, 432

unhiding columns (Excel), exercise, 203

Uniform Resource Locator. ***See*** **URL**

updating tables (Access), 527

URL (Uniform Resource Locator), 311

V

value axis (PowerPoint), 377

values (Excel), 251–253

exercise, 271

vertical scrollbars, 745–746. ***See also*** **scrollbars**

vertical WordArt (PowerPoint), exercise, 366

View menu commands, Toolbars, 775

View menu commands (Access)

Form Header/Footer, 474

Toolbars, 414

View menu commands (Excel), Customize, 187

View menu commands (Office 2000)

as Web Page, 745

Details, 743

Toolbars, 743

View menu commands (PowerPoint)

Notes Page, 446

View menu commands (Word)

Header and Footer, 146

Ruler, 131

Toolbars, 103

views

Access

Datasheet, 408

Design, 408

Design (exercise), 479

Form Design, 473

modifying, 414–416

My Computer, 752

PowerPoint

Normal, 328

Outline, 328

Slide Show, 328

Slide Sorter, 328

Word, 87

VLOOKUP (Excel), exercise, 275

W

watermarks (PowerPoint), exercise, 363

Web

Help, 782–783

worksheets (Excel), 322

Web pages (Access)

data pages

creating (exercise), 524, 526

editing (exercise), 526

filtering (exercise), 526–527

sorting (exercise), 526–527

forms, 516–518

Web pages (Excel)

summary sheets (exercise), 317

workbooks (exercise), 320–321

worksheets, 311–312

viewing, 312–314

white space (Word). ***See also*** **margins**

configuring, 143–144

exercise, 162–163

widths (Access), 430–432

exercise, 438–441

Window menu commands (Excel), Unfreeze Panes, 233

windows

maximizing, 746, 772

minimizing, 746

mouse, 738–741

multiple taskbars, 747–748

navigating, 736, 738, 741, 746

resizing, 743–744

restoring, 746

scrolling, 745–746

Start button, 741–742

Windows Explorer

disks, 754

interface, 743

modifying files, 743–744

wizards

Access

adding tables (exercise), 421

Form, 465

Lookup (exercise), 422

Page, 517

Report, 488–491

Report (exercise), 500

Simple Query, 445

Answer, 781

Excel, Chart, 280

Word (exercise), 88–89

Word

AutoFormat, 173–174

exercise, 180

clip art

inserting, 151–152, 162–164

modifying, 153–156

Clipboard (exercise), 112

columns of text (exercise), 111

commands

Break (Insert menu), 150

Bullets and Numbering, 123

Clip Art (Insert menu), 151

Header and Footer (View menu), 146

Insert Table (Table menu), 170

Options (Tools menu), 74

Page Numbers (Insert menu), 145

Page Setup (File menu), 143

Paragraph (Format menu), 124

Picture (Format menu), 155

Print (File menu), 106, 778

Ruler (View menu), 131

Save As (File menu), 94

Select Column (Table menu), 175

Table AutoFormat (Table menu), 173

Table Properties (Table menu), 177

Tabs (Format menu), 131

Toolbars (View menu), 103

dialog boxes

Break, 150

Date and Time, 147

Format Picture, 155

Insert ClipArt, 152

Insert Table, 170

Mail Merge Wizard, 511

Open, 93, 773

Options, 74

Page Setup, 143

Pages Numbers, 145

Paragraph, 120, 125

Print, 106, 779

Save As, 82, 777

Spelling and Grammar, 82

Table AutoFormat, 173

tabs, 131

documents

adding spaces, 119–120

aligning text, 118–120

applying Paste Special to Excel worksheets (exercise), 319–320

Click and Type feature, 97

closing, 82–83

copying text (exercise), 110

creating bulleted lists, 122–124

creating numbered lists (exercise), 137–139

deleting text, 79

drag-and-drop, 104–106
editing (exercise), 87
Format Painter, 126–127
formatting paragraphs (exercise), 136
grammar checking, 80–82
hanging indents, 127–128
indenting paragraphs, 124
inserting text, 95–96
inserting text in existing (exercise), 109
modifying fonts, 116–117
modifying fonts (exercise), 136
modifying line spacing, 120–122
modifying to two columns (exercise), 166
moving text, 102–103
naming, 93–95
navigating, 76–78
opening, 73–76, 773–774
opening different file formats (exercise), 111
opening existing, 93–95
pasting Excel charts (exercise), 320
pasting Excel worksheets (exercise), 318
pasting text (exercise), 110
printing, 82, 106–107, 778–779
renaming, 777–778
replacing text (exercise), 109
saving, 82–83, 774
selecting text, 98–102
sorting bulleted lists (exercise), 139
spell checking, 80–82
tabs, 130–133
Undo/Redo, 103–104
form letters
linking tables (Access), 511–513
merging tables (Access), 513–514
headers/footers
adding (exercise), 162–166
creating, 146–149
dates, 147
formatting text, 148
Help (exercise), 88
landscape layout (exercise), 89
Letter Wizard (exercise), 88–89
margins, 143–144
configuring (exercise), 162, 165
outlines
creating PowerPoint presentations (exercise), 343
importing to PowerPoint (exercise), 342
page breaks, 150–151
inserting (exercise), 163
page numbers, 145
inserting (exercise), 162
Print Preview, 156–159
exercise, 163
reports (exercise), 341
subscripts/superscripts (exercise), 138
tables
adding rows/columns (exercise), 180
aligning cells (exercises), 181–182
aligning numbers (exercise), 180
aligning text, 175–177
entering data, 170–171
formulas (exercise), 182
inserting, 169–170
merging cells (exercises), 181
sorting (exercise), 182
text (exercise), 182
thumbnails (exercise), 112
title pages, 87
underlining words (exercise), 137
word wrapping feature (Excel), 215
WordArt (PowerPoint)
adding, 353–355
exercise, 362, 364
animating (exercise), 399
circular (exercise), 367–368
moving, 355
resizing, 355
WordArt Gallery dialog box, PowerPoint, 353
WordPad (exercise), 752
workbooks (Excel)
cell references, 251–253
creating formulas (exercise), 271
mathematical calculations, 249–251
cells
editing, 191–192
entering data, 190–191
filling with absolute formulas, 257–259
filling with formulas, 253–257
filling with relative formulas, 257–259
selecting, 188–190
closing, 196–197
exercise, 200
columns, 194–195
summing (exercise), 201
editing (exercise), 200
hyperlinks, 308–309, 311
inserting (exercise), 321
navigating, 186–188
numbers
formatting, 210–211
modifying cells/columns, 211–213
renaming, 219
saving, 196–197
saving as Web pages (exercise), 320–321
summary sheets
creating, 304
linking, 305–308
saving as Web pages (exercise), 317
Web pages (exercise), 320–321
worksheets
editing (exercise), 223
moving, 303
previewing printing, 238–239
printing, 235–237
saving as Web pages, 311–312
XML, 312–314
worksheets (Excel)
borders, 217–219
adding (exercise), 222–223
built-in financial formulas, 261–262
calculating statistics (exercise), 274–275
cell references, 251–253
creating formulas (exercise), 271
mathematical calculations, 249–250
cells
aligning text, 213–215
copying, 233–234
editing, 191–192
entering data, 190–191
filling with absolute formulas, 257–259
filling with formulas, 253–257
filling with relative formulas, 257–259
modifying formatting (exercise), 321–322
protecting, 226
selecting, 188–190, 206–209
charts
creating, 282–284
editing, 284, 286–290
modifying types, 288
printing, 290–291
closing, 196–197
exercise, 200
colors (exercise), 222–223
column charts (exercise), 295–298
columns
hiding/unhiding (exercise), 203
summing, 194–195
inserting (exercise), 200, 202–203
conditional formulas, 264–266
COUNTIF function (exercise), 273
counting formulas, 264–266
creating (exercise), 199–200
dates (exercise), 225
documents
Paste Special (exercise), 319–320
pasting (exercise), 318
editing (exercise), 200, 223
existing (exercise), 221–222
fill handles (exercise), 246
fill lists (exercise), 245
fonts, 216–217
formulas
applying, 260–261
exercise, 274
recalculating, 266–268
trend lines (exercise), 299
frequency distribution (exercise), 275
Goal Seek (exercise), 274
headers/footers (exercise), 245
hyperlinks, 308–311
inserting (exercise), 321
lease reports (exercise), 242
line charts, 279–282
creating (exercise), 294–297
lines, 217–219
adding (exercise), 222–223
moving, 303
navigating, 186–188
numbers
formatting, 210–211
modifying cells/columns, 211–213

series, 229–231
opening, 206–209
panes, 231–233
printing, 196–197, 235–237
exercise, 245
previewing, 238–239
projecting population growth (exercise), 244
renaming, 219
schedules (exercise), 243–244
shading, 217–219
Solver (exercise), 276
summary sheets
creating, 304
linking, 305–308
saving as Web pages (exercise), 317
tables (exercise), 223–224
updating (exercise), 527
text
creating sequential headings, 228–229
modifying colors, 216–217
time reports (exercise), 243
VLOOKUP (exercise), 275
Web (exercise), 322
Web pages
saving as, 311–312
XML, 312–314
workbooks, 196–197
X-Y charts
adding trend lines (exercise), 299
data labels (exercise), 298
zoom, 231–232
World Wide Web. *See* WWW
wrapping
words (Excel), 215
WWW (World Wide Web), 47–68
information
emailing, 59, 61–62
printing, 59, 61
saving, 59, 60
search
access, 52–55
engine, 48
parameters, 55–57
refining, 57–59
subject directory, 48
subject index
access and search, 49–52
web site
adding (favorites list), 62–63

X

X-Y charts (Excel)
adding data labels (exercise), 298
trend lines (exercise), 299
XML (Extensible Markup Language), 311

Y

y-axis (Excel), 286
Y2K (exercise), 276
year 2000. See Y2K

Z

Zip drives, copying, 764
zoom (Excel), modifying, 231–232